LIABILITY FOR PRODUCTS

Liability for Products

English Law, French Law, and European Harmonisation

by

SIMON WHITTAKER

OXFORD
UNIVERSITY PRESS

OXFORD
UNIVERSITY PRESS

Great Clarendon Street, Oxford OX2 6DP

Oxford University Press is a department of the University of Oxford.
It furthers the University's objective of excellence in research, scholarship,
and education by publishing worldwide in

Oxford New York

Auckland Cape Town Dar es Salaam Hong Kong Karachi
Kuala Lumpur Madrid Melbourne Mexico City Nairobi
New Delhi Shanghai Taipei Toronto

With offices in

Argentina Austria Brazil Chile Czech Republic France Greece
Guatemala Hungary Italy Japan Poland Portugal Singapore
South Korea Switzerland Thailand Turkey Ukraine Vietnam

Oxford is a registered trade mark of Oxford University Press
in the UK and in certain other countries

Published in the United States
by Oxford University Press Inc., New York

British Library Cataloguing in Publication Data
Data available

Library of Congress Cataloging in Publication Data
Whittaker, Simon.
Liability for products: English law, French law, and European
harmonization / by S. Whittaker.
p. cm.
ISBN 0–19–825613–2 (hardcover: acid-free paper)
1. Products liability—England. 2. Products liability—France.
3. Products liability—European Union countries. I. Title.
KJC1688.W47 2005
346.2403'8—dc22

2005012361

Typeset by Newgen Imaging Systems (P) Ltd., Chennai, India
Printed in Great Britain
on acid-free paper by
Biddles Ltd., King's Lynn

ISBN 0–19–825613–2 978–0–19–825613–7

For my parents,
Edmund and Margaret Whittaker

Preface

The idea for a book on liability for products comparing the approaches of English and French lawyers and the wider context of the two legal systems, came to me soon after the enactment of the EC Product Liability Directive in 1985, but its appearance has taken very much longer than I anticipated. This is due in part, no doubt, to a number of other projects which have caught my attention, but it is also due to the fact that, as I worked, I felt that I needed to explore further into first French law and then (so as to compare what I found there) English law, looking beyond the private laws of contract and tort and into the laws of administrative liability, criminal law, and criminal and civil procedure and including material on the EC Consumer Guarantees Directive in 1999 (which added a second European dimension to the study).

I would like to start by thanking the editors at Oxford University Press who have been both encouraging and very patient over the years in relation to this work: Richard Hart, John Louth and, most recently and in particular, Gwen Booth. At times a work of this kind can become a strain rather than a joy and Gwen has been a great and practical help in getting the work finished. I have also had the benefit of and am most grateful to a number of research assistants who have helped me in particular to keep the work up-to-date and by checking references: Jonathan Bremner, Charles Clarke, Hadrien Costa de Beauregard, Lydie Reiss, and Andrew Scott. Given the range of its subject-matter, I have set a cut-off date of 1 January 2004 and while I have included some primary material after this date, I have not included new secondary material.

I have also had the benefit of many discussions with friends and colleagues both at home and abroad. Of these, I would particularly mention the following: Denis Baranger, John Bell, John Cartwright, Sergio Camára Lapuente, Bénédicte Fauvarque-Cosson, Michele Graziadei, Denis Mazeaud, Rebecca Williams, and Reinhard Zimmermann. I must make particular mention of my colleagues at St. John's, Paul Craig and Mark Freedland, whose influence is very visible in my developing interest in public law and whose moral support has been invaluable. I also owe a considerable intellectual debt to my former doctoral supervisor and, later, colleague for a number of years, Bernard Rudden, with whose wise support my interest in comparative law first flourished. I am most grateful to them all. Needless to say, though, all faults which remain are my responsibility alone.

I could not have completed this work without the help and support of my wife, Judith, and my children during unknown numbers of weekends of my absence while I have worked. I would also like to thank my parents, Margaret and Edmund Whittaker, without whose encouragement and support I would not have embarked on an academic career. To them, this book is dedicated with my love and respect.

St. John's College,　　　　　　　　　　　　　　　　　　　　　Simon Whittaker
Oxford　　　　　　　　　　　　　　　　　　　　　　　　　　20 December, 2004

Contents

PART V GENERAL CONCLUSION

Abbreviations

French Law

The Codes are referred to in the body of the text in full, the most commonly cited being in English translation, thus, the *Code civil* becomes the Civil Code. References to the Codes in the footnotes are abbreviated as follows:

A.c. pén.	*Ancien Code pénal*
C. assur.	*Code des assurances*
C. civ.	*Code civil*
C. com.	*Code de commerce*
C. consom.	*Code de la consommation*
C. constr. et hab.	*Code de la construction et de l'habitation*
C. éduc.	*Code de l'éducation*
C.G.C.T.	*Code général des collectivités territoriales*
C. santé pub.	*Code de la santé publique*
C. rur.	*Code rural*
C. org. jud.	*Code de l'organisation judiciaire*
C. séc. soc.	*Code de la sécurité sociale*
C. pén.	*Code pénal*
C.P.P.	*Code de procédure pénale*
N.c.pr.civ.	*Nouveau Code de procédure civile*

French Cases

French cases are referred to by their deciding body and date, together with any reference where a report of the decision may be found. Sometimes this is supplemented by the name of a party (e.g. *affaire Jand'heur*), this being standard practice as regards decisions of administrative courts. I have abbreviated the month of the date to three letter English abbreviations. Many decisions of the Cour de cassation and Conseil d'Etat (as well as all codified law and many individual *lois*) are available from the *service public* website, <http://www.legifrance.gouv.fr>.

The highest court judging civil and criminal cases is the Cour de cassation, which is divided according to the subject matter of the case. These are abbreviated in the notes as follows:

Ass. plén.	Assemblée plénière of the Cour de cassation
Ch. mixte	Chambre mixte of the Cour de cassation
Ch. réun.	Chambres réunies of the Cour de cassation
Civ. (1)	First civil chamber of the Cour de cassation
Civ. (2)	Second civil chamber of the Cour de casssation
Civ. (3)	Third civil chamber of the Cour de cassation
Com.	Commercial chamber of the Cour de cassation
Req.	Chambre des requêtes of the Cour de cassation
Soc.	Chambre sociale of the Cour de cassation

The Cour de cassation's plenary sessions which are now called the Assemblée plénière, used to be called the Chambres réunies; until 1947 the Cour de cassation possessed a Chambre des requêtes which acted as a filter for the main court. The Chambre mixte sits to resolve divergences of interpretation and case law.

Abbreviations used for other courts

CAA	Cour administrative d'appel
CE	Conseil d'Etat
CE Ass.	Assemblée du contentieux (or Assemblée) of the Conseil d'Etat
CE Sect.	Conseil d'Etat, Section du contentieux
TC	Tribunal des conflits
TGI	Tribunal de grande instance
Trib. corr.	Tribunal correctionnel

The decisions of courts of appeal are cited simply by the place of the court in question.

Where a report includes the *conclusions*, the *Commissaire du gouvernement* or *rapport* of the judge assigned to report on the case to the court, this appears as 'concl.' or 'rapp.' respectively followed by the name of the judge in question.

English Cases

The abbreviated citations to the law reports to the official reports and to the *English Reports* follow the standard practice. Abbreviations of unofficial reports are contained in the general abbreviations, below p. xix.

Special abbreviations

1993 Directive = Council Directive 93/13/EC of 5 April 1993 on unfair terms in consumer contracts.

'Amending Directive' = Directive 99/34/EC of the European Parliament and of the Council of 10 May 1999 amending Council Directive 85/374/EEC on the approximation of the laws, regulations and administrative provisions of the Member States concerning liability for defective products.

'Case C-203/99, *Veedfald*' or '*Veedfald*' = Case C-203/99 of 10 May 2001, *Veedfald v Århus Amtskommune*, [2001] ECR 1–3569.

'*Commission v UK*' = Case C-300/95 of 29 May 1997, *Commission v UK* [1997] ECR I-2649.

'Consumer Guarantees Directive' or '1999 Directive' = Directive 1999/44/EC of the European Parliament and of the Council of 25 May 1999 on certain aspects of the sale of consumer goods and associated guarantees.

'Council Resolution 2002' = Council Resolution of 19 December 2002 on the amendment of the liability for defective products Directive (2003/C 26/02) OJ C 26/2 4 February 2003.

'EU Parliament Resolution 2000' = European Parliament Resolution on the Commission Green Paper 'Liability for Defective Products' PE 289.426 (30 March 2000).

'EU Parliamentary Decision 1999' = EU Parliamentary Decision of 23 March 1999 on the common position EC No. 3/1999, OJ C 177 of 22 June 1999.

'European Convention' or 'Convention' = European Convention on products liability in regard to personal injury and death of 27 January 1977, E.T.S. No. 91.

'European Court decisions of 2002' = Case C-52/00 of 25 Apr. 2002, *Commission v France* [2002] I-3827 ('Case C-52/00'); Case C-154/00 of 25 Apr. 2002, *Commission v Greece* [2002] ECR I-3879 ('Case C-154/00'); Case C-183/00 of 25 Apr. 2002, *Gonzàlez Sanchez v Medicina Asturiana SA* [2002] ECR I-3901 ('Case C-154/00' or '*Gonzàlez Sanchez*').

'General Product Safety Directive' or 'GPSD 2001' = Directive 2001/95/EC of the European Parliament and of the Council of 3 December 2001 on general product safety.

'Product Liability Directive' or '1985 Directive' = Council Directive 1985/374/EEC of 25 July 1985 on the approximation of laws, regulations and administrative provisions of the Member States concerning liability for defective products.

'Vienna Convention' = United Nations Convention on Contracts for the International Sale of Goods of 1980.

UK statutes and statutory instruments

1977 Act = Unfair Contract Terms Act
1978 Act = Civil Liability (Contribution) Act 1978
1979 Act = Sale of Goods Act 1979
1987 Act = Consumer Protection Act 1987
1994 Act = Sale and Supply of Goods Act 1994
2000 Act = Powers of the Criminal Courts (Sentencing) Act 2000
2002 Regulations = Sale and Supply of Goods to Consumers Regulations 2002 SI No. 3045
GPSR 1994 = General Product Safety Regulations 1994 SI No. 2328

French Legislation

Constitution of 1958 = Constitution of the Fifth Republic of France of 4 October 1958

loi of 1978 = *loi* no. 78–12 of 4 January 1978 *relative à la responsabilité et l'assurance dans le domaine de la construction*

loi of 5 July 1985 = *Loi* no. 85–677 of 5 July 1985 *tendant à l'amélioration de la situation des victimes d'accidents de la circulation et à l'accélération des procédures d'idemnisation*

loi of 1996 = *loi* no. 96–393 of 13 May 1996 *relative à la responsabilité pénale pour des faits d'imprudence ou de négligence*

loi of 1998 = *loi* no. 98–389 of 19 May 1998 *sur la responsabilité du fait des produits défectueux*

loi of 2000 = *loi* no. 2000–647 of 10 July 2000 *tendant à préciser la définition des délits non intentionnels*

loi no. 2002–303 = *Loi* no 2002–303 of 4 March 2002 *relative aux droits des malades et à la qualité du système de santé*

Avant projet de loi = G. Viney (président du comité), *Avant-projet de loi sur la garantie de conformité due par le vendeur* (May, 2002) <http://www.justice.gouv.fr/publicat/RappGTIDF.htm>.

projet de loi of 2004 = *Projet de loi relative à la garantie de la conformité du bien au contrat due par le vendeur au consommateur et à la responsabilité du fait des produits défectueux*, Sén. No. 358 (16 Jun. 2004)

loi of 9 December 2004 = *loi de simplification du droit* no. 2004–1343 of 9 December 2004

Ordonnance of 17 February 2005 = *Ordonnance* no. 2005 of 17 February 2005 *relative à la garantie de la conformité du bien au contrat due par le vendeur au consommateur*

Other Abbreviations

AJDA	*Actualité juridique du droit administratif*
Am. J. Comp. L.	*American Journal of Comparative Law*
Ass. nat.	Assemblée nationale de la République française
BLR	Building Law Reports
BMLR	Butterworths Medico-Legal Reports
Bull. civ.	Bulletin des arrêts des Chambres civiles de la Cour de cassation (a selection of the decisions of various civil chambers of the Cour de cassation which are reported in four different sections, designated by the appropriate Roman numeral. The references in the text refer to their numbers rather than the page).
Bull. crim.	Bulletin des arrêts de la Chambre criminelle de la Cour de cassation
CA	Court of Appeal (England and Wales)
CJD	Creutzfeld–Jakob disease
CPR	Civil Procedure Rules
CJEG	Cahiers juridiques de l'électricité et du gaz
CLJ	*Cambridge Law Journal*
CLY	Current Law Yearbook
Comm. gouv.	*Commissaire du gouvernement*
Cont., Conc., Cons.	*Contrats, concurrence, consommation*
Cr App R	Criminal Appeal Reports
Crim LR	*Criminal Law Review*
D	Recueil Dalloz
DA	Recueil Dalloz analytique
D. adm.	*Droit administratif* (a review annexed to Juris-Classeur Droit Administratif (Editions techniques, Paris))
DC	Recueil Dalloz critique
Déc.	*Décret*
DH	Recueil Dalloz hebdomadaire
Dig.	The Digest of Justinian
DP	Recueil Dalloz périodique
Dr. mar. fr.	*Droit maritime français*
Dr. soc.	*Droit social*
Droit pénal	*Droit pénal* (a review annexed to Juris-Classeur Pénal (Editions techniques, Paris))
ECHR	European Convention on Human Rights
ECJ	European Court of Justice
ECR	European Court Reports
EDCE	*Etudes et documents du Conseil d'Etat*
EDF	Electricité de France
ERPL	*European Review of Private Law*
E.T.S.	European Treaty Series
GDF	Gaz de France
fasc.	fascicule, i.e. a division of large-scale work such as the Juris-Classeurs, q.v.
GP	Gazette du palais
HC Deb.	House of Commons Debates (Hansard)
HGH	Human growth hormone
HL Deb.	House of Lords Debates (Hansard)

HLR	Housing Law Reports
HSE	Health and Safety Executive
ICLQ	*International and Comparative Law Quarterly*
IHL	In-House Lawyer
JBL	*Journal of Business Law*
JCP	Jurisclasseur périodique (otherwise known as *La Semaine Juridique*)(Edition générale)
J.O. Rép. fr.	*Le Journal officiel de la République française*
Jur.-Cl. Civ.	Juris-Classeur Civil (Editions techniques, Paris)
Jur.-Cl. Proc. Civ.	Juris-Classeur Procédure Civile (Editions techniques, Paris)
Jur.-Cl. Adm.	Juris-Classeur Administratif (Editions techniques, Paris)
Jur.-Cl. Pén.	Juris-Classeur Pénal (Editions techniques, Paris)
Jur.-Cl. Proc. pén.	Juris-Classeur Procédure pénale (Editions techniques, Paris)
Jur.-Cl. Contrats Distribution	Juris-Classeur Contrats Distribution (Editions techniques, Paris)
J. Crim. Law	*Journal of Criminal Law*
J. Leg. Hist.	*Journal of Legal History*
KIR	Knights Industrial Reports
LSG	Law Society Gazette
Leb.	Recueil Lebon or Recueil des décisions du Conseil d'Etat
LQR	*Law Quarterly Review*
LS	*Legal Studies*
Lloyd's Rep Med	Lloyd's Law Report Medical
Med. LR	Medical Law Reports
Med.L.Rev.	*Medical Law Review*
MLR	*Modern Law Review*
NLJ	*New Law Journal*
OJLS	*Oxford Journal of Legal Studies*
Ord.	*Ordonnance*
OUCLJ	*Oxford University Commonwealth Law Journal*
PD	Practice Direction
PIQR	Personal Injuries and Quantum Reports
PL	*Public Law*
rapp	*rapport*
RDP	*Revue de droit public et de science politique*
Resp. civ. et assur.	*Responsabilité civile et assurances* (a review annexed to Juris-Classeur Responsabilité et assurance (Editions techniques, Paris)
Rev. crit.	*Revue critique de législation et jurisprudence*
Rev. marché commun	*Revue du Marché commun et de l'Union européenne*
RFDA	*Revue française de Droit administratif*
RGAT	Recueil général des assurances terrestes
RIDC	*Revue internationale de droit comparé*
RSC	Rules of the Supreme Court
RTDCiv.	*Revue trimestrielle de droit civil*
RTDCom.	*Revue trimestrielle de droit commercial*
RTR	Road Traffic Reports
S	Sirey
Sén.	Sénat de la République française
SI	Statutory Instrument

SNCF	Société nationale des chemins de fer
Somm. comm.	Sommaires commentés
Tul LR	*Tulane Law Review*
Tr L	Trading Law
Washburn LJ	*Washburn Law Journal*
Web JCLI	Web Journal of Current Legal Issues
WL	Westlaw (on-line resource) (Sweet and Maxwell)

Author Abbreviations

Analysis of Replies = College of Europe, *Analysis of the Replies to the Commission Green Paper on Product Liability* (13 September 2000) <http://europa.eu.int/comm/internal_market/en/goods/prodliability.htm>

Archbold = Archbold, *Criminal Pleading, Evidence and Practice* (2004)

Ashworth, *Principles* = A. Ashworth, *Principles of Criminal Law* (OUP, 4th. edn., 2003)

Bell, *French Legal Cultures* = J.Bell, *French Legal Cultures* (Butterworths, London, 2002)

Bell, Boyron and Whittaker = J. Bell, S. Boyron and S. Whittaker, *Principles of French Law* (OUP, 1998)

Bénabent, *Contrats spéciaux* = A. Bénabent, *Droit civil, Les contrats spéciaux civils et commerciaux* (Montchrestien, Paris, 5th. edn., 2001)

Bénabent, *Obligations* = A. Bénabent, *Droit civil, Les obligations* (Montchrestien, Paris, 8th. edn. 2001)

Benjamin = A.G. Guest (gen. ed.), *Benjamin's Sale of Goods* (Sweet and Maxwell, London, 6th. edn., 2002)

Benjamin, Special Supplement = C. J. Miller (gen. ed.), *Benjamin's Sale of Goods, Special Supplement to the 6th edition* (Sweet and Maxwell, London, 2003)

Bianca and Grundmann, *EU Sales Directive* = M.C. Bianca and S. Grundmann (eds.), *EU Sales Directive* (Intersentia, Antwerp, 2000)

Bihl, *Droit pénal* = L. Bihl, *Le droit pénal de la consommation* (Nathan, n.p., 1989)

Bihl, *Vente* = L. Bihl, *Le droit de la vente (vente mobilière)* (Dalloz, Paris, 1986)

Braibant and Stirn, *Droit administratif français* = G. Braibant and B. Stirn, *Le droit administratif français* (Presses de Sciences Po et Dalloz, Paris, 6th. edn., 2002)

Bridge, *Sale of Goods* = M.G. Bridge, *The Sale of Goods* (OUP, 1997)

Brown and Bell = L. Neville Brown and J. Bell, *French Administrative Law* (OUP, 5th. edn., 1998)

Calais-Auloy and Steinmetz = J. Calais-Auloy and F. Steinmetz, *Droit de la consommation*, (Dalloz, Paris, 6th edn., 2003)

Carbonnier, *Introduction* = J. Carbonnier, *Droit Civil, Introduction* (PUF, Paris, 26th. edn., 1999)

Carbonnier, *Obligations* = J. Carbonnier, *Droit Civil, Tome 4, Les obligations* (PUF, Paris, 22nd. edn., 2000)

Chapus, *Droit administratif general,* Tome 1 = R.Chapus, *Droit administratif général,* Tome 1 (Montchrestien 15th. edn., 2001)

Chapus, *Droit administratif général,* Tome 2 = R.Chapus, *Droit administratif général,* Tome 2 (Montchrestien, Paris, 15th. edn., 2001)

Chapus, *Responsabilité publique et responsabilité privée* = R. Chapus, *Responsabilité publique et responsabilité privée: les influences réciproques des jurisprudences administrative et judiciaire* (LGDJ, Paris, 1954)

Chitty on Contracts = H. Beale (gen. ed.) *Chitty on Contracts* (Sweet and Maxwell, London, 29th. edn., 2004) 2 vols. (with specialist editors)

Clerk and Lindsell on Torts = A.M. Dugdale (gen.ed.),*Clerk and Lindsell on Torts* (Sweet and Maxwell, London, 18th. edn., 2000)

Craig, *Administrative Law* = P.P. Craig, *Administrative Law* (Sweet and Maxwell, London, 5th. edn., 2003)

Craig and de Búrca, *EU Law* = P.P. Craig and G. de Búrca, *EU Law, Text, Cases, and Materials* (OUP, 3rd. edn., 2003)

Cranston's Consumers and the Law = C. Scott and J. Black, *Cranston's Consumers and the Law* (Butterworths, London, 3rd. edn., 2000)

de Laubadère and Gaudemet, *Droit administratif,* Tome 2 = A. de Laubadère and Y. Gaudemet, *Traité de droit administratif,* Tome 2, *Droit administratif des biens* (LGDJ, Paris, 11th. edn., 1998)

de Juglart, *Vente* = H., L. and J. Mazeaud et F. Chabas, *Leçons de droit civil,* Tome 3, vol. 2 *Principaux contrats: Vente et échange,* 2e Partie by M. de Juglart (Montchrestien, Paris, 7th. edn., 1987)

Delmas-Marty and Guidicelli-Delage = M. Delmas-Marty and G. Guidicelli-Delage, *Droit pénal des affaires* (PUF, Paris, 4th. edn., 2000)

Desportes and Le Gunehec = F. Desportes and F. Le Gunehec, *Droit pénal général* (Economica, Paris, 10th. edn., 2003)

Dicey, *Introduction to the Study of the Law of the Constitution* = A.V. Dicey, *Introduction to the Study of the Law of the Constitution* (Macmillan, 10th. edn., 1965 by E.C.S. Wade). The first edition was published in 1885.

EC Commission, *First Report* = EC Commission, *First Report on the Application of the Council Directive on Approximation of Laws, Regulations and Administrative provisions of the Member States concerning Liability for Defective Products (85/374/EEC)* Com(95)617 final (13 December 1995)

EC Commission, *Green Paper* = EC Commission, Green Paper, *Liability for Defective Products* Com(1999)396 final (28 July 1999)

EC Commission, *Second Report* = *Report from the Commission on the Application of Directive 85/374/EEC* [etc.] Com/2000/0893 final (2001)

Fairgrieve, *State Liability* = D. Fairgrieve, *State Liability in Tort: A Comparative Law Study* (OUP, 2002)

Flour, Aubert and Savaux, *Fait juridique* = J. Flour, J.-L. Aubert and E. Savaux, *Droit civil, Les obligations, 2 Le fait juridique* (Armand Colin, Paris, 10th. edn., 2003)

Flour and Aubert, *Rapport d'obligation* = J. Flour and J.-L. Aubert, *Les obligations, 3 Le rapport d'obligation* by J.-L. Aubert, Y. Flour, and E. Savaux (Armand Colin, Paris, 1999)

Fontaine and Viney = M. Fontaine and G. Viney (eds.), *Les sanctions de l'inexécution des obligations contractuelles, Etudes de droit comparé* (Bruyant, Bruxelles and LGDJ, Paris, 2001)

Gaudemet, *Droit administratif,* Tome 1 = Y. Gaudemet, *Traité de droit administratif,* Tome 1, *Droit administratif général* (LGDJ, Paris, 16th. edn., 2001)

Ghestin, Goubeaux and Fabre-Magnan, *Introduction générale,* = J. Ghestin (dir.), *Traité de droit civil;* J. Ghestin, G. Goubeaux, and M. Fabre-Magnan, *Introduction générale* (LGDJ, Paris, 1994)

Ghestin, *Conformité* = J. Ghestin, *Conformité et garanties dans la vente (Produits mobiliers)* (LGDJ, Paris, 1983)

Ghestin, *La formation du contrat* = J. Ghestin (dir.) *Traité de droit civil;* J. Ghestin, *La formation du contrat* (LGDJ, Paris, 3rd. edn., 1993)

Ghestin, *Sécurité des consommateurs* = J. Ghestin (ed.) *Sécurité des consommateurs et responsabilité du fait des produits défectueux,* Colloque (LGDJ, Paris, 1987)

Ghestin (1986) = J. Ghestin, 'La directive communautaire du 25 juillet 1985 sur la responsabilité du fait des produits défectueux' D 1986 Chron. 135

Ghestin (1988) = J. Ghestin, 'L'avant-projet de loi sur la responsabilité du fait des produits défectueux: une refonte partielle du code civil' *Revue du jurisprudence commerciale* (1988) 201

Ghestin (1998) = J. Ghestin, 'Le nouveau titre IVbis du Livre III du Code civil "De la responsabilité du fait des produits défectueux:" L' application en France de la directive sur la responsabilité du fait des produits défectueux après l'adoption de la loi no. 98–389 du 19 mai 1998' JCP 1998.I.148

Ghestin and Desché, *Vente* = J. Ghestin (dir.) *Traité des contrats,* J. Ghestin and B. Desché, *La vente* (LGDJ, Paris, 1990)

Guinchard and Buisson = S. Guinchard and J. Buisson, *Procédure pénale* (Litec, Paris, 2nd. edn., 2002)

Harris and Tallon = D. Harris and D. Tallon (eds.), *Contract Law Today: Anglo-French Comparisons* (OUP, 1989)

HL Select Committee, *Tenth Report* = House of Lords Select Committee on European Communities, *Tenth Report on Consumer Guarantees* (4 March 1997)

Hodges, *Report* = C.J.S. Hodges, *Report for the Commission of the European Communities on the Application of Directive 85/374/EEC on Liability for Defective Products* (May 1994)

Huet, *Principaux contrats spéciaux*, = J. Ghestin (dir.) *Traité de droit civil*; J. Huet, *Les principaux contrats spéciaux* (LGDJ, Paris, 2nd. edn., 2001)

Huet, *Responsabilité du vendeur* = J. Huet, *Responsabilité du vendeur et Garantie contre les vices cachés* (Litec, Paris, 1987)

Ibbetson, *Historical Introduction* = D. Ibbetson, *A Historical Introduction to the Law of Obligations* (OUP, 1999)

Lambert-Faivre, *Droit des assurances* = Y. Lambert-Faivre, *Droit des assurances* (Dalloz, Paris, 9th. edn., 1995)

Lambert-Faivre, *Droit du dommage corporel* = Y. Lambert-Faivre, *Droit du dommage corporel: Systèmes d'indemnisation* (Dalloz, Paris, 4th. edn., 2000)

Larroumet, *Contrat* = C. Larroumet, *Droit civil*, Tome 3, *Les obligations, Le contrat* (Economica, Paris, 4th. edn., 1998)

Larroumet, D 1998 Chron. 311 = C. Larroumet, 'La responsabilité du fait des produits défectueux après la loi du 19 mai 1998' D 1998 Chron. 311.

Law Com. No. 160 = Law Commission, *Sale and Supply of Goods*, Law Com. No. 160 (1987)

Le Tourneau and Cadiet, *Droit de la responsabilité* = P. Le Tourneau and L. Cadiet, *Droit de la responsabilité et des contrats* (Dalloz, Paris, 2000)

Lovells, *Report* = Lovells, *Product Liability in the European Union: a Report for the European Commission* (February 2003)

MacCormick, *Report* = D.N. MacCormick, *Report on the Commission Green Paper 'Liability for defective products'* PE 232.108 (1 March 2000)

Malaurie, Aynès and Gautier, *Contrats spéciaux* = P. Malaurie, L. Aynès and P.-Y. Gautier, *Les contrats spéciaux* (Defrénois, Paris, 2003)

Malaurie, Aynès and Stoffel-Munck, *Obligations* = P. Malaurie, L. Aynès and P. Stoffel-Munck *Droit civil: les obligations* (Defrénois, Paris, 2003)

Malinvaud (1988) = P. Malinvaud, 'L'application de la directive communautaire sur la responsabilité du fait des produits défectueux et le droit de la construction ou le casse-tête communautaire' D 1988 Chron. 85

Malinvaud (1999) = P Malinvaud, 'La loi du 19 mai 1998 relative à la responsabilité du fait des produits défectueux et le droit de la construction' D 1999 Chron. 85

Markovits = Y. Markovits, *La directive C.E.E. du 25 juillet 1985 sur la responsabilité du fait des produits défectueux* (LGDJ, Paris, 1990)

Markesinis and Deakin's *Tort Law* = S. Deakin, A. Johnston and B. Markesinis, *Markesinis and Deakin's Tort Law* (OUP, 5th. edn., 2003)

Marty and Raynaud, *Obligations* = G. Marty and P. Raynaud, *Droit civil, Les obligations, Tome I: les sources* (Sirey, Paris, 2nd. edn., 1988)

Mazeaud, *Les victimes* = D. Mazeaud, 'Les victimes et les dommages réparables' in *La responsabilité du fait des produits défectueux (loi du 19 mai 1998) Petites affiches, La Loi* No. 155 (28 December 1998)

Mazeaud and Chabas, *Obligations* = H., L. and J. Mazeaud, *Leçons de droit civil,* Tome II, Premier Volume, *Les obligations théorie générale* (Montchrestien, Paris, 9th. edn, 1998 by F. Chabas)

Merle and Vitu, *Droit pénal* = R. Merle and A. Vitu, *Traité de droit criminel, Problèmes généraux de la science criminelle, Droit pénal général* (Eds. Cujas, Paris, 6th. edn., 1984)

Merle and Vitu, *Procédure pénale* = R. Merle and A. Vitu, *Traité de droit criminel, Procédure pénale,* (Eds. Cujas, Paris, 6th. edn., 1984)

Moreau, *Droit administratif* = J. Moreau, *Droit administratif* (PUF, Paris, 1st. edn., 1989)

Nicholas = B. Nicholas, *The French Law of Contract* (OUP, 2nd. edn., 1992)

O'Hare and Hill, *Civil Litigation* = J. O'Hare, K. Browne and R. N. Hill, *Civil Litigation* (Sweet and Maxwell, London, 10th. edn., 2000)

Opinion of the Economic and Social Committee = *Opinion of the Economic and Social Committee on the 'Proposal for a European Parliament and Council Directive amending Council Directive 85/374/EEC* [etc.] (98/C 95/17) (30 March 1998)

Pacteau, *Contentieux administratifs* = B. Pacteau, *Contentieux administratifs* (PUF, Paris, 5th. edn., 1985)

Pothier, *Obligations* = R. J. Pothier, *Traité des obligations* (Paris, 1761) in *Oeuvres complètes de Pothier* (Thomine et Fortic, Paris, 1821), Vol. I

Pothier, *Vente* = R. J. Pothier, *Traité du contrat de vente* in *Oeuvres complètes de Pothier* (Thomine et Fortic, Paris, 1821), Vol. 3

Pradel, *Droit pénal* = J. Pradel, *Manuel de droit pénal général* (Eds. Cujas, Paris, 14th edn., 2002)

Pradel, *Procédure pénale* = J. Pradel, *Manuel de procédure pénale* (Eds. Cujas, Paris, 11th edn., 2002)

Pradel, *Sang et droit pénal* = J. Pradel (ed.), *Sang et droit pénal, A propos du sang contaminé . . .* (Eds. Cujas, Paris, 1995)

Richer, *Droit des contrats administratifs* = L. Richer, *Droit des contrats administratifs* (LGDJ, Paris, 2nd. edn., 1999).

Rivero and Waline, *Droit administratif* = J. Rivero and J. Waline, *Droit administratif* (Dalloz, Paris, 18th. edn., 2000)

Roselli, *Report* = F. Roselli, *Analysis of the Economic Impact of the Development Risk Clause as provided by Directive 85/374/EEC on Liability for Defective Products*

Roth-Behrendt, *Opinion* = D. Roth-Behrendt, *Opinion for the Committee on Legal Affairs and the Internal Market* PE 232.108

Roth-Behrendt, *Report* = D. Roth-Behrendt, EU Parliament, Committee on the Environment, Pubic Health and Consumer Protection, *Report on the proposal for a European Parliament and Council Directive amending Council Directive 85/374/EEC* [etc.] PE 225.962fin. (28 September 1998)

Smith and Hogan = *Smith and Hogan Criminal Law* (Butterworths, London, 10th. edn., 2002) by J.C. Smith

Stapleton, *Product Liability* = J. Stapleton, *Product Liability* (Butterworths, London, 1994)

Starck, Roland and Boyer, *Responsabilité délictuelle* = B. Starck, H. Roland and L. Boyer, *Obligations*, 1. *Responsabilité délictuelle* (Litec, Paris, 5th. edn., 1996)

Taylor, *Harmonisation communautaire*, = S. Taylor, *L'Harmonisation communautaire de la responsabilité du fait des produits défectueux, Etude comparative du droit anglais et du droit français* (LGDJ, Paris, 1999).

Terré, Simler, Lequette, *Obligations* = F. Terré, P. Simler, Y. Lequette, *Droit civil: Les obligations* (8th. edn., Paris, Dalloz, 2002).

Testu and Moitry = F.X. Testu and J.-H. Moitry, 'La responsabilité du fait des produits défectueux, Commentaire de la loi 98-389 du 19 mai 1998' Dalloz Affaires (16 July 1998) Supplement to No. 125

Treitel, *The Law of Contract* = G.H. Treitel, *The Law of Contract* (Sweet and Maxwell, London, 11th. edn., 2003)

Treitel, *Remedies* = G.H. Treitel, *Remedies for Breach of Contract, A Comparative Account* (OUP, 1988)

Vedel and Delvolvé, *Droit administratif,* Tome 1 = G Vedel and P Delvolvé *Droit administratif,* Tome 1 (PUF, Paris, 12 th. edn, 1992)

Véron (4th edn.) = M. Véron, *Droit pénal spécial* (Masson, Paris, 4th. edn., 1995)

Véron (9th edn.) = M. Véron, *Droit pénal spécial* (Armand Colin, Paris, 9th. edn., 2002)

Vincent and Guinchard, *Procédure civile* = J. Vincent and S. Guinchard, *Procédure civile* (Dalloz, Paris, 27th. edn., 2003)

Viney, *Introduction à la responsabilité* = J. Ghestin (dir.) *Traité de droit civil*; G. Viney, *Introduction à la Responsabilité* (LGDJ, Paris, 2nd. edn., 1995)

Viney and Jourdain, *Conditions* = J. Ghestin (dir.) *Traité de droit civil*; G. Viney and P. Jourdain, *Les conditions de la responsabilité* (2nd. edn., LGDJ, Paris, 1998)

Viney and Jourdain, *Effets de la responsabilité* = J. Ghestin (dir.) *Traité de droit civil*; G. Viney and P. Jourdain, *Les effets de la responsabilité*, (2nd. edn., Paris, LGDJ, 2001)

Wade and Forsyth, *Administrative Law* = W. Wade and C. Forsyth, *Administrative Law*, (OUP, 8th edn., 2002)

Weatherill = S. Weatherill, *EC Consumer Law and Policy* (Longman, 1997)

Whittaker (1985) = S. Whittaker, 'The EEC Directive on Product Liability' 5 Yearbook of European Law (1985) 234

Whittaker (1989) = S. Whittaker, 'European Product Liability and Intellectual Products' (1989) 105 *LQR* 125

Zimmermann, *Liability for Non-Conformity* = R. Zimmermann, *Liability for Non-Conformity, The new system of remedies in German sales' law and its historical context, John Maurice Kelly Memorial Lecture* (Faculty of Law, University College, Dublin, Dublin, 2004)

Zimmermann, *Obligations* = R. Zimmermann, *The Law of Obligations, Roman Foundations of the Civilian Tradition* (Juta & Co. Ltd., 1990)

Note: All references in the footnotes are to page numbers unless otherwise indicated. All translations are the author's own unless otherwise indicated.

Table of Cases

Commonwealth and UK

European Court of Justice

European Court of Human Rights

France

Note: French civil or criminal cases are not generally so well known by their dates as to appear in a table in treatises, but some works do list the most significant and well known decisions. This table will follow this lead and list here the most significant decisions, placing in parentheses a few words to indicate their subject matter. By contrast, French administrative cases are well-known typically by the name of one or both of their parties and for this reason, I shall list all the French administrative cases to which reference is made.

French civil cases

Criminal cases

Administrative cases

A note on the cases arising out of the affaire du sang contaminé

This *affaire* arose out of the supply in France of blood contaminated with the HIV virus in the 1980s. In its broadest sense, the *affaire* found expression in three sets of proceedings, which are described in the text as indicated below.

(i) proceedings brought in the ordinary or the administrative courts claiming damages against blood transfusion centres, hospitals or clinics in respect of the supply of contaminated blood:

    in the ordinary courts: Civ. (1) 12 Apr. 1995, *Dupuy, Martial*, JCP 1995.II.22467 note Jourdain;

in the administrative courts: CE Ass. 26 May 1995, *Pavan, Consorts N'Guyen, Jouan,* Leb. 221, AJDA 1995.577-78, AJDA 1995.508 note Stahl and Chavaux, JCP 1995.II.22468 note Moreau.

These are discussed in the text at pp. 149–51.

(ii) criminal proceedings brought against individuals allegedly responsible for the deaths and injuries caused by the contamination of the blood:

against the officers of the National Blood Transfusion Centre: Paris (Chambre d'accusation) 19 Sept. 1991 and Trib. corr. Paris 23 Oct. 1992, D 1993.222; Paris 13 Jul. 1993, D 1994.18 note Prothais; Crim. (2) 26 Jan. 1994, Bull. civ. II no. 41; Crim. 22 Jun. 1994, JCP 1994.II.41 note Rassat;

against government ministers: Haute Cour de justice (Commission d'instruction) 5 Feb. 1993, D 1993.261 note Pradel; Cour de justice de la République 9 Mar. 1999, D 1999 IR 86.

against a range of others: Paris (Chambre d'instruction) 4 Jul. 2002, D 2003.164 note Prothais; Crim. 18 Jun. 2003, Bull. crim. no. 127, JCP 2003.II.10122 note Rassat.

These are discussed in the text at pp. 394–401.

(iii) proceedings brought in the administrative courts for damages alleging that the State was responsible for the failure of the government to control the safety of blood products: TA Paris 20 Dec. 1991, 8 RFDA (1992) 566, concl. Stahlberger, ibid. 552; CAA Paris 16 Jun. 1992, JCP 1992 Actualité no. 33–37; CE Ass. 9 Apr. 1993, Req. no. 138652, D 1993.312, concl. Légal, obs. Maugüé and Touvet, AJDA 1993 Chron. 344. These are discussed in the text at pp. 315–19, 324.

Netherlands

United States of America

Table of Legislation

United Kingdom

Statutes

Secondary legislation

Other Materials

European Union

EC Directives

France

Constitutions and constitutional legislation

Codes

Ancien Code pénal

Code civil

Germany

Spain

1

General Introduction

1. The Starting Point for this Study

The EC Product Liability Directive of 1985 can be seen as the first European legislation which touched the heartland of the private laws of the Member States, affecting cases which previously had been dealt with by their established rules of contract or of tort. In the two subsequent decades there have been a string of directives affecting contracts in general,[1] dealing with aspects of public contracts,[2] commercial contracts[3] and most especially consumer contracts.[4] Moreover, the effect of these directives in the laws of the Member States has sometimes been considerably wider than their terms have required, the national systems using their implementation as an occasion for wider reform on the basis (at least in part) of the legal concepts which they contain.[5] Of these directives, two are particularly prominent: the Unfair Terms in Consumer Contracts Directive[6] and the Consumer Guarantees Directive;[7] and while the latter is itself fairly limited in scope, at times its implementation in the laws of the Member States has proved highly controversial.

At the same time as these legislative initiatives, there has also been very considerable academic and European institutional interest in questions of the future direction or

---

[1] EC Dir. 2000/31/EC of 8 Jun. 2000 on certain legal aspects of information society services, in particular electronic commerce, esp. arts. 9–11.

[2] E.g. Dir. 92/50/EEC of 18 Jun. 1992 relating to the coordination of procedures for the award of public service contracts.

[3] Dir. 2000/35/EC of the European Parliament and of the Council of 29 Jun. 2000 on combating late payment in commercial transactions; Dir. 86/653/EEC of 18 Dec. 1986 on the coordination of the laws of the Member States relating to self-employed commercial agents.

[4] Dir. 85/577/EEC of 20 Dec. 1985 to protect the consumer in respect of contracts negotiated away from business premises; Dir. 90/314/EEC of 13 Jun. 1990 on package travel, package holidays and package tours; Dir. 93/13/EEC of 5 Apr.1993 on unfair terms in consumer contracts; Dir. 94/47/EC of the European Parliament and of the Council of 26 Oct. 1994 on the protection of purchasers in respect of certain aspects of contracts relating to the purchase of the right to use immovable properties on a timeshare basis; Dir. 97/7/EC of the European Parliament and of the Council of 20 May 1997 on the protection of consumers in respect of distance contracts; Dir. 98/6/EC of the European Parliament and of the Council of 16 Feb. 1998 on consumer protection in the indication of the prices of products offered to consumers; Dir. 99/44/EC of the European Parliament and of the Council of 25 May 1999 on certain aspects of the sale of consumer goods and associated guarantees; Dir. 98/27/EC of the European Parliament and of the Council of 19 May 1998 on injunctions for the protection of consumers' interests.

[5] The most prominent example of this has been the amendment of the German Civil Code, the B.G.B., on implementation of the Consumer Guarantees Directive: see Zimmermann, *Liability for Non-Conformity*.

[6] Dir. 93/13/EC of Apr. 5 1993 on unfair terms in consumer contracts.

[7] Dir. 99/44/EC, above n. 4 (the 'Consumer Guarantees Directive' or '1999 Directive').

directions in which EC legislation should go, whether quite modestly focusing on the quality and consistency of legislation of the 'sectoral' character as has already been enacted, or more radically looking towards a European contract law or European Civil Code.[8] Various academic initiatives have been undertaken to construct or to start to construct sets of legal propositions which *may* form the basis of more general future legislation, the two best known being the *Principles of European Contract Law* and work of the Study Group for a European Civil Code chaired by Professor Von Bar.[9]

There has also arisen lively academic discussion as to the proper nature and function of comparative legal studies. At one end of the spectrum some scholars see in developments of the legal systems of western Europe a 'gradual convergence'; those at the other end instead argue against the possibility of any true debate between lawyers raised in different systems owing to the fundamental incommensurability of different laws (and in particular, the common law and civil law) and the different ways of thinking in different legal cultures.[10] Many comparative lawyers in Europe (of which the present writer is one) find themselves somewhere between these two pole positions: unconvinced by the idea that there is any *general* convergence, but acknowledging the presence of new points of contact and interaction between national laws, not least as a result of the work of the European Union and of the European Court of Human Rights; seeing the justice of criticisms of those who too readily see similarity between laws, ('whether at a doctrinal level or at a functional level the laws use different words or techniques but come to the same results'[11]) without looking more carefully at the wider legal institutional context in which these substantive laws function, but nevertheless seeing the comparative law enterprise as fundamentally possible and worthwhile. For, in my view, this enterprise is essentially concerned with an attempt at understanding the way in which lawyers in other legal systems see legal questions,

---

[8] Communication from the Commission to the European Parliament and Council, *A More Coherent European Contract Law: An Action Plan* Com. (2003) 68 final; EC Commission, Communication from the Commission to the European Parliament and the Council: European Contract Law and the revision of the *acquis*: the way forward (2004) Com (2004) 651 final.

[9] The Commission on European Contract Law (eds. O. Lando and H. Beale), *The Principles of European Contract Law: Parts I and II* (Kluwer, 2000); id. (eds. O. Lando, E. Clive, A. Prüm and R. Zimmermann) *The Principles of European Contract Law: Part III* (Kluwer, 2003). *Study Group on a European Civil Code*, (work in progress, which includes draft provisions on tort law, is published at <http://www.sgecc.net/>).

[10] The following works will give a sense of the debate: O. Kahn-Freund, 'On Uses and Misuses of Comparative Law' (1974) 37 *MLR* 1; R. Schlesinger, 'The Past and Future of Comparative Law' (1995) 43 *American J. Comparative Law* 477; T. Koopmans, 'Towards a new "Ius Commune" ' in B. de Witte and C. Forder (eds.), *The Common Law of Europe and the Future of Legal Education* (Deventer, 1992) 43; A. Watson, *Legal Transplants: An Approach to Comparative Law* (Univ. Georgia Press, Athens, Georgia, 2nd. edn., 1993) Chap. 4; B. Markesinis, 'Learning from Europe and Learning in Europe' in B. Markesinis (ed.), *The Gradual Convergence: Foreign ideas, Foreign Influences and English Law on the Eve of the 21st Century* (OUP, 1994) 1, esp. at 11–32; H. Patrick Glenn, 'La civilisation de la common law' [1993] *RIDC* 559; P. Legrand, 'European Legal Systems are not Converging' (1996) 45 *ICLQ* 52; R. Zimmermann, 'Savigny's Legacy, Legal History, Comparative Law and the Emergence of a European Legal Science' (1996) 112 *LQR* 576; P. Legrand, 'Against a European Civil Code' (1997) *MLR* 44; J. Bell, 'Mechanisms for Cross-fertilisation of Administrative Law in Europe' in J. Beatson and T. Tridimas (eds.), *New Directions in European Public Law* (Hart Publishing, Oxford, 1998) 147; Bell, *French Legal Cultures*, Chap. 1; E. Örücü, *The Enigma of Comparative Law: Variations on a Theme for the Twenty-first Century* (Martinus Nijhoff, Leiden, 2004) 179–202.

[11] Cf. K. Zweigert and H. Kötz, *An Introduction to Comparative Law* (OUP, 1998) 34.

attempt to resolve them, deal with the resolution of disputes, and relate legal questions to other types of question (political, economic or social). Comparative law may concern legal doctrine ('principles', rules, the significance of particular cases), legal theory, legal history; it may involve empirical work, for example, investigating the way in which different 'legal actors' behave within a system or in one part of a system. In all this, a 'foreign lawyer' (that is, someone whose first training is in a system other than the system being studied) is clearly at a considerable disadvantage, maybe knowing a little (or even quite a lot), but at risk of not knowing what he or she does *not* know; and not sharing the assumptions of, and missing many of the allusions caught by, those native to the system. On the other hand, a foreign lawyer also has a certain advantage stemming from these same characteristics: he or she can see with fresh eyes what the lawyers and others within a legal system are doing as well as saying. But comparative law necessarily requires debate, and particularly debate between lawyers from the two or more systems which are under examination where both have a certain understanding of the other. In this respect, comparative legal work does not differ fundamentally from legal work *within* any particular legal system, for lawyers brought up in the same legal system (and even having studied at the same university or working in the same professional environment) can bring considerably different ways of thinking to bear on the same legal issues (or even argue that these legal issues should not be the starting point of discussion). These differences in intellectual background, political or ideological starting point do not invalidate the debate within a legal system; they enrich it. So too, differences in ways of thinking between lawyers from other legal systems can enrich debates both as to what we would wish to be doing with our laws and how we should be doing it, issues of policy and of technique. In this respect, modern European legal systems are not 'closed systems', unaffected by external influences, whether direct or indirect, technical, political or economic—though the extent of their openness may differ significantly between each other and over time.

How then can such a comparative law dialogue be undertaken without talking at cross purposes or encountering other significant misunderstanding? At a practical level a comparative lawyer needs to attempt to understand quite a sizeable chunk of another legal system before attempting to offer comparative observations. Certainly, if one's focus of attention is a relatively contained conceptual or doctrinal question, it is all too possible to miss the ways in which the other system deals with the question or (more insidiously) miss the fact that the question is not posed or not posed in the same form in the other system and why. This is one of the reasons why undertaking comparative legal studies at an undergraduate student level is so difficult: the student often simply does not know enough about the way in which his or her *own* legal system fits together (or does not fit together) to be able to appreciate the different patterns of another system.

Secondly, though, we need to embrace the diversity of approach which different scholars can bring to the comparative law enterprise, rather than be quick to point out the limited nature of other people's investigations. There are, indeed, a number of levels at which or ways in which comparative law can be undertaken. At a first level, one can look at the legal norms themselves—the principles and rules—and see how they compare to what appear to be their counterparts; one can then look at their legal context—the other principles or rules to which they are related or with which they conflict; in both respects, one is concerned with the function or functions of the rules, either as these are attributed by those within the system or can otherwise be detected. But other scholars will be more concerned with the historical development of the law or of its institutions; with methods, styles or forms of legal reasoning; with perceptions of the law or particular laws and lawyers' mentalities, either as a matter of empirical study or by reflection upon the different language which lawyers and others use in their debates. Others will be concerned instead with legal institutions, legal proce-dures; their studies may relate to the sociology, the economics or the political thought influencing the two or more systems under consideration. Each of these elements (and no doubt a number of others) help to create a fuller picture of any legal system; but we cannot expect any single comparative legal study to undertake all of them, any more than we expect every national legal study to do so. The nature and type of study reflect the skills and intellectual taste of the student or scholar.

Having said this, it is not my purpose to attempt to expose a theory of comparative law nor to argue for a particular vision of what comparative lawyers should or should not be doing, but rather to explain my own starting point for a much more particular study. The first purpose of this book is to investigate how the law implementing two EC directives—the Product Liability Directive of 1985[12] and the Consumer Guarantees Directive of 1999—relates to and reacts with the surrounding laws of two domestic legal systems, those of England and France, and how these compare. In my view, the great advantage of undertaking a comparative study which includes within it law subject to EC legislative intervention is that it provides points of contact and ref-erence between the two systems, around which wider contrasts and comparisons can be explored. It also will allow me to offer some observations on the significance of the 'harmonisation' of law which these directives promise and on which their competence rests, not merely from the point of view of their particular provisions but more widely. On the other hand, my focus on just two legal systems is very restricted compared to comparative legal undertakings which compare or draw on the laws of western Europe, or, increasingly after enlargement of the EU, of Europe more generally.[13] The reasons for this stem in part from the limited nature of my own work, but even more from the wide range of issues which my topic requires within these two systems. This will become apparent from the way in which I shall interpret 'liability for products' and my approach to the comparison of the two laws, as it will include a good deal of the private and administrative law of liability, the relationship between criminal and civil liability and aspects of civil and criminal procedure, as well as an analysis of the sub-stantive provisions of the two European directives. In this way, I wish to use a particular topic as a way into exploring much broader features of the two legal systems.

---

[12] Dir. 1985/374/EEC (the 'Product Liability Directive' or '1985 Directive').

[13] E.g., the works undertaken under the Trento 'Common Core' of European Private Law project (directed by Professors M. Bussani and U. Mattei). The published results so far are: R. Zimmermann and S. Whittaker (eds.), *Good Faith in European Contract Law* (CUP, 2000); J. Gordley (ed.), *The Enforceability of Promises in European Contract Law* (CUP, 2001); M. Bussani and V.C. Palmer (eds.), *Pure Economic Loss in Europe* (CUP, 2003). For an account of a wide range of jurisdictions' laws on product liability see G. Howells, *Comparative Product Liability* (Dartmouth Publishing Co., 1993).

2. 'Liability for Products'

Many European lawyers would see the category of 'liability for products' (or more often 'product liability') as being a relatively new and still rather alien legal category.

For a civil lawyer, the traditions of Roman law did not identify 'liability for products' as a distinct ground of delictual liability and while the law of sale possessed in the aedilitian remedies a special set of actions in relation to defective property, this was both wider than 'product liability' (the property being of any type according to the later Romanists) and not focused on claims for damages.[14] So while French jurists wrote on the liability of manufacturers for their products from the middle of the 1950s, often inspired in doing so by the existence of the category in US law,[15] before the Product Liability Directive there was no distinct legal treatment of the category either by the Civil Code, or in the *jurisprudence* of the Cour de cassation or the Conseil d'Etat, though the former can be seen to have tailored some more general bases of liability for the particular situation of manufacturers or 'business sellers' ('*vendeurs professionnels*').[16] Instead, for reasons which I shall explain, French lawyers (both private and public) long concentrated their attention on liability for fault conceived in a myriad of ways and on liability for things, whether under private law of liability for the 'deeds of things' under article 1384 alinéa 1 of the Civil Code or in public law for 'dangerous things'.[17]

Broadly similarly, for an English common lawyer 'product liability' was first seen as a recognised type of case within the wider category of liability in the tort of negligence, and while it did and still does retain a degree of distinctiveness there, the focus of the liability is not on the state of the product, but rather on the nature of the defendant's conduct (negligent or not)[18] and the law belongs to and is affected by wider developments in the law governing that tort. In this it contrasts strikingly with US law where the famous section 402A of the *Second Restatement of the Law of Torts*[19] which sought to impose liability without negligence in respect of products has given the law a more distinctive character.[20] In both common law contexts, the core concern of 'product liability' has been the liability of the manufacturer of a product (that is, goods which a manufacturer has produced from their raw materials) for personal injuries or death; liability could be contractual (often arising under the law of sale of goods) or tortious, but in the English common law it often needed to be the latter given the absence of privity of contract between the person injured and the manufacturer in modern arrangements of production and distribution. There were (and are) a number of

---

[14] Below, p. 70.

[15] E.g. J.-F. Overstake, 'La responsabilité du fabricant de produits dangereux' 1972 *RTDCiv.* 485; H. Mazeaud, 'La responsabilité civile du vendeur-fabricant' *RTDCiv.* 1955.64.

[16] Below, pp. 84–5.   [17] Below, pp. 52–4, 118–21.

[18] Most famously, *Donoghue v Stevenson* [1932] AC 562 (referring to the liability of manufacturers or retailers of products, but not 'product liability' as such).

[19] American Law Institute (1977). This provision was replaced in 1997 with 21 separate rules.

[20] For an introduction to the US law and legal theory see: Stapleton, *Product Liability*, chaps. 4–8; J. Stapleton, 'Restatement (Third) of Torts: Products Liability, an Anglo-Australian Perspective' (1999–2000) 39 Washburn LJ 363; D. Owen, *Products Liability Law* (West, 2005); W. Page Keeton, D.G. Owen and J.E. Montgomery, *Product Liability and Safety; Cases and Materials* (Foundation Press, 3rd. edn., 1996) with supplements.

penumbral cases where 'product liability' may or may not also be said to arise. These
include cases of liability for different types of harm (notably damage to property or
pure economic loss); liability towards those other than persons within the chain of
distribution of the product ('bystanders'); and liability of persons within the chain of
distribution other than manufacturers, notably sellers or suppliers. While in English
law the involvement of a 'product' in the causing of harm cannot be said to have
constituted a distinct *legal* ground for the imposition of liability before implementation of the 1985 Directive, this was not the case in the US where its independence
was assured by its special treatment in the highly influential (if not binding) *Restatement
of Torts*.

The enactment of the EC Product Liability Directive in 1985 required the introduction into the laws of the Member States of a distinct body of law imposing liability
for certain types of harm (but principally personal injuries or death) caused by 'defective products' on certain categories of persons involved in their production and distribution. The principal purpose of the Directive was the 'approximation of the laws of
the Member States' which was 'necessary because . . . existing divergences may distort
competition and affect the movement of goods within the common market',[21] though
it also claimed that its provisions were enacted in the interests of consumer protection.[22]
The Directive clearly intended that liability should be channelled towards the producer
of the product (though it defines 'producer' to include Community importers and
own-branders as well as manufacturers), imposing liability on mere suppliers only
where they cannot identify their own supplier or the producer within a reasonable
time.[23] And so by harmonising the rules of liability in producers and suppliers it can
help to create a level playing field for them in the internal market.

However, in my view this is much too narrow a vision of 'liability for products' and
rests on assumptions which misunderstand the patterns of liability within legal systems,
as I shall explain from the particular examples of English law and French law, before
and after implementation of the 1985 Directive.[24] For the way in which liability is
channelled within a legal system is a function of two issues in particular: the relative
attractiveness of suing one or other potential defendant and the means of recourse and
basis of apportionment of liability available between potential defendants.

(a) The relative attractiveness of claiming against different defendants

In some types of case involving products, one or more persons other than their
manufacturer or supplier may be liable for the harm suffered by a claimant, whether or
not the involvement of the product is formally significant in the imposition of that
liability. The relative attractiveness of claiming against one or other of these various
potential defendants is an important factor in determining where liability will *first* fall,
for while in both the English and French systems a claimant *may* be able to sue more

---

[21] Recital 1.   [22] Below, pp. 438–9.
[23] Art. 3. And see below, p. 443. Case C-52/00, paras. 36–40 where the ECJ held that French implementing legislation which imposed liability on suppliers without such a possibility of escape to be in breach
of the Directive.   [24] See further Chap. 18 below.

than one defendant in the same litigation,[25] this both complicates the case (factually and legally) and risks increasing its costs. For this purpose, the relative attractiveness to a claimant of one defendant over another is a function of a number of factors, but these can be grouped together in terms of the difficulty of establishing the fundamental basis of liability (does it require proof of fault or negligence, establishing the 'defectiveness' of the product or is liability fully strict?), the particular application of its incidental rules on the facts (for example, does it allow a defence of contributory negligence in the claimant or has its limitation period expired?) and the question whether or not the defendant is able to pay any award which the court makes (whether as a matter of the defendant's own resources or insurance). Where a claimant has a sound claim against a particular defendant who is able to pay, then he or she does not need to address the question whether any other person is also liable, but can leave this to that defendant's own recourse, whether within the same proceedings by that defendant's joining that other person or in subsequent proceedings.[26] A claimant is not concerned with whether or not liability is channelled onto a product's 'producer', but simply with achieving full compensation. Even where a claimant sues two or more defendants (one being the 'producer'), and all are held liable to him jointly in respect of the harm, the question who bears the cost of this liability *as between* these unsuccessful defendants remains open: it may fall at least in part on the producer, but it may not.[27]

This means that, in order to assess whether or not the Product Liability Directive is successful in its aim of channelling liability on the legal basis which it specifies onto 'producers' in the interests of fair competition, one needs to examine the full range of persons who may be liable for harm caused by products and seek to track the course or courses of claims which are likely to be made, and establish the wider patterns of liability. Clearly, this may include possible defendants within the chain of distribution of products who may be liable on other grounds apart from those prescribed by the Directive itself. Of these, sellers of products are clearly of particular significance, whether or not they have sold the product directly to the claimant, but a number of other contractual suppliers or providers of products may be liable for the harm which they cause (notably, hirers of goods, landlords or other occupiers of premises, and employers) as may those who have put some intellectual or physical input into the product but who are neither producer or supplier (such as designers or repairers).

However, for the purpose of establishing the patterns of liability, three other categories of defendant must be included within the investigation of 'liability for products' who do not often appear within the traditional *dramatis personae* of 'product liability': those who own or use products, the public suppliers of products and the public regulators of products.

The liability of those who own or use products is particularly prominent in French law as it has attracted distinct legal categories of liability in both private and public law. In French private law, this liability centres on the famous general liability for the 'deeds of things'.[28] This strict liability, constructed by the courts in the first half of the

---

[25] See below, pp. 547–8, 558. In the French system, there is an important exception where one defendant's liability is a matter for the ordinary courts and the other's is for the administrative courts, below, p. 320.
[26] Below, pp. 547–8, 558.   [27] Below, pp. 33–4, 172–3, 546–53, 557–63.
[28] Below, p. 51–61.

twentieth century at the suggestion of *la doctrine* from a very unpromising provision of the Civil Code,[29] is imposed on the 'thing's' *gardien*, technically a person with its 'use, direction or control' but often its owner.[30] Surprisingly, there are very few restrictions on the types of things which attract this liability: all physical movables and immovables are included, and no distinction is made as to whether or not the thing is dangerous or defective.[31] The main spur and for long the typical example of this was the liability of car owners or drivers for the 'deeds' of their vehicles, its typical nature only being qualified when in 1985 legislation made liability even stricter than is the case as regards other 'things'.[32] What this means is that where a person is injured in a motor vehicle accident, he or she is likely to be best advised to claim damages from its driver as *gardien* of the vehicle, rather than entering the question whether or not the vehicle was 'defective' and therefore whether any claim should instead or also be brought against the car's manufacturer. This liability for the 'deeds of things' has remained very wide and has had (and continues to have after implementation of the Product Liability Directive) a very important effect on the channelling of liability in respect of defective products.

French administrative law does not possess a general 'liability for the deeds of things' which matches that recognised by the ordinary courts as a matter of private law, but it has recognised special and strict liabilities which arise from the use and/or supply of products, which are attractive from the point of view of a claimant and which therefore can vie successfully with liabilities of producers under the 1985 Directive. Of these, two have been prominent: the liabilities imposed for harm caused by particular examples of dangerous things (though the liability also extends to liability for some dangerous activities and is not as important in practice as at first sight appears) and liability arising from 'public works' (*travaux publics*).[33] Where these liabilities apply, a claimant is likely to prefer to claim damages against the defendant designated by administrative law (who may or may not be a public body) before the administrative courts, rather than against the person potentially liable under the legislation implementing the Product Liability Directive.

By contrast with the French public and private laws, apart from under the law of sale and related contracts which remain constrained by privity, English law has recognised relatively few situations where a claimant injured by an allegedly defective product would generally prefer to sue someone other than its manufacturer, this reflecting its increasingly exclusive reliance on the tort of negligence to deal with claims for death, personal injury and damage to property.[34] An English victim of a product might well, therefore, need to claim against a 'producer' of the product as long as he or she can satisfy the conditions of liability imposed by the 1985 Directive.

Secondly, public bodies (or others on their behalf) may supply or put at a citizen's disposal particular types of products as part of a public service. The public nature of this supply *may* attract special public rules of liability, distinct from those applicable to producers in the commercial sector; even where it does not and the ordinary rules (of 'private law') apply, the public nature of the supply may nevertheless have an incidental

---

[29] Art. 1384 al. 1 C. civ.   [30] Below, pp. 52–4.   [31] Below, p. 27 but cf. pp. 54, 56–7.
[32] Below, pp. 60–1.   [33] Below, pp. 118–21, 121–31.   [34] Below, pp. 162–3, Chap. 9.

effect on liability.[35] I shall look at how the public nature of a service understood in a broad and non-technical sense may impact on liability for products, looking at this problem generally and at the examples of the supply of public utilities, transport and health care.

This public dimension to the law of liability for products is even more overtly reflected in the third category of person who can be liable for harm caused by products, that is, public regulators of product safety. For in both English and French law, public authorities have come to play a considerable role in the policing of the safety of products produced or supplied by others. In order to do so, they possess broad powers to regulate the attributes of products, to prosecute those who supply unsafe products, to order unsafe products off the market and even to prevent unsafe products from coming onto the market, some of these powers finding their origins in European legislation concerning the safety of products, whether general or particular.[36] From the point of view of the ability to pay, a public authority is a very attractive defendant, but can a public authority be liable to a person injured by a product on the ground of its regulatory failure? Here, English and French law appear to give very different responses, the English being generally hostile to such claims, the French apparently much more open,[37] but the real position is more complex as the English law is controversial and unsettled and in French law there are a number of factors which militate against the actual imposition of liability in a public authority in this sort of context.[38]

(b) Recourse between potential defendants

In neither French nor English law does liability necessarily rest with any defendant first sued, nor, indeed, is a claimant necessarily restricted to claiming against a single, most attractive defendant. So the second major element of the way in which (or the extent to which) liability is channelled within the French and English laws concerns the existence of means of recourse between potential defendants and the basis of the allocation of their responsibility. Where a case would attract liability under the Product Liability Directive but a claimant prefers to sue another defendant (the 'first defendant') on some other ground, to what extent does liability stick with this defendant or will it instead flow on, channelled towards those whom the Directive designates as producers? As I shall explain, the answer to this question differs significantly in French and English law and, moreover, within each system depends in part on whether or not the first defendant is within the contractual chain of distribution, on the legal ground on which liability is imposed and (in the case of French law) on whether the liability is private or administrative.[39] Overall, the channelling of liability in cases of allegedly defective products is a function of a complex of factors, many of which do not rest on any feature of the rules set for producers and the other defendants envisaged by the 1985 Directive itself.

It will be seen, therefore, why this work has been entitled 'liability for products' rather than 'product liability': for while 'product liability' suggests concern with the

---

[35] Below, Chaps. 7, 11. [36] Below, pp. 307–10, 334–5, 370–1, 405–7.
[37] Below, pp. 310–11, 315–19, Chap. 13. [38] Below, pp. 319–25, 168–9, Chap. 13.
[39] Below, Chap 19.

liabilities of those within the chain of production and distribution, my concern is much wider and encompasses all those who may be liable in respect of harm caused by products. It will also be clear why my explanation of the laws of England and France, which form the setting into which this legislation implementing the Product Liability Directive falls and to which it relates, must include administrative as well as private law.

3. Broadening the Investigation Further

However, in my view, there are four further important features of the setting within which liability for products so understood must be set: the relationship between criminal responsibility and civil liability and the role of the criminal process; the significance of key differences in the French and English *civil* processes when deciding important substantive issues; the relationship of the Consumer Guarantees Directive of 1999 to questions of liability for products; and the characteristics of the processes by which the two EC directives have been implemented in France and England.

First, the relationship between criminal responsibility and civil liability has been particularly important in the French context in two ways: in part because of the direct relationship between the substantive criminal law affecting the manufacture and supply of unsafe products and the imposition of liability to persons injured by them; and, in part because of the practical and indeed sociological importance of the criminal process in the investigation and adjudication of claims for compensation of people injured by products.[40] The importance of the criminal process to liability for products (and in other situations of recovery of personal injury and death) stems from a complex and heady mix of elements, including the breadth of civil liability for fault provided by the Civil Code; the power of victims of criminal offences to trigger the judicial investigation of alleged criminal offences and then, if proceedings continue, to be involved in the criminal trial as a party to the proceedings; and the extensive powers of investigating magistrates (the *juges d'instruction*), particularly when compared to the relatively restricted evidence which may be summoned to civil courts.[41] Moreover, the role of the criminal courts in the investigation, characterisation and award of compensation for crimes involving defective products became very prominent in France in the course of the 1990s in the *affaire du sang contaminé*, in the course of which various public health officials and, ultimately, the prime minister and two other government ministers were charged with offences relating to the public supply of blood products infected with HIV which caused the death of many haemophiliacs and others who received them.[42] Quite apart from the political fallout of this prominent *affaire*, it led directly to a change in the Constitution of the Fifth Republic;[43] affected legislation attempting to change the basis on which public officers could be made criminally liable for acts done in the performance of their duties;[44] had a major influence on the *jurisprudence* of both the civil and administrative courts

---

[40] Below, Chap. 14.   [41] Ibid.   [42] Below, pp. 394–401.   [43] Below, p. 399.
[44] Below, pp. 388–93.

concerning liability for products;[45] and created a very difficult climate for implementation of the Product Liability Directive.[46] Indeed, it would not be going too far to say
that the echoes of this *affaire* can still be heard in any French discussion of liability
(civil, criminal or administrative) in respect of products.

The contrast here with English law is very striking, for there one looks in vain for any
significant connection between the very extensive criminal offences relating to the production, supply or use of unsafe products and the imposition of civil liability.[47] And
while in theory it is possible for a victim of a product to gain compensation from an
English criminal court as part of the criminal process, in fact this rarely occurs, except
in the least serious of cases.[48] This is to be explained by reference to a complex of factors: the absence of general criminal offences of negligent causing of death or personal
injuries; the lack of any necessary doctrinal connection between criminal and civil
liability; the absence of a direct role for the victims of crime in the criminal process; and
the restrained powers of relevant courts to award compensation coupled with a judicial
perception that awards of damages are essentially a matter for the civil courts.[49]

This involvement of the criminal process and institutions as well as the substantive
criminal law in my depiction of liability for products led me back to assess the impact
of features of the civil processes in French and then in English law on key aspects of
civil liability for products; and so certain characteristics of the civil processes provide
the second further feature of the setting into which I wish to place liability for products. Of course, there are a number of ways in which the civil procedure may impact
on issues of liability for products, including questions relating to the financing of
access to justice and to special arrangements for the disposal of group claims where a
number of persons have suffered injury or death caused by the same category of product: these are important issues but for reasons of space are not pursued here.[50] My
concern is rather with how the civil processes of France and England differ in their
approach to the determination of such key issues as 'fault', 'negligence' or 'defect', these
approaches stemming from the nature of the civil process itself, the relative roles of the
parties and the court in relation to evidence (and the range of evidence available), and
the finality or otherwise of decisions made by lower courts. Issues such as these are
neither simply factual nor purely legal and in English law are thereby sometimes
termed rather weakly 'mixed' questions of fact and law, but they have in common that
they require the court to make an assessment or an evaluation (caught nicely in the
French term, *une appréciation*) as to whether or not a certain normative standard has
been reached. In my view, these differences in the processes by which decisions are
reached can have profound effects on the quality and nature of the substantive decision reached by a court, so that even where a French and an English court purport
to apply an identical ('completely harmonised') legal test of liability as set out in
European legislation, their decisions may well differ on apparently identical facts.[51]

---

[45] Below, pp. 149–51, 315–19, 324.   [46] Below, pp. 454–5, 457–8.   [47] Below, Chap. 15.
[48] Ibid.   [49] Below, pp. 403–4.
[50] For a comparison in the French and English context: Taylor, *Harmonisation communautaire*, 174–81.
[51] There is a further difficulty here, as a significant difference between the two systems is that the range
of evidence before a court available for deciding an issue of fact (and therefore, in a sense, the facts themselves) is different: below pp. 46–50, 208–14. The importance of differences in civil process in the practical
impact of the EC Product Liability Directive (in particular in contrast with product liability in the US) is

Moreover, the European Court of Justice is not likely to see it as its role to resolve such divergences in the substantive impact of even perfectly harmonised rules of liability: for while the European Court would be willing to interpret the criteria of normative standards (such as 'defect' in product liability) set by European legislation, it is likely to see issues of their application as ones of fact for the evaluation of the courts of Member States.[52] Furthermore, in principle the European Court accepts that questions of civil procedure are for the laws of Member States, this sometimes being elevated to a 'principle of procedural autonomy' of the Member States,[53] though the Court has on occasion made inroads into this 'autonomy' when this is justified by particular legislation and Community principle.[54] To the extent to which an issue is treated as one of fact or of judicial evaluation, there is no room for harmonisation: laws can be harmonised, legal concepts can be subjected to 'autonomous' interpretations, but facts and their legal significance remain fundamentally particular and therefore local.

The third further feature of the wider setting of liability for products concerns the role of the Consumer Guarantees Directive of 1999, the second directive whose implementation is the subject of this study.[55] Indeed, this directive could even be seen as the contractual counterpart of the extra-contractual Product Liability Directive, though the latter does not classify the liability which it requires Member States to impose according to the Gaian scheme. Both directives require the creation of legislation which imposes 'liability' on suppliers of movable physical things ('goods' under the 1999 Directive, 'products' under the 1985 Directive) when they fail to attain a composite standard either of safety (the 1985 Directive) or quality and fitness for purpose (the 1999 Directive[56]) and both make important provision for the timescale within which any claim must be brought. On the other hand, as I shall explain, there are very important differences between the two directives: in their degree of purported harmonisation; in the 1985 Directive's concern with the safety of products in contrast to the 1999 Directive's concern with the quality or fitness of goods; in the 1999 Directive's restriction to the protection of consumers, whereas the 1985 Directive protects all those injured or killed by unsafe products; and especially in the remedial expression of the 'liabilities' which the two directives create.[57] For, as to the last of these, while the 1985 Directive is concerned only with liability in damages to compensate a claimant for personal injuries, death or (in certain quite narrow circumstances) damage to property, the 1999 Directive does *not* require the imposition of liability in damages, but instead creates an elaborate hierarchy of other rights against sellers of goods: rights to repair or replacement, price reduction, and rescission and

noted by M. Reimann, 'Product Liability in a Global Context: the Hollow Victory of the European Model' (2003) 11 *ERPL* 128, 151–53.

[52] Below, pp. 492–4.

[53] E.g. *R (on the application of Delena Wells) v Secretary of State for Transport, Local Government and the Regions* Case C-201/02 [2004] ECR, at para. 65.

[54] E.g. *Océano Grupo Editorial SA v Murciano Quintero* (Joined Cases C-240/98 to C-244/98) [2000] ECR I-4941 where the ECJ held that a national court was entitled to raise the question of the unfairness of a term in a consumer contract of its own initiative; *Cofidis SA v Jean-Louis Fredout* Case C-473/00 [2002] ECR I-10875.   [55] Below, Chap. 19.

[56] 'Contractual conformity' is rather wider than this description indicates: see below, pp. 591–604.

[57] Below, pp. 481, 502, 566–73, 591–2.

restitution. While in a certain sense both directives arise from a general sense of a need to protect consumers in relation to products, the nature of the interests which they are concerned to protect and the way in which they are protected are very different. In this way, the Consumer Guarantees Directive provides a counterpoint to the Product Liability Directive.

However, ironically, one of these differences between the two directives coupled with the understandable concern of national legislators to preserve a certain consistency of treatment and coherence of regulation within their laws after implementation leads to the potential for a direct clash between them. For while the Product Liability Directive has been held by the European Court to require the creation of a 'completely harmonised' set of rules governing liability for products (in the way which it circumscribes this notion),[58] the Consumer Guarantees Directive allows the retention or creation of greater protection for consumers.[59] Given the limited nature of the remedies which the Consumer Guarantees Directive requires by contrast to those already provided by many Member States (and notably by existing English and French law), a Member State may prefer to implement the Consumer Guarantees Directive either by amending its existing law governing liability for qualitative defects in the sale of goods (and thereby incidentally changing the ambit of liability *in damages* for these defects) or by overhauling its law governing liability in contracts of sale (and possibly other related contracts) more generally, using the Directive to set the basis of liability ('contractual non-conformity') but adding to and/or 'improving' the remedies for a defendant's failure to reach this standard for the benefit of *all* categories of buyer—private, commercial or consumer. As I shall explain, the former was the route adopted by the English legislator in implementing the 1999 Directive, thereby creating fairly marginal changes to the incidence of liability in damages for the benefit of consumers.[60] In France, by contrast, there was a dispute as to whether the 1999 Directive should be implemented by reforming the law of sale contained in the Civil Code or instead by merely creating another set of rights for consumers of goods in the *Code de la consommation*. This dispute is revealing of a number of characteristics of the French legal scene, not least the conflicting attitudes towards European influences on private law and the proper functions of modern contract law. While France finally took a minimalist approach in its *loi* of 9 December 2004 to implementing the 1999 Directive in the *Code de la consommation* with only an apparently very minor amendment of the period in which rights must be exercised under the law of sale, the surrounding French juristic debate shows how a wider and apparently permitted implementation of the 1999 Directive could make practical nonsense of the 'completely harmonised' character of the 1985 Directive.[61] For while the European Court of Justice has held that it is wrong for a Member State to impose liability for defective products on their 'supplier' beyond the conditions which the 1985 Directive sets, it expressly allowed the maintenance or even the creation of contractual liabilities 'such as liability for latent defects' under the law of sale.[62] This suggests that the uniformity required by the 1985 Directive is not merely partial (as the Directive itself concedes) but is also essentially

---

[58] European Court decisions of 2002, below, pp. 440–4.   [59] Below, p. 568.
[60] Below, pp. 583–8.   [61] Below, pp. 574–83.   [62] Below, pp. 441–3.

formal, since a Member State remains entitled to impose liability in damages on persons coming within the Directive's ambit as long as they are called something else and the 'legal ground' of their liability is described in a different way. Such an artificial distinction undermines the justification given by the European Court for its view that the 1985 Directive creates a uniform law, for this rested on the economic effects of divergences in rules of liability in terms of distorting competition and impeding the free movement of goods between Member States:[63] such economic considerations cannot rest on differences of classification or formal legal differences in the basis of liability, but on the practical effects which these rules have on the costs of liability to producers and suppliers in fact caught by its provisions. But it shows that while the Product Liability and Consumer Guarantees Directives themselves are concerned with different subject matters, their implementation in the laws of the Member States may be interrelated. While the 1985 Directive seeks to impose a 'completely harmonious' scheme of liability within its domain, and the 1999 Directive merely minimal requirements, the potential for substantive conflict remains.

What all this means is that the present work is concerned with many issues which are not usually seen as bearing directly on product liability as it is generally understood. In my view, though, the laws surrounding these two directives offer an opportunity to explore and compare a number of different areas of liability in the two systems and to attempt an explanation of their complex interrelationship. For in undertaking the research for this book, I have been very much struck by the extent to which apparently disparate areas of the law relate to as well as contrast with each other; and the extent to which the relationships differ as between the French and English systems. To many continental civil lawyers in particular, this observation may seem axiomatic as regards private law, coming as they do from legal traditions which see private law as a genuine legal category, given unity and integrity in modern times by the Civil Codes; but it is much less so as regards the relationship between administrative and civil liability, and particularly as regards French law where public and private appear so sharply divided. And while ancient common law saw profound connections between its laws of crime and torts, the modern English lawyer generally sees very much fewer connections between criminal and civil liability than does the French lawyer and certainly does not see the criminal law or the criminal process as major factors in the allocation of compensation of death, personal injuries or damage to property caused.

4. The Limits of the Study

On the other hand, this study does not deal with a number of things which it could usefully have included, quite apart from those already indicated in relation to the certain procedural aspects of liability for products. Of these, five are prominent.

First, it is primarily concerned with liability for movable products and while at times this does require consideration of liabilities imposed in respect of buildings, my

---

[63] Below, p. 441.

concern is to explain how these affect the channelling of liability for movable products rather than in their own right. Secondly, while I am concerned with civil liability for defects of quality or function as well as defects of safety in the two systems, my explorations of the relationship of civil and criminal liability and of civil and administrative liability are restricted to defects of safety. This is in part because it is here that these relationships are most interesting, but it is also necessary owing to considerations of space. Thirdly, and for the same reason, I do not include discussion of two very important areas which impact practically on the burden of liability on producers and suppliers: the quantification of damages and their general relationship to social security payments.[64] Fourthly, while I shall look at the proper interpretation of the two directives under consideration, I shall not look at questions of their interpretation or application raised outside the contexts of the French or English systems (or published in French or English). For while I am concerned with the way in which the European Court of Justice is likely to interpret these directives, I am primarily concerned with their impact on the laws of these two Member States: this book is not intended to be a comprehensive exposition of the considerable literature or national case law on these two directives and their implementation in Europe. Fifthly, this is not a theoretical work in the sense of being primarily concerned with theories of the fundamental functions of the law of liability, whether tortious or contractual (for example, the attribution of moral responsibility, the achievement of compensation or economic deterrence); nor am I concerned with the reasons why a legal system should choose to impose 'liability for fault' or 'strict liability' in this or that context, though I shall refer from time to time to the justifications advanced by courts or writers for their views as to the interpretation or future direction of the law.

5. The Structure of the Work and its Treatment of the Material

The present work is divided into five parts. Within the first part, I shall look at considerable length at the way in which the two systems impose liability in respect of the manufacture, supply or use of products (whether classified as belonging to private or to administrative law) *apart from* their laws implementing the two directives, setting out first the French position (Chapters 2 to 7) and then the English (Chapters 8 to 11); the second part concerns liability in the administration in respect of failures to regulate or control product safety in French law (Chapter 12) and in English law (Chapter 13); the third part, the relationship of criminal responsibility for product safety and compensation in French law (Chapter 14) and then in English law (Chapter 15).

In all this, I shall first expose and explain the position in French law and then explain the position in English law, at this second stage drawing comparisons between the two systems as I do so. Having set out the law's general approaches to the area in question, whenever possible I shall use a particular case or two as the context for

---

[64] For a recent comparative study of awards of damages see L. Reiss, *Le juge et le préjudice: Etude comparée des droits francais et anglais* (P.U. d'Aix-Marseille, 2003).

elucidation of the points which I have to make, hoping that by doing so I shall also give a sense of the feel of the legal argumentation and the nature of the process in the two systems. As regards the French law, the same set of facts come up again and again, the *affaire du sang contaminé* finding expression in the civil, criminal and administrative courts.[65] My general approach in these discussions is that I do not assume any specialist knowledge on the part of the reader, nor make any assumption that he or she comes from an English (or common law) or French (or civil law) background. One consequence of this is that either an English or a French lawyer may at times consider that some of the points which I shall make are somewhat elementary; but elementary or not, they need to be made in order to depict the full picture and set up the means of making the comparison.

In the fourth part of the work, I shall look at the Product Liability Directive and Consumer Guarantees Directive and how they relate to English and French law. In Chapter 16, I shall look first at the creation of the Product Liability Directive, at its review at the European level; at its crucial interpretation by the European Court in 2002 as creating a 'completely harmonious' scheme of liability; at the processes and difficulties of its implementation in French and English law. In the following chapter (Chapter 17) I shall look further at the significance of its provisions in the light of the jurisprudence of the European Court and from the points of view of English and French lawyers, and in Chapter 18, I shall seek to explain how the implementation of this Directive has affected the patterns of liability in the two laws. In Chapter 19 I shall look at the Consumer Guarantees Directive, comparing it to the Product Liability Directive and explaining the difficulties of its implementation in French and English law. In the final part (Part V, Chapter 20) of the work, I shall offer more general conclusions to the work as a whole in terms of the relationships between the broad bodies of law under consideration and any lessons to be drawn for the harmonisation of laws in Europe.

[65] Below, pp. 149–51, 315–19, 324, 394–401.

PART I

CIVIL LIABILITY IN RESPECT OF THE MANUFACTURE, SUPPLY OR USE OF PRODUCTS APART FROM IMPLEMENTATION OF THE EC DIRECTIVES

2

Introduction to the Private and Public Laws of Liability in France

French law is famous for the sharpness with which it draws the distinction between private law and public (and particularly administrative) law, revealed at the level of the courts' jurisdiction, as well as at the levels of substantive law and legal procedure.[1] For, the jurisdictional divide between the 'ordinary courts' (the *ordre judiciaire*, at the apex of which is the Cour de cassation) and the administrative courts (the *ordre administratif*, at the apex of which is the Conseil d'Etat) has made it necessary for French lawyers to construct criteria for the distribution of cases between the 'civil' and 'administrative'. In general, French law allocates cases between these two jurisdictions by reference to the criterion of the relationship of the defendant's activities to the 'public service' (*le service public*), the courts combining for this purpose both institutional elements (whether or not a party is a public body) and functional elements, that is the relation of a party's activities to the 'public service' itself.[2] However, in other cases, either special legislation or the courts have constructed particular rules for the allocation of cases between the two jurisdictions which do not conform to these general criteria, for example, in relation to motor vehicle accidents or harm caused by 'public works'.[3] While the jurisdictional allocation of cases typically also determines the substantive law to be applied to the case, this is not universally true[4] and exceptionally the ordinary courts apply administrative legal principle to the cases before them, as in the case of liability in respect of the *police judiciaire*.[5]

The French law of liability demonstrates many of the key features of this wider division between administrative and civil, public and private. Indeed, the *arrêt Blanco* of 1873,[6] which established the distinct and separate ('autonomous') nature of administrative law did so in this very context; but the fact that *Blanco* involved a traffic accident, whose perpetrator was a member of the administration acting in the course

---

[1] See generally, Brown and Bell, Chap. 3; Bell, Boyron and Whittaker, chap. 2; J. Allison, *A Continental Distinction in the Common Law—A Historical and Comparative Perspective on English Public Law* (revised edn., OUP, 1996).

[2] See further Brown and Bell, Chap. 6 and esp. 129–35; Gaudemet, *Droit administratif*, Tome 1, 390 referring to *le service public* as the general criterion, but explaining the nuances of the modern law. See further Chapus, *Droit administratif général*, Tome 1, 3–6; and the key work by J. Rivero, 'Existe-t-il un critère du droit administratif?' (1953) RDP 279.   [3] See below, pp. 115, 121–31 respectively.

[4] Chapus, *Droit administratif général*, Tome 1, 764–6.

[5] Civ. (1) 10 Jun. 1986, *cons. Pourcel*, JCP 1986.II.20683 rapp. P. Sargos.

[6] TC 8 Feb. 1873, DP 1873.3.17.

of his duties, also shows that some of the cases which have attracted the jurisdiction of the administrative courts and the application of administrative law do not involve the exercise of special public powers or consideration of the legitimacy of administrative action. This means that some factually similar categories of case have stretched across the public and private jurisdictions, and have led to different applicable rules and results, as in the case of medical liability, road accidents and accidents on another person's property.[7] Sometimes, these substantive differences result from a different vision in the Conseil d'Etat as to the relevant principles or considerations to be applied in the public context, for example, as regards medical liability where for long it imposed liability only on the ground of *faute lourde* ('gross fault') when the ordinary courts imposed liability on the ground of *faute simple* ('ordinary fault').[8] However, the differences go deeper than the level of substantive legal argument, for not merely do administrative judges reject the regimes of liability provided by the Civil Code: there remains a genuine intellectual and cultural divide between public and private *lawyers* in France, perpetuated both by the training and career paths of judges and by the interests and teaching practices of university jurists.[9]

Having said this, differences between the two sets of rules of civil liability should not be exaggerated. So while it is true that the Civil Code does not govern administrative liability, in the absence of such a code and, indeed of much legislation, the administrative courts are sometimes 'inspired' by the rules or ideas of private law. This is universally acknowledged as regards the administrative law of contract, where the core ideas of private law are qualified or recast according to the perceived needs of the public interest;[10] conversely, some jurists have seen the private law of contract as having undergone a process of 'publicisation'.[11] The connections between private and public law are less widely acknowledged as regards administrative extra-contractual liability.[12] In some cases, it is true, the connections are direct and obvious, for example, in the developments in medical liability before it was placed (or apparently placed) on a unified basis.[13] Moreover, since the closing years of the nineteenth century, private and public lawyers have taken as their starting point an assumption that in general 'fault' is the foundation of liability for harm, but that exceptions should be made, in particular on the ground that the defendant's action or activities created a special risk: in both regimes of liability, liabilities are based on *la faute*, some arise *sans faute*. However, this similarity in fundamental approach can itself be misleading as the understanding of what constitutes 'fault' changes significantly under the two regimes

---

[7] Below, pp. 144–55; 33, 60–1, 115; 111, 126–7.   [8] Below, pp. 144–5.

[9] Bell, *Legal Cultures*, 37–42; 46–8.

[10] Richer, *Droit des contrats administratifs*, 25–6, below, p. 33.

[11] L. Josserand, 'La "Publicisation" du Contrat' in *Recueil d'Etudes en l'honneur d'Edouard Lambert* (Paris, 1938) Tome 3, 143 and below, p. 23.

[12] 'Extra-contractual liability' here typically refers to what in private law would be delictual liability, but it also includes a rather restrained body of law governing cases which in private law would attract liability under one of the *quasi-contrats* or *enrichissement sans cause*.

[13] See below, pp. 140–6, 150–1. Another example can be found in the influence of the administrative treatment of liability for the harm caused by escaped mental patients in CE Sect. 3 Feb. 1956, *Thouzellier*, Leb. 49, D 1956.596 note J.-M. Auby on the acceptance of a general principle of liability for another's deeds in Ass. plén. 29 Mar.1991, *Blieck*, D 1991.324 note Larroumet, JCP 1991.II.21673 conc. Dottenwille.

and with it, of course, the understanding of liability 'without fault'.[14] So while 'illegality' is equated with 'fault' by both the administrative and the ordinary courts, the 'illegality' in question differs, the administrative lawyer's understanding resting on breach of administrative principle, the civil lawyer's on breach of duty and criminality.[15] Moreover, while the Civil Code boldly declares that 'fault causing harm attracts liability' and private lawyers assert that any type of fault will do, administrative law is more circumspect, setting out the situations where different degrees of fault will give rise to liability.[16] Similarly, while the ordinary courts had to rely on radical interpretations of the Code itself in order to give effect to liability for risk,[17] the Conseil d'Etat could use the idea 'neat', but also go beyond it, constructing an original law of liabilities *sans faute* based on more specifically public ideas, such as the need to preserve the 'equality of public burdens'.[18] As a result, while lines are drawn between liability for fault and without fault in both regimes, these categories mean different things and the lines between them are drawn in different places and, sometimes, for different reasons.

In the remainder of this chapter, I shall outline the very basic features of the regimes of liability, note the influence of liability insurance in their development and outline how insurers and others who pay compensation to primary claimants may themselves have a claim for an indemnity in respect of these payments. As I have explained, these latter features are important in forming an understanding of how liability is channelled in the system.

1. The Private Law

(a) Contract

The Civil Code's provisions on the law of contract and delict represent a triumph of the generalising tendency of the natural lawyer Romanists of the previous two centuries.[19] So, the Code declares that 'a contract is an agreement by which one or more persons undertake obligations to one or more others, to transfer property, to do or not to do something'.[20] Contractual obligation was founded on simple agreement and, unlike its Roman antecedents, there was no need for an agreement to be reduced to any special form or to fall into any substantive category of contract before it would be enforced. In the course of the nineteenth century, the rationale for this consensual basis of contractual obligation was referred to by French jurists as the 'autonomy of the will'[21] and this idea soon became the dogmatic starting point of discussion for contractual problems. While English discussions of the 'meeting of minds' and the importance of intention in the formation of contracts may be thought of as similar,

---

[14] See below, pp. 40–50, 311–15.   [15] Below, pp. 45–6, 313–4.
[16] Below, pp. 30–2, 311–15.   [17] Below, pp. 24–7.   [18] Below, pp. 32, 119–21.
[19] Notably, Jean de Domat, *Les lois civiles dans leur ordre naturel* (ed. de Héricourt), Paris, 1715) and Pothier, *Obligations;* and see Zimmermann, *Obligations*, 544–5; J. Gordley, *The Philosophical Origins of Modern Contract Doctrine* (OUP, 1991) 217 *et seq.*   [20] Art. 1101 C. civ.
[21] V. Ranouil, *L'autonomie de la volonté, Naissance et évolution d'un concept* (PUF, Paris, 1980).

indeed, historically related to the French approach,[22] French lawyers took and have continued to take the parties' intention seriously, preferring to keep to the 'subjective' intentions of the parties and taking remarkably broad approaches to pre-contractual 'defects in consent,' such as improper pressure (*violence*) or mistake (*erreur*).[23] Nevertheless, general statements on the centrality of party autonomy must be qualified in at least two ways, both of which are reflected in the treatment by the courts of the problems of liability for products.

First, drawing on the legacy of the Roman nominate contracts, the draftsmen of the Code set out rules which describe the normal legal incidents of a number of important, typical contracts, notably, sale, hire, partnership and agency.[24] As article 1135 explains, 'agreements obligate a party not only as to what is there expressed, but also to all the consequences which equity, custom or the law give to the obligation according to its nature'. For the most part the provisions governing 'special' contracts were understood as being susceptible to contrary agreement (*lois supplétives*), but in the modern law there is an increasing tendency, felt particularly in the context of liability for defective products, for the courts to find some means to prevent their exclusion by the parties (thereby awarding them the status of *lois impératives*).[25] Moreover, French lawyers have gone beyond the categories which they found in the Code, sometimes sub-dividing them (for example 'medical contracts', which are special examples of *louage d'ouvrage*), sometimes creating new categories which cut across the old ones (for example contracts relating to the supply and setting up of a computer system).

Secondly, the courts have developed various ways of regulating the relationship of contractors which can be justified only rather remotely from the Code and are at most only tenuously related to the parties' agreement. Two examples of this, both of which have been significant in the context of liability for products, are obligations to inform, advise and warn the other party (*obligations d'information ou de renseignement*) and obligations concerning the safety of the other party to the contract or his property (*obligations de sécurité*).[26] An example of the former may be found in the obligation of a trader to advise his customers of the uses and capabilities of the products which he offers for sale.[27] Obligations concerning the safety of the other party have a wider compass and include ones on fairground-keepers or restaurants to their customers, doctors to their patients, and carriers to their passengers.[28] The effect of these contractual obligations as to safety is sometimes to impose liability for fault (here meaning lack of care) and sometimes without fault, this turning on whether the obligation is held to be *de moyens* or *de résultat*.[29] With this background, it is not surprising that when French courts sought an established mechanism by which to 'implement' the Product Liability Directive after ten years of legislative inaction, it was to *obligations de sécurité* which they turned.[30]

---

[22] Nicholas, 32–6.   [23] Below, p. 64.   [24] Nicholas, 33–4.   [25] Below, pp. 93–5, 105.
[26] Below, pp. 64–9 and 28, 72, 100, respectively.   [27] Below, pp. 68–9.
[28] Civ. 12 Feb. 1975, JCP 1975.II.18179 note Viney; Civ. 20 May 1936, DP 1936.1.88 rapp. Josserand, concl. Matter (though see below, p. 152); Paris 9 Feb. 1968, JCP 1968.II.15653 note R. Prieur and Civ. 21 Nov. 1911, S 1912.1.73 note Lyon-Caen, D 1913.1.249 note Sarrut, respectively.
[29] Below, pp. 100–1.   [30] Below, pp. 72, 455–7, 461–2.

These general developments of contract law have at times been justified by reference to the implied intentions of the parties to the contract, to the requirements of equity in the circumstances or to contractual good faith.[31] However, more straightforwardly, they have been recognised as simply being the result of the courts' view of the proper regulation of the contractual relationship which the parties have created,[32] and while they have suffered their share of juristic criticism (particularly owing to their lack of substantial textual support), most modern jurists recognize the useful purpose they play, sometimes in enabling a victim of personal injuries to avoid the need to prove fault and sometimes protecting a defendant from liability without fault. Indeed, since the middle of the twentieth century, these developments, taken together with special legislation governing particular types of contractual relations (such as in employment, tenancies or insurance) have been seen as indicating a shift away from the principle of autonomy of the will and towards a more social view of contract, imbued with considerations of the public interest.[33] Famously described by Louis Josserand as early as 1930 as the 'publicisation' of contract,[34] this much wider view of the proper function of contract law explains the adventurousness of the courts in developing contractual techniques to deal with problems of liability for death or personal injuries which have been important in imposing liability for products and also the imposition, and the extension beyond the parties, of liability for qualitative defects in products, whether goods or buildings. Here, as we shall see,[35] the status of the parties (in particular where one or other is in business or otherwise *professionnel*) is an important factor: from forming the legal underpinning of the expression of market power, contract law has become one of the means by which that power is controlled. Equality between citizens is no longer presumed, but rather requires the intervention of the law for its achievement.

(b) Delictual liability

The Civil Code's famously few provisions on delictual liability followed closely the work of the natural lawyer Romanists of the previous two centuries, which had rationalised and generalised the Roman materials almost beyond recognition.[36] So, according to article 1382 'any human action which causes harm [*un dommage*] to someone else obliges the person by whose fault it occurred to make it good' and article 1383 adds that 'everyone is liable for the harm which he has caused not only by his act,

---

[31] Arts. 1134 al. 3, 1135 C. civ. For criticism of this 'forcing' of contract see L. Josserand, 'L'essor moderne du concept contractuel' in *Recueil d'études sur les Sources du Droit en l'honneur de François Gény*, (Librairie du Recueil Sirey, Paris, 1935), Tome II, 333 at 340, 345. As to the role of good faith in French law, see R. Zimmermann and S. Whittaker (eds.), *Good Faith in European Contract Law* (CUP, 2000) 32–39; Terré, Simler, Lequette, *Obligations*, 182–3; 434–41.

[32] Josserand, *ibid.*; G. Marty and P. Raynaud, *Droit civil*, Tome II, Vol. I (2nd. edn., Sirey, Paris, 1988), 250.

[33] For an excellent introduction, see Terré, Simler, Lequette, *Obligations*, 39 *et seq.* and for a developed communitarian position: D. Mazeaud, 'Loyauté, solidarité, fraternité: la nouvelle devise contractuelle?' in *Mélanges en hommage à François Terré: L'avenir du droit* (PUF, Dalloz & Ed. Juris-Classeur, Paris, 1999) 603.

[34] L. Josserand, 'La "publicisation du contrat"', in *Recueil d'études en l'honneur d'Edouard Lambert* (LDGJ, Paris, 1938) Tome 3, 143.   [35] Below, pp. 65–7, 84–5.

[36] Zimmermann, *Obligations*, 1032–5.

but also by his negligence or by his carelessness'.[37] These provisions make no use of a concept approaching the English duty of care in the tort of negligence in order to delineate the ambit of its imposition of liability for fault,[38] nor do they, like the more recent German B.G.B. provisions, enumerate those interests of a person which are deemed worthy of delictual protection.[39] Not merely do the French provisions make clear that there is no restriction as to the type of fault (no distinction is made between *faute lourde* and *faute simple*), but, even more surprising to a common lawyer, they do not exclude from the scope of delictual liability any particular types of harm: *dommage* is broad enough to cover what an English lawyer would treat as personal injury, death (and its consequential losses), loss of reputation, psychiatric injury, distress, damage to or loss of property and economic loss, whether 'pure' or 'consequential'.[40] Indeed the width of the concept of *dommage* has meant that French lawyers have not in general felt it necessary to make the sort of distinctions between different types of harm suffered by a claimant, in particular not dealing with 'pure economic loss' as a peculiar or distinct category.[41] In principle, all categories of injury and all injured persons, whether foreseeable or not, are included with the protection of this general and basic law of delictual liability (*le droit commun de la responsabilité civile*). Moreover, in principle *all* a claimant's harm is recoverable in damages, whether direct or not, under the principle of *réparation intégrale*.[42] Unsurprisingly, French lawyers have at times rejoiced in this generality, while at others struggled to escape its consequences.[43] But if the classical French approach to the law of contract rests on the principle of the 'autonomy of the will', its classical approach to the law of delict rests on the moral principle of responsibility for fault.

However, echoes of some of the examples of delictual liability without fault of Roman law survived into the Civil Code.[44] Article 1384 alinéa 1 introduced these by stating that

One is liable not only for the harm which one causes by one's own deed, but also for that which is caused by the deed of persons for whom one is responsible, or of things which one has in one's keeping.

The Code then continued by describing the circumstances in which someone is liable in these two types of way.

---

[37] Below, pp. 40–6.   [38] Cf. below, pp. 159–62.

[39] 823 I BGB and see B. Markesinis and H. Unberath, *The German Law of Torts: A Comparative Treatise* (Hart Publishing, Oxford, 4th. edn., 2002) Chap. 2.   [40] Viney and Jourdain, *Conditions*, 11 *et seq.*

[41] French discussions generally refer to three types of losses: *préjudice matériel, préjudice corporel* and *dommage moral*, though the first of these is sometimes called '*préjudice économique, pécuniare, patrimonial ou financier*'. *Préjudice corporel* may be translated as 'personal injury' and *dommage moral* includes what a common lawyer would term mental distress, grief, psychiatric injury or damage to reputation. French law treats all losses other than these indiscriminately as *préjudice matériel*, including those which English law categorises as physical damage to property or pure economic loss: P. Prud'homme, *La réparation du préjudice non-corporel en droit français et en droit anglais: un aperçu des rapports de la responsabilité contractuelle et de la responsabilité délictuelle* (*thèse*, Paris II, 1990), 1–3.

[42] Terré, Simler, Lequette, *Obligations*, 860–2. This principle is qualified as regards contractual liability where in general harm must have been foreseen or forseeable at the time of contract: arts. 1150–1 C. civ. According to Bénabent, *Obligations*, 475–6 the principle of *réparation intégrale* is tempered in practice by the power of assessment of the lower courts.   [43] Bell, Boyron and Whittaker, 357 *et seq.*

[44] Arts. 1384–1386 C. civ.

The first way concerns a person's liability for another's harmful actions. The Code originally recognised three groups of cases here: the liability of parents for minor children living with them;[45] the liability of teachers and craftsmen for their pupils and apprentices;[46] and the liability of masters and principals for their servants or agents.[47] While French law sees this as a category (*la responsabilité du fait d'autrui*), the substantive legal foundation differs between its members, some being truly vicarious (as an English lawyer would see this) and some personal, and has changed over the years. So, parental liability was long based on a rebuttable presumption of fault,[48] the parent being able to escape liability if he or she showed proper supervision, control, education and instruction of the child, but in 1997 the Cour de cassation held instead that it arises whenever their child causes harm unless they show *force majeure* or contributory fault in the injured party.[49] The Code originally imposed liability on teachers for their pupils' actions also on the basis of a presumption of fault,[50] but, first, liability based on this presumption was imposed on the State rather than on the teacher personally, and then, in 1937, the basis of the State's liability was changed to one of proven fault in the teacher.[51] As will be clear from this, neither of these are cases of true vicarious liability: parental liability is personal, though based on the act of the child; the principal liability in respect of the pupil's action does not fall on teachers, but directly on the State.

The third and most important example of liability for another's action is of employers or principals (*commettants*).[52] This liability is truly vicarious and arises on fulfillment of three conditions. First, there must be a 'relationship of subordination' between the person whose act causes the harm and the person to be held liable, the typical, but by no means exclusive example of this being of employment (for convenience I shall refer to the employer or employee).[53] Secondly, the employee must have caused the harm in question 'in the course of the functions for which they are employed',[54] a requirement very similar to the common law's notion of the 'course of employment'. Thirdly, the employee's action must have constituted a delictual fault:[55] vicarious liability is not imposed on employers in respect of any apparent stricter delictual liabilities of the employee.[56] Employers' vicarious liability is, of course, very important in practice and we shall see some examples of it in the context of liability for products in those cases where *faute* can be proved.[57]

Until 1991, the courts had held that these were the only instances of liability for another's actions, though liability could otherwise be imposed on a basis of proven

---

[45] Art. 1384 al. 4 C. civ. (as amended).   [46] Art. 1384 al. 6 C. civ.   [47] Art. 1384 al. 5 C. civ.
[48] Art. 1384 al. 7 C. civ.
[49] Civ. (2) 19 Feb. 1997, D 1997.265 note Jourdain. The child need not be liable for the harm: Civ. (2) 10 May 2001, JCP 2001.II.10613 note J. Mouly.
[50] This still applies to the liability of a craftsman for his apprentice: arts. 1384 al. 6 & al. 7 C. civ.
[51] *Loi* of 5 Apr. 1937, now art. L. 911-4 C. éduc.; Malaurie, Aynès and Stoffel-Munck, *Obligations*, 73.
[52] Art. 1384 al. 5 C. civ.   [53] Malaurie, Aynès and Stoffel-Munck, *Obligations*, 76–7.
[54] Art. 1384 al. 5 C. civ.   [55] Civ. (2) 8 Oct. 1969, Bull. civ. II No. 269.
[56] Notably, under art. 1384 al. 1 C. civ. and art. 1385 C. civ., since these liabilities are imposed on the *gardien*, who in these circumstances is the employer: Civ. 30 Dec. 1936, D 1937.1.5 rapport Josserand, note R Savatier ('deeds of things'); Civ. (2) 15 Dec. 1976, *Laclergerie*, JCP 1977.IV.34 (animals).
[57] Notably, in the criminal courts: below, pp. 376, 381.

fault under articles 1382 and 1383.[58] In that year, though, in the *arrêt Blieck*, the Assemblée plénière held that there could be other examples, apparently on the basis of a general principle of liability for another's action itself drawn from article 1384 alinéa 1 and based on a 'relationship of control'.[59] The impact of the decision is still not entirely certain, but the new approach may apply, for example, to child-minders, leisure centres or holiday clubs for children, sports clubs for their players[60] and even to a local authority for squatters living in its property.[61] The Cour de cassation has affirmed that it establishes a strict liability which arises by operation of law (*une respon-sabilité de plein droit*) which may apparently be avoided by proving *cause étrangère* or contributory fault in the victim,[62] but not by proving merely an absence of fault.[63]

The second type of special liabilities provided for by the Civil Code were particular examples of 'liability for things'. Thus, article 1385 governs liability for animals and article 1386 for ruinous buildings and, following the position in Roman law,[64] dispensed the injured party from any need to prove fault. These two examples of liability for things may seem of somewhat minor importance, but the terms of article 1384 alinéa 1, which was apparently intended merely as a preface to the specific provisions which followed, were later interpreted so as to impose a very general liability on the *gardien* (keeper) of any thing which causes harm.[65] This reinterpretation is a remarkable feat of judicial activism on a very slim legislative basis.[66] The motivation of both the jurists who advocated it and judges who accepted it was to allow the victims of personal injuries or death to gain compensation without any need to prove fault, many accidents of the machine age remaining unexplained or, as it was sometimes put, 'anonymous'.[67] The context for its application was first accidents at work[68] and then accidents on the roads.[69] So, in the case of the latter a vehicle owner could be held liable as its *gardien* for the harm which it caused without needing to prove any fault in the driver, his only defences being *force majeure* or contributory fault.[70] However, the

---

[58] Flour, Aubert and Savaux, *Fait juridique*, 227.

[59] Ass. plén. 29 Mar. 1991, *Blieck*, D 1991.324 note Larroumet, JCP 1991.II.21673 concl. Dottenwille. For the text of art. 1384 al.1 C. civ., above, p. 24.

[60] Civ. (2) 22 May 1995, JCP 1996.II. 22550 note Mouly (injury to rugby player by unidentified member of opposing team).

[61] Civ. (2) 22 May 1995, JCP 1995.I.3893 n. 5 note Viney, D 1996.453 note Le Bars and Buhler.

[62] Malaurie, Aynès and Stoffel-Munck, *Obligations*, 68.

[63] Crim. 26 Mar. 1997 (3 cases): (1st. case) JCP 1998.II.10015 note M. Huyette, (2nd. case) JCP 1997.II.22868, rapp. F. Desportes; (3rd. case) D 1997.496 note P. Jourdain.

[64] J.A.C. Thomas, *A Textbook of Roman Law* (North-Holland, 1976), 382–3 (*pauperies*) & pp. 378–9 (*actio de posito et suspenso*).

[65] A. Tunc, ' "It is wise not to take the Civil Codes too seriously" Traffic accident compensation in France', in *Essays in Memory of Professor F. H. Lawson* (ed. P. Wallington & R. M. Merkin) (Butterworths, London, 1986), 71 at 72 *et seq*. *Cf*. A. Watson, *Failures of the Legal Imagination* (Scottish Academic Press, Edinburgh, 1988) 7–8.

[66] *Cf*. F.H. Lawson and B.S. Markesinis, *Tortious Liability for Unintentional Harm in the Common Law and the Civil Law* (CUP, 1982) Vol. I., 146–57.

[67] Josserand note to Lyon 12 Dec. 1902, Req. 3 Jun. 1904, D 1907.1.177.

[68] Civ. 16 Jun. 1896, S 1897.1.17 note Esmein.

[69] Civ. 29 Jul.1924, D 1925.1.5 note Ripert is an early example of its application. *Cf*. Req. 19 Apr. 1914, D 1914.1.303 (exploding soda syphon at café).

[70] In Req. 13 Apr. 1934, D 1934.1.41 note Savatier, it was established that fault in the victim which did not amount to *force majeure* could lead to a partial reduction of damages.

use of article 1384 alinéa 1 to achieve this result did not allow its impact to be restricted to these or to other specific contexts, as the text itself makes no distinction according to the type of 'thing' for which liability is imposed, not even distinguishing between things which are or are not dangerous.[71] Therefore, after the courts accepted the reinterpretation in 1930 in the famous *arrêt Jand'heur*,[72] they found themselves grappling with a general delictual provision of liability without fault, the only apparent limiting factor on which was the causal intervention of a 'thing'. In this way, French courts imposed a strict liability for physical things some 65 years before implementation of the EC Product Liability Directive imposed strict liability for defective products.

(c) The relationship between contractual and delictual liability

The final strand in this general pattern of civil liability of private law, and one which is prominent in our discussion of liability for products, is its special approach to the relationship between contract and delict, both as between parties to a contract and beyond them. There are four aspects of this relationship to which I wish to draw attention here, these revealing a curious combination of highly conceptual and contrastingly functional views of the law involved.[73]

First, towards the end of the nineteenth century, a group of jurists argued that the special rules governing contractual liability found in the Civil Code and the binding force of contractual obligation both necessitated a rule forbidding delict from intruding into the 'private law' created by parties to a contract, so as to deny a party to a contract the possibility of claiming on the basis of delict, a position which became known as *non-cumul des responsabilités contractuelle et délictuelle* and since the 1920s has been accepted by both courts and writers.[74] Its significance is very considerable, not least owing to the overweening generality of French law's principle of liability for delictual fault:[75] to allow the French law of delict to apply between parties to a contract would not merely offend French lawyers' sense of juridical aesthetics, but would indeed threaten the effectiveness of agreements and of the Code's regulation of particular contracts.[76]

However, the second aspect of the relationship between contract and delict between contracting parties contrasts sharply with the conceptual flavour of much juristic writing on *non-cumul* and illustrates the willingness of French lawyers to manipulate their classifications in order to give effect to a particular policy. For the desire to allow victims of personal injuries to be compensated without a need to prove fault, which led to the reinterpretation of article 1384 alinéa 1,[77] found a contractual expression in the

---

[71] Cons. Le Marc'hadour rapp. DP1930.1.57 at 64; L. Josserand, 'Le travail de refoulement de la responsabilité du fait des choses inanimes', DH Chron. 1930.5. Cf. G. Ripert who had argued that only dangerous things required *la garde*: note, Civ. 29 Jul. 1924, D 1925.1.5.

[72] Ch. réun. 13 Feb. 1930, S 1930.1.121 note Esmein, DP 1930.1.57 note Ripert.

[73] S. Whittaker, *The Relationship between Contract and Tort: a Comparative Study of French and English Law* (Oxford, D. phil. thesis, 1987).

[74] Civ. 11 Jan. 1922, S 1924.1.105 note Demogue, DP 1922.1.16; Civ. (2) 9 Jun. 1993, Bull. civ. II, no. 204 and see Viney, *Introduction à la responsabilité*, 403 *et seq.*   [75] See above, pp. 23–4.

[76] T. Weir, 'Complex Liabilities' in *International Encyclopedia of Comparative Law*, (A. Tunc, chief ed.) (1982), Vol XI, Chap. 12, 28.   [77] Above, pp. 26–7.

creation of *obligations de sécurité*, obligations owed by one party to a contract to look after the personal safety of the other. This was a controversial technique whose effectiveness in imposing strict liability rested on a misconception as to the nature of contractual liability, for at the time most French lawyers thought that the 'contractual fault' on which liability was based could be established whenever a party to the contract did not achieve what he had to.[78] Thus, for example, if an employer owed his employee a contractual obligation as to his safety at work, injury there would establish contractual fault, unless the employer could show *force majeure*.[79] This was misconceived because it made no distinction between those contractual obligations whose performance requires some degree of care (*obligations de moyens*), and those which require a particular result (*obligations de résultat*),[80] but before 1925 when this distinction was clearly drawn, a shift in classification from delict to contract was generally considered to entail a shift from fault (under articles 1382 or 1383) to liability without fault in the sense of *imprudence* (under article 1147).

Where reclassification of liability as contractual was generally more favourable to an injured party than its delictual alternative there was little practical need to invoke the rule of *non-cumul* to prevent that party from choosing to rely on delict, but by the mid 1930s, jurists and courts realised that use of *obligations de sécurité* combined with the rule of *non-cumul* enabled them to control the basis of liability of one party to a contract to the other who has suffered physical harm: some *obligations de sécurité* could be held to be fault-based (*obligations de moyens*) and some strict (*obligations de résultat*). In this way, the courts acquired a major way of controlling the recently created strict liability for the 'deeds of things', for their imposition of an *obligation de sécurité de moyens* would forbid recourse to liability under article 1384 alinéa 1 because of the rule of *non-cumul*. So, for example, a surgeon could not be liable for the 'deed' of his scalpel where his contractual obligation to his patient was *une obligation de moyens*.[81] The *jurisprudence* on the line between these two types of *obligations de sécurité* is very unsettled, the courts nuancing their decisions from case to case[82] and resorting to Byzantine distinctions,[83] with the additional complication that sometimes they impose obligations somewhere between the two (notably, *obligations de résultat atténuées*) or contractual 'liability for the deeds of things'.[84]

Thirdly, French law has extended the idea of *non-cumul* beyond privity of contract.[85] For, it is thought, if the law recognizes the existence of a contractual right in one person against another, the special nature of this right (and, conversely, of the

---

[78] E.g. M. Sauzet, 'De la responsabilité des patrons vis-à-vis des ouvriers dans les accidents industriels', (1883) *Rev. crit.*, 596, 614.   [79] J.-E. Labbé, note, S 1885.4.25.

[80] This distinction was first drawn by R. Demogue in 1925: *Traité des obligations en général* (Arthur Rousseau, Paris,1925), Tome V, no. 1237 *et seq. Force majeure* is a defence to *obligations de résultat*.

[81] Civ. 20 May 1936, DP 1936.1.88 rapp. Josserand, concl. Matter. On the fate of this *jurisprudence*, see below, pp. 151–2.

[82] Bénabent, *Obligations*, 204. For further discussion, see Viney and Jourdain, *Conditions*, 457 *et seq.* For examples, see below, pp. 72, 100.

[83] Malaurie, Aynès and Stoffel-Munck, *Obligations*, 476 (concerning the position of carriers).

[84] E.g. Civ. (1) 17 Jan. 1995, D 1995.350 note P. Jourdain (school liable under contractual *obligation de sécurité* which extends to the 'deed of things which are used for the performance of the obligation'). More generally see Bénabent, *Obligations*, 271 *et seq.* referring to the 'disorder' in the law.

[85] S. Whittaker, 'Privity of Contract and the Law of Tort: The French Experience' (1995) 15 *OJLS* 327.

other person's liability) should not be usurped by the application of the general law of delict: to allow delict here would lead to the overturning of the 'contractual equilibrium' established by the parties.[86] Although this way of thinking suffered a major setback in 1991,[87] it still affects the law governing the contractual liability of manufacturers and others in the chain of distribution to purchasers of either movables or buildings, especially as regards qualitative defects,[88] where in principle a purchaser may sue those in the chain of distribution in contract, but only in contract.[89] Interestingly, though, implementation of the Product Liability Directive required French law to create an exception to *non-cumul*, for it requires a beneficiary of the rights which it creates to be enjoyed by those whom products injure, whether or not they possess a contractual claim against the producer or supplier.[90]

A final twist in the relationship between contract and delict in French law may also be found in the context of liability for products. The traditional and 'logical' view of the courts was that non-performance of a contractual obligation which causes harm to a third party may or may not constitute a *faute délictuelle* so as to give rise to liability to that third party, depending on the nature of the fault apart from the contract: 'as a third party cannot take advantage of the contract, any fault in a party to the contract should not be assessed by reference to the contractual standard'.[91] However, from 1998 the Cour de cassation has sometimes held that non-performance of a contractual obligation (even an *obligation de résultat*) in itself constitutes delictual fault so as to attract liability to a person not party to or otherwise within the domain of protection of the contract,[92] an approach which threatens to redraw the boundaries of contract and delict at the cost of 'denaturing' the concept of delictual fault. One of these cases concerned a claim for damages by the daughter of a person who contracted and died of AIDS having received blood contaminated by HIV from the national blood transfusion service. Here, the Cour de cassation clearly wished to extend the benefit of the very strict contractual liability which it had constructed for this purpose for the benefit of this victim *par richochet* in respect of facts long before French legislative implementation of the Product Liability Directive. This case forms, therefore, an example of the unsettling impact of the *affaire du sang contaminé* on fundamental principles of French law and to the extent to which it forms part of the French 'judicial implementation' of the 1985 Directive, it may not survive the combined effects of the *loi* of 1998 and the European Court's decisions in 2002.[93] Certainly, this fundamental issue does not appear to have been settled as the Cour de cassation has also on occasion upheld the traditional demarcation between the two liabilities.[94]

---

[86] Ibid., 345.

[87] Ass. plén.12 Jul. 1991, *Besse*, JCP 1991.II.21743 note Viney (abandoning the theory of 'groups of contracts').

[88] Ass. plén. 7 Feb. 1986, D 1986.293 note Bénabent (liability based on 'contractual non-conformity'); Civ. (1) 21 Jan. 2003, Bull. civ. I no. 18; Art. 1792 C. civ. and see below.

[89] Civ. (1) 9 Oct. 1979, *Lamborghini*, D 1980.IR.222 obs. Larroumet; GP 1980.1.249 note Planqueel.

[90] Art. 1386-1 C. civ.

[91] Bénabent, *Obligations*, 369 and see Civ. (3) 18 Apr. 1972, Bull. civ. III no. 233; Civ. (1) 11 Apr. 1995, Bull. civ. no. 171.

[92] Civ. (1) 15 Dec. 1998, Bull. civ. I. no. 368; Civ. (1) 18 Jul. 2000, Bull. civ. I no. 221; Civ. (1) 13 Feb. 2001, Bull. civ. I no. 35.　　　　　[93] Civ. (1)13 Feb. 2001, *cit.* and see below, pp. 150, 461–5.

[94] Com. 8 Oct. 2002, JCP 2003 Chron. 152 no. 3 obs. Viney.

2. The Administrative Law of Liability

It has been seen as a 'miraculous' paradox that the Conseil d'Etat, set up by Napoleon as a bureaucratic control on executive action in the interests of efficiency, instead developed into a forum for the hearing and settling of disputes relating to maladministration and created a special system of administrative law,[95] parallel to and distinct from the system of private law. While there remains disagreement as to the defining characteristic or characteristics of administrative law,[96] most French public lawyers would agree that the modern law combines 'extraordinary powers' (*prérogatives exorbitantes du droit commun*) and 'extraordinary controls' (*sujétions exorbitantes*).[97] The recognition that the administration has powers greater than and different from ordinary citizens is an important one, reflecting the idea drawn from the principle of the separation of powers that it is the role of the executive to govern and that it must therefore have the means available to do so. As I shall explain, the inherent power of the executive to govern is fully reflected in French law's treatment of the powers exercised in the interests of health and safety, including as regards products, and contrasts markedly with the starting point of English law.[98]

The 'extraordinary' controls on the exercise of these powers have two distinct aspects: control on the legality of *actes* and the imposition of *responsabilité* for both *actes* and activities. The first subjects administrative rule-making and 'decisions'[99] to a requirement of legality which requires them to conform to a set of 'general legal principles'(*principes généraux du droit*), which concern both the procedure and the substance of administrative *actes*, as well as to legislation itself.[100] No less important, however, has been the second, a system of special rules governing administrative liability; for although at first the construction of a special set of rules governing liability in the administration was viewed as necessary in order to protect its work from the inappropriately wide principles of private law (whether of delict or contract), subsequently the picture has become more diverse.[101] So, while in some areas French administrative liability law still has a protective effect, in other respects it has gone further than private law or in different directions.

(a) Administrative extra-contractual liability

While the French administrative law of liability remains distinct from its private law counterpart, the function of this 'autonomy' has changed over the nearly two centuries since the Revolution; for it was conceived as a regime of privilege, but appears now as a regime of special, public responsibility.[102]

Before 1873, the rule was that of a general State immunity, French doctrinal writers carrying on the approach of the ancien régime caught in the maxim, *Le roi ne peut mal faire*:[103] as Laferrière put it, 'it is the nature of sovereignty to impose its will on

---

[95] Brown and Bell, 25, referring to P. Weil, *Le droit administratif* (Paris, 1980) 8.
[96] Above, p. 19.   [97] Vedel and Delvolvé, *Droit administratif*, Tome 1, 35–6.
[98] Below, pp. 306–10, 332–5.   [99] See below, p. 313.
[100] Brown and Bell, Chap. 9.   [101] See below, Chap. 6.
[102] For an excellent comparative discussion see Fairgrieve, *State Liability*.
[103] Braibant and Stirn, *Droit administratif français*, 315.

everyone, without the possibility of any claim for compensation'.[104] Only particular legislative support for the imposition of liability allowed an exception to be made to this position, as in the liabilities arising from 'public works' which grew up around a provision of 1799.[105] This State immunity was complemented by the existence of a personal immunity in public servants in respect of acts done in the performance of their duties, an immunity guaranteed by the Constitution of 1799.[106] This last rule, which was so disparaged by Dicey,[107] has had a remarkable tenacity in French law, surviving changes of constitution and forms of government, even being revived in 1873 after its formal repeal by the Tribunal des conflits on the basis of the principle of the separation of powers.[108]

However, the Tribunal des conflits in the *arrêt Blanco* took a remarkable step in a new direction, recognising that the State itself *could* be liable for the deeds of the persons whom it employed in the public service even in the absence of specific legislative authority. In holding that the administration could be liable on the basis of fault for the injuries caused in a traffic accident, it declared that its liability was 'neither general nor absolute... it has its own special rules which vary according to the needs of the service and the necessity to reconcile the rights of the state with private rights'.[109] Thus, the Tribunal des conflits' consecration of the 'autonomy' of the liability of the administration was aimed at preventing the Civil Codes' broad delictual liability for fault and vicarious liability of employers for employees[110] from applying to the administration; but while this is indeed restrictive, it came in a decision which cautiously accepted liability.

Since *Blanco* the administrative law of liability has been extended considerably, in a number of ways.

First, there has been a gradual extension of the range of situations where fault will attract liability. In some situations, the courts have replaced an established immunity in the administration with the recognition of liability, as long as very serious fault (*faute lourde*) is established;[111] in others, and increasingly, they have replaced a requirement of *faute lourde* with one of *faute simple*.[112] They have also developed special, 'public' understandings of the notion of fault itself, holding that any 'defective functioning of the administration' from the point of view of the citizen[113] and any illegality of an administrative *acte*, such as a decision or an enactment, themselves constitute *faute de service* so as to attract liability.[114] Moreover, while individual public servants have in principle remained immune, the administrative courts have taken a

---

[104] E. Laferrière, *Traité de la juridiction administrative et des recours contentieux* (Berger-Levrault, Paris, 2nd. edn., 1896), Vol. 2, 13 and 183 *et seq*.   [105] *Loi du 28 pluviôse*, art. 4 and see below, pp. 121–31.

[106] Art 75 of Constitution 22 Frimaire an VIII (1799).

[107] Dicey, *Introduction to the Study of the Law of the Constitution*, 345–8.

[108] TC 30 Jul. 1873, *Pelletier* DP 1874.3.5 (the rule had been repealed during the Paris Commune in 1870). An exception is found where the public servant commits a fault 'detachable from the public service'. For further discussion, see Fairgrieve, *State Liability*, 20 *et seq*.

[109] TC 8 Feb. 1873, S 1873.153 (trans. Brown and Bell, 183).   [110] Above, pp. 23–7.

[111] Here, the leading decision was CE 10 Feb. 1905, *Tomasco-Greco*, DP 1906.3.81.

[112] E.g. as regards medical liability (below, p. 144). For other examples, see below, pp. 315–18.

[113] Gaudemet, *Droit administratif*, Tome 1, 806.

[114] Ibid., 807–8; CE Sect 26 Jan. 1973, *Driancourt*, Leb. 78 and see further Fairgrieve, *State Liability*, Chap. 3.

generous view of the necessary connection between the activities of the public servant and the 'functioning of the public service', so as to impose liability on the administration itself in respect of their actions.[115]

Perhaps even more remarkable, though, has been the creation of various bases of liability in the administration which do not require proof of fault in any of the above senses.[116] These are as varied as the different understandings of 'fault' itself. The first example arose in 1895 in a case where a public servant had been seriously injured by a machine while working in a State arsenal. The Conseil d'Etat held simply that the State was liable for the consequences of the claimant's injury because he had undertaken a risk of danger in the public service.[117] This decision reflected the same concern that victims of the machine age should be compensated without the need to prove fault which in private law found expression in juristic suggestions that employers owed their employees obligations as to their safety under their contract of employment and which found judicial recognition in 1896 when the Cour de cassation accepted the idea of a general 'liability for the deeds of things' under article 1384 alinéa 1 of the Civil Code.[118] But, unlike the private lawyers, the Conseil d'Etat was unfettered by the need to pin this new liability to any particular legislative provision and felt able to justify its decision directly on the notion of risk.

However, many other instances of the imposition of liability without fault on the administration have been developed by the Conseil d'Etat, each one with its own justification, ambit and rules. For our own concern of liability for products, the most obviously significant are those cases which recognise liability without fault where the administration's things or activities are particularly dangerous and have caused an 'abnormal harm'.[119] However, perhaps most strikingly original (and 'public') in their basis are those cases where liability is imposed on the administration on the basis that its action in the public interest has caused a claimant particular harm, thereby upsetting the 'equality of public burdens to be imposed on citizens', an idea which is directly linked to the central constitutional notion of equality of citizens.[120] This has been applied to cases involving administrative *actes* (such as a 'decision' or *règlement*) which may therefore give rise to liability even if legally valid, such as the refusal of a local authority to remove squatters from the claimant's property even after a court order.[121] The law of administrative liability without fault lacks even the *formal* homogeneity of the private law, where it arises either from the 'deed of a thing' or of another person.[122]

Another important area of liability may be found in the law governing 'public works'.[123] In the modern law this consists of a complex of liabilities, differing in basis (proof of fault, presumption of fault or no fault) and according to the category of claimant in question ('participant', 'user' or 'third party').[124] It is a significant area of law for liability for products, even though at first sight it rests on a relationship with

---

[115] Vedel and Delvolvé, *Droit administratif,* Tome I, 550 *et seq.*
[116] Fairgrieve, *State Liability,* Chap. 5.
[117] CE 21 Jun. 1895, *Cames,* D 1896.3.65 concl. Romieu.
[118] Civ. 16 Jun. 1896, D 1897.1.433 note Saleilles, S 1897.1.17 note Esmein and see above, pp. 26–7.
[119] Below, pp. 118–21.   [120] Chapus, *Droit administratif général,* Tome 1, 1363 *et seq.*
[121] CE 30 Nov. 1923, *Couitéas,* D 1923.3.59 concl. Rivet.   [122] Above, pp. 24–7.
[123] Below, pp. 121–31.   [124] Below, pp. 124–9.

immovable property. Strikingly, it governs the liabilities of some categories of *private* person, where they are involved in 'public works' it is an administrative law of liability, but not exclusively a law of liability in the administration.[125]

(b) Liability arising from administrative contracts

French law distinguishes between private law and administrative contracts both for jurisdictional and substantive legal purposes. The line between the two is complex, but in general the courts treat as administrative those contracts in which one of the parties is a public authority or person acting on behalf of a public authority and which closely concern the provision of a *service public* or those contracts whose contracts reserve to the administration special powers by terms known as *clauses exorbitantes du droit commun*.[126] Where a contract is held to be 'administrative,' any dispute arising from it is a matter for the administrative courts, but the law which those courts apply is based on the concepts of the Civil Code, modified so as to take into account the needs of the public interest.[127] In particular, the Conseil d'Etat recognizes 'extraordinary powers' in the administration (such as the power to vary the terms of its contracts reflecting the principle of the 'mutability' of the public service[128]) but also subjects particular types of administrative contracts to special controls.

However, unlike its private law counterpart, the administrative law of contract has not been important in French law's treatment of liability for products. As I shall later explain,[129] this results from the greater flexibility of administrative extra-contractual liability as compared with the private law of delict; from the Conseil d'Etat's view of some relationships as essentially non-contractual;[130] and from the treatment by French law of some contractual liabilities of public bodies as belonging to private law and the jurisdiction of the ordinary courts.[131] This illustrates the complexity of the division between private law and public law in France, for neither the nature of the body nor the nature of the function themselves determine the law applicable and it is for this reason that I shall treat the liability of those who supply products in the course of a public service (in a very general sense) as a matter both of private and administrative law.[132]

3. 'Solidary Liability' in Private and Public Law

As I shall later explain, a very important issue in determining the patterns of liability for products is the way in which the law treats the question of the position of two or

---

[125] Below, pp. 129–30.

[126] Brown and Bell, 202 *et seq.*; Gaudemet, *Droit administratif,* Tome I, 671 *et seq.*; Richer, *Droit des contrats administratifs,* 84 *et seq.* Some types of contracts concluded by the administration are classified as administrative by legislation: e.g. public works contracts (*marchés de travaux publics*): *loi* of 28 pluviôse an VIII, art. 4.   [127] Brown and Bell, 203 *et seq.*

[128] E.g. the recognition of *clauses exorbitantes* and the principle of *imprévision* so as to allow the modification of administrative contracts in the light of supervening circumstances: and *cf.* below, p. 133.

[129] Below, pp. 116–18.

[130] E.g. where a claimant is a 'user' of a *service public administratif:* below, p. 135.

[131] E.g. the liability of *services publics industriels et commerciaux* to their customers: below, pp. 135–6.

[132] Below, Chap. 7.

more persons (the 'co-authors') liable for the same harm. The basic position in French private law here is a simple one, accepting a principle of 'solidary' liability, so that all co-authors are liable in full as against a person who has suffered the harm (the claimant who thereby possesses the *droit de poursuite du créancier*), but providing for recourse between them either by way of contribution or contractual indemnity.[133]

By contrast, since 1937 the Conseil d'Etat's position has differed here significantly, denying that the 'co-authors of the same harm' are necessarily liable *in solidum* towards the person suffering that harm.[134] So, it has generally refused to hold a public body liable in full to a person harmed by its *fault*, where this harm has also been caused by a person liable in private law, and instead grants to the public body a defence known as *fait d'un tiers* or *fait d'une tierce personne*, the effect of which is to reduce or even to exclude liability in the administration.[135] On the other hand, where the liability of the administration is imposed *without* fault or under the special rules applicable to 'public works' (whether or not liability is based on fault), the Conseil d'Etat accepts that the administration may be liable in full, even if another person is also liable for the same harm as a matter of private law.[136] This difference in treatment of the liability of co-authors has important consequences on the liability of the administration for products, particularly as regards the exercise of their powers of control and supervision of the safety of products.[137]

4. The Time Element

The periods within which particular types of claim must be brought have had a significant effect on their attractiveness and, indeed, in French law have often been a reason for the acceptance by the ordinary courts of a different analysis so as to avoid what they see as too short a period.

The present position in private law distinguishes broadly between general periods of prescription of rights and special periods of prescription or *délais* within which a claim must be brought. Although there is a general prescription rule of 30 years which in principle governs contractual rights, this does not apply to contracts made between *commerçants* (traders as defined by commercial law) or between *commerçants* and non-*commerçants*, whoever bears the obligation,[138] where instead a period of 10 years applies.[139] In the case of claims for damages for non-performance of a contract, the prescription runs from the date of the event giving rise to the right, such as the date of the accident, or the manifestation of the damage.[140] Since 1985, these rules have not applied to delictual liability where prescription is always 10 years from the date of the 'manifestation or aggravation' of the harm.[141] This means that *generally* there is no difference in the time period between contract and delict.

---

[133] As I shall explain, French private law is complicated by a division between the position where obligations are *solidaires* (this being termed *solidarité*) and where they owe *obligations in solidum* (sometimes termed *solidarité imparfaite*): below, pp. 546–7.   [134] Below, pp. 322–4, 551–3.

[135] Ibid.

[136] CE Sect. 14 Jun. 1978, *Mutuelle générale française accident*, Leb. 528 and see below, p. 126.

[137] Below, pp. 322–5.   [138] Art. 2262 C. civ.; Flour and Aubert, *Rapport d'obligation*, 300.

[139] Art. 110-4 C. com.

[140] Flour and Aubert, *Rapport d'obligation*, 304.   [141] Art. 2270-1 C. civ.

However, French law possesses many special periods within which a claim must be brought in respect of particular contractual liabilities. Of these, in this book the *bref délai* which governs the seller's classical liability for latent defects is very prominent, both in its application and in its avoidance: it is described as 'short' but may allow a claim to be brought many years after the contract is made and performed.[142] Other special periods apply to claims against builders (where they differ according to the seriousness and nature of the defect) and these differ from the general contractual position in their starting point as well as in the period set.[143]

Claims for damages under French administrative law also have their own special time periods. First, a claimant who has applied to the administration for compensation and been refused must initiate proceedings within *two months*.[144] Secondly, in principle he must bring any claim against the administration within four years of the first day of the year following that in which his rights arose.[145] As I shall explain, these two periods together (and in combination with other factors) have had a major effect on the practical impact of the administrative liabilities which the Conseil d'Etat has in principle recognised.

5. The Significance of Insurance, Social Security and *Fonds de Garantie*

French private lawyers accept that the development of the rules of civil liability have been influenced by the practice of insurance and, in particular, liability insurance, and they have long realised that this has led to a decline in individual responsibility (for *faute*) and the expansion of liabilities *sans faute*.[146] Indeed, some changes (particularly but not exclusively affecting those in business[147]) could not have been envisaged without the development of liability insurance. The relationship between liability insurance and the development of civil liability has worked both ways: sometimes the courts have been willing to impose a very extensive liability on a particular class of defendant because that class generally insures against liability already, as was the case in the *arrêt Jand'heur* itself in relation to motor accidents,[148] whereas at other times a class of defendant takes up a practice of insurance after a change in law makes it seem necessary.[149] Moreover, it would seem that, even though formally irrelevant, *juges du fond* (the courts of first instance and of appeal[150]) do take into account the fact that the defendant actually happens to be insured in their decision on questions of liability,[151] though the extent to which they do so is difficult to assess given that so many important issues are left to their 'sovereign power of assessment'.[152]

Moreover, French law has increasingly resorted to imposing a duty on particular categories of persons to insure themselves against liability. The first example of this

---

[142] Art. 1648 C. civ., below, pp. 91–3.   [143] Art. 1792 *et seq.* C. civ. below, p. 105.

[144] Below, p. 320.   [145] Below, p. 320.

[146] Viney, *Introduction à la responsabilité*, 24 *et seq. Cf.* Flour, Aubert and Savaux, *Fait juridique*, 81 *et seq.* who accept the influence but appear less happy with the outcome.

[147] This is not the case as regards the *gardien* of private motor vehicles: above, pp. 26, 60–1.

[148] Above, p. 27.   [149] Starck, Roland and Boyer, *Responsabilité délictuelle*, 46–7.

[150] Below, pp. 40–1.   [151] Malaurie, Aynès and Stoffel-Munck, *Obligations*, 12.

[152] E.g. delictual fault; causation; 'defect' in sale: below, pp. 44–5, 55 and 75–6 respectively.

was as regards third party liability in motor vehicle accidents, which was made compulsory in 1958, a year after legislation had set this area of liability on the same legal basis whether the vehicle was private or administrative.[153] More recent examples are to be found particularly in the areas of transport, professional liabilities and the leisure industry.[154] However, there are important exceptions to this: thus, while builders must insure against the strict liabilities which they bear,[155] a commercial seller or manufacturer does not have to insure against the liabilities which may arise in respect of their products.

Of course, many businesses which risk burdensome liabilities do take out insurance even though it is not compulsory. There are standard types of liability insurance, for example, '*assurance R.C.* [*responsabilité civile*] *du chef d'entreprise*' and '*assurance R.C. produits*'. In the case of private individuals, the existence of liability in the Civil Code of parental liability for children and the development of liability on *gardiens* under article 1384 aliéna 1, which applies equally to private individuals as to businesses, has led to the existence of a standard policy for heads of households (known as *assurance R.C. 'père de famille*'),[156] though this is often included in a more general insurance policy, notably '*assurance multirisque-habitation.*'[157] Of course, these insurance policies are not free nor are they unlimited in the sums against which they insure, nevertheless in many cases the practice of insurance in France has evolved to protect potential defendants, but with the concomitant effect that claimants are more likely to achieve a satisfied award.[158]

While the most conspicuous area of influence of liability insurance has been in the area of civil liability, it can be seen elsewhere. So, while insurance cannot cover a person's liability to pay a fine, it may cover his liability to pay compensation to the victim of crime claiming in a criminal court as *partie civile*: indeed, a defendant's liability insurers may be party to the proceedings.[159] As regards administrative liability, a distinction must be made between the State itself (which acts as its own insurer and does not enter contracts for this purpose) and other public bodies, many of which have turned to insurance to cover their increasingly extensive liabilities.[160] This has been particularly the case as regards the smallest category of local authorities, the *communes*, for some of which the imposition of liability for an accident causing personal injuries or death may otherwise represent a significant proportion of its annual budget.[161] Generally,

---

[153] *Loi* of 27 Feb. 1958 (now art. L. 211-1 C. assur.).

[154] Lambert-Faivre, *Droit des assurances*, 16–17.   [155] Below, p. 104.

[156] Bénabent, *Obligations*, 355, n.10 sees Civ. (2) 19 Feb. 1997, D 1997.265 note Jourdain making parental liability even more strict as reflecting the practice of this insurance.

[157] On this type of policy, see the Commission des clauses abusives, Recommendation No. 85–04 (6 Dec. 1985).

[158] Since 1930 (*loi* of 13 Jul. 1930) a victim has been able to claim against a liability insurer directly, thereby avoiding any insolvency in the policy-holder: see now art. 124-3 C. assur; Lambert-Faivre, *Droit du dommage corporel*, 545.   [159] Below, p. 381.

[160] F. Vincent, 'Assurance de responsabilité des collectivités territoriales et de leurs élus' Jur.-Cl. Adm., Fasc. 740, 3.

[161] See CE 25 Sept. 1970, *Tesson*, D 1971.55 where Comm. gouv. M. Morisot noted that the defendant *commune*'s annual budget was smaller than the claimant's damages, but had been supplemented by a special State grant.

however, French public lawyers have not seen liability insurance as a very significant influence on the development of the rules of administrative liability. Rather, they have instead seen the imposition of administrative liability (especially when *sans faute*) as itself a form of insurance.[162]

However, as I shall explain, recent experience in France has led to a realisation that the existence of liability insurance is not necessarily a full answer to the imposition of strict or otherwise burdensome liabilities. For when in 2002 legislation created a new set of rules for liability in respect of both public and private health care and an obligation to insure against this liability on those medical practitioners and institutions which could bear liability (with the exception of the State itself), within months further legislation had to be rushed through in order to 'reassure' insurers sufficiently to enter or renew their contracts with a sizeable number of health care providers by shifting some of the risks to a publicly financed fund.[163]

While coverage of liability by insurance usually removes the need for either the victim or defendant to look elsewhere for compensation, in principle an insurer held liable may claim contribution from any other person also liable for the victim's harm,[164] even where an insurer has been held liable under the rules of private law and claims recourse against the State under administrative law.[165] This recourse is generally founded on the idea of subrogation, the insurer taking over whatever rights the primary victim had against such other persons.[166] Generally, the effect of subrogation is that the insurer's claim follows the rules incidental to the notional claim of the primary claimant, including as to prescription and competent jurisdiction, with the exception that an insurer of a defendant may not claim before a criminal court as subrogated to the rights of any possible *partie civile*,[167] even though insurers are otherwise able to become party to civil proceedings before criminal courts.[168] However, the insurer's recourse cannot exceed either the amount which it has itself actually paid out under the policy *or* the amount for which the other person responsible is *ultimately* liable.[169] So, for example, if A is the insurer of B, who is liable to C (the primary claimant) for compensation of 1000 Euros, A may recover an amount against D (a person also liable for C's harm) to the extent to which the court considers that D is responsible to C *as compared* to B's responsibility to C.

Personal or first party indemnity insurance has been available in France since the nineteenth century, but its relevance for a claim for damages depends on the nature of the loss. In the case of damage to property, any payments made to the primary claimant by his insurer are considered to be *indemnitaire* and therefore reduce pro rata any claim which he may make against the defendant. This does not reduce a defendant's overall liability, but instead transfers it to the primary claimant's insurer by way of subrogation,

---

[162] P. Le Tourneau and L. Cadiet, *Droit de la responsabilité et contrats* (Dalloz, Paris, 2000) 77–8.

[163] Below, pp. 151–5.

[164] Viney and Jourdain, *Effets de la responsabilité*, 780 *et seq.* Exceptions are made as regards members of the insured's family or employees: art. L. 121-12 al. 3 C. assur.

[165] CE 22 Nov. 1985, RGAT 1986.374. Cf., below, pp. 326–30.

[166] Viney and Jourdain, *Effets de la responsabilité*, 784–5 interpreting art. 121-12 C. assur.

[167] Crim. 3 Jun. 1992, Bull. crim. no. 218.　　　　[168] See below, p. 383.

[169] Viney and Jourdain, *Effets de la responsabilité*, 787.

whose claim for recourse follows the same pattern as regards the position of the liability insurer.[170] On the other hand, in the case of first party insurance against personal injury or death, any payments made by an insurer to the assured (the would-be primary claimant) do not affect any right to recover against a person potentially liable: the payments are said to be *forfaitaires* unless the contract provides the contrary, with the result that the insurer has no right to recover these payments against the defendant.[171]

Social security and *fonds de garantie* (special compensation funds) have been very important in France in effecting compensation for personal injuries,[172] but at least since 1985 in law their incidence does not reduce the potential liability of someone whether in the law of delict or contract.[173] For French law allows the bodies which administer and make the various types of social security payment (in particular, *Caisses de sécurité sociale*) to reclaim these amounts from anyone civilly liable to their recipient on the basis of subrogation to the rights of the primary victim.[174] These *tiers payeurs* can take advantage of any liability in a civilly liable defendant, apart from that which is attributable to compensation of a personal character.[175]

6. How do these General Frameworks of Liability and Recourse Impact on 'Liability for Products'?

In the following chapters, I will look at how these general frameworks of liability, whether public or private, impact on liability for products.

In Chapters 3 to 5 I shall look at private law. In Chapter 3, I shall start by looking at the way in which the law of delict has governed French liability for products, whether this liability rests on members of the chain of distribution (such as manufacturers or suppliers) or on others, notably, on their *gardiens*. In this respect, I shall spend some time exploring the significance of 'delictual fault' in French law, from an institutional and procedural as well as juristic point of view. I shall then look at the complex law governing liability for the 'deeds of things'. In Chapter 4 I shall examine the way in which the law of sale has been used to govern many issues of liability for products, looking at the various foundations of liability and the range of remedies available to a buyer or sub-buyer. In Chapter 5, I shall look at a range of examples of other categories of person liable in private law in respect of things. Some of these liabilities arise in a defendant in the context of the supply of the property in question (such as those who contribute to the construction of buildings or who hire property); some arise instead owing to the intellectual input into the property, such as designers or architects; for some, liability is imposed owing to their failure to advise accurately as to the safety or

---

[170] Terré, Simler, Lequette, *Obligations*, 852; art L. 121-12 C. assur.

[171] Ibid.; art. L. 131-2 C. assur.   [172] Viney, *Introduction à la responsabilité*, 41–6.

[173] The position was considerably clarified by the *loi* no. 85–677 of 5 Jul. 1985, arts. 28–34. For an example of such a fund, see the *loi* no. 91–1406 of 31 Dec. 1991 providing a special scheme for the transfusional victims of HIV, below, p. 316.

[174] Art. L 376-1 al. 2 C. séc. soc. Viney and Jourdain, *Effets de la responsabilité*, 280 *et seq*. Where legislation creates a general immunity in a person otherwise liable (as in the case of accidents at work), any *tiers payeurs* cannot recover by way of subrogated claim.   [175] Art. L 376-1 al. 3 C. séc. soc.

quality of property neither supplied or used by themselves (as is the case with certifiers).

By contrast with this treatment of private law, my treatment of the impact of public law on liability for things is rather more complex. For example, on what basis or bases are public *bodies* liable for the things which they employ in the public service? As ever, 'things' for this purpose are as varied as military explosives, blood products in public hospitals, mains electricity, cars used by civil servants or a public monument such as the Paris Opera House. While *sometimes* French law treats liability in these sorts of situation as belonging to public law, this is by no means always the case.

Here, I distinguish three types of situations. In the first (dealt with in Chapter 6), I shall look at the impact of administrative *law* on the use or supply of things, these things typically, but not exclusively, being used or supplied by public bodies. Here, I shall look at the application of the administrative law of liability for fault, liability without fault and governing 'public works' in this context.

By contrast, in Chapter 7 I shall look at a number of situations which straddle the categories of administrative and private law. This straddling can either take the form of the use of private law to govern the liabilities, or at least some of the liabilities of certain classes of public bodies in respect of the use or supply of things. Here, a prime example is the complex of liabilities governing the supply of 'public utilities' such as gas, water and electricity. Sometimes, though, this straddling of the categories of public and private law takes the form of looking at a factual or functional category of activity which is recognisably the same whether carried on by a public and or a private body. Here, an example may be found in the case of liability in respect of the use or supply of products in the course of medical care.

Thirdly, however, I wish to distinguish cases of liability imposed on a public authority for failing to exercise its powers of supervision or control over the safety of things, again whether these are movable or immovable. In French law, this liability clearly falls to be governed by public law. In my view, this law is distinctive in a more profound way, for this situation involves the exercise by a public body of powers which are peculiarly public. They are public not merely in the sense that they are granted for the furtherance of the public interest, but also in the sense that they include powers which ordinary citizens do not enjoy. It is for this reason that I deal with this area in a separate section of this work, where I shall compare the position in English law.[176]

---

[176] Below, Chaps. 12 and 13.

3

Droit Privé: Delictual Liability for Fault and for the 'Deeds of Things'

How does liability for products fit into the traditional picture of the private law of delict? The answer is by no means straightforward, but there are two key points.

First, liability for delictual fault has played a more restrained role in the imposition of liability for products in the civil (as opposed to criminal) process than its extraordinary breadth would suggest. Moreover, even where liability is based on fault, an English lawyer needs to take care as the understanding and functions of the notion of fault differ significantly from the tort of negligence. For while negligence or intentional conduct may constitute *une faute*, they will not always do so; conversely, a person may commit *une faute* even in the absence of negligence (in the English sense) or deliberate conduct: *la faute* has a wide range of meanings, this being clear from French juristic 'definitions' which talk merely of its 'wrongfulness' or the 'abnormality' of a person's behaviour.[1] Moreover, even where French law accepts that a defendant's liability can be based on a lack of care (*imprudence* or *manque de diligence*), this concept has not been explored and structured in a way at all like the English notion of 'negligence', with its rules on the applicable standard of care in different contexts and evaluation of a range of relevant factors.[2] Secondly, liability for the 'deeds of things' under article 1384 alinéa 1 of the Civil Code plays an important role in the pattern of liabilities for products, a role which is not affected by the implementation of the Product Liability Directive by the *loi* of 1998.[3]

In order to appreciate these liabilities, whether for fault or without fault, I need to look more closely at the notion of fault itself, but also at the institutional and procedural context in which it is imbedded. This context is also important for an understanding of the application of other important concepts on which liability is founded, notably, defect, whether for the purposes of the law of sale or the *loi* of 1998.[4]

1. Defining and Finding Delictual Fault

(a) The institutional context

The key element of this setting is the division of function between the lower courts (courts of first instance and cours d'appel) which are together known as the

---

[1] Bell, Boyron and Whittaker, 358–9. [2] Below, pp. 186–200.
[3] Below, pp. 539–41. [4] Below, pp. 78–9, 482–4.

juges du fond (courts deciding on the merits on the basis of both fact and law) and the Cour de cassation. While there is a system of appeals from decisions of first instance to the cours d'appel, the latter's judgments are subject only to *pourvoi en cassation* ('application for quashing') to the Cour de cassation. The starting point for understanding the relative roles of the Cour de cassation and the *juges du fond* is that the Cour de cassation is the 'guardian of the law' and in principle, therefore, is concerned with ensuring the proper application of the law to facts by the lower courts throughout France. The importance of this purpose and of citizens receiving justice according to the law means that French litigants have both a right of appeal (by way of the re-opening of issues appealed as a matter of fact and law)[5] and also a right to apply to the Cour de cassation to ask it to see the law properly applied by the *juges du fond*.[6] So, on dealing with a *pourvoi en cassation*, the Cour cassation does not re-decide cases submitted to it having corrected the legal rules to be applied[7] and certainly does not re-assess evidence or re-open issues of fact; rather it reviews the decision below and, if this was defective, 'quashes' it, sending the case back to a lower court to make any new factual findings or 'assessments' of these facts as necessary.[8] From this perspective, the Cour de cassation is a court of review of the legitimacy of the decisions of the lower courts subjected to its control.

The importance of this system of *cassation* for an understanding of French private law cannot be overestimated. For it means that all propositions of private law have to be analysed so as to distinguish between issues or aspects of issues to be treated as ones of fact for the 'sovereign power of assessment' (*pouvoir souverain d'appréciation*) of the *juges du fond* and of law for the control of the Cour de cassation. And while modern legislation occasionally makes clear that in coming to a particular decision (or in exercising a power of assessment) the lower courts have a 'sovereign power', for the most part it is the Cour de cassation itself which determines which propositions fall within its control: it intervenes on grounds, in ways and to an extent of which it is itself the master. Thus, whole tracts of the legal landscape (or what to an English lawyer would be the legal landscape) are all but abandoned by the Cour de cassation to the lower courts,[9] while in other places, the Cour de cassation is careful to restrict their room for manoeuvre with rules of law whose non-observance will attract its intervention. In the result, it is one of the most salient but also one of the most frustrating aspects of French private law that many issues are decided by the lower courts behind this impenetrable veil of their 'sovereign power of assessment'. This division of function between the *juges du fond* and Cour de cassation is of singular importance both as regards our present concern with determining the issue of delictual fault, and also with other key concepts such as 'defect' in the law of sale.[10]

---

[5] Art. 543 N.c.pr.civ. An exception is made for small claims at present set at €3,800: Art. R 311-2 C. org. jud.   [6] Arts. 604–5 N.c.pr.civ. (from decisions of last resort).

[7] It does have the power to decide the case on the basis of facts 'sovereignly found': art. 627 N.c.pr.civ.

[8] Vincent and Guinchard, *Procédure civile*, 1064–5.

[9] Striking examples may be found in French treatment of the interpretation of contracts and the measure and quantification of damages: Bell, Boyron and Whittaker, 332–3, 349–51 and 395–7.

[10] Below, pp. 78–9.

(b) The definition of *la faute délictuelle*

I have already drawn attention both to the breadth of provisions in articles 1382 and 1383 of the Civil Code concerning liability for delictual fault and to their absence of restriction either as to the type of conduct included (beyond that it constitutes *une faute*) or the type of harm recoverable (*any harm*).[11] Nor do these provisions tell us very much about French law's understanding of *la faute* itself, except to the extent that it makes clear that it may be seen in a lack of care as well as in malice or intention and that no formal distinction is drawn according to the seriousness of a defendant's fault between *faute intentionnel* ('intentional fault'), *faute lourde* ('gross fault') and *faute légère* ('ordinary fault').

But what does *la faute* mean? While Planiol famously suggested that fault should be defined as the non-performance of a pre-existing legal duty,[12] this definition has not generally found favour, being considered inaccurate (there being no need for a claimant to establish any such duty), unnecessary and unhelpful.[13] Instead, many French jurists looking for a general definition of *la faute délictuelle* end up by using such very broad expressions as 'abnormal behaviour' or simply 'failing to do what one ought to do',[14] definitions which are helpful only to the extent to which they emphasise how open the question of fault may be. But while there is certainly no shortage in French *doctrine* of discussions of the concept of *la faute*, much of their focus and concern appears very alien to English law's concern with the analysis of negligence in the sense of a lack of reasonable care in the circumstances and one looks for any equivalent of such an analysis in vain. In my view, there are four reasons for this.

First, doctrinal debate as to the conception of *la faute* in France has long been dominated by an underlying argument as to whether or not *faute* does or should stand as the basis of all civil liability (or rather, *responsabilité*) delictual or contractual, special or general. In this debate, a central focus of attention has been the question whether or not the test for *faute* is 'subjective' (assessed '*in concreto*', by reference to a moral judgment as to what the particular defendant was in a position to do)[15] or 'objective' (assessed '*in abstracto*' by reference to a standard such as the *bon père de famille*). A key context for argument about this question was the liability of the mentally incompetent: should their 'fault' be judged by reference to their own capacities or by reference to those of a fully competent person? While particular questions relating to this 'subjective/objective' debate have been settled either by legislation (as in the case of the

---

[11] Above, pp. 23–4.   [12] M. Planiol, 'Etudes sur la responsabilité civile' (1905) *Rev. crit.* 277, 287.
[13] Malaurie, Aynès and Stoffel-Munck, *Obligations*, 28; Flour, Aubert and Savaux, *Fait juridique*, 94. Cf. Viney and Jourdain, *Conditions*, 326 *et seq.* who explain cases where no legal duty is broken or legal right violated as ones of 'extra-contractual duties created by *la jurisprudence*'.
[14] Flour, Aubert and Savaux, *Fait juridique*, 95; Tourneau and Le Cadiet, *Droit de la responsabilité*, 1047.
[15] An important supporter of this position was P. Esmein: see 'Le fondement de la responsabilité contractuelle rapproché de la responsabilité délictuelle' 1933 RTDCiv. 627 and his edition of Aubry et Rau, *Droit civil*, Vol. VI (Lib. Techniques Juris-Classeurs, Paris, 6th. edn, 1951), 396 where *la faute délictuelle* is defined as '*un acte donnant lieu à reproche*'. A very different definition appears in the 7th edition of 1975 (by A. Ponsard and N. Dejean de la Batie, Vol. VI, 520) where *la faute* is said not to involve a moral assessment but rather to consist of '*faits défectueux générateurs d'un trouble social auquel le droit se doit se remédier*'.

mentally incompetent)[16] or by settled judicial practice (as in the case of those with special skills[17] or children[18]) and while the vast majority have adopted an objective position at least as regards *non-intentional* fault, the nature of this debate has distracted attention away from any fuller exploration of the content of *imprudence* itself. While jurists may sometimes state that '[non-intentional] fault consists sometimes in not having foreseen the possibility of harm, sometimes, if it has been foreseen, in not having taken the necessary precautions to avoid its occurrence',[19] they do not develop further discussion of these elements or their possible balancing. For a traditionally-minded French lawyer, the common law's balancing of cost against benefit would have the ring of economic pragmatism about it, a ring out of tune both with traditional Catholic and with Enlightenment individualistic assumptions of what morality means in the context of responsibility for personal behaviour.[20] Some French lawyers *were* concerned with the proper allocation of risk between the perpetrators and the victims of accidents, but their ideas were seen as essentially hostile to arguments based on fault; in such a milieu, it is unsurprising that an aspect of fault (*imprudence*) should not be explained in terms of the avoidance of the risk of harm. It may well also be that the 'superabundance and diversity' of opinions in *la doctrine* helps to explain the courts 'timidity' in coming to a universal definition of civil fault themselves.[21]

A second reason for the very different treatment of delictual fault in French *doctrine* from analyses of English negligence lies in the former's role within the system of the substantive law of liability. As I have said, the ambit of liability for *la faute délictuelle* is far broader than that imposed by the tort of negligence even in the hands of the most expansive English judge. In the absence of defined areas of application or a controlling concept such as the English 'duty of care' in the tort of negligence, *la faute* is forced to play a number of roles, setting out not merely the 'mental' element (*l'élément moral*) necessary for the imposition of liability (intention or negligence) but at least in some types of case also the situations where this should give rise to liability (a 'wrongfulness' aspect). French law has in effect had to invent the particularity of treatment usually associated with those legal systems which recognize only 'special delicts' or a law of torts under the umbrella of the general principle of liability for fault found

---

[16] Art. 489-2 C. civ. enacted by the *loi* no. 68–5 of 3 Jan. 1968, which declares that 'a person who has caused harm to another while under the influence of a mental problem is on that ground not the less obliged to make compensation of the harm'.

[17] Civ. (2) 8 Jul. 1954, JCP 1954.IV.122 (profession); Paris 25 Jan. 1956, D 1956.184.

[18] Ass. plén. 9 May 1984, JCP 1984.II.20256 note Jourdain, D 1984.525 note Chabas.

[19] Flour, Aubert and Savaux, *Fait juridique*, 107. Malaurie, Aynès and Stoffel-Munck, *Obligations*, 30–1 refer to 'degrees of foreseeability', but in the context of the different types of *faute*.

[20] See M. Villey, 'Esquisse historique sur le mot responsable' in *Archives de philosophie du droit*, Tome 22, *La responsabilité* (Paris, 1977), 45 at 55–6 (attributing the traditional position in responsibility for fault to a starting point in the morality of Aquinas, the Spanish scholastics and the 'professors of morality' of the seventeenth century supplemented by an influence of Kant). Esmein, argued for its link to sin: *op. cit.* n. 15, 1933 RTDCiv. 627, 631–2. Moreover, most French jurists continue to justify *la responsabilité contractuelle* on the basis of *une faute contractuelle*, where the fault consists simply in the failure to perform the contractual obligation as the debtor ought, a characterisation of the basis of contractual liability which operates at a higher level of generality than the distinction between *obligations de résultat* and *obligations de moyens* (where *une faute* in the sense of *manque de diligence* is necessary for liability to arise): Larroumet, *Contrat*, 594 *et seq.*   [21] Viney and Jourdain, *Conditions*, 318.

in the Civil Code. So, for example, while *imprudence* may count as delictual fault, interference by a third party in the performance of a contract will not give rise to liability in that third party in the absence of *une faute intentionelle*: in this situation, lack of care does not supply the requisite fault element.[22] Having said this, in French law these are islands of special treatment in a sea of liability, rather than (as in the English law of torts) islands of liability in a sea of immunity.[23]

It is this broader functional context that explains in part the Cour de cassation's view that while it is for the *juges du fond* to find the facts (what happened), it is for itself to control their classification (as properly *faute* or not).[24] Without such a power of control, the Cour de cassation would not be in a position to use *la faute* as a technique for holding certain types of fault necessary for liability in particular contexts.

However, this division of function between the *juges du fond* and Cour de cassation provides the third reason for the lack of exploration of what fault means by the courts. For while formally the Cour de cassation reserves to itself a power of review of the characterization of the defendant's behaviour as *une faute* and requires the *juges du fond* to explain their decisions on *la faute* so as to allow this control,[25] this still leaves its evaluation on the facts in large measure to the *juges du fond*, especially in the context of *imprudence*.[26] As Carbonnier puts it:

Fault is no more the sum of physical, psychological and social elements than life is the sum of oxygen, hydrogen, carbon etc. There must be something more: a spontaneous and intuitive judgment by the court seen as morally self-evident. Nowhere more than in relation to fault do the judges proceed by way of a judgment based on fairness [*équité*] condemning or pardoning in the name of society . . . The Cour de cassation's assessment is a global one, acting as a court of *review of excesses of fairness*. Rather than ensuring that the law is respected, its role here appears to be to prevent (in the interest, most often, why shouldn't one say it? of insurance companies and parties with deep pockets) an over-charitable fairness, which would let the evaluation of needs and resources come before consideration of the morality of the case.[27]

So, the Cour de cassation sometimes chooses to intervene in the decision making of the lower courts on *la faute délictuelle*, not merely where it can identify a contradiction in the lower court's position,[28] but also where it takes the view that the facts relied on

---

[22] Malaurie, Aynès, and Stoffel-Munck, *Obligations*, 376; e.g. Com. 13 Mar. 1979, Bull. civ. IV no. 100. Another example may be found in the law governing civil liability for *concurrence déloyale* as here competitive behaviour will not be held 'at fault' unless it is *unfair* (*déloyal*): Starck, Roland, and Boyer, *Responsabilité délictuelle*, 114, who refer to the fact that '*la concurrence doit être déloyale, la grève illicite, la critique malveillante, la séduction dolosive, la rupture de fiançailles intempestives, etc*'.   [23] See below, p. 159.

[24] Flour, Aubert, and Savaux, *Fait juridique*, 114; Civ. 28 Feb. 1910, S 1911.1.329 note Appert, DP 1913.1.43; Civ. (2) 7 Jun. 1962, D 1962.721 note Savatier; Civ. (2) 25 Nov. 1965, Bull. civ. II no. 935.

[25] Civ. (2) 7 Mar. 1973, D 1973.IR.104, JCP 1973.IV.153.

[26] Flour, Aubert and Savaux, *Fait juridique*, 95. '*Mieux vaut donc convenir, de façon moins ambitieuse, que la notion de faute est inévitablement assez vague. Elle constitue ce que l'on appelle parfois un "standard", c'est-à-dire une directive relativement générale pour l'application de laquelle le juge ne peut pas ne pas bénéficier d'un large pouvoir d'appréciation.*' According to G. Ripert, '*ce mot[la faute], venu au droit de la morale, n'a pu acquérir la précision technique de certains termes juridiques*' and for this reason has not received any satisfactory definition: *La règle morale dans les obligations civiles* (LGDJ, Paris, 4th. edn., 1949) 199.

[27] Carbonnier, *Obligations*, 414 (emphasis added).

[28] E.g.Civ. (2) 29 Jun. 1972, Bull. civ. II no. 204.

by the lower court should not be seen as *une faute*.[29] But this 'considerable role' which 'marries strangely' with its function as a court of review, has not led to a true definition of *faute civile*: 'the supreme court [is content]...in the majority of cases to decide disputes on a case by case basis without formulating any guidelines of a general nature.'[30] Moreover, while we see the occasional re-evaluation in terms of *la faute* by the Cour de cassation of the facts as found below, we do not see the reassessment of the evidence which was put before the court below as to the issue of *faute*. Indeed while the *arrêt* of a lower court must set out the factual circumstances of the case, the courts do not see it as part of their function in the *arrêt* to explain why they rely on this or that piece of evidence rather than on another: the court refers to the competing claims and allegations of the parties, and then simply announces its view of the facts and their legal significance. Often complex factual and especially technical issues are not discussed in the judgment, but are instead taken from the report of judicially appointed experts as a given.[31] For some authors the breadth of 'appreciation' which this gives to the *juges du fond* allows them to qualify the 'objective nature' of their assessment of non-intentional fault and take into account personal factors affecting the individual defendant, such as his physical abilities or age.[32]

Fourthly, while *la jurisprudence* is immensely important in French law (and particularly in the law of civil responsibility with its mere handful of codal provisions), there is no sense in which a particular decision of a higher court or even the settled practice of a higher court *binds* a lower court.[33] This absence of a binding force of previous decisions similar to the English doctrine of precedent and its concomitant doctrine of *ratio decidendi*, means that French lawyers look at their *jurisprudence* with different eyes than an English lawyer looks at case law. French lawyers look at affirmations of principle, the interpretation of legislation in question and the general context, but do not see the same sort of need to connect the facts of the case to the law as is felt in England. In my view, one consequence of this is that French lawyers do not tend to look for patterns in the decision making of the courts which then gradually attract a degree of legal force: there is much less tendency towards the juridification of facts.[34]

On the other hand, there is one particular feature of French understanding of delictual fault which illustrates very clearly its difference from the English conception of negligence. For while French lawyers reject the need for any breach of a legal, regulatory or professional duty to found *une faute civile*, they accept that breach of such a duty *will* provide *une faute civile* so as to provide a basis for civil liability.[35] This means, first, that the commission of any criminal offence itself constitutes a civil fault so as to give rise to liability in damages for any harm which it causes, even as regards criminal offences which do not themselves require any negligence, being committed by a person's mere 'physical' action or failure to act:[36] the commission of an 'offence of strict

---

[29] E.g. Civ. 25 Nov. 1965, Bull. civ. II no. 935 (no fault in the owner and driver of a car in failing to check whether a competent garage replaced his vehicle's wheel properly).

[30] Viney and Jourdain, *Conditions*, 318.   [31] Below, pp. 48–50.

[32] Terré, Simler, Lequette, *Obligations*, 701.   [33] Bell, Boyron, Whittaker, 27–8.

[34] Cf. below, pp. 201–2, 245.   [35] Terré, Simler and Lequette, *Obligations*, 695.

[36] Ibid., 698 and see below, p. 373. Cf. Bénabent, *Obligations*, 364–5 who suggests tentatively that Civ. (1) 7 Oct. 1998, Bull. civ. I, no. 286 suggests that these offences form an exception, but this case is a

liability' (*une infraction purement matérielle*) can constitute *une faute civile*.[37] Furthermore, there is no need for a duty to be contained in legislation or sanctioned by the criminal law for its breach to constitute *in itself* a civil fault: 'any breaking of an explicit mandatory rule is in itself illicit and therefore *fautif*, without it being necessary to find negligence, imprudence, lack of care, or any deficiency of behaviour whatsoever in the person in question'.[38] This means that breach of professional duties or even rules of a game constitute 'fault' so as to give rise to liability in damages for any harm that it causes.[39] On the other hand, the performance of duties contained in legislation does not mean that some further fault cannot be found, as a defendant may still be at fault for failing to abide by a customary standard.[40]

(c) Establishing fault in the French civil process

I wish now to turn to the process by which the French legal system decides the issue of a defendant's delictual fault, both in terms of its understanding of the notion of burden of proof and in terms of the range of materials before the *juges du fond*. In order to do so, I need to examine briefly French law's conceptions of the relative roles of the parties and the court in relation to fact and law.

A traditional way of thinking of the French civil process starts with a rigid demarcation between the roles of the parties (to define their dispute by their respective allegations and to bring forward evidence of the facts on which they rely) and for the court to apply the law to the facts as they find them: 'the court decides the case according to the rules of law applicable'.[41] According to this way of thinking, ' the court being neutral, it is for each party to prove the facts necessary for the success of their allegations'.[42] However, this simple model does not fit the reality of the process under the New Code of Civil Procedure in a number of ways, as 'the evolution of [French] civil procedure towards the inquisitorial model tends... to tone down the importance of the burden of proof... the essential thing is to arrive at the truth'.[43]

So, first, while the parties may be invited to make submissions on the law applicable to their case,[44] a court is not restricted to the legal materials cited to it: the court 'knows the law'.[45] On the other hand, the question whether a court can or must re-characterize a claim in different legal terms from those proposed by a litigant is more difficult as there is clearly a tension between the principle that it is for the parties to define the subject matter of their dispute and for the courts to apply the law. For while

---

contravention de grande voirie which is not strictly a criminal offence. This position has not been changed by the *loi* no. 2000–647 of 10 Jul. 2000, below, pp. 393–4, which has at least in part led to the abandonment of the 'unity of criminal and civil faults'.

[37] Cf. below, pp. 387–90, 393–4 on the effect of changes to the definition of *délits*.

[38] Viney and Jourdain, *Conditions*, 327–8. See similarly, Terré, Simler and Lequette, *Obligations*, 695.

[39] Carbonnier, *Obligations*, 418–19.   [40] Ibid., 419.

[41] Art. 12 al. 1 N.c.pr.civ. ('*le juge tranche le litige conformément aux règles de droit qui lui sont applicables*').

[42] Carbonnier, *Introduction*, 336; Cf. art. 9 N.c.pr.civ.

[43] Ibid., 346. see further G. Couchez, *Procédure civile* (Armand Colin, Paris, 12th edn., 2002), 189–91.

[44] Art. 13 N.c.pr.civ.

[45] '*Curia novit legem*. (*Le juge est censé connaître [le droit]*)': Carbonnier, *Introduction*, 348. see also Bell, *French Legal Cultures*, 89–91.

the parties adduce a 'complex of facts' to the court which then characterizes them, they are free to support their factual allegations with their allegedly legal consequences.[46]

Secondly, the facts are established before a French court through the 'administration of *les preuves*'. There is, though, a particular difficulty in translating *preuve*, as it combines elements of the English terms 'proof' and 'evidence'. In English law, rules of evidence set out what types or sources of evidence may be admitted for assessment by the fact-finding body and, on occasion, what weight should be given to them. The (persuasive or legal) burden of proof has been defined as 'the obligation of a party to meet the requirement that a fact in issue be proved (or disproved) either by a preponderance of the evidence or beyond reasonable doubt'[47] and in the civil context the 'standard of proof' is the balance of probabilities.

In the French context, these notions are not as sharply distinguished. The more prominent distinction is between the facts (*les faits*) on which a litigant relies and their *preuve* and here the sense of *preuve* seems to be similar to the English 'proof', The starting point is that the burden of proof ('*le charge de la preuve*') as to delictual fault under articles 1382 and 1383 of the Civil Code lies on the person claiming it and may be established 'by any means',[48] being typically contrasted with those liabilities found in the Civil Code where the burden of proof is reversed creating a (rebuttable) presumption of fault.[49] Some jurists make clear that strictly speaking the claimant's burden of proof applies only to the simple facts (what happened, the *éléments matériels*), the legal characterization of these facts being for the court, 'an operation of legal classification which is controlled by the Cour de cassation'.[50]

However, on turning to French works on civil procedure, one finds that the parties to civil litigation are said to *share* the practical responsibility for gathering evidence (*les preuves*) with the court itself.[51] For the *juges du fond* have the power to order any necessary 'procedural measures'[52] and have an explicit power to order of their own initiative the production of a document, the examination of a witness or the commissioning of an expert report.[53] Furthermore, French lawyers do not recognise different (or any) standards of proof, but simply say, for example, that 'the proof of fault, like any other proof, does not necessarily attain certainty; a sufficient probability

---

[46] Claimants must support their allegations in this way: art. 56 2° N.c.pr. civ. See further Vincent and Guinchard, *Procédure civile*, 524 *et seq.* and esp. 537–8 discussing art. 12 N.c.pr.civ. to the effect that the courts *must* classify the parties' claims (i) if the parties have not done so; (ii) where the parties have done so but wrongly; and (iii) where a court has exercised its discretion to pick up and rely in its decision on facts from the material before it which have *not* been specifically relied on by the parties in their submissions (so-called *faits adventices*). On the other hand, where the parties have not relied on particular facts in their submissions and the court has not picked them up from the *faits adventices*, then the court *may* but need not classify the facts in question, for these are facts or legal transactions which the court may legitimately ignore.

[47] *Cross and Tapper on Evidence* (Butterworths, 9th. edn., 1999) 108 and see below, pp. 208–9.

[48] Flour, Aubert and Savaux, *Fait juridique*, 113.The formula that '*la preuve...peut être faite par tous moyens*', often called, '*libre preuve*' has the significance that there are no restrictions as to the type of evidence or type of reasoning from which a decision may be made. See below, p. 78.

[49] E.g. liability of parents for their children before 1997, above, p. 25.

[50] Bénabent, *Obligations*, 350.

[51] Arts. 10, 11, 143, 144 N.c.pr.civ.; Ghestin, Goubeaux and Fabre-Magnan, *Introduction*, 561–2; Vincent and Guinchard, *Procédure civile*, 540–1.   [52] Art. 3 N.c.pr.civ.

[53] Art. 10 N.c.pr.civ.

('*une vraisemblance suffisante*') can be considered as proof by a court'.[54] While the *juges du fond* in civil cases are not said to decide according to their 'intimate conviction',[55] they may simply conclude that the factual elements of a case convince them that a defendant was or was not at fault.[56]

(d) The gathering of evidence

However, even more different from the English process are the ways in which *les preuves* (in the sense of evidential materials) are presented to the *juges du fond*. There are two main features here.

(i) *The distrust of orality and the absence of documentary disclosure*

The French civil process reflects a longstanding distrust of orality and a preference for written evidence[57] and French civil hearings typically do not consist of the hearing of witnesses, their cross-examination and the lengthy exposition of legal arguments.[58] As to non-technical matters, witnesses may be heard by a court directly, but it is more common for the parties (not their lawyers) to obtain written depositions from witnesses.[59] On the other hand, there is a striking paradox in French reliance on written evidence, for its civil process does not possess what a common lawyer would recognise as a power to order disclosure.[60] For while French law gives its courts an apparently wide power to order the production of documents, in reality this is rarely exercised, since the parties can ask only for the production of an identified document and must also show its relevance, both of which assume that they already know of its existence and its content;[61] there is no duty of disclosure of a list of relevant documents in either the parties or their lawyers. The exchange of documents is seen as part of the right of a party to see the other's case, rather than as a mechanism for the discovery of facts prejudicial to the other side from their own documents; and the weight of professional ethics is balanced in favour of not revealing any document prejudicial to one's own client's case, rather than the revealing of any relevant document in a quest for the truth.[62] In the result, relevant documentary evidence often does not come before civil courts because opposing parties do not know what to ask for and will not volunteer it in the absence of specific, judicial instruction.

(ii) *The* expertise

French courts do not take 'evidence' of technical facts in the way in which much controversial technical evidence is taken in the English civil process, viz. by competing

---

[54] Starck, *Responsabilité délictuelle*, 151–2.   [55] Cf. below, p. 385, concerning criminal offences.
[56] Civ. (1) 6 Jan. 1971, Bull. civ. I, no. 5.   [57] Bell, Boyron and Whittaker, 84–5.
[58] J. Beardsley, 'Proof of Fact in French Civil Procedure' (1986) 34 *Am. J. Comp.L.* 459.
[59] Bell, Boyron and Whittaker, 98–100. Evidence by deposition is called *attestation*, by oral evidence *enquête*; where the parties themselves give evidence, the process is termed *comparution*.
[60] Ibid., 93–6.
[61] Arts. 138–142 N.c.pr.civ. Art. 132 N.c.pr.civ. also provides that the parties must provide the other side with documents but this applies only to documents *which they intend to rely on* ('*communication des pièces*'): Bell, Boyron and Whittaker, 94–6.   [62] Beardsley, *op. cit.* n. 58, 474–5.

evidence, whether oral or in writing.[63] Instead, technical issues are the object of an independent written report by judicially appointed technical experts, this process being termed the *expertise*. However, technical experts often go well beyond the merely technical and, inevitably, give their own judgments on issues which are strictly of mixed law and fact, such as the existence of *une faute*. There are four key features to *expertises*.

First, while a French court has the power to order an *expertise* of its own initiative, it rarely does so and can refuse a party's request for an *expertise* for no more specific reason than that it considers it of no use.[64] A court has a complete discretion as to whom to appoint to advise on technical issues,[65] although they may refer to lists, approved for different areas of France by the administration. The parties may challenge an expert's appointment only on very narrowly defined grounds of relationship to the parties themselves or involvement in the subject matter of the litigation.[66] The court has a 'sovereign power of assessment' in the definition of the expert's task[67] and the timescale for submitting the report (which is usually in writing).[68] In all, the court controls the questions and to whom they are addressed.

Secondly, the expert or experts receive copies of any relevant documents from the parties and choose the method which he or they consider appropriate for the investigation of the issues in question. They can examine any physical thing (such as the scene of an accident or a product involved) and can hold a hearing with both parties (and their lawyers) present[69] and invite their and others' accounts of what actually occurred.[70] For some, this hearing is closer to a common law trial than is the court's hearing itself, though even here no cross-examination occurs.[71]

Thirdly, while in principle courts are not bound to follow the views of the expert,[72] they very rarely do not, since, as one writer puts it, it is difficult for a judge to contradict an expert in his own field without recourse to the advice of another expert.[73] The court may, to this end, order a further *expertise* to examine or to re-examine issues whose treatment it considers unsatisfactory, but this is only rarely done.[74] Although a party may claim that the *expertise* be annulled either on formal or on substantive grounds,[75] again this is rare.[76] On the other hand, if the *juges du fond* fundamentally misinterpret the conclusions reached by an *expertise*, their decision will be quashed.[77]

---

[63] Below, pp. 211–12.

[64] R. Genin-Méric, 'Mesures d'instruction exécutés par un technicien. Les trois modalités de l'intervention du technicien', Jur.-Cl. Proc. Civ., Fasc. 662 (1995), 7–8; Req. 15 Jun. 1880, DP 1881.1.62. The decision to appoint an expert can be subject to appeal under art. 272 N.c.pr.civ. There are exceptions to this power to reject requests for an *expertise*, notably in the case of the *action aestimatoire*: art. 1644 C. civ.

[65] Arts. 232 and 265 N.c.pr.civ.

[66] Arts. 234 and 341 N.c.pr.civ. The grounds of challenge are the same as those of judges themselves.

[67] Soc. 29 Nov. 1984, JCP 1985.IV.50.   [68] Art. 282 N.c.pr.civ.   [69] Art. 276 N.c.pr.civ.

[70] Genin-Méric, *op. cit.* n. 64 Jur.-Cl. .Proc. Civ. Fasc. 662, 16.   [71] Beardsley, *op. cit.* n. 58, 483.

[72] Art. 246 N.c.pr.civ.

[73] R. Genin-Méric, 'Mesures d'instruction exécutées par un technicien, Dispositions communes, L'intervention d'un technicien dans l'instruction des litiges', Jur.-Cl. Proc. Civ. (1988), Fasc. 660, 12 (this passage does not appear in the more recent edition of this work).   [74] Beardsley, *op. cit.* n.58, 484.

[75] It is *not* a ground for nullity that an *expert* has not heard the evidence of all those whom the parties request should be heard, as it is for him to choose his sources of information, Genin-Méric, *op. cit.* n. 64, Jur.-Cl. .Proc. Civ. Fasc. 662, 20.   [76] Genin-Méric, *op. cit.* n. 64, Jur.-Cl.Proc. Civ., Fasc. 662, 19–21.

[77] This fundamental misinterpretation is known as *dénaturation* and see Civ. (3) 4 Jan.1979, JCP 1979.IV.79.

Fourthly, although an expert is appointed by and reports to the court, the cost of the *expertise* is not paid for out of public funds.[78] Instead, the court decides on an appropriate fee for the expert[79] and which party or parties to the litigation should provisionally pay this amount into court in advance,[80] a decision for which the court need give no reasons.[81] If this sum is not paid, the *expertise* lapses.[82] The question which of the parties ultimately bears the costs of the *expertise* is not decided until the court gives judgment,[83] and then it is the losing party, unless the court otherwise decides for a specified reason.[84] What this means is, therefore, that if, as often happens, a claimant makes a provisional payment in respect of the likely cost of an *expertise*, he risks losing this if the defendant proves insolvent. As we shall see, this aspect of the costs of civil proceedings has tempted claimants to bring their claim where possible before a criminal court, where costs are differently handled.[85]

What all this means is that in practice the French civil process severely limits the range of factual material which is put forward for the consideration of the *juges du fond* on an issue such as delictual fault. As will be seen, these characteristics of the French process have been fully reflected in its treatment of the key concept of *vice* or *défaut* for the purposes of contractual liabilities and will also be reflected at least in part in their treatment of the concept of 'defect' for the purposes of the Product Liability Directive.[86]

2. The Restricted Significance of Delictual Fault for Liability for Products

The extraordinary generality of liability under articles 1382 and 1383 of the Civil Code would suggest that it would have been important in governing liability for defective products and indeed it has been, but not in ways which would suggest themselves readily to the common lawyer. As I have previously indicated, this is because many of the cases of harm caused by products are in French law dealt with either by liability for the deeds of things, which is more attractive to a claimant, or by contractual liability, which is exclusive within its own domain. Liability for delictual fault, therefore, is significant only in the gaps between these two 'special' liabilities.

As I shall explain, where a person has bought property, he enjoys a number of different contractual actions in respect of harm caused by its defects, not merely against his own contractor, the seller, but against any other person higher up the chain of distribution;[87] and where a buyer possesses a contractual claim he may not instead claim on the basis of delictual fault owing to the operation of the rule of *non-cumul*.[88] Secondly, many people who enjoy the use of a product which has caused them injury or loss do so under a contract (for example, of hire or for the provision of services) and again where this is the case they are likely to enjoy a contractual claim against the provider of

---

[78] An unpaid expert can recover his costs against the State only if he shows a *faute de service* in the court: Civ. (1) 21 Dec. 1987, D 1988.578 note Moussa.

[79] Art. 284 al. 1 N.c.pr.civ. This may be increased after the report is submitted: art. 280 al. 2 N.c.pr.civ.

[80] Art. 269 N.c.pr.civ.　　　　[81] Soc. 2 Apr. 1981, GP 1981.2 Pan. Jur. 315.

[82] Art. 271 N.c.pr.civ.　　　　[83] Art. 695 al. 4. N.c.pr.civ.　　　　[84] Art. 696 N.c.pr.civ.

[85] Below, pp. 385–6.　　　　[86] Below, pp. 78, 484.　　　　[87] Below, pp. 96–8.　　　　[88] Above, pp. 27–9.

the product, again excluding recourse to delict.[89] On the other hand, claims for damages for personal injuries and damage to property caused to those who have neither bought the product nor enjoy it under a contract are usually brought against its *gardien* under article 1384 aliéna 1 of the Code, which does not require any formal proof of fault, rather than liability for proven fault under article 1383.[90] The relationship between these two liabilities will be examined in more detail in the following section as in the modern law here article 1384 alinéa 1 creates the larger category.[91]

Where does this leave liability for delictual fault ?

First, delictual fault remains important as the basis for liability for the compensation of personal injuries and death where claims are brought by victims of offences before the criminal courts as *parties civiles*. This is because French lawyers have long considered that the commission of any offence, whatever its *mens rea* and of whatever type itself constitutes delictual fault.[92] Both the specific and the general regulation of product safety and product quality by the criminal law have been used as the basis for a claim for damages for the victims of these crimes. Moreover, there are practical and procedural reasons why the victims of such product crimes should wish to claim before the criminal rather than civil courts.[93] While more recently, this relatively simple picture has become more complex, delictual fault remains the legal basis for the imposition of civil liability where this is tied to a criminal offence. I shall return to this topic in Chapter 14.

Secondly, sometimes a person who has suffered harm caused by a product may prefer *not* to sue its *gardien* or any person with whom he is in contractual relations but instead go against some other, perhaps more substantial, defendant, notably the product's manufacturer claiming the latter's delictual fault.[94] In this situation, as early as the 1970s French courts appeared to adopt a very particular interpretation of delictual fault, holding it established in a manufacturer (though apparently *not* in a mere supplier) merely by the act of putting a defective product onto the market.[95] Some older cases concern, for example, the victim of a road accident who chooses to sue the manufacturer of the car whose faulty brakes caused the accident, a choice possibly made because the driver was uninsured.[96] Other cases in which a claimant has relied on delictual fault seem to be based on a desire to avoid the complications to which the definition of *la garde* can give rise, in particular, its 'dualist division'.[97] While in principle delictual fault can be relied on in this way to sanction design as well as manufacturing defects and obligations to warn or to inform against a manufacturer,[98] by comparison

---

[89] Above, pp. 28–9.   [90] Below, pp. 100–1, 108–11.   [91] Below, pp. 51–9.

[92] See below, pp. 374–5.   [93] Below, pp. 384–6.

[94] A buyer or sub-buyer is barred from such a claim in delict by the rule of *non-cumul*: below, pp. 96–7.

[95] G. Viney, 'L'indemnisation des atteintes à la sécurité des consommateurs en droit français,' in Ghestin, *Sécurité des consommateurs*, 71 at 80; Ghestin, *Conformité*, 261, Civ (3) 5 Dec. 1972, D 1973.401 note J. Mazeaud.

[96] Req. 7 Oct. 1940, D.H.1940.180 (a case of *faute lourde* in the design of the vehicle's brakes). A *Fonds de garantie* now covers the victims of personal injuries caused by unidentified or uninsured drivers: art. L. 421-1 C. assur.

[97] Cf. Civ. (1) 22 Jun. 1971, JCP 1971.II.16881 (claimant injured by an exploding beer bottle succeeded against retailer for fault) and see below, p. 54.

[98] Viney, *op. cit.* n. 95, Ghestin, *Sécurité des consommateurs*, at 80, citing Civ. 17 Oct. 1984, JCP 1984.IV.355. On *obligations d'information*, see below, pp. 64–9.

to the incidence of cases based on contract or liability under article 1384 alinéa 1 it has not been very commonly invoked. Moreover, the continuing tendency of the domain of contract to expand beyond the parties ensures that the range of the potential application of delict is to the same degree reduced. It is for this reason that those cases of delictual liability for fault which remain in relation to products will be considered in the context of the particular contractual categories which may concern liability for things, as the 'special law of contract' increasingly ousts the *droit commun* of delict.[99]

Thirdly, while generally in French law delictual fault has retained its importance in relation to the compensation of pure economic loss, this is not as true as regards liability for products, for most of the economic losses caused by products are due to their defectiveness and are suffered by the person who needs as a result to repair or replace the product. In the vast majority of this sort of case the person who suffers a loss of this sort will possess a contractual action for this purpose (and, as ever, rely on this alone as against any co-contractor). On the other hand, where economic losses are caused by a product's *position* (for example, blocking a highway and causing delays to its business users), then delict, whether article 1382 or 1384 alinéa 1, may indeed apply.[100]

3. Liability without Fault for Harm Caused by Things

In 1930, the *arrêt Jand'heur* established that article 1384 alinéa 1 of the Civil Code imposed a 'presumption of liability' for the 'deeds of things' which applied to all types of physical thing,[101] whether or not they were defective, dangerous or merely the instrument of human action.[102] This decision also established, much to the displeasure of those who contended that fault was the basis of *all* civil liability,[103] that a *gardien* could not escape this liability by showing a lack of fault, but only by showing the existence of *force majeure*, that is, that the harm was unforseeable and unpreventable.[104] However, this apparently stark picture becomes more complex when one turns to the developing understanding of the key notion of *la garde* and to the treatment by the courts of the requirement of a causal connection between the thing and the claimant's harm.

(a) Who is liable?

One important question which remained after *Jand'heur* was on exactly whom this presumption of liability should rest: what is *la garde*? This question lies at the heart of the attribution of liability for things.

---

  [99] Below, pp. 100–4, 111–12.   [100] E.g. Civ. (2) 19 Mar. 1980, D 1980. IR. 414 note Larroumet.
  [101] So, e.g., televisual images are not themselves 'things' but may be produced by physical things: le Tourneau, note, Paris 27 Feb. 1991, JCP 1992.II.21809. The particular cases dealt with by arts. 1385 and 1386 C. civ. have remained outside the general liability of art. 1384 al. 1.
  [102] Ch. Réun. 13 Feb.1930, rapp. Le Marc'hadour, concl. Matter, S 1930.1.121 note Esmein, DP 1930.1.57 note Ripert.   [103] See the notes of Ripert and Esmein, ibid.
  [104] As will be seen, this simple definition of *force majeure* was refined in response to its use in the context of art. 1384 al. 1 C. civ.: below, pp. 57–8.

The story of the development in understanding of *la garde* parallels the controversy as to the basis of liability for the 'deeds of things'.[105] At first, both the context (employers' liability) and the theoretical justification (the creation of a risk—*risque créé*—or the profiting from use of the thing which created the risk—*risque-profit*[106]—both pointed to the owner of the things, such as machinery and plant, which injured their workers.[107] However, by the 1920s the most important context for the imposition of this new liability was in respect of road accidents and it was in this context that the definition of *la garde* reached its crisis. For, in the *arrêt Franck* the question arose whether the owner of a vehicle which had been stolen and then caused an accident remained *gardien*. The Chambres réunies held not, defining *la garde* in terms of the possession of 'the use, direction and control'.[108] After this decision, therefore, while an owner of a thing is presumed to be its *gardien*, he can rebut this presumption by showing that *garde* has been transferred,[109] which is a particular example of his being no longer in a position to prevent the thing from doing harm. In this way, liability under article 1384 alinéa 1 became attributive of responsibility and not merely a mechanism for the allocation of risk.

The definition of *la garde* established by the Chambres réunies has also caused considerable difficulty, in particular where the particular elements of this definition are not united in one person. Thus, in general, a person who hires a thing, whether a movable or an immovable, becomes the *gardien* in substitution to the person who lets it.[110] Sometimes the distinctions in the case law are difficult to explain. For example, it has been held that a customer becomes *gardien* of a supermarket trolley put at his disposal by the store,[111] but not of a bottle which he has taken from the shelves and dropped (injuring another customer).[112] In the case of employees or other *préposés*,[113] the courts have held that even if they have possession of the 'thing' and appear to have its 'direction', they cannot have *la garde*, which remains in the employer.[114] The technical justification for this is that being a *préposé* necessarily involves subordination to the *commettant*, and this is inconsistent with the existence of the *droit de la garde*, but the practical outcome is the retention of liability for things on the employer

---

[105] Viney and Jourdain, *Conditions*, 644 *et seq.*

[106] See the discussion in Starck, Roland and Boyer, *Responsabilité délictuelle*, 31–6.

[107] R. Saleilles's note to Civ. 16 Jun. 1896, D 1897.1.433. Cf. Req. 19 Jan. 1914, D 1914.1.303 (owner of a café liable as *gardien* of soda-syphon).

[108] Ch. Réun. 2 Dec. 1941, S 1941.1.217 *rapp.* Lagarde note Mazeaud, DC 1942 25 note Ripert, S 1943.51. This left the possibility of liability in the owner for proven fault under art. 1383 C. civ., but the courts have denied the directness of the causal link between any fault in the owner and the thief's victim's injuries: Civ. 6 Jan. 1943, D 1945.117 note Tunc.

[109] Malaurie, Aynès and Stoffel-Munck, *Obligations*, 99–100; Terré, Simler and Lequette, *Obligations*, 741–2; Viney and Jourdain, *Conditions* 651–2 (who note that the presumption applies only in cases where the owner is identified).

[110] Civ. (2) 18 Jun. 1975, *Dame Luchet*, D 1975.IR.211 and see also Starck, Roland and Boyer, *Responsabilité délictuelle*, 256 *et seq.*   [111] Civ. (2) 14 Jan. 1999, JCP 1999.IV.1418.

[112] Civ. (2) 28 Feb. 1996, JCP 1996.IV.940.   [113] See above, p. 25.

[114] Civ. 30 Dec. 1936, *arrêt Garibaldi*, DP 1937.1.5 rapp. Josserand note Savatier, S 1937.1.137 note Mazeaud; Civ. (3) 20 Oct. 1971, D 1972.414 note Lapoyade Deschamps. The position is less clear where the employee acts outside the scope of his employment or the 'thing' in question does not belong to his employer: Viney and Jourdain, *Conditions*, 654. Both minors (Ass. plén. 9 May 1984, *Gabillet*, D 1984.525 note Chabas) and those with reduced mental capacity (art. 489-2 C.civ.) may be *gardiens*.

(who is more likely to be insured) and the avoidance of the question whether vicarious liability under article 1384 alinéa 5 and liability under article 1384 alinéa 1 can co-exist.[115] What all this means is that it is not infrequent for someone injured by a 'thing' to be himself its *gardien* and where this is the case, the *gardien*/victim will often have to look to *contract* to recover damages for his own injury, many of these contractual claims being founded on the defectiveness of the thing in question.[116]

However, the position is yet more complicated, for the courts have at times recognized that *la garde* may be split, one person being *gardien du comportement* (responsible for harm caused by the thing's handling) and the other *gardien de la structure* (responsible for harm caused by its defects or even its normal characteristics).[117] In general, this distinction has been applied only to cases where the thing in question possesses 'its own dynamism capable of manifesting itself in a dangerous way',[118] a restriction which in practice has often meant that the injury has been caused by the thing's explosion or where the thing is flammable or corrosive.[119] It is by no means clear why a distinction should be drawn between this type of case and other situations where things cause harm.[120] Where it has been applied, it certainly looks as though the courts have abandoned a truly strict liability for harm caused by things and instead impose liability according to whether the thing in question is inherently defective or whether it has been mis-handled or ill-treated.

(b) Causation and attribution

Perhaps, though, even more important in understanding the relationship between liability for things and liability for defective products in French law is the role of causation in attributing liability for a thing under article 1384 alinéa 1. Here, I wish to start by making four preliminary observations.

First, French lawyers and French courts have not in general shown a taste for the development or application of grand theories of causation, in contrast to their German counterparts.[121] Although there is some discussion in *la doctrine* of the various theories which have been advanced—equivalence of conditions, 'adequate causation', theories of risk—most writers are content to conclude that no one theory is

---

[115] Above, p. 25.   [116] Below, p. 69 *et seq.*

[117] Civ.(1) 12 Nov. 1975, JCP 1976.II.18479 note Viney; Terré, Simler, Lequette, *Obligations*, 746–8; Viney and Jourdain, *Conditions*, 663–70. This idea is to be distinguished from situations in which two or more persons are held to be *co-gardiens*: e.g. members of a hunting party as regards one hunter's gun: Civ. (2) 15 Dec. 1980, D 1981.45 note Poisson-Drocourt.

[118] Civ. (1) 12 Nov. 1975, JCP 1976.II.18479 note Viney.

[119] Viney and Jourdain, *Conditions*, 665. But while it has not been applied to pharmaceuticals (below, p. 147) it has been applied to trees: Civ. (2) 18 Jun. 1975, Bull. civ. II no. 190, RTDCiv. 1976.146 note Durry. It has not been applied to motor vehicles: Versailles 27 Jan. 1983, JCP 1983.II.20094 note Dupichot.

[120] P. Dupichot, note to Versailles 27 Jan.1983, JCP 1983.II.20094.

[121] F. Lawson and B. Markesinis, *Tortious Liability for Unintentional Harm in the Common Law and the Civil Law* (CUP, 1982), Vol. 1, 106. For a discussion of these theories, see H.L.A. Hart and T. Honoré, *Causation in the Law* (OUP, 2nd. edn., 1985), chaps. XVI–XVII. For a comparative discussion of their application to French and English law see P. Catala and J.A. Weir, 'Delict and Torts: a Study in Parallel, Part IV, Causation,' (1965) 39 *Tul. L.R.* 701.

reflected in the positive law,[122] even though on occasion the courts have adopted the terminology of one or the other theory to describe the results which they have reached.

Secondly, and clearly related to this, the purposes for which a causal relationship needs to be established vary considerably even within the private law of obligations,[123] and while there is an attempt to treat causation generally in the treatises, its treatment in the cases reflects these different purposes. The courts' general position is found in relation to the causal connection required to exist between a defendant's fault and a claimant's harm for the purposes of articles 1382 and 1383 of the Civil Code and here there is a rich *jurisprudence* relating to the classic problems of causation, for example, multiple causes or the 'loss of a chance'.[124] However, particularly difficult questions have arisen in relation to liability for the 'deeds of things' for where *responsabilité* is based on fault, issues of causation and fault tend to merge,[125] but where liability is divorced from fault, more weight is thrown on causation. As we shall see, this is particularly true of the liability for the 'deeds of things'.

Thirdly, the Cour de cassation in general leaves the interpretation and assessment of evidence (*les éléments de preuve*) to the lower courts,[126] but 'exercises its control with the view to verifying whether the facts found by the *juges du fond* are to be characterised as establishing the existence or the absence of a causal relationship',[127] this including cases where they have 'denatured' the terms of the *expertise*,[128] where their reasoning is considered unsound,[129] or simply in order to review their interpretation of the evidence on the ground that they have 'not deduced the proper consequences from their findings'.[130] On the other hand, as Carbonnier observes, an element of judgment is inevitable because a claimant's harm often possesses many causes between which a choice must be made and so the courts proceed 'empirically'.[131]

Fourthly, in principle a claimant bears the burden of proof as to the causal relationship between his harm and the defendant's act, but the Cour de cassation has sometimes allowed the use of presumptions, which are particularly important in situations where the full sequence of events or their explanation is not clear. Unfortunately, it is sometimes unclear whether or not a person subject to a presumption is entitled to rebut it.

(i) The 'deeds of things'

The main reason for inventing the liability for the 'deeds of things' was to enable victims of 'anonymous accidents' of the machine age to obtain compensation without having to establish any person's fault[132] and its proponents considered that the mere physical causation (*causalité matérielle*) between a thing (notably, industrial machinery) and an injury would be easier to establish.[133] While in many situations physical

---

122 Carbonnier, *Obligations*, 395–6.
123 The criminal courts take a different approach again: below, pp. 375–6, 388–91.
124 Viney and Jourdain, *Conditions*, 151 *et seq.*   125 Carbonnier, *Obligations*, 391, 397.
126 Viney and Jourdain, *Conditions*, 167.   127 Marty and Raynaud, *Obligations*, 680.
128 Viney and Jourdain, *Conditions*, 215.
129 E.g. Civ. (2) 6 Feb. 1980, *Duplissy*, JCP 1980.IV.157.
130 Civ. (2) 6 Feb. 1980, *Laydacia*, JCP 1980.IV.157.   131 Carbonnier, *Obligations*, 391.
132 Above, p. 26.   133 Saleilles, note to Civ. 16 Jun. 1896, D 1897.1.433.

events are more easy to prove than issues involving evaluative judgments, French courts soon found that the wider and stricter they made liability under article 1384 alinéa 1, the more stress was placed on the element of causation.

What then is meant by the 'deed of a thing' (*le fait d'une chose*)? It is very rare for a person to suffer physical harm, whether personal injuries or damage to property, without a physical thing being 'involved' in a broad sense and it was soon recognised by French jurists that the new principle of liability would 'displace the centre of delictual liability, transporting it from article 1382 to article 1384.1'.[134] The approach of the courts to the causal relation between the thing and the injured person's harm has been complex and at times casuistic, the courts using causation to reflect a normative sense of the proper attribution of responsibility for the claimant's harm. They have thereby come close on occasion to a return to liability for fault.

The judicial starting point in relation to the causal role of things was that 'as soon as it is established that the thing contributed to the occurrence of the harm, it is presumed that it is an effective cause [*cause génératrice*] unless the *gardien* proves the contrary',[135] but it soon became clear that different approaches were taken by the courts according to whether the thing in question was stationary at the relevant time, for if it were its *gardien* could escape liability by proving that it had played only a 'passive role'.[136] Over the last half century or so the courts have established a steady if complex pattern of practice, which links the causal potency of things to the idea of their abnormality.[137]

First, where the thing of which the defendant was *gardien* was in motion and impacted on the person injured or property damaged, then proof of these physical circumstances gives rise to a presumption of causation. The typical case, though now overtaken by the provisions of the *loi* of 5 July 1985,[138] was of a motor vehicle which knocks over a pedestrian or crashes into another vehicle: the pedestrian will not have to show anything more to establish the necessary causal element.[139] Secondly, where the thing of which the defendant was *gardien* was moving at the time of the injury, but did not itself come into contact with the person injured or property damaged, the claimant has to show that the thing played an 'active role' in causing his injury and in practice the courts look for a defect in the thing itself or an 'anomaly in its position or behaviour'.[140] Thirdly, where the thing is stationary, an injured party also has to show that it played an 'active role' in causing his harm and to do so jurists and courts again refer to whether it was 'abnormal' or 'behaved abnormally'. Two sorts of case

---

[134] H. Capitant, 'La responsabilité du fait des choses inanimées d'après des Chambres réunies du 13 février 1930' DH Chron. 1930.29 at 32.   [135] Civ. 9 Jun. 1939, DH 1939.449.

[136] Cf. Civ. 19 Feb. 1941 and Civ. 24 Mar. 1941, DC 1941.85 note Flour.

[137] See J. Boré, note to Civ. (2) 29 May 1964 (2 cases), JCP 1965.II.14248, followed by Viney and Jourdain, *Conditions*, 635–44; Terré, Simler and Lequette, *Obligations*, 753–5.

[138] Below, pp. 60–1.

[139] For an example outside the context of road accidents see Paris 9 Feb.1968, JCP 1968.II.15653 note Prieur.

[140] Viney and Jourdain, *Conditions*, 640. E.g. Civ. (2) 8 Jul. 1971, D 1971.690; Civ. (2) 11 Jan. 1995, JCP 1995.I.3853 no. 7 note Viney. Cf. Malaurie, Aynès and Stoffel-Munck, *Obligations*, 96 arguing that the requirement of 'abnormality' has been abandoned by the courts, at least for moving things, pointing to Civ. (2) 2 Apr. 1997, Bull. civ. II no. 109.

are typical. *Immovables* are almost always stationary.[141] So a person who claims damages from the *gardien* of a floor must show that it played an 'active role' in causing his injuries and therefore, where a claimant slipped and was injured on a slight incline in the defendant's supermarket, her claim was rejected on the ground that she had not shown that the floor, rather than her own carelessness or the state of her shoes, was the real cause of her injury.[142] On the other hand, a stationary thing's 'abnormality' can be shown if it is defective or badly positioned.[143]

What are we to make of these strange 'arabesques in the caselaw'?[144] Does the courts' appeal to the concept of normality to determine the causal significance of the thing mean that they have surreptitiously transformed an apparently strict liability for things into a liability for *defective* things or even a liability for fault? Certainly, defectiveness can be relevant to establishing the thing's causal role, though it is merely one example of abnormality. And certainly abnormality is, as Carbonnier observes, a notion 'tainted with morality' which can lead to the re-introduction of something very much like fault.[145] On the other hand, in cases where a thing's defectiveness suggests its causal significance, its *gardien* cannot escape liability by showing himself innocent of fault nor even that the defect existed through circumstances entirely beyond his control, as an internal defect cannot constitute *force majeure*.[146] Thus, although in some cases the courts look as though they are returning to liability to fault, this is not a general phenomenon.[147] Indeed, as long as the thing does behave 'abnormally', the injured party does not have to show *why* this is the case[148] and only where the facts allow the *gardien* to establish *force majeure* or the claimant's contributory negligence will the causes of this abnormality need to be investigated.

(ii) Force majeure and contributory fault[149]

While a *gardien* cannot escape liability simply by showing that he was not at fault, he can do so by showing *force majeure* and he may reduce or even exclude his liability by establishing the claimant's contributory fault. Both these defences have proven important, to the extent that some jurists have argued that where the courts have interpreted them broadly, liability is really based on something not far from fault.

In the Civil Code, *force majeure* appears as a defence to liability in damages for non-performance of a contractual obligation, where it was traditionally held to consist of some event or act of either the claimant or a third party which was unforeseeable,

---

[141] Not always: art. 1384 al. 1 has been applied to a landslide: Civ.(2) 15 Nov. 1984, *Lantonnais Van Rhodes*, D 1985.20 *concl.* Charbonnier.

[142] Civ. (2) 19 Nov. 1964, JCP 1965.II.14022 note Rodière, D 1965.93 note Esmein. See also Civ. (2) 11 May 1966, D 1966.735 note Azard; Civ. (2) 7 Mar. 1979, D 1980.IR.35 note Larroumet.

[143] Civ. (2) 19 Jul. 1972, D 1972 Somm. 212, JCP 1972.IV.234, RTDCiv. 1973. 352 obs. Durry; Civ. (2) 30 Nov. 1994, JCP 1995.IV.283; Civ. (2) 7 May 2002, Bull. civ. I no. 92 (staircase not 'dangerous'). Typical older examples concerned stationary motor vehicles, but this context is no longer current after the *loi* of 5 July 1985, below, p. 60.   [144] Terré, Simler and Lequette, *Obligations*, 702.

[145] Carbonnier, *Obligations*, 477.   [146] Below, p. 58.

[147] A. Tunc, 'Force majeure et absence de faute en matière délictuelle,' RTDCiv. 1946.171, 194–5.

[148] E.g. Civ. (2) 29 May 1996, JCP 1996.IV.1633.

[149] French courts have accepted that a claimant's acceptance of risks may affect recovery, but in practice this has been applied to participants in sporting competitions and has the effect of subjecting liability to a proof of very serious breach of the rules: Malaurie, Aynès and Stoffel-Munck, *Obligations*, 61–3.

could not be prevented and was not otherwise 'imputable' to the debtor of the contractual obligation.[150] Nevertheless, when in 1896 the Cour de cassation first recognised article 1384 alinéa 1 as an independent source of liability, it accepted that *force majeure* could be a defence,[151] including for this purpose cases where the event was a human act (*fait d'un tiers*) or natural occurrence (*force majeure* in a narrow sense). However, having established that a defect in the thing was not a condition of liability under article 1384 alinéa 1, the courts sought to avoid allowing the presence of an unforeseeable and unpreventable defect as a means of *escaping* liability and so they added to the definition of *force majeure* a requirement that any occurrence or condition must be 'exterior to the thing'.[152] As a result, a defect in the thing itself 'is included within the risks for which the *gardien* assumes liability towards third parties'.[153]

More generally, however, with the movement away from the idea of liability for risk which can be discerned in the later 1930s and 1940s, French courts were more ready to find *force majeure*, and this was reflected in their acceptance that it was enough if the event or act was *normally* or *reasonably* unforeseeable.[154] This was particularly notice-able as regards the liability of a *gardien* of a motor vehicle for accidents precipitated by external factors, such as a dog running to the road[155] or oil spilt on the road and not visible.[156] Even the bad driving of other road users was on occasion held to be *force majeure*,[157] though it was more commonly treated as a concurrent cause.[158] A claimant's own 'behaviour' could also be held to be a *force majeure*, notably where, for whatever reason and quite apart from any question of contributory *fault* on his part, he was lying prone in the road.[159]

In the result, although in some cases proof of *force majeure* may look very close to proof of an absence of fault, the two are not the same: a *gardien* cannot simply rely on his own lack of fault, but must point to some other cause, for which he is not responsi-ble and which bears the characteristics of *force majeure*. For this purpose, the role of the *juges du fond* in determining whether an event or act is 'unforseeable and unpre-ventable' allows them to nuance their decision so as to fit their view of the facts as a whole including the comparative fault of the claimant and defendant.[160] On the other hand, where the alleged *force majeure* consists of an act of a third party, especially where a third party is also *gardien* of a thing, the courts have been more ready to

---

[150] Art. 1148 C. civ. The Code itself refers to *cas fortuit* and *cause étrangère*, but it is generally accepted that there is no substantial difference between these terms and *force majeure*. More recently writers and courts have reduced the significance of the requirement of 'unforeseeability', considering it relevant only where it allows a *gardien* or contractual debtor to avoid the event allegedly constituting *force majeure*: Terré, Simler, Lequette, *Obligations*, 560; Com. 1 Oct. 1997, Bull. civ. IV no. 240.

[151] Civ. 16 Jun. 1896, S 1897.1.17 note Esmein, D 1897.1.433 note Saleilles.

[152] Req. 22 Jan. 1945, S 1945.1.57. This was later applied to *obligations contractuelles de résultat*: Poitiers 16 Dec. 1970, GP 1971.1.264, below, p. 100.   [153] Civ. (2) 6 Mar. 1959, GP 1959.2.12.

[154] E.g. Civ. (2) 25 Jan.1956, JCP 1956.II.9153 and see further Viney and Jourdain, *Conditions*, 242–4; Malaurie, Aynès and Stoffel-Munck, *Obligations*, 97.

[155] Civ. (2) 10 Apr. 1964, D 1965.169 note Tunc.

[156] Civ. (2) 28 Oct. 1965, D 1966.137 note Tunc.   [157] Civ. 30 Nov. 1960, S 1961.142.

[158] Civ. 2 Jul. 1969, JCP 1971.II.16582.   [159] Civ. (2) 17 Dec. 1963, D 1964.569 note Tunc.

[160] F. Leduc, 'L'état actuel du principe général de responsabilité délictuelle du fait des choses' in F. Leduc et al., *La responsabilité du fait des choses, réflexions autour d'un centenaire* (Economica, Paris, 1997) 54–5.

exclude *force majeure* and instead hold the two contributors to the injury jointly liable, so as to allow recovery from either in full.

The other defence for a *gardien* of a thing is to show that an act of the claimant contributed to his own harm. Where the claimant's act constitutes *force majeure* then it is a complete defence, but otherwise, his contributory *fault* was long held capable of reducing the damages recoverable against the *gardien* to an extent within the 'sovereign power of assessment' of the *juges du fond*.[161] This was much criticised.[162] So, for Carbonnier:

> By detaching the defence of contributory fault of a victim from the notion of *force majeure* and applying it to any type of fault, the Cour de cassation has encouraged the *juges du fond* in their long-held tendency to slice the cake in two as soon as they cannot otherwise see a clear result—and, as a consequence, to encourage in legal advisers their propensity to put in as a matter of form against all claims an allegation that the defendant is only partly responsible. This itself has led claimants, worn down by disputes, to settle on conditions imposed on them by the other side's insurers. The liability for the *fait des choses* was thus emptied of the quasi-automatic character which under *Jand'heur* ensured its considerable effectiveness.[163]

This sort of criticism did not fall on deaf ears and in 1981 the French Government set up a working group under the auspices of the new Minister of Justice, Badinter, on the reform of the law relating to road accident injuries,[164] but before it could reach any decision, the Cour de cassation in the *arrêt Desmares* changed its approach, asserting that an injured party's behaviour could affect a liability under article 1384 alinéa 1 *only* where it qualified as *force majeure* where it excluded liability.[165] This change was made in the context of a traffic accident injuring a pedestrian, where criticism of its earlier attitude was sharpest, but a year later the Cour de cassation applied it to cases outside this context.[166]

However, the confusion and contradictions to which this *jurisprudence* continued to give rise in the lower courts prompted the legislature to intervene swiftly in respect of road traffic accidents in the *loi* of 5 July 1985,[167] which then triggered a further *revirement* outside its context, the Cour de cassation renouncing its approach in *Desmares* and declaring that fault in an injured party may reduce a claimant's damages whether or not it was unforeseeable and unpreventable.[168] This *jurisprudence* remains current.[169] With this history, it is unsurprising that the proper ambit of this defence was one of a number of points of debate in relation to implementation of the Product Liability Directive in France.[170]

---

[161] Ass. plén. 9 May 1984, *Derguini*, D 1984. 525 concl. Cabannes, note Chabas.

[162] Notably, by A. Tunc, 'Les causes d'exonération de la responsabilité de plein droit de l'article 1384 alinéa 1er du Code civil' D 1975 Chron. 83.

[163] Carbonnier, *Obligations*, 476 (citations omitted). See also A.Tunc, ' "It is wise not to take the Civil Codes too seriously." Traffic accident compensation in France' in P. Wallington and R.M. Merkin, (eds.) *Essays in Memory of Professor F.H. Lawson* (London, 1986) 71 at 78.   [164] Tunc, ibid. at 79.

[165] Civ. (2) 21 Jul. 1982, D 1982.449 *concl.* Charbonnier, note Larroumet.

[166] Civ. (2) 15 Nov. 1984, D 1985.20 *concl.* Charbonnier (3 cases).

[167] No. 85–677 and below, p. 60.

[168] Civ. (2) 6 Apr. 1987, *Chauvet, Bardèche, Belzedhoune*, GP 1987.1.440; Civ. (2) 6 Apr. 1987, *Waeterinckx*, JCP 1987.II.20828 note Chabas, D 1988.32 note Mouly.

[169] Malaurie, Aynès and Stoffel-Munck, *Obligations*, 96.   [170] Below, p. 511.

4. Reform of the Law of Motor Vehicle Accidents

Since 1957, liability for 'harm caused by vehicles' has been subject to the rules of private law and the jurisdiction of the ordinary courts even though it involves the administration,[171] but the *loi* of 5 July 1985 reformed the rules applicable to the liability of *gardiens* of motor vehicles, creating new rules governing the defences of *force majeure* and contributory fault in the victim and specifying that these apply to 'victims of a traffic accident in which a motor vehicle is implicated'.[172] This legislation created a new regime for the harm caused by traffic accidents, a regime which is distinct from and exclusive of liability for the 'deeds of things' in general.[173] Apart from the new rules governing defences, the legislation's great innovation was that it attempted to avoid any causal link between the vehicle (the 'thing') and the accident, substituting instead a requirement of 'involvement.' However, this brave and radical move has not been a complete success.

First, neither a driver nor a *gardien* of a motor vehicle can rely on the defence of *force majeure* against any injured party and this rule applies to those who suffer damage to property as well as those who suffer personal injuries, and to drivers as well as to passengers or pedestrians.[174] As a result, a driver is liable for injuries caused when his car spins out of control on hidden ice or where it crashes owing to an 'unforseeable and unpreventable' act of a third party.

Secondly, though, the treatment of the injured party's fault is really rather bizarre. Where a person who suffers personal injuries is *not a driver* of a motor vehicle, his fault can affect the liability of the *gardien* of any implicated vehicle only if it was 'inexcusable' and the 'exclusive cause' of his injury and here liability is excluded.[175] This test is a generous one and the courts have been slow to find it satisfied.[176] However, the fault of road accident victims who are less than 16 or more than 70 years old or who suffer from a registered disability of 80 per cent or more will extinguish their claim only where they 'voluntarily sought the injury suffered',[177] for example, as a result of an attempt to commit suicide.[178] On the other hand, *drivers* of motor vehicles, and those who claim through them including their dependants,[179] are treated with less sympathy, as *any fault* on their part can reduce or extinguish any other vehicle driver's liability,[180] and this is also the test for *any* person's claim for damage to property caused by a vehicle accident.[181]

---

[171] *Loi* of 31 Dec. 1957.

[172] *Loi* no. 85–677 arts. 1–6 ('*loi* of 5 Jul. 1985'); R. Redmond-Cooper, 'The Relevance of Fault in Determining Liability for Road Accidents : The French Experience', (1989) 38 *ICLQ* 502.

[173] Viney and Jourdain, *Conditions*, 1100–04; Civ. (2) 28 Jan. and 4 Feb. 1987, D 1987.187 note Groutel. The new regime does draw on earlier *jurisprudence*, notably as to the definition of *gardien* and for issues such as the assessment of damages.

[174] F. Chabas, *Le droit des accidents de la circulation* (2nd. edn., Paris, 1988), 155.

[175] *Loi* of 5 Jul. 1985, art. 3 al. 1.

[176] 'Inexcusable fault' has been defined as 'a voluntary fault of an exceptional seriousness which exposes without any valid reason the injured party to a danger which he ought to have been aware of': Civ. (2) 20 Jul.1987 (11 cases) GP 1988.1.26 note Chabas. [177] *Loi* of 5 Jul. 1985, art. 3 al. 2 & 3 al. 3.

[178] Chabas, *op. cit.*, n. 174, 176. [179] *Loi* of 5 Jul. 1985, art. 6. [180] Ibid., art. 4.

[181] Ibid., art. 5.

Thirdly, a vehicle no longer has to cause a claimant harm as long as it is 'implicated' in the accident.[182] Some jurists argue that the legislation's use of 'implication' means that there is no need for a claimant to show that the particular vehicle whose *gardien* is sued caused the accident.[183] Others consider that its use merely suggests that a more generous approach should be taken to determining the causal role of a vehicle in the accident.[184] The Cour de cassation has distinguished between cases where the victim's body or vehicle was in physical contact with the defendant's vehicle, where the latter is necessarily implicated, whether stationary or not,[185] and cases where no such physical contact occurs, where the dominant approach is that the vehicle's disruption of the traffic is required.[186] This is distinctly reminiscent of earlier judicial use of the concept of 'normality' in establishing causation, absent the reference to the stationary nature of the vehicle.[187] Moreover, there must be a causal link between the accident and the claimant's damage.[188] In the result, '[b]y degrees and in various forms, causation has reappeared'.[189]

5. Compensation for Accidents at Work

Both *obligations de sécurité* and liability for the 'deeds of things' were invented by French jurists so as to allow employees injured at work to recover compensation without the need to prove fault.[190] It is ironic, therefore, that despite their later success neither still govern this area, as legislation has gradually replaced employer's liability with a special regime of social insurance to which the employer contributes.[191]

Under the present scheme, which has its origins in 1946,[192] liability for accidents at work rests on a public social fund, the *Caisse de sécurité sociale*, and employers enjoy an all but complete immunity, bearing liability only in the case of intentional or inexcusable fault[193] or an intentional fault on the part of an employee.[194] An employee's intentional fault will exclude recovery under the scheme and his 'inexcusable fault' may reduce it.[195]

---

[182] Viney and Jourdain, *Conditions*, 1121–8.

[183] H. Groutel, 'L'implication du véhicule dans la loi du 5 juillet 1985' D 1987 Chron. 1.

[184] Chabas, *op. cit.* n. 174, 97; Flour, Aubert and Savaux, *Fait juridique*, 330–40.

[185] Civ. (2) 23 Mar. 1994, D 1994.IR.96.

[186] Civ. (2) 5 Jan. 1994, *Zemmour*, JCP 1994.IV.79; Civ. (2) 15 Jan. 1997, JCP 1997.II. 22883 note Chabas.   [187] Above, pp. 56–7.   [188] Bénabent, *Obligations*, 417–19.

[189] Viney and Jourdain, *Conditions*, 1122; P. Jourdain 'Implication et causalité dans la loi du 6 juillet 1985' JCP 1994.I.3794.   [190] Above, pp. 26, 28.

[191] For earlier legislation, see *loi* of 9 Apr. 1898 and A. Tunc, *La responsabilité civile* (Economica, Paris, 2nd ed., 1989), 27–8.

[192] *Loi* of 30 Oct. 1946, integrating the scheme into art. L 411-1 *et seq.* C. séc. soc.; Terré, Simler and Lequette, *Obligations*, 872. For a comparative discussion M. Voirin, 'De la responsabilité civile à la sécurité sociale pour la réparation des dommages corporels: extension ou disparition de la branche accidents du travail?' 1979 *RIDC* 541.

[193] This has been defined as a 'fault of exceptional gravity, deriving from a deliberate act or omission, with an awareness of its dangerousness and the absence of any justification for it': Ch. réun. 15 Jul. 1941, DC 1941.117 note Rouast and see art. L. 231-8 C. trav.

[194] Art. L. 452-5 C. séc. soc. An employer may insure against this liability: art. L. 452-4 al. 3 C. séc. soc.

[195] Art. 453-1 C. séc. soc.

Compensation by the *Caisse* is partial, being fixed according to a fixed scale (*forfaitaire*): in particular it does not cover non-pecuniary losses.[196] The ambit of the scheme is a wide one, applying both to 'accidents' and to certain illnesses caused by the conditions of work.[197] 'Accidents at work' covers those which occur during working hours at the workplace and those which occur during a task outside the workplace, for example, a car accident while a company representative on his rounds.[198] The scheme also applies to injuries to employees while on their way to and from work (*accidents de trajet*),[199] including, of course, those resulting from motor vehicle accidents. This means that an employee injured in a motor vehicle accident in the course of employment can recover *some* compensation from the *Caisse*, but he will not be able to recover damages for any uncompensated losses against his own employer as *gardien* of the vehicle, thereby losing the benefit of the very strict regime of liability for motor vehicle accidents put in place in 1985 (though exceptionally and rather oddly, an employee injured on the way to or from work may do so).[200]

However, this regime of compensation does not rule out liability arising by application of the general law of civil liability in someone *other than* the employer in respect of injuries occurring at work or while on the way to work.[201] Two examples of such a 'third party' may be found in the case of the *gardien* (other than the employer himself) of a motor vehicle which is implicated in the accident injuring the employee and in the case of the manufacturer of machinery which has injured the employee. Where such a defendant can be made out, both the injured employee himself (to recover the difference between their social security payments and damages recoverable under the general law[202]) and the *Caisse de sécurité sociale* (to recover damages to cover the cost of any payments it has made) may claim.[203] Where a 'third-party' is liable in this way, he may not claim contribution from the employer unless the latter committed an 'intentional fault':[204] here, therefore, an employer's residual liability differs as between a claim by the employee himself and a third party claiming contribution.

---

[196] Terré, Simler and Lequette, *Obligations*, 878–9; art. 431-1 C. séc. soc. *et seq.*

[197] Only those *maladies professionnelles* which are on a list drawn up by regulation are included: art. R. 461-1 *et seq.* C.séc. soc.   [198] Terré, Simler and Lequette, *Obligations*, 873–4.

[199] Art. L. 411-2 C. séc. soc.   [200] *Loi* of 6 Aug. 1963.   [201] Art. 454-1 C. séc. soc.

[202] Ass. plén. 22 Dec. 1988, JCP 1989.II.21236, concl. Monnet, obs. Saint-Jours.

[203] Cf. above, p. 38.   [204] Art. 452-5 C. séc. soc.

4

Droit Privé: The Law of Sale

1. Introduction

Even before implementation of the Consumer Guarantees Directive, French law possessed six distinct conceptual bases for finding a seller liable to his buyer in respect of failures of safety, quality or usefulness in the property sold, four of which are contractual, one delictual and one either contractual or delictual depending on its context. This complexity is in part a legacy of history and in part a function of modern French juristic conceptual speculation and judicial pragmatic instrumentalism. The confusion which it has caused is made worse by the fact that neither the jurists nor the courts have proved sure for very long whether these various bases possess their own discrete domains or whether they can apply at the option of the claimant. While there were two attempts to reform this situation, one at the time of implementation of the Product Liability Directive and one at the time of implementation of the Consumer Guarantees Directive, neither has succeeded.[1]

So, a buyer may wish to rely on the general doctrines of *erreur* (mistake) and *dol* (dishonest dealing) and of obligations to supply information or to advise (*obligations d'information*) to avoid the contract and return the property or as the basis of a claim for damages. While none of these expressly rely on the defectiveness of the property or loss caused by the property as their legal basis, they have proved significant in this context, especially in the case of *obligations d'information*. A buyer may also wish to rely on the classic liability for latent defects under the *garantie légale* or for 'non-conforming property', both of which are tied to the contract of sale and are based on 'defects' in the property, though this is understood differently.[2] To these the courts added in the 1990s *obligations de sécurité*, thereby using a French contractual technique to 'implement' the Product Liability Directive while the French legislator failed to do so.[3]

Each of the conceptual bases has a different or somewhat different focus: the quality of the consent of the buyer; the wrongful conduct of the seller; the defectiveness of the property or its implications for safety. Each of them possesses its own conditions of application and effects which make them sometimes more, sometimes less attractive to a buyer, but over the last 40 years or so French courts have been torn between allowing their development and relationship to become a function of these practical

---

[1] Below, pp. 453, 574–83. [2] Below, pp. 69–72.
[3] Below, p. 72. For the history of these developments used as an example of the influence of doctrinal legal writing and case law on private law development, see Bell, *French Legal Cultures*, 89–91.

features (with particular emphasis on differences in the periods within which claims must be brought) and following juristic views of the conceptual correctness of one or other position. This is why much of the *jurisprudence* in this area has long looked unsettled if not actually contradictory: judges apply the law which yields the outcome which they consider 'right' for reasons which do not appear on the face of the legal reasoning which they use.[4] While the position became somewhat more settled after 1993 when the Cour de cassation ruled latent defects which render property unfit for its normal purpose give rise only to liability under the *garantie légale*,[5] their relationship became controversial again in the French debates on how properly to implement the Consumer Guarantees Directive.[6] In this discussion, I shall look first at *obligations d'information* and then at the *garantie légale* and its rivals.

2. *Obligations d'Information*

The Civil Code provided for two grounds of vitiation of contracts founded on imbalances of information between the parties: *erreur sur les qualités substantielles de la chose* (mistake as to the substantial quality of the subject matter) and *dol* (dishonest conduct).[7] In the hands of French jurists and courts, both of these have been expanded far beyond their Roman antecedents.[8] As a result, in general a party can escape a contract for *erreur* for mistake as to any aspect of the contract (except *mere value*) if it formed a determining element in a party's decision to enter the contract,[9] and as long as both parties were aware of the factual circumstances which give rise to the essential quality of the mistake.[10] A party may escape a contract on the ground of *dol* where any dishonest dealing by the other party causes his 'determining mistake', that is, one without which he would not have entered the contract.[11] It therefore includes fraudulent misstatements, but is rather wider, extending to any chicanery intended to deceive as long as it was effected by the other party to the contract. Where a party's *dol* has caused the other party harm, it attracts liability in delict under article 1382 of the Civil Code irrespective of whether the contract is annulled.[12] So stated there is a considerable overlap between *erreur* and *dol*, though it is said that where a defendant is dishonest it is easier for a claimant to establish his own mistake.[13] They differ, however, in that *dol* necessarily constitutes a delictual fault so as to attract liability in damages as well as annulment,[14] whereas *erreur* does not rest on any wrongful conduct in the other party.[15] While the courts long allowed a claimant to choose

---

[4] But see below, p. 72, as to whether there has been a degree of settling down since the mid-1990s.

[5] Civ. (1) 5 May 1993, D 1993.506, below p. 72.   [6] Below, p. 580.

[7] Arts. 1110, 1116 C. civ.   [8] Nicholas, 84–5.

[9] Ibid., 85–6; J. Cartwright, 'Defects of Consent and Security of Contract: French and English Law Compared' in P. Birks and A. Pretto (eds.), *Themes in Comparative Law in Honour of Bernard Rudden* (OUP, 2002) Chap. 11.

[10] Civ. 23 Nov. 1931, *affaire de la Villa Jacqueline*, DP 1932.1.129, note Josserand, GP 1932.1.96.

[11] Malaurie, Aynès and Stoffel-Munck, *Obligations*, 241.   [12] Civ. (1) 4 Feb. 1975, D 1975. 405.

[13] Larroumet, *Contrat*, 305.   [14] Civ. (1) 4 Feb. 1975, D 1975.405.

[15] Such a mistake may be caused by a pre-contractual and therefore delictual fault of negligence and so give rise to damages: Terré, Simler and Lequette, *Obligations*, 229; Civ (3) 29 Nov. 1968, GP 1969.1.63.

whether to claim annulment of the contract for *erreur* or instead termination of the contract under the *garantie légale*,[16] in 1996 the Cour de cassation held that where there was a 'latent defect' within the meaning of the *garantie légale*, a buyer could not instead claim annulment on the ground of substantial mistake.[17] On the other hand, where a buyer's mistake has been induced by the *dol* of the seller, then the courts still appear to allow a buyer to claim annulment for *dol*.[18]

Moreover, since the 1960s the courts have accepted that *dol par réticence* (a knowing and dishonest failure to disclose a relevant matter) can give rise to annulment of the contract[19] and it was in this context that the presence of an *obligation d'information* first became important, for where such an obligation exists any knowing silence will constitute *dol par réticence* without more.[20] However, *obligations d'information* soon took on a much wider significance. For it was argued that sometimes a party to a contract *ought* to have been aware of information of significance to the other and ought to have told him about it: where this is the case, silence or the (honest) giving of mis-information constitutes breach of an 'obligation to inform'.[21] The main significance of this development was that any failure in the provision of information which caused harm would necessarily give rise to liability in damages.[22]

The Civil Code makes no explicit mention of *obligations d'information* and their development illustrates the willingness of French courts and jurists to develop practical legal devices on apparently shaky legislative foundations.[23] Sometimes they have been founded on the requirement of good faith[24] or the demands of equity[25] and, in the context of sale, a seller's obligation to inform is sometimes seen as 'accessory' to the obligation to deliver the property.[26] The legitimacy of the case law was confirmed by legislation in 1992 which imposed obligations on 'business sellers of property or suppliers of services ... before the conclusion of the contract, to put a consumer in a position to know the essential characteristics of that property or those services'.[27]

For long manufacturers and, later, business suppliers of goods were seen as the prime examples of those bearing an *obligation d'information*, both of whom were held by the courts liable in damages for their failure to supply information concerning the

---

[16] Civ. (1) 28 Jun. 1988, D 1989.450 note Lapoyade-Deschamps; Civ. (1) 28 June 1989, Bull. civ. I no. 268, D 1991 Somm. 318 and see Ghestin, *La formation du contrat*, 509–13 (setting out the doctrinal controversy).

[17] Civ. (1) 14 May 1996, Bull. civ. I no. 213, D 1998.305 note F. Jault-Seseke; JCP 1997.I.4009 note C. Radé.   [18] Civ. (1) 22 Apr. 1997, Bull. civ. I no. 129; Civ. (3) 29 Nov. 2000, Bull. civ. III no. 182.

[19] Carbonnier, *Obligations*, 113–14.   [20] E.g. Civ. (1) 15 May 2002, Bull. civ. I no. 132.

[21] The idea is attributed to M. de Juglart, 'L'obligation de renseignements dans les contrats' (1945) RTDCiv. 1 and see for a general comparative discussion, J. Ghestin and B. Nicholas, 'The Pre-contractual Obligation to Disclose Information', in D. Harris and D. Tallon (eds.), *Contract Law Today* (OUP, 1989) 151.

[22] Below, pp. 67–9.   [23] Huet, *Principaux contrats spéciaux*, 238.

[24] Malaurie, Aynès and Stoffel-Munck, *Obligations*, 366.

[25] Art. 1135 C. civ.; e.g. Civ. (1) 3 Jul. 1985, Bull. civ. I no. 211, JCP 1985.IV.320.

[26] Arts. 1603, 1615 C. civ.; Civ. (1) 20 Mar. 1989, D 1989.IR.178. Malaurie, Aynès and Gautier, *Contrats spéciaux*, 226 *et seq.* at 227 refer to 'the *devoir d'information*... which enlarges the obligation to deliver and relates it to the *garantie [légale]*'. Cf. Ghestin, *op. cit.* n. 21, who argues that the general doctrine can be constructed on the basis of a number of particular examples of *obligations d'information* found in legislation and case law.   [27] *Loi* no. 92–60 of 18 Jan. 1992, art. 2; now art. L. 111-1 C. consom.

goods to their buyers.[28] Within this context, the obligations have not been restricted to warnings of danger, but have included duties to give proper instructions as to the effective use of products, to advise a customer of the disadvantages of the goods offered or even the availability of a more suitable product on the market.[29] As a result, *obligations d'information* have been 'one of the most effective ingredients in the development of the liability of manufacturers and business sellers'.[30]

However, even after this legislation the legal classification of *obligations d'information* and the consequences of their non-performance remain uncertain. The formal position is clear: a *pre*-contractual *obligation d'information* turns a knowing silence into *dol par réticence* so as to allow annulment on this ground;[31] whereas breach of a contractual *obligation d'information* (for example, forming part of the seller's *obligation de conformité*) attracts the possibility of *résolution* for non-performance under the *droit commun*, depending on its seriousness.[32] As between parties to a contract, liability in damages for breach of *pre*-contractual duties is delictual, whereas breach of contractual obligations can only be contractual.[33] However, while attempts have been made to find a basis for distinguishing between pre-contractual and contractual *obligations d'information*,[34] they are difficult to distinguish in practice.[35] This even remains true beyond the parties to a contract, for some argue that the benefit of the contractual obligation to inform can be transmitted with the thing as its 'accessory' as does the benefit of the *garantie légale*,[36] while others hold that beyond the parties to the contract, breach of an obligation to inform gives rise only to liability in delict.[37] The courts have themselves taken no very firm line on the issue of classification, preferring to take whichever conceptual basis appears to them the more convenient, an approach made less significant by the fact that the content of the duty is not affected by its classification.[38]

A key influence on the incidence of judicial imposition of *obligations d'information* has been the status of the parties. The legislation of 1992 imposed an *obligation d'information* only on business suppliers of property and services to consumers, but

---

[28] Viney and Jourdain, *Conditions*, 427.   [29] Below, pp. 68–9.

[30] Viney and Jourdain, *Conditions*, 426 (writing in 1998).   [31] Above, p. 65.

[32] Art. 1184 C. civ. and see e.g. Com 12 Apr. 1995, *Cont., conc., cons.* 1995 no. 125 obs. Leveneur.

[33] Above, p. 27.

[34] See notably, M. Fabre-Magnan, *De l'obligation d'information dans les contrats* (LGDJ, Paris, 1992), 224 *et seq.*, who suggests a distinction between those obligations whose purpose is to enlighten a party's consent (which are pre-contractual) and those whose purpose is to ensure a satisfactory performance of the contract (which are contractual).

[35] Ghestin and Desché, *Vente*, 920; Terré, Simler and Lequette, *Obligations*, 237.

[36] Cf. below, pp. 95–8. According to this line of argument, an *obligation d'information* is considered merely as part of the *obligation de délivrance* giving rise to liability under the *droit commun contractuel* and an action based explicitly on an *obligation de livrer une chose conforme* has been transmitted in this way: Ass. plén. 7 Feb. 1986, JCP 1986 II 20616 note Malinvaud, D 1986.293 note Bénabent.

[37] Malinvaud, note to Com. 16 Oct. 1973, JCP 1974.II.17846 and see, eg. Civ. (1) 11 Oct. 1983, Bull. civ. I no. 228, RTDCiv. 1984.731 obs. Huet.

[38] E.g. Civ. (1) 31 Jan. 1973, JCP 1974.II.17846 note Malinvaud (manufacturer's liability to consumer for personal injuries caused by a failure to warn properly of the product's dangers is 'necessarily contractual'); Civ. (1) 11 Oct. 1983, *cit.*; Com 25 Jun. 1980, Bull. civ. IV no. 276, RTDCiv. 1981.157 obs Durry (contractual liability for failure to warn about undiscoverable quality of paint); Paris 2 Feb. 1990, D 1990.IR.51 (pre-contractual liability in delict).

the courts have imposed one also on one business to another even in the absence of any danger.[39] As between businesses, the courts have steered a middle course,[40] either imposing an obligation to inform on business sellers, but then reducing liability on the basis that the buyer ought also to have known of the matter and that a failure to do so constitutes contributory fault,[41] or refusing to impose the obligation where a business buyer is found also to have the competence to understand the matter.[42] In this way, the courts have nuanced their decisions so as to take into account the relative status, skill and means of knowledge of the parties to the contract in question, rather than simply accepting or denying the imposition of *obligations d'information*.

Generally, the jurists and courts accept that *obligations d'information* (where contractual) are classed as *obligations de moyens*,[43] with the result that a buyer has to show a failure to provide appropriate information by the seller and that this resulted from a lack of care[44] or that the information supplied was insufficient given the risk or the interest of the user.[45] However, the Cour de cassation has held that it is for a person owing an *obligation d'information* to show that he has fulfilled it,[46] which reduces the significance of its classification as *obligation de moyens* to an indication that a seller need supply only that information which he could normally know: he does not have to indicate the properties of a product or characteristics of property which are capable of being discovered at some later date.[47] Moreover, the courts themselves vary the content of the obligation according to the status of the parties and the subject matter of the information in question, being much stricter where safety is in issue and where the buyer is inexperienced or unknowledgeable.

Many cases of *obligations d'information* imposed on sellers of goods have consisted of a duty to warn of the dangers of the product to person or property, whether generally or in the absence of certain precautions. So, for example, a manufacturer was held liable in damages to his crop for failing to inform a farmer of the need to water the plants after treating them with its artificial fertilizer (though liability was reduced on the basis that the farmer ought also to know about the use of fertilizers).[48] Similarly, the manufacturer of an insecticide was held liable to a farmer when the product blew

---

[39] Malaurie, Aynès and Gautier, *Contrats spéciaux*, 227–8; Civ. (3) 21 Jul. 1993, D 1994 Somm. 237 note Tournafond (sale of building); Cf. Civ. (3) 29 Nov. 2000, Bull. civ. III no. 182.

[40] Malaurie, Aynès and Gautier, *Contrats spéciaux*, 229–30; P. Jourdain, 'Le devoir de "se" renseigner' D 1983 Chron. 139 and P. Le Tourneau, 'De l'allégement de l'obligation de renseignements ou de conseil' D 1987 Chron. 101.

[41] Civ. (1) 9 Dec. 1975, JCP 1977.II.18588 note Malinvaud, D 1978.205 note Savatier; Civ. (1) 11 Jun. 1980, JCP 1980.IV.324 (claimant's exclusive fault).

[42] Civ. (1) 20 Jun. 1995, D 1995.IR.200; Civ. (1) 3 Jun. 1998, JCP 1998.IV.2684. Cf. Civ. (1) 7 Jun. 1989, D 1989.IR.200 (manufacturer of veterinary pharmaceuticals under a legislative duty to inform vet of a contra-indication of its product held liable for failing to do so).

[43] G. Viney, 'L'indemnisation des atteintes à la sécurité des consommateurs en droit français', in Ghestin, *Sécurité des consommateurs*, 78; Huet, *Responsabilité du vendeur*, 55 and see Civ. (1) 23 Apr. 1985, Bull. civ. I no. 125, RTDCiv. 1986.367 obs. Huet. Where liability is delictual, the legal basis is proven fault under arts. 1382 or 1383 C. civ.   [44] Malaurie, Aynès and Stoffel-Munck, *Obligations*, 474.

[45] Huet, *Principaux contrats spéciaux*, 241.

[46] Civ. (1) 25 Feb. 1997, *Hédreul*, JCP 1997.I.4025 note Viney (medical obligation to warn of risks of operation); Malaurie, Aynès, and Gautier, *Contrats spéciaux*, 228.

[47] Bénabent, *Contrats spéciaux*, 130.

[48] Civ. (1) 9 Dec. 1975, JCP 1977.II.18588 note Malinvaud, D 1978.205 note Savatier.

into his eye, the Cour de cassation declaring roundly that 'a maker of a product must furnish all indispensable information for its use and notably warn the user of all the precautions to be taken where it is dangerous'.[49] And where a householder had used glue for tiling in his kitchen and vapour from the glue was ignited by a gas cooker, killing his daughter, injuring several other members of his family and damaging the kitchen, the glue's manufacturer was held liable in contract to the householder and in delict to the other victims on the basis of its failure to warn adequately of the product's dangers and necessary precautions for use.[50]

French courts have also relied on *obligation d'information* in sellers and manufacturers to impose liability where a product proved ineffective rather than unsafe: 'a *vendeur professionnel* has by reason of this status an obligation to inform the buyer of the conditions of use of the product',[51] though this is true only where meaningful instructions can be given.[52] Sometimes, a seller must advise a buyer as to the choice of the product, pointing out if there are any difficulties in its use,[53] whether the buyer is a private individual or is also in business,[54] though not where a buyer is in a position to appreciate the matter himself.[55] French courts have even held sometimes that a seller ought to have informed his customer that there is a *better* product on the market which he should use or that for some other reason he should not use the product offered for sale.[56] For example, a winemaker engaged a mason to paint the inside of a wine vat and the mason bought a paint termed '*Registrat alimentaire*' which suggested that it was suitable for use with food.[57] Once painted and filled, however, the wine took the taste and smell of the paint. The winemaker recovered damages against the mason, who then recovered a partial indemnity against the retailer and manufacturer: according to the Cour de cassation, even if used perfectly the paint would have spoiled the wine and the seller, knowing the use to which it was to be put, had failed to indicate that its product was unsuitable for the job.[58] On the other hand, where a seller was unable to have foreseen his buyer's particular use of the property, no *obligation*

---

[49] Civ. (1) 14 Dec.1982, D 1983.IR.131, GP 1983 Pan. Jur. 119.

[50] Civ. (1) 11 Oct. 1983, Bull. civ. I, no. 228, RTDCiv. 1984.731 obs. Huet. See also Civ. (1) 3 Jan. 1973, JCP 1974.II.17846, note Malinvaud; Civ. (1) 10 Jun. 1980, *Cie d'installation*, JCP 1980.IV.324 (restaurant liable to a child for injuries caused by a rotating dessert trolley recovered an indemnity against its installer and its manufacturer for failure in their *obligations de renseignements*).

[51] Com. 11 Jul. 1988, Bull. civ. IV no. 250, JCP 1988.IV.343; Civ. (1) 4 May 1994, Bull. civ. I no. 163, D 1994.Somm.236 note G. Paisant.   [52] Civ. (2) 17 Nov. 1976, Bull. civ. I no. 355.

[53] The duty is particularly extensive where the product is complex or technical and needs to be suitable to the particular needs of the purchaser, as in the case of a computer system. However, even here, the seller is not under a duty to recommend a product other than for the purchaser's present or perhaps foreseeable, needs at the time of contract and so a supplier of a business computing system has been held not liable when it proved unable to cope with an increased workload, itself the consequence of a considerable expansion in the buyer's business: Com 14 Mar. 1989, Bull. civ. IV no. 89, JCP 1989.IV.185.

[54] Civ (1) 3 Jul. 1985, JCP 1985.IV.320 (individual); Civ. (3) 13 May 1987, JCP 1987.IV.244 (business); Civ. (1) 23 Apr. 1985, Bull. civ. I no. 125, RTDCiv. 1986.367, obs. Huet (paint used by professional artist became detached from canvas); Civ. (1) 4 May 1994, Bull. civ. I no. 163, D 1994.Somm.236 note G. Paisant (newly marketed seeds sold to farmer).

[55] Civ. (1) 7 Jun. 1995, Bull. civ. I no. 251; Com. 17 Mar. 1998, Bull. civ. IV no. 105.

[56] Com. 11 Jul. 1988, Bull. civ. IV no. 250.   [57] Com. 15 Apr. 1975, Bull. civ. IV no. 106.

[58] See also Civ. (1) 22 Nov. 1978, *affaire Quinoléine*, JCP 1979.II.19139 note Viney (manufacturer of pesticides liable for damage to vines caused by product difficult to use in local conditions).

d'information is imposed, this leading to a distinction between the buyer's immediate supplier (who knows his particular purpose) and a more remote seller (who does not).[59] So, for example, a manufacturer of a computer system may not be liable for failing to inform its ultimate purchaser of its unsuitability for his needs, where only its immediate seller was in a position to evaluate them.[60]

Many (if not all) of these cases on *obligation d'information* pre-date the decisions of the mid-1990s which prevented the 'general law of contract' (*le droit commun contractuel*) and particularly *obligation de conformité* from encroaching on the domain of the *garantie légale* and which treated liability for defects in safety separately.[61] However, they still appear in the footnotes of the jurists and are treated as reflecting current practice. This resilience of *obligations d'information* even where their ambit overlaps with the *garantie légale* in sale may be attributed in part to their wider significance, especially in relation to the incidence of *dol par réticence*,[62] but there is also a sense that cases of failures to inform, warn or advise are different from cases of liability for latent defects and may therefore rightly be treated by their own doctrine distinct from the *garantie légale*. On the other hand, from the mid-1990s the courts do appear to have preferred to treat claims for personal injuries based on failures to warn either on *obligations de sécurité* or on the new provisions of the Civil Code which implemented the Product Liability Directive. As I shall explain, however, the problems encountered by French implementation of this Directive may revive the significance of *obligations d'information* on *vendeurs professionnels*.[63]

3. Liability under the *Garantie Légale* and its Rivals

The oldest and still central basis for a seller's liability for failures in quality or utility of the property sold remains the liability for latent defects imposed by articles 1641 to 1649 of the Civil Code, the so-called *garantie légale*. This liability has always been distinctive in a number of ways. From its origins in Roman law, it was imposed by special legislative provision, distinct from more general sanctions for contractual failures in performance and special to the law of sale[64] and possessing its own set of remedies with their own limitation periods, reflected in the Civil Code for two centuries in article 1648's *bref délai* (short delay).[65] However, the special nature of these features

---

[59] Versailles 13 May 1988, *Epoux Bouju*, D 1988.IR. 203.

[60] Com. 5 Dec. 1989, Bull. civ. IV no. 306, D 1990 Somm. 322 note Huet. Cf. Civ. (1) 26 Nov. 1981, Bull. civ. I no. 354, JCP 1982.IV.63.   [61] Below, p. 72.   [62] Above, p. 65.   [63] Below, p. 463.

[64] Liability for latent defects arose from the edict of the curile aediles in the late second century BC and originally concerned the rules applicable to the public sale of slaves and certain types of livestock: Zimmermann, *Obligations*, 311 *et seq.*; Zimmermann, *Liability for Non-Conformity*, 9 *et seq.*

[65] In Roman law this was six months as regards the *actio redhibitoria* (Dig. 21.1.19.6), twelve months as regards the *actio quanti minoris* (Dig. 21.1.38 pr.). Liability in damages for loss caused by a defect was developed as the principles laid down in the aedilitian edict became absorbed by the general action on the purchase, the *actio empti*, which enjoyed a prescription period of 30 years: Zimmermann, *Obligations*, 321–2, 324. In the modern law, the starting point and length of the 'short delay' was assessed by the *juges du fond*, see below, pp. 91–93.

should not give the impression of narrowness, for once again, there was a process of generalisation from the ancient concepts, a gradual whittling away of ancient restrictions. In the result, the *garantie légale* applies to sales of *all* types of property: all movable property (including goods, incorporeal movables such as contractual rights or intellectual property[66]) except *res extra commercium*,[67] and all immovable property,[68] to second-hand goods as much as to new ones,[69] and to property incorporated into other property.[70] It also concerns a wide range of types of 'defects' (including defects of functioning and not merely physical imperfection) and usually attracts liability in damages and not merely termination of the contract and restitution or a reduction in the price.[71]

However, as I noted earlier, this picture has been complicated in modern French law by the development and expansion of two other analyses. The first reflects old problems of the relationship between the special liability of sellers for latent defects and their more general liability for contractual failures in performance.[72] Under the Civil Code, a seller is bound to deliver 'the property sold'[73] and this implies that the property conforms to the terms agreed by the parties as to what *was* sold, so that the obligation to deliver includes an obligation of contractual conformity (*obligation de conformité*). Breach of these contractual obligations (*non-conformité* or *un défaut de conformité*) gives rise to liability under the general contractual regime provided by the Code, both as to damages[74] and termination of the contract[75] and any action is subject to the general rules of prescription of 10 or 30 years, rather than the *bref délai* of the *garantie légale*.[76]

Now, the traditional French way of drawing the line between these two grounds of seller's liability was to say that contractual non-conformity dealt with cases where the buyer had not received the thing which he had agreed to buy, whereas liability for latent defects dealt with cases where the buyer had received the thing, but where it possessed defects of a type which would have prevented him from buying it.[77] However, this distinction was not destined to remain neat. For while liability for delivering non-conforming property can arise from breach of stipulations as to the time of delivery, the quantity of goods,[78] or the type of goods where bought generically,[79] it can also arise from stipulations governing other aspects of the property, including

---

[66] The *garantie légale* has been said to apply to the supply of computer software, at least if it is a standard program, as much as to the supply of computers themselves: Huet, *Responsabilité du vendeur*, 171.

[67] Notably, parts of the the human body, which neither in whole or in part can be the subject of a contract: Savatier note to Civ. 17 Dec. 1954, JCP 1955.II.8490. Malaurie, Aynès and Gautier, *Contrats spéciaux*, 139–40.

[68] This follows from the terms and structure of the Civil Code itself, see arts. 1598, 1641–1649 and the declaration in Com. 11 Jun. 1954, D. 1954.697. There are special rules for *ventes d'immeubles à construire* similar to the regime applicable to builders generally: art. 1646-1 C. civ. and below, p. 104 *et seq.*

[69] Com. 11 Jun. 1954, D 1954.697.

[70] Com. 20 Jan. 1970, JCP 1972.II.17280 note Boitard et Rabut (mechanical component of ship).

[71] Below, p. 73 *et seq.* and 79 *et seq.*   [72] See generally, Zimmermann, *Obligations*, 319–22.

[73] Arts. 1603–1604 C. civ.   [74] Arts. 1147–1148 C. civ.

[75] Arts. 1183–1184 C. civ. (*résolution*).   [76] Above, p. 69 and below, p. 91 *et seq.*

[77] O. Tournafond, 'Les prétendus concours d'actions et le contrat de vente (erreur sur la substance, défaut de conformité, vice caché)' D 1989 Chron. 237, 238.

[78] J. Schmidt-Szalewski, 'Vente, Obligations du vendeur. Obligation de délivrance Généralités. Etendue,' Jur. Cl. Civ. arts. 1603–1623 (2003), Fasc. 210. In the case of sales of land, the Code contains special provisions as to the conveyance of property of a different size than was stipulated: arts. 1616–1619 C. civ.

[79] Civ. (1) 11 Oct. 1966, JCP 1967.II.15193 note Géraud de la Pradelle.

those concerning its quality or fitness for purpose[80] which are the traditional concern of the *garantie légale*. This is therefore where the distinction between the two grounds of liability begins to break down, for in French law a contractual agreement as to the property sold need not be express, issues of the content of agreement and interpretation being in principle a matter for the 'sovereign power of assessment' of the *juges du fond*.[81] Moreover, where a seller has an obligation to deliver property of a defined type, it is generally required to be of 'average quality' or, as it is traditionally put, '*marchande et loyale*',[82] its significance again being a matter for the 'assessment' of *juges du fond*.[83] Where property sold is not up to quality in this way its buyer may claim damages,[84] even if this failure has no impact on the property's fitness for its purpose. So, for example, the Cour de cassation has declared that an 'order for a new item is to be understood normally as one for something without *any* defect [*sans défaut*]'.[85]

Since the middle of the last century some French jurists have gone further and argued that the 'contractual conformity' of property sold should include elements of the fitness for the purpose for which it was sold.[86] At the same time as this was being realised, writers and the courts also began to accept that the notion of 'defect' for the purposes of the *garantie légale* might be understood 'functionally, so that a defect exists *if* the property sold is found unfit for the purpose for which the buyer intended it' rather than in more physical terms.[87] With this double expansion, many cases could be analysed either in terms of the *garantie légale* or contractual non-conformity,[88] and for claimants the latter had the advantage of avoiding the *bref délai*.[89]

For a number of years, French courts seemed quite happy to build a second law of liability for latent defects on the framework of 'contractual non-conformity'[90] and even considered it for the court to raise of its own initiative the possibility of this basis of liability instead of the *garantie légale*.[91] The courts appeared to choose one or other analysis as a function of the prescription period which they thought

---

[80] Ghestin and Desché, *Vente*, 750 citing Civ. (1) 1 Dec. 1987, Bull civ. I no. 324.

[81] Civ. (3) 28 Nov. 1968, JCP 1969 II 15797.

[82] C. Aubry and C. Rau, *Cours de droit civil français*, Tome V (Eds. Techniques, Paris, 6th. edn., 1947 by P. Esmein) 60; Malaurie, Aynès and Gautier, *Contrats spéciaux*, 217.

[83] This is often supported by reference to art. 1246 C. civ.: de Juglart, *Vente*, 247; Req. 18 Dec. 1934, GP 1935.1.271 (where the court took into account the parties' previous dealings).

[84] Under arts. 1147 and 1603 C. civ. There may be other remedial effects, see below, p. 79 *et seq.*

[85] Civ. (1) 4 Apr. 1991, *affaire de la Renault neuve*, Bull. civ. I no. 130, D 1992 Somm. 201 obs: Tournafond (emphasis added).

[86] Notably, Ghestin, *Conformité et garantie*, 134, echoing Pothier, *Vente*, 161–162. Ghestin argued for a 'chronological' basis for distinguishing between liability arising from the *obligation de délivrance* (to be applied to defects before the property has been accepted) and from the *garantie légale* (to be applied to latent defects arising after the property has been accepted): Ghestin and Desché, *Vente*, 820 *et seq.*

[87] Again, see Ghestin and Desché, *Vente* 764 *et seq.* This represented a change in interpretation of art. 1641 C. civ.

[88] Tournafond, *op. cit.* n. 77, D 1989 Chron. 237 who dates these developments to the 1950s.

[89] Above, p. 70.

[90] This approach was implicitly endorsed by the Assemblée plénière: Ass. plén. 7 Feb. 1986 JCP 1986.II.20616 note Malinvaud, D 1986.293 note Bénabent. See also Civ. (1) 5 Nov. 1985, Bull. civ. I no. 287 (damages in respect of damage caused by defect in design of motorcycle against its manufacturer); Civ. (1) 13 Dec. 1989, Bull. civ. I, no. 393 (*résolution* of sale of car with design and manufacturing defects against its retailer).　　　[91] Art. 12 al. 1 N.c.pr.civ.; Civ. (1) 16 Jun. 1993, D 1994.210.

appropriate[92] in particular given the seriousness of the defect.[93] In practice, therefore, the courts took not merely a 'functionalist' view of the concept of defect, but also a functionalist approach to its application. However, in the mid-1990s French courts instead started to draw a firm line between the two analyses of defects in sale, holding that hidden defects which render property unfit for its normal purpose may be the subject only of the *garantie légale*,[94] leaving liability for contractual non-conformity to cases where property supplied does not conform to 'agreed specifications',[95] whether express or implied.[96] Whether or not this line holds for very long is a matter of doubt: its juristic basis has remained controversial,[97] as can be seen in its significant role in the dispute as to French implementation of the Consumer Guarantees Directive.[98]

However, the picture became further complicated by judicial recourse to the *obligations de sécurité* in the context of the seller's liability to buyer. *Obligations de sécurité* belong to the 'general law of contract', having been attached 'forcibly' to contracts since the beginning of the twentieth century,[99] but their use in the context of sale seems to have been caused by a combination of judicial discomfort with using 'contractual non-conformity' to avoid the *bref délai* of the *garantie légale* and judicial embarrassment at France's continued failure to implement the Product Liability Directive.[100] As a result, French courts themselves 'implemented' the core concerns of the Directive under the aegis of a native French technique, though they adapted it considerably for its new context, subjecting the *obligation de sécurité* to a requirement of defect and extending its protection for the benefit of those not party to the contract of sale.[101] As I shall later explain, the status of this *jurisprudence* after French *legislative* implementation remains controversial.[102]

In the following discussion, I shall not delve further into the controversies as to the proper line between liability for latent defects and for 'defects of conformity', nor the legitimacy of the judicial extension in this sphere of *obligations de sécurité*, but instead will look in more detail at the ambit of the *garantie légale*, with sideways glances as to the differences which these other bases of liability offer.

---

[92] Ghestin and Desché, *Vente* 830–31; P. Le Tourneau, 'Conformités et garanties dans la vente d'objets mobiliers corporels' RTDCom. 1980.231, 271–2.   [93] Huet, *Responsabilité du vendeur*, 47.

[94] Civ. (1) 5 May 1993, D 1993.506 note Bénabent; Civ. (1) 16 Jun. 1993, D 1994.210; Civ. (1) 13 Oct. 1993, D 1994.211; Civ. (1) 27 Oct. 1993, D 1994.211; Com. 26 Apr. 1994, Bull. civ. IV no. 159; P. Jourdain, 'Les actions des acquéreurs insatisfaits ou victimes de dommages' GP 1994.2.826; Civ. (1) 20 Feb. 1996, Bull. civ. I no. 86.

[95] Civ. (1) 16 Jun. 1993, D 1994.210; Civ. (1) 17 Jun. 1997, Bull. civ. I no. 206 (taxi to be specially adapted to take disabled passengers).

[96] E.g. civ. (1) 30 March 1999, Bull. civ. I no. 118, *Cont. Conc. Cons.* (1999) 110 note L. Leveneur (crop seeds which became diseased held to be a matter of 'contractual non-conformity' rather than *vice caché* as the price and previous course of dealings between the parties led the *juges du fond* to hold that *treated* seeds had been ordered).

[97] Huet, *Principaux contrats spéciaux*, 199 *et seq.* esp. at 202. Malaurie, Aynès and Gautier, *Contrats spéciaux*, 208 ask whether the distinction required is not 'over-subtle'.   [98] Below, pp. 580–1.

[99] Above, p. 22–3.

[100] Jourdain, obs. RTDCiv. 1991.539, 540. Some influence may also have been felt from the enactment of a general duty as the safety of products and services in 1983: *loi* no. 83–660 of 21 Jul. 1983, art. 1, now art. L. 221-1 C. consom., below, p. 309

[101] Civ. (1) 17 Jan. 1995, D 1995.350 note Jourdain and see below, pp. 455–7.

[102] Below, pp. 461–3.

(a) 'Defect'

The concept or concepts of a defect have been central to the liabilities of a seller, whether as *vice caché* under the *garantie légale*, as *défaut de conformité* under the *obligation de conformité* or as *défaut de sécurité* under the 'judicial implementation' of the Product Liability Directive.[103] Here, I wish to look at the types of defect which have attracted liability, at how serious they need be before liability results, the significance of their hidden nature and *who* decides these issues.

(i) *Types of defects*

Although the approach of French courts to the understanding of a *vice* under the *garantie légale* has not been uniform, there have been examples of its application to a very wide range of types of defect.

The traditional example of a *vice* is where property suffers from some physical defect, for example, rotten meat,[104] or where manufactured goods suffer from a manufacturing defect.[105] In 1986 the Assemblée plénière recognised that a physical defect could constitute a *défaut de conformité* so as to give rise to liability under the general law,[106] though subsequently the Cour de cassation has denied its application where it overlaps with the *garantie légale* in this way.

Secondly, poor design has been held to render something defective either for the purposes of the *garantie légale* or contractual 'non-conformity'.[107] For example, in one case a passenger in a motor vehicle was injured when an aerosol can left in its glove compartment exploded: the court held that its manufacturer was liable under the general law of contract for its defective design in the car in that the compartment was too close to the fuses.[108]

Thirdly, the property's defect may stem from the inadequacy of its accompanying information. Sometimes, this consists of a claim made by a seller about the property which proves false. Where the claim is held to have formed part of the definition of the property, liability may arise on the basis of the property's 'non-conformity',[109] but liability may arise under the *garantie légale*, as long as this 'defect' is sufficiently serious.[110] For example, where a car manufacturer's publicity material supplied by an accredited

---

[103] While not universal in French usage, I shall restrict *vice* for defects giving rise to liability under the *garantie légale*, *défaut* for defects giving rise to liability under the general law.

[104] Angers 30 Oct. 1951, D 1952.60.

[105] Com. 17 Dec. 1973, GP 1974.1.429 note Planqueel, JCP 1975.II.17912 note Savatier; Civ. (1) 9 Oct. 1979, *affaire Lamborghini*, GP 1980.1.249 note Planqueel, D 1980.IR.222, obs. Larroumet; Civ. (1) 28 Nov. 1979, D 1985.485 note Huet, D 1980.IR.566 obs. Larroumet; Civ. (1) 14 May 1996, Bull. civ. I no. 213.

[106] Ass. plén. 7 Feb. 1986, JCP 1986.II.20616 note Malinvaud, D 1986.293 note Bénabent (an insulating product which corroded the pipes into which it was placed).

[107] Viney, *op. cit.* n. 43, in Ghestin, *Sécurité des consommateurs*, at 76–77; Huet, *Responsabilité du vendeur*, 163. E.g. Civ. (5) Nov. 1985, Bull. civ. I no. 287 (design of motorcycle and *défaut de conformité*); Civ. (1) 23 May 1995, Bull. civ. I no. 217, (motor vehicle and *vice caché*); Civ. (1) 17 Jun. 1997, Bull. civ. I no. 206 (motor vehicle and *défaut de conformité*); Civ. (1) 20 Feb. 1996, Civ. I no. 86 (electric equipment and *vice caché*).   [108] Civ. (1) 24 Apr. 1985, Bull. civ. I no. 128, RTDCiv. 1986.366 obs. Huet.

[109] E.g. Com. 6 Oct. 1975, D. 1976 IR 20 (provenance of apparatus specified). The definition need not be express: e.g. Paris 27 Nov. 1967 JCP 1968.II.15531 note J.H.   [110] Below, pp. 75–6.

seller made a false claim about its petrol consumption, this led to a finding that the car itself suffered from a 'latent defect'.[111] Sometimes misstatements can affect the safety of something sold. For example, in another case the claimant had bought from the defendant a new Opel motor car fitted with tyres described as 'puncture-proof'.[112] Just over a fortnight and 800 kilometres later, one of the tyres burst while driving and the car was severely damaged in the ensuing accident, although no-one was seriously hurt. The court gave judgment for the buyer, who was entitled to think that the tyres were in good condition given their newness, and that their description as 'puncture-proof', even making some allowance for the exaggeration common in promotional material, entitled him to place a greater confidence than he would in a standard tyre.[113] Here, then, a buyer's *higher* expectations of a product can (if induced by the seller and disappointed) lead to it being held defective. Conversely, if a seller makes clear that the property suffers from impurities otherwise not to be expected in a product of its description, it will not be held defective by reason of these impurities:[114] here, a similar result can be reached by saying that the property sold was defective, but that this defect was drawn to the attention of the buyer and therefore was not 'hidden.'[115]

Sometimes, though, a seller's failure to inform or warn the buyer has led to the finding of a *vice*,[116] and here liability under the *garantie légale* comes very close to liability for failing to fulfil an *obligation d'information*,[117] which, if contractual, arises under the general law of contract.[118] In common with *obligations d'information*, the case law on the *garantie légale* provides examples of failures to warn of a product's dangers and failures to advise or instruct the buyer in a way to prevent the product's effectiveness for its task. So, for example, a manufacturer was held liable to indemnify a builder in respect of his liability arising from use of roofing material which failed to remain transparent as was required: the manufacturer should have expressed reservations about the material's effectiveness or sent accompanying instructions.[119] A seller who fails to warn his buyer of the dangers of the product sold or fails to instruct him as to the proper precautions to be taken in order to avoid injury to person or damage to property has also been held liable under the *garantie légale*,[120] though where a buyer is interested principally in the recovery of damages, it is usually advantageous to claim breach of an *obligation d'information*[121] and, as has been said, from the 1990s the courts tended to base liability here on an *obligation de sécurité*.[122]

While most 'defects' come within one of these groups, the courts have sometimes held that property sold suffers from a *vice* consisting solely in the property's lack of fitness for its purpose. This is particularly clear in the case of sales of immovable property, notably where sellers are held liable under the *garantie légale* on the ground that their

---

[111] Paris 3 May 1967, GP 1967.2.34 note J.-P. D. See similarly Com. 23 Jan 1978, Bull. civ. IV. no. 33 (vehicle not manufactured in the year stated by seller).

[112] Paris 18 Jan. 1971, GP 1972.1.289 note Kosossey. See also Civ. (1) 21 Mar. 1962, Bull. civ. I no. 174.

[113] The buyer was held not to have been contributorily negligent in not checking his tyres.

[114] Com. 29 Nov. 1977 Bull. civ. IV no. 284.   [115] Below, p. 76.

[116] E.g. Com. 3 Jan. 1977, GP 1977.2.461 note Planqueel, D 1977 IR 176.   [117] Above, pp. 64–9.

[118] Above, p. 66.

[119] Civ. (3) 2 Oct.1979, D. 1980.IR.224 obs. Larroumet. See also Com. 3 Jan. 1977, D 1977.IR.176.

[120] E.g. Com. 15 Apr. 1975, Bull. civ. IV no. 106 (damage to property).   [121] Above, pp. 66, 70.

[122] Above, p. 72 and below, pp. 461–3 on the present status of this case law.

buyers cannot use the land for the purposes which they envisage, for example land sold for building where the seller knows that no planning permission for building will be given.[123]

(ii) The seriousness of the defect

Article 1641 of the Civil Code provides that a seller is liable only for latent defects in the property which 'render it unfit for the use for which it is intended, or which so diminish this use that, had he known of them, the buyer would not have acquired it, or would have acquired it only at a lesser price'. Traditionally, this article contains two elements, that there be a defect and that it renders the property unfit for its purpose or diminishes its fitness to the extent that the buyer would not have entered the contract, at least at the price paid,[124] but the modern, 'functional' interpretation of defect reads its requirements conjunctively, the property's defectiveness being defined by reference to its lack of fitness for purpose.[125]

Both the existence and seriousness of a property's 'defect' are within the 'sovereign power of assessment' of the *juges du fond* and this means that we can gain only a rather general impression of its understanding or application.[126] Nevertheless, for liability under the *garantie légale* the defect must have *some* effect on the property's use. A recurring example in *la doctrine* concerns the sale to a dealer of a second-hand Renault car which suffered from vibrations in its gearbox and wind noise: these minor defects were held to reduce the car's attractiveness but not to affect its utility to the dealer and so not to attract the *garantie légale*.[127] On the other hand, the court may have taken a different view if the pleasure drawn from the property is central to the reason for its purchase, as in the case of sale of perfume, a Hi-fi set or 'luxury products' to an individual.[128] French courts have sometimes referred to the ease of repair of property or the temporary nature of a defect in holding that a defect is not sufficiently serious to give rise to the *garantie légale*,[129] but some commentators have argued that these features do not necessarily have this effect.[130]

While the terms of article 1641 themselves suggest that an objective approach should be taken to the issue of the buyer's purpose for which the property is not fit,[131] so that the *garantie légale* applies to cases where the property is unfit for the *normal* purpose to which property of the type in question is put,[132] most jurists say that a buyer can rely on his particular purpose for the property where this is known to the seller:[133] here, it becomes part of their agreement, and if it is unfit for this purpose the

---

[123] Civ. (1) 16 Jun. 1966, Bull. civ. I no. 374.

[124] This interpretation was based on the Roman position: Dig. 21.1.1.8. For a valuable discussion of these issues, see Ghestin and Desché, *Vente*, 764 *et seq.*   [125] Above, p. 72.

[126] Req. 22 May 1900, DP 1900.1.454; Civ. (1) 21 Jul. 1987, JCP 1987.IV.361 (existence of defect); Com. 16 Nov. 1976, GP 1977.1.Pan. Jur. 43 (seriousness of defect). Cf. above, pp. 40–1.

[127] Nîmes 18 Dec. 1980, D 1983.29 note Larroumet.

[128] Huet, *Responsabilité du vendeur*, 164; Malaurie, Aynès and Gautier, *Contrats spéciaux*, 266.

[129] E.g. Com. 16 Nov. 1976, GP 1977.1. Pan. Jur. 43.; Paris 3 Dec. 1976, JCP 1977.II.18579 note Boitard et Dubarry (computer system with teething problems).

[130] Ghestin and Desché, *Vente*, 769–70.   [131] *'l'usage auquel on l'a destiné.'*

[132] Malaurie, Aynès and Gautier, *Contrats spéciaux*, 266.

[133] Ghestin, *Conformité*, 187–89; Huet, *Responsabilité du vendeur*, 164; Bénabent, *Contrats spéciaux*, 152.

seller may be liable.[134] Given this explanation, some jurists suggest that the proper legal basis of liability here is non-performance of a contractual undertaking, attracting liability under the general law rather than under the *garantie légale*,[135] but the cases do not all bear this out.[136]

Where the seller was not aware of a buyer's special purpose, a distinction appears to have been drawn between dangerous and non-dangerous defects. So, where a buyer used a product for a purpose dangerous to persons or property then, as long as this use is not too far-fetched, the courts held that a seller's failure to warn either attracts liability under the *garantie légale* or for breach of an *obligation d'information*. Since the mid-1990s, though, liability here became subsumed under the judicial 'implementation' of the Product Liability Directive.[137] On the other hand, French courts have been much less likely to impose liability where property simply fails to achieve an unusual, unspecified but foreseeable purpose. So, for example, where a vehicle was bought as a 'collectors' car', its buyer cannot complain when it is not fit for normal use on the roads.[138] And, as I have explained, a seller is not generally under an obligation to inform the buyer as to a product's effectiveness for unforeseeable and unspecified uses.[139]

(iii) A hidden defect?

While a buyer must show that the defect existed at the time of delivery for liability under the *garantie légale* and for contractual non-conformity,[140] they appear to differ as to whether the defect must be hidden at this time.

Under the *garantie légale*, a buyer must show that the defect was 'not apparent' to him on sale,[141] the *juges du fond* having a 'sovereign power of assessment' as to whether this is achieved.[142] Clearly, a buyer will fail if he is shown to have known of the defect on sale and so a seller may avoid liability by informing the buyer of any defect both 'in its cause and its extent'.[143] But French courts do not allow a seller to escape liability by making general statements apparently informing the buyer of the defectiveness of the property, which they have treated as exemption clauses.[144] Where a buyer ignores a

---

[134] Req. 31 Jul. 1905, S 1907.1.437; Req. 18 Dec. 1934, GP 1935.1.271.

[135] Malaurie, Aynès and Gautier, *Contrats spéciaux*, 267.

[136] E.g. Com. 15 Apr. 1975, Bull. civ. IV no. 89.　　　　　[137] Above, p. 72.

[138] Civ. (1) 24 Nov. 1993, Bull. civ. I no. 347.　　　　　[139] Above, pp. 68–9.

[140] Com. 3 Dec. 1980, Bull. civ. IV no. 409 (contractual non-conformity); Com. 9 Dec. 1981, Bull. civ. IV no. 438 (*garantie légale*); Bénabent, *Contrats spéciaux*, 159–60. It is not enough for a claimant to show the existence of a defect at the time of claiming: Com. 27 Nov. 1984, GP 1985 Pan. Jur. 80 obs. Dupichot; Civ. (1) 22 Jun. 1971, JCP 1971.II. 16881. The issue of the timing of the defect remains in the hands of the *juges du fond*: e.g. Civ. (1) 28 Nov. 1979, D 1985.485 (1er. esp.) note Huet, D 1980 IR 566 obs. Larroumet.

[141] Com. 24 Jan. 1984, JCP 1984.IV.107. Most authors say that it is the time of contract (de Juglart, *Vente*, 304) but Ghestin and Desché contend that strictly speaking it is the time of the transfer of risk in the property: Ghestin and Desché, *Vente*, 780. In most cases, these times will be the same: arts. 1138 and 1624 C. civ.　　　　　[142] Req. 22 May 1900, DP 1900.1.454.

[143] Com. 3 Nov. 1972, GP 1973.1 Pan.jur. 31; Civ. (3) 14 Jun. 1989, Bull. civ. III no. 140. A defect which results from the technical specifications of the buyer will also not be 'hidden': Malinvaud, note to Paris 18 Feb. 1977, JCP 1977.II.18675 and cf. Com. 29 Nov. 1977, Bull. civ. IV no. 284, above, p. 74.

[144] Ghestin, *Conformité*, 21 and see below, p. 93–5.

defect which has been drawn to his attention, the 'apparent nature' of the defect will often coincide with a lack of care in the buyer, with the difference that the defence of *faute de la victime* allows a court to reduce a claimant's damages to the extent which it considers appropriate, whereas a finding that the defect was not hidden excludes liability altogether.

However, a defect may also be found to have been apparent where the buyer *ought* to have known of the defect at the relevant time.[145] Here, the *juges du fond* take into account the relative status and technical knowledge of the parties as well as the nature and the extent of the investigations necessary to reveal the defect.[146] So, where the buyer is not technically expert, the courts take a fairly generous view of what is required of him, though a defect will be held 'apparent' if a little attention would have revealed it to a person of average prudence.[147] Where a buyer possesses skill or knowledge in relation to the property, then it is more likely that a court will hold that its defect is apparent to him,[148] though it will not rule it out. So, for example, where a buyer ran a dry-cleaning business and bought a chemical product for use in her machines, her claim for damages based on its abnormal composition was accepted as the court found that this defect could have been discovered only by a laboratory analysis.[149] In these cases, there is a clearer link between the hidden nature of the defect and the buyer's contributory fault, and giving the flexibility of result which a finding of *faute de la victime* allows, the courts have sometimes preferred to hold a defect 'hidden' but then reduce the buyer's damages. For example, where a buyer bought a second-hand tractor sold 'as seen' without taking the precaution of having it checked by an engineer and ten days later the tractor went out of control and caused him serious injuries, the court held the seller liable but reduced the buyer's damages on the ground of *faute de la victime*.[150] This approach has also been taken where the seller actually knew of the defect at the time of sale but did not reveal it.[151]

At first sight, though, the *garantie légale*'s restriction to hidden defects marks a difference with liability for *défauts de conformité* which is not so restricted. However, this difference lessens on examination, for if goods suffer from a *défaut de conformité* which is apparent on delivery but the buyer nevertheless accepts them without qualification, the buyer's claim to *résolution* is lost on the ground of the goods' acceptance.[152] As regards complex products (such as computers) a buyer's assessment of whether they conform to their specifications may take a period of time and is therefore held *not* apparent on delivery, a *défaut de conformité* which is 'easily discoverable' by a buyer on delivery will be held apparent.[153] In this way, the sorts of considerations which the courts take into account as part of the 'hidden' nature of the *vices* under the *garantie légale* can also be taken into account by them for the purposes of their lack of the property's contractual conformity.

---

[145] Ghestin and Desché, *Vente*, 771–6.   [146] Bénabent, *Contrats spéciaux*, 154–5.

[147] E.g. Seine 21 Dec. 1956, D 1957.47.   [148] E.g. Civ. (1) 18 Dec. 1962, D 1963.114.

[149] Com. 30 Nov. 1982, Bull. civ. IV no. 391.   [150] Com. 4 Nov. 1970, D. 1971.188.

[151] Civ. (3) 3 May 1989, D 1990.117 note Tournafond.

[152] De Juglart, *Vente*, 299 note 1; Malaurie, Aynès and Gautier, *Contrats spéciaux*, 237; Com. 12 Feb. 1980, D 1981.278 note Aubertin.   [153] Malaurie, Aynès and Gautier, *Contrats spéciaux*, 237–38.

(iv) How are issues of defectiveness decided?

As I have said, the issues of the existence, hidden nature and seriousness of a defect for the purposes of the *garantie légale* are all placed within the 'sovereign power of assessment of the lower courts'[154] and in contrast to the position as to findings of delictual fault, the Cour de cassation has not reserved for itself control over the characterization of the facts for this purpose.[155] Lower courts do not therefore have to explain their decisions on the defectiveness of the property as long as they identify its presence and necessary attributes.[156]

Moreover, while the books state clearly that the burden of proof (*le charge de la preuve*) as to the issue of the existence and seriousness of a defect lies on the buyer and may be established 'by any means',[157] in the context of establishing the defectiveness of property, the role of the *expertise* is particularly important.[158] As I have explained in relation to findings of delictual fault,[159] judicially appointed experts often go well beyond the merely technical and express their own judgments on issues which are in strict law of mixed law and fact. As Malinvaud strikingly put it:

[v]ery often hidden defects can only be brought to light by way of a technical *expertise*, this sometimes being very complex . . . One can even say that the burden of proof rests on the *experts*, who bring to the court the technical elements of the assessment.[160]

This means that in many cases, it is not the *juges du fond* nor indeed any judge or lawyer who decides the issue of defectiveness: it is the expert.[161]

In practice, in claims alleging the defectiveness of property, a buyer often requests an *expertise* at a interlocutory stage before a single judge, the *juge des référés*,[162] the expert being asked to investigate whether the defect existed, when, its seriousness and whether it could be discovered by the buyer. Such a request had the advantage of counting as bringing an action so as to satisfy the *bref délai* of the *garantie légale*[163] and allows a buyer to obtain clear evidence of the defective state of property where he

---

[154] Req. 22 May 1900, DP 1900.1.454; Civ. (1) 21 Jul. 1987, JCP 1987.IV.361 (existence of defect); Com. 16 Nov. 1976, GP 1977.1.Pan. Jur. 43 (seriousness of defect); Civ. (1) 7 Jan. 1982, Bull. civ. I no. 8 (hidden nature). [155] Above, p. 44.

[156] E.g. *cassation* of a decision below where the *juges du fond* allowed a buyer's action without identifying how the defect was hidden: Com. 5 Feb. 1974, Bull. civ. IV no. 50.

[157] Bénabent, *Contrats spéciaux*, 159; Malaurie, Aynès and Gautier, *Contrats spéciaux*, 278; Civ. (1) 13 Dec. 1965, JCP 1966.II.14643. On the significance of this, see above, p. 47. [158] Cf. above, pp. 48–50.

[159] Above, p. 49.

[160] Note to Com. 10 Dec.1973, JCP 1975.II.17950 and see Ghestin and Desché, *Vente*, 782 as to the 'anteriority' of the defect to the sale.

[161] E.g. Com. 15 May 1972 and Com. 16 Jul. 1973, JCP 1974.II.17864 note Ghestin; Com. 17 Feb. 1976, JCP 1976.II.18482 note Malinvaud; Com. 15 Apr. 1975, Bull. civ. IV no. 106; Reims 3 Jul. 1975, JCP 1976.IV.183 note J. A; Paris 24 Mar. 1982, D 1984.IR.188 obs. Wagner; Com. 12 Dec. 1984, Bull. civ. IV no. 349; Com. 17 Oct. 1977, GP 1978.I.221 note Plancqueel; Civ. (1) 4 Apr. 1991, D 1992 Somm. 201 obs. Tournafond; Civ. (1) 11 Jun. 1991, Bull. civ. I no. 201; Civ. (1) 20 Feb. 1996, Bull. civ. I no. 86.

[162] Art. 484 N.c.pr.civ.; R. Genin-Méric, 'Mesures d'instruction exécutées par un technicien, Intervention du technicien dans l'instruction du litige' Jur.-Cl. Proc. Civ. Fasc. 660 (1995). These proceedings are inter partes. [163] Art. 2244 C. civ.; below, p. 92.

wishes to resell or repair.[164] While in principle the *juges du fond* do not have to follow the view taken by the *expertise*,[165] if they fundamentally misinterpret its conclusions, their decision will be quashed.[166]

4. The Buyer's Rights in Respect of Defects

The Civil Code followed ancient Roman law in providing three particular actions to the buyer under the *garantie légale* in respect of latent defects: for the restitution of the price with return of the property (the *action rédhibitoire*); for the reduction of the price (the *action estimatoire*); and an action for damages (the *action en responsabilité*).[167] On the other hand, the consequences of 'contractual non-conformity' of the property in principle follow those of the general law of contractual non-performance, and include specific enforcement, *résolution* and damages, but their significance in the context of sale needs explanation and they are supplemented in the case of commercial sales. This parentage in the general law is also true of the non-performance of contractual *obligations d'informa-tion* and *obligations de sécurité*, though their particular utility has been in the context of the imposition of liability in damages.[168] In this way, the terminology used by modern French lawyers to describe the consequences of the *garantie légale* still reflects the proce-dural bias of ancient Roman law, referring to 'actions' rather than the more substantive thinking which generally dominates French law and describes the law in terms of various effects of contractual obligation (including the *obligation de conformité*), the rights of which they are the correlative, and the sanctions of their non-performance. The language of 'remedy' (*les remèdes*) which so dominates English discussions of the consequences of breach of contract has been almost altogether absent from French discussions.[169]

(a) Does the buyer have a right to the replacement or repair of the goods?

It may seem odd to a common lawyer that I start my discussion with the question whether a buyer possesses a right to the repair or replacement of the defective property, but from a French perspective, this question reflects general possibility of 'specific enforcement' or 'enforcement in kind' of the seller's obligations (*exécution en nature*), itself related to the binding force of contractual obligations.[170]

In principle, therefore, where a seller has not performed his obligation to deliver conforming property, the buyer may demand that he does so, and for French law this holds good whether the seller has failed to perform altogether or has performed

---

[164] Cf. Com. 22 Jan. 1968, D 1968 Somm. 65 where the buyer of a second-hand car had it repaired and the *juges du fond* rejected his claim on the ground of *vice caché* as he had not sought in time '*vérifications contradictoires*'.   [165] Art. 246 N.c.pr.civ.   [166] Civ. (3) 4 Jan.1979, JCP 1979.IV.79.

[167] Arts. 1641, 1644–1646, 1648 C. civ.

[168] However, examples of termination of a contract (*résolution*) on the ground of non-performance of a seller's *obligation de sécurité* may be found in Civ. (1) 11 Jun. 1991, Bull. civ. I no. 201 and of a seller's *oblig-ation d'information* in civ. (1) 25 Jun. 1996, Bull. civ. I no. 274.

[169] See D. Tallon, 'Remedies: 2. French Report' in Harris and Tallon, 263–4. But see below, p. 604 *et seq*.

[170] Bell, Boyron and Whittaker, 346 *et seq*.

defectively by delivering property which does not 'conform'.[171] In the latter case, this 'right to performance' consists of a right to the replacement of the goods and, possibly, to their repair. Here, though, we have to be particularly careful, for this suggests a right in the buyer to have the property repaired or replaced *by the seller*, whereas in some French discussions what is intended is that a buyer should have the right to recoup from the seller the cost of replacement or repair by a third party.[172] This ambiguity reflects a wider difference in approach between French and English law: to a common lawyer, claims by a buyer for the cost of repairs or replacement are seen as particular examples of claims for damages; but to a French lawyer, they can be seen as examples of the 'enforcement in kind' of the seller's contractual obligation as the buyer receives the 'performance' owed by the seller, even if not *from* the seller.[173]

The mechanism by which the property is to be repaired or replaced by another person is found in article 1144 of the Civil Code, which provides that a creditor of a contractual obligation may ask the court to authorise him to engage a third party to undertake performance of the debtor's obligation at the latter's expense: under this provision, a buyer may ask for such an authorisation for the replacement of defective goods.[174] However, this apparently facilitative provision also reflects a concern that in general a creditor may not obtain a substitute performance elsewhere without prior judicial authorisation and so should not (as in English law) simply obtain a substitute performance and claim damages for its cost.[175] In this way, French law protects both the creditor's right to performance and the debtor's right to perform.[176] There are two important exceptions, though, to this requirement of judicial intervention. The first exception applies to any case (civil or commercial) where the courts consider that the debtor's performance needs to be 'replaced' as a matter of urgency.[177] The second is found in commercial sales, where a unilateral right of replacement, known as *rachat*, exists in relation to generic goods, as long as the buyer has given the seller notice and a period of time to perform.[178] In this case, where the buyer has to spend more than the original price of the goods on their replacement, the difference is recoverable from the seller.[179] By contrast, a buyer cannot require a seller to replace property suffering from a latent defect within the meaning of the *garantie légale* which he discovers after the property's acceptance, for the *obligation de garantie* gives rise only to the system of actions which the Code itself prescribes.

In looking at the availability in a buyer of a right to repair defective property, we need again to distinguish according to whom it is intended should effect the repair. The difficulty with imposing an *obligation* on a seller to repair defective property is

---

[171] Malaurie, Aynès and Gautier, *Contrats spéciaux*, 239; Bihl, *Vente*, 225–6. Such an order would normally be backed by *astreintes*. This follows the general approach of French law to the availability of orders for specific enforcement of a contract which are available except for cases of physical or 'moral' impossibility: Bell, Boyron and Whittaker, 346–8.   [172] E.g. Huet, *Responsabilité du vendeur*, 316.

[173] S. Whittaker, 'Les sanctions de l'inexécution des contrats, Droit anglais' in Fontaine and Viney, 977 at 1011–16.   [174] E.g. Com. 20 Jan. 1976, Bull. civ. IV no. 26.   [175] Below, p. 86.

[176] S. Whittaker, 'Performance of another's obligation: French and English law contrasted' in D. Johnston and R. Zimmermann (eds.), *Unjustified Enrichment, Key Issues in Comparative Perspective* (CUP, 2002) 433 at 452.

[177] Ibid., 448 *et seq*. The possibility is sometimes referred to as the *faculté de remplacement*.

[178] Malaurie, Aynès and Gautier, *Contrats spéciaux*, 242–3.   [179] Ibid., at 242.

that the seller never agreed to do so: a seller's obligation is to deliver conforming property or to guarantee it against latent defects, not to repair it if it is delivered in breach of either of these obligations.[180] Despite this, it has been said that a buyer has a legal right to have defective goods repaired by the seller, though some of the cases used to support this are concerned with the recovery of the cost of repairs by way of damages.[181] Overall, the position has not been clear, though this will apparently change on implementation of the European Consumer Guarantees Directive, though only as regards consumer buyers.[182]

(b) Termination, restitution and price reduction

In the English law of sale of goods, one of the buyer's most important remedies is the rejection of non-conforming goods and recovery of their price.[183] The arrangement of the French law here is quite different, distinguishing more sharply between a right to reject the delivery of the goods, liability to pay an unpaid price, recovery of a price once paid, and reduction of the price. The relationship between these various possibilities and termination of the contract is not straightforward.

First, French law recognises that sometimes a buyer can reject the delivery of defective property tendered by the seller on the ground of its contractual non-conformity (but not *ex hypothesi* on the ground of its *latent* defects),[184] but there is some discussion as to when. Some jurists argue that the right of rejection is generally available, as the Civil Code provides that a creditor of an obligation 'should not be forced to accept property other than that which is due to him',[185] but others say that a buyer can reject 'non-conforming' property only in commercial contracts for the sale of goods (that is, where the goods are bought for resale)[186] under the procedure known as *laissé pour compte*.[187] Under *laissé pour compte* a buyer may reject non-conforming goods and leave them at the risk of the seller or of the carrier, even for a short time after receipt of the goods,[188] without putting an end to the contract as a whole, for example, because he wishes to claim a substitute from the seller.[189] So while in theory a buyer who has rejected goods and wishes nothing more to do with the contract should bring an action to terminate the contract (an *action résolutoire*)[190] in practice this never

---

[180] This is often discussed in terms of the availability of *réparation en nature*: Terré, Simler and Lequette, *Obligations*, 579–80; Malaurie, Aynès and Stoffel-Munck, *Obligations*, 499. Some decisions deny *réparation en nature* in the contractual context: Civ. 4 Jun. 1924, S 1925.1.97, and Civ. 15 Mar. 1948, S. 1948.1.100, though cf. Com. 5 Jul. 1984, Bull. civ. IV, no. 219 (the *juges du fond* have a 'sovereign power' as to the '*mode de réparation*').

[181] Huet, *Responsabilité du vendeur*, 316–19; J. Gatsi, 'Vente commerciale, Obligation de délivrance du vendeur, sanction de l'inexécution' in Jur.-Cl. Contrats Distribution (1999) Fasc. 310, 7. Contra P. Ancel, 'La garantie conventionelle des vices cachés dans les conditions générales de vente en matière mobilière,' RTDCom. (1979) 203, 213.   [182] Below, pp. 616–18.   [183] Below, pp. 251–5.

[184] Above, p. 76.   [185] Art. 1243 C. civ.; Ghestin and Desché, *Vente*, 757.

[186] Art. 110-1 al. 1° C. com.

[187] Gatsi, *op. cit.*, 12; Malaurie, Aynès and Gautier, *Contrats spéciaux*, 243.

[188] Malaurie, Aynès and Gautier, *Contrats spéciaux*, 243.

[189] Ghestin, *Conformité*, 140 & 162; Huet, *Principaux contrats spéciaux*, 232–3 who see this as an example of the *exception d'inexécution*.

[190] P. Le Tourneau, 'Conformités et garanties dans la vente d'objets mobiliers corporels' RTDCom. (1980) 231, 238–40.

happens: it is left to the seller to contest the issue of conformity by testing the lawfulness of the buyer's rejection.

Secondly, if a seller delivers on credit goods which suffer from a 'defect of conformity', the buyer can refuse to pay the price by way of application of the 'defence of non-performance' (*l'exception d'inéxecution*)[191] as long as the seller's contractual non-performance is sufficiently serious.[192] While the matter is not free from doubt,[193] in principle a buyer can also claim the benefit of this defence in respect of 'non-performances' of a seller's *obligation de garantie*.[194]

Thirdly, in the case of apparent defects of 'contractual non-conformity', a buyer has the right to ask a court to rescind the contract and to order the return of the price by *action en résolution* as long as the non-performance is sufficiently serious, no distinction being made according to the status of the parties to the contract, whether *professionnel* or not.[195] In the case of latent defects, the buyer has a free choice between returning the goods and claiming back their price with expenses or keeping them and claiming a reduction in price in an extent to be calculated by *expertise*.[196] These actions under the *garantie légale* also lie whatever the status of the seller or buyer.

To a common lawyer, the most striking aspect of these actions is that termination of the contract and recovery of the price requires the buyer to go to court.[197] On the other hand, the actions under the *garantie légale* and for 'non-conformity' have their differences. Under the *garantie légale*, a buyer has a free choice whether to return the property and claim back its price or to keep the property and claim a reduction in price: a buyer need give no reason,[198] and may change his mind until either the court gives judgment or the seller agrees to his claim;[199] and a court is not entitled to substitute, for example, a reduction in the price where a buyer has claimed its restitution nor may a seller avoid restitution by arguing that the defect is reparable,[200] by offering a partial refund, or replacement of the property sold.[201] By contrast, where a buyer asks a court for *résolution* of a contract of sale with restitution of the price on the grounds of the property's 'non-conformity', the court may agree and order the return of the price

---

[191] See generally, Nicholas, 213–16 and Ghestin, *Conformité*, 138–49 in the context of the *obligation de conformité*.

[192] Com. 16 Jul. 1980, Bull. civ. IV no. 297, RTDCiv. 1981.398 obs. Chabas; Malaurie, Aynès and Gautier, *Contrats spéciaux*, 292; Treitel, *Remedies*, 300 *et seq*. The issue of seriousness is within the 'sovereign power of assessment of the *juges du fond*': Civ. 26 Nov. 1951, GP 1952.1.72.

[193] Treitel, *Remedies*, 302.

[194] Bihl, *Vente*, 252. This appears from cases in which a buyer raises the seller's liability for latent defects by way of defence to an action for the price: e.g. Rennes 30 Apr. 1952, D 1952.588.

[195] Art. 1184 C. civ. While some jurists refer to the *action rédhibitoire* as an action for *résolution*, I shall reserve *résolution* for termination under art. 1184 C. civ.

[196] Arts. 1644 & 1646 C. civ. After the courts imposed liability in damages on all *vendeurs professionnels*, the courts have taken a strict view of 'expenses', an example in the case of sale of a vehicle being the cost of its *carte grise*: Bihl, *Vente*, 256; Civ. (1) 4 Feb. 1963, JCP 1963.II.13159 note Savatier.

[197] Art. 1184 al. 3 C. civ. (*résolution*); art. 1648 C. civ. (which required an action to be brought within a *bref délai*). Exceptionally, a consumer buyer of movable property may repudiate the contract by registered letter if the seller fails to deliver the property within seven days of the due date: art. L. 114-1 C. consom.

[198] Civ. (1) 11 Jun. 1980, JCP 1980.IV.326, RTDCom. 1981.351 obs Hémard.

[199] Com. 22 Jul. 1953, D 1953.587.

[200] Civ. (1) 23 May 1995, Bull. civ. I no. 216, D 1996 Somm. 15 obs. Tournafond.

[201] Huet, *Responsabilité du vendeur*, 303; Civ. (1) 11 Jun. 1980, Bull. civ. I no. 185.

or may instead declare the contract subsisting and award a 'reduction in the price' by way of damages.[202] However, this difference does not mean that the same set of facts would be decided differently according to which of these two analyses a court adopts, as French courts do not refuse to rescind contracts of sale for 'non-conformity' where this renders the property unfit for its purpose and only here can an action under the *garantie légale* arise.[203]

In principle, any claim for restitution of the price under the *garantie légale* is conditional on a buyer's ability to return the property.[204] Where the buyer can no longer do so because the property has perished, a distinction is drawn between the situation where this is caused by its own defect, where the seller remains liable to restore the price, and the situation where this is caused by *cas fortuit*, where the buyer loses his action for the return of the price.[205] A buyer also loses his right to sue for the return of the price where his inability to return the property stems from his own act, notably, by having resold it to a third party.[206] On the other hand, a seller is not entitled to refuse the property back on the ground of its use and enjoyment or any resulting normal wear and tear,[207] though a court may award some recompense to a seller in good faith in respect of such a use,[208] but where a buyer's own act has caused the goods to deteriorate, courts sometimes award a sum lesser than the price so as to take account of its depreciation in value[209] or award damages.[210] Since it is unlikely that minor defects will fall within the *garantie légale*,[211] a buyer will not often wish to choose to keep the property and claim back part of its price, but where he does, the claim for price reduction remains available even where he is unable to return the property or is unable to claim damages.[212] By contrast with all this, a buyer's right to ask a court for *résolution* for contractual non-conformity of the goods is not conditional on their restoration to the seller.[213]

---

[202] De Juglart, *Vente*, 262; Ghestin, *Conformité*, 194 and see Civ. 27 Nov. 1950, GP 1951.1.132. Technically such a reduction of the price is an award of damages, but it is sometimes termed *réfaction* after the procedure applicable to commercial sales by which the court may refuse to terminate the sale because the non-performance is not sufficiently serious but then reduce the price: Malaurie, Aynès and Gautier, *Contrats spéciaux*, 241–2, e.g. Com 23 Mar. 1971, D 1974.40 note Alter. The Cour de cassation will on occasion quash a decision of a lower court which refuses *résolution* where it considers this unjustified on the terms of the contract and facts as they have found them: Civ. (1) 1 Dec. 1987, *Belghazi*, Bull. civ. I no. 324, D 1987.IR.262.　　　　　[203] Bihl, *Vente*, 227.　　　　　[204] Art. 1644 C. civ.; Bihl, *Vente*, 255.

[205] Art. 1647 C. civ. E.g. Angers 30 Oct. 1951, D 1952.60.

[206] Ghestin and Desché, *Vente*, 817. If he regains the property through his sub-buyer's own *action rédhibitoire*, then his own right to claim the price revives: Huet, *Responsabilité du vendeur*, 307.

[207] Bihl, *Vente*, 255; Civ. (1) 22 Nov. 1988, Bull. civ. I no. 334.

[208] Ghestin and Desché, *Vente*, 801, citing Civ. (3) 12 Jan. 1988, JCP 1988.IV.109 (seller of land recovering indemnity for buyer's occupation). Cf. Civ. (1) 11 Mar. 2003, Bull. civ. I no. 74 (no indemnity for use in the case of a private sale of a second-hand car).

[209] Civ. (1) 23 Oct. 1974, D 1975.424; Civ. (1) 4 Oct. 1988, JCP 1988.IV.375, RTDCiv. 1989.539 obs. Mestre.　　　　　[210] Paris 3 May 1967, GP 1967.2.34 note J.-P. D.　　　　　[211] Bihl, *Vente*, 263.

[212] See below, p. 84 *et seq*. Moreover, the basis for a reduction in price and an award of damages is not identical, as a claim for a reduction in price is proportionate to the price as a whole, which also fixes the ceiling of recovery; damages are based on the buyer's loss: Huet, *Responsabilité du vendeur*, 311.

[213] Huet, *Responsabilité du vendeur*, 305–06, citing Req. 14 Dec. 1875, S 1877.1.21 (*résolution* and recovery of the value of the goods sold where they could not be returned) though cf. Paris 3 May 1967, GP 1967.2.34 note J.-P. D. in which the buyer attempted to rely on the property's 'non-conformity' to avoid this restriction on the *garantie légale*, but the court 'reformulated' his claim as an *action rédhibitoire* and thereby kept him to its conditions.

The *garantie légale* and contractual non-conformity also differ in relation to the circumstances in which the right to sue for return of the price will be lost. Under the *garantie légale*, a buyer retains the right to return the property and claim back the price until *judgment* or until the seller has agreed to his request that he should keep them at a reduced price;[214] he does not lose his right merely because he has repaired the goods,[215] nor because the seller repairs or offers to repair its defects or even to replace them.[216] On the other hand, where a court finds that the parties have agreed that the buyer will not exercise his right to return the property, this agreement ('renunciation') will be upheld[217] and a buyer's use of the property over a long period after the discovery of a defect may be treated as the tacit renunciation of this right.[218] And of course until the *ordonnance* of 17 February 2005 *all* actions under the *garantie légale* had to be brought within the *bref délai*.[219]

When does a buyer lose his right to claim *résolution* of the contract on the ground of the property's 'non-conformity'? In general discussions, it is often stated it is lost by renunciation,[220] but this usually refers to a choice by the injured party to enforce the contract, whether specifically or by claiming damages.[221] Such a formal renunciation would certainly have the same effect in the context of sale.[222] However, a failure in the buyer to denounce this non-conformity on delivery is sometimes said to prevent any subsequent claim, whether for *résolution* or damages.[223] In the case of *résolution*, this may be supported on the ground that its effect is to restrict later termination of the contract to the *garantie légale*,[224] though a court could instead simply reject a claim for *résolution* in these circumstances as a matter of its discretion.[225] However, to claim that a right to damages is lost on acceptance of the property without reservation is incompatible with the case law of the 1980s and early 1990s which allowed claims for damages for contractual 'non-conformity' long after the acceptance of delivery of the goods.[226]

(c) Actions for damages

In the modern law all sellers who are aware of defects in the property sold[227] and 'business sellers' (*vendeurs professionnels*) who are presumed to be so aware, are liable in damages under the *garantie légale* for the loss caused to their buyers by latent defects in the property.[228] In principle this liability arises whether the buyer is a consumer or in

---

[214] Above, p. 82. [215] Civ. (3) 17 Feb. 1988, Bull. civ. III no. 38 (immovable property).

[216] Civ. (1) 11 Jun. 1980, RTDCom. 1981.349 obs. Hémard; Civ. (1) 7 Jan. 1982, GP. 1982.1 Pan.Jur. 184. Cf. sale of *immeubles à construire*: art. 1642-1 al. 2. C. civ.

[217] Com. 3 Dec. 1975, D 1975.IR.36 (no such agreement found by the *juges du fond*).

[218] Grenoble 2 Oct. 1967, GP 1968.1.Tab. 196. [219] Below, pp. 91 *et seq.*

[220] Malaurie, Aynès and Stoffel-Munck, *Obligations*, 425.

[221] Mazeaud and Chabas, *Obligations*, 1154. [222] Ghestin and Desché, *Vente*, 739.

[223] Ibid., 760; Huet, *Principaux contrats spéciaux*, 233; Com. 12 Feb. 1980, D 1981.278 note Aubertin.

[224] Bordeaux 23 May 1977, GP 1978.1.94; cf. Paris 3 May 1967, GP 1967.2.34 note J.-P. D.

[225] Treitel, *Remedies*, 400. [226] Above, p. 71. [227] Art. 1645 C. civ.

[228] For an early example, see Civ. 19 Jan. 1965, *l'affaire de Pont-Saint-Esprit*, D 1965.389. More recently, Civ. (1) 8 Jun. 1999, Bull. civ. I no. 198. The idea that traders of the type of goods in question are liable because they ought to know of their defects may be found in the medieval law and was picked up by Pothier, *Vente*, 168; Zimmermann, *Obligations*, 334–6.

business,[229] although where a business buyer is in the same 'speciality' as a business seller, he may lose his right to damages on the ground that he should have discovered the defect.[230] By contrast in principle liability for 'non-conforming property' is imposed on all types of sellers and for the benefit of all types of buyers, as it arises from non-performance of the express or implied stipulations of the contract as to the nature and quality of the goods,[231] though in practice French courts have not extended 'contractual non-conformity' so as to impose liability on *non*-business sellers.[232]

I have so far translated *vendeurs professionnels* as 'business sellers', but this key expression needs further explanation, particularly given that it is also used in determining the effectiveness of contract terms attempting to exclude liability under the *garantie légale*.[233] While the lower courts are given considerable leeway in applying this expression, the Cour de cassation requires them to justify their decisions[234] and will intervene if it considers they have got it wrong.[235] '*Vendeur professionnel*' was first used to describe those sellers who should be treated as though they knew of a defect because they *ought* to have known of it,[236] and in the case of goods, therefore, typically a *vendeur professionnel* is someone whose business is selling goods of the same general type as the ones sold,[237] so that manufacturers, distributors and retailers are all included.[238] On the other hand, it is not enough for a seller to be in business and entering the contract for the purposes of the business: so, for example, a road haulier who sold a towing vehicle to the claimant, who was also in the transport business, was held by the Cour de cassation not to be a *vendeur professionnel* apparently on the basis that, while he had used the vehicle in the course of his business, he was not in the business of selling vehicles.[239]

How do French courts assess the damages to be awarded in respect of defects in the property? Here, we find the normal, rather opaque statements generally adopted by French lawyers as regards damages, stating a principle of 'full compensation' (*réparation intégrale*) but then placing the question of the quantification of the buyer's harm within the 'sovereign power of assessment' of the *juges du fond*.[240] It is clear, though, that under the *garantie légale* or the general law, a buyer may recover damages in respect of personal injury,[241] damage to other property[242] and what a common lawyer

---

[229] Huet, *Responsabilité du vendeur*, 342; Com. 27 Nov. 1991, JCP 1992.IV.409.

[230] Above, p. 77.

[231] These propositions result from this liability's inclusion within the 'general law' of liability for non-performance of contract: arts. 1142 and 1147 C. civ. and see Ghestin, *Conformité*, 194–5.

[232] E.g. Civ. (1) 11 Mar. 2003, Bull. civ. I no. 74 (no damages under the *garantie légale* or under art. 1184 C. civ. against a *non-professionnel*). [233] Below, p. 94.

[234] Civ. (1) 12 Mar. 1980, JCP 1980.IV.208.

[235] Ghestin and Desché, *Vente*, 896–7; e.g. Com. 12 Dec. 1984, Bull. civ. IV no. 349.

[236] For a summary of the proper basis of this assimilation: Bihl, *Vente*, 258–9.

[237] Huet, *Principaux contrats spéciaux*, 328. In the case of sale of land, some sellers are treated as *professionnels*: e.g. property developers: e.g. Civ. (3) 27 Mar. 1969, D 1969.633 note Jestaz. Sellers of newly built property are governed by art. 1646–1 C. civ.

[238] Bihl, *Vente*, 257–8; Huet, *Principaux contrats spéciaux*, 326.

[239] Com. 12 Dec. 1984, Bull. civ. IV no. 349.

[240] De Juglart, *Vente*, 311. For the relative roles of the *juges du fond* and Cour de cassation for this purpose see Viney and Jourdain, *Effets*, 125–38; Treitel, *Remedies*, 175–6.

[241] Civ. (1) 24 Nov. 1954, JCP 1955.II.8565. [242] Com. 17 Feb. 1987, D 1987.543 note Jourdain.

would term pure economic loss, including any difference in the property's value as it should have been and in its defective state[243] or the cost of repairs and consequential losses.[244] A buyer may also recover an indemnity in respect of any liabilities incurred to a third party, whether under a further contract of sale or as *gardien* of the goods.[245] Moreover, while under the *garantie légale* a buyer must choose between restitution of the price or its reduction, he may combine either claim with one for damages, although not in a way which grants both damages for loss of its value and a reduction in its price.[246] On the other hand, in French law in general a buyer may not himself terminate the contract of sale on the ground of the defectiveness of the goods, buy substitute goods elsewhere and then claim their cost by way of damages as this substitution of performance requires judicial authorisation.[247]

(d) Causation and defences

A seller cannot escape liability under the *garantie légale* by showing that he was not at fault nor that the defect arose by circumstances beyond his control (*force majeure*), though a buyer's contributory fault may reduce any award of damages. And unlike their approach to liability for the 'deeds of things',[248] French courts have not appeared to use the requirement of causation between the defect and a claimant's harm nor defences based on causation to temper the strictness of liability which the *garantie* imposes. This strictness remains central to the future role of the *garantie légale* in compensating death, personal injury and damage to property after implementation of the Product Liability Directive.[249]

(i) Proof of causation in general

In principle, a buyer must show that the defect caused his harm,[250] but in keeping with the position as to the existence of a defect, the assessment of the possible 'factual elements' of causation is a matter for the *juges du fond*,[251] and in this they are often guided by *experts*,[252] who may draw inferences from circumstancial evidence and even presume that a proven defect on sale played a causal role in the buyer's harm in the absence of some other more convincing explanation.[253] Nevertheless, the *juges du fond* must explain how a defect they find was causally related to the claimant's harm[254] and should not impose liability on a seller where a buyer's harm may have been caused by a number of circumstances, only one of which is tied to a defect in the property. So,

---

[243] De Juglart, *Vente*, 312.

[244] Com. 20 Jan. 1971, JCP 1972.II.17280 note Boitard et Rabut (loss of use of property while being repaired).   [245] Below, pp. 97–8.   [246] Bihl, *Vente*, 262.   [247] Above, p. 81.

[248] Above, pp. 55–7.   [249] Below, p. 464.

[250] Ghestin, note, Com. 15 Mar. 1976, JCP 1977.II.18632. Some decisions appear to require a claimant to demonstrate *how* or *why* the property was defective, i.e. to explain the cause of a defect (e.g. Com 18 Jan. 1984, JCP 1984.IV.97) but these cases are concerned with the question of the timing of the defect: cf. above, p. 76.   [251] Civ. (1) 18 Mar.1986, Bull. civ. I no. 75, JCP 1986.IV.155.

[252] Cf. above, pp. 48–50.

[253] Huet, *Principaux Contrats*, 300. E.g. Civ. (1) 30 Jan. 1996, JCP 1996.IV.689.

[254] Com. 15 Mar. 1976, JCP 1977.II.18632 note Ghestin.

for example, in one case a company had bought a bottle of chlorine some 20 years before it exploded, injuring a number of people working in an adjacent factory.[255] While the lower court accepted evidence showing that the bottle was not entirely satisfactory, it found that the explosion could have been caused by its overfilling, exposure to sunlight or by the corrosive effect of the acid over a long time. In these circumstances, the *juges du fond* were entitled to hold that the buyer had failed to show that any defect in the bottle had caused the explosion. As I shall explain, this relatively more cautious approach to the requirement of causal connection has long marked a difference with the practice of the French *criminal* courts.[256]

(ii) Fault in the buyer

While courts can reduce or exclude an award for damages under the *garantie légale* on the ground of the buyer's 'fault', they have rarely done so except where liability is based on the seller's failure to supply the appropriate information or warnings, following here their approach to *obligations d'information*,[257] or where liability is based on the property's contractual non-conformity.[258] Although the Cour de cassation controls the nature of the behaviour which is capable of constituting fault on the part of the buyer for this purpose, as it does generally,[259] in practice it often leaves it to the lower courts,[260] and they to their expert advisors.[261] Where such a 'fault' is found, a lower court may reduce the claimant's damages to an extent which lies within its 'sovereign power of assessment'.[262] By contrast, where a buyer's own act is held to be both unforeseeable and unpreventable by the seller (and thereby constitutes *force majeure*), liability is extinguished.[263]

In French law, a buyer's fault is relevant to a seller's liability either in relation to the purchasing or to the use of the property.

As to 'fault in purchasing', on occasion the Cour de cassation has allowed a lower court to find a buyer at fault in going to the wrong class of seller and purchasing an inappropriately cheap product, given the importance of the job to which he wishes to put it.[264] Other cases in this category are closely related to other aspects of liability. So, French courts sometimes prefer to hold that a buyer's failure to detect a defect in the property which he has purchased constitutes 'contributory fault' on his part, rather than depriving the defect of its 'hidden character'.[265] Similarly, some jurists treat cases in which a buyer has ordered property to his own design or specification which then does not fulfill the buyer's intended purpose as instances of fault in the buyer, going to the issue of causation, rather than on the basis that the property was not defective.[266]

---

[255] Civ. (1) 4 Dec. 1973, GP 1974.1.444 obs. Planqueel.   [256] Below, pp. 375–6; cf. pp. 389–93.

[257] Above, p. 67.   [258] Huet, *Responsabilité du vendeur*, 352–6.

[259] Civ. 17 Nov. 1936, S 1937.1.53 (*faute de la victime* in the context of liability under art. 1384 al. 1 C. civ.) and see Com. 15 May 1972, JCP 1974.II.17864 note Ghestin.

[260] Viney and Jourdain, *Conditions*, 296.   [261] Above, pp. 48–50.

[262] Civ. (2) 27 Apr. 1979, *Dame Remolu*, JCP 1979.IV.213.

[263] Below, pp. 89–90. Cf. Civ. (1) 31 Jan. 1973, D 1973.149 note Schmelck (decision which confused these two grounds of defence quashed).

[264] Com. 17 Feb. 1976, JCP 1976.II.18482 note Malinvaud. Cf. Com. 15 May 1972, JCP 1974.II.17864 note Ghestin.   [265] Above, pp. 76–7.

[266] Ghestin and Desché, *Vente*, 803–04, who cite as example Paris 12 Apr. 1983, *inédit*, (company sells metal components made with a mould supplied by the buyer and to its design).

By contrast, the cases of buyer's fault in the use of the property are closer to what a common lawyer would see as contributory negligence. Perhaps the clearest example is where a buyer fails to follow the instructions which accompany a product: here French courts have tended to exclude rather than reduce liability.[267] In other cases, a buyer may simply have failed to show the care of a *bon père de famille* in using the product[268] and here the courts are likely to reduce rather than exclude the seller's liability, their attitude depending on the relative knowledge or expertise of the buyer and seller,[269] in both respects in keeping with their approach to breach of a seller's *obligation d'information*.[270] Even so, where a buyer's care falls below the standard expected of anyone, specialist or mere consumer, *faute de la victime* may be established. So, a car driver's fault in driving too fast may reduce his damages for the consequences of an accident, partly caused by the vehicle's defective steering.[271]

Distinctions according to the degree of expertise or skill of the buyer may also be relevant in cases where a buyer has used a product for a purpose for which it is claimed that it was not intended. Here, it is said that a seller will not be liable where the buyer has put the thing sold to an abnormal use,[272] but what of an abnormal but forseeable use? At least in the context of the defects which have injured persons or other property, a French court may hold a seller under an obligation to warn the buyer against any foreseeable misuse of the product,[273] but the distinction between normality and foreseeability is not discussed in the French texts.[274]

Sometimes a buyer's failure to maintain or repair the property properly will be said by a seller to have contributed to his own harm. Here, a court may hold the failure to repair excusable or causally irrelevant (and the seller liable in full)[275] or, conversely, that the defect in the property may have resulted from the buyer's failure to repair after delivery (and the seller not liable).[276] Sometimes, though, a court will find that a buyer has, by failing to remedy the defect, partly caused his own loss and so reduce the buyer's award. So, for example, where a buyer of an electric iron continued to use it after realising that it had a malfunction, her damages for personal injuries when it exploded were reduced by a quarter.[277] And where a buyer discovers a defect in the property and then resells it, without warning the sub-buyer, he will not be able to recover an indemnity from his own seller for any liabilities to the sub-buyer which he incurs as a result.[278] But a buyer would appear to have no duty to check property for defects before re-sale and so any failure to do so cannot be the ground of a reduction of his claim for an indemnity from his own seller.[279]

---

[267] Com. 6 Nov. 1972, GP 1973.1 Pan. Jur. 31 (farmer's use of pesticide contrary to clear instructions).
[268] Rouen 17 Apr. 1969, GP 1969.2 Somm.31 (alleged fault in buyer in installing defective equipment badly).   [269] Huet, *Responsabilité du vendeur*, 174–5.
[270] Above, pp. 67–8.
[271] Civ. (1) 4 Feb. 1963, JCP 1963.II.13159 note Savatier. See also Lyon 26 Feb. 1962, GP 1962.1.401; Com. 25 Nov. 1997, *Cont., conc., cons.* 1998 no. 43 note Leveneur, RTDCiv. 1998.386 obs. Jourdain.
[272] Bihl, *Vente*, 245. Cf. above pp. 68–9.   [273] Above, pp. 67–8.   [274] Above, p. 76.
[275] Paris 18 Jan. 1971, GP 1972.1.289 note Kosossey (failure to check 'puncture-proof' vehicle tyres) and see above, p. 74.   [276] Cf. above, p. 87.   [277] Civ. (1) 21 Mar. 1962, Bull civ. I, no. 174.
[278] Civ. (1) 3 Jul. 1985, D 1985.IR.482.
[279] Com. 17 Oct. 1977, GP 1978.1.221 note Plancqueel.

(iii) Force majeure

The effect of *force majeure* on a seller's liability under the *garantie légale* is complicated by difficulties of terminology. For some jurists, a seller's liability for latent defects is a prime example of an *obligation de garantie*, which differs from an *obligation de résultat* by the very fact that it entails liability for non-performance, regardless of *force majeure*.[280] However, a distinction should be drawn between two questions: first, can a seller escape liability under the *garantie légale* on the ground that the defect arose through *force majeure*? And, secondly, can a subsequent event constitute *force majeure* so as to break the chain of causation between the property's defect and the claimant's harm?

The answer to the first question is unequivocal: a seller is liable for the defects in the property which he sells *however* they got there and to this extent, the *garantie légale* covers liability for *force majeure*.[281] Until the 1960s this feature of the *garantie* affected only a seller's liability to make restitution or return part of the price, for *ex hypothesi* a seller would not be actually aware of the defect, but when the courts held *vendeurs professionnels* liable in damages on the basis of their presumed knowledge of the property's defect,[282] this feature of liability under the *garantie légale* became much more important, for it meant that liability in damages extended to cases where the defect in the property arose owing to circumstances beyond the seller's control and to cases where it was impossible for him to have discovered the defect before sale. As a result, French law imposed liability in damages on all 'business sellers' (and not just on seller/manufacturers) to all buyers in the chain of distribution for what later became known as 'development risks'.[283] A nice example of this may be found in a decision of the Cour de cassation in 1971.[284] Here, the claimants ran a nursery garden and had bought a large quantity of chrysanthemum cuttings from the defendant company. Two or three months later, the claimants experienced problems with the plants and they therefore asked a *juge des référés* to appoint experts to investigate the causes of the plants' problems. About a year later, the experts reported that the cuttings had clearly suffered from a defect on delivery, but that they (the *experts*) were unable to discover either its nature or its cause, but the court nevertheless held the seller of the cuttings was liable under the *garantie légale* to return their price and in damages. The seller challenged this decision on the ground that it was absolutely impossible ('*une impossibilité objective*') for them to have detected the defect in question arguing that even a *vendeur professionnel* should not be liable for losses caused by *force majeure*: this was certainly a very strong case on the facts, for even after a year of investigation, the *expertise* had been unable to explain the defects. Nevertheless, the Cour de cassation upheld the decision of the *juges du fond*, holding that such impossibility was legally

---

[280] Bénabent, *Obligations*, 273. For this view of the law of sale: Larroumet, *Contrat*, 615–16; Nicholas, 56.
[281] Larroumet, *Contrat*, 615.   [282] Above, p. 84.

[283] Malinvaud, note to Com. 10 Dec. 1973, JCP 1975.II.17950; Huet, 'Le paradoxe des médicaments et les risques de développement,' D 1987 Chron. 73, 76–7; Bihl, *Vente*, 259. Cf. J. Revel, 'La prevention des accidents domestiques: vers un régime spécifique de responsabilité du fait des produits?' D 1984 Chron. 69, 71; Civ. (1) 9 July 1996, D 1996.610 note Lambert-Faivre.

[284] Com. 15 Nov. 1971, D 1971.211. See also Com. 27 Apr. 1971, JCP 1972.II.17280 note Boitard et Rabut; Rouen 22 Feb. 1974, D 1974 Somm. 68.

irrelevant, for 'business sellers' are deemed to know the defects in the property which they sell.[285]

At first sight, liability for breach of a seller's obligations of conformity differs from liability under the *garantie légale*, as these obligations are classified as *obligations de résultat* which generally allow a defence of *force majeure*, but this difference is illusory, owing to an addition to the definition of *force majeure* that an act or event must be 'exterior to the thing',[286] a condition which spread from delict to the applications of *force majeure* in contract.[287] What this means is that where a contractual *obligation de résultat* has as its object a physical thing, its non-performance may not be excused by any event which makes performance impossible and unforseeable, unless it is also 'exterior to the thing'.[288] So even though a seller's *obligation de conformité* is an *obligation de résultat*, the fact that the defect arose through circumstances which were unforseeable and beyond the control of the seller is no excuse: any defect in the property is by definition 'not exterior' and cannot therefore constitute *force majeure*. This characteristic has been noticeable as regards the supply of blood products contaminated with HIV where the contract is not one of sale and so liability was imposed on the basis of *obligation de sécurité de résultat*.

On the other hand, an event occurring *after* delivery of the defective property may constitute *force majeure* so as to excuse a seller from liability under the *garantie légale*, since it may break the causal link between the property's defect and the buyer's harm.[289] While such an event may be an act of nature, it will more typically be a supervening act of the claimant (which I have already discussed)[290] or of a third party. An example of the latter may be found in an intervening action of a repairer or installer of a defective product which may be held to break the chain of causation,[291] although the seller and repairer may instead be held jointly liable to the buyer in these circumstances.[292] Resale by a retailer of property known to be defective would break the chain of causation so as to prevent a customer suing the retailer's own supplier by *action directe* under the *garantie légale*;[293] and *force majeure* could arise where a vehicle manufacturer contracts with its appointed 'agents' on the basis that they buy its products, and reserves to itself the power to instruct them to repair or withdraw defective vehicles from the market.[294] However, in the *arrêt Lamborghini* the failure of an agent instructed to recall a particular model for repair was not held to constitute *force majeure*, the *juges du fond* preferring to hold the manufacturer, importer and retailer of the car in question jointly liable (though in *delict*) to the ultimate

---

[285] See similarly Civ. (3) 7 Mar. 1990, JCP 1990.IV.174 (liability of 'builder').   [286] Above, pp. 57–8.

[287] Terré, Simler and Lequette, *Obligations*, 558–61 and e.g. Civ. 20 Nov.1968, GP 1969.1.119.

[288] Mazeaud and Chabas, *Obligations*, 667–8 and see e.g. Poitiers 16 Dec. 1970, GP 1971.1.264; Civ. (1) 12 Apr. 1995, JCP 1995.II.22467 note Jourdain, below, p. 150.

[289] Malinvaud, note to Com. 10 Dec. 1973, JCP 1975.II.17950.   [290] Above, p. 88.

[291] Huet, *Responsabilité du vendeur*, 361–2. See, e.g., Civ. (3) 26 Oct. 1977, GP 1978.1.339 note Planqueel (action brought under art. 1721 C. civ.).

[292] Huet, *Principaux contrats spéciaux*, 333. Cf. Civ. (1) 16 Jul. 1971, GP 1971.2.810 in which garage A repaired a motorbike and sold it to garage B, which failed to notice the fault, and then resold it to C, a private individual. C drove the motorbike and injured D, whose action in delict under art. 1382 C. civ. was successful against both A and B jointly.   [293] Below, pp. 96–7.

[294] Huet, *Principaux contracts spéciaux*, 334.

buyer of the car for the consequences of an accident which resulted from the unrepaired defect.[295]

Finally, even where a third party's action is the immediate cause of a buyer's harm, it may not constitute *force majeure* so as to prevent a claim under the *garantie légale*. So, the seller and installer of a burglar alarm in a villa was held liable for the consequences of a burglary some two years later on the ground that the defectiveness of the alarm played a causal role in its owner's loss, as the burglars would not have stayed in the villa for the considerable time which they did had the alarm sounded.[296] Clearly, where the purpose of the product in question is to prevent the action of a third party of a particular type, liability for its defective functioning ought not to be excluded when this intervention occurs.

5. The *Bref Délai* and its Avoidance

For 200 years article 1648 of the Code required that any claim brought under the *garantie légale* must be brought within a 'brief delay'. In 2001 Bénabent described this provision as:

one of the most troublesome of the present law of sale and constitutes a breeding-ground for litigation so active that today it threatens to poison the whole organisation of actions brought against a seller: it is the wish to avoid this provision which has been the cause of the disorder in the case law in this respect.[297]

Certainly, differences in the rules as to the time within which claims must be brought have often predominated in the minds of claimants and of courts in deciding on which legal basis of a seller's liability to rely. Here, I wish to look briefly at how French courts applied this infamous *bref délai* and to compare it with corresponding rules of prescription applicable to contractual actions generally. Only then can the significance of its reform by the *ordonnance* of 17 February 2005 on the occasion of implementation of the Consumer Guarantees Directive be appreciated.[298]

Article 1648 required a buyer to bring any action based on the property's defects within a short period, taking into account the nature of the defect and the custom of the place where the contract was made, but it did not set a fixed period nor say when it starts to run. However, most jurists agree that the *bref délai* started from the time of *effective* discovery of the defect by the buyer,[299] that is, not merely its existence, but also its extent, these being for the *juges du fond* to decide.[300] As a result, while a buyer might have discovered

---

[295] Civ. (1) 9 Oct. 1979, GP 1980.1.249 note Planqueel, D 1980.IR.222 obs. Larroumet. The Cour de cassation quashed their decision, though on the basis of the classification of liability.

[296] Civ. (1) 18 Mar. 1986, Bull. civ. I no. 75.   [297] Bénabent, *Contrats spéciaux*, 157.

[298] Below, p. 583.

[299] Malaurie, Aynès and Gautier, *Contrats spéciaux*, 277. Ghestin suggested that the 'brief delay' should commence when the buyer *should* have discovered it: *Conformité*, 34.

[300] Bénabent, *Contrats spéciaux*, 158; Huet, *Principaux contrats spéciaux*, 305; Civ. (3) 14 Jun. 1989, Bull. civ. III no. 140; Com. 15 Nov. 1971, D 1972.211. Some older cases held that the starting point of the *bref délai* was entirely within the 'sovereign power of assessment' of the *juges du fond*: Ghestin, *Conformité*, 33; Civ. 11 Dec. 1884, DP 1885.1.357, S 1886.1.149; Civ. (1) 15 Dec. 1982, GP 1983 Pan. Jur. 120.

that, for example, a motor vehicle is not working properly or that seeds are not growing as they should, he was not held to have 'discovered the defect' in the property so as to set time running, this being sometimes delayed until receipt of an expert's report, whether privately commissioned or judicially appointed,[301] though this became no longer necessary after it was provided that an interlocutory application for the appointment of an expert interrupted any prescription period.[302] Moreover, in some situations the courts held that the *bref délai* started running from a point later than discovery, notably where a buyer claimed an indemnity in respect of his own liability to a sub-buyer where it was held to start only once the sub-buyer had brought an action.[303] What all this meant was that while the *bref délai* might be short, it might sometimes start running years after the contract of sale had made:[304] as one supportive jurist put it, 'the *garantie légale* is almost imprescribable, at least during the useful life of the property'.[305]

Secondly, the length of the *bref délai* was for the *juges du fond* to decide,[306] an approach which gave rise to considerable uncertainty.[307] Here, article 1648 required the courts to take into account the nature of the defect (so that the period might be longer where problems took some time to emerge)[308] and of any local customs, (though this factor was more important in the nineteenth century where many cases of liability under the *garantie légale* concerned livestock).[309] More generally, the courts used to take a more generous view of the appropriate length of time where damages for death or personal injuries or damage to other property were claimed,[310] though from the mid-1990s such claims could be brought instead under the *obligation de sécurité*.[311] Overall, however, the period averaged around six months, usually no more than nine months and rarely as long as a year.[312] While negotiations with a view to settlement did not interrupt the running of time,[313] sometimes the courts found a suspension in these circumstances by finding an implicit agreement of the parties to this effect.[314]

As I have already explained, judicial avoidance of the 'brief delay'[315] was at its most apparent in those cases where the courts allowed a buyer to claim for failures in quality

---

[301] Bénabent, *Contrats spéciaux*, 158. Com. 12 Mar. 1979, Bull. civ. IV no. 98; Civ. (1) 11 Jan. 1989, Bull. civ. I no. 12, RTDCom. 1989.711 obs. Bouloc.

[302] Art. 2244 C. civ. (amended by *loi* no. 85–677 of 5 Jul. 1985, art. 37); Ghestin and Desché, *Vente*, 791, 795. Once the *bref délai* was interrupted in this way, the rules of prescription of the 'general law' apply: Civ. (1) 21 Oct. 1997, D 1998.409 note Bruschi.

[303] Com. 19 Mar. 1974, D 1975.628 note Malinvaud; Com. 17 Dec. 1973, GP 1974.1.429 note Planqueel, JCP 1975.II.17912 note Savatier and see below, p. 967. Where a seller was being prosecuted for *tromperie* or *falsification* in respect of the same facts from which the buyer's claim arises, the latter was justified in waiting for the outcome of the criminal proceedings before suing in the civil court: Civ. (1) 15 Dec. 1982, GP 1983 Pan. Jur. 12.   [304] Civ. (3) 2 Feb. 1999, *Cont., conc., cons.*, 1999 no. 71 note Leveneur (9 years).

[305] D. Mainguy, 'Propos dissidents sur la transposition de la directive du 25 mai 1999 sur certains aspects de la vente et des garanties des biens de consommation' JCP 2002.I.183 at 2110.

[306] Ghestin and Desché, *Vente*, 785–6 (with copious citations).   [307] De Juglart, *Vente*, 313.

[308] Civ. (1) 11 Mar. 1980, JCP 1980.IV.208.

[309] E.g., M.Troplong, *Le droit civil expliqué, De la vente* (3rd. edn., 1837) Tome 2, Table between 14 and 15, who notes the various customary periods concerning 'special redhibitory defects' in livestock.

[310] Huet, *Responsabilité du vendeur*, 265.   [311] Above, p. 72.

[312] Huet, *Responsabilité du vendeur*, 294; Bénabent, *Contrats spéciaux*, 158–9.

[313] Bénabent, *Obligations*, 592; Civ. (1) 13 Nov. 1996, JCP 1997.IV.6.

[314] Paris 3 May 1967, GP 1967.2.34 note J.-P. D.

[315] Cf. below, p. 106 for similar techniques in the law of construction.

or safety of the property under the general law of contract, whether this was put in terms of a failure in contractual non-conformity of the property, breach of an *obligation d'information* or breach of an *obligation de sécurité*.[316] Where this 'general' law applies, it attracts a prescription period of 10 years for commercial and 'mixed' cases (i.e. where one of the parties is a *commerçant*) and of 30 years for entirely non-commercial ('civil') cases.[317] In both cases time runs from the date of due performance of the obligation in question, rather than the discovery of the defect.[318] By contrast with these periods, once started the *bref délai* was brief indeed.

6. The Contractual Exclusion of Liability

Despite their acceptance of the binding force of contractual obligations, French lawyers have long shown themselves hostile to exemption clauses, whether they attempt to exclude or to limit liability.[319] For long this was seen as reflecting the requirements of civil morality, for even the terminology of *responsabilité* is more redolent of morality than is the English 'liability', and the traditional view of many French lawyers was that all *responsabilité* is based on *la faute*: surely the law should not allow people to avoid their proper responsibilities? Moreover, from the 1960s most French lawyers have accepted the need to protect consumers as the weaker party to contracts from 'abusive terms' (*clauses abusives*) of which exemption clauses long stood as the prime examples.

This hostility has been expressed in a variety of ways, some general across the board of civil liabilities, whether contractual or delictual, some special to particular contexts; some the creatures of judicial invention, some of legislative intervention.[320] All may be found in the modern law governing a seller's liability, despite the less moralistic terminology of *obligation de garantie* rather than *responsabilité* and despite its principal traditional concern with rescission and restitution rather than with damages. While the resulting controls differ according to the legal basis of liability, broad distinctions can be seen according to the status of the contracting parties.

---

[316] The following are examples of recourse to the 'general law' of contract where prescription was in issue: for contractual 'non-conformity': Com. 3 Jan. 1971, JCP 1973.II.17300 note Leloup; Civ. (1) 9 Mar. 1983, JCP 1984.II.20295 note Courbe; Ass Plén. 7 Feb. 1986, JCP 1986.II.20616 note Malinvaud, D 1986.293 note Bénabent; Civ. (1) 8 Nov. 1988, JCP 1989.IV.15; Com. 22 May 1991, D 1991 Somm. 200 obs. Tournafond; for *obligation de sécurité*: Civ. (1) 11 Jun. 1991, D 1991.IR.56, RTDCiv. 1992.114 obs. Jourdain.

[317] Art. 2262 C. civ.; art. 110-4 C. com. (which excepts those cases where a shorter period obtains).

[318] Malaurie, Aynès and Gautier, *Contrats spéciaux*, 208 (obligation to deliver conforming property).

[319] Larroumet, *Contrat*, 658. Exemption clauses appear to have come into practice in France as a result of their use by the English merchant navy and this added little to the favour with which they were viewed: J.E. Labbé, 'Nouvelle communication sur les clauses de non responsabilité particulièrement dans les connaissement', in *Annales de droit commercial* (1886–7) *Correspondance*, 251 at 252.

[320] P. Delebecque and D. Mazeaud, 'Les clauses de responsabilité: clauses de non responsabilité, clauses limitatives de réparation, clauses pénales, Rapport francais', in Fontaine and Viney, 361. Apart from the techniques mentioned in the text, exemption clauses must be 'accepted' by the other party (Civ. (1) 28 Apr. 1971, JCP 1971.IV.148) and are interpreted strictly: Civ. (1) 31 Mar. 1954, D 1954.417; Civ. (3) 19 Oct. 1971, JCP 1971.IV.267.

First, a person who sells property other than in the regular course of a business (that is, someone who is not a *vendeur professionnel*)[321] may exclude his liability under the *garantie légale* unless he was aware of the defect on sale,[322] though in the case of liability for contractual 'non-conformity', he may do so only in the absence of *dol* (here in the sense of deliberate non-performance or performance in bad faith) or *faute lourde* ('*gross fault*').[323]

Secondly, a *vendeur professionnel* selling to a consumer or *non-professionnel* may not exclude or limit his liability, whatever the legal basis on which it arises, (whether the *garantie légale*, contractual 'non-conformity', breach of an *obligation d'information* or of an *obligation de sécurité*), a position proclaimed by decree in 1978,[324] though earlier achieved by the courts as regards the *garantie légale* by saying that *vendeurs professionnels* are deemed irrefutably to be aware of any defect in the property.[325] However, French courts have interpreted 'consumer' for this purpose fairly restrictively. So, taking the lead from legislation regulating 'doorstep selling',[326] they see a consumer as someone who makes a contract which is 'not directly related' to any business which he may operate, though this suggests a somewhat wider meaning than that of the 'final end-user' generally taken as to the position under the European Directive on unfair terms in consumer contracts, as it allows the possibility of a business to gain the benefit of the protection where the contract does not relate *directly* to its business.[327] As we shall see, this formulation appeared in an early draft of the Consumer Sales Directive, but was later rejected. [328] While this ban on exemption clauses is complete, a seller may avoid liability by informing his buyer of any defect[329] and may define the subject matter of the contract in a restrictive way, so as to restrict any liability on the basis of contractual 'non-conformity',[330] though a court may hold such a term to be unfair under the general controls on unfair contract terms in consumer contracts in the *Code de la consommation* unless it defines the main subject matter of the contract.[331]

---

[321] Above, p. 85.   [322] Art. 1643 C. civ. Malaurie, Aynès and Gautier, *Contrats spéciaux*, 292.

[323] Terré, Simler, and Lequette, *Obligations*, 596–9; Larroumet, *Contrat*, 661–2.

[324] *Loi* no. 78–23 of 10 Jan. 1978, art. 35; Déc. 78–464 of 24 Mar. 1978, art. 2. The administration's general failure to exercise this power led to its being taken over by the courts: Civ. (1) 14 May 1991, D 1991.449 note Ghestin. Since the creation of the C. consom. the courts have enjoyed a general power to strike out unfair contract terms in consumer contracts, the relevant provision being amended in 1995 to give effect to the EC Dir. 93/13 on unfair terms in consumer contracts: art. L. 132-1 C. consom. The *décret* of 1978 has not been rescinded.

[325] Civ. (1) 24 Nov. 1954, JCP 1955.II.8565 note H.B; Civ. (3) 27 Mar. 1969, D 1969.633 note Jestaz.

[326] *Loi* no. 77–1137 of 22 Dec. 1972, art. 8-1-e, amended in 1989 to take account of Dir. 85/577/EEC of 20 Dec. 1985 to protect the consumer in respect of contracts negotiated away from business premises and now contained in art. L. 121-23 C. consom.

[327] For the French approach see Civ. (1) 23 Feb. 1999, Bull. civ. I no. 59; Civ. (1) 5 Mar. 2002, Bull civ. I no. 78; Civ. (1) 22 May 2002, Bull. civ. I no. 143. For the position under the 1993 Directive (arguatur) see *Chitty on Contracts* paras. 15–022—15–023 arguing from *France v Di Pinto* Case 361/89 of 14 March 1991 [1991] ECR 1-1189; *Benincasa v Dentalkit* Case C-269/95 of 3 July 1997 [1997] ECR I-03767. While in the French context it had been argued that a 'non-professional' (as distinct from a consumer) is a person who enters a contract in a course of a business but not within 'the same speciality' as his contractual partner, this interpretation is not now followed by French courts, who therefore treat 'consumer' and 'non-profes-sional' as synonymous: see Civ. (1) 3 & 30 Jan. 1996, JCP 1996.II.22664; Larroumet, *Contrat*, 403–07 and G. Paisant, 'A la recherche du consommateur: Pour en finir avec l'actuelle confusion née de l'application du critère du "rapport direct"' JCP 2003.I.121.   [328] Below, pp. 576, 591.   [329] Above, p. 76.

[330] Malaurie, Aynès and Gautier, *Contrats spéciaux*, 293.   [331] Art. 132-1 al. 7 C. consom.

Thirdly, the question of the validity of exemption clauses is more complicated as regards sale by a business to other businesses. As regards the *garantie légale*, the assimilation by French courts of 'business sellers' to those with knowledge of defects in the property ruled out in principle contractual exemptions of liability for *vices cachés*.[332] And while the courts have made an exception for cases where the buyer in question is 'in the same speciality' as his seller,[333] in this situation a buyer is unlikely to be able to rely on the *garantie légale* at all on the ground that he should have discovered any defects.[334] As a result, exemption clauses are valid only where they are redundant.[335] On the other hand, a much more liberal approach governs exclusions of liability for contractual 'non-conformity'. Here, a seller can avoid liability by defining what will count as 'conforming' property,[336] may specify that the property is suitable only for a particular purpose,[337] and may in principle exclude liability for any non-conformity of the property, with the exception of *dol* (here in the sense of deliberate or knowing breach of contract) and *faute lourde*, the latter marking a significant difference from the position under the *garantie légale*.[338] However, the practical consequence of this contrast should not be overestimated, since the courts can find *faute lourde* in a 'business seller' relatively easily so to invalidate contract terms purporting to exclude liability for contractual non-conformity, even where the buyer is also in business.[339] On the other hand, liability arising from breaches of a seller's *obligation de sécurité* or *obligations d'information* where safety is in issue are said to be incapable of exclusion by contract, because issues of personal safety are a matter of public policy.[340]

What this means in practice is that a *vendeur professionnel* can limit liability for contractual non-conformity of the property against non-consumer buyers (excepting *dol* and *faute lourde*), but not liability under the *garantie légale*, a difference which is hard to justify given the difficulties which French lawyers have experienced in drawing the line between these two bases of liability. As shall be seen, these effects of the distinction between the two bases of liability became an element in the argument as to how properly to implement the Consumer Guarantees Directive in France.[341]

7. Liability beyond Privity

In looking at the way in which French law has used the law of contract to govern the relationships between parties in the chain of distribution of products *beyond* privity, it

---

[332] Civ. (3) 27 Mar. 1969, D 1969.633 note Jestaz; Com. 17 Dec. 1973, GP 1974.1.429 note Planqueel, JCP 1975.II.17912 note Savatier; Com. 27 Nov. 1991, Bull. civ. IV no. 367, JCP 1992.IV.409. The issue is for the *juges du fond* to decide: Civ. (1) 20 Feb. 1996, Bull. civ. I no. 86, *Cont. conc. cons.* 1996.96 note Leveneur.
[333] Com. 8 Oct. 1973, JCP 1975.II.17927 note Ghestin; Com. 3 Feb. 1998, Bull. civ. IV no. 60.
[334] Above, p. 77.   [335] Malaurie, Aynès and Gautier, *Contrats spéciaux*, 294.
[336] Huet, *Responsabilité du vendeur*, 392.   [337] Malaurie, Aynès and Gautier, *Contrats spéciaux*, 293.
[338] P. Le Tourneau, 'Conformités et garanties dans la vente d'objets mobiliers corporels,' RTDCom. 1980.231 at 267; Ghestin and Desché, *Vente*, 928; Malaurie, Aynès and Gautier, *Contrats spéciaux*, 241. Important decisions in this respect include Civ. (1) 20 Dec. 1988, JCP 1989.II.21354 note Virassamy (no need for buyer to be 'of same speciality'); Civ. (1) 24 Nov. 1993, JCP 1994.II.22334 note Leveneur.
[339] Ghestin and Desché, *Vente*, 928–32 esp. at 928. Cf. Com. 3 Apr. 1990, Bull. civ. IV no. 108.
[340] Viney and Joudain, *Conditions*, 435–7.   [341] Below, pp. 581–2.

is helpful to distinguish between the general position without special contract and recourse to special contract, notably in the form of manufacturers' guarantees.

(a) The general position: *actions directes* and *actions récursoires*

Despite the unpromisingly restrictive provisions in the Civil Code,[342] French law has taken a very liberal approach to the acceptance of contractual rights beyond the parties to a contract, recognizing a wide law of contracts for the benefit of third parties (*stipulations pour autrui*) and a range of other mechanisms.[343] In the context of sale, the courts have long accepted the idea that the various rights of the 'initial' buyer in a chain of distribution against his own seller (typically, their manufacturer) in respect of its latent defects attach to the property as its 'accessory', with the result that any buyer in the chain may sue *any* seller further up the chain by way of a 'direct action' (*action directe en garantie*): there is no restriction that the buyer must be a consumer nor that the seller must be *professionnel*.[344] This analysis in terms of 'accessory rights' avoids formal conflict with the principle of the 'relativity' of contracts,[345] since the sub-buyer becomes the initial buyer's 'successor in title', and is treated as though he were party to the original contract.[346] In this way, a buyer of a defective product has been held able to sue not merely his own retailer, but also its distributor or its manufacturer in *contract*.[347]

As against any buyer, all sellers are jointly liable ('*in solidum*'),[348] so that the buyer can recover in full from any one, leaving it to these sellers to claim an indemnity (whether whole or in part) by recourse claim (*action récursoire*).[349] Such an indemnity claim may itself be brought under one of the bases of a seller's liability against any person higher in the chain of distribution, with the twist that his deemed knowledge of the defect used to impose liability as seller is not used so as to deny his claim as buyer. Owing to the impact of the rule of *non-cumul*,[350] this extension of contract results in the exclusion in these situations of all the various liabilities in delict, although an exception to this exclusion had to be made for the liabilities introduced to implement the Product Liability Directive into French law.[351]

---

[342] Arts. 1119–1121, 1165 C. civ.

[343] S. Whittaker, 'Privity of Contract and the Law of Tort: the French Experience' (1995) 15 *OJLS* 327 and see above, pp. 28–9.

[344] Civ. 12 Nov. 1884, S 1886.1.149, DP 1885.1.357; Civ. (1) 9 Oct. 1979, *affaire Lamborghini* D 1980.IR.222 note Larroumet, GP 1980.1.249 note Planqueel. For an extended discussion of the various analyses: Ghestin and Desché, *Vente*, 1046 *et seq.*   [345] Art. 1165 C. civ.

[346] *Ayant cause à titre particulier* (i.e. successor in title to a particular right or thing) as distinct from *ayant cause à titre universel* (i.e. general successor in title, such as the legal heir): Nicholas, 172.

[347] Civ. (1) 8 Jun. 1999, Bull. civ. I no. 198, (even where a manufacturer delivers products directly to its sub-buyer, the intermediate buyer remains liable as *vendeur professionnel*). A person who commissions or who acquires a building possesses an *action directe* against a number of those involved in the construction, these contractual liabilities beyond privity possessing a legislative basis: see arts. 1792 *et seq.* C. civ. and below, p. 104.

[348] Civ. (1) 9 Oct. 1979, *affaire Lamborghini*, D 1980.IR.222 obs. Larroumet, GP 1980.1.249 note Planqueel; Civ. (1) 6 Jul. 1988, Bull. civ. I no. 231, below, pp. 546–9.

[349] Ghestin and Desché, *Vente*, 1026 *et seq.*

[350] Above, pp. 27–9 and Civ. (2) 30 Nov. 1988, Bull. civ. II no. 240.   [351] Art. 1386-1 C. civ.

It is clear that the original purpose of the recognition of these *actions directes en garantie* was to create a direct contractual claim for a sub-buyer against the original seller (often the manufacturer of goods or the builder of premises) at a time before *any* claim in delict had been established.[352] Such a direct right avoided the circuity of action of suit up the chain of contracts[353] and had the advantage for claimants of side-stepping the insolvency of any intervening member of the chain.[354] Clearly, the importance of these *actions directes* grew when liability in damages under the *garantie légale* was extended to all *vendeurs professionnels*, for this made possible many more claims for damages, which are the principle concern of these *actions directes*.[355] While they were not recognised so as to impose liability for personal injuries in particular, at one time they have had a considerable impact in this area.[356] While recognition of this *action directe* for latent defects taken with the rule of *non-cumul* appeared to have the disadvantage of keeping it to the *bref délai*,[357] its worse effects were avoided by holding that the delay starts running in recourse claims only from the date of themselves being sued.[358]

Despite the attractions which *actions directes en garantie* have held for French lawyers, use of the idea that a buyer's rights run with the property can present difficulties. For the logic of the technique is that a claimant's rights are derivative rather than personal, stemming from the contract of sale made by the member of the chain of distribution sued. To take the simplest example, if A, a manufacturer, sells goods to B, a retailer, who resells them to C, a consumer, C's rights against A under the *action directe* will be those which B possessed under his contract with A and were transmitted by him to C. Reliance on these 'initial rights' causes several problems, some of which are special to the French legal context and some of which are inherent in the technique of transmission itself.[359] So, for example, claims under the *garantie légale* require the existence of a latent defect in the property on delivery and both defectiveness and its latency are to an extent relative to the particular agreement between the parties.[360] Where, therefore, a sub-buyer's direct claim against a manufacturer alleges that a product was not fit for its purpose, the manufacturer may escape liability by establishing that the product *was* fit for the purpose specified by its own buyer, an intermediate member of the chain.[361] On the other hand, French courts have refused to allow the logic of the 'transmission' of the buyer's rights with the property to lead to the denial of a recourse claim by a seller who has sold the property, holding that an intermediary seller may still sue where he has a 'direct and certain interest' in doing so.[362]

---

[352] C. Jamin, 'Une restauration de l'effet relatif du contrat,' DS Chron 1991 257, 259.

[353] Ghestin and Desché, *Vente*, 1036.   [354] Jamin, *op. cit.* n. 352, 259.

[355] Above, p. 84. On claims for termination of the contract see cf. above, p. 79, n. 168.

[356] G. Viney, 'L'indemnisation des atteintes à la sécurité des consommateurs en droit français', in Ghestin, *Sécurité des consommateurs*, 71 esp. at 74–6.

[357] Civ. (1) 9 Oct. 1979, *affaire Lamborghini*, D 1980.IR.222 obs. Larroumet, GP 1980.1.249 note Planqueel.   [358] Above, p. 92.

[359] For further discussion: Whittaker, *op. cit.* n. 343, 348–51.   [360] Above, pp. 73–4, 77.

[361] Civ. (1) 3 Dec. 1996, Bull. civ. I no. 440. While decided as a matter of 'contractual non-conformity', the particularity of a buyer's purpose is equally relevant to claims under the *garantie légale*: above, pp. 74–5.

[362] Civ. (1) 28 Nov.1979, D 1985.484 note Huet (sale); Civ. (3) 20 Apr.1982, JCP 982 IV 230 (*responsabilité décennale*); Ghestin and Desché, *Vente*, 1039.

Overall, these *actions directes* have been a potent way of permitting those who suffer from defects of quality or safety to recover compensation, whether their loss is their own (damage to property, personal injury or costs of repair) or results from themselves being held liable to others, notably where they are *gardiens* of the product and are held liable on this basis to third parties.[363]

(b) Manufacturers' guarantees

French textbooks often distinguish between the *garantie légale* (the guarantee which is required of sellers by the law itself) and *garanties conventionnelles* (guarantees which result from agreement). As between the parties to a contract of sale, express guarantees form an example of the express setting of 'contractual conformity'.[364] To the extent to which they add to a buyer's rights, they take effect according to their terms; to the extent to which they purport to reduce the buyer's rights either in so many words or by excluding the seller's liability, they are treated as exemption clauses and subjected to the controls of this type of terms which I have already discussed.[365] In the case of manufacturers' guarantees, there appears to be no doubt among French lawyers that they can create direct contractual relations between those that give them and their beneficiaries.[366] A buyer's claim under a *garantie conventionelle* is governed by the general law and therefore was not caught by the *bref délai*.[367]

While there is relatively little up-to-date work published on French practice in relation to manufacturers' guarantees, they appear to rely on quite different concepts and principles from their 'legal' counterparts.[368] So, while they do require a buyer to show the defectiveness of a product, the concern is that it *appears* within a set period from the time of sale: there is no need for a buyer to show that the defect existed earlier. Typically, the seller or guarantor offers the repair of the goods supplied and, sometimes, their replacement, but no reduction in price nor damages. A buyer who benefits from such a guarantee may choose instead to claim under the *garantie légale* even having renounced the benefit of the contractual guarantee.[369]

---

[363] Below, p. 549.   [364] Above, pp. 70–1.   [365] Above, p. 95.

[366] Malaurie, Aynès and Gautier, *Contrats spéciaux*, 295–6.

[367] So, e.g., where a *clause de garantie* provides that a guarantee will extend for 10 years, the *bref délai* does not apply: Com. 2 May 1990, Bull. civ. IV no. 132, RTDCiv.1991.136 obs. Rémy.

[368] The following is principally drawn from P. Ancel, 'La garantie conventionnelle des vices cachés dans les conditions générales de vente en matière mobilière' RTDCom. 1979.203. See also Huet, *Principaux contrats spéciaux*, 354 *et seq*.   [369] Com. 28 Jun. 1994, Bull. civ. IV no. 248.

5

Droit Privé: Liability for the Provision of Services Involving Products

Apart from liability under the general law of delictual fault, so far I have looked at the way in which French law imposes liability for products on two particularly important categories of person: their *gardiens* (typically their owners)[1] through the law of delict and on their sellers, whether immediate or more remote, through the law of contract.[2] In this chapter, I shall look at how French private law governs the liabilities of a number of other categories of person for products which are involved in the provision of a service in a very broad sense. This involvement may consist of the transfer of a product from one person to another, as where goods are provided as part of the provision of a wider service, as in a restaurant meal, building a house or hiring a boat; while sometimes the product is the subject matter of the service in a different sense, as in the case of the designer of a car, or the consultant surveyor of a new building. In French law, all the cases treated here find a common basis in the *contrat de louage* ('hire' in a very general sense), which, following its Romanist origins, then divides into the hire of things (*louage des choses*, whether these are movable or immovable); the hire of services (*contrat de louage d'ouvrage*, but now more frequently *contrat d'entreprise*); and contracts of employment (*louage de service*, now termed *contrat de travail*). In this chapter, I shall look at examples of the first two,[3] my present discussion being restricted to private law: I shall look later at the law governing the provision of public services (whether this law is private or administrative).[4] Very little of the private law governing liability of the provider of a service stems from the Civil Code as originally drafted, but rather reflects modern legislative and judicial developments.

1. The General Approach to Liability for the Provision of Services

While French law treats all contracts for the provision of services as *contrats d'entreprise*, this category is very diverse, though some jurists discern a broad distinction as to the basis of liability between contracts for 'intellectual services', which give rise merely to *obligations de moyens*, and 'physical services', which give rise to *obligations de résultat*.[5] Here, I shall look at three more particular situations affecting liability for products by way of illustration.

---

[1] Above, pp. 51–61.   [2] Above, Chap. 4.
[3] For compensation for accidents at work, see above, pp. 61–2.
[4] Below, Chap. 7.   [5] Bénabent, *Contrats spéciaux*, 338–40.

(a) Suppliers of products and services

Sometimes products are supplied under contracts which are neither sale (as they involve an element of service) nor hire (as property in the goods passes). In French law, these are all *contrats d'entreprise*, but their context varies considerably and with it so does the attitude of French courts to issues of liability, sometimes preferring liability to be strict, sometimes based on fault. As regards liability for personal injuries or damage to property, the way in which liability of the supplier of the product is expressed is through the technique of *obligation de sécurité*, but in keeping with their general approach to this technique, the reasons for the courts' decisions as to the strictness of the liability are often elusive and difficult to generalise.[6] Here, I would like to look at two examples.[7]

A well-known question relates to the standard of liability of a *restaurateur* in respect of food supplied. As to the safety of the food, liability is based on an *obligation de sécurité de résultat*: so, in the well-known case of the poached turbot which contained botulism, a restaurant was held liable for the food poisoning which this caused to its customer, even though the court accepted that the restaurant could not have detected or removed the offending organism.[8] On the other hand, the court noted that the restaurant owed its customers a mere *obligation de diligence ordinaire* as to the 'quality of the taste' of the dishes which it served, a duty whose actual content would vary according to the class of restaurant in question.[9]

By contrast, hairdressers are apparently treated by French courts more leniently than *restaurateurs*, since they are generally said to be liable only under an *obligation de moyens* even as to the safety of the products with which they treat their customers. Thus, in one case, a hairdresser had treated the customer with a bleaching agent, as a result of which she suffered a skin complaint, but the lower court's decision which held the hairdresser liable in damages to her was quashed as it had found that the product had been used in accordance with its instructions and a hairdresser is not under an *obligation de résultat*, but only *de moyens*.[10] Perhaps the court considered that the more appropriate defendant was the manufacturer of the product, and that the hairdresser should not be burdened with liability even if later he can recover an indemnity from the manufacturer.[11] If so, this approach contrasts strikingly with the position governing sale, where all members of the chain of distribution are liable for any 'defects' in the products which they have sold directly to any purchaser harmed by them.[12]

---

[6] Above, pp. 27–8.

[7] An important example of this category *used* to be found in the case of doctors and dentists, on which see below, pp. 142–4, 151–3.

[8] TGI Poitiers 7 Jan. 1969, D 1969.174 note Pradel; Poitiers 16 Dec. 1970, GP 1971.1.264 obs. Mémèteau. The botulism could not constitute *force majeure* as it was not 'exterior to the thing': cf. above, p. 90. The court did not distinguish between the various customers who suffered from the poisoning on the basis of who paid the bill.   [9] Poitiers 16 Dec. 1970, cit.

[10] Civ. (1) 4 Oct. 1967, D 1967.652.

[11] Cf. Civ. (2) 5 May 1959, JCP 1959.II.11159 (manufacturer held liable to the customer injured by a permanent wave lotion on the basis of fault under arts. 1382–3 C. civ.).   [12] Above, pp. 96–8.

(b) The liability of repairers

Where a product has been repaired and then causes harm either to the person who commissioned the work (typically and for convenience, its owner) or to others, what recourse do they have against the person who undertook the repairs?[13] Here, the French courts have been relatively conservative.

Under a contract to repair, for example, a motor vehicle by a mechanic, the repairer owes his client a contractual obligation to do the work, but the courts have fluctuated in their view as to its content, sometimes treating it as an *obligation de résultat*, sometimes *de moyens* and sometimes something in between, usually known as an *obligation de résultat atténuée*.[14] However, some points do emerge from this uncertain picture. First, while it is for the *juges du fond* to decide what the repairer agreed to do for the owner,[15] a repairer of a product like a motor vehicle will normally be found to have undertaken its putting into running order and will be excused from liability when it breaks down only if he shows that his client refused to allow a necessary repair or was warned as to its incomplete or temporary nature.[16] In one case, for example, A, who had been held liable as *gardien* of his vehicle when it swerved into B's vehicle, succeeded in his recourse claim against C, a garage mechanic, to whom he had taken his vehicle for repair shortly before the accident, on the ground that a repairer of a vehicle must put it into correct running order and do the work to a proper standard, warning his client of the temporary nature of any repairs and in particular of any dangers which could thereby result;[17] sometimes, though, a mere warning as to a risk may not be enough, as a repairer can be held at fault for allowing a dangerous vehicle back onto the road, in contract to the client and in delict to any third parties who are injured as a result.[18] Moreover, some cases have held that a garage mechanic is liable to the owner in respect of harm caused by the vehicle or merely its breakdown on the basis of a rebuttable presumption of fault and of causal significance.[19] So, for example, where after repair a car broke down some 1,500 kilometres from the garage for reasons which remained obscure, the Cour de cassation held that it was for the repairer to show that he had performed his obligation and that he had not been at fault.[20]

By contrast with their adventurousness in the context of sale and the construction of buildings,[21] French courts have not extended the benefit of contracts of repair

---

[13] Very similar issues arise in relation to someone who installs but does not sell a product. An installer working under a *contrat d'entreprise* (rather than as an employee) owes an *obligation de moyens* to the customer as to the quality and safety of the work (Lyon 2 Jul. 1975, JCP 1975.IV.339) and on the basis of delictual fault under arts. 1382–3 C. civ. to third parties (Civ. (2) 8 Jun. 1979, DS 1980.563 note Espagnon, D 1980 IR 33 obs. Larroumet) even where the claimant is the commissioner of construction work and the installer is a sub-contractor: Ass. Plén. 12 Jul. 1991, *arrêt Besse*, JCP 1991.II.21743 note Viney (which concerned the analogous case of a plumber).

[14] Malaurie, Aynès and Gautier, *Contrats spéciaux*, 471; Viney and Jourdain, *Conditions*, 489–90.

[15] Civ. (1) 18 Jul. 1972, Bull. civ. II no. 189.

[16] Durry, RTDCiv. 1983.142 obs. to Douai 5 Feb. 1982.

[17] Civ. (1) 16 May 1960, D 1960.737 note Tunc. Other courts have used the technique of *obligation d'information* in order to impose liability on a garage repairer: Bénabent, *Contrats spéciaux*, 341, 343.

[18] Durry, *op. cit.* n. 16.　　　[19] Bénabent, *Contrats spéciaux*, 339.

[20] Civ. (1) 22 Jun. 1983, Bull. civ. I no. 181, RTDCiv. 1984.119, obs. Rémy; and see similarly also Civ. (1) 9 Jun. 1993, *Cont., conc., cons.* 1993.205 note Leveneur; Civ. (1) 8 Dec. 1998, Bull. civ. I no. 343 (liability to client, referring to a presumption of fault and of causation).

[21] Above, pp. 96–8, below, p. 104.

beyond their parties, leaving a traditional division of roles between contract and delict. So, a person who buys property which has been badly repaired cannot sue its repairer on the basis of the contract of repair made with its former owner, his seller,[22] but must prove the repairer's delictual fault under article 1383 of the Code. Similarly, anyone other than the person for whom the repairs were done who is injured, for example, by a badly repaired vehicle, may sue the repairer but only for delictual fault; but given the very strict liability imposed on a *gardien* of a motor vehicle, he is much more likely to sue its *gardien*,[23] leaving it to the latter to claim an indemnity from the repairer either in contract, if he commissioned the work, or in delict, if he did not.[24]

While the liability imposed on the *gardiens* of motor vehicles is particularly strict,[25] this picture is of wider significance. Typically, a person who engages someone to repair a product is either its owner or, possibly, its hirer and *typically* will therefore also be its *gardien*.[26] This means that where the product causes harm to anyone else, they will prefer to sue its *gardien* under article 1384 alinéa 1 of the Code, leaving its *gardien* to sue either in contract (if he or she did indeed commission the work) or, if not, for delictual fault if it can be established. So, while the repairer may be responsible for the harm caused by an inadequate repair based on a presumption of fault, any third party will prefer to leave such questions of attribution for the product's *gardien*.

(c) Designers, advisers and certifiers

A wide range of people contribute an intellectual, rather than a physical input into the construction of products. While many manufacturers design their own products, some use engineers or consultants to advise them as to a suitable design and as to the safety, quality or effectiveness of existing products. The general rule in French law is that all those who give such advice are liable only if their fault is shown, in contract to the person who commissions the advice and in delict to anyone else who suffers loss as a result,[27] though a large exception is made in the context of the construction of buildings.[28]

Let us take a simple example. If a manufacturer engages a specialist engineer to advise on the efficiency or safety of its products, the engineer does so under a *contrat d'entreprise* under which he owes an *obligation de moyens* as to any advice or information which he supplies to the manufacturer. The only exception to this rule requiring a proof of fault is where the designer can be said to have sold the plans for the design of a product, in which case the courts impose liability on the designer for any 'latent defects' in the design under the *garantie légale*.[29] Similarly, if the product in question causes loss or injury to a third party—for example, a consumer is injured by a badly

---

[22] Com. 25 May 1982, JCP 1982.IV.276.　　　[23] Above, pp. 60–1.

[24] E.g. Civ. (1) 16 May 1960, D 1960.737 note Tunc (contract).　　　[25] Above, pp. 60–1.

[26] Above, p. 53.

[27] G. Viney, 'La responsabilité des entreprises prestataires de conseil,' JCP 1975.I.2750; A. Bénabent, 'Contrat d'entreprise' Jur.-Cl. Contrats Distribution (1992) Fasc. 425, no. 139, p. 18; D. Veaux, 'Contrats de conseil' Jur.-Cl. Contrats Distribution (1992) Fasc. 430, 21 & 23.　　　[28] Below, pp. 104–8.

[29] Civ. (3) 6 Dec. 1972, D 1973.IR.7 (*cassation* of decision holding *bureau d'études* liable as seller of a plan on the basis that such a person is liable only for hidden defects). Cf. below, pp. 69 *et seq.*

designed car—the product's designer can be liable to that third party only on condition of a proof of fault, generally in delict.[30] Moreover, there is no evidence here of the courts taking the view that the mere design of a defective product itself constitutes fault, in contrast to their view of the position of a manufacturer.[31]

A similar position applies to those who advise a buyer as to the suitability of a particular product (which turns out to be unsuitable) or the certifier of a product (which turns out not to be not as stated). For example, where A gives specialist advice as to the suitability of a particular computer system for B's business, but does not itself supply either the hardware or software for the system,[32] then A will only be liable on the basis of fault under an *obligation de moyens*. Commercial practice in the context of ships provides an example of the possible liability for advice. In France, the Bureau Veritas[33] keeps a register of ships and classifies and values them after survey, principally for the purposes of insurance.[34] The person who commissions such a survey can claim in contract if he suffers loss due to its fault in the making of its report.[35] Moreover, if a prospective purchaser of a ship relies on a valuation or other statement made by the Bureau Veritas which he has *not* commissioned and as a result buys a ship for an inflated price, he can recover damages in delict against the Bureau Veritas for any loss suffered by this bad bargain, again, though, only if he can establish fault.[36] Inaccuracy in the certification of a ship may cause personal injuries or death, which again can be the subject of a claim in delict for fault. Thus, in another case, the Bureau Veritas had certified that the Dredger '*Cap-de-la-Hague*' could be loaded to a particular extent.[37] After the vessel sank, causing the death of most of its crew, the president and director of maritime services of the Bureau were prosecuted for involuntary homicide[38] and the 49 relatives and dependents of those drowned as well as the National Seamen's Union claimed damages for the harm which their death caused them before the criminal court as *parties civiles*.[39] Both the prosecution and the claim for damages succeeded against the director of maritime services, since the Bureau Veritas had misclassified the ship. The court clearly took a very strict view of the director's behaviour in order to find his fault and of his fault's causal role in causing the ship to founder,[40] though it is by no means clear that a *criminal* court would take the same view today.[41]

---

[30] Arts. 1382–3 C. civ. There is an exception where the claimant has bought the product from the person who commissioned the design, where the action has been held contractual: Civ. (1) 21 Jan. 2003, Bull. civ. I no. 18.　　　　　　　　　　　　　　　　　　　　　　　　　　　　　　　[31] Above, p. 51.

[32] Where either of these elements are supplied, the courts apply the rules governing the law of sale or sometimes impose an *obligation de résultat* which comes to a very similar result: see Huet, *Responsabilité du vendeur*, 102–09; Veaux, *op. cit.*, 22–3.

[33] According to its web-site (www.bureauveritas.com), the Bureau Veritas, a commercial company, also offers services 'in the areas of Conformity Assessment' relating, inter alia, to industry, consumer products, health and food.

[34] In this respect, its position has been compared by one writer to the Lloyd's Register: Veaux, *op. cit.* n. 27, 17.　　　　　　　　　　　　　　　　　　　　　　　　　　　　　　　　　　[35] Ibid.

[36] Paris 12 Dec. 1968, *Navire 'Emergo'* Dr. mar. fr. 1969.223 note Le Clère (though the court found that these conditions were not satisfied on the facts).

[37] Crim. 30 May 1980, Bull. crim. no. 166, Dr. mar. fr. 1981.146.　　　[38] Below, p. 372 *et seq.*

[39] On the role of the *partie civile*, see below, pp. 380–7.

[40] See the criticisms in E. Langavant and P. Boisson, 'L'affaire du naufrage de la drague "Cap-de-la-Hague" et le problème de la responsabilité des sociétés de classification' Dr. mar. fr. 1981.131.

[41] This results from reform to the law of involuntary homicide, below, pp. 387–93.

It can be seen that for someone who suffers personal injuries caused, for example, by a badly designed product, the remedies which he would possess against persons other than its designer are much more attractive. If he has bought the product, then he will have several possible routes to recovery against those in the chain of distribution, based on proof of its defect, but without the need to show fault.[42] If he has not bought the product, then he could sue its owner as *gardien*,[43] or possibly its manufacturer as *gardien de la structure*[44] or based on the delictual fault of supplying a defective product.[45] The main reason, therefore, for any attempted claim by a person suffering injury or death caused by a product against its designer, rather than against these other possible defendants, would be of deeper pockets.[46] More commonly, designers, advisers or certifiers are likely to find their liability put in issue by a product's manufacturer, owner or *gardien* by way of recourse for a liability imposed on some stricter ground.

2. The Law of Construction

The Civil Code as first enacted made special provision for the liabilities of builders and architects to their clients,[47] and, after some years of judicial and legislative development, in 1978 this was taken further by the creation of an elaborate system of liabilities for a range of those responsible for the construction of buildings, including builders, architects, specialist advisers (*techniciens* or *bureaux d'études*), manufacturers of certain prefabricated parts,[48] 'any other person who owes duties to the employer under a contract for services' and 'any person who has a building constructed and then sells it'.[49] So, it is not merely builders in the ordinary sense who are liable under this regime, but also the designers (architects) and technical advisers who would normally be liable only on the basis of proven fault.[50] Moreover, the benefit of these liabilities is enjoyed by any successor in title to the employer who commissioned the work, this being a legislative recognition of the *action directe en garantie* also found in the context of sale.[51] All those who bear liabilities under this regime have a legal obligation to insure themselves and where liability insurance is taken out by a builder, the employer has a 'direct action' against the insurer to escape that builder's insolvency.[52]

---

[42] Above, Chap. 4.   [43] Above, pp. 52 *et seq*. E.g. Civ. (1) 21 Jan. 2003, Bull. civ. I no. 18.

[44] Above, p. 54.   [45] Above, p. 51.

[46] Another reason could be where the fault is clearly established by a criminal court and the claimant can simply join these proceedings as *partie civile*: see Crim. 30 May 1980, Dr. mar. fr. 1981.146 and below, pp. 380–7.

[47] Art. 1792 C. civ. This provision was expressed as a consequence of the *contrat d'entreprise* between the builder and client.

[48] Art. 1792-4 C. civ. This provision is difficult and somewhat obscure: see for further discussion, G. Liet-Veaux, 'Construction, Diverse garanties légales: généralités. Ouvrages, travaux et personnes en cause', Jur.-Cl. Civ., Arts. 1788–94, Fasc. 6 (2002) 30.

[49] Art. 1792-1 C. civ. created by *loi* no. 78–12 of 4 Jan. 1978 *relative à la responsabilité et l'assurance dans le domaine de la construction* ('*loi* of 1978'). On the range of those liable see Liet-Veaux, *op. cit.*, Jur.-Cl. Civ., Arts. 1788–94, Fasc. 6, 23 *et seq*.

[50] Civ. (1) 9 Apr. 1962, Bull civ. I no. 201 (*bureau d'études* held liable for design defects in a heating system). For the general position, see above, p. 102.

[51] Art. 1792 al. 1 C. civ. and see above, pp. 95–8. This transmissibility does not apply to liability for failure in the *obligation de parfait achèvement*, below, p. 105.

[52] Arts. L. 241-1 C. assur. The duty to insure is backed by criminal sanctions: art. L. 243-7 al. 2 C. assur.

There are three distinct grounds of liability under this legislative scheme, these depending principally on the seriousness of the problems with the building, though they are known rather by the time for which they remain current after the completion and formal acceptance of the building.[53] First, there is the 'ten-year liability' (*la responsabilité décennale*). This concerns 'harms' (*dommages*) caused by hidden defects in the building existing at the time of its acceptance which threaten the soundness of the building *or* which affect one of its constituent elements in such a way as to make it unfit for its purpose, even if these defects[54] result from 'defects in the soil',[55] these requirements being within the 'sovereign power of assessment' of the *juges du fond*.[56] As often in French law, the notion of 'harm' is interpreted very broadly and includes not merely losses caused by the need to remedy the defects, but also losses consequential on the defects, such as personal injury or death,[57] damage to other property[58] or economic losses in general. Liability is very strict, the legislation referring to a 'presumption of responsibility' and giving as a defence only *force majeure*.[59] In this respect, and in keeping with the strict application of this notion in the context of the *garantie légale* in sale,[60] *force majeure* is not established where a builder uses a defective technique, even if this had been approved by a public advisory body and its defect was not known at the time.[61] However, the courts also accept that a builder's liability may be reduced on the ground of the employer's own fault, in particular where he was involved in the direction or the plans of the building.[62]

Secondly, the special regime provides a 'two-year liability' in respect of defects in fixtures and fittings which do not make the building unfit for its purpose.[63] This liability is otherwise similar to the 'ten-year liability', except that it is even stricter, there being no defence of *force majeure*.[64] Neither this liability nor the 'ten-year liability' may be excluded by agreement, whether or not the employer or his successor in title are in business.[65]

Thirdly, 'builders' owe their employers a 'guarantee of perfect achievement', which arises in respect of any defect notified to the builder either on completion of the building or subsequently in writing and this lasts for a period of a year from that acceptance.[66] This guarantee is intended as a means by which fairly minor defects are remedied and in the first instance imposes an obligation on the builder himself to put them right, though if he does not do so, the employer may after a certain time engage another builder to do the work instead.[67]

[53] This is termed *la réception*: art. 1792-6 C. civ. Before acceptance, liability arises only under the general law of delictual or contractual liability: e.g. Aix 11 Jan. 1962, D 1962.496.

[54] The requirement of a latent defect is not found in the legislation, but is universally acknowledged: G. Liet-Veaux, 'Construction, Responsabilité décennale, dommages couverts', Jur.-Cl. Civ., Arts. 1788–94, Fasc. 7 (2004) 2 *et seq*. [55] Art. 1792 al. 1. C. civ.

[56] Liet-Veaux, *op. cit.* n. 54, Jur.-Cl. Civ., Arts. 1788–94, Fasc. 7, 6.

[57] Civ. (3) 15 Oct. 1970, Bull. civ. III no. 514. [58] Civ. (3) 22 Feb. 1978, JCP 1978.IV.135.

[59] Art. 1792 al. 2 C. civ. (referring to *cause étrangère*); art. 1792-2 al. 1 C. civ. The terminology of 'presumption of liability' is reminiscent of that used by the *arrêt Jand'heur*, above, p. 52. [60] Above, pp. 89–91.

[61] Civ. (3) 17 May 1983, Bull. civ. III no. 115. The advice was given by the Centre scientifique et technique du bâtiment, an *établissement public à caractère industriel et commercial*.

[62] Civ. (3) 21 Dec. 1982, JCP 1983.IV.80. [63] Art. 1792-3 C. civ.

[64] Bénabent, *Contrats spéciaux*, 376.

[65] Art. 1792-5 C. civ. Cf. above, pp. 93–5 (sale).

[66] Art. 1792-6 al. 2 C. civ. [67] Art. 1792-6 al. 4 C. civ. Cf. art. 1144 C. civ.

While this legislative system of liabilities in respect of the construction of buildings has much in common with the *garantie légale* of the law of sale, in particular in its reliance on the notion of defect and its strictness,[68] there are a number of differences. The most striking one is that the time periods within which claims must be brought differ according to the seriousness of the defect in question and start to run from a fixed point, the 'acceptance' of the building by the employer, whereas in sale differences in time periods have rested on complex, and not altogether convincing, distinctions according to the character of the defect[69] and run in general either from the occurrence of the harm or its discovery.[70] A second difference is that the courts have long settled that, *where it applies*, this regime of liabilities in respect of the construction excludes recourse to other grounds of recovery.[71] In this context, therefore, not only is recourse to delict excluded, but so is recourse to the general law of contractual liability,[72] whether this is put in terms of a failure to fulfill an obligation of 'contractual conformity'[73] or even a failure to perform an alleged *obligation de sécurité*.[74]

However, despite this exclusive domain, even 'builders' may be liable other than on the basis of this special regime of liability. This is most obviously the case where the person harmed by the defect in the building is neither their employer nor his successor in title for here, delict 'regains its sway'[75] resulting in a builder being liable in delict for proven fault.[76] However, a 'builder' may also be liable to the employer other than under the special regime where the defect in question falls outside the net of all three liabilities, in particular, where it relates to the structure of the building (as distinct from its fixtures and fittings which may give rise to 'two-year liability') but is not suffi-ciently serious to fall within the 'ten-year liability'.[77] In this situation, a builder is liable under the general law of contract, apparently only on the basis of fault,[78] but with the exception that liability ceases ten years after the formal acceptance of the building (in the absence of *dol* but not *faute lourde*).[79]

Secondly, a number of persons concerned with the construction of buildings do not count as 'builders' within the meaning of this special regime, this being true, in partic-ular, of the vast majority of sub-contractors.[80] Where a sub-contractor also counts as a 'seller', for example, of defective tiles incorporated into a building's roof by a main

---

[68] Above, pp. 73, 86–91.   [69] Above, pp. 91–3.   [70] Above, pp. 91–2, 93.

[71] Cf. above, pp. 64, 69–72.

[72] Civ. (3) 10 Apr. 1996, Bull. civ. III no. 100, RTDCiv. 1996.918 obs. Jourdain, D 1997 Somm. 349 note Tournafond.

[73] Civ. (3) 4 Oct. 1989, *L'Harmet*, Bull. civ. III no. 178, JCP 1989.IV.385; Civ. (3) 13 Apr. 1988, JCP 1989.II.21315 note Martin.

[74] Civ. (3) 10 Mar. 1981, Bull. civ. III no. 49, GP 1981.1.694 note Leneveu.

[75] The courts sometimes use the phrase that the delictual provisions of the Code '*reprennent leur empire*'.

[76] Civ. (1) 9 Oct. 1962, D 1963.1 note Liet-Veaux. It would seem that the employer himself would be the *gardien* of the premises so as to exclude any claim against a builder on this basis: see Civ. (3) 21 Feb. 1984, GP 1984.2.Pan.Jur. 180 obs. Jestaz (employer held liable under art. 1384 al. 1 C. civ. to neighbour).

[77] Defects of this type are sometimes termed '*vices intermédiaires*': Bénabent, *Contrats spéciaux*, 377.

[78] Malaurie, Aynès and Gautier, *Contrats spéciaux*, 474–5 e.g. Civ. (3) 10 Jul. 1978, JCP 1979.II.19130, note Liet-Veaux, GP 1979.I.122 note A. Planqueel.

[79] Civ. (3) 16 Oct. 2002, Bull. civ. III no. 205; Bénabent, *Contrats spéciaux*, 377.

[80] This exclusion stems from art. 1792-1's definition of 'builders'. An exception is found in the position of manufacturers of prefabricated components under art. 1792-4 C. civ., see above, p. 104.

contractor, then the courts have accepted that an employer may sue that sub-contractor by way of *action directe* on the basis of the various liabilities which a seller owes in respect of defects.[81] However, a sub-contractor who does not 'sell' any product which is incorporated into the building because he works under a contract for the provision of services (which may not indeed involve the supply of any product), is liable to the employer or others *only* in delict and on the basis of proven fault.[82] This means that in theory at least most sub-contractors can be liable to a person who commissions a building for ten years from the appearance of the harm whatever its nature or seriousness.[83]

Thirdly, the construction legislation of 1978 created a special regime of liability in respect of the inspection and checking of buildings by a new category of professional adviser, the *contrôleur technique* (building inspector).[84] These *contrôleurs* are engaged under a contract, typically by the employer (though sometimes with an insurance company), to advise in relation to any technical problems, notably those which relate to the solidity of the work or as to safety,[85] and is compulsory for certain categories of building.[86] A *contrôleur technique* who works under a contract with and is paid by the employer, is liable to the employer and to any subsequent purchaser, on the basis of the 'ten-year liability' applicable to 'builders', that is, in respect of serious, structural defects 'within the limits of the mission with which he is entrusted by the employer',[87] though an inspector informs the employer of a defect in the building, he will not be liable for any damage which results from it.[88] By contrast, where a *contrôleur technique* works under a contract with someone other than the employer, for example, an insurance company or builder, the 'ten-year liability' does not apply, even if the employer ultimately pays for the work[89] and the *contrôleur technique* is liable only for fault, again in contract to the person who engaged him and in delict to others (including the employer).[90]

Clearly, therefore, these inspectors play an important role in the safety of buildings in France but while this system of control was clearly set up in the public interest, and while the independence of their views is protected by a system of licensing and by a rule that they may not take part in any activity relating to the design or construction of the building,[91] they are not members of the administration, nor, indeed, is their work

---

[81] Ass. plén. 7 Feb. 1986, D 1986.293 note Bénabent (liability based on 'contractual non-conformity'); Civ. (1) 21 Jan. 2003, Bull. civ. I no. 18. Cf. Civ. (3) 28 Nov. 2001, Bull. civ. III no. 137, RTDCiv. 2002.104 obs. Jourdain.   [82] Ass. plén. 12 Jul. 1991, *arrêt Besse*, JCP 1991.II.21743 note Viney.

[83] Art. 2270-1 al. 1 C. civ.

[84] *Loi* of 1978, arts. 8–11; Liet-Veaux, *op. cit.* n. 48, Jur.-Cl. Civ., arts. 1788–94, Fasc. 6, 29–30. The origins of this sort of control of buildings can be traced to 1929, but before the *loi* of 1978 the role of *contrôleurs techniques* was primarily to give advice to insurers: B. Boubli, '*Contrat d'entreprise*', in *Encyclopédie Dalloz, Civil* (2003) 32.   [85] *Loi* of 1978, art. 8.

[86] Ibid., art. 11; art. R. 111-38 *et seq.* C. constr. et hab. which makes inspection compulsory for buildings open to the public whose capacity exceeds 300 persons, for very tall buildings and for non-industrial buildings with special technical difficulties.

[87] *Loi* of 1978, art. 9. See, e.g., Paris 29 Jan. 1987, D 1988.Somm.115, RGAT 1987.233 obs. Bigot.

[88] Civ. (3) 30 Mar. 1989, *Soc. Sopire Intermarché*, JCP 1989.IV.206.

[89] Liet-Veaux, *op. cit.* n. 48, Jur.-Cl. Civ., Arts. 1788–94, Fasc. 6, 29.

[90] In one case, a manufacturer had asked the advice of a *contrôleur technique* only because this was a condition of obtaining the benefit of a particular group insurance: the report states somewhat enigmatically that the court held that the *contrôleur* was under no *obligation de conseil* to the manufacturer: Civ. (3) 3 Jan. 1980, GP 1980.1.Pan.Jur.225.   [91] *Loi* of 1978, art. 10.

treated as an expression of any *service public*.[92] their work and their liability belong firmly to private law.

In all, therefore, this special system of liability in construction is both itself complex and is supplemented by a complicated set of rules governing the potential liabilities of others involved in some way in the construction of buildings. While not free from doubt, the basic position is that where those potentially liable under the special regime have committed 'a common fault' (*une faute commune*) which causes the whole of a claimant's harm, they are liable *in solidum* and so each liable to the claimant for the whole loss.[93] Nevertheless, these various special liabilities only rarely require any proof of fault and extend both to a very wide range of defendant and to all types of buildings. Moreover, in France, this system of liabilities of builders is all the more important because of the wide practice and frequent effectiveness of clauses in contracts of sale of immovable property attempting to exclude the seller's liability for latent defects in the property:[94] a purchaser of a new building will often need to claim against the property's builder or architect rather than its seller.

How does this relate to liability for products? Where a building's defects are caused by the defectiveness of the materials or components of which it is made, an employer or its purchaser is likely to seek recovery from one of the 'builders' under this special regime based on the defects in the *building*, rather than needing to identify the source of this defect and then claim against the supplier or manufacturer of the particular materials or components: the 'builders' are strictly liable and cannot escape liability by pointing to a defect in their own materials. Again, the liability of the manufacturer or supplier of the component product is likely to arise only as regards any indemnity claim by a builder.

3. Hire of Property

The Civil Code subjected the hire of movable and immovable property to the same Romanist framework, not making any formal distinction between the hire of movables and leases of immovables similar to that found in English law, nor giving any proprietary interest to tenants of immovable property. While this framework has been qualified or by-passed by modern legislation in many contexts and for many purposes to an extent that the general rules of the Code have become of only secondary importance,[95] the law governing the liability of a person who hires out property (for convenience, the 'owner') to the person hiring it (the 'hirer') has remained largely unaffected.

(a) The owner's liability to the hirer

The basic pattern of the owner's liability is reminiscent of the system of liability imposed on sellers, but differs from it at a number of points. It may be based on at least

---

[92] Cf. below, p. 133.

[93] For further discussion, see Liet-Veaux, *op. cit.* n. 48, Jur.-Cl. Civ., Arts. 1788–94, Fasc. 6, 32–34 and, e.g., Civ. (3) 31 Mar. 1978, Bull. civ. III no. 142.   [94] Huet, *Principaux Contrats spéciaux*, 338, 349.

[95] In particular, French legislation has given very considerable protection to tenants of premises, whether residential, agricultural or commercial: Malaurie, Aynès and Gautier, *Contrats spéciaux*, 378 *et seq.*

four special grounds of contractual liability, quite apart from any liability arising under the general law governing all contracts, for example, for *dol* or for breach of an *obligation d'information*.[96] It has long been established that the rule of *non-cumul des responsabilités* prevents a hirer from relying on delict against the owner.[97]

First, in principle, the owner must deliver the property[98] in a good state of repair in *all* respects,[99] even those which are the responsibility of the hirer during the term of the contract.[100] This liability is more onerous for the owner than the law governing the liability of a seller, who must simply deliver the property agreed in the state existing at the time of sale and without hidden defects.[101] While in principle it may be excluded by the parties' agreement (and, indeed, frequently is by a term stipulating that property is taken 'as found'[102]), the courts interpret any such exclusion strictly.[103]

Secondly, after delivery, the owner[104] is under an obligation to effect those repairs on the property which are necessary for the use for which it has been hired,[105] as long as those repairs are not classed as the responsibility of the hirer ('*réparations locatives*').[106] While the issue of responsibility for repair has attracted considerable litigation, in general the owner's responsibility concerns repairs to the property's structure or other essential elements, whereas the tenant's concerns more minor matters.[107] Again, although the responsibility for repair may be allocated and the obligation to repair excluded by agreement, the courts interpret these agreements strictly.[108] While an owner's duty to repair hired property was at first considered an *obligation de moyens*, more recently the courts have interpreted it more strictly.[109] Certainly, the courts have sometimes imposed liability to a person injured by hired property who suffers personal injury as a result of a failure to repair for which the owner is responsible without showing any lack of care,[110] though in 1987 the Cour de cassation required proof either of fault or a defect in the property.[111]

---

[96] For liability for *dol*, see above, p. 64. As to breach of an *obligation d'information*, see de Juglart, *Principaux Contrats*, 442; Viney and Jourdain, *Conditions*, 425.

[97] Paris 17 Jan. 1905, D 1907.2.97 note Planiol; Civ. (2) 7 Jan. 1955, JCP1955.IV.22.

[98] In the case of immovable property, 'delivery' as required by art. 1719 1° C. civ. is understood in the broad sense of putting the property into the possession of the hirer.

[99] Arts. 1719 1° and 1720 al. 1 C. civ.

[100] Malaurie, Aynès and Gautier, *Contrats spéciaux*, 424 and see below, p. 109.

[101] De Juglart, *Principaux contrats*, 432.

[102] Such a term is known as a *clause de location 'en l'état'*: Bénabent, *Contrats spéciaux*, 229.

[103] Malaurie, Aynès and Gautier, *Contrats spéciaux*, 424–5 who note that the normal exceptions made to the effectiveness of exemption clauses apply (notably, where a party has committed *dol*) and that for residential tenancies the premises must fulfill minimum standards of comfort and fitness for habitation: *loi* no. 89-462 of 6 Jul. 1989, art. 6(a) and, where it is a person's principal residence, it must provide 'a decent home' (*un logement décent*): art. 1719 1° C. civ. (as amended in 2000). Any such exclusion may be ineffective as a *clause abusive* if the contract of hire constitutes a consumer contract within the meaning of art. L. 132-1 C. consom.

[104] The obligation is personal and does not bind the owner's successors in title: de Juglart, *Principaux Contrats*, 434. [105] Art. 1719 2° C. civ.

[106] Art. 1720 al. 2 C. civ. [107] Malaurie, Aynès and Gautier, *Contrats spéciaux*, 425.

[108] Bénabent, *Contrats spéciaux*, 230; Malaurie, Aynès and Gautier, *Contrats spéciaux*, 426. An old example is Req. 19 Jan. 1863, S 1863.1.185. Again, a lessor of residential premises may not exclude his duty to make those repairs which are necessary to maintain them in the normal state of repair of rented accommodation: *loi* no. 89–462 of 6 Jul. 1989, art. 6 (c). [109] Viney and Jourdain, *Conditions*, 724–5.

[110] Civ. (1) 14 Dec. 1966, D 1967.340 (tenant's small child injured).

[111] Civ. (3) 29 Apr. 1987, GP 1987.2.Pan. Jur.164, RTDCiv. 1988.149 obs. Rémy.

Thirdly, an owner is liable in damages to the hirer for any harm caused by defects in the property let which prevent its use, even if the owner was unaware of them at the time of the contract.[112] While the Code does not say so explicitly, courts and jurists agree that this liability applies only to latent defects,[113] thereby echoing the position under the *garantie légale* in sale.[114] But there are a number of significant differences between these two liabilities for latent defects. So, in the context of hire the courts apparently take a wide, 'functionalist' view of the notion of defect,[115] in contrast to the narrower view taken more recently in the context of sale;[116] an owner's liability applies only to those defects which prevent the property's use, whereas a seller's liability extends also to those defects which so affect its use that the buyer would have bought it only at a lesser price;[117] reflecting the continuing nature of contracts of hire, there is no requirement that the hidden defect exists at the time of making the contract[118] and it is for this reason that it is easily confused with liability arising from a failure to repair; an owner is liable in damages to his hirer for loss caused by a defect whether or not he was aware of the defect,[119] whereas a seller is liable in damages under the *garantie légale* only if he knew of the defect on sale or sold the property in the course of a business.[120] Moreover, while liability is strict, an owner may rely on a defence of *force majeure* against his hirer, even as regards the prevention of defects in the property hired (in contrast to the position in sale),[121] though the decision which recognizes this concerns defects arising after delivery of the property, for example, resulting from the installation by a third party of defective central heating,[122] a situation not falling within the *garantie légale* at all.[123] The courts allow recovery of damages in respect of any harm caused by defects in the property hired, whether personal injuries, damage to other property or losses caused by its lesser usefulness,[124] and apply their general approach to the effectiveness of exemption clauses to the owner's liability, holding them valid in the absence of *dol* (here, knowledge of the defect) or *faute lourde*;[125] but they have not transferred from sale to hire the technique which deems those hiring property in the course of business to know of its defects in order to invalidate exemption clauses.[126] Finally, an owner's liability for latent defects in hire runs for the prescription periods of the general law: there is no 'brief delay', for so long so characteristic of liability under the *garantie légale* in sale.[127] For some writers, these various differences between liability arising under contracts of hire and of sale shows that the former has more in common with liability for breach of contract under the 'general law', rather than the special regime of the *garantie légale* in sale.[128]

---

[112] Art. 1721 C. civ.   [113] De Juglart, *Principaux Contrats*, 439.   [114] Above, pp. 76–7.

[115] Viney and Jourdain, *Conditions*, 717.   [116] Above, p. 72.

[117] Art. 1641 C. civ. and see above, p. 75.   [118] De Juglart, *Principaux contrats*, 439.

[119] Art. 1721 C. civ.; Huet, *Principaux contrats*, 758.   [120] Above, p. 84.

[121] Above, pp. 89–91.   [122] Civ. (3) 26 Oct. 1977, D 1978 IR 41.   [123] Above, p. 90.

[124] Huet, *Principaux contrats*, 759–61 e.g. Civ. (1) 25 Jan. 1961, JCP 1962.II.12429 (action by injured husband of tenant on basis of implied *stipulation pour autrui*).

[125] The courts take a strict interpretation to such a clause: see Civ. (1) 25 Jan. 1961, JCP 1962.II.12429.

[126] Malaurie, Aynès and Gautier, *Contrats spéciaux*, 429. However, where a contract of hire constitutes a consumer contract within the meaning of art. L. 132-1 C. consom., an exemption of liability may constitute a *clause abusive*. Again an exception to the general position exists for residential tenancies where no exclusion of liability for latent defects is permitted: *loi* no. 89–462 of 6 Jul. 1989, art. 6 (c).

[127] The period is therefore in principle for 30 years, 10 years where either party is a *commerçant*, above, pp. 34 and 91–3.   [128] Bénabent, *Contrats spéciaux*, 231.

Fourthly, some jurists argue that an owner owes the hirer an *obligation de sécurité*, that is, a contractual obligation to care for the safety of his person or property.[129] However, in common with the position in the contract of sale, it is not clear whether this obligation is distinct from the others which I have already described which are imposed on the owner by the Civil Code, notably, liability for hidden defects.[130] A possible difference between the two would be that the latter requires the proof of a defect by the hirer, whereas this is not in principle necessary for an *obligation de sécurité*, though it has been required in the context of sale.[131] While it has been suggested that at least in the context of buildings the courts distinguish between cases where an owner is sued for the loss of a tenant's property stolen from the premises, where liability rests on a proof of fault (*obligation de moyens*), and cases where an owner is sued for personal injury or death by the hirer, where liability is strict (*obligation de résultat*),[132] a more recent decision of the Cour de cassation affirmed the existence of any *obligation de sécurité de moyens* as regards the hire of premises in a case where the hirer had been injured by a gas cooker in unexplained circumstances.[133] The effect of this was to deny liability, either for the premises' 'latent defects' or against the landlord as their *gardien*.

(b) Other liabilities arising in the context of hire

French courts have not extended the benefit of the liabilities arising for breach of the various contractual obligations in hire beyond the parties by *action directe*.[134] This means that in principle any third party to the contract may sue in delict, whether on the basis of fault[135] or, as regards the hire of buildings, the presumption of liability imposed on their *owners* by article 1386 of the Civil Code in the case of their 'ruin'.[136] By contrast, any claim by a third party to a contract of hire of movable property brought under article 1384 alinéa 1 of the Code is likely to be focused on the hirer who is more likely to qualify as its *gardien* than the owner,[137] leaving the hirer to claim an indemnity on one of the bases of owner's liability which I have just outlined. The only exception to this traditional approach to the domain of contractual liability is found in the case of contracts for the hire of residential property, where French courts have extended the benefit of the liabilities imposed on an owner to the tenant for the benefit of other persons who live on the premises by way of implied *stipulation pour autrui*.[138]

Conversely, a hirer may sue persons other than the owner in respect of harm caused by the property, but only in delict.[139] So, for example, a tenant of premises cannot sue their

---

[129] Malaurie, Aynès and Gautier, *Contrats spéciaux*, 427; Bénabent, *Contrats spéciaux*, 232.

[130] De Juglart, *Principaux contrats*, 440–2; Huet, *Principaux contrats*, 761–2. For the rejection of an *obligation de sécurité* independent of the owner's liabilities imposed by the Code: Civ. (3) 29 Apr. 1987, *Lecreux*, JCP 1987.IV.221, GP 1987.2 Pan. Jur. 164. Bénabent, *Contrats spéciaux*, 232, notes the possibility of liability under French law's implementation of the Product Liability Directive. [131] Above, p. 72.

[132] De Juglart, *Principaux contrats*, 441; Civ. 4 Jun. 1959, S 1961.329 note Planqueel.

[133] Civ. (2) 2 Dec. 1998, RTDCiv. 1999.407 obs. Jourdain.

[134] Huet, *Principaux contrats*, 762–4. Eg. Civ.(1) 11 Oct. 1967, D 1968.106, RTDCiv. 1968.362 obs. Durry. [135] Arts. 1382–3 C. civ. and e.g. Paris 8 Feb. 1896, D 1896.2.457 note Planiol.

[136] Above, p. 26. [137] Above, p. 53. [138] E.g. Civ (1) 25 Jan. 1961, JCP 1962.II.12429.

[139] Malaurie, Aynès and Gautier, *Contrats spéciaux*, 429.

'builder' under the special regime of liability already described,[140] nor the manufacturer of any defective materials used in the building by way of a contractual *action directe*, since any rights in the owner of the property against the manufacturer arising under the law of sale are not transmitted under the contract of hire.[141] Any claim by a hirer in delict against a builder or supplier would typically rest on proof of fault, given that the hirer is likely to become *gardien* of the property as a result of the contract.[142]

To conclude, apart from any claims under French law's implementation of the Product Liability Directive, for a person who hires property the best chance of recovery for loss caused by the property will be against the owner, but this will in general require proof that the property required repair or possesses hidden defects. The hirer's claims against any other person will usually rest on the proof of delictual fault.

[140] Civ. (1) 9 Oct. 1962, D 1963.1 note Liet-Veaux, RTDCiv. 1963.332, obs. Tunc; Civ. (3) 25 Jan. 1989, *Moreau*, JCP 1989.IV.111, RTDCiv. 1989.551 obs. Jourdain.
[141] Above, p. 111.   [142] Ibid.

6

Droit Administratif and Liability for Products

In this chapter, I shall start to explain how administrative law may govern liability for products by looking generally at how liability is imposed for fault and then at the special rules governing liability for dangerous things and for *travaux publics* ('public works').[1] In the following chapter, I shall look at how some of these liabilities relate to particular contexts (brought together loosely by the idea of the provision of public services), and in a later chapter at the particular case of liability in the administration for failures in its exercise of powers affecting the safety of products.[2]

As I have explained, a very important way in which the Cour de cassation gave effect to its desire to impose liability without fault for personal injuries and death was by constructing a liability for the 'deeds of things' based on article 1384 alinéa 1 of the Civil Code.[3] In French private law, therefore, 'liability for things' is a distinct legal category with a broad unity of treatment of the position of a particular class of defendants (*gardiens*), even if the courts have nuanced this treatment by sometimes dividing *la garde* and by manipulation of the concept of the 'deed' of a thing.[4] This law has considerable importance for liability for products, given that all physical things and therefore all 'products' are included within it.[5]

By contrast, denial of the Civil Code as a basis for development of the law of administrative liability has profoundly affected the way in which it governs liability for products, for this denial has led to the rejection by the Conseil d'Etat of a distinct legal category governing liability for physical things.[6] So instead of the division of liability between liability for personal deeds (for fault), for the 'deeds of things' and the 'deeds of others' which we find in private law,[7] the basic division in administrative law is between cases where liability is imposed on the basis of *faute* and cases where liability is imposed *sans faute* (or on *risque*), with liability for 'public works' forming a further distinct heading of liability straddling this dichotomy. As I indicated earlier, these broad categories of liability are not at all homogenous, for within them distinctions are made on a variety of bases.[8] Thus, within liability for *faute*, a distinction may be drawn between liability for *actes* (which includes administrative rule-making and many

---

[1] Below, as to the terminology here: pp. 121–2.   [2] Below, chaps. 7 and chap. 12.

[3] Above, pp. 51–61. The other main means was *obligations de sécurité de résultat*, above, pp. 22, 27–8.

[4] Above, pp. 52–4, 55–7.   [5] With the exception of 'incorporeal products': above, p. 52.

[6] A. de Laubadère, 'Le problème de la responsabilité du fait des choses en droit administratif français', (1959) EDCE 29; R. Chapus, 'Principes généraux et concepts fondamentaux de la responsabilité administrative' in Jur.-Cl. Admin. Vol. 7, fasc. 700 (1984) § 14. Cf. R. Chapus, *Responsabilité publique et responsabilité privée* (LGDJ, Paris, 1954), 265 *et seq.* where the author previously adopted such a category.

[7] Above, pp. 23–5.   [8] Above, p. 32.

decisions), where *faute* is simply equated with administrative illegality, and liability for administrative activities,[9] where it rests sometimes on *faute simple* ('ordinary fault') while in others it is the more demanding *faute lourde* ('gross fault').[10] Examples of administrative liability without *faute* are even more heterogeneous,[11] with their own rationale, ambit and usual context, the *jurisprudence* of the Conseil d'Etat often looking markedly *ad hoc*.[12] In all this, the involvement of a physical thing (whether movable or immovable) in the production of a claimant's harm forms an element in the imposition of liability in two bases of liability: administrative liability for *dangerous* things or activities, and liability for 'public works'.

Here, I shall start by looking briefly at how liability for fault may govern liability for products and explain why the specifically administrative law of contracts has had relatively little impact on it.[13] I shall then look at administrative liability for dangerous things and activities and how liability for 'public works' relates to liability for products.

1. Administrative Liability for Products Based on Fault

Liability for 'fault' is both the starting point and the broadest basis of liability in administrative law, as it is in private law.[14] While the Conseil d'Etat in 1873 in the *arrêt Blanco* was careful to point out that liability in the administration should not be 'general nor absolute',[15] since then it has greatly reduced the number of situations in which liability is not imposed even though fault in the administration (*faute de service*[16]) can be established as the cause of the claimant's harm and of situations where liability will be imposed only if a very serious fault (*faute lourde*) can be established. Despite the sometimes tortuous course of these developments, certain general propositions can be stated.

First, where a public servant (*agent de service* or *fonctionnaire*) commits a fault which is 'not unconnected' with the public service, then the administration is liable to a person harmed as a result, but the individual public servant enjoys a personal immunity.[17]

Secondly, where a public servant has committed a fault which either owing to its lack of connection with the 'public service' (*service public*) or its seriousness falls outside the scope of this legal immunity, (a so-called '*personal* fault'[18]), then he may be

---

[9] Below, p. 313.   [10] See below, pp. 312–5.

[11] F. Vincent, 'Responsabilité sans faute' in Jur.-Cl. Admin. Vol. 8, Fasc. 824 (2000) 3.

[12] Gaudemet, *Droit administratif*, Tome I, 819 referring to the 'empiricism' of the courts. These other bases of liability may affect liability for products as in the cases concerning the liability of *communes* to those amateurs who undertake the lighting of fireworks at public firework displays: see Braibant and Stirn, *Droit administratif français*, 304. Here, liability would not be imposed under the head of 'dangerous things' as fireworks have been held to be 'non-dangerous': CE 30 Mar. 1979, DS 1979.552 note Richer.

[13] Cf. above, p. 33.

[14] As to administrative law, Gaudemet, *Droit administratif*, Tome I, 877 who describes liability for fault as the general position (*le droit commun*). For the role of liability for fault in private law, see above, pp. 40–50.

[15] TC 8 Feb. 1873, S 1873.153, above, p. 31.   [16] Fairgreave, *State Liability*, 102 *et seq*.

[17] Chapus, *Droit administratif général*, 1385.

[18] 'Personal fault' or '*une faute détachable de la fonction*' is typically found by the courts where the servant's fault has nothing to do with his public functions or where his fault is intentional and, possibly, where it counts as *faute lourde*: Gaudemet, *Droit administratif*, Tome I, 784–8.

personally liable in the ordinary courts under the rules of private law. In this situation, the administration will also be liable in the administrative courts (an 'accumulation' of liability), as long as the individual public servant's fault was not 'committed outside the public service' or 'detachable from the public service'.[19] To this end, the Conseil d'Etat has taken a very liberal view of the degree of connection with the public service necessary to attract the administration's liability, imposing liability where the ordinary courts would not impose vicarious liability on an employer.[20]

Thirdly, in some cases the administrative courts do not consider it necessary to establish a fault in any one identified public servant so as to impose liability on the administration, but instead find a fault in the administration itself, either in that it has acted illegally or has failed to create a suitable system for the administration of the area in question or otherwise fallen short of the legitimate expectations of the citizen to good government: in these circumstances, there is a 'fault' in the service itself (*faute du service public*),[21] an institutional failure.

But how do these general bases of liability affect liability for products in the broad sense in which I have defined this? This is, I think, best explained by way of a few illustrations.

Of all the products which are used by the administration one of the most frequently harmful are motor vehicles and many of the cases testing the limits of administrative liability for fault were decided in this context. Where liability was imposed on this basis, fault was understood in the sense of recklessness or negligence in the public servant driving the vehicle and the involvement of the administration's vehicle in occasioning a claimant's harm was merely a factor in finding the necessary connection between the public servant's fault and the public service in order to attract liability.[22] However, this example of liability in the administration for products was removed in 1957 when 'harm caused by vehicles' was unified under the rules of private law and submitted to the jurisdiction of the ordinary courts.[23] This has been interpreted very broadly with the result that private law governs the recovery of all types of harm caused by any 'machine which moves by its own means' or is towed,[24] whether or not it is used for the carriage of goods or persons.[25] In the result, cases of harm caused by administrative vehicles remain an example of liability in the administration, but are no longer an example of administrative liability. Similarly, the liability of the public providers of medical care involved an important example of liability for the use or supply of products, liability evolving from a standard of *faute lourde*, through one for *faute simple* to a presumption of fault (at least in certain situations), but again legislation has (at least apparently) placed liability on a common basis for the public and private sectors, though it has left its assessment to the distinct jurisdictions.[26]

---

[19] Gaudemet, *Droit administratif,* Tome I, 791 *et seq.* The leading decisions were CE Ass. 18 Nov. 1949, *Dlle Mimeur, Defaux, Bethelsemer,* Leb. 491, D 1950.667, JCP 1950.II.5286 concl. Gazier.

[20] Vedel and Delvolvé, *Droit administratif,* Vol. 1, 571.

[21] Gaudemet, *Droit administratif,* Tome I, 806–07.

[22] CE Ass. 18 Nov. 1949, *Mimeur,* Leb. 491, D 1950.667, JCP 1950.II.5286 concl. Gazier (use of military vehicle used on personal detour not detachable from public service for which it was entrusted to him).

[23] *Loi* of 31 Dec. 1957.   [24] Vedel and Delvolvé, *Droit administratif,* Tome 1, 700.

[25] TC 11 Dec.1972, *Spathis,* JCP 1974.II.17669 note Moderne; TC 15 Oct. 1973, *Barbou,* AJ.1974.94 concl. Braibant.   [26] Below, p. 141 *et seq.*

There remain, however, some situations in which public bodies are liable on the ground of *faute de service* in respect of harm caused by the products which they use. I shall give one example in the context of the provision of a 'leisure service' and another in the provision of an emergency service.

In my first example, a *commune*[27] had provided a floating diving stage for public use at a beach.[28] A group of young people see-sawed up and down on it until it overturned, hitting and injuring a diver. The Conseil d'Etat held that liability in the *commune* could be only on the basis of fault, whether in providing the diving stage or in its management, neither having been shown on the facts,[29] a decision which makes clear its rejection of a general liability for the deeds of things as found in private law.[30] In my second example, *Millet*,[31] a young apprentice became stuck while working at the bottom of a well. The local rescue services were called in to help, but the apprentice was injured in the course of being pulled out. His employer's claim for the medical expenses and maintenance which he had paid to his apprentice by reason of these injuries was successful before the Conseil d'Etat, on the ground that the equipment (especially the ropes) which the service used was insufficient for the job and these deficiencies, coupled with the absence of proper leadership constituted *faute lourde* so as to attract liability in the commune which ran the service.

It must be said, though, that since the removal of vehicle accidents from the domain of administrative law, cases in which harm is caused in the course of the use of physical things and in which liability is imposed on the basis of fault under the general rules of administrative liability have not been very important. The main reason for this is that most cases of this type are dealt with either by administrative liability for dangerous things (where a claimant would normally prefer to rely on this liability without fault) or for 'public works' (where a claimant is not as a matter of law able to rely on the general law of liability for fault).[32] Before looking at these two special grounds of liability, I wish to explain the reasons for the restrained importance of contractual liability to govern administrative liability for things.

2. A Restrained Role for the Administrative Law of Contract

The private law of contract has been immensely important in imposing liability for products, the ordinary courts developing the liabilities which were already provided by the Civil Code (as in the case of the *garantie légale* in sale), imposing new liabilities and extending them beyond the parties to a contract.[33] By contrast, the administrative law of contract is relatively unimportant in governing liability for products. There are two main reasons for this.

First, many cases of liability arising from the use or supply of things in a public context are governed by the administrative law of extra-contractual liability, even though

---

[27] The *commune* is the smallest unit of local authority.

[28] CE 12 Oct.1973, *Commune de Saint-Brévin-les-Pins*, RDP 1974.1137 note Waline.

[29] The CE rejected the diver's claim on the basis of 'public works' on the ground that the diving stage was not an immovable, cf. below, p. 124.   [30] RDP 1973.1137.

[31] CE 18 Jan. 1974, Leb. 48.   [32] Below, pp. 118–21, 121–31.   [33] Above, Chaps. 4 and 5.

on similar facts in the private context liability would be considered contractual. There are two factors at work here. The first is that in some situations French law views the provision of a public service as giving rise to a special relationship of public law, between its provider and its 'user,' the citizen.[34] Where this is the case, the Conseil d'Etat refuses to see any contract between the provider of the service and its recipient, even if this provision arises from their agreement and its users incur a charge. So, for example, a person who uses a public ferry service may count as its 'user' rather than as party to a contract[35] as are patients in public hospitals.[36] This means, among other things, that any liability arising from the way in which the public service is provided, including as regards any products used or even supplied to its recipients, can only be extra-contractual: the public law analysis of the relationship ousts contract, even administrative contract. The second factor relates again to the absence of the Civil Code as the basis of the Conseil d'Etat's development of liability and can be seen clearly by contrasting the position in private law. I have earlier explained that the ordinary courts have tended to expand the domain of contractual liability at the expense of the delict and *obligations de sécurité* were a prominent means of achieving this.[37] While their particular purpose has varied over time and according to context, their imposition allows the courts to avoid the requirement of proof of delictual fault found in articles 1382 and 1383 of the Civil Code or, by contrast, the strictness of liability for the 'deeds of things'.[38] By contrast, French administrative judges have not needed to invoke contract for either of these purposes: they do not need to use contract to avoid the law of extra-contractual liability, which is entirely in their hands, unfettered by legislative texts. So, for example, when the Conseil d'Etat wished to impose liability without fault for accidents at work, it did not need either to find an *obligation de sécurité* in the contract of employment under which its employees worked[39] nor re-interpret existing legislation (as was done by the ordinary courts in the case of article 1384 alinéa 1 of the Civil Code),[40] but instead could rely directly on the idea that the administration should be liable for any harm caused to someone who risks danger in the public service.[41] So too, in the absence of any 'liability for the deeds of things' of the strictness and generality of that recognised by the ordinary courts, administrative courts did not feel the need to use contract to protect some classes of defendant from an inappropriately strict liability:[42] the Conseil d'Etat was free to recognise

[34] Below, Chap. 7.
[35] TC 22 Jan. 1921, *Bac d'Eloka*, Leb. 91. *Cf.* CE 10 May 1974, *Denoyez*, AJDA 1974.298, chron. Jurisp. Franc et Boyon where a ferry service was held to be a *service public administratif.*
[36] Below, p. 135.   [37] Above, pp. 27–8.   [38] Above, p. 28.
[39] This had been suggested by some members of *la doctrine* but was not adopted by the ordinary courts: above, p. 28. A strictly *contractual* approach to workers' compensation was not open to the Conseil d'Etat given that not all public servants in a broad sense work under contracts: Chapus, *Droit administratif,* Tome 2 (1999), 17–18, 53 *et seq.*
[40] Civ. 16 Jun. 1896, S 1897.1.17 note Esmein, D 1897.1.433 note Saleilles and see above, p. 26.
[41] CE 21 Jun. 1895, *Cames*, D 1896.3.65 concl. Romieu. While this example of the imposition of administrative liability without fault became redundant when pensions for permanent public servants were introduced by legislation (*loi* of 26 Dec. 1964 and *déc.* of 28 Oct. 1966; Vedel and Delvolvé, *Droit administratif,* Tome 1, 602–03) it inspired other examples where liability without fault is imposed for the benefit of *collaborateurs occasionnels du service public*: e.g. CE 25 Sept. 1970, *Tesson*, D 1971.55 concl. Morisot.
[42] Above, p. 28.

extra-contractual strict liability where and on the basis which it thought fit without the resort to reclassification.[43] Overall, therefore, the Conseil d'Etat sometimes has positive reasons for seeing the provision of a public service as non-contractual (as it treats the recipient of such a service as in a relation of public law exclusive of contract) and sometimes simply has no reason to see liability as other than non-contractual.

A second reason for the restrained impact of the administrative law of contract on liability for products is that most contracts for the supply of property, whether goods or land, which are entered by public bodies, whether as supplier or recipient, are classed as 'civil contracts', attracting both the jurisdiction of the ordinary courts and the application of private law. Of these, perhaps the most important examples are contracts of supply made by *sociétés publics industriels et commerciaux*, which are public bodies, institutionally governed by public law, but whose operations are in general a matter for private law. Included within this category are the main suppliers of gas[44] and electricity,[45] whose liability to their customers is therefore placed *en bloc* in the private law domain.[46] On the other hand, the activities of these corporations can attract liability to *non*-customers in administrative law, notably under the special rules relating to 'public works'. As I shall later explain, liability in respect of the supply of these products is a complex combination of public and private law.[47]

Finally, even where French law treats a particular contract as being administrative, the substantive law which the Conseil d'Etat chooses to apply is often not particularly 'administrative' in its character, sometimes being virtually identical with that applied by the ordinary courts. This is notably the case as regards the commissioning of building works by public bodies, the contracts for which are 'administrative', but the liability regime for which has been inspired by the principles of the relevant provisions in the Civil Code.[48]

3. Dangerous Things and Activities

One of the earliest categories of situation in which liability *sans faute* was imposed was where a dangerous thing used by the administration caused physical injury.[49] At first sight, it is here that French administrative law comes closest to private law's liability for the 'deeds of things', but the similarity is only very superficial.

First, since the *arrêt Jand'heur* the ordinary courts have not restricted liability for the 'deeds of things' to *dangerous* things, in part because it is not mentioned in article 1384 alinéa 1 and in part because of the difficulty of its definition.[50] While public lawyers also recognised the difficulty of defining dangerousness,[51] the Conseil d'Etat

---

[43] Below, pp. 118–21.   [44] Gaz de France ('GDF').   [45] Electricité de France ('EDF').

[46] Below, p. 136. See also the liability of SNCF, the French railway company, below, pp. 139–40.

[47] Below, p. 136 *et seq.*

[48] CE Ass. 2 Feb.1973, *Trannoy*, Leb. 94, concl. Rougevin-Baville; arts. 1792 and 2270 C. civ.

[49] See generally, Fairgrieve, *State Liability*, 138–42.

[50] Above, p. 52. Cf. those cases where they require the 'thing' to possess its own 'dynamism': above, p. 54.

[51] J. Moreau, 'Rapport sur les choses dangereuses en droit administratif français', in *Travaux de l'Association Henri Capitant*, Tome XIX (1967), 256, 258.

dealt with this by avoiding a definition and instead constructing a list of dangerous things.[52] In drawing up this list, the Conseil d'Etat has been both distinctly cautious and clearly influenced by factors other than the special danger which the thing in question may be said to possess.[53]

Secondly, though, the Conseil d'Etat has extended liability under this heading beyond things to dangerous activities, in particular so as to impose liability without fault for the harm which young offenders or mental patients cause when they escape from their detention.[54] This means that the only common element to this collection of examples of administrative liability without fault is the notion of special danger: a 'thing' may or may not be involved.

Most writers trace this head of liability to the *arrêt Regnault-Desroziers* of 1919,[55] which concerned a large explosion of munitions in a fortress during the First World War. The Conseil d'Etat held that neighbouring property owners were entitled to recover damages from the State for the damage caused by the explosion without showing any fault in the military, since these military operations 'entailed risks exceeding those which normally result from being a neighbour'. Nevertheless, its practical impact has been quite modest, as in many cases compensation may be obtained from the State under legislative schemes for the compensation of war damage.[56]

A second and at one time important type of 'dangerous thing' could be found in motor vehicles.[57] While liability without fault might be justified here on the basis of their special danger to persons and property, they are not dangerous to the same degree as an ammunition dump! It is clear, though, that their inclusion reflects the Conseil d'Etat's desire to avoid substantial differences between its own and the ordinary courts' approach to liability for traffic accidents, both jurisdictions sharing the view that this liability should be strict.[58] However, since the unification of the law of vehicle accidents in 1957, they have not featured as an example of 'dangerous things' in administrative law. Another transitory example of this head of administrative liability was at one time found in liability for harm caused by electricity, gas and water in the course of 'public works', but by the 1950s this approach had been abandoned in favour of the more general scheme of liability under 'public works'.[59]

Of more lasting significance was the imposition by the Conseil d'Etat in 1949 of strict liability for harm caused by the use of 'firearms or devices which entail exceptional risks for persons or property, where the harm is suffered in circumstances that its

---

[52] Cf. Chapus, *Droit administratif général*, Tome I, 1337–41; F. Vincent, 'Responsabilité sans faute' in Jur.-Cl. Admin. Vol. 8, Fasc. 824 (2002) 3. Chapus, *Responsabilité publique et responsabilité privé*, 278–9 attributed this difference of approach between two jurisdictions to their institutional differences: whereas at the time the Conseil d'Etat was practically the sole forum for the imposition of administrative liability and could itself control its practical expression, if the Cour de cassation had defined dangerousness, this would have led to '*anarchie jurisprudentielle*' in the lower courts.   [53] Below, pp. 119–21.

[54] Below, pp. 120–1.   [55] CE 1 Aug. 1919, D 1920.III.1 note Appleton.

[56] Moreau, *op. cit.* n. 51, (1967), 256, 283–284. Where no legislative scheme covers the claimant's harm the *jurisprudence* of *Regnault-Desroziers* has been applied: CE Ass. 21 Oct. 1966, *SNCF*, D 1967.164.

[57] CE 22 Dec. 1924, S 1926.3.1 note Hauriou, D 1925.3.9 note Appleton, which used the terminology of presumption of *fault*, but allowed it to be rebutted only on proof of *force majeure* or *faute de la victime*.

[58] For the ordinary courts, see above, pp. 52–61.

[59] CE 17 Oct. 1952. *Ville d'Arras*, Leb. 453 and below, p. 121 *et seq*.

gravity exceeds the burdens which ought normally to be borne by private individuals as the counterpart to the advantages which result from the existence of the public service in question'.[60] This was a big change as liability in these circumstances had previously been imposed only on the basis of *faute lourde*, but this category has been fairly restrictively interpreted, its benefit being denied to any person who is the object of police activity.[61] Moreover, the rationale for its imposition is not entirely settled, for when in 1986 the Cour de cassation applied it to a case involving injury to a bystander by the firearm of a criminal suspect in a shoot-out with the *police judiciare*,[62] it did so on the basis of the principle of *égalité devant les charges publiques*,[63] rather than on the special dangerousness of firearms.

In general, though, French administrative courts have taken a very restrictive approach to their list of 'dangerous things'. Thus, while it includes all types of firearms used by the police, it does not include their use of tear gas in the quelling of a riotous demonstration.[64] On the other hand it is open to the Conseil d'Etat to add further examples to the list of 'dangerous things',[65] and in 1995 at the height of the *affaire du sang contaminé* it added blood products potentially contaminated with HIV as supplied by the French blood transfusion centres.[66]

Moreover, as has been said, the Conseil d'Etat has imposed liability without fault in respect of certain classes of dangerous activities, notably to cases where young offenders or mental patients detained under open systems have escaped and caused harm to other persons or property,[67] though not to others, for example, where a young person was not detained under the open system in question[68] and where an unemployed person was doing work experience in a company.[69] It is interesting to note that this development had a later broad parallel in private law, but when the Cour de cassation came

---

[60] CE 24 Jun. 1949, *Lecomte et Daramy*, JCP 1949.II.5092 concl. Barbet, note George.

[61] CE Sect. 27 Jul. 1951, *Aubergé et Dumont*, Leb. 447, D 1952.108, concl. Gazier, note Morange. Here *faute simple* is enough to establish liability.

[62] Claims against the *police judiciaire* fall within the jurisdiction of the ordinary courts but are governed by administrative law principles: Vedel and Delvolvé, *Droit administratif*, Tome I, 662–3.

[63] Civ. (1) 10 Jun. 1986, JCP 1986.II.20683. The Cour de cassation did not distinguish in this respect between cases where the claimant was injured by a police or by a suspect's bullet.

[64] CE 16 Mar. 1956, *Domenech*, Leb. 124 (*faute lourde* required).

[65] Brown and Bell, 177, give CE 19 Oct. 1990, *Ingremeau*, Leb. 284 as an example of this category, but in this decision a local authority was held liable for the injury caused by a bow and arrow used by a child in its foster care on the basis of a presumption of fault and no mention was made of the danger of either this thing or any activity. These authors rightly point out that the decision in *Ingremeau* is ' not all that surprising because, in private law, parents would be liable to the victim for the acts of the child', citing Ass. plén. 9 May 1984, *Fullenwarth* D. 1984.525 note Chabas, which imposed liability under art. 1384 al. 4 C. civ.

[66] CE Ass. 26 May 1995, *N'Guyen, Jouan, Pavan*, Leb. 221, 222, AJ 1995.508 Chron. Stahl and Chavaux, JCP 1995.II.22468 note Moreau; CE 16 Jun. 1997, *Assist. Publ.-Hospitaux de Paris*, Leb. 242 and see below, p. 150. Cf. TA Paris 20 Dec. 1990, JCP 1991.IV.395 (nurse in Ministry of Defence psychiatric hospital contracted HIV virus after one of her patients deliberately turned a tube of his infected blood over scratches on her hand).

[67] CE 3 Feb. 1956, *Thouzellier*, D 1956.596 note Auby, JCP 1956.II.9608 note Lévy; CE 13 Jul. 1967, *Département de la Moselle*. Leb. 341 (respectively).

[68] CE 14 Jun. 1978, *Soc. de construction pour le bâtiment*, Leb. 259.

[69] CE 15 Oct. 1990, *SA Paris Touraine automobile*, Leb. 279.

to impose strict liability for harm caused by escaped mental patients, it did so by invoking the generality of the terms of article 1384 alinéa 1 of the Civil Code in order to recognise a general liability for the deeds of persons in one's keeping.[70]

Exploding munitions, guns, electricity, motor vehicles, 'poisoned' blood and escaped mental patients or prisoners have all been included as 'dangerous things' or revealing dangerous activities at one time or another, but they have little in common apart from the fact that the Conseil d'Etat has considered them appropriate for liability without fault. Moreover, the practical importance of this head of strict administrative liability is not now very great. Of the various 'things' which have been included, only really firearms remain—the others being overtaken by special legislative schemes (wartime munitions), transferred to private law (vehicles), or subsumed under another head of administrative liability (electricity, gas and water) and blood overtaken by more general legislative changes governing medical liability.[71] Certainly, administrative liability for dangerous things does not possess either the generality or the importance of private law's liability for the 'deeds of things', instead serving as one possible basis among others for the ad hoc approach of the Conseil d'Etat to the line between strict liability and fault.

4. Liability in Respect of 'Public Works'

The French law relating to 'public works' (*travaux publics*[72]) possesses a certain 'autonomy' within its administrative law, having its own distinct concepts and rules.[73] Following pre-revolutionary precedent,[74] in 1799 legislation placed issues of liability arising in respect of public works within the jurisdiction of the administrative courts[75] which then found it necessary to develop rules of liability for this area long before the *arrêt Blanco* in 1873.[76] The rules governing liability arising from public works are of considerable importance for liability for products, for they govern many cases involving physical things which cause harm, whether those things are movable or immovable. Moreover, while they are primarily concerned with liability of the administration, this is an area where the Conseil d'Etat has accepted jurisdiction and set the liability of private persons (the *entrepreneur* or 'works contractor') to other private persons harmed

[70] Ass. plén. 29 Mar.1991, *Blieck*, D 1991.324 note Larroumet, JCP 1991.II.21673 concl. Dottenwille, above, p. 26.   [71] Below, p. 151 *et seq.*

[72] See below, p. 122 for discussion of the terminology used.

[73] Chapus, *Droit administratif général*, Tome 2, 545; de Laubadère and Gaudemet, *Droit administratif*, Tome 2, 437. Cf. Vedel and Delvolvé, *Droit administratif*, Tome 1, 171–2 who consider that the development of general administrative law has reduced the real distinctiveness of the law relating to *travaux publics*.

[74] Fairgreave, *State Liability*, 8.

[75] *Loi du 28 pluviose, An VIII*, art. 4; Chapus, *Droit administrative général*, Tome 2, 545. At the time, the 'administrative court' was the Conseil de préfecture. There are exceptions to this jurisdictional position, a particularly important one being where the liability in issue is that of a *service public industriel et commercial* towards its customers: see below, p. 138. Another example may be found in cases where harm is caused by a vehicle in the course of a *travail public*. Here, the Tribunal des conflits has held that since 1957 by *loi* the ordinary courts have possessed an exclusive jurisdiction: TC 11 May 1964, *Guibert*, Leb. 791.

[76] TC 8 Feb. 1873, DP 1873.3.17, above, p. 31.

by their activities.[77] Where this law applies, it excludes reliance on the general law of administrative liability, whether or not based on fault.[78]

Here, I shall explain briefly the notion of public works and the related notion of an *ouvrage public* ('*a* public work'), look at the legal bases of liability and defences and then at the range of defendants affected and at the special rules by which responsibility is distributed among them.

(a) *Travaux publics* and *ouvrage public*

The terminology used here is confusing, for in the expression '*travail public*' *travail* designates either the work in operation (*travail public* in the strict sense) or a 'thing' once it has been constructed or otherwise worked on, though this can also be termed *ouvrage public*.[79] I shall refer generally to the law governing 'public works', keeping *travail public* and *travaux publics* to describe the work in operation and *ouvrage public* to describe its result (though sometimes an *ouvrage public* exists without any *travail public*).[80] So, for example, the work of constructing a motorway is a *travail public*, whereas the motorway once completed is an *ouvrage public*.

A *travail public* possesses two elements: the work must concern immovable property and it must have a public element.

First, there must be work concerning immovable property. While work done on movable property, however large or important (for example, an aircraft carrier) cannot constitute a *travail public*, the Conseil d'Etat has taken a fairly extensive view of the necessary connection to immovable property, borrowing for this purpose its definition in the Civil Code.[81] As a result, *travaux publics* can include the cutting of a lawn in a park as well as the construction of a road or building and covers situations where work is done on *movable* property as long as it is to be incorporated into an immovable (for example, an organ built for installation in a broadcasting studio).[82] The Conseil d'Etat has also taken a broad view of the notion of 'work' for this purpose, which may be of any type, including both 'positive' works of construction or repair and 'negative' works, such as a failure to repair the results of earlier work (such as repair of a public road) or even a failure to do work on immovable property which *should* have been effected.[83] In practice, the operation of public works often involves the use of machinery or tools and in this way the law of *travaux publics* can govern liability for harm caused by *movable* property (and therefore products). For example, where a works contractor digs a hole with a mechanical digger which causes subsidence to nearby houses, their

---

[77] Below, pp. 129–31.

[78] Vedel and Delvolvé, *Droit administratif*, Tome 1, 668 (liability for fault); Chapus, *Droit administratif général*, Tome 2, 652 (where a person 'participates' in a *travail public* he may recover only on the basis of proof of fault and not on the basis of liability without fault for 'dangerous things').

[79] Chapus, *Droit administratif général*, Tome 2, 527.   [80] Below, p. 124.

[81] M. Waline, note to CE 12 Oct 1973, *Commune de Saint-Brévin-les-Pins*, Rev. dr. pub.1974.1137; Art. 517 C. civ. and see J. Carbonnier, *Droit civil, 3—Les biens* (PUF, Paris, 19th. edn., 2000) 90.

[82] CE 10 Feb. 1978, *Société Muller*, Leb. 65. This follows art. 517 C. civ. according to which '*[l]es biens sont immeubles... par leur destination*'.

[83] E.g. CE 18 Dec. 1931, *Robin*, S 1932.3.41 concl. Ettori, note Bonnard (failure to warn of submerged rock in naturally navigable river).

owner can (as a 'third party' to a *travail public*) sue the contractor or the public body for whom the work was done: the work concerns immovable property, even though the thing which caused the harm is a movable.[84]

Secondly, the Conseil d'Etat distinguishes the public element in a *travail public* in one of two ways, as a *travail public* must either (i) be done on behalf of account (*'pour le compte'*) of a *public* body and in the general interest or (ii) while undertaken on behalf of a *private* person, must 'concretize the performance of a *service public* by a public body'.[85] In the first, more common situation, the work must be effected on or result in property belonging to a public body, even though it is actually undertaken by a private contractor,[86] but the 'general interest' requirement is interpreted broadly, it not being necessary that the work is done in the exercise of a *service public*.[87] For example, in *Commune de Monségar*[88] a claim was brought by the parents of a child injured in the course of gymnastic exercises at his local church by the collapse of the marble holy-water basin: here the Conseil d'Etat held that the *commune* which owned the church could be liable on the basis of its failure to maintain the property since public worship was in the general interest even though there was no ecclesiastical *service public*.

However, work done 'on behalf of' a private person may also constitute a *travail public* as long as it puts into effect the provision of a *service public* by a public body. For example, in *Grimouard*,[89] in implementing a reforestation scheme (which was by law a 'public service') the Minister of Agriculture agreed with two landowners for work to be done on their land and engaged a contractor to do it. In the course of the work, a tractor which was used by the contractor backfired, causing a fire which damaged both the landowners' own property and property belonging to their neighbours. Since the work in question was done in furtherance of a 'public service' for the Minister, the Conseil d'Etat held that it constituted a *travail public*, even though at no stage was it intended that a public body would own the immovable property which was the subject of the work. As a result, the neighbouring owners recovered damages against the Minister without needing to prove fault in either the contractor or the administration.[90] Again, the physical cause of the claimants' harm was a product (the tractor), although this fact was not the legal basis for the imposition of liability (as it would be in the private law liability for the 'deeds of things');[91] and while liability was imposed on a public person (the Minister), it resulted from use of product by a private person (the works contractor).

An *ouvrage public* is defined as immovable property which is 'the result of human endeavour' and 'set aside for use in the general interest'.[92] The first aspect of this

[84] See below for further examples. An exception is made where the 'thing' used in the course of public works is a vehicle, for here the ordinary courts have an exclusive jurisdiction: TC 11 May 1964, *Guibert'* Leb. 791 (street-cleaning vehicle spraying and damaging frontage of claimant's shop).

[85] Chapus, *Droit administratif général*, Tome 2, 548.   [86] Ibid., 550–3.

[87] The notion of *service public* ('public service') is a legal and not merely a descriptive category in French administrative law: see above, p. 19; below, pp. 133–4.

[88] CE 10 Jun. 1921, D 1922.3.26, concl. Corneille.   [89] CE 20 Apr. 1956, Leb. 168.

[90] As 'third parties' to the work: see below, p. 128. By contrast, the landowners who had agreed to participate in the scheme were held entitled to recover against the Ministry on the basis of contractual fault.

[91] Above, pp. 51–61.   [92] Chapus, *Droit administratif général*, Tome 2, 557–61.

definition is closely related to the 'immovable' aspect of *travaux publics*,[93] though here the concern is with immovable results rather than work on immovable property. So, the Eiffel Tower, public roads, ports, bridges, sports fields or gardens as well as buildings proper are all included: even a ski-run may be an *ouvrage public* if it possesses constructed elements,[94] although a floating diving-stage at a beach has been held *not* to be an *ouvrage public* since it was not fixed to the ground.[95] The second, 'public' aspect of the definition of an *ouvrage public* differs from that required of a *travail public*, since it must be 'set aside for use in the public interest',[96] though this does not necessarily mean that any member of the public can use it.[97]

Thus, while in the vast majority of cases an *ouvrage public* is the result of a *travail public*, this is not necessarily the case; some immovable property which is set aside for use in the public interest was purchased from private hands ready for use; and work done on an *ouvrage public* is not a *travail public* where it is done by a private person on his *own* account.[98] Conversely, some *travaux publics* do not result in an *ouvrage public*, either because they have no concrete result or because the result is not set aside for use in the public interest.[99]

Finally, the actual running (*'fait d'exploitation'*) of a 'public service' which uses an *ouvrage public* on this ground alone counts as a *travail public*.[100] For example, in *Lemaire* a tugboat owned by the French State collided with a privately owned motorboat while performing a manoeuvre ordered by the Harbour Master of the Port of Rouen with the view to allowing a third vessel to moor.[101] The Conseil d'Etat held that the motorboat's owners were entitled to claim damages in respect of this collision in the administrative courts as it related to the 'functioning of an *ouvrage public*'. In the result, what at first sight appears to be a case of harm caused by a product (the tugboat) was treated as caused by the 'exploitation' of some larger immovable thing (the port). Similarly, in *Del Carlo* the claimant's vehicle was hit on a one-way bridge by an oncoming car whose driver had been instructed by a temporary roadsign to proceed.[102] The Conseil d'Etat held the minister responsible for the roadworks liable for this failure in its normal maintenance of an *ouvrage public* (the road), even though the immediate cause of the claimant's harm was the other (private) vehicle.

(b) The bases of liability for harm caused by 'public works'

Where public works cause harm, most modern authors distinguish according to whether the harm is 'permanent' or 'accidental'.[103] The first need not detain us here as

---

[93] Chapus, *Droit administratif général*, Tome 2, 559.

[94] CE 27 Jun. 1986, *Grospiron*, D 1987. 113 note Excoffier.

[95] CE 12 Oct. 1973, *Commune de Saint-Brévin-les-Pins*, RDP 1974.1137 note Waline.

[96] There is no requirement that the property in question is owned by a public body, though it often is: Chapus, *Droit administratif général*, Tome 2, 564–6.

[97] CE Sect. 30 Sep. 1955, *Caisse rég. de séc. soc. de Nantes*, Leb. 459 (railway turntable belonging to SNCF held to be an *ouvrage public* as set aside for use in the public railway service).

[98] Chapus, *Droit administratif général*, Tome 2, 561–2.

[99] E.g. CE 20 Apr. 1956, *Grimouard*, Leb. 168.

[100] Vedel and Delvolvé, *Droit administratif*, Tome I, 668; de Laubadère and Gaudemet, *Droit administratif*, Tome II, 439.

[101] CE 27 Nov. 1931, DH 1932.88. Cf. CE 25 Apr. 1958, *Barbaza*, Leb. 228.

[102] CE 5 Oct. 1966, Leb. 522.

[103] Chapus, *Droit administratif général*, Tome 2, 650 *et seq.*; Vedel and Delvolvé, *Droit administratif*, Tome 1, 670 *et seq.* Some authors prefer to apply the distinction between 'users' and 'third-parties'

it concerns cases where a person's immovable property has suffered and is likely to continue to suffer harm from the creation, extension or running of an *ouvrage public*.[104] The second category of 'accidental harm' includes all cases of death, personal injury or damage to property which are caused by either *travaux publics* or an *ouvrage public* and these cases sometimes involve liability for products. Their factual variety is considerable and the law involved quite complex, the courts distinguishing in particular according to the 'status' of the claimant in relation to the public works, whether a 'participant', a 'user' or a 'third party'.

Where a person is harmed in the course of executing *travaux publics*, that person (a 'participant') may recover damages from the person responsible only on the basis of proven fault,[105] even where his or her harm is caused by a dangerous thing.[106] In practice, participants are of two types: workers and non-workers. A worker employed on a *travail public* by a works contractor[107] is covered by the standard workers' compensation scheme and is entitled to a fixed-rate compensation from his local *Caisse de sécurité sociale*.[108] In these circumstances, his employer enjoys a wide immunity, but the *Caisse* may recoup the compensation which it pays and the worker may recover any uncompensated losses from any 'third party' who contributed to his injury, including other works contractors or the public authority for whom the work was undertaken subject to a proof of fault.[109] As to non-workers, the works contractors themselves and sometimes even their suppliers are held to 'participate' in public works. For example, in one case, the claimant owned a lorry which was hit while stationary on the hard shoulder of a motorway prior to delivery of materials to be used in surfacing. The Conseil d'Etat held that he was a participant in the motorway *travaux publics* even though he was not involved in the processing or application of the material which he delivered and as a result he had to prove fault in order to recover.[110]

While proof of fault is required in these cases, unlike the general law of liability for *faute de service*, a public body may not reduce its liability for *travaux publics* by pointing to a causally relevant act of a third party (*fait d'un tiers*), whether or not this act is unforeseeable or unpreventable.[111] Thus, for example, if an excavator belonging to one works contractor (a participant) is damaged partly as a result of the fault of another works contractor and partly of the fault of the public authority who commissioned the

---

(see below, pp. 124–9) equally to cases of permanent harm: de Laubadère and Gaudemet, *Droit administratif,* Tome 2, 482–4.

[104] Vedel and Delvolvé, Tome 1, 670; Chapus, *Droit administratif général,* Tome 2, 665. E.g. CE 11 Jul. 1960, *SNCF c. Goncet,* Leb. 476 (houseowner recovered damages for disturbance to his enjoyment of property caused by SNCF's extension of nearby marshalling yards).

[105] Chapus, *Droit administratif général,* Tome 2, 652 *et seq.* Issues relating to harm to participants arise only in relation to their involvement in *travaux publics,* as one cannot participate in a thing (an *ouvrage public*) anymore than one can use work in operation (a *travail public*): C. Lavaille, 'Le dommage causé au participant à l'opération de travail public', AJ 1975.540, 543. On the range of persons responsible, see below, p. 129 *et seq.*

[106] CE 15 Feb. 1963, *Minotto,* Leb. 95 (electricity).

[107] If the worker is an 'agent' of the public service, then if injured he is compensated by way of an invalidity pension, rather than by imposition of liability: see above, p. 117 n. 41.

[108] See above, pp. 61–2.   [109] CE 15 Feb. 1963, *Minotto,* Leb. 95.

[110] CE 24 Apr. 1981, *Soc. des autoroutes du Nord et de l'Est de la France,* Leb. 953.

[111] Chapus, *Droit administratif général,* Tome 1, 1251–2; Tome 2, 677–78.

works (in failing to organise the site properly), the excavator's owner may sue either the works contractor or the public authority and recover in full, leaving it to that person to his own recourse claim. In practice, therefore, where a public authority which commissions work commits a fault which is even partly to blame, it acts as 'guarantor' of any liability engendered by the works contractors.[112]

Those who benefit from an *ouvrage public* by using it (*usagers*[113]) are somewhat better off than participants in *travaux publics* as they can take advantage of a rebuttable presumption of fault which rests on the contractors who have done the work and on the public body for whom it is done.[114] Indeed, a user has only to show a causal relationship between the *ouvrage public* and his own harm, it being for the defendant then to show that it has done all that can normally be expected of it to ensure the 'normal maintenance' of the public work in question or the normal execution of the *travaux publics*[115] and a 'failure in normal maintenance' can consist of an *ouvrage public*'s design as well as its poor execution or repair.[116] Apart from showing that it was not at fault, a defendant may escape or reduce its liability as the case may be if it can show that the claimant's harm was caused by his own contributory fault[117] or by *force majeure* (this notion being here restricted to 'acts of nature'),[118] but again may not reduce its liability by pointing to an act of a third party (*fait d'un tiers*).[119] A few illustrations will make this clearer.

Many cases of a 'failure in normal maintenance' of an *ouvrage public* consist of bad workmanship or use of the wrong materials in construction of a building or other structure or a failure to keep it in proper repair. For example, in *Goutines*, a suspension bridge collapsed in the course of its operational trials owing to the use by its builders of

---

[112] There is an exception for the case where the public body sued possesses *no* recourse as a matter of law against a person jointly responsible for the harm, as here it will be liable only to the extent of its responsibility (e.g. where the public authority has no recourse against a private law employer): Lavaille, *op. cit.* n. 105, 555.

[113] At one time, the Conseil d'Etat held that a person who used an *ouvrage public* without permission or abnormally could not count as a 'user' and therefore should be submitted to the regime of liability of 'third parties' with the paradoxical result that they benefited from a strict liability: Chapus, *Droit administratif général*, Tome 2, 641–2. However, more recently it has held that such a person must prove fault: CE Sect. 20 Jun. 1984, *Motheron*, DA 1984. no. 335 and may recover nothing if the claimant's own fault is held to be the only cause of injury: CE 12 Jun. 1998, *Masse c. EDF*, CJEG 1999. 36 note R. Savigant (young trespasser ignoring clear warning and climbing 2m gate of electricity station and being electrocuted). A 'user' of an *ouvrage public* is to be distinguished from a '*usager d'un service public*' an administrative law relationship to be distinguished from the relationship of private law which a customer of a *service public industriel et commercial* enjoys: see below, pp. 134–6.

[114] O. Renard-Payen, 'Responsabilité du fait des travaux et ouvrages publics, Dommages subis par les usagers', Jur.-Cl. Admin. Fasc. 932 (1994), 3.

[115] Braibant and Stirn, *Droit administratif français*, 336. This is not to suggest that a person may 'use' *travaux publics*, but rather that a user of an *ouvrage public* may impugn the execution of the work done (itself often a *travail public*, see above, p. 124) by the contractor.

[116] Chapus, *Droit administratif général*, Tome 2, 660.

[117] E.g. CE 18 Jan. 1980, *Commune d'Echirolles*, Leb. 35.

[118] CE 8 Nov. 1968, *Connac*, Leb. 566.

[119] E.g. CE Sect. 27 Nov. 1987, *Soc. provençale d'équipement*, Leb. 383 (owner and tenant of premises on an industrial estate commissioned by the local *commune* able to recover damages for the losses which they suffered due to flooding, whether or not that flooding was caused in part by the diversion of local streams to the estate's drains by third parties).

supports and suspension rods which were too weak for the job and by their failure to make proper calculations as to the load.[120] The builders of the bridge were therefore held liable for the consequences of its collapse, but their liability was shared with the public body which commissioned the bridge as it was held not to have exercised proper control over its design and construction.[121] A typical example of an injury caused by the failure to maintain a public building may be seen in a case in which part of the balustrade of the Paris Opera House fell down and injured a person walking underneath: the Conseil d'Etat held the Minister responsible for the upkeep of the building liable for these injuries since he had not shown an absence of fault in allowing the balustrade to decay.[122] In *Gentili*,[123] a pupil at a state school suffered injuries to his hand when the glass in his classroom door broke on being slammed: the Conseil d'Etat held the local authority responsible for the upkeep of the school liable for this 'failure in its normal maintenance' given that the glass in question did not correspond to relevant safety standards and that other accidents of the same type had already occurred, but it reduced the liability by a quarter to take into account the contributory fault of the pupil in the accident. Here, then, liability resulted from the local authority's failure to install appropriate glass.

However, even more prominent are cases concerning injuries and damage caused by the state of public roads and, again, French administrative courts take a wide view of the responsibilities of both works contractors and the administration itself. We therefore find cases included of injuries caused by the ill-repair of a road, but also those caused by the responsible person's failure to deal sufficiently quickly with ice or a flood affecting a road, whether by removing the danger or warning the public about it.[124] Again, the administrative courts have impugned the design as well as the physical maintenance of roads where this has contributed to an accident, as in the case where a road layout and its accompanying signs are confusing.[125]

Finally, where an 'exceptionally dangerous' *ouvrage public* causes harm, liability can be imposed irrespective of any absence of fault on the part of the defendant.[126] The leading example of this approach is *Dalleau*,[127] in which the claimant's car was crushed by a fall of rocks as he drove along a road on the island of Réunion in the Indian Ocean.[128] The Conseil d'Etat found that the road suffered from no defect of design or construction, but its susceptibility to rock falls made it 'exceptionally dangerous' and this justified holding the State liable without fault for the consequences of a fall. However,

---

[120] CE 16 Dec. 1953, Leb. 552.

[121] CE Sect. 27 Nov. 1987, *Soc. provençale d'équipement*, Leb. 383 is another example of liability of a *bureau d'études* for its bad design of an *ouvrage public*.

[122] CE 24 Apr. 1963, *Ablesom*, Leb. 239.   [123] CE 5 Nov. 1980, RDP 1981.1108.

[124] CE 17 Apr. 1991, *Thévenet* & CE 21 Jun. 1991, *Christ.* 1991 RDP 1440 (failure to warn of floods on road); CE 25 Mar. 1988, *Société des autoroutes du sud de la France*, Leb. 1062 (failure to mobilise de-icing machines at night on motorway in time or to warn drivers of the risk). The CE has been less strict as regards trees growing by the highway whose fall occasions an accident, holding that there is no 'failure in normal maintenance' where the tree's rottenness is invisible: CE 8 Nov. 1968, *Connac*, Leb. 566.

[125] CE 21 Jun. 1991, *Ridoin*, 1991. RDP 1439. See also CE 5 Oct. 1966, *Del Carlo*, Leb. 522 (inadequate temporary traffic signals) and CE 18 Jan. 1980, *Commune d'Echirolles*, Leb. 35 (traffic lights gave insufficient time to manoeuvre safely).   [126] Chapus, *Droit administratif général*, Tome 2, 656-7.

[127] CE 6 Jul. 1973, D 1973.740 note Moderne.

[128] *La Réunion* is an overseas *département* of France.

this exception has had a very limited impact,[129] and has not been applied to another case of a mountain road, to a toboggan run in a public park or falling trees by the highway.[130] This suggests that the Conseil d'Etat merely wishes to reserve to itself the possibility of imposing liability without fault where it thinks that the facts demand it, even where they come within a legal category where liability is established on another basis.

Someone who is neither a participant in a *travail public* nor a user of an *ouvrage public* is termed a 'third party' (*un tiers*). A person in this category who suffers harm as a result of either *travaux publics* or an *ouvrage public* benefits from a liability *sans faute* imposed on both public bodies and works contractors involved in the public works, the only defences being *force majeure* or contributory fault of the claimant:[131] and the fact that some other person has also contributed to the claimant's harm is not a ground for reducing the liability of either the works contractor or public body sued, '*fait d'un tiers*' not being a defence.[132] Again, a wide variety of cases comes within this heading, many of which involve harm involving products. A very common type of case may be illustrated by *Commune de Saintes*, where a town engaged a contractor to construct an underground carpark and the work damaged a neighbouring property: the latter's owner recovered damages from the town in respect of this damage without the need to show fault in either the contractor or the town.[133] The decision in *Grau*, however, shows that the connection with a *travail public* may be less direct.[134] Grau was a works contractor engaged to quarry stone by a public body, using explosives to do so. On one occasion, an explosion caused a high-tension electricity cable to fall onto a telephone cable, which then transmitted a surge of current to the earpiece of a telephonist working for PTT, the French public telephone company. The Conseil d'Etat held Grau liable to the telephonist without proof of fault as she was a 'third party' to a *travail public* (the quarrying), but held PTT liable to indemnify Grau as himself a 'third party' to the *telephone equipment* (a distinct *ouvrage public*) for which it was responsible and through which the telephonist had suffered her injuries, though it reduced his indemnity on the ground of his own contributory fault. This decision also illustrates that accidents causing harm to third parties may be causally related to an *ouvrage public* as well as to *travaux publics*.

Finally, it should be recalled that while *travaux publics* need to concern immovable property,[135] they need not result in any work of construction. So, for example, in *Alban* the defendant company had undertaken to spray an insecticide from the air as part of an anti-mosquito programme instituted by *loi*.[136] The claimants, landowners

[129] O. Renard-Payen, 'Responsabilité du fait des travaux et ouvrages public, Dommages subis par les usagers', Jur.-Cl. Adm. Fasc 932 (1994) 3.

[130] CE Sect. 5 Jun. 1992, *Epoux Cala*, Leb. 224; CE 20 Apr. 1966, *Rivière*, Leb. 276; CE 8 Nov. 1968, *Connac*, Leb. 566 respectively.   [131] CE 10 Feb. 1961, *Ville de Béziers*, Leb. 113.

[132] CE 7 Nov. 1952, *Grau*, JCP 1953.II.7448 note PL.

[133] CE 15 Oct. 1986, *Commune des Saintes*, D 1987 Somm. 283 obs. Terneyre. See also CE 22 Oct. 1971, *Ville de Fréjus*, Leb 630 (claimants' properties damaged when a dam burst); CE. 13 Jul. 1965, Leb. 442, *Arbez-Gindre*, D 1966.88 concl. Braibant (fire in school belonging to *commune* spread to neighbours' properties). For more examples, see below, p. 138 concerning the liability of *services publics industriels et commerciaux* for harm caused by water, gas or electricity to non-customers.

[134] CE Sect. 7 Nov. 1952, Leb. 503, JCP 1953.II.7448 note PL.   [135] Above, p. 122.

[136] TC 4 Feb. 1974, DS 1975.214 note Despax.

whose crops had suffered owing to the nature of the product sprayed, recovered damages as 'third parties' to the spraying which was categorised by the *loi* as a *travail public*. Again, we see liability for damage caused by a product (the insecticide spray) subsumed under the category of liability for public works.

(c) The defendants and their recourse

As has been seen, 'administrative' liability for public works may be imposed not merely on the public body responsible but also on those private persons who were or are involved in them, but does an injured person have a choice whom to sue? And what recourses for defendants are provided?

There are two basic rules as to whom a claimant may sue. First, a person harmed by a *travail public* may sue either any one of the works contractors involved in the project or the public body for whom the work is done or both jointly (*'solidairement'*),[137] subject to establishing the conditions of liability applicable to his status as 'participant', 'user' or 'third party'. In this respect, 'works contractor' includes all those physically involved in the work (whether directly or as sub-contractors[138]) and all those whose advice or other intellectual input has contributed to the work (such as architects or other specialist advisers)[139] and their liability is not extinguished on completion of the work.[140] So, for example, a 'participant' injured in the course of a building project partly owing to the fault of the architect and partly of one of the builders may opt to sue either, being able to recover in full from the person actually sued. Secondly, a claimant who suffers accidental harm caused by an *ouvrage public* can sue either the person who commissioned it (its *maître d'ouvrage*) or the person who bore the responsibility for maintaining it.[141]

In all, therefore, the combination of the range of persons both private and public potentially liable for public works and their inability to excuse themselves by pointing to someone else more directly responsible (there being no defence of *fait d'un tiers*[142]) has led to a remarkably generous system of compensation from a claimant's point of view. However, the widely applicable joint liability of those involved in *travaux publics* gives rise to complex issues as to their means of recourse for contribution between each other. The procedural expression of such a recourse may either be an *appel en garantie* (where a defendant brings the other person allegedly responsible into the proceedings brought against him) or an *action récursoire* (where a person already held liable in full brings independent proceedings for recovery of contribution or an

---

[137] CE 4 Mar. 1955, *Ville d'Orléans* Leb. 140 and see Chapus, *Droit administratif général,* Tome 2, 673 *et seq.* There is an exception where a public body concedes by *contrat de concession* a *travail public* to a private person, as here anyone harmed by the work can sue either the works contractors or the 'concessionary' who (if solvent) is substituted to the public body itself: CE 10 Feb. 1961, *Ville de Béziers,* Leb. 113.

[138] CE 13 Nov. 1987, *Dame Cabrera,* DA 1987 no. 679.

[139] Chapus, *Droit administratif général,* Tome 2, 674–5.

[140] CE 27 Nov. 1987, *Soc. provençale d'équipement,* Leb. 383.

[141] De Laubadère and Gaudemet, *Droit administratif,* Tome 2, 456. On the complex issues which arise concerning which public body bears this responsibility, see O. Renard-Payen, 'Responsabilité du fait des travaux et ouvrages publics, Mise en œuvre de la responsabilité', Jur.-Cl. Adm. Fasc. 930 (1994), 3 *et seq.*

[142] Above, pp. 126, 128.

indemnity).[143] In either case, a distinction is drawn according to whether the person seeking recourse is a public body or a works contractor.[144]

A public body which has paid compensation to someone harmed by public works may sue any of the works contractors which it has employed for a full indemnity under an indemnity clause ('*clause de garantie*') in any contract between them, for contribution on breach of any contractual obligation by a works contractor, or on the basis of any extra-contractual fault committed in the course of the work.[145] Where the works contractor's action was the sole cause of the harm for which the public body has been held responsible, the latter can recover a complete indemnity from that contractor even in the absence of any breach of contract or extra-contractual fault on its part.[146] On the other hand, where a person *other than* a works contractor has contributed to the harm for which a public body has been held fully liable to a claimant under the law of *travaux publics*, that public body is subrogated to any rights which that claimant possessed against that other person, and so can claim contribution in the administrative courts if that other person is a public body or otherwise subject to the administrative jurisdiction,[147] but in the ordinary courts where he is not. For example, in *Del Carlo* the claimant was a private individual whose vehicle was damaged when another vehicle driven by another private individual, L, was directed to cross a one-way bridge at the wrong time. The Conseil d'Etat held the State liable in full to the claimant for his damage even though this was partly caused by L' s negligence, but observed that the State would be subrogated to the claimant's rights against L.[148] Such a claim would be governed by private law and be a matter for the jurisdiction of the ordinary courts.

A works contractor held liable in full for harm caused by a *travail public* has a similar system of possible recourse against others responsible for it. Such a recourse for contribution would lie in the administrative courts against the public body responsible, either under the terms of the contract under which the contractor works (though not after final completion of the work)[149] or in respect of any fault either in its design or its supervision committed by the public body which commissioned work.[150] On the other hand, the proper jurisdiction for a recourse claim by one works contractor against another is more complex. Where the claim is based on a contract between them the proper jurisdiction depends on the question on whose account the defendant contractor acted: if for a public authority, the claim lies in the administrative courts,[151] but if on its own account, then before the ordinary jurisdiction and under

---

[143] A broader term for the latter can be *recours en garantie* and this enables *actions récursoires* to be used to describe 'independent claims' as distinct from subrogated claims (*actions subrogatoires*).

[144] Chapus, *Droit administratif général*, Tome 2, 679 *et seq.*

[145] CE 4 Mar. 1955, *Ville d'Orléans*, Leb. 140; Chapus, *Droit administratif général*, Tome 2, 697 *et seq.* A public authority cannot claim an indemnity by way of subrogation to the rights of a works contractor where the latter acts on behalf of another public body: CE 27 Nov. 1987, *Soc. provençale d'équipement*, Leb. 383.

[146] CE 5 Feb. 1988, *Epoux Le Baot*, Leb 51.   [147] CE 9 Dec. 1964, *GDF c. Flecq*, Leb. 632.

[148] CE 5 Oct. 1966, *Del Carlo*, Leb. 522.

[149] CE 27 Nov. 1987, *Soc. provençale d'équipement*, Leb. 383.

[150] CE 6 Jan. 1971, *Soc. Enterprise Cracco*, Leb. 1126, 1232. There is an exception in the case of a works contractor of one *travail public* suing a public body responsible for a distinct *ouvrage public*, on which see CE 7 Nov. 1952, *Grau*, JCP 1953.II.7448, above, p. 128.

[151] CE 27 Nov. 1987, *Soc. provençale d'équipement*, *cit.* and see the discussion in Chapus, *Droit administratif général*, Tome 2, 680–1.

the rules of private law.[152] Where the claim is extra-contractual, for example, by one works contractor employed by a public body and held liable entirely for harm caused jointly with another works contractor with whom it is not contractually bound, then it comes within the jurisdiction of the administrative courts if the litigation 'arises from the performance of a public works contract' and opposes 'participants in the performance of public works'.[153]

In all, the law governing public works shows the workings of the substantive and jurisdictional divide between French public and private law at its most complex. Public law governs the parties' relations not simply because one or more of them are public bodies (for sometimes the law of public works applies to the relations between private persons), nor because the activity in question is peculiarly public, such as the enactment of legislation or the making of a decision affecting an individual's rights, for constructing a building or making a road is not inherently public in this way. Instead, the 'public element' is defined more subtly by the definitions of *travail public* or *ouvrage public* which relate the work either to a public body or to a *service public*.[154]

While the significance of this body of law for liability for products is considerable, it is not at all obvious. For liability is overtly connected to *immovable* property, but in practice may be imposed for products, either when they are to be incorporated or have been incorporated into a building or (and more frequently) where they are used in the operation of public works. However, in striking contrast to private law liability for the 'deeds of things', the basis of liability for 'public works' ranges overtly from liability for fault to liability without fault and the range of defendants is considerable (rather than placing liability on the thing's *gardien*). This means that this impact of this special body of law in attracting claims for compensation for damage caused by an allegedly defective product depends very much on the particular circumstances in which the product was used.

[152] TC 20 Jan. 1986, *Soc. Bouillet Ingénierie*, D. adm. 1986 no. 159.

[153] CE 24 Nov. 1997, *Soc. de Castro c. Bourcy et Sole*, Leb. 540 (claim by works contractor against architect) and see Chapus, *Droit administratif général*, Tome 2, 601–02. [154] Above, pp. 123–4.

7

Public Services, *Service Public* and Liability for Products

In this chapter, I shall explore further the involvement of public elements in French law's approach to liability for products. My starting point is the idea of the provision of a public service, a notion which I have chosen for its openness and general lack of technicality in the English context and its elusiveness and technical importance in the French. As will be seen, French law's approach to the regulation of the provision of public services in a very general sense gives rise to a kaleidoscope of liabilities: some general and some special; some private and some public; some the work of the courts and some of national legislation or international convention. Furthermore, while in some of these situations the involvement of a product (or even a 'thing') is not formally the basis of liability, in others it is of central importance.

What then may be the significance of the notion of 'public service'? In a first sense, calling a service 'public' may refer to its free availability to the public generally or to any member of the public, rather than being restricted to certain persons or by way of special arrangement. So, a passenger bus service or an amusement park may be 'public' in this sense, whether it is owned or operated by a public or a private body: the service is public in terms of its accessibility.

Secondly, a 'public service' may refer to its ownership or operation by a public body, whatever its accessibility or its subject matter. So while many public services in this sense are generally available, some may not be, for example, a particular educational service may be restricted to children with special needs. Here, the service is public in a proprietary or managerial sense. Where such a service is provided directly by a public body (in a technical public law sense, such as a French *établissement public* or an English local authority), rather than through a private law intermediary, the service may also be seen to be public in an institutional sense. On the other hand, some services may be operated by a body whose institutional nature is private, but which is owned (wholly or in part) by a public body, as in the case of an English company incorporated under the Companies Act a majority of whose shares are owned by the Crown.

Thirdly, whether or not a service is provided by a public body, directly or indirectly, a service may be public in the sense that at least certain aspects of its provision are considered sufficiently important to be regulated in the public interest. This is partly a matter of degree. In one sense, in western legal systems *all* services offered by one person to another are 'public' in the sense that they are subject to a minimum of regulation by the law, notably the general law of contract and the criminal law (for example, concerning fraud). Moreover, like other laws, French law goes very much further, regulating the effects of contracts in an elaborate way, even while still treating this as *private* law.[1] In this regulation, the legislature or courts may at times seek to give effect to the typical expectations of the parties, but even more they give effect to their view of the proper balance of the rights and obligations of the parties taking account of the wider interests of society.

However, in French law the public interest has played a more overt role, for its administrative law has identified a distinct category of 'public services' (*services publics*[2]), a notion whose significance dominated much of the theory of administrative law for the first half of the twentieth century. Classically *un service public* is defined as 'any activity of a public body whose purpose is to satisfy a need in the general interest'.[3] This combines two elements: the first is institutional (the service must count as an activity of a public *body*); the second is 'functional' (the service must satisfy a need in the general interest). In the course of the twentieth century, the necessary connection between a public body and the activity to qualify as a *service public* became less and less direct, so that, notably, a public body did not itself need to provide the service, which could be 'delegated' to a private body.[4] As a result, in the modern law the public nature of a *service public* rests ultimately on its function, that is, whether the service is aimed at satisfying a need in the general interest.[5]

While the main use of the notion of *service public* has been as a criterion to distinguish between activities within the jurisdiction of the Conseil d'Etat and those within the jurisdiction of the ordinary courts,[6] it has also attracted a set of legal principles regulating these services partly in the interest of their citizen recipients and partly in the interest of society more generally, known as the *lois de Rolland*.[7] On the other hand, the institutional characteristics of the bodies which provide a *service public* follow their legal form, whether public (such as an *établissement public*) or private (such as a *société anonyme*).[8] And the mere fact that a service is 'public' for this purpose does not mean that the relationship between its provider and its '*recipient*' belongs to public law: it *may* do so, but it may instead belong to private law. The rules governing

---

[1] Above, pp. 22–3.

[2] I shall restrict *services publics* to this special French usage, using the English 'public services' in one of the other meanings which I have identified.

[3] Gaudemet, *Droit administratif,* Tome 1, 34 *et seq.* See also Chapus, *Droit administratif général,* Tome 1, 578 *et seq.*   [4] Brown and Bell, 131–4.

[5] This means both that some services provided by private bodies may count as *services publics* and that certain services provided by public bodies may not count as *services publics*. Examples of the latter may be found in the management of public property known as the *domaine privé* (Chapus, *Droit administratif général,* Tome 1, 585–6) and the activities of *entreprises publiques,* such as Regie Renault.

[6] For criticism of this role: Rivero and Waline, *Droit administratif,* 164–9.

[7] Named after Louis Rolland, these are a principle of continuity of the *service public,* its 'mutability' in the public interest and equality in its application to citizens: Moreau, *Droit administratif,* 333 *et seq.*; Chapus, *Droit administratif général,* Tome 1, 603 *et seq.*

[8] See the discussion in Chapus, *Droit administratif général,* Tome 1, 167 *et seq.* who also draws attention to the special privileges accorded to public bodies against the normal methods of the execution of judgments (*voies d'exécution*), the special prescription period for their debts (*la prescription quadriennale*) and the impossibility of recourse to arbitration.

the provision of *services publics* may therefore possess aspects of public law and private law.

In this chapter, I shall look at the way in which French law treats the imposition of liability incurred in the provision of public services in *all* the different senses which I have identified, for only in this way can a sense be gained of the variety of regulatory treatments to which they are subject. I shall start by explaining how French law distinguishes between different categories of *services publics*, how this affects the legal position of their recipients and how this in turn affects the substantive law governing liability in respect of the provision of the public service and its impact on liability for products. Then I shall examine three major examples of public services which have cut across the public and private law divide in French law: the supply of public utilities, transport and health care.

1. The Key Distinction: 'Users of a *Service Public*' and 'Contractual Customers'

As I have said, where a service represents the activity of a public body and 'satisfies a need in the general interest' and therefore qualifies as a *service public*, at least some of its aspects are governed by public law.[9] In this way, French law can apply to public services its administrative law's combination of 'extraordinary powers' in the administration and 'extraordinary controls' on their exercise,[10] and yet can allow them to operate in a recognisably private, even 'market' setting.

How does a *service public* straddle the two realms (and legal regimes) in this way? French lawyers approach this problem by drawing a key distinction within the category of *services publics* between *services public administratifs* and *services publics industriels ou commerciaux*. Historically, the category of *services publics administratifs* grew out of the traditional *services publics* of the State and of local authorities, such as the army, the police and the diplomatic service ('*services régaliens*'), though in the modern law it is not restricted to these examples.[11] By contrast, the category of *services publics industriels ou commerciaux* was created later to describe those *services publics* which have much in common with services provided by commercial operators (*entreprises privées*). Where legislation does not otherwise provide, the Conseil d'Etat distinguishes between the two types of *services public* taking into account three factors:[12] the subject matter of the service, so where a body's activities are similar to those of private traders it is more likely to perform a *service public industriel ou commercial*;[13] the way in which it is financed, notably, whether from taxation or grant as opposed to payment by the

---

[9] Above, p. 133.   [10] Above, p. 30.

[11] A *service public administratif* need not even be provided by a public body (*établissement public*), e.g. the activities of *ordres professionnelles*: Chapus, *Droit administratif général*, Tome 1, 537–40.

[12] Chapus, ibid., 591 *et seq.*

[13] E.g. the leading case of TC 22 Jan. 1921, '*Bac d'Eloka*', Leb. 91, D 1921.3.1 concl. Matter; Cf. CE Sec. 10 May 1974, *Denoyez et Chorques*, Leb. 274 (both ferry services).

recipient of the service;[14] and the 'modalities of its functioning', so that a free service is unlikely to be 'industrial or commercial' and one which enjoys a legal monopoly is likely to be 'administrative'.[15] Some jurists consider the Conseil d'Etat's decision making on this borderline to be rather *ad hoc*.[16]

What is the effect of classifying a *service public* as 'administrative' or 'industrial or commercial' on any liability in the provider of the service to those harmed in the course of its provision?

First, in the case of *services publics administratifs*, public law dominates the legal relations with persons with whom their provider comes into contact. So, where a person is the direct beneficiary or 'recipient' of a *service public administratif*, then he is in a 'legal and regulatory situation of public law' with the provider of the service and designated its 'user' (*usager*).[17] Typically, such a relationship is non-contractual,[18] and this means that any liability in the provider of the service either to the recipients *or* to third parties is extra-contractual as well as belonging to public law. So, for example, the Conseil d'Etat has held that the relationship between visitors to a public museum or the users of French *autoroutes* or toll bridges are 'users' rather than parties to a contract, even if they pay for access.[19] The relationship between public hospitals and their patients forms a key example of this situation, though its significance for liability appears to have disappeared.[20]

However, there are important exceptions to this general picture and for our purposes two are significant. First, the fact that a particular *service public* is 'administrative' does not prevent it being *operated* by a private body, for the *service public* may be 'delegated' (for example, to a private law company, whether or not its shares are owned by the State) or may be the object of a contract, typically a contract of concession.[21] Where this is the case, the *service public* does not cease to be 'administrative' in its character, but, at least for some jurists, the relations between its provider and its recipient are in principle governed by the private law of contract.[22] The second exception arises in relation to '*Logements HLM*' ('*Habitations à loyer modéré*' or housing with reduced rents). This residential accommodation is constructed, bought or improved with the aid of State finance and is owned by designated organisations (either *Offices publics d'HLM* or *sociétés anonymes*). However, even though by law this provision is a *service*

---

[14] E.g. CE Ass. 16 Nov. 1956, *Union syndicale des industries aéronautiques*, Leb. 434, D 1956.759 concl. Laurent.   [15] TC 22 Feb. 1960, *Soc. Pétronaphte*, Leb. 857.

[16] Gaudemet, *Droit administratif,* Tome 1, 756 ('*assez empirique*').

[17] If the citizen is not yet a recipient of the service but wishes to be, he is termed a *candidat*. Notice that *usager* here is used in a different sense from *usager* in the context of liability for 'public works': cf. above, pp. 126–8.

[18] Cf. the former exception as regards PTT, the French telephone corporation which was classed as a *service public administratif* but whose customers received the service under contracts 'with regulatory effects': CE Sect. 29 Jun. 1979, *Mme Bourgeois*, Leb. 293. This was changed by the *loi* no. 90-568 of 2 Jul. 1990 arts. 25, 26 which placed the relationship between the 'public operators' of the telephone service in the private law domain.   [19] TC 28 Jun. 1965, *Ruban c. Société de l'Autoroute Estérel-Côte d'Azur*, Leb. 816.

[20] Below, p. 151 *et seq.*   [21] Chapus, *Droit administratif général*, Tome I, 554.

[22] Moreau, *Droit administratif,* 343 and see CE 2 Oct. 1985, *Jeissou*, Leb. Tab. 544, AJDA 1986.1.38 concl. Jeanneney. Where a private body provides a *service public administratif* and this takes the form of decisions (*actes*), these will be subject to control by the administrative courts under the law of *excès de pouvoir*: see, e.g., as regards the bodies regulating French professions (*ordres professionnels*): Rivero and Waline, *Droit administratif,* 442.

public administratif and even if the property is owned by a public body (belonging to the *domaine privé*) and is classed as an *ouvrage public*,[23] the relations between these 'public sector' landlords and their tenants is governed by the private law of contract and the ordinary courts.[24] This means, inter alia, that any claim for compensation by a French 'public sector' tenant under the *HLM* scheme in respect of the safety or quality of the residential provision is governed by the provisions of the Civil Code which I have already described.[25] At least as to the landlord's liability, the presence of the *service public administratif* is irrelevant.

Secondly, where a *service public* is classed as 'industrial or commercial', then its relations with the recipients of the service (their 'customers') belong en bloc to private law and the jurisdiction of the ordinary courts and typically take the form of contracts,[26] though this does not prevent the terms and sometimes even the tariffs of these contracts being set by administrative regulation or even the inclusion of a *clause exorbitante de droit commun*.[27] On the other hand, while in general the liability of a *service public industriel ou commercial* to *non-customers* is also governed by private law and subject to the ordinary courts,[28] where 'public works' are involved in the circumstances which give rise to liability, this regime of administrative liability instead applies.[29] Both these may be found in the context of *services publics industriels ou commerciaux* (for example in the supply of public utilities or public railway services) and this means that the provider of such a *service public* may be liable in private law to its customers, but under the administrative law of 'public works' to non-customers.[30]

2. Liability in Respect of the Supply of Public Utilities

The supply of piped water and gas and networked electricity in France constitutes *services publics* but their combinations of public and commercial elements are reflected in the complex of rules by which they are governed. In terms of their institutional status, gas and electricity have long been supplied by Gaz de France (GDF) and Electricité de France (EDF), both of which are public bodies (*établissements publics*) and enjoyed legal monopolies in respect of the supply, though this is changing as the French gas and electricity markets are liberalised in accordance with EC directives.[31] By contrast,

[23] CE Sect. 10 Mar. 1978, *Office public d'HLM de Nancy*, Leb. 121. For *ouvrage public* more generally, see above, pp. 123–4.   [24] TC 22 Apr. 1985, *Maret*, D. adm. 1985 no. 282.
[25] Above, pp. 118–21.
[26] CE 25 Apr. 1958, *Barbaza*, Leb. 228; CE 22 Jan. 1960, *Gladieu*, Leb. 52; TC 17 Oct. 1966, *Veuve Canasse*, Leb. 834. There are exceptions, e.g., a person who travels by train without a ticket belongs to private law even though there is no contract: TC 5 Dec. 1983, *Niddam*, Leb. 541.
[27] Rivero and Waline, *Droit administratif*, 446.
[28] TC 11 Jul. 1933, *Dame Mélinette*, Leb. 1237.
[29] Further exceptions exist in the case of harm caused by 'decisions organising the service' ('*actes d'organisation du service*') and where a body exercises distinctly public powers ('*prérogatives de puissance publique*'): Chapus, *Droit administratif général*, Tome 1, 840.   [30] Below, pp. 137–9, 140–1.
[31] In the case of gas, the change was made by *loi* no. 2003–8 of 3 Jan. 2003 *relative aux marchés du gaz et de l'électricité et au service public de l'énergie*, implementing Dir. 98/30/EC of 22 Jun. 1998 concerning common rules for the internal market of natural gas. In doing so, the French legislature specifically applied a reinforced set of *obligations de services publics* on all those operating in the French market: by *loi* no. 2003-8, art. 16.

piped water is supplied either directly by local authorities (*en régie*) or by private companies (*sociétés de capitaux privés*),[32] typically under contracts of concession with central or local government.[33] Thus, both public and private bodies perform a *service public* of the supply of products, a service which is considered as 'industrial or commercial' rather than 'administrative' in character.

Following the general position, French courts accept that those who receive gas, water and electricity do so under contracts, despite the existence of a duty of supply in their provider (as with EDF and GDF), the setting of many of their terms by decree, and the possibility of unilateral variation of the terms of the supply by their supplier.[34] For the supplier's obligation to be contractual it is 'enough in fact that the obligation to do the thing in question arises from the agreement on a particular purpose, even if the exact determination of the latter is the work of a third party, and even if one of the parties is forbidden by reason of its monopolistic position from refusing its consent'.[35] While for the most part the courts have not felt the need to classify these contracts and have simply described their obligations, sometimes they have been treated as contracts of sale.[36] This has left the courts more free to work out the consequences of the suppliers' obligations.

First, EDF and GDF owe their customers an *obligation de résultat* as to the maintenance of the supply of the electricity or gas and are therefore liable for any failure in supply in the absence of *force majeure* or contributory fault in the customer. Thus, in one case, an action for damages was organised by an association of some 4,500 commercial companies against EDF in respect of losses caused by a power cut resulting from a strike by its employees.[37] The Cour d'appel de Paris held EDF bound to an *obligation de résultat* in respect of the supply of electricity to its customers, though it found *force majeure* in the intervention of the government's role in relation to the causes of the strike.[38]

Secondly, the courts have imposed liability on these public suppliers in respect of the quality or safety of the products which they supply. For example, in one case a manufacturer of edible ice sued the *Lyonnaise des Eaux* alleging that its water contained ferrous elements which gave the ice a reddish colour, apparently caused by rust in the company's old pipes.[39] Despite the somewhat special use to which the claimant put the water, the Cour de cassation agreed that 'a customer... has the right to demand that water supplied by the public service is not only drinkable but also suitable for the various uses... to which it is usually employed', an analysis similar to the obligation of conformity of the property in the contract of sale.[40]

---

[32] Traditionally, the most important companies have been *Cie générale des eaux* (which as 'Vivendi Water' forms part of the Vivendi Universal group) and *La Lyonnaise des Eaux.*

[33] Chapus, *Droit administratif général,* Tome 1, 641–2 who notes that sometimes the distribution of water is placed by a local authority in the hands of a private company by *affermage.*

[34] Such a unilateral right of variation stems from the principle of the 'adaptation' or 'mutability' of the public service: Gaudemet, *Droit administratif,* 749–50.

[35] J.-P. Gridel, note to Angers 11 Mar. 1986, JCP 1987.II.20789.

[36] E.g. Civ. (1) 26 May 1994, Bull. civ. I no. 190.

[37] Paris 4 Jun. 1980, JCP 1980.II.19411 concl. Bernard.

[38] Cf. Anger 11 Mar. 1986, JCP 1987.II.20789 obs. Gridel.

[39] Civ. (1) 26 Oct. 1964, Bull. civ. I no. 468.   [40] Above, p. 71.

Thirdly, the courts have held EDF, GDF and the water companies to an *obligation de sécurité de résultat* in respect of the safety of the installations (equipment, branch circuits, etc.) necessary to supply their products. For example, in one case, the claimant's building was seriously damaged by a fire caused by a short circuit in an electrical circuit which had been left under tension.[41] Where water or gas escape owing to deficiencies in the installations or apparatus by which the product is supplied, the courts distinguish between cases involving the 'particular branch' of a customer, where private law applies, and those involving the main pipes or electricity network where the fact that the harm is suffered by a customer is considered irrelevant and where administrative law applies.[42]

Fourthly, French law has subjected claims by non-customers (*tiers*[43]) for harm caused by the activities or products of these service providers to the jurisdiction of the ordinary courts and to the rules of private law, with the exception of cases involving 'public works'.[44] Here the courts have taken a broad view of the ambit of this exception. So, for example, in one case a driver was killed when he lost control of his car on the failure of the lighting of the public road; his widow and child claimed damages in the ordinary courts against EDF as *gardien* of the electrical current, but the Cour de cassation denied jurisdiction holding that 'public lighting constituted a fitting of the public highway' (an *ouvrage public*) so that their claim should have been brought in the administrative courts.[45] If it had been, the law of 'public works' would have seen the driver as a 'user' of the public road with the result that he (and those claiming through him) would benefit from a presumption of fault in the public authority or 'works contractor' responsible for the lighting.[46] On the other hand, where a 'third party' to an *ouvrage public* used by EDF to supply electricity was electrocuted owing to the modification of the voltage, his widow could claim damages on the basis of a stricter liability without fault.[47]

Overall, therefore, this discussion shows that the similarity of activity of 'industrial or commercial' *services publics* to ordinary commercial suppliers has generally led to the application of a similar regime of liability, but where a claimant is not a customer and yet suffers harm (typically, therefore, for a reason other than the *quality* of the product), liability is usually imposed on the basis of the special regime of administrative liability for 'public works'. Given that many (though not all) 'non-customers' for these purposes will also count as 'third parties' under the law of 'public works', the result is that EDF or GDF is liable to them without proof of fault or defect in either the thing supplied (water, electricity or gas) or in the *ouvrage public* with which it is associated.[48] To this extent, therefore, liability is very strict, whether it is

---

[41] Civ. (1) 9 Dec. 1986, JCP 1987.II.20790 obs. Gridel.

[42] Chapus, *Droit administratif général*, Tome 2, 649; CE 13 Mar. 1959 Leb. 182; CE 22 Jan. 1960, *Gladieu*, Leb. 52.

[43] So, for example, a workman brought in by a customer to repair an electrical installation (CE 14 Jun. 1961, *Dame Bayer*, Leb. 406) counts as a 'third party' as much as a mere passer-by injured when an escape of gas explodes (CE 22 Jan. 1960, *Gladieu*, Leb. 52).

[44] CE 14 Jun. 1961, *Dame Bayer*, Leb. 406. On 'public works', see above, p. 121 *et seq.*

[45] Civ.(1) 17 Nov. 1987 (unreported) pourvoi no. 86-12926 (legifrance).

[46] Above, p. 126–8.   [47] CE 14 Jun. 1961, Leb. 406.   [48] Above, p. 128.

classified as private and contractual (as in the case of customers) or administrative and non-contractual (as in the case of non-customers).

Finally, this area illustrates that the designation of a situation as sufficiently public to attract the application of administrative law is not an all or nothing decision: instead, French law possesses different layers of 'publicness', each of which possess their own criteria and entail their own consequences. So, a service offered to the public may count as a *service public,* where the 'public' aspect is defined principally in functional terms and attracts a set of specifically public principles as to their provision;[49] a *service public* may then be classed as 'administrative' or 'industrial or commercial', where this further 'public' aspect of the service's operation is decided according to a further set of factors and has important effects on the legal relations between its provider and its recipients;[50] and the activities of a *service public* may involve 'public works', with again a different understanding of what the 'public' element requires and a set of legal consequences, including as to the basis of liability.[51] And at each stage of the layering, the resulting classifications affect the regime of liability, but in the context of the supply of public utilities they very much favour the imposition of liability without either defect in the product supplied or fault in the supplier.

3. Public Transport

In the case of public transport (in the sense of transport available to the public generally), the provider of the service does not supply any product to any member of the public,[52] but does use products in the provision of the service, notably, the vehicle of transport itself. In France, there has long been considerable public involvement in the provision of transport services in a proprietary or institutional sense, this being true of rail, air and road transport, the nature of this involvement changing so as to reflect more general shifts in public 'ownership'.[53] Quite apart from this kind of public involvement, where transport is made available to the public in general, the carrier is often held to operate a *service public,* usually 'industrial or commercial', but sometimes 'administrative'.[54] This means that in principle the general, private law of contract still governs the relations between carriers and their passengers, though it has been supplanted as regards carriage by air and by sea by special regimes of liability,[55] and in the case of carriage by motor vehicle, legislation governing road accidents has transformed it.[56] While these special regimes differ considerably from the norm (sometimes to the advantage and sometimes the disadvantage of a claimant passenger) I shall restrict my discussion to the 'general position', and focus on travel by rail.[57]

---

[49] Above, p. 133.   [50] Above, pp. 134–6.   [51] Above, p. 121 *et seq.*
[52] But cf. below, pp. 523–7, esp. at p. 524.   [53] Below pp. 140–1 (rail).
[54] Above, n. 13 (ferry services).
[55] As regards air transport, liability is governed by international convention and in particular the Warsaw Convention of 12 October 1929, whose system was applied to internal carriage by air by the *loi* of 2 Mar. 1957. As regards carriage by sea, French law has taken its own position principally by the *loi* no. 66-420 of 18 Jun. 1966.   [56] Above, pp. 60–1.
[57] Below, pp. 140–1.

The Civil Code provides that a carrier of goods is liable for their loss or damage, unless this is caused by *force majeure*[58] or a defect in the goods themselves,[59] a liability which may be limited by agreement, but not excluded.[60] While the Code makes no special provision for the carriage of passengers, in 1911 the Cour de cassation held that a carrier must carry passengers 'safe and sound' to their destination,[61] thereby recognising what was later known as an *obligation de sécurité de résultat*.[62] This means that a person injured in the course of carriage can recover damages against the carrier, unless the latter proves the injured person's contributory fault or *force majeure*:[63] there is no need to show either fault in the carrier or its employees or that the vehicle or any other 'thing' used was defective. French courts have extended the protection of this very strict contractual liability to the legal dependents of passengers killed in the course of carriage by fictitious *stipulation pour autrui*.[64]

Most modern examples of *obligations de sécurité* in carriage are found in the context of rail travel, where there is an elaborate case law defining when the obligation starts and finishes[65] and what constitutes *force majeure* in the context.[66] There is, though, here something of a paradox. For while *obligations de sécurité* appear as a classic example of the inventiveness of French private lawyers, since its inception in the mid-nineteenth century French rail transport has constituted a *service public*[67] and since 1937 French railways have been nationalised as the *Société nationale des chemins de fer français* (SNCF).[68] Despite these public features, the relationship between travellers and SNCF has been consistently held to belong to private law and the jurisdiction of the ordinary courts, following the classic pattern of 'industrial and commercial' *services publics*. On the other hand, the public underpinning of SNCF has clearly influenced the very strict attitude of the courts to contractual liability in railway

---

[58] Art. 1784 C. civ.   [59] Art. 103 C. com., Com. 25 Jan. 1954, GP 1954.1.423.

[60] Art. 103 al. 3 C. com.

[61] Civ. 21 Nov. 1911, S 1912.1.73 note Lyon-Caen, D 1913.1.249 note Sarrut.

[62] Above, p. 28.

[63] Civ. (1) 27 Apr. 1976, JCP 1976.II.18477 note Rodière, RTDCiv. 1977.138 obs. Durry.

[64] Civ. 6 Dec.1932 & Civ. 24 May 1933, S 1934.1.81 note Esmein. The dependent may renounce the benefit of this stipulation and sue instead in delict: Com. 19 Jun. 1951, *affaire Lamoricière*, S 1952.1.89 note Nerson (claimants avoiding an exemption clause in the contract of carriage).

[65] So accidents on station platforms do not concern the performance of the contract of carriage and therefore give rise only to liability in delict: Civ. (1) 7 Mar. 1989, D 1991.1 note Malaurie, RTDCiv. 1989.548 obs. Jourdain (art. 1384 al. 1 C. civ. applicable as *gardien* of the train).

[66] The general law also applies to carriage in trams and by horse, both of which fall outside the categories of special regulation. Sometimes French administrative law has governed the liability of the provider of a public water transport service as in the famous case TC 22 Jan. 1921, *Bac d'Eloka*, Leb. 91, D 1921.3.1 concl. matter; cf. CE 26 Jul. 1930, *Benoit*, 840.

[67] The first French railways were built and operated by private companies under 'concessions' granted by the State, which exercised control on the fares on the basis that the services constituted *services publics*: Chapus, *Droit administratif général*, Tome 1, 173; *loi* of 11 Jun. 1842; SNCF 'Naissance des chemins de fer en France', <http://www.sncf.com>.

[68] On nationalisation in 1938, SNCF was formed as a *société d'économie mixte*, 51% of whose capital belonged to the State and the rest to the shareholders of the five former private rail companies, but in 1982 it became an *'établissement public à caractère industriel et commercial:'* SNCF 'Création de la SNCF' and 'Création de l'établissement public SNCF' <http://www.sncf.com>.

accident cases.[69] For example, in a case decided in 1953 in which a person injured in a train crash which had been deliberately caused by unknown striking railway employees claimed damages against SNCF,[70] the court held that SNCF could not rely on the act of strikers as *force majeure* so as to exclude its liability as the latter should have foreseen their acts and should have taken greater precautions to prevent them, even though on the facts as found by the *juges du fond* it is by no means clear what precautions could have been taken. In the view of one leading commentator, in this sort of case the courts treat SNCF as a sort of public compensation fund (*fonds de garantie*) in respect of railway transport accidents.[71]

However, this subjection of the liability of SNCF to private law is not complete. For if a person injured by its operations does not count as a 'user' of the *service public* which it provides (so as to attract private law), then in an appropriate case he or she may rely on the administrative law of 'public works'.[72] Where this is the case, the strictness of the liability faced by SNCF will depend on the claimant's 'status' as 'user', 'participant' or 'third party' to the public works in question.[73] Here, then, SNCF's liability will be administrative and may or may not be strict.

4. Liability for Medical Services and Medical Products

In France, the provision of health care belongs both to the public and private sectors of the economy. Historically, most provision was private, by doctors exercising their 'liberal profession' and by private clinics; public hospitals were reserved for the poor. While private care remains very important, the increasing sophistication of modern health care has meant that some types of intervention are found only in the public sector, so that (as of 1998), some 65 per cent of hospital beds were in public hospitals.[74] However, the financing of the public and private sectors rests on a fundamentally different basis from the publicly financed UK National Health Service. For in France, in principle, patients pay for their health care whether it is provided in the public or private sectors, but are then reimbursed *in part* by their medical insurer (though in certain cases the insurer pays direct).[75] In France, medical insurance (*assurance maladie*) is compulsory, different categories of the population and their families being insured with different bodies.[76] The remaining five per cent of the population have recently been included within a 'universal illness cover' for all French residents.[77] In addition, most people also take out supplementary private health insurance.

[69] Ripert and Roublot, *Traité de droit commercial,* Tome 2, (14th. edn., LGDJ, Paris, 1994), by P. Delebecque and M. Germain, 781–2.   [70] Civ. 30 Jun. 1953, D 1953.642.

[71] G. Durry, obs. to Civ. (1) 26 Jan. 1971, RTDCiv. 1971.863.

[72] E.g. CE 14 Mar. 1990, *Mme Declerck,* Leb. 965, CJEG 1990.217, concl. Daël, note D.D. (claimant injured riding a bicycle across a manual level crossing held to be a 'user' of the *ouvrage public* for which SNCF was responsible).   [73] Above, pp. 124–9.

[74] *Le système de santé en France* (2003) § 1.3 published at <http://www.sante.gouv.fr>.

[75] Ibid., § 2.1.

[76] 80% of the population of 'commercial employees' are insured by the Régime général de la Sécurité sociale; other groups are covered by more specialised bodies, e.g. agricultural workers by the Mutualité sociale agricole: ibid.   [77] Ibid.

In both the public and private sectors, medical treatment (whether diagnostic or surgical) is often accompanied by the use of products. The most obvious and wide-spread example is the use of pharmaceutical drugs, but other products are used, for example, X-ray machines or blood plasma. Typically, these products are manufactured by commercial companies, whether national or international, though their use in the French market is closely regulated. In the case of pharmaceuticals, they are supplied to patients either by a hospital or by pharmacists (*pharmaciens officines*) which are pri-vate, professional businesses. However, some types of 'medical product' are produced and/or supplied by public bodies or by private bodies exercising a recognisably public function. Of these, the supply of blood products in France is a striking example, as it was thrust into the limelight by the *affaire du sang contaminé*.

Here I wish, therefore, to look at the way in which French law has dealt with issues of liability in respect of the products used and supplied in the course of medical treat-ment. This is a complex subject made more difficult by the division of the substantive law between private and administrative law, by a series of changes in approach by the courts and by a legislative declaration of the basis of liability for both public and pri-vate health care in 2002 which sought to clarify but leaves some questions unan-swered, particularly as regards products, whether these are supplied to patients or otherwise used in treatment.[78] In these developments, the role of medical liability insurance has become central, for while it has long been common in France, in 2002 it was made compulsory for all private practitioners, for private clinics and hospitals, for public hospitals (though not for practitioners working in public hospitals who enjoy a personal immunity[79]), and for the producers and suppliers of 'health products,'[80] but within a few months the refusal of insurance companies to cover some clinics and doctors led to the State agreeing to undertake a proportion of the risk.[81] I shall also look at the liabilities incurred by others in the chain of distribution of medical products, notably pharmacists and manufacturers.

(a) The liability of doctors and hospitals

From 1936, the general rule of private law was that doctors were liable to their patients for harm suffered in the course of treatment only in contract and on the basis of a proof of fault, the doctor being bound to an *obligation de sécurité* later seen typical of *obligations de moyens*.[82] Where a medical practitioner was employed by a hospital or clinic under a contract of employment, it was liable for his or her fault, again in

---

[78] *Loi* no. 2002-303 of 4 Mar. 2002 *relative aux droits des malades et à la qualité du système de santé* ('*loi* of 4 Mar. 2002') creating art. L 1142-1 C. santé pub.   [79] Below, p. 143.

[80] Below, p. 151.

[81] *Loi* of 4 Mar. 2002 creating art. L 1142-2 C. santé pub.; *loi* no. 2002-1577 of 30 Dec. 2002 *relative à la responsabilité médicale*, art. 1 (*infections nosocomiales*), below, pp. 154–5.

[82] Civ. 20. May 1936, DP 1936.1.88, rapp. Josserand, concl. matter. Doctors working in either the pub-lic or private sectors have also been prosecuted for involuntary homicide or causing personal injuries but only those in the private sector (or their hospital employers) can be held liable in damages by the criminal courts to their patients present as *parties civiles* owing to the separation of jurisdictions: TC 14 Jan. 1935, S 1935.3.17 note Alibert (not in the medical context).

contract,[83] though most doctors in the private sector work independently so that only the doctor was likely to be liable.[84]

This contractual obligation was generally expressed as an obligation to provide 'conscientious and attentive care, which accords (save exceptionally) with the accepted scientific position'.[85] In principle, therefore, fault was not seen merely in a mistaken diagnosis nor should it be deduced from the 'abnormality and seriousness' of a patient's harm,[86] though sometimes the courts found fault so that a patient who had suffered harm in an unusual way should recover compensation, one author going as far as to refer to this as *faute virtuelle*.[87] Doctors have a duty to inform their patients of the possible risks of any treatment proposed,[88] and in 1998 the normal burden of proof here was reversed so that a doctor must show that he or she informed the patient.[89] Finally, where a patient contracted an infection which did not exist before entering hospital (*une infection nosocomiale*), the courts held that both the doctors and the clinic were bound to an *obligation de sécurité de résultat*.[90] Taking this approach one stage further in 1999 the Cour d'appel of Paris declared that while the general basis of liability was an *obligation de moyens*, where 'acts are needed to repair the consequences of a previous surgical act' it became an *obligation de sécurité de résultat*.[91] In practice this meant that where a patient's harm did not relate to his or her anterior condition nor to its foreseeable consequences liability was strict.[92]

Liability arising from the public provision of medical care has long been treated as a matter for the administrative courts and for long possessed a distinct administrative law.[93] This meant that while the State or other public bodies providing health services could be liable for harm caused by medical practitioners in public health institutions, the doctors themselves possessed a general immunity common to all public servants where their behaviour is linked to their employment in the public service.[94] For many years a patient had to show that the doctor's behaviour constituted *faute lourde* ('gross fault', such as recklessness or a serious lack of care) for liability in the authority to arise,[95] but in 1992 the Conseil d'Etat substituted a basis in ordinary fault, *faute simple*.[96]

---

[83] Civ. (1) 4 Jun. 1991, JCP 1991.II.21730 note Savatier, RTDCiv. 1992.123, obs. Jourdain which also held that the employer's liability excludes that of the doctor personally.

[84] J. Penneau, 'La réforme de la responsabilité médicale: responsabilité ou assurance', *RIDC* 1990.525, 536, who notes that doctors are also liable for any auxiliary staff who work under them, whether or not they are employed by the hospital; Malaurie, Aynès and Stoffel-Munck, *Obligations*, 472.

[85] Civ. 20. May 1936, DP 1936.1.88, rapp. Josserand, concl. matter. For a more recent example, see Civ. (1) 27 May 1998, Bull. civ. I no. 185.

[86] Cf. Civ (1) 27 May 1998, Bull. civ. I no. 185 and Civ. (1) 13 May, 1998, Bull. civ. I no. 174.

[87] J. Penneau, *op. cit.* n. 84, 532.   [88] Civ. (1) 29 May 1984, D 1985.281 note Bouvier.

[89] Civ. (1) 27 May 1998, Bull. civ. I no. 187.

[90] Civ. (1) 29 Jun. 1999, rapp. Sargot, JCP 1999.II.10138.

[91] Paris (1) 15 Jan. 1999, JCP 1999.II.10068 note Boy.   [92] Boy, ibid., at 738.

[93] Where a patient was treated privately by a doctor in a public hospital, liability in the doctor is a matter for the ordinary courts, liability in the hospital or its auxiliary staff for the administrative courts: CE. 10 Oct. 1973, *Mlle de Saint-Louvent*, Leb. 556.

[94] Vedel and Delvolvé, *Droit administratif,* Tome I, 562–3, above, pp. 31–2.

[95] R. Chapus, *Droit administratif général,* Tome 1 (Montchrestien, Paris, 4th. edn., 1988) 811–12.

[96] CE 10 Apr. 1992, JCP 1992.II.79027 note Moreau, Leb. 1992 171, concl. Legal.

However, while sometimes the Cour de cassation and the Conseil d'Etat required proof of fault for medical liability even where products were used or supplied,[97] more recently they imposed much stricter liabilities in these types of situation. The theoretical bases for these exceptional approaches varied between private and public law and in practice according to whether the product was *used by* the doctor in treating the patient or whether it was *supplied to* the patient (as in the case of serum, blood or medicines).

First, after 1936 the ordinary court's classification of medical liability as contractual together with the rule of *non-cumul* prevented recourse by patients to liability for the 'deeds of things' in respect of the products used by doctors or other medical staff,[98] but it allowed the possibility of strict contractual liabilities outside the context of diagnosis or surgery.[99] For example, in a case decided in 1984 a patient suffered burns after being treated with a compress by a physiotherapist.[100] The court held that while in general those who give medical treatment bear only an *obligation de moyens*, this was not the case as regards injuries caused by the instruments which they use, where they owe an *obligation de sécurité (de résultat)*: here, the patient's suffering of burns as a result of treatment was enough to establish liability, even though how this occurred remained unknown, a decision which came very close to imposing in the medical context a 'contractual liability for the deeds of things'.[101] This *jurisprudence* was confirmed in 1999 by the Cour de cassation, which declared that doctors owe their patients an *obligation de sécurité de résultat* as to the equipment which they use in the course of their investigations and treatment.[102]

The approach of the Conseil d'Etat to liability for injuries caused by products used in the course of treatment by public hospitals was different in its arrangement, but fairly similar in its result, the standard of liability moving away from a requirement of fault, let alone 'gross fault'. So, even while public medical liability was generally based on *faute lourde*, in cases other than those relating to strictly medical activities,[103] including ones involving liability for defective apparatus, liability was based on *faute*

---

[97] E.g. Civ. (1) 30 Oct. 1962, D 1963.57 note Esmein, JCP1962.II.12924 note Savatier, RTDCiv. 1963.329. obs. Tunc (patient injured when the step of an examining table gave way).

[98] Civ. 27 May 1940 DC 1941.53, GP 1940.2.81 (lower court's decision holding doctor liable as *gardien* of the X-rays quashed on the basis that a doctor's liability to his or her patient was exclusively contractual). Cf. the position where the patient's relatives sued where delict was allowed: Civ. (1) 1 Apr. 1968, D 1968.653, note Savatier, JCP 1968.II.15547 note Rabut (anaesthetic apparatus); Civ. (1) 25 May 1971, JCP 1971.IV.175 (doctor liable only if the injected agent was defective).

[99] Viney and Jourdain, *Conditions*, 470–5. At times the courts used factual presumptions of fault in this context, e.g. Civ. (1) 28 Jun. 1960, JCP 1960.II.11787 note Savatier, RTDCiv. 1961.112, obs. Tunc (presumption that the defective nature of medical apparatus was due to some fault in those who used it).

[100] Rouen 7 Feb. 1984, DS 1985.IR 405 obs. Penneau. See also Seine 3 Mar. 1965, JCP 1966.II.14582 note Savatier (which imposed an *obligation de résultat* on the medical team collectively as to the safety of an anaesthetic machine for the benefit of the deceased patient's relatives); Pontoise 28 Nov. 1986, D 1987.31 note Larroumet.　　　　　　　　　　　　　　[101] Penneau, obs. DS 1985.IR. 405, 406.

[102] Civ. (1) 9 Nov. 1999, Bull. civ. I no. 1; D 2002.117 note Jourdain (no recovery on the facts as the equipment in question (an examination table) had not been shown to be causally related to the patient's harm).

[103] A. de Laubadère, J.-C. Venezia and Y. Gaudemet, *Traité de droit administratif*, Tome 1 (LGDJ, Paris, 10th. edn., 1988) 778.

simple which could be found in the organisation or the functioning of the hospital[104] or even 'revealed' by the courts from the facts themselves, for example, where a premature baby suffered severe burns which could have been caused only by apparatus used by the hospital.[105] However, the Conseil d'Etat's approach was not uniform and so in one case in which the end of a probe used for an internal examination broke off, it held the hospital could be liable for fault in the organisation of its service only if the patient established that the probe in question was 'obviously defective, insufficiently tested or worn'.[106]

The approaches of French courts to liability in respect of products *supplied by* doctors or hospitals to their patients differed as between medicines and serum on the one hand (which I shall look at here) and blood products on the other (which I shall look at later given its special features).[107]

In most cases the ordinary courts held that a doctor's or clinic's liability for the medicines supplied or serum injected should be based only on fault. For example, in one case one doctor prescribed and another administered a dose of methodol before radiography as a result of which the patient suffered from sciatica.[108] The court held the prescribing doctor not liable as he had given proper consideration to her case and could not have foreseen her intolerance of the drug, but held the doctor who administered the injection liable as at fault in giving a dosage of nearly twice as much as both the manufacturer and works of authority recommended.[109] But occasionally exceptions were made to this requirement of proof of fault. For example, in one case a child patient suffered harm apparently as a result of impurities in the serum with which she had been injected.[110] Even though it was unclear whether the impurity was caused by a mistake in the nurse as to the type of serum, a mistake in the manufacturer, a crack in its container or insufficient sterilisation of the needle, the clinic was held liable as it had failed to supply to its patient a substance 'in accordance with its proper nature and purpose', an approach reminiscent of the law of sale.[111]

The Conseil d'Etat took an even stricter approach to the liability of public hospitals in respect of the serum and medicines which they supplied to their patients. At first it did so by presuming the existence of a fault in the organisation or functioning of the public medical service,[112] first in the context of compulsory vaccinations,[113] but later

---

[104] R. Chapus, *Droit administratif général*, Tome 1, (4th. edn., 1988) 812.

[105] CE 1 Mar. 1989, *Epoux Peyres*, Leb. 65.

[106] CE 4 Mar. 1988, *Godoy*, GP 1988.1.Pan.Jur.226.

[107] In the case of protheses, the courts accepted that, for example, a dentist's liability for diagnosis or fitting was governed by an *obligation de moyens*, but its manufacture an *obligation de résultat*: Paris 8 Feb. 1991, JCP 1992.II.21788 note Mémeteau; Poitiers 8 Apr. 1992, DS 1993.Somm. 27; Civ. (1) 29 Oct. 1985, Bull. civ. I no. 273.

[108] Civ. (1) 23 May 1973, JCP 1975.II.17955 note Savatier, GP 1973.2.885 note Doll. See similarly Civ. 6 Mar. 1945, D 1945.J.217; Civ. (1) 29 Jun. 1977, JCP 1977.IV.225; Civ. (2) 30 Jun. 1976, JCP 1979.II.19038.   [109] On the patient's claim against the drug's manufacturer, see below, p. 147.

[110] Civ. (1) 4 Feb. 1959, JCP 1959.II.11046 note Savatier, D 1959.153 note Esmein.

[111] Above, p. 69 *et seq.*   [112] Chapus, *Droit administratif général*, (*op. cit.* n. 104) 807–808.

[113] CE Ass. 7 Mar. 1958, *Dejous*, Leb. 153, AJDA 1958.2.220, chron. Fournier et Combarnous, RDP 1958.1087 concl. B. Jouvin. By *loi* no. 64–643 of 1 Jul. 1964, as amended by *loi* no.75-401 of 26 May 1975 a system of State liability for vaccinations in public hospitals was created: P.-J. Doll, 'Des responsabilités en matière de vaccinations obligatoires', JCP 1975.I.2736.

more generally in cases of injections which caused abnormal reactions in the patient. For example, in *Dame Derridj* a patient who suffered spinal paralysis after a course of antibiotic injections recovered because where a routine and benign medical procedure causes abnormal results this 'can only be regarded as revealing a fault in the organisation or functioning of the service'.[114] In practice rebuttal of such a presumption of fault was difficult except where a defendant could point to some external cause as to blame.

However, in 1993 in *Bianchi* the Assemblée of the Conseil d'Etat went further.[115] There the claimant suffered from tetraplegia after arteriography of the vertebrae at a public hospital. The *expertise* advised the court that the 'contrast product', iodine, which had been injected prior to the procedure, had itself played no role in causing the patient's injuries and that their most likely cause was the formation of an air or blood clot in the course of the introduction of the iodine into his body, an inherent risk in the treatment. However, the absence of any fault in the medical team did not prevent the Assemblée from holding the public hospital authority liable, for in its view:

where a medical act which is necessary for the diagnosis or treatment of a patient presents a risk whose existence is known but whose occurrence is exceptionally rare and where there is no reason to think that the patient would be particularly exposed to such a risk, the public hospital service is liable if the performance of this medical act is the direct cause of a patient's later harm as long as the latter bears no relation to his initial condition nor to its foreseeable development and as long as it is extremely serious.

This was a small but considerable departure for the Conseil d'Etat as it expressly admitted the possibility of an overt and very strict liability for harm suffered in consequence of medical intervention,[116] though somewhat fenced in by conditions (an exceptional, known risk; a 'direct' cause of a patient's 'extremely serious' harm). But while *Bianchi* itself concerned harm caused by medical treatment involving the supply of a product (the iodine) to the patient, the terms of the *arrêt* were broader, the expression 'medical act' (*acte médicale*) including diagnosis as well as treatment. While, French public lawyers attempted to fit this new example of public liability without fault into the traditional patterns of liability in the administration,[117] *Bianchi* made clear that the Conseil d'Etat had gone further than the Cour de cassation in imposing liability without a need to prove fault.[118]

(b) The liability of manufacturers and pharmacists

The liability of manufacturers of medicines and serum and of pharmacists for their supply was governed by private law and until 1998 formed an exception to the willingness of French courts to impose liability for products without proof of fault.

---

[114] CE 22 Dec. 1976, *Dame Derridj*, Leb. 576, JCP 1978.II.18792 note J.-M. Auby.

[115] CE Ass 9 Apr. 1993, *Bianchi*, JCP 1993.II.22601 note Moreau, AJDA 1993.349 note Mangüé and Touvet. Cf. the earlier decision in CAA Lyon 21 Dec. 1990, *Gomez*, AJDA 1993.349.

[116] Moreau, note, JCP 1993.II.22601.

[117] E.g. liability for 'dangerous things' or for the infliction of an 'abnormal and direct loss': see Moreau JCP 1993.II.22601.   [118] Mangüé and Touvet, *op. cit.* n. 115, 351.

For until that year, the liability of pharmaceutical manufacturers was based only on delictual fault: a patient could not claim against a manufacturer based on the *garantie légale* of the law of sale extended by way of *action directe* or a contractual *obligation de résultat* extended by way of *stipulation pour autrui*,[119] nor on article 1384 alinéa 1 of the Civil Code as *gardien* of the drugs, even where their container exploded![120]

What counted as 'delictual fault' for this purpose and how strictly was it assessed? Certainly, putting onto the market a 'defective medicine' was not treated as in itself a fault,[121] but the courts did hold that manufacturers should take 'exceptional care in developing their products',[122] even if they did not guarantee that they would in no circumstances cause their users harm.[123] More concretely, according to one court, where a product is causally related to a claimant's harm, its manufacturer's liability 'is conditional on the existence of fault in the conception, manufacture or presentation of the medicine',[124] but it should not be liable for harm which was abnormal or unforeseeable at the time of putting it onto the market, even where unrelated to any special reaction.[125]

On the other hand, a manufacturer of a pharmaceutical product was found to have been at fault in failing to withdraw it from the market. For example, in one case the claimant had suffered an intestinal blockage after taking the defendant's tablets, which had been prescribed by her doctor.[126] Their manufacturer argued that over 130,000 boxes of the tablet had been sold in France without problems since its introduction, but an *expertise* reported that in the few months preceding the claimant's own use of it, several cases of injuries had been reported, possibly due to a modification in its formula. The court therefore held that the manufacturer was at fault in failing to undertake further research as to its product before offering it for sale to the public and in failing to give more detailed and clearer warnings to alert its consumers to the risks of the product. It further held that the manufacturer could not escape its liability by pointing to a failure in either the claimant or her doctor to follow the instructions which had been given, given that these were incomplete and not of a type to strike the attention of a patient.[127]

---

[119] Civ. (1) 8 Apr. 1986, *arrêt Thorens*, JCP 1987.II.20721 note Viala and Viandier, RTDCiv. 1987.777, obs. Huet (*pourvoi en cassation* against Paris 15 Dec. 1983, D 1985.228 note Penneau). See also Paris 4 Jul. 1970, D 1971.73 note Plat and Duneau; Rouen 14. Feb. 1979, *affaire Nimaol*, JCP 1980.II.19360 note Boniet, D 1979 IR 25 obs. Larroumet (liability for *contractual* fault) and J. Huet, 'Le paradoxe des médicaments et les risques de développement (question suscitée par des décisions de jurisprudence récentes et quelques articles de presse: la responsabilité pharmaceutique est-elle une responsabilité pour faute?)' D 1987 Chron. 73.

[120] Civ. (2) 30 Jun. 1976, JCP 1979.II.19038 (manufacturer of an elderly ampoule held not liable under art. 1384 al. 1 C. civ. as it did not possess ' the powers which characterise *la garde*' of the ampoules).

[121] Cf. above, p. 51. [122] Nanterre 12 Dec. 1985, extracts reported D Chron.1987.78–79.

[123] Paris 4. Jul. 1970, D 1971.73 note Plat and Duneau.

[124] Nanterre 12 Dec. 1985, extracts reported D Chron.1987.78.

[125] Paris 4 Jul. 1970, D 1971.73 note Plat and Duneau; Civ. (1) 23 May 1973, JCP 1975.II.17955 note Savatier, GP 1973.2.885 note Doll; Civ. (1) 8 Apr. 1986, *arrêt Thorens, cit.*

[126] Pau 12 Mar. 1958, S 1958.397 note F. G., GP 1958.1.322.

[127] For other cases concerning liability for warnings in the pharmaceutical context, see Civ. (2) 23 Feb. 1983, D 1983 IR 497 obs. Penneau (manufacturer gave sufficiently detailed information as to its product implanted by a doctor); Nanterre 12 Dec. 1985, extracts reported D Chron.1987.78–79 (manufacturer liable for failing to inform medical profession of risks to teeth of antibiotic); Rouen 14 Feb.1979,

However, in 1998 the Cour de cassation took a different view, 'implementing' the Product Liability Directive just before the legislator.[128] There the claimant had in 1988 taken a medicine wrapped in indigestible sponge, which was aimed at allowing the pharmaceutical to be absorbed gradually but which had to be surgically removed. The manufacturer of the medicine argued that it owed the patient an *obligation de sécurité* to deliver 'a product having a therapeutic effect conforming to accepted scientific practices, without usually presenting for its user disadvantages or dangers higher than the therapeutic effect which it bears', so that in the absence of any defect (*défectuosité*) being found by *expertise*, the lower court should not have held it liable. However, the Cour de cassation held that 'the manufacturer must deliver a product exempt of any defect [*défaut*] of a nature to create a danger for persons or property, that is to say, a product which offers the safety which one is legitimately entitled to expect'. So, the lower court was right to hold the manufacturer of the medicine liable as their findings made clear that the claimant's harm was caused by the very characteristics of the non-digestible wrapping of the medicine which stuck in his intestine which was a defect in the relevant sense. Interestingly, in upholding liability, the Cour de cassation rejected the manufacturer's argument which articulated clearly that the product was not defective because on balance its benefits outweighed its costs.

The position of the suppliers of pharmaceuticals to the general public was treated in a similar way to the liability of their manufacturers, though without the final twist towards liability without fault. In France, all medicines and other pharmaceutical products are supplied only by pharmacists or dispensing chemists (*pharmaciens officines*), who are subject to considerable legislative control, both as to their organisation and their professional duties, though acting within the private sphere conducting a 'liberal profession'.[129] Patients pay the pharmacist the full price of the prescription drugs, but may claim the reimbursement of the cost or some of the cost from their insurers. While this supply looks like a contract of sale, the courts have not imposed liability under the *garantie légale*,[130] but instead only on the basis of proven (usually contractual) fault to their customers for harm caused to those to whom they supply medicines.[131] However, the standard of care imposed on them is a high one, and pharmacists must check the input of others (such as doctors or manufacturers) into their own practice, though they are not expected to verify a branded product, which is received ready-packaged and which it would be impracticable to check.[132] Pharmacists must also give proper advice as to the products which they supply, this being particularly important where the customer is not under the care of a medical practitioner.[133]

JCP 1980.II.19360 note P. Boniet, D 1979.IR.25 note Larroumet (information insufficiently brought to doctors' attention); Paris 20 Jun. 1963, GP 1963.2.319, D 1964.30 (criminal court found manufacturer of a concentrated antiseptic supplied neat by a pharmacist and applied neat by its customer had clearly and explicitly attached a warning against its undiluted use).

[128] Civ. (1) 3 Mar. 1998, Bull. civ I, no. 95, JCP 1998.II.10049 rapp. P. Sargos and see below, pp. 455–7.
[129] Art. L. 4211-1 *et seq.* C. santé publ.
[130] B. Harichaux de Tourdonnet, 'Santé, Responsabilité du pharmacien, Pharmacien-fabricant, Pharmacien d'officine, Laboratoire d'analyse de biologie médicale', in Jur.-Cl. Responsabilité civile, Arts. 1382 à 1386, (Eds. Techniques, Paris), Fasc. 442, 24–25.   [131] Ibid., 10.
[132] Paris 4 Jul. 1970, D 1971.73 note Plat et Duneau.
[133] Art. R. 5015-48 C. santé publ.; Cf. Agen 3 Apr. 1950, GP 1950.2.59 (pharmacist not guilty of criminal fault as user's reaction was 'totally inexplicable and unforeseeable').

(c) The *affaire du sang contaminé*: Part I—civil liability of the producers and suppliers

From 1952 to 1993 the supply of blood and blood products in France was governed by legislation which created 'a quasi-public organisation of a hybrid nature', constituting 'a sort of *service public* of human blood'[134] and subjecting it to a form of monopoly, no blood being collected or supplied outside the framework of its scheme. At the centre of the French blood transfusion service was an 'association', with various representatives, including those of the Minister of Health, but blood was collected, processed and supplied by some 180 licensed local blood transfusion centres, some of which were private bodies and some of which formed part of local departmental or municipal public bodies. 'In this nebula, each local centre was independent and responsible for its own activities',[135] but, ruthlessly following the bifurcation of the French system, each centre was liable for harm caused to those receiving blood or blood products either in the administrative courts under public law (if the centre formed part of a public body) or in the ordinary courts under private law (if the centre was a private body). However, in the wake of the *affaire du sang contaminé*, the French blood transfusion service has twice been reorganised, in 1993 and again in 1998.[136] Here, I shall explain how French courts decided issues of liability for harm caused by blood infected with HIV, whether in the blood transfusion centres or the doctor or hospital supplying the blood or blood product under this earlier organisational scheme and then consider how this will change in part as a result of these organisational changes. I shall look later at the liability of the French State to the victims of HIV for failing properly to organise the National Blood Transfusion system[137] and at the alleged criminal responsibilities of individuals for their part in the tragedy.[138]

The approach of the ordinary courts demonstrates a willingness to stretch contractual concepts to a very surprising extent. For they analysed the relationship of the 'parties' to the supply of blood in contractual terms, even though French regulation of the supply of blood meant that someone to whom it is supplied does not *buy* it (blood being '*hors de commerce*') so as to attract the various claims arising from the contract of sale.[139] In this respect, perhaps the most interesting aspect was their treatment of the liability of blood transfusion centres. In a well-known case of 1954, a patient had been supplied in a *public* hospital with blood infected with syphilis, apparently 'arm to arm' from a donor, this having been arranged by the hospital with the Oeuvre de la transfusion sanguine d'urgence, one of the private law bodies which organised the distribution of blood before the 'monopolistic' system set up in 1952 took effect.[140] The Cour de cassation agreed that the Oeuvre should be liable in damages, even in the absence of fault, on the ground that the hospital had made a contract with it for the supply of blood for the benefit of the patient claimant which required that the blood be '*loyale*', thereby in effect imposing an *obligation de résultat* as to its safety. This was a remarkable

---

[134] Y. Lambert-Faivre, *Le droit du dommage corporel*, (Dalloz, Paris, 1st. edn., 1990), 440. The main legislation was the *loi* no. 52-854 of 21 Jul.1952.   [135] Lambert-Faivre, ibid., 441.

[136] Above, p. 10. *Loi* no. 93-5 of 4 Jan. 1993; *loi* no. 98-535 of 1 Jul. 1998.

[137] Below, pp. 315–19, 324.   [138] Below, pp. 394–401.

[139] R. Savatier, note to Civ. 17 Dec. 1954, JCP 1955.II.8490.

[140] Civ. 17 Dec. 1954, JCP 1955.II.8490, note Savatier, GP 1955.1.54, D 1955.269 note Rodière.

decision, remarkable for its treatment of the Oeuvre's liability as belonging to the ordinary courts given its involvement in the *service public* of supplying blood in a context far from 'industrial or commercial';[141] for its reliance on an administrative law contract between a public hospital and the Oeuvre as the basis of a private law claim; and, even as a matter of private law, for its fictitious finding of a contract between the hospital and the Oeuvre for the benefit of the patient.[142] In the result, the Oeuvre was liable to the patient without proof of either fault or defect in the blood and with no defence that the infection in the blood was caused by circumstances beyond its control.

In 1995 in a pair of cases concerning the supply of blood contaminated with HIV the Cour de cassation followed this very strict contractual approach to the liability of private law blood transfusing centres, holding that they were 'bound to supply to recipients products free from defects and unable to escape liability under this *obligation de sécurité* except by showing *cause étrangère*, which would not include an internal defect in the blood, even if undetectable.[143] So, while the Cour de cassation placed liability in the mould of an *obligation de sécurité de résultat*, unlike its decision in 1954 it did not appear to consider it necessary to overcome the lack of privity of contract between a patient in a private clinic and the transfusion centre by finding a contract for the benefit of a third party.[144] On the other hand, the Cour de cassation held that the clinics in which the blood was supplied to the patients owed them only an *obligation de prudence et diligence* in respect of the blood products, explicitly requiring the *juges du fond* to decide whether or not a clinic had the possibility of checking the quality of the products received from the transfusion centre.[145] Taken together, it is clear that the Cour de cassation considered that (absent any fault) liability should be borne by the transfusion centres *rather than* the private clinics or doctors.

It was also in 1995 that the Assemblée of the Conseil d'Etat reviewed its own treatment of the liability of blood transfusion centres and hospitals,[146] in the context of some 600 claims for harm caused by blood contaminated with HIV which had been supplied in public hospitals.[147] The Assemblée agreed with the approach of the Cour de cassation: the blood transfusion centres, whether public or private, possessed a monopoly over the collection of blood and a supervisory role over the treatment, preparation and supply of blood products and this together with the inherent risks of these products justified imposing liability on them without fault,[148] but a public hospital which merely supplied blood and which did not include such a centre should be liable only for proven fault.[149] So while the Cour de cassation used its control over

---

[141] Cf. above, pp. 134–5.   [142] Savatier, note JCP 1955.II.8490.

[143] Civ. (1) 12 Apr. 1995, *Dupuy, Martial*, JCP 1995.II.22467 note Jourdain. Cf. the earlier Paris 1 Jul. 1991, JCP 1991.II.21762 note Harichaux.

[144] In 2001, the Cour de cassation extended the benefit of this contractual liability to a deceased patient's relatives on the basis that third parties to contracts may properly rely on a breach of contract of one of the parties where it causes them harm: Civ. (1) 13 Feb. 2001, Bull. civ. I no. 35.

[145] Civ. (1) 12 Apr. 1995, *affaire Dupuy*, JCP 1995.II.22467 note Jourdain.

[146] CE Ass. 26 May 1995, *Pavan, N'Guyen, Jouan*, Leb. 221, AJDA 1995.577–78, AJDA 1995.508 note Stahl and Chavaux, JCP 1995.II.22468 note Moreau. See also M.-A. Peano and D. Peano 'Les centres de transfusion sanguine devant le juge judiciaire et le juge administratif' (1995) Resp. civ. et assur. no. 31, 3; J.-S. Bergé, 'Risque et faute dans la contamination transfusionelle' GP 1996.2.737.

[147] Peano and Peano, ibid., 5.   [148] CE Ass. 26 May 1995, *N'Guyen, cit.*

[149] CE Ass. 26 May 1995, *Pavan, cit.*

the content of contractual obligations whereas the Conseil d'Etat preferred a more direct approach, at this stage there was considerable harmony between the two jurisdictions in their allocation of liability, imposing very strict liability on the blood transfusion centres but relieving hospitals or clinics of liability except on the basis of proven fault. This pattern has, however, been the subject of three distinct disruptive influences.

The first was France's decision in implementing the Product Liability Directive to impose liability for defects of safety on all 'business suppliers' without the restrictions which article 3(3) of the Directive contained.[150] This suggested that private (and possibly also public) hospitals would be liable without proof of fault despite this earlier *jurisprudence.* However, this potential effect did not survive the amendment of the French implementing legislation following its censure by the European Court of Justice in April 2002.[151] The second disruptive influence was the reorganisation of the French blood transfusion service in 1998 which created a new public body, the Établissement française du sang (EFS), whose role is to supervise and organise the provision of blood within France.[152] While this body acts through 'local establishments', they do not possess legal personality[153] and this means that any future liability in a blood transfusion centre will fall on the EFS and within the jurisdiction of the administrative courts.[154] So an institutional reorganisation led necessarily to the abandonment of the ordinary courts' role in imposing liability on this category of defendant. Thirdly, however, legislation in March 2002 was enacted which *appears* to unify the basis of medical liability, including of hospitals and doctors in respect of the supply of blood, but whose effect remains not entirely clear.

(d) Legislative intervention in 2002

Following some 30 years of pressure for change and a growing concern that the courts were too free in their imposition of liability without fault on medical practitioners and hospitals, in March 2002 important legislation governing health care was enacted.[155] It had three main relevant aspects: it provided for the basis of the liabilities of medical practitioners and establishments, whether public or private; it required *all* those providing medical services, whether private or public, and the producers or suppliers of medical products, to insure against their liability, with the exception of the State itself;[156] and it set up a special fund for the compensation of those suffering very

---

[150] Below, pp. 458–9.
[151] *Commission v France,* Case C-52/00 of 25 Apr. 2002, [2002] I-3827, paras. 36–47; *loi* of 9 Dec. 2004, art. 29, below, p. 459.   [152] *Loi* no. 98-535 of 1 Jul. 1998, art. 18.
[153] Art. 1223-1 C. santé pub.   [154] CE 27 Oct. 2000, *Torrant,* Leb. 147.
[155] *Loi* no. 2002-303 of 4 Mar. 2002 *relative aux droits des malades et à la qualité du système du santé,* ('*loi* no. 2002-303') art. 98 creating new tit. IV of book 1 of the legislative part of the C. santé pub.
[156] Art. L. 1142-2 C. santé pub. See P. Mistretta, 'La loi no. 2002-303 du 4 mars 2002 relative aux droits des malades et à la qualité du système du santé, Réflexions critiques sur un droit en pleine mutation', JCP 2002.I.141; P. Sargos, 'Le nouveau régime juridique des infections nosocomiales, loi no. 2002-303 du 4 mars 2002' JCP 2002 Actualité, 1117; Y. Lambert-Faivre, 'La loi no. 2002-303 of 4 Mar. 2002 relative aux droits des malades et à la qualité du système du santé III—L'indemnisation des accidents médicaux' D 2002 Chron. 1367.

serious harm as a result of contracting a 'nosocomial infection' or a medical accident where liability was not established.[157] It also dealt with an number of other important medico-legal issues and of more particular problems: so, for example, it created retroactively a presumption of causation between the supply of blood infected with Hepatitis C and a patient's own infection.[158]

(i) *The basis of liability and its relationship to liability for products*

The legislation's key provision governing liability states that:

> Outside the case where their liability is incurred by reason of a defect in a medical product [*produit de santé*], [doctors, dental surgeons and midwives], and any establishment, service or bodies in which individual acts of prevention, diagnosis or care take place are liable for the harmful consequences of acts of prevention, diagnosis or care only in the case of fault. The above establishments, services or bodies are liable for harm resulting from nosocomial infections, unless they establish the existence of a *cause étrangère*.[159]

The purpose of this provision was to clarify and to unify the rules (but not the jurisdictions) governing medical liability in public and private law, which was seen as unstable and uncertain and as discriminating unfairly between patients in the public and private sectors.[160] In parliament, it was recognised that there was a tension between the rights of patients to compensation and the need to avoid unsupportable and uninsurable liabilities in doctors and hospitals and defensive medicine *à l'Americaine*.[161] The legislation also provided for a special prescription period for actions for damages against medical practitioners and establishments of ten years from the time of 'consolidation' of a claimant's harm.[162] Nevertheless, a number of uncertainties remain.

First, while the legislation states as a general principle that the liabilities of both individuals and institutions in respect of health care are based only on fault, it is not clear whether this refers to proven fault or may also include presumed fault.[163] As has been seen, in their earlier *jurisprudence* both the Cour de cassation and the Conseil d'Etat had recourse to presumptions of fault in some situations of medical liability, though these did not coincide.[164] In this respect, the legislation's *travaux préparatoires* are ambiguous as an earlier draft referred to the ability of the courts to find fault, whether proved or presumed, but this was later simply omitted.[165] Commentators on the legislation have argued for either position.[166]

---

[157] Art. L. 1142-1 al. II C. santé pub.

[158] *Loi* no 2002-303, art. 102 and see Ass. Nat. No. 3688, *Rapport d'information* by C. Evin, B. Charles et J.-J. Denis, Troisième partie, 39.   [159] Art. L. 1142-1 al. 1 C. santé pub.

[160] Ass. Nat. No. 3263, *Rapport* (28 Sept. 2001) by C. Evin, B. Charles et J.-J. Denis; and see Sén., (2001–2002) no. 174, *Rapport* by F. Giraud, G. Dériot and J.-L. Lorrain, p. 221; Sén. No. 175, *Avis* by P. Fauchon, 14; Ass. Nat. No. 3688, *Rapport d'information* by C. Evin, B. Charles et J.-J. Denis, Troisième partie.   [161] Ass. Nat. Déb. (2nd séance of 2 Oct. 2001), J.O. Rép. f., 5322.

[162] New art. L. 1142-28 C. santé publ.   [163] Mistretta, *op. cit.* n. 156, 1080.

[164] Above, pp. 143, 145–6.

[165] Ass. Nat. Texte No. 705 (4 Oct. 2001), *projet de loi*, draft art. L. 1142-1 al. 1 C. santé pub.; Ass. Nat. No. 3263, *Rapport*, 3–4.

[166] Sargos, *op. cit.* n. 156, 1118 (proven fault); Mistretta, *op. cit.* n. 156, 1080–1 (presumed as well as proven fault); Lambert-Faivre, *op. cit.* n. 156, D 2002 Chron. 1367 at 1368 (*loi* confirms previous 'remarkable developments' of notion of fault).

Secondly, though, the *loi* of March 2002 provides that the general rule of liability for fault does not apply to liability in respect of defects in 'medical products'.[167] In the *travaux préparatoires* this provision was said to have been included so as to ensure compatibility with the Product Liability Directive and the legislation which implemented it in France,[168] though at the time the French legislative extension of the Directive's provisions so as to impose liability on all business suppliers of products on the same terms which the Directive required for producers and importers meant that its significance appeared much larger than it will be after amendment of the implementing legislation so as to conform to the Directive.[169] On the other hand, it has been said that the provision in the 2002 legislation concerning the liability of hospitals and doctors in respect of defective medical products is broad enough to cover cases where products are *used* in the course of treatment and not merely where they are supplied,[170] thereby preserving earlier *jurisprudence* of the Cour de cassation and the Conseil d'Etat where liability without fault was imposed. This view would retain a liability without fault where a provider of health care is neither the producer nor the supplier of a product in the ordinary sense as, for example, in the case of anesthetic apparatus.[171] Finally, the exclusion of liability for *medical* products from the general rule leaves the possibility of liability (whether under the Product Liability Directive or under the previous *jurisprudence*) in respect of harm caused by products other than 'medical products', for example, food cooked and supplied to patients containing salmonella or a chair which breaks when used.

Thirdly, the *loi* provides exceptionally that institutional (but not individual) providers of health care are to be liable in respect of harm caused by 'nosocomial infections', their only defence being *cause étrangère*.[172] While the *loi* does not define 'nosocomial infections', the courts may well use the definition in a ministerial circular of 2000 which refers to them as any infection contracted in a health care establishment;[173] if so, they could include infections which are transmitted via medical products, for example, through use of an aseptic needle, prothesis or implant or even blood infected with a virus. Liability is indeed strict here, modelled on the *obligation de sécurité de résultat* developed by the Cour de cassation, but to be used by administrative courts as well.[174] But this liability would certainly go further than the Product Liability Directive's provisions as to the liability of those who merely supply products and could be vulnerable to challenge on this ground.[175]

(ii) Compensation for medical accidents

Perhaps more radical were the new legislation's provisions governing compensation for medical accidents. Here, the legislation of March 2002 was concerned to ensure compensation for the most serious consequences of medical accidents and thereby remove

---

[167] Art. L. 1142-1 al. 1 C. santé pub.   [168] E.g. Ass. Nat. No. 3263, *Rapport*, 22–3.
[169] Below, p. 459.   [170] Lambert-Faivre, *op. cit.* n. 156, D 2002 Chron 1367 at 1368.
[171] Above, pp. 144–5.   [172] Art. L. 1142-1 al. 1 C. santé pub. *in fine*.
[173] Sargos, *op. cit.* n. 156, 1117–8. The category is therefore wider than 'iatrogenic conditions' which are any conditions directly related to health care. Cf. the definitions given in Sén. No. 174, *Rapport*, 229.
[174] Sén. No. 174, *Rapport*, 224.   [175] Below, p. 523.

the need for the courts to impose liabilities other than for fault.[176] The legislation set up a fund from which payments would be made in respect of nosocomial infections, iatrogenic conditions or medical accidents where these cause a patient abnormal consequences to the state of his or her health, the seriousness having a threshold of 25 per cent incapacity (whether permanent or temporary).[177] The justification for this compensation of the most serious consequences of 'medical risks' was 'national solidarity', that is the idea that the State as collective representative must support those of its citizens who have some special need. The legislation makes clear that this right to compensation arises only where there is no liability in any medical professional, health care provider *or producer of products*:[178] the new rights should not lead to the 'irresponsibility' of those concerned in health care.

At a practical level, the legislation set up new mediation mechanisms for patients suffering very serious harm (as earlier defined) allegedly as a result of their health care, with the idea that these will channel a claim either towards those liable or towards the new compensation fund.[179] This creates a 'one-stop access' for the settlement of claims to be administered by regional committees, though leaving the possibility of recourse to the courts (either civil or administrative) at any stage.[180] After an investigation, if a Commission finds a person (such as a hospital authority) liable for the patient's harm, then its insurer must make an offer of compensation within four months; the patient is free either to accept this offer or proceed to litigation. If no offer is made, then the new national fund pays the compensation and may itself proceed against the person responsible.[181] On the other hand, where the commission finds that the patient was a victim of a 'medical accident', then it will itself pay the compensation. The Commission follows the general law as to its manner of assessment of a patient's harm.

(iii) The hasty legislative sequel: the State 'sharing' the liability risks

The legislative changes of March 2002 sought to strike a balance between the interests of patients, of doctors and of institutional providers of health care, but the reaction of the insurance industry was dramatic. For while all persons and institutions who could be liable under the new provisions had to insure, some insurers left the French market and others refused to renew the cover for some half of private health care institutions and some public hospitals: there was a real likelihood that some hospitals and clinics would have to stop work for want of insurance cover.[182] Further legislation was therefore introduced in Parliament later in 2002 to 'reassure' medical insurers and this passed into law on 30 December 2002, two days before some of the insurance coverage was due to end.[183] The effect of this new legislation was to transfer the liability for

---

[176] Sénat, No. 174, *Rapport*, 223.   [177] Art. 1142-1-II C. santé pub.   [178] Ibid.

[179] The provisions are contained in new arts. L 1142-4—1142-24 C. santé pub.

[180] Ass. Nat. No. 3688, *Rapport d'information*, 34 *et seq.* describes this new procedure.

[181] New art. L. 1142-15.3 C santé pub.

[182] Sén. No. 33, *Proposition de loi relative à la responsabilité civil médicale, Exposé des motifs* (24 Oct. 2002).

[183] *Loi* no. 2002-1577 of 30 Dec. 2002 *relative à la responsabilité civile médicale* on which see P. Mistretta, 'La Loi no. 2002-1577 of 30 Dec. 2002 relative à la responsabilité civile médicale. Premiers correctifs de la loi no. 2002-303 du 4 mars 2002' JCP 2003 Actualité 165.

compensation in three situations to the national compensation fund; first, liability for Creuzfeld-Jakob disease (CJD) transmitted to some 2,000 patients treated with human growth hormone (HGH) between 1973 and 1988;[184] secondly, liability for the intervention of medical practitioners 'in exceptional circumstances' (for example, at a roadside accident);[185] and, thirdly, liability for 'nosocomial infections' contracted in a health establishment, service or body (but apparently not in a private doctor's surgery[186]) where this causes an incapacity of 25 per cent, leaving only relatively minor cases to these bodies' insurers.[187] This means that the national fund and the assurers share the cost of harm caused by nosocomial infections.

The first and third of these impact on liability for medical products. The first is an example of a particularly prominent case of the supply of a harmful product, the first civil case having recently succeeded against those bodies responsible for the supply of HGH in France,[188] proceedings in the criminal courts being still in progress.[189] Here, the financial responsibility for the consequences of the product were simply transferred from the supervisory body of this supply (the Association France-Hypophyse, subsequently dissolved) to the new national compensation fund, though this apparently leaves the possibility of claims being made against other persons potentially liable for the supply (notably, the Institut Pasteur and the hospitals providing the treatment). As regards liability for 'nosocomial infections', the December legislation transferred a proportion of the cost of the strict liability which the March legislation had imposed from the insurers of the institutional providers of health care to the national compensation fund. As I have explained, this may also have an effect on some cases of their liability for products.[190] For the national compensation fund is given a right of recourse against the providers of health care (and their insurers) only where that provider has committed a proven fault (*une faute établie*) and in particular breach of one of its duties imposed by the rules enacted to prevent nosocomial infection.[191] To the extent, therefore, to which this applies to infections contracted by patients as a result of products supplied to them by these establishments, it changes the basis of their liability to a particular demanding degree of fault, *un manquement caracterisé*.[192] As I have noted, producers and suppliers of medical products were included in the earlier requirement of insurance against liability and so also stand to benefit from this shift in the extent of liability by the State's undertaking of the risk of harm for nosocomial infections.

---

[184] New art. L. 1142-22 al. 2 C. santé pub.   [185] New art. L. 1142-1-1 2° C. santé pub.
[186] Mistretta, *op. cit.* n. 183, JCP 2003 Actualité 165.   [187] New art. 1142-1-1 1° C. santé pub.
[188] TGI Montpellier 9 Jul. 2002 No. 02/00565 reported <http://www.editions-legislatives.fr/aj/actualites/>.
[189] The bodies responsible for the supply of HGH in France were the Association France-Hypophyse and the Institut Pasteur. In April 2004, the dossier was still before the *juge d'instruction*: *Le Quotidien du médecin*, 28 Apr. 2004.
[190] Above, p. 153.   [191] New art. L 1142-17 and L. 1142-21 C. santé pub.
[192] Mistretta, *op. cit.* n. 183, JCP 2003 Actualité 165.

8

Introduction to Private and Public Liability in English Law

At a formal level, the English law of liability is at once more unified and more fragmented than its French counterpart. It is more unified because English law does not traditionally distinguish an entirely discrete category of the administrative law of liability any more than the legal system itself recognises a distinct jurisdiction for the disposal of disputes involving public bodies or of a specially public nature. On the other hand, English law is more fragmented owing to the process of 'individuation' which has resulted from the steady accretion of 'implied' terms for particular contracts and from the disparate nature of its law of torts. Thus, a French jurist first looking at the English law of liability would fail to see familiar distinctions, but would see instead many others, cutting here and there across the law in a really rather bewildering fashion. In all this, there is apparently little which would be recognisable as a special law of 'liability for things', but there has long been a distinct treatment of product liability, by which is typically meant the law governing the liability of manufacturers and possibly other suppliers for physical damage caused by their products.

It is the purpose of this chapter and the following chapters to go beyond this somewhat opaque series of propositions and explain how English law has treated the practical issues of liability for products which I have already discussed in relation to French law, and to compare and contrast them. I shall start in this chapter by explaining the general framework of analysis of the English law of liability; in the following chapters I shall look at the torts which are significant in relation to the imposition of liability for products and notably the tort of negligence, liability arising from the contract of sale, and liability for products in the context of the supply of private or public services (whether contractual or tortious). As can be seen, this treatment reflects in a very general way the structure of my arrangement of the French material. I shall start by explaining English law's framework for the law of torts and breach of contract and then look at how English law deals with questions of liability in the administration.

1. The Legal Bases of Civil Liability

While English law does not distinguish as sharply or as neatly as French law between contract and tort, where *non-cumul* stands guard on this boundary against any blurring or overlap,[1] its treatment of the bases of liability differs considerably according to whether liability arises for breach of contract or from the commission of a tort.[2] The starting point for the 'classical' analysis of contract is broad, for any agreement supported by consideration may be a contract[3] and liability in damages may arise for breach of any of the terms of a contract, whether express or implied. To a considerable extent, this breadth of analysis is the legacy of the generalising influence of English nineteenth-century jurists, such as Anson or Pollock,[4] who themselves borrowed from earlier civilian writers in recasting the common law materials into a general law of contract based on the intention of the parties.[5]

It is noticeable, moreover, that a sense of the particular or 'special' law of contract has been all but lost in many modern English texts on contract law, certainly as compared to French law, whose Civil Code enshrines both grand, generalising principles and considerable sets of rules drawn from the nominate contracts of Roman law.[6] This persistent generality of approach of many English contract lawyers has tended to obscure the importance of the categorisation of contracts in their regulation, and this is particularly prominent as regards the duties and potential liabilities flowing from the relationship created by contract. For while some types of contract possess legal rules attaching to a contract by reason of its nature (for example, common law rules as to the effect of disclosure in contracts of insurance[7] or statutory rules governing contracts of consumer credit[8]), for many contracts their regulation results from the implication of terms. Here, there is a certain paradox, for while the 'implication' of terms is a technique which is general to all types of contract and formally justified by reference to the intention of the parties, in practice its application is very specific, the courts delineating the particular circumstances in which a term should be implied in the contract before them and may therefore be implied in the future in similar cases.[9] Indeed, we can often see a process of the refinement of implied terms in the hands of the courts. So, for example,

---

[1] Above, p. 27–9. At one stage in English law, the courts appeared to be saying that any breach of contractual duty could give rise to liability in tort (*Brown v Boorman* (1842) 3 QB 511, (1844) 11 Cl. & Fin. 1, HL) or, conversely, that a party to a contract could not be liable in the tort of neligence to the other party even if the tort's constituent elements were present (*Tai Hing Cotton Mill Ltd v Liu Chong Hing Bank Ltd.* [1986] AC 80, 107) but in *Henderson v Merrett Syndicates Ltd.* [1995] 2 AC 145 the House of Lords established that a party to a contract may opt whether to sue the other party on the basis of an independent tort as long as this is not inconsistent with the contract: see further *Chitty on Contracts*, para. 1–105 *et seq.*

[2] On the historical development see Ibbetson, *Historical Introduction*. For more detailed discussion of the modern relationship between tort and contract see *Chitty on Contracts* para. 1–096 *et seq.*

[3] There remains a dispute as to the proper definition of contract in English law, whether in terms of promises supported by consideration (or contained in a deed) or agreements giving rise to obligations which the law will enforce: *Chitty on Contracts* paras. 1-001–1-004.

[4] Sir Frederick Pollock, *Principles of Contract at Law and in Equity* (Stevens, London, 1st. edn., 1876); Sir William Anson, *Principles of the English Law of Contract* (OUP, 1st. edn., 1879).

[5] A.W.B. Simpson 'Innovation in Nineteenth Century Contract Law' (1975) 91 *LQR* 247; J. Gordley, *The Philosophical Origins of Modern Contract Doctrine* (OUP, 1991) Chap. 6.   [6] Above, pp. 21–2.

[7] *Carter v Boehm* (1766) 3 Burr. 1905.   [8] Consumer Credit Act 1974.

[9] A distinction is usually drawn between terms implied 'in fact', that is, from an appreciation of what the parties would have agreed to in the particular circumstances (which must satisfy the 'officious bystander' test in *Shirlaw v Southern Foundries (1926) Ltd.* [1939] 2 KB 206, 227) and terms implied in law, which must be 'necessary' and not merely reasonable and which have been developed to create the legal incidents of the type of contract in question: *Lister v Romford Ice and Cold Storage Co Ltd.* [1957] AC 555; *Liverpool CC v Irwin* [1977] AC 239 and see further Treitel, *The Law of Contract*, 201 *et seq.*

while some terms are implied in contracts of employment generally, others are restricted to particular types of employment situation.[10] And while at first sight the content of some statutory implied terms is the same across a fairly large category of contract (for example contracts for the sale of goods by businesses), further distinctions may be drawn by the legislation as to the impact of these implied terms according to whether or not a buyer is a consumer.[11] Indeed, whereas French law has a unified set of approaches to all types of contracts of sale for the purposes of liability in the seller,[12] English law distinguishes between contracts of sale of goods and of land, within contracts of sale of goods between consumer and non-consumer buyers and within contracts of sale of goods to consumers between different but overlapping conceptions of consumer.[13] The law of sale of goods remains an important part of the English law of liability for products, both as regards the primary victim who has suffered personal injury, damage to property or economic loss and as a means of recourse by a person held liable to the primary victim.

To this regulation of contractual relations by the legislature and the courts must be added regulation (or attempted regulation) by contractual practice through the use of standard forms. For the most part, these standard sets of terms are set by one of the parties to the contract—the business, if the contract is with a consumer or one or other business where the contract is commercial. Sometimes, though, they result from multilateral negotiations between interested groups (as is the case as regards standard terms in the building industry[14]) or take into account imput from public regulatory bodies (such as the National Conditions of Carriage by Rail).[15] On the other hand, what is not common in English contractual practice is the setting of the terms of contracts by legal regulation or administrative decree, a mechanism which has long formed part of the French contractual scene and which indeed gave rise to the idea of a *contrat d'adhésion*.[16]

By contrast with the adventurousness of French courts, English courts have taken a very strict view of English law's principle of privity of contract and confined contractual rights to the parties, so that it was only in 1999 and by statute that a third party could be granted rights under a contract by the parties.[17] One reflection of this approach has been that English law has not extended the benefit of contractual liabilities beyond the parties through the law of contract, thereby leaving liability here to be governed by tort.[18] However, this is an area where formal principle and judicial reality have long since parted company, since while formally upholding the principle of privity of contract, the courts developed a number of mechanisms, some transparently fictitious and some remarkably complicated (and some both) in order to give a non-party some right of recourse against a party to a contract in respect of the latter's (contractual)

---

[10] Cf. the general implication of a term requiring good faith and loyalty in the parties (see *Johnson v Unisys Ltd* [2001] UKHL 13, [2003] 1 AC 518 at [24]) and the restrictive definition of the range of features regarding the contract of employment required before implication of the term in question in *Scally v Southern Health and Social Services Board* [1992] 1 AC 294, 307.

[11] Sale of Goods Act 1979, ss. 14, 15A and see below, pp. 253–4, 261.   [12] Above, p. 70.

[13] Below, pp. 227–8, 261–2.   [14] *Chitty on Contracts*, Vol. II, paras. 37 *et seq.*   [15] Below, p. 285

[16] Above, p. 137.   [17] Contracts (Rights for Third Parties) Act 1999.

[18] S. Whittaker, 'Privity of Contract and the Law of Tort: The French Experience' (1995) 15 *OJLS* 327; *id.*, 'Privity of Contract and the Tort of Negligence: Future Directions' (1996) 16 *OJLS* 191.

non-performance.[19] In particular, while privity of contract is strictly preserved, English courts have extended liability in the tort of negligence, first in the context of liability for personal injuries and damage to property and later as regards pure economic loss, that is, financial losses not consequential on the claimant's own personal injuries or damage to property in which he has a proprietary or possessory interest.[20] In this respect, cases of a manufacturer's or supplier's liability for the financial consequences of defects in the products which they supply have been at different stages central areas.[21]

This leads on to the law of torts itself, an area which must strike any modern civilian jurist as revealing the common law at its most gothic. For instead of the classical statements of principle found in articles 1382 to 1384 of the French Civil Code or even the more restrained, but nevertheless finite provisions of the German Civil Code,[22] the English law of extra-contractual liability consists of a collection of particular nominate torts, each a civil wrong with its own basis, structure, rules and sometimes context, a collection whose only common element is that they do not belong to any other category, such as breach of contract, breach of trust or liability to make restitution. The particular 'nominate torts' of which these grounds of liability are comprised certainly do not possess any systematic starting point for attracting the cases which they include: so, some torts focus on the way in which harm is inflicted (for example, harm caused by words in the torts of deceit, malicious falsehood and defamation); some focus on a particular type of fault (notably, the tort of negligence); one focuses on the legal source from which liability is said to arise (breach of statutory duty); some focus on the type of interest of the claimant which is prejudiced (for example, interference with contractual relations); and many simply arise out of a particular factual context (notably, private nuisance). The law of torts does indeed appear to be no more than the 'unanalysed remainder' of the common law, devoid of unifying principle or structure,[23] together with some more recent statutory additions each enacted on a distinctly ad hoc basis and often following the basic categorisation of the common law itself.[24]

Of all these torts the most general (and the most important for our later discussion) is the tort of negligence and here at first a French lawyer may be tempted to see a counterpart to liability for fault found in articles 1382 and 1383 of the Civil Code. It is true that English judges have in the context of this tort come closest to the promulgation of a principle of liability for fault: the famous 'neighbour principle' of Lord Atkin in *Donoghue v Stevenson* which appeals to the reasonable forseeability of harm as a ground for imposing a 'duty of care' (and therefore liability for harm negligently caused)[25] or Lord Wilberforce's 'two-stage' approach which starts by looking at the 'sufficient promixity' of the parties and then asks whether there are any considerations which ought to exclude or limit the duty,[26] are both potentially very general in their application and

---

[19] Law Commission, *Privity of Contract: Contracts for the Benefit of Third Parties* (Law Com., 1996) 242, para. 2.8 *et seq.*   [20] Below, p. 183.

[21] Below, pp. 161, 184–5.   [22] Art. 823 *et seq.* B.G.B.

[23] This phrase is Sir F. Pollock's (*The Law of Torts* (London, Stevens, 1st. edn., 1887) 5) though he attempted to argue the contrary position.

[24] E.g. Occupiers Liability Acts 1957 and 1984 (below, pp. 182–3) and Animals' Act 1971.

[25] [1932] AC 562, 580.   [26] *Anns v Merton LBC* [1978] AC 728, 751–2.

have been used to extend liability in various directions. Nevertheless, any simple comparison would be misleading, since the tort of negligence differs from the *droit commun délictuel* both in its understanding of 'fault' and in its scope of application.

For, of course, the tort of negligence rests on proof of a particular type of fault, that is, negligence, in the sense of a lack of reasonable care as determined according to a balancing of factors, some general and some special to particular contexts.[27] By contrast, while delictual fault certainly may include negligence in the sense of a failure to take the care which a *bon père de famille* would show (best expressed as *imprudence* or *manque de diligence*) it is much wider, French jurists resorting to definitions in terms of 'abnormal behaviour' or simply 'failing to do what one ought to do',[28] definitions which reveal that this French concept of fault leaves very open what actually counts as 'abnormal behaviour' or what one ought to do in any given situation.[29] As a result, first, while in French law negligence or deliberately harmful behaviour may constitute fault for this purpose, neither will *necessarily* do so, for in some contexts, French courts consider that negligence is not enough to attract liability and that even deliberately harmful behaviour may not be wrongful.[30] So while fraud (*manoevres dolosives*) will always constitute fault, competitive market practices will do so only if they are 'unfair'.[31] On the other hand, conduct which is neither negligent nor intentional may constitute delictual fault. So, any breach of duty, including the commission of any criminal offence of any strictness, will constitute fault so as to attract liability.[32] Finally, the open nature of the French understanding of delictual fault allows French courts on occasion simply to hold that a certain type of behaviour is 'at fault' without more, as in the case of those decisions which hold that a manufacturer is at fault by putting a defective product onto the market.[33] In the result, while delictual fault may include negligence in a similar sense to the common law concept, this reveals only a very small part of the picture, for French courts and writers rely on the concept of fault in order to delineate what constitutes *wrongful* behaviour, what kinds of behaviour should give rise to liability. Put into the language of the common law, fault defines the scope of the tort as well as founding the basis of liability.

This brings me to the second key distinguishing feature between liability for delictual fault and in the tort of negligence: their radically different scopes of application. The analytical framework of the tort of negligence is often broken down into five questions:

(i) Was there a duty of care?

(ii) Was this duty broken (was the defendant negligent)?

(iii) Did this breach cause the claimant's harm?

(iv) Was this harm too remote?

(v) What defences are available?

In this familiar analysis, the function of the duty of care has become clear. For since the later nineteenth century, English lawyers have used the idea of a 'duty to take care' or

---

[27] Below, p. 186 *et seq.*   [28] Above, p. 42.   [29] Above, pp. 42–3.   [30] Above, pp. 43–4.
[31] Above, p. 44 n. 22.   [32] Above pp. 45–6 and see below, pp. 374, 393–4.   [33] Above, p. 51.

'duty of care' first to collect together those situations in which negligence causing harm would give rise to liability, and then as a tool for defining when negligence causing harm should give rise to liability.[34] So while the House of Lords' famous decision in *Donoghue v Stevenson* in 1932[35] was important in freeing the tort of negligence from the idea that liability should not be imposed beyond privity of contract (the so-called 'privity of contract fallacy'[36]) and in adding manufacturers' liability for personal injury caused by their products to the list of situations where negligence would give rise to liability, its greatest importance was its invitation to courts to expand the situations in which negligence could give rise to liability, this being expressed in terms of situations in which a 'duty of care' would be imposed.[37]

While English courts now invoke a number of different formulae in their decision making as to the existence of a duty of care in the tort of negligence (including simply whether given reasonable foreseeability, and 'proximity', it is 'just, fair and reasonable' to do so[38]), its function has remained the definition of the scope of the tort, answering the question when negligence causing harm *may* give rise to liability. However, in striking contrast to the position as regards French delictual liability for fault, the scope of the tort is confined in a number of ways and directions, some of whose boundaries are by no means certain: unlike the French law, under the duty of care distinctions are drawn as to the type of harm which a claimant has suffered, the type of behaviour which a defendant has committed and the factual or legal context.[39] So, while in general it can be said that English courts are more likely to hold that a duty of care exists where a defendant's negligence has caused physical harm (personal injuries and death or damage to property owned by the claimant),[40] they have proved much more hesitant as regards liability for 'pure' economic loss and 'psychiatric injury' not consequential on one's own personal injuries. This hesitation has sometimes been expressed as a blanket rejection of liability in these sorts of situations,[41] but more recently it has instead been reflected in special approaches or criteria for the imposition of liability. So, liability for pure economic loss is most unlikely to be imposed in the absence of an 'assumption of responsibility' by the defendant;[42] liability for psychiatric injury is restricted by a distinction between 'primary victims' (persons who were aware of imminent danger or

---

[34] The conscious use of duty of care as a defining element of the tort can be clearly seen in the earlier textbooks on torts, notably in Pollock's work, *The Law of Torts, op. cit.* n. 23.   [35] [1932] AC 562.

[36] *Greene v Chelsea BC* [1954] 2 QB 127, 138.

[37] E.g. *Rimmer v Liverpool City Council* [1985] QB 1 (restricting the impact of the restrictive rule in *Cavalier v Pope* [1906] AC 428 and see Occupiers Liability Act 1957, s. 4; Defective Premises Act 1972, s. 4 (1). See also *Herrington v British Railways Board* [1972] AC 877, 899, 909, 920 refusing to follow its earlier decision in *R. Addie & Sons (Collieries) Ltd. v Dunbreck* [1929] AC 358.

[38] See esp. *Caparo Industries plc v Dickman* [1990] 2 AC 605, 618 (where Lord Bridge also notes the so-called 'incremental approach' by which the court proceeds by analogy with established categories). In some areas, the courts find it best to apply *all* the available approaches to the establishment of the duty of care in turn: see Sir Brian Neill in *Bank of Credit and Commerce International (Overseas) Ltd (in liquid.) v Price Waterhouse* [1998] PNLR 564, 583 in the context of auditors' liability.

[39] For general discussions see Markesinis and Deakin's *Tort Law*, 85 *et seq.*; *Clerk and Lindsell on Torts* para 7–05 *et seq.*   [40] But see below, p. 162.

[41] This was generally seen as the position as regards pure economic loss before the landmark decision in *Hedley Byrne & Co Ltd. v Heller & Partners Ltd.* [1964] AC 465: see *Cattle v Stockton Waterworks Co.* (1875) LR 10 QB 453.   [42] *Henderson v Merrett Syndicates Ltd.* [1995] 2 AC 145.

participated in a traumatic event) who recover under the same conditions as those suffering personal injury and 'secondary victims' (typically bystanders to traumatic events or their immediate aftermath) who recover only if certain further conditions are fulfilled, notably as to relationship with those injured or killed, their proximity in space and time and the nature of the shocking event in question.[43] As in French law, distinctions are drawn between liability for action and for omission, though the English approach is more restrictive and more highly regulated.[44]

Finally, though, even if a defendant's lack of reasonable care causes a claimant physical harm, a duty of care may be denied if the defendant can convince the court that in the circumstances of the case negligence should *not* give rise to liability. Such a denial of a duty of care may sometimes be the result of earlier precedent,[45] but it may simply be argued as a matter of 'fairness, justice and reasonableness' or on the basis of considerations of policy against the imposition of liability in the context.[46] Here, then, whatever the particular form of words used by the court, the 'proximity' of a claimant to a defendant or the 'reasonable foreseeability' of the claimant's harm by the defendant is not enough for the imposition of liability for negligence. Indeed, while the 'fairness, justice and reasonableness' formula has sometimes been put forward as a test for the existence of a duty of care in negligence, its very terms acknowledge that there is no test: the scope of the tort results from an elaborate casuistry, sometimes simply based on precedent and sometimes on a sophisticated balancing of factors, some legal and some overtly of policy.[47] In the result, the scope of the tort of negligence is not susceptible to definition by formulae or rigid rule, but rather by patterns of substantive considerations woven together by the courts in the fabric of the case law. In this way, the tort of negligence reproduces within itself something of the complexity of the law of torts in general.

If French private law's principle of liability for delictual fault finds a certain echo in the English law of negligence, its general liability for the 'deeds of things' is reflected in near silence in the English law of torts.[48] Nor does English law possess an open list of 'dangerous things' such as is used by French administrative law for the imposition of liability without fault.[49] The closest which the English common law has come to recognition of strict liability for dangerous things was in the heyday of liability under the so-called rule in *Rylands v Fletcher*, according to which a 'person who, for his own purposes, brings on his land, and collects and keeps there anything likely to do mischief if it escapes, must keep it in at his peril, and, if he does not do so, he is prima facie answerable for all the damage which is the natural consequence of its escape'.[50] However, even on the face of this form of words, it can be seen that this liability for

---

[43] *Page v Smith* [1996] 1 AC 155, itself the subject of critical discussion in *White v Chief Constable of South Yorkshire* [1999] 2 AC 455.

[44] In principle, there must be a duty to intervene, an assumption of responsibility or a relationship of control: see *Smith v Littlewoods Organisation Ltd* [1987] 2 AC 241; *Stovin v Wise* [1996] AC 923 and generally *Clerk and Lindsell on Torts*, paras. 7–45 *et seq.*

[45] *Cavalier v Pope* [1906] AC 428 (landlord's liability) but see above, n. 37.

[46] E.g. *Marc Rich & Co. AG v Bishop Rock Marine Co.* [1996] AC 211 (no duty of care in classification agency surveying safety of ship); *McFarlane v Tayside Health Board* [2002] 2 AC 59 (no duty of care in respect of financial cost to parents of healthy child born after failed vasectomy).

[47] Below, Chap. 13.   [48] Above, pp. 51–61.   [49] Above, pp. 118–21.

[50] (1865–66) LR 1 Ex. 265, 279 affirmed (1868) LR 3 HL 330, 338, 339.

dangerous things ('likely to do mischief')[51] is restricted to the context of things escaping from land and the courts have interpreted its constituent elements increasingly narrowly.[52] More radically, since 1994 the House of Lords has taken the view that the liability imposed in *Rylands v Fletcher* should not be seen as a distinct and innovatory tort, but rather as an expression of liability in the tort of private nuisance,[53] a tort which has been held to concern the mutually reasonable behaviour of neighbouring landowners and is for this reason not to be a basis for liability for personal injuries or death.[54] As a result, the 'strict' liabilities of private nuisance and *Rylands v Fletcher* are not relevant to the imposition of liability for products for personal injury or death and are relevant to liability for damage to property only to a very limited extent. Apart from liability under *Rylands*, English law does impose liabilities in respect of harm caused by particular types of thing, for example, for animals,[55] for defective premises (whether in their occupier,[56] their builder or their landlord[57]) or for 'defective equipment' provided by an employer for the purposes of his business.[58] Here, though, there is considerable diversity as to the bases, conditions and attributes of liability, some being very closely related to the tort of negligence itself, some being more distant.

What all this means is that in English law (and apart from implementation of the Product Liability Directive in the Consumer Protection Act 1987) the vast majority of cases which in French law could attract liability for the 'deed of a thing' are governed by torts where the involvement of a 'thing' is not a condition of liability, but merely forms part of the factual matrix from which other conditions of liability may be satisfied. In this respect, both the tort of breach of statutory duty (which allows the imposition of civil liability in respect of *some* breaches of statutory duty[59]) and of public nuisance (an unsatisfactorily portmanteau crime where harmful activity affects a large number of 'Her Majesty's subjects' which may give rise to liability in tort if 'special damage' is suffered)[60] have played a certain role, though in different contexts. So, for example, an employer may be liable, sometimes without proof of negligence, in the tort of breach of statutory duty to his employee for injury caused by unprotected machinery;[61] the supplier of piped water to the general public may be liable for the illness caused to a person in a locality as a result of the water's contamination.[62]

However, the tort of negligence is by far the most important of the torts in relation to compensation for harm involving products, in particular by its absence of any formal restriction as to the category of defendant on whom and type of situation in which liability may be imposed. So, liability in this tort may be imposed on the *users* of

---

[51] There is also a requirement that the presence of the thing on the defendant's property constituted a 'non-natural user' of the land: (1868) LR 3 HL 330, 338, 339.

[52] *Read v J Lyons & Co. Ltd.* [1947] AC 156; *Transco plc v Stockport MBC* [2003] UKHL 61, [2004] 2 AC 1, below.

[53] *Cambridge Water Co. v Eastern Counties Leather plc.* [1994] 2 AC 264, 297–300 (Lord Goff).

[54] *Hunter v Canary Wharf Ltd.* [1997] AC 655. *Transco plc v Stockport MBC, cit.*

[55] Animals Act 1971.   [56] Occupiers Liability Acts 1957 and 1984.

[57] Defective Premises Act 1972, s. 4.

[58] Employer's Liability (Defective Equipment) Act 1969, below, p. 182.   [59] Below, pp. 219–24.

[60] Below, pp. 224–5.   [61] Below, p. 219.   [62] Below, pp. 211–12.

products, such as the driver of a car involved in a road accident or the organiser of a cricket match whose ball causes injury,[63] as well as on manufacturers, designers, distributors or specialist consultants of products.[64] Before implementation in English law of the Product Liability Directive, the tort of negligence was the most important extra-contractual route to compensation for harm involving products, though liability rests not on the state of the product or its causal relationship to the claimant's harm, but rather on the characteristics of the defendant's conduct.

Clearly, this means that the decision as to what constitutes 'negligence' in these different categories of situation is of central importance and there are striking contrasts here with French law both in terms of the substantive law and of the procedural mechanisms by which decisions are reached. The 'negligence issue' in the tort of negligence is a complex one, the subject of a general standard of considerable abstraction (the 'reasonable person test'), but then involving the balancing of a number of considerations, some economic and some social.[65] In English law, 'fault' in the tort of negligence involves a basically utilitarian calculus known as the 'cost/benefit analysis', rather than the much broader moral judgment which lies at the heart of *la faute*.[66]

Perhaps even more striking, though, are the contrasts in legal process. Despite recent reforms which have introduced into English civil procedure a degree of judicial 'managerialism' into the traditionally party-led civil trial process,[67] English civil trials differ very considerably from the decision making of French civil tribunals.[68] Three aspects of this are very important for the practical adjudication of issues such as negligence, defectiveness or the fitness of purpose for the purpose which goods are sold, these relating to the allocation of decisions on facts within the court hierarchy, the rules and practice of adducing expert evidence and the availability of effective mechanisms for the 'discovery' of documents from opposing parties adverse to their position.[69] Thus, even where French law bases liability on *imprudence* and English law on 'negligence', the ways in which decisions on these apparently similar concepts are reached remain radically different.

The third principle of liability in French private law concerns harm caused by other persons in one's control.[70] This principle arose from a process of generalisation from examples found in the Code and, even if it becomes fully established, its generality will remain significantly qualified by the different rules which these particular examples possess.[71] These liabilities are by no means all vicarious in the common law sense (that is, a liability imposed on one person because of the tort of another with whom he is in a particular category of relationship), for while some do share these characteristics (as in the case of employers and principals) others are based on a presumption or even proof of fault in the defendant.[72] Moreover, in French law, their background is the general possibility of liability for proven fault under articles 1382 or 1383 of the Civil Code, the other person's action forming part of the factual background of the defendant's causally relevant

---

[63] *Bolton v Stone* [1951] AC 850, below, p. 193.   [64] Below, p. 181.   [65] Below, p. 186 *et seq*.
[66] Above, pp. 42–5 and below, pp. 189–202.   [67] Civil Procedure Rules (CPR) below, p. 206.
[68] Above, pp. 205–8.   [69] Below, pp. 208–18.   [70] Above, pp. 25–6.   [71] Above, p. 26.
[72] Above, p. 25.

fault.[73] So, for example, in the leading case in which the Cour de cassation appeared to accept a general principle of liability for another's deed and which concerned damage to property caused by an escaped mental patient, the underlying issue was not whether liability could be imposed, but whether liability should be based on a 'presumption of liability' or merely on proven fault.[74]

Even more disparate is the treatment of these sorts of issue by French administrative law. Clearly, the liability of the Administration in respect of maladministration by public servants is one of the main concerns of liability based on *faute de service*,[75] but this liability is not seen as an example of liability for another person's deeds especially where fault is found not in any individual public servant, but rather in the 'defective functioning' of the public service itself (*faute du service*).[76] Moreover, some cases which in private law attract 'liability for another's deeds', for example, where damage is caused by an escaped mental patient, are in administrative law typically governed by a distinct basis of liability without fault, such as 'equality of public burdens'.[77] Indeed, in this particular example, the public law *result* (liability without fault) may well have inspired the private law development, even though the conceptual techniques are different. For French administrative law, therefore, a person may be liable in circumstances where the claimant's harm results (in part) from the intervention of another person, but this does not form the legal ground of liability.

English law possesses no principle of liability for the deeds of others within one's control and in general it has restricted its true vicarious liability almost entirely to cases of employers liable for the torts of their employees committed in the course of employment.[78] There is in general no vicarious liability for the torts of 'independent contractors', that is, those working for a defendant under a contract for services rather than a contract of employment.[79] In this context, though, liability in the employer is truly strict: given the relation of 'employment' and the requisite connection between the employee's tort and his employment, liability arises in the employer without more. While technically the employee's liability is not *transferred* to the employer (since the employee in principle remains jointly liable[80]), the employer is liable if and to the same extent as the employee is liable,[81] though this will often subject the employer's liability to a proof of negligence in the *employee*. In the result, vicarious liability is very important in English practice because it extends liability to defendants who are more likely to be solvent and/or insured than are the majority of the individuals whom they employ, but it appears as exceptional and even anomalous as an example of a very strict

---

[73] Above, p. 23.   [74] Ass. plén. 29 Mar. 1991, JCP 1991.II.21673 concl. Dottenwille, above, p. 26.
[75] Above, p. 114.   [76] Above, p. 115.   [77] Above, p. 120.
[78] See generally, *Clerk and Lindsell on Torts*, Chap. 5. Vicarious liability is also imposed in respect of some cases of a principal's liability for his agent's torts and where a borrower of a chattel harms another person through its use: *Morgans v Launchbury* [1973] AC 127.
[79] There are, however, important qualifications on this general position, but these exceptions are generally said to involve special personal strict liabilities (based on 'non-delegable duties') rather than true exceptions. For examples, see below, pp. 284–5, 290–1.   [80] *Clerk and Lindsell on Torts*, para 4–130.
[81] *ICI v Shatwell* [1965] AC 656 (employee's defence of *volenti non fit iniuria* benefitted employer vicariously liable).

liability unrestricted by factual context and not tied to special danger, justifiable only by reference to convenience and public policy.[82]

Beyond the situations where English law imposes this truly vicarious liability, it does not explicitly impose liability for another's deeds, but liability may still be imposed on one person for harm more directly caused by another person's action on the basis of particular torts (and notably the tort of negligence) subject to their own conditions. So, for example, parents or school authorities are liable for harm caused by the acts of the children in their keeping, if negligence is proved in the parent or school.[83] In this sort of case, the physical involvement of another person in the occurrence of the harm may influence a court's decision whether or not to impose a duty of care (if another person has caused the harm, then the defendant's liability may be for an omission); on negligence (in terms of the standard of care required to prevent another person's harmful act[84]) or on the question of the requisite causal connection between any breach of duty in a defendant and the claimant's harm (a third party's act may 'break the chain of causation') or the question of remoteness of damage.[85] Rather differently, an occupier of premises may be liable to his visitors for harm caused to them by the state of the premises where the danger was due to their faulty construction or repair by an independent contractor engaged by him[86] or for harm caused to neighbouring owners by dangers created by acts of trespassers on his land and of which he knew or ought to have known.[87] Whereas French law has recognised an overarching category of liability for another's action (even if one uniting a disparate set of particular liabilities), English law has taken a piecemeal approach, dealing specially with a central category of situation which could be covered by such a principle (through its law of vicarious liability), but leaving other examples to be governed by the rest of its medley of torts.

2. The English Law of Administrative Liability

For the great constitutional theorist, A.V. Dicey, English law's rejection of a distinct set of rules governing public servants was central to the English constitution, being an expression of the rule of law itself: as he put it, 'every man, whatever be his rank or condition, is subject to the *ordinary law* of the realm and amenable to the jurisdiction of the ordinary tribunals'.[88] In this respect, Dicey contrasted and criticised the position in French law at

---

[82] Ibbetson, *Historical Introduction*, 181–2 quoting J. Story, *Commentaries on the Law of Agency* (A. Maxwell, London, 1st. edn., 1839) 404 para 452 and see *ICI v Shatwell* [1965] AC 656, 685 'social convenience and rough justice' (Lord Pearce). For recent discussion of vicarious liability see *Lister v Hesley Hall* [2001] UKHL 22; [2002] 1 AC 215.

[83] *Gorely v Codd* [1967] 1 WLR 19; *Lewis v Carmarthenshire CC* [1955] AC 549 and cf. *Dorset Yacht Co. Ltd. v Home Office* [1970] AC 1004 (liability of prison officers for escaped borstal boys).

[84] *Smith v Littlewoods Organisation Ltd.* [1987] AC 241, 268–70, below, p. 197.

[85] *Home Office v Dorset Yacht* [1970] AC 1004, 1027–8.

[86] Occupiers Liability Act 1957, s 1(4)(b).

[87] *Sedleigh-Denfield v O'Callagan* [1940] AC 880 (private nuisance).

[88] A.V. Dicey, *Introduction to the Study of the Law of the Constitution*, 193 and see 334 (emphasis added). The first edition was published in 1885.

the time of his writing, which 'privileged' both the administration itself and its servants.[89] Rather than being 'autonomous',[90] English law's general approach to liability for administrative action has been to subsume it within the framework of the 'ordinary' law of torts and contracts, though with the striking if narrow exception of the specifically public tort of misfeasance in public office.[91] Again, in contrast to the French position, there was no general immunity from liability in tort for public servants (whether of the Crown or of local corporations) simply on the basis that they acted within the scope of their public functions, though the Crown itself could not be liable in tort[92] and could be sued only indirectly by proceedings being brought against a nominated servant,[93] until legislation in 1947 brought Crown immunity to an end.[94]

This starting point remains true for the modern law: apart from misfeasance in public office, there is no distinctive ground of liability in the administrative *law*, which may arise only from breach of a term of its contracts or under one of the nominate torts, all of which are in principle capable of applying to public as well to private persons, public or private activities. Indeed, when Crown immunity was abolished in 1947, this framework of the 'ordinary law' was extended to the Crown's liability, it being explicitly provided that 'the Crown shall be subject to all those liabilities in tort to which, if it were a private person of full age and capacity, it would be subject'.[95]

However, this gives only a very partial and unhelpful picture of English law's treatment of the liability of public authorities. For while the frameworks of liability may be the same for public authorities as for other persons, their significance in the two contexts can differ very considerably. In particular, English law has long hesitated to impose a duty of care in the tort of negligence in respect of harm caused by a person in the exercise of a statutory power, even where this harm is physical and therefore generally recoverable.[96] Unlike French law which recognises considerable inherent powers in its administrative bodies,[97] English law generally requires statutory and, therefore, Parliamentary authority for public action.[98] This has had a considerable effect on the development of public liability, for the courts have been concerned to ensure that the imposition of liability should not impede the proper exercise of the powers which Parliament has entrusted to the body concerned. Nevertheless, the relative willingness of the courts to impose liability has ebbed and flowed. So, from 1970, the courts for a while accepted the possibility of imposing a duty of care in respect of harmful activities caused in the exercise of a statutory power as long as this did not interfere with the statutory discretion, so linking with the doctrine of *ultra vires* which was developed for

---

[89] Ibid., esp. Chap. XII.   [90] Above, pp. 19–20.

[91] This tort dates back to the end of the seventeenth century: *Three Rivers DC v Bank of England (No.3)* [2003] 2 AC 1, 29 (where the HL held that liability in this tort required proof either of action involving the exercise of public power for improper or ulterior motives or which arose where a public officer acted knowingly or recklessly beyond his powers and in the knowledge that such actions would probably result in injury to the claimant).

[92] Sir William Holdsworth, *A History of English Law*, Vol. IX (Methuen & Co, London, 1926) 19–20, 42 *et seq*.   [93] *Adams v Naylor* [1946] AC 543.

[94] Crown Proceedings Act 1947 (which sets some exceptions).   [95] Ibid., s. 2(1).

[96] See generally, Fairgrieve, *State Liability*, 58 *et seq*.   [97] Below, pp. 306–7.

[98] Craig, *Administrative Law*, 4–5. The exceptions are where a power arises from the royal prerogative or otherwise at common law (for example, under the law of corporations) or under the law of contract.

the purpose of review of the legality of administrative action.[99] However, in the 1980s and 1990s, they increasingly considered 'public policy' as an overt ground for denial of a duty of care in the tort of negligence where the defendant was a public body or exercised a public function, quite apart from any (protective) statutory discretion, a development which went hand in hand with wider judicial concern not to allow the tort of negligence to expand too readily into new contexts[100] reflected in their general approaches to the duty of care which expressed caution and the need for a positive justification for liability.[101] By the mid-1990s, the House of Lords had reached a position which was very protective of public bodies as regards their direct civil liability for negligence,[102] and had declared their general unwillingness to impose liability in the tort of breach of statutory duty in the context of public bodies.[103]

However, this very restrictive approach was challenged from two European directions. The first was that the jurisprudence of the European Court of Justice in the *Francovich* litigation,[104] established that where a Member State acted unlawfully as a matter of EU law, the effectiveness of EU law and of a citizen's remedy could be achieved only by recognition of a claim for damages and not merely achieving the annulment of the action in question. While this did not formally affect the English law on liability of public authorities outside the European context, the distinction which it created to the detriment of citizens prejudiced by illegal administrative action under domestic English law was glaring and the object of criticism.[105] However, the second challenge was even more remarkable, for in the *Osman* decision the European Court of Human Rights ruled that the striking out of claims by citizens against public authorities on the ground that public policy required that in the circumstances there should be no duty of care in the tort of negligence was a breach of the European Convention's right to due process.[106] As the European Court of Human Rights itself later realised, this unfortunate decision was based on a misunderstanding, for the Court treated the denial of a duty of care as giving a procedural immunity to defendants, whereas its function is to delineate the substantive conditions for the existence of liability.[107] While English judges viewed *Osman* with a degree of perplexity[108] and appeared relieved when the misunderstanding was cleared up,[109] the episode had a longer-lasting effect first in a much greater judicial reluctance to strike out claims for negligence against public authorities before trial of the facts, a reluctance which lingered in part on the ground that the area of the law was still 'developing'.[110] *Osman* and *Z v United Kingdom*

---

[99]   *Dorset Yacht Co Ltd v Home Office* [1970] AC 1004, 1031 and below, p. 339.

[100]   So, liability in the tort of negligence for pure economic loss and for psychiatric injury were also controlled: above, pp. 161–2.   [101]   Above, p. 161.

[102]   *X v Bedfordshire CC* [1995] 2 AC 633; *Stovin v Wise* [1996] AC 923.

[103]   Craig, *Administrative Law*, 883–5; *Stovin v Wise, cit.*; *Barrett v Enfield LBC* [2001] 2 AC 550; *Phelps v Hillingdon BC* [2001] 2 AC 619, 652; *Gorringe v Calderdale MBC* [2004] 1 WLR 1057, below, p. 335 *et seq.*

[104]   Case C-6/90 & C-9/90 *Francovich and Banfaci v Italy* [1991] ECR 1-5357; Cases C-46/93 and C-48/93 *Brasserie du Pecheur SA v Germany; R v Sec. of State for Transport, ex p Factortame* [1996] ECR 1-1029.

[105]   Fairgrieve, *State Liability*, 52–3.   [106]   *Osman v United Kingdom* [1999] 1 FLR 193.

[107]   *Z v United Kingdom* [2001] 2 FLR 612.

[108]   *JD v East Berkshire Community Health NHS Trust* [2003] EWCA Civ 1151 [14], [2004] 2 WLR 58, *per* Lord Phillips MR.   [109]   Ibid. at [22].

[110]   *Thames Trains v The Health and Safety Executive* [2002] EWHC 1415 (QB) [8], [2003] PIQR 202 quoting Lord Browne-Wilkinson in *X v Bedfordshire CC* [1995] 2 AC 633, 740–1.

also drew attention to the vulnerability of English law's overtly restrictive approach to the liability of public authorities in negligence as a matter of the *substantive* provisions in the European Convention on Human Rights, which has become more significant since the Human Rights Act 1998 requirement that public authorities must act compatibly with Convention rights (for example, a person's right to a private life) and that these rights must be given effective protection.[111]

Secondly, even if a duty of care exists, English courts are able to take into account the public value of a defendant's activity as a matter of the decision on the existence of negligence itself. Unlike French law, which has distinguished between *faute* and *faute lourde* and sometimes presumed fault,[112] English law has not done this overtly, reserving different degrees of fault for different contexts, but is instead able to take into account questions of the public interest or public policy as part of the 'cost/benefit' analysis used in determining whether or not a defendant was negligent. This can certainly be seen in the courts' approach to services (whether public or private) aimed at the saving of life,[113] and the approach of English courts to the standard of care of medical practitioners, which has been somewhat special and quite protective, could also be seen in this light.[114] It has been suggested, that the degree of expansion of the scope of the duty of care in the tort of negligence set in motion by *Osman* and its emphasis on assessment of the facts after trial will mean that the courts will place reliance on these techniques in the future.[115]

How then does the English law of administrative liability compare to the law of France? Certainly, it remains the case that, with the exception of misfeasance in public office, English law retains the same frameworks of liability whether the defendant or its function is public or private in nature. So, for example, there never has been any distinct category or treatment in English law of liability for road accidents simply because they are 'administrative',[116] nor any generally distinct treatment of the liability of the public occupiers of land or public works remotely similar to the French law of 'public works'.[117] Nor does English law recognise any special torts imposing strict liability on public bodies on the basis of public law principle, such as has been seen in relation to liability for 'dangerous things and activities', or 'equality of public burdens' in French law,[118] with the sole exception of the tort of misfeasance in public office which requires a deliberate abuse of power and which has been cautiously defined.[119]

3. Public Contracts

Dicey's denial of a distinct administrative law can still be seen very clearly in English law's approach to contracts made by public authorities: there is very little law which

---

[111] Human Rights Act 1998, s. 6; *JD v East Berkshire cit.* [55] *et seq.* [112] Above, pp. 20, 115, 119–20.
[113] *Watt v Hertfordshire CC* [1954] 1 WLR 835, 838 (fire service).
[114] *Bolam v Friern Barnet HMC* [1957] 1 WLR 582, below, p. 188. [115] Below, p. 342.
[116] Cf. above, p. 115. [117] Above, pp. 123–31.
[118] Above, pp. 118–21. The CA's tentative move in this direction in *Marcic* was later rejected by the HL: *Marcic v Thames Water Utilities Ltd.* [2002] EWCA Civ. 64 [2002] QB 929 [115]–[118]; [2003] UKHL 66 [37]–[46], [2004] 2 AC 42. [119] Above, p. 167.

governs contracts simply on the basis of their 'public' character, no corpus of distinctively administrative law of contracts: here, the 'ordinary law' remains very much in force.[120] Moreover, until the increase in importance of statutory public bodies in the course of the nineteenth century, there did not even arise a question of the capacity (or *vires*) of a public body to make a contract: the Crown itself possesses full contractual capacity;[121] Crown servants acting within their authority enjoy the same capacity;[122] and chartered corporations, whether public (such as cities or towns) or private (such as the London guilds or trading companies) were held at common law to enjoy the same contractual capacity as natural persons.[123] However, once the majority of powers enjoyed by public authorities became statutory, the question of their capacity to conclude contracts turned on construction of the statute in question, the courts struggling with the problems now dealt with in terms of contractual *ultra vires*, either directly in relation to its power to contract or in relation to other discretionary powers whose exercise must not be fettered.[124] As a result, traditionally the only significant 'public law' question is whether or not a public body has the *vires* to enter the contract in question and this can be fitted easily into the framework of the ordinary law of contract as an instance of the more general issue of contractual capacity.[125] The general lack of specific legal control of the making of contracts by public bodies is all the more remarkable given the importance which it has gained in the provision of public services.[126]

However, this position has never reflected the full picture. First, there are true exceptions, the most important of which arises from implementation of the European directives on public procurement and which governs a particular range of public contracts.[127] This can either be seen as the beginning of a distinctively administrative *law* of contracts or, less radically, an example of the special legal regulation of a distinctively administrative *contract*.

Secondly, public authorities have often been in a position owing to their market power to set the terms on which they deal with others. Historically, this has been used to give effect to government policies against 'sweated labour' or on the control of pay[128] and can be seen in the prevalence of standard term contracts.[129]

Thirdly, public authorities have sometimes been given the power by statute to enter 'agreements' with other persons on terms which they then set in the form of byelaws.

---

[120] Wade and Forsyth, *Administrative Law*, 787.   [121] *Chitty on Contracts*, para. 10–004.

[122] *Town Investments v Dept. of the Environment* [1978] AC 359, 380–1.

[123] *Sutton's Hospital Case* (1613) 10 Co Rep 1, 30b; *Riche v The Ashbury Railway Carriage and Iron Co. Ltd.* (1874) LR 9 Ex. 224, 262–3.

[124] The leading recent discussion is *Hazell v Hammersmith and Fulham LBC* [1992] 2 AC 1.

[125] See e.g. *Chitty on Contracts*, Chap. 10; Treitel, *The Law of Contract*, 563–7 (under 'corporations incorporated by special statute' as a sub-set of corporations). Cf. *Crédit Suisse v Allerdale BC* [1997] QB 306, 350 where Hobhouse LJ restricted the 'public law' issue to the existence of capacity thereby leaving to 'private law' (by which he appears to have meant the ordinary, general law) the consequences of any incapacity. (The substantive point was altered by the Local Government (Contracts) Act 1997.)

[126] Craig, *Administrative Law*, Chap. 5.

[127] See generally S. Arrowsmith, *The Law of Public and Utilities Procurement* (Sweet and Maxwell, London, 1996).   [128] Wade and Forsyth, *Administrative Law*, 789.

[129] E.g. *Rice v Great Yarmouth BC* [2003] 3 LGLR 4 (standard form contract drafted by the Association of Metropolitan Authorities for use by local authorities for the maintenance of sports facilities and parks).

This was true of the auction sales held by the East India Company from their merchant ships on docking in the eighteenth and early nineteenth century,[130] and was also sometimes the case as regards the great public works undertakings of the nineteenth century, such as the conditions on which ships used docks constructed and maintained by statutory dock companies.[131] These conditions take effect as laws rather than as contract terms and are, as a result, not subject to contractual requirements, for example, of notice.[132] In the twentieth century, a power to enact regulations was on occasion used by public utilities to set the terms on which they dealt with their customers (for example, water or gas companies), though after the privatisations of these services in the 1980s, the preferred technique has been to allow the provider of a service to set its terms subject to statutory duties and a wider regulatory framework of control.[133] In these types of situation, whether older or more recent, the degree of intervention in the relationship has raised the question whether it may still count as contractual or should instead be 'statutory' and, arguably, for this reason belonging to public law *rather than* to contract law. As I shall later explain, the decision on this point may have an impact on whether or not liability in respect of the supply of these public services rests on proof of negligence.[134]

Fourthly, the courts have on a number of occasions taken into account (overtly or covertly) the fact that a contract is made with a public authority in their application of the 'ordinary' common law contractual rules. So, for example, in the leading authority on contractual implied terms, the particular and public nature of the contract before the House of Lords was considered relevant to its application of the test of 'necessity'.[135] And a local authority which invited tenders for the contracts of licence to operate pleasure flights from the airport which it owned and managed was held bound by a contractual duty to consider all tenders submitted in accordance with its advertisement, this being in part a function of the form of advertisement and the reasonable expectations which this engendered and partly on the basis of the authority's own standing orders.[136]

Moreover, some legal frameworks for particular types of contracts do distinguish between the private and public sectors. Thus, the relations between some public 'employees' and their 'employers' were formally classified as non-contractual ('Crown service')[137] and this resulted in a number of distinctions from the position applicable to the employment relationship more generally. While it has been argued that the relationship should now be seen as contractual, it has also been said that there is a specifically public dimension to the relationship.[138] While both are contractual, the

---

[130] *Eagleton v East India Co.* (1802) 3 Bosanquet and Puller 55.

[131] *London Association of Shipowners and Brokers v London and India Docks Joint Committee* [1892] 3 Ch 242.

[132] S. Whittaker, 'Public and Private Law-making: Subordinate Legislation, Contracts and the Status of "Student Rules"' (2001) 21 *OJLS* 103, esp. 119–120.

[133] E.g. the provision of piped gas to domestic premises, below, pp. 276–80.   [134] Below, pp. 276–7.

[135] *Liverpool CC v Irwin* [1977] AC 239, 259–60 (distinguishing public and private sector tenancies).

[136] *Blackpool and Fylde Aero Club v Blackpool City Council* [1990] 1 WLR 1195, 1201.

[137] *Ridge v Baldwin* [1964] AC 40, 65.

[138] Craig, *Administrative Law*, 162–5; S. Deakin and G. Morris, *Labour Law* (Butterworths, London, 2nd. ed., 1998) 182–8.

relations between landlords and tenants in the private sector are governed (in part) by the Housing Act 1988, those in the public sector by the Housing Act 1985 Part IV (the distinction between 'public' and 'private' being specially defined for this purpose).[139] Furthermore, towards the end of the twentieth century, there has been a greater awareness of the need to consider the use of contracts by public bodies, in particular as a mechanism of government and also the possibility of their being specially regulated.[140]

There are, therefore, both differences and similarities to the approaches of English law and of French law to contracts made by public authorities. At first, they seem radically different, for French law recognises a distinct category of administrative contracts, which attract their own specifically public law and which are subject to the jurisdiction of the administrative courts;[141] but the division is not carried through into fundamental differences in the substantive law in the same way as it is as regards its extra-contractual liability. Indeed, unlike the famous declaration in *Blanco* of the autonomy of the rules governing administrative liability, the substantive law governing administrative contracts starts with the principles of the Civil Code, qualifying them and supplementing them so as to give effect to the different requirements of the public interest as is necessary according to the issue in question or the type of context of the contract.[142] As a way of thinking, this is not very different from the *approach* of English law, which also qualifies or supplements its 'ordinary' law of contract for some types of issue and some types of public contract, as I have broadly indicated. The difference then is perhaps rather one of degree, though a considerable degree, for the French administrative law is more elaborate than its piecemeal and limited English counterpart. Moreover, in keeping with its more general development, the Conseil d'Etat recognises special powers and special controls in relation to administrative contracts.[143] By contrast, while some English rules governing public contracts can be seen as restrictive (notably, in the area of procurement), there is no *general* recognition that in the making or performance of contracts a public body may need powers which an ordinary citizen does not enjoy. Reflecting English law's general stance, any special contractual powers must be granted by parliamentary legislation.

4. A Crucial Unity: The Joint Liability of Tortfeasors and Contract Breakers

While French private law has accepted a principle of the joint liability of those liable for the same harm (either in terms of solidarity or *obligation in solidum*), its general administrative law of liability for fault has rejected this principle and holds instead

---

[139] Housing Act 1985, ss. 79–81 and see S. Bright and G. Gilbert, *Landlord and Tenant Law—The Nature of Tenancies* (OUP, 1995) Chap. 6.
[140] M. Freedland, 'Government by Contract and Public Law' [1994] PL 86.   [141] Above, p. 33.
[142] Ibid.   [143] Ibid.

that a public body may not be liable for more than the harm which its fault has itself caused (this being put in terms of a defence of *fait d'un tiers*).[144] English law's approach here is very different, for it applies its law of joint and several liability equally to private and to public bodies.[145] As a result, where a public authority is liable to a person in respect of the same damage for which another person (whether public or private) is also liable, each person is liable in full vis-à-vis the person who suffered the damage, whatever the legal foundation of liability. This rule and the ability of public bodies to satisfy claims if liability is imposed, makes them very attractive defendants for inclusion within a primary victim's claim; on the other hand, the absence in English law of the sort of indirect protection from liability which the defence of *fait d'un tiers* and other systemic considerations provides in French law throws more weight on its threshold requirement of the existence of a duty of care.[146]

5. Insurance and its Practice; Social Security and Recourse

(a) The significance of liability insurance in the development of liability

While commentators on English law and, though less frequently, the judges themselves have sometimes drawn attention to the importance of the incidence of insurance on the development of liability, both the extent and the legitimacy of its influence remain controversial.[147] As in France, contracts of insurance may be taken out either by a potential claimant ('first-party insurance') or by a potential defendant ('liability insurance'), but while the availability of first-party insurance has sometimes been used as an argument as to the proper incidence of liability,[148] most attention has been focused on the role of liability insurance. Certainly, liability *insurers* play a fundamentally important role in the modern English tort process: from the point of view of a claimant who sees that any claim once established will be satisfied; from the point of a defendant who will not have to find the funds to satisfy any claim (subject to any minimum or maximum as to the cover in question); and from the point of view of the

---

[144] Above, pp. 33–4, which notes the exceptions as regards liability without fault and under the law of 'public works'.

[145] E.g. *Dutton v Bognor Regis UDC* [1972] 1 QB 373 (builder and local authority liable in respect of same harm) though subsequently overruled as to the existence of a duty of care in the local authority by *Murphy v Brentwood DC* [1991] 1 AC 398; *George Wimpey & Co. Ltd. v British Overseas Airways Corp.* [1955] AC 169 (where a public authority was not liable to contribution even though *once* liable to the primary claimant as able to benefit from a specific limitation period then applicable to claims against public authorities); *Levine v Morris* [1970] 1 WLR 72 (car driver and highway authority: 75/25% split). This is specifically enacted in relation to the liability of the Crown by the Crown Proceedings Act 1947, s. 4. Notice also that a 'public authority' against which an award of damages is made under the Human Rights Act 1998, s. 8 is specifically enabled to claim contribution from any other person also 'liable' for the same harm: Human Rights Act 1998, s. 8(5).   [146] Below, pp. 318–25.

[147] See P. Cane, *Atiyah's Accidents, Compensation and the Law* (Butterworths LexisNexis, London, 6th. edn., 1999), 190 *et seq.*; Markesinis and Deakin's *Tort Law*, 24; cf. J. Stapleton, 'Tort, Insurance and Ideology' (1995) 58 *MLR* 820.

[148] *Lamb v Camden Council* [1981] QB 625, 635, 637 (Lord Denning MR). Cf. *Transco Plc v Stockport MBC* [2003] UKHL 61; [2004] 2 AC 1 [46], [47] (Lord Hoffmann) and [60] (Lord Hobhouse).

process itself, the liability insurer taking a prominent role in negotiations towards any settlement. But in what ways has the incidence of liability insurance affected the development of liability?

First, English judges accept that the *actual* incidence of liability insurance should not be taken into account in deciding individual cases[149] and while civil cases were still decided in part by juries, the latter were not told whether or not the defendant was insured owing to the prejudicial effect this would have.[150] To do otherwise would be unfair and counterproductive, creating an incentive for defendants *not* to take out insurance. While it may be contended that the judges nevertheless do take the defendant's insurance into account in deciding borderline issues of fact or law, this is unverifiable and, it is submitted, unlikely given their declared views on the matter.

On the other hand, secondly, the *availability* to a certain category of defendant to protect himself and spread the risk by insurance (and *a fortiori* the incidence of compulsory insurance) has been seen as an important influence on the development of modern English tort law by jurists[151] and on some occasions it has been seen as a proper factor to take into account in developing the law by the judges themselves.[152] If this is true, there is nevertheless a marked contrast as to its relative impact of development of liability in England and France. For in French private law, over the course of the twentieth century there was a shift in the basis of many liabilities for death, personal injury and damage from fault to something stricter, and this was often comforted by the increasing practice of liability insurance, which has quite frequently been made compulsory.[153] The law governing road accidents is a striking example,[154] but less obviously so too is the liability of parents for their children which in French law was made increasingly strict by the courts in recognition of the widespread practice (and fairly modest cost) of the insurance cover known as '*R.C. père de famille*'.[155] And both public and private courts in France sometimes imposed liability on medical practitioners without the need to prove fault, and here the incidence of liability insurance (or, in the case of certain public bodies, self-insurance) was clearly of central importance.[156]

By comparison, while the modern English law of torts could not be envisaged without the widespread practice of liability insurance,[157] English developments of liability for accidental physical harm have been *relatively* restrained,[158] being all but restricted

---

[149] E.g. *Lister v Romford Ice and Cold Storage Co. Ltd.* [1957] AC 555, 576–7, Viscount Simonds referring to *Mason v Sainsbury* (1782) 3 Doug 61 (which concerned first-party insurance); *Davie v New Merton Board Mills Ltd.* [1959] AC 604, 626–7; *Hussain v New Taplow Paper Mills Ltd.* [1988] AC 514, 530.

[150] *Gowar v Hales* [1928] 1 KB 191, 197; *Harman v Crilly* [1943] 1 KB 168, 170.

[151] Cane, *op. cit.* n. 147, 203 *et seq.*; Markesinis and Deakin's *Tort Law, loc. cit.*

[152] In particular, Lord Denning: *Nettleship v Weston* [1971] 2 QB 691, 699 (in the context of motor vehicle accident); *Launchbury v Morgans* [1971] 2 QB 245, 253. See also, e.g. *Smith v Eric S. Bush* [1990] 1 AC 831, 858–9 (Lord Griffiths). Cf. *Marc Rich & Co. AG v Bishop Rock Marine Co. Ltd.* [1996] AC 211, 228, 229 (Lord Lloyd of Berwick); *Hunt v Severs* [1994] 2 AC 350, 363 (Lord Bridge); Stapleton, *op. cit.* n. 147, 823–4.   [153] Above, pp. 35–6.

[154] Above, p. 60–1.   [155] Above, p. 36.   [156] Above, pp. 142, 151.

[157] Cane, *op. cit.* n. 147, 203.

[158] Apart from expansion of the duty of care, other important developments were the reform of the law of contributory negligence by the Law Reform (Contributory Negligence) Act 1945 and the abolition of the 'doctrine of common employment' by the Law Reform (Personal Injuries) Act 1948, s. 1(1).

to a requirement of a standard of reasonable care (even where liability insurance is compulsory),[159] the courts rejecting the possibilities offered to them of imposing liability without negligence through the tort of breach of statutory duty, private nuisance or the rule in *Rylands v Fletcher*.[160] For example, while English law required that any person using a motor vehicle on a highway must take out insurance covering risks of injury or death to third parties some 20 years earlier than did French law,[161] English law has kept liability to a requirement of negligence and while at times a fairly demanding attitude has been taken to this, nevertheless 'fault' has remained a genuine hurdle to the imposition of liability.[162] Similarly, the general rule has remained that a person injured by an employee must prove negligence (if not in the employer) despite the compulsory nature of the employer's liability insurance,[163] the main exception being liability for breach of statutory duty which had been well established by the end of the nineteenth century.[164] And, as I have said, outside the context of employment proper, English law has remained shy of imposing true vicarious liability or, indeed, liability without fault for the harm caused by others. So, for example, in 1957 Parliament kept the liabilities of occupiers of premises to their visitors in respect of work done by independent contractors subject to proof of negligence, even though it might have been thought that householders (the occupiers) could easily spread this risk through their household insurance;[165] and in 1978 the House of Lords rejected Lord Denning's suggestion that there should be a new category of vicarious liability so as to impose liability on the person who had insured a family car, preferring to keep the law of vicarious liability outside employment within established and fairly narrow bounds.[166] As Cane has put it, '[d]espite the influence of widespread liability insurance on the common law of torts, it must be said that there has been no really deep-seated change such as might have been expected if judges or law reformers had wished to rebuild the law on the foundations of the liability insurance system'.[167]

(b) Recoupment of sums paid to primary claimants from tortfeasors

After legislation in 1985, the French approach to recoupment by those who have compensated a would-be claimant (*tiers payeurs*) has been put on a fairly integrated basis so that, apart from payments made by first-party insurers in respect of personal injuries and death (which do not reduce the primary victim's recovery), any person paying a third party and thereby reducing the damages recoverable may recoup against

---

[159] Above, pp. 162–3.   [160] Above, p. 163.

[161] Road Traffic Act 1930, s. 35 now contained in Road Traffic Act 1972, s. 143 *et seq*.

[162] See below, p. 186 *et seq. Roberts v Ramsbottom* [1980] 1 WLR 823 and *Mansfield v Weetabix Ltd.* [1998] 1 WLR 1263 specifically criticised by Markesinis and Deakin's *Tort Law*, 44, n. 184 on the basis that the courts made 'little use of insurance arguments'.

[163] See the common law's retention of this rule as to defective equipment at work in *Davie v New Merton Board Mills Ltd.* [1959] AC 604 and its quite modest legislative amendment in the Employers' Liability (Defective Equipment) Act 1969.   [164] *Groves v Lord Winborne* [1898] 2 QB 402, below, p. 219.

[165] Occupiers Liability Act 1957, s. 2(4)(b); Cane, *op. cit.* n. 147, 201.

[166] *Morgans v Launchbury* [1971] 2 QB 245, 253–7; [1973] AC 127, 136.

[167] Cane, *op. cit.* n. 147, 206.

any person liable by way of a legislative claim for subrogation.[168] This is true of private insurers of damage to property; institutions which pay social security (including contributions to medical costs and expenses) (*Caisses de sécurité sociale*) and special funds set up for particular situations (such as compensation for crimes or infection with HIV after receipt of blood products). In this way, a person liable for a primary victim's harm remains liable for the same amount whether or not another person compensates that victim wholly or in part.

By contrast, the position in English law regarding the impact of payments by third parties on the occurrence of accidental loss or damage is very complex, though changes over the last 20 years or so are leading in the same direction as the French position. For an English lawyer, the first issue is whether payment by a third party to the victim of an accident is to be deducted from the claim of that victim against the tortfeasor.

In principle any sum paid under a contract of accident insurance to the primary victim (the assured) will not be deducted from his recovery against the tortfeasor, on the basis that these sums were paid for by the assured as a result of his foresight;[169] but where the contract of insurance is one of indemnity, that is, where its intention is to compensate the policyholder to the extent of his loss quantified in advance,[170] the insurer may recoup any amount paid by him to the assured who has been compensated in full by a tortfeasor or, if not yet paid, can claim directly for such amounts from the tortfeasor by way of subrogation before payment to the assured.[171] This means that whether or not the contract of insurance is one of indemnity in the above sense, the cost of liability to the tortfeasor (or *his* insurer) remains constant.

In other cases where a person pays compensation to a primary victim in respect of their injury, loss or damage, a distinction is drawn between payments which are seen as reducing the claimant's loss (which are to be deducted from any award and therefore reduce the tortfeasor's liability) and other payments (which are not deducted from any award and do not reduce the tortfeasor's liability).[172] However, this has proved a difficult line. So, while payments by an employer in lieu of wages such as sick pay will reduce the primary victim's recovery,[173] charitable payments by a third party will not.[174] Where a deduction is made from the primary victim's recovery, in effect the tortfeasor will get the benefit, for the common law denies any recourse for the person paying whether personally or by way of subrogation.[175] This odd result is justified by

---

[168] Above, pp. 37–8.   [169] *Bradburn v Great Western Railway* (1874) LR 10 Exch 1 (personal injury).

[170] *Chitty on Contracts* para. 41–002.

[171] Ibid., paras. 41–081, 41–083. This is the case as regards the contracts of insurance against the cost of medical expenses run by the two principal private medical insurance schemes, BUPA and PPP: H. McGregor, *McGregor on Damages* (Sweet and Maxwell, London, 16th. edn., 1997) para. 1674.

[172] See Markesinis and Deakin's *Tort Law*, 796 *et seq.* for a helpful introduction. For further discussion of this law, see both Law Com. No. 147 (1997) and Law Com. No. 262.

[173] Cf. *Hussain v New Taplow Paper Mills Ltd.* [1988] AC 514; *Parry v Cleaver* [1970] AC 1 (occupational disability pension held by a majority *not* deductable) confirmed in *Smoker v London Fire and Civil Defence Authority* [1991] 2 AC 502.   [174] *Parry v Cleaver* [1970] AC 1, 14.

[175] *Metropolitan Police District Receiver v Croydon Corp.* [1957] 1 QB 154.

saying that the tortfeasor's liability is only to compensate a claimant's loss which these types of payment reduce.[176]

The English law governing the relationship between social security payments and the provision of medical care by the NHS is difficult to summarise, having been subject to change on a number of occasions over the last 20 years or so, the result being 'as complex as it is intellectually contradictory'.[177] At common law any payments made to the victim are not deducted from any award of damages and while therefore the tortfeasor remains liable in full, there is an element of double compensation.[178] However, this position has been all but ousted by successive legislative changes. Until 1989 the basic position was that a claimant's damages would be reduced by *half* as regards a certain number but not all of the significant social security benefits for up to five years:[179] here the effect of such a deduction was to benefit the tortfeasor in part as there was no recovery of the cost of the benefits by the State. The current position is that almost all social security benefits[180] are to be deducted from a primary claimant's award of damages (or at least as to those heads of damages considered relevant to the benefits in question, and so leaving out damages representing the claimant's pain and suffering or loss of amenity).[181] However, these deductions will be made only as regards the receipt of benefits for a period of five years or until a final payment by the tortfeasor;[182] and they do not take effect in certain types of situation, notably, where the victim's award is for a loss of dependency caused by the death of a person for which the tortfeasor is liable[183] or where compensation is made under the criminal injuries compensation scheme.[184] Where a deduction *is* made from the victim's award, then the payer of the benefit in question may recoup this payment from the tortfeasor under a scheme run by the Compensation Recovery Unit of the Department of Health and Social Security, by which a tortfeasor's insurer must obtain a certificate from the department that it has reimbursed the department in respect of payments before the primary claimant is paid.[185] In 2003 this approach was extended to the provision of health care under the NHS, so that where the victim has received public medical care or ambulance services, a sum may be recovered by the Compensation Recovery Unit on behalf of the DHSS from any person liable to the victim for the injuries which required the NHS's intervention.[186] The DHSS must then pay over sums so received to the responsible bodies of the relevant NHS hospital or ambulance services which have provided the care in question.[187]

---

[176] *Parry v Cleaver* [1970] AC 1, 32 *per* Lord Morris of Borth-y-Gest (dissenting).

[177] Markesinis and Deakin's *Tort Law*, 801.   [178] *Clerk and Lindsell on Torts*, paras. 29–38.

[179] Law Reform (Personal Injuries) Act 1948, s. 2(1); Social Security Act 1989 and see *McGregor on Damages* paras. 1634–44, 1690–2.

[180] The benefits in question are listed: Social Security (Recovery of Benefits) Act 1997, s. 29 and Sched. 2.

[181] Social Security (Recovery of Benefits) Act 1997, s. 8 and Sched. 2,   [182] Ibid., s. 3.

[183] Social Security (Recovery of Benefits) Regulations 1997, SI No. 2205 reg. 2(2)(a).

[184] Ibid., reg. 2(2)(d). On this scheme, see below, p. 403 n. 2. Payments made under the Macfarlane Trusts set up to compensate haemophiliacs infected with HIV by transfusion are also excluded: reg. 2(2)(a)–(c). On this trust, see further below, p. 359.   [185] Social Security (Recovery of Benefits) Act 1997, ss. 4, 6.

[186] Health and Social Care (Community Health and Standards) Act 2003 Part 3.

[187] Ibid., s. 162.

Overall, therefore, from a position by which the tortfeasor indirectly gained the benefit of the provision of social security (whether wholly or in part), English law has moved much further in the direction taken by French law in relation to the relationship between damages for personal injuries and the provision of benefits (whether in kind through the NHS or by way of social security), increasingly following a pattern by which the victim's damages are reduced but the tortfeasor's liability is preserved but towards the public provider of support. Nevertheless, the English picture remains more complex and restricted.

9

The Tort of Negligence, its Adjudication and its Satellites

1. The Dominance of the Tort of Negligence

Since the middle of the twentieth century, negligence has dominated the English law of liability for death, personal injury and damage to property. This has resulted from judicial expansion of the tort of negligence itself and its attraction into its orbit of a number of satellite liabilities by judicial interpretation of other formally distinct liabilities towards a basis in negligence[1] and by legislative creation of liabilities for statutory negligence.[2] As a result, the need for a claimant to prove a defendant's lack of reasonable care is general for the recovery in respect of death, personal injury and damage to property.

Moreover, since the decision of the House of Lords in *Hedley Byrne v Heller Partners* in 1963,[3] the tort of negligence has provided the forum for arguments as to the ambit of recovery of a range of non-physical harms designated as 'pure economic losses', where these are (a) not intentionally inflicted (this being the subject matter of the 'economic torts'[4]), (b) not brought within a claim *for* breach of contract and (c) not consequential on the claimant's own personal injuries or damage to property.[5] From a stark position which denied any recovery for such losses outside the law of contract,[6] the courts have accepted that it may *sometimes* be allowed, more recently where the defendant is said to have assumed responsibility for the circumstances from which the loss has arisen.[7] Two prominent contexts for recovery of pure economic loss have been negligent advice in relation to buildings to be sold and losses caused by *qualitative* defects in either goods or buildings sold.[8]

In contrast to the French position whose private law recognises a general principle of liability for the 'deeds of things' and whose public law recognises a category of

---

[1] Notably, liability in private nuisance and under the rule in *Rylands v Fletcher*, above, pp. 162–3.

[2] E.g. Occupiers Liability Acts 1957 and 1984. The metaphor is Ibbetson's, *Historical Introduction*, 199.

[3] [1964] AC 465.

[4] E.g. The tort of interference with contractual relations: see further Markesinis and Deakin's *Tort Law*, 506 *et seq.*   [5] Below, pp. 183–5.

[6] *Cattle v Stockton Waterworks Co.* (1874–75) LR 10 QB 453; *Weller & Co. v Foot & Mouth Disease Research Institute* [1956] 1 QB 569.

[7] *Hedley Byrne & Co. Ltd. v Heller Partners Ltd.* [1964] AC 465; *Henderson v Merrett Syndicates Ltd.* [1995] 2 AC 145 and see below, p. 184.   [8] Below, p. 185.

liability for dangerous things, before implementation of the Product Liability Directive English law did not treat liability for things or liability for products as a *formally* distinct legal category. True, in *Donoghue v Stevenson*, the leading case on the tort of negligence, the House of Lords did recognise the existence of a duty of care in a manufacturer of products towards those physically injured by them, but by doing so it merely added a further case to the legally recognised situations where negligence would give rise to liability, subsuming this example of liability for products into the general framework of the tort of negligence.[9] Moreover, the tort of negligence began to recognise a full range of possible defendants to be liable for the harm which products may cause, whether they made, designed, supplied, gave advice about or used the product in question. Here, though, while a product may provide the 'instrument' of the claimant's injury (for example, a vehicle in a road accident or an electric iron which explodes), the focus of the law remains the defendant's failure to conform to the 'negligence standard' (the requirement of reasonable care in the circumstances) rather than on the state of the product itself or its role in causing a claimant's damage. Indeed, one of the reasons why English courts have been so reluctant to allow recovery in tort for economic losses caused by the qualitative defectiveness of property (whether goods or buildings) has been because it involves a shift of attention towards the quality of the 'thing' and away from the defendant's conduct which lies at the heart of the tort of negligence.[10]

Much of the English textbook discussions on the tort of negligence concern the ambit of the duty of care, and rightly given the size and complexity of the case law and its juristic as well as its practical interest, but as regards liability for physical harm caused by action or activity, in my view it is the significance and assessment of the breach of duty or 'negligence issue' which is really interesting, for with certain notable exceptions, the courts do recognise the existence of a duty of care covering a defendant's positive action which causes physical harm.[11] What this leaves for our purposes are the difficult areas of liability for pure economic loss in relation to products and the liability of public bodies or others for failing to intervene in the interests of the claimant's safety or for failure in their exercise of powers of regulation or control over safety, which I shall discuss later.[12] Having looked briefly at the duty of care, I wish therefore to explore at some length English law's treatment of the 'negligence' issue: First, because the apparently broad and unified scheme of the tort of negligence hides a varied and complex treatment of what is actually required of the defendant in relation to the safety of products according to the particular context and, secondly, because its analysis of and process of deciding the issue of negligence contrasts sharply with French law's treatment of *la faute*, *vice* or *défaut*.[13] Having done so, I shall turn to two satellite liabilities of negligence, liability for breach of statutory duty and in public nuisance.

---

[9] There has been discussion as to whether the duty of care is owed only in the absence of an opportunity for intermediate intervention, but the probability of such an intervention goes not to the existence of a duty of care but rather to the question whether any breach of it caused the claimant's harm: see *Clerk and Lindsell on Torts*, paras. 9.-29–9.-31.   [10] Below, p. 185.

[11] Below, pp. 181–3.   [12] Below, Chap. 13.   [13] Above, pp. 46–50, 78–9.

2. Liability for Physical Damage

While it is always open to a defendant to argue that no duty of care should be imposed as a matter of policy, in general where a person's positive conduct leads to physical harm in another person, the courts recognise an existence of a duty of care.[14] There are many cases where the imposition of a duty of care may be seen to involve liability for a product in the broad sense in which I have defined this notion.[15] Most obviously, such a duty of care has been held to exist not merely as regards the manufacturer of goods,[16] but also their designer (where not also their manufacturer),[17] their distributor,[18] supplier[19] or repairer.[20] Similarly, builders,[21] architects,[22] and engineering consultants[23] owe a duty of care to those who suffer personal injury or damage to property caused by their negligence in relation to the building in respect of which they work. In all these cases, there could be said to be something 'wrong' with the property (whether movable or immovable) which is involved in causing the claimant's damage and the claim seeks to establish a lack of reasonable care in the person or persons responsible for the problem. However, in many other cases a product may be involved in the production of a claimant's harm because it has been *used* in such a way as to cause the claimant harm, whether or not there is anything 'wrong' with the product itself. So, in English law (and in striking contrast with French law), the compensation of death, injuries or damage to property caused by road accidents remains subject to the general law of the tort of negligence, and vehicle drivers owe duties of care to their passengers, pedestrians, road users and neighbouring owners of property, whether or not the vehicle is motorised and whether it is moving or stationary.[24]

Also of very considerable practical importance and again in sharp contrast with the French position,[25] compensation for injuries at work remains within the sphere of the law of torts in English law: it has been supplemented rather than ousted by the provision of social security.[26] Employers themselves owe a duty of care to their employees in respect of their personal safety;[27] moreover, employees owe each other duties of care in the tort of negligence with the consequence that an employer may be liable vicariously

---

[14] J. Stapleton 'Duty of Care Factors: a Selection from the Judicial Menus', Chap. 4 in P. Cane and J. Stapleton (eds.) *The Law of Obligations: Essays in Honour of John Fleming* (OUP, 1998) 72. Cf. the approach of the majority of the House of Lords in *Marc Rich & Co. AG v Bishop Rock Marine Co. Ltd.* [1996] AC 211, 235 (Lord Steyn) (liability of a marine classification society).

[15] Above, pp. 5–10.

[16] *Donoghue v Stevenson* [1932] AC 562; *Grant v Australian Knitting Mills* [1936] AC 85; *Carroll v Fearon* [1998] PIQR P416 (duty to warn about product after putting on the market).

[17] *Kaye v Alfa Romeo* (1984) 134 NLJ 451 (manufacturer and designer of seatbelt anchorage).

[18] *Watson v Buckley, Osborne, Garrett & Co. Ltd. & Wyrovoys Products Ltd.* [1940] 1 All ER 174.

[19] *Roe v Minister of Health* [1954] 2 QB 66 (duty of care owed by anaesthetist in respect of impure anaesthetic injection).

[20] *Stennett v Hancock* [1939] 2 All ER 578 and cf. *Haseldene v CA Daw & Son Ltd.* [1941] 2 KB 343.

[21] *D. & F. Estates Ltd. v Church Commissioners for England* [1989] AC 177 esp. *per* Lord Bridge at 206; *Murphy v Brentwood DC* [1991] 1 AC 398, 462, 475, 487–8.

[22] Cf. *Clay v A.J. Crump & Sons Ltd.* [1964] 1 QB 533.

[23] *Haseldene v C.A. Daw & Son Ltd. cit.*; *George Hawkins v Chrysler (UK) Ltd. and Burne Associates* (1986) 38 Build LR 36.   [24] E.g. *Ludgate v Lovett* [1969] 1 WLR 1069. Cf. above, pp. 60–1.

[25] Above, pp. 61–2.   [26] Below, pp. 176–7.   [27] *Wilsons & Clyde Coal Co. Ltd v English* [1938] AC 57.

for the negligence of an employee causing another employee harm as long as the former was acting in the course of his employment.[28] While in these cases, the legal basis of liability at common law is negligence in either employers personally or their employees, in many cases a product, such as machinery, tools or the substances with which the employees work will be involved.[29] This position was only moderately modified by legislation in 1969 which imposes liability on employers without proof of negligence *in the employer* but retains a requirement of causally relevant 'fault' in a third party.[30]

We can also see a number of situations where French law looks at the involvement of a 'thing' in the production of the claimant's harm under article 1384 alinéa 1 of the Civil Code which are left in English law simply to the ordinary law of the tort of negligence.[31] So, children who play 'sword-fights' with plastic rulers owe each other a duty of care[32] and sports players owe duties of care to each other and to spectators in respect of balls or other objects which go astray.[33] Doctors owe their patients duties of care in respect of their health care: in their pre-treatment advice,[34] in their diagnosis, in their surgery and in aftercare, and, apart from any impact of the Consumer Protection Act, medical liability remains based on the tort of negligence whether or not a product such as a pharmaceutical or X-ray machine is involved in the production of the claimant's harm.[35] And, quite apart from any other basis of liability, a person who stores or uses a product which is likely to cause harm if it 'escapes' is held to a duty of care in respect of death, personal injury or damage to property which it may cause.[36]

On the other hand, liability in respect of the state of or things done on premises[37] to persons *on the premises* who suffer harm owing either to their state or to what occurs on them is governed by English law by the closest of the satellites of the tort of negligence, the 'negligence' liabilities imposed on occupiers in respect of premises by the Occupiers Liability Act 1957 in respect of 'visitors' and the Occupiers Liability Act 1984 in respect of non-visitors.[38] For this purpose, no formal distinction is drawn

---

[28] For the distinction between this and personal liability in the employer see ibid. and *Staveley Iron and Chemical Co. Ltd. v Jones* [1956] AC 627.

[29] E.g. *Davie v New Merton Board Mills Ltd.* [1959] AC 604.

[30] Employers' Liability (Defective Equipment) Act 1969, s. 1. Fault is defined as negligence, breach of statutory duty or any other act or omission which gives rise to liability: s. 1(3) 'fault'.

[31] Above, pp. 51–61.   [32] *Mullin v Richards* [1998] 1 WLR 1304.

[33] *Bolton v Stone* [1951] AC 850 (cricket ball); *Pearson v Lightning* The Times, 30 April 1998 (golf ball); *Wilks v Cheltenham Homeguard Motor Cycle & Light Car Club* [1971] 1 WLR 668 (motorcyclist in a 'scramble' crashed into spectator).

[34] *Sidaway v Board of Governors of the Bethlem Royal Hospital* [1985] AC 871.

[35] *Gold v Essex County Council* [1942] 2 KB 293 (treatment with Grenz rays); *Roe v Ministry of Health* [1954] 2 QB 66 (care of ampoules containing anaesthetic), below, p. 286 *et seq.*

[36] *Overseas Tankship (UK) Ltd v Miller Steamship Co. Pty. Ltd.* (*The Wagon Mound No. 2*) [1967] 1 AC 617 (spillage of furnace oil); *British Celanese Ltd. v A.H. Hunt (Capacitors) Ltd* [1969] 1 WLR 959 (metal foil strips). Liability may also be imposed on the basis of public or private nuisance or under the rule in *Rylands v Fletcher*.

[37] The same liabilities are imposed in respect of a person occupying or having control over 'any fixed moveable structure, including any vessel, vehicle or aircraft': Occupiers' Liability Act 1957, s. 1(3)(a); similarly, Occupiers' Liability Act 1984, s. 1(2).

[38] In the case of visitors, the 1957 Act makes particular provision for certain elements in the determination of the issue of negligence: Occupiers' Liability Act 1957, s. 2(4); in the case of non-visitors, the 1984 Act imposes a special set of conditions for the existence of such a duty: Occupiers' Liability Act 1984, s. 1(3).

between 'occupation' by public and by private bodies.[39] Moreover, while occupiers of immovable property may owe duties of care in the tort of negligence to persons not present on the property (and notably, to their neighbours),[40] they may also bear liabilities arising under the Defective Premises Act 1972 or the torts of nuisance, and many of the examples where liability is imposed concern cases where products have 'escaped' from the premises and caused harm (whether or not these products were attached to or formed part of the immovable property).[41] Very broadly speaking, therefore (and apart from liability under the 1987 Act), the involvement of a product in the production of a claimant's injury is irrelevant to the categorisation of a defendant's liability, but the occupation of premises does give rise to a series of distinct grounds of liability, some of which are 'negligence liabilities' but *outside* the formal boundaries of the common law tort and some of which are typically dealt with by distinct tortious liabilities.

3. Liability for 'Pure Economic Loss'

'Pure economic loss' may be defined as that financial loss which is not consequential on damage to property owned by the claimant[42] or on personal injuries suffered by the claimant.[43] Pure economic loss caused by the death of another person is also irrecoverable at common law, but important exceptions were made for 'dependents' of the deceased by the Fatal Accidents Acts.[44] Where economic loss is consequential on a claimant's damage to property it is in principle included within the duty of care, but may be irrecoverable on the ground that it is too remote.[45] The test of remoteness in the tort of negligence is one of a lack of reasonable foreseeability of the type of harm suffered by the claimant,[46] and its function can be seen as a way of controlling liability even in respect of types of harm in principle included within the scope of the tort and otherwise falling within the scope of a duty of care.

---

[39] 1957 Act, s. 6; 1984 Act, s. 3 (Crown liability). For the application of the Act to local authorities, see *Jolley v Sutton LBC* [2000] 1 WLR 1082. Issues of social utility (and therefore the public interest) may go to the question of the content of a public authority's duties under the Acts: *Tomlinson v Congleton BC* [2003] UKHL 47; [2003] 3 WLR 705 and see above, p. 169.

[40] *British Celanese Ltd. v A.H. Hunt (Capacitors) Ltd.* [1969] 1 WLR 159 (metal foil blowing from defendant's land and causing power failure which damaged plaintiff's machinery).   [41] Below, pp. 224–5.

[42] A possessory right in the claimant has been said to be enough: *Leigh and Sillivan Ltd. v Aliakmon Shipping Co. Ltd.* (*The Aliakmon*) [1986] AC 785.

[43] For an extremely useful discussion, see J. Stapleton, 'Duty of Care and Economic Loss—A Wider Agenda' (1991) 107 *LQR* 249. For further discussion of liability for pure economic loss and defective products see S. Whittaker 'Defective Products and Economic Loss' 49 *MLR* 369 (1986); *id.*, 'Privity of Contract and the Tort of Negligence: Future Directions' (1996) 16 *OJLS* 191, 223–39.

[44] Originally the Fatal Accidents Act 1846; currently the Fatal Accidents Act 1976. It has been held that a business loss suffered by a dependent is not recoverable under the Act: *Burgess v Florence Nightingale Hospital for Gentlewomen* [1955] 1 QB 349.

[45] *Spartan Steel & Alloys Ltd v Martin & Co (Contractors) Ltd.* [1973] QB 27.

[46] *Overseas Tankship (UK) Ltd. Appellant v The Miller Steamship Co. Pty.* (*The Wagon Mound No. 2*) [1967] 1 AC 617.

Quite apart from the question of remoteness of damage, we could distinguish further between the types of pure economic losses relevant to liability for products. In the case of *defective* products, losses may be caused by the devaluation of the product or its need of repair or replacement (though English courts treat the case where the product is simply defective and where its defect has caused its own damage or destruction both equally as giving rise to 'pure economic loss');[47] or as a result of a product's causing some other harm to a person's other economic interests, notably by triggering a liability to a third party under a contract (for example, where the purchase of defective machinery disrupts a claimant's industrial process and so causes his failure to perform a contract with a third party or even then triggers a liability in his buyer to a fourth party).[48]

However, English courts do not distinguish between these different types of loss in coming to a firm general rejection of liability for pure economic loss caused by defective products nor between whether the product in question is a movable or an immovable.[49] To this general picture, there is only one caveat, as there remains the *possibility* of liability under the case law set in motion by *Hedley Byrne*.[50] While this case law first centred on cases where a defendant's misstatement caused the claimant pure economic loss (so, in the context of liability for products, in cases concerning the liability of surveyors, architects or designers),[51] in *Henderson v Merrett Syndicates Ltd*.[52] Lord Goff saw the basis of liability under *Hedley Byrne* in a 'broad doctrine' of assumption of responsibility capable of applying equally to liability for the negligent performance of services and for misstatements,[53] and this suggests that liability for pure economic loss caused by defective products may be imposed as long as the defendant can be said to have agreed to do the work for the claimant and possessed or held himself out as having special skill in doing so.[54] On the other hand, Lord Goff distinguished the 'ordinary case' of the liability of a building sub-contractor who would not be liable for sub-standard work to the commissioner of the building beyond privity of contract because the parties had chosen to structure their relationship in a way inconsistent with such a direct relationship.[55]

This observation explains in part why English courts have taken such a restrictive attitude to the imposition of liability for pure economic loss caused by defective products in tort of negligence. For while they are generally concerned with opening the 'floodgates' to claims which would be over-burdensome to defendants and sometimes have seen limited Parliamentary intervention as a reason against judicial creativity,[56] in the context of defective products there is also a strong sense that recovery in respect

---

[47] *Murphy v Brentwood DC* [1991] 1 AC 398.   [48] Cf. *Lambert v Lewis* [1982] AC 225.

[49] *Muirhead v Industrial Tank Specialities Ltd.* [1986] QB 507; *Simaan General Contracting Co. Ltd. v Pilkington Glass Ltd.* [1988] QB 758 (movable product); *Murphy v Brentwood DC* [1991] 1 AC 398 (building).   [50] [1964] AC 465.

[51] *Smith v Eric S. Bush* [1990] 1 AC 831 (surveyor); *IBA v EMI Electronics Ltd.* [1980] 14 BLR 1 (designer of radio mast).   [52] [1995] 2 AC 145.   [53] Ibid. at 180–1.

[54] For this interpretation of the judicial understanding of 'assumption of responsibility' see S. Whittaker 'The application of the "broad principle of *Hedley Byrne*" as between parties to a contract' (1997) 17 LS 169.   [55] [1995] 2 AC 145, 195–6.

[56] E.g. *Murphy v Brentwood DC* [1991] 1 AC 398, 457, 472, 482, 491, 498 in relation to the Defective Premises Act 1972.

of qualitative defects (as opposed to dangerous defects) should be left to the law of contract. This idea lies behind judicial concern that the tort of negligence should not disrupt the contractual structure which the parties have put in place[57] and that imposing liability in tort may nullify the protection with which the defendant was provided by a contractual exemption clause.[58] Even more fundamental, though, is the difficulty of determining the appropriate standard of liability to be required of a defendant. For the tort of negligence bases liability on a defendant's lack of reasonable care, as judged by an assessment of the balance between the risk of harm against the cost of its avoidance,[59] whereas the contractual basis of liability for products rests either on the express terms of the contract in question or on the achievement of a standard of quality or utility.[60] Where express or implied contract terms require the attainment of a particular result, the defectiveness of a product is surely to be judged by reference to these standards rather than by reference to the degree of care which the defendant used in trying to achieve this result.[61]

However, the reluctance of the courts to use the tort of negligence to impose liability for pure economic loss caused by defective products has not prevented its occasional recovery by other means. So, products (and particularly buildings) can be constructed under a scheme of arrangements by which an express direct contract is made to create a basis of liability in the event of defect;[62] a right of recovery in respect of defects under a contract may be assigned to its subsequent purchaser;[63] and the parties to a contract under which a product is made may create a right in a non-party in respect of any subsequent defects.[64] The courts themselves have also sometimes used circumventing techniques, either by finding 'collateral contracts'[65] or by allowing the person who commissioned a product to recover substantial damages in respect of its defects which they hold on trust for the benefit of a person who actually suffers the loss as a result (such as a sub-purchaser).[66]

All this contrasts very strikingly with the position in French law, where in principle 'pure economic loss' may be recovered under the general provisions for delictual fault, but where many cases which English law would see as concerning liability for pure economic loss caused by defective products would be governed *exclusively* by

---

[57] *Simaan General Contracting Co. Ltd. v Pilkington Glass Ltd.* [1988] QB 758.

[58] *Henderson v Merrett Syndicates Ltd.* [1995] 2 AC 145, 195–6. See also *White v Jones* [1995] 2 AC 207, 294. [59] Below, p. 189 *et seq.*

[60] Cf. below, pp. 232–42 in relation to the Sale of Goods Act 1979, s. 14.

[61] See, e.g., the dissent of Lord Brandon in *Junior Books Ltd. v Veitchi Co. Ltd.* [1983] 1 AC 520, 551–2 and further Whittaker, *op. cit.* n. 43, (1996) 16 *OJLS* 191, 207–11.

[62] For example, the 'duty of care deed' used in *Alfred McAlpine Construction Ltd. v Panatown Ltd* [2001] 1 AC 518 (esp. at 593 *per* Lord Millett).

[63] Such an assignment is subject to contrary exclusion in the first contract: *Linden Gardens Trust Ltd v Lenesta Sludge Disposals Ltd.* [1994] 1 AC 85.

[64] Contracts (Rights for Third Parties) Act 1999, s. 1.

[65] *Shanklin Pier Ltd. v Detel Products Ltd.* [1951] 2 KB 854.

[66] *Alfred McAlpine Construction Ltd. v Panatown Ltd.* [2001] 1 AC 518. It is to be noticed that there were at least two judicial views as to the basis of the recovery allowed, on which see A.S. Burrows, 'No Damages for a Third Party's Loss: *Alfred McAlpine Construction Ltd. v Panatown Ltd*'. (2001) *OUCLJ* 197; E. McKendrick, 'The Common Law at Work: The Saga of *Panatown Ltd. v Alfred McAlpine*' (2003) 3 *OUCLJ* 145.

special contractual rules extended beyond the parties either by the courts themselves (in the case of the law of sale) or by legislation (as regards liability for buildings).[67] As a result, French law subjects liability to the contractual standards and to any exemption or limitation clauses which it considers should be effective as a matter of public policy.[68]

4. Defining Negligence

The 'fault' element of the tort of negligence contrasts sharply with the French conception of *la faute délictuelle* in a number of important ways and for a number of reasons: first, the concepts of *faute* and 'negligence' have different functions in their respective systems of substantive law; secondly, the decision making of English courts is elaborately structured by the law in contrast to the relatively unstructured 'assessments' made by the *juges du fond*; and thirdly, the procedural contexts of judicial decision making in the two systems are profoundly different.

(a) Negligence as a lack of reasonable care

The English understanding of the concept of 'negligence' pre-dates the emergence in the latter half of the nineteenth century of a recognisably distinct tort of negligence, but the modern approach which became established in the 1950s reflects long-gone arguments as to the division of functions between judge and jury, borrowings from American law, and a general intellectual tendency of seeking to structure the judicial discretion created by broad and open-textured concepts. The historical development of the English understanding of negligence also shows that it flirted with but then resolutely rejected the idea that the breach of *any* legal duty in itself constitutes negligence so as to give rise to liability, a rejection which contrasts sharply with French acceptance that any breach of a duty itself constitutes *une faute*.[69]

In contrast to French law,[70] English law's starting point was the concept of negligence rather than the concept of fault, and it is negligence which has been the subject of definition and elucidation. In my view, it is for this reason (as well as for reasons of intellectual taste) that many English lawyers have not been as concerned to see a personal, moral fault as the basis for liability in the tort of negligence as French lawyers have been with regards to *la faute*. Of course, one does see in English and particularly older discussions of liability for negligence reference to the 'fault' of the defendant, sometimes in overtly moralising terms.[71] But while it could be simply asserted that a

---

[67] Above, pp. 97, 104.   [68] Above, pp. 97, 105.   [69] Above, pp. 45–6.
[70] Above, pp. 42–6.
[71] An example is Lord Atkin himself in *Donoghue v Stevenson* [1932] AC 562, 580 where he observed that negligence is based 'upon a general public sentiment of moral wrong-doing for which the offender must pay'. However, in a LEXIS search of the cases where morality and negligence were close together, the vast majority of the mere 52 cases retrieved concerned a dictum of Lord Bridge in *McCloughlin v O'Brian* [1983] 1 AC 410, 441–2 where he denied that making a 'defendant liable for reasonably foreseeable

failure to come up to the law's objective standard is in some sense a fault, it is generally acknowledged that there is no personal moral failure involved where a person does all that he or she is able to do and yet falls short of an externally set standard.[72] And for many writers, the justification of setting the standard of liability at 'negligence' does not lie in a moral judgment of the behaviour of the defendant, but rather in a balance between the interests of claimants to compensation and defendants to liberty and initiative, or, conversely, in the deterrence of unreasonably unsafe conduct.[73] If one were to need to choose a moral basis for the modern tort of negligence it would have to lie in some sort of rough and ready utilitarianism (perhaps sometimes qualified to take into account the importance of individual rights), rather than in a moral credo which sees the defendant's failure as a moral wrong. If there is a traditional morality of the English law of torts, it is that of Bentham, rather than as in French law of Aquinas or Kant.[74]

The scene was set for the legal definition of negligence in 1837 in *Vaughan v Menlove*, where the defendant's hayrick spontaneously ignited and the fire spread to the closely neighbouring cottages owned by the plaintiff.[75] The judge at trial had put to the jury the question whether the defendant had committed a 'gross negligence', a concept familiar to English lawyers from the law of bailment which distinguished between *dolus*, *culpa lata* and *culpa levissima* in emulation of the Roman law of contract.[76] However, Tindal CJ rejected the need for such a special fault on the facts:[77] the standard of behaviour for negligence ought not to be 'co-extensive with the judgment of the individual', as the law requires 'in all cases a regard to caution such as a man of ordinary prudence would observe'.[78] So English law drew on the *bonus paterfamilias* of the Roman law of contract in order to create its objective conception of negligence developed for the purposes of liability in tort.[79]

---

psychiatric illness caused by his negligence would be to impose a crushing burden on him out of proportion to his moral responsibility'; and of Viscount Simonds in *Overseas Tankship (UK) Ltd. v Morts Dock & Engineering Co. Ltd. (The Wagon Mound)* [1961] AC 388, 422–3 where 'current ideas of justice and morality' were used to limit the extent of liability by a more restrictive test of remoteness. No judge assimilated a finding of negligence to a finding of a moral wrong in the defendant.

[72] *Nettleship v Weston* [1971] 2 QB 691 below, p. 85, is often cited as an example of a finding of negligence where no moral fault could be imputed.

[73] For differing views see: T. Honoré, 'The Morality of Tort Law—Questions and Answers' in D.G. Owen (ed.), *Philosophical Foundations of Tort Law* (OUP, 1995) 73; R.W. Wright, 'The Standards of Care in Negligence' ibid., 249 (who argues against the utilitarian basis of liability for negligence); A. Burrows, *Understanding the Law of Obligations* (Hart, Oxford 1998) 123–6.

[74] For the French approach, see above, pp. 42–3 and also L. Josserand, 'Un ordre juridique nouveau' DH 1937 Chron. 41, 44 who, in the course of criticising legislation allowing the courts broad powers to give debtors time to pay 'taking into account the economic situation', observed that '*les idées de Bentham et de William James peuvent être mises à la base du mouvement juridique actuel, bien plutôt que celles de Platon, de Descartes ou de Kant; et le concept du droit naturel est menacé d'un discrédit grandissant*'. And Josserand wrote the seminal work, *La responsabilité du fait des choses inanimées* (Paris, 1897) and was one of the key figures in the creation of a 'presumption of liability' applying to the deeds of things, thereby divorcing the imposition of liability from *la faute*. [75] (1837) 3 Bing NC 468.

[76] *Coggs v Bernard* (1704) 2 Ld Raym 909. Ibbetson, *Historical Introduction*, 164.

[77] (1837) 3 Bing NC 468, 474.   [78] Ibid. at 474.

[79] See also *Blyth v Birmingham Waterworks Co.* (1856) LR 4 Ex 32.

(b) The standard of care

Since *Vaughan v Menlove*,[80] the general standard of care imposed by the tort of negligence has been the objective standard of the reasonable person, but there are some qualifications on this where the *category* of person to which the defendant belongs (or professes to belong) requires either a higher or a lower standard of care than that expected of people generally.

Most importantly, the standard expected of professionals is the standard of a reasonable professional of the speciality in question, this being justified on the basis that one can expect more of those who profess special skill than those who do not.[81] In practice, a defendant will often bring forward expert evidence to the effect that his conduct conformed to the standard required by 'a competent body of professional opinion'(the '*Bolam*' test),[82] and this argues very strongly against a finding of negligence, though the courts are entitled to find that a current professional practice is not 'reasonable or responsible'.[83] The *Bolam* test is, therefore, both more and less demanding than the ordinary standard of the reasonable person. Conversely, English law has accepted that the standard of care may sometimes be lowered, notably as regards children, where the standard is of the reasonably prudent child of the age of the particular defendant in the situation.[84]

Another key example of the way in which English courts have nuanced the standard of care according to the category of defendant may be seen in their attitude to drivers' negligence. Here, the standard is reasonable care required of drivers generally, and this standard is not lowered for a learner driver,[85] a strict approach which Lord Denning MR justified by the presence of compulsory third party insurance.[86] How far can this objectivity go? In *Mansfield v Weetabix Ltd.* a driver, unaware of a condition which caused his brain not to function properly yet not fully unconscious, suffered a series of minor collisions before crashing into the plaintiffs' shop.[87] In these circumstances the Court of Appeal held that a driver should not be liable in negligence where a disabling event occurred in a gradual rather than sudden manner provided that the driver is unaware of it occurring.[88] For Leggatt LJ, 'the standard of care that [the defendant there] was obliged to show in these circumstances was that which is to be expected of a reasonably competent driver unaware that he is or may be suffering from a condition that impairs his ability to drive'.[89] To take any more objective a view would be to impose strict liability.[90]

Finally, is the standard of care higher where a particular (and reasonable) expectation is induced in a victim (or others) by a defendant's behaviour? For example, where a manufacturer represents that his product is particularly safe (owing to some special feature) does this increase the standard of care as compared with the standard applicable to manufacturers generally? While it has been said (in the context of the *lowering* of

---

[80] (1837) 3 Bing NC 468, above, p. 187.

[81] Cf. *Adams v Rhymney Valley DC* (2001) 33 HLR 446, 450–1 *per* Sedley LJ.

[82] *Bolam v Friern Barnet HMC* [1957] 1 WLR 582, 590 *per* McNair J.

[83] *Bolitho v City and Hackney HA* [1998] AC 232, 243.

[84] *Mullin v Richards* [1998] 1 WLR 1304, 1311 approving the approach of the HC of Aus. in *McHale v Watson* [1966] 115 CLR 199 (children aged 15 playing 'sword-fights' with plastic rulers at school when ruler broke and injured eye of one child).   [85] *Nettleship v Weston* [1971] 2 QB 691.

[86] Ibid. at 699–700.

[87] [1998] 1 WLR 1263. The CA disapproved the stricter approach at first instance in *Roberts v Ramsbottom* [1980] 1 WLR 823.   [88] [1998] 1 WLR 1263, 1268.

[89] Ibid.   [90] Ibid.

the standard in the context of a learner driver) that a claimant's actual or reasonable expectations as to a defendant's competence are irrelevant to the standard of care in the interests of certainty,[91] the representation of a product as 'absolutely safe' and 'positively needing no preliminary tests' has been held relevant to the question of breach where it caused injury in normal use.[92]

(c) Breach of duty: from jury verdicts to a judicial cost/benefit analysis

For about a century after *Vaughan v Menlove*,[93] there was little elucidation of what the standard of 'reasonable man' actually required (or when breach of the duty would be found) and this was primarily a result of the division of responsibility as to the issue of negligence, for while it was for the judge to define negligence (in terms of a failure to act as a reasonable man would have done), it was for the jury to assess whether or not the defendant had attained this standard or breached his duty.[94] However, from the middle of the nineteenth century English judges sought ways of gaining a degree of control over the discretion which this gave to juries, concern being openly expressed that otherwise they would too readily find negligence in order to see compensation awarded, in particular against railway companies whose operations took their toll in terms of death and personal injury.[95] The main mechanism used by the courts was to ask whether the trial judge should have withdrawn the issue of negligence from the jury on the ground of insufficiency of evidence.[96] A striking example may be found in *Blyth v Birmingham Waterworks Co.*[97] where a fire-plug installed by a waterworks company had frozen in an exceptionally long and hard frost causing flooding to the plaintiff's property. Alderson B expressed the view that a reasonable man would act with reference to the average circumstances of the temperature in ordinary years taking into account the reasonableness of the precautions (two of the elements later more formally designated as factors in the determination of the issue of negligence)[98] but on this basis on the facts as found, there was no evidence of negligence to go to the jury. However, in numerous cases of withdrawal of the issue of negligence in the second half of the nineteenth century, the judges can be seen to remain genuinely concerned to preserve the jury's role in finding negligence, while making appropriate provision to avoid arbitrariness.[99] As Sir Frederick Pollock remarked approvingly,[100] it would be 'a serious burden for the Court to

---

[91] *Nettleship v Weston* [1971] 2 QB 691 at 700 (*per* Lord Denning MR); 707–08 (*per* Megaw LJ).

[92] *Watson v Buckley, Osborne, Garrett & Co. Ltd.* [1940] 1 All ER 174 (distributor which advertised hairdressing product). Cf. the claim for indemnity in the tort of negligence in *Lambert v Lewis* against a manufacturer of a trailer coupling described in its publicity as 'foolproof' and requiring no maintenance, though this issue was left open by the HL: [1982] AC 225, 277.   [93] (1837) 3 Bing NC 468, above, p. 187.

[94] *Vaughan v Menlove* (1837) 3 Bing NC 468, 475.   [95] Ibbetson, *Historical Introduction*, 174–5.

[96] *Stubley v LNW Rly. Co.* (1865–66) LR 1 Ex. 13; *Smith v LSW Rly. Co.* (1870–71) LR 6 CP 14; *Bridges v LN Rly. Co.* (1874–75) LR 7 HL 213; *Metropolitan Rly. Co. v Jackson* (1877–78) LR 3 App Cas 193.

[97] (1856) 11 Ex 781.

[98] Ibid. at 784. Martin and Bramwell BB agreed. On these elements, see below, pp. 193–8.

[99] See esp. *Metropolitan Rly. Co. v Jackson* (1877–78) LR 3 App Cas 193, 197 (Lord Cairns LC); 207–08 (Lord Blackburn).

[100] M. De Wolfe Howe (ed.) *The Pollock–Holmes Letters: correspondence of Sir Frederick Pollock and Mr Justice Holmes, 1874–1932* (CUP, 1942) Vol. I, 13, 92. Pollock observed in 1887 that the judicial tendency was 'if not to enlarge the province of the jury, to arrest the process of curtailing it': *The Law of Torts* (Stevens & Sons, 1st. edn., 1887) 360.

take judicial notice of what a reasonable man's conduct would be in every variety of circumstances':[101] and the juryman represented the reasonable man in person.

Clearly, while the jury's broad role was preserved, English judges had little occasion to develop more elaborate explanations of what 'reasonable care' required. So, while in deciding whether or not there was evidence of negligence to go to a jury, a judge may refer to the need to consider the cost of precautions to be undertaken to avoid *most* accidents,[102] we do not really see any more articulated balancing of factors. Even Pollock was content simply to state that 'the caution that is required is in proportion to the magnitude and the apparent imminence of the risk'.[103]

However, in the middle of the twentieth century the next stage in the development of the English understanding of negligence led to its much more formal articulation. There were four elements at work here.

A first element can be seen in English law's rejection of the idea that breach of any duty (of whatever content) constituted negligence, a position strikingly different from French law's approach to delictual fault.[104] At first, judicial discussions in the context of the tort of breach of statutory duties in factory safety legislation suggested the contrary, the breach of the statutory duty being referred to as 'statutory negligence' so as to emphasise 'that the Legislature erects a standard of carefulness' so that it is not 'left to the chance opinion of a jury to decide whether these precautions may properly be omitted'.[105] Moreover, in the late 1930s and 1940s the question arose whether breach of a statutory duty constituted 'negligence' for the purposes of an exception to a scheme of social insurance for accidents at work where the injury was caused 'by the personal negligence or wilful act of the employer or of some person for whose act or default the employer is responsible'.[106] Here, the House of Lords held that breach of any statutory duty of safety provided 'all the essentials of negligence': to decide otherwise would be to attach too much importance to the forms of action.[107] As a result, an employee could still claim compensation in tort despite the existence of the scheme.

However, this equation of breach of a statutory duty of safety and negligence was short-lived in English law. For in *Caswell v Powell Duffryn Associated Collieries Ltd.* in 1940 the House of Lords had to determine whether the defence of 'contributory negligence' in a plaintiff (which at the time acted as a bar to liability rather than as a ground for its reduction[108]) applied to claims for breach of statutory duty on the ground that they were actions for negligence.[109] In this context, the House of Lords

---

[101] M. De Wolfe Howe, *op. cit.* n. 100, 92–3.

[102] *Stubley v LNW Rly. Co.* (1865–66) LR 1 Ex 13, 20 (Channel B); Cf. *Smith v SW Rly. Co.* LR 5 CP 98, 6 CP 14 (1870) at 23 *per* Lush J.   [103] *The Law of Torts, op. cit.* n. 100, 353.

[104] Above, pp. 45–6.

[105] *David v Britannic Merthyr Coal Company Ltd.* [1909] 2 KB 146, 164 *per* Fletcher Moulton LJ affd. *Britannic Merthyr Coal Company Ltd. v David* [1910] AC 74 (though some of the reasons of the CA were doubted).   [106] Workmen's Compensation Act 1925, s. 29(1).

[107] *Lochgelly Iron and Coal Co. Ltd. v M'Mullan* [1934] AC 1, 9, 10 *per* Lord Atkin. Even more striking was Lord Warrington of Clyffe's view that while an employer owed an 'absolute obligation on the owner to make secure the roof', breach of this obligation itself constituted negligence: ibid. at 13–14 and see ibid. 23 *per* Lord Wright.

[108] This remained the case until the Law Reform (Contributory Negligence) Act 1945.

[109] *Caswell v Powell Duffryn Associated Collieries Ltd.* [1940] AC 152.

distinguished negligence and breach of statutory duty very firmly, recognising that the latter 'belongs to the category often described as that of cases of strict or absolute liability'.[110] It also reaffirmed the traditional English refusal to distinguish between 'mild' and 'gross' negligence for the purposes of liability in tort: as Lord Wright memorably put it, 'generally speaking in civil cases "gross" negligence has no more effect than negligence without an opprobrious epithet'.[111] After this decision and after the social insurance arrangements for workers were changed in 1948,[112] the mere breach of a statutory duty of safety is not seen as itself constituting negligence, though it may provide good evidence of it.[113]

A second factor in the elucidation of the concept of negligence was that by the middle years of the twentieth century the use of juries had gradually died out in the vast majority of English civil cases and entirely as regards claims for death, personal injuries or damage to property.[114] The beginnings of this process can be seen in the later nineteenth century in a possibility for the parties to agree that their case should be tried by a judge alone,[115] but the immediate cause of the first removal of the right to jury trial in civil cases was the difficulty during the Great War of sparing men[116] from their military or other work to undertake jury service,[117] a change which was retained after the war, the judge possessing a discretion whether or not to empanel a jury.[118] While, after some legislative vacillation, this has remained the formal position, the courts have made completely clear that they will not exercise their discretion in favour of a jury trial for claims for personal injury or death.[119] While some judges expressed regret for the end of what they saw as a valuable constitutional right,[120] others saw its removal as desirable to ensure a degree of uniformity in fact-finding in the application of the standard of care[121] and in assessing damages,[122] and more generally because claims for personal injuries and death were too complex to be assessed by laymen.[123] As a result, the opaque and unreasoned general verdicts of juries on negligence were replaced with judicial decision making, which lends itself to overt explanation as to

[110] Ibid. at 177–8, *per* Lord Wright.   [111] Ibid. at 175, *per* Lord Wright.

[112] The National Insurance (Industrial Injuries) Act 1946 came into force in that year.

[113] *Bux v Slough Metals* [1973] 1 WLR 1358, 1365 *et seq.* and below, p. 203. Cf. the unsuccessful attempt by Williams to revive the idea that breach of a statutory duty of *any* content itself constitutes negligence on the basis that 'the standard of conduct has been fixed by the legislature instead of by the judge': G. Williams, 'The Effect of Penal Legislation in the Law of Torts' (1960) 23 *MLR* 233, esp. at 236, finding support for this view in Lord Atkin's speech in *Lochgelly Iron and Coal Co. Ltd. v M'Mullan, cit.*

[114] Ibbetson, *Historical Introduction*, 188–9.

[115] Common Law Procedure Act 1854, s. 1; Rules of the Supreme Court 1883, Order 36 rule 6. For details, see Lord Devlin, *Trial by Jury* (Stevens and Sons Ltd., London, revised edn. 1966), 130 *et seq.*

[116] Women were able to serve as jurors after the Sex Disqualification (Removal) Act 1919, s. 1.

[117] Juries Act 1918, s. 1; *Hope v Great Western Railway Co.* [1937] 2 KB 130, 136 *per* Lord Wright MR.

[118] *Ford v Blurton* (1922) 38 Times LR 801. The key provision was the Administration of Justice (Miscellaneous Provisions) Act 1933, s. 6 and see *Hope v Great Western Railway Co.* [1937] 2 KB 130, 138. The present provisions are found in the Supreme Court Act 1981, s. 69.

[119] *Ward v James* [1966] 1 QB 273; *H. v Ministry of Defence* [1991] 2 QB 103.

[120] *Ford v Blurton* (1922) 38 Times LR 801, 805 *per* Atkin LJ.

[121] *Ward v James* [1966] 1 QB 273, 296 *per* Lord Denning MR.

[122] *Sims v William Howard & Son Ltd.* [1964] 2 QB 409, 415 *per* Lord Denning MR.

[123] This reason was reaffirmed in denying a jury trial to a claim arising from the King's Cross Fire: *Singh v London Underground* (1990) The Independent, 25 April 1990.

how the facts relate to the applicable legal standard. This gave an added impetus to the need to explain which factors drawn from the facts ought to be taken into account in decisions on negligence.

Ironically, however, a third factor in the elucidation of negligence can be seen in an influence from America, which itself partly formed a reaction to the *continuing* presence of juries. Oliver Wendell Holmes had argued in 1881 that juries should be guided by judges in their decisions on negligence,[124] and while US courts rejected the idea of framing standards of behaviour for particular situations which amounted to inflexible rules of law,[125] by the 1930s American jurists had set out the factors to be taken into account in deciding whether a defendant had breached his duty to take reasonable care, notably the likelihood of harm and its seriousness as against the cost of precautions.[126] This elucidation of the nature of the decision on the issue of breach of duty, which was in 1947 to be formulated in simple algebraic form so famously by Learned Hand J,[127] was picked up by English textbook writers in the early 1950s,[128] even though in England by this stage juries were becoming much rarer in trials on negligence.

This brings me to the final element in the elucidation of negligence, which is that at least for the last 50 years or so English lawyers have often looked for ways of structuring wide judicial discretions, whether these discretions are set by statute or inherent in the open-textured nature of the concepts of the common law itself.[129] In part this stems from a concern to achieve a degree of consistency reminiscent of earlier judicial controls on jury decision making; in my view, though, it goes deeper and reflects the way in which English lawyers have interpreted the doctrine of precedent so as to involve the facts of previous decisions in the construction of the law itself, for the binding aspect of a decision (its *ratio decidendi*) is found in that proposition of law, or those propositions of law, which are necessary for the decision on the facts. As a result, while English judges are concerned to expound legal principle and sometimes to explain any legal policy also at play, their treatment of the legal propositions found in previous decisions is always sensitive to their facts. This means that even where the substantive law itself gives judges a broad discretion, English lawyers tend to seek patterns in the way in which they have exercised the discretion so as to draw from them the sorts of consideration properly to be taken into account in future decisions. In my view, this tendency can be seen clearly in the establishment of a range of proper factors

---

[124] *The Common Law* (Boston, 1881) 123–4 and see John. G. Fleming, *The American Tort Process* (OUP, 1988) 117.

[125] Fleming, ibid., citing the judgment of Cardoza J. in *Pokora v Wobash Rly* 292 US 98 (1934), esp. at 105.

[126] American Law Institute, *First Restatement of the Law of Torts* (1934) para. 283 (which refers to the 'weighing of interest') and W.L. Prosser, *Handbook on the Law of Torts* (West Pub. Co., St. Paul, Minn., 1st. edn., 1941) 220–3.   [127] *United States v Carroll Towing Co. Inc.* (1947)159 F.2d 169, 173.

[128] E.g. P.H. Winfield, *Winfield on Tort: a textbook of the Law of Tort* (Sweet and Maxwell, London, 6th. edn., 1954) by T. Ellis Lewis (who makes clear in the preface his general reliance on US scholarly literature).

[129] See further S. Whittaker, 'Theory and Practice of the "General Clause" in English law: General Norms and the Structuring of Judicial Discretion' in S. Grundmann and D. Mazeaud (eds.), *Theory and Practice of the 'General Clause'* (forthcoming).

to be taken into account in deciding the issue of negligence;[130] the resulting law retains the flexibility provided by a large and open-textured concept but also ensures a degree of adjudicative consistency.

These four elements all influenced the way in which the modern concept of negligence came to be elucidated from the 1950s, seen first in *Bolton v Stone*[131] and then again in the important (if somewhat confused) decision of the Privy Council in *The Wagon Mound (No. 2)*.[132] In the first of these cases, which concerned the liability of a cricket club for a ball which was struck far beyond the ground and happened to cause personal injury, the House of Lords accepted that the ability for a defendant to foresee a slight risk of a slight harm would not lead to a finding of negligence: the degree of likelihood and the size of harm were both relevant as were the cost of precautions (here assumed to be the cessation of cricket on the ground in question).[133] In *The Wagon Mound (No. 2)* the Privy Council considered that *Bolton v Stone* had established that an infinitesimal chance of harm justified a defendant in taking no steps to avoid it, but it did not always follow that small risks can be neglected. So, where oil had been spilt in Sidney Harbour, while the likelihood of harm through its ignition by the use of oxyacetylene welding tools in the vicinity was very slight, its likely magnitude was very great[134] and the cost of avoiding it was slight.[135] In these circumstances, the balance of factors pointed to the existence of negligence.[136]

While the modern understanding of negligence was set in place by these decisions, the process of structuring of the judicial discretion in finding negligence has continued both as regards these central factors and the recognition of a number of further factors relevant for some types of case.

(i) The probability of harm, the knowledge of the defendant and the time factor

While the language of foreseeability of the claimant's harm has often disguised a real concern with its likelihood, it also draws attention to the relevance of the defendant's ability at the time to appreciate the risk of harm to the claimant in the judicial assessment of negligence.

At common law, the starting point for the assessment of the defendant's ability is an objective one: what *ought* a reasonable person in the position of the defendant to have known of the risk of injury? In some cases, the courts have regard to what they consider to be 'common knowledge', of which all reasonable people are expected to be

---

[130] This tendency can also be seen in legislation: e.g. Misrepresentation Act 1967, s. 2(2) (damages in lieu of rescission of the contract); Unfair Contract Terms Act 1977, s. 11, Sch. 2 ('reasonableness' of certain contract terms). It can be seen in a procedural context, e.g. the award of interim (formerly, interlocutory) injunctions: *American Cyanamid Co. v Ethicon Ltd* [1975] AC 396.   [131] [1951] AC 850.

[132] *Overseas Tankship (UK) Ltd v Miller Steamship Co. Pty. Ltd.* [1967] 1 AC 617.

[133] [1951] AC 850, 862–3 *per* Lord Normand. Cf. ibid. at 867 (Lord Reid); 863 (Lord Oaksey).

[134] [1967] 1 AC 617, 643 *per* Lord Reid.   [135] Ibid., 643–4, *per* Lord Reid.

[136] *Overseas Tankship (UK) Ltd. v The Miller Steamship Co. Pty. Ltd. (The Wagon Mound No. 2)* [1967] 1 AC 617. The oddity of the discussion of the decision in *Bolton v Stone* by the Privy Council was that it considered it relevant to the question of foreseeability for the purposes of remoteness of the type of damage (damage by fire rather than damage by pollution) rather than for the purposes of breach of duty. For a recent judicial acceptance of this approach see *Tomlinson v Congleton BC* [2003] UKHL 47 at [34]; [2004] 1 AC 46.

aware, for example, the presence of blind people walking unaccompanied on the streets of London (though it is to be noted that the court itself had the benefit of national statistics in this respect).[137] In other cases, they look instead to the knowledge to be expected of the category of person to which the defendant belongs, so, in the case of medical practitioners, what a particular practitioner should have foreseen as a risk is determined by the standard of a reasonably competent practitioner in the area of expertise professed at the time of the conduct in question.[138]

Similarly, in *Vacwell Engineering Co. Ltd. v B.H.H. Chemicals Ltd.*, a manufacturer of chemicals supplied to the plaintiffs, who were electrical manufacturers, ampoules containing boron tribromide, a chemical whose vapour they knew to be harmful (and which they so labelled) but which they did not know to be explosive on contact with water.[139] The ampoules exploded in the course of being handled and in deciding the issue of their manufacturer's negligence, the question arose as to whether or not they should have known of the explosive property of the chemical. The court considered the extent of the defendant's duty to undertake research in this respect before putting a product on the market and heard expert evidence that while the explosive nature had been known since the nineteenth century, four modern textbooks did not refer to it.[140] The court concluded that

it was the duty of [the defendants] to have established and maintained a system under which adequate investigation and research into the scientific literature took place in order to discover, inter alia, what hazards were known before a new, or little known, chemical was marketed.[141]

Reliance on the modern textbooks was not enough. Moreover, quite apart from the existing literature, an expert chemist should have carried out suitable theoretical chemical calculations which would have conveyed at least a warning which might well have led him to carry out further (if themselves dangerous) experiments which would have demonstrated the risk of explosion.[142] Both reasoning from first principles and practical experimentation might be required.[143]

The duty on a manufacturer to undertake original research into the risks created by a new product or a new context for an existing product was explicitly recognised by the House of Lords in *IBA v EMI*.[144] There the plaintiffs had commissioned the construction of an aerial television mast by EMI, who had themselves brought in BICC to design it. The mast collapsed after three days of intense cold some three and a half years later and the question arose whether BICC's design, which was completely new and untried in UK conditions, was negligent.[145] Lord Edmund-Davies accepted that 'the law requires even pioneers to be prudent' and that there may be circumstances

---

[137] Cf. *Haley v London Electricity Board* [1965] AC 778, 791 *per* Lord Reid.

[138] *Roe v Ministry of Health* [1954] 2 QB 56 (doctor storing glass ampoule containing anaesthetic in phenol which leaked in through imperceptible cracks).

[139] *Vacwell Engineering Co. Ltd. v B.D.H. Chemicals Ltd.* [1971] 1 QB 88.   [140] Ibid. at 95–6.

[141] Ibid. at 99.   [142] Ibid. at 100.

[143] The CA approved a settlement by which the defendants were liable for 80% of the plaintiffs' harm: [1971] 1 QB 111.   [144] [1981] 14 BLR 1.

[145] The House of Lords held that the designers owed the owners of the mast a duty of care in tort under *Hedley Byrne* directly to the plaintiffs, the commissioners of the mast.

when the only way to eliminate a manifest and substantial risk is to abandon a project altogether.[146] On the facts, the designers' lack of empirical knowledge or expert advice required them to identify and think through the problems so as to assess adequately the dimensions of their 'venture into the unknown'.[147] So, where the likelihood and magnitude of harm justify it, a reasonable manufacturer must sometimes look further than the existing state of scientific and technical knowledge.

On the other hand, the standard does remain that of a reasonable person in the defendant's position so that what the law of negligence requires of a manufacturer or a designer differs from what is required of an employer or mere supplier of a product. So, for example, an employer which exposed its employees to contact with hardwood dust which caused one of them to contract dermatitis was held not to have been negligent, for while a reasonable employer has a duty to take reasonable steps to keep his knowledge up to date concerning the risks involved in his own operations, including reading trade journals and government safety bulletins, normally he has no duty to undertake research of his own.[148] Similarly, a mere supplier is unlikely to be held negligent in supplying a product with hidden dangers where he reasonably relied on the competence of his own reputable suppliers.[149]

However, there is a subjective qualification to this objective position. Where a defendant was actually aware of a particular risk he cannot argue that a reasonable person in his position may not have been and that therefore his failure to take steps to avoid the claimant's harm did not constitute negligence: a reasonable person acts on his own knowledge, even if others in his position would not be held liable for failing to act similarly.[150] It is for this reason, as well as in order to establish the probability of harm, that claimants bring forward evidence as to the history of previous accidents occasioned by the defendant's activity or inactivity.[151]

What is the position where the defendant failed to consider the risks of his own course of action, but then in fact acted in a way which was 'reasonable', given the likelihood of harm, its magnitude and the cost of avoiding it?[152] In *Adams v Rhymney Valley District Council*, which concerned the alleged negligence of a local authority in its choice of window locks for residential property, the Court of Appeal considered whether the fact that no-one in the authority had balanced the factors for and against the use of two types of lock constituted negligence, even though a reasonably competent professional in the field would have recommended the decision actually made by the authority.[153] In Sedley LJ's view, the mere failure to consult a professional adviser did not constitute negligence, but where the advice *might* have recommended conduct

---

[146] [1981] 14 BLR 1 at 28.   [147] Ibid. at 31.

[148] *Graham v Co-operative Wholesale Society Ltd.* [1957] 1 WLR 511, 517–18.

[149] *Davie v New Merton Board Mills Ltd.* [1959] AC 604; *Watson v Buckley, Osborne, Garrett & Co. Ltd.* [1940] 1 All ER 174; *Mason v Williams & Williams Ltd.* [1955] 1 WLR 549; *Fisher v Harrods Ltd.* [1966] 1 Lloyd's Rep 500.

[150] E.g. *Wright v Dunlop Rubber Co. Ltd.* (1972) 13 KIR 255 (employer knew of carcinogenic nature of elements of its product but failed to warn the employers of its customers).

[151] E.g. *Bolton v Stone* [1951] AC 850.

[152] If a defendant fails to consider the risk of harm of his action in circumstances where, if he had done so, he would have acted differently and in a way to avoid the claimant's harm, then there is negligence: e.g. *Levine v Morris* [1970] 1 WLR 72, 80.   [153] (2001) 33 HLR 446.

which in fact was taken, a defendant's decision should not be judged as if they had done the very thing which they neglected to do.[154] However, the majority of the Court of Appeal disagreed: the local authority's failure to consult others or itself to consider the design from the point of view of fire safety was irrelevant if its actual choice was one which a reasonable person in its position would have made: to decide otherwise would be 'to prefer form to substance',[155] for negligence requires the assessment of a defendant's conduct 'not the thought processes which preceded it'.[156] With respect to Sedley LJ, the majority view is to be preferred, for while English administrative law requires a public authority possessing a discretionary power to consider whether or not to exercise it, the tort of negligence does not require individuals to consider how to act reasonably as long as they do so.

Finally, in assessing what the defendant knew or ought to have known as to the risk of harm and its avoidance, English courts have emphasised that these issues are to be judged as at the time at which it is alleged that the defendant ought to have acted: foreseeability rules out the benefit of hindsight. As Denning LJ memorably observed in 1954 in relation to the alleged negligence of a hospital anaesthetist in respect of the leaking of a sterilisation liquid through cracks in a glass ampoule of anaesthetic: '[w]e must not look at the 1947 accident with 1954 spectacles'.[157] If the standard of the reasonable person is personally objective, it remains temporally relative.

(ii) The magnitude of harm

The Wagon Mound (No. 2) made clear that the seriousness of harm likely to be caused by the neglect of a relevant precaution is relevant to the issue of negligence,[158] but there is a striking absence in the cases of any *financial* calculation of the 'value' of the harm which either would not or could not have occurred. In the hands of English judges, there is no explicit economic calculation of the type which would require the actual estimated cost of precautions to be put against the actual (or potential harm) caused and the statistical probability of the actual (or potential) harm: the balancing of these factors remains at large. Instead, typically there is an implicit assessment of the probability (usually without statistics)[159] and a rough sense of the cost of precautions (often with no figures adduced) as against the harm likely to be caused, but with the harm *actually* caused to the claimant present in the minds of the judges. This non-mathematical nature of the judicial calculation is important because it allows courts to take into account factors which could not form part of a purely economic calculation, such as the utility of the defendant's conduct other than in economic terms. As a result, the courts clearly consider that a defendant is justified in taking a greater risk of injury in promoting the interests of personal safety.[160]

---

[154] (2001) 33 HLR 451.   [155] Ibid. at 458, *per* Sir Christopher Staughton.
[156] Ibid. at 460, *per* Morritt LJ.   [157] *Roe v Minister of Health* [1954] 2 QB 66, 84.
[158] *Overseas Tankship (UK) Ltd. Appellant v The Miller Steamship Co. Pty. Ltd. (The Wagon Mound No. 2)* [1967] 1 AC 617, above, p. 193.
[159] *Haley v London Electricity Board* [1965] AC 778 forms an exception, see below p. 197.
[160] Below, pp. 198–9.

(iii) The cost of precautions

The cost of the precautions which a defendant is expected to have undertaken so as to avoid likely harm is an important factor in the assessment of negligence. For example, in *Latimer v A.E.C. Ltd*.[161] where a claimant had suffered minor injuries on slipping at work, it was held that an employer was not negligent in allowing its employees to continue working in its large factory despite the slipperiness of the floor after heavy rain given the drastic nature of closing the factory,[162] though this may be required of a reasonably prudent employer 'if the peril to his employees is sufficiently grave'.[163]

Three further points arise. The first is the importance of looking at the correct basis on which to assess the cost of precautions. For example, *Haley v London Electricity Board*[164] concerned the precautions to be undertaken by the defendants to protect blind people from injuring themselves as a result of the excavation which they had constructed in the highway. Here, should the court balance the cost of providing fencing appropriate to protect blind pedestrians for *the one* excavation where the particular plaintiff had been injured or for *all* its excavation works in pavements? The answer is that the point of reference of the cost of precautions needs to tally with the point of reference of the probability of harm. So, in a case like *Haley*, if a court were to focus on the probability of a blind pedestrian walking along *the particular street* where the defendants were working (a very low probability), then the appropriate cost would be the cost of the *one* fencing needed for that excavation: but if the probability of blind pedestrians walking in London were taken as the measure of this factor (as it was in *Haley* itself), then the appropriate cost of precautions should be the cost of preventing such injuries in London.[165]

Secondly, while generally the standard of the practicability of precautions is an objective one based on the costs incurred by a reasonable person in the situation of the defendant given the risk of harm, in some situations and especially where a danger has been thrust upon the defendant, a more subjective approach to the cost of precautions has been held appropriate, sometimes referred to as a standard of 'measured' negligence.[166] So, for example, in *Goldman v Hargrave*,[167] lightning struck a tree on the land of the defendant in Western Australia and the fire spread to the plaintiff's closely neighbouring property. In these circumstances, the Privy Council held that the plaintiff could succeed only on proof of negligence (whether under the tort of negligence itself or in nuisance), and that where a hazard is thrust upon a defendant, negligence must be judged according to 'what it is reasonable to expect of him in his individual circumstances'.[168] A similar approach has been taken by the majority of the House of Lords to the liability of an occupier for harm done by trespassers to his neighbour's land: here, the practicability of avoiding a very probable danger must be assessed by the standard of the particular occupier.[169]

---

[161] [1953] 3 WLR 259.   [162] Ibid. at 262, *per* Lord Porter.
[163] Ibid. at 267, *per* Lord Tucker.   [164] [1965] AC 777.   [165] See further, below, p. 199.
[166] For other examples, see below, p. 342 concerning the modern approach to the liability of public authorities.   [167] [1966] 3 WLR 513.
[168] Ibid. at 524, *per* Lord Wilberforce following *Sedleigh-Denfield v O'Callaghan* [1940] AC 880 (a nuisance created by a trespasser).
[169] *Smith v Littlewoods Organisation Ltd*. [1987] AC 241, esp. 268–70 *per* Lord Mackay. Cf. ibid. at 270, 274 (Lord Goff preferring to restrict liability by denying the existence of a general duty of care).

Thirdly, can a defendant escape liability in negligence by arguing that he relied on the skill, judgment or competence of another person? Unsurprisingly, English law's response is 'only when it is reasonable to do so', taking into account the usual balance of risk against precautions: reliance on another person's competence should be seen as a practical expression (or part of a practical expression) of a defendant's precautions.[170] So, for example, in *Davie v New Merton Board Mills*[171] it was held that an employer is not liable in negligence for personal injuries caused by a tool which had been negligently manufactured 'provided that he has been careful to deal with a seller of repute and has made any inspection which a reasonable employer would make'.[172]

(iv) The utility or social value of the defendant's conduct

The utility of the defendant's conduct can be relevant to the issue of breach, making reasonable the taking of greater risks.[173] The most obvious cases involve the emergency services acting in the interests of saving life (for example a fire-engine driving to a road accident[174]) or more generally in the public interest (for example, a police constable in a high-speed car chase of a suspected car-thief[175]). These sorts of cases could, of course, be treated as examples of the relevance of the 'cost of precautions' but it is clear that the 'cost' here is not a financial one of avoiding harm but rather the sacrificing of another's health or of the public interest in the deterrence of crime. It is a cost to society at large rather than to the pocket of the defendant (or even his insurer).

The balancing becomes particularly difficult where the defendant's behaviour brings certain risks of injury (which have transpired) but avoids other risks of injury (which have not). Here, both individuals and the courts are faced with competing considerations of safety. For example, in *Adams v Rhymney Valley District Council*[176] the claimant was a tenant of a terraced house whose landlord had replaced all the windows with ones with locks with removable keys. The windows were sufficiently large to allow escape in the event of fire but they were kept locked so as to prevent the tenant's children from falling out and the key kept downstairs; in the course of a fire, the tenant's wife could not open the upstairs windows and their three children died. In these circumstances, the Court of Appeal recognised that there was a conflict between the need to provide a means of escape or rescue in the case of fire and the need to prevent children climbing or falling out of the window and it was unwilling to interfere with the trial judge's view that the choice between the two types of lock was not negligent in the circumstances.[177] Similarly, in *Levine v Morris*, which involved a claim against the highway authority responsible for the road on which the claimant had suffered a car accident, Widgery LJ noticed that a designer of a road 'may be faced with

---

[170] Under the Occupiers Liability Act 1957, s. 2(3) particular provision is made concerning the relevance of recourse by occupiers to independent contractors and performance of their 'common duty of care'.

[171] [1959] AC 604.

[172] Ibid. at 646, *per* Lord Reid. The result was changed for the context of employers by the Employers Liability (Defective Equipment) Act 1969.

[173] *Watt v Hertfordshire County Council* [1954] 1 WLR 835, 838, *per* Denning LJ.

[174] *Daborn v Bath Tramways Co. Ltd.* [1946] 2 All ER 333, 336; *Watt v Hertfordshire County Council* [1954] 1 WLR 835.   [175] *Marshall v Osmond* [1983] QB 1034, 1038.

[176] (2001) 33 HLR 446.   [177] Ibid. at 455–6; 459–60 (Sedley LJ dissenting).

a conflict between considerations concerned with the functional efficiency of the road and considerations of safety...[or] with conflicting considerations each of which affects safety, as where a warning sign, which must be visible if it is to provide safety, cannot be placed in a position of visibility unless its situation presents some risk of injury to the driver of a car which may collide with it'.[178]

So, the courts understand that the utility of a defendant's conduct may not just relate to the safety of the claimant or others, but may also relate to the effective functioning of the activity itself: roads need to be reasonably safe, but they also need to handle large numbers of travellers. While personal safety is extremely important, it cannot be the touchstone of social utility.[179]

(v) Vulnerable or careless claimants

English courts have increasingly shown themselves willing to take into account the vulnerability of a claimant in determining what a defendant should do to prevent his injury. For this purpose, vulnerability may result either from the claimant's physical circumstances or from his mental or intellectual capabilities.

In some types of case, the claimant's vulnerability stems from circumstances which suggest a greater likelihood of harm occurring and for this reason this factor could be seen as a special example of probability. So, a reasonable person must expect a child to take less care of his own safety than an adult,[180] but others can be at greater risk of injury from their mental state and so require extra care. For example, the police owe a duty of care to a person detained in their custody to take precautions to prevent him from committing suicide, where they are alerted to this risk.[181] In both these situations, a claimant's recovery may be reduced on the ground of contributory negligence.[182] Furthermore, an adult's *physical* vulnerability may be relevant to the precautions to be taken to avoid injury, as in *Paris v Stepney Borough Council*, where the existing blindness of the claimant in one eye was held relevant to the precautions to be taken to protect his other eye.[183] And in *Haley v London Electricity Board*[184] the House of Lords held that the precautions reasonably needed to avoid injury from a trench in the pavement increased given the likely presence of blind persons, and its decision finding breach (and in particular its treatment of the cost of precautions[185]) suggests a concern to ensure that blind people can walk the streets as safely as the sighted.

---

[178] [1970] 1 WLR 72, 79–80, *per* Widgery LJ.

[179] Cf. *Tomlinson v Congleton BC* [2003] UKHL 47 at [40]–[43]; [2004] 1 AC 46 where Lord Hoffmann expressed concern that the imposition of too high a standard of care on a local authority in respect of the potential risk of injury in its country park could tend to reduce citizens' liberties.

[180] *Phipps v Rochester Corpn.* [1955] 1 QB 450, confirmed by Occupiers Liability Act 1957, s. 2(3)(a); *DE (A Child) v S Garages Ltd.* (QBD) (28 Nov. 2000), WL 33281292; Cf. *B. v Cardiff CC* [2001] EWCA Civ 703; [2002] ELR 1.

[181] *Reeves v Metropolitan Police Commissioner* [2000] 1 AC 360 (the defendants had admitted negligence).   [182] Ibid.; *DE (A Child) v S Garages Ltd, cit.*

[183] *Paris v Stepney BC* [1951] AC 367. See *Johnstone v Bloomsbury HA* [1992] QB 333, 344–5, *per* Stuart-Smith LJ.   [184] [1965] AC 777.

[185] The HL noted the statistics of blindness in the adult population (1 in 500) but then assumed that the cost of precautions was the cost of a fence for the *particular* trench dug by the defendants on the facts, rather than the cost of protecting all such escavations in the same manner: cf. above, p. 197.

As regards adults with no special physical or mental needs, there has been an evolution, parallelling the changing attitude of English law to the defence of contributory negligence. So, in 1865 Bramwell B held that a railway company could not be negligent in failing to take precautions against the injury of people crossing a railway line by a footpath since they had twenty seconds to check to see that nothing was coming and to return to safety! The company should not bear any duty 'to warn people against the consequences of their own folly'.[186] However, this highly individualistic way of thinking diminished significantly in the course of the twentieth century and particularly after 1945 when the significance of the defence of contributory negligence changed from being a bar to liability to triggering a judicial power of reduction of the claimant's damages,[187] for otherwise a claimant's lack of care for his own safety would rule out a defendant's liability by denial of any breach of duty.[188] So, for example, in *Levine v Morris* in 1970[189] a highway authority was held negligent in its design of the road where the plaintiff was injured in a road accident, though liability was reduced on the ground of contributory negligence: 'a prudent man will guard against the possible negligence of others when experience shows such negligence to be common' and the highway authority must not design its roads on the assumptions that no driver will make mistakes.[190]

As Bramwell B foresaw, the modern approach can be seen particularly in cases where a defendant's alleged negligence consists of a failure to warn the claimant of the risk of injury to himself, and this is clearly reflected in a manufacturer's liability to a person using its product, where it must take reasonable steps to discover the properties of the product which it markets and then warn the user against reasonably avoidable risks.[191] On the other hand, a person is under no duty to warn of an entirely obvious risk of harm[192] and there can be seen signs elsewhere in the law of negligence of judicial reluctance to impose liability where its effect is to require a person to take action to prevent the foolhardy actions of others.[193]

(vi) Comparisons with French law

It can be seen, therefore, that modern English law sets out the factors which a court must take into account in deciding whether or not a defendant has broken his duty to take reasonable care. While the process of weighing up these factors is often referred to as a 'cost/benefit' analysis, it can be seen that this is no mere economic calculation, but requires the evaluation of different considerations, some financial and some social,

---

[186] *Stubley v The London and North Western Rly. Co.* (1865–66) LR 1 Exch 13, 18.

[187] Law Reform (Contributory Negligence) Act 1945, s.1. (reduction 'to such an extent as the court thinks just and equitable having regard to the claimant's share in the responsibility for the damage').

[188] A similar evolution in the significance of *volenti non fit injuria* (voluntary acceptance of the risk of injury) can be seen after the enactment of the 1945 Act, the courts generally preferring to apportion liability under the Act rather than rule it out on the basis that the claimant had accepted the risk of his own injury: Markesinis and Deakin's *Tort Law*, 756–7.   [189] [1970] 1 WLR 72.

[190] Ibid. at 79, Widgery LJ quoting Lord du Parcq in *London Passenger Transport Board v Upson* [1949] AC 155 at 176.

[191] *Vacwell Engineering Co. Ltd. v B.D.H. Chemicals Ltd.* [1971] 1 QB 88. It is to be noted that while the chemical was typically sold to specialised users, there was no restriction by the defendants on the class of customer purchasing it.   [192] *Staples v West Dorset DC* [1995] PIQR 439.

[193] This is particularly clear in *Tomlinson v Congleton BC* [2003] UKHL 47; [2004] 1 AC 46.

reflecting broadly a philosophy of utilitarianism. At a practical level, though, a court in deciding negligence must balance a particular set of factors; while other English liabilities also require the balancing of factors, these factors sometimes differ slightly (one or more being omitted or substituted), sometimes being almost entirely different.[194] In the English context, therefore, the language of 'fault' (whether used in the context of negligence or elsewhere) serves only to confuse, being too vague and unspecific for the particularity of the English techniques.

At this stage, it can be appreciated how very different is the approach of an English court to deciding negligence and a French court in deciding *une faute*.[195] In part, this results from the different functions of these concepts in the two systems of substantive law: for the breadth of the French understanding of *la faute délictuelle* is required by the different roles which it must play under the all-embracing articles 1382 and 1383 of the Civil Code, both in terms of defining the limits of liability (a role played in English law by the defining characteristics of the nominate torts and in the tort of negligence by the concept of a duty of care) and in terms of the different types of 'fault' appropriate for different contexts. However, even if we restrict our comparison with French law to its understanding of *imprudence* or *manque de diligence* (its nearest equivalent to the English negligence) we find very different treatments which I would describe as a French contentment to leave the issue to a global judicial assessment and an English concern to structure its judicial assessment and thereby to create a more complex and specifically *legal* understanding of the concept of negligence. So, while the Cour de cassation retains for itself the issue of the characterisation of *une faute délictuelle* of facts by the lower courts, its intervention has been ad hoc rather than based on a set of general, legal guidelines. This allows a number of considerations to be taken into account by the lower courts covertly, under the cloak of their 'sovereign power of assessment' and in particular permits expression to be given to their 'moralising' tendencies.[196] By contrast, the English approach to negligence requires the considerations to be taken account of by a court to be argued by the parties, decided upon as to relevance and then assessed by the court.

These differences are in part explained by the different institutions of French and English civil adjudication: in the French, the distinction between the *juges du fond* and the Cour de cassation and in the English the presence or absence of juries. But they also stem from even more fundamental differences in understandings of the appropriate line between issues of law and of fact. For, as I explained earlier, the English doctrine of precedent links fact and law together in the process of ascertaining the common law itself and this has created an intellectual tendency towards the juridification of facts, that is, the construction of legal issues from patterns of judicial decision making on facts. By contrast, while French case law is highly important for an understanding of French delictual liability, French private lawyers do not see previous judicial decisions in the same way as English lawyers and, in particular, do not see the factual context of a decision as essentially relevant to the validity of the legal

---

[194] Cf. the set of factors to be used by a court in assessing the reasonableness of a neighbour's use of land for the purposes of private nuisance: *Clerk and Lindsell on Torts*, paras. 19-06–19-19.

[195] For discussion of the French approach, above, pp. 42–6.   [196] Above, p. 43.

propositions which it proclaims. French judicial decisions do not *bind* and for a French lawyer, the validity of any legal proposition comes from its relation to *la loi* or to legal principle: is it right, rather than was it relevant? There is therefore much less reason for a French lawyer to seek out the pattern of application of a concept such as *imprudence*, no need to 'distinguish' one decision from another, and so no juridifying tendency of the sort which we see in English law.

(d) The relevance of crimes, statutory and other duties, and safety standards

While English law has rejected the idea that breach of a statutory duty itself constitutes 'statutory negligence' so as to give rise to liability *for* negligence,[197] breach of a statutory or other duty, or of some other standard remain significant in establishing negligence.

In striking contrast to the French position,[198] English law does not hold that a criminal offence which causes harm necessarily gives rise to civil liability: there has been no doctrine of the 'unity of criminal and civil fault'.[199] There are a number of reasons for the English position. First, while there is an overlap between some common law crimes and specific torts,[200] very many modern criminal offences are statutory and so (following the special nature of statutory intervention[201]), each offence is special, requiring to be interpreted according to its own provisions and purposes. In our own context, the particular nature of statutes is reflected in the rule that the question whether the commission of a particular statutory offence also gives rise to civil liability is a matter of parliamentary intention, this process of divination taking place under the auspices of the tort of breach of statutory duty.[202] Secondly, unlike French law, English law does not possess a general or unified concept of 'civil fault' at all: while the language of fault is used to refer to the standard of liability of certain torts, in English law without more a defendant's 'fault' does not give rise to liability. Thirdly, in the English context there are no institutional or procedural reasons for equating criminal and civil faults: there is no *partie civile* in the English criminal process.[203] Finally, most English lawyers would see the distinction between crimes and torts as resting on a difference in their functions: crimes exist to prevent, deter, punish and impose retribution; all torts exist to compensate, some torts have an element of prevention, torts on occasion deter and exceptionally punish. The equation of crime and tort would be seen as cutting across these distinct functions in the interests of conceptual tidiness.[204]

On the other hand, all this does not mean that the commission of a crime is irrelevant to the finding of a breach of duty in the tort of negligence. For a conviction 'is a

---

[197] Above, pp. 190–1.

[198] Above, pp. 45–6 and for the practical importance of this, below, Chap. 14.

[199] Below, p. 374.

[200] Markesinis and Deakin's *Tort Law*, 416, 417 (assault and battery exist as common law crimes and torts). [201] Cf. below, pp. 337, 469.

[202] This remains the case even though the tort of breach of statutory duty rests on the notion of a 'statutory duty' rather than a statutory offence, see below, pp. 218–20. [203] Below, p. 419 *et seq.*

[204] Some French lawyers also draw attention to the different functions of the criminal law and *la responsabilité civile* in criticising the doctrine of the 'unity' of criminal and civil fault, below, p. 368 n. 5.

weighty piece of evidence of itself'.[205] So, where an offence of negligence (such as driving without due care and attention) has been committed by a defendant this will be a very considerable help to a claimant in establishing civil liability in the defendant for negligence.[206] Breach of a statutory duty may also be evidence of negligence, though it can not itself constitute negligence if the duty is strict.[207] Conversely, the Court of Appeal has denied that an employer's provision of safety goggles to its employees in compliance with safety regulations meant that it did not need to go further and take reasonable steps to see that these goggles were used to avoid liability in negligence.[208] Compliance with a relevant regulatory duty may be 'of evidential value' of reasonable care, but it may not be enough,[209] as this depends on the nature and the degree of risk involved.[210] Moreover, '[t]here is . . . no presumption that a statutory obligation abrogates or supersedes the employer's common law duty or that it defines or measures his common law duty either by clarifying it or by cutting it down—or indeed by extending it'.[211]

However, a strikingly different approach was taken by the Court of Appeal in *Albery and Budden v BP Oil Ltd. & Shell UK Ltd*, where the plaintiffs brought proceedings on behalf of their infant children against the defendant oil companies alleging that their manufacture and supply to motorists of petrol with a certain proportion of added lead was negligent and risked the children's health.[212] The plaintiffs adduced evidence of increasing scientific concern with the effect of lead in petrol on the atmosphere for the health in particular of young children[213] and that other countries had provided for the reduction of lead in petrol to a much lower limit than the 'maximum permitted amount' fixed in the United Kingdom by legislative order and with which the defendant petrol companies complied.[214] However, the Court of Appeal saw the 'maximum permitted amount' (which had not been challenged as *ultra vires*) as the expression of the government's policy of phased and continuing reduction of lead content in petrol.[215] In these circumstances, the court considered it 'difficult to believe that there is . . . any reason to suppose that a different standard should be, or would be, applied in fixing the permitted limit by reference to criminal or civil liability'.[216] So, a court could hold that the permitted limit was not limitative of liability for negligence only where circumstances *other than* the mere statutory limits were in issue,[217] for a judicial decision holding that the supply of petrol containing lead to an extent permitted by law was in itself negligent would slight the authority of Parliament. As a

---

[205] *Stupple v Royal Insurance Co. Ltd.* [1971] 1 QB 50 at 72, *per* Lord Denning MR. Under the Civil Evidence Act 1968, s. 11 (1) and (2) a person proved to have been convicted of an offence 'shall be taken to have committed that offence unless the contrary is proved' in any subsequent civil proceedings.

[206] Similarly, where a claimant commits an offence by failing to take precautions for his own safety this will be of considerable help in establishing his contributory negligence: *Froom v Butcher* [1976] QB 286 (failure to wear seatbelt); *Capps v Miller* [1989] 1 WLR 839 (failure to wear secured crash-helmet).

[207] *Clerk and Lindsell on Torts*, para. 7–188.   [208] *Bux v Slough Metals* [1973] 1 WLR 1358.

[209] Ibid. at 1364.   [210] Ibid. at 1367.   [211] Ibid. at 1369–70, *per* Edmund-Davies LJ.

[212] LexisNexis unpaginated script P No. 78 11469/90 11470.   [213] Ibid.

[214] The order was made under the Control of Pollution Act 1974, s. 75.   [215] *Cit.* n. 212.

[216] Ibid., *per* Megaw LJ.

[217] The example given was of a driver travelling at 29 miles per hour in a 30 miles per hour limit which *could* constitute negligence depending on the circumstances.

result, the defendant oil companies could not be negligent in acting in reliance on the statutory prescribed limit.[218]

At a formal level, *Albery* can be reconciled with the general approach by saying that, on a proper interpretation, the statutory order in question was intended to set the level of safety required of the suppliers of petrol in relation to its lead content, thereby 'taking from the courts their duty of deciding' whether supplying petrol in this context demonstrated reasonable care for the safety of persons likely to be affected; but if this argument holds good, it is of much wider application. What is clear is that the Court of Appeal was unwilling to undertake the review of the administrative decision setting the maximum as well as minimum safety to be expected by persons in relation to the lead content of petrol by application of the law of negligence rather than by application of the law of judicial review. While *Albery and Budden v BP Oil Ltd. & Shell UK Ltd.*, which has not been widely reported, has not been subsequently discussed by an English court we shall see again the idea that judgments implicit in the exercise of public regulatory powers should not be overturned by judicial decisions under the law of negligence in the context of the liability of public regulatory authorities themselves,[219] and the idea that regulatory requirements may set limits on the safety actually required of an undertaking in article 7(d) of the Product Liability Directive itself.[220]

English law sees non-legislative standards as relevant to but not conclusive of the existence of negligence. In some cases, the question of the applicable standard of care and the question of breach of duty run together. For the '*Bolam* test' requires specialists to observe the standard of care of the reasonable professional in the field in question, but accepts that a reasonable professional may without negligence take a different view of the appropriate course of action from others within the field.[221] So where a professional association or regulatory body expresses publicly the view that a particular set of precautions should properly be taken to avoid a particular risk, this will be potent evidence *against* the negligence of a member of a profession who has caused harm despite keeping to the precautions so set.

On the other hand, failure to comply with a non-legislative standard will not determine the issue of negligence: the criterion of reasonableness prevails.[222] In practice, the courts distinguish between private individuals and defendants who are in business or are otherwise in a position where it is reasonable to keep up-to-date with relevant standards and put them into effect (such as a local authority).[223] However, even where the defendant's business or other position requires it to be aware of the relevant safety standard, breach of the standard does not *necessarily* lead to a finding of negligence as other factors, such as the proper balance of risks of different courses of

---

[218] *Cit.* n. 212.   [219] Below, pp. 339–40.   [220] Below, p. 435.   [221] Above, p. 188.

[222] *Greaves & Co. (Contractors) Ltd. v Baynham Meikle & Partners* [1975] 1 WLR 1095 (British Standards Institution circular).

[223] *Ward v The Ritz Hotel* [1992] PIQR P315 (non-compliance of hotel with British Standard); *Billington v Maguire* [2001] EWCA Civ 273; 2001 WL 513024 (lorry driver parked on highway blocking cycle lane contrary to the applicable Code of Practice ('Safety at Street Works and Road Works') and the clearway regulations). Cf. *O. v Wilson* [1999] CLY 4004 (failure to conform to British Standard in respect of glass in door not negligence in private householder).

conduct and the practicability of fulfilling the standard remain relevant.[224] And in some contexts the law requires even non-expert individuals to know the safety standards applicable to the particular activity which they undertake, as is the case regarding the provisions of the Highway Code.[225]

5. Establishing Negligence: Burdens of Proof, Evidence and the Finality of Decision Making

In order to understand the process by which decisions on negligence are reached, I need to explain certain fundamental characteristics of the English civil process, the nature of evidence and of the burden of proof as well as the mechanisms by which it is assessed whether at trial or on appeal. In all this, the English civil process differs markedly from the French.[226]

(a) The roles of the parties and of the court

The traditional conception of the English civil process combines the ideas of the adversarial character of the parties and the relative passivity of the judge.[227] This has a number of consequences, but for present purposes the most important is that it is for the parties by their pleadings to define the issues both factual *and legal* in dispute between them to be determined by the court.[228] As I have earlier explained, until the middle of the twentieth century, in general the body by which these determinations were made differed according to whether an issue was factual (for determination by the jury) or legal (for determination by the judge) and this division has affected the English understanding of the notions of burden of proof and standard of proof. But the most striking point is that it is for the parties not merely to advance the facts which give rise to the dispute and the legal characterisation which they wish to give to those facts, but also to advance the legal authorities (whether statutory or judicial) which, in their view, justify this characterisation. The court's role is to decide whether the facts as

---

[224] E.g. *Hawkyard v North Yorkshire CC* [1999] CLY 2887 (local authority's responsibility to maintain footpaths in wintry weather).

[225] Since 1960, statute has provided that breach of the Highway Code is relevant to civil liability (now Road Traffic Act 1988, s. 38) but this creates no presumption of negligence: *Powell v Phillips* [1972] 3 All ER 864 (when statute specifically made breach of the Code relevant to negligence). Cf. *Arnot v Sprake* [2001] EWCA Civ 341; 2001 WL 239773 (relevance of absence from Highway Code of requirement for defendant to act otherwise than as he did). [226] Above, pp. 46–50.

[227] In *Jones v National Coal Board* [1957] 2 WLR 760, 766 Denning LJ noted that: '[i]n the system of trial which we have evolved in this country, the judge sits to hear and determine the issues raised by the parties, not to conduct an investigation or examination on behalf of society at large, as happens, we believe, in some foreign countries. Even in England, however, a judge is not a mere umpire to answer the question "How's that?" His object, above all, is to find out the truth, and to do justice according to law; and in the daily pursuit of it the advocate plays an honourable and necessary role. Was it not Lord Eldon L.C. who said in a notable passage that "truth is best discovered by powerful statements on both sides of the question"?'

[228] Sir William Holdsworth, *History of English Law*, Vol. IX, 264, 328.

pleaded are established and whether the propositions of law as advanced hold good and therefore justify the remedy which is sought. The parties do not simply submit a factual dispute to which the court then applies its relevant consequences in law.

Has this position been altered by the Civil Procedure Rules which have widely been seen as introducing into English law a fundamentally different conception of the relative roles of the parties and of the court in the civil process?[229] For under these rules, the parties are under a duty to help the court in furthering its overriding objective of dealing with cases justly[230] and the court has the task of encouraging the parties to cooperate with each other in the conduct of the proceedings.[231] To help courts further the overriding objective, they have a number of powers of management of the process, including powers to strike out a statement of case or to pare down the issues to be tried or appealed.[232] There has indeed been a shift away from traditional judicial passivity towards a degree of judicial interventionism in the civil process. These changes are certainly radical if not indeed revolutionary.

Nevertheless, there is no reason to think that the new rules, either in text or spirit, have changed the relative roles of the parties and the court in *defining* the nature of the issues to be tried. For while a court now has a power to eliminate issues considered unworthy of trial or appeal, those issues which are to be tried or appealed remain defined by the parties, both factually and legally. This can be seen by the courts' continuing views of the function of pleadings (or 'statements of case' as they are now termed) and by the doctrine of cases decided *per incuriam*.

As to pleadings, the Civil Procedure Rules encourage the simplification of the particulars of claim and defence used by parties to set out before trial the facts on which they would rely by a requirement that they be concise and clear,[233] but the purpose of pleadings under the new regime remains 'to mark out the parameters of the case that is being advanced by each party' being 'critical to identify the issues and the extent of the dispute between the parties'.[234] Moreover:

> even in relation to evidence and proof, [the Civil Procedure Rules] do not confer on the court the powers which are to be found in other jurisdictions—commonly called inquisitorial or investigative—by which the court itself decides the areas of enquiry and what facts it wishes to establish and, in some cases, by whom the facts are to be established. [Nor do they] signal a major departure from the general principle that it is primarily for each party to decide what its case is and how best it is to be presented to the other party or parties or to the court.[235]

So while a court can order a party to put forward a clear and concise claim on pain of its being struck out, it should not take the case out of a party's hands or require a party

---

[229] See the observations of R.L. Turner (Senior Master) in the Preface to the Civil Procedure Rules, pp. vii, x quoted by M.N. Howard (gen. ed.) *Phipson on Evidence* (Sweet and Maxwell, London, 15th. edn., 2000) 13. The Civil Procedure Rules were made under the Civil Procedure Act 1997, s. 1.

[230] CPR 1.1 & 1.3.   [231] CPR 1.4 (2)a.   [232] CPR 3.4(1); CPR 52.3(7) respectively.

[233] Part 16.2(a) and see *St. Albans Court Ltd. v Daldorch Estates Ltd.* The Times, 24 May 1999, *per* Arden J; *McPhilemy v Times Newspapers Ltd.* [1999] 3 All ER 775.

[234] *McPhilemy v Times Newspapers Ltd.* [1999] 3 All ER 775 at 793, *per* Lord Woolf.

[235] *Circuit Systems Ltd. v Zuken-Redac (UK) Ltd.* [2001] BLR 253 at [22], and [58]–[63], Aldous LJ, quoting with approval the observations of H.H. J. Humphrey Lloyd QC in para. [40] of his judgment below.

to put forward a case which is not its preferred case.[236] There is nothing in the Rules to suggest that the courts are entitled to re-characterise the legal basis of the parties' claims, though they do possess a power to award a remedy not claimed by a party in its statement of case.[237]

Moreover, that it is for the parties to advance the law on which they rely as well as the facts is reflected in an aspect of the doctrine of precedent, for a court is not bound by the decision of an earlier court where it was made *per incuriam*, that is, where it was 'reached . . . in the absence of knowledge of a decision binding on it or a statute' where 'it is shown that, had the court had this material, it *must* have reached a contrary decision'.[238] Underlying this doctrine is a rejection of the fundamental principle well-known in other western European legal systems (and accepted by French law) that the 'court knows the law', the main significance of which is that while it is for the parties to present the facts it is for the courts to apply the law to the facts.[239] While English judges are exceptionally learned in the law and are traditionally recognised as its 'oracles',[240] in principle they do not 'know the law' in the sense that they are entitled to apply it to the facts put forward by the parties without the parties themselves advancing the authorities in question.[241]

How does this affect the determination of an issue such as negligence? First, it remains the case under the Civil Procedure Rules that a claimant will need to set out either in the pleadings or at trial *how* he says that the defendant's conduct was negligent as a matter of fact (what happened, when and where) but also how these facts ought to be characterised as negligent given the applicable standard of care and the balance of the relevant factors. It is not for a court to 'pick up' from the facts as apparent from the evidence an aspect of the defendant's behaviour which it considers negligent where this was not pleaded by the claimant.[242] Similarly, it is not for the court to note that the defendant's conduct fell short of an applicable legislative standard, as the relevance of such a standard must be pleaded by a party (and then will be used as evidence by the court).[243]

The differences here with the relative roles of the parties to the French civil process are considerable but should not be exaggerated. The French *civil* process under the New Code of Civil Procedure follows neither a simplistically inquisitorial nor an adversarial model.[244] The starting point is that civil litigation concerns a *private* dispute invoking the application of *private law* and this means that the initiative for starting it and much of the course of proceedings are the parties' responsibility, but also that 'the subject-matter of the litigation is determined by the respective claims of

---

[236] [2001] BLR 253 at [22].   [237] CPR 16.2(5).

[238] *Duke v Reliance Systems Ltd.* [1988] QB 108, 113, *per* Sir John Donaldson MR.

[239] Above, p. 46.

[240] W. Blackstone, *Commentaries on the Law of England* (OUP, 1st. edn., 1765–1769) Book I, 69 describes judges as 'the depositaries of the law, the living oracles'.

[241] Cf. C.K. Allen, *Law in the Making* (OUP, 7th. edn, 1964), 246 who remarks that 'in practice *per incuriam* appears to mean *per ignorantiam*. It would seem that *ignorantia juris neminen excusat*—except a court of law'.

[242] Cf. the treatment by the CA in *Zucchi v Waitrose Ltd.* (30 Mar. 2000), 2000 WL 345171 of the judge who held the defendant negligent in a way unpleaded by the claimant and unsupported by the evidence.

[243] Above, pp. 202–3.   [244] See above, pp. 46–8.

the parties';[245] 'the court must reach a decision on everything which is claimed but only on what is claimed'.[246] Nevertheless, the courts may take on a managerial role over the preparation of the case before it is heard and generally 'oversee the proper running of the case';[247] and the courts share with the parties the responsibility for collecting evidence so as to see whether or not the facts claimed by the parties are established.[248]

(b) The notion of evidence, proof and burdens of proof

How, then, in the English context do the parties proceed in placing facts and law before the courts? Put simply, facts are alleged in the parties' statements of claim and then supported by evidence; legal propositions are the subject of argument supported by citation.[249] Evidence of a fact is defined as 'that which tends to prove it—something which may satisfy an inquirer of the fact's existence',[250] and may be used to prove either facts in issue or facts from which facts in issue may properly be inferred;[251] the *law* of evidence fixes the types of evidence which, while relevant for this purpose, should be excluded from consideration.[252] Further, the *proof* of a particular fact is its establishment to a particular degree of probability. It is at this stage that an English lawyer resorts to the twin notions of the burden of proof and the standard of proof. The *persuasive* burden of proof lies on the party who has to establish the existence or the non-existence of a fact: generally, it is for a party claiming something to establish it and therefore to bear this burden.[253] English law accepts that in civil cases the degree (or 'standard') of proof is that a fact must be established as more likely than not or on a 'balance of probabilities',[254] this being contrasted with the position in the criminal law where issues must (generally) be established beyond reasonable doubt.[255]

For a common lawyer, this is all very basic, but it is to be noticed that while propositions of law are clearly not the subject of burdens of proof (though they are the subject of submission and counter-submission by the parties), English law also uses the notion of burden of proof to cover the legal characterisation of facts in issue.[256] So, in the context of the tort of negligence, while the definition of the standard of care and

---

[245] Art. 4 al. 1 N.c.pr.civ.   [246] Art. 5 N.c.pr.civ.   [247] Art. 3 N.c.pr.civ.

[248] Above, p. 47.

[249] There is no need for the parties to adduce *evidence* of English law, whether this be statutory or case law.

[250] C. Tapper, *Cross and Tapper on Evidence* (Butterworths, London, 9th. edn., 1999) 1.

[251] Ibid., 20.

[252] Ibid., where the exclusionary form of the law of evidence is explained by its origins in rules which remove types of evidence from consideration by the jury.

[253] Ibid., 118. The persuasive burden of proof is sometimes referred to as the 'legal' burden of proof: ibid., 108. English lawyers also refer to the *evidential* burden of proof, meaning 'the obligation to show... that there is sufficient evidence to raise an issue as to the existence or non-existence of a fact in issue', a notion of particular significance in the context of trial by jury, for where a party fails to discharge such an evidential burden the issue in question will be withdrawn from the consideration of the jury: ibid., 109.   [254] Ibid., 140–1.

[255] *Woolmington v DPP* [1935] AC 462, 481; *Doyle v Olby (Ironmongers) Ltd.* [1969] 2 QB 158.

[256] E.g. placing of the burden of proof as to the reasonableness of a contract term on the person relying on the term by the Unfair Contract Terms Act 1977, s. 11(5).

the set of factors to be taken into account on breach are a matter of law for argument on the authorities, a claimant bears the burden of proof of showing that the defendant was negligent, that is, that by doing X or failing to do Y the defendant failed to attain this legal standard taking into account the relevant factors: it is not for the claimant merely to establish the facts of X or non-Y and for the court to make a ('neutral') evaluation of their character as negligence.[257] In proving negligence, therefore, the claimant is not merely establishing facts according to the relevant degree of probability but also that the proper inference from these facts is one of negligence as it is defined in law. As we shall see, this idea of the evaluation as negligence by inference from 'primary' facts is an important one in the law governing the limits of the appellate jurisdiction.[258]

On the other hand, the power of the courts to 'infer' negligence from the circumstances has led to an important practical distinction in English judicial practice in relation to manufacturers' liability in the tort of negligence. In the view of some commentators, where a product suffers from a manufacturing defect compromising its safety, the courts often presume negligence, so leading to 'a covert area of strict liability masquerading as negligence liability'.[259] However, the difference remains that even here the manufacturer may escape liability if he adduces convincing evidence that the defect was unforeseeable or not reasonably avoidable.[260]

At this stage, though, I need to explain the significance of the maxim *res ipsa loquitur* which applies in some circumstances to claims for negligence and is sometimes said to give rise to a 'presumption of negligence' and even 'reverse' the burden of proof. This maxim has been the subject of considerable disagreement and at times confusion, but its present understanding by English courts is fairly clear.

The original significance of the maxim concerned the question whether there was sufficient evidence for an allegation of negligence to be put to the jury[261] and in this context Earle CJ famously observed that:

> where the thing is shewn to be under the management of the defendant or his servants, and the accident is such as in the ordinary course of things does not happen if those who have the management use proper care, it affords reasonable evidence, in the absence of explanation by the defendants, that the accident arose from want of care.[262]

This dictum has subsequently been taken as the basis for the application of the maxim which therefore applies to factual situations where the defendant has control of the circumstances from which the claimant's harm has arisen and this harm would not

---

[257] Cf. the likely position as to the 'fairness' of a contract term under Dir. 93/13/EC argued for by *Chitty on Contracts*, paras. 15-62–15-063.   [258] Below, pp. 215–17.

[259] J. Stapleton, 'Products Liability in the United Kingdom: The Myths of Reform' (1999) 34 *Texas International Law Journal* 45, 50; Taylor, *Harmonisation communautaire*, 49. The classic example is *Grant v Australian Knitting Mills* [1936] AC 85.

[260] *Clerk and Lindsell on Torts*, para. 9–24; similarly, Markesinis and Deakin's *Tort Law*, 607 and see *Evans v Triplex Safety Glass Co. Ltd.* [1938] 1 All ER 283; *Daniels and Daniels v R White & Sons* [1938] 4 All ER 258; *Hill v James Crowe (Cases) Ltd.* [1978] ICR 298 (which partly rested on vicarious liability for negligence in the manufacturer's employees).

[261] It therefore concerned the *evidential* burden, see above, p. 208.

[262] *Scott v London & St. Katherine Docks Co.* (1865) 3 H & C 596, 601. Cf. *Easson v L.N.E.Rly.* [1944] KB 421, 425, *per* Du Parcq LJ.

usually arise without negligence. So, for example, it has been applied against the manager of a steelworks where there was an explosion of gas 'of such a violence to cause fear of imminent danger to the workers'[263] and against the suppliers of a re-conditioned motor car whose wheel fell off in the course of being driven the day after it was supplied.[264] On the other hand, the maxim does not apply where more than one defendant is indicated as the possible cause of the claimant's harm,[265] for example, where a claimant is injured by a product which has been manufactured and then sold on through a distributor or retailer.[266]

More difficult has been the precise effect of the application of the maxim. Sometimes it has been said to create a presumption of negligence which a defendant needs to rebut either by explaining how the accident happened in a way consistent with an absence of negligence on his part or by establishing on the balance of probabilities that he was *not* negligent, or that it shifts the burden to the defendant to show the same things:[267] it is not enough for a defendant to show that the accident is inexplicable.[268] Use of the language of presumption and requiring (if only sometimes) that a defendant shows a lack of negligence does look as though the persuasive burden of proof on negligence shifts where the maxim applies.[269] However, the better and more recent view is that *res ipsa loquitur* makes no change to the persuasive burden of proof and is, in Steyn LJ's words, 'not a doctrine, nor a principle, nor a rule. It is simply a convenient label for a group of situations in which an unexplained accident is, as a matter of common sense, the basis for an inference of negligence':[270] this means that the burden of proof remains on the claimant to show negligence in all cases and it is misleading to talk of the shifting of this burden.[271] What the factual situations where *res ipsa loquitur* has been said to apply have in common is that the evidence as a whole gives support to a proper *factual* inference of negligence on the part of the defendant.[272] In this light, *res ipsa loquitur* is simply a Latin tag given to a particular group of cases where the evidence of negligence is circumstantial rather than direct— it does not lead to the imposition of liability without proof of negligence.

(c) The collection and trial of evidence

In English law, the complexity of the nature of the decision making on the issue of negligence is reflected in the potentially elaborate and wide-searching nature of the

---

[263] *Colvilles Ltd. v Devine* [1969] 1 WLR 475, 477, *per* Lord Guest.
[264] *Herschtal v Steward and Ardern Ltd.* [1940] 1 KB 155.
[265] *Pritchard v Clwyd CC* [1993] PIQR P21, P27, *per* Beldam LJ.
[266] *Donoghue v Stevenson* [1932] AC 562, 622, *per* Lord Macmillan.
[267] *Moore v R. Fox & Sons* [1956] 1 QB 596, 607, *per* Evershed MR; similarly *Ludgate v Lovett* [1969] 1 WLR 1016, 1277.   [268] *Moore v R. Fox & Sons* [1956] 1 QB 596, 608.
[269] For the view that the *evidential* burden of proof shifts see: *Henderson v Jenkins & Sons* [1970] AC 282, *per* Lords Reid and Donovan respectively; *Ward v Tesco Stores Ltd.* [1976] 1 WLR 810. However, in the absence of an application to the court that there is no issue to be tried (either by a jury or for the purposes of summary judgment under the former RSC Or. 14) it is difficult to see what this means.
[270] *Bergin v David Wickes Television Ltd.* [1994] PIQR P167, P168 applying the approach taken by the Privy Council in *Ng Chun Pui v Lee Chuen Tat* [1988] RTR 298.
[271] *Ng Chun Pui v Lee Chuen Tat* [1988] RTR 298.   [272] Ibid.

civil process. As I have explained, while in some respects English judges have taken on a more interventionist role, it remains overwhelmingly for the parties to gather and prepare the evidential materials from which the court must decide.[273] Here, I wish to look at how three key aspects of the modern English process apply to an issue like 'negligence' and to highlight the differences from the French position. While the procedures differ considerably between the three 'tracks' (procedural routes by which a case is resolved) put in place by the Civil Procedure Rules, I shall look at the position for cases concerning larger personal injury litigation.[274]

First, the French civil process has long been characterised by a distrust of orality of evidence, whereas the English has relied heavily on oral evidence both of facts and of expert opinions, which have been treated as factual. Here, while English practice is moving towards the French, there remains a very considerable gulf between the two.

As to evidence of facts, 'the general rule is that any fact which needs to be proved by the evidence of witnesses is to be proved ... at trial, by their oral evidence given in public',[275] but no evidence is to be given orally unless a written 'witness statement' has been served on the other side in advance of the hearing without the court's permission.[276] So, what is generally intended is that a witness makes a 'witness statement', and swears at the trial to its veracity so that this statement forms his 'evidence in chief'.[277] The oral process therefore concentrates on the cross-examination of witnesses of fact, which remains key to the trial of contentious issues of fact, though subject to an overall judicial power of control.[278]

Secondly, there remain very considerable differences between the approach of French and English law to the determination of technical issues. I have explained how in the French process, the court appoints its own *expert* or *experts* from an official list (though typically at the request of one or both of the parties) and defines the questions for their determination: the *expertise* is seen as the provision to the court of technical advice which may form part of the *éléments de la preuve*, that is, the materials from which a determination may be made.[279] In practice the *expertise* determines many factual issues formally within the 'assessment' of the *juges du fond* and notably the element of *vice* in sale or 'fault' under article 1383 of the Civil Code.[280] Expert advice is therefore inherently uncontroversial in the French process in the sense that it is not for the parties to advance opposing expert's views, to be tested in oral cross-examination by the parties' counsel and then resolved by judicial judgment.[281]

The approach of English law to the resolution of technical matters is that it is a matter for *evidence*, and for this reason remains for the parties to advance and to establish. This basic conception was long expressed by a highly adversarial attitude in many lawyers involved in litigation and in a number of the experts who gave evidence. So, traditionally, expert evidence on an issue was provided by an appropriately qualified person engaged by one side whose views could be adopted or discarded by that

---

[273] Above, pp. 205–6.

[274] The three tracks are the 'small claims track', the 'fast track' and the 'multi-track': see CPR 27, 28, 29 respectively. A claim for personal injuries for £15,000 and above would follow the 'multi-track' procedure.

[275] CPR 32.2 (1)(a).　　[276] CPR 32.10.　　[277] O'Hare and Hill, *Civil Litigation*, 573.

[278] CPR 32.1 (3).　　[279] Above, pp. 48–50.　　[280] Above, pp. 78, 48–9 respectively.

[281] Cf. below, p. 384 concerning the criminal process.

party,[282] and if adopted offered to the other side for its agreement or contest. If agreement on a technical issue was not reached by the parties, the parties' experts gave their evidence orally and were then subjected to cross-examination. This manner of proceeding was the object of some of Lord Woolf's most severe criticisms in *Access to Justice*, both in terms of its cost and in terms of the damaging effect on the quality of justice of expert witnesses becoming too closely associated with one or other side to a dispute.[283] The Civil Procedure Rules addressed these criticisms in a number of ways: overall, they explicitly provide that the duty of an expert is to help the court on the matters within his expertise, this overriding any duty to the person from whom he has received instructions or by whom he is paid.[284] Secondly, the Civil Procedure Rules make provision for the encouragement of parties to agree on the appointment of a 'jointly appointed expert' and may even order such an appointment against their wishes,[285] though it is not likely that the court will do so except where the issue 'falls within a substantially established area of knowledge and where it is not necessary for the court to sample a range of opinion',[286] and so not where there is likely to be controversy. Even where an expert is jointly appointed by order of the court, the expert remains instructed by the parties who define the issues to be addressed, though subject to advice by the court in case of need.[287] While, therefore, joint experts can be appointed by order of a court, they are not 'court experts': the courts do not possess their own list of experts and will select them either from a list agreed by the parties or (on default of agreement) in such a way as they direct, for example, by request for a nomination by the relevant professional body.[288] Moreover, whether experts are instructed by one of the parties or jointly, their input into the decision making remains *evidence* and while, in principle, it must be in writing, it may be the subject of written questions or (in the case of another party's expert) the subject of oral cross-examination at trial.

As a result, even after the Civil Procedure Rules, where technical matters are in dispute an English judge will receive competing expert views and will therefore have to decide between them. As regards negligence, a court may well be faced with expert views on the factors to be balanced in coming to its decision, such as the probability of harm, the state of technical knowledge, or the availability and cost of precautions which would have averted the risk. These technical disputes are then fully reflected in the analysis by the trial court in the text of its judgment, where the competing positions are summarised, the points of agreement or dispute identified and the reasons set out for the court's own position.[289] In this way, the evidential materials from which the court's evaluation of the defendant's conduct are drawn are set out for public and higher judicial scrutiny.

The third important aspect of the English civil process which remains very different from the French is its approach to the production of relevant documents. The

---

[282] If a party received expert evidence which ran contrary to his own case, he could (and still can) simply ask another expert, the earlier prejudicial advice not coming to court: O'Hare and Hill, *Civil Litigation*, 408.

[283] *Access to Justice*, Interim Report to the Lord Chancellor on the civil justice system in England and Wales (June, 1995) Chap. 23.   [284] CPR 35.3.

[285] CPR 35.7.

[286] Notes to CPR 35.7 in *The White Book from Sweet and Maxwell* (online resource updated to Jan. 2004).   [287] CPR 35.8 & 35.14.

[288] CPR 35.7(3).

[289] E.g. in *Carroll v Fearon* [1998] PIQR P416, P422 the trial judge was reported as describing the defendant manufacturer's expert's theory to be 'nonsense'.

traditional English approach to what was called 'discovery' required '*all* relevant documents' to be produced for the inspection of the other side even if they damaged their own case.[290] The parties to the litigation themselves had a duty to search for and disclose all these documents and solicitors for parties had a legal duty to give full effect to this process, backed up by a powerful professional culture of conformity.[291] Neither a party nor his lawyers were allowed to retain any document which was prejudicial to his case, the main exceptions being documents themselves generated for the purposes of the litigation (which are protected by legal professional privilege) and those which benefit from 'public immunity' privilege.[292] As Lord Woolf noted, this aspect of the English process 'comes as a surprise, sometimes a painful surprise, to litigants from abroad'.[293] While discovery was a very powerful means of finding out facts and was sometimes said itself to 'win cases',[294] it was also extremely expensive.[295]

The Civil Procedure Rules retain all these distinctive features of discovery in their provisions on 'disclosure' and inspection of documents, but attempt to cut down the net to be cast over a party's records. So, under 'standard disclosure' (which is ordered by a court unless it directs otherwise),[296] a party must disclose 'only (a) the documents on which he relies; and (b) the documents which (i) adversely affect his own case; (ii) adversely affect another party's case; or support another party's case'.[297] However, in doing so, a party does not have to disclose *all* relevant documents but is required only to make a reasonable search for documents falling within these rules, taking into account the number of documents involved, the nature and complexity of the proceedings, the ease and expense of retrieval of any particular document; and the significance of any document likely to be located during the search.[298] Nevertheless, many cases of claims for negligence remain destined to produce very considerable documentary bundles and the English rules still require spontaneous disclosure of documents by a party prejudicial to his own case. Here, the key difference with the French position does not lie in the formal power of the courts, for a French court may order the production of any relevant document, but rather in the rule that the French court will order production only where a party has identified a document held by the other party as relevant to an issue in dispute, in the absence of a duty in the parties themselves to disclose relevant documents and in a legal professional ethic against doing so to the prejudice of one's own client.[299] It is a difference in understanding of the proper roles of the protagonists to the process.

---

[290] The test of 'relevance' was a very broad one, including documents which 'may fairly lead [a party] to a train of inquiry' which may directly or indirectly advance the case of his opponent or damage his own case: *Compagnie Financière du Pacifique v Peruvian Guano Co.* (1882) QBD 55, 63, *per* Brett LJ.

[291] So, notably, a solicitor must refuse to act if his client refuses to produce documents which ought to be the subject of discovery and cf. below, p. 297.

[292] On the latter, see below, pp. 356–60.   [293] *Access to Justice, op. cit.* n. 283, 164.

[294] E.g. *Wright v Dunlop Rubber Co. Ltd.* [1972] 13 KIR 255, (manufacturer of chemical product disclosing documents which revealed its own state of knowledge some 30 years previously).

[295] *Access to Justice, op. cit.* n. 283, 165.   [296] CPR 35.5(1).   [297] CPR 31.6.

[298] CPR 37.1(1) & (2) and see A. Pertoldi, 'From discovery to disclosure: neither quicker nor cheaper?' (2001) IHL 38.

[299] Above, p. 48. Cf. the critical comments as to the 'lamentable' approach of the defendant manufacturers to discovery in *Carroll v Fearon* [1998] PIQR P416, 424 and the robust attitude of the court to their negligence in part as a result.

Taken together, these English rules governing the production and treatment of evidence can give rise to a very different range of factual material coming before the courts for their decision than is the case in France. As to questions of simple facts relevant to the issue of negligence—who did what, knew what and when?—English law provides the double weapons of the cross-examination of witnesses and disclosure of prejudicial documents. From this perspective (and despite the court's new managerial role), the English civil process remains fiercely adversarial, any inquisition being conducted not by the judge, but rather by the parties acting as each other's confessor (through disclosure) as well as their inquisitor (through cross-examination).[300] By contrast, French courts are limited to the factual evidence put by the parties themselves in a documentary form unmoulded by their lawyers and not subject to the fire of cross-examination.

As to the characterisation of facts (such as a finding of negligence), English substantive law sets both the standards and the factors from which a court comes to its view, whereas in French law, many questions of characterisation (including those as to the existence of delictual fault) remain broad and at large without explicit guidelines, legal or judicial. Whereas in the English process, expert input in the court's decision making is evidential and controversial, in the French process while the parties can argue their positions before the *expert*, the latter's report expresses views which are all but unchallengeable either by the judges themselves or the parties.[301] Indeed, where there is more than one body of scientific or technical opinion of importance in determining issues of liability, in the French context, the outcome will depend to a considerable extent on the court's choice of expert. By contrast, in the English process, while the views of experts are highly regarded, any controversy is likely to be exposed and the competing views tried before the court, the judge taking into account the experts' personal distinction and experience as well as the nature of and manner of delivery of their evidence.

(d) The finality of decisions on negligence

A further very significant contrast is to be found in the way in which the French and the English processes make a *final* determination of issues such as negligence and defect, though the English position after reforms in 2000 is not fully clear.[302] Two aspects of these rules are significant for present purposes.

First, there used to be a general *right* of appeal as far as the Court of Appeal[303] but no right of appeal to the House of Lords even on matters of law.[304] Appeal to the House of Lords remains unchanged, an appeal lying either with the permission ('leave') of the court whose decision is appealed or with the permission of the House of Lords itself[305] and this was (and still is) granted taking into account the general public

---

[300] Written questions may also be put to the other side, these now being known as requests for further information: see CPR Part 18.   [301] Above, p. 49.

[302] This law is fully described in the notes to the Rules of the Supreme Court Orders 55 and 59.

[303] Supreme Court Act 1981, s. 16 (appeals from the High Court); County Courts Act 1984, s. 77 (appeals from County Courts). There were, of course, numerous exceptions, in particular where appeals to the Court of Appeal were restricted to points of law.

[304] Administration of Justice (Appeals) Act 1934, s. 1(1).   [305] Ibid.

importance of the case, its likelihood of success and the degree of dissension the case may have previously caused among judges already.[306] However, after concern was expressed that the civil work of the Court of Appeal was hampered by unmeritorious appeals,[307] a new system of rules was put in place in 2000 governing appeals other than to the House of Lords. Under these rules,[308] in general permission is required for an appeal and this will be given where the court considers that it will have a realistic rather than fanciful prospect of success,[309] or where there is some other compelling reason why it should be heard.[310] Appeal from a court or tribunal is in principle to be heard by the 'next level of judge in the court hierarchy',[311] any second appeal being available only exceptionally.[312] As a result, there is no longer any general right of appeal from the High Court to the Court of Appeal.

Secondly, under the former regime, decisions of lower courts in civil cases were susceptible to challenge by way of appeal rather than review, in the sense that the appellate court undertook a re-opening of the issues put to it for appeal, whether these were factual or legal, rather than looking merely at the quality or procedure of the decision making.[313] Under the new regime, the function of a court hearing an appeal is 'limited to a *review* of the decision of the lower court',[314] but the grounds of this review are very wide, the court being required to 'allow an appeal where the decision of the lower court was (a) wrong; or (b) unjust because of a serious procedural or other irregularity in the proceedings in the lower court'.[315] On the other hand, the new regime is clearly aimed at the creation of a system of review of the decision making of lower courts on the basis of a dossier, as it requires the filing of papers on appeal to include documentation from the decision appealed,[316] and in principle the appellate court will not receive 'oral evidence or evidence which was not before the lower court'.[317]

How, though, did the former regime of appeals apply to issues such as the negligence of a defendant and how, if at all, does the new regime differ?

Under the former regime, English appellate courts were surprisingly willing to intervene in the decisions of lower courts on negligence, denying to judicial determinations the protection from appeal which had been established for jury verdicts.[318] According to Viscount Cave LC speaking in the context of an appeal on a finding on negligence:

it is the duty of the Court of Appeal to make up its own mind, not disregarding the judgment appealed from and giving special weight to that judgment in cases where the credibility of

---

[306] O'Hare and Hill, *Civil Litigation*, 791.

[307] Review of the Court of Appeal (Civil Division) chaired by Sir Jeffrey Bowman (1997) available at <http://www.lcd.govuk/civil/bowman/bowfr.htm>.

[308] Access to Justice Act 1999, s. 54, CPR 52; Practice Direction 52—Appeals.

[309] CPR 52.3(1), CPR 52.3(6)(a); *Swain v Hillman* [2001] 1 All ER 91, 92, cited with approval in *Tanfern Ltd. v Gregor Cameron-Macdonald* [2000] 1 WLR 1311, 1316, *per* Brooke LJ.

[310] CPR 52.3(6).

[311] *Tanfern Ltd. v Gregor Cameron-Macdonald* [2000] 1 WLR 1311, 1314 , *per* Brooke LJ who notes the exceptions.   [312] Access to Justice Act 1999, s. 55(1).

[313] RSC Or. 55 r. 3(1) (appeals to the High Court); RSC Or. 59 r. 3(1) (appeals to the Court of Appeal).

[314] CPR 52.11 (emphasis added).   [315] CPR 52.11(3).   [316] PD 52 5.6(b); PD 52 5.6 (i).

[317] CPR 52.11 (2). This has resulted in a 'significant change in practice' as regards interlocutory appeals: *Tanfern Ltd. v Gregor Cameron-Macdonald* [2000] 1 WLR 1311, 1317, *per* Brooke LJ.

[318] Above, pp. 189–90.

witnesses comes into question, but with full liberty to draw *its own inference from the facts* proved or admitted, and to decide accordingly.[319]

This liberal approach to intervention by appellate courts in decisions on negligence can be seen consistently at least until the late 1990s. Sometimes, the courts distinguished between the 'primary' or 'simple' facts (what a defendant said, knew or did all fall in the first category) and 'secondary' facts (for example, the characterisation of these as 'negligence'), the appellate court intervening more readily in the latter; but other judges preferred to be less categorical on the basis that 'it may often be difficult to say what is simple fact and what is inference from fact, or . . . what is perception, what evaluation'.[320] This approach was reflected in the Rules of the Supreme Court under which appellate courts had the power to draw inferences of fact[321] and in numerous decisions of the Court of Appeal and House of Lords where the judges re-opened the findings on negligence. In this respect, while appellate judges showed respect for the views of the judge at trial (especially as to issues of the credibility of witnesses which only he was in a position to assess), they showed themselves remarkably willing to set out the relevant evidence as garnered from the judgments appealed and reassess it, criticising the judge below for giving too much weight here or too little there, as well as for failing to take into account some relevant piece of evidence or taking into account some irrelevant one.[322] Appellate judges even set out part of the transcript of a cross-examination of witnesses, including expert witnesses, with comments on their treatment at trial.[323]

In this respect, the courts use the expression 'inference of fact or from the facts' in two ways. First, they use it to refer to the process of deducing from the facts a second fact, for example, the deduction that a person found seriously hurt by a busy road with injuries consistent with impact by a motor vehicle was involved in a traffic accident.[324] Secondly, however, the courts use 'inference from the facts' to denote the characterisation of the facts as found in terms of the law's understanding of negligence, which is neither a mere determination of a fuller factual picture nor simply the application of a straightforward legal proposition to a set of facts: it involves an evaluation and not merely a perception.

Under the new regime, appeals will be allowed on the ground that the decision below was 'wrong'[325] and that '[t]he appeal court may draw any inference of fact

---

[319] *Mersey Docks and Harbour Board v Procter* [1923] AC 253, 258–9 (emphasis added).

[320] *Benmax v Austin Motor Co. Ltd.* [1955] AC 370, 375, *per* Viscount Simons.

[321] RSC Or. 55 r. 7(3) (appeals to the High Court); RSC Or. 59 r. 10(3) (appeals to the Court of Appeal).

[322] E.g. *Wheat v E. Lacon & Co. Ltd.* [1966] AC 552, 569, *per* Viscount Dilhorne ('There being in this case no dispute as to the primary facts and no direct evidence as to the cause of [the plaintiff's] fall, it is . . . the duty of your Lordships not to shrink from the task of evaluating the evidence and to decide what inference, if any, can properly be drawn from the undisputed evidence'); *Whitehouse v Jordan* [1981] 1 WLR 246 (in the context of medical negligence).

[323] E.g. *Hawkins v Chrysler (UK) Ltd.* [1986] 38 BLR 26 (claim for negligence against employer and specialist flooring engineer on whose floor the plaintiff slipped).

[324] Where a case attracts *res ipsa loquitur*, the inference will typically have both elements: the circumstances of control justify a deduction of the existence of other facts (acts or omissions) which justify a qualification as negligence: cf. above, pp. 209–10.   [325] CPR 52.11 (3), above, p. 215.

which it considers justified on the evidence';[326] and, reading these two provisions together, an appellate court should feel entitled to allow an appeal on the ground that a decision below was 'wrong' on the basis that the lower court did not draw the proper inferences from the facts which it established. If an 'inference from the facts' includes the legal characterisation of facts found below, appellate courts will remain able to overturn a decision below on negligence which they consider 'wrong' because they differ in the evaluation of the facts as found below. However, it remains unclear whether appellate courts will be more or less reluctant to overturn decisions on negligence. While judicial decisions on negligence involve the balancing of factors according to a general standard and this may be thought to give rise to a certain discretion, it is not a judicial discretion in the same sense as is found in judicial powers to determine interlocutory questions which were the main target (and so far the main victim) of the change from re-hearing to review.[327] While the House of Lords has recently expressed the view that appellate courts should hesitate before re-opening issues similar to negligence,[328] the Court of Appeal has continued to overturn decisions at first instance on negligence, intervening on the basis that the judge 'misdirected himself'[329] or simply where it felt that it was not open to the judge below on his own findings of fact to find the defendant not guilty of any negligence.[330]

A comparison with French law here reveals a number of contrasts, but also some similarities. In French law, there is a right of appeal from decisions of first instance to a cour d'appel,[331] and the latter's role is to reassess the issues submitted to it as a matter of law, fact and evaluation without any sense of deference to the views of the judges of first instance such as is seen in the English context; this reflects the fact that (at least in this sort of case) the judges of appeal are in just as good a position to decide and evaluate issues of fact as are judges of first instance: all the facts, basic and technical, are contained in the *dossier*. Indeed, if anything, a French lawyer would see the judges of the cour d'appel as better able to make a judgment, given that they are more senior and more experienced in the profession of judging. By contrast, the role of the Cour de cassation is very different, for while access to it is available as of right, its principal role is to ensure the proper interpretation and application of the law to the facts, leaving the facts within the 'sovereign power of assessment' of the *juges du fond*. While in this respect the Cour de cassation will intervene in decisions of the *juges du fond* on the existence of *une faute délictuelle* this takes place on a somewhat ad hoc basis rather than on the basis of developed guidelines.[332]

---

[326] CPR 52.11(4) echoing RSC Or. 55 r. 7(3) (appeals to the High Court); RSC Or. 59 r. 10(3) (appeals to the Court of Appeal).

[327] *Tanfern Ltd. v. Gregor Cameron-Macdonald* [2000] 1 WLR 1311, 1317; Court of Appeal, *Review of the Legal Year 2001–2002*, 16.

[328] *Jolley v Sutton LBC* [2000] 1 WLR 1082, 1089. See also *Barber v Somerset CC* [2004] UKHL 13; [2004] 1 WLR 1089 where the HL by a majority preferred to reinstate the decision on negligence at trial rather than the CA's substitution of its own judgment on the issue.

[329] *Zucchi v Waitrose Ltd.* (30 March 2000) 2000 WL 345171. Cf. *Hawkins v Chrysler (UK) Ltd.* [1986] 38 BLR 36, 46 (where Fox LJ considered that the judge below had not 'misdirected' himself).

[330] *Billington v Maguire* [2001] EWCA Civ 273, 2001 WL 513024 at [35]. Aldous LJ dissented on the ground that the judge's 'informed opinion' was one to which he was entitled to come on the primary facts: ibid. at [74]. [331] Above, p. 41.

[332] Above, pp. 44–5.

(e) The relationship between the civil process and decisions on negligence or fault

In the previous paragraphs I have identified a number of ways in which differences between English and French law in their understandings of the roles of the courts and the parties, in the nature and methods of evidence coming before the courts and the nature of appeals reflect and are reflected in the nature of the substantive decision making undertaken by the courts. So, in the English context the once broad and open standard of the reasonable man has been elaborated into a complex of rules and factors, each of which may require particular and sometimes controversial factual input, sophisticated legal argument and judicial analysis and evaluation. This degree of legal refinement invites recourse to the range of evidential materials caught by disclosure and the trial of issues through adversarial evidence, whether purely factual or scientific and technical—indeed, sometimes, it is difficult to see how it could be undertaken without them. Moreover, while the fundamentally oral and still adversarial nature of the English trial gives decisions at first instance a particular status (particularly where they rest in part on the credibility of witnesses), more generally appellate courts (including the House of Lords) are willing to reconsider and re-evaluate the evidence on issues such as negligence and substitute their own views.

By contrast, in the French context, and even taking into account the self-proclaimed role of the Cour de cassation, issues of the determination of delictual fault and even more of *imprudence* remain considerably at large: broad standards of behaviour are kept broad in the process of their assessment and, if appealed, their reassessment by the *juges du fond*. Moreover, technical and complex factual determinations and their consequential evaluation in legal terms (for example, whether a 'fault' has been committed or whether a product is 'defective') are generally taken by experts, whose views are then proclaimed and typically accepted rather than discussed by the courts in their judgments: technical issues are taken on trust, rather than subjected to trial. Moreover, the absence of any duty of spontaneous disclosure of prejudicial documents means that in some cases French civil courts decide on the basis of limited and sometimes incomplete information, though neither we (nor they) can know what they do not know. This, then, is the converse in terms of the nature and likely quality of justice of the costs incurred by English parties by the process of disclosure of documents; it also explains in part the popularity of the French *criminal* process in the adjudication of claims for personal injury and death.[333]

6. Breach of Statutory Duty

The tort of breach of statutory duty is particularly revealing of English law's choices of policy as well as technique in relation to the compensation of personal injuries and death, and these choices are fully reflected in its application to liability for products. It is also interesting from a comparative perspective: in its mixture of two legal sources,

[333] Below, Chap. 14.

statute and common law; in its interaction between crime and tort; and between the exercise of administrative power and civil liability. Here, I shall consider these points, with the exception of the last which I shall discuss in its wider context of the liability of those who exercise powers of safety in relation to products.[334]

While earlier cases had accepted that breach of a duty imposed by statute would give rise to a claim for damages by a person harmed as a result,[335] it was the decision of the Court of Appeal in *Groves v Lord Wimborne* which made clear the distinct existence of the 'tort of breach of statutory duty' decided as regards an accident at work.[336] At the time, the main need for its distinctive nature was the avoidance of restrictive defences to liability in an employer in the tort of negligence (notably, by reason of the doctrine of common employment and *volenti non fit injuria*).[337] As a result, by the end of the nineteenth century, English courts were asking whether breach of a particular statutory duty would give rise to civil liability in addition to any sanction or remedy provided by the legislation itself (notably, by way of criminal sanction), looking for an answer in the interpretation of 'parliamentary intention'. Except where the statute in question makes express provision for the issue of civil liability (either positively or negatively), the courts have constructed a number of considerations to help them decide whether or not Parliament 'intended' civil liability to result from breach of the particular duty, these considerations sometimes being expressed in the language of 'presumptions': notably, whether the duty was intended to protect the (restricted) category of person such as the claimant,[338] whether it is intended to avoid the particular harm suffered by the claimant,[339] and whether the remedy or sanction provided by the Act is sufficient.[340] For many English lawyers, there is considerable doubt as to the helpfulness of these considerations in determining the incidence of civil liability for breach of statutory duties: 'if results can be predicted it is because of factors other than the presumptions'.[341] As Lord Hoffman has observed:

[w]hether a statutory duty gives rise to a private cause of action ... requires an examination of the policy of the statute to decide whether it was intended to confer a right to compensation for breach. Whether it can be relied upon to support the existence of a common law duty of care is

---

[334] Above, p. 168 and below, Chap. 13.

[335] E.g. *Britton v Great Western Cotton Co.* (1872) LR 7 Exch 130. In *Couch v Steel* (1854) 3 E & B 402, Lord Campbell accepted in very general terms that a breach of a statutory duty would give rise to liability (in the context of a failure in a ship's captain to provide medicines for the crew of a ship during a voyage), but its generality was doubted by the CA in *Atkinson v Newcastle Waterworks Co.* [1877] 2 Ex D 441, 448. Cf. *Stovin v Wise* [1996] AC 923, 952 where Lord Hoffman noted that the common law courts refused to award compensation to those injured by the breach of the *common law* duty on inhabitants of a parish to maintain the highway. Lord Denning MR's attempt in *Ex p Island Records* [1978] Ch 122, 135 to enunciate a broader principle was rejected by the HL in *Lonrho Ltd. v Shell Petroleum Co. Ltd. (No. 2)* [1982] AC 173, 187.

[336] [1898] 2 QB 402.

[337] Markesinis and Deakin's *Tort Law*, 362. *Groves v Lord Wimborne* [1898] 2 QB 402 itself rejected the application of the doctrine of common employment.

[338] E.g. *Cutler v Wandsworth Stadium Ltd.* [1949] AC 498.

[339] *Gorris v Scott* (1873–74) LR 9 Ex 125.

[340] E.g. where judicial review is available: cf. *Phelps v Hillingdon LBC* [2001] 2 AC 619, 652 (Lord Slynn) and the differing views of members of the HL in *Cullen v Chief Constable of the Royal Ulster Constabulary* [2003] UKHL 39, [14], [34] and [66]–[67]; [2003] 1 WLR 1763.

[341] K.M. Stanton, *Breach of Statutory Duty in Tort* (Sweet and Maxwell, London, 1986) 52.

not exactly a question of construction, because the cause of action does not arise out of the statute itself. But the policy of the statute is nevertheless a crucial factor in the decision.[342]

This dictum nicely illustrates the mixture of legal sources on which liability is based in these cases: the duty is set by the statute, which is also 'crucial' to the question of the incidence of civil liability; but liability is imposed at common law under the general framework of 'the tort' of breach of statutory duty.

In practical terms, throughout the twentieth century the tort of breach of statutory duty grew up in the shadow of the emergent and later dominant tort of negligence. Apart from its advantages in terms of defences (which were considerably reduced on their reform in the mid century),[343] two other features have allowed it to retain its significance. First, liability does not necessarily rest on negligence in the sense of a lack of reasonable care in the circumstances. As I have explained, while sometimes breach of a duty of safety was termed 'statutory negligence',[344] the courts have accepted that the standard of liability (whether strict or based on negligence) varies according to the content of the particular statutory duty,[345] sometimes imposing a rebuttable presumption of negligence[346] or a duty of accomplishment (notably, to see that machinery is safely fenced).[347]

Secondly, the tort of breach of statutory duty may allow a claimant to avoid restrictive aspects of the scope of the tort of negligence, in particular relating to the nature of the defendant's conduct or the claimant's harm. So, for example, in *Monk v Warbey* the plaintiff recovered damages from the owner of a car which he had permitted to be driven by an uninsured person (in breach of a statutory duty), where that person had then caused the plaintiff personal injuries:[348] here, the car owner had caused the plaintiff the pure economic loss of failing to recover compensation from the driver's insurer.[349] Pure economic loss may be recovered in the tort of breach of statutory duty (depending on the nature and purpose of the duty in question); the limiting conditions of its recovery in the tort of negligence are not present.[350] Similarly, claimants have tried to avoid the restrictions on recovery in respect of negligence in the exercise of a statutory power by arguing that the statute in question imposed a *duty* and that this gave rise to a distinct liability at common law. These attempts have, however, been met with a very cold judicial reception.[351]

---

[342] *Stovin v Wise* [1996] AC 923, 952.

[343] The doctrine of common employment was abolished by the Law Reform (Personal Injuries) Act 1948, s. 1(1); the Law Reform (Contributory Negligence) Act 1945 turned contributory negligence from a complete defence to liability to a ground of possible reduction or extinction of a claimant's damages; the defence of *volenti non fit injuria* (which still acts as a complete defence) has been narrowed in its practical scope: *Wooldridge v Sumner* [1963] 2 QB 43, 69–70; *Nettleship v Weston* [1971] 2 QB 691, 701 and *Morris v Murray* [1991] 2 QB 6, 7, *per* Fox LJ. [344] Above, p. 190.

[345] E.g. *Britton v Great Western Cotton Co.* (1872) LR 7 Exch 130 and see the examples collected in *Clerk and Lindsell on Torts*, paras. 11-49–11-51(M. Jones). For a recent example see *Palmer v Marks and Spencer plc* [2001] EWCA Civ 1528 2001 WL 1135094.

[346] E.g. *Nimmo v Alexander Cowan & Sons Ltd.* [1968] AC 107 (duty to maintain a safe workplace 'so far as is reasonably practicable').

[347] E.g. *Britton v Great Western Cotton Co.* (1872) LR 7 Exch 130 ('unqualified duty to fence' fly-wheel connected to steam-engine). [348] [1934] 50 Lloyd's Rep 33.

[349] Ibid. at 36 (though not expressed in terms of 'economic loss').

[350] E.g. as regards breaches of EC law: *Clerk and Lindsell on Torts*, paras. 11-37–11-39, who note that otherwise the courts are cautious about recovery here. [351] Above, p. 168.

Where, then, have English courts accepted that the breach of a statutory duty will give rise to civil liability? Many writers have historically drawn a broad distinction between cases involving accidents at work (where liability is imposed) and other cases (where liability *may* be imposed but often is not).[352] The Law Commission has suggested that a principle of interpretation should be enacted which would give rise to a presumption of actionability in tort for breaches of statutory duty in the absence of express provision to the contrary,[353] but unless this occurs, such authorities as exist in the context of statutory provisions relating to the safety of products suggest that they will not be interpreted as implicitly giving rise to civil liability in tort.

For, in general the courts have not proved willing to find that breach of statutory duties enacted in the interests of health and safety, including the safety of products, will implicitly give rise to civil liability.[354] So, for example, it was held that breach of a provision which required of the owners of motor vehicles that their fittings be 'in such a condition as not to cause, or to be likely to cause, danger to any person on the motor car or on the highway' did not give rise to an action in respect of damage to another road user's vehicle when the wheel of the defendant's vehicle came off on the highway: a member of the public using the highway was not a member of a particularly protected class.[355] Similarly, the statutory offence of selling a motor vehicle for driving on the road in such a condition that it would be unlawful to use it for this purpose has been held not to give rise to a civil action for damages, this time on the ground that the penalty provided for by the Act was prima facie enough.[356] The English courts did not choose to use this tort to impose liability without negligence on either owners or suppliers of motor vehicles for accidents on the roads.

Nor have the courts chosen to impose civil liability for breach of the numerous statutory duties concerning the safety and quality of food even though their clear purpose is the protection of personal safety. In *Square v Model Farm Dairies (Bournemouth) Ltd.*,[357] a householder had suffered distress and expense due to the infection of several members of his household with typhoid which they had contracted from the defendant's milk, but the Court of Appeal rejected their claims for damages for breach of statutory duty founded on the offence of selling food to the prejudice of its purchaser 'which is not of the nature, substance, or quality of the article demanded'.[358] This provision simply made criminal what would otherwise be a breach of contract and it was 'impossible to think' that anyone other than the purchaser himself was intended to be protected; and he should rely on his contractual remedy.[359] By contrast, in *Read v Croydon Corporation*[360] the defendant local authority owned and maintained two

---

[352] E.g. G.L. Williams, 'The Effect of Penal Legislation in the Law of Tort' (1960) 23 *MLR* 233.

[353] *The Interpretation of Statutes: Report of the Two Commissions*, Law Com. No. 21, Scot. Law Com. No. 11 (HC 256, 1969).

[354] R. Cranston, *Consumers and the Law* (Weidenfield and Nicolson, London 2nd. edn. 1984) 276 who considered this regrettable.

[355] *Phillips v Britannia Hygienic Laundry Co. Ltd.* [1923] 2 KB 832 at 840, *per* Bankes LJ. Similarly, *Herschtal v Stewart and Ardern Ltd.* [1940] 1 KB 155 (supplier of a reconditioned motor car not liable civilly for breach of duties in the Road Traffic Act 1934, s. 38 and the Motor Vehicles (Construction and Use) Regulations 1937, s. 67). [356] *Badham v Lambs Ltd.* [1946] KB 45.

[357] [1939] 2 KB 365. See also *Buckley v La Reserve* [1959] Crim L Rev 451.

[358] This offence is now contained in the Food Safety Act 1990, s. 14.

[359] [1939] 2 KB 365 at 380, *per* Slesser LJ.   [360] [1938] 4 All ER 631.

wells supplying the locality with water. The first plaintiff was a rate-payer who suffered loss caused by the illness of his daughter, the second plaintiff, who had contracted typhoid from drinking the defendant's water.[361] They claimed damages for breach of a statutory duty owed by the defendants to 'provide...a supply of pure and wholesome water sufficient for the domestic use of all the inhabitants of the town... who...shall be entitled to demand a supply, and shall be willing to pay a water rate for the same'.[362] Stable J upheld the father's claim, observing that 'it is difficult to think of a duty which more concerns the individual, and each individual as such, than does the supply of domestic water',[363] but denied the daughter's claim on the ground that the duty was on its terms owed only to rate-paying occupiers.[364] However, these decisions on the tort of breach of statutory duty did not affect the result, as the judge also held that the local authority's duty was limited to the exercise of care and skill and on the facts, negligence was established.[365]

On the other hand, there appears to be an emerging legislative strategy in this sort of case which expressly deals with the question of the imposition of civil liability and distinguishes between breach of general duties regarding safety (which do not give rise to civil liability) and breach of particular safety regulations (which do).[366] A notable example may be found in Part II of the Consumer Protection Act 1987, for breach of its general safety requirement for consumer products is expressly stated *not* to give rise to civil liability,[367] it being thought that to introduce civil liability for breach of this general duty would duplicate needlessly the provisions concerning product liability enacted by Part I of the Act in implementation of the Product Liability Directive, particularly given that their ambit and contents are not the same.[368] A similar legislative approach was taken to breach of the duties underlying the general offence in the Health and Safety of Work Act of manufacture or supply of unsafe articles or substances for use at work which is also expressly stated not to give rise to civil liability.[369] By contrast, breach of *regulations* made under the very wide administrative powers provided for this purpose by both of these Acts is expressly stated to give rise to civil liability unless the regulation provides otherwise.[370] There have been a number of regulations made under these powers, particularly in the work context. Although there is no reported example of the application of these provisions in relation to

---

[361] In fact, the proceedings were a test case: there had been 43 deaths caused by the outbreak of typhoid.

[362] Waterworks Clauses Act 1847, s. 35. Their claims in contract failed in the absence of a contract: [1938] 4 All ER 631, 648.   [363] [1938] 4 All ER 631 at 653.

[364] [1938] 4 All ER 631, 649.

[365] For the present position here, below, pp. 276–9.

[366] Cf. the Food Safety Act 1990 which recognises various general offences relating to the supply of unsafe food (ss. 7, 8 and 14) and creates wide powers to make regulations concerning food safety (s. 16), but leaves open the question whether breach of the statutory duties thereby imposed gives rise to civil liability.

[367] Consumer Protection Act 1987, ss. 10(1) and 41(2).

[368] Department of Trade and Industry, *Implementation of EC Directive on Product Liability, An explanatory and consultative note* (985), 9 and see further, below, pp. 474–5.

[369] Health and Safety at Work Act 1974, ss. 6 and 47(1)(a), 47(2) (expressly enacting the result reached by the courts in relation to one of its predecessors: see *Biddle v Truvox Engineering Co. Ltd.* [1952] 1 KB 101). Cf. The Management of Health and Safety at Work Regulations 1999, SI 1999 No. 3242, r. 22.

[370] Consumer Protection Act 1987, ss. 11 and 45 (1); Health and Safety at Work Act 1974, ss. 15 and 47(2). See also P. Cane, 'Civil Liability under the Consumer Safety Act 1978,' 3 *JPL* 215 (1980) discussing the earlier law.

product safety, they are of considerable potential use given that breach of the particular and concrete provisions of a regulation may well be easier to prove than the more general 'defectiveness' of a product under Part I of the Consumer Protection Act or negligence at common law.[371] It is also interesting to note the relationship between the statutory duties provided by the 1987 Act and the criminal offences which support them. Here, it is provided that 'where safety regulations prohibit a person from supplying... any goods..., that person shall be guilty of an offence if he contravenes the prohibition',[372] but the conditions for the existence of the criminal offence are not identical to those required for civil liability; so, for example, the crime may possess a defence of 'due diligence',[373] whereas defences to civil liability follow the general rules of liability in tort.[374]

It is difficult to compare the tort of breach of statutory duty with French law. At a fundamental level, French law does not recognise a distinction approaching that between common law and statute, each of which provide valid sources of law, common law providing the general legal position, statute being seen as superior but exceptional.[375] For a French private lawyer, the general or underlying position is found in a code, that is, a general, integrated and potentially all-embracing scheme of legislation of which the Civil Code remains the archetype. In this mindset, civil liability may be imposed either under the provisions of the Civil Code or by any special legislation *directly*, without any interposition of a body of law created by the courts: *jurisprudence* in private law remains theoretically (and constitutionally) derivative, always needing to find a basis (somewhere, somehow) in legislation or in a legal principle drawn from it. This means that when French law asks whether breach of a legal duty or the commission of a criminal offence gives rise to civil liability, this question is seen in terms of whether these lapses constitute *une faute délictuelle* for the purposes of the general liabilities found in articles 1382 and 1383 of the Civil Code. French law has long held the view that *all* breaches of duty and *all* criminal offences constitute such a fault so as to attract liability where they cause harm, though the so-called 'unity of civil and criminal fault' of which this proposition formed part has itself been significantly qualified.[376] As a result, a French lawyer would see no room and no need for the recognition of any specific or distinct wrong of breach of a legislative duty. By contrast, an English lawyer does not feel comfortable with the idea that breaches of all statutory duties give rise to civil liability; for if statutory intervention is by its nature exceptional, how can one generalise in this way without explicit statutory support?[377] Instead, each statute creates its own miniature normative world distinct from the general common law, with which it interacts to the extent to which and the way in which Parliament is found to have intended. And an English lawyer would be even less

---

[371] For the question whether the imposition of civil liability for breach of product safety regulations is unlawful in EC law, see below, pp. 474–5. [372] Consumer Protection Act 1987, s. 12(1).
[373] Ibid. ss. 12, 39(1) and (5). [374] Ibid., s. 41(1).
[375] Cf. below, p. 469 on the effect of different roles of legislation in the two systems in the context of implementation of the 1985 Directive. [376] Above, pp. 45–6; below, pp. 393–4.
[377] Hence the suggestion of the Law Commission which wished to see such a generalised starting point to enact legislation creating a presumption of civil liability for breach of statutory duties: *The Interpretation of Statutes: Report of the Two Commissions*, Law Com. No. 21, Scot Law Com. No. 11 (HC 256, 1969).

happy with the assimilation of statutory 'criminal wrongs' and 'civil wrongs', partly because it is realised that many statutory criminal offences do not involve any genuine wrongdoing (*mens rea*), partly for lack of a recognition of an overarching category of 'civil wrongs' itself (possessing instead a law of *torts*), and partly from a sense that the purposes of civil and criminal liability are different.

However, I am also struck by the neglect by English courts of the potential of the distinct tort of breach of statutory duty, in particular as a mechanism for the imposition of liability for personal injuries or death without proof of negligence, even in contexts such as road accidents where insurance has been first common and then compulsory.[378] English judges have preferred to retain negligence as the basis of these liabilities and have therefore developed the tort of negligence as the basis of liability, leaving differences in its practical impact to variations in the standard of care and to the assessment of the factors relevant to breach of duty. Judicial willingness to impose liability for breach of statutory duties owed in the context of accidents at work remains strikingly exceptional.

7. Public Nuisance

'Public nuisance' is both a crime and a tort at common law and has classically been defined as 'an act not warranted by law or an omission to discharge a legal duty, which act or omission obstructs and causes inconvenience or damage to the public in the exercise of rights common to all His Majesty's subjects'.[379] Since the late seventeenth century, English courts recognised that a person who suffers 'special damage' as a result of a public nuisance can sue its perpetrator for damages in the civil courts,[380] damage being 'special' if it is over and above that which is suffered by the general public[381] this clearly being satisfied where a claimant suffers personal injury or property damage.[382] On the other hand, it has been said that the courts do not consider that personal injuries or death should be recovered in public nuisance, but should be left to the tort of negligence, in common with private nuisance.[383]

Public nuisance covers a wide and varied range of activities whose effect is to endanger the life, health, property, morals or comfort of the public, and its criminal manifestation has been applied to cases involving unsafe products.[384] The sort of situation to which it can been applied may be seen in the civil proceedings which arose out of the 'Camelford water' affair. There, the defendant was a local water authority whose piped

---

[378] *Phillips v Britannia Hygienic Laundry Co. Ltd.* [1923] 2 KB 832.

[379] Sir J.E. Stephens, *A Digest of the Criminal Law* (Sweet and Maxwell, London, 9th. edn., 1950, by L.F. Sturge), 179.

[380] J.R. Spencer, 'Public Nuisance—a Critical Examination' (1989) 48 *CLJ* 55, 73, e.g. *Iveson v Moore* (1699) 1 Lord Raym 486.

[381] G. Kodilinye, 'Public nuisance and particular damage in modern law' 6 *LS* (1986) 182. Recovery for pure economic loss may be recovered in public nuisance as long as it constitutes 'special damage': e.g. *Tate & Lyle v Greater London Council* [1983] 2 AC 509.   [382] Kodilinye, *op. cit.* n. 381, 182–3.

[383] *Hunter v Canary Wharf Ltd.* [1997] AC 655, 692 (Lord Goff of Chieveley).

[384] Below, pp. 414–6.

water had been contaminated by the accidental addition of a quantity of aluminium sulphate at a water treatment works.[385] The claimants were some 180 of the authority's customers who claimed compensation in respect of injuries sustained as a result of drinking the contaminated water, putting their claim, *inter alia*, on the basis of public nuisance,[386] the water authority having previously been convicted of the crime of public nuisance.[387] In these circumstances, the defendant conceded the issue of liability for compensatory damages, though it convinced the Court of Appeal that it should not be liable to exemplary and/or aggravated damages as regards liability in public nuisance or negligence.[388]

Whether there would be any advantage in relying on public nuisance in a case like this rather than, in particular, on the tort of negligence (or indeed the product liability provisions of the Consumer Protection Act 1987), depends on the difficult question of the fault element required for public nuisance. Generally it is said that where the defendant has created the public nuisance which caused the claimant's special damage, the burden is on him to show that it occurred without default on his part,[389] but it is far from clear whether this means proof of no negligence or instead that the apparent nuisance was in fact reasonable (and so not a nuisance at all) as, for example, in cases of obstruction of the highway.[390] Indeed, the continued utility of the tort has been doubted: as Howarth has observed, 'if public nuisance were no longer to be a recognized tort, few would mourn its passing'.[391]

---

[385] *AB and Others v South West Water Services Ltd.* [1993] QB 507.

[386] Claims were also made on the basis of the tort of negligence, breach of statutory duty, liability under Part I of the Consumer Protection Act 1987, liability under *Rylands v Fletcher* and for breach of contract.

[387] Below, p. 415.

[388] [1993] QB 507, 524. The CA's decision on punitive damages was overruled by *Kuddus v Chief Constable of Leicestershire Constabulary* [2002] 2 AC 122 on the ground that it is wrong to restrict them to torts in respect of which they had been granted before *Rookes v Barnard* [1964] AC 1129.

[389] *Dymond v Pearce* [1972] 1 QB 496; *Southport Corporation v Esso Petroleum Co. Ltd.* [1954] 2 QB 182, 197; Markesinis and Deakin's *Tort Law*, 490.

[390] As in *Dymond v Pearce* [1972] 1 QB 496.

[391] D. Howarth, *Textbook on Tort*, (Butterworths, London, 1995 edn.) 365.

10

The English Law of Sale of Goods

The English law governing the sale of goods is an important area for the imposition of liability for products, important both for their primary victim and for those who wish to claim compensation in respect of having themselves been held liable to another person. From a starting point of a general immunity enjoyed by sellers expressed by the catchy (if un-Roman) tag *caveat emptor*, English law has developed a number of different bases of liability based on the law of sale or appearing in its context. As in the French law under the *garantie légale* or for *défauts de non-conformité*, liability is strict in the sense that the buyer does not need to show 'fault' or negligence for liability to be established; as in French law, 'liability' extends to rights in a buyer to claim termination of the contract and restitution of the price as well as to damages. And as regards both systems, we can see the growing significance of consumer sales in the development of the rules and concepts used by the law.

However, under these broad similarities are found a number of important, if at times quite subtle, differences. Of these, in my view, four are most prominent.

The first differences are to be found in the conceptual frameworks used by the law to impose liability. In France the Civil Code reflected a legacy of the Roman law of sale, governing all property (whether movable or immovable) and making specific provision for the imposition of liability in sellers for latent defects even in the absence of any statement or promise by them.[1] In English law, there was no such starting point in a codification, no real sense of the distinctiveness of contracts of sale as distinct from other types of contract and a general absence of common law regulation of the consequences of contracts by the law itself.[2] One response to this regulatory vacuum has been for the parties themselves to make express provision to govern the issues which are dealt with by a Civil Code's provisions on special contracts: this approach has in many respects remained the general position as regards sales of land.[3] The other response visible from the nineteenth century, though, was for the courts to develop implied terms to govern the consequences of contract, a technique formally justified by reference to the parties' implicit intention but gradually evolving into a recognisably legal regulation. This was the main path chosen by the courts for the sale of goods and it was given a statutory imprimatur by the Sale of Goods Act 1893. As I shall explain, differences in the historical sources of the English and French laws governing sale of goods have had a continuing influence on their substantive content, not least in

---

[1] Above, pp. 69–70.
[2] B. Nicholas, 'Rules and Terms—Civil Law and Common Law' (1974) 48 Tul LR 947.
[3] Below, p. 228.

the absence of the sort of bifurcation of liability seen in French law between liability under the *garantie légale* and for contractual non-conformity under the *droit commun contractuel*.

A second prominent difference between the English and French laws is found in the range of persons who may benefit from the liabilities imposed on sellers of goods. While in French law a seller may be liable not merely to his own buyer but to any sub-buyer in the chain of distribution by *action directe*, English law has restricted the benefit of claiming under the implied terms owed by sellers in respect of the quality and fitness for purpose of the goods to their immediate buyer.[4]

Thirdly, while the majority of claims brought for damages for breach of the implied terms imposed on sellers of goods under the Sale of Goods Act have been for what an English lawyer would call 'pure economic loss', there is no doubt and no discomfort with including claims for damage to property and personal injury or death. In striking contrast with more recent French developments which have tried to divorce issues of contractual non-conformity and of safety,[5] English law has long accepted that a lack of safety in goods may constitute a failure in their quality or fitness for purpose and this was made irrefutable by legislation in 1994.[6]

Fourthly, while in common with French law, English law provides for remedies of rescission and restitution as well as for damages for failures of quality or fitness for purpose, both the rules for the availability of these remedies and their 'hierarchy' are significantly different, reflecting more general differences in understanding of the notion of contractual obligation and in the proper balance of interests between contractual 'creditors' and 'debtors'.

Apart from these particular differences, the English law of sale reveals a number of English law's more general features as compared to the French: in its techniques, in its preferred forms of legal reasoning and in the impact of its institutional arrangements. In this respect, some of the usual remarks often made about English law hold good: noticeably, the prominence of remedies and the relative complexity of its regulation, whether this is legislative or by case law. On the other hand, as we shall see, from a starting point which was first decidedly non-interventionist and then became commercially oriented, the law has moved increasingly towards a consumerist model of contract.

In the following discussion, I shall attempt to keep to a similar division of issues as I used in setting out the French law, though this has to be modified in some respects.

1. The Disunity of the English Law of Sale

French law inherited from Roman law a unified approach to its law of sale, including movable property (whether tangible or intangible) and immovable property within one legal framework both as to the creation and the effects of the contract.[7] But when

---

[4] Below, p. 264.   [5] Above, p. 72.
[6] Sale of Goods Act 1979 (the '1979 Act'), s. 14(2B)(d) as inserted by the Sale and Supply of Goods Act 1994 ('the 1994 Act'), s. 1.   [7] Above, p. 70.

English courts started considering whether and how to use the technique of the implication of terms to regulate the consequences of contracts of sale, they took very different approaches to contracts for the sale of land and of goods. For, while at the beginning of the nineteenth century, implied terms as to the quality or fitness for purpose of goods and land were both denied,[8] by the mid-century this was changing for goods but not for land.[9] The enactment of the Sale of Goods Act 1893 set the seal on this distinctiveness of the law of sale of goods as opposed to sale of interests in land.

In the English law, 'goods' are defined as including 'all personal chattels other than things in action and money'.[10] This includes 'all things which are at once tangible, movable and visible, and of which possession can be taken', but excludes choses in action such as shares, negotiable instruments and all forms of intellectual property, such as copyrights or trade marks,[11] which are transferred by assignment, rather than sale. On the other hand, electricity and other forms of energy are thought capable of being bought and sold,[12] as are water, oil and gases.[13] Moreover, in contrast to the French position which holds that body parts are not capable of being the object of a contract,[14] English law appears to accept that they may be the subject of ownership once worked on so as to be distinguished from a mere corpse awaiting burial.[15] And while it has been said that a disk containing software does constitute 'goods' for the purposes of the Sale of Goods Act 1979, though the program itself does not,[16] this has been criticised on the basis that the medium of supply of the programme (by disk or by electronic transfer) should make no difference in its regulation.[17] As will be seen, however, the courts often imply terms at common law as to quality and fitness for purpose in contracts which do not count as 'sale of goods' but which involve the transfer of property.[18]

2. The Legal Bases of a Seller's Liability

English law shares with French law a complexity in its regulation of liability in sellers to their buyers in respect of failures of quality or safety of the property sold, whether this liability gives rise to a right to terminate the contract, damages or both. In French law, the complexity may be seen both at the pre-contractual stage and the stage of

---

[8]   *Parkinson v Lee* (1802) 2 East 314.

[9]   *Hart v Windsor* (1843) 12 M & W 68 (lease); *Bottomley v Bannister* [1932] 1 KB 458, 468; *Lynch v Thorne* [1956] 1 All ER 744; *Southwark LBC v Tanner* [2001] 1 AC 7, 17.

[10]   1979 Act, s. 61(1) and see *Benjamin* § 1-078 *et seq.*   [11]   *Benjamin* § 1-080.

[12]   Ibid., § 1-085 but see below, pp. 278–9.   [13]   *Benjamin* § 1-087.   [14]   Above, p. 70.

[15]   *Benjamin* § 1-089; *Dobson v North Tyneside Health Authority* [1996] 4 All ER 474. American decisions are divided as to whether the supply of blood by transfusion constitutes the supply of services or sale of goods: *Belle Bonfils Memorial Blood Bank v Hansen* 579 P 2d 1158 (1978); *Perlmutter v Beth David Hospital* 123 NE (2d) 792 (1955).

[16]   *St. Albans City & District Council v International Computers Ltd.* [1996] 4 All ER 481, 493 *per* Sir Iain Glidewell. A contract for the transfer of software would contain a similar implied term at common law: ibid., 494.

[17]   *Benjamin* § 1-086 citing M. Chissick and A. Kelman, *Electronic Commerce Law and Practice* (Sweet and Maxwell, London, 2nd. edn., 2001), 62–4.   [18]   Below, pp. 271–3.

non-performance of the contract. At the pre-contractual stage, the Code's unpromising provisions on *dol* and *erreur* applicable to all types of contracts were developed very considerably and supplemented by *obligations d'information* which are typically imposed on business sellers to their non-business buyers.[19] While *erreur* gives rise only to a right to rescind the contract,[20] and the failure to perform a pre-contractual obligation to inform gives rise only to a claim for damages,[21] *dol* may give rise to either or both, but is restricted to dishonest conduct by the other party.[22] These liabilities all have in common, though, that their foundation is the existence of some inbalance of information between the parties to the contract, whether or not this is caused by one party's conduct, as in the case of *dol*. This being so, cases of failures in quality, safety or fitness for purpose of property are not at the forefront of the grounds of liability, but are sometimes covered by them.

While English law also uses its general contract law to deal with informational imbalances in the context of the law of sale, its scope is rather different.[23] So, while English law has a wide law of misrepresentation inducing contract which can include both fraudulent and innocent false statements of fact and which can lead to rescission and/or damages, in general (and in the specific context of sale) it does not impose pre-contractual duties of disclosure or information, nor does it allow the contract to be set aside on the ground of mistake save in the most extreme cases (and not ones which arise in respect of the failure of property to conform to standards of quality, fitness for purpose or safety).

It is rather at the level of the performance of the contract where the English law of sale of goods has chosen to deal with failures of quality, safety and fitness for purpose. Here, the courts carved out exceptions to *caveat emptor* by implying terms which were in 1893 crystallised by Parliament in the provisions of sections 13 and 14 of the Sale of Goods Act. While the wording of these provisions was considerably altered in the last quarter of the twentieth century, their division into three terms has remained constant: terms as to conformity with the goods' description, their 'merchantable' or, later, 'satisfactory' quality and their reasonable fitness for their purpose.[24] Moreover, while the conditions for the implication of these terms or their breach may differ, the *consequences* of their breach do not.[25] So, breach of any of these terms gives rise to a right in the buyer to reject the goods and rescind the contract, a right which may be lost by 'acceptance' of the goods in the same ways; and any claim for damages by a buyer for breach of these terms is subject to the same regime of liability, notably, as regards their measure and limitation of actions.[26] This means that the differences between the statutory implied terms have not mattered in the way in which in French law the differences between liability under the *garantie légale* (which has its distinct system of remedies and (until 2005) its notorious *bref délai*) and under the general law for non-performance of a contractual obligation attached to sale, whether an *obligation de conformité*, *obligation d'information* or *obligation de sécurité*.[27] As a result, the English courts have not been tempted to manipulate the basis of contractual liability

---

[19] Above, pp. 64–9.

[20] Rescission must be demanded of a court and is not a unilateral right in the party in error: art. 1117 C. civ. and above, p. 64.

[21] Above, p. 66.   [22] Above, p. 65.   [23] Below, pp. 230–2.

[24] Below, pp. 234–42. Sale of Goods Act 1979, s. 13; s. 14(2) and 14(3) respectively.

[25] Below, p. 251.   [26] Below, pp. 251–7.   [27] Above, pp. 69–72.

in sale to gain or to avoid a particular incidental rule of the sort which has plagued the French law due to the *bref délai* of the *garantie légale*. There are, however, differences in English law between liability for breach of the statutory *implied terms* and for breach of any *express* terms as to the quality or fitness for purpose of goods sold, notably as to the circumstances in which the right to rescind the contract will arise and be lost.[28]

(a) Misrepresentation, non-disclosure and mistake

The English law governing liability for informational imbalance arising in the context of sale of goods for which the seller may be liable is strikingly different from the French from a number of points of view.[29] These differences are not particular to the context of sale, but in both systems this type of contract has been at the forefront of lawyers' minds in determining the limits of the law.

Setting out the bare legal position in English law governing pre-contractual informational imbalance is now relatively straightforward.[30] Where a seller makes a positive misrepresentation of fact which induces the buyer to enter the contract, in principle the buyer may rescind the contract (with consequential restitution of the price if paid) whatever the nature of the misrepresentation (whether fraudulent, negligent or purely innocent),[31] and/or he may claim damages unless the seller establishes that he honestly believed and had reasonable grounds for believing the truth of his own statements.[32] However, where the seller makes no representation of fact, in general the buyer will have no remedy either on the ground that he was seriously mistaken as to the nature or condition of the goods nor on the ground that the seller knew of their defect or inappropriateness for the use to which he intended to put them and failed to inform him: the law of mistake as to the substance is extremely narrow in English law and a duty of disclosure is imposed only in exceptional situations which have little impact on sellers' liability.[33]

A first difference between this English position and the French law relates to the historical roots of the law. For French law inherited from the Roman tradition not merely vitiation of contracts on the ground of *dol*, but also an explicit doctrine of *error in substantia*, taken from the law of sale but generalised to all contracts;[34] it also included a tradition that contracts must be made as well as performed in good faith, even if the draftsmen of the Civil Code felt it necessary to include only the latter explicitly within its terms,[35] and good faith has been seen as the foundation of

[28] Below, p. 253.

[29] J. Cartwright, 'Defects in Consent and Security of Contract: French and English law Compared' in P. Birks and A. Pretto, *Themes in Comparative Law in Honour of Bernard Rudden* (OUP, 2002), 153.

[30] See generally Treitel, *The Law of Contract*, Chaps. 8 and 9; *Chitty on Contracts*, Vol. I, Chaps. 5 and 6.

[31] *Redgrave v Hurd* (1881) 20 Ch D 1.

[32] Misrepresentation Act 1967, s. 2(1). He may also be able to recover damages in the tort of negligence (*Hedley Byrne & Co. Ltd. v Heller & Partners Ltd.* [1964] AC 465; *Esso Petroleum Co. Ltd. v Mardon* [1976] QB 801) or the tort of deceit (*Derry v Peek* (1889) 14 App Cas 337, 374–5).

[33] *Smith v Hughes* (1871) LR 6 QB 597; *Bell v Lever Bros Ltd.* [1932] AC 161; *Great Peace Shipping Ltd. v Tsavliris Salvage (International) Ltd.* [2002] EWCA Civ 1407; [2003] QB 679 rejecting the existence of a wider doctrine of mistake in equity as accepted in *Solle v Butcher* [1950] 1 KB 671. And see B. Nicholas, 'The Pre-contractual Obligation to Disclose Information, 2. English Report' in D. Harris and D. Tallon (eds.), *Contract Law Today* (OUP, 1989) 166.   [34] Above, p. 64.

[35] Art. 1134 al. 3 C. civ.

obligations d'information.[36] While the law of fraud has deep roots in the common law, the idea that a contract is vitiated on the ground of mistake can be seen clearly only in the nineteenth century as the result of a late wave of continental influence on the development of the English law of contract.[37] But while English judges might have been willing to quote passages on mistake in contracts from Pothier's *Traité des obligations* or from Justinian's *Digest*,[38] in the context of mistake as to the subject matter of the contract they gave a distinctly narrow (and classical) interpretation to them in the interest of the need for certainty in commercial transactions.[39] Moreover, Lord Mansfield's declaration that 'good faith forbids either party by concealing what he privately knows, to draw the other into a bargain, from his ignorance of that fact, and his believing the contrary' which he said was 'applicable to all contracts'[40] was restricted to its context of contracts of insurance.[41] So, while distinctly civilian elements were available to nineteenth-century English writers and courts, they were not developed in the directions in which they were taken by French lawyers.

A further contrast between the general approaches of English and French law is found in their different conceptions of contract and different priorities of policy. So, French law has developed a greater concern with the protection of the quality of consent of the parties to a contract, on occasion *despite* the terms of the Civil Code and the tradition of Roman law, reflecting the long domination of a 'subjective' theory of contract; whereas English law has taken an 'objective' view of agreement and has been concerned more with preserving the reasonable reliance of a party on the continuation of a contract and with the need to promote certainty of transactions rather than with the protection of the quality of an individual's consent.[42] Perhaps the most striking manifestation of the modern French approach is in *obligations d'information*, a doctrine with no explicit basis in the Civil Code but which has been used to explain in what circumstances a failure to speak will attract vitiation for *dol* and to help impose liability in damages for delictual *faute*.[43]

However, in the specific context of seller's liability to a buyer for failures in quality, safety or fitness for purpose the main difference between the English and the French law is one of technique. In English law, where a seller has made a statement as to one of these aspects of the goods, it will readily impose liability on the ground of misrepresentation; but where he has said nothing, neither the law of mistake nor the law of non-disclosure applies. By contrast, in French law, a buyer may well be able to seek rescission of the contract on the ground of the seller's knowing failure to speak and possibly on the basis of his own mistake as to the goods' essential quality.[44] And in

---

[36] Above, p. 65.   [37] Ibbetson, *Historical Introduction*, 227–9.

[38] *Kennedy v The Panama, New Zealand and Australian Royal Mail Co. Ltd.* (1867) LR 2 QB 580, 587–8, Blackburn J citing D 18.1.9-11; approved in *Bell v Lever Bros Ltd.* [1932] AC 161, 207, 219–20 and 233–4.

[39] Cf. R. David, 'La doctrine de l'erreur dans Pothier et son interprétation dans la Common law d'Angleterre', *Etudes de droit civil à la mémoire de Henri Capitant* (Dalloz, Paris, 1939) 145.

[40] *Carter v Boehm* (1766) 3 Burr 1905, 1910.

[41] *Ormrod v Huth* (1845) 14 M & W 652, 655 (Tindal CJ rejected Lord Mansfield's dictum as to good faith in the context of misrepresentation of quality in sale of goods).   [42] Cartwright, *op. cit.* n. 29.

[43] Above, pp. 64–9.   [44] Above, p. 64.

these circumstances French courts have imposed liability in damages for loss caused by inadequate warnings, instructions or even advice as to a suitable alternative for non-performance of a seller's *obligation d'information*, where this non-performance consists of saying nothing at all or saying something but getting it wrong.[45] Under the law of *obligations d'information*, French law deals with a number of cases which are governed in English law by misrepresentation as well as those left without remedy by its general refusal to impose duties of disclosure.

However, even more important a contrast of technique between the English and the French laws is to be found in the former's reliance on its law of implied term rather than on pre-contractual liability. For if *caveat emptor* is a false maxim for modern English law, its falseness stems from the breadth of the statutory implied terms as to quality and fitness for purpose, rather than from its law of misrepresentation, non-disclosure or mistake. Indeed, while an English claimant may choose to rely alternatively on the law of misrepresentation and on breach of one or more of these implied terms where quality or fitness for purpose are in issue, the former is usually of significance only where one of its incidents differs from the law of implied term.

(b) Contract terms as to the quality of goods

Two years before the promulgation of the French Civil Code, the Court of King's Bench in *Parkinson v Lee* held that in the absence of fraud or an express warranty, there is no liability in a seller of goods for their defects, refusing to imply a warranty that the goods would be 'merchantable' merely on the ground that their price was one for merchantable goods.[46] Nevertheless, the courts later distinguished from this position cases where the buyer could not exercise his own judgment and so relied on his seller's judgment as to the quality or fitness for purpose of the goods, and implied terms to this effect.[47]

On the 'codification' of the law of sale of goods in 1893, the position taken by the common law on the definition and consequences of contracts of sale of goods was reduced to a series of fairly simple and formally coherent statutory propositions.[48] While it involved some substantive changes, the 1893 Act was not intended to introduce radical innovation and did not prevent the application of rules of the common law, as long as they were not inconsistent with the Act's provisions.[49] These general features were reflected in the terms implied as to the quality or fitness for purpose of the goods, where the Act confirmed earlier common law developments and introduced the three-fold structure of implied terms which remains to this day: in section 13 that goods sold by their description should correspond to their description and in section 14 that, while generally there is no implied term as to the fitness or quality of the goods,[50] in certain circumstances terms are to be implied that the goods were of merchantable quality[51] and reasonably fit for their purpose.[52] This has had considerable advantages

---

[45] Above, pp. 65–8.   [46] (1802) 2 East 314, 321–2.

[47] In *Jones v Just* (1867–1868) LR 3 QB 197, 202–04 Mellor J summarised nicely the position at the time.   [48] Sale of Goods Act 1893.   [49] Sale of Goods Act 1893, s. 61(2).

[50] Ibid., s. 14(1).   [51] Ibid., s. 14(2).

[52] Ibid., s. 14(3). To this can be added the special provisions for sale by sample found in s. 15.

in terms of clarity and simplicity, but the wording has had to be revised on several occasions, not counting implementation of the Consumer Guarantees Directive.[53] While the substantive elements used by Parliament in setting these texts and by the courts in their interpretation have remained remarkably constant, the balance between them has shifted significantly.

Before looking, though, at the statutory implied terms, I shall look briefly at English law's approach to express terms relating to the quality of the goods.

(i) Express warranties

An express term of a contract of sale concerning the description, quality or fitness for purpose of the goods takes effect according to its terms.[54] So, if the term is broken, liability in damages will arise, but the question whether breach gives rise to a right to reject the goods and rescind the contract depends first on the interpretation of the parties' intention on the issue (for example, they may have used technically the language of 'condition'[55]), but if no clear intention is discernible the courts instead ask whether breach substantially deprives the buyer of the benefit of the contract.[56] Where such a statement concerning the goods is made by a seller but does not clearly form part of the contract (for example, by forming part of a signed written document), the courts decide whether the parties intended it to have contractual effect under the general law of warranty,[57] though as ever an objective view is taken of their intention for this purpose.[58] While the ambit of liability in damages for misrepresentation was narrow, the courts were ready to find such an intention so as to incorporate a pre-contractual statement into the contract or to find a 'collateral warranty', especially where the seller is in business and the buyer has no special skill,[59] but since the creation of a statutory right to damages for misrepresentation in 1967 there has been far less need to do so.[60]

Express stipulations as to the quality or fitness for purpose of goods may be useful in some commercial contexts despite the underlying standards of the statutory implied terms[61] and are common in some consumer contexts, for example, as regards electrical goods, where retailers offer 'extended warranties' which are sometimes free and sometimes require an extra charge.[62] Extended warranties may take the form of an undertaking by the retailer itself of some liability beyond that imposed by the statutory implied terms

---

[53] The Supply of Goods (Implied Terms) Act 1973, ss. 2 & 3; the Sale of Goods Act 1979, s. 14; 1994 Act, s. 1. For implementation of the EC directive, below, pp. 585–8.

[54] Eg. *VAI Industries (UK) Ltd. v Bostock & Bramley* [2003] EWCA Civ 1069; [2003] BLR 359 (a continuing express warranty of goods as 'free from defect').

[55] The question remains one of construction: 1979 Act, s. 11(3); *L Schuler AG v Wickman Machine Tool Sales Ltd.* [1974] AC 235; *Rice v Great Yarmouth BC* [2003] 3 LGLR 4 (both contracts for the provision of services over an extended period).

[56] *Hongkong Fir Shipping Co. Ltd. v Kawasaki Kisen Kaisha Ltd.* [1962] 2 QB 26; *Bunge Corpn. v Tradax Export SA* [1981] 1 WLR 711; *Cehave NV v Bremer Handelsgesellschaft mbH* [1976] QB 44 and see *Chitty on Contracts*, Chap. 24.   [57] *Heilbut Symons & Co. v Buckleton* [1913] AC 30.

[58] *Benjamin* § 10-017.

[59] *Oscar Chess Ltd. v Williams* [1957] 1 WLR 370; *Dick Bentley Productions Ltd. v Harold Smith (Motors) Ltd.* [1965] 1 WLR 623.   [60] Misrepresentation Act 1967, s. 2.

[61] *VAI Industries (UK) Ltd. v Bostock & Bramley* [2003] EWCA Civ 1069.

[62] Office of Fair Trading, *Extended Warranties on Domestic Electrical Goods* (July 2002), published on the internet at <http://www.oft.gov.uk/>.

(often under a 'service agreement') or an undertaking by a third party, typically an insurer, to the same or similar effect. Typically, extended warranties provide consumers with protection by way of replacement or repair of goods within a specified period, usually after any manufacturer's guarantee has expired.[63] In law, these warranties take effect on their terms, except that they may not restrict a seller's liability under the statutory implied terms.[64] The practice of extended warranties in the context of electrical goods has been the subject of investigation both from the point of view of competition and the fairness of retailer practices towards consumers, not least because their cost to the consumer appears to bear little relationship to the risks encountered.[65]

(ii) 'Sale by description'

Section 13(1) of the 1979 Act provides that 'where there is a contract for the sale of goods by description, there is an implied term that the goods will correspond with the description', this term being classed as a 'condition'. This provision is the least altered since 1893 and appears to be the most straightforward of the three implied terms. It could be thought to give a contractual basis for liability for statements describing goods sold, unrestricted to sales in the course of a business,[66] but it has been given a narrow interpretation by the courts, so that it does *not* give contractual force to any description emanating from a seller concerning the goods.[67]

In practice, the most usual and straightforward cases of the application of this implied term are where *unascertained* goods are described before sale, such as a certain quantity of iron or corn of a particular grade and type, where the seller will be held to have sold the goods by this description;[68] it will also apply to *ascertained* goods bought unseen, as here the buyer can be said to be relying on the goods' description alone.[69] However, a sale of ascertained goods which have been seen by the buyer may or may not be held to be by description: 'the description must have a sufficient influence in the sale to become an essential term of the contract and the correlative of influence is reliance'.[70] The buyer's reliance must have been 'within the reasonable contemplation of the parties',[71] which is not the case where a seller makes clear that he has no expertise in the matter of the statement, whereas the buyer does.[72]

As I shall explain, this restrictive interpretation of section 13 is balanced by the significance of the 'description' of the goods (here in a wide sense) to their 'satisfactory quality' or their reasonable fitness for their purpose within the meaning of section 14.[73] This means that a court has sometimes held the goods' description to have been satisfied for the purposes of section 13, leaving 'more delicate questions' of the satisfactory nature of the goods as so described to the more sophisticated evaluations put in

---

[63] On manufacturers' guarantees, see below, pp. 264–5.

[64] The statement in the text assumes that the buyer 'deals as consumer' for the purposes of the Unfair Contract Terms Act 1977 ('the 1977 Act'), s. 6 and see *Benjamin*, § 14-043.

[65] Office of Fair Trading, *Extended Warranties on Domestic Electrical Goods*, 5.

[66] Unlike the terms implied by the 1979 Act, s. 14, below, pp. 236–7, 240.   [67] *Benjamin*, § 11-012.

[68] *Berger & Co. Inc. v Gill & Duffus SA* [1984] AC 382 and see *Benjamin* §§ 11-008, 11-012.

[69] *Varley v Whipp* [1900] 1 QB 513, 516.

[70] *Harlingdon and Leinster Enterprises Ltd. v Christopher Hull Fine Art Ltd.* [1991] QB 564, 574, *per* Nourse LJ.   [71] Ibid. Slade LJ agreed.

[72] Ibid. at 571, 574.   [73] Below, pp. 237, 240.

place by section 14.[74] For example, in one case in 1936,[75] the plaintiff was an aviator who had bought some goggles fitted with 'safety-glass', but whose lens broke in a crash and injured his eye. The Court of Appeal rejected his claim for damages under section 13, holding that use of the expression 'safety-glass' could not amount to an absolute guarantee that the glass would not splinter,[76] a decision clearly influenced by its view that the goggles were of 'merchantable quality' given that a buyer has a 'right to expect, not a perfect article, but an article which would be saleable in the market'.[77]

(iii) From 'merchantable quality' to 'satisfactory quality'

The evolution of the implied term as to the quality of the goods marks the shift in orientation of the law towards a model of consumer rather than commercial sales of goods and also illustrates nicely the modern tendency of English law to structure the discretion given to judges in the application of broad evaluative concepts by setting out factors for them to take into account and the 'aspects' of the facts for which they should look.

From 1893 to 1994, the statutory standard required of *some* sellers was one of 'merchantable quality', this notion having been used previously by the common law. Section 14(2) as originally enacted provided that :

Where goods are bought by description from a seller of goods who deals in goods of that description (whether he be the manufacturer or not), there is an implied condition that the goods shall be of merchantable quality; provided that if the buyer has examined the goods, there shall be no implied condition as regards defects which such examination ought to have revealed.

As enacted, therefore, the ambit of the term was restricted as to goods ('bought by description') and as to the sellers ('who deals in goods of that description') and its standard of merchantable quality focused firmly on the commercial utility of the goods, especially in terms of their potential for resale.[78] At the time, the decision as to merchantable quality lay in principle within the province of the jury, which could sometimes be a 'special jury' of merchants,[79] and where it was they would be in a good position to assess the 'merchantable quality' of the goods without need for any judicial explanation.[80] Even after the disappearance of juries from the civil process by the 1960s,[81] some judges continued to think it impossible to frame a definition of 'merchantable quality' 'except in the vaguest terms',[82] though others had a go, it becoming accepted that account should be taken of the goods' description[83] and (where appropriate) their price.[84]

---

[74] *Ashington Piggeries Ltd v Christopher Hill Ltd.* [1972] AC 441, 489, *per* Lord Wilberforce (claim that mink food made up to the buyer's formula did not correspond to its description because it contained an impurity rejected). [75] *Grenfell v E.B. Meyrowitz Ltd.* [1936] 2 All ER 1313.

[76] Ibid. at 1317, *per* Slesser LJ.

[77] Ibid., quoting Willes J, in *Wieler v Schilizzi* (1856) 17 CB 619, 674.

[78] 'Merchantable can only mean commercially saleable': *Henry Kendall & Sons v William Lillico & Sons Ltd.* [1969] 2 AC 31, 75, *per* Lord Reid.

[79] J. Oldham, 'Special Juries in England: Nineteenth Century Usage and Reform' (1987) *J Leg Hist* 148.

[80] Cf. *Tronson v Dent* (1853) 8 Moore 419. [81] Above, p. 191.

[82] *B. S. Brown & Son Ltd. v Craiks Ltd.* [1970] 1 WLR 752, 754, *per* Lord Reid.

[83] *Henry Kendall & Sons v William Lillico & Sons Ltd.* [1968] AC 31, 75.

[84] *B. S. Brown & Son Ltd. v Craiks Ltd.*, *cit.*, 754–5. On this law, see Law Commission Report *Sale and Supply of Goods*, Law Com. No. 160 (1987) ('Law Com. No. 160') 7 and Bridge, *Sale of Goods*, 293 *et seq.*

Despite its terminology, the courts felt able to use the implied term of 'merchantable quality' outside the commercial context, so as, for example, to impose liability on a seller to a consumer in respect of a second-hand car described as in good condition but having been written-off by its insurer.[85] However, the focus of this term on the goods' utility could require a buyer to tolerate considerable defectiveness. For example, in *Townsley v Langton* a horse bought for showjumping and represented as 'sound' but which suffered from a lung infestation (which was not reasonably discoverable by a buyer on examination) was held to have been of 'merchantable quality' as it could still be ridden in competitions, even though it was resold 'without warranty' at less than half its cost.[86]

Although subject to some earlier amendment, section 14(2) was completely recast in 1994 as a result of the recommendations of the Law Commission.[87] On the eve of implementation of the Consumer Guarantees Directive in 2002, section 14(2) read:

> (2) Where the seller sells goods in the course of a business, there is an implied term that the goods supplied under the contract are of satisfactory quality.

> (2A) For the purposes of this Act, goods are of satisfactory quality if they meet the standard that a reasonable person would regard as satisfactory, taking account of any description of the goods, the price (if relevant) and all the other relevant circumstances.

> (2B) For the purposes of this Act, the quality of goods includes their state and condition and the following (among others) are in appropriate cases aspects of the quality of goods—
> > (a) fitness for all the purposes for which goods of the kind in question are commonly supplied,
> > (b) appearance and finish,
> > (c) freedom from minor defects,
> > (d) safety, and
> > (e) durability.

> (2C) The term implied by subsection (2) above does not extend to any matter making the quality of goods unsatisfactory—
> > (a) which is specifically drawn to the buyer's attention before the contract is made,
> > (b) where the buyer examines the goods before the contract is made, which that examination ought to reveal, or
> > (c) in the case of a contract for sale by sample, which would have been apparent on a reasonable examination of the sample.

What changes were thereby introduced?

First, the category of seller was extended to all those selling goods 'in the course of a business', which has been interpreted 'at their wide face value' so as to include all sales by a business as part of its business without any restriction to sales which form any regular part of the business: only 'purely private sales of goods' were intended to be

---

[85] *Shine v General Guarantee Co. Ltd.* [1988] 1 All ER 911. Similarly, *Lee v York Coach and Marine* [1977] RTR 35.

[86] Milmo J, 5 July 1982 (Lexis). The buyer recovered damages on the ground of misrepresentation under the Misrepresentation Act 1967, s. 2(1).   [87] Law Com. No. 160.

excluded.[88] The Act provides that 'business' includes 'a profession and the activities of any government department or local or public authority' and this suggests that the activity need not be with the view to profit.[89]

Secondly, a standard of 'satisfactory quality' was substituted for 'merchantable quality', principally to avoid a test appropriate only for some types of commercial transaction.[90] While it retains a unique standard for all types of contracts of sale of goods, in particular whether commercial or consumer,[91] 'satisfactory quality' is not a simple broad test but possesses three levels of elaboration. At a first level, it states that 'goods are of satisfactory quality if they meet the standard that a reasonable person would regard as satisfactory'. While this formulation seems circular,[92] its reference to the 'reasonable person' makes clear that it is in principle an objective test though qualified as regards the *position* in which the buyer finds himself,[93] an objectivity which is carried through to the test's treatment of the goods' fitness for their purpose:[94] the courts should not inquire whether or not the goods were seen as satisfactory by or for the particular buyer. 'Satisfactory' suggests that the goods have to be 'good enough', being preferred to a test of 'acceptable quality' to avoid the argument that goods were 'acceptable' even though they were objectively unsatisfactory[95] and to a test referring to the 'reasonable expectations of the buyer' for fear of encouraging a decline in standards of quality, consumer expectations being quite low in particular contexts.[96]

At a second level, in assessing the satisfactory quality of the goods a court is required to take into account 'any description of the goods, the price (if relevant) and all the other relevant circumstances'. These factors had been used by the courts in assessing the 'merchantable quality' of goods and were introduced into section 14 in 1973,[97] being 'essential in setting the required standard of quality'.[98] Here, the better view is that the 'description' of the goods should be interpreted to refer to any descriptive statements and not merely to those recognised under the law of sale by description.[99] As to their price, Lord Reid earlier explained (in relation to the same wording under the former test of 'merchantable quality') that where 'the market price for the better quality is substantially higher than that for the lower quality... [t]hen it could not be right that, if the contract price is appropriate for the better quality, the seller should be entitled to tender the lower quality and say that, because the lower quality is commercially saleable under the contract description, he has fulfilled his contract'.[100] More simply, what is 'satisfactory quality' must depend on the place in the market at which the goods are aimed as reflected in their price: 'the buyer [is] entitled to value for money'.[101] On the other hand, a lower price for a second-hand vehicle may not necessarily justify a lowering of the standard as it may simply reflect the buyer's good bargain.[102] As to

---

[88] *Stevenson v Rogers* [1999] QB 1028, 1039, *per* Potter LJ. The change had been made by the Supply of Goods (Implied Terms) Act 1973, s. 4. [89] *Benjamin* § 11-046.

[90] Law Com. No. 160 § 2.10, 8. [91] Cf. below, p. 238. [92] *Benjamin*, § 11-049.

[93] *Chitty on Contracts*, para. 43-086. [94] Below, p. 238.

[95] HC Deb. (2 Feb. 1994) Vol. 237 Col. 633; Law Com. No. 160 §§ 3.19–3.22.

[96] Law Com. No. 160, § 3.26. [97] Supply of Goods (Implied Terms) Act 1973, s. 7(2).

[98] Law Com. No. 160 § 3.27 and see above, pp. 234–5. [99] *Benjamin* § 11-040.

[100] *B. S. Brown & Son Ltd. v Craiks Ltd.* [1970] 1 WLR 752, 754.

[101] *Rogers v Parish Ltd.* [1987] QB 933, 944, *per* Mustill LJ.

[102] *Keeley v Guy McDonald Ltd.* (1984) New LJ 522.

relevant 'other circumstances', while these will depend on the particular case, they have been held *not* to include the 'buyer's personal agenda', which is relevant instead to liability under section 14(3).[103] On the other hand, it has been held that the relative ease of repair of any defect in the goods should *not* prevent their quality being held inadequate if the defect is sufficiently serious.[104] And the existence of an additional manufacturer's warranty is not a reason to require a buyer to put up with defects which would otherwise render the goods unsatisfactory: in taking out such a warranty, a buyer is adding to rather than subtracting from his existing rights.[105] It has also been said that compliance with a relevant public standard is an important but not a conclusive factor in determining the standard of quality.[106]

At a third level of elaboration, the Act also notes that the quality of the goods includes their 'state and condition',[107] and then sets out five 'aspects' of their quality to which the courts should have regard in appropriate cases: the fitness of the goods for all the purposes for which goods of the kind in question are commonly supplied; their appearance and finish; their freedom from minor defects; their safety and their durability.[108] This further elaboration addressed difficulties experienced by the courts under the earlier law by clarifying that these features of goods *can* contribute to a judgment of their 'unsatisfactory quality', depending on the circumstances. So, for example, while 'minor defects' (which may or may not affect the goods' appearance) may well render unsatisfactory a new car sold to a consumer, they are not likely to do so where the car is second-hand and are less likely to do so where the buyer is not a consumer.[109] This also marks the first occasion when the notion of 'defect' is used by the statute as an element in imposing liability on a seller.[110]

Changes were also made to the significance of the goods' fitness for purpose, the new formulation addressing the problem of goods reasonably fit for one or more purposes for which the goods were commonly supplied, even though this did not happen to be the buyer's actual (and private) purpose.[111] But more importantly the goods' fitness for common purposes is expressed to be merely one aspect among many of the goods' quality, rather than (as under the 1979 enactment) a necessary feature.[112] While the inclusion of the goods' fitness for purpose as relevant to their satisfactory quality makes clear the continuing potential for overlap between this implied term and the term implied in section 14(3), it has been held that it is the function of section 14(2) to provide a 'general standard of quality' not 'to ensure that goods are fit for a particular purpose made known to the seller which is the function of section 14(3)'.[113]

---

[103] *Jewson Ltd. v Boyhan* [2003] EWCA Civ 1030 at [78]; [2004] 1 Lloyd's Rep. 505, *per* Sedley LJ.

[104] *Rogers v Parish Ltd.* [1987] QB 933, 944 (under the law of 'merchantable quality' as amended in 1973).   [105] Ibid. 944–5.

[106] *Medivance Instruments Ltd. v Gaslane Pipework Services Ltd.* [2002] EWCA Civ 500; 2002 WL 1876274 § 37.

[107] This change had been made previously by the 1979 Act, s. 61(1) 'quality' (as enacted).

[108] 1979 Act, s. 14(2B) as inserted by the 1994 Act, s. 1.   [109] Law Com. No. 160 § 3.38 *et seq.*

[110] Cf. Sale of Goods Act 1893, s. 14(2) (no liability where 'defect' ought to have been discovered on examination).

[111] *Henry Kendall & Sons v William Lillico & Sons Ltd.* [1969] 2 AC 31; *Aswan Engineering Establishment Co. v Lupdine Ltd.* [1987] 1 WLR 1.

[112] 1979 Act, s. 14(6) as enacted.   [113] *Jewson Ltd. v Boyhan, cit.* at [68] *per* Clarke LJ.

While there were cases under the old law holding that goods were 'unmerchantable' owing to their lack of safety,[114] the new formulation in section 14(2B) made the 'safety' of the goods explicitly relevant to the issue of their 'satisfactory quality'.[115] According to the Law Commission, 'it [is] clearly an important element in the implied [term of quality] that goods should be reasonably safe when used for any of their normal purposes',[116] especially as regards consumer goods.[117] And the new provision makes

clear that hazardous things or substances, which can be safely used only when unusual precautions are taken, will not be of the required standard of quality if appropriate warning is not given or if they are more hazardous than they should be.[118]

This raises the question more generally of the significance of failures in information or warnings accompanying the goods, which has been such an important and prominent feature of the French law.[119] Apart from the description of the goods,[120] are instructions or warnings accompanying goods and directed to their use relevant to their 'satisfactory quality'? While there is no reason in principle why they should not be, most cases of this sort would involve consideration of the adequacy of the information in relation to the reasonable fitness of the goods to achieve their purpose and for this reason there is a tendency to treat them under the implied term of fitness for purpose found in section 14(3).[121]

A final possible 'aspect' of the goods' 'satisfactory quality' which is omitted from the statutory test is their design, whether a failure in design affects their safety or their more general utility.[122] However, even more than in the case of warnings or instructions, any failure in a product's design is likely to be seen as going to their fitness for purpose and therefore mentioned in this way as an aspect of their 'satisfactory nature' or being dealt with under the distinct implied term of reasonable fitness for purpose.

(iv) The reasonable fitness of the goods for their purpose

According to section 14 (3) of the 1979 Act:

where the seller sells goods in the course of a business and the buyer, expressly or by implication, makes known . . . to the seller . . . any particular purpose for which the goods are being bought, there is an implied term that the goods supplied under the contract are reasonably fit for that purpose, whether or not that is a purpose for which such goods are commonly supplied, except where the circumstances show that the buyer does not rely, or that it is unreasonable for him to rely, on the skill or judgment of the seller.[123]

This provision, which has changed relatively little since 1893, has formed a very important basis of the seller's liability to his buyer, long being seen as broader and less

---

[114] *Watson v Buckley, Osborne, Garrett & Co. Ltd.* [1940] 1 All ER 174 (hairdye); *Godley v Perry, Burton & Sons (Bermondsey) Ltd.* [1960] 1 WLR 9 (dangerous toy catapult); *Lee v York Coach and Marine* (1977) RTR 35 (unsafe second-hand vehicle). [115] 1979 Act, s. 14(2B)(d).

[116] Law Com. No. 160 § 3.44–3.46.

[117] The Law Commission was not concerned by any overlap with liability under Part I of the Consumer Protection Act 1987 as this would 'perform an essentially different function': ibid., § 3.46.

[118] Ibid. § 3.45.   [119] Above, pp. 65–9.   [120] Above, p. 237.

[121] *Wormell v R.M.H. Agriculture (East) Ltd.*, [1987] 1 WLR 1091.

[122] *Clegg v Andersson* [2003] EWCA Civ 320i; [2003] 1 All ER (Comm) 721 (design of keel for yacht rendering it 'unsatisfactory').

[123] The omissions include equivalent provisions as regards credit sellers.

problematic than the test of 'merchantable quality'.[124] In the modern law it is also restricted to sales in the course of a business,[125] and does not apply 'where the circumstances show that the buyer does not rely, or that it is unreasonable for him to rely, on the skill or judgment of the seller',[126] though reliance is presumed unless contrary proof is established, for example from evidence of sole reliance on the goods' manufacturer rather than their immediate seller or of the buyer's reliance on his own skill and judgment.[127]

Moreover, the implied term as to fitness of the goods for their purpose differs from the term as to their 'satisfactory quality' in its overtly and exclusively functional concern, a concern which has both objective and subjective aspects.[128] Its subjective aspect is the more obvious on a first reading, for it provides that the term will be implied where the buyer makes known to the seller his *particular* purpose; where this is the case, it does not matter that the buyer's purpose is unusual or not generally foreseeable. So, in a leading case, the defendant manufacturer of motor vehicles sold buses to the plaintiff, a bus company, for use in Bristol, which entailed heavy use in a hilly district.[129] The buses as supplied were suitable for touring purposes, but were built too lightly for this particular and known purpose, breaking down a lot and finally becoming useless: they were held to have been not reasonably fit for their purpose. However, soon after its enactment in 1893, the courts accepted that there could be an objective aspect of this implied term, the reference to a buyer making known his purpose 'impliedly' allowing them to hold that a normal purpose for use of the type of goods in question would be impliedly conveyed. In this way, the courts imposed liability for goods not reasonably fit for their normal or ordinary purpose, some of the early cases concerning claims for personal injuries or death caused by food, the courts holding that food and drinks sold must be fit for human consumption.[130] On the other hand, where a buyer has in mind a particular, unusual purpose which he does not communicate to the seller, the latter will not be liable if the goods are not reasonably fit for this purpose. For example, in one case, the plaintiff contracted dermatitis from wearing a tweed coat sold by the defendant, the plaintiff having abnormally sensitive skin: as she had not told the seller of her sensitivity, she could not recover as the goods were reasonably fit for their ordinary purpose.[131]

In either situation, the standard to be attained is one of *reasonable* fitness for the purpose. This qualification creates a threshold of significance or importance, but there is no requirement that the lack of fitness is such that the buyer (had he known of it) would not have bought the goods or would have paid a different price of the sort stipulated by French law's liability for latent defects.[132] Rather 'reasonableness' creates a mid-way point: the goods do not have to achieve the buyer's purpose perfectly, but any slight fulfilment will not be enough.[133] So 'a second-hand car is "reasonably fit for the

---

[124] Bridge, *The Sale of Goods*, 316–17.   [125] Above, p. 236.   [126] 1979 Act, s. 14(3) *in fine.*
[127] *Teheran-Europe Co. Ltd. v S.T. Belton (Tractors) Ltd.* [1968] 2 QB 545, 555.
[128] Above, p. 237.
[129] *Bristol Tramways Carriage Co. Ltd. v Fiat Motors Ltd.* [1910] 2 KB 831.
[130] *Frost v Aylesbury Dairy Co.* [1905] 1 KB 608, esp. at 612 (milk described as 'pure and unadulterated' infected with typhoid); *Jackson v Watson & Sons* [1909] 2 KB 193 (tinned salmon causing death). Cf. *Preist v Last* [1903] 2 KB 148 (hot-water bottle burst causing scald).
[131] *Griffiths v Peter Conway Ltd.* [1939] 1 All ER 685.   [132] Above, pp. 75–6.
[133] Law Com. No. 160 § 2.18 ('the seller does not guarantee that his goods are absolutely suitable').

purpose" if it is in a roadworthy condition, fit to be driven along the road in safety, even though not as perfect as a new car',[134] the reason for this distinction being that a buyer's reasonable expectations are lower as regards second-hand as opposed to new goods.[135] At times, moreover, the courts have described the significance of the reasonable fitness of the goods for their purpose in terms reminiscent of the cost/benefit analysis in the tort of negligence. So, in *Henry Kendall & Sons v. William Lillico & Sons Ltd.* Lord Pearce observed, considering a sale of a touring car to a consumer:

I would expect a tribunal of fact to decide that a car sold in this country was reasonably fit for touring even though it was not well adapted for conditions in a heat wave; but not, if it could not cope adequately with rain. If, however, it developed some lethal or dangerous trick in very hot weather, I would expect it to be found unfit. In deciding the question of fact *the rarity of the unsuitability would be weighed against the gravity of its consequences*. Again, if food was merely unpalatable or useless on rare occasions, it might well be reasonably suitable for food. But I should certainly not expect it to be held reasonably suitable if even on very rare occasions it killed the consumer.[136]

This indicates that the implied term requires a buyer to tolerate some inadequacies in the goods and suggests that in determining their significance the likelihood and gravity of harmful consequences of any inadequacy must be assessed. What it does not say (unlike the position in negligence) is that these elements are to be balanced against the cost of any precautions to be taken to avoid the inadequacy.[137]

More generally, in common with the position as regards 'satisfactory quality', both the price of the goods and their description may be relevant to the reasonableness of their fitness for purpose: cheap goods should not be useless, but their price is relevant to what can be expected of their efficiency. In some types of case, this is related to a judgment as to the nature of their job, and therefore the question of the disclosure of his purpose by the buyer.[138] Similarly, any description of the goods will be relevant to the question of breach as it will sometimes be enough to designate its purpose: for example, sale of a rubber 'hot-water bottle' imports a term that the goods should be 'fit for use as a hot-water bottle under any circumstances in which such bottles are usually applicable, including the purpose of applying heat to any part of the human body'.[139] And where a person sells a second-hand car, if sold as a vehicle, then it must be reasonably fit for the purpose of being driven on the road and not dangerous,[140] but if it is sold as scrap, its unroadworthy character would not make it unfit for its purpose. Information accompanying the goods in the form of warnings or instructions may also be relevant to their fitness for purpose: for example, where a manufacturer of a chemical could reasonably foresee that it would be used in a context where it may be in contact with water, its lack of a warning that it would explode on such contact

---

[134] *Bartlett v Sidney Marcus Ltd.* [1965] 1 WLR 1013, 1017, *per* Lord Denning MR.
[135] Bridge, *The Sale of Goods*, 321.
[136] *Henry Kendall & Sons v William Lillico & Sons Ltd.* [1969] 2 AC 31, 115 (emphasis added).
[137] Cf. above, pp. 192–200.
[138] Cf. *Henry Kendall & Sons v William Lillico & Sons Ltd.* [1969] 2 AC 31, 79, *per* Lord Reid.
[139] *Preist v Last* [1903] 2 KB 148, 154, *per* Collins MR.
[140] *Lee v York Coach and Marine* [1977] RTR 35.

rendered the chemical not reasonably fit for its purpose.[141] However, here 'a warning of a defect, however clear and unambiguous, is not necessarily decisive.... [Section 14(3)] sets a standard that must be judged by considering the article concerned, the purpose for which it was, and was known to the seller, to be used, and all other relevant circumstances, including any warning about any particular defect in the article concerned'.[142]

English courts have therefore seen the safety of the goods, their effectiveness for practical use and for commercial utility all as potentially relevant to their reasonable fitness. So, for example, mineral water is not reasonably fit for its purpose if it generates gas to an extent that the bottle containing it bursts and injures its buyer.[143] Sometimes, however, safety may not be enough. In *Britvic Soft Drinks Ltd. v Messer UK Ltd.*,[144] the defendant had sold carbon dioxide in bulk to the claimants for use in the preparation of soft and alcoholic drinks. It was later discovered that the gas had been contaminated by benzene, a carcinogen, owing to a leak in the heat exchanger in its manufacture. It was held that this contamination rendered the gas not reasonably fit for its purpose, even though it was not present in such quantities as to be injurious to health, because the presence of any carcinogen rendered the drinks into which the gas was to be incorporated un-saleable to the public who would not knowingly buy a food product accidentally containing a carcinogen in any quantities.[145] Interestingly, Tomlinson J thought that the public would take a different view of such a contamination where the carcinogen served a useful purpose such as preservation and had been 'deliberately introduced as a result of a considered value judgment that its anti-bacterial properties outweigh its carcinogenic effects'.[146]

We can see, therefore, that the term implied as to the satisfactory quality of the goods and as to their fitness for purpose have a very good deal in common: they both impose a standard which is explicitly relative—the quality must only be *satisfactory*, the goods *reasonably* fit; a number of factors *may* be relevant in judging the fulfilment of these standards, of which the goods' description are important for both, but their price appears as rather more important for their 'quality' than their fitness for purpose; and there are different aspects of these standards, of which safety is clearly an important one. So, while the statutory form of the implied term as to the fitness of the goods for their purpose is left at large by the legislation, both factors and aspects are present in its application.

(v) Comparisons with French law

How do the English and French treatments of the bases of a seller's liability to his buyer for failures in quality, safety and fitness for purpose compare?

---

[141] *Vacwell Engineering v BDH Chemicals* [1971] 1 QB 88, 105. The lack of any knowledge of this characteristic was not relevant to the issue of breach of the implied term, unlike the position in negligence: cf. above, p. 194. See similarly, *Wormell v RHM Agriculture (East) Ltd.* [1987] 1 WLR 1091.

[142] *Medivance Instruments Ltd. v Gaslane Pipework Services Ltd.* [2002] EWCA Civ 500; 2002 WL 1876274 [45], *per* Neuberger J.   [143] *Geddling v Marsh* [1920] 1 KB 668 esp. at 673.

[144] *Britvic Soft Drinks Ltd. v Messer UK Ltd.* [2002] 1 Lloyd's Rep 20, affd. on other grounds [2002] 2 Lloyd's Rep. 368. The court also held that the gas was not of satisfactory quality for the same reason. See similarly *Bacardi-Martini Beverages Ltd. v Thomas Hardy Packaging Ltd.* [2002] EWCA Civ 549; [2002] 2 All ER (Comm) 335.   [145] [2002] 1 Lloyd's Rep. 20 at p. 41.   [146] Ibid.

First, the law in both systems has changed considerably and in a number of ways, particularly since the 1960s or 1970s. English law's traditional commercial model of sale has given way to an increasing concern to tailor the bases of liability to the requirements of consumer sales, as can be seen in the reshaping of the term as to the goods' quality, in the presumption of reliance on the seller's skill in the term as to their fitness for purpose,[147] and the extension of the categories of those sellers caught by the first of these terms to all those selling in the course of a business.[148] If there is a traditional model for the French law of sale visible from its bases of seller's liability, it is simply a reflection of the domain of *droit civil*, applicable to all private law contracts and with no particular assumptions made as to the commercial or individual nature of the contract, a generality reinforced by the law's application to immovable as well as to movable property.[149] While we do not see the sort of overt shift in orientation towards consumer sales in the French *jurisprudence* which is visible in English law, many of the developments of the last 40 years have been particularly important for consumers, notably, the imposition of liability in damages on all *vendeurs professionnels*,[150] and the development of *obligations d'informations* and *obligations de sécurité*.[151]

Secondly, while the conceptual starting points of the two systems were very different, there is a degree of convergence. So, the traditional understanding of liability under the *garantie légale* was that it rested on a latent physical defect which was sufficiently serious that the property was no longer fit for its purpose, but this evolved so that lack of fitness is now used to define when the property suffers from a defect.[152] Liability for 'contractual non-conformity' is also said to rest on a *défaut*, the defect here being simply the failure of the property to conform to an express or implied contractual stipulation[153] (there is no reference as such to defect in the law of *obligations d'information*).[154] By contrast, while the English law of implied term did not take as its foundation the presence of a defect, whether physical or otherwise, but rather either a failure to keep to what was promised (as in sale by description) or a failure in the commercial usefulness of the goods (as in 'merchantable quality' and fitness for purpose),[155] there has been a noticeable shift towards use of the language of defect, appearing as an explicit 'aspect' of the standard of the goods' satisfactory quality ('minor defects').[156] This shift in part reflects the concern to ensure that the law is suitable for consumer sales of new goods, but it may also reflect a concern in the courts to enable suit up the chain of supply so as to allow liability to rest with the person responsible for the inadequacy of the goods.[157] The modern English law, therefore, combines a strong functionalist approach with a recognition that some defects should give rise to a remedy even if the goods *are* fit for their purpose.

This leads me, thirdly, to consider the different treatments of 'aspects' of inadequacy of the goods. Here, English law has taken a very open approach, firmly including the safety of goods as a possible aspect of their quality or of their fitness for purpose[158] and seeing failures in the supply of information by a seller relating to the goods (warnings,

---

[147] Above, pp. 237, 240.   [148] Above, p. 286.
[149] Cf. above pp. 80, 81, concerning remedies where the commercial nature of the contract is significant.
[150] Above, p. 85.   [151] Above, pp. 65–9, 72.   [152] Above, p. 71.
[153] Above, p. 70.   [154] Above, p. 66.   [155] Above, pp. 234, 235, 240.
[156] Above, p. 238.   [157] Bridge, *The Sale of Goods*, 293.   [158] Above, pp. 239, 240.

instructions or descriptions) as possible elements in their quality or fitness for purpose.[159]
By contrast, French law has taken a rather more compartmentalised approach. While
French courts have accepted that 'defects' in goods includes physical defects, defects in
design or failures in the supply of information relating to them,[160] from their inception
obligations d'information have tended to attract those cases where the substance of a
claimant's case is that the seller has failed to inform or warn him properly, whether as to
the utility or the safety of the goods.[161] And while earlier cases concerning liability for
latent defects could concern unsafe as well as unsuitable goods,[162] since the 1990s
French courts have channelled cases concerning unsafe goods towards the law of *obligations de sécurité*, and away from either *obligation de conformité* or the *garantie légale*.[163]
This judicial approach has been supported by a body of jurists, arguing against the 'mixing up' of issues of safety and contractual conformity.[164]

Fourthly, where it is concerned with the buyer's purpose, French law starts from an
objective view, looking at the normal purpose of the type of property in question, but
where the buyer has communicated a special purpose, any failure of fitness for this purpose can give rise to liability either under the *garantie légale* or for non-conformity,[165]
a position very similar to that in the English law of implied term of fitness for purpose.[166]
And in both systems, a seller may in appropriate circumstances be liable in respect of the
goods' failure to fulfil the *foreseeable special* purpose of the buyer: in English law, if the
buyer's purpose was 'impliedly made known' to the seller; in French law, by holding that
the seller ought to have informed the buyer of the inappropriateness of the goods for his
purpose under the law of *obligations d'information*.[167]

Fifthly, one apparent difference between French and English laws disappears significantly on examination. In French law, liability under the *garantie légale* is restricted to
hidden defects, meaning that a defect was not known and should not have been known
to the buyer on sale, taking into account his degree of expertise.[168] While in English
law there is no general requirement that any failure in quality or function should be
hidden from the buyer, its apparent nature may be significant. So, it is provided that
the implied term as to satisfactory quality 'does not extend to any matter making the
quality of goods unsatisfactory (a) which is specifically drawn to the buyer's attention
before the contract is made [or] (b) where the buyer examines the goods before the
contract is made, which that examination ought to reveal'.[169] This differs from the
French position only as regards the case where a buyer did not examine the goods, but
ought to have done so in circumstances where this would have revealed the goods'
unsatisfactory quality.[170] The hidden nature of any defect is less prominent as regards
the implied term as to the fitness for purpose, but a warning or instructions for use
of otherwise unsafe or unsuitable goods may make them reasonably fit for their

---

[159] Above, pp. 237, 239.   [160] Above, pp. 73–4.   [161] Above, pp. 65–9.
[162] Above, p. 74.   [163] Ibid.
[164] e.g. J. Calais-Auloy, 'Ne mélangeons plus conformité et sécurité', D 1993 Chron. 130.
[165] Above, pp. 70–1.   [166] Above, p. 240.   [167] Above, pp. 68–9, 240.
[168] Above, pp. 76–7, which explains the position as regards liability for 'contractual non-conformity'.
[169] 1979 Act s. 14(2C)(a) and (b). It is further provided that 'in the case of a contract for sale by sample,
which would have been apparent on a reasonable examination of the sample': ibid., s. 14(2C)(c).
[170] Cf. Bridge, *The Sale of Goods*, 314–5; *Benjamin* § 11-054.

purpose,[171] and where a buyer ought to have known that the goods are not reasonably fit for his own purpose, a court is likely to hold that he has not relied or that it was unreasonable for him to rely on the skill and judgment of the seller.[172]

Finally, and perhaps most strikingly, while in French law failures in safety and the supply of information have been separated off from the mainstream of contractual quality, its standards of quality which rest on 'defect' (*vice caché* or *défaut de conformité*) remain very broad and open compared to the English. French courts are not provided by their Code with any factors to take into account in establishing the existence of a defect nor any guidance as to what 'aspects' such a defect may possess. This does not mean that French courts do not take into account similar factors in deciding the question of 'defect' as English courts do under the statutory implied terms (for example, any description of the goods and whether they were new or second-hand),[173] but this is a matter of extrapolation rather than forming an explicit element in the legal justification of their decision. For in French law, the existence and seriousness of the defect are treated as issues of fact for the 'sovereign assessment' of the *juges du fond*, and are decided in practice by *expertise* in all but the simplest cases.[174]

Overall, the evolution of the English implied term of 'satisfactory quality' has remarkable similarities at a level of legal technique with the 'negligence issue' in tort.[175] At one time juries had made a global and unexplained assessment of the quality of goods (as they did of negligence),[176] but their disappearance led to a judicial exploration of the circumstances which would argue for or against breach of the implied terms of quality or fitness for purpose. While it is said that breach remains an issue of fact,[177] this did not prevent the courts from carving out elements to which future courts should look in making their evaluation of future facts. But unlike the structuring of what is required of a reasonable person in negligence,[178] in the codified law of sale of goods, the legislator set out and sought to improve the structuring which the courts had created. Here again, English lawyers have found further legal elements as a result of treating different cases differently (distinguishing 'factors' and 'aspects'); French courts are content with the law more general and open, leaving distinguishing features between cases as differences of fact.

(vi) Strict liability and defences: reasonable standards and reasonable care

Liability under the statutory implied terms is a well-known example of a contractual strict liability in the sense that negligence in the seller is irrelevant to their breach. This position was established by the courts at common law[179] and then applied to liability

---

[171] *Vacwell Engineering v B.D.H. Chemicals* [1971] 1 QB 88; *Medivance Instruments Ltd. v Gaslane Pipework Services Ltd.* [2002] EWCA Civ 500; 2002 WL 1876274 [40] *et seq.*   [172] Above, p. 240.

[173] Above, pp. 73–4, 75.   [174] Above, p. 78.   [175] Above, pp. 189–202.

[176] Above, pp. 189–90, 235.

[177] *Rogers v Parish Ltd.* [1987] QB 933, 943, *per* Mustill LJ. This was intended to encourage appellate courts to be slow to interfere with decisions at trial, though they have done so where the approach taken by the judge is seen as incorrect or insufficient weight was given to expert evidence: e.g. *Clegg v Andersson* [2003] EWCA Civ 320 [2003]; 1 All ER (Comm) 721; *Jewson Ltd. v Boyhan*, cit.

[178] Cf. liability under the Occupiers Liability Acts 1957 s. 2(2) and 1984 s. 1(4) and (5) where the assessment of 'negligence' is partly structured.

[179] *Randall v Newson* (1876–1877) LR QBD 102 (CA) (jury verdict that goods not reasonably fit for their purpose but against negligence upheld).

under section 14 of the Sale of Goods Act in *Frost v Aylesbury Dairy Co. Ltd.* in 1905.[180] There the defendant sold milk to the plaintiff and his family on the basis that it would be 'pure and unadulterated', but which was infected with typhoid with the result that his wife died. The Court of Appeal upheld the jury's verdict for the plaintiff on the ground of breach of the statutory implied terms, holding that it was no defence for the sellers to establish that the typhoid in the milk was a 'latent undiscoverable defect'.[181] This strict approach has been applied equally to non-manufacturing sellers, such as distributors or retailers.[182] As Lord Diplock later observed in relation to the implied term as to fitness for purpose, it does not matter 'that in the then state of knowledge no one could by exercise of skill or judgment detect the particular characteristic of the goods which rendered them unfit for that purpose'.[183]

On the other hand, the standards imposed by the statutory implied terms are not themselves absolute standards: goods need only be of '*satisfactory* quality' and *reasonably* fit for their purpose.[184] So, as regards safety, some judges have said that goods do not have to be absolutely safe, even if they are described in terms which draw attention to their safety.[185] In 2002 in *Medivance Instruments Ltd. v Gaslane Pipework Services Ltd.*, a gas-fired convector heater had overheated and ignited adjacent packaging, causing a large fire in a factory. The factory owners who had bought the heater alleged that their seller was in breach of both statutory implied terms because it had not been supplied with sufficient protection in the event of overheating on fan failure, either by a thermostat device or a suitable guard, and they pointed out that other similar heaters did possess such protection and this could be supplied relatively cheaply and easily.[186] On the other hand, the sellers noted that the relevant British Standard contained no such requirement or recommendation, despite running to 30 pages of fairly small print.[187] At trial, the judge found that the heaters were both of merchantable quality and reasonably fit for their purpose, being 'satisfied that the degree of risk does not require the installation of a different sort of heater than that provided'.[188] This decision was upheld by the Court of Appeal on the basis that the clear and unambiguous warnings which accompanied the heaters would (if followed) have enabled the fire to have been avoided. So, in determining what is 'satisfactory' or 'reasonably fit for its purpose' the courts sometimes look at the same sort of balancing of considerations of risk and precaution as they do under the tort of negligence.

At a formal level, these decisions and the 'strictness of liability' can be reconciled by saying that while the courts may sometimes need to follow a cost/benefit analysis in determining whether goods are of 'satisfactory quality' or reasonably fit for their purpose, having come to that view, the presence or absence of negligence in the seller is irrelevant to liability. Moreover, while 'foreseeability' is relevant in the sense that the *normal* purpose of the buyer for the goods goes to breach of the term as to their

---

[180] [1905] 1 KB 608.	[181] Ibid. at 613.	[182] E.g. *Priest v Last* [1903] 2 KB 148.

[183] *Ashington Piggeries Ltd v Christopher Hill Ltd.* [1972] AC 441, 505; *Henry Kendall & Sons v William Lillico & Sons Ltd.* [1969] 2 AC 31, 84, *per* Lord Reid.	[184] Above, pp. 237, 239.

[185] E.g. *Grenfell v E.B. Meyrowitz Ltd.*, above, p. 235.

[186] [2002] EWCA Civ 500, 2002 WL 1876274 esp. at [24].	[187] Ibid. at [30].

[188] Ibid. at [39] quoted by Neuberger J. The test of merchantable (rather than satisfactory) quality applied as the facts pre-dated the amendment in 1994 of the Sale of Goods Act which made this change.

'satisfactory quality',[189] and may form the basis of the implication of the term as to the in fitness for purpose, once a court has come to a view that the goods are not 'satisfactory' or reasonably fit for their purpose, the seller's knowledge or reasonable foresight of the circumstances which bring this about are irrelevant: the seller undertakes that the goods *will be* of satisfactory quality and reasonably fit for their purpose and is not (as in the tort of negligence) held liable only for a failure to act reasonably in the face of a risk of a particular type and degree.

However, in my view, these neat reconciliations offer little true explanation of the contrast of approach to be seen in the cases. Instead, it appears that where safety is in issue, the courts in fact have sometimes distinguished between cases of manufacturing or processing defects, such as typhoid in milk, where negligence is truly irrelevant to liability as the seller is held to have promised their absence, and cases of failures in design (including any warnings or instructions accompanying a product), where a cost/benefit analysis is relevant as the seller cannot be expected to promise a *perfect* design. This could be seen to lie behind the position of Tomlinson J in *Britvic Soft Drinks Ltd. v Messer UK Ltd.* who distinguished the case before him (in which a carcinogen had been *accidentally* introduced into a substance used in making drinks) and the case of the *deliberate* use of a carcinogen for a useful purpose:[190] the first case is a defect in process, the second an alleged defect in design.

How does this rather variable approach compare to the French view of the various bases of seller's liability? Liability under the *garantie légale*, for contractual non-conformity and for failure to perform an *obligation de sécurité* under the case law of the 1990s all rest on proof of a defect and while these defects are variously described, French law clearly asserts that liability arises without the need for the buyer to show *faute* and without the possibility of the seller escaping liability by proving its absence.[191] If one were to go further and ask whether French courts actually take into account the sorts of considerations of risk and cost which English courts have in determining the existence of such defects, the only sure response is that one cannot tell as we cannot draw aside the veil of the *pouvoir souverain d'appréciation* nor read the reports of the *experts*. On the other hand, there is much more ambiguity of approach as regards the duties required of sellers under contractual *obligations d'informations*, where the formal position is that fault is needed for liability to be established, though the courts have reversed the burden of proof.[192] And French courts take different views of the practical content of these obligations according to the status of the parties to the contract and the subject matter of the information (in particular, whether it goes to the safety of the goods or merely to the effectiveness).[193]

I have earlier described how French law's treatment of the defences to liability form an important element in the degree of strictness of the liability in the seller and that this focuses on *force majeure* or the *faute* of the buyer.[194] What is the position of English law with regard to these sorts of situation?

---

189 Above, p. 240.
190 *Britvic Soft Drinks Ltd. v Messer UK Ltd.* [2002] 1 Lloyd's Rep. 20, 41 quoted above, p. 242.
191 Above, pp. 72, 90 and as to *force majeure*, see below, p. 248.   192 Above, p. 67.
193 Ibid.   194 Above, pp. 87–91.

First, French law defines *force majeure* as an event, action or circumstances which make performance of an obligation impossible, which are unforeseeable and which are 'exterior to the thing'.[195] *Force majeure* is not a defence to liability under the *garantie légale*[196] and where liability under the 'general law' is based on *obligations de résultat, force majeure* cannot be seen in defects in the property supplied as they are not 'exterior to the thing'.[197] For this reason, it is said that under the *garantie légale* or the law of 'contractual non-conformity', the seller is liable for 'development risks' in the property sold.[198] On the other hand, a supervening event or action may break the chain of causation between any defect in the property sold and a claimant's harm,[199] though sometimes French courts prefer to hold jointly liable those involved in the chain of failure which has led to the claimant's harm.[200] In sum, while the way in which the defect arose is irrelevant to liability, the defect must contribute to the claimant's harm.

While English law does not possess a notion of *force majeure* as a defence to non-performance of a contractual obligation,[201] the undiscoverable or unpreventable characteristic of any failure in quality or fitness for purpose of the goods is no defence to liability under section 14 of the 1979 Act.[202] On the other hand, as in French law, English law requires that a claimant's harm was caused by the defendant's breach of contract. In English law, many of the cases in which the causal link has been said to have been broken concern claims for an indemnity by a buyer where it is alleged that the buyer's own fault caused the harm,[203] but in other cases an English court may choose to impose joint and several liability rather than say that a seller's breach of contract was causally unrelated to the buyer's harm. For example, a seller sells a second-hand vehicle described as in want of minor repair and its buyer sends it to another person for repair; the buyer drives the car whose brakes fail causing injury; here, the seller would be in breach of the terms implied by section 14 in delivering an unroadworthy vehicle and this could well be seen as contributing to the buyer's harm, even if the intervening repairer were found negligent in failing to detect and repair the defective brake.

By contrast, at first sight the English and French approaches to the defence of contributory negligence are radically different. For French law accepts that a seller may escape or reduce his contractual liability under any legal basis on the ground of the buyer's fault, whereas English law denies a seller the defence of contributory negligence in respect of liability for breach of the statutory implied terms in the 1979 Act.[204] However, a closer look shows that the two laws are not as far apart as this suggests.

In French law, a first category of situation concerns 'fault' committed by a buyer in the course of purchasing the goods. For example, French courts have reduced a seller's liability in damages on the ground that the buyer *ought* to have been aware of the

---

[195] Above, p. 58.   [196] Above, p. 89.   [197] Above, p. 90.   [198] Above, p. 89.

[199] Above, pp. 90–1.   [200] Above, p. 91.

[201] In some situations, *force majeure* may find a broadly functional equivalent in the law of frustration: Bell, Boyron and Whittaker, 342–3.   [202] Above, p. 246.

[203] Below, pp. 249–50.

[204] This stems from the decision that the Law Reform (Contributory Negligence) Act 1945 does not apply to claims for breach of contract unless they are founded on the breach of a contractual obligation to take reasonable care *concurrent with* breach of a tortious duty to take reasonable care: *Forsikringsaktieselskapet Vesta v Butcher* [1989] AC 852; *Barclays Bank plc v Fairclough Building Ltd.* [1995] QB 214; *Barclays Bank plc v Fairclough Building Ltd. (No. 2)* [1995] IRLR 605.

defect on sale, a compromise between full liability and its denial on the ground that the defect was not 'hidden' from the buyer.[205] Here English law would distinguish between cases where the buyer examined the goods before sale and ought from such an examination to have discovered their defect (where the seller is not liable),[206] and cases where the buyer did not examine the goods even where he had an opportunity to do so (where the seller is liable in full): in English law in neither case is liability reduced.

Secondly, French courts sometimes hold a purchaser to have been 'at fault' in using goods for an unspecified and unsuitable purpose, this allowing them to reduce or exclude liability in the seller.[207] In English law, where a buyer's use is not an ordinary one, a court would deny liability not on the ground of 'fault' in the buyer, but rather on the ground that there is no breach, since any *particular* purpose to which the goods are to be put must be communicated, expressly or impliedly, to the seller.[208] So, for example, where market gardeners bought water which contained a tiny concentration of a herbicide for use on their tomatoes which were grown hydroponically and which were damaged as a result, there was no breach of the implied term that the water be reasonably fit for its purpose as the growers had not communicated their special needs to the sellers.[209]

Thirdly, French courts have sometimes held the buyer at fault where his own design for the product sold by the seller proved unsatisfactory.[210] Here, English law would say that while the goods are not reasonably fit for their particular purpose, the buyer has relied on his own skills and judgment rather than on the seller's and on this ground cannot recover.[211]

Fourthly, French courts have excluded or reduced a seller's liability on the ground of the buyer's 'fault' in using the goods. This fault may take a number of forms. In some cases, it consists of failing to follow instructions or warnings accompanying the goods, whether these are clear or unclear and inadequate.[212] Here, an English court is likely first to consider whether there is breach of any of the implied terms, which would depend on the need for and adequacy of the information supplied in the context. So, for example, in one case the plaintiff bought raw pork but failed to cook it through: the court held that there was no breach of the implied terms in respect of the food-poisoning that resulted since the pork was 'merchantable' if cooked properly according to accepted standards.[213] On the other hand, if there is a breach, the question arises squarely as to the effect of a buyer's failure to act carefully in using the goods. Here, an English court cannot reduce the seller's liability on the ground of the buyer's contributory negligence, but can exclude it altogether if the buyer's conduct is so unreasonable as to break the chain of causation between the seller's breach and his own harm, this sometimes being treated as an example of the general duty in an injured party to mitigate his own damage.[214] Sometimes, though, the courts have preferred to express their decision in terms of the ambit of the implied term, rather than the requirement of causation. So, for example, in *Lambert v Lewis* an owner of a trailer bought a

---

[205] Above, p. 87.   [206] Above, p. 244.   [207] Above, p. 88.   [208] Above, p. 240.
[209] *Hamilton v Papakura District Council* [2002] UKPC 9.   [210] Above, p. 87.
[211] Above, p. 240.   [212] Above, p. 88.   [213] *Heil v Hedges* [1951] 1 TLR 512.
[214] E.g. *Biggin & Co. Ltd. v Permanite Ltd.* [1951] 1 KB 422, 435, *per* Devlin J.

coupling from a retailer and the coupling broke causing an accident.[215] In these circumstances, the House of Lords held that the statutory implied terms did not extend as far as 'a warranty that the coupling could continue to be safely used to tow a trailer on a public highway notwithstanding that it was in an obviously damaged state'.[216] There was therefore no need to hold that the failure in the owner to stop using the coupling after he could see that it was damaged broke the chain of causation between any breach of contract by the retailer and the loss which he suffered as a result of the accident.[217]

On the other hand, knowledge of a defect in the goods by a buyer who then uses them harming himself or others may not be necessary for a break in the causal link.[218] In *Bostock & Co. Ltd. v Nicholson & Sons. Ltd.* the plaintiffs had contracted to buy from the defendants sulphuric acid, commercially free from arsenic, for use in the manufacture of glucose.[219] The plaintiffs used the acid and then sold the glucose to brewers who used it to make beer, which poisoned a large number of persons, some of whom died.[220] Here, the court held that the plaintiffs by the exercise of ordinary care might have discovered the presence of arsenic in the acid. So, while they could recover damages for the cost of the acid and the value of the other goods mixed with it and spoilt on the ground of breach of an implied term that the goods would correspond with their description, they were not entitled to damages in respect of their liability to the brewers nor to damage to the goodwill of their business as these did not flow ordinarily from the breach of contract but rather from the act of the plaintiffs in manufacturing and selling poisonous glucose to brewers for use in the brewing of beer.[221]

Overall, therefore, we can see that French law's acceptance of the defence of *faute de la victime* to claims by buyers against their sellers gives to its lower courts a power to apportion liability on the basis of what they consider fair in the circumstances. In English law, 'there [is] no room for contributory negligence [in contract], although, in the assessment of damages, causation and the plaintiff's duty to mitigate his loss [are] very relevant'.[222] While English courts do possess a certain flexibility in apportioning losses under the law of mitigation, use of causation tends to result in all or nothing for a claimant. And in other cases where a French court apportions liability by invoking *faute de la victime*, English law denies liability for absence of any breach.

3. Buyer's Remedies for Failures in Quality, Safety and Fitness for Purpose

At the start of this discussion, I need to point out a central difference in the way in which the bases of liability in the French and English laws relate to their remedial consequences. In French law, following Roman law, the traditional remedial focus of the *garantie légale*

---

[215] [1982] AC 225.   [216] Ibid. at 276 *per* Lord Diplock.   [217] Ibid. at 276–7.
[218] Cf. *Chitty on Contracts* paras. 43-443–43-445.   [219] [1904] 1 KB 725.
[220] *Wren v Holt* [1903] 1 KB 610 (claim for personal injuries by beer drinker).
[221] [1904] 1 KB 725, 741–2. The court had referred to the Sale of Goods Act 1893, s. 53(2) which it treated as framed on the general law of *Hadley v Baxendale* (1854) 9 Ex 341. Cf. *Mowbray v Merryweather* [1895] 2 QB 640 (successful claim for an indemnity by an employer in respect of damages for negligence in respect of defective equipment supplied under a contract for services which injured employee).
[222] *Basildon District Council v J.E. Lesser (Properties) Ltd.* [1985] QB 839, 849, *per* Judge Newey QC.

was a right to return the property and to recover the price or a right to a reduction in the price if the property is kept: damages were available only where the defect was known by the seller on delivery.[223] This focus was reflected in the *bref délai*, a restrictive time element appropriate to where a contract is to be unravelled. When liability in damages was extended in the 1960s to *vendeurs professionnels*, the *bref délai* became increasingly inappropriate and its avoidance the motive for the development of less restricted bases for the imposition of liability *in damages*, notably *obligations d'information* and *obligations de conformité* (though either could also found a claim for *résolution* of the contract).[224]

By contrast, the technique of implied term used by English courts and then adopted by the legislature had a very different remedial impact from the beginning: for breach of any term of a contract which causes loss will in principle attract liability in damages. Of course, the Sale of Goods Act 1893 went further, designating its implied terms as 'conditions' and providing that their breach would give rise to a right to reject the goods and terminate the contract (whether on tender or at some later stage), but the Act subjected this right to a restrictive set of rules as to its loss by 'acceptance' of the goods. Unlike French law, therefore, English law has not needed to develop new bases of seller's liability *in damages* so as to escape restrictive rules primarily concerned with the rights of rescission or price reduction. This central difference accounts for the relative unity of regime of the English law of implied terms in sale, differences in the bases of liability having no necessary impact on the nature or timescale of the remedies available.

(a) The right to reject the goods and repudiate the contract

According to the scheme of classification accepted by the Sale of Goods Act 1893, the statutory implied terms are all 'conditions' with the result that their breach entitles the buyer to reject the goods on tender by the seller or after delivery and to repudiate the contract.[225] In both situations and following the general position as regards rescission or repudiation for breach of contract, in principle the buyer has a right to act unilaterally, without any need to invoke the aid or any order of the court, though the seller may subsequently challenge the buyer's right so to act. Where a buyer has lawfully rejected the goods for breach of condition, he ceases to be liable to the price and may recover the price if already paid subject to the requirement of a 'total failure of consideration'.[226]

Until 1994, these rights of rejection and repudiation in the buyer were entirely unfettered: the breach of the term did not have to be serious,[227] nor the exercise of the right fair.[228] This absoluteness gave a very powerful remedy to a buyer of goods, useful

---

[223] Above, pp. 69, 84.   [224] Above, p. 71.

[225] The 1979 Act, s. 11(4) refers to a buyer 'rejecting the goods and treating the contract as repudiated' on the ground of breach of condition. *Benjamin* § 12–028 notes the qualifications on this identity of incidence of the rights of rejection and repudiation, notably where a seller has the possibility of re-tender of goods within the time fixed for performance after tender of non-conforming goods: ibid. §§ 12–022 and 12–031.   [226] See below, p. 254.

[227] *Lombard North Central PLC v Butterworth* [1987] QB 527, 535 and see Law Com. No. 160, § 4.1.

[228] *Glencore Grain Rotterdam BV v Lebanese Organisation for International Commerce* [1997] 2 Lloyd's Rep 386, 398 Evans LJ. A buyer may not reject goods where he is unable to return them in the same state as they were delivered, unless this inability was caused by the seller's breach of contract: for further discussion, see *Benjamin* § 12–057.

both as a threat to encourage a seller to deliver goods conforming to the standards set by the statutory terms and as a means of getting out of the contract if the terms were in fact broken. In its best light, the remedy allows a buyer who receives unsatisfactory goods to avoid the contract and purchase a substitute elsewhere, any difference between their cost and the contract price being made up by way of damages.[229] It requires no waste of time (by making any requirement of recourse to court) and may therefore be thought of as peculiarly appropriate to commercial contexts where the buyer requires conforming goods to perform his own obligations to a sub-buyer. On the other hand, the remedy sacrifices the interest of the seller in performing the contract and, after delivery, may upset any reliance he may have on the stability of the transaction. Moreover, in this classic form, an unscrupulous buyer may take advantage of an unimportant breach of condition to avoid a bad bargain or to take advantage of a changed market and buy a substitute more cheaply.[230]

English law has therefore put in place two important restrictions on the buyer's right of rejection for breach of the implied terms. The older one excludes rejection and repudiation where the buyer has affirmed or is deemed to have affirmed the contract. Under the general law, affirmation of a contract on breach is an act by which the injured party chooses to maintain the contract rather than to rescind it and, for this reason, an injured party must know of the right to rescind before he can be said to have affirmed.[231] While the law of sale of goods allows a buyer aware of a breach of condition by his seller to elect to maintain the contract while retaining any claim for damages,[232] it makes special provision for 'deemed acceptance' of the goods by the buyer with a concomitant loss of the right to rescind the contract for breach of condition. The law provides that a buyer will lose his right to reject by acceptance (i) by intimating to the seller that he accepts the goods; (ii) where he 'does any act in relation to them which is inconsistent with the ownership of the seller', or (iii) he retains the goods after the lapse of a reasonable time without intimating to the seller that he has rejected them.[233] None of these situations of 'deemed acceptance' are conditional on any requirement that the buyer is aware of any breach of the statutory implied conditions which would give rise to a right of repudiation, though as regards the first two no acceptance will be deemed to have taken place where a buyer has not had a reasonable opportunity of examining the goods so as to ascertain whether they are in conformity with the contract.[234] '[A]cts inconsistent with the ownership of the seller' typically consist of cases where the buyer cannot return the goods (though it no longer includes cases where they are delivered under a sub-sale)[235] and the mere fact that the buyer 'asks for, or agrees to, their repair by or under an arrangement with the seller' does not justify a finding that the buyer is deemed to have accepted the goods.[236]

---

[229] Below, p. 255.   [230] Below, p. 253.   [231] *Peyman v Lanjani* [1985] Ch 457.

[232] 1979 Act, s. 11(2). Waiver of the condition is to be distinguished from waiver of the breach itself, the latter referring to a choice by the buyer not to maintain any remedy for the breach: *Chitty on Contracts*, para. 22–046.   [233] 1979 Act, s. 35.

[234] Ibid., s. 35(2). This second limitation was introduced so as to avoid a buyer losing the right where he signs a paper on their delivery stating that he has 'accepted' the goods as well as having 'received' them: Law Com. No. 160 §§ 5.20 *et seq*. Section 35(3) prevents avoidance of this rule by agreement as against those 'dealing as consumer'.   [235] *Benjamin* § 12–047; 1979 Act, s. 35(6)(b).

[236] 1979 Act, s. 35(6)(a).

Nevertheless, a buyer may lose his right to reject the goods for breach of the statutory terms on the lapse of a reasonable time, even though he was unaware of his right to rescind at any time during the relevant period,[237] and while the length of time considered reasonable depends on the circumstances including the discoverability of any defect by the buyer, it tends to be measured in days or weeks rather than months.[238] Despite this apparent unfairness, the Law Commission has rejected the idea that there should be a longer-term right to reject goods in sale, recognising the importance of the existing policy which 'favours finality',[239] and preferring to 'retain a relatively short-lived right to reject with a corresponding automatic right to return of the purchase price' unabated to take into account any use by the buyer.[240] It also rejected the introduction of an 'arbitrary' fixed period to replace the 'reasonable time'[241] and the creation of statutory guidelines to be taken into account in assessing reasonableness for this purpose on the basis that they would either be so general as to be 'obvious and unhelpful' or so detailed as to be 'inappropriate and misleading' for some situations.[242] On the other hand, following the Law Commission's recommendation, the availability of a reasonable opportunity for examining the goods was made explicitly relevant to the determination of a 'reasonable time',[243] and the buyer's arranging for the goods to be repaired by the seller must not settle the issue,[244] which 'shows that time taken merely in requesting or agreeing to repairs, and…for carrying them out, is not to be counted'.[245]

Secondly, since 1995 a buyer who does *not* 'deal as consumer' cannot reject the goods for breach of the statutory implied terms where 'the breach is so slight that it would be unreasonable for him [to do so]'.[246] Given the wide interpretation which has been given by the courts to the phrase 'dealing as consumer', this provision restricts the right of rejection to buyers who have bought goods in the course of their business of a type which forms a regular part of their business[247] and, given this context, it is not surprising that the restriction may be excluded by the express or implied intention of the parties.[248] The change was expressly made to avoid an unjustifiable or market-oriented rescission to the prejudice of the seller in cases of minor defects and, conversely, to avoid the temptation for a court to hold that there is no *breach* in order to avoid rescission, this also ruling out any remedy in damages.[249] On the other hand, the Law Commission felt that those 'dealing as consumer' should retain their absolute right to reject inadequate goods since they are not usually in the position easily to dispose of defective goods and it may be difficult to quantify their loss in money terms, especially where a defect is minor.[250] An absolute right to reject puts a

---

[237] 1979 Act, s. 35(4).   [238] *Benjamin* § 12–054.   [239] Law Com. No. 160 § 5.6.
[240] Ibid. § 5.7.   [241] Ibid. § 5.16.   [242] Ibid. § 5.19, note 19.
[243] 1979 Act, s. 35(5) as inserted by the 1994 Act, s. 2(1).
[244] 1979 Act, s. 35(6)(a) as inserted by the 1994 Act, s. 2(1).
[245] *Clegg v Andersson* [2003] EWCA Civ 320 [63], *per* Sir Andrew Morritt V-C.
[246] 1979 Act, s. 15A(1) as inserted by the 1994 Act, s. 4.
[247] The 1979 Act, s. 6(5A) provides that this phrase is to be construed in accordance with the 1977 Act, s. 12 which defines 'dealing as consumer', itself interpreted in *R. & B. Customs Brokers Co. Ltd. v United Dominions Trust Ltd.* [1988] 1 WLR 321. The Court of Appeal noted that a firm would also fail to 'deal as consumer' if it 'held itself out' as making the contract in the course of a business, but the mere use of the corporate name, list of directors etc. was not enough: ibid., 328–9.   [248] 1979 Act s. 15A(2).
[249] Law Com. No. 160 § 4.1 *et seq*.   [250] Ibid., § 4.4.

consumer in a stronger and clearer bargaining position with a seller, and he can purchase goods of the same description from someone else if he has lost confidence in the original seller.[251]

The Law Commission also considered the possibility for consumer sales of substituting a right to repair or replacement ('cure') of the goods by the seller for the buyer's right of rejection, the seller having 'the right to "cure" any defect but if he did not do so the buyer could reject'.[252] While this proposal found considerable support among those the Law Commission consulted, the idea was somewhat reluctantly dropped as it gave sellers a ground upon which they could argue that the buyer was not entitled to return the goods and recover the price and that many questions of the detail of the scheme remained unsettled, leading to dispute and uncertainty, almost certainly to the detriment of consumers.[253] For all these reasons, the absolute nature of the right of rejection of inadequate goods was retained for consumers.

(b) Restitution of the price

The question whether breach of a statutory implied term as to the quality or fitness for purpose of the goods gives rise not merely to a right of rejection but also a right of restitution of the price (if paid) forms part of a much wider question as to the availability of restitution of money or property 'on a failure of consideration'.[254]

From the buyer's point of view, a claim for restitution (if established) has the advantage over damages that he would not have to establish or mitigate his loss and can even avoid a bad bargain, but it has the disadvantage of not allowing any recovery for loss of a good bargain.[255] At present, the law as to its availability remains that even after rejection of goods on the ground of breach of condition, a buyer can recover the price only on a *total* failure of consideration,[256] by which is generally meant a failure of the 'bargained-for counter-performance'.[257] In the context of hire-purchase, this requirement has been held to mean that a hirer failed to recover back the price on the ground that he had used and enjoyed the goods for a period of time,[258] whereas in the context of breach of the implied term as to the seller's title to the goods, some considerable use by a buyer (and his own purchaser) has been held *not* to prevent a total failure of consideration[259] and it has been argued that this approach should be followed in the context of breach of implied terms as to quality and fitness for purpose, possibly

---

[251] Law Com. No. 160 § 4.9.   [252] Ibid., § 4.11.

[253] 'For example, did the seller have to redeliver the 'cured' goods to the buyer or did the buyer have to collect them? What if by this time the buyer had moved far away? How promptly should the cure be effected? At whose risk were they to be while being redelivered to the buyer?': Law Commission, § 4.13.

[254] A. Burrows, *The Law of Restitution* (Butterworths, London, 2nd. edn., 2002), Chap. 10 and esp. 324 *et seq.*; R. Goff and G. Jones, *The Law of Restitution* (Sweet and Maxwell, London, 6th. edn., 2002) Chap. 19; *Chitty on Contracts* para. 29–54 *et seq.*

[255] There are other advantages: *Chitty on Contracts*, para. 29–059.   [256] 1979 Act s. 54.

[257] Burrows, *op. cit.* n. 254, 324 *et seq.*

[258] *Yeoman Credit Ltd. v Apps* [1962] 2 QB 508 (this use was coupled on the facts with an intention to keep the car on the part of the hirer).

[259] *Rowland v Divall* [1923] 2 KB 500; Treitel, *The Law of Contract*, 1049 *et seq.*

subject to a right to counter-restitution for any benefits received.[260] Given the contentious state of the law and the frequency of *some* use by a buyer of goods in cases of rejection after delivery, the Law Commission's reference to the buyer's 'short-lived right to reject with a corresponding *automatic* right to return of the purchase price'[261] may be over-optimistic.

(c) Damages

Unlike the French position, breach of the implied terms as to description, quality and fitness for purpose have always allowed a buyer to recover damages for losses occasioned by their breach, the knowledge or otherwise by the seller as to the existence of any defect being irrelevant.[262] In terms of the measure and quantum of damages, the Sale of Goods Act 'codified' the common law, expressing the general law of breach of contract in the context of the buyer's remedies for failures in quality of the goods.[263] In common with English law generally, there is a complex law governing the measure and quantification of damages, unlike the French position where this is all but left to the assessment of the *juges du fond*.[264]

Where the buyer rejects the goods and repudiates the contract, he is said to be able to treat the seller's failure to deliver conforming goods as a simple failure to deliver, with the result that, where there is an available market for the goods,[265] damages will *prima facie* be assessed by reference to the difference between the contract price and the market or current price of the goods at the time or times when they ought to have been delivered.[266] So, on rejection, the buyer is entitled to go into the market, buy substitute or near-substitute goods and recover their cost by way of damages, but this is the *prima facie* basis of his damages even if he chooses not to buy any substitute.[267] Underlying these rules one can see the law of mitigation of damage, both empowering a buyer and creating an incentive for a buyer who has rejected the goods to obtain their substitute elsewhere.[268] In this way, English law recognises a right in the buyer to replacement goods, but these are to be obtained from a third party and then charged to the seller's account as damages rather than required from the seller himself.

Where the buyer is not entitled to reject the goods or has chosen not to do so, the *prima facie* measure of damages for breach of the statutory implied terms is the difference in value of the goods if they had conformed to standard and their actual value.[269] While English law does not distinguish a separate right in the buyer to the reduction of the price on the account of the goods' defects (such as the *action aestimatoire* of

---

[260] *Benjamin* § 12–068. The requirement of 'total' failure of consideration has been much criticised: see notably Burrows, *op. cit.* n. 254, 333 *et seq.* and P. Birks, 'Failure of Consideration' in F.D. Rose (ed.) *Consensus Ad Idem: Essays in Honour of Guenter Treitel* (Sweet and Maxwell, London, 1996) Chap. 4.

[261] Above, p. 253.   [262] Above, p. 84.   [263] 1979 Act, ss.51 and 53.

[264] Above, pp. 85–6. The main qualification in French law relates to the requirements contained in arts. 1149–1150 C. civ.

[265] For discussion of the meaning of this phrase, see *Benjamin*, paras 16–062 *et seq.*

[266] 1979 Act s. 51(3).   [267] *Chitty on Contracts* para. 43–416.

[268] A buyer does not have to accept non-conforming goods from the seller by way of mitigation of damage: *Heaven and Kesterton Ltd. v Establissements Francois Albiac & Cie.* [1956] 2 Lloyd's Rep 316, 321.

[269] 1979 Act s. 53(3).

French law[270]), he is entitled to set off any damages based on the difference in value against the seller claiming an unpaid price.[271] But this measure of damages is only a *prima facie* rule and the buyer may instead claim damages for the reasonable cost of repair of the goods[272] or of their replacement. Indeed, he may be under a 'duty' to replace the goods under the law of mitigation of damage if doing so reduces any consequential losses.[273]

Moreover, a buyer can recover any loss of profits or other consequential losses subject to a statutory version of the test of remoteness of damage established in *Hadley v Baxendale*,[274] that is, losses 'directly and naturally arising, in the ordinary course of events, from the breach' as well as 'special damages', that is, one's compensating losses arising from facts within the special knowledge of the seller. In either case, these may include damages for personal injury, and for damage either to the goods themselves or to other property.[275] Furthermore, damages for breach of the implied terms may include the recovery of an indemnity loss, that is a loss caused by the buyer being held liable either to his sub-buyer under the law of sale or to a third party.[276] In both cases, the effect of the law of remoteness of damage restricts the range of recovery. So, an indemnity is recoverable in respect of a sub-sale where at the time of making the contract the buyer would or probably would resell the goods and that this contract would or probably would contain the same or similar terms as to the goods and it was not unlikely that breach of the seller's undertakings would cause the buyer to be liable to his own sub-buyer.[277] Similarly, an indemnity in respect of liability in the tort of negligence to a third party may be recovered as long as the third party was not unlikely to be injured as a result of the defect and as a result the buyer was not unlikely to be held legally liable.[278] Other consequential damages may be available to a buyer, for example, for the disappointment caused to a buyer of a vehicle to be used for a holiday,[279] or a consumer buyer may recover modest damages for his loss of pleasure in receiving goods conforming to their standard.[280]

Finally, I should note that actions for damages for breach of the statutory implied terms and of any corresponding express conditions are subject to the general law of

---

[270] Above, pp. 79, 82.   [271] 1979 Act, s. 53(1)(a) and (4).

[272] The cost of repair may sometimes be seen as representing the likely difference in value: *Keeley v Guy McDonald Ltd.* (1984) 134 New LJ 522. Following the general principle explained in *Ruxley Electronics and Construction Ltd. v Forsyth* [1996] AC 344, the cost of repairs or replacement cannot be recovered if unreasonable in the circumstances. Where no market value of the defective goods can be determined, the cost of repairs may be awarded: *Minster Trust Ltd. v Traps Tractors Ltd.* [1954] 3 All ER 136.

[273] *British Westinghouse Electric and Manufacturing Co. Ltd. v Underground Electric Railways Co. of London Ltd.* [1912] AC 673.

[274] (1854) 9 Exch 341; 1979 Act ss. 53(2) and 54. E.g. *H. Parsons (Livestock) Ltd. v Uttley Ingham & Co. Ltd.* [1978] QB 791.

[275] *Randall v Newson* (1877) 2 QBD 102; *H. Parsons (Livestock) Ltd. v Uttley Ingham & Co. Ltd.* [1978] QB 791 (damage to other property); *Bostock & Co. Ltd. v Nicholson & Sons* [1904] 1 KB 725 (property itself contaminated by defect and contaminating other property).   [276] *Benjamin* § 17–074 *et seq.*

[277] *Chitty on Contracts*, para. 43–459.

[278] *Chitty on Contracts*, para. 43–457; *Lambert v Lewis* [1982] AC 225 (claim rejected on the facts).

[279] *Jackson v Chrysler Acceptances* [1978] RTR 474.

[280] By analogy with damages for 'loss of amenity' in *Ruxley Electronics and Construction Ltd. v Forsyth* [1996] AC 344 (swimming pool not built to specification).

limitation of actions for breach of contract. The action becomes barred after six years[281] and time runs from the delivery of the goods rather than the time when the defect is or could have been discovered or when damage results.[282] However, this law does not apply to claims for personal injuries or death which possess their own regime.[283] Here, the limitation period is only three years, but it starts *either* from the date of delivery *or* from the date of the claimant's knowledge of the significance of his injury and its attribution to the defendant's act in delivering inadequate goods, although his knowledge of the significance of the latter in law is irrelevant.[284] It is to be noted that the special and restrictive provisions as to the buyer's 'deemed acceptance' of the goods have no bearing whatever on the time within which claims for damages may be brought.[285]

(d) Comparative observations

The comparison of the remedies available in respect of failures in quality, safety and fitness for purpose in English and in French law is by no means straightforward, given the complexities of legal basis and remedy within each system and differences in understanding of a number of the apparently similar concepts used.

(i) *The significance of the seller's business*

While in both English and French law the business status of a seller justifies an increased responsibility, its understanding and its significance differ.

The French understanding of *vendeur professionnel* is relatively narrow, referring either to a seller whose business is to sell the general type of property sold in the relevant transaction or who otherwise possesses a special skill or expertise in relation to the type of property sold,[286] whereas the English understanding of a seller 'acting in the course of a business' is broader, applying to *any* sale made as part of the seller's business, whether regular or not.[287]

The primary significance of being a *vendeur professionnel* is that it justifies the imposition of liability in damages under the *garantie légale*,[288] whereas other sellers (including those businesses who sell things outside their regular trade) may be liable in damages on this basis only if they were aware of the defect on sale.[289] A similar pattern is found as regards pre-contractual liability, any seller being liable in damages for knowingly misinforming or failing to inform the buyer of a significant aspect of the property sold (*dol*), but *vendeurs professionnels* also being liable under the law of *obligations*

---

[281] Limitation Act 1980, s. 5 (unless the contract is contained in a deed, when the period is 12 years: Limitation Act 1980, s. 8). It is to be noted that there can be no extension of time under the Latent Damage Act 1976, creating Limitation Act 1980, s. 14A as claims for breach of the implied terms are not claims for negligence.   [282] *Battley v Faulkner* (1820) 3 B & Ald 288.

[283] Limitation Act 1980, s. 11. Cf. below, p. 528 as to liability under Part I of the Consumer Protection Act 1987.

[284] Limitation Act 1980, ss.11 and 14. Claims under the Fatal Accidents Act 1976 must be brought within three years from the date of death or the date of knowledge of the person for whose benefit the action is brought, whichever is the later: Limitation Act 1980, ss. 12, 13 and 14.   [285] Above, pp. 252–3.

[286] Above, p. 85.   [287] Above, p. 236.

[288] Above, p. 84. For its effect on exemption clauses, see above, p. 94 below, p. 262.

[289] Above, p. 84.

d'information.[290] Moreover, while liability for 'contractual non-conformity' can in principle apply to *all* sellers of goods given that its legal basis is the express or implied agreement of the parties, French courts do not appear to use this 'general law' to impose liability in damages for failures in general quality of the goods on *non-professionnels.*[291]

In English law, sale in the course of business is a condition of the existence of any remedy under the statutory implied terms of quality and fitness for purpose, whether rejection of the goods, restitution or damages.[292] Its broad understanding of 'the course of business' is therefore of considerable importance, as it leaves aside from their protection only sales by private individuals, which can give rise to liability only under the law of sale by description,[293] under an express contractual warranty[294] or under the law of misrepresentation.[295] All these bases of liability have in common a prerequisite that the seller has to have *said* something before liability will be imposed: in principle, a knowing silence is not enough to ground liability.[296] On the other hand, the breadth of application of the statutory implied terms of quality and fitness for purpose and the expansion of the ambit of remedies for misrepresentation in English law have reduced the need to expand either the law or the practice of *express* warranty for commercial and consumer sales.

(ii) Buyer's right of rejection and the hierarchies of remedies

For the most part English law treats a buyer's right to reject the goods and to repudiate the contract to the same regime.[297] In contrast to the position in French law apart from commercial sales, the English right of repudiation requires no judicial authority.[298] For English law, the right is central to the system of remedies available for breach of the statutory implied terms and so, while it has been subject to a test of reasonable exercise in the case of commercial buyers,[299] its free exercise for other buyers has been retained despite the risk of unfair prejudice to sellers.[300] In principle, a buyer is entitled to end his dealings with the failing seller and go elsewhere and he does not have to mitigate by accepting his own seller's offer of repair or replacement of the goods. Even more, the availability and exercise of the right of repudiation has an impact on the measure of damages: where the goods are rejected, English law's general assumption is that the buyer will buy a reasonable substitute in the market and either claim back his money by way of restitution or damages for his lost bargain; where goods are retained, the buyer will usually recover either the difference in value between the goods as they are and as they should have been or the cost of remedial action, subject to a criterion of reasonableness.[301]

However, while potent, the buyer's right of repudiation is short-lived. Under the law of 'acceptance of the goods,' a buyer may lose his right of repudiation of the contract after acceptance of *delivery* of the goods, by 'intimating' to the seller that he has accepted them, by using them in a way inconsistent with the seller's ownership or after a 'reasonable lapse of time', even if he did not know of the goods' inadequacy at the

---

[290] Above, pp. 64, 65–7. (though on occasion an *obligation d'information* has been imposed on a *non-professionnel*).   [291] Above, pp. 70–2, 85.

[292] 1979 Act s. 14(2) and (3), above, pp. 236, 239.   [293] Above, p. 234.

[294] Above, pp. 233–4.   [295] Above, p. 230.   [296] Above, p. 230.

[297] Cf. above, p. 251 n. 225.   [298] Above, p. 82.   [299] Above, p. 253.

[300] Above, pp. 253–4.   [301] Above, p. 255.

relevant time.[302] While a reasonable time will depend on the nature of the goods in question, and any other relevant circumstance (so, for example, time spent in discussions of possible repairs will not be included), it is to be measured in days or weeks, rather than months.[303] On the other hand, none of these restrictive rules on 'acceptance' affect the seller's liability in damages: these rules are aimed at securing the finality of transactions, leaving open the possibility of a subsequent financial adjustment via damages.

By comparison with repudiation for breach of the statutory implied terms, rescission for misrepresentation also provides a general right for a buyer to escape the contract, return the property and gain restitution of the price, but a misrepresentee will not lose his right to rescission by affirmation without knowing of it and the delay within which this time must be exercised is rather longer. On the other hand, while a right to rescind for *innocent* misrepresentation is subject to a general discretion in the court where rescission would be inequitable,[304] a right to reject the goods for breach of condition is subject to a test of reasonableness only in the case of commercial buyers.[305]

There are also a number of differences between the remedies for breach of the statutory implied terms and for breach of any express term governing the quality or fitness for purpose of the goods. In principle, if the parties have made clear that breach of such an express term should give rise to a right to terminate the contract, this stipulation will be given effect:[306] there is no formal discretion in the court to refuse rescission for breach nor does the buyer lose the right after a 'reasonable time', though he can do so after knowledge of the right by renunciation.[307] On the other hand, where the parties have not made clear whether or not the breach is intended to give rise to a right to rescind, the courts determine its availability according to whether the breach has substantially deprived the buyer of the benefit of the contract.[308]

The French law differs here in a number of respects. First, it distinguishes more sharply between the right of a buyer to reject the goods on delivery on the ground of their lack of conformity and to terminate the contract after receipt of the goods, return them and claim back the price.[309] In French law, rejection of the goods on delivery must be on the ground of 'contractual non-conformity' since any 'defect' must be patent so as to give a buyer a reason for their rejection,[310] but it is not clear that a *non-commercial* buyer is entitled to reject the goods without first asking the court to 'dissolve' the contract.[311] Here, as elsewhere, French law seeks to maintain the contract in the interest of protecting the right of a debtor (the seller) to perform.[312] This looks very restrictive next to the English position, but it should be recalled that the buyer has the right in French law to require the delivery of conforming goods from the seller and so, on receipt of non-conforming goods, may demand their exchange, if necessary by action and court order: the creditor (the buyer) has a right to performance.

The French approach appears rather less restrictive than the English to termination of the contract on the ground of (latent) defects in the goods after they have been delivered, providing the *action rédhibitoire* of the *garantie légale*[313] for all categories of

---

[302] Above, p. 253.   [303] Above, p. 253.   [304] Misrepresentation Act 1967, s. 2(2).

[305] Above, p. 253.   [306] Above, p. 233.   [307] Above, p. 252.   [308] Above, p. 233.

[309] Above, pp. 81–4.   [310] Above, p. 81.   [311] Above, pp. 81–2.   [312] Above, p. 80.

[313] Above, pp. 82–3. A buyer has sometimes 'resolved' the contract on the ground of the goods' 'contractual non-conformity' even after their delivery: ibid.

buyer and all types of seller.[314] While until February 2005 in French law a buyer used to lose this right to terminate the contract after expiry of a *bref délai*,[315] in English law a buyer is likely to do so by 'accepting' the goods, which can be deemed to have occurred after a fairly short ('reasonable') period after their delivery.[316]

Overall, however, English and French law have adopted very different policies in relation to the buyer's remedies in respect of deficiencies in the goods, reflecting wider differences in relation to the relative interests of the parties on non-performance. In general, English law gives the buyer faced with breach of one of the statutory implied terms a free choice whether to repudiate the contract or claim damages, but no right to claim repair or replacement of the goods by the seller; if the buyer wishes to obtain a substitute performance, he need not and has no right to look to the seller, but must instead seek the substitute elsewhere, whether by replacement or repair. And if he does not terminate the contract, his remedy in damages *may* be limited to the difference in value of the goods as delivered and as they should have been.[317] If there is a hierarchy of remedies in respect of breach of the seller's obligations, it is rejection of the goods first; damages second, with specific enforcement not featuring.

By contrast, French law, before the implementation of the Consumer Guarantees Directive, possesses *two* patterns of remedies, one under the 'general law', and in particular on the ground of 'contractual non-conformity', and one under the *garantie légale*. So, where a buyer claims that goods delivered fail to conform to the contract under the 'general law', in principle, he can claim delivery of a substitute: the buyer has the right to proper performance and the seller has a right to perform. Termination of the contract, with the concomitant loss of the seller's right to perform and gain the price, must be sought from a court and may be refused;[318] similarly, non-commercial buyers must seek judicial authorisation before they can obtain a substitute for the goods elsewhere.[319] Otherwise, damages may be recovered in French law (subject to the conditions already set out) and are important for the recovery of consequential losses.[320] Here, the traditional concern of French law to maintain performance of contractual obligations can be seen, termination and damages being seen as distinctly second-best for *both* parties.

By contrast, the *garantie légale* places termination of the contract (by the *action rédhibitoire*) at the forefront of its analysis and makes it generally available, supplemented by the more modest *action aestimatoire* which one can see as a partial rescission.[321] Of course, damages are important, especially for consequential damage, but they remain less widely available than termination. Under the *garantie légale*, therefore, the French hierarchy of remedy is much more like the English, the seller risking losing the contract for a short time after delivery of property with latent defects.

4. Contractual Exclusion of Liability

At common law a contract term which on its construction purports to exclude liability for breach of contract or in tort is effective, with the exception of liability

---

[314] Above, p. 82.   [315] Above, pp. 91–3, 583 where the reform to this period is noted.
[316] Above, p. 253.   [317] Above, pp. 255–6.   [318] Above, pp. 82–3.
[319] Above, p. 80.   [320] Above, pp. 84–6.   [321] Above, p. 82.

for fraud.[322] This general position applied fully to the liability of sellers to buyers, whether on the basis of breach of an express warranty, breach of one of the statutory implied terms[323] or under the law of innocent misrepresentation.[324] However, this position was radically changed in 1977 for sellers acting 'in the course of a business' as regards claims for breach of contract and for all sellers as regards liability for misrepresentation.[325] While this English statutory control of exemption clauses was supplemented in 1994 on implementation of the Unfair Terms in Consumer Contracts Directive 1993,[326] little has changed as regards the effectiveness between the parties of exemption clauses in contracts of sale of goods.[327]

First, a contract term which purports to exclude or restrict any remedy for breach of an *express* warranty as to the quality of goods will be subject to control only where (i) the seller makes the contract in the course of his business and (ii) the term is contained in the seller's written standard terms *or* is relied on as against someone 'dealing as consumer'.[328] Where these conditions are fulfilled, the contract term is subject to a test of 'reasonableness', i.e. that it was 'a fair and reasonable [term] to be included having regard to the circumstances which were, or ought reasonably to have been, known to or in the contemplation of the parties when the contract was made'.[329] The courts have developed a number of factors to be taken into account in determining the issue of reasonableness, adopting where appropriate those specifically provided by the Act for the exclusion of liability under the statutory implied terms in contracts of sale of goods.[330] The 1977 Act provides that the burden of proof as to the issue of reasonableness rests on the seller for this purpose.[331] On the other hand, where an express warranty is made other than in the course of the seller's business, and neither in the other's written standard terms or as against a buyer dealing as consumer, any exemption clause is in principle valid.

Secondly, a contract term which purports to exclude or restrict any remedy under the law of misrepresentation, whether for rescission or damages, is also subject to a test of reasonableness, the burden of proof again being on the seller as to this issue.[332] Here, this control is not limited to sale in the course of a business, to sales made on standard terms or with those 'dealing as consumers'.

---

[322] *Nicholson v Willan* (1804) 5 East 507 (the general rule); *S. Pearson & Son Ltd. v Dublin Corporation* [1907] AC 351; *HIH Casualty & General Insurance Ltd. v Chase Manhattan Bank* [2003] UKHL 6; [2003] 1 All ER (Comm) 349 (fraud). The courts for long used the construction of exemption clauses *contra proferentem* as a limited technique for their control, but this has become less necessary and appropriate since the enactment of the 1977 Act.

[323] Sale of Goods Act 1893, s. 55; Sale of Goods Act 1979, s. 55(1) stating the general position.

[324] *Boyd and Forrest v Glasgow Rly.* 1915 SC (HL) 20, 36.   [325] 1977 Act, ss. 3, 6 and 8.

[326] Dir. 93/13/EEC on unfair terms in consumer contracts.

[327] The EC directive was implemented in English law by the Unfair Terms in Consumer Contracts Regulations 1994 SI No. 3159, revoked and replaced by the Unfair Terms in Consumer Contracts Regulations 1999 SI No. 2083. Their limited impact in the context of sale of goods results from the usually wider definition of protected buyer in the 1977 Act as opposed to the 1999 Regulations ('dealing as consumer' rather than 'consumer') and the complete ban imposed by the Act as opposed to the 'test of fairness' put in place by the Regulations.

[328] 1977 Act, s. 1(3); s. 3. On 'dealing as consumer,' see above, n. 247.   [329] 1977 Act, s. 11(1).

[330] 1977 Act, s.11(2) and Sch. 2.   [331] 1977 Act, s. 11(5).

[332] Misrepresentation Act 1967 s. 3, as substituted by the 1977 Act, s. 8. A similar test of control applies to liability under *Hedley Byrne* at common law: 1977 Act, s. 2(2).

Thirdly, and perhaps most importantly, a contract term which purports to exclude or restrict any right or remedy[333] arising for breach of the statutory implied terms as to the description, quality or fitness for purpose of the goods in a person selling in the course of business[334] will be totally ineffective as against a buyer who 'deals as consumer'[335] and subject to a test of reasonableness as against other buyers,[336] given a number of specified considerations and factors, including (where relevant) the relative strength of the bargaining positions of the parties, any inducement given to accept a term, the extent to which the party knew or ought reasonably to have known of the term, the practicability of compliance with any condition whose non-compliance excludes or restricts liability and whether the goods were manufactured, processed or adapted to the special order of the customer.[337]

In determining the effectiveness of clauses purporting to exclude a seller's liability for defects French law, like English law, distinguishes between sellers and buyers in business and those who are not. But as I explained in the context of the ambit of liability in damages,[338] the notion of *vendeur professionnel* requires that any contract is of a type regular in the business, while the English selling 'in the course of a business' does not;[339] and 'dealing as consumer' under the English legislation is broader than '*consommateur ou non-professionnel*' under the French.[340]

All this means that, first, in the case of a sale of goods which forms a regular part of the seller's business (for example, a retailer) to a person who buys other than as any part of their business (a consumer in a narrower sense), in both French and English law any exclusion of liability for failures in quality, safety or fitness for purpose is absolutely forbidden, without the need for any argument as to the fairness or reasonableness of the contract term in question.[341]

---

[333] The varieties of exemption clause for this purpose are set out broadly in the 1977 Act, s. 12.

[334] A very broad view has been taken of this phrase in the context of the 1979 Act, s. 14 so as to extend the incidence of its statutory implied terms, excluding only 'purely private sales' (above, pp. 236–7), but for the purposes of the 1977 Act , s. 12, a narrower view requiring a degree of regularity in making contracts of the type in question has been taken so as to extend the Act's stricter controls to a wider category of contractor: *R. & B. Customs Brokers Co. Ltd. v United Dominions Trust Ltd.* [1988] 1 WLR 321). It is submitted that the broader view is right for s. 1(3) of the 1977 Act as this applies the same test to the incidence of the statutory implied terms and to controls on their exclusion and this reflects the legislative history, for the 1977 Act replaced earlier provisions which simply provided that the statutory implied terms could not be excluded against a consumer or against others unless reasonable: Supply of Goods (Implied Terms) Act 1973, s. 4, new 1979 Act , s. 55(4).   [335] Above, n. 247.

[336] 1977 Act , s. 6(2) (those 'dealing as consumer' within the meaning of s. 12); s. 6(3) (others). *After* implementation of the Consumer Guarantees Directive, an individual (as opposed to a company) does not 'deal as consumer' for these purposes if the goods are second-hand and sold at a public auction at which individuals have the opportunity of attending in person: 1977 Act, s. 12(2)(a), below, p. 588. Such a person may prefer to rely on the test of unfairness of terms contained in the Unfair Terms in Consumer Contracts Regulations 1999, SI No. 2083 rather than the test of reasonableness contained in the 1977 Act , s. 11. On the differences between these two tests of control, see *Chitty on Contracts*, 15-068.

[337] 1977 Act , s. 11 and Sch. 2. The burden of proof is on a person claiming the reasonableness of a term: ibid., s. 11(5). The courts have added other factors: *Benjamin* § 13-083.   [338] Above, p. 85.

[339] Above, pp. 236–7.   [340] Above, pp. 94, 253.

[341] In French law, this falls within the ban in Déc. 78-465 of 24 Mar. 1978, art. 2; in English law, this would be sale in the course of a business to someone 'dealing as consumer' within the 1977 Act , s. 6(2) (implied terms). An exception is found as regards the exclusion of liability under an express term, where the test is one of reasonableness: s. 3(2).

Secondly, though, the English statutory controls on exemption clauses apply to sales of goods made by a person acting 'in the course of a business' where in the same circumstances in French law the sale would not be made by a *vendeur professionnel* and so any exemption clause would be valid except for *dol* (in the case of pre-contractual liability), actual knowledge of the defect (as regards liability under the *garantie légale*) or *dol* or *faute lourde* (as regards liability for 'contractual non-conformity').[342] Moreover, a buyer may in English law 'deal as consumer' when in the circumstances he would not count as '*consommateur ou non-professionnel*' in French law, as the English phrase includes business buyers of goods of a type which do not form a regular part of the business.[343]

Thirdly, French and English law both possess controls on the effectiveness of exemption clauses governing a business seller's liability for defects or failures in quality to business buyers, but the ambit and pattern of their controls differs significantly. The French law takes a categorical approach here, distinguishing different types of buyers, different legal bases of liability and different types of conduct by the seller.[344] So, for example, a *vendeur professionnel* may not exclude liability under the *garantie légale* unless he does not know of the defect *and* the buyer is in business 'of the same speciality' as the seller, a notion which has been interpreted narrowly by French courts,[345] but he may exclude liability for 'contractual non-conformity' in the absence of deliberate non-performance (*inexécution dolosive*) or *faute lourde*.[346] By contrast, English law subjects all clauses excluding liability for breach of the statutory implied terms or for breach of express terms to a single test of reasonableness as against those 'not dealing as consumers'.[347] There are no distinct situations where such a clause is upheld or invalidated, but rather a flexible standard which allows a court to take into account some of the sorts of consideration which lie behind the French distinctions (for example, the 'same speciality' of the parties may be thought relevant to their relative bargaining power). But the focus of the English test of control is the reasonableness of the inclusion of the exclusion clause in the contract at the time,[348] whereas the focus of the French invalidating rules is the wrongfulness of the seller's behaviour, reflecting its more 'moralising' approach to non-performance. So, in striking contrast to French law's treatment of *inexécution dolosive*, English law specifically provides that 'it is immaterial for any purpose of [the statutory controls] whether the breach was inadvertent or intentional'.[349] The French law's concern is with the standard of behaviour of the parties in performance, which is capable of being seen as part of its wider concern with contractual good faith;[350] the English concern is with the reasonableness of the term itself, rather than the reasonableness of any behaviour under the contract.[351]

---

[342] Above, p. 94.   [343] Above, pp. 236–7.   [344] Above, p. 95.   [345] Ibid.
[346] Ibid.   [347] Above, p. 262.
[348] 1977 Act, s. 11(1), the question being whether 'the term shall have been a fair and reasonable one to be included having regard to the circumstances which were, or ought reasonably to have been, known to or in the contemplation of the parties when the contract was made'.   [349] 1977 Act, s. 1(4).
[350] Art. 1134 al. 3 C.civ.
[351] In this respect, there was a change from a test of 'reasonable reliance' on an exemption clause found in the Supply of Goods (Implied Terms) Act 1973, s. 4, creating new Sale of Goods Act 1893, s. 55(4) to the present test found in the 1977 Act, s. 11(1).

5. Seller's Liability beyond Privity and Indemnity Actions

In general, English courts have not allowed the development of true exceptions to privity of contract, the effectiveness of contracts for the benefit of third parties coming only in 1999 by statutory intervention.[352] At one level, this may be seen as no more than a reflection of the extraordinary strictness with which English courts have interpreted its principle of privity of contract, but it is noticeable that liability for failures of quality or performance has not really attracted any of the circumventions of privity visible in other contexts, notably, the courts not allowing 'transmissible warranties' in the law of sale of goods.[353] This means that in general a buyer can sue only his own seller in respect of the failures in quality or fitness for purpose of goods and this has the secondary consequence that those further up the chain of distribution, such as importers or manufacturers will be liable on this ground only if their own buyer has been held liable.

On the other hand, there is a very widespread practice of manufacturers giving express 'guarantees' of their products for the benefit of their purchasers, especially but not exclusively where these are consumers.[354] For long, a main purpose of these guarantees was actually to *reduce* the manufacturer's liability under the general law of the tort of negligence, but this practice was rendered ineffective in 1977.[355] Now, these guarantees function as one among many selling points of the goods in question and their purpose is to increase the rights of the purchaser of goods, usually by allowing him to require their replacement or repair on the grounds of their defect (often termed 'fault') within a set period: typically, though, the guarantees do not create any liability in damages for any other losses caused by the defectiveness of the goods.[356] While a one-year manufacturer's guarantee is fairly standard, two-year, five-year or even 'life-time' guarantees are sometimes offered. It is often the case that while the guarantee is expressed as being made by the manufacturer, the latter entrusts the actual work of dealing with claims and even the putting into effect of repairs to retailers.[357] While at common law there are technical problems with the legal validity of these guarantees, there is no reported case of a manufacturer refusing to act under them on this basis (or indeed more generally)[358] and

---

[352] Contracts (Rights for Third Parties) Act 1999 and see Law Commission, *Privity of Contract: Contracts for the Benefit of Third Parties*, Law Com. no. 242 (1996), above, pp. 158–9.

[353] The absence of any 'transmissible warranty of quality' was noted by Lord Keith of Kinkel in arguing against the imposition of a duty of care in the tort of negligence with a similar effect in *Murphy v Brentwood DC* [1991] AC 398, 469. The idea of rights running with property has been used in the context of covenants concerning land: for a summary of the position, see Law Commission, *Privity of Contract: Contracts for the Benefit of Third Parties*, Law Com no. 242 (1996), §§ 2.10–2.12. Occasionally English courts have found a 'collateral contract' between parties beyond ordinary privity of contract so as to impose liability in a manufacturer directly where the manufacturer has made a direct representation to the buyer: *Shanklin Pier Ltd. v Detel Products Ltd.* [1951] 2 KB 854. The courts have not used the tort of negligence to avoid privity in this context: above, p. 184.

[354] See generally, C. Twigg-Flesner, *Consumer Product Guarantees* (Ashgate, Aldershot, 2003).

[355] 1977 Act, s. 5.   [356] Twigg-Flesner, *op. cit.* n. 354 Chap. 2.

[357] C. Twigg-Flesner, 'Network Liability for Manufacturer's Guarantees—Remedying Legislative Shortcomings with a Legal Jigsaw' [1999] JBL 568.

[358] At common law, a manufacturer's guarantee could be effective if agreed *after* the sub-purchaser completes the purchase only if he incurs some detriment, but the main example of this (the surrender of other rights against the manufacturer) may fall foul of the invalidity of any such surrender by way of the application of the 1977 Act, s. 5.

their validity as regards 'consumers' is ensured after implementation of the Consumer Guarantees Directive.[359]

Given the general denial of liability in sellers beyond privity, any channelling of liability towards the business responsible for the failure in the quality of the goods must take place by suit up the chain, each intermediate contractor claiming damages so as to be indemnified in respect of the liability which he has incurred.[360] This does not require separate litigation as the defendant sellers can bring in their own seller by what used to be termed 'third party proceedings' and are now an example of 'Part 20 Claims'.[361] Any channelling of liability will be frustrated by a break in the chain of litigation and this may happen for a number of reasons, some legal and some practical. The main practical reason is where an intermediate contractor becomes insolvent, but legal obstacles to the channelling of liability are more varied.[362] So, some claims for an indemnity by an intermediate contractor may fail on the ground that no breach of the statutory implied terms can be shown. For English law does not focus on the existence of a defect in the goods traceable to its source (typically being the manufacturer), but instead looks to sets of factors concerning the goods in relation to the particular contract under which they are supplied,[363] in particular, any description of the goods, their price and their general or particular purpose made known to the seller. Even if an intermediate seller can establish a breach of contract, he will also need to show that his indemnity loss was both caused by this breach (rather than by his own actions) and was not too remote.[364] Suit up the chain may also become impossible owing to the effectiveness of an exemption clause in one of the contracts: for while exclusion of liability by a retailer will not be effective against a buyer who 'deals as a consumer', it may be effective when relied upon by a distributor, importer or manufacturer against another intervening business contractor (who would not usually be dealing as consumer) if 'reasonable', this last condition being assessed by reference to criteria applicable to each individual contract.[365] Finally, any claim for an indemnity by an intermediate seller on the ground of breach of the statutory implied terms may be time-barred, since the applicable limitation period of six years starts running from the time of breach of the contract (here, the delivery of non-conforming goods by the relevant seller) so that the longer the chain of distribution, the more likely it will be that this period will have expired before any claim for an indemnity by an intermediate contractor is made.

The pattern here is, therefore, radically different from that which is found in relation to French law.[366] There a sub-purchaser (whether the ultimate purchaser or an intermediate contractor) may claim against a manufacturer or *any* other member of the chain of distribution of goods by way of *action directe* either under the *garantie légale* or on the basis of their 'contractual non-conformity', whatever the solvency or otherwise of any intervening contractor. Such an *action directe* is said to be brought on

---

[359] Below, pp. 624–5.

[360] E.g. *Mowbray v Merryweather* [1895] 2 QB 640 (claim by an employer in respect of liability to his employee for negligence); *Lambert v Lewis* [1982] AC 225 (owner of vehicle claims indemnity from retailer, who in turn claims indemnity from manufacturer).

[361] CPR 20.6. E.g. *Lambert v Lewis, cit.*; *Muirhead v Industrial Tank Specialities Ltd.* [1986] QB 507.

[362] Bridge, *Sale of Goods*, 371–2.   [363] Above, pp. 237–8, 240.

[364] Above, pp. 249–50, 256.   [365] Above, p. 262.   [366] Above, pp. 95–8.

the basis (or bases) of the contractual rights of which *that person's buyer* held against the seller (or sellers) whom a buyer chooses to sue and so is contingent on proof of the existence of a defect at the time of delivery by the member of the chain sued, but this would appear to cause no particular difficulty where the goods suffer from problems of design or manufacture.[367] Given this background of the imposition of liability directly on manufacturers and distributors towards sub-purchasers through the ordinary law of sale and given the consensualist nature of French contract, it is not surprising that manufacturers' express guarantees are readily viewed as enforceable. While they are certainly prevalent in French practice, their function is merely to supplement the existing legal liabilities rather than (as in English law) to form the sole basis of liability.[368]

In my view, though, when contrasted with the English strict adherence to privity of contract, the importance of *actions directe en garantie* in forming the legal basis for recourse actions by intermediate contractors becomes clear. Apart from avoiding intervening insolvency, any claim for an indemnity by *action directe* under the *garantie légale* could be brought within a *bref délai* of the time when the individual claimant has himself been sued,[369] whereas in the English context an intermediate contractor is much more at risk of being out of time.[370]

---

[367] Above, p. 97.   [368] Above, p. 98.
[369] Above, p. 92. On reform of the *bref délai* see below, p. 583.   [370] Above, p. 265.

11

The English Law Governing Public Services, Private Services and Liability for Products

In looking at the way in which French law has governed liability for products used or supplied in the course of the provision of public services, I distinguished three senses in which the expression 'public services' may be used: services may be public in terms of their general availability; the institutional nature of their provider; or the legal nature of the regime by which they are governed.[1] I explained the way in which French law divides the provision of public services understood in any of these senses and how this affects the legal nature of liability in the provider of the service. In this respect, two key features emerged. The first was that French administrative law has developed a notion of *service public* in a technical legal sense to describe those services which involve public bodies (either directly or indirectly) and which are provided in the public interest and it has used this notion as the general touchstone of its jurisdictional and substantive division between administrative and private law. Secondly, however, the designation of a service as a *service public* does not necessarily remit all aspects of its provision to regulation by administrative law. So, while all *services publics* must respect a set of administrative legal principles, the *lois de Rolland*, the institutional governance of their provider follows the legal form in which it is cast, whether this belongs to public or private law.[2] Moreover, French courts determine the legal basis of liability in a provider of a *service public* to its recipient by distinguishing within *services publics* between 'administrative' services (where the relationship is governed by administrative principle) and 'industrial or commercial' services (where the relationship is governed by private law and normally by contract law).[3] I then looked at the working out of this distinction in the context of the liability of three public services (in a broad sense) where the supply or use of products is important: the supply of utilities, transport services and health care.

In turning to English law, I find it relatively straightforward to describe and compare the treatment of issues of liability in the provider of these same particular public services, but more difficult to describe its general approach. We can certainly see the existence of public services in each of the first two senses which I have identified as much in the English as in the French context. Clearly many services are public in the sense that they are offered to the public generally and, indeed, the common law itself treated distinctly certain types of public provision in this sense, as 'common' or

---

[1] Above, pp. 132–3.   [2] Above, p. 133.   [3] Above, pp. 134–6.

'public carriers' and innkeepers bore specially strict liabilities as regards their custodial duties;[4] and in the modern law the provision of goods or services to the public or a section of the public brings particular responsibilities, for example, duties of non-discrimination on the grounds of race, nationality or ethnic group.[5] So too, in the UK there has been a very considerable involvement of public bodies in the provision of all sorts of services, ranging from those which look peculiarly public (such as judicial and prison services) to those which do not (such as transport or health care). In the UK, too, there have been many changes in the mechanisms by which public bodies (whether the State, local authorities, special statutory bodies, public corporations or 'Next Step Agencies') are involved in the provision of public services and themselves then involve private sector bodies, their variety and the nature of their involvement changing with political and economic fashion.[6] So, some services are provided by organs of central government (as in civil and criminal justice), some by public 'agencies' or corporations of various types and some by private sector companies under 'contracting-out' arrangements.[7] As with France, both public and private sector involvement can be seen in the provision of utilities, transport and health over the last century or so in England.

Apart from what I have already mentioned, we also see in the English context as in the French very considerable regulation in the public interest of the provision of services in either of the first two senses, the law using a variety of techniques, some direct (as in the regulation of the consequences of contracts by common law or statute) and some less direct (as in the regulation of the way in which the provider of a service does business, for example, in the regulation of financial services by the Financial Services Authority).[8] This regulation in the public interest can affect services provided to the public whether they belong to the 'private sector' or 'public sector' of the economy. However, what we do not see in the English context is any overarching use of the notion of 'public service' by the law itself of the sort seen in French law's *service public*: in English law the designation of a service as 'public' does not itself have any distinct set of legal consequences. This is all the more striking in contrast to the centrality of reform of public services in many government initiatives, whether this is sought in improved efficiency in their provision by public bodies, in encouraging various types of 'public/private partnerships' or in their 'contracting-out' to the private sector.[9] How should we account for this absence of legal significance to the public service when this notion is clearly of immense administrative and political importance?

First, there is no jurisdictional division in English law between private and public law courts of the sort which exists in France and therefore no need to establish a criterion for the distribution of cases between the two. Even though English courts do have to distinguish between the public and private for the purposes of the availability of judicial review, here they are concerned only with this one aspect of public law, where

---

[4] As to common carriers, see below, pp. 281–2. As to innkeepers, see *Lane v Cotton* (1702) 1 Salk 17, 18.

[5] Race Relations Act 1976 s 20 (no discrimination on the grounds of race, nationality or ethnic group in respect of the provision of goods or services to the public or a section of the public).

[6] Craig, *Administrative Law*, Chap. 4.   [7] Ibid.

[8] This is now governed by the Financial Services and Markets Act 2000.

[9] Craig, *Administrative Law*, 138–41.

the lawfulness of an enactment, decision, action or failure to act in the exercise of a public function is raised.[10] As a result, the way in which the distinction is drawn is shaped by the differences in the procedures (notably, the requirement of judicial permission in proceedings for judicial review) and by reference to concepts other than a general notion of a 'public service'. To this extent, therefore, there has been no need for a general legal notion of the public service.

Secondly, in terms of substantive law, the fundamental *starting point* of English law has remained that the 'ordinary law' (notably, relating to contract, tort and property) applies to all persons equally: Dicey's view of the rule of law is a powerful intellectual legacy, even if it is one which some try to renounce![11] This does not mean, of course, that there are no distinctive English administrative laws (there clearly are), but rather that these are still seen as special areas of regulation to be justified by the nature of the powers exercised (and controlled) or by other particular considerations, qualifying the general position set out at common law. In this respect, modern English administrative law grew around the doctrine of *ultra vires*, which in its modern form sought to control the exercise of *statutory* powers given by Parliament to bodies (whether institutionally public or private) and applied less comfortably to the exercise of the other specifically public source of power, the prerogative.[12] Here, there are two senses in which these controls are special: first, on the ground that they relate to the control of powers whose legal source (statute) has long been seen as an exception, an 'intervention' in the general picture of the common law[13] and, secondly, on the ground that each judicial assessment of the exercise of statutory powers starts with a careful analysis of their particular ambit. On the other hand, from this somewhat unpromising start, English courts have developed a recognisably distinct and general body of grounds of judicial review, true principles of administrative legality. And having done so, the appropriateness of their justification in terms of the doctrine of *ultra vires* has increasingly been questioned.[14]

From this perspective, therefore, while English law has developed a genuinely distinctive administrative law, its ambit is determined not by any overarching notion (such as in the French *service public*) but rather on more particular criteria, which can differ from context to context; so, for example, English law may take different views of the notion of a 'public authority' for the purposes of the Human Rights Act 1998 and for judicial review more generally.[15] And the English law governing the constitutions and powers of public bodies other than the State itself is complex and diverse, being sometimes the creature of particular statute and sometimes administrative arrangement or 'agreement'.[16] Moreover, in my view, the way in which its administrative law has arisen means that English law's sense of a distinctive *private* law remains rather hazy, since for most purposes it does not matter whether or not a case is designated as 'private', except in the negative sense of being non-public: it is not that there is

---

[10] CPR Part 54.2; Craig, *Administrative Law*, Chap. 23. [11] Above, pp. 166–7.

[12] Craig, *Administrative Law*, 5–9, 15–16.

[13] Nicholas in Harris and Tallon, Chap. 4, 'The Pre-contractual Obligation to Disclose Information, English Report', 178 and see below, pp. 336–7. [14] Craig, *Administrative Law*, 12–20.

[15] This is suggested by the Human Rights Act 1998, s. 6 which has its own definition of 'public authority' for these purposes. [16] Craig, *Administrative Law*, 93–5.

something distinctively private about the law itself, as this remains the general, 'ordinary' law. This fundamental way of thinking is reflected in the way in which most English textbooks on contract law are presented: they describe the law applicable to contracts generally, possibly including some discussion as to the special features involved for contracts made by public bodies, but often leaving this to works on administrative law. For most English lawyers, there is at most a distinct category of public contracts, rather than a distinct category of public contract law.

The consequence of this for our present purposes is that the liability of the suppliers of public services in respect of their use or supply of products is governed by the ordinary law of contract and of tort, rather than by any specifically public regimes of liability such as we have seen in French law, though with notable exceptions where there is some particular statutory ground to qualify this treatment. This means that the law itself is not divided between the public and private, but paradoxically it does not mean that the ordinary law applies identically in the public and private spheres. So, I shall explain how English courts have sometimes developed special treatments within the 'ordinary' framework to govern the liability of the public providers of services[17] and sometimes how the same 'ordinary framework' applies differently where the provision is private rather than public.[18] Moreover, in some contexts, English courts have held that the statutory (and I would add public) nature of the relationship between the provider and recipient of a service is inconsistent with the existence of a contract, thereby leaving the provider's liability to be based on tort. This reclassification of liability makes an important difference as regards a provider's liability in respect of the supply of a product, for here contractual liability is strict, whereas liability in tort would require proof of negligence: in this way, therefore, liability for the public supply of products to their recipients may be less onerous than for their private supply. Finally, where a public body is exclusively responsible for the manufacture and supply of a particular product, the basis of its liability comes close to the situation where a public body exercises powers of control of the safety of products which I shall discuss in Chapter 13.[19]

In the following discussion, therefore, I shall start by looking briefly at the way in which the ordinary law governs liability in respect of the provision of services and how this compares to French *private* law, and then how this has been applied in the context of the supply of public utilities, transport services and health care.

1. Services and Products under the 'Ordinary Law'

The general law governing liability in respect of the supply of services can be simplified to four fundamental propositions. First, where a supplier acts under a contract, liability to the other party may either be based on the contract or in the tort of negligence, but liability to third parties will only be in tort and notably the tort of negligence, unless the parties contracted for the third parties' benefit.[20] Secondly, in the absence of

---

[17] Below, p. 289.   [18] Below, pp. 284–5.   [19] Below, pp. 295–9.
[20] This final qualification results from the Contracts (Rights of Third Parties) Act 1999.

express provision in the contract, a supplier's contractual obligation in respect of the quality or safety of the services provided is merely to take reasonable care, *unless* it relates to goods supplied under the contract, where it becomes an obligation that the goods are of satisfactory quality and reasonably fit for their purpose analogously to sale of goods.[21] This remains true whether the contract counts as a 'contract for services' in a technical sense or more loosely, as in the case of hire of goods.[22] Thirdly, while at common law suppliers of services could limit or exclude their liabilities for death, personal injury, physical damage or economic loss, whether or not caused by negligence and whether to the other party to any contract or to third parties, this power has been severely limited by legislation in the last quarter of the last century, in particular protecting very strongly those who suffer personal injury or death by negligence or who deal as consumers.[23] Fourthly, however, some services provided in relation to land are different. This can be seen both as regards liability arising from the hire of land (termed in English law contracts of tenancy or leases) and from the provision of buildings on land.

(a) Liability in respect of the supply of goods and services

I described earlier how English courts in the course of the nineteenth century developed implied terms relating to the quality of the goods in contracts of sale, how these were first set in legislative form and how this legislative form has evolved in the course of the second half of the last century.[24] By contrast, until 1982 the implication of terms relating to the quality of goods or services to be implied in other contracts was left to the courts, which they readily undertook despite the restrictive tenor of the general tests for the implication of terms which required them to be 'necessary' and not merely reasonable.[25] However, the courts were faced with an important choice as regards the content of the terms which they implied as regards the basis of liability: should the party be held to a duty to take reasonable care in the accomplishment of the contractual task or a duty to see that the task is accomplished? Unlike French law, English law had no tradition of appeal to the concept of fault as the basis for liability for breach of contract and so in determining this issue each term, whether express or implied, fell to be interpreted by the courts so as to establish the standard to be required.

In this respect, the terms implied in contracts of sale of goods soon became a powerful exemplar of *implied* terms which imposed liability for failure to accomplish the contractual task (defined principally in terms of reasonable fitness of the goods for their purpose) without proof of negligence, even before their statutory crystallisation in 1893.[26] Perhaps the nearest to contracts of sale (and sometimes hard to be distinguished from them) are contracts for work and materials, where a person undertakes to create goods and supply them. So, for example, in *Samuels v Davis* the plaintiff had been seen by a dental surgeon whom he had asked to make a dental prosthesis: the Court of Appeal held that it made no difference as to the implication of a term that the

---

[21] Supply of Goods and Services Act 1982, s. 4.   [22] Ibid. s. 9.

[23] Unfair Contract Terms Act 1997, s. 2 and s. 3.

[24] Above, pp. 232, 235–6.   [25] See above, p. 157.   [26] Above, p. 245.

prosthesis be reasonably fit for its purpose whether the contract was classed as sale of goods or for work and materials.[27] A similar approach was taken to the liability of a restaurant in respect of the safety of the food served.[28] However, the courts also applied this approach to contracts where the supplier of services had no physical or intellectual input into the make-up of the product in question. So, for example, in *Watson v Buckley* the plaintiff was treated by the first defendant, a hairdresser, with a hairdye distributed to the hairdresser by a second defendant and manufactured by a third defendant.[29] The distributors had advertised the hairdye as safe, harmless even to 'the most sensitive skin' and the plaintiff was shown these assurances; the hairdresser applied the product according to the manufacturer's instructions but it nevertheless caused the plaintiff dermatitis, as it was over twice as acidic as had been thought. In these circumstances, the court held the *distributors* liable in the tort of negligence for failing to test the product and in representing it as safe, but it also held the hairdresser liable for breach of contract despite her lack of negligence. As Stable J straightfor- wardly put it, where the contract 'is really half the rendering of service and, in a sense, half the supply of goods, the implied warranty is no less than it would be in the case of the sale of goods simply'.[30] A similar approach was taken to a case where a builder stipul- ated that a sub-contractor should use a tile made by a particular manufacturer, for though this prevented the implication of a term that the tile would be reasonably fit for its purpose on the part of the sub-contractor to the builder, it left an implied term that the tiles would be of merchantable or proper quality (which they were not, having an undiscoverable manufacturing defect).[31] And in the case of the hire of goods (or chattels as they are still sometimes termed) it was held that a contract for the hire of a carriage for a specific journey contained an implied term that the carriage would be reasonably fit for its purpose,[32] though other cases suggested that liability required negligence in the hirer or those for whom he was responsible.[33]

On the other hand, where a contract was for the provision of services without any transfer of possession of goods to the other party to the contract, then the courts gen- erally refused to imply a term more onerous than reasonable care, often put in terms of rendering services 'in a proper and workmanlike manner'.[34] This was applied to situations where no products were involved in the provision of the service,[35] but was also applied where products were involved. So, as I shall explain, carriers were held liable to their passengers for any injury incurred during transport only on proof of negligence, even where the means of transport was not reasonably fit for its

---

[27] [1943] 1 KB 526. Cf. *Lee v Griffin* (1861) 1 B & S 272 (distinguishing the two types of contract in the context of formal requirements). See also *IBA v. EMI Electronics Ltd.* (1980) 14 BLR 1 (designer and supplier of television aerial mast).

[28] *Lockett v A & M Charles Ltd.* [1938] 4 All ER 170.   [29] [1940] 1 All ER 174.

[30] Ibid., 179–80; *GH Myers & Co. v Brent Cross Service Co.* [1934] 1 KB 46; *Dodd v Wilson* [1946] 2 All ER 691.   [31] *Young & Martin Ltd. v McManus Childs Ltd.* [1969] 1 AC 454.

[32] *Hyman v Nye* (1880–81) LR 6 QBD 685, 689–90 though cf. 687–8 (hirer as 'insurer against all defects which care and skill can guard against'). See also *Reed v Dean* [1949] 1 KB 188 (hire of Thames motor launch); *Yeoman Credit Ltd. v Apps* [1962] 2 QB 508 (hire-purchase).

[33] *Jones v Page* (1867) 15 LT (NS) 619, 620, *per* Pigott B.

[34] *Kimber v William Willett Ltd.* [1947] KB 570.

[35] E.g. the supply of medical services of diagnosis, see below, p. 288.

purpose.[36] However, this standard of negligence has also been applied to the contractual liabilities of those whose input into a product is purely intellectual, as in the case of designers of goods or architects of buildings[37] or whose physical input has been applied to the other party's property, such as in the laying of a person's carpet once cleaned[38] or the inspection of or advice on their property from the point of view of its safety.[39]

However on the recommendation of the Law Commission,[40] in 1982 legislation was enacted which crystallised the terms to be implied in business contracts of supply of goods, partly to clarify the law and partly to reflect more exactly the terms to be implied by the existing statutory model set by the law of sale of goods.[41] Accordingly, it was provided that in contracts for the transfer of goods made in the course of business terms were to be implied as to their description, their 'merchantable quality' and reasonable fitness for their purpose, with similar content and caveats as in the law governing sale of goods.[42] Contracts of transfer were defined as those 'under which one person transfers or agrees to transfer to another the property in goods', whether or not services are also provided or to be provided under the contract, though certain contracts in this category (notably sale of goods and hire-purchase) were excepted as they were regulated elsewhere.[43] Similar provision was made as regards the hire of goods in the course of a business.[44] On the other hand, it was provided (confirming the common law position) that in contracts for the 'supply of a service where the supplier is acting in the course of a business, there is an implied term that the supplier will carry out the service with reasonable care and skill': here, therefore, the standard of liability is negligence.[45]

In this way, statute set out the distinction between contracts where goods are transferred to another party (whether permanently or temporarily) where liability for the quality and fitness for purpose is strict and other contracts for the provision of services, even where goods (or products) are involved in their accomplishment. Moreover, when subsequent changes have been made to the content of the statutory implied terms in contracts of sale of goods (for example, moving from 'merchantable quality' to 'satisfactory quality') and to their susceptibility to exclusion by express provision, parallel changes have been made to the law governing contracts of transfer and of hire of goods,[46] including on implementation of the Consumer Guarantees Directive, which did not itself require these wider changes.[47]

---

[36] *Readhead v Midland Rly. Co.* (1867) LR II QB 412, (1869) LR IV QB 379, below, pp. 283–4.

[37] *Greaves & Co (Contractors) Ltd. v Baynham Meikle & Partners* [1975] 1 WLR 1095 (though a stricter term implied on the facts); *George Hawkins v Chrysler (UK) Ltd.* (1986) 38 BLR 36 (designer and supervisor of refurbishment held only to reasonable care).

[38] *Kimber v William Willett Ltd.* [1947] KB 570.

[39] *Driver v William Willett (Contractors) Ltd.* [1969] 1 All ER 665 (consultant engineers and employer's compliance with safety rules).

[40] *Implied Terms in Contracts for the Supply of Goods* (1979) Law Com. No. 95.

[41] Above, pp. 235–6.   [42] Supply of Goods and Services Act 1982, ss. 3 and 4 (as enacted).

[43] Ibid., s. 1.   [44] Ibid., ss. 8 and 9.   [45] Ibid., s. 13.

[46] Unfair Contract Terms Act 1977, ss. 6 and 7; Sale and Supply of Goods Act 1994, ss. 1, 7(1) and Sch. 2, para 6.

[47] Sale and Supply of Goods to Consumers Regulations 2002, rr. 7 and 10 and see below, p. 588.

However, given the approach of the English common law to privity of contract, the strict liabilities for the quality and fitness for purposes of goods transferred whether permanently (as in contracts for work and materials) or temporarily (as in contracts of hire) could not be enjoyed by third parties. In English law, for long this left the generality of third parties to tort and to a requirement of proof of negligence and also excluded them from recovery in respect of pure economic loss.[48] And while legislation in 1999 allows parties to contracts to create contractual rights in third parties, its requirements as to the existence of their intention were drawn so as to prevent the courts from extending the benefit of contractual obligations to third parties unless the contract expressly so provides or itself 'purports' to be for their benefit and the evidence justifies a finding that the parties intended to grant them contractual rights.[49]

This picture is considerably more clear-cut than the position in French private law. First, as regards the basis of liability under *contrats d'entreprise*, the courts have used the distinction between *obligations de resultat* and *obligations de moyens* to nuance the basis of liability from very strict (with a defence only of *force majeure*) to proof of fault, and sometimes something in between.[50] While there may be thought to be a certain tendency towards the imposition of liability without fault where a product is supplied (as with the restaurant's liability for its food), there are counter-examples even here (as with the hairdresser's liability for hairdye used).[51] On the other hand, it has been rare for French courts to extend the contractual obligations which they have recognised to third parties in these contexts,[52] leaving third parties to the various possibilities of the law of delict, including liability under article 1384 alinéa 1 as to harm caused by things.[53]

(b) Contracts involving buildings: tenancies and building contracts

However, both English courts and the legislature have taken very different approaches to contracts concerning buildings, whether of sale, hire (leases or tenancies and licences) and the liability of builders.

First, the law governing liability under contracts for the sale of land (and therefore of the buildings attached to land) remains strikingly different from the law of sale of goods. In principle, a seller of land is subjected to no implied term as to the state of the land or its fitness for its purposes, even to the extent that in principle a seller of residential premises is not under any duty as regards their fitness for habitation.[54] This stark position was qualified in 1972 by statute, according to which 'a person taking on work for or in connection with the provision of a dwelling' owes a duty to see that the work is done in a 'workmanlike' or 'professional' manner 'so that as regards that work the dwelling will be fit for habitation when completed'.[55] While this does not change the position for sellers of premises in general, it does create a new and strict liability in those 'taking on work' (which would include builders and architects) in respect of 'dwellings' (that is, residential properties), it being provided that this liability

---

[48] Above, p. 179.   [49] Contracts (Rights for Third Parties) Act 1999, s. 1.
[50] Above, pp. 99–104.   [51] Above, p. 100.   [52] Above, pp. 101–2, 103, 111–12.
[53] Ibid.   [54] Above, p. 228.   [55] Defective Premises Act 1972, s. 1(1).

benefits the person who commissioned the work and extends 'to every person who acquires an interest (whether legal or equitable) in the dwelling'.[56] On the other hand, for many years this liability had little practical relevance as it did not apply to most new housing as it was excluded in respect of houses built under the National House Builders Protection Scheme.[57] Even after the discontinuation of this scheme in 1990, the short limitation period of six years from the completion of the work is likely to have a restrictive effect on its impact.[58]

Moreover, after *Murphy v Brentwood District Council*[59] the courts have firmly rejected the imposition of liability in either a seller or a builder in respect of defects in quality in a building sold in the tort of negligence.[60] It is partly for this reason that in the English context a buyer of premises almost always instructs a surveyor to inspect any premises which are intended for purchase, this also being required as a condition of the loan of money by building societies and banks concerned to lend only on a reasonably safe security. This general immunity of sellers of real property also explains the importance attached to the liability of surveyors of property in respect of inspections and reports with a view to purchase.[61]

The common law's attitude to the liability of landlords in respect of the state of the premises was also restrictive. So, at common law there is no implied term in contracts of tenancy that the leased premises are or will be fit for habitation or for any particular use,[62] though an exception was made as regards tenancies of furnished accommodation where there is an implied term (usually called an implied covenant) that they are reasonably fit for habitation *when let*.[63] At common law, this general contractual immunity in landlords to their tenants was paralleled by a rejection of any duty of care in the tort of negligence in landlords to their tenants or others even as regards personal injuries or death,[64] though in the second half of the last century the courts cut down this immunity where the landlord had designed or built the premises in question.[65]

However, there are important exceptions to this common law position. First, as regards houses or flats let at a low rent, there is an implied term that the premises will be at the start of the tenancy and will remain during its life fit for human habitation;[66] and as regards houses or flats let for a period of less than seven years, a landlord owes a number of obligations to repair and maintain the premises.[67] Secondly, by statute by virtue either of an obligation or a *right* to repair premises a landlord owes a duty to take reasonable care to maintain or repair the premises 'to all persons who might reasonably be expected to be affected by defects in the state of the premises'.[68] This duty may therefore be owed either to a tenant or a non-tenant,[69] but it is expressly limited to recovery in respect of personal injury, death or damage to their own property and requires proof of negligence in the landlord.[70]

---

[56] Ibid., s. 1(1)(a) and (b).   [57] Markesinis and Deakin's *Tort Law*, 356–7.
[58] Defective Premises Act 1972, s. 1(5).   [59] [1991] 1 AC 398.   [60] Above, p. 184.
[61] See especially *Smith v Eric S. Bush* [1990] 1 AC 831 and above, p. 228.
[62] *Bottomley v Bannister* [1932] 1 KB 458, 468; *Edler v Auerbach* [1950] 1 KB 359, 374.
[63] *Collins v Hopkins* [1923] 2 KB 617.   [64] *Cavalier v Pope* [1906] AC 428.
[65] *Rimmer v Liverpool City Council* [1985] 1 QB 1.
[66] Landlord and Tenant Act 1985, s. 8 and see also ss. 9–10.   [67] Ibid., ss. 11–17.
[68] Defective Premises Act 1972, s. 4(1).
[69] *Alderson v Beetham Organisation Ltd.* [2003] EWCA Civ 408; [2003] 1 WLR 1686.   [70] Ibid.

This complex and somewhat patchy pattern of liability contrasts strikingly with the English law governing the liability of a business supplier of goods, where liability is imposed strictly to the transferee. Even more, though, it contrasts with the rules governing the liabilities of sellers of immovable property, of landlords to their tenants and of builders in French law. As I have explained, all these can be liable for the harm caused by the defects in the buildings which they supply, either by way of the general law of the Civil Code (as in the case of sale, where the rules governing immovable and movable property share a common framework) or by way of special legislation distinguishing different types of defect (as in the case of the liabilities of *constructeurs*).[71] As regards builders, the French liability is both very strict and runs happily beyond privity to subsequent purchasers of the property, though within set prescription periods.[72] While in part these differences can be seen as a practical consequence of the historic divorce in English law between the law governing real and personal property and the harmony of treatment of the laws of sale and *louage* in French law, they also reflect very different choices of policy as regards the proper liabilities in particular of builders, including the decision by the French legislature in imposing liability in 1978 that all 'builders' must be insured.[73]

2. The Public Supply of Gas, Electricity and Water

The supply in England and Wales of networked electricity, piped gas and piped water has long been the subject of statutory control, whether under mixed regimes of supply by both public and private bodies (as before the nationalisations in the late 1940s), under regimes of public monopoly after them,[74] or under the privatised regimes of the 1980s.[75] While in English law the public or private nature of the bodies supplying these products has not had any formal effect on the nature of their liability, the arrangements surrounding their distribution have done so as regards their liability to their customers.

(a) Liability to customers

Since the nineteenth century, suppliers of water and later of gas and electricity were subjected by statute to broad general duties of supply to 'tariff' customers (including domestic customers but not being restricted to consumers) leaving non-tariff customers to make special contractual arrangements without the benefit of such a duty. Where a supplier of these products did so under a statutory duty, the courts held that this was incompatible with the voluntary nature of contract in its inception, in the setting of its terms and especially in the setting of the payment which was by tariff,

---

[71] Above, pp. 70 (sale), 104–8 (builders), 108–11 (hire).   [72] Above, pp. 104–5.
[73] Above, p. 104.
[74] This was true of electricity and gas (Electricity Act 1947, Gas Act 1948) but not water which remained divided between public suppliers and privately owned statutory undertakers even after the Water Act 1945.   [75] Gas Act 1986; Electricity Act 1989; Water Act 1989; Water Industry Act 1991.

so that the relationship was 'statutory' and not contractual.[76] On the other hand, where gas, electricity or water were supplied *other than* under a statutory duty (principally to larger commercial customers), then the courts accepted that this could be under contract.[77] Where this was the case, then a customer could claim damages in respect of financial losses caused by interruptions in the supply.[78]

Where there was no contract, this left the possibility of claims for damages by customers based on the failure of the supply, whether in terms of its interruption or a failure in its quality, to the law of torts. In this respect, the courts generally took the view that the statutory duties of supply did not give rise to civil liability under the tort of breach of statutory duty, the main reason being that their failure was also sanctioned by a penalty.[79] This appeared to leave only the possibility of claiming damages in the tort of negligence. So, while claims for personal injuries and death resulting from the supply of infected drinking water have sometimes succeeded,[80] claims for financial losses caused by failures in supply or in the quality of these products have failed.[81] However, as I have already noted in relation to the contamination of the water supply at Camelford,[82] there is a possibility of a person who has suffered 'special damage' as a result of the supply of gas, water or electricity recovering damages under the tort of public nuisance as long as the supply constituted a 'nuisance' (which could be satisfied by the supply of contaminated water or a fluctuating voltage of electricity) to a sufficient range of 'Her Majesty's subjects'.[83] If liability for public nuisance is established, then it can cover the compensation of financial as well as physical losses and does not rest on proof of negligence.[84]

However, this pattern of relationships changed as regards gas and electricity from the late 1980s. At this time, the gas, electricity and water industries were privatised in the sense that the creators, 'transporters' and suppliers of these products became trading companies susceptible to private investment, but their supply remained subject to a considerable amount of statutory regulation and institutional regulatory control.[85] The present position as regards gas and electricity is that while there remains a statutory duty of *connection* to the mains supply in private operators, these operators are not the same as those who supply the product in question: there is a division between the provision of the infrastructure of supply (which is subject to a statutory

---

[76] *Stevens v Aldershot & District Gas Water & Lighting Co.* (1933) 102 LJKB 12; *Willmore & Willmore v South Eastern Electricity Board* [1957] 2 Lloyd's Rep 375; *Norweb plc v. Dixon* [1995] 1 WLR 636 (all electricity); *Clegg, Parkinson & Co. v Earby Gas Co.* [1896] 1 QB 592 (gas); *Read v. Croydon Corpn.*[1938] 4 All ER 631 (water).   [77] *Morris & Bastert Ltd. v Loughborough Corpn.* [1908] 1 KB 205.
[78] Ibid.
[79] *Stevens v Aldershot & District Gas Water & Lighting Co. cit.* On the other hand, sometimes the courts assumed or held that breach of safety regulations could give rise to liability, especially where these related to the safety of places of work: *Hartley v Mayoh & Co and the North-Western Electricity Board* [1953] 2 All ER 525.
[80] *Read v Croydon Corpn., cit.*; *Barnes v Irwell Valley Water Board* [1939] 1 KB 21 (CA) (water contaminated by lead pipes).
[81] *Stevens v Aldershot & District Gas Water & Lighting Co, cit.*; *Clegg, Parkinson & Co. v Earby Gas Co, cit.*
[82] Above, pp. 224–5.   [83] Above, p. 224.
[84] Cf. *Tate and Lyle v GLC* [1983] 2 AC 509.
[85] So, for example, the gas and electricity industry markets are regulated by the Office of Gas and Electricity Markets ('OFGEM') and the water industry by the Office of Water Services ('OFWAT').

duty) and the supply of the product itself (which is not).[86] However, no person may supply piped gas or electricity (whether to domestic or to non-domestic customers) without a licence and the terms of the standard conditions of these licences impose on the suppliers duties of supply to *domestic* customers as soon as is reasonably practicable after a supply has been requested.[87] On the other hand, the terms on which domestic or other customers receive electricity or gas are generally a matter for their supplier and the licences themselves assume that the suppliers will act under contracts with their customers.[88] In my view, the courts are also likely to see the relationship of the supply of gas and electricity as contractual given the absence of any *statutory* duty, even in the presence of a licensing condition imposing such a duty. For while the supplier is said to owe a 'duty' under the licence, its true legal nature is one of a set of conditions for conducting the business, whose acceptance is voluntary. If the courts do so, the contracts of supply of gas are likely to count as contracts of sale of goods or for the transfer of goods,[89] and so attract the statutory implied terms to the quality and fitness for purpose of the products supplied and the complete ban on any restriction of liability in their supplier,[90] but this is less clear as regards the supply of electricity which may not count as a 'corporeal movable' as it is not tangible.[91] If the supply of electricity is not a sale of goods or contract for the transfer of goods, then it is most likely that it would be classed as a contract for the supply of services, with the consequence that the suppliers would owe duties to carry out the service with reasonable care, rather than any stricter obligation.[92] However the contracts are classified, claiming for breach of contract would allow a gas or electricity customer to recover damages not merely for physical damage caused by failures in the safety of the supply, but also for pure economic losses caused by its poor quality or interruption. By contrast, even after privatisation, there remains a duty to supply in the suppliers of water ('water undertakers') to supply piped water to domestic premises on request.[93] This being the case, the

---

[86] In the case of gas, the distinction is between 'gas transporters' (who bear the duty to connect) and gas suppliers (who supply the product): Gas Act 1986, s. 10 as substituted by Gas Act 1995, s. 10(1), Sch. 3, para. 4 and then amended by Utilities Act 2000, s. 80 and Sch. 6(1) para. 2(1). In the case of electricity, the distinction is between the distributors of electricity (who bear the duty to connect) and electricity suppliers (who supply the product): Electricity Act 1989, ss. 16 and 17 as substituted by the Utilities Act 2000, s. 44.

[87] Gas Act 1986, s. 7A; Electricity Act 1989, s. 7 as amended by Utilities Act 2000, ss. 32 and 81. See also the *Gas Suppliers Licence: Standard Conditions*, condition 32; *Electricity Supply Licence: Standard conditions*, condition 32; both approved by the Dti in September 2001 and available at <http://www.dti.gov.uk/>.

[88] The Gas Act 1986 and the Electricity Act 1989 (as amended) both provide that the supply of gas otherwise than under a contract is supplied under a 'deemed contract' on terms which are determined by a scheme for this purpose: Gas Act 1986, Sch. 2B para. 8 (as inserted by Gas Act 1995, s. 9(12), Sch. 2 and amended by Utilities Act 2000, Sch. 6, Part 1, paras. 1, 2, 23, Sch. 8; Electricity Act 1989, s. 24, Sch. 6, para. 3. The typical example of their application is where a new owner or tenant of premises takes over the supply of gas or electricity from their predecessor without entering a contract with the supplier.

[89] 'Gas' may count as a 'personal chattel' for the purposes of the Sale of Goods Act 1979, s. 61(1); *Benjamin* § 1–087. The definition of 'goods' is identical for the purposes of the strict implied terms in contracts for the transfer of goods: Supply of Goods and Services Act 1982, ss. 4, 18.

[90] Above, pp. 235–42, 273; The 1977 Act, s. 6(2). In the following discussion, it would also be a question whether the customers under 'deemed contracts' would be treated in the same way as customers under actual contracts.

[91] *Benjamin* § 1–085. *East Midlands Electricity Board v Grantham* [1980] CLY 271 held that electricity was not 'goods' for the purposes of the Companies Act.

[92] Supply of Goods and Services Act 1982, s. 13.   [93] Water Industry Act 1991, s. 52.

legal basis of its supply remains non-contractual, with the result that liability for failures in the supply must rest on tort, whether negligence or nuisance.[94] In practice, liability for physical damage rests on negligence and so there can be no recovery for mere failures in quality nor more generally in respect of pure economic loss.

(b) Liability to non-customers

In English law liability in the suppliers of gas, electricity or water to non-customers could only be founded on tort, given the absence of privity of contract. While the courts have on occasion imposed liability for breach of a statutory duty in relation to the equipment or installation necessary for the supply of the product (for example the inadequacy of earthing[95]) and while in the case of escapes of water liability is imposed specially by statute,[96] it is again the tort of negligence which is the likely basis for this liability. So, a supplier of electricity has been held liable in negligence to a fireman called to a fire who was electrocuted by a wire which should not have been under tension if the wiring for which the supplier was responsible had been properly checked.[97] A supplier of water is liable for any personal injuries or damage to property (notably, animals) caused by its contamination even where this is suffered by non-customers where this results from negligence.[98] However, where the supply of a utility is cut off and causes merely financial loss, inconvenience or discomfort, these losses are not recoverable in the tort of negligence from their supplier or from anyone else responsible, even if negligent.[99] Again, there is a possibility of the imposition of liability on the ground of public nuisance here,[100] but liability in *private* nuisance is even less likely given the restrictive approach which the courts have taken to this tort, seeing it as appropriate for the balancing of interests between neighbours or harm to their proprietary interests in land; there have been no cases in which a court has imposed liability in nuisance on a utility undertaker or a works contractor for *non-physical* harm.[101]

(c) Comparisons with French law

These English approaches to the liabilities of the public suppliers of water, gas and electricity differ significantly from those taken by French courts. First, French lawyers have not allowed the nature of the institutions or legal framework by which utilities are supplied to determine the basis of liability to customers. In France, the supply of piped gas, water and electricity has been undertaken by public, private and 'mixed' bodies over the years, but the institutional nature of the suppliers has not affected their being considered a part of the *service public*.[102] While English law has no *legal* concept of the 'public service', it is here similar to the extent to which the supply of utilities has

---

[94] Above, pp. 163, 179–83, 224–5.
[95] *Sellars v Best* [1954] 1 WLR 913 (Electricity Supply Regulations 1937).
[96] Water Industry Act 1991, s. 209(1).
[97] *Hartley v Mayoh* [1953] 2 All ER 525 affd. as to liability in negligence [1954] 1 QB 383.
[98] *Read v Croydon Corpn.*, *cit.*
[99] *Spartan Steel & Alloys v Martin* [1973] 1 QB 27; *Anglian Water Services Ltd v Crawshaw Robbins & Co. Ltd.* [2001] BLR 173 [115]–[117].   [100] Above, pp. 224–5.
[101] *Anglian Water Services Ltd v Crawshaw Robbins & Co. Ltd.*, *cit.* [125].   [102] Above, pp. 136–7.

remained the subject of considerable regulation in the public interest, though the mechanisms of this regulation have changed considerably with privatisation.

While French law recognises that the relationship between the recipient of a 'public service' may be either a matter for private law and typically contractual or for public law and non-contractual, it has long included the relationship of the suppliers of gas, water and electricity to their customers within private law and treated it as typically contractual, even though many of the terms on which these utilities are supplied are set by administrative decree and can be varied in the public interest.[103] The Cour de cassation has taken a very strict view of the content of the contractual obligations which the suppliers of these products bear, both as to the products themselves and to related work and installations.[104] What this means is that liability for the continuity, quality and the safety of water, gas and electricity is very strict, there being no requirement that any of these products be defective.[105]

Furthermore, French law generally subjects the liability of these suppliers of public utilities to *non-customers* to the private law of delict, whether this be for fault or, more likely, for the 'deeds of a thing',[106] but with the important exception where liability can be connected to 'public works', where it will be subjected to this special administrative regime of liability.[107] Here, the basis of liability (whether requiring proof of fault, resting on a presumption of fault or being imposed without fault) turns on the status of the claimant, whether 'participant' in the work, 'user' of the work or a 'third party'. So, for example, where a surge in an electrical current causes personal injuries or death to a non-customer, in French law that person may be able to claim damages against EDF without needing to show any fault.[108] Here, in English law, in the absence of any statutory duty held to give rise to civil liability,[109] liability rests only on proof of negligence.

Here, then, the classic characterisations of French and English law prove only partly true. For while French law does sometimes impose special rules to govern the liability of public utilities to non-customers, English law does not. By contrast, while French law treats their relationship to their customers as contractual and belonging to private law, English law *sometimes* sees the public regulation (in the form of statutory duties) as special and exclusive of contract. As we shall see, though, the Product Liability Directive and the Consumer Guarantees Directive have different effects on this area, for while the first applies here as elsewhere, the public supply of gas, water and electricity was specifically excluded from the second.[110]

3. The Liability of Carriers

The roots of the modern English law of liability for carriage can be found in the early eighteenth century, when the courts adopted a Romanist framework, the central focus was on the carriage of goods and the typical mode of public transport was stagecoach.[111] When the railways came in the nineteenth century, this same

---

[103] Above, p. 137.   [104] Above, pp. 137–8.   [105] Ibid.   [106] Above, p. 138.
[107] Ibid.   [108] Ibid.   [109] Above, pp. 218–21.   [110] Below, pp. 476, 589.
[111] *Coggs v Bernard* (1703) 2 Ld Raym 909, 913, 917–18.

framework was applied, though attempts were made to supplement it so as to reflect the different technical and organisational context.[112] By contrast, in the twentieth century air transport and the international transport of passengers were subjected to their own regulatory regimes, reflecting the UK's adherence to international conventions and EU legislation.[113] As with my treatment of the French law, here I shall look at the law apart from these special areas.

In the course of the nineteenth century and for most of the twentieth century, public bodies were very much involved in the provision of transport by road and rail. This was sometimes local, where a town or county took upon itself the operation of bus or tram services; in the case of the railways, it was national. So while until 1921 there were many small railway companies, each operating their own trains on their own (and other companies') tracks, in that year these companies were consolidated into four new companies,[114] and then in 1948 these were nationalised under a new statutory body, the British Transport Commission, which was also made responsible for the provision of most other major transport operations, such as long-distance road haulage.[115] The railways continued in State ownership, though undergoing a number of institutional changes,[116] until 1993 when the railways were privatised.[117] To do so, the legislation distinguished broadly between three functions: the ownership and responsibility for the track, signals and stations (first Railtrack plc and then Network Rail); the operation of passenger and goods services (the train companies operating under franchises); and the regulatory institutions created to ensure fair competition and the protection of consumers.[118] The provision of local and national bus services have followed a similar process of privatisation.[119]

What is particularly noticeable, though, is that the public involvement and even ownership of transport services has had very little impact on the law governing their operators' liability. In general the imposition of statutory duties on the public bodies responsible for the provision of these services has not led to a denial of the existence of contracts between them and their customers,[120] and so the general liability rule has remained a requirement of proof of negligence, whether the liability is classified as contractual or tortious. On the other hand, changes in the organisation of rail transport have affected the way in which the law of contract has applied so as to extend the range of carrier liability.

(a) The general position

The common law distinguishes between 'common' or 'public' carriers, who by way of trade offer themselves willing to carry any goods or persons on a particular route and

---

[112] Below, pp. 283, 284.   [113] On this see *Chitty on Contracts*, Chap. 35.
[114] Railways Act 1921, s. 1, Sch. 1.   [115] Transport Act 1947, Part II and s. 39.
[116] Under the Transport Act 1962, the British Transport Commission was abolished and the British Railways Board created.   [117] Railways Act 1993.
[118] The primary regulator at the time of writing is the Strategic Rail Authority set up by the Transport Act 2000, Part IV, but in July 2004 a further restructuring of the rail industry was announced by the Minister of Transport.   [119] The leading legislation was the Transport Act 1985.
[120] See below, p. 282 for the exception.

are therefore bound to accept any would-be customer,[121] and all other carriers, but the importance of this distinction for liability concerned only the carriage of goods. In that context, it was early established that a common carrier is liable for the loss of or damage to the goods, the only defence being 'act of God' or of the King's enemies.[122] However, English courts refused to extend this 'insurer's liability' to the carriage of passengers, whether by road (and notably by stagecoach) or by rail,[123] and here liability was instead based on negligence, whether or not the carrier was a common carrier, whether or not the passenger paid for the journey and whether the claim was brought in contract or in the emerging tort of negligence: the common carrier's duty to accept goods or passengers was not thought incompatible with the existence of a contract.[124] Apart from legislative exceptions, it was accepted that any exemption or limitation clause could validly exclude a carrier's strict liability as common carrier in respect of goods or liability for negligence in respect of passengers.[125]

While the special liability of common carriers of goods has been eclipsed in the modern law,[126] the wider requirement of proof of negligence established by the nineteenth century remains applicable in the twenty-first, so that in principle a passenger injured during travel must prove the negligence of the carrier in order to establish liability, whether as a matter of contract or tort. So, for example, where a mother bought a ticket for herself and for her child, the latter could not claim damages for breach of contract but could do so in tort subject to a proof of negligence.[127] This also means that there is no significant distinction between the liability of carriers to their passengers and to bystanders injured by a transport accident[128] and that a statutory context of carriage inconsistent with contract makes no difference to the basis of liability. For example, in *Clarke v West Ham Corporation* it was held that where a local authority operated a tram service under statute which gave it the power to levy 'tolls' and imposed on it a duty to run a number of services on the lines in question, it was not entitled to exclude its liability for negligence, unless it offered some further consideration for the relinquishment of the passengers' rights to travel and to compensation for negligence at common law, such as by a reduction in the tariff.[129] Here, without such a special contract, the relationship of passengers to carrier was clearly seen as non-contractual and liability therefore rested on negligence.

However, there have been two ways in which qualifications have been suggested to this position, the first unsuccessful, the second successful.

---

[121] *Clarke v West Ham Corpn.* [1909] 2 KB 858, 882, *per* Kennedy LJ and see generally *Chitty on Contracts*, §§ 36-007 *et seq.*   [122] *Coggs v Bernard* (1703) 2 Ld Raym 909, 917–18.

[123] *Readhead v Midland Rly. Co.* (1867) LR II QB 412, (1869) LR IV QB 379; *O'Connor v British Transport Commission* [1958] 1 WLR 346.

[124] *Ansell v Waterhouse* (1817) 6 M & S385; *Bretherton v Wood* (1821) 3 Brod and Bing 54; *Foulkes v Metropolitan District Rly.* (1880) 5 CPD 157; *O'Connor v British Transport Commission, cit.*

[125] *Nicholson v Willan* (1804) 5 East 507; *Shaw v York & North Midland Rly. Co.* (1849)13 QB 347; *Peek v North Staffs Rly. Co.* (1862–3) 10 HLC 473, 494.

[126] Since 1963 neither the nationalised railways nor the modern train operators are 'common carriers' by express legislative exclusion: Transport Act 1962, s. 43(6); Railways Act 1993, s. 123.

[127] *O'Connor v British Transport Commission, cit.*; *Barkway v South Wales Transport Ltd.* [1950] 1 All ER 392.

[128] E.g. *Chadwick v British Railways Board* [1967] 1 WLR 912 (which concerned liability for the plaintiff's 'nervous shock' after acting as a rescuer at a railway accident which claimed 90 lives).

[129] *Clarke v West Ham Corpn.* [1909] 2 KB 858, 875, 880.

(b) The rejection of a strict liability for products used by carriers

As I have explained, by the 1860s English courts were using the implication of terms to regulate the liabilities of parties to contracts, sometimes on the basis of negligence and sometimes on a stricter basis, the liability of sellers of goods in respect of their quality and suitability for purpose being typical of the latter.[130] In *Readhead v Midland Railway Co.*[131] the question arose whether a term should be implied into contracts for the carriage of passengers analogous to the terms already implied in contracts of sale of goods.

In *Readhead*, the plaintiff was injured when the railway carriage in which he was travelling overturned, it being found that this was caused by the breaking of a tyre of a wheel of the carriage which suffered from a latent defect, which was not attributable to any fault in the manufacturer and which was not detectable before it broke. The plaintiff claimed damages against the railway company, his carrier, on the basis of a term implied into the contract that the carriage in which he travelled was reasonably fit for its purpose. However, a majority of the Queen's Bench and the Exchequer Chamber disagreed, rejecting the plaintiff's suggested analogies with the common carrier's strict liability for goods[132] and with the terms implied in sales of goods.[133] Here, the judges were motivated by a fear of the consequences of acceptance of such a strict implied term, which could be argued in 'a variety of other cases'.[134] For as the court realised, if the plaintiff's argument were accepted, then the carrier's strict liability would also apply to 'the roadworthiness of the other carriages in the same train and of the engine drawing them, ... the soundness of the rails, of the points, of the signals, of the masonry, in fact of all the different parts of the system employed and used in his transport'.[135] Moreover, in the court's view it would be a 'plain injustice' to impose on the defendant an obligation to compensate someone injured by a defect which no human skill or care could either have prevented or detected.[136] The standard of liability must therefore be negligence even where an injury is caused by the defectiveness of the means of transportation.[137]

While it has been said that the standard of care required of a carrier of passengers is a high one,[138] nevertheless it is subject to the balancing of considerations required generally in the assessment of negligence. So, for example, in one case a child of four years had fallen out of the door of a guard's van in a train and was killed, apparently being able to open the door from the inside.[139] It had been argued that since modern passenger-carrying coaches had no internal handles at all the defendant carrier had failed to comply with modern standards, but the Court of Appeal held that while the carrier had to have regard to passenger safety in providing suitable door handles for guards' vans to which they have access,[140] there was no 'universal law that every railway or omnibus

---

[130] Above, p. 232.   [131] (1867) LR II QB 412, (1869) LR IV QB 379.
[132] (1869) LR IV QB 379, 383–4.   [133] Ibid., 386.   [134] (1869) LR IV QB 379, 385.
[135] Ibid., 384, *per* Montague J for the court.   [136] Ibid., 393.
[137] While a carrier can be the 'occupier' of the means of carriage as 'premises' it is unlikely that this changes the basis of liability except as regards unlawful passengers: Occupiers Liability Act 1957, s. 2; Occupiers Liability Act 1984, s. 1.
[138] *O'Connor v British Transport Commission* [1958] 1 WLR 346, 351.   [139] Ibid.
[140] Ibid., 349.

or taxicab or passenger aircraft undertaking which trades for reward must have the latest standard of design . . . Economically and practically it would be impossible'.[141]

(c) A special vicarious liability via contract

Under the general law of vicarious liability, carriers are liable for the torts of their employees in common with other employers.[142] Where a carrier operates not merely the means of transport, but also other elements necessary for the service, as in the case of a railway company which runs the services, provides and is responsible for the maintenance of the track, engines, and rolling stock, then the impact of vicarious liability is very considerable, for while it may be difficult to point to which of that single company's employees is negligent, it may be much easier to show that one or more of them were. Moreover, where all the circumstances from which injury or damage are within the control of a single defendant, a claimant may rely on the maxim *res ipsa loquitur* so as to help establish negligence, though the utility of this maxim disappears where an explanation of how the injury was caused is given.[143]

However, the structure of rail transport in the nineteenth century led to English courts going further than this classic form of vicarious liability and accepting a special form of vicarious liability for the benefit of passengers under cover of interpretation of the contracts of carriage. The idea first appeared in *GWR v Blake*.[144] There the plaintiff had bought a through-ticket from London to Pembrokeshire from a first railway company which provided the train all the way, but whose track stopped halfway, after which the journey continued on track belonging to a second railway company. The plaintiff was injured in an accident during this second part of his journey, when his train collided with an engine left on the track by the employees of the second company: no negligence was found in the first company's driver. In these circumstances, the court held that the first company had an obligation to use reasonable care to maintain the *whole line* in a condition fit for traffic, so as to make it liable for the negligence of the second company over whose track its train travelled.[145] In Cockburn CJ's words:

It would be inconsistent with public convenience and safety to put any other construction on such a contract than that the [first railway company] should be primarily liable to the [plaintiff], and should take their remedy against the [second company], whose servants have caused the accident.[146]

The courts later made clear that the liability of a carrier from whom a passenger bought a through-ticket extended to the negligence of *all* other persons from whom care was necessary for the transport in question: there was no need for any contractual relationship between that carrier and any other railway company, though they would not be liable for the acts of strangers, for example, the placing of a log on the line by a 'mischievous person'.[147] In this way, the courts imposed a special form of vicarious

---

[141] *O'Connor v British Transport Commission* [1958] 1 WLR 351, *per* Sellers LJ.
[142] Above, p. 165.   [143] *Barkway v South Wales Transport Ltd*, *cit.* and cf. above, pp. 209–10.
[144] (1862) 7 H & N 987.   [145] Ibid., 992.   [146] Ibid., 993.
[147] *Thomas v Rhymney Rly. Co.* (1871) LR 6 QB 266, 274.

liability, for its effect is to make carriers liable for the negligence of people other than their employees or even independent contractors. While, though, there need be no contract, whether of employment or otherwise, between the carriers and those others for whose negligence they are liable, this special liability was founded on the construction of the contracts between carriers and their passengers and this suggests that the doctrine does not apply for the benefit of passengers who travel other than under a contract, for example, under a free pass.[148]

While the railways were nationalised this special doctrine was not needed, since all those working for the safe travel of rail passengers were employed by the nationalised service, but after the 're-privatisation' of the railways, its significance revives. For under the present arrangements, a rail passenger travels under a contract with a first passenger transport company to travel over track operated by Network Rail in trains operated by one or more other companies, leased from further companies and manufactured by still others. If the nineteenth-century doctrine of *GWR v Blake* were applied to this new set of arrangements, it would mean that a passenger injured during a railway journey could recover from the carrier from whom he bought his ticket on proof of negligence in any of these other companies or their employees, quite apart from any recovery against those companies themselves.

It would appear, moreover, that this potential liability has not gone unnoticed by the train companies. For the standard minimum terms of all contracts of carriage of persons by rail in the UK, the National Rail Conditions of Carriage, provide that a passenger makes a contract not merely with the train company from which he or she buys a ticket, but also with any other train company whose train services (or other goods or services) are needed for the journey.[149] They further provide that the train company which issues the ticket is not responsible for any losses that occur while travelling on another company's trains.[150] Even if this provision is interpreted as referring only to liability for losses other than caused by personal injuries or death, given the imposition of the special vicarious liability which I have described, these provisions must be vulnerable to challenge under modern legislative controls of unfair contract terms.[151]

(d) Comparisons with French law

The general basis in English law of carriers' liability in negligence (whether in tort or contract) makes a striking contrast to the very strict liability developed by French courts in the early twentieth century for carriers to their passengers via *obligations de sécurité* and still applicable to transport by rail.[152] So, while English carriers are liable for the safety of the products which they use only on proof of negligence, French carriers are liable for any injuries to their passengers during transit, it being no *force majeure* to show that any defect in the products which they use to accomplish the journey were undiscoverable or arose beyond their control.[153] Moreover, the French carrier's *obligation de sécurité* is also likely to apply so as to impose liability in situations

---

[148] *Chitty on Contracts*, para. 36-057.
[149] National Rail Conditions of Carriage (ed. 2000), clause 5, § 1.   [150] Ibid., clause 5, § 2(c).
[151] Unfair Contract Terms Act 1977, s. 3; Unfair Terms in Consumer Contracts Regulations 1999.
[152] Above, pp. 139–41.   [153] Above, pp. 90, 141.

where English law holds contractual carriers liable for the negligence of those who contribute to the accomplishment of the journey (their special vicarious liability), since it is unlikely that the actions of these persons would be held unforeseeable, unpreventable and beyond the sphere of control of the carrier as is required by the defence of *force majeure*.[154] In short, where a person is injured in a rail crash in France, they are likely to claim damages from SNCF, leaving it to the latter to claim an indemnity against any other person (including the producer or supplier of any product involved); in English law, such a person would have to establish negligence in an identified person, whether the carrier itself or some other person contributing to the process of carriage.

Secondly, the substantive harmony of the English law around negligence contrasts markedly with the French law, which draws distinctions as to the basis of liability between passengers injured in the course of transport itself and otherwise, and between passengers and non-passengers (who may be able to rely on liability for the 'deeds of things' or liability in respect of 'public works', both of which hold out the possibility of recovery without proof of fault). On the other hand, French law shares with English law a general rejection of any difference as to the basis of liability for injury to passengers depending on whether the transport constitutes a 'public service', either in institutional or legal terms: French lawyers generally consider that public transport services are carried on in an 'industrial and commercial' manner. Indeed, the main difference as regards liability between public and private transport services is found in the *English* context, where the practical arrangements of a shared (private) railway transport network gave rise to the imposition of the special vicarious liability.

4. Medical Liability and Medical Products

English courts have consistently held medical practitioners to the same general standard of liability of reasonable care since at least the middle of the eighteenth century, whether their patients paid for their services under a contract or instead were treated for free as a matter of private charity, (as in the famous London hospitals of St Bartholomew's or St Thomas's) or public provision (which became increasingly common in the nineteenth century and then general with the founding of the National Health Service (NHS) in 1948). But while English law, unlike traditional French law,[155] does not appear to distinguish between liability in respect of public and private health care, the picture is more complicated.

First, for a period of some 30 years at the beginning of the last century, the courts took a restrictive view of the liability of public (and typically charitable) hospitals as opposed to private clinics, denying that the ordinary law of vicarious liability applied. With the increasing governmental role in the provision of health care in the middle of the century, the courts first applied the ordinary law and then went further, imposing a 'non-delegable' duty.[156]

---

[154] Above, p. 141.   [155] Above, pp. 141–6, 149–51.   [156] Below, pp. 289–91.

Secondly, the way in which its 'ordinary law' of tort and contract applies to the liabilities of providers of health care differs according to the public or private nature of the provision. For English courts have held that hospital authorities, medical practitioners (whether in hospital or in general practice), and pharmacists when acting under the NHS do not provide care to their patients under contracts, even if they make some payment for it, whereas private health care is provided under contracts with their patients. While generally the same standard of care is imposed as regards the services which are given, these contracts brings with them strict liability in respect of the medical products which they supply.[157] In the result, the legal structure of the provision of health care means that the application of this ordinary law of contract and tort leads to a distinction between public and private liability for products supplied.

Thirdly, while the ordinary law of the tort of negligence applies to the liabilities of manufacturers and suppliers of medical products to those beyond privity of contract, owing to the central role of the NHS, public bodies themselves have sometimes been seen as the manufacturers and not merely the suppliers of medical products. Where they have, their public role has increased rather than diminished the standard of care which they have been held to owe.

Fourthly, while liability insurance is not compulsory in the UK, systems of indemnity exist in respect of most medical acts. The NHS has taken on responsibility for clinical negligence of its employees employed by health authorities, the individual authorities contributing to a central fund in a way which emulates insurance.[158] The general medical or dental practitioners who are not covered by this scheme, including those undertaking private practice, either take out indemnity insurance or (in the case of individuals) belong to one of two mutual societies.[159]

(a) The personal liability of medical practitioners

The general rule is that the personal liability of medical practitioners, whether surgeons, physicians, nurses or ancillary staff, rests on proof of negligence whether put as a matter of contract or tort. In *Slater v Baker* of 1767 the plaintiff engaged the defendant surgeon for a fee of a guinea to treat his broken leg, but the surgeon fitted him with a metal instrument as a result of which the leg became useless.[160] The plaintiff claimed damages from the surgeon for his 'ignorance and lack of skill' in carrying out his undertaking to him, that is, in contract. While three surgeons gave evidence as to the surgeon's general competence, they agreed that he had not followed normal practice, one witness having not 'the least idea of the instrument' used.[161] The jury's verdict holding the surgeon guilty was upheld by the Court of King's Bench, which noted that even very skilful professional men can act ignorantly and unskilfully in particular cases and here 'it seems as if Mr Baker wanted to try an experiment with this new instrument'.[162] At this stage, therefore, a medical practitioner could be liable in

---

[157] Below, pp. 291–2.
[158] National Audit Office, *Handling clinical negligence claims in England* (3 May 2001), 6.
[159] Ibid., 5. These are the Medical Defence Union and the Medical Protection Society.
[160] (1767) 2 Wils KB 359.   [161] Ibid., 360.   [162] Ibid., 362.

Civil Liability

contract only for negligence even as regards a product supplied for the purposes of treatment. However, English courts held medical practitioners liable for the consequences of their negligence even in the absence of a contract with their patients:[163] for if payment had to be shown 'in all cases of surgeons retained by any of the public establishments, it would happen that the patient would be without redress'.[164] So, neither the absence of privity of contract nor even the absence of any payment should prevent a patient for claiming in tortious negligence.[165]

This general founding of the personal liability of medical practitioners on negligence has continued until the present day. As I have earlier explained, the courts have set out in the *Bolam* test a standard of care which is both more demanding than for persons generally (in that greater skill is required of those who profess it or accepted positions which require it) but also more generous (in that negligence will not normally be found if a competent body of professional opinion holds that the action taken by a defendant was reasonable, even if others would take a different view).[166] This approach applies to medical practitioners in respect of diagnosis, treatment and advice[167] and makes clear the continuing crucial role of expert evidence in determining the content of medical duties of care. Moreover, while on occasion a court has found that the circumstances in which a patient has suffered injury do allow for the application of the maxim *res ipsa loquitur*,[168] more recently the usefulness of the maxim in this context has been doubted where expert and factual evidence has been called at trial,[169] in keeping with the more general decline in acceptance of its usefulness.[170]

Moreover, though the authorities conflict, more recent authority denies any difference in the standard of care owed either by individual practitioners or service providers in a public context, even where this is the prison service. So, while it has been held that the prison service did not owe the same standard of care to a prisoner known to have suicidal tendencies as would be required of a mental hospital,[171] later it was held that a pregnant woman prisoner was entitled to expect the same level of care for herself and her child as a person at liberty, subject to the constraints of escort or control on her movement.[172]

Conversely, the courts have avoided the imposition of any stricter liability on the basis of contractual warranty in respect of diagnosis or treatment generally. So, for example, the Court of Appeal has refused to interpret a contract to perform a vasectomy as importing an obligation that the patient would be rendered sterile even though he was told that the operation was 'irreversible', instead finding only an obligation to take reasonable care in warning of the possibility of future fertility, as a reasonable person would not have expected a guarantee given the inexact nature of medical science.[173]

---

[163] *Pippin v Sheppard* (1822) 11 Price 400.   [164] Ibid., 409, *per* Garrow B.

[165] See also *Seare v Prentice* (1807) 8 East Rep 348; *Gladwell v Steggall* (1839) 5 Bing (NC) 733.

[166] Above, p. 188.

[167] *Sidaway v Bethlem Royal Hospital* [1985] AC 871; *Bolitho v City and Hackney HA* [1998] AC 232.

[168] *Mahon v Osbourne* [1939] 2 KB 14 (CA) (swab left in patient after surgery).

[169] *Ratcliffe v Plymouth and Torbay HA* [1998] PIQR P170, P189–P190.

[170] Above, pp. 209–10.   [171] *Knight v Home Office* [1990] 3 All ER 237 (QBD).

[172] *Brooks v Home Office* [1999] 2 FLR 33 (QBD).   [173] *Thake v Maurice* [1986] 1 QB 644, 685.

(b) The liability of hospital authorities

The legal basis of the liability of hospital authorities to their patients first became prominent in cases where a patient suffered injuries in the course of medical treatment in hospital but could not show which doctor or member of the nursing or other staff was negligent. Here, the law of vicarious liability appeared to offer a solution by suggesting that the hospital be liable for its servants' proven negligence, even where the identity of the individual to blame was not established, but nineteenth-century judges felt unable to take this approach, in part because many doctors working in the hospitals of the day did so voluntarily (as in the great charitable hospitals) or under contracts for services rather than of service and in part because they wished to protect the charitable ('public') hospitals which were dependent on voluntary contributions from liability which they could not afford.[174]

Both motivations can be seen in the decision of the Court of Appeal in 1909 in *Hillyer v The Governors of St Bartholomew's Hospital*, where a patient who had suffered burns during the course of a free operation sued the charitable hospital as vicariously liable for those who performed the operation, whether doctors or nurses.[175] While Farwell LJ accepted that hospital authorities were liable for the negligence of their servants even though they acted in performance of public duties (such as local boards of health) or of charitable functions, like a public hospital, he restricted this liability only to *servants*, which did not include any 'professional men, employed by the defendants to exercise their profession to the best of their abilities according to their own discretion',[176] nor even to nurses who acted under doctors' instructions at the time even where they were generally employed by the hospital.[177] Kennedy LJ went further, holding that the duty to a patient treated gratuitously was limited, not being 'the ordinary duty of a person who deals with another through his servants'.[178] In his view, the governors of a public hospital do have a duty to exercise reasonable care in the selection of the medical staff and in providing 'fit and proper apparatus and appliances', but are not liable for the negligence of the members of staff in the exercise of their professional skill.[179] Cozens-Hardy MR agreed with both his fellow judges so that the patient failed in his claim. While the basis of the decision was the subject of considerable controversy, for some 30 years it enshrined a distinct approach to the liability of public (and in particular, charitable) as opposed to private, 'commercial' hospitals or clinics.[180]

However, as the importance of public bodies as opposed to charitable foundations in the provision of 'public' health care increased in the course of the century, so attitudes to liability changed and in 1942 in *Gold v Essex County Council* the Court of Appeal refused to follow the approach of either Lord Justice in *Hillyer*.[181] In *Gold's* case the plaintiff had been treated with Grenz rays in a local authority hospital (which charged a small fee) and suffered burns by the admitted negligence of a competent but non-medically qualified radiographer in failing properly to screen her face. The local

---

[174] See in particular *Perionowsky v Freeman* (1866) 4 Foster and Finl 977, 981, *per* Cockburn CJ; *Cassidy v Ministry of Health* [1951] 2 KB 343, 361, *per* Denning LJ.   [175] [1909] 2 KB 820.
[176] Ibid., 825.   [177] Ibid., 826.   [178] Ibid., 828–9.   [179] Ibid., 829.
[180] *Cassidy v Ministry of Health* [1951] 2 KB 343, 360.   [181] [1942] 2 KB 293.

authority denied that they were liable for the radiographer's negligence as they did not run the hospital as a business, relying on *Hillyer*,[182] but for the Court of Appeal the extent of a hospital's obligation did not depend on whether it was contractual (as with a nursing home for profit) or non-contractual (as in the case of a hospital giving free treatment);[183] and the limited duty contended for by the defendant authority was inconsistent with the statutory powers it acted under which required the provision of hospital accommodation to sick persons in their area.[184] As a result, the hospital was held vicariously liable for its radiographer's negligence, though the court accepted that it would not have been for the negligence of medical practitioners *not* employed by the hospital, as with visiting surgeons or physicians, whether the hospital was voluntary or run by a local authority.[185]

However, after the Second World War and especially with the coming of the NHS in 1948,[186] judicial attitudes changed again. First, it was accepted that hospitals could be liable *personally* for their own institutional negligence, for example in failing to put in place a reasonably safe system as to the provision of dangerous drugs.[187] This avoided the need either to establish the identity of the particular persons responsible for the harm or the nature of their relations with the hospital. Then in *Cassidy v Ministry of Health*[188] the Court of Appeal confirmed that the approach in *Gold* applied to all those employed under contracts of service (or employment), whether doctors or other medical or non-medical staff. Denning LJ went further, holding that a patient should expect that reasonable care would be taken of him in hospital, whether paying directly or not.[189] In his view, the hospital's duty of reasonable care could not be discharged by engaging professional people; it would be liable for the negligence of *all* on their permanent staff, whether or not working under contracts of service, as long as they were not employed and paid for by the patient.[190] In this way, Denning LJ's approach stepped aside from the normal law of vicarious liability and imposed a personal non-delegable duty on the hospital authority.[191]

Under the present arrangements in place in the NHS, this difference in approach in the Court of Appeal in *Cassidy* does not matter as *all* medical staff (whether full-time or part-time) in NHS hospitals work under contracts of employment on standard terms,[192] with the result that public hospital authorities are vicariously liable for their negligence except where they act as part of their 'private practice'.[193] However, increasing recourse by the NHS to the contracting out of medical and other work by public sector providers to the private sector, often trading companies which engage their own

---

[182] [1942] 2 KB 293, 296–7.   [183] Ibid.   [184] Ibid., 303–04, 309.   [185] Ibid., 310.

[186] National Health Service Act 1946.

[187] *Collins v Hertfordshire CC* [1947] KB 598. Cf. *Lindsey CC v Marshall* [1937] AC 97 (patient in public nursing home not warned of previous cases of serious infectious disease).

[188] [1951] 2 KB 343.   [189] Ibid., 359–60.   [190] Ibid., 362.   [191] Ibid., 364.

[192] National Health Service Hospital Medical and Dental Staff and Doctors in Public Health Medicine and the Community Health Service (England and Wales) Terms of Conditions of Service (updated to 2003), approved by the Secretary of State for Health.

[193] Ibid., conditions 40–43 allow all employees to engage in private practice, subject to certain conditions. By contrast, from 2003 NHS general practice has taken place under contracts with group practices rather than with individual practitioners under a particular form of contract for services: New General Medical Services Contract for General Practitioners: see <http://www.nhsconfed.org/gmscontract/>.

staff, whether medical or otherwise, produces a new context in which the classic law of vicarious liability fails to channel liability onto the public authority; for these private sector providers work under contracts for services, whether their own staff act under contracts of employment or for services. Here, then, Denning LJ's approach in *Cassidy* again becomes significant, for it would not permit a public sector provider to escape its 'non-delegable' duty as a result of the contractual arrangements by which the service is provided. And so it has been held that a public health authority which arranged for an operation to be performed by a private surgical hospital was liable for the negligent performance of this operation on the basis of its non-delegable duty.[194]

In my view, therefore, the history of the liability of hospital authorities demonstrates that English courts have been sensitive to the different and changing character of the providers of hospital care. From a position concerned to protect the finances of voluntary hospitals and resting on the idea that a professional practitioner could not be their 'servant', the courts have come to see the public providers of health care as owing special duties in respect of the quality and safety of the care actually provided. While the courts appear to apply the 'ordinary law', in fact they have taken first a more generous and then a stricter view of the liability of 'public' providers.

(c) Contractual liability and medical products

There is, moreover, a further way in which English law (apart from the Consumer Protection Act 1987) in practice distinguishes between liability for the provision of public and private health care and this relates specifically to the supply of products. For the House of Lords has held that NHS patients are not treated or supplied with drugs under contracts, as the statutory provisions which underpin the NHS are inconsistent with the existence of contracts between the service providers (hospitals and general practitioners) and their patients, even where the patient contributes some payment to the cost of the provision.[195] When treated under the NHS a patient has a statutory right to the medicine and the hospital or pharmacist has a statutory duty to supply it and this is inconsistent with the existence of a contract which rests on the parties' express or implied agreement.[196] The courts have consistently upheld this position and have applied it to the relationship between general practitioners and their NHS patients.[197] The logical consequence of this denial of contract is that a NHS patient supplied with a product in a hospital or by a general practitioner, or even a prescribed drug by a commercial pharmacist must claim on the basis of the tort of negligence and not on the basis of the strict statutory terms implied in any contract for services which includes the transfer of goods,[198] even where a charge is made. By contrast, where a private patient is supplied with a product in the course of his or her treatment,

---

[194] *M v Calderdale and Kirklees HA* (Huddersfield County Court) [1998] Lloyd's Rep Med 157 cited with approval by *Clerk and Lindsell on Torts*, para. 8–64.

[195] *Pfizer Corpn. v Ministry of Health* [1965] AC 512.   [196] Ibid., 535–6 (Lord Reid).

[197] *Re Medicaments Ref. (No. 2)* [1970] 1 WLR 1339; *Reynolds v Health First Medical Group* [2000] Lloyds' Rep Med 240 (Hitchin County Court).

[198] Supply of Goods and Services Act 1982, s. 4, above, p. 273.

their provider will be liable where they were not reasonably fit for their purpose or of satisfactory quality.[199] So too will a pharmacist or a supermarket who supplies non-prescription medicines. In the result, where products are supplied under the public health service their supplier will liable only for negligence, whereas where they are supplied by way of private health care liability will be strict.

So, in common with the position which applies to the liability of public utilities, while the liability rules themselves distinguish liability for negligence in tort and strict liability in contract, the courts' view that contracts are incompatible with relationships shaped by statutory rights and duties leaves public liability for products to negligence and private liability as strict.

(d) The liability in negligence of manufacturers and suppliers

There are few English decisions imposing liability on manufacturers of medical products in general and none in the area of pharmaceuticals.[200] Given the absence of privity of contract between manufacturers and those who suffer personal injury and death as the alleged result of use of a product, the basis of liability remained the tort of negligence until the passing of the Consumer Protection Act. This means that a description of the application of the tort of negligence to manufacturers of medicinal products generally consists of extrapolation from decisions in other contexts. And while generally *Donoghue v Stevenson* established the existence of a duty of care,[201] claimants have found it difficult to establish a causal link between use of a medicinal product and their own harm, even before the question of negligence in their manufacturer is argued.[202]

Nevertheless, it is clear that a manufacturer's duty to take reasonable care has a number of elements. Some relate to the state of the product itself: its design, instructions or warnings for use; the range of tests carried out before it is released onto the market (for example, whether it is reasonable to rely on testing on animals or on limited numbers of human subjects).[203] In this respect, compliance with the terms of a product licence or even particular legal requirements (for example, as to package inserts accompanying pharmaceuticals) is not conclusive of the issue of reasonable care, following the general position.[204] Where a manufacturer of a product already marketed later discovers some risk relating to its use, it must take reasonable care in deciding whether or not to issue public warnings, to suspend or to terminate production and order its withdrawal from use:[205] in the pharmaceutical context withdrawals

---

[199] Above, p. 273.
[200] I. Dodds-Smith and M. Spencer, *Product liability for medicinal products* in Powers and Harris, *Clinical Negligence* (3rd. edn., 2000) 835, 842 *et seq.* There have been a number of cases where claims for negligence against a manufacturer of a pharmaceutical have been settled: e.g. claims against Glaxo in respect of 'myodil' referred to in *Rawlinson v North Essex HA* [2000] Lloyd's Rep Med 54. For an example of liability, see below, pp. 295–9 concerning the Creutzfeldt Jakob Disease Litigation.
[201] [1932] AC 562. For recovery for psychiatric injury see below, pp. 298–9.
[202] E.g. *Loveday v Renton* The Times, 31 March 1988 (transcript) (no causal link established between 'whooping cough' vaccine and brain damage in young children).
[203] Dodds-Smith and Spencer, *op. cit.* n.200, 860.   [204] Above, p. 203.
[205] *Wright v Dunlop Rubber Co. Ltd.* (1972) 13 KIR 255.

are common and sometimes controversial.[206] However, there are two particular features in assessing negligence in relation to medical products.

First, use of a particular medical product may be a better or even the only way to treat a particular condition which is itself painful, distressing, disabling or even life-threatening and so the 'cost/benefit' analysis required in assessing the require-ments of reasonable care must include the human cost of withdrawal of a product from use.[207] Secondly, there are difficult questions as to the relative responsibilities of the manufacturer of a medical product and the medical practitioner who prescribes its use.[208] Clearly, it is for a physician to diagnose and to assess whether an individual patient requires a particular medicine and, sometimes, in what quantities and com-bined with what other medicines. To this end, a manufacturer must put medical practitioners in a position to make a proper assessment, but on the understanding that the practitioner is trained, has recourse to published pharmacological guides and can take specialist advice if need be. In the case of medicines available only on prescription, it is this combination of information and expertise which allows a medicine to be put to its effective and safe use. From this perspective, it may be thought enough for a manufacturer to furnish information only to prescribing professionals, rather than requiring information to be brought directly to a patient.[209] On the other hand, man-ufacturers of medicines are required by specific laws to provide some information about their products direct to their users.[210] Given this practice, the law of negligence would require that any information is accurate, clear and enough to inform and warn non-specialist users of any particular risks. For example, where a medicine has serious risks when taken by a pregnant woman, a manufacturer should not be able to rely merely on prescribing doctors asking their female patients about their present or intended condition, given that a simple direct warning accompanying the product may avert serious harm caused by a doctor's own inadvertance.

As I earlier explained, the law of negligence is typically much less demanding of those in the chain of distribution other than manufacturers.[211] So, generally the care expected of a mere supplier or distributor, such as a wholesaler will not usually extend to the design of the products in which they deal, whether this consists of their compo-sition or the information which accompanies them. Mere distributors may reasonably rely on the reputable manufacturer of a product in respect of these matters and do not have to undertake research for themselves, though they must use care in ensuring that no damaged or out-of-date product is supplied.[212] This liability in tort is of greater significance in the context of provision under the NHS, since those who supply med-ical products to patients will not owe them strict contractual obligations. On the other hand, pharmacists purchase prescription medicines from wholesalers under contracts,

---

206 Dodds-Smith and Spencer, *op. cit.* n. 200, 864–5.

207 Cf. above pp. 198–9, and see below, pp. 354–6.

208 Dodds-Smith and Spencer, *op. cit.* n. 200, 863–5.

209 Cf. *Holmes v Ashford* [1950] 2 All ER 76 (hairdye manufacturer entitled to rely on warnings given with product and ignored by hairdresser).

210 This results from a complex of EU legislation and practice set out conveniently in *Guideline on the Packaging Information of Medicinal Products for Human Use authorised by the Community* (August 2002), published at <http://pharmacos.eudra.org>.   211 Above, p. 195.

212 Dodd-Smith and Spencer, *op. cit.* n. 200, 867.

the wholesalers in turn purchasing from manufacturers or importers and then the pharmacist charges the NHS the cost of the medicine supported by the prescription; and hospitals buy medicines in large amounts, requiring manufacturers to tender for contracts to supply at discounted rates directly.[213] This leads to the rather odd position that while an NHS supplier of a medicine is liable only on the basis of negligence (apart from liability under the Consumer Protection Act 1987), they can themselves claim under the strict implied terms in the Sale of Goods Act.

(e) The State as manufacturer and supplier of medical products

However, the dominance of the NHS in the provision of the health care for the last half century has led public bodies themselves on occasion to take on the role of manufacturer as well as supplier of certain medical products. I shall give two very different examples, the first concerning the use in NHS hospitals of a generic spray for burns which caused deafness; the second the production and supply of human growth hormone (HGH) which was found to be infected with Creutzfeldt-Jakob disease (CJD).

(i) The NHS as commissioner of the manufacture of generic medical products

In *Mann v Wellcome Foundation Ltd*[214] the two plaintiffs had been treated as children in 1968 and August 1969 in two NHS hospitals for serious burns with a polybactrin spray; both later suffered deafness. The unpatented product in question, whose active agent was neomycin, had been marketed in the UK from 1952 by a small pharmaceutical company and had been sold to many hospitals through wholesalers. In 1963 in the interests of cutting costs the regional health authority in which the two hospitals were situated engaged another company to make up the spray to their specification and supply it to their hospitals. The plaintiffs were unsure which spray had been used in their own treatment and so sued the health authority and both manufacturers, though the manufacturers both fell out of the picture, the first owing to the lack of evidence that their product had been used and the latter on the basis that they had no role in determining the spray's chemical formulation.[215]

This left the health authority in the firing line, it being found that there was a strong probability that the plaintiffs had been treated with the generic spray and it being admitted that the plaintiffs' deafness had been caused by their treatment with the spray. Waterhouse J had no doubt that the health authority owed the plaintiffs a duty of care 'having taken over the role of the original manufacturer of the spray as supplier . . . and being responsible for managing, in effect, the use of the drug in their hospitals'. The plaintiffs argued that the health authority failed to carry out clinical

---

[213] Association of British Pharmaceutical Industry, *The Cost of Medicines—Good Value for Patients* (2001) 4, available at <http://www.abpi.org.uk/publications>.

[214] (20 Jan 1989) (QBD) 87 NLJ 938 (LexisNexis transcript).

[215] The plaintiffs also sued three other manufacturers against whom no arguments were made in the hearing; the Wellcome Foundation Ltd. joined the proceedings as the parent company of the first manufacturing company which had ceased in trading.

tests, failed to consider the optimum balance of the chemicals, failed to warn of the risk of ototoxicity (poisoning of the ear) and failed to establish any safe regime for administration of the spray, for example, with maximum limits for applications. The defendants countered, *inter alia*, that at the relevant time reasonably informed medical opinion believed that neomycin was not absorbed to any significant extent by the body and had been established as a safe and satisfactory treatment of burns: the health authority could not reasonably have been expected to carry out further tests when it switched to a virtually identical generic substitute for a product which had been in use for about six years and was considered appropriate by the medical profession.

Waterhouse J decided that the 'overwhelming weight of the evidence' was in favour of a finding that until the autumn of 1969 the health authority could not reasonably have foreseen that neomycin might be absorbed to a significant extent when applied by spray to a burn: the health authority 'cannot reasonably be expected to be wiser or to have greater prophetic vision than the doctors and scientists who advise it, subject only to consideration of what was available additionally in medical and scientific literature and the state of knowledge in the relevant expert branches of those professions'. Waterhouse J rejected all the plaintiffs' allegations of negligence and their claims failed.

Here, therefore, we can see that the special position of the NHS in commissioning the manufacture of a generic product and then arranging for its use in its own hospitals owes duties which extend beyond those of the 'mere supplier'. By undertaking responsibility for the composition, supply and administration of the product the NHS authorities thereby owed a combination of the practical duties normally associated with manufacturers, suppliers and the supervisors of medical practice. While in *Mann* there was the special feature that the NHS authority specified the composition of the product, Waterhouse J's judgment also indicates that the standard of care expected of the bodies responsible for the supply of products within the NHS owe a duty of care whose content is anyway more akin to a manufacturer's than a commercial distributor's, a more onerous duty justifiable given the importance of their decision and their access to expertise and advice. In this respect, the tort of negligence is able to accommodate this range of duty by the flexibility of the requirements of reasonable care. As we shall see, though, this marks a striking contrast with the Product Liability Directive which distinguishes sharply between 'producers' and mere suppliers.[216]

(ii) The Creutzfeld-Jakob Disease Litigation

My second example of a public body being treated as manufacturer as well as supplier of a medical product is found in the litigation surrounding the contamination by the agent (a prion, but sometimes termed a 'slow virus') which causes Creutzfeld-Jakob disease ('CJD') in the human growth hormone ('HGH') supplied under the NHS until 1985. This litigation is instructive both as regards its application of the 'ordinary' law of negligence to the public manufacture, control and supply of products and the process by which it was achieved.

Between 1959 and 1985 some 2,000 children who suffered from a defective pituitary gland and as a result suffered extreme shortness of stature (or 'dwarfism') and

---

[216] Below, pp. 521–7.

some 10 per cent of whom also suffered serious ill-health, were treated with a course of injections with HGH extracted from the pituitary glands of cadavers and then processed. The therapeutic effects of the treatment were remarkable, children achieving a normal height and being able to lead a full life. Clinical trials of the treatment were undertaken from 1959 by the Medical Research Council ('MRC'), an independent body financed from public funds, with the approval of the Department of Health ('the Department'), but were continued by it on an increasingly therapeutic basis until 1977, when responsibility for the treatment was taken over directly by the Department. The MRC and the Department had entrusted responsibility for the oversight of the programme to committees, one of which, the Health Service Human Growth Hormone Committee ('the Committee'), composed of scientific experts, was responsible for supervision of the collection and processing of the material into HGH and surveillance of its safety. The HGH used in the programme was obtained from a number of sources and by several processes, one of which (the Hartree process) was later found to be the source of the contamination. Under the programme, some 940,000 pituitaries were collected from cadavers in the UK[217] and it was later accepted that the general natural incidence of CJD was 1 or 2 deaths per million population worldwide. Unfortunately, though, the HGH used in treatment was infected with the prion which causes CJD and by the time the case came before the courts some sixteen of its recipients had died of the disease and some three more were expected to do so.

The recipient patients claimed damages from the MRC and the Department in the tort of negligence,[218] claiming that they had been informed of the risk of infection of HGH by CJD as early as late 1976 and had failed to act until 1980 when changes in production methods were introduced. The claimants were divided between those who had contracted the disease or their personal representatives (the 'Group A plaintiffs') and those who had received HGH at the relevant time, had not contracted the disease but who had suffered psychiatric injury for fear of infection (the 'Group B plaintiffs'). The litigation's successive stages took place between 1994 and 1998.[219]

---

[217] It was later alleged that this collection had generally been unlawful since no protocol had been developed to gain appropriate consents and that the removal had not complied with the provisions of the Human Tissue Act 1961: The *Creutzfeldt-Jakob Disease Litigation* (1995) (2000) 54 BMLR 1.

[218] Their claim based on the tort of battery (unlawful physical touching) on the ground that their consents to the injections of HGH had been invalid owing to the unlawful collection of pituitaries was struck out as 'deplorable' and 'insupportable in law': The *Creutzfeldt-Jakob Disease Litigation* (1995) (2000) 54 BMLR 1.

[219] The main decisions are: The *Creutzfeldt-Jakob Disease Litigation, Plaintiffs v United Kingdom Medical Research Council* (July, 1996) [1996] 7 Med. LR 309; (2000) 54 BMLR 8 (main trial and decision on Group A plaintiffs); The *Creutzfeldt-Jakob Disease Litigation, Newman v United Kingdom Medical Research Council* (November, 1997) (2000) 54 BMLR 85 (Court of Appeal, appeal on aspects of main trial decision); The *Creutzfeldt-Jakob Disease Litigation, Newman v Secretary of State for Health (No. 2)* (2000) 54 BMLR 95; The *Creutzfeldt-Jakob Disease Litigation, Group A and C Plaintiffs* (April and May 1998) (2000) 54 BMLR 100 and 104 (both 'straddlers' claims'); The *Creutzfeldt-Jakob Disease Litigation, Group B Plaintiffs v United Kingdom Medical Research Council* (December, 1997) [2000] Lloyd's Rep. Med. 161, (2000) 54 BMLR 92; The *Creutzfeldt-Jakob Disease Litigation, Andrews v Secretary of State for Health (Damages Assessments)* (June, 1998) (2000) 54 BMLR 111. The significance of these descriptions will appear from the following text. Subsequent references to these cases will omit the reference to the CJD litigation.

The main trial before Morland J took 25 days, and involved a considerable number of witnesses of fact and of expert witnesses from either side as to the state of scientific knowledge some 25 or 30 years earlier. There were 50 ring-binders of documentation, most of which were administrative memoranda, letters and minutes disclosed by the MRC and the Department. While Morland J observed that 'litigation of this scientific complexity, on a subject of general public importance, might be better resolved by an inquisitorial rather than an adversarial system', he was satisfied that the defendants had not withheld any witness with worthwhile evidence and had made a full disclosure of relevant documents 'under the firm guidance' of their own leading counsel.[220] The final judgment ran to some 37,000 words, engaging in detail with the arguments of counsel, and with the oral and documentary evidence.

The MRC and the Department accepted that they owed a duty of care to the Group A plaintiffs, who had contracted CJD[221] under which they had duty to take 'all reasonably practicable steps ... to minimise dangers and side-effects' of the treatment.[222] The basis of this duty appears from the way in which Morland J approached the *standard* of care as he expressly denied that:

a government department or a quasi-government agency such as the MRC can discharge this duty by a *lower standard* of care than a commercial pharmaceutical company.... [S]hortage and limitation of funding and the fact that the collection of pituitaries, the production of H.G.H. and the supervision of the committees manned by unpaid volunteers are irrelevant.[223]

So, the public nature of the defendants should not lessen the standard of care applicable, which must be the same as for commercial producers of 'organic medicinal products'.[224] On the other hand, later Morland J observed that:

the standard of care ... to be imposed in respect of a committee is that of a reasonably competent and carefully enquiring group of professionals of the relevant disciplines of sufficient standing to be entrusted with the membership of that committee bearing in mind that it is a committee which is not merely advisory but is carrying out executive and administrative functions.[225]

The decisive role of the committee therefore increased the degree of care which it had to take and made its access to available information all the more important. So the central role of the defendants in the research, production, supply and use of HRH justified the imposition of duties akin to those owed by a commercial manufacturer, but extending further. On the other hand, Morland J was careful to assess the evidence of scientific and medical knowledge 'objectively, transposing [himself] backwards in time 15, 20, 25 years ago, applying the standards of care, ethics and knowledge to be reasonably expected all those years ago'.[226] He acknowledged that the case could not be determined on 'scientific proof' but only on the basis of what the plaintiffs could establish on the balance of probabilities.[227]

In looking at the issue of the defendants' negligence, Morland J noted that the MRC officers had been alerted to the possible risk of CJD in HGH from late 1976 by a leading agricultural scientist but had taken few steps to follow this up. Furthermore

---

220 [1996] 7 Med LR 309, 317.   221 Cf. the position of the Group B plaintiffs, below, pp. 298–9.
222 [1996] 7 Med LR 309, 318.   223 Ibid.   224 This term was used ibid., 311.
225 Ibid., 318.   226 Ibid., 317 and see above, p. 196.   227 Ibid.

towards the end of 1977 they received two very clear letters from leading scientists one of which referred to 'the gruesome possibilities and their imponderable probabilities' of infection of HGH with CJD,[228] which the officers did not put to the Committee, though some discussion of a summary of their contents took place.[229] This behaviour on the part of the responsible officials from mid-1977 and 1980 Morland J found to be negligent, characterising their behaviour as lethargic[230] and explaining it in part as resulting from the dislocation caused by the transfer in responsibility for the programme from the MRC to the Department which was 'long drawn out and piecemeal'.[231] However, he also found that at times the responsible officials deliberately withheld information from the Committee,[232] partly because they wrongly considered that the Committee was not concerned with such matters,[233] but partly as a result of a more general attitude. According to Morland J:

an unwise philosophy pervaded both the Department of Health and the Medical Research Council that the risk of slow virus contamination of human growth hormone was too awful to contemplate or at least should not be the subject of public knowledge and discussion, even among clinicians.[234]

He concluded that 'there was no good reason why the changes in production methods ... should not have been made in early 1977 if proper advice had been sought'[235] and therefore held the defendants liable in negligence to those Group A plaintiffs who had been supplied with HGH for the first time after 1 July 1977. This decision was not the subject of appeal.[236]

Later the position of claimants who were in the course of being treated in July 1977 was specifically considered (termed the 'straddling plaintiffs'). While Morland J had declared himself not satisfied that if properly informed of the risk the Committee would have ordered the cessation of supply of the processed HGH in question to this class of patient,[237] he later held that if the Committee had ordered the cessation of the supply of HGH to *new* patients, on the balance of probabilities no UK medical practitioner would have continued to supply those already in the course of treatment.[238] As a result, these claimants were also able to recover damages where they could establish on the balance of probabilities that a majority of their treatments pre-dated 1 July 1977, given that each supply of HGH carried a risk of infection rather than there being any cumulative effect.[239]

Finally, the claims of the Group B plaintiffs who had suffered psychiatric harm for fear of infection by CJD were tried.[240] The existence of a duty of care as regards this type of harm had been the subject of considerable judicial discussion, the leading

---

[228] [1996] 7 Med. LR 337.   [229] Ibid.   [230] Ibid., 334.   [231] Ibid., 332.

[232] Ibid., 335.   [233] Ibid., 334.   [234] Ibid., 315.   [235] Ibid., 332.

[236] *Newman v United Kingdom Medical Research Council* (2000) 54 BMLR 85 (CA).

[237] [1996] 7 Med LR 309, 316.

[238] *Newman v United Kingdom Medical Research Council* (November, 1996) (2000) 54 BMLR 12 (CA); *Newman v Secretary of State for Health (No. 2)* (2000) 54 BMLR 95; *Group A and B Plaintiffs* (April, 1998) (2000) 54 BMLR 104.   [239] *Group A and C Plaintiffs* (2000) 54 BMLR 100.

[240] *Group B Plaintiffs v United Kingdom Medical Research Council* (2000) BMLR 92, [2000] Lloyd's Rep Med 161. For the decisions as to the assessment of their damages see *Andrews v Secretary of State for Health* (2000) 54 BMLR 111.

decision in the House of Lords distinguishing between 'primary victims' (persons who were aware of imminent danger or participated in a traumatic event) where a duty of care is imposed, and 'secondary victims' (typically bystanders to traumatic events or their immediate aftermath) where a duty of care is imposed only if further conditions, notably as to relationship with those injured or killed, are established.[241] Morland J accepted that the Group B plaintiffs should not be treated as 'primary victims' as their psychiatric illnesses resulted from fear of a future 'ghastly untreatable terminal brain disease'.[242] Here, he was concerned that such an automatic imposition of a duty of care in respect of psychiatric injury sustained through fear of a future disease would impact on other spheres, such as exposure to asbestos or radiation, bringing huge numbers of claims and making insurance difficult or impossible. Moreover:

[i]t could inhibit producers, prescribers and suppliers of a product from warning the public of the danger of a product. For example, if a potentially lethal substance had been negligently introduced into a production batch of canned food. It would be disastrous if a supplier or producer were inhibited from warning the public of danger for fear that some of those who had already eaten the canned food might bring a claim as a primary victim for psychiatric injury triggered by the warning.[243]

However, Morland J then held that Group B plaintiffs were owed a duty of care, even if not 'primary victims'. In so holding, he took into account the nature of the relationship of the parties (described as 'akin to doctor and patient'); their relative fewness; the terrible and terminal nature of CJD; their lack of effective personal choice in their treatment; and the defendants' actual awareness of the risk that withdrawal of HGH could cause widespread panic among its recipients.[244] He saw no public policy reasons against imposing liability in these circumstances.[245]

Here, then, we find an English court prepared to hold the public producer and supplier liable in negligence for the death, personal injury and psychiatric injury caused by a medical product. In this respect, the key findings of negligence related to an administrative failure to investigate a risk to which they had been alerted and a decision that the risk should not be communicated even to the responsible Scientific Committee, rather than that this Committee had looked squarely at the risk involved and considered it inappropriate to suspend or terminate the programme. Moreover, the case also illustrates the fact that sometimes a public body may be producer, supplier and itself regulator of a particular product. For while commercial manufacturers' views of the safety of their products may be the subject of public and therefore exterior supervision or control, in the case of HGH the same public bodies were responsible for both.

(f) Comparative observations

There are a number of similarities but also of striking differences between the evolution of the English and French laws governing medical liability and liability for medical products apart from liability under the Product Liability Directive.

At the very broadest level, there is a very striking paradox. For while English law formally treats all cases of medical liability to the 'ordinary' law and does not appear to distinguish according to whether health care is provided in the public or the private sectors, the way in which it applies to these two sectors in the context of liability for products is different, imposing a strict liability on all suppliers for the quality and safety of the products supplied in the private sector, but not the public sector.[246] By contrast, while French law for perhaps a century recognised very different bases of liability for public and private sector health care, over the last decade or so the *jurisprudence* of the Cour de cassation and the Conseil d'Etat moved closer and closer, and then in 2002 legislation placed the liability of medical practitioners and institutions on the same legal bases.[247]

Secondly, however, English law's treatment of medical liability has been remarkably stable. Apart from the contractual liabilities in private sector suppliers of medical products (which have not figured prominently in the case law owing to the dominance of the NHS), liability requires proof of negligence either in individual medical practitioners in the provision of care or in medical institutions in their organisation and systems of care.[248] English law has not developed any special strict liabilities in hospitals or doctors regarding the use or supply of products nor in respect of particular categories of medical risk (such as are found in French law in relation to nosocomial infections). On the other hand, after a degree of hesitation in the context of charitable hospitals, English law first applied its general law of vicarious liability and then extended it to construct a personal and 'non-delegable' duty at least in hospitals as to the provision of health care.[249] In these cases, therefore, while proof of negligence is still required (in the action of the hospital's employee, contractor or the latter's own employees), from the point of view of the hospital itself, liability is very strict indeed.

By contrast, the law governing French medical liability has not been stable for some 40 or more years. While the general basis of liability in private law has remained constant, more and more examples of presumed fault or strict contractual liabilities were accepted, especially as regards the use or supply of products, even before the courts 'implemented' the Product Liability Directive.[250] The general basis of liability in administrative law itself changed from a requirement of *faute lourde* to *faute simple*, to which were again added particular cases of liabilities without fault, these echoing but not exactly matching those recognised by the ordinary courts. On the other hand, neither jurisdiction has had much recourse to the notion of vicarious liability. As regards the Conseil d'Etat the reason is obvious, as it has no general recourse to this notion in attributing liability to the administration.[251] But while in principle the individual civil servant enjoys an immunity, the administration may be liable directly, particularly for their fault in the organisation of the public service (*faute du service*).[252] In the case of private sector health care, there are cases in which hospitals are held liable for the fault of their employees, but doctors are not generally *employed* by private hospitals but rather work under contracts with their patients.[253] A patient in a private hospital may therefore need to sue either the doctor or the hospital or both (all in

---

[246] Above, pp. 291–2.   [247] Above, pp. 142–6, 151–3.   [248] Above, pp. 287–91.
[249] Above, pp. 289–91.   [250] Above, pp. 143–6.   [251] Above, pp. 31–3.
[252] Ibid.   [253] Above, pp. 142–3.

contract).[254] It should be in this light that we should see the imposition of liability in respect of 'nosocomial infections', for where a patient has contracted an infection during his or her stay in hospital, it may be impossible to show how it arose or who was at fault.[255] To this extent, this direct strict liability could play something like the role which in English law is played by vicarious liability.

Fourthly, apart from implementation of the Product Liability Directive, neither English law nor French law imposed liability on the manufacturers of pharmaceutical or other medical products except on the basis of fault or negligence. In the case of English law, this fits perfectly well into the general framework; in French law, it was difficult to reconcile with its strict approach either to liability in sale beyond privity of contract nor to its approach in other contexts to the application of liability for the 'deeds of a thing'.[256] This was also true of the liability of pharmacists in respect of prescription medicines in both systems, with the exception in English law of those which are supplied under contracts of sale.[257]

Fifthly, the cost of liability of medical practitioners and hospitals remains very differently spread in the two systems. In the French context, both public and private providers of health care have to take out contracts of liability insurance, with the consequential problems which we have seen hurriedly dealt with in late 2002. By contrast, the NHS acts as its own insurer and other providers, such as NHS general practitioners or doctors working in private practice are mostly covered by their special 'mutual societies' or by insurance.[258]

Finally, the Creutzfeld-Jakob Disease Litigation illustrates very dramatically the differences in the nature of the civil processes in the two jurisdictions, the English trial judge reading vast quantities of documentary evidence and scientific literature and hearing days of controversial scientific evidence and argument. While Morland J himself pondered whether an inquisitorial approach would have been better, it can be seen that the combination of rules, practices and professional ethics led to a full investigation of the facts. In my view, if we are to find any equivalent of this sort of treatment in the French system, we need to look at the criminal process, rather than the civil.[259]

---

[254] Ibid.   [255] Above, p. 143.   [256] Above, pp. 146–7.   [257] Above, pp. 148, 291–2.
[258] Above, pp. 151–5, 287.   [259] Below, pp. 380–6.

PART II

ADMINISTRATIVE LIABILITY FOR FAILURE TO REGULATE OR CONTROL PRODUCT SAFETY

12

French Law: Formal Bases of Liability and Practical 'Irresponsibility'

In this part, I shall look at what may be thought by an English lawyer to be a more specifically 'public' topic, the question of liability in the administration for failures in the organisation or control of product safety. For example, where a local authority or a government minister has power to regulate or control a product in the interests of safety (for example, by ordering its withdrawal from the market), can the public body in question, whether national or local, be liable to a person who suffers harm as a result of its exercise or failure to exercise the power in question? I shall look in this chapter at the response to this question in French law and in the following chapter at the response of English law, drawing there comparisons between the two.

This is a particularly revealing topic as regards the general picture of liability for products in France in a number of ways. First, the issue of liability for failures in the exercise of safety powers requires an understanding of the sources of public power in French law, sources which are very different from their English 'equivalents'. Secondly, it is an area where the Conseil d'Etat has revised the law very considerably, moving from a denial of liability, to a requirement of *faute lourde* and, increasingly but somewhat patchily, towards a requirement merely of *faute simple*. In this last respect, the *affaire du sang contaminé* provides both a very striking example and may well have a wider influence on the law's development, a public scandal provoking a significant *revirement*. Thirdly, however, the area shows the difficulty of assessing the practical impact of the formal rules of administrative liability. For even where liability for failures in the exercise of powers of control in the interests of safety may in theory be established (given the standard of liability required by the Conseil d'Etat), in practice it may not actually be imposed. The reasons for this are found in a number of particular rules relating to the comparative attractiveness as a matter of substantive law of claiming against any *private* persons also liable for the harm caused by an unsafe product coupled with the approach of the administrative courts to recourse actions by private persons against the administration in this context; in the rules concerning the time within which claims against the administration must be brought; and in the general rule denying joint liability between a private person and a public person liable to a claimant in respect of the same harm.[1] These systemic reasons for the non-imposition of liability on the administration in respect of the exercise of public safety powers are

---

[1] Below, pp. 319–30.

strikingly illustrated by their *circumvention* by the Conseil d'Etat in the *affaire du sang contaminé*.[2]

There are four further preliminary points. First, this chapter is concerned with the possession by *public* bodies of powers relating to product safety which give rise to *administrative* liability: I have already noted that some private persons may bear liability in respect of their control of product safety, as in the case of the certification of ships[3] and *contrôleurs techniques* of buildings.[4] Secondly, it is concerned with the imposition of liability in respect of failures in the exercise of powers of control by a public body over *other* persons, whether public or private, rather than over its own activities. Where a public body itself provides a service involving the use or provision of products, this brings different issues of liability which I have already explained.[5] Thirdly, my discussion will be concerned with questions of liability in the administration in respect of the safety of products, rather than their quality. Fourthly, I shall discuss later how the exercise of public powers of safety have influenced the development of *criminal* responsibility for death and personal injury more widely and, indirectly, the incidence of criminal responsibility of other, private 'decision makers'.[6]

1. Sources of French Administrative Power and Product Safety

According to the French way of thinking, the executive's constitutional role is to govern and it must therefore possess the powers to do so: in principle, executive power is not granted by parliamentary legislation, it is inherent. This position results from a potent combination of political history and constitutional principle.

Its historical basis is found in the way in which succeeding post-revolutionary governments were careful to take over the powers formerly enjoyed by the kings of France and their servants.[7] So, though early republican draft constitutions declared roundly that national sovereignty resides in the whole people,[8] post-revolutionary governments were keen to attribute to the State administration a similar set of powers as had previously been possessed by their former sovereign, the king, a position which Napoleon Bonaparte was keen to follow in his own brand of dictatorship. There is, therefore, a good deal of truth in Dicey's gibe that '[Napoleon] fused together what was strongest in the despotic traditions of the monarchy with what was strongest in the equally despotic creed of Jacobinism'.[9]

However, this historical continuity in relation to the position of the executive before and after the Revolution was reinforced and perpetuated even after the beginnings of a truly democratic Republic in the late nineteenth century by the pervasive influence of the principle of the separation of powers. For while Montesquieu's prime concern was to ensure that no one public power went beyond the bounds of its function, it was nevertheless seen as implicit in the principle that each of the three 'powers' have

---

[2] Below, pp. 315–9.   [3] Above, p. 103.   [4] Above, p. 107.   [5] Above, Chaps. 6 and 7.
[6] Below, pp. 378, 387–93.
[7] M. Waline, *Traité de droit administratif* (Sirey, Paris, 9th. edn., 1963), 16.
[8] E.g. *Projet de déclaration des droits naturels, civils et politiques des hommes*, art. 27 in the *Constitution Girondine* of 1793.   [9] Dicey, *An Introduction to the Study of the Law of the Constitution*, 336.

inherent and legitimate as well as distinct roles under the constitution. And this argues for the recognition of the independence of executive power (*le pouvoir exécutif*).[10]

Moreover, a common lawyer who merely reads the provisions of post-revolutionary constitutions concerning the *pouvoir exécutif*[11] or of the present Constitution of the Fifth Republic, which states simply that the Prime Minister 'ensures the execution of laws',[12] would not gain a true impression of the breadth of the powers which the notion embraces. In the modern law the *pouvoir exécutif* includes the power to publish laws and to use force to ensure their application, but it goes very much further and includes very considerable administrative powers, including to ensure 'the minimum conditions necessary for the continuity of national life, *i.e.* the maintenance of *ordre public* and the running of public services[13], and these both independently of any formal legislative provisions'.[14] It is the duty but also the right of French governments to govern.[15]

Moreover, for these purposes *ordre public* is not restricted to public order in a narrow sense (the prevention of riots or crime in general), but extends to 'public welfare' including the 'health of the nation', such as the safety of property or persons or the maintenance of public health, as well as to such matters as the maintenance of proper business conduct and the protection of national monuments.[16] Administrative action aimed at the protection of *ordre public* in this very wide sense is known as *la police administrative*, an expression which is significant in the context of its liability.[17] Moreover, executive power to maintain *ordre public* is not restricted to physical intervention (for example, policing a riot), but also includes the making of administrative *actes*, whether by coming to decisions affecting the rights or duties of citizens, enacting rules or entering administrative contracts.[18] French public law has, therefore, long recognised an inherent power in the administration to make legal rules (a *pouvoir réglementaire*) if they are demanded by *ordre public*.[19]

What this means is that any public body with a general responsibility for the maintenance of *ordre public* may intervene in the interests of product safety. So, for example, in one case the Minister for Health had issued a public warning regarding

---

[10] The key discussion is found in C. de S. Montesquieu, *De l'esprit des lois* (1748), Book XI, Chap. 6.

[11] E.g. *Loi* of 25 Feb. 1875 art. 3 (the constitutional legislation of the Third Republic).

[12] Constitution of 1958, art. 21.

[13] While the administration may not be able to create a *service public* without legislative authority, (Chapus, *Droit administratif général*, Tome I, 625–6) its *pouvoir exécutif* allows it to set up bodies and to employ people in order to carry out those tasks which are necessary to give effect to a *service public*.

[14] Vedel and Delvolvé, *Droit administratif*, Tome 1, 31.

[15] Cf. the reference in the *arrêt Blanco* to the '*droits de l'Etat*' as needing to be reconciled with '*droits privés*' in the context of the liability of the administration: TC 8 Feb. 1873, DP 1873.3.17, above, pp. 19–20.

[16] Vedel and Delvolvé, *Droit administratif*, Tome 1, 31.

[17] Chapus, *Droit administratif général*, Tome I, 665.

[18] The notion of *acte administratif* is of crucial importance as only this type of action of the administration is subject to annulment on the grounds of illegality: Gaudemet, *Droit administratif*, Tome 1, 513 *et seq.*

[19] For a striking example see CE 8 Aug. 1919, *Labonne*, D 1920.3.23 (inherent power in President of the Republic as *Chef de l'Etat* to enact road traffic regulations for the whole of France). The power of *maires* to intervene on the grounds of *ordre public* has long been codified, now appearing as art. L. 2212-2 C.G.C.T., on which see below, p. 308. There is a further complication as the Constitution of the Fifth Republic created a distinct and *exclusive* area for administrative law-making (the *pouvoir autonome réglementaire*) as distinct from the parliamentary *pouvoir législatif*, on which see Bell, *French Constitutional Law*, 78 *et seq.*

two batches of pâté in which botulism had been found. Here, the Conseil d'Etat refused their manufacturer's claim for damages for the losses which he suffered as a result given the absence of any *faute* in the Minister and roundly declared that it was for the Minister 'even in the absence of any legislative provision giving express authority, to take those measures permitting him to warn the public against products whose consumption presented a serious risk to health'.[20]

However, while inherent administrative power to intervene in the interests of *ordre public* is very broad, it has frequently been supplemented by parliamentary legislation creating powers to create institutions, make rules or come to decisions. Some of these powers have the advantage of particularity, as to the focus and limits of the power but also as to the person who bears it. To some extent, this allocation is geographical: so the prime minister has a national remit, the *prefet* and president of the Conseil général share a remit in respect of *départements* and the *maire* has a remit within his or her *commune*,[21] but this picture is complicated by the fact that the *maire*'s activities are under the supervision of the *préfet* (known as a *pouvoir de tutelle*) and this entitles the *prefet* to intervene where the *maire* is thought to be failing properly to act.[22]

At this stage, I wish to give two important illustrations of the powers possessed by administrative bodies which are significant for product safety: the first, the general powers possessed by *maires* in respect of public health and safety; and the second, a special set of powers for departmental and national officers regarding the safety of products and services.

French law gives very wide powers to and imposes considerable responsibilities on *maires* in relation to public health and safety within their locality, the *commune*. While these powers may be seen as an expression of their local *pouvoir exécutif*, they have long been set in legislation according to which the *maire* has an obligation to ensure within the *commune* 'good order, security, safety and public health'.[23] This general power includes matters of health and safety relating to the use or distribution of products,[24] but is supplemented by specific powers, for example, relating to the inspection of food exposed for sale, where a *maire* can forbid its continuing sale, order its destruction, and put in motion a prosecution if regulations are broken.[25]

This example of the *maire*'s powers leads me to its counterpart at the national level. Food is a product with a long, if broken, history of regulation in France. Important legislation in 1905 gave to the central administration considerable powers to regulate the sale or supply of food and drinks and to define particular products (such as 'pure beef')[26] and other legislation provides for the control or definition of other types of product, notably as regards the licensing and regulation of pharmaceuticals.[27] However, in 1978 a

[20] CE 30 Jul. 1997, *Boudin*, D 1999 Somm. 59 obs. Bon and de Béchillon.

[21] Chapus, *Droit administratif général*, Tome 1, 712 *et seq.*			[22] Art. 2215-1 C.G.C.T.

[23] '*Le bon ordre, la sûreté, la sécurité et la salubrité publique*': Art. 2212 al. 2 C.G.C.T (formerly art. L. 131-2 of the Code des communes).

[24] See below, pp. 328–9, concerning CE 7 Mar. 1980, *affaire du 'Cinq-Sept'*, D 1980.320 note Richer, concl. Massot, AJDA 1980.423 note Albertini.

[25] Art. L. 2212-2 4° C.G.C.T. and see C. Gabolde, 'Hygiene publique' Jur.-Cl. Adm. Fasc. 220 (2000) 220, 27.

[26] *Loi* of 1 Aug. 1905, art. 11. The *loi* also created criminal offences, on which see below, pp. 369–70.

[27] Arts. L. 5111-1 *et seq.* C. santé pub.

general law on the safety of products and services was passed, being amended and recast in 1983[28] and then incorporated in 1992 into the *Code de la consommation*.[29] This roundly declares that:

In normal conditions of use or in other circumstances which are reasonably foreseeable by the *professionnel*, products and services must offer the safety which people are legitimately entitled to expect and must not harm human health.[30]

This formulation, which echoed a draft of the Product Liability Directive of the time, requires an objective standard of safety, 'a safety compatible with the state of technical means and the conditions of use of the product or service'.[31] In interpreting it, the Conseil d'Etat has relied on the 'precautionary principle' according to which the absence of scientific certainty as to a risk should not delay effective and proportionate measures to prevent serious and irreversible harm[32] and has referred to the need for the public body to examine both the probability and seriousness of the harm in question.[33]

While this general declaration is couched in the language of duty, it has no independent bite, its function being rather to set the standard on which future administrative activities should be based and according to which they may ultimately be judged.[34] These subsequent provisions create a power in the Conseil d'Etat to enact by decree rules regulating:

in so far as there is the need, by product or category of product, the conditions in which the manufacture, importation, export, offer for sale, sale or free distribution, physical detention, labelling, packaging, distribution or mode of use of the product in question.[35]

The Conseil d'Etat also possesses powers to make rules concerning the conditions under which products are made or services offered from a health and safety point of view.[36] These powers must be exercised in a manner 'proportionate to the danger presented by the products or services in question',[37] and only in the interests of safety (and not, therefore, in the interests of quality or of standardization) and 'respecting France's international obligations',[38] notably under the EU treaties. Furthermore, before

---

[28] *Loi* no. 83–660 of 21 Jul. 1983.

[29] Art. L. 221-1 *et seq.* C. consom. France did not amend this legislation so as to implement the Dir. 92/59/EEC of 29 Jun. 1992 on general product safety, but a government *ordonnance* has implemented its reformulated version, Dir. 2001/95/EC of 3 Dec. 2001 on general product safety: *ord.* no. 2004–670 of 9 Jul. 2004, JO Rép. fr. no. 159, p. 12520 made under *loi* no. 2004–237 of 18 Mar. 2004 *portant habilitation du Gouvernement à transposer, par ordonnance, des directives communautaires et à mettre en oeuvre certaines dispositions du droit communautaire*. According to Calais-Auloy and Steinmetz, 287 while the 2001 Directive uses a different formulation to describe the general safety requirement (referring to the European version as 'gibberish'), in their view it has the same significance as the existing French version. Unlike the present European directives, the French legislation extends to services generally rather than being restricted to those involving the provision of products.

[30] Art. L. 221-1 C. consom. The provisions following this statement of principle were amended by *ord.* no. 2004–670 of 9 Jul. 2004 J.O. Rép. fr. 12520 by way of implementation of EC Dir. 2001/95/EC of 3 Dec. 2001 on general product safety. [31] Calais-Auloy and Steinmetz, 293.

[32] Ibid., 294, quoting art. L. 200-1 C. rur. [33] CE 11 Sept. 2002, D 2002 IR 2579.

[34] This is made clear by art. L. 221-2 C. consom. which states that 'products which do not satisfy the general obligation of safety . . . are to be forbidden or regulated under the conditions hereafter provided'.

[35] Art. L. 221-3 1 ° C. consom. [36] Art. L. 221-3 2 ° C. consom.

[37] Art. L. 221-9 C. consom. [38] Art. L. 221-9 C. consom.

promulgating a regulation, the Conseil d'Etat must consult the Commission de la sécurité des consommateurs,[39] a body set up in 1983 principally to collect and to provide information and advice on the safety of products and services.[40] What is envisaged is that this Commission is first seized either by an individual or a public body with a complaint about a product; the Commission makes inquiries of the businesses in question and undertakes any necessary technical investigations and then makes a recommendation to the minister with responsibility for consumer affairs as to how to act to stop any danger to the public. A final restriction on these powers is that they do not apply to products or services which are otherwise specifically regulated.[41]

The second type of control is more administrative than regulatory. So, the Conseil d'Etat may by decree order that products or a category of products be 'withdrawn from the market or recalled with the view to their modification, to total or partial refund of their cost or their exchange' and that products be destroyed where this constitutes the only means of stopping the danger.[42] Decrees may also provide for the distribution of information concerning products to be made available to consumers.[43] These powers are very wide, but they are tied to the making of a decree by the Conseil d'Etat which is both slow and cumbersome.[44] There is, therefore, an emergency procedure by which the minister responsible for consumer affairs or other relevant ministers may issue a business with a warning, require it to make its products safe or order that they be subjected to expert testing.[45] Moreover, in the case of a serious or immediate danger, a minister may suspend the manufacture, import or export of a class of products for a period of no more than one year, order their recall or their destruction, or the publication of warnings or instructions concerning a product,[46] though any businesses affected must be given a chance to comment within 15 days of any suspension.[47]

2. Liability in the Administration in Respect of Failures in the Exercise of Product Safety Powers

How then do French administrative courts treat the liability of the administration in respect of the exercise of its powers regarding product safety? At first a relatively straightforward picture emerges. For there are a number of cases where liability has been imposed on local authorities in respect of their officers' failures in the exercise of their general powers over public health and safety, the Conseil d'Etat sometimes imposing liability on the basis of *faute simple* (ordinary fault) and sometimes *faute lourde* (very serious fault),[48] any attempt to define the difference between the two

---

[39] Art. L. 221-3 C. consom.   [40] Arts. L. 224-1–224-6 C. consom.
[41] Art. L. 221-8 C. consom.   [42] Art. L. 221-3 3°C. consom.   [43] Ibid.
[44] L. Bihl, 'La loi du 21 juillet 1983 sur la sécurité des consommateurs,' in Ghestin, *Sécurité des consommateurs*, 49, 60.   [45] Art. L. 221-7 C. consom.
[46] Ibid., art. L. 221-5.
[47] Ibid., art. L. 221-5 al. 4. A *préfet* may also use these emergency measures within the Department, subject to review by the relevant national minister: ibid. art. L. 216 al. 2.
[48] Above, p. 31. E.g. CE 23 Oct. 1959, *Doublet* (no.1), Leb. 540, D 1960.191 note Lavroff (*faute lourde*); CE 28 Apr. 1967, *Lafont*, JCP 1967.II. 15296 note Rabinovitch (*faute simple*); CE 9 Feb. 1966, *Ville de Touquet-Paris Plage*, Leb. 91, AJDA 1966.439 note Moreau (*faute lourde*); CE Sect. 13 May 1983, *Lefebvre*, Leb. 194, AJDA 1983. 476 concl. Boyon (*faute simple*).

being limited to the proposition that '*faute lourde* is more serious than *faute simple*'.[49] Moreover, some French jurists state firmly that the administration may be liable on the same legal basis or bases for failures to exercise the powers contained in the legislation on consumer safety, though these assertions are not developed.[50] However, there is no corpus of *jurisprudence* relating to the imposition of liability in respect of the exercise of product safety powers, with the striking exception of the decision of the Assemblée of the Conseil d'Etat in the *affaire du sang contaminé*.[51]

There are, in my view, two reasons for this dearth of case law. First, it results in part from the understandings of *la faute* which apply to cases of this sort and, in particular, its relation to the concept of illegality. This is the more obvious reason, but is nevertheless difficult to pin down given the various distinctions which the courts make for this purpose and the degree of uncertainty as to the standard of fault required by the Conseil d'Etat before liability will be imposed. Secondly, though, there are a number of legal and systematic reasons (stemming from both private and public law) which, in the first place, make it less attractive from the point of view of someone injured by a product to sue the administration as opposed to a private person responsible for his injuries and, in the second place, in this context make any recourse claim by any such private person against the administration either unlikely to succeed or only to succeed in part. The upshot is that even in those circumstances where an administrative court would hold that a public body has committed the sort of *faute* which is capable of giving rise to liability, in the majority of cases the administration would never actually have to pay up in respect of any harm caused (in part) by this fault. These legal reasons for the practical 'irresponsibility' of the administration in this area take as their starting point the strict jurisdictional division between the ordinary and administrative courts, but they include such apparently unrelated areas as the administrative rules governing joint liability, limitation and foreclosure periods (and their causes of interruption) and the treatment of recourse claims by private persons held liable in a private court against a public body in the administrative courts.

My discussion will therefore be divided into three parts. The first will examine the nature of fault required in respect of failures in administrative bodies in the exercise of their powers affecting the safety of products; the second will explain the significance of the *affaire du sang contaminé*; and the third set out the complex of rules which in practice tends towards the 'irresponsibility' of the administration.

(a) *Faute simple, faute lourde* and illegality

As has already been seen in relation to the former administrative law relating to the use or supply of products by public hospitals,[52] the French law of administrative liability for fault combines the use of different notions of fault with a willingness to manipulate them to suit what the Conseil d'Etat perceives to be the justice of the case or, as

---

[49] Chapus, *Droit administratif général*, Tome I, 1303.

[50] G. Cas and D. Ferrier, *Traité du droit de la consommation* (PUF, Paris, 1986), 221, 227; Bihl, *Droit pénal*, 132; J.-Cl. Vindreau, *La responsabilité pénale du fabricant* (Thèse, Lille, 1984) 369.

[51] CE Ass. 9 Apr. 1993, Req. no. 138652 D 1993.3.12, concl. Légal, obs. Maugüé and Touvet, AJDA 1993 Chron. 344 and see below, pp. 315–19.   [52] Above, pp. 144–6.

Gaudemet more elegantly puts it, 'the theory as to administrative fault is, like many of the theories adopted by the case law, nuanced and noted for its empiricism'.[53] This is certainly true of liability in respect of the control of product safety, whether this consists of a failure to intervene (sometimes termed *la carence de la puissance publique*) or an inadequate intervention.

My starting point is that French public lawyers generally treat the liability of public authorities in respect of the exercise of their powers to maintain *ordre public* as a category of liability, even if not an altogether homogeneous one. As I have explained, *ordre public* extends to public health and safety,[54] though particular instances within this broad heading are often quite differently treated: so liability in the exercise of 'police powers' in the narrow sense[55] tends to be treated differently from the liability of a *commune* for a failure to supervise a public swimming area,[56] the granting by a public authority of a license to an unsafe pharmaceutical[57] or the failure in a regulatory authority to control the financial affairs of a *société mutualiste*.[58] At one time, liability in respect of these *pouvoirs administratifs de police* would in general only give rise to liability for *faute lourde*, but this clearly does not reflect the variety of modern judicial practice, which sometimes imposes liability for *faute simple* and sometimes for *faute lourde*, with *faute simple* apparently becoming increasingly common.[59] Indeed, it has been questioned how long liability for *faute lourde* will be retained by the Conseil d'Etat.[60]

Two suggestions have been put forward as to the basis on which the Conseil d'Etat decides between these two. The first distinguishes according to the difficulty of the particular activity undertaken by the administration, difficulty leading to the more lenient standard of *faute lourde*.[61] Certainly, there are many cases in which a particular administrative activity presents considerable difficulty and in which a standard of *faute lourde* has at one time been fairly consistently applied, notably cases involving rescues by the fire service[62] or police action against terrorists.[63] However, if the 'difficulty' of a public body's activity refers indirectly to the cost of an effective public provision owing to the physical difficulty or complexity of the task or tasks to be undertaken, then these factors could clearly be taken into account in determining whether *faute simple* existed rather than in determining the formal standard of liability[64] and this no doubt has been one of the reasons for the change in 1998 of the

[53] *Droit administratif,* Tome 1, 808.   [54] Above, p. 307.
[55] CE 4 Mar. 1932, *Ville de Versailles,* Leb. 274 (police directing traffic: *faute grave*); CE 3 Apr. 1981, *Ville de Bayonne,* Leb. 905 (police directing traffic: *faute lourde*); CE 20 Oct. 1972, *Marabout,* Leb. 664, AJDA 1972.625 concl. Guillaume, GP 1973.1.265 note Rougeaux, JCP 1973.17373 note Odent (police failure to enforce parking restrictions: *faute lourde*).
[56] CE 9 Feb. 1966, *Ville de Touquet-Paris Plage, cit.* (*faute lourde*); CE Sect. 13 May 1983, (*faute simple*). *Cf.* CE Sec. 28 Apr. 1967, *Lafont,* Leb. 182.
[57] CE 28 Jun. 1968, *affaire Stalinon,* JCP 1968.II.15578 note anon and see below, p. 315.
[58] CE 23 Dec. 1981, *Andlauer,* D 1982 IR 450 obs. Moderne and Bon.
[59] Chapus, *Droit administratif général,* Tome 1, 1303 *et seq.*   [60] Ibid., 1313.
[61] Vedel and Delvolvé, *Droit administratif,* Tome 1, 583 *et seq.* An example of this criterion being adopted by the CE may be found in CE 20 Oct. 1972, *Marabout, cit.*
[62] CE 21 Feb. 1964, *Ville de Wattrelos,* Leb. 118 concl. G.Braibant; CE 18.1.1974, *Millet,* Leb. 48 (rescue from a well).   [63] CE 28 May 1984, *Soc. française de production,* Leb. 736.
[64] J.-H. Stahl, concl. CE Sect. 20 Jun. 1997, *Theux,* Leb. 253 (liability of emergency medical services).

general standard for the liability of rescue services to *faute simple*.[65] Moreover, *faute simple* may sometimes disguise a very strict approach. In one case, for example, the Conseil d'Etat held a *commune* liable for harm caused by a delay in the use of fire equipment by the fire service, on the basis that 'where it was not shown that the equipment's malfunction was attributable to *cas fortuit*, this delay itself constitutes a fault of a nature to attract liability'.[66] The difference between tying liability to *faute simple* rather than to *faute lourde* therefore lies in the fact that with the former 'the characterization of the facts shall no longer be influenced by the preoccupation *a priori* to restrain the possibility of liability arising'.[67] Conversely, the maintenance of a standard of *faute lourde* may reflect a concern to discourage 'defencive practices' especially in relation to regulatory authorities.[68]

A second approach distinguishes between those 'acts' of the administration which have legal consequences ('*actes administratifs*') which attract a standard of *faute simple*, and physical activities ('*activités*' or '*opérations sur le terrain*') which attract a standard of *faute lourde*.[69] Here, it is important to understand the significance of holding that the standard of liability for *actes* is mere 'ordinary fault'. For, while all enacted *règlements* count as *actes administratifs*, by no means all administrative decision making will so qualify, but only those which count as *décisions*, i.e. promulgated norms whose purpose is to modify or to maintain a person's legal position.[70] In general the illegality of an *acte administratif* is equated with *faute* (*simple*) sufficient to attract liability for any consequential harm and conversely, making a legal *acte* does not constitute *faute*.[71] However, while the requirements of administrative legality are numerous, the main test as to the substantive appropriateness of a public authority's decision requires something very like serious fault as here the Conseil d'Etat holds an administrative *acte* illegal only if it rests on a 'manifest error of assessment' of the matter in question. And where the illegality of an *acte* is not concerned with its substantive appropriateness, then this illegality, while constituting *faute*, will often be held causally unrelated to a complainant's harm.[72] So, for example, if a ministerial decision not to exercise product safety powers contained in the *Code de la consommation* were held illegal for

---

[65] CE Sect. 13 Mar. 1998, *Améon*, D 1998 no. 535 note Lebreton, JCP 1998.I.181 chron. Petit; CE 29 Apr. 1998, *Comm. de Hannappes*, Leb. 185, D 1998.535 note Lebreton, JCP 1999.II.10109 note Genovèse.   [66] CE 29 Apr. 1998, *Comm. de Hannappes, cit.*
[67] Chapus, *Droit administratif général*, Tome 1, 1312.   [68] Fairgrieve, *State Liability*, 115–16.
[69] Chapus, *Droit administratif général*, Tome 1, 1313; Braibant, concl. CE 21 Feb. 1964, *Ville de Wattrelos, cit.*
[70] Chapus, *Droit administratif général*, Tome 1, 502. As a result, some administrative decisions in a loose sense do not constitute *décisions* in this technical sense: e.g. a failure to provide a proper life-saving service at a beach. However, the notion of a *décision* is an open-textured one, in the view of some jurists conditioned by the rule that only *actes administratifs* are subject to review on the grounds of illegality.
[71] Chapus, *Droit administratif général*, Tome 1, 1295–96; Vedel and Delvolvé, *Droit administratif*, Tome 1, 584; CE Sect. 26 Jan. 1973, *Driancourt*, Leb. 78; CE 28 Mar. 1980, *Iverneau*, RDP 1980.1744 obs. de Soto. There are exceptions where the CE has required *faute lourde* even as regards *actes*: e.g. CE 7 Jul. 1971, *Gérard*, Leb. 513. For a very useful comparative discussion see Fairgrieve, *State Liability*, Chap. 3.
[72] See CE Sect. 19 Jun. 1981, *Carliez*, concl. Genevois, AJDA 1982.103; CE Sect. 25 Jun. 1999, Leb. 215, but cf. CE 17 Jun. 1983, *SCI Italie-Vendrezane*, Leb. 267 (substantial damages awarded for expenses incurred in reliance on illegal planning decision); CE 20 Jan.1989, *Arbet*, Leb. 907 (interested person recovered damages for loss of opportunity to put his view and consequential inconvenience).

failing to consult the Commission de la sécurité des consommateurs,[73] any loss caused by this lack of consultation is unlikely to be related to harm caused to a citizen using the product in question.

The approach of the Conseil d'Etat to the substantive appropriateness of administrative decision making in the context of product safety may be illustrated by its decision in 1982 in *Union fédérale des consommateurs*.[74] In this case, the *Union*, a national federation of local consumers' groups, requested the Minister of the Economy to order the withdrawal under consumer safety powers of a particular model of car tyre and, when he refused to do so, applied to the administrative courts to annul this refusal. However, the Conseil d'Etat refused to do so since the Minister had decided in reliance on a scientific and technical study and not on any materially inaccurate facts that the tyres did not present a danger to vehicle safety of a nature to justify their withdrawal from the market and, in so doing, had not made any 'manifestly erroneous assessment of the circumstances of the case'.[75] The Conseil d'Etat has taken a similar approach to a public authority's failure to enact regulations governing a product.[76] Indeed, it has been said that the Conseil d'Etat will not intervene where technical matters are involved as it 'does not recognise in itself a power to check whether or not a shampoo is dangerous'.[77] While these cases concerned refusals to intervene, it is clear that the Conseil d'Etat would take the same approach to an allegedly inappropriate decision to intervene.[78] If, therefore, an administrative court views a public body's exercise of a product safety power as an *acte administratif*, there is little difference between a standard of liability in *faute simple* and *faute lourde*: *faute simple* requires illegality, and where substantive illegality requires 'manifest error' it looks very like *faute lourde*.

However, French courts appear to prefer to treat cases involving the exercise of safety powers (and in particular those concerning the general powers which *maires* possess within their *communes*),[79] not in terms of the illegality of any decisions or failures to decide but rather in terms of the degree of care taken, whether *faute simple* (in the sense of lack of ordinary care) or *faute lourde* (some grosser form of fault). For example, in *Doublet*[80] a local householder sued the *commune* as responsible for its *maire's* failure to enforce regulations regarding the health and safety of a camping site opposite his house. The Conseil d'Etat held that the *maire's* 'systematic failure' to enforce the regulations constituted a *faute lourde* so as to entail liability in the *commune*.

---

[73] Above, pp. 309–10.   [74] CE 30 Jun. 1982, Leb. 249.

[75] On this basis of 'illegality' more generally, see Braibant and Stirn, *Droit administratif français*, 281–3; Brown and Bell, 256 *et seq*.

[76] CE 28 Jan. 1987, *Union fédérale des consommateurs*, No. 37945 (unreported) (failure to regulate caustic soda). In CE 23 Oct. 1959, *Doublet*, Leb. 540, D 1960.191 note Lavroff it was held that a *maire's* refusal to regulate a camping site in the interests of public health would be annulled only if 'by reason of the seriousness of the peril resulting from a situation which was particularly dangerous for good order, public safety or public health, this authority, by not promulgating those measures which were indispensable to stop the serious peril, failed to recognise his legal obligations'. Cf. CE 27 Nov. 1964, *Dame Renard*, Leb. 590 where the State was held liable in damages for failing to enact a regulation which would have set the terms on which the claimant's rights under a *décret* could be exercised.

[77] Braibant and Stirn, *Droit administratif français*, 281–3.

[78] CE 27 Apr. 1988, D 1988 IR 147 (erasers to look like sweets); CE 21 Apr. 1994, D 1997 IR 123 (beef products).   [79] Above, p. 308.

[80] CE 14 Dec. 1962, D 1963.117.

In the *affaire Stalinon*, decided in 1968, the Conseil d'Etat upheld this approach to the basis of liability in the context of product safety, but did not impose liability in the circumstances.[81] At the time, pharmaceuticals had to be approved and licensed by an administrative committee, the Commission des spécialités pharmaceutiques, and this had been done in respect of a drug called '*Stalinon*'. After *Stalinon* caused many deaths and serious injuries, the company director and scientific consultant responsible for its composition were convicted of offences of involuntary homicide and causing personal injuries and held liable in damages in full to the drug's many victims, despite an argument that their liability should reduced on account of the 'irregularity' of the public committee's operations which had led to the granting of the drug's licence.[82] Ten years later the insurers of the company which manufactured and marketed the drug and of its promoter claimed contribution from the State in respect of these liabilities on the basis that they were subrogated to their policyholders' claims.[83] While the Conseil d'Etat accepted that the public committee might well have committed a *faute lourde* in its decision to license *Stalinon*, it held that this would not give rise to liability towards the insurers whose losses were the 'direct consequence' of the faults of those who had promoted the drug and had been convicted.[84]

However, following the general trend, the Conseil d'Etat appears to be moving away from a requirement of *faute lourde* towards *faute simple* in the sense of 'ordinary fault' even in the context of the control of 'activities' undertaken or neglected which affect product safety. So, while in earlier decisions, *faute lourde* was held to be the appropriate basis for the claims in respect of the persons drowned when vessels sank even after public inspectors had declared them seaworthy,[85] in 1998 the Conseil d'Etat imposed liability in a similar case merely for *faute simple*.[86] This trend appears to be confirmed by its approach to liability in the administration for failures in regulation and safety in the *affaire du sang contaminé*.[87]

(b) The *affaire du sang contaminé*: Part II—State liability for failures in the control of safety

The important decision of the Assemblée of the Conseil d'Etat in 1993 in the *affaire du sang contaminé* is perhaps the most striking example of this changing basis of

---

[81] CE 28 Jun. 1968, JCP 1968 II 15578 note anon. See similarly, CE 7 Mar. 1980, *affaire du 'Cinq-Sept,'* D 1980.320 note Richer, concl. Massot, AJDA 1980.423 note Albertini, below, pp. 327–9.

[82] Paris 3 Jan. 1958, S 1958.336 note Bredin. For the Paris Criminal Court of Appeal, it appeared from the documents submitted to it by the Minister of Health relating to the Commission's workings that its investigation of the drug was 'too superficial', but the court concluded that in the absence of fraud, it was not for it to assess the scientific validity of the Commission's controls: ibid., 338–9. For further discussion of the criminal court's decision, see below, pp. 373–4.

[83] CE 28 Jun. 1968 (2 cases), JCP 1968.II.15578 note anon.   [84] Below, p. 327.

[85] CE 26 Feb. 1954, *Vacher*, Leb. 132; CE 1 Oct. 1976, *Cie d'assurances*, Leb. 388 (recourse claim by the shipowners and their insurers).

[86] CE Sect. 13 Mar. 1998, *Améon*, D 1998 no. 535 note Lebreton, JCP 1998.I.181 chron. Petit.

[87] Fairgrieve, *State Liability*, 109 points to decisions which reaffirm the basis in *faute lourde*, notably as regards the supervision of banks: e.g. CE 30 Nov. 2001, *Kechichian*, AJDA 2002 136. There may here be a distinction between liability for personal safety (based on *faute simple*) and for economic harm (based on *faute lourde*): Fairgrieve, ibid., 119–20 referring to M. Guyoma and P. Collin AJDA 2002.133 at 134.

liability.[88] The claimants were three haemophiliacs who had been transfused with blood in the course of 1983, 1984 and 1985 and who had been diagnosed HIV positive in January, March and June of 1985 and the public body which administered a special legislative fund for the compensation of the transfusion or haemophiliac victims of HIV.[89] The defendant was the State, as responsible for the Minister of Health.[90] The basis of the claims was that the Minister of Health had failed in the exercise of his legal powers of control over the safety of the blood distributed and regulated by the National Blood Transfusion Centre and distributed via local Blood Transfusion Centres to hospitals and clinics:[91] these were not claims in respect of the supply or manufacture of the blood.[92] The State had two types of power: a power to regulate the collection of blood and the conditions of use of blood products in France (including a power to order the withdrawal of any products from distribution) and a power of supervision over the National and local blood transfusion centres, this being an example of what is termed a *pouvoir de tutelle*.[93]

According to the Conseil d'Etat, before October 1984 information as to the possible risks and prevention of infection by HIV was uncertain, but by that time the scientific community accepted that the HIV virus could be transmitted by blood transfusion but could be de-activated by heat treatment; it was also known that if blood products were not so treated, at least 10 per cent of those who contracted the HIV virus would develop AIDS, of whom 70 per cent would die.[94] The Conseil d'Etat noted that these facts had been drawn to the attention of the relevant State authority in writing by an epidemiologist at the Direction générale de la Santé in November 1984. By March 1985 the relevant public authority had been clearly told of the exceptional risk of contamination by blood transfusion,[95] but it was not until October 1985 that the State ordered the withdrawal of the affected blood and blood products from the distribution service.[96] According to M. Légal, the *Commissaire du gouvernement*, this failure to intervene in the State authorities was explained by a concern about the

---

[88] TA Paris 20 Dec. 1991, 8 RFDA (1992) 566, concl. Stahlberger, ibid. 552; CAA Paris 16 Jun. 1992, JCP 1992 Actualité nos. 33–37; CE Ass. 9 Apr. 1993, Req. no. 138652, D 1993.312, concl. Légal, obs. Maugüé and Touvet, AJDA 1993 Chron. 344. Other cases came before the CE in the *affaire* concerning the liability of public hospitals or blood transfusion centres, see above, pp. 150–1.

[89] This was established by the *loi* no. 91-1406 of 31 Dec. 1991 which set up a special body to administer a fund from which payments were to be made to those who contracted the HIV virus after transfusion or an injection with blood derivatives: between April and December 1992, it made awards to some 6,600 people: Y. Lambert-Faivre, 'Principes d'indemnisation des victimes post-transfusionnelles du sida (Cour d'appel de Paris, 27 novembre 1992 (20 arrêts)' D 1993 Chron. 67. The fund is financed half by the State and half by contributions from insurance companies: J.-M. Pontier, 'Sida, de la responsabilité à la garantie sociale (à propos de la loi du 31 décembre 1991)' RFDA 8 (1992) 533, 544–5.

[90] The Minister of Health was later found guilty of involuntary homicide: Cour de Justice de la République 9 Mar. 1999, below, p. 399.

[91] The legal regime was based on the *loi* of 21 Jul. 1952, on which see above, p. 149.

[92] For this type of claim see above, pp. 149–51.

[93] Comm. gouv. Légal, concl. D 1993.312, 314. Such a *pouvoir de tutelle* may be over either public or private bodies. The classic example of a *pouvoir de tutelle* was of the State over local authorities, but this supervision was significantly changed by the laws of decentralisation in 1982: Chapus, *Droit administratif général*, Tome 1, 408 *et seq.*   [94] D 1993.312, 321.

[95] Ibid., 317.   [96] Circular of 20 Oct. 1985.

unknown effects of heat treatment on blood, a desire not to make a fuss which might lead to the ostracism of HIV-positive persons and a misplaced confidence in French blood products.[97]

In holding the State liable to all the claimants before it, the Conseil d'Etat dealt firmly with both issues of the standard of fault applicable and difficulties of causal connection between any fault in the State and the harm caused to transfusional victims of HIV.[98]

First, should the appropriate standard of fault in relation to the exercise of the State's powers be *faute simple* or *faute lourde*? All the courts through which this litigation progressed were willing to find *faute lourde* in the State in its failure to act as of March 1985 when it had been informed of the exceptional risk of infection, but before this date (and after November 1984) they found only *faute simple* owing to the remaining degree of uncertainty as to the risks involved. The question whether *faute lourde* was required for liability therefore remained significant, for if it were, only those persons who received blood and were diagnosed HIV-positive *after* March 1985 could recover and one of the claimants in the case itself (and, no doubt, others not actually party to it) had been diagnosed HIV-positive before this date.[99]

For both the courts below, the relevant standard was *faute lourde*: as Mme Stahlberger, the Commissaire du gouvernement at first instance explained, the exercise of the powers in question was difficult[100] or involved difficult questions of assessment of a situation or a finely-balanced control, citing the *affaire Stalinon*, in the context of the licensing of pharmaceuticals.[101] However, in the view of the *Commissaire du gouvernement* of the Conseil d'Etat, M. Légal, the administrative courts had not always required *faute lourde* in respect of the exercise of powers of this type,[102] 'distinguishing' the decision in the *affaire Stalinon* on the basis that the State has no control over the research activities of pharmaceutical companies in the development of a new drug, whereas:

blood derivatives are developed under the administration's control (like a vaccine which has been made compulsory), their products and their manner of manufacture are, or ought to be, known in advance by the Minister of Health.[103]

---

[97] D 1993.312, 319. It was also later alleged that the decision reflected a preference for a French test: below, pp. 398, 400.

[98] For the decision of the Conseil d'Etat on the defence of '*fait d'un tiers*', see below, p. 324.

[99] The TA Paris, which imposed liability on the State only after March 1985, refused compensation for those who had already been diagnosed HIV-positive at that date in respect of the physiological consequences of this recontamination on the ground that these were totally hypothetical given the existing state of scientific knowledge and that, therefore, their loss was 'purely contingent': TA Paris 20 Dec. 1991, 8 RFDA (1992) 552, 566.

[100] Stahlberger, concl., TA Paris 20 Dec. 1991, 8 RFDA (1992) 552, 554–5 citing CE 29 Mar.1946, *Caisse départementale d'assurances sociales de Meurthe-et-Moselle*, RDP 1946.490 concl. Lefas (exercise by a *préfet* of *pouvoirs de tutelle* over a local financial institution).

[101] CE 28 Jun. 1968, *affaire Stalinon*, JCP 1968.II.15578 note anon and see above, p. 315.

[102] CE Sect. 4 May 1979, *Gail*, Leb. 190 (failure to modify instructions for compulsory vaccine). He also cited examples of the exercise by public authorities of powers of health and safety (CE 28 Apr. 1967, *Lafont*, Leb. 182, JCP. 1967.II. 15296 note Rabinovitch) or of *pouvoirs de tutelle* (CE 26 Jun. 1970, *Bartoli*, Leb. 441 concl. Vught) also based on *faute simple*. [103] D 1993.312, 316.

These arguments (together, one suspects, with their practical effect on compensation for those diagnosed with HIV earlier and otherwise left only partially compensated) convinced the Conseil d'Etat, which held that:

having regard to the extent of the powers which [the relevant provisions] confer on the State services as regards the general organization of the public blood transfusion service, the control over those bodies which are charged with the performance of this service and the promulgation of rules appropriate to ensure the quality of human blood, its plasma and derivatives, and the purposes for which these powers have been granted to them, the liability of the State may arise where *any fault* is committed in the exercise of these powers.[104]

By so deciding, the Conseil d'Etat followed its general tendency away from a require-ment of *faute lourde* to one of *faute simple*, but it did so in cautious and qualified terms, relying on the State's special powers over and the special organisation of the blood transfusion service. Public powers over the manufacture and distribution of blood were (and are) very different from more general public powers over the design or marketing of a commercial product by a private company or private companies and so it is possible that cases such as the *affaire Stalinon* may therefore remain subject to a requirement of *faute lourde*,[105] although the Conseil d'Etat's subsequent decision in *Améon* required only *faute simple* in respect of the safety certification of sea-going vessels.[106]

The second issue which the Conseil d'Etat had to determine in the *affaire du sang contaminé* related to the causal connection required between the State's fault and any individual claimant's harm. At first instance, the Minister of Social Affairs argued that it was for the claimants to show that their infection with the HIV virus was caused by their receipt of transfusions with contaminated blood and thereby with any alleged administrative fault, although it was for the court to order any *expertise* to this end: it was not enough to adduce statistical data connecting receipt of blood with diagnosis of the infection as there were other possible sources of infection with the virus.[107] While this argument reflects the established burden of proof as to causation as regards the liability of public authorities, it was rejected by all three of the administrative courts before whom the litigation came. For Mme Stahlberger at first instance, where an expert report pointed with 'sufficient certainty' to transfusion as the source of infec-tion at a particular period, then a court should apply a *presumption* of causation[108] and the Conseil d'Etat took a similar view, simply recording the receipt by a claimant of blood in late 1984 and early 1985 and his diagnosis as HIV-positive. As was observed at the time, this was a very generous view of the requirement of causation.[109]

Thirdly, the Conseil d'Etat also rejected the State's argument that it should not be liable beyond the proper share of its responsibility, by way of application of the defence of *Fait d'un tiers*. Here, as I shall note in explaining the more general significance of this defence, the Conseil d'Etat was at its most radical.[110]

---

[104] D 1993.312, 321 (emphasis added).
[105] Cf. CE 6 Oct. 2000, *Comm. de Saint-Florent*, AJDA 2001.201 note M Cliquennois (*faute lourde* in respect of *pouvoir de tutelle* of *préfet* over decentralised local authorities).
[106] CE 13 Mar. 1998, *Améon*, D 1998 no. 535 note Lebreton, JCP 1998.I.181 chron. Petit.
[107] Stahlberger, concl., TA Paris 20 Dec. 1991, 8 RFDA (1992) 552, 561.
[108] Ibid., 562 and see Légal, D 1993.312, 320–1.
[109] Maugüé and Touvet, AJDA 1993 Chron. 344, 348.   [110] Below, p. 324.

Overall, this decision of the Conseil d'Etat was an important one, but its importance was as much symbolic and political as legal and far-reaching. Its symbolic importance was as a recognition of the State's *responsibility* for the failures in the ministries charged with the regulation and control of the Blood Transfusion Service: to establish this responsibility was as much a reason for the case being brought by the haemophiliac recipients of the blood as the recovery of damages which they would thereby receive supplementary to the sums awarded under the special legislative compensation scheme.[111] For, at much the same period when the Conseil d'Etat imposed responsibility on the *State* in respect of *faults* in the administration and control of the blood transfusion service, the criminal process was, at least in the views of many of the victims of the infected blood, proving singularly inadequate in attributing responsibility to the *individuals* involved, whether in the management of the blood transfusion service or in the government itself.[112] It is understandable that in the highly charged atmosphere surrounding this *affaire* in the early 1990s, the Conseil d'Etat would wish to avoid deciding that, while at fault in supervising the blood transfusion service, the State's fault was not bad enough to attract responsibility; or, secondly, that even if its fault had been bad enough, it was for those who had received blood transfusions to show that it was the receipt of this blood which caused their HIV, rather than their 'lifestyle'; or, finally, that the State could escape its own responsibility in part by pointing to other people's fault.

(c) Systemic tendencies towards the 'irresponsibility' of the administration

In principle, therefore, an administrative authority which has failed in its control of the safety of a product may be liable to a person injured by it, whether on the basis of *faute lourde* or *faute simple*. However, there are a number of reasons why in this context (and in others like it) in practice this fairly liberal approach to the imposition of liability does not result in liability actually being imposed on public authorities. These reasons are complex, and involve the relative substantive bases of liability in public and private law; the administrative law rules as to delay and prescription; the administrative law defence of *fait d'un tiers*; and the Conseil d'Etat's restrictive attitude to recourse actions by private persons held liable by the ordinary courts. While none of these rule out the possibility of a public body being held liable for its failures in control of product safety, their effect, either singly or in combination, works against this happening: some create disincentives, some create legal tripwires. In all this, the jurisdictional division between the ordinary courts and the administrative courts is of key importance.

Let me start my explanation of this by posing a simple hypothetical case. Let us say that a defective product is put onto the market by a French manufacturer and this product causes numerous injuries owing to its design or lack of warnings. After a while, these injuries come to the notice of its manufacturer and of the public authorities responsible for product safety, either at the national or departmental level.[113] However, for a period of six months, the relevant public authorities fail to take any action in respect of the product in question, neither warning the public nor ordering its withdrawal from the market. Our hypothetical claimant is a person who suffers

---

[111] Above, p. 316 n. 89.   [112] Below, pp. 394–401.   [113] See above, pp. 307–10.

serious personal injuries caused by a newly purchased product's defect four months after its dangers have come to the attention of the manufacturer and public authorities.[114] In these circumstances, the claimant has a potential claim against the manufacturer in the ordinary courts and against the public authority in the administrative courts. However, she cannot claim damages in either jurisdiction against *both* types of defendant, but must choose whether to bring actions in *both* jurisdictions or elect which defendant to sue in the latter's appropriate jurisdiction.

In French law, there is no legal reason why a claimant should not bring parallel proceedings in both jurisdictions against different (appropriate) defendants in respect of the same harm[115] and, unlike the position as regards criminal and civil proceedings,[116] proceedings in the ordinary courts do not suspend proceedings in the administrative courts or vice versa. If the proceedings are allowed to run their course, one will come to judgment prior to the other and, once satisfied, such a judgment will go to reduce or extinguish the loss in respect of the claim in the other jurisdiction; on the other hand, bringing parallel proceedings possesses the obvious disadvantage of cost and time spent by a claimant; and if a claimant recovers in full in one jurisdiction and then terminates the litigation in the other, he may be faced not merely with his own wasted costs in that jurisdiction, but also those of the other side.[117]

What, then, of limiting one's proceedings to the ordinary courts? There are a number of good reasons why a claimant would prefer to claim in the ordinary courts *rather than* the administrative courts,[118] but if he chooses to do so, there is no sure way in which he can protect his position in relation to any future claim against a public authority in the administrative courts against the risk of being out of time under the 'four-year prescription' rule (*la prescription quadriennale* formerly termed *la déchéance quadriennale*).[119] For while a written application for compensation to a public authority by a person will interrupt the running of time for this purpose,[120] making such an application creates its own risk. If it is accepted in full, then well and good; if the public authority fails to respond to the claim, this silence does not trigger a short period within which proceedings must be brought[121] (even though it is deemed to be a rejection for the purposes of allowing proceedings to be brought);[122] but if the public authority expressly rejects the application for compensation, either wholly or in part, the applicant then has only two months in which to contest this by bringing proceedings for damages in the administrative courts.[123] So, applying for compensation to a public body runs the risk of accelerating the period in which a claim must be brought from four years to two months.

---

[114] Cf. the facts of *Smith v Sec. of State for Health* (15 Feb. 2002) 2002 WL 45404, below, pp. 354–5.

[115] An example may be found in the litigation in Civ. 17 Dec. 1954, JCP 1955.II.8490 note Savatier, GP 1955.1.54 where the claimant, who had contracted syphilis from the blood with which he had been supplied, brought a claim against the blood transfusion service in the ordinary courts and a claim against the public hospital in the administrative courts: above, pp. 149–50.   [116] Below, p. 374.

[117] Where a claimant loses a claim, he may be ordered to pay the costs of the winning side by the court in either jurisdiction: Brown and Bell, 125; R. Chapus, *Droit du contentieux administratifs* (Montchrestien, Paris 10th. ed., 2002) 961–6.   [118] Below, pp. 321–4.

[119] Below, p. 321.

[120] *Loi* no. 68-1250 of 31 Dec. 1968, art. 2 al. 1.   [121] Pacteau, *Contentieux administratifs*, 178–9.

[122] This is necessary so as to fulfill the rule of the *décision préalable* required before a claim for compensation may be brought before the administrative courts: Chapus, *Droit du contentieux administratifs, op. cit.* n. 117, 483 *et seq*.   [123] Pacteau, *Contentieux administratifs*, 163–4.

In the following discussion, I shall explain the reasons why my hypothetical claimant is likely to choose to claim in the ordinary courts rather than the administrative courts and, secondly, how this choice is likely to affect the ultimate imposition of liability in the public body.

(i) The relative attractiveness of claiming in the ordinary courts and in the administrative courts

There are at least five different factors which might weigh with a claimant in deciding whether to sue in the ordinary courts or the administrative courts in circumstances such as our hypothetical case of a failure of a public authority to intervene appropriately in the interests of product safety.

First, a private law claim brought in the ordinary courts will often not require him to prove a defendant's fault, whereas the basis of this claim in the administrative courts will do so. I do not need to stress this point, for I have already explained the many ways in which French courts have imposed liability on private persons in respect of harm caused by the things which they use, supply or manufacture, whether this liability is put in terms of liability for the 'deeds of things', under the *garantie légale* or contractual 'non-conformity' in sale, or for breach of an *obligation de sécurité de résultat*.[124] By contrast, a public authority will not be liable in respect of its exercise of powers of control over product safety without proof of fault, whether *faute simple* or *faute lourde*.[125]

Secondly, in general (though by no means universally), a claimant will have more time within which to bring a claim before the ordinary courts than before the administrative ones. For in private law the general period of prescription is 10 years either from the 'manifestation of the harm' for extra-contractual claims or from the non-performance for contractual claims against a trader,[126] though with the awkward exception of the *bref délai* which has governed claims brought under the *garantie légale* in the law of sale.[127] By contrast, as I mentioned earlier, any action for damages brought against a public authority is subject to a delay of two months from the time of rejection of the claimant's application to that authority[128] and to an overall four-year prescription period which extinguishes *all debts* owed by the majority of French public bodies,[129] a rule which has been said to dominate all litigation against the administration.[130] The prescription period starts from the first day of the year following that in which the rights were acquired,[131] this being

---

[124] Above, pp. 52–61, 69–72, 100–1.   [125] Above, pp. 311–19.   [126] Above, p. 34.

[127] Above, pp. 91–3, 620–1.   [128] Above, p. 320.

[129] It applies (with legislative exceptions) to the French State, Departments, *communes*, and those *établissements publics* which are subject to state financial control through a '*comptable public*': *loi* no. 68-1250 of 31 Dec. 1968, art. 1 and see J.-M. Auby and R. Drago, *Traité de contentieux administratifs*, (LGDJ, Paris, 1984) Tome 2, 515. Its origins lie in the financial instability of the French State after the revolution and during the First Empire and the desire of early nineteenth-century French governments to prevent a backlog of public debt from arising in the future: Braibant and Stirn, *Droit administratif français*, 317.

[130] A. Plantey, 'Prescription quadriennale; Domaine, maniement, effets, contentieux' Jur.-Cl. Adm. Fasc. 111 (2004), 4. Cf. Braibant and Stirn, *Droit administratif français*, 357 who describe it as 'an important institution which often applies in practice and which has caused the loss of large sums of money to persons who have been in the right on the merits'.

[131] *Loi* no. 68-1250 of 31 Dec. 1968, art. 1 and see Plantey, *op. cit.*, 27 *et seq.*

seen as the time of death as regards claims in respect of a person's death,[132] and either the date when injuries occur or when they become fully apparent ('consolidated') as regards claims for personal injuries. Although time does not run 'against a person who may be legitimately regarded as unaware of the existence of the *créance*',[133] the Conseil d'Etat has taken a rather narrow approach to the discretion to allow more time which this offers. For example, in its decision in 1987 in *Chartrousse & Soc. Normand* the claimant had been injured and his car damaged in a road accident and, having failed to recover damages against another driver in the ordinary courts, he claimed damages from the Minister of Transport alleging a failure to maintain the road.[134] However, his claim was held barred by expiry of the four-year prescription period: the accident had occurred in 1972, and in the view of the Conseil d'Etat, the claimant's injuries were 'consolidated' by 1973. Furthermore, the state of the road was known at the time of the accident so that he could not be said to have been unaware of his possible claim against the Ministry, even though the ordinary court had rejected his claim only in 1977. The Conseil d'Etat also held that bringing proceedings in the *ordinary* courts does not interrupt the running of time for the purposes of the four-year prescription rule.[135]

This strict and relatively short period for claims in the administrative courts might suggest that it is in a claimant's interest to claim first against the public body, leaving litigation against the private person until later; but given the general balance of advantage in favour of suing in the ordinary courts, where a claimant claims first against a private person, its likely effect is that any later administrative claim is barred; it is rare for a claim (and in particular a serious claim) in respect of death or personal injuries to be concluded by the ordinary courts within four years of the accident or 'consolidation' of a claimant's injuries.[136]

The third factor in a claimant's choice whether to sue a private defendant in the ordinary courts rather than a public defendant in the administrative courts is that he is likely to recover more money in the ordinary courts.[137] Here, the most important cause is the Conseil d'Etat's rejection for the last half century of the joint liability of private and public persons in respect of the same harm caused by their respective faults or, to use the French terminology, the various 'co-authors of the harm' are not liable *in solidum* for fault.[138] The

---

[132] CE 28 Sep. 1990, *Centre hospitalier spécialisé d'Armentières*, AJDA 1991.60 obs. Prétot.

[133] *Loi* no. 68-1250 of 31 Dec. 1968, art. 3.

[134] CE 23 Dec. 1987, Leb. 422, AJDA 1988.II.361 note Prétot. Cf. above, pp. 122–31.

[135] Ibid., interpreting *loi* no. 68-1250 of 31 Dec. 1968, art. 2 al. 2.

[136] This may be less true as regards claims for damages brought in criminal courts by way of *actions civiles*, on which, see below, p. 385.

[137] Formerly, in part this was because the Conseil d'Etat refused to award damages for *dommage moral*, a position which it formally abandoned in 1961: CE 25 Nov. 1961, *Letisserand*, S 1963.59 note Hamon. French administrative courts are also said to take a very strict approach to a claimant's contributory fault: Fairgrieve, *State Liability*, 177–81.

[138] Vedel and Delvolvé, *Droit administratif*, Tome I, 618–20; CE 16 May 1951, *Veuve Pintal*, D 1951.511 note F.M.; CE 15 Oct. 1976, JCP 1980.II.19319 note Brard. For a decade before liability *in solidum* had been accepted: CE Sect. 23 Dec. 1941, *Ville de Montpellier*, DC 1942.156 note J.D; CE 9 Nov. 1937, *Cie d'assur. 'La Préservatrice'* Leb. 919. The position is more complicated as regards contribution between two public bodies: J. Moreau, 'Détermination du patrimoine du personne responsable' Jur.-Cl. Adm. Fasc. 836, 7–8 (1994) notes that in two situations of contributory faults by public authorities, there is 'a true solidarity': liability for 'public works' (on which see above, pp. 121–31) and where there is a 'strict collaboration between several public services'. See also F. Roques, 'L'action récursoire dans le droit administratif de la responsabilité', AJDA 1991.75, esp. 76 *et seq.* and below, pp. 326–30.

practical expression of this rejection is that where a public person is sued for harm which is partly its responsibility (based on its fault) and partly the responsibility of a private person (whether based on the latter's fault or otherwise) the public authority possesses a defence known either as *fait d'un tiers* or *fait d'une tierce personne*, the effect of which is to reduce or exclude liability in the administration.[139] Moreover, the decision whether and to what extent to reduce liability is based on the relative 'responsibilities' of the public and private 'co-authors' of the claimant's harm in the view, of course, of the *administrative* courts, who take into account both their comparative fault and the comparative causal significance of their behaviour. For example, in *Ville de Rueil-Malmaison* the claimant and his son were injured and his wife killed in a fire at a privately owned cinema.[140] Here, the Conseil d'Etat took into account the relative fault of the cinema's owner, to whom the necessary refitting of the cinema had been pointed out, and of the town, which had failed to serve a formal notice on him to perform these changes and had failed to close the cinema pending their performance. In the result, the Conseil d'Etat imposed liability on the town for half the harm caused to the claimants by the fire.[141] This decision has much in common with our hypothetical product safety case, for it concerns the liability of a public authority for failing in its *police administrative* to control the failures in safety of a private and commercial operator.

Two reasons have been advanced for this defence. The first is that there can be no *joint* liability (*solidarité*) where liability in the two co-authors of the harm is judged according to different sets of legal principles, the one public, the other private,[142] but this is a circular argument as it rests on a preconceived idea of which liabilities may be joint which sits uneasily with the Conseil d'Etat's earlier acceptance of liability *in solidum*. More convincingly, there is said to be general principle of law (*principe général de droit*) that a public authority should not be made to pay more than it owes and that this prevents the application of the solidarity rule under which one co-author of a harm pays out in full to a claimant, even though he is *responsable* only in part, an argument which gives weight to one's suspicion that the rule was conceived to protect public finances. However, French jurists have been very critical of the defence of *fait d'un tiers*, Vedel and Delvolvé calling it one of the 'carbuncles disfiguring the law of administrative liability'.[143] First, it creates an unjustified difference from the law applied in the ordinary courts; secondly, it is inconsistent with the rights of victims as it puts on them the risk of insolvency in a third party; thirdly, the private and public jurisdictions may disagree as to the proper division of responsibility between the two

---

[139] Chapus, *Droit administrative général*, Tome 1, 1251–3; CE 15 Oct. 1976, *District urbain de Reims*, CE Sect. 5 Oct. 1977, *Gazup*, CE 28 Oct.1977, *Commune de Flumet*, CE Sect 14 Jun. 1978 reported together JCP 1980.II.19319 note Y. Brard; CE 14 May 1986, *Commune de Cilaos*, Leb. 716, AJDA 1986.466 obs. L. Richer; CE 30 Nov. 2001, *Kechichian*, AJDA 2002.136 (liability for *faute lourde* of banking regulator). Cf. CE 1 Feb. 1974, *Commune de Sainte-Anastasie*, Leb. 79 (*commune*'s liability for damage to property caused by rockets left in an unlocked and unguarded cowshed and let off by a young boy accidentally not reduced on the ground of the boy's contributory fault). [140] CE 10 Jul 1957, Leb. 457.

[141] Ibid. See also CE 9 Jul. 1975, *Ville de Cognac*, Leb. 413 (accident at a public swimming baths partly caused by the fault of a young diver and partly by the local authority's failure to provide proper supervision or organisation of the baths: town's liability assessed at one half).

[142] P.L., note CE 7 Nov. 1952, JCP 1953.II.7448.

[143] Vedel and Delvolvé, *Droit administratif*, Vol. 1, 620.

persons both liable; and, fourthly, the rule is inconsistently applied, not applying to liability in respect of 'public works' even where this is based on fault.[144]

At a first reading the decision in 1993 of the Assemblée of the Conseil d'Etat in the *affaire du sang contaminé* suggests a move away from use of the special defence, perhaps in part owing to these criticisms.[145] While the recipients of contaminated blood sued the administration for its alleged failures to regulate and supervise the distributors of blood products, they certainly could have sued a number of other people or bodies: local blood transfusion centres, public hospitals, private sector clinics and doctors.[146] Should the State's liability for its failures to supervise properly the supply of blood in France be reduced so as to take into account the contribution to the claimant's harm of the National Blood Transfusion Centre,[147] a private body, whose liability was governed by private law, even though it acted in furtherance of a *service public*?[148] The Conseil d'Etat thought not, owing to the close collaboration between the blood transfusion centres and the State's own general organisation of the *service public* regarding blood products and the distribution of their respective roles.[149] In so holding, the Conseil d'Etat went further than its earlier case law, where it had rejected the defence where two *public* bodies had collaborated in the same *service public*.[150] For some jurists, the Conseil d'Etat's decision may be a welcome signal towards its abandonment of the defence of *fait d'un tiers* altogether,[151] but it may rather be an expression of its unwillingness to rely on a technical rule to protect the State from full responsibility for its part in the *affaire du sang contaminé*: certainly, the defence has been subsequently upheld in other contexts.[152] While it still exists, it creates a strong disincentive to a person harmed by both a private person and a public person from suing the latter first.

Fourthly, a common reason for an English claimant to sue a public authority where a private person is also liable (such as in the famous line of cases concerning liability of local authorities in respect of their powers under the Public Health Acts),[153] is that the private person cannot pay, whereas the public person is insured or has 'deep pockets'. This may also be a reason for a French claimant to sue a public authority rather than a private person[154] and the question of insolvency actually attracts special rules governing

[144] Vedel and Delvolvé, *Droit administratif*, Vol. 1, 620; Y. Brard, note JCP 1980.II.19319.

[145] CE Ass. 9 Apr. 1993, Req. no. 138652 D 1993.312, concl. Légal, obs. Maugüé and Touvet, AJDA 1993 Chron. 344, above, pp. 315–18.　　　　　　　　　　　　　　　　　　　　　[146] Above, pp. 149–51.

[147] The *Commissaire du gouvernement*, M. Légal, dismissed any possible causal role in the doctors who prescribed the transfusion on the basis of their not having at their disposal the same means or the same information as either level of the transfusion service: D 1993.312, 320.

[148] The *Commissaire du gouvernement*, Mdme. Stahlberger, thought so: TA Paris 20 Dec. 1991, (1992) AJDA 552, 564; Paris 16 Jun. 1992, JCP 1992 Actualité no. 33-37.　　　　　　　　[149] D 1993.312, 321.

[150] CE Ass. 13 Jul. 1962, *Lastrajoli*, Leb. 507 (State and *département*); CE 24 Mar. 1978, *Laporta*, Leb. 159 and see Moreau, *op. cit.* n. 138, Jur.-Cl. Adm. Fasc. 836 (1994) 7–8; F. Roques, 'L'action récursoire dans le droit administratif de la responsabilité', AJDA 1991.75, 79 *et seq*. Légal argued that the CE's decision on this point was within this line of *jurisprudence*: D 1993.312, 317.

[151] Chapus, *Droit administratif général*, Tome 1, 1280–2.

[152] CE 22 Nov. 2000, *Appaganou*, Leb. 557. Cf. CE 15 Jan. 2001, *Assistance publique-Hôpitaux de Paris*, Leb. 15 (defence rejected as between blood transfusion centres).

[153] *Anns v Merton LBC* [1978] AC 728.

[154] E.g. CE 9 Jul. 1975, *Ville de Cognac*, Leb. 413; CE 1 Feb. 1974, *Commune de Sainte-Anastasie*, Leb. 79; CE 5 Dec. 1952, *Renon et Fichaut*, S 1953.3.63; CE 5 Oct. 1977, *Gazup*, JCP 1980.II.19319 note Brard.

liability in the French law of 'public works'.[155] However, in many situations of liability for products, French *private* law provides a number of possible defendants and thereby spreads the risk of insolvency in any one. So, a buyer may sue not merely his own seller, but *any other* seller in the line of distribution of the property in question directly, avoiding any intervening insolvency;[156] an employer commissioning a building or its relatively recent buyer may sue a range of persons responsible for its construction, all of whom are liable jointly in respect of their contribution.[157] Others may in principle sue any person by whose fault his harm has arisen, but more helpfully may sue the product's *gardien*.[158] And this extensive potential list of private law defendants should be seen in the light of the incidence of liability insurance, which is sometimes compulsory.[159]

Fifthly, the procedural incidents of claiming in the ordinary courts or the administrative courts are fairly evenly balanced for this purpose. Certainly, the Conseil d'Etat's power to order the production of documentary evidence from public bodies is much broader than its *civil* court counterpart's powers to order the disclosure of documents, for it recognises a general power in administrative courts to 'demand from the appropriate public body the production of all documents susceptible to establish the court's view and to allow the determination of the claims of the applicant'.[160] While French law accepts that a court may not order the production of a document protected by 'legal secrecy',[161] including medical secrecy and national secrecy, since 1998 an independent administrative authority decides whether or not material falls within this category.[162] However, these powers in the administrative courts are on a par with those enjoyed by a *criminal* court's *juge d'instruction*.[163] And the position as to both costs and legal aid is much the same in the ordinary civil and administrative courts.[164]

Given all these factors, it can be seen that in many cases involving a failure in a public authority to control a private person in relation to the safety of their products, a claimant is likely to prefer to claim damages first in the ordinary courts (whether civil or criminal) from any private law defendant rather than from the public body in the administrative courts. On the other hand, if such a person does sue in the ordinary courts and fails (or fails in part), he is very likely to be faced with an expired prescription period. Overall, therefore, suing the administration in this sort of case risks recovering too little or being too late.

---

[155] Above, p. 129. [156] Above, pp. 96–8. [157] Above, p. 108. [158] Above, Chap. 3.
[159] Above, pp. 35–7.

[160] CE Sect. 1 May, 1936 *Couespel du Mesnil*, Leb. 485 and see Gaudemet, *Droit administratif*, Tome 1, 462; R. Chapus, *Droit du contentieux administratif* (Montchrestien, Paris, 10th. edn., 2002), 798. In the absence of a law of contempt, the sanction for the administration's refusal to comply with such an order is that the facts as alleged are deemed to be established: ibid., 801.

[161] CE Sect. 23 Dec. 1988, *Banque de France*, Leb. 464.

[162] *Loi* no. 98-567 of 8 Jul. 1998, *instituant une Commission consultative du secret de la défense nationale*.

[163] On civil courts' restrained powers in this respect, see above, p. 48. On the wider powers of criminal courts in *instruction*, see below, pp. 384–5.

[164] The same regime of *aide juridictionnelle* applies to claims in the ordinary courts as in the administrative courts: Pacteau, *Contentieux administratifs*, 203. As to the relative costs between criminal and civil courts, see below, pp. 385–6.

(ii) Recourse actions by private persons in the administrative courts

So far I have argued that in cases of a public authority's failure to control product safety, the public authority is unlikely to find itself sued by a person injured by a product where, as often, he has an alternative claim against a private person. However, this likelihood would not be enough to lead to the practical 'irresponsibility' of the public authorities in this sort of case if they could be sued for contribution by any private person held liable in full to the product's victim. In principle such a right of recourse by private law defendants (and their insurers) has existed since the late 1940s,[165] but it is complicated in three ways, the last of which has a particularly protective effect on public authorities.

First, any recourse by a person held liable in the ordinary courts may have as its legal basis either the rights of the primary claimant to which he is subrogated or an independent right on the ground that his loss was caused by the public authority's fault.[166] The main disadvantage in this context with reliance on the primary claimant's rights against the administration is that they may well have ceased to exist owing to the expiry of the four-year prescription period.[167] By contrast, any independent right of recourse does not suffer from this disadvantage, for here time runs from the beginning of the year after it was acquired and this has been held not to take place until settlement[168] or final judgment in favour of the initial claimant.[169]

Secondly, however, when a recourse claim by a person held liable in full by an ordinary court comes before the administrative courts, the latter do not consider themselves bound by the view taken earlier by the ordinary court as to the liability, share in responsibility or causal role of the action of the public authority.[170] This is understandable given the 'autonomy' of the liability of public authorities, for in principle it is only for the administrative courts applying special public law rules to determine the existence and extent of administrative responsibility.[171] Having said this, in many cases the Conseil d'Etat has been content to follow the earlier judgment on these matters,[172] but on occasion has taken a very different view, as may be seen in a case decided in 1962.[173] There the primary victim owned a house in a narrow street to which was attached an electricity console which was hit by a lorry, damaging the house wall. A few years later, the house owner rebuilt the wall and recovered damages in the ordinary courts to cover

---

[165] CE 30 May 1947, *Soulié et Daraux* and CE 26 May. 1948, *Cie d'assur. 'La Préservatrice'*, D 1949.J.30 note C.L.; CE 7 Nov. 1952, *Cie. 'L'Urbaine et la Seine'*, JCP 1953.II.7448 concl. Bernard. More recently, CE 22 Nov. 1985, RGTA 1986.374.

[166] Moreau, *op. cit.* n. 138, Jur.-Cl. Adm. Fasc. 836, 10 *et seq.*   [167] Above, pp. 321–2.

[168] CE 24 May 1964, *Min. des Travaux publics*, Leb. tab. 869.

[169] CE 26 Apr. 1963, *Centre Hospitalier de Besançon*, Leb. 243 (date of judgment of Cour d'appel) and Auby and Drago, *op. cit.* n. 129, 516–17.

[170] CE 30 May 1947, *Soulié & Daraux*, CE 26 May 1948, *Cie d'assur. 'La Préservatrice'*, D 1949.J.30 note C.L.   [171] Above, pp. 19–20.

[172] E.g. CE 7 Nov. 1952, *Cie 'L'Urbaine et Seine'*, JCP 1953.II.7448 (where the point was conceded by the State). Since this decision the approach of the administrative courts to the assessment of damages has become more liberal, thus reducing the range of possible differences.

[173] CE Sect 16 Mar. 1962, *Cie d'assur. 'L'Urbaine et La Seine'*, AJDA 1962.320.

its cost from the owner of the lorry. However, the Conseil d'Etat rejected the lorry owner's claim for contribution against the State as responsible for the position of the electricity console, on the basis that the cost of rebuilding the wall was not a direct consequence of the accident as it been incurred too long afterwards. In the result, therefore, the civil defendant (or rather his insurer) bore all the loss and the public body escaped liability altogether.

Thirdly, the Conseil d'Etat has sometimes refused a person held liable in the ordinary courts *any* recourse against a public authority simply on the basis of the wrongful character of that person's behaviour. This can be seen in two important cases which concerned product safety and which had led not merely to the imposition of liability but also to the criminal conviction of the private persons involved: the *affaire Stalinon*[174] and the *affaire du 'Cinq-Sept'*.[175]

In the *affaire Stalinon* a company director and a scientific consultant responsible for the composition of the licensed pharmaceutical of that name were convicted of involuntary homicide and held liable in damages for the many deaths and serious injury which its use had caused.[176] Ten years later, the insurers of the director and the company which marketed *Stalinon* claimed to be indemnified by the State owing to its fault in granting the drug a licence, relying on their subrogated rights from their assured.[177] In rejecting this claim, the Conseil d'Etat catalogued the faults in the director and the company in the drug's research, in their application for its licence, in its manufacture and in post-marketing care and concluded that they:

could not effectively take advantage of the *fautes lourdes* which the State might have committed, by giving [the drug] a licence without any investigation and by failing to withdraw its ministerial licence soon enough . . . or by failing to supervise its manufacture.

And their insurers could be in no better position than those (the original criminal defendants) to whose rights they were subrogated. So, while the Conseil d'Etat accepted that the State could have been liable in respect of its *fautes lourdes* in relation to its licensing of *Stalinon*, any person who was directly responsible for the promotion of a drug (and those who claimed through them) had no right of recourse against the State.

Exactly the same attitude may be found in the administrative law aftermath to the *affaire du 'Cinq-Sept'*, where a fire killed and injured many young people at a discotheque. A criminal court had held the managers of the companies which owned the discotheque, the suppliers of its heating system and the managing director of the manufacturers of a polyeurethane-based product which had been used in its decoration guilty of involuntary homicide and condemned all of the companies responsible for these individuals to pay damages in respect of the deaths and personal injuries which

---

[174] CE 28 Jun. 1968, *affaire Stalinon*, JCP 1968.II.15578 note anon.

[175] CE 7 Mar. 1980, *affaire du 'Cinq-Sept'*, D 1980.320 note Richer, concl. Massot, AJDA 1980.423 note Albertini. See similarly also CE 1 Oct. 1976, *Cie d'assurances*, Leb. 388 (recourse claim by ship owners and their insurers against public body in respect of the inspection of a ship which sank).

[176] For the criminal proceedings, see Paris 3 Jun. 1958, S 1958.336 note Bredin, below, pp. 373–4.

[177] CE 28 Jun. 1968 *cit*.

their crimes had caused.[178] However, while the criminal court also found the local *maire* guilty of the same crimes, it did not impose liability on either him or the *commune*, following the general rules excluding the imposition of liability on public bodies and public servants by the ordinary courts.[179] So again, the issue of liability in either the *commune* or the State[180] for the failure in their respective officers to exercise their powers of control of public health and safety arose in the Conseil d'Etat a decade after the tragic fire had taken place and by way of a claim for contribution by the liquidators and liability insurers of the companies which ran the discotheque.[181]

The Tribunal administratif de Grenoble held that the *maire* had indeed committed a *faute* in failing to exercise his powers concerning the construction, opening and health and safety of the discotheque, and in particular in passing on to the *prefet* an application for operation of the discotheque at night with his approval, despite knowing that it was already operating without proper permission. The Tribunal also accepted that, despite having been informed by a police report of the irregular operation of the discotheque, the *State* services failed to close the discotheque or to require its operators to conform to legal requirements, had failed to ensure that the safety aspects of its planning controls were enforced, and had failed to invite the *maire* to attend the Departmental Safety Commission, even though a member of it. Nevertheless, neither the Tribunal nor the Conseil d'Etat considered that these faults—even though in the case of the *commune* they were characterised as *fautes lourdes*[182]—were ones on which the liquidators of the companies which had built and run the discotheque or their insurers could rely so as to obtain contribution, since the faults of the private persons through whom they claimed were the 'determining cause' of the fire and of all the harm which it caused.[183]

The formal basis of the decision denying a causal role to the *maire's faute lourde*, was thought unconvincing even by its contemporary commentators, which saw it as merely a way of justifying its decision to refuse recovery.[184] In Richer's view the key motivation of the court was the seriousness of the faults of the persons through whom the companies' insurers claimed,[185] these being 'deliberate and inexcusable' and, of course, criminal. Indeed, the decisions in the *affaire du 'Cinq-Sept'* and in the *affaire Stalinon* could be seen as examples of the maxim *nemo auditur propriam turpitudinem*

---

[178] For the criminal proceedings, see Lyon 13 Jul. 1973, GP 1973.2.830; Crim. 14 Mar. 1974, GP 1974.1.417, below, pp. 375–8.

[179] Above, pp. 19–20. A public servant may be liable there for a 'fault separable from his public role', (see CE 26 Jul. 1918, *Ep. Lemonnier*, D 1918.3.9 concl. Blum, S 1919.3.41 note Hauriou) but this had apparently not been argued.

[180] The State was brought into the litigation by the *commune* by way of a claim for contribution in respect of any liability with which it may itself be charged. The CE has accepted claims for contribution by a *commune* in respect of the failure in the relevant State authority to exercise the control of its own conduct, for example, in relation to its own financial management: CE 27 Dec. 1948, *Commune de Champigny-sur-Marne*, D 1949.408 concl. Guionin.

[181] CE 7 Mar. 1980, D 1980.320 note Richer, concl Massot, AJDA 1980.423 note Albertini.

[182] The TA appeared to consider that *faute simple* would have been enough to establish liability in principle.

[183] As the liability of the State was in issue only by way of a recourse claim by the *commune*, the Conseil d'Etat's decision on the latter's liability made any discussion of the State's liability redundant.

[184] Richer, D 1980.320 and P. Albertini, 1980 AJDA 423, 425.   [185] D 1980.320.

allegans,[186] or a general 'defence of illegitimacy' (*exception d'illégimité*) available to the administration to prevent a person who suffers harm caused by it to recover damages where this occurs 'in an illegitimate situation arising from his own irregular behaviour'.[187]

Both the *affaire du 'Cinq-Sept'* and the *affaire Stalinon* appeared to have concerned claims for recourse based on the private law defendant's own 'independent' right, as distinct from any subrogated right taken over from the *primary victims* of the two tragedies.[188] Could reliance on the primary victims' rights lead to any different outcome? In my view, this is unlikely. In the first place, in some cases any rights in the primary victims will have expired owing to the four-year prescription period.[189] For example, in *'Cinq-Sept'* the fire occurred in 1970; the criminal proceedings (in which liability in damages was imposed) were concluded in 1974;[190] claims for recourse against the administration were introduced in 1976 and final adjudication given in 1980.[191] Moreover, even if a subrogated recourse claim were introduced within the prescription period, it is likely that the Conseil d'Etat would still reject it for the same substantive reason (that is, that the private law defendants' wrongdoing should bar their recovery) either by manipulation of causation or by more openly invoking the *nemo auditur* maxim.[192]

However, denial of any recourse in this type of case leads to a rather strange position. For if those injured in the fire at the *'Cinq-Sept'* Discotheque had started by claiming damages against the *commune* in the administrative courts, they would have recovered (even if only in part),[193] and then would have been able to recover any residue from the private law defendants in subsequent civil or criminal proceedings (subject to the applicable rules of prescription there). This means that the question whether a public authority in this sort of case will actually bear any financial responsibility for the harmful consequences of its failure to intervene on the grounds of public health and safety so as to prevent a private person from causing harm will depend on the decision of the primary victim as to the jurisdiction in which to bring his or her first claim, as well as the degree of 'wrongfulness' of the conduct of the private person.

---

[186] Albertini, 1980 AJDA 423, 425.

[187] Chapus, *Droit administratif général*, Tome 1, 1254–5.

[188] This appears from the judgments' references to the insurers not being in any better position than their *assured* and not being able to take advantage of any *faute lourde* in the public authority for which the State was responsible: above, p. 328.   [189] Above, p. 320.

[190] Crim. 14 Mar. 1974, GP 1974.1.417 note anon.

[191] CE 7 Mar. 1980, AJDA 1980.423.

[192] Cf. CE 22 Nov. 1985, RGTA 1986.374 where a recourse claim by the insurers of the *parents* liable strictly under art. 1384 al. 7 C. civ. for the acts of arson of their children which destroyed a school killing several pupils was upheld against the State as responsible for the personal fault of members of the administration who had been involved in the design and construction of the school. Here, the CE held the State liable up to one fifth of the cost of liability to the primary victims as the 'serious faults' of the administration had facilitated the spread of the fire and made it impossible to escape it in time and these faults had 'directly led' to the loss in question. Here, it is to be noticed, while the damage was caused by criminal acts, the insurers claimed through the parents (whose liability was strict) and the administration's faults did not consist of a failure to control either the parents or their children, but in their distinct failures as regards the building.

[193] This was accepted by the *Commissaire du gouvernement*, M. Massot in the *affaire du 'Cinq-Sept'*: Albertini, 1980 AJDA 423, 425.

Where, as often, a primary victim prefers to claim first in the ordinary courts, the public authority will not have to pay, however bad its own failures. Despite allowing liability in public authorities in this sort of case for either *faute simple* or *faute lourde*, the system as a whole does indeed tend to lead to their practical 'irresponsibility'. To this complex and contradictory position, therefore, the *affaire du sang contaminé* forms a notable and very striking exception.

13

English Law: Recurrent Themes and Endemic Casuistry

In examining the position of English law governing liability for the regulation or control of the safety of products and comparing it to French law, we are faced with very considerable difficulty caused by the nature of the modern English case law. For this topic forms an example or series of examples of the potential liability of public authorities in respect of the exercise of their powers, an area which the courts have themselves described as 'developing' and in which it is difficult to see any very clear overall direction or pattern. For while each judgment appears sensible and rational within its own frame of reference and context and attempts to place itself within the corpus of other decisions, the overall picture remains obscure.

In this chapter, I shall not attempt to describe the complexities of the general case law in this area nor make any general description or comparison with the French law of administrative liabilities.[1] Instead, I shall do five things. First, I shall explain how the sources of power in English administrative bodies relate to their potential liabilities. Secondly, I shall set out the recurrent themes which have been used by the courts in their overall decisions in finding or refusing to find a basis for liability in the tort of negligence in public authorities. Thirdly, I shall examine the types of situation which can arise in relation to the exercise of powers affecting the safety of products and illustrate how an English court is likely to view issues both of the existence of a duty of care and of breach of duty. Fourthly, I shall note the possible impact of a special 'public interest immunity' against the disclosure of documents in these sorts of cases in the context of the English litigation brought by the haemophiliac recipients of blood products infected with HIV. Fifthly and finally, I shall attempt to relate these approaches in the English law to the French position which I have already described.[2]

At the outset, though, I think it helpful to explain how the sort of situation with which I am concerned relates to wider features of the English legal system. As will be recalled, here I am concerned with the situation where it is claimed that a public authority should be liable for the harm caused by the lack of safety of a product owing to its failure to control or prevent another person (notably, the product's manufacturer or distributor) from acting in a way which causes the claimant's harm. There are three key features of English law which differ from the French and which impact on the way in which liability is channelled in this sort of case.

---

[1] See further Fairgrieve, *State Liability*, for a general comparative treatment.   [2] Above, Chap. 12.

First, in English law the lack of any jurisdictional division in the courts which decide public or private cases of the sort existing in France means that a claimant injured by a product can sue a private defendant (such as a product's manufacturer) and a public defendant (such as the public body which licensed the product or failed to warn of its dangers) before the same tribunal and in the same litigation. Unlike a French litigant in this sort of case, an English claimant does not need to choose whether to sue one or other potential defendant first in their appropriate courts.[3] Secondly, as I have explained, where a public authority is liable for the same harm in respect of which a private person is liable, then each may be held liable in full vis-à-vis the victim of the harm: in English law there is no special treatment of the joint liability of public and private persons and so, if the elements of liability can be made out, public authorities make attractive defendants from a claimant's point of view, having deep pockets and/or insurance.[4] Moreover, thirdly, English law has no special rule or set of rules governing the time within which claims against which public authorities must be made.[5] In all, therefore, English law does not possess the three key elements which in French law militate against the imposition in practice of liability for failures in product safety: its divided jurisdiction, denial of full recovery against a public authority jointly liable for fault with a private person, and special rules governing the prescription of actions for damages against public authorities.[6] In the absence of such features, English law's control of liability in public authorities in this sort of situation must be more direct and overt.

1. Sources of English Administrative Powers and Product Safety

The starting point of modern English law regarding the sources of administrative powers is fundamentally different from the French. In French law, the executive's function is to govern and it possesses the inherent power to do so—the *pouvoir exécutif:* the principle of the separation of powers assumes the existence of independent powers in each institution of the State, executive, legislative and judicial. So, while modern French administrative bodies do possess many particular powers granted by special parliamentary legislation, these powers may be seen as special expressions of more general and inherent powers which surround and support them. As was explained, this picture is fully reflected in the French administration's powers in respect of the safety of products, as both central and local governments enjoy an inherent and general power to further the health and safety of citizens in the interest of maintaining *ordre public*, and they also enjoy a number of powers, particular either to type of product or to type of administrative intervention.[7]

---

[3] Above, p. 320.

[4] Formerly, there were shorter periods of limitation applicable where a person acted in pursuance or execution or intended execution of an Act of Parliament, but these were abolished by the Law Reform (Limitation of Actions etc.) Act 1954. The Public Authorities Protection Act 1893 had imposed a limitation period of six months. After the 1954 Act public authorities are in this respect treated in the same way as all other defendants: *Birkett v James* [1978] AC 296, 332.   [5] Above, pp. 172–3.

[6] Above, pp. 319–25.   [7] Above, pp. 306–10.

By contrast, in English law the idea of an inherent power in the government (that is, ministers of the Crown) to govern as seen in the royal prerogative can be seen as out of keeping with the increasing arrogation by Parliament to itself of the monopoly of non-judicial power: royal prerogative may still exist but it does so only to the extent to which it is recognised by the common law (that is, the courts)[8] and only as regards the more traditional fields of governmental activity, such as the granting of charters, the concluding of treaties and the making of war.[9] By the nineteenth century, the reduction of the prerogative's importance was confirmed both at a theoretical and a practical level. At a theoretical level, one of the consequences of Dicey's claims for parliamentary competence was that executive power should be channelled through Parliament;[10] at a practical level, there was an increasing realisation of the need for government to intervene in areas not previously thought to merit attention, such as in the relief of poverty and safety at work.[11] Increasingly, governmental power at the national level was seen to require statutory authority and therefore took its focus and shape from each particular statute; and the source of the powers of local government shifted from the common law of corporations to statute, this reaching a conclusion in their becoming statutory bodies in 1972.[12] While in the latter part of the twentieth century, central government has sought to act through its power to make contracts, it still remains the case that 'the dominating source of power is Parliament'.[13] A major consequence of this has been that the judicial control of administrative action for long took as its basis the doctrine of *ultra vires*, seeing in each parliamentary statute not merely the granting of particular administrative powers, but also the imposition of implicit and general limitations on the exercise of those powers. While the claims of this doctrine have been subject to challenge by those who see the basis of judicial review of administrative action in the protection of fundamental rights and the subjection of government to principles of good administration recognised at common law,[14] no-one would deny that where a body's powers derive from statute, the court's starting point in judicial review is the construction of the particular powers in question. This means that with the eclipse of the royal prerogative, most English administrative power has become necessarily special, for statutory powers are by their nature particular, even where they are extremely broad.

However, as shall be seen, this particularity of English administrative powers has also directly affected the question of the imposition of liability in their exercise. In common with judicial review under the doctrine of *ultra vires*, more recent judicial approaches to liability in the tort of negligence in the exercise of statutory powers have been to start by looking very carefully at the scheme and purposes of the statute in question.[15] So, while the framework of the tort is shared with claims not involving any

---

[8] As Sir Edward Coke CJ put it, 'the King hath no prerogative, but that which the law of the land allows him': *The Case of Proclamations* (1610) 12 Co Rep 74, 76.

[9] See Sir William Blackstone, *Commentaries on the Laws of England* (Clarendon Press, Oxford, 1st. edn., 1765–1769). Book I, chap. 7, esp. 240, 272–3; Sir W. Wade and C. Forsyth, *Administrative Law* (OUP, 8th. edn., 2000), 219–23.

[10] Above, Dicey, *Introduction to the Study of the Law of the Constitution*, 83–4; Craig, *Administrative Law*, 4–5.

[11] Craig, *Administrative Law*, 48–52.   [12] Local Government Act 1972.

[13] Wade, *op. cit.* n. 9, 219.   [14] Notably, Craig, *Administrative Law*, 21 *et seq.*

[15] Below, pp. 336–8.

public element, where a case concerns the exercise of public (statutory) powers, this legal context bears directly both on the question of the existence of a duty of care and of its breach.

This general picture is fully reflected in the law empowering different English administrative bodies to act in the interests of the safety of products. Unlike the French position,[16] there is no inherent general power in government to act in furtherance of the health and safety of citizens, but there are very many particular statutory powers to do so. Of these, very important sets of powers may be found in Part II of the Consumer Protection Act 1987 and the General Product Safety Regulations 1994[17] implementing the European Directive on General Product Safety of 1992[18] and itself due to be amended so as to conform to this directive's amendment in 2001.[19] Both these sets of provisions adopt a standard of safety of the products within their area of application and then create a series of powers in relevant administrative authorities to intervene in the interests of upholding these standards. So, the relevant minister has the power to issue regulations governing consumer goods in the interest of their safety and these regulations may include requirements as to their composition, design, construction or packaging:[20] this power, which finds its origin in legislation in 1961,[21] has been considerably exercised.[22] Secondly, where he considers that consumer goods are unsafe, the relevant minister has the power to make different types of orders against those supplying or offering products for supply,[23] including notices prohibiting a person from supplying a particular product or requiring a person to publish a warning about a product.[24] And, thirdly, both the relevant minister and local authorities (in practice local trading standards officers) have the power to issue notices prohibiting a person from supplying a product for a period of up to six months.[25] In practice, the power to issue suspension notices has been quite heavily used and appears to have been effective, whereas notices to warn have been seen as too cumbersome and not very effective.[26]

Implementation of the General Product Safety Directive 2001 will add to these powers a power to order a producer or distributor to recall a product and, if necessary, to organise a recall themselves.[27] The Department of Trade and Industry's consultation document has noted, however, that producers of consumer products have a generally good track record of carrying out voluntary recall of dangerous products in a timely and appropriate way and it does not therefore anticipate the need for the enforcement of the producers' obligations to recall their products:[28] one may think,

---

[16] Above, p. 307. [17] SI 1994 No. 2328.

[18] Council Dir. 92/59/EEC of 29 Jun. 1992 on general product safety.

[19] Dir. 2001/95/EC of the European Parliament and of the Council of 3 Dec. 2001 on general product safety ('GPSD'). [20] Consumer Protection Act 1987, s. 11(2).

[21] Consumer Safety Act 1961, s. 1.

[22] E.g. The Plugs and Sockets Etc. (Safety) Regulations 1994, SI 1994 No. 1768; The Gas Appliances (Safety) Regulations 1995, SI 1995 No. 1629.

[23] The 1987 Act's scheme of measures in response to lack of safety in 'consumer goods' provided in Part II of that Act was extended in 1994 to the 'products' governed by the General Product Safety Regulations 1994 ('GPSR 1994'): ibid., r. 11. [24] 1987 Act, s. 13; GPSR 1994, r. 11(a).

[25] 1987 Act, s. 14; GPSR 1994, r. 11(b).

[26] Department of Trade and Industry, Consumer Affairs Directorate, *Transposing the revised General Product Safety Directive* (Nov. 2001) 25. [27] GPSD 2001, art. 8(1)(f)(ii).

[28] Department of Trade and Industry, *op. cit.* n. 26, 15.

therefore, that a public order to recall a product may be a means of last resort. Implementation of the 2001 Directive also requires public authorities acting under these powers to act 'in such a way as to implement the measures in a manner proportional to the seriousness of the risk, and taking due account of the precautionary principle'.[29] The 'precautionary principle' 'applies in situations where preliminary scientific evaluation indicates that there are reasonable grounds for concern about health and safety, but where the scientific evidence is insufficient or inconclusive', having been used particularly in the context of environmental liability.[30]

However, there are also very many more particularly focused statutory provisions, whether particular to the context of use of a product (as is the case with legislation governing health and safety at work) or to a particular type of product (as in the case of the safety of food and of medicines), some of which are of national origin and some of which result from European legislative initiatives. On implementation of the 2001 Directive, the general provisions of the General Product Safety Regulations will still apply 'in so far as there are no specific provisions with the same objective in rules of Community law governing the safety of the products concerned'.[31] This means that even where there are special rules governing a particular type of product (such as toys) deriving from EU law, the general provisions governing product safety apply where those rules do not cover all aspects of control provided by the general product safety scheme.[32] Examples of some of the types of special powers entrusted to public authorities which affect the safety of products will be encountered in the ensuing discussion of cases determining whether their exercise should give rise to liability.

To this extent, therefore, while the constitutional starting points of French and English law are very different, they have in common that their respective public bodies enjoy a considerable range and breadth of powers by which they may intervene in relation to the safety of products, this commonality in part being derived from the EU directives on general consumer safety.

2. Recurring Themes Concerning Duty of Care in Respect of the Exercise of Statutory Powers

As I have explained, in modern practice the central tort for the imposition of liability in the administration in respect of the exercise of their powers has been in the tort of negligence rather than, notably, the tort of breach of statutory duty,[33] and over the last half century the concept of the duty of care has borne the brunt of the court's attention in controlling liability in this situation. While the so-called 'tests' for the imposition of a duty of care have varied over this period, in the context of the exercise of public powers most courts now follow the approach of the House of Lords in *Caparo* and so look

---

[29] GPSD 2001, art. 8(2).   [30] Department of Trade and Industry, *op. cit.* n. 26, 26.
[31] GPSD 2001, art. 1(2).   [32] Department of Trade and Industry, *op. cit.* n. 26, 8.
[33] Above, p. 168. For a general discussion of this tort, see above, pp. 219–24. Its use of parliamentary intention as a criterion for the imposition of civil liability has been borrowed by some judges in the context of the tort of negligence: see below, pp. 336–7.

at the foreseeability of the claimant's harm, 'proximity' and whether it would be 'fair, just and reasonable' for there to be liability for negligence.[34] While sometimes the courts have denied the existence of a duty of care against a public authority on the ground of the lack of forseeability or proximity,[35] in many cases, the crucial question for the courts is whether it is 'fair, just and reasonable' to impose a duty of care or whether there are convincing policy reasons to the contrary given the particular factors present in the case before them and in the light of previous authorities.[36] There are, nonetheless, a number of recurring themes in judicial discussions of these very open issues.[37]

(a) The statutory context

The most important theme emerging from the case law of the last decade has been the concern of the courts to relate the issue of liability for negligence to the particular statutory context of the power whose exercise is impugned. This was most succinctly expressed by Lord Browne-Wilkinson in *X v Bedfordshire CC*, who considered that, even if the defendant's action was 'justiciable' and so not a matter of policy for its own decision:

[t]he question whether there is . . . a common law duty and if so its ambit, must be profoundly influenced by the statutory framework within which the acts complained of were done . . . [A] common law duty of care cannot be imposed on a statutory duty if [its] observance . . . would be inconsistent with, or have a tendency to discourage, the due performance by the local authority of its statutory duties.[38]

This idea has a number of variants. So, sometimes the courts express concern that the imposition of liability should not defeat the purpose for which the statutory power in question was created or, even more demandingly, that the purpose of the statutory power should be (at least in part) aimed at the protection of the interest of the claimant before the court. This last variant has been used both positively and negatively. Positively, a court may say that the purpose of the statutory power being to protect the claimant from the type of harm suffered by him is a good reason for the finding of a duty of care, as in *Perrett v Collins*[39] in the context of the safety of aircraft. However, this variant has also been used to argue against the existence of a duty of care as, for example, in the *East Berkshire* case, where the Court of Appeal held that statutory powers in local authorities to remove children at risk of abuse from their

---

[34] *Caparo Industries plc v Dickman* [1990] 2 AC 605, 617–18 and see above, p. 161. This approach has been followed in *X v Bedfordshire CC* [1995] 2 AC 633, 729, 739, 749; *Stovin v Wise* [1996] AC 923, 931–2, 949; *Barrett v Enfield LBC* [2001] 2 AC 550 ('*Barrett*') 564, 566; *Phelps v Hillingdon LBC* [2001] 2 AC 619 ('*Phelps*'), 653; *JD v East Berkshire Community Health NHS Trust* [2003] EWCA Civ 1151 [1]; [2004] 2 WLR 58.

[35] E.g. *K v Home Office* [2002] EWCA Civ 775 (2002) 152 NLJ 917 (no proximity between Home Secretary's release of a repeat offender and subsequent victim of crime).

[36] Craig, Administrative Law, 899. E.g. *Hill v Chief Constable of West Yorkshire* [1989] AC 53; *Yuen Kun-Yeu v Att.-Gen. of Hong Kong* [1988] AC 175; *X v Bedfordshire CC* [1995] 2 AC 633.

[37] There has also been an important influence of the law of human rights, above, pp. 168–9.

[38] *X v Bedfordshire CC* [1995] 2 AC 633, 739. See also *Stovin v Wise* [1996] AC 923, 935.

[39] [1998] 2 Lloyd's Rep. 255, below, pp. 352–3.

families were aimed at the protection of children, with the result that while a duty of care could be owed by the local authorities to any child harmed by the exercise of these powers, no such duty could be owed to their parents.[40] Sometimes, a court focuses not so much on the person harmed, but on the nature of the harm suffered. So, for example, in *Harris v Evans* the claimant ran a business providing 'bungee jumping' and who suffered lost business ('pure economic loss') after the Health and Safety Executive's ('HSE'[41]) decision led to a prohibition on use of bungee with a mobile crane: here the HSE did not owe any duty of care to the business in question.[42]

This theme is a very important one and reflective of a number of fundamental features of English law. First, it shares with the traditional approach to the incidence of civil liability for breach of statutory duty a starting point in interpretation of implied parliamentary intention, but unlike this tort, it does not focus so much on the question of an implied and indeed fictitious imposition of liability in damages (adding a 'private right' to whatever sanctions or remedy are provided for breach of the 'public law duty'),[43] but rather on the consistency of imposing civil liability with the purpose of the statute, a teleological interpretation of the powers actually created.[44]

Secondly, it reflects the fundamentally exceptional nature of English legislation: for statutes are seen traditionally as interventions, departing from a position generally established at common law only to the extent to which they themselves provide.[45] While one could argue with the appropriateness of this vision as regards the nature of some English statutes (where they purport to govern a large area of the law, exclusively and systematically), it is fully reflected in the piecemeal nature of English law's statutory public powers, which are particular and carefully drawn even if numerous and varied. This marks a striking contrast to the French approach to administrative powers, for French public law accepts that its administration has an inherent power to govern, notably under the idea of the *pouvoir exécutif des lois*.[46] So, in the context of *police administrative*, the administration has a general power to intervene in the interests of *ordre public*, whether or not particular bodies are given particular powers by *loi*, for example to regulate a product or recall it from the market in the interest of citizens' safety.[47] So, too, the starting point of French law to liability in the administration for the exercise of its *police administrative* is a general one, though the decisions of the Conseil d'Etat themselves reflect a degree of 'empiricism'.[48] By contrast, by holding that the existence of a duty of care in the tort of negligence for public authorities depends on the particularities of the powers which they exercise, English judges allow their vision of the special nature of statutes and therefore the particular nature of administrative powers, to spill over into their treatment of the common law of liability.

---

[40] *JD v East Berkshire Community Health NHS Trust* [2003] EWCA Civ 1151; [2004] 2 WLR 58.

[41] This is the public body charged with the policing of legislation governing health and safety at work under the Health and Safety at Work Act 1974 (as amended).

[42] [1998] 1 WLR 1285, below, pp. 350–1.   [43] Above, pp. 219–20.

[44] Cf. *Gorringe v Calderdale MBC* [2004] UKHL 15 [3], [2004] 1 WLR 1057 *per* Lord Steyn.

[45] Cf. B. Nicholas, in Harris and Tallon, Chap. 4, 'The Pre-contractual Obligation to Disclose Information, English Report', 178.   [46] Above, p. 307.

[47] Above, pp. 307–8.   [48] Above, p. 312.

The English judicial approach also reflects a second fundamental characteristic of the English common law: the temptation towards casuistry, by which I mean, towards distinguishing ever more finely between the contexts of decision making rather than appealing to broader rules. Modern English judicial treatment of precedents reflects the tension on the one hand between the need for consistency and legal certainty and on the other the practical limitations of constructing legal propositions in the context of the civil process, where arguments are focused on particular facts (or sets of facts) and necessarily restricted both in their nature and in the type of evidence with which they may be supported. While English judges *do* take into account policy considerations in their development of the law, they are also conscious of these limitations and on their relative position to Parliament in terms of democratic legitimacy. In this tension, the vice of casuistry is found at one extreme of the spectrum of compromises between these tensions, paralysing the attempt to construct useful (because more generally applicable) legal propositions, at the other end of which is the vice of legal formalism, where legal rules are applied to inappropriate contexts or with inappropriate results out of a bare appeal to authority.

In my view, the English temptation towards casuistry was encouraged by judicial rejection of 'blanket immunities' for certain categories of administrative activities, a rejection seen (at one time) as necessary to give effect to the decisions of the European Court of Human Rights in *Osman* and *Z*.[49] It is reflected in two elements of the case law governing administrative liability. First, it is seen in the invocation in this context of the idea that any extension of liability to new situations (that is, ones whose facts have themselves not previously been the subject of judicial decision) must be 'incremental', that is, based on analogy with other decisions and rather cautious, an invocation used from time to time in other types of problem areas of the tort of negligence.[50] Secondly, the major decisions of the last decade concerning the liability of public authorities have been liberal in their use of distinguishing the approaches to liability in previous cases by reference to their statutory context or facts, or both.[51] Of course, distinguishing previous cases is as much a part of the doctrine of precedent as following them, but the extent to which the courts distinguish previous judicial statements of the law differs significantly in different legal contexts and at different historical periods. The extent to which earlier cases have been distinguished in the law governing the liability of public authorities reflects a lack of confidence in the formulation of general rules or even guiding principles for the imposition of a duty of care in this area. In this way, the repeated question whether the imposition of a duty of care is 'fair, just and reasonable' is used merely as a cover for deciding each slightly different set of facts or differently characterised claim *de novo*, on the basis of a fresh assessment of the relevant factors or considerations of policy.

---

[49] *Osman v United Kingdom* [1999] 1 FLR 193; *Z v United Kingdom* [2001] 2 FLR 612, above, pp. 168–9.

[50] The phrase originates in a dictum of Brennan J in *Sutherland Council v Heyman* (1985) 60 ALR 1, 43–4 and is found in *Caparo* [1990] 2 AC 605, 618, 628, 633–4; *X v Bedfordshire CC* [1995] 2 AC 633, 751; *Barrett v Enfield LBC* [2001] 2 AC 550, 564.

[51] See e.g., the treatment of *Dorset Yacht Co. Ltd. v Home Office* [1970] AC 1004, *Stovin v Wise* [1996] AC 923 and *X v Bedfordshire CC cit.* n. 50 by the HL in *Barrett v Enfield LBC* [2001] 2 AC 633, at 572, 578–80, 586 and 584–6 respectively and of *Stovin v Wise* and *X v Bedfordshire CC* in *Phelps* [2001] 2 AC 619, 673, 657–8 respectively.

(b) The relationship between the illegality of a public body's action and the need to protect 'policy decisions'

The relationship between the illegality of a public body's action and the need to protect 'policy decisions' has often been seen as central to judicial decisions as to the imposition of a duty of care in the tort of negligence. There have been a number of variations on this theme.[52]

The first clear signs of the courts' relating their approaches to judicial review of administrative decisions and to the imposition of liability can be seen in the House of Lords' decision in *Dorset Yacht*.[53] In principle where Parliament has given a discretionary power to a public body, the courts should not interfere with its exercise, except to the extent to which it acted *ultra vires*, that is, beyond the ambit of its powers as defined by the grounds of review of administrative decision making; a duty of care may also be a potential interference in the exercise of a discretionary power and so should not be imposed except where the action in question was *ultra vires*. In this way, administrative illegality was made a condition for the imposition of a duty of care as regards the exercise of discretionary powers. On the other hand, a distinction was drawn between the sort of decision which involved the assessment of policy and 'operational decisions', which merely involved the putting into effect of decisions of policy already made. As to the latter, there was no reason why the courts should not impose a duty of care, subject to any other applicable considerations, such as the nature of the harm suffered by the claimant. Unlike the position in French law, the administrative illegality of a public body's decision making was not a ground of liability but a mere threshold to be crossed.[54]

However, the courts soon became dissatisfied with this approach to the relationship between administrative illegality and liability in negligence. For they found the distinction between 'policy' and 'operational' decisions difficult to use as a touchstone of liability, and also considered that certain types of administrative illegality (notably, procedural ones, such as breach of the principle *audi alteram partem*) were not relevant to the question whether or not a public body's discretion should be protected. For this reason, from the late 1980s, the courts preferred instead either to focus attention on the most general substantive ground of administrative review, *Wednesbury* unreasonableness, as a necessary hurdle for the imposition of a duty of care in negligence in this situation, or instead (and sometimes as well) to assess the 'justiciability' of the public body's decision, that is, the appropriateness for judicial assessment of the various factors which a public body would have to consider in coming to its view as to how to act.[55] While 'justiciability' is a flexible concept, it accepts that while *some* policy decisions may be appropriate for assessment by the court, others must remain with the public bodies to which a power of decision is entrusted; in particular, courts have avoided imposing duties of care in respect of decisions where these impinge on the allocation of resources between different public functions or services.

---

[52] Fairgrieve, *State Liability*, 41 *et seq.*

[53] *Dorset Yacht Co. Ltd. v Home Office* [1970] AC 1004, 1031 and see also *Anns v Merton LBC* [1978] AC 728, 755. [54] Above, p. 313.

[55] *Rowling v Takaro Properties Ltd.* [1988] AC 473, 501; *X v Bedfordshire CC* [1995] 2 AC 633, 739.

More recently, moreover, the House of Lords has appeared to go further. For, in *Barrett* and *Phelps*, it was accepted that a duty of care could be imposed in respect of the decision making under statutory powers even in the absence of any administrative illegality, though they also accepted that a decision to exercise a statutory discretion is likely not to give rise to liability in negligence, 'unless it is wholly unreasonable so as not to be a real exercise of the discretion, or if it involves the making of a policy decision involving the balancing of different public interests', whereas 'acts done pursuant to the lawful exercise of the discretion can . . . be subject to a duty of care, even if some element of discretion is involved'.[56] Given this acceptance, it is difficult to know how lasting this rejection of the link between administrative illegality and liability will be, for the courts have remained concerned to say that their imposition of duties of care must not interfere with the 'policy decisions' of public authorities in their exercise of statutory powers and this way of thinking provides a natural link to the question of the legality of these decisions themselves.[57] Moreover, the administrative illegality of a public body's decision making may be relevant to the imposition of a duty of care in another way. For sometimes a court draws attention in refusing to impose such a duty to the existence of means of recourse open to the claimant other than in damages in tort. So, for example, where a person adversely affected by an administrative decision has the right to challenge that decision by appeal or judicial review, this may reduce the need to use the tort of negligence to create *some* remedy.[58] On the other hand, there is judicial support for the view that the presence of a statutory discretion should remain relevant, but to breach of duty, rather than to the existence of a duty of care.[59]

Finally, it should be remembered that a court may refuse to impose a duty of care on the ground that it would not be 'fair, just and reasonable' to do so even where the hurdle of administrative illegality or interference with the policy decisions of a public authority has been overcome. Here, 'policy factors' come into account in the court's own assessment of the appropriateness of finding a duty of care. So, at times, the courts have assessed whether a duty of care would impose too great a financial burden on the defendant or defendants in its category more generally, whether it would adversely affect their behaviour (by encouraging 'defensive' decision making) or conversely would create an incentive to more careful behaviour.[60] These ultimately highly individuated decisions on duty of care are not particular to the public context and can be seen in relation to private bodies acting in a commercial setting.[61]

(c) The relationship to 'private law'

English law did not traditionally distinguish a separate public law and I have suggested earlier that for this reason it has a residual and rather hazy sense of its own private

---

[56] *Barrett* [2001] 2 AC 550, 572 *per* Lord Slynn; cf. *Phelps* [2001] 2 AC 619, 653; *Gorringe v Calderdale MBC* [2004] UKHL 15 [5]; [2004] 1 WLR 1057. See further Fairgrieve, *State Liability*, 46 *et seq.*

[57] See Fairgrieve, *State Liability*, 49–51 for criticisms.

[58] *S v Gloucestershire CC* [2001] 1 Fam. 313, 329–30.

[59] *Gorringe v Calderdale MBC, cit.*, [5] quoting Craig, *Administrative Law*, 898 with approval.

[60] Cf. *Hill v Chief Constable of West Yorkshire* [1989] AC 53, 63; *Phelps* [2001] 2 AC 619, 672.

[61] *Marc Rich & Co. AG v Bishop Rock Marine Co.* [1996] AC 211.

law: [62] its starting point is the 'ordinary law' of the land (the common law) from which statute derogates, including statutes which define the special powers and responsibilities of public bodies. [63] While it is indeed true that English courts have seen the liability of public bodies in the exercise of their statutory powers as a distinct legal problem, at least since *Dorset Yacht*, [64] it is still set in the wider framework of the law of torts in general and of the tort of negligence in particular, and the vast majority of this body of law is concerned with cases between private individuals or companies outside situations involving public bodies or public powers. This belonging of the law governing administrative liability to a wider structure dominated by private law cases has affected it in a number of ways, but two are particularly prominent.

First, even where the particular hurdles associated with the imposition of a duty of care in respect of the exercise of public powers are overcome, a claimant may face further hurdles shared by the general law, notably, as to the type of conduct of the defendant and the type of harm which he suffers.

As to the former, the general law of negligence distinguishes between liability for action and for omission, subjecting the latter to additional requirements of the existence of a special duty, a relationship of control or an 'assumption of responsibility'. [65] This issue of liability for omissions was particularly prominent in the House of Lords' decision in *Stovin v Wise*, where a bare majority of the House of Lords held that a highway authority did not bear a duty of care in respect of failing to make a junction safer. [66] Given that the case concerned an omission, the question then became whether the public nature of the defendant's powers, duties and funding imposed on it a positive duty to take action. [67] So, where a public authority fails to exercise its powers, a claimant must overcome the general (private) law's restrictive attitude to liability for omissions, this creating particular problems in the administrative context. [68]

Perhaps, though, the nature of a claimant's harm is an even more difficult hurdle to overcome. For while the courts since *Donoghue v Stevenson* have showed themselves fairly ready to impose duties of care in respect of a person's death, personal injury or damage to property, they have been much more restrictive as to his psychiatric injury or pure economic loss. [69] In a number of important decisions concerning administrative liability, the claimants have sought damages in respect of these more contentious types of harm and while sometimes the courts have refused recovery either explicitly on the ground of the irrecoverable nature of the harm in the circumstances, in other cases it has formed the background to their reluctance to find a duty of care on the public nature of the defendant's action. So, for example, when in *Murphy v*

---

[62] Above, pp. 269–70.   [63] Above, p. 333.   [64] [1970] AC 1004.

[65] The leading case outside the context of public authorities is *Smith v Littlewoods Organisation Ltd.* [1987] AC 241.   [66] [1996] AC 923, 943–4.

[67] Ibid., at 946. Lord Hoffmann considered that in these circumstances it was a minimum precondition for the imposition of a duty of care that any decision made whether or not to intervene was irrational so that there was in effect a public law duty to act: 950, 953. However, in *Calderdale v MBC* [2004] UKHL 15; [26] [2004] 1 WLR 1057, Lord Hoffmann accepted that this 'controversial' suggestion may have been ill-advised.

[68] Cf. Craig, *Administrative Law*, 903–04 criticising this application of the 'ordinary approach' on the basis that 'the position of a public body vested with a discretionary power is not the same as that of a private individual who simply 'happens upon some accident'.

[69] On these topics in general see above, pp. 161–2, 183–6, 298–9.

Brentwood DC[70] the House of Lords departed from its own previous decision imposing a duty of care on local authorities in respect of the inspection of building foundations in *Anns v Merton LBC*,[71] it did so on the ground that the harm suffered by the claimant house owners was 'pure economic loss' rather than that the local authority was acting under and within its statutory powers (though the public nature of the defendant was not irrelevant to this issue).[72] More recently, when in the *East Berkshire* case[73] the Court of Appeal had to decide the question of liability in the exercise of local authority powers to remove children from their families it distinguished between claims by children and by their parents on grounds which related to the function and purpose of the statutory powers in question, but it did not go unnoticed that any harm suffered by the parents would be psychiatric and financial,[74] the recovery of both of which have proved problematic in the tort of negligence more generally.[75] In this way, a person's claim in negligence against a public authority may be affected by judicial attitudes to the nature of his harm common to negligence claims generally.

However, the connection with private law sometimes pulls in the opposite direction, for where a public servant undertakes an activity which an ordinary citizen may do, such as the provision of health care or driving a vehicle, the courts have readily imposed a duty of care.[76] Moreover, recently, English courts have sometimes had recourse to private law notions in order to escape the confines which they have imposed as a matter of public law. This approach first became apparent in *X v Bedfordshire*, and was then picked up and considered in *Phelps*. The starting point was a contrast between the imposition of a duty of care on a public body directly and the imposition of a duty of care on a public servant for whose tort a public body is then vicariously liable. In both of these cases, the courts imposed liability on public bodies vicariously by imposing a duty of care on 'professionals' employed by them, seeing no reason why a doctor, psychologist or teacher employed by a public body should be treated differently from any other professional.[77] This allows a court to impose liability on a public body, even though it has refused to impose liability through a direct duty of care on the ground that this would not be 'fair, just and reasonable'. In doing so, the courts are often comforted by the fact that the liability of professionals is restrained by the *Bolam* test to the standard of care required of them.[78] In this way, judicial control over liability is shifted from the stage of recognition of a duty, to the stage of breach of duty.[79] A very important aspect of this is that under the Civil Procedure Rules,[80] written evidence may be used to support a claim by a defendant to have a claimant's case struck out, rather than proceeding on the assumption that the claimant's alleged facts are true: so that in some cases a defendant may succeed in strike out on the ground of lack of breach of duty.[81]

---

[70] [1991] 1 AC 398.   [71] [1978] AC 728.   [72] [1991] 1 AC 398.

[73] [2003] EWCA Civ 1151; [2004] 2 WLR 58.   [74] Ibid., [1], [106].   [75] Above, pp. 161–2.

[76] Fairgrieve, *State Liability*, 66. On medical liability, see above, pp. 286–92.

[77] *X v Bedfordshire CC* [1995] 2 AC 633, 763; *Phelps v Hillingdon LBC* [2001] 2 AC 619, 670–2, 653–5; *Gorringe v Calderdale MBC* [2004] UKHL 15 [38]; [2004] 1 WLR 1057.

[78] [2001] 2 AC 619, 655 and for this test see above, p. 188.

[79] P. Craig and D. Fairgrieve, '*Barrett*, Negligence and Discretionary Powers' [1999] PL 626; Craig, *Administrative Law*, 902; Fairgrieve, *State Liability*, 84–6.   [80] CPR Part 24.5.

[81] Fairgrieve, *State Liability*, 85–6 giving *S v Gloucestershire CC* [2001] 1 Fam 313 as an example.

It is difficult, however, to assess how far the courts will have resort to this escape into private law. First, it relies on the notion of 'professional liability', which appears comprehensible but nevertheless possesses no legally defined ambit: in one sense, any person who exercises any degree of skill (or holds themselves out as so doing) can be said to be 'professional'. Secondly, as Lord Slynn recognised in *Phelps*, sometimes the same considerations which lead a court to reject a direct duty of care apply equally to the imposition of liability indirectly through the torts of public servants.[82]

(d) The distinction between persons primarily and secondarily responsible

In some decisions on the liability of public authorities a distinction has been drawn between the position of those primarily responsible and those secondarily responsible for a claimant's harm, a distinction of potentially great importance for liability for the regulation of product safety. The idea of the distinction is that where a public authority's powers relate to the control of behaviour of another (typically private) person, and the latter's behaviour causes the claimant's harm, the private person is primarily responsible for the harm, the public authority being at most secondarily responsible. The same idea is sometimes cast in the language of causation, so that the private person is said to have 'directly' caused the claimant's harm, whereas the second person has only 'indirectly' caused it.

The question of the liability of a public authority in respect of the actions of others arose squarely in 1970 in *Dorset Yacht*, where it was alleged that borstal officers in charge of young offenders had been negligent in failing to prevent them from escaping and causing damage to the plaintiff's property.[83] In this case itself, the House of Lords found that there was a relationship of control between the officers and the boys, stemming from the situation itself created as a result of the exercise by the Home Office of its statutory powers in relation to young offenders, whose purpose was in part the control of the boys' actions. For this reason, a duty of a care could be found.[84]

However, in other cases the distinction between a person primarily responsible and the defendant sued who is (at most) secondarily responsible has been seen as a reason for rejection of a duty of care in the latter. So, in *Marc Rich*, one of the reasons for the denial of a duty of care in a classification society of a ship to the owner of cargo which was lost when the ship went down was that the primary responsibility for the seaworthiness of the ship rested on its owners, rather than on the society, whose role was 'subsidiary'.[85] A similar line of thinking can be seen in the distinction drawn in *Capital & Counties* as regards the duties of care of fire services between cases where their intervention creates a fresh danger (for which they should be responsible) and where it merely fails to deal with a danger created by a third person (who started a fire).[86]

This idea may be particularly potent in the context of the regulation by a public body of a private person's conduct. So, for example, in *Yuen Kun Yeu v A-G of Hong Kong*[87] it was held that a statutory regulator of the provision of financial services in

---

[82] [2001] 2 AC 619, 653.   [83] [1970] 1 AC 1004.   [84] See esp. ibid. at 1030 (Lord Reid).
[85] *Marc Rich & Co. Ag. v Bishop Rock Marine Co.* [1996] AC 211, 237, *per* Lord Steyn.
[86] *Capital & Counties plc v Hampshire CC* [1997] QB 1004, 1031–2, 1042.   [87] [1988] AC 175.

Hong Kong should not owe a duty of care to those who incurred loss as a result of the fraudulent conduct of a deposit-taking business, in part on the ground that the 'immediate cause' of the plaintiff's loss was the conduct of the business and that there was no relationship of control of the sort which existed between the borstal officers and the boys in *Dorset Yacht*.[88]

3. The Context of the Safety of Products

There are four recognisably different types of failure of response by a public authority to a product risk:

(i) a failure to enact appropriate rules to regulate the manufacture, distribution or access to market of a particular category of product;

(ii) a failure in respect of the enforcement of rules affecting the safety of products, whether these are general rules (such as the general safety requirement[89]) or special to a particular type of product;

(iii) a failure in the provision of information concerning the safety or risks of particular products;

(iv) a failure to control access to the market of a particular class of product or a particular individual product where it has the power to do so.

Of course, in a particular case a claimant may allege that more than one of these types of failure in the administration have contributed to his harm. And in some cases, of which *Smith v Secretary of State for Health* is a striking example,[90] a defendant public authority may argue that its approach to one type of response (for example, an order of recall of a product from the market) is related to its view as to another type of response (for example, the provision of public warnings): here, therefore, the public authority's defence to an allegation of negligence is in part that it made a reasonable choice as between a number of possible regulatory responses.

In the following discussion, I shall look at these four types of failure in turn, both from the point of view of the existence of a duty of care and the issue of negligence.

(a) A failure to enact appropriate rules

While English law possesses general requirements for the safety of consumer products,[91] it also possesses very considerable sets of regulations for the control of particular categories of product, such as in the case of food or medical products (including pharmaceuticals).[92] These rules may specify the necessary characteristics of a particular product (for example, providing that motor vehicles are manufactured with seat belts for their passengers), or may make special provision for the licensing of new products before they are marketed (as in the case of pharmaceuticals),[93] or the

---

[88] Ibid., 195–6.   [89] See below, pp. 354–6.
[90] [2002] EWHC 200; [2002] Lloyd's Rep Med 333, below, pp. 354–6.
[91] 1987 Act, s. 10; GPSR 1994, r. 2 and r. 10(2), below, p. 406.   [92] Below, p. 405.
[93] Below, p. 354.

inspection of old products before they can continue to be used (as in the case of the requirement of motor vehicles to be tested annually under the MOT scheme).

Let us take by way of example a case where a claimant is injured in a road accident while being driven in a coach and it is accepted that her injuries are attributable to the absence of any seat belt in the coach in question. She alleges, *inter alia*, that the coach should have been fitted with seat belts and that the defendant public authority should have issued regulations which required that a coach of the type in question should be used for the transport of passengers only if it has been certified by a responsible body as fitted with appropriate seat belts. How would an English court approach the questions of duty of care and breach of duty in this sort of circumstance?

In my view, even within a set of facts such as this, a number of distinctions could be drawn. First, there is a distinction between the situation where no regulations have been made to govern the aspect of passenger restraint in the category of vehicle in question (a 'pure omission') and the situation where regulations have been made to govern this issue, but where their observance could not (and did not) prevent injury of the type suffered by the claimant (where the defendant's conduct could be thought of more in terms of inadequate action).[94] Secondly, where a body has not taken any action in relation to the risk of injury of the sort suffered by the claimant, a distinction could be drawn between cases where a competent public authority considers whether or not to intervene and chooses not to do so, and cases where it fails to consider the question of intervention, perhaps owing to some administrative oversight or delay. Thirdly, a distinction could be drawn between the question whether *some* protective measures should be required of those running passenger coaches, perhaps in relation to the cost of the safety measures as against other considerations, such as the cost of public transport (this question appearing to be one of 'policy') and issues relating to the technical details of the measures, given what is known about the nature of accidents in question, their incidence and their likely effects (this appearing to be more 'operational' in its nature).

In all these different variables, the courts are likely to be concerned with two main considerations in determining whether to impose a duty of care. The first is a concern to protect the legitimate exercise of the public authority's discretion in deciding whether or not or how to regulate passenger safety in coaches. In this respect, it may be thought of as peculiarly a matter of policy for a body to determine the appropriateness of enacting secondary legislation. Indeed, unlike French law, English law does not furnish any example of a successful challenge to a public body in respect of the failure to make a relevant bye-law or issue delegated legislation by way of judicial review nor any claim for damages against a public body in respect of the same type of failure, although the latter would clearly be possible if it consisted of the non-implementation of an EC Directive.[95] This is not to say that a court would never interfere in such a decision, if, for example, a body with rule-making power adopted a policy for its exercise which was irrational or inconsistent with higher constitutional principle. On the other hand,

---

[94] Cf above, p. 341.

[95] Cases C-6/90 and 9/90, *Francovich and Bonifaci v Italy* [1991] ECR 1-5357; Cases C-178-9/94, 188-190/94 *Dillenkofer and others v Germany* [1996] ECR 1-4845 paras. 26–27. For French law, see above, p. 314 n. 76.

while enacted subordinate legislation may be challenged on the ground of its substantive *ultra vires* (on the ground that it falls outside the powers of the enabling legislation, conflicts with a person's primary legislative rights, or with constitutional principle or is otherwise unreasonable), this last criterion has not been used as a ground for declaring subordinate legislation invalid where the court considers it unnecessary or inconvenient.[96]

However, while judicial concern to protect a public body's law-making discretion will be a strong one, situations may be envisaged where other considerations would pull strongly in the opposite direction. So, where a competent public body was aware of the very serious nature of a risk to health or safety and the enactment of a rule or rules (such as requiring seat belts in my example) was relatively straightforward and uncontroversial and yet failed to intervene as a result of administrative incompetence (such as a breakdown in communications within the public body[97]) or for an improper reason (such as a desire not to impose a burden on the coach-building industry based in a marginal parliamentary constituency[98]), then the courts may well consider both that the considerations to be taken into account were 'justiciable' and that the imposition of a duty of care was 'fair, just and reasonable'. Again, it can be seen that the questions traditionally associated with determining the existence of a *breach* of duty (the magnitude of risk and the cost of precautions and more generally the nature of the negligence on the facts) would figure as factors in deciding whether or not to impose a duty of care, but with the difference that the courts would be swayed by evidence of obvious negligence. It is not merely, therefore, that the courts are not willing to determine the issue of duty of care in this developing area without looking at the facts of any alleged negligence (and so not usually on an application of striking out), but rather that once established, the nature and degree of the defendant's negligence becomes relevant to whether or not a duty of care should be recognised. Here, therefore, English law does seem to be moving towards an approach which imposes liability only for serious fault at the same moment when French law appears to be abandoning this approach, but the two systems are moving in the same direction, that is, toward more liberal approaches to liability than they formerly possessed.

(b) The enforcement of rules

In this situation, a claimant does not impugn the content of rules governing the safety of a product on the market, but rather the policing of those rules by the appropriate public authority. In other contexts, English courts have held that there are good reasons for refusing to impose a duty of care in respect of the investigation and prosecution of criminal offences. So, the House of Lords has held that as a matter of public policy the ordinary police are not liable in negligence in respect of their activities in the investigation and suppression of crime.[99] The Court of Appeal took a

---

[96] Craig, *Administrative Law*, 389–92.
[97] For an example of such a breakdown between *two* public bodies, see *The Creutzfeldt-Jakob Disease Litigation*, above, pp. 295–9.   [98] Cf. below, p. 356.
[99] *Hill v Chief Constable of West Yorkshire* [1989] AC 53 cited with implicit approval though distinguished by Lord Slynn in *W v Commissioner of the Police of the Metropolis* [2000] 1 WLR 1607, 1611–13.

similar approach to the liability of the Crown Prosecution Service to a defendant in relation to the conduct of a prosecution, on the basis that the prosecution service should not have to spend time and use scarce resources in dealing with threatened litigation which should be concentrated on their prime function of prosecuting offenders, even though its actions could lead to the imprisonment of people subsequently not prosecuted.[100]

However, in 2002 in *Thames Trains Ltd v The Health and Safety Executive* the existence of a duty of care in relation to the policing of requirements of safety arose in a context not dissimilar to product safety.[101] This case concerned the Ladbroke Grove Junction railway crash, in which 31 people were killed and 259 injured when a westbound Thames train passed through a signal at danger and collided with an eastbound high speed train. The accident was probably caused partly by the failure of the driver of a train operated by Thames Trains and partly by a failure in Railtrack, the private company which controlled the infrastructure and which was primarily responsible for the signalling system at the junction which was confusing and to a degree obscure.[102] Thames Trains and Railtrack agreed to settle the claims of those injured or the dependants of those killed,[103] but Thames Trains then claimed contribution from the Health and Safety Executive (HSE), alleging breaches of a number of its statutory duties in relation to the supervision of safety on the railway and of a duty of care at common law. On an application by HSE for the claim against them to be struck out, Morland J accepted that there was no reasonably arguable case that the HSE owed a statutory duty giving rise to a private right to passengers on trains, a decision confirmed on appeal.[104] Morland J also recognised a number of considerations arguing against such a common law duty of care in the HSE: notably that there was no indication in the legislation that Parliament intended that it should be liable for any failure in its supervisory role; that the rail companies were primarily responsible for safety of the railways; that its position could be seen as analogous to prosecuting authorities who were not liable to the persons primarily responsible and that there was no 'policy imperative' to impose liability on the HSE given the accident's victims' claims against the companies; that the HSE's powers of intervention were discretionary; and that any liability in the HSE would be borne by the taxpayer.[105] Nevertheless, Morland J refused to strike out the claim in the circumstances. For he noted that it was alleged that Railtrack had undertaken a major remodelling of the railway infrastructure in the area of the crash and had sought approval of these changes from the HSE, which nevertheless neither gave its approval nor prevented trains from running through the altered scheme and that the HSE had known through inspection that the sighting of the signals in question 'was inadequate and created a risk of collision'.[106] Therefore, although the HSE is a 'regulatory, supervisory, licensing body' and therefore unable to carry out or to duplicate the primary duties of Railtrack and the train operators to

---

[100] *Elguzouli-Daf v Commissioner of the Police of the Metropolis* [1995] QB 335, 348.

[101] See *Thames Trains plc v Health and Safety Executive* [2002] EWHC (QB) 1415; [2003] PIQR 202 (Morland J), [2003] EWCA Civ 720; (2003) 147 SJLB 661, 2003 WL 21047574 (app. dismissed).

[102] Ibid., [3]–[4].

[103] Thames Trains were convicted on 5 Apr. 2004 of offences under the Health and Safety at Work Act 1974 and fined £2 million: The Times, 6 Apr. 2004.   [104] [2003] EWCA Civ 720 [9].

[105] [2002] EWHC (QB) 1415 [16], [25], [28], [34], [38].   [106] Ibid., [54].

manage the railways safely, nevertheless it does have a specific, long-stop purpose of safety from personal injury.[107] In Morland J's view, therefore, the case differed both from *Yuen Kun Yeu v A-G of Hong Kong*[108] (which concerned a regulator's liability for pure economic loss) and *Marc Rich*[109] (which concerned a classification society's liability for loss of property). The learned judge cited with evident attraction the Canadian decision in *Swanson v The Queen in right of Canada*[110] which upheld a duty of care in the Canadian regulatory of air safety to family members of those killed in an air crash in respect of its failures in supervision of air safety on the basis that its decisions had not involved any considerations of policy.[111] He concluded that, even with the state of the authorities as they were,[112] it could reasonably be argued that 'the Executive should be made liable not for failing to use statutory powers involving expenditure of money but for failing negligently to use, as the public would expect, their statutory powers through the Railway Inspectorate in carrying out routine duties of inspection and supervision'.[113] Moreover, the possibility of a duty of care being recognised was more likely given the Railway Inspectorate's 'alleged close involvement in and knowledge of the dangerous situation at Ladbroke Grove junction with inaction over a period of three years'.[114]

The Court of Appeal also upheld Morland J's decision as to the reasonably arguable existence of a common law duty, noting, *inter alia*, the fact that the HSE's behaviour may well be found at trial to have gone beyond 'pure omissions' and so outside the impact of the denial of a duty of care in *Stovin v Wise*,[115] in an arguable reliance of the public or of passengers in the role of the HSE in relation to rail safety, and in the possible existence of exceptional factors which would apply on the facts once revealed.[116] Given the 'strong tide of modern authority' against striking out claims before full trial of the facts,[117] the application to strike out this claim should be denied without any more elaborate review of the authorities.[118]

Here, then, we can see two of the more general themes in the case law of the last decade (in the concern with the protection of the exercise of discretion involving consideration of policy and the lack of need for liability in a public regulatory body where there is another body who is primarily responsible), but these themes are capable of being counterbalanced by the nature of the harm in respect of which liability is sought (personal injuries and death as opposed to damage to property or pure economic loss) and the degree of involvement of the public body in the circumstances leading to the harm. And Morland J saw the facts allegedly constituting breach of any duty to be imposed as significant to the question of duty of care, for, according to the claimant's allegations, the defendant had *actual* knowledge of the grave risk and the length of time during which it took no action and it permitted the risk to be run.[119]

---

[107] Ibid., [60], [63].

[108] [1988] 1 AC 175, above, pp. 343–4. *Harris v Evans* [1998] 1 WLR 1285 was distinguished on similar grounds: [81]–[83]. [109] [1996] 1 AC 211, above, p. 343.

[110] [1991] 80 DLR741. [111] *Thames Trains*, [2002] EWHC (QB) 1415 [66]–[67].

[112] The claimants argued that *Stovin v Wise* [1996] AC 923 should not be followed: [2002] EWHC (QB) 1415 [71]. [113] Ibid., [79].

[114] Ibid., [87]. [115] *cit.* [116] [2003] EWCA Civ. 720 [24–29].

[117] Ibid., [34], *per* May LJ. [118] Ibid., [11], [35].

[119] [2002] EWHC (QB) 1415 [54]–[55].

(c) Supplying information about products

A failure in the provision of information about the risks to health or person of a product already in circulation may itself take a number of forms: a total failure to inform people of the risk associated with use of a particular category of product or individual product; a failure to inform people adequately of such a risk, whether this relates to the content of any information or the way in which it is conveyed; or the positive promotion of a product for use where this involves risks which are not specified or not explained to its users.

In 1984, the position as to liability for advice as to the use of a product by central government by way of exercise of a statutory power appeared to be fairly clear, for in that year a claim by children harmed allegedly by 'whooping cough vaccine' against the Department of Health for its alleged negligence in promoting the use of the vaccine was struck out by Stuart-Smith J.[120] There, the Department relied on its Minister's general powers and duties for the promotion of physical and mental health under the National Health Service Act 1946 and a specific power to make arrangements with local health authorities for vaccination or immunisation of diseases.[121] Applying the then current distinction between the policy and operational spheres, Stuart-Smith J held that the Department's allegedly negligent action in failing to warn the public of the risks was plainly within the limits of a discretion *bona fide* exercised under these statutory powers and was therefore protected, though he accepted that it could be argued that the advice given by NHS doctors as to how or in what circumstances the vaccine should be administered fell within the operational sphere.

Danns v Department of Health is a more recent and particularly good example of the courts' approach to liability for the provision of information by central government, though not in the context of products.[122] In that case, the male plaintiff had undergone a vasectomy operation in 1983 and, following current practice, had been advised by his doctor that its effect would be to render him sterile. In 1991, however, his wife, the second plaintiff, gave birth to his son. The plaintiffs claimed damages for pain, distress and the financial costs of this unwanted child against the Department of Health, alleging that from the publication of a particular survey in 1984, it had become known that after vasectomy a man had a 1 in 2,000 chance of later becoming fertile. As a result, the Minister should have disseminated this information directly via newspapers to the some three quarters of a million men affected and not merely have left it to doctors to warn their patients.

The Court of Appeal affirmed the decision at trial holding the Department not liable in the tort of negligence in these circumstances.[123] Leggatt LJ considered that

---

[120] *DHSS v Kinnear* 134 *NLJ* 886, The Times, 7 July 1984, 1984 WL 281999. The children also claimed damages against their local area health authorities and the manufacturers of the vaccine in the UK. The subsequent history of this litigation, which was representative of some 200 claims, is complex, but it was concluded by a trial decision holding that on a balance of probabilities the vaccine did not cause the claimant's condition: *Loveday v Renton* The Times, 31 March 1988, 1988 WL 624143 (Stuart-Smith LJ).

[121] National Health Service Act 1946, ss. 1, 26(2).   [122] [1998] PIQR P226.

[123] The claim for breach of statutory duty was abandoned before the CA.

the judge below was right to hold that as regards future patients the Department was 'fully entitled to leave it to the [medical] profession to decide what advice or counselling it should give'.[124] As to their own position, the plaintiffs had alleged that the Department had not considered the 1984 survey which had escaped the attention of those dealing with such matters there; the Department contended that they had considered it and decided to do nothing. Here, Leggatt LJ considered that even if the plaintiffs' case had been accepted, they would still have had to show that, 'if the Department had exercised its discretion, it would have been bound to decide to disseminate the information', which it was clear was not the case.[125] However, the Court of Appeal accepted the Department's contention that it *had* considered whether or not to disseminate this information and that this decision, *bona fide* made could not be challenged (as was indeed accepted by the plaintiffs themselves), applying the approach of Lord Browne-Wilkinson in *X v Bedfordshire CC* in this respect which tied the possibility of liability in negligence in respect of the exercise of a statutory discretion to a condition of illegality.[126] Given that this view has itself been overtaken by subsequent decisions in the House of Lords,[127] it may be thought that the Court of Appeal's approach in *Danns* is to this extent vitiated. However, the Court of Appeal was clearly influenced by its view of the substance of the Department's decision making, it being 'sensible' in 1984 for it to refrain from disseminating the information about the risk of fertility:[128] confining one's attention to the single subject of 'the remote possibility' of the risk of fertility in determining what information to provide 'is to ignore the scope and volume of medical research'.[129]

In *Harris v Evans* in 1998 the question of liability for the public provision of information concerning the safety of a product arose in very different circumstances, but it also resulted in denial of the existence of a duty of care.[130] There the plaintiff ran a business of 'bungee jumping' from a mobile telescopic crane in an area whose local authority was advised by an HSE inspector that it should not be used for this purpose until certified as fit by some competent person or the manufacturer of the crane. The plaintiff failed to fulfill these conditions and so was ordered not to use the crane by the local authority, but this was later withdrawn. The plaintiff claimed damages for lost business against the inspector personally and against the HSE in negligence arguing that they were liable for his allegedly negligent misstatement under *Hedley Byrne*, but this claim was struck out by the Court of Appeal. In its view, in such a context appeal to authorities governing 'assumption of responsibility' in respect of pure economic loss[131] (as suffered by the plaintiff) could not take place outside the context of the statutory framework. Here, statute created extensive powers in the inspectors in the interest of safety and also provided a system of appeals against any act taken by the statutory enforcing authority (which the

---

[124] [1998] PIQR P226, P229–P230.   [125] Ibid., at 230.
[126] Ibid., 232–3 and see [1995] 2 AC 633, 738.   [127] Above, pp. 339–40.
[128] [1998] PIQR P226, P233, *per* Leggatt LJ.   [129] Ibid., *per* Roch LJ.
[130] [1998] 1 WLR 1285.
[131] *Hedley Byrne & Co. v Heller & Partners* [1963] AC 465; *Spring v Guardian Assurance plc* [1995] 2 AC 296; *White v Jones* [1995] 2 AC 207.

plaintiffs had not chosen to exercise).[132] In these circumstances, no duty of care should be imposed in respect of the economic consequences of any decision made unless it created a new risk or danger.[133]

This decision makes an interesting contrast with *Danns v Department of Health*.[134] The two decisions have in common a concern with the protection of the purposes of the two sets of statutory powers whose exercise or non-exercise is impugned, but whereas in *Danns* the plaintiffs claimed that the Department had not done enough to protect their personal interests, in *Harris v Evans* the plaintiff claimed that the HSE had done too much in a mistaken belief that it was in the interests of safety and that this had prejudiced his economic interests. Whereas in *Danns*, it could be said that the parties were not 'proximate' (the male plaintiff being a member of a class of three-quarters of a million),[135] in *Harris* the HSE could clearly see that its advice would principally affect the plaintiff's business. Nevertheless, in both cases the courts were concerned to give room to the defendant public bodies to advise or not to advise on matters of safety as they thought fit, as had been provided by statute. As I shall explain in relation to *Smith v Department of Health*,[136] this concern is likely to remain one which the courts will see as all but conclusive of the issue of duty of care in negligence in this sort of case, even after the degree of liberalisation in approach to the liability of public authorities after *Barrett* and *Phelps*.[137]

(d) Controlling access to or continuance on the market of a particular product

Perhaps the most important supervisory control which public authorities possess in relation to product safety is found in their control over access to or continuance on the market of a category of a product or, indeed, an individual product. This takes two main forms: pre-circulation control (licensing, inspection or certification) and post-circulation control (exercising powers to order a product's recall).

Two contrasting decisions in the context of the certification of aircraft reflect the changing focus of judicial concerns. In *Philcox v Civil Aviation Authority* in 1995 the plaintiff owned a light aircraft which had been repaired by his club, a limited company, and then inspected and certified for airworthiness by the Civil Aviation Authority ('CAA') under statutory powers: without such a certificate, the aircraft could not lawfully fly.[138] A month later the aircraft crashed and while neither the plaintiff nor his passenger were seriously injured, the plaintiff claimed damages from his club, an action later settled. The plaintiff then brought an action for damages for the necessary repairs to the aircraft for the loss he suffered owing to the air crash, that is, damage to the aircraft not recompensed by his insurer and for loss of revenue from hire of the aircraft while it was unable to fly. While the Court of Appeal was not altogether clear as to the nature of the plaintiff's harm (whether damage to property,

---

132 *Harris v Evans* [1998] 1 WLR 1285, 1296–8, *per* Scott V-C.   133 Ibid., at 1302.
134 Above, pp. 349–50.   135 [1998] PIQR P226, P233.
136 [2002] EWHC 200 (QB); 67 BMLR 34, below, pp. 354–6.   137 Above, pp. 340, 342.
138 (1995) 92(27) LSG 33, The Times, 8 June 1995, (unpaginated *LexisNexis* transcript used).

economic loss, or economic loss 'associated with physical damage to the aircraft'[139]), all the judges agreed that no duty of care arose in the CAA in respect of its certification, on the basis that it was not 'fair, just and reasonable' to impose a duty in the circumstances, principally on the ground that a person such as the plaintiff whose action is supervised by a public regulator should not be able recover damages against that regulator[140] or, put another way, the statutory scheme of control in question was constructed for the protection of people other than the aircraft's owner, such as passengers, cargo-owners or other members of the public.[141] The primary responsibility for the maintenance of the aircraft rested on the plaintiff as owner.

In *Perrett v Collins*, decided just three years later, the Court of Appeal took a rather different approach.[142] There the first defendant had purchased a kit aircraft and in the course of its construction had decided to substitute a different gearbox without making the necessary alteration to the aircraft's propeller. This construction was carried out under the occasional supervision of an inspector (the second defendant) generally employed by a flying club (the third defendant) of which the first defendant was a member but who was paid a small fee by him for this purpose. On completion of the aircraft, the second defendant signed a permit to allow the aircraft to fly as provided for under rules made under statutory powers contained in the Civil Aviation Act. However, the aircraft crashed on its test flight and injured the plaintiff, the first defendant's passenger.

On these facts, the Court of Appeal upheld the trial judge's decision below and held that both the second defendant inspector and the flying club owed the plaintiff duties of care in respect of his inspection and certification, despite the presence of the construction fault: the plaintiff's harm was physical (personal injury) which was a 'potent factor' pointing to the existence of a duty of care, whereas the harm in *Philcox* was treated as 'purely economic';[143] there was no concern with either the foreseeability of the plaintiff's harm (which the defendants had conceded[144]); the statutory scheme of control was constructed for the safety of aircraft and persons, that is, with the view to avoid the type of harm which in fact occurred;[145] and the role of the surveyor was not 'secondary' but was 'independent' of the role of the owner/builder who was merely an amateur.[146] In this respect, it clearly weighed with the court that the inspector was very closely involved in the construction of the plane and the flying club was very closely involved 'in organisational terms' with the owner/builder;[147] that the inspector was paid by the owner and that, while the flying club might not be profit-making, its purposes were both recreational and potentially extremely dangerous to third parties.[148] Finally, Buxton LJ was unimpressed by the policy reasons against liability put forward by the defendants, whether in terms of an increase in their insurance premiums, the danger of 'defensive surveying' or that the withdrawal of the flying club would put a burden on the CAA, 'with greater expense to small aircraft operators or the taxpayer or both'.[149] These assertions were unsupported by evidence and the increase of costs to

---

[139] Staughton LJ and Millett LJ considered it damage to property; Ward LJ did not express a view on the matter.   [140] Staughton LJ.
[141] Staughton LJ and Millett LJ (who also saw no 'proximity').   [142] [1998] 2 Lloyd's Rep 255.
[143] Ibid., 276, 265.   [144] Ibid., 257.   [145] Ibid., 258.   [146] Ibid., 259, 272, 274.
[147] Ibid., 274.   [148] Ibid. 275.   [149] Ibid., 276–7.

defendants from liability should not be seen as a reason for denying relief where a person had been negligently injured.[150]

In this case, therefore, the defendant inspector was held liable for failing to take reasonable care before giving a permission necessary for the lawful use of a particular example of a product of a type whose use entails a high risk of injury or death. The safety defect in the aircraft was one of manufacture (by an amateur builder/owner), the inspector's negligence a failure to discover and/or act reasonably in response to that defect. Quite apart, though, from the special features of the case (notably, that the defendant inspector was a private person acting professionally and for reward even if within a statutory framework and the 'close involvement' in the product's construction[151]), the central thesis of the case which distinguishes on the one hand between liability for physical damage (and in particular personal injury) in which a duty is more likely to be imposed and pure economic loss on the other reveals a striking paradox in the law more generally.

For if held liable the first defendant, the owner/builder whose negligence contributed to the plaintiff's personal injuries, could claim contribution from either or both of the two other defendants, the inspector and the club under the law governing joint and several tortfeasors. This may not seem objectionable on the facts as the owner/builder had engaged the inspector and joined the club in part to prevent himself from building an unsafe aircraft, but behind the parties present in *Perrett v Collins* one could see other possible defendants, notably, the seller and the manufacturer of the kit of the aircraft. While the facts necessary to take a view on the potential liabilities of these parties are not available in the judgments (notably, as regards the person from whom the owner/builder bought the substitute gearbox) one could imagine a situation where one or other of such persons should have warned the amateur owner/builder of the aircraft of the risk of changing the gearbox but not the propeller. Even at common law, if negligence could be made out in either seller or manufacturer, they could be liable to the passenger injured when the aircraft crashed and could, therefore, also claim contribution from the inspector and flying club in respect of any liability incurred. In this way, a decision imposing liability on a certifier of a product to a victim of personal injuries can lead to a claim for contribution by the person controlled by the process of certification in respect of the economic loss caused by his own civil liability for personal injuries.

Perrett v Collins, therefore, shows that the distinction between compensating the primary victims of personal injuries from regulatory failures by a public body and compensating a person regulated by such a body which suffers economic loss breaks down when juxtaposed with the law of contribution between tortfeasors. For where liability is imposed in a regulator to a primary victim of this kind, then the regulated party stands to benefit by way of contribution towards any liability for which he is 'primarily responsible' (as indeed was the situation in *Thames Trains v HSE*).[152] Of course, such a claim for contribution by a regulated person may not lead to a very large

---

[150] Ibid.
[151] See similarly, *Robinson v Dept of Environment* [1988] 6 NIJB 24 (QBD) (duty of care in department in respect of MOT certification of motor vehicles).   [152] Above, pp. 347–8.

actual award against a regulator in the regulated person's favour, as the court possesses a discretion under the Civil Liability (Contribution) Act 1978 to award what is just and reasonable taking into account the relative fault and causal significance of the fault in the production of the primary victim's harm.[153] But a claim for contribution will exist.

(e) Choosing between regulatory responses

Perhaps, however, the most rewarding discussion in the area of the liability of regulators of products in the interests of their safety may be found in *Smith v Secretary of State for Health*,[154] particularly in relation to the issue of breach of duty. There in late May 1986 the plaintiff when four years old suffered from chicken pox, had been given aspirin by her mother and as a result of this medicine developed Reye's syndrome, and became grievously permanently disabled. On 10 and 11 June 1986, the Committee on the Safety of Medicines ('CSM') issued warnings against the use of aspirin in children under the age of 12 which were reported in a national newspaper. The plaintiff's basic case was that this warning should have been given earlier, and in particular within a week or two of a meeting of the CSM in March 1986 when it had been advised of the risk of death or serious injury from Reye's syndrome in children on taking aspirin, for if a warning had been given, the plaintiff's mother would not have given her aspirin and she would not have been injured.

A number of preliminary issues came for trial before Morland J, including both the existence of a duty of care and of breach of duty, which he set in the statutory framework in which the Department and CSM worked. In law, it was for the Secretary of State for Health to determine the granting, renewal and revocation of licenses for all medical products in the UK, including 'proprietary medicines', that is, those available over the counter without prescription,[155] though his power to revoke or vary a medicine's licence once granted was 'circumscribed and [could] involve very lengthy consultation and appeal processes'.[156] The CSM was established by statutory instrument to advise the Secretary of State as to the 'safety, quality and efficacy' of medicines for human use,[157] and in reality laid down the policy which the Department implemented.[158]

In the larger part of his judgment, Morland J addressed the question whether the Secretary of State had been negligent in failing to issue public warnings about aspirin earlier. In this respect, he contrasted the approach of the UK authorities to the US experience, where in 1982 the authorities had issued warnings as to the use of aspirin by children even though at the time its validity was disputed by the pharmaceutical industry and their action opposed:[159] it was only in 1985 that the US industry started to cooperate with the authorities' concerns.[160] In Morland J's view, the US experience formed an object lesson to the CSM on how the problem should *not* be dealt with:

The lesson was that clear informative warnings fully supported by the whole pharmaceutical industry were required. Otherwise a mixed and confused message would come across not

---

[153] Below, pp. 557–61.   [154] [2002] EWHC 200 (QB); 67 BMLR 34.
[155] Medicines Act 1968, s. 6(1).   [156] [2002] EWHC 200 (QB), at [20].
[157] Medicines (Committee on Safety of Medicines) Order SI 1970 No. 1257, para. 3.
[158] [2002] EWHC 200 (QB) [90].   [159] Ibid., at [38].   [160] Ibid., at [42].

stopping aspirin being given to febrile children but at the same time causing loss of confidence in aspirin when it should be taken by children and adults.[161]

For while aspirin in children possessed the risk of Reye's syndrome, aspirin remained an effective antipyretic and analgesic.[162]

In March 1986 the CSM accepted the possible causal link of aspirin to Reye's syndrome in children and it recommended that warnings should be issued, possibly to include letters to prescribing doctors, pharmacists, advertisements and product labelling, but did not recommend that paediatric preparations should be withdrawn from the market.[163] However, once the CSM's secretariat met industry representatives (which they quickly did), the difficulty and scale of the problem became apparent, for aspirin had been 'a panacea in every medicine cupboard of every home since Edwardian times' and there were some 40 million packs already in circulation.[164] In response to this, the Department decided to postpone further discussion of the issue by the CSM until May in the 'reasonable belief and expectation that there was the likelihood of the full cooperation of the industry thus circumventing the cumbersome statutory procedures [of withdrawal of its licence] and achieving a more effective result',[165] in particular so as to avoid the US route which led to a complete loss of public confidence in aspirin. In Morland J's view, this positive cooperation by the industry was crucial to the success of any decision relating to aspirin and children,[166] but establishing unanimity among producers required effort.[167] When the CSM met in late May it endorsed the strategy proposed by the industry, that is, to amend dosage instructions on adult products, to warn against use by children under 12 without medical advice and to run a public education campaign funded by the Aspirin Association and developed in conjunction with the Department: this advice was followed by the Department.[168] In the result, there was a 'concerted and successful campaign' to stop children under 12 being given aspirin except on doctor's orders,[169] with 'excellent results but tragically too late to save [the plaintiff] from catastrophic disability'.[170] In Morland J's judgment, there was, therefore, no fault in either the Department or the CSM in dealing with the risk caused by aspirin: the delay of an extra month 'created a window of opportunity for a far better overall result',[171] and the risk that two or three children might die or be gravely disabled had to be balanced against the 'undoubted benefit of a coherent coordinated comprehensive campaign including the withdrawal of paediatric aspirin with the full weight of the Department of Health, the CSM and the industry behind it thus giving a clear definitive unambiguous message to both professionals and the general public'.[172]

This is a very important illustration of the way in which an English court applies the 'cost/benefit' analysis in assessing the existence of negligence,[173] even when balancing the cost in terms of death and disability against a benefit of other possible death or disability. In coming to his view, Morland J looked extremely carefully at the development of the public authority's view as to how to proceed and how it changed once the

---

[161] Ibid., at [45].   [162] Ibid., at [61] (expert evidence at trial).   [163] Ibid., at [57]–[58].
[164] Ibid., at [99], *per* Morland J and [79] respectively.   [165] Ibid., at [72].   [166] Ibid., at [76].
[167] Ibid., at [78].   [168] Ibid., at [81].   [169] Ibid., at [86].   [170] Ibid., at [82].
[171] Ibid., at [87].   [172] Ibid., at [106].   [173] Above, pp. 192–200.

difficulty of achieving an effective result in the particular context was appreciated. In the context, the Department was right *not* to issue public warnings nor to start the process by which the product's licence would be revoked, but rather to come to an agreed joint solution in partnership with industry. In these circumstances, even though those responsible *knew* of the risk that a child may suffer as a result of the necessary delay, this risk was worth taking; therefore, they were not negligent. This decision makes an interesting factual contrast with Morland J's earlier imposition of liability for negligence in the Department and the Medical Research Council in relation to Human Growth Hormone and CJD, though there these public bodies both produced and supplied as well as regulated the product in question.[174]

Having come to this view as to the absence of negligence, Morland J's decision in *Smith v Department of Health* on the existence of a duty of care became hypothetical and he treated it briefly. His conclusion was that no duty was owed as the decisions to postpone the CSM's final decision on action in relation to aspirin and the content of any warning were 'well on the "discretionary/policy" side' of the line between discretionary/policy decisions and operational decisions and were not justiciable,[175] though Morland J added that he was not saying that the public bodies before him could never be liable for a failure to exercise or an improper exercise of their statutory powers, for example if the Secretary of State had delayed implementation of a decision until after a bye-election in a marginal constituency where there was a large aspirin factory or the CSM had postponed its meeting to avoid the Epsom Derby meeting: special circumstances clearly demand a remedy, as the House of Lords in *Phelps* had acknowledged.[176]

4. The *HIV Haemophiliac Litigation* and the Disclosure of Documents

In my general discussion of the issue of breach of duty in negligence, I emphasised the importance in the English context of disclosure of documents and contrasted it to the mechanisms for obtaining documents in the French civil process.[177] Here, I wish to draw attention to an important qualification on the general scheme which I previously described, potentially significant for claims against public authorities in respect of product safety, known as 'public interest immunity'. This special rule played a central part in the English litigation brought by haemophiliac recipients of HIV-infected blood against a range of public bodies whose negligence they alleged was responsible for their harm, for soon after disclosure was ordered against the Department of Health, the government (though a *new* government) agreed to a settlement.[178] This accounts for the absence of any civil decision determining liability for the provision of HIV-infected blood to haemophiliacs, in very striking contrast to the position in France.[179]

The HIV haemophiliac litigation would have led to a spectacularly complex trial estimated to last six months:[180] 962 haemophiliacs (or their dependants) claimed

---

[174] See especially *The Creutzfeldt-Jakob Disease Litigation, Plaintiffs v United Kingdom Medical Research Council* (July, 1996) (2000) 54 BMLR 8, above, pp. 295–9.
[175] [2002] EWHC 200 (QB) at [91]–[93].
[176] Ibid., at [95] citing *Phelps v Hillingdon LBC* [2000] 3 WLR 776, 790 and 808.
[177] Above, pp. 213–14.   [178] Below, p. 359.   [179] Above, pp. 149–51, 315–19, 394–401.
[180] The Times, 21 September 1990, 1 and 4.

damages in respect of harm suffered from their infection by HIV from Factor VIII blood products supplied to them under the NHS in the course of the 1980s. Their claims were directed against central regulatory bodies (the Department of Health, the statutory licensing body for blood products, and the CSM, known collectively as the 'central defendants') and 220 regional and local health authorities and special bodies, such as the Central Blood Laboratories Authority.[181] They claimed damages for breach of statutory duty and in the tort of negligence, claiming (*inter alia*[182]) that the failure of the central defendants to achieve self-sufficiency in blood products for England and Wales was negligent as it caused many haemophiliac patients to be treated with Factor VIII concentrate imported from the USA which was infected with HIV; that the Department knew or should have known of the risk to the plaintiffs from this imported concentrate; and that practical steps could have been taken to eliminate or reduce this risk.[183]

While the central defendants had disclosed a very large number of documents relating to the plaintiffs' claims, the Minister of Health supplied a list of some 600 documents for which public interest immunity was claimed, that is, documents which would pass the applicable test of relevance to the facts on which the plaintiffs relied but which the Minister refused to disclose on the ground that it was 'necessary for the proper functioning of the public service that these documents should, except in the most exceptional circumstances, be withheld on the grounds of public interest'.[184] The documents included submissions to ministers, communications between civil servants and position papers which related to decisions described by the Minister as issues of policy, notably as to the adoption of a policy of self-sufficiency in blood products and the resources to be allocated to the provision of blood products more generally.[185]

The plaintiffs applied to the court for an order that the Minister should nonetheless produce the documents in question. The Court of Appeal noted that while it was entirely proper for the Department in the circumstances to raise the issue of public interest immunity against disclosure of these documents,[186] it was for the court to determine whether the documents should be produced[187] and '[t]he task of the court is properly to balance the public interest in preserving the immunity, on the one hand, and the public interest in the fair trial of the proceedings, on the other'.[188] In coming to its view, a court should be satisfied that the documents in question are very likely to contain material which would give substantial support to his contention on an issue so

---

[181] The nature of the claims appears from the decision of the Court of Appeal on 'public interest immunity': *HIV Haemophiliac Litigation* (1998) 41 BMLR 171; [1996] PIQR. P220.

[182] The main statement of claim extended to 117 pages: [1996] PIQR P220, P223.

[183] Ibid., at P242.　　　[184] Ibid., at P228, quoting the terms of the Minister's certificate.

[185] Ibid., at P226.

[186] Subsequently, the House of Lords has held that a minister has a discretion whether or not to claim public interest immunity in proceedings, though once a court has accepted the claim, the 'immunity' cannot be renounced: *R v Chief Constable of the West Midlands Police ex p Wiley* [1995] 1 AC 274.

[187] [1996] PIQR P220, P229. On 'public interest immunity' generally, see Craig, *Administrative Law*, 857–70.

[188] [1996] PIQR P220, P229, *per* Ralph Gibson LJ. This principle was affirmed by the House of Lords in *Conway v Rimmer* [1968] AC 910.

that without them he might be deprived of the means of proper presentation of his case.[189]

At first instance, Rougier J considered that he should refuse to order the production of the documents if he was wholly satisfied that the plaintiffs had as a matter of law no arguable case against the central defendants[190] and in this way the question whether these defendants owed a duty of care in the tort of negligence on the facts as alleged became relevant to the question of the availability of disclosure. The Court of Appeal agreed with this basic approach, being prepared to hold that there was no valid cause of action for these limited purposes where this was sufficiently clear, but not where (as in the case before it) a case raises novel questions of public importance, where the decisions in law are better made after trial.[191] For in the Court of Appeal's view, while it might be rare for a case for negligence to be proved against the Department of Health in respect of the exercise of its general functions in relation to the NHS, this was not enough to deny the possibility in law for the purposes of the court's decision as to the disclosure of documents.[192] As Bingham LJ observed, given the avoidable nature of the tragedy which had afflicted the plaintiffs, if their allegations of fact could be made out, 'the law might arguably be thought defective if it did not afford redress'.[193] In the result, the plaintiffs had a 'good arguable claim' in common law negligence.[194]

The Court of Appeal then looked at the nature of the plaintiffs' allegations in order to help determine which documents *should* be disclosed. According to the plaintiffs, the central defendants had made 'grave errors of judgment'. Moreover, if the evidence was later found to support the plaintiffs' claims, the court considered that the defendants' failure to act upon their knowledge of the risk to the plaintiffs was likely to have been

the result of failure at some level within the department to pass that available information to those who were required to make the decisions. If that is not in fact the explanation, but it is proved that the information as to the nature and gravity of the risk, and of the steps available to eliminate or reduce it, was supplied to those who were required to make the decisions, then . . . the plaintiffs would have a prima facie case for asserting that the decisions were such that no reasonable or responsible person could properly make them.[195]

In this way, the Court of Appeal was clearly prepared to countenance a claim against a public body responsible for making decisions on product safety in the tort of negligence, subject to a criterion of *Wednesbury* unreasonableness.[196]

Given this view of the hypothetical facts, the court held that it was highly likely that the documents in respect of which public interest immunity had been claimed would give substantial support to the plaintiffs' contentions, as they related to the explanation of how the department had failed to protect the plaintiffs from the risk of infection from contaminated blood.[197] The Court of Appeal did not consider the need for a fair trial which this represented to be outweighed in the circumstances

---

[189] Ibid., at P229, quoting Lord Fraser in *Air Canada v Sec. of State for Trade (No.2)* [1983] 2 AC 394, 436.   [190] [1996] PIQR P220, P230.

[191] Ibid., at P233–34, P247–8.   [192] Ibid., at P240, P248–9.   [193] Ibid., at P249.

[194] It considered the claim for breach of statutory duty 'at best of uncertain validity': ibid., at P234.

[195] Ibid., P243, *per* Ralph Gibson LJ.   [196] Cf. above, p. 339.

[197] [1996] PIQR P220 at P243.

either by the need for 'effective, candid and uninhibited advice to ministers' nor by any 'public interest in protecting from possible critics the inner workings of government in the formulation of important government policy'.[198] For this reason the Court of Appeal ordered the production of all those documents in the Minister's certificate, apart from some whose substantive content would be otherwise available (some 204 documents in total),[199] subject to their prior inspection by the judge to whom the trial of the case had been allotted so as to apply the criterion for production enunciated by the Court of Appeal.[200]

The Court of Appeal's approach and decision on public interest immunity fits well into the general trend both in the courts and in government itself away from the withdrawal of documents from the civil process on this ground, this trend being encouraged by the implications of article 6 of the European Convention and the Human Rights Act.[201] Moreover, while the more restrictive general criteria for disclosure of documents introduced by the Civil Procedure Rules could be seen as pulling against this liberalising tendency in relation to public interest immunity as they encourage the reduction of documentation principally in the interest of cost, under 'standard disclosure' a party must still disclose all documents which adversely affect his own case or which support or adversely affect another party's case, and while a defendant need only undertake a 'reasonable search' for such documents, the criteria of reasonableness would not suggest that many of the documents in contention in the *HIV Haemophiliac Litigation* would fall outside this test.[202] This English law governing the disclosure of documents whose retention is allegedly in the public interest contrasts with the approach of the Conseil d'Etat to the production of documents, which does not recognise any system by which a defendant claims an 'immunity' from revealing documents relevant to a claimant's case.[203]

The sequel to the decision of the Court of Appeal in the *HIV Haemophiliac Litigation* on 20 September 1990 on disclosure was an extra-judicial one. While in late October, the then Prime Minister, Margaret Thatcher, was reported as denying any more funds for compensation of the haemophiliac victims of HIV beyond the £34 million *ex gratia* already pledged,[204] after John Major became Prime Minister on 28 November 1990, the government announced that it had agreed to settle the haemophiliacs' claims by making available £42 million for their benefit to the Macfarlane Trust, a fund set up by the government in 1987 with a grant of £10 million,[205] and by paying their costs (already estimated at some £2 million), though it still denied any negligence.[206] While for some this reflected the government's 'basic humanitarian instinct',[207] for others it reflected its wish to avoid disclosure of sensitive information relating to the importation of blood products from the US which would

---

[198] Ibid., at P249, *per* Bingham LJ.   [199] Ibid., at P249.   [200] Ibid., at P246–7.

[201] Craig, *Administrative Law*, 863.   [202] On the criteria, see above, p. 213.

[203] Brown and Bell, *French Administrative Law*, 95–7.

[204] The Times, 17 October 1990, 8 and 19 October 1990, 9.

[205] The Times, 12 December 1990, 1 and 3.

[206] The Times, 12 December 1990 and see The Times, 30 January 1991, 6. In June 1991, the High Court approved the settlement of all but a handful of the claims by the *haemophiliac* recipients of blood products infected with HIV: The Times, 11 June 1991, 3.

[207] C. Miller, 'Victims missed in the HIV payout', The Times, 10 September 1991, 31.

have revealed the nature of the decisions made.[208] While at first the government refused to make any money available to compensate those who had contracted HIV by transfusion with infected blood who were not haemophiliac,[209] in February 1992 it made some £10 to £12 million available for this purpose. In the result, the haemophiliacs' civil litigation led to the creation of a special fund for the compensation of certain victims of blood products, rather than either damages in the ordinary sense or any judicial decision adjudicating on the alleged negligence of the public defendants.

5. Comparative Observations

The differences between the starting points of the English and French laws of administrative liability are very striking, but their full force is not reflected in the reality of the imposition of liability in cases such as the regulation of product safety. Here, I wish to make five main comparative observations.

First, the starting point in the sources of administrative power remain fundamentally different, reflecting differences in constitutional principle and the sources of the law in the two legal systems. So, as a matter of French constitutional principle, it is the role of the executive to govern and this brings with it among other things an inherent power to intervene in the interests of the health and safety of citizens: the *pouvoir exécutif* justifies intervention in the interests of *ordre public* conceived in a very broad sense. For a French public lawyer, the existence of powers in the executive of a type and a range which are not enjoyed by ordinary citizens (*prérogatives exorbitantes du droit commun*) does not need to rest on special legislative authority, but does require 'special controls', both in terms of review by reference to principles of legality and by the imposition of special administrative *responsabilités*, some of which are stricter, some less onerous than the liabilities imposed by private law.[210] These general starting points are reflected in the law governing the powers and liabilities of the administration as regards the safety of products, for central and local authorities enjoy general powers of intervention and can be liable to a person harmed as a result of their exercise or non-exercise, certainly on the basis of *faute lourde* and possibly merely *faute simple*.[211] On the other hand, as in many other areas, there is a good deal of special legislation in France creating special powers for the administration in the area of product safety and where this is the case, the starting point for the administrative courts' analysis of liability is an examination of the nature and extent of these powers. Moreover, while French public lawyers consider the question of liability for this *police administrative* under this heading, they admit that there is a good deal of 'empiricism', that is, sensitivity to context and the practicalities of that context.[212] The decision of the Assemblée of the Conseil d'Etat in the *affaire du sang contaminé* can be seen as a perfect example of such sensitivity, the court overtly relying on the particular involvement and degree of control of the central authorities in the blood transfusion service

---

[208] B. Levin, The Times, 13 August 1990, 10.   [209] The Times, 30 November 1991, 5.
[210] Above, p. 30.   [211] Above, pp. 312–15, 319.   [212] Above, pp. 311–12.

in requiring mere *faute simple*, though perhaps also taking into account the wider impact of its decision in a highly politically charged case.[213]

By contrast, the starting point of the English courts to both the sources of administrative power and to the liabilities which may result from its exercise is fundamentally particular. This may be seen to result from two interconnected aspects of the role of statutes in the English constitutional and legal context. For, first, it has been a consequence of Dicey's claims for parliamentary competence that executive power should be channelled through Parliament, leaving Crown prerogative as exceptional and somewhat anomalous.[214] This way of thinking has placed statutes at the head of the sources of administrative powers, though more recently the Crown's inherent power to enter contracts and possibly to act otherwise as a 'person of full age' have become prominent.[215] Secondly, moreover, in the English way of thinking statutes are necessarily special, however broad.[216] And while generally statute intervenes exceptionally in the context of a body of regulation already provided by the common law, in the case of special statutory powers for public authorities, statute intervenes so as to create a basis for action in the absence of any general common law provision. Let me emphasise, this is not to deny the importance and the breadth of modern legislation empowering the executive, but, however broad, modern statutory powers exist in the context and for the purposes of the statute in question. As I have described, this particularity of approach is fully, one could even say *too* fully, reflected in the approach of the English courts to the imposition of liability in negligence for harm caused in the exercise of statutory powers, aided and abetted by the very open nature of the *Caparo* 'test' for the existence of a duty of care in the tort of negligence.[217] As a result, taken together, the law governing the liability of the administration has descended into an increasingly impenetrable casuistry as to this threshold requirement for the existence of liability.

Overall, secondly, even after the degree of liberalisation in the English approach to duty of care after *Osman, Phelps* and *Barrett*,[218] French law remains much more open in principle to the imposition of liability in cases such as the supervision of the safety of products than does English law. For the French law sees this sort of case as falling within the category of liability for activities, rather than for *actes* and as a result avoids the technical link between administrative illegality and administrative liability: liability can simply rest on ordinary fault (*faute simple*) or serious fault (*faute lourde*)— it is as to these different bases rather than the existence of liability where the 'empiricism' of the Conseil d'Etat is found.[219] And while French lawyers do draw attention in deciding between *faute simple* and *faute lourde* to the relative difficulty of the task entrusted to the administration in respect of which liability is sought, they do not appear overtly concerned that the imposition of liability will itself interfere with the proper exercise of administrative powers. Indeed, rather the contrary: the imposition of liability is seen as part of the controls which form the corollary to the recognition of 'extraordinary powers' in the administration.[220]

By comparison, English courts have been very much concerned to prevent the imposition of a duty of care from interfering with the free and effective exercise of statutory

---

[213] Above, pp. 315–19.   [214] Above, p. 333.   [215] Above, p. 268.
[216] Above, p. 337.   [217] Above, pp. 336–8.   [218] Above, pp. 168, 336.
[219] Above, p. 312.   [220] Above, p. 30.

powers. The language by which this concern has been expressed has changed over the course of the last quarter of the twentieth century. At first a distinction was drawn between the 'operational sphere' where a duty of care can be imposed without risk to the administration's discretion and the sphere of 'policy' where administrative illegality (acting *ultra vires*) was seen as a threshold before any duty of care could be imposed, but later the question was put more broadly in terms of the lack of 'justiciability' of the issues which a court would have to decide before imposing a duty of care, and even more broadly simply in terms of the public policy *against* such a duty. Even after dicta in the House of Lords in *Barrett* and *Phelps* appear to have divorced the issues of administrative illegality and liability,[221] English courts are likely to remain concerned with the risk of an inhibiting effect on the proper exercise of statutory powers. And, even outside the public context, the tort of negligence itself does not take as its starting point a principle that 'fault causing harm attracts liability': outside established authorities, new situations for the imposition of a duty of care must be justified as a matter of 'fairness, justice and reasonableness' and can be denied as a matter of policy, even where the harm consists of death, personal injuries or damage to property.[222] By contrast, the French law of administrative liability is 'autonomous' from a private law of delict whose articles 1382 and 1383 of the Civil Code do indeed accept a principle of liability for fault of extraordinary generality.

Thirdly, at first there appears to be a marked contrast in the approach of English and French courts to the question of liability for the regulation of the behaviour of others in cases such as the safety of products. For some English decisions reflect a perception that while a regulator may be negligent in its exercise of powers of control over an enterprise, it is nevertheless the enterprise which is 'primarily responsible' for any harm which its own negligence causes.[223] This perception may be seen as a reason for the rejection of a duty of care in the public authority towards a person injured by the enterprise's negligence, but has been seen even more as a reason for refusing a claim by an enterprise for pure economic loss caused (it alleges) by the public authority's own regulatory failure.[224] This perception is sometimes linked to judicial statements that they would look more favourably on a claim by a person who has suffered personal injuries or death against a public authority in respect of its negligent failure in the exercise of regulatory powers than it would on a claim for financial loss. As has been explained, however, to an extent the validity of this last distinction breaks down in English law because of the availability of claims for contribution between tortfeasors, an enterprise 'primarily' liable to a victim of personal injuries being able to claim contribution from the regulator 'secondarily' liable for failing to control its own action.[225]

By contrast, French administrative courts have proved willing to impose liability on a public authority to a person harmed by its failure to control other people, the issue being whether this situation justifies the imposition of liability only on the ground of *faute lourde* or merely *faute simple*.[226] On the other hand, I earlier explained that a number of characteristics and rules of the French system as a whole work together so as

---

[221] Above, p. 340.   [222] Above, p. 162.   [223] Above, pp. 343–4, 347.   [224] Ibid.
[225] Above, pp. 353–4.   [226] Above, pp. 310–15, 319.

to lessen the practical impact of this general position, including the divided jurisdiction, the relative attractiveness of private and administrative law claims, rules as to the prescription of administrative law claims and the attitude of the Conseil d'Etat to recourse claims brought by private defendants held liable by the ordinary courts.[227] Taken together, in general if a person is injured by the failure of a public authority to control the activities of a manufacturer or a supplier of a product, then he is likely to sue the private person in the ordinary courts; and any claim for contribution by that private person in the administrative courts may well fail. Given French acceptance of liability in the administration (whether for *faute lourde* or *faute simple*), this has the odd result that a claimant's choice of defendant (and therefore jurisdiction) impacts directly on the channelling of liability.

Fourthly, though, I am struck by the considerable differences in treatment of the concept of fault in the two laws, quite apart from their different treatment of the relationship between fault and illegality. So, while French administrative law differs from its private law by distinguishing between *faute simple* and *faute lourde*, they have in common a very open understanding of what constitutes 'fault' for these purposes: neither set out any criteria for elucidation of this concept nor for distinguishing between *faute lourde* and *faute simple*.[228] On the other hand, the *affaire du sang contaminé* furnishes an example of French judicial understanding of these concepts in the context of product safety; there the court found that after a certain date when the State authorities had been informed of the exceptional nature of the risk of infection with HIV through the provision of blood products they had committed *faute lourde*, but before this date it found only *faute simple* owing to the degree of uncertainty as to the risks involved.[229] Clearly, then, the nature and degree of risk of the harm which their exercise of powers could avert is significant for this purpose.

By comparison, though, and in common with their approach to establishing breach of duty in the tort of negligence more generally, in the English context we find that the criteria for negligence are much more clearly articulated, the courts looking at the costs and benefits of the defendant's behaviour. In this respect, cases involving the public regulation of product safety share with the generality of cases in negligence a concern with the foreseeability of a risk and the cost of precautions, but the concept of 'cost' needs to be understood in broad terms, including considerations of the substantive public interest in question (for example, wider costs to society of removing a particular product from the market). So, for example, in *Smith v Department of Health* the court accepted that the overall end of securing an effective withdrawal of aspirin from use for children, had to take into account the need not to undermine confidence generally in aspirin as it remained a useful medicine.[230] On the other hand, in other cases English courts accept that breakdowns in administrative communication,[231] unexplained delays when acquainted with a risk[232] and acting for improper purposes can constitute negligence of a sort to encourage the acceptance of a

---

[227] Above, pp. 319–25.   [228] Above, pp. 42–6, 309–12.   [229] Above, pp. 317–18.
[230] [2002] EWHC 200 (QB); 67 BMLR 34, above, pp. 354–6.
[231] *The Creutzfeldt-Jakob Disease Litigation*, above, pp. 297–8.
[232] *Thames Trains v Health and Safety Executive* [2002] EWHC (QB) 1415 at [87], above, pp. 347–8.

duty of care.[233] If the courts' more liberal approach to duty of care foreseen in *Barrett* and *Phelps* continues and is attended by a tendency to control the ambit of liability of public authorities at the level of breach of duty rather than duty of care,[234] then increasingly the courts will need to take into account the public interest in a public authority's action or inaction in their assessing whether or not it is negligent.[235] On the other hand, in some cases bringing in the public interest to the assessment of breach of duty will require the consideration of circumstances which genuinely lack 'justiciability'. For example, where a public body charged with the monitoring of products on the market fails to detect a seriously dangerous defect in a product, it may well argue that it did not have sufficient resources to police the market as effectively as it would have liked, but it was doing its best within the resources allocated to it by central or local government. In these circumstances, it may be foreseen that a court would not wish to address the question whether the allocation of resources to the product safety body was sufficient for its task, for the allocation to a particular body cannot be divorced from the distribution of resources as between different public purposes and services, a sort of decision which is archetypically 'non-justiciable'. On the other hand, if a court were to accept such an argument from a public authority, it would mean applying a different, more subjective standard to the issue of the 'reasonableness of precautions' to be taken in the face of the risk than is normally applied in the tort of negligence, where the actual resources of a defendant are usually irrelevant.[236] Perhaps in this way, the courts would take into account that public authorities have no choice as to the roles which are entrusted to them by statute and so in a sense have the need to deal with danger thrust upon them.[237] It may well be, however, that the sort of difficulties which these questions reflect would be seen by courts as a reason to draw the line more firmly against liability than qualification of the standard of negligence in this way would allow and return to a greater willingness to deny the existence of a duty of care. In this light, the concept of a duty of care can be seen to play a double function. In one sense, it continues to define the scope of the tort of negligence, delineating in which circumstances negligence will give rise to liability. But in another sense, the *denial* of a duty of care serves rather to enable a defendant to avoid the costly and disruptive process of disclosure before trial and the examination and cross-examination at trial as to the issue of negligence itself. As Lord Woolf has recognised, striking out actions on the ground that the legal position is clear and an investigation of the facts would provide no assistance, is a useful mechanism for saving costs[238] and avoiding the courts being faced with unmeritorious claims very much in keeping with the overriding objective of the Civil Procedure Rules.[239] Striking out on the ground of a lack of a duty of care is certainly more straightforward than on the ground of the absence of breach of duty.

---

[233] *Phelps v Hillingdon LBC* [2000] 3 WLR 776, 790 and 808.
[234] Above, p. 340.   [235] Cf. above, p. 198.   [236] Above, p. 197.
[237] Cf. above, p. 197 in relation to *Goldman v Hargrave* [1966] 3 WLR 513.
[238] *Kent v Griffiths* [2001] QB 36 at 51 and see *JD v East Berkshire Community Health NHS Trust* [2003] EWCA Civ 1151 [15]; [2004] 2 WLR 58.   [239] CPR Part I.

PART III

CRIMINAL RESPONSIBILITY FOR UNSAFE PRODUCTS AND ITS RELATIONSHIP TO COMPENSATION

14

Fraudes, Homicides and the Role of the *Partie Civile*

1. Introduction

In France, very many claims for damages in respect of death or more serious personal injuries have been brought by the injured party in the criminal courts. This prominent and traditional role for the criminal process results from a jigsaw puzzle of different elements. First, the victim of a crime is able to set in motion a prosecution as well as join one started by the public prosecutor, the *ministère public* (or *parquet*), participating fully in the process as the *partie civile*.[1] Secondly, there are a number of advantages for an injured person in claiming in the criminal rather than the civil courts, in terms of cost, relative speed, the quality of the investigation and the nature of the trial itself. Thirdly, there are very broad offences of involuntary homicide and causing personal injuries.[2] Fourthly, a range of defendants can be included within the criminal process—traditionally, individuals (whether private or those with public office), but more recently private companies and sometimes even public authorities.[3] Fifthly, a criminal court's finding a defendant guilty of an offence determines the issue of fault so as to award damages under articles 1382 or 1383 of the Civil Code, this forming one aspect of a doctrine known as the 'unity of criminal and civil faults'.[4]

This traditional importance of the criminal process in imposing liability in damages for death and personal injuries was fully reflected in relation to cases involving liability

---

[1] Below, pp. 380–7.

[2] 'Causing personal injuries' will be the name given to the French offences of '*blessures et coups involontaires*' and see below, pp. 372 *et seq.*   [3] Below, pp. 376–80.

[4] Below, pp. 374–5, 393–4. In France, compensation for personal injuries or death caused by a crime may also be available from a public fund (the *Fonds d'indemnisation des victimes des actes de terrorisme et d'autres infactions*) as provided for by arts. 706-3–706-15 C.P.P. Under the scheme, a person who has suffered harm caused by the facts giving rise to an offence may obtain full compensation (*réparation intégrale*) for this harm, where it results from offences against the person and causes either death, permanent incapacity or a total inability to work of a month or more (art. 706-3. C.P.P.). There is no restriction as to the nature of the criminal offence, it being specifically provided that compensation is available for loss caused by 'voluntary or involuntary acts which constitute the physical characteristics of an offence' (art. 706-3 al. 1 C.P.P.). While there are various excluded situations (including in respect of cases which fall within the special legislation governing motor vehicle accidents (art. 706-3 1° C.P.P.)) there is no general requirement that the victim cannot obtain compensation elsewhere. Instead, after payment the fund is subrogated to any rights of successful claimants and may sue in any court to recover in respect of sums paid out, this including the right to *initiate* criminal proceedings by 'constituting itself' *partie civile*: art. 706-11 C.P.P., below, p. 383.

for products. Moreover, it was here that the *affaire du sang contaminé* was most dramatic, affecting public and professional attitudes to liability for products and product safety. It was also in this *affaire* where some very difficult questions were asked as to the type of offence appropriate to a case of a defendant who supplies a product *knowing* of its very high risk to life and health: where death results, should this be seen as akin to murder? While in French law the characterisation of a defendant's offence does not have any direct impact on liability to compensate its victim, it has very important other effects—on the process, on the punishment and on public perception of the seriousness of the crime.

On the other hand, by no means all voices in France have favoured the criminalisation of negligent conduct which causes death or injury nor the link between criminal responsibility and compensation for death and personal injury.[5] In particular, the French national association of *maires*, the elected and unpaid heads of the smallest administrative districts, who often found themselves found guilty of involuntary homicide for the slightest 'speck of fault'[6] in the exercise of their many powers and duties, campaigned for a 'decriminalisation' of their honest efforts, particularly in the provision of public services and the exercise of their powers of safety.[7] At first *maires* and some other officials were protected directly by requiring that they could be prosecuted only with official permission (and thereby circumventing the normal role of *parties civiles*), but this special treatment was swept away by the new Criminal Code of 1994.[8] However, the political pressure did not go away and two years later it led to legislation which tried to 'subjectivise' the fault element required of *anyone* for the offences of involuntary homicide and causing personal injuries[9] and then in 2000 to broader legislative reform of the definition of fault for certain cases and of the procedural relationship between criminal and civil liability.[10] These changes have affected and will continue to affect the impact of the criminal law in imposing criminal responsibility for products, though it is unlikely to do so in many cases where the manufacturer's design or construction of the product or warnings accompanying it are in issue.[11] Moreover, while the *loi* of 2000 has partly broken the so-called 'unity of criminal and civil faults', ironically it is likely to increase the importance of the criminal process in compensating death and personal injuries.[12] These reforms can be seen only in the context of the earlier law, so I shall start by looking at the traditional picture and its application to liability for products before looking at their impact.

2. The Traditional Picture and its Application to Liability for Products

I shall distinguish two broad questions in setting out the pieces of the traditional picture of the involvement of the criminal process in imposing liability in damages for death and personal injuries: the substantive criminal law and whom it governs and the

---

[5] In doctrine for long a lone voice against the link was found in A. Pirovano, *Faute civile et faute pénale* (thèse, Aix-en-Provence, 1966).   [6] The phrase is Mlle. Geneviève Viney's, below, p. 374.

[7] Above, p. 308.   [8] Below, p. 378.

[9] *Loi* no. 96-393 of 13 May 1996 ('*loi* of 1996'), below, pp. 387–8.

[10] *Loi* no. 2000-647 of 10 July 2000 ('*loi* of 2000'), below, pp. 388–94.   [11] Below, pp. 391–3.

[12] Below, pp. 393–4.

role of the *partie civile*. I shall illustrate these points with cases in which liability for products has been in issue.

(a) The substantive criminal law and whom it governs

French law divides criminal offences into three categories,[13] and this has important effects for the courts in which and procedures according to which they are prosecuted, as well as the penalties inflicted.[14] They are, in descending order of seriousness: *crimes*, tried by the Cour d'assises[15] where judgment is made by a mixed bench of professional and lay judges or '*jury*'[16]; *délits*, tried by the Tribunal correctionnel;[17] and *contraventions*, tried by the Tribunal de police.[18] Most French lawyers further distinguish as regards any criminal offence between its *élément materiel* (what the defendant did or failed to do); its *élément légal* (the classification of those facts as a matter of law) and its *élément moral* (the 'fault' element, whether intention, negligence or without fault).[19]

The general criminal law, which consists of its fundamental principles and its most important offences, is found in the Criminal Code of 1994, [20] which thoroughly revised its predecessor enacted in 1810.[21] The new Code left all but intact the previous laws of voluntary and involuntary homicide and causing personal injuries (though it made the deliberate nature of a breach of an *obligation de sécurité* an aggravating factor in sentencing),[22] but it created a new offence of the *deliberate* placing of a person in danger in breach of an *obligation de sécurité*.[23] More importantly, it accepted in principle (as the previous law had not) that *personnes morales* ('legal persons') could commit criminal offences, though this is qualified considerably as regards public bodies.[24] The remainder of French criminal law (its 'special part') is found scattered among particular special laws or *règlements* and in particular provisions of other codes; this body of law includes the offences of *tromperie* and *falsification*, which particularly concern products and which were created by a special *loi* in 1905, later being incorporated in the Consumer Law Code.[25]

I shall start by explaining briefly the pattern of offences special to the product context, though their role has not been large in permitting compensation for personal injury and death; then the law of *voluntary* homicide, both because of its significance in the *affaire du sang contaminé* and in order to understand the importance of the changes made to the 'fault element' for *involuntary* homicide and causing personal injuries.

---

[13] Arts.111-1, 121-3 C. pén.; Pradel, *Droit pénal*, 240 *et seq.*

[14] This tripartite distinction also possesses a constitutional dimension, for *crimes* and *délits* can be created only by *loi*, whereas *contraventions* may be created by *règlement*: art.111-3 C. pén. reflecting art. 34 of the Constitution of 1958.   [15] Arts. 214 & 231 C.P.P.   [16] Art. 240 C.P.P.

[17] Art. 381 C.P.P.   [18] Art. 521 C.P.P.

[19] For a useful discussion, see M.-L. Rassat, *Droit pénal général* (PUF, Paris, 2nd. edn., 1999), 273 *et seq.* Cf. Pradel, *Droit pénal*, 270 who sees the *élément moral* as going to the culpability of the offender rather than the definition of an offence.

[20] All the provisions of the new code came into force on 1 Mar. 1994.

[21] Ancien Code pénal (A.C. pén.).

[22] Art. 221-6 al. 2, 222-19, 222-20, art. R 622-1 C. pén. respectively.   [23] Art. 223-1 C. pén.

[24] Art. 121-2 C. pén., below, pp. 378–80.   [25] *Loi* of 1 Aug. 1905; arts. L 213-1–213-4 C. consom.

(i) Criminal offences particularly concerning products

While criminal law plays a very significant and varied role in reinforcing the very many norms governing products generally and individual types of products in particular, there is a surprising absence of an overall criminal offence overtly dealing with the supply of unsafe products, even after implementation in France of the General Product Safety Directives of 1992 and 2001.[26] So, while French law has since 1983 contained a general duty on business suppliers to supply products and services offering 'the safety which people are legitimately entitled to expect',[27] breach of this duty does not of itself constitute a criminal offence, its role being rather to set the conditions on which the administration can intervene, whether by regulation or otherwise.[28] There are instead a multitude of interconnecting offences, the only common element of which is that they do not require any harm to have been caused before criminal responsibility is established.

Historically, the two most important offences have been *tromperie* and *falsification*, together known as *fraudes* and classed as *délits*.[29] Their primary aim was the elimination of the unfair effects of fraudulent trade practices on competition endemic at the turn of the twentieth century,[30] but they have played a significant role in controlling the safety of products.[31]

Tromperie is committed where a person, whether or not party to a contract, deceives or attempts to deceive a contractor concerning the substantial quality, type, suitability for purpose, or risks in use of goods or services.[32] Despite the principle of strict interpretation of the criminal law,[33] its elements have been interpreted broadly and so, for example, 'goods' are understood as any corporeal movable property which can be counted, weighed or measured.[34] The thrust of the offence is deception, but it has been used to protect citizens from unsafe products, for example, where a dealer fails to warn a customer that a car which he sells has been in an accident,[35] it being '*tromperie par abstention*' to do an act which suggests that a product does not possess certain defects which it has.[36] It was *tromperie* of which the senior officers of the French National Blood Transfusion Centre were convicted in the *affaire du sang contaminé*.[37]

Falsification is committed by a maker or supplier of adulterated goods destined for sale of certain types, i.e. food and drink, animal feeds, medicines and agricultural or natural products.[38] For this purpose, 'adulteration' includes any improper alteration of the characteristics of the product in question from its natural state or any difference between their actual composition and its 'proper' composition, the 'proper'

---

[26] Ordonnance No. 2004 of 9 Jul. 2004, J.O. Rép. fn. 10 Jul. 2004.

[27] *Loi* no. 83-660 of 21 Jul. 1983, now art. L 221-1 C. consom.

[28] Arts. L. 221-2–221-9 C. consom. and see above, pp. 308–9.

[29] *Loi* of 1 Aug. 1905; revised by the *loi* no. 78-23 of 10 Jan.1978; arts. L. 213-1 *et seq.* C. consom.

[30] Bihl, *Droit pénal,* 7.

[31] B. Bouloc, 'La loi de 1905 en tant qu'instrument de la sécurité des consommateurs' in Ghestin, *Sécurité des consommateurs,* 13; Bihl, *Droit pénal,* 108–15.

[32] Art L. 213-1 C. consom. The reference to 'substantial quality' has clear echoes with *erreur sur la substance* under art. 1110 C. civ.: cf. above, p. 22.   [33] Now found in art. 111-4 C. pén.

[34] Delmas-Marty and Guidicelli-Delage, 579; Crim. 22 Jun.1977, D 1977.IR.481. It has been applied to electricity: Crim. 22 Oct. 1959, JCP 1959.II.11376.

[35] Calais-Auloy and Steinmetz, 237, 299.   [36] Delmas-Marty and Guidicelli-Delage, 579.

[37] Below, pp. 395–6.   [38] Art. L. 213-3 C. consom.

elements defined in terms both of any specific legal rules governing the product (which are numerous, especially as regards food) and in terms of the practices of the particular trade.[39] So, for example, a baker was convicted of *falsification* for offering for sale bread containing letherine since this was not added to bread according to the 'fair and continuous customs of the trade'.[40]

What is the *élément moral* of these related offences? In the case of *tromperie*, its core meaning and the original intention of its creators requires proof that a defendant knew that the characteristics of the goods or services in question did not conform to their description of them, that is, an intentional fault.[41] However, in the case of manufacturers and importers, the Cour de cassation allows lower courts to *deduce* bad faith from a failure to check the goods for their conformity to their description and in this way to reduce the fault element to negligence.[42] A similarly strict approach is taken to *falsification*, though in practice a distinction is drawn between the person who tampered with the product and a person who merely supplies it in an already adulterated state, who is more likely to succeed in a defence of good faith.[43]

Apart from these two offences, the criminal law sanctions directly the supply of products in breach of administrative regulations by *contraventions*,[44] but these offences have not appeared frequently as the basis of prosecution, partly because breach of a regulation can form the basis of a charge of *falsification* or *tromperie*[45] and partly because breach of a regulation which causes death or personal injury has often attracted a charge of the more serious offences of involuntary homicide or causing personal injury.[46]

(ii) Voluntary homicide

The distinction between voluntary and involuntary homicide reflects the fundamental difference between intentional and unintentional criminal fault. While the Criminal Code has defined unintentional fault for this purpose (and in an increasingly complex manner),[47] neither the code nor the courts have defined intentional fault, notably for the crime of murder, with the striking exception of the Tribunal correctionnel in the first criminal case in the *affaire du sang contaminé*.[48] The jurists have, however, to an extent taken up the baton. Pradel, for example, distinguishes within *dol* (deliberate wrong-doing) between *dol général* (the intention to accomplish an act which one knows to be forbidden) and *dol spécial*, where there is a further element either of awareness of the causing of a harm or the seeking of a particular result[49] and of which murder

---

[39] Delmas-Marty and Guidicelli-Delage, 583.

[40] Seine 17 Nov. 1966, JCP 1967.II.15009 note Gondre. Cf. Agen 23 Jan. 1975, D 1975.748 note Fourgoux (calves fattened with illegal injection of oestrogen).

[41] Delmas-Marty and Guidicelli-Delage, 581.

[42] Ibid., 581-2; Calais-Auloy and Steinmetz, 250–52; Pradel, *Droit pénal,* 112.

[43] Delmas-Marty and Guidicelli-Delage, 583–4; Bouloc, *op. cit.*n. 31, 17.

[44] Art. L. 214-1 C. consom. This also applies to EC regulations which fall within the scope of Chaps. II to VI of the C. consom., see art. L. 214-3 C. consom.

[45] E.g. Paris 7 May 1968, GP 1968.2.151 (breach of regulation in treating pans with chemical which its manufacturer had indicated was corrosive and dangerous for use with kitchen equipment).

[46] Below, pp. 372–5.   [47] Below, pp. 372, 387, 389.

[48] Pradel, *Droit pénal,* 440, below, 397.   [49] Ibid., 441, 445.

furnishes the typical example as it requires an intention to kill.[50] He also sees a distinction within *dol général* between *dol direct* (where a person seeks a particular result) and *dol indirect* (where he knows that his chosen act will lead—certainly or almost certainly—to a result which is not sought), but he considers this distinction more used outside France and that the two are assimilated by French courts.[51] On the other hand, in general a person's motive in acting is irrelevant to their criminal responsibility: euthanasia is a crime in France, the 'good' motive leaving untouched a defendant's intention to kill.[52]

While the Cour de cassation has declared that an intention to kill must be shown for murder,[53] it allows this to be 'deduced' from the circumstances by the Cour d'assises (for example, from the vulnerability of the part of a body which the defendant has attacked[54]), and this 'power of deduction' allows the line between intending an act (which kills) and intending to kill to be blurred. For example, in a case in 1880, an apprentice baker incorporated a compound of arsenic into the dough in order to cause difficulties to his employer, but thereby killed 280 people who consumed it: he was convicted of the crime of poisoning (which is generally considered to have the same *élément moral* as murder[55]) even though he bore no malice to the bread's consumers.[56] It was to the crime of poisoning to which some of the victims of the *affaire du sang contaminé* turned when they heard that some of those responsible for the supply of the blood had known of its deadly risks at the time.[57]

(iii) The traditional law of involuntary homicide and causing personal injury

Between 1810 and 1996 it was a criminal offence classed as a *délit* for a person to cause serious injury or death by negligence or breach of any rule, legislative, regulatory or otherwise. Article 221-6 of the Criminal Code of 1994 (reflecting closely earlier provisions[58]) as enacted stated that:

The act of causing by clumsiness, imprudence, inattention, negligence or breach of an obligation of safety or care imposed by *loi* or by *règlements* the death of another person constitutes involuntary homicide and is punished by three years imprisonment and a fine of 300,000 F.

It also provided for a *délit* of causing serious personal injuries, their seriousness being defined in terms of a total incapacity for work for three months or more, its companion regulations providing for *contraventions* where the injury was less serious.[59] Under the Code of 1994 most *délits* were to be crimes of intention, but these offences were included within this category because of the importance of the interests which they protect.[60] I shall look first at their 'fault element' and at a criminal court's interpretation of the requirement of a causal link between the defendant's fault and the victim's injury. Both

---

[50] Art. 221-1 C. pén. This is seen as implicit in its 'voluntary nature' and in the presence of a distinct offence of deliberate assault causing another's death 'without the intention to do so': art. 222-7 C. pén.; H. Angevin, 'Atteintes volontaires, Meutre, Empoisonnement', Jur.-Cl. pén. Arts. 221-1 à 221-5 (2000), 11.

[51] Pradel, *Droit pénal*, 441.   [52] Merle and Vitu, *Droit pénal*, 571–2, 715–16.

[53] Crim. 8 Jan. 1991, D 1992.115 note Croisier-Nerac.   [54] Angevin, *op. cit.* n. 50, 13.

[55] See below, p. 397.

[56] This case is described by J.-P. Delmas Saint-Hilaire, 'Un crime d'empoisonnement: la double tromperie de l'affaire du sang contaminé cessera-t-elle enfin?' in Pradel, *Sang et droit pénal*, 39 at 56.

[57] Below, pp. 395–8.   [58] Arts. 319, 320 A.C. pén.   [59] Art. R. 622-1, 625-2 A.C. pén.

[60] Desportes and Le Gunehec, 433.

these were very significant for the victim's choice of the criminal process for claiming damages and both were changed (in part and in some circumstances) on reform of the law in 1996 and 2000. The following law, therefore, remains valid for *some* types of case, but not others.[61]

First, the 'fault element' was very broadly defined and was very broadly interpreted by the courts: not merely negligence or lack of care, but breach of any rule or regulation was enough. So, for example, a manufacturer was held guilty of 'negligence' in the design of the packaging of a product for failing to leave an appropriate margin for expansion of a corrosive product which therefore burst out of its plastic bottle on use and injured a customer[62] and another manufacturer was held guilty of causing serious injury through negligence by failing to recall earlier versions of a product (a toy chemistry set) once he had changed its design in response to reported accidents, even though he was not in a position to contact his customers.[63] There was no requirement of any degree of seriousness of the negligence established.

Even more extensive was the courts' interpretation of the phrase 'breach of *règlements*', for they accepted that this included not merely administrative regulations (*règlements* in the constitutional sense), but 'any prescription of an obligatory character whose lack of respect has caused the harmful result in question'.[64] So, for example, breach of professional standards[65] or even of the rules of rugby football[66] were held sufficient to provide the necessary 'fault element' to establish these offences. Moreover, the mere breach of a legal regulation constituted *in itself* a fault so as to attract criminal responsibility, without any additional carelessness or negligence needing to be shown, with the result that the 'fault element' was reduced to nothing, the offence being effectively strict (*une infraction matérielle*).[67] This approach meant that where the law provided many specific regulations (as in the case of products, road traffic and the workplace)[68] it was very much easier for the 'fault element' required for these serious crimes to be established.[69]

This may be illustrated by the *affaire Stalinon*, where over 100 people were killed and injured when they used a drug of that name.[70] The drug was conceived by a qualified pharmacist, who entrusted the necessary research before marketing it to a chemist. After various tests, the pharmacist applied to the French pharmaceutical licensing authority on the basis that it was a modified version of an already licensed drug (which it was not), the rights to which he had acquired. The licence was granted and it was made up by a laboratory and marketed. The pharmacist was charged with involuntary homicide and causing personal injuries, against which he argued that he had fulfilled his various regulatory duties to ensure that suitably qualified persons tested and made the drug and was not responsible for the way in which this was put into effect by the laboratory. However, the court held that the regulations in question imposed a duty of direct control on manufacturers of drugs at all stages of their manufacture and his breach of this duty and his

---

[61] Below, pp. 388–94.   [62] Crim. 13 Nov. 1962, D 1963.Somm.30.

[63] Crim. 27 May 1972, GP 1972.2.719. For other examples relating to manufacturers see: Crim. 6 Jun. 1999 and Crim. 11 Apr. 1999, *Droit pénal* (Nov. 1991), 5.   [64] Merle and Vitu, *Droit pénal*, 739.

[65] Rouen 26 Feb.1969, JCP 1971.II.16849.   [66] Crim. 24 Jan. 1956, D 1956.197.

[67] Merle and Vitu, *Droit pénal*, 738.   [68] Bihl, *Droit pénal*, 135 and above, p. 370.

[69] Véron (9th. edn.), 74.

[70] Paris 3 Jun. 1958, S 1958.336 note Bredin. For the administrative law sequel to the case, see above, pp. 315, 327.

failure to act when Stalinon's difficulties were drawn to his attention were the direct cause of the catastrophic results.[71] He was therefore convicted and ordered to pay damages to the drug's victims who were *parties civiles* to the proceedings.

Apart from the words used by the Code to define the crimes of involuntary homicide and causing personal injuries, French criminal courts were very strict in their assessment of their 'fault element' because of its significance for compensation for the person injured by the alleged offence. While this relationship was typically expressed in terms of the 'unity of criminal and civil faults', in fact this doctrine has a number of distinct aspects.[72] The first and most important aspect, so much assumed as to be taken as axiomatic, was that any finding of a 'criminal fault' also establishes the existence of a civil fault for the purposes of civil liability under articles 1382 or 1383 of the Civil Code. In the case of involuntary homicide and causing personal injuries, this is readily comprehensible, given that their traditional definition used very similar words to the definition found in article 1383, but the significance was and is wider, for both the criminal and the civil courts consider that *any* offence of whatever seriousness or *élément moral* constitutes *une faute civile*, just as a civil court would find *any* other breach of duty as constituting *une faute civile*: while delictual fault *includes* a lack of care it is broader than a common lawyer would understand by 'negligence'.[73] This French position clearly worked (and still works) as a fundamental pillar of the criminal courts' imposition of liability to compensate the victim of any criminal offence which they find.

However, further elements of the 'unity doctrine' could have a less favourable effect on the victim's chances of achieving compensation. One of these (a rule which subjected all claims for damages based on a criminal offence to the much shorter prescription periods of the criminal prosecution) was abolished in 1980,[74] but there remained a further rule, known as *l'autorité de la chose jugée au criminel sur le civil*,[75] according to which the decision of a criminal court as to a defendant's 'fault' (whether guilty *or not guilty*) bound any subsequent civil court,[76] a rule made more potent by the duty of civil courts to stay their proceedings once a criminal court is seized of the same facts.[77] This meant that a criminal court's acquittal of a person of the offence of involuntary homicide or causing personal injuries prevented both the criminal court and any subsequent civil court from imposing liability in damages on the basis of *civil* fault. In the result, as Viney famously observed in 1982, this combination of rules meant that the criminal judges:

> often feel constrained, even in cases where the suppression of crime appears not at all necessary for the protection of *ordre public*, to find a 'speck of fault' with the sole aim of saving the victim's right in any civil court.[78]

---

[71] Paris 3 Jan. 1958, S.1958.336 note Bredin. For the administrative law sequel to the case, at 338.

[72] Viney, *Introduction à la responsabilité*, 260 *et seq*. The leading case was Civ. 19 Dec. 1912, S 1914.1.249 note Morel.   [73] Above, pp. 45–6.

[74] *Loi* no. 80–1042 of 23 Dec. 1980, new art. 10 C.P.P.

[75] Guinchard and Buisson, 773. If a victim of a crime claims first in the civil jurisdiction in principle he cannot then claim as *partie civile* unless he was ignorant of the criminal nature of the defendant's behaviour and the criminal proceedings were initiated by the *ministère public*: ibid. 771–2.

[76] Since 1972, decisions of tribunaux de police have not had the force of *chose jugée* in respect of any *action civile*: art. 528-1 al. 2 C.P.P.   [77] Art. 4 al. 2 C.P.P.

[78] G. Viney, *Les obligations, La responsabilité: conditions* in J. Ghestin (ed.) *Traité de droit civil* (LDGJ, Paris, 1982) 186. The phrase 'speck of fault' was frequently used in the *travaux préparatoires* of the *loi* of 2000 below, pp. 388–9.

This situation was improved by legislation in 1983 which allowed a criminal court to impose liability in damages on a defendant acquitted of involuntary homicide or causing personal injuries towards a *partie civile* on some civil law basis *other* than fault, notably for the 'deeds of things' or breach of an *obligation contractuelle de résultat* or *de moyens*.[79] Nevertheless, the potentially distorting effect on criminal responsibility of its necessary connection with civil liability was a key reason for their partial divorce by the *loi* of 2000.[80]

Secondly, the criminal courts took an extensive approach to the causal relationship necessary between a defendant's 'fault' and a victim's injury for the purposes of involuntary homicide and causing personal injury, an approach seen as wider than the approach taken by the civil courts to liability for delictual fault.[81] This difference created a very real advantage for the victims of these offences in bringing their claims for damages before the criminal rather than civil courts, because the criminal courts applied their finding on criminal causation to the issue of a defendant's liability in damages as well as to his criminal responsibility.

The difference of approach to causation in the two courts is difficult to pin down exactly, because their decisions are often cloaked behind their 'sovereign power of assessment' as the *juges du fond*.[82] The jurists often try to catch the difference by saying that the criminal courts follow a theory of causation based on the theory of the 'equivalence of conditions' whereas the civil courts follow the theory of 'adequate causation',[83] but this suggests a more systematic approach than has been favoured by either jurisdiction. Indeed, as Carbonnier observed, there has been a general tendency on the part of *both* the civil and criminal courts to confuse the issue of causation and of the gravity of fault, so as to give extra causal potency to an act or omission which also constitutes an offence.[84] Certainly, for the criminal courts their approach to causation made 'the extreme importance of moral culpability stand out'.[85]

While, therefore, the Chambre criminelle of the Cour de cassation required the causal relationship between a defendant's fault and the victim's injury to be 'certain',[86] sometimes criminal courts found one where it was 'very conjectural, and even improbable'.[87] An example given by Merle and Vitu of where this was the case concerned the supply of a glazing product to a mason who had been engaged by some wine makers to resurface a storage vat in their cellar.[88] The court held the technical director of the product's manufacturer negligent in failing to warn of the product's inflammability

---

[79] *Loi* no. 83–608 of 8 Jul. 1983, new art. 470-1 C.P.P. E.g. Crim. 17 Feb. 1987, Bull. crim. no. 74 (*loi* of 5 Jul. 1985); Crim. 3 Mar. 1993, Bull. crim. no. 96 (*obligation de moyens*).   [80] Below, pp. 393–4.

[81] Bihl, *Droit pénal*, 137; Merle and Vitu, *Droit pénal*, 680 *et seq*. P. Fauchon, *Rapport sur la proposition de loi de M. Pierre Fauchon, tendant à préciser la définition des délits non intentionnels*, Sén. No. 177 (20 Jan. 2000) ('Fauchon, *Rapport*, Sén. No. 177') para. I (B)4.

[82] E.g. Crim. 23 Oct. 1931, GP 1931.2.934; Crim. 20 Nov.1969, GP 1970.1.97.

[83] H. L. and J. Mazeaud, *Leçons de droit civil*, Tome II, Vol. I *Obligations, théorié générale* (Montchrestien, Paris, 8th. edn., 1991 by F. Chabas) 651–2 and see below, p. 390.

[84] J. Carbonnier, *Droit civil*, Tome 4, *Les Obligations* (PUF, Paris, 18th. edn., 1994), 352.

[85] Merle and Vitu, *Droit pénal*, 691.

[86] Crim. 9 Jan.1979, JCP 1980.II.19272 note Chabas; Crim. 14 Feb. 1996, Bull. crim. no. 78; Véron (9th. edn.) 78 *et seq*.   [87] Merle and Vitu, *Droit pénal*, 688.

[88] Dijon 4 Jul.1958, JCP 1958.II.10714.

and of its dangers when used in a confined space and that this negligence was a cause of the *mason's* failure to warn the vine growers, one of whom smoked in the cellar and caused an explosion: presumably the conjectural element was the question whether the mason would have passed on the warning to the wine makers. Perhaps more clear are cases where the criminal courts held that the alleged offender's behaviour was merely one of several *possible* factors or actions which led to the accident, there being (until 2000) no requirement that the causation be either 'direct or immediate'.[89] For example, in one case a water company had undertaken the provision of water for a small town under a contract of concession under which it had a duty to maintain the town sewers which ran close to the wells.[90] The town suffered an epidemic of typhoid, some of whose victims died. The company's head of operation's conviction for involuntary homicide was upheld on appeal on the ground that he had not taken any precautions to ensure the soundness of the sewer walls through which waste had leaked into the water supply: his suggestion that the epidemic was caused by a deliberate act of an unknown third party was dismissed as ingenious speculation. The Cour de cassation refused to interfere with this decision, as it resulted from a sovereign assessment of the facts of the *juges du fond* as to causation. Again, the defendant was held civilly liable to the victims, as was the water company as vicariously liable for his actions. Similarly, in the *affaire Stalinon*, the court held that the drug's manufacturer could not escape conviction on the ground that the public licensing agency was to blame for the deaths and injuries which the drug caused because it had not taken proper care in testing the product before allowing it onto the market (though it took care not to pronounce upon the existence of such an 'administrative fault').[91]

On the other hand, while the criminal courts have considered that the 'contributory fault' of a victim of involuntary homicide or personal injuries excludes a defendant's *criminal* responsibility only where it constitutes *force majeure* or is the exclusive cause of his own harm,[92] since 1972 the criminal courts have not applied this approach to the defendant's civil liability, it being for the *juges du fond* to decide whether an injured party was at fault, whether this was causally related to his injury and, if so, to what extent the damages recovered should be reduced.[93]

(iv) The defendants

Until 1993 it was a fundamental rule of French criminal law that only human persons could be guilty of offences[94] and this left people who ran trading companies (including those producing or selling products) or elected representatives or administrative officials (whose duties included the supervision of product safety) in the firing line of prosecution. While the Criminal Code of 1994 departed from this fundamental rule, it did not abolish it entirely but rather created a number of important exceptions which at first distinguished according to particular offences and which still distintinguish between different types of *personnes morales*.[95]

---

[89] Crim. 11 Dec. 1957, JCP 1958.II.10423. Cf. below, pp. 389–93.
[90] Crim. 23 Oct. 1931, GP1931.2.934. The deputy engineer and chief mechanic were acquitted.
[91] Paris 3 Jun. 1958, S.1958.336 note Bredin, above, pp. 315, 327, 373.   [92] Véron (9th. edn.), 80.
[93] Ch. Mixte 28 Jan. 1972, JCP 1972.II.17050 concl. Lindon.
[94] Merle and Vitu, *Droit pénal*, 776 *et seq.*   [95] Below, pp. 378–80.

As regards human defendants, in general French courts considered that the *chef d'entreprise* or *dirigeant* (the 'factual boss', usually the managing director) of a company was the most appropriate defendant where its product caused death or serious personal injury[96] and they held *dirigeants* of a firm criminally responsible for offences committed by the firm's employees even though he himself did nothing and knew nothing about them.[97] While this has been seen as a vicarious criminal liability, it is generally treated as an example of responsibility for negligence by omission, the *dirigeant* being liable for failing to prevent the offence from being committed. It remains difficult for a *dirigeant* to rebut this presumption of fault,[98] and so while a *dirigeant* may sometimes escape criminal responsibility where he shows that he 'delegated his powers of control', for example, as to health and safety,[99] even here a court may hold him responsible by finding some more personal fault in him.[100] While sometimes other members of the company staff have been convicted in this sort of context, it was rare for a junior member of staff to be prosecuted, even if he was the person 'physically responsible' for an injury or death.[101]

In the case of unsafe products, criminal responsibility has been imposed not merely on their manufacturer, but also on their supplier.[102] The range of defendants who can be involved in a prosecution for involuntary homicide and causing personal injuries may be illustrated by the *affaire du 'Cinq-Sept'* which concerned the criminal responsibilities for the deaths of nearly 150 young people and a similar number of injuries in a fire at a discotheque outside a small French town.[103] The discotheque had been newly built out of concrete and was owned and run by two companies, controlled by three businessmen. The immediate cause of the fire lay in the heating system, which allowed hot air and gas to escape, but its devastating effects resulted from the decoration of public areas with a highly inflammable polyurethane-based product, which, when alight, emitted lethal fumes, and from the main exit being blocked by a pedal-operated turnstile. A number of people who had contributed to this tragedy were held guilty of involuntary homicide and causing serious personal injuries: the businessmen who ran the discotheque and those who made and installed the central heating on the basis of their breach of building regulations and their personal lack of care; and the managing director of the company which made the polyurethane-based product on the ground that he knew that it would be used for decorating public rooms and ought to have warned of its potential dangers. All these defendants were also held liable in damages to the victims of their crimes present as *parties civiles*.

---

[96] J.-C. Vindreau, *La responsabilité pénale du fabricant de produit* (thèse, Lille, microfiche, 1984) 165 and see Crim. 19 Dec. 1977, JCP 1979.II.19227 note Robert.

[97] Pradel, *Droit pénal*, 369 *et seq.*; Delmas-Marty and Guidicelli-Delage, 50 *et seq.*

[98] Desportes and Le Gunehec, 487 *et seq.*　　　[99] Ibid., 492–4.

[100] E.g. Crim. 27 May 1972, GP 1972.2.719.

[101] Delmas-Marty and Guidicelli-Delage, 67–8. Cf. below, pp. 390–1.

[102] Crim. 20 Oct.1971, JCP 1971.IV.267 (car dealer who sold a car with a damaged chassis which caused an accident liable for the injuries to road user); Trib. corr. Pointoise 11 Feb. 1980, Versailles 5 Dec. 1980, noted by J. Nguyen Thanh-Bourgeais, 'La sécurité des consommateurs. Réflexions sur l'affaire du talc Morhange' D 1981 Chron. 87 (where a baby-talc killed 36 babies and injured 167 others because it contained a very high proportion of a toxic bactericide—individuals from the companies which supplied the bactericide, manufactured the talc and owned its trademark were all convicted and ordered to pay damages to the *parties civiles*).

[103] Trib. corr. Lyon 20 Nov. 1972, GP 1973.1.3, Lyon 13 Jul. 1973, GP 1973.2.830, Crim. 14 Mar. 1974, GP 1974.1.417.

Perhaps most interesting was the position of the local *maire*. The *maire* had granted planning permission for the construction of the discotheque and this imposed on him certain specific duties in respect of the safety of the establishment seen by the court as examples of his more general duty 'to ensure good order, security, safety and public health'.[104] On the facts, it was held that the *maire* had failed to perform his public duty by not taking proper care in the supervision of the construction and operation of the discotheque and was therefore guilty of involuntary homicide and causing personal injury, despite his argument that, as an elected official with no special training, he could not possibly know and in fact was not aware of all his legal duties and that he should not be convicted in the absence of moral fault. However, the criminal court's conviction of the *maire* did not lead to the imposition on either him or the *commune* of civil liability in damages since as part of the 'ordinary jurisdiction' (*ordre judiciaire*) it lacked the competence to impose liability on an individual member of the administration in respect of a fault connected with the exercise of his public functions or on the administration itself.[105] Here, therefore, the principle of the separation of powers and the division between the public and private jurisdictions prevented the court from giving effect to the normal consequences of a criminal conviction for the benefit of the victims of a crime.

While the *maire*'s argument in the *affaire du 'Cinq-Sept'* did not allow him to avoid conviction, the association of *maires* lobbied the government to introduce a special legislative immunity to protect them from prosecution in respect of any alleged failure to fulfil their many public duties, though the *loi* as enacted instead only made their prosecution subject to a special vetting procedure by the local *préfet*.[106] This procedure was, however, swept away in 1993 in the interest of simplifying procedure and removing what looked to the general public like an unjustified protection for elected officials.[107]

Turning to the position of *personnes morales* as defendants, the Criminal Code of 1994 introduced the possibility of their criminal responsibility for three main reasons: to increase the deterrent and preventative effect of the criminal law, particularly in the case of serious offences affecting public health, the environment, company affairs and social legislation;[108] conversely, to deflect criminal prosecutions away from the individuals who ran them and who in practice bore a 'presumption of criminal responsibility . . . in respect of offences of whose existence they are often unaware'.[109] Under the present law:

Legal persons, with the exception of the State, shall be criminally responsible according to the distinctions provided by articles 121-4 to 121-7 for offences committed on their behalf, by their governing bodies or officers [*organes*] or their representatives.

[104] These are now found in art. 2212 al. 2 C.G.C.T. and see above, p. 308.

[105] Above, p. 167. For the administrative law sequel in which some of the defendants' insurers claimed contribution from the *commune* and the State, see CE 7 Mar. 1980, DS 1980.320 note Laurent Richer, above, pp. 327–9.

[106] *Loi* no. 74–646 of 18 Jul. 1974; J. Robert, 'La loi du 18 juillet 1974 et les crimes et délits imputables aux maires dans l'exercice de leurs fonctions' JCP 1975.I.2714.

[107] *Loi* no. 93-2 of 4 Jan. 1993, art. 102.

[108] F. Desportes and F. Le Gunehec, *Le Nouveau droit pénal*, Tome. I, *Droit pénal général* (Economica, Paris, 1994) 421–2.

[109] R. Badinter, the *Garde des sceaux* in introducing the Criminal Code bill, quoted by M.-E. Cartier, contribution to '*La responsabilité pénale des personnes morales*' in P. Méhaignerie (ed.) *Le nouveau code pénal, enjeux et perspectives* (Dalloz, Paris, 1994), 37 at 42.

Nevertheless, local authorities and their groupings shall be criminally responsible only in respect of offences committed in the exercise of activities which may be the object of an agreement to delegate a public service.

The criminal responsibility of legal persons does not exclude that of physical persons who are the authors or accomplices of the same acts.[110]

This is a complex provision and has given rise to much doctrinal discussion,[111] but there are three important points.[112]

First, in principle *all* legal persons may be convicted of crimes, the only absolute exception being the State itself, the reason for the latter being said to be its monopoly of the right to punish.[113] While it was discussed in Parliament whether other exceptions should be made, notably in the case of trade unions or political parties, the French legislature felt constrained to take this very inclusive approach, for fear that any special immunity retained for a particular type of body would be held unconstitutional by the Conseil constitutionnel on the grounds of inequality before the law.[114] Thus, all private law bodies, including non-profit-making companies, trade unions, political parties and charitable foundations, as well as commercial companies are included, as are most public law bodies, such as *établissements publics industriels et commerciaux.* On the other hand, local authorities can be criminally responsible only in respect of criminal offences committed 'in the exercise of activities which may be the object of an agreement to delegate a public service'. This last expression has a technical meaning in French administrative law which has apparently been adopted by the Cour de cassation for this purpose, rather than simply distinguishing between offences committed in areas which do not concern their special public powers (*prérogatives de puissance publique*).[115] Thus, a *commune* could be responsible in respect of such matters as its own running (*en régie*) of a school bus service, refuse collection or the distribution of water,[116] but would not be in respect of activities such as the exercise of its powers in the areas of public order, health and safety, its *pouvoirs de police administrative.*[117] This means that, for example, a *commune* in circumstances such as the *affaire du 'Cinq-Sept'*[118] remains incapable of being prosecuted in respect of the deaths and injuries caused in part by its *maire's* failures to exercise safety powers and nor could any local authority in respect of any alleged failure in its powers of control of unsafe products. As a result, the criminal responsibility of local authorities has been very little invoked.[119] And of course many administrative powers of control of the safety of products[120] belong to *State* authorities, whether a minister or the *préfet,*[121] and these authorities remain immune from criminal responsibility.

---

[110] Art. 121-2 C. pén.

[111] The following discussion draws heavily on Desportes and Le Gunehec, 525 *et seq.*

[112] While originally the criminal responsibility of legal persons only concerned certain crimes, it applied from its inception to involuntary homicide and causing personal injuries and legislation gradually extended its application to more and more criminal offences until in 2004 it was applied to all offences of whatever type and nature: *Loi* no. 2004-204 of 9 Mar. 2004, art. 54.   [113] Desportes and Le Gunehec, 536–7.

[114] Cartier, *op. cit.* n. 109, 38; Pradel, *Droit pénal,* 475.

[115] Desportes and Le Gunehec 537–41 and see Crim. 12 Dec. 2000, *affaire du Drac,* Bull. crim. no. 371.

[116] Desportes and Le Gunehec, 541–2.   [117] Ibid., 542.

[118] Above, pp. 377–8.   [119] Fauchon, *Rapport,* Sén. No. 177, para. I(B)2.

[120] Above, pp. 307–10.   [121] Above, p. 309–10.

Secondly, in order for a legal person to be convicted, the offence must have been committed either by one of its *organes* or by its human representative on behalf of the legal person.[122] The term *organe* is used to describe various senior officers and governing bodies who are by law charged with the administration or direction of the various types of legal persons: for example, in the case of a *commune*, the *organes* are the *maire* and municipal council.[123] However, the significance of the term 'representative' is far from clear,[124] though it certainly includes the *dirigeant* and others who 'represent' a company, for example, as its contractual agents, but excludes mere employees.[125] Moreover, even where committed by a legal person's *organe* or representative, an offence must be committed 'on its behalf' in order to lead to its criminal responsibility, this being understood as being 'in the exercise of activities aimed at ensuring the organisation, the functioning or the objectives of the grouping with legal personality', even if the legal person has no interest in the activity and does not benefit from it.[126]

Finally, despite the fact that one of the purposes of the introduction of criminal responsibility for legal persons was to deflect prosecutions for non-intentional offences away from individuals, article 121-2 alinéa 3 of the Criminal Code specifically retains the criminal responsibility of those 'human persons who are the authors or accomplices of the . . . facts' for which the legal person is held responsible. It is clear, moreover, from the discussion of the *loi* of 2000 that individuals remained very much in the firing line, particularly given that the choice of whom to prosecute remains shared between the public prosecuting authorities and the victims of crimes.[127]

(b) The role of the *partie civile*

Apart from the presence of substantive criminal offences and both human and corporate defendants, the importance of the criminal process in France for the compensation of personal injuries and death (including in the context of products) rests on French law's recognition of a special role for the victim as *partie civile* in the prosecution and trial of crimes.[128]

(i) The double role of the partie civile

French criminal law is perceived as an expression of the demands of *ordre public* and in principle, therefore, a representative of the State, the *ministère public* or *parquet*, decides whether the prosecution of an offence is appropriate as a matter of the public interest and, if it is, sets criminal proceedings (the *action publique*) in motion.[129] *Ministères publics* are formally a type of judge (*magistrat*) and are recruited in the same

---

[122] Art. 121-2 al. 1 C. pén.

[123] Desportes and Le Gunehec, 571. In the case of a *société*, these are the *gérant, président-directeur-général*, the *conseil d'administration* or the *directoire*, the *directeurs généraux*, the *conseil de surveillance* and the *assemblé générale.*   [124] Ibid., 573–5.   [125] Cartier, *op. cit.* n. 109, 41.

[126] Desportes and Le Gunehec, 577.   [127] Below, pp. 381–2, 388.

[128] For introductions to the French criminal process see J.R.R. Spencer, 'French and English Criminal Procedure: A Brief Comparison' in B.S. Markesinis (ed.) *The Gradual Convergence* (OUP, 1993) 33; Bell, Boyron, Whittaker, 122 *et seq.*

[129] Arts. 1 al. 1 & 31 C.P.P. The *ministère public* is represented by different officers in the different courts, e.g. *procureur de la République* in the Tribunal correctionnel.

way as are other judges, though they belong to the administration and are under the ultimate control of the Minister of Justice.[130] In some areas, specialist public agencies investigate 'regulatory offences,' such as those relating to health and safety at work[131] and 'consumer offences', including *tromperie* and *falsification*,[132] where investigation is in the hands of the *Direction générale de la concurrence, de la consommation et de la répression des fraudes*.[133] While these public agencies do not formally decide whether or not a prosecution should be made, in many cases they choose not to report their findings to the *ministère public* (who does decide on prosecution) even where they consider that an offence has been committed, preferring instead to warn the offender, leaving prosecution only to very serious cases.[134] Where a prosecution is brought, any victim of the alleged crime may join the proceedings as *partie civile* by bringing an *action civile*,[135] his most obvious purpose in doing so being that, if the defendant is found guilty, the court has the power to award him damages against the defendant (or against any person responsible for the defendant, such as his employer[136] or insurer[137]) for any harm caused by the offence.[138] However, the role of *parties civiles* is much larger than this suggests, for they are full parties to the proceedings and may call evidence and put arguments as to a defendant's criminal responsibility as well as to his liability to pay damages.

Moreover, French law gives the victim of a criminal offence the power to decide whether or not criminal proceedings are commenced, for by 'constituting himself *partie civile*'[139] he places a case directly in the hands of the *juge d'instruction* ('investigating magistrate') and so effectively overrides the discretion of the *ministère public* as to whether proceedings should be initiated:[140] the victim's decision has the 'effect of triggering indirectly (but necessarily) the *action publique*'.[141] This does not mean, however, that the

---

[130] Pradel, *Procédure pénal*, 123 *et seq.*

[131] The *inspecteurs de travail*: art. L. 611-1 *et seq. Code du travail.*   [132] Art. 215-1 C. consom.

[133] Arts. L. 215-3–215-4, 222-1–222-3 C. consom. Various other administrative officers are given the same powers. In principle, the ordinary police are not excluded from the investigation of these offences special to the product context: Crim. 22 Jun. 1977, D 1977.IR.496 (in the context of misleading advertising).

[134] Bihl, *Droit pénal*, 171; Calais-Auloy and Steinmetz, 252.

[135] I shall use *action civile* to refer to a civil claim brought by a victim in respect of a crime in a criminal court, though it is sometimes used more broadly so as to include a claim brought by such a victim in a civil court.

[136] Arts. 388-1, 531 C.P.P. The courts apply art. 1384 als. 4–7 C.civ. to determine the liabilities of these non-criminals: Pradel, *Procédure pénale*, 283–4, above, pp. 25–6.   [137] Art. 388-1 C.P.P.

[138] Arts. 2 & 85, C.P.P.

[139] '*plainte avec constitution de partie civile*'. The procedure in respect of a *contravention* is termed *citation directe.*

[140] This effect of a victim's declaration of himself as *partie civile* was first established by the courts: Crim. 8 Dec. 1906, *arrêt Thirion*, D 1907.1.207, rapp. Laurent-Attalin and Crim. 28 May 1925, *arrêt Bencker*, DP 1926.1.121, note Leloir. And see arts. 1 al. 2, 85 *et seq.* C.P.P. Its roots are in pre-revolutionary practice: Viney, *Introduction à la responsabilité*, 112–13, 128.

[141] Pradel, *Procédure pénale*, 180. There are two further preventative controls on this power in the victim: (i) where the *ministère public* considers the claim insufficiently justified he may require the victim to be heard by a *juge d'instruction* (art. 86 al. 3 C.P.P.); and (ii) he may set in motion a procedure by which proceedings start against an unknown defendant with the person accused by the victim appearing as a witness (*réquisition non dénommée*); art. 86 al. 2 C.P.P. For other restraints on the *action civile*, see below, pp. 386–7. For more general discussion of the role of the *parquet* and *juge d'instruction*, see Bell, *French Legal Cultures*, 110–12, 115, 135–9.

victim's decision necessarily means that the person he accuses will go to trial for the crimes of which he accuses him: the *juge d'instruction* investigates the case against the accused[142] and must independently decide whether the facts give rise to an offence[143] and if so, what charges are appropriate to be brought and in which court.[144] If he finds that no crime has been committed, that there is insufficient evidence or that the culprit remains unknown, he may order the proceedings to cease ('*non-lieu*').[145] While the *juge d'instruction*'s decisions are fully appealable by the public prosecutor[146] and the accused,[147] a *partie civile* may appeal from them only where they involve no charges being brought or to the extent that they prejudice his 'civil interest'.[148] These rules became prominent in the course of the *affaire du sang contaminé*, as we shall see.[149]

French lawyers recognise that the *action civile* therefore has a double purpose: to permit the victim of a crime to gain damages from the offender but also to allow the victim to participate in the enforcement of the criminal law and so give vent to private vengeance.[150] It is for this reason that the victim of a crime may 'corroborate the *action publique*' where he could not in law claim damages owing to some civil immunity in the accused, as in the case of many accidents at work.[151]

Given this power to initiate criminal proceedings, it is obviously very important to determine who is to be treated as a 'victim' of an offence. At times, French courts have restricted this notion so as to exclude from the *action civile* some people who could have claimed damages for their harm in the civil courts, for example, the relatives of a person injured by an offence.[152] On the other hand, legislation has extended the definition of a victim of an offence in the context of crimes against consumers so as to include recognised consumers' associations, who may claim damages in respect of 'a direct or indirect harm prejudicing the collective interest of consumers' and as *parties civiles* may initiate and participate in the prosecution of offences affecting consumers.[153] In this way, consumers' associations play a semi-public policing role, being concerned neither with personal compensation nor private vengeance.[154] All three roles of the *action civile* can be seen in relation to the French criminal law which affects the safety of products, though my present concern is with its role as a vehicle of compensation.

Apart from delineating who counts as a 'victim' of a crime, French law restricts the availability of the *action civile* in three further ways. First, on occasion, the courts have refused to allow it in relation to offences which protect the general interest rather than

---

[142] The victim of a crime can also trigger an investigation where the offender is unknown at the time: Pradel, *Procédure pénale*, 230.　　　　　　　　　　　　　　　　[143] Arts. 176, 177 C.P.P.

[144] Arts. 178 al. 1, 179 al. 1, 181 al. 1 C.C.P.　　　[145] Art. 177 al. 1 C.P.P.　　　[146] Art. 185 C.P.P.

[147] Art. 186 al.1 C.C.P.　　　[148] Art. 186 al. 2 C.C.P.　　　[149] Below, pp. 395–6.

[150] Viney, *Introduction à la responsabilité*, 128 *et seq.*; Pradel, *Procédure pénale*, 225–6 and F. Boulan, 'Le double visage de l'action civile exercée devant la juridiction repressive' JCP 1973.I.2563.

[151] E.g. Crim. 15 Mar. 1977, JCP 1979.II.19148. For the immunity, see above, pp. 61–2.

[152] Crim. 29 Nov. 1966, JCP 1967.II.14979 note P.C.

[153] *Loi* no. 73–1193 of 27 Dec.1973 ('*Loi Royer*') art. 46. These provisions, much amended, now appear in art. L. 411-1 *et seq.* C. consom. On the wider role of other types of associations as *parties civiles*, see Bell, *French Legal Cultures*, 140–2.

[154] Nguyen Thanh-Bourgeais, *op. cit.* n. 102, D 1981.Chron.87, 92 referring to consumers' association as '*auxiliaires au ministère public*'. See further Calais-Auloy and Steinmetz, 597–9 who note that usually consumers' associations join existing proceedings rather than initiate their own.

the interests of individuals and therefore are said to give rise only to a *préjudice social*,[155] for example, the offence of failing to report a crime.[156] This has, however, been much criticised by *la doctrine*, in particular because the search for a criterion to distinguish this category of offence is 'similar to divination'.[157] It has not been applied to offences of involuntary homicide and causing personal injuries nor to other offences affecting product safety, such as *tromperie* and *falsification*.[158]

Secondly, no *action civile* can be brought if no *action publique* can lie,[159] for example, where the alleged offender has died, where the offences have been amnestied or where the prescription period for the *action publique* has elapsed.[160] The prescription periods set by French law are ten years for *crimes*, three years for *délits* and one year for *contraventions*, all from the commission of the offence.[161] In the case of *délits* (which include involuntary homicide, causing personal injury and the two *fraudes*),[162] this period is much shorter than that applicable to delictual claims in civil courts which must be brought within ten years from the 'manifestation or aggravation' of a claimant's damage.[163] As a result, the expiry of the prescription period of the *action publique* prevents the victim of an alleged offence from claiming by way of *action civile* in the criminal courts, but it does not prevent him from suing in the civil courts, where the prescription periods of the civil law apply even though the action is 'founded' on an offence.[164]

Thirdly, article 2 of the Code of Criminal Procedure allows the *action civile* only to those who have *personally* suffered harm *directly* from an offence, in contrast to claims in the civil courts where in principle *any* type of harm is recoverable.[165] A person who has suffered personal injuries has always been able to bring the *action civile*, as has the heir of a person who has been the victim of involuntary homicide,[166] and they may also claim damages for any damage to property caused by the defendant's fault.[167] While the mere relatives of a person injured or killed by an offence could not use the *action civile* to recover either their financial losses or their *dommage moral*,[168] since 1989 this has been allowed.[169] Moreover, a number of bodies which have paid compensation to the direct victim of a crime may claim damages for this loss from the offender in the criminal court, notably, *Caisses de sécurité sociale*[170] or private insurers,[171] though these *parties civiles* may only *join* existing criminal proceedings and do not possess the power to initiate them.[172]

---

[155] Pradel, *Procédure pénale*, 249–52.

[156] Art. 434-1 C. pén. and see Crim. 2 Mar. 1961, D 1962.121 note Bouzat.

[157] Merle and Vitu, *Procédure pénale*, 95.   [158] Above, pp. 370–1.

[159] Pradel, *Procédure pénale*, 237, 292–3; art. 10 al.1 C.P.P.   [160] Arts. 3 and 6 al. 1. C.P.P.

[161] Arts. 7–9 C.P.P. respectively. For this tripartite distinction see above, p. 369.

[162] Above, pp. 370–2.   [163] Art. 2270–1 C. civ., above, p. 34.

[164] Art. 10 al.1 C.P.P., as modified by *loi* no. 80–1042 of 23 Dec. 1980.   [165] Above, p. 24.

[166] Guinchard and Buisson, 598, 613.

[167] Art. 3 al. 2 C.P.P. A person who suffers damage to property alone may not claim as *partie civile* in respect of these offences against the person: Crim. 16 Mar. 1964, JCP 1964.II.13953 obs. P.C.

[168] Crim. 29 Nov. 1966, JCP 1967.II.14979 note P.C. So, in the *affaire Morhange* (above, n. 102) the relatives of the babies who died were denied damages for their grief: Nguyen Thanh-Bourgeais, *op. cit.* n. 102, 91.

[169] Crim 9 Feb. 1989 and Crim 21 Mar. 1989, D 1989.614 note Bruneau (*dommage moral* in respect of witnessing serious injury to members of the family).

[170] Pradel, *Procédure pénale*, 248–9. On their right of recourse in general, above, p. 38.

[171] Ibid., 247–8.   [172] Art. 388-2 C.P.P.

(ii) Advantages of claiming by way of action civile

I have already explained that a victim of a crime may prefer to claim damages by way of *action civile* so as to take advantage of the criminal court's generous view of 'fault' and of causation,[173] but there are three other more procedural reasons.

First, a major practical advantage for a victim of an offence in claiming as *partie civile* is that he may take advantage of the methods of gathering evidence of the criminal process which are seen as more effective than those available in the civil process and reflect the fundamentally different nature of the two types of proceedings. Traditionally, as Merle and Vitu observe:

> In the civil context, the case is a matter for the parties, something which they bring before a neutral and passive judge; the proceedings are an activity *before* the court. In the criminal context, by contrast, it is completely different: the proceedings are a matter for the State owing to the public interests which are at stake, and they are an activity *of* the court, which is active in the search for the truth.[174]

While the contrast between the civil and criminal processes has been narrowed somewhat owing to changes in the relative roles of the parties and the court in civil proceedings,[175] there remain considerable differences, the criminal process retaining a predominantly 'inquisitorial' spirit.[176] As regards *délits*,[177] the *ministère public* may choose to set in motion an investigation of the facts by a *juge d'instruction*, whose function is to gather evidence and compile the dossier with the aid of the *police judiciaire*[178] and then to determine on the basis of the evidence if there is a case to go before a trial court.[179] Where a *partie civile* initiates proceedings this *instruction* is automatic.[180] To fulfil his mission, the *juge d'instruction* possesses considerable powers: he may make any investigations or inquiries which are not expressly forbidden by law.[181] These powers, which may be exercised either on the request of a party to the proceedings (including the *partie civile*) or on the judge's own initiative, include the taking of evidence from witnesses or the victim and examining possible defendants,[182] ordering a judicial *expertise*,[183] visiting the scene of the alleged crime, and conducting searches.[184] The *juge d'instruction* has the right to examine and, if necessary, seize any document, whether confidential or not.[185] Moreover, a party can call an expert to give evidence which he can then use to counter the official *expertise*.[186] These powers of investigation can lead to a very much wider range of evidence being available to a criminal court than can be reached by way of the methods provided by the civil process and commentators agree that they play a

---

[173] Above, pp. 372–6. [174] Merle and Vitu, *Procédure pénale*, 16 (authors' emphasis).

[175] Above, pp. 46–8. [176] Pradel, *Procédure pénale*, 306.

[177] Art. 85 C.P.P. This stage is compulsory for *crimes*, and only possible for *contraventions* if required by the *procureur de la République*: arts. 79 and 44 C.P.P.

[178] This term includes all those public authorities whose duties include the investigation of offences: arts. 14–16 C.P.P. [179] Art. 179 C.P.P. [180] Above, p. 381.

[181] Art. 81 al. 1 C.P.P. [182] Art. 80-1 C.P.P. (which sets its conditions).

[183] Pradel, *Procédure pénale*, 564–5; art. 156 C.P.P. The court nominates an expert normally from an official list: art. 157 al. 1 C.P.P. [184] Arts. 92 and 94 C.P.P.

[185] Art. 97 C.P.P. ('*perquisition*'). This rule is qualified in order to protect the defendant's rights: Pradel, *Procédure pénale*, 356 et seq. [186] Pradel, *Procédure pénale*, 408.

significant role in attracting claims for damages for personal injuries and death away from the civil courts.[187]

But what about the burden of proof? In criminal proceedings the burden of proof lies either on the *procureur de la République* (who represents the State at the trial) or on the *partie civile* to prove the necessary elements of any criminal offence in the defendant,[188] this reflecting the principle of the presumption of innocence.[189] This principle is seen as requiring the acquittal of someone where there remains 'a sufficient doubt that prevents the judge arriving at a certainty'.[190] Rather oddly to a common lawyer used to distinguishing different standards of proof in civil and criminal trials,[191] French law does not use any particular formula to describe *how* well established any fact must be to justify a conviction: to a French lawyer this is both unnecessary and inappropriate given the recognition of a 'sovereign power of assessment' in the *juges du fond* as to the relative weight of the evidence: as the Code puts it, ' *[l]e juge décide d'après son intime conviction*'.[192] Clearly, therefore, the presumption of innocence can work to the disadvantage of a *partie civile*,[193] particularly at a time when the result of the criminal prosecution determined entirely the availability of liability in damages.[194]

Secondly, French commentators agree that it is in general quicker and cheaper for a person to sue in the criminal courts rather than in the civil.[195] This relative speed of the criminal process stems from the idea that 'the certainty and speediness of prosecution and conviction rather than the severity of punishment are indispensable to its effectiveness,' whereas delays are part of the fabric of civil procedure.[196] A victim of a crime's claim for compensation benefits from this relative speed because the criminal court normally gives its decision on this issue at the same time as on criminal responsibility itself.[197] Where a court finds itself unable to do so, notably for lack of information as to the victim's loss, it may suspend its decision on the award of compensation until it is able to do so, for example, having ordered an *expertise* on the victim's injuries.[198]

As to the cost, since 1993 in principle the State *always* bears the costs of prosecution (which include the cost of attendance of witnesses and any *expertise*[199]) and does not attempt to recover them from the defendant,[200] with the exception of very small fixed amounts to be recovered either from the convicted person or from the *partie civile* where he has initiated proceedings which have failed.[201] On the other hand, in principle

---

[187] Ibid., at 230.   [188] Guinchard and Buisson, 444 *et seq.*

[189] *Déclaration des Droits de l'Homme* of 27 Aug. 1789, art. 9; Guinchard and Buisson, 444 *et seq.*; Spencer, *op. cit.* n. 128, 33 *et seq.*

[190] Merle and Vitu, *Procédure pénale*, 155. Cf. Guinchard and Buisson, 446 ('the slightest doubt must benefit the accused').   [191] Below, p. 423.

[192] Art. 427 C.P.P. ('The court decides according to its intimate conviction') and see Guinchard and Buisson, 463 *et seq.*

[193] E.g. Paris 7 May 1968, GP 1968.2.151 (two defendants acquitted of *tromperie* as there was doubt as to their bad faith).   [194] Above, pp. 374–5.

[195] Pradel, *Procédure pénale*, 230; G. Stefani, G. Levasseur and B. Bouloc, *Procédure pénale* (Dalloz, Paris, 19th. edn., 2000), 247.   [196] Merle and Vitu, *Procédure pénale*, 20.

[197] Art. 464 C.P.P.   [198] Ibid.

[199] Arts. R. 92–93 C.P.P. This also applies to *expertises* ordered after judgment on the *action publique* and concerned solely with a victim's harm as these remain subject to the rules governing criminal procedure: Paris 19 Oct. 1968, D 1969 Somm. 31.   [200] Art. 800-1 N.C.P. (*loi* no. 93-2 of 4 Jan. 1993, art. 120).

[201] E.g. €90 in the case of proceedings in the Tribunal correctionnel: art. 1018-A *Code général des impôts*.

all private parties to the proceedings (whether the defendant, his insurer or employer, or the *partie civile*) bear their own costs, notably for the employment of legal counsel,[202] though a *partie civile* can recover them from any convicted defendant subject to the court's consideration of 'equity or the economic position of the person convicted',[203] and on an order of no case to answer (*non-lieu*) or an acquittal, an accused's costs may be borne by the State or by a *partie civile* who initiated the proceedings.[204] The important difference between civil and criminal proceedings is not, therefore, so much in the rules which apply to the recovery of costs by a successful claimant, but rather in the State's shouldering of a considerable part of the burden of the expenses of the case in criminal proceedings whatever its outcome. Where the case is long or complicated, this is no inconsiderable advantage.

Thirdly, the *action civile* possesses an advantage stemming from the very nature of criminal trials themselves, which are very different from French civil hearings, having much more of the character of English trials (whether civil or criminal).[205] In particular (and unlike French civil hearings) a good deal of evidence in a French criminal trial is oral,[206] the accused, witnesses of fact and (if a party calls them) expert witnesses being asked questions in person by the court and (since 2000 and under the control of the court) by the *ministère public* and the parties' counsel,[207] allowing the possibility of a 'type of cross-examination *à la française*'.[208] Clearly, some victims of crimes prefer this 'real trial' in which they are face-to-face with the accused and can hear him give evidence; this may indeed form part of a process of closure after the death of a relative.[209]

(iii) Further restraints on the exercise of the action civile

So described, the *action civile* is clearly open to abuse. Apart from the liminary control exercised by the *juge d'instruction*,[210] there are a number of further restraints on its exercise. First, a *partie civile* who *initiates* proceedings must, if without legal aid, deposit a sum deemed sufficient to cover the possibility of being ordered later to pay up to €15,000 as a 'civil fine' if a *juge d'instruction* considers his initiation of proceedings to have been 'abusive or dilatory'.[211] Secondly, a *partie civile* may find himself ordered to pay a defendant's costs if the *juge d'instruction* ends the proceedings or on an acquittal.[212] And thirdly, a defendant who is acquitted may himself initiate proceedings as *partie civile* against the *partie civile* in the earlier proceedings on the basis of the offence of malicious prosecution (*dénonciation calomnieuse*) where the original *partie civile* knew that his

---

[202] Pradel, *Procédure pénale*, 854 *et seq.*

[203] Arts. 216, 375, 475-1, 543 C.P.P. Cf. art 700 N.c.pr.civ.

[204] Art. 800-2 C.P.P. (as inserted by *loi* no. 2000-516 of 15 Jun. 2000, art. 88).

[205] Bell, Boyron, Whittaker, 133–4.

[206] Guinchard and Buisson, 1056–7. There is an even greater reliance on oral evidence for the most serious offences tried by the Cour d'assises: ibid., 1070.

[207] For the Tribunal correctionnel: arts. 442, 442-1 C.P.P. The accused and the *partie civile* can put questions to witnesses only through the court: art. 442-1 al. 2 C.P.P.   [208] Guinchard and Buisson, 1081.

[209] C. Roca, 'Nouvelle définition de l'infraction non intentionnelle: une réforme qui en cache une autre plus importante' *Petites affiches* (26 Oct. 2000) no. 214, 4, 4–5.   [210] Above, pp. 381–2.

[211] Art. 88, 177-2 C.P.P.   [212] Above, p. 382.

complaint was untrue.[213] However, where a person has suffered serious personal injuries or his relative has been killed and there is some suggestion of fault in a person whom he names in his complaint, these restraints are unlikely to be considered appropriate.

3. Reform, Complexity and Uncertainty

In the mid-1990s, there was continued concern about the unfairness of the very strict approach of both the criminal law and the criminal courts to involuntary homicide and causing personal injuries. In common with the aftermath of the *affaire du 'Cinq-Sept'*,[214] an important concern was with 'public decision-makers' ('*décideurs publics*') and an important pressure group was the association of *maires*, who had apparently found themselves even more at risk of conviction after the decentralisation of powers from Paris to local authorities in the 1980s.[215] There were two legislative attempts to deal with this problem, the first, in 1996, fairly minor and the second, in 2000, much more considerable. Together they have made quite a number of legal and procedural changes affecting the role of the criminal courts in the imposition of liability in damages for death and personal injuries.

(a) Making criminal fault more subjective

The first legislative attempt at reform was an amendment of the definition of the *élément moral* for all *délits*. So, while article 121-3 of the Code as enacted had stated simply that a *délit* could be committed by *imprudence* or *négligence*,[216] in these cases and where there is breach of a duty of safety provided by *loi* or *règlements*, it was further required that the defendant had not taken 'normal care [*les diligences normales*] taking into account, where appropriate, the nature of his mission or his duties, of his abilities as well as of the power and means which he possessed'.[217] Similar (but not identical) amendments were made to provisions dealing with the criminal responsibilities of *maires*.[218] The purpose of these changes was to remove the possibility of a person being held guilty of a *délit* (notably, involuntary homicide or causing serious personal injuries) by the commission of an offence of strict liability and to move from an objective assessment of the negligence of the defendant for the purposes of these criminal responsibilities to a subjective assessment (*'une appréciation* in concreto').[219]

It is difficult to assess whether these changes had any appreciable effect before they were overtaken by wider reform some four years later.[220] For example, in the criminal proceedings arising out of the stadium disaster at Furiani, when a stand collapsed during a football cup match owing to its design and its overloading, killing 15 people and

---

[213] Art. 226-10 C. pén. Art. 91 C.P.P. provides a further independent ground for recovery of damages against a *partie civile* who initiates proceedings which are negligent or in bad faith where the *juge d'instruction* orders that there is no case to be tried.   [214] Above, pp. 377–8.

[215] J. Pradel, evidence to the Sénat's Commission des Lois in Fauchon, *Rapport*, Sén. No. 177, Annex 1.

[216] Cf. above, p. 369 on the jurisdiction for *délits*.   [217] *Loi* no. 96-393 of 13 May 1996, art. 1.

[218] Arts. 2123-34, 3123-28, 4123-28 C. G.C.T.: Desportes and Le Gunehec, 441–2.

[219] Desportes and Le Gunehec, 439–40.   [220] Ibid., 442–3.

injuring nearly 2,000 more, the *juges du fond* felt able to convict various officials of the football league and a senior administrator in the office of the *préfet*, the latter for his failure in his various legal responsibilities as to premises open to the public, on the basis that they had not acted with 'normal diligence... taking account of their duties, powers and means at their disposal', a decision with which the Cour de cassation did not interfere.[221] Even those commentators who see the changes made in 1996 as ridding the law of '*délits matériels*' (that is, *délits* of strict liability[222]) accept that breach of a duty (whether or not this constitutes a *contravention*) will still create at least in fact a presumption of fault.[223] However, others have been more critical. Pradel considers the change useless as the courts had previously taken into account the 'normal care' to be required of a defendant in assessing responsibility[224] and because it does not constitute a ground for intervention by the Cour de cassation and so cannot lead to any systematic change.[225] Certainly the association of *maires* was not content.[226]

(b) Protecting 'public decision makers'—and some others

However, much wider reforms were put in place by the *loi* of 2000, sometimes known as the *loi Fauchon* after the senator who proposed it.[227] Their motivation was again principally to protect public decision makers from being convicted of involuntary homicide and causing personal injuries where they were not really to blame,[228] but again it did not go about this directly for fear of falling foul of the constitutional principle of equal treatment of citizens.[229] As proposed by Fauchon the reforms had three major elements:

(i) breaking the necessary connection between a criminal court's decision on criminal responsibility and the imposition of civil liability in damages for fault;

(ii) redefining the fault element for *délits* committed by individuals whose action had played only an indirect causal role; and

(iii) extending the criminal responsibility of local authorities to all their activities so as to provide a substitute for the individual elected officers and public servants who would escape conviction as a result of (ii).[230]

However, the last of these elements did not win the support of the government and was dropped in the course of the bill's parliamentary progress, partly because it was

---

[221] Crim. 24 Jun. 1997, Bull. crim. no. 251.   [222] Above, p. 373.

[223] Desportes and Le Gunehec, 443 citing Crim. 2 Apr. 1997, Bull. crim. no. 132.

[224] J. Pradel, 'De la véritable portée de la loi du 10 juillet 2000 sur la définition des délits non intentionnels' D 2000 *Point de vue*, V. Similarly, Y. Mayaud, 'Intervention sur la loi du 10 juillet 2000' GP 31 Jul. 2000, 1193, 1194; Véron, (9th. edn.) 71, 75 (who sees the change as 'purely formal').

[225] S. Petit (*Conseiller référendaire* at the Cour de cassation) 'La responsabilité pénale des agents publics et des élus' GP 1999. 2. 1746, 1749–51.

[226] J.-P. Gauzer (representing the Association des maires de France), evidence to Sénat's Commission des Lois in Fauchon, *Rapport*, Sén. No. 177, Annex 1.   [227] *Loi* no. 2000–647 of 10 Jul. 2000.

[228] *Proposition de loi tendant à préciser la définition des délits non intentionnels, exposé des motifs*, Sén. No. 9 (7 Oct. 1999).

[229] This was the view of the report to the *Garde des sceaux* by J. Massot (chair), *Le groupe d'étude sur la responsabilité pénale des décideurs publics* (8 Jun. 1999) (available at <http://www.sante-publique.org/Massot/massot. htm>) Chap. II (2)(A) 2° and 3°. Fauchon himself was unconvinced: Fauchon, *Rapport*, Sén. no. 177, I (B) (4).   [230] Ibid. III(C).

thought to give the civil courts too much control over the activities of public authorities contrary to the principle of the separation of powers,[231] partly because the investigation and prosecution of a local authority was thought likely to lead to the same traumatic experience for the *maire* as would his own prosecution, and partly owing to a background fear that it could lead to the State itself becoming capable of being criminally responsible.[232] Once in place the reform to the 'fault element' was held to be retroactive as it favoured defendants.[233]

(i) Redefining 'criminal fault' (sometimes)

Apart from minor changes, the *loi* of 2000 added a further provision to the definitions provided by article 121–3 of the Criminal Code, to the effect that as regards *délits* by negligence:

physical persons who have not directly caused the harm but who have created or contributed to the creation of the situation which allowed the occurrence of the damage or who have not taken measures allowing it to be avoided, are criminally responsible if it is established that they have either manifestly deliberately broken a particular obligation of care or safety provided by *loi* or *règlement*, or have committed an 'aggravated fault' [*une faute caractérisée*] and exposed another person to an especially serious risk of which they could not be unaware.[234]

This is quite a complex provision which has attracted a good deal of critical comment in *la doctrine*.[235] Its first distinction is between *personnes morales* (where the definition of fault for the purposes of *délit* is not changed[236]) and individuals, where the definition of fault depends on whether or not their action or omission has caused a person direct or indirect harm. As regards 'direct harm', again the definition of fault remains the same, but as regards 'indirect harm' a defendant may be convicted of a *délit* only on proof *either* of a manifestly deliberate breach of a legal duty of care or safety *or* of *une faute caractérisée* which exposed another person to an especially serious risk *and* was one of which they could not be unaware.[237]

The application of the new definition of fault therefore turns in part on whether or not the victim's death or injury was 'directly' caused by a defendant. The *loi* gives some guidance as to what is meant by this, explaining that a person causes indirectly where he has 'created or contributed to the creation of the situation which allowed the occurrence of the damage or who [has] not taken measures allowing it to be

---

[231] S. Petit, evidence to Commission quoted in Fauchon, *Rapport*, Sén. No. 177, Annex 1.

[232] J.-D. Nuttens, 'La loi Fauchon du 10 juillet 2000 ou la fin de la confusion de la faute civile et de la faute pénale d'imprudence' GP 2000.2.1740, 1744–5 referring to J.O. Rép. fr. 2nd séance of 5 Apr. 2000, 3125 (speech of the *garde des Sceaux*).   [233] Crim. 12 Dec. 2000, *affaire du Drac*, Bull. crim. no. 371.

[234] Art. 121–3 al. 4 C. pén. as inserted by the *loi* of 2000, art. 1.

[235] It was extended to govern the fault element of the *contravention* of causing less serious personal injuries in 2001: art. R. 610-2 al. 2 C. pén. On the debate see in particular: Pradel, *op. cit.* n. 224, D 2000 *Point de vue*, V; Mayaud, *op. cit.* n. 224, 1193; Nuttens, *op. cit.* n. 232.

[236] The *loi* of 2000 made a *possibly* significant change to art. 121–3 al. 3 by replacing '*règlements*' with '*règlement*', this being seen as changing its significance from rules generally to *règlements* in the constitutional sense: cf. above, p. 387. However, this change is very small given the breadth of *imprudence* and *négligence*: Ministre de la justice, *Présentation des dispositions de la loi no. 2000–647 du 10 juillet 2000*, Circulaire No. 1796–6B of 11 Oct. 2000 ('*Circulaire* of 2000'), para. 1.2.1.   [237] Below, pp. 391–2.

avoided'. The underlying idea is that the criminal courts are to abandon (for these cases) their traditional understanding of causation for the purposes of involuntary homicide and causing personal injuries (based on a sense of the 'equivalence of conditions') and instead apply a more restrictive understanding based on a theory of 'adequate causation'.[238] It was clearly intended that most of the actions or omissions of 'public decision makers' would cause only 'indirect harm' (in that they contribute to situations which allow the occurrence of damage) and so would be criminally responsible for their administrative failures which cause death or personal injuries only on proof of one or other of the more serious faults which the new legislation creates.

However, the criterion of 'direct' or 'indirect' causation is by no means straightforward and was, indeed, convincingly criticised at the time of the *loi*'s parliamentary progress on the ground that 'it would be very difficult to put in place a consistent *jurisprudence* on the basis of an apparently elusive notion of causation',[239] and even that the discretion which it gives to the courts in determining the conditions of criminal responsibility contravenes the constitutional principle that *délits* should be defined by *loi*.[240] It is thought that in most road accidents[241] and cases of injury or death as a result of medical treatment,[242] the harm will be considered 'directly' caused and so the test of fault remains the same. On the other hand, the new law has been applied so as to relieve a *maire* of criminal responsibility for homicide, holding that while at fault in his duties of supervision, his behaviour had only indirectly contributed to the victim's death and was not within either definition of serious fault.[243] Moreover, the application of the new test of fault is not restricted to *public* decision makers. For example, it may be thought capable of protecting company bosses (*chefs d'entreprises*) for failing to prevent accidents at work directly caused by one employee to another or to a non-employee, though (owing to particular features of the law governing the duties of employers here) the courts are still likely to impose criminal liability in respect of accidents at work causing death or serious injury.[244] On the other hand, the mere failure to take safety precautions to prevent injury or death will not necessarily be classed as an 'indirect cause' of a victim's death or injury.[245] To the extent, though, to which the *loi* of 2000 does protect 'decision makers' such as *maires*, senior officials or senior company officers, it may deflect criminal charges downwards onto junior employees

---

[238] Y. Mayaud, 'Retour sur la culpabilité non intentionnelle en droit pénal' D 2000 Chron. 603, 606. For the courts' earlier and still general approach, above, pp. 375–6.

[239] G. Viney, evidence quoted in Fauchon, *Rapport*, Sén. No. 177, Annex 1. For other critics, see C. Ruet, 'La responsabilité pénale pour faute d'imprudence après la loi du 10 juillet 2000 tendant à préciser la définition des délits non intentionnels' *Droit pénal* (Jan. 2001); P.J. Pansier and C. Charbonneau, 'Commentaire de la loi sur la responsabilité pénale des élus' *Petites affiches* (Jul. 2000).

[240] J. Pradel, evidence quoted in Fauchon, *Rapport*, Sén. No. 177, Annex 1; Constitution of 1958, art. 34.

[241] Ibid., para. 2.3.1.

[242] P. Mistretta, 'La responsabilité pénale médicale à l'aune de la loi du 10 juillet 2000. Evolution ou révolution?' JCP 2002.I.149. E.g. Crim. 29 Oct. 2002, Bull. crim. no. 196; Crim. 13 Nov. 2002, Bull. crim. no. 203.

[243] For examples: TGI La Rochelle 19 Sept. 2000, Rennes 19 Sept. 2000, *Petites affiches* no. 234 (23 Nov. 2000) 11 note Vital-Durand.   [244] *Circulaire* of 2000, para. 2.3.2.

[245] Rennes 19 Sept. 2000, *cit.*, (headteacher and junior teachers criminally responsible for death of child on expedition for failing to take appropriate precautions).

('*lampistes*' or 'dogs-bodies') whose physical actions or omissions are closest to the victim's death or injury.[246]

Apparently, the legislator was concerned to avoid any decrease in responsibility in the area of health and public safety;[247] but where would the position of individuals who manufacture or supply a product which causes personal injury or death come in this discussion? Given the uncertainty as to 'directness', there can be no simple answer, but it is likely that their actions which have failed in the design, manufacture, warning or recall of a product are likely to be considered 'direct', except in cases where the action of a person using the product and who should have known better looks instead to be its 'direct cause'. Three cases may illustrate this.

In one case in the early 1990s, a microlight aircraft crashed owing to pilot error, but the Cour de cassation nevertheless accepted that the manufacturer of the aircraft could be convicted of involuntary homicide in respect of the cheap safety belts which the *expertise* considered too fragile, as there was no requirement that the victim's harm be 'direct and immediate'.[248] After the legislation, the manufacturer's fault could be thought only an 'indirect cause', the pilot's the 'direct cause' of the passenger's death. Similarly, in a case before the Cour de cassation in 2001 a professional cleaner of water pipes used a chemical product based on hydrochloric acid in a house without telling its occupants to take the necessary precautions (such as keeping rooms ventilated), as a result of which an occupant died from the release of hydrogen sulphide.[249] Here, the managing director and the scientific director of the company which manufactured the product which the cleaner used alleged that her death was caused solely by the cleaner's fault in failing to warn the occupants of the risks,[250] but the court held that their behaviour had 'contributed to the creation of the situation which allowed the occurrence of the damage' and then convicted them on the basis of '*faute carac-térisée*'.[251] On the other hand, in a case decided well before the *loi* of 2000, a manufac-turer of clasps used in mountain climbing was convicted of involuntary homicide when climbers fell to their deaths when the clasps broke.[252] In the absence of any causally relevant lack of care in the climbers, on these facts the manufacturer's fault which consisted in failing to provide a sufficient resistance in the clasps in foreseeable conditions of use looks 'direct.'

Moreover, as my earlier example concerning the product used in cleaning pipes illus-trates, even if a person's action or omission is held to be the 'indirect cause' of a victim's death or injury, he may still be convicted if either one of the new tests of 'fault' are satis-fied. Here, again, there is a good degree of uncertainty and a good deal of discretion in the *juges du fond*. The first new test of fault requires the existence of a legal duty (which is something on which the Cour de cassation can pronounce) but then requires that it must have been 'manifestly deliberately broken' by the defendant, an issue of fact for

---

246 P. Conte, 'Le lampiste et la mort' *Droit pénal* (Jan. 2001) 10.
247 *Circulaire* of 2000, para. 2.3.4 referring to R. Dosière, *Rapport*, AN no. 2266 (22 Mar. 2000) 41.
248 Crim. 11 Apr. 1999, *Droit pénal* (Nov. 1991), 5.   249 Crim. 10 Jan. 2001, Bull. crim. no. 2.
250 The cleaner did not appeal from his conviction.
251 Cf. Com. 20 Mar. 2001, Bull. crim. no. 71. (shipbuilder convicted of involuntary homicide for deaths when ship sank for fault in the design of one of the electrical panels allowed water in, thereby stop-ping the pumps; case sent to be re-tried on the basis that the new law provided for a special test of fault where damage was indirect).   252 Crim. 6 Jun. 1999, *Droit pénal* (Nov. 1991), 5.

the *juges du fond* with which the Cour de cassation is unlikely to wish to interfere. The second test of fault requires that the fault be 'aggravated' (*une faute caracterisée*), that it exposed another person to a serious risk *and* that this was a risk of which the defendant 'could not be unaware',[253] though while these appear as three distinct conditions, the courts are likely to use the second and third elements as a guide to the existence of an 'aggravated fault'.[254] This second test resulted from a political compromise: the earlier test of fault of an 'exceptional gravity' had to be dropped after associations of the victims of crime contacted the press and denounced the legislation as a disguised amnesty for public decision makers at the time when their liability was very much at issue as regards 'contaminated blood' and asbestos.[255] However, even though the legislation attempts to define when a serious fault is to be found, its assessment is apparently entirely left to the *juges du fond*,[256] and this has led some commentators to consider that little has changed. So, the *juges du fond* are to some extent able to manipulate the line between 'direct' and 'indirect' harm so as to lead to the ordinary test of fault or the more demanding new tests, but even having arrived at the new tests they are able to decide broadly on the basis of whether or not they consider that the defendant should or should not be criminally responsible: this is what they always did do.[257]

What then is the overall position, after the new law, of people whose actions or omissions affect the safety of products? First, central or local authorities cannot be convicted of involuntary homicide or causing personal injuries in respect of failures in the exercise of their powers of health and safety,[258] and that the individuals who work in them (elected or unelected officials) are unlikely to be convicted unless their actions constitute a deliberate breach of a legal duty or a really serious lack of care.[259] This position as regards criminal responsibility makes a striking contrast with the evolution of the law of the liability in damages of the administration in the hands of the Conseil d'Etat, which has moved away from a requirement of serious fault, there termed *faute lourde*.[260] Secondly, where a product is manufactured, supplied or used by a private company or by a public body distinct from the State itself and not forming part of a local authority, the action or omission of individuals within these bodies can attract criminal responsibility for death or personal injury either on the basis of 'ordinary fault' following the more subjective standard set in 1996 or the more serious faults provided in 2000, depending on the 'directness' of the injury.[261] Thirdly, in the same situations, the corporation (whether public or private) can itself be criminally responsible on the basis of 'ordinary fault' even where the death or personal injury was 'indirect'.[262] For while under the previous law the courts subjected the criminal responsibility of *personnes morales* to a condition of the commission of an offence in its *organes* or 'representatives',

---

[253] Art. 121-3 al. 4 C. pén. *in fine*.   [254] Desportes and Le Gunehec, 453.

[255] Ibid., 453 and see J.-M. Bizat, 'Les députés corrigent la réforme sénatoriale de la pénalisation des fautes non intentionnelles', *Le Monde* 7 Apr. 2000.   [256] Crim. 4 Jun. 2002, D 2003.95 note Petit.

[257] Pradel, *op. cit.* n. 224, D 2000, VII.

[258] The central authorities on the basis that the State cannot be criminally responsible; the local authorities on the basis that these powers are not ones which they can 'delegate' within the meaning of art. 121-2 al. 2 C. pén.   [259] Above, p. 390.

[260] Above, p. 315.   [261] Above, pp. 391–2.

[262] Crim. 24 Oct. 2000, (no. 00–80.378) in Y. Mayaud, 'Sommaire de jurisprudence sur les violences non intentionnelles après la loi du 10 juillet 2000', *Revue de science criminelle* (2001) 156, 162–3.

this has not been interpreted to mean that they will be criminally responsible after the *loi* of 2000 *only* if these same individuals satisfy the *new* tests of criminal responsibility which it provides, an 'illogical' position justified by the legislator's intention of retaining the responsibility of corporations as it was.[263] Taken together, therefore, in a case where a defective product has caused death or personal injury, the victims are likely to be able to find suitable persons (whether human or corporate) against which they need allege no more than 'ordinary fault' in order to establish criminal responsibility.

(ii) Breaking the 'unity of criminal and civil faults'?

By requiring different substantive tests for criminal fault and for civil fault even if only in some situations, the *loi* of 2000 has been said to break their essential unity, for there will be some cases where a court considers that a defendant has committed an 'ordinary' fault, but not the more aggravated fault required of individuals whose action indirectly contributed to the victim's personal injuries or death.[264] However, perhaps equally important for the legislation's general strategy of partial decriminalisation was its creation of a new rule according to which a criminal court's acquittal of a person of a criminal offence does not prevent a civil court from holding him liable in damages on the basis of civil fault in respect of the same action or omission.[265] For this change removes the link between criminal responsibility and civil liability for fault which had led the criminal courts to hold defendants guilty of criminal offences of involuntary homicide and causing personal injuries in order to award the 'victims' compensation.[266] It is for this reason that this apparently procedural change contributes further to the divorce of criminal and civil fault.

However, the break between the two faults is both indirect and partial.[267] It is indirect because the law does not as such state that fault for the purposes of criminal responsibility and for the purposes of civil liability is to be assessed according to different criteria bearing in mind the different purposes for which they are imposed. It is partial first because in most cases criminal fault remains the same as civil fault, the exception being where an indirect harm is caused by an individual,[268] but, more importantly, secondly, because the divorce only works one way: for while not all civil faults constitute criminal faults, all criminal faults still necessarily constitute civil faults.[269] This means that where a criminal court finds a defendant guilty of a criminal offence of involuntary homicide or causing personal injuries it will still have both the power and the substantive legal foundation for the imposition of civil liability in damages on the defendant (or those who are responsible for him) to the victim. Moreover, while the *loi* of 2000 refers merely to the power of the *civil* courts to impose civil liability for fault after an acquittal, the Chambre criminelle of the Cour de cassation has declared that the criminal courts also

---

[263] Mayaud, ibid., 163; *Circulaire* of 2000, para. 1.2.2.1; Ruet, *op. cit.* n. 239, 8–9.

[264] So, Mayaud, *op. cit.* n. 224; Nuttens, *op. cit.* n. 232; A. Dorsner-Dolivet, 'Que devient le principe de l'identité des fautes civiles et pénales après la loi du 10 juillet 2000?' *Revue de la recherche juridique* (Aix-en-Provence, 2002–1) 199.   [265] Art. 4-1 C.P.P. inserted by *loi* of 2000, art. 2.

[266] Cf. above and see Fauchon, *Rapport*, Sén. no. 177,

[267] P. Jourdain, 'Autorité' de la chose jugée au pénal et *principe* d'unité des fautes: la rupture est consommée entre faute civile et faute pénale, mais l'est-elle totalement' D 2001 Somm. comm. 2232, 2233; *Circulaire* of 2000, para. 1.1.1.   [268] Pradel, *Droit pénal*, 462.

[269] Jourdain, *op. cit.* n. 267, 2233.

have the power to impose liability in damages for 'civil fault' in similar circumstances,[270] a power of particular importance where the defendant's criminal fault has to be special (whether a deliberate breach of an obligation or 'aggravated'). In the result, while the *loi* of 2000 has removed the distorting link between the conviction of a person for involuntary homicide or causing personal injuries and civil liability in damages, it has if anything made the use by a victim of personal injuries or death of an *action civile* before the criminal courts more attractive.[271] For the existing advantages of a victim's claiming before the criminal court (in terms of judicial powers of investigation, cost and the speed of the process) remain,[272] and are no longer clouded by the risk that the criminal court's failure to convict will deprive him of the award of damages which a civil court would have allowed. So while some of the pieces of the jigsaw puzzle have been changed, the overall picture remains remarkably the same. The criminal law and the criminal process will retain their important roles in the compensation of personal injuries and death, including in cases involving products.

4. The *Affaire du Sang Contaminé*: Part III—Criminal and Constitutional Dimensions of Product Safety

Perhaps the most prominent proceedings relating to the continued supply of HIV-infected blood products in France in the course of late 1984 and 1985 were those brought to seek to establish criminal offences in those allegedly responsible.[273] Certainly, the *affaire* has had a very important effect on French attitudes to responsibility for products (whether in terms of product safety or product liability) and for some involves *two* scandals: the first, the knowing supply of contaminated blood products and the second, the denial of justice in relation to the offences. Much of the debate surrounding the affair occurred at a political and journalistic level, bringing the facts, their significance and the political responsibilities involved to the attention of the French public. However, from a lawyer's and particularly a comparative lawyer's point of view, the most important manifestation of the *affaire* were the three sets of criminal proceedings to which it gave rise: the first in the ordinary criminal courts against the scientists who ran or advised the National Blood Transfusion Centre;[274] the second against the Prime Minister and two other ministers in first one and then a second special constitutional criminal court; and the third back in the ordinary courts against a collection of 30 administrative officers and medical practitioners.[275] However, after some 15 years of investigations and proceedings, only the officers of the National Blood Transfusion Centre and one of the ministers were convicted of any criminal offence; and in the case of the former the basis of their conviction led to a storm of protest from some of the victims, and in the case of the latter no punishment was imposed.[276]

---

[270] Crim. 28 Sept. 1999, Bull. crim. no. 198 (absence of criminal fault does not prevent civil liability for contractual fault); art. 470-1 C.P.P.; Roca, *op. cit.* n. 209, 5.   [271] Roca, ibid., passim.

[272] Above, pp. 384–6.

[273] For proceedings in the civil and administrative courts, see above, pp. 149–51, 315–19, 324.

[274] Below, pp. 395–8.   [275] Below, pp. 398–401.   [276] Below, pp. 396–7, 399.

(a) The first stage: proceedings against the officers of the National Blood Transfusion Centre in the ordinary courts

At first, there were two principal defendants charged with offences: Dr. M. Garetta, the former director of the French National Blood Transfusion Centre and Dr. L.-P. Allain, its director of research and development.[277] The facts as found by the *juges du fond* were that from 1983 the responsible officers of the Centre had become progressively aware that use of unheated blood products could result in the contamination of their recipients with HIV, the 'causal agent' of AIDS, and from 21 March 1985 they were informed of massive contamination of batches on the market; but they failed to take steps to prevent the use of the products in France by warning haemophiliacs and doctors of the mortal danger, to stop their distribution or to substitute treated blood products of foreign or French origin, all these decisions being based on a desire to exhaust existing stocks for economic reasons.[278] It was only in October 1985 that a government circular forbade the supply of untreated blood products in France.

The human cost of this was terrible. By early 1993 some 250 French haemophiliacs had died of AIDS and 1,200 were diagnosed HIV-positive.[279] In late 1991, some haemophiliacs initiated proceedings as *parties civiles* against Allain and Garetta alleging the *délit* of *tromperie* in respect of the blood products with which they had been supplied, but after it became known publicly that they had *known* that the blood products were contaminated at least from May 1985, claims were brought by haemophiliacs, their relatives and the French Association of Haemophiliacs on the ground of the *crime* of poisoning.[280] The difference between these offences related to the punishments available and the court of trial, for *délits* are tried by the Tribunal correctionnel with a bench of professional magistrates, whereas *crimes* are tried by the Cour d'assises with a mixed bench of professional judges and lay jurors.[281] The *ministère public* opposed charges on the ground of poisoning and sought to have them declared inadmissible before investigation, though on this he was overruled by the Cour d'appel of Paris, on the ground that the appropriate criminal offence could not be determined before the *juge d'instruction* had investigated the facts.[282]

When the case came to court, it was to the Tribunal correctionnel and on charges of *tromperie* and of failing to assist a person in danger,[283] only Garetta being prosecuted for involuntary homicide.[284] Given that the *parties civiles* could not appeal against the decision of the *juge d'instruction* to send the case for trial on this lesser ground,[285] some

---

[277] Two others were charged with refusal to prevent the commission of a *délit* under art. 63 al. 1 A.C. pén.: the former Director General of Health and the former Director of the National Health Laboratory. The former was found guilty and sentenced to four years' suspended sentence of imprisonment; the latter was acquitted. Their part in the proceeds is omitted in the following discussion.

[278] Crim. 22 Jun. 1994, JCP 1994.II.41 note Rassat quoting the decision of the Cour d'appel of 13 Jul. 1993.   [279] H. Légal, concl. to CE Ass. 9 Apr. 1993, D 1993.312 (above, pp. 315–19).

[280] Arts. 301, 302 A.C. pén. and see A. Prothais, note to Paris (Chambre d'accusation) 19 Sept. 1991 and Trib. corr. Paris 23 Oct. 1992, D 1993.222, 223. They had also earlier alleged a failure to assist someone in danger under art. 63 A.C. pén.   [281] Above, p. 369.

[282] Paris (Chambre d'accusation) 19 Sept. 1991 D 1993.222 note Prothais.

[283] Art. 63 al. 1 A.C. pén. (now art. 223-6.1 C. pén.).

[284] Under art. 319 A.C. pén. (and see above, p. 372).

[285] Art. 186 C.C.P.; Crim. 1 Dec.1964, Bull crim. no. 318 and see above, p. 382.

of them argued before the tribunal itself that it had no *jurisdiction* to try the charges as the facts before it constituted the *crime* of poisoning, but this argument lost at first instance, on appeal and was declared inadmissible *en cassation*, though the issue was somewhat briefly considered.[286] The decision to proceed on these limited bases can therefore be seen as a striking example of what is known in France as the '*correctionali-sation*' of the prosecution process, according to which lesser charges leading to trial in the Tribunal correctionnel are preferred by *ministères publics* and *juges d'instruction* rather than those which lead to trial in the Cour d'assises, a phenomenon which, though 'illegal' (as cases should be tried by the courts according to the proper character-isation of the facts as these officers find them), is very widespread.[287]

As to the charges which *were* brought, both Garetta and Allain were found guilty of *tromperie* and sentenced respectively to four years' imprisonment and a fine of FF500,000 and four years' imprisonment (two of which were suspended):[288] these sentences were confirmed on appeal and by the Cour de cassation.[289] The Tribunal also imposed liability in damages on them.[290] The proceedings raised four controver-sial issues: the propriety of reliance on *tromperie*; the 'fault element' of the crime of poisoning; the marginalisation of involuntary homicide; and issues relating to the *actions civiles* themselves.

First, some *parties civiles* were shocked that charges were brought for *tromperie* rather than for poisoning.[291] *Tromperie* was seen as a 'grocer's offence', a 'criminal charge written for the sale of pots of jam', belittling the seriousness of the crimes and the terribleness of their consequences, since the central element of the *affaire*—the death of hundreds of people—is entirely absent.[292] Moreover, the case demanded trial by the Cour d'assises, the appropriate forum for a case of national importance owing to its involvement of lay jurors.[293] Clearly, the penalties available were also very differ-ent, as *tromperie* can lead at most to a sentence of four years' imprisonment, whereas poisoning could lead to a maximum sentence of life imprisonment.[294] On the other hand, some *parties civiles* actually favoured charges for *tromperie* in part on the basis that proceedings in the Tribunal correctionnel were thought quicker and more certain to succeed, but in part on financial grounds.[295] For by the time the case came to appeal, the French Parliament had set up a compensation scheme for the haemophiliac and transfusional victims of HIV which promised them 'full compensation' for their

---

[286] Below, pp. 397–8.

[287] Merle and Vitu, *Procédure pénale*, 686 *et seq.*; Pradel, *Procédure pénale*, 105–108.

[288] Trib. corr. Paris 23 Oct. 1992 (extracts), *2éme esp.*, D 1993.222 note Prothais. Garetta's sentence was the most severe which the law allowed in the aggravating circumstances found in art. 2 al. 1 of the *loi* of 1 Aug. 1905.

[289] Paris 13 Jul. 1993, D 1994.18 note Prothais; Crim. 22 Jun. 1994, JCP 1994.II.22310 note Rassat (Allain's *pourvoi*). The *réquisitions* of A.-G. Perfetti and the *rapport* of the *conseiller* Blin are reported in Pradel, *Sang et droit pénal*, 111 and 145 respectively.   [290] Ibid.

[291] Prothais, note, D 1993.222 at 224 and cf. above, pp. 370–1.

[292] Delmas Saint-Hilaire, *op. cit.* n. 56, in Pradel (ed.), *Sang et droit pénal*, 39 at 41; J.H. Robert, *Droit pénal* 1994.somm. no. 12.   [293] Delmas Saint-Hilaire, *op. cit.* n. 56, 58–9.

[294] Art. 302 A.C. pén. specified the death penalty, but this was generally abolished in France and replaced by life imprisonment by the *loi* no. 81–908 of 9 Oct. 1981. Under 221-5 C. pén., poisoning is punished by a maximum sentence of 30 years' imprisonment.   [295] Delmas Saint-Hilaire, *op. cit.* n. 56, 58.

losses.[296] This suggested that they would get no damages by *actions civiles* in respect of an offence based on the harm caused to them by their contamination,[297] whereas damages caused by *tromperie* could be said to be aimed at compensation of a 'totally independent' *dommage moral* stemming from the 'attack made on the integrity of their consent'.[298]

Secondly, a key aspect of the controversy concerned the *élément moral* of the crime of poisoning. On the one hand, both the Tribunal correctionnel and the Cour d'appel of Paris considered poisoning to be a form of murder, thereby requiring an intention to kill, explaining that what is required is not merely an intended act, but a:

wilful act accomplished with the view to a precisely-sought result by its perpetrator, here the death or the attack on the corporeal integrity of another person.[299]

This position could be supported by poisoning's position in the Criminal Code of 1810,[300] its definition in the Code[301] and from traditional *doctrine*.[302] As to both courts, none of the officers of the National Blood Transfusion Centre had acted with the aim of causing the deaths of the haemophiliacs to whom the infected blood would be supplied. On the other hand, for others, the crime of poisoning has its own *élément moral*, the 'intention to poison', i.e., that a person intentionally administers a substance to a person knowing it to be deadly:[303] as the courts had found that the defendants administered a substance known to be deadly, their lack of motive in seeking its recipients' deaths was irrelevant.[304] However, a third position was suggested by Delmas Saint-Hilaire in the course of a scathing attack on the decision of the Cour d'appel.[305] The Cour d'appel had noted that an intention to kill in murder may be inferred from the circumstances,[306] and continued:

if an intention to kill may be inferred from a person's knowledge of the deadly character of the product which he administers to another, this inference is possible only where the factual circumstances justify it—as is the case where, for example, a relationship of conflict exists between the agent and the victim; . . . it is not the same in the case in hand where the facts in issue belong to the category of a relationship of a manufacturer of a therapeutic product/doctor/patient.[307]

---

[296] *Loi* no. 91-1406 of 31 Dec. 1991, art. 47 on which see S. Durfort, 'La procédure légale d'indemnisation des victimes' in B. Feuillet-Le Mintier (ed.) *Le Sida, Aspects juridiques* (Economica, Paris, 1995), 111; J.-M. Pontier, 'Sida, de la responsabilité à la garantie sociale (à propos de la loi du 31 Décembre 1991)' RDFA 8 (1992) 533.

[297] It was later so decided: Crim. (2) 26 Jan. 1994, Bull. civ. II no. 41. Some of the *parties civiles* were infected by HIV *before* the time when the defendants were aware of its dangers and reliance on *tromperie* avoided the problem of whether their 'sur-contamination' had caused them any harm. On this idea, cf. below, p. 400.　　　　　[298] Trib. corr. Paris 23 Oct. 1992, quoted by Blin, *op. cit.* n. 289, 168.

[299] Trib. corr. Paris 23 Oct. 1992, *cit.*

[300] It fell within a section headed 'Murder, assassination, parricide, infanticide, poisoning' which starts by defining murder as '*homicide commis volontairement*': art. 295 A.C. pén.

[301] Art. 301 A.C. pén. used the phrase 'an attempt on the life' of a person: M. Danti-Juan, 'Sang contaminé, tromperie et empoisonnement. Trop et trop peu n'est pas mésure . . .' in Pradel, *Sang et droit pénal*, 61 at 66.　　　　　[302] Prothais, note, D 1993.222 at 226.

[303] Prothais, ibid., and note D 1994.118; Delmas Saint-Hilaire, *op. cit.* n. 56; *id.*, 'Homicide Assassiné (à propos de l'arrêt de la Cour de Paris rendu le 13 juillet 1993 dans l'affaire dite "du sang contaminé")' GP 1994.1.173.　　　　　[304] Delmas Saint-Hilaire, *op. cit.* n. 56, 54.

[305] *Op. cit.* n. 303.　　　　[306] Above, p. 372.　　　　[307] Paris 31 Jul. 1993, D 1994.118.

According to Delmas Saint-Hilaire, this approach to cases where there was no 'relationship of conflict' was wrong in principle, contrary to established *jurisprudence* and dangerous in its potential effects on the crime of voluntary homicide in general.[308] The Advocate-General of the Cour de cassation, M. Perfetti, came to a similar conclusion,[309] and proposed that the Cour de cassation should send the case for retrial by the Cour d'assises.[310]

However, the Cour de cassation held that the Cours correctionnelles were not entitled to consider whether the *crime* of poisoning had been committed, though this could be considered in separate proceedings.[311] So the convictions stood, but other proceedings on other grounds remained possible.

(b) The second stage: proceedings against government ministers

In the course of the trial of the National Blood Transfusion Centre officers, the two ministers who were responsible for overseeing the National Blood Transfusion Service gave evidence that they were aware in mid-1985 that there was a danger in relation to the blood products being supplied in France,[312] and it had earlier been reported that the *cabinet* of the Prime Minister had delayed approval to a *dépistage* test produced by an American firm from early May to late June 1985, apparently in order to allow a French test to be fine-tuned.[313] As a result, some of those infected with HIV as a result of their receipt of blood products attempted to set in motion a prosecution against the former Prime Minister, M. Laurent Fabius, and two former ministers, Mme. G. Dufoix, the *ministre des Affaires sociales et de la Solidarité nationale*, and M.E. Hervé, the *secrétaire d'Etat chargé de la Santé* in office in 1985 as allegedly criminally responsible for the serious injury and death which the blood products caused.[314] However, under article 68 of the Constitution of the Fifth Republic of 1958 members of the French government could be prosecuted for *crimes* or *délits* committed in the course of their duties only by impeachment ('*mise en accusation*') by both the Assemblée nationale and the Sénat, confirmed by the President of the Republic and, if impeached, would be tried by a specially constituted tribunal, the Haute Cour de justice, composed of an equal number of *deputées* and senators.[315]

Towards the end of 1992 proceedings were commenced under this special procedure against the three ministers for their alleged part in the *affaire* on the charges of failing to assist a person in danger,[316] rather than for involuntary homicide.[317] However, when the case came before the investigating committee (the Commission d'instruction of the Haute Cour, which fulfilled a role somewhat similar to a *juge d'instruction*) the latter

---

[308] *Op. cit.* n. 303, at 175.   [309] *Op. cit.* n. 289, 138–142.   [310] Ibid., 140–2.

[311] Crim. 22 Jun.1994, whose judgment is published in full in Pradel, *Sang et droit pénal*, 171 *et seq.*

[312] J.Y. Chevallier, 'L'affaire du sang contaminé' in Pradel, *Sang et droit pénal*, 23 at 35.

[313] Ibid., 30–2 and see *Le Monde* 11 Sept. 1999.   [314] Blin, *op. cit.* n. 289, 151.

[315] Constitution of 1958, art. 67 (as promulgated).

[316] Under art. 63 al. 2 A.C. pén. now arts 223-6.1 & 223-7 C. pén.

[317] The possibility of charges on this basis had been raised in the Sénat but expressly excluded from the motion by which the special criminal proceedings were commenced: P. Truche, *procureur général* before the Commission d'instruction of the Haute Cour de Justice, *réquisitions* reported in *Droit pénal* Mar. 1993. Chron. no. 8, 3.

held as a preliminary issue that prosecutions for the offences alleged were time-barred as they related to facts more than three years after their occurrence, i.e., at the latest March 1986 when the three ministers left office.[318] For Pradel, this decision was 'embarassing, for it may give the impression to an ill-informed public that justice was stifled',[319] but proper given that 'judges [are] charged with ensuring that the law is respected and not with twisting it according to the advantages of the moment'.[320] Perhaps more open to criticism was the choice of charges brought, for prosecutions for involuntary homicide would not have been time-barred, given that this offence is complete only on the death of its victim and many persons had died as a result of the supply of the infected blood within three years of the proceedings.

However, soon after this decision was made, a Bill was introduced to revise the Constitution so as to remove the criminal responsibility of members of the government (but not of the President of the Republic[321]) from the Haute Cour and place it in the hands of a new special tribunal, the Cour de justice de la République, a change enacted by a *loi constitutionnelle* in July 1993.[322] Under the new arrangements, any person prejudiced by a *crime* or *délit* allegedly committed by a minister in the course of his duties could complain to a special committee composed of judges,[323] which would then decide whether or not to instruct the *procureur général* of the Cour de cassation to bring proceedings before the new court.[324] The new court would consist of twelve members of parliament (six from either chamber) and three judges of the Cour de cassation, one of whom would preside.[325] Unlike its predecessor, the new court must follow the definitions of criminal offences set out in legislation and would be subject to the control of the Cour de cassation.[326] It is to be noted, however, that the victim of any alleged crime would not be able to become party to the proceedings as *partie civile*.[327] This represented a compromise between those who considered that ministers should face only a political responsibility and those who considered that they should face trial in the ordinary courts in the ordinary way.

Given that the new arrangements were retroactive,[328] proceedings under them were set in motion against the same three ministers as before, who were this time charged with the *délit* of involuntary homicide. Some six years later and after some three weeks of trial, the Cour de justice de la République acquitted M. Fabius and Mme. Dufoix, noting that the former had actually accelerated the decision in favour of requiring a *dépistage* test for blood products, but it convicted M. Hervé on the basis that he had failed in his duties under the *Code de la santé publique*, though it did not impose any punishment.[329] The Cour did not pronounce on the significance of the

---

318 Haute Cour de Justice (Commission d'instruction) 5 Feb. 1993, D 1993.261 note Pradel.

319 Ibid., 264.   320 Ibid., 264–5.   321 Constitution of 1958, art. 68.

322 *Loi constitutionnelle* no. 93-952 of 27 Jul. 1993.

323 *Loi organique* no. 93-1251 of 23 Nov. 1993, art. 12.   324 Constitution of 1958, art. 68-1.

325 Ibid., art. 68-2.

326 Ibid., art. 68-1 al. 3; *Loi organique* no. 93-1251 of 23 Nov. 1993, arts. 33, 34.

327 *Loi organique* no. 93-1251 of 23 Nov. 1993, art. 13 al. 2; C. Lienhard 'La Cour de justice de la République et sa procédure à l'épreuve de sa première expérience' JCP 1999.I.505, 506.

328 Constitution of 1958, art. 68-3.

329 Cour de justice de la République 9 Mar. 1999, D 1999 IR 86, and see the comments in *Le Monde*, 10 Mar. 1999, 6–7 which records the size of majority of the votes cast by the judges and comments on the political aspects of the decision.

question of the delay in approving the American test of *dépistage* or on the possible protection of the French test.[330] This decision provoked considerable debate in the public arena as well as within political and legal circles.[331]

(c) The third and final stage: thirty defendants discharged by the Cour d'appel of Paris

However, there remained a third stage in the criminal courts' role in the *affaire*. Various *parties civiles* had instigated further proceedings against senior and junior officers of the National Blood Transfusion Service, against various senior civil servants in the ministries concerned, and against some doctors who had continued to prescribe blood to their patients in the course of 1985. The *juge d'instruction* of Paris finished her investigation in May 1999 and sought to have serious charges brought before the Cour d'assises, including poisoning (against the senior officers of the National Blood Transfusion Services), involuntary homicide and failing to rescue from danger, but the *ministère public* considered that they should be charged with lesser offences and tried by the Tribunal correctionnel. In the meantime, the *loi* of 2000 had intervened, redefining the *élément moral* for non-intentional *délits*: given that the courts accepted that its provisions applied retroactively, counsel for the defendants argued that the charges should be abandoned in the light of its changes.[332] However, when the Chambre d'instruction of the Cour d'appel of Paris gave judgment it did not refer to the changes made by the *loi* of 2000, nor did it choose between the two routes proposed by the *juge d'instruction* and the *ministère public*, but held instead that none of the defendants should face any charges, and that, indeed, no criminal offences had been committed, pronouncing a general *non-lieu*.[333] First, it held that the *doctors* did not commit any crime of poisoning as they did not know at the time that the blood had a *necessarily* fatal character and therefore they could not have had the requisite intention for this crime. Secondly, at the relevant time there remained a doubt as to the capacity of the American firm to supply its *dépistage* test in sufficient quantities for the whole of France and it had not been established that the various officers responsible for the delay in authorising the American test nor those who had continued to collect blood in France had committed a fault or that any such fault had caused any injury. Thirdly, it held, given that the date of contamination of those who became HIV-positive through receipt of the blood products could not be established, that therefore their 'sur-contamination' by contaminated products during the relevant time had not been shown to have any *certain* causal relationship between their injuries or death and any fault in *any* of the defendants. All these decisions were confirmed by the Cour de cassation which treated the issues of the existence of fault and of causation as within the 'sovereign power of assessment' of the *juges du fond*.[334] As a result, the criminal aspect of the *affaire*

---

[330] *Le Monde*, 11 Mar. 1999.

[331] J. Pradel, 'Cour de justice de la République: oui mais . . .' JCP Dernière actualité (15 Apr. 1999) no. 15, 1.   [332] C. Prieur, *Le Monde*, 14 Nov. 2000. On the *loi* of 2000, see above, pp. 389–93.

[333] Paris (Ch. instr.) 4 Jul. 2002, D 2003.164 note Prothais.

[334] Crim. 18 Jun. 2003, Bull. crim. no. 127, JCP 2003.II.10121 note Rassat. And the Cour de cassation declared that 'the crime of poisoning can be constituted only if the defendant has acted with the intention to bring about death, this *élément moral* of poisoning being in common with other voluntary offences against human life'.

du sang contaminé came to an end some 15 years after the first criminal proceedings had commenced. As was to be expected, it was greeted by the recipients of the infected blood with claims that it marked a failure of justice and an editorial in *Le Monde* which regretted that the courts had failed to inquire genuinely into the reasons why, of all the western European countries, France had the highest proportion of transfusional victims of HIV (over 4,000).[335]

5. Conclusion

While the criminal proceedings in the *affaire du sang contaminé* were extraordinary as regards the number of victims and their vulnerability, the number and variety of alleged roles of the accused and the complexity of the proceedings, they have had a profound effect on attitudes to the responsibilities of individuals in government and the administration for safety generally and on product safety and product liability in particular. In the course of the 1990s, attention became very firmly focused on the role of individual victims of the *affaire* in the criminal process in terms of their claims for compensation, but even more in terms of their seeking to establish *responsabilité* according to the crimes which they saw as most appropriate. While their views on the characterisation of the offences were not allowed to go to trial, their power to initiate proceedings in the ordinary criminal courts was crucial to the airing of the *affaire* and their absence was particularly noticeable as regards proceedings in the special criminal tribunals provided by the Constitution for government ministers, whether before or after its amendment.

However, what is particularly interesting from a legal point of view is the consideration given by the courts and even more by French jurists to the problem of the proper characterisation of the criminal liability of a person who supplies a product which he knows has a very high risk of causing death. When death occurs, why is this not murder? For, while murder requires an intention to kill, this is not normally understood as requiring a desire to cause death. For the Cour d'appel of Paris in 1993, the answer lay in the nature of the relationship between the supplier or manufacturer of a product and its recipient, which is not one from which a court should infer an intention to kill even if the product was known to be potentially deadly.[336] And the overall sense of the way in which the criminal proceedings in the *affaire* progressed suggests that the majority judicial view was that even in these circumstances the appropriate way of looking at these sorts of facts was in terms of *faute par imprudence* even if the *faute* should prove a very serious one.

Of more general significance were the changes to the definition of the fault element governing involuntary homicide and causing serious personal injuries made by the *loi* of 2000. While it is as yet difficult to assess with certainty their effect on the substantive basis of the criminal responsibility of manufacturers, suppliers and users of products, they are likely to reduce very considerably the incidence of the criminal responsibility

---

[335] *Le Monde*, 20 Jun. 2003.   [336] Paris 31 Jul. 1993, above, p. 397.

of the public controllers of the safety of products, subjecting it to more onerous tests of fault. Conversely, however, the *loi* of 2000's changes to the institutional relationship between criminal and civil decisions on fault may instead enhance the role of the criminal process in the compensation of personal injuries and death as long as a good case can be made out against *non-administrative* defendants.[337]

Finally, in this discussion I am struck by the pervasive significance of competing constitutional principles. On the one hand, the principle of equal treatment of citizens requires that the substantive criminal law should not distinguish between 'public deciders' and others; but on the other it can distinguish between the responsibilities of local authorities according to whether or not their particularly public functions are in issue.[338] Moreover, while the subjection of the Cour de justice de la République to the ordinary criminal law and control by the Cour de cassation suggests a proper sense of the principle that France is an *Etat de droit*, its distinctive nature both in terms of procedure and composition reflects a residual sense of the separation of powers.

[337] Above, pp. 388–94.   [338] Above, pp. 378–9, 388.

15

English Law: Crime, the Criminal Process and 'Essentially Civil Claims'

English law possesses an elaborate and wide-ranging series of criminal offences which sanction the manufacture or supply of an unsafe product (whether or not it causes personal injury or death) and its criminal courts possess broad powers to order any person convicted of a criminal offence to compensate the victim of the crime.[1] Nevertheless, the criminal law and the criminal process in England play only a very marginal role in providing compensation for accidental death and personal injury, including in cases involving unsafe products. This marks a very striking contrast with the position which I have just described as regards France.

Accounting for the absence of a phenomenon in a legal system as contrasted with its presence in another is often difficult, but the main reason for the relative insignificance of the criminal process in compensating accidental personal injuries and death in England and Wales is fundamentally a simple one: most English lawyers do not see the criminal law as a proper basis nor a criminal court as the proper forum for argument as to the recovery of compensation for harm of this kind—these roles are better performed by the law of torts and the civil courts. Instead, the proper purposes of the criminal law are prevention, deterrence, punishment and (possibly) retribution, and the criminal process's primary concern is with their putting into effect in a just and fair manner: compensation for the victim of the crime remains an afterthought, a possible response to the offender's commission of the crime. These attitudes both reflect and are reflected in the institutions, procedures and practices of English criminal courts.

However, the explanation of how this all takes shape within English law is not as straightforward, for in the same way that there are a number of elements necessary to make the French criminal process significant in awarding compensation, there are a number of elements in English law which prevent it from doing so.[2] First, while in

[1] Below, pp. 404–7, 423–7.

[2] There is a further divorce between compensation and the commission of non-deliberate criminal offences such as those affecting product safety. For, unlike the French criminal injuries compensation scheme (above, p. 367 n. 4) in the UK the Criminal Injuries Compensation Scheme 2001 (made under the Criminal Injuries Compensation Act 1995, ss. 1–6, 12) is all but restricted to 'crimes of violence' (Scheme, para. 8). This concept has been defined as 'any crime in respect of which the prosecution must prove as one of its ingredients that the defendant unlawfully and intentionally or recklessly, inflicted or threatened to inflict personal injury upon another': *R v Criminal Injuries Compensation Board, ex p Webb* [1986] 1 QB 184, 198, *per* Watkins LJ. Moreover, '[t]he mere endangering of safety, without more, does not in itself import violence, whether on the railway or on the factory floor': ibid. at 195. And see A. Ashworth, 'Punishment and Compensation: Victims, Offenders and the State' (1986) 6 *OJLS* 86, 100 *et seq.*

theory any person (including the victim of a crime) may seek to enforce the criminal law by bringing a private prosecution, this traditional right does not exist in relation to many offences, and is otherwise generally subject to control by the prosecuting authorities: private vengeance is not considered to be a proper role of the criminal law or the criminal process.[3] Secondly, the attitude of the primary enforcement authorities in cases of product safety (as with other 'regulatory crime') is one of education and compliance, rather than of prosecution, though the presence of injury weighs in favour of prosecution.[4] Thirdly, while, as I have said, English criminal courts possess wide powers to order a defendant guilty of an offence to compensate its victim of personal injuries, their powers in relation to death are strictly limited. Fourthly, the victim is not a party to the criminal process and has no *right* to compensation. English courts often lack sufficient information to make an award of compensation for personal injuries and they lack the procedural mechanisms to acquire it. And English judges do not consider it appropriate to order compensation for personal injuries except in the most straightforward (and therefore typically least serious) cases.[5] Fifthly, while there are many strict liability offences against product safety, there are no general criminal offences of homicide or causing serious personal injuries based on simple negligence. This has two main consequences on compensation: it affects the size of award of compensation available in principle, the courts' powers differing according to the classification of the offence, and it marginalises the consequences of a defendant's actions and therefore removes the need for evidence of a victim's injuries sufficient to enable a court to order compensation.[6]

In this chapter, I shall, therefore, explain these features of the English system a little more—but by necessity almost without illustration drawn from the context of the responsibility of manufacturers or suppliers in respect of their products. However, the comparison with the French law would, I think, be incomplete without explaining rather more the English law governing homicide, which is so significant and has been so controversial in French law in this context.

1. The Substantive Criminal Law and Product Safety

First, English criminal law remains as yet uncodified, despite proposals from the Law Commission that at least its main elements should be.[7] While in practice the vast majority of the law is statutory (this including all the offences which are special to product safety), some important offences (notably murder, manslaughter and public nuisance) remain fundamentally based on the common law.[8]

Secondly, English lawyers distinguish between the *actus reus* (the event) and the *mens rea* (the state of mind) required for any offence.[9] Within *mens rea*, they

---

[3] Below, p. 419.   [4] Below, pp. 420–1.   [5] Below, pp. 423–7.

[6] Below, pp. 411–14, 425–6.

[7] Law Commission, *A Criminal Code for England and Wales* (1989) Law Com. No. 177.

[8] Sometimes aspects of the crimes have been changed by statute, e.g. the rule for murder that death must occur within a year and a day of an accused's action: Law Reform (Year and a Day Rule) Act 1996.

[9] Smith and Hogan, Chap. 4.

distinguish between intention (to cause specific results), recklessness, negligence and blameless inadvertence; but there is a much greater sophistication than in French law in the tests which have been developed by the courts to identify the different *mens rea* applicable to different offences.[10]

Thirdly, English law does not distinguish sharply between different categories of criminal offence according to their gravity in the way in which French law distinguishes between *crimes*, *délits* and *contraventions*,[11] but it does distinguish according to the nature of the 'mode' of trial which different crimes attract. So, crimes are tried 'on indictment' in the Crown Court (where a jury decides issues of fact if a defendant does not plead guilty to the offence); 'summarily' by a Magistrates' Court (where decisions of law and fact are taken either by a professional judge or by a panel of trained lay adjudicators[12]); and 'either way' as between these two modes of trial, this being decided by the court on the basis of guidelines as to the relative appropriateness of the two modes of trial, though if the court opts for summary trial, the defendant must consent.[13] Broadly speaking, the mode of trial reflects the perceived gravity of the offence and is matched by differences in the sentencing powers of the Crown Court and Magistrates' Courts, but the categories of crime are not as sharply delineated as in French law, nor do they possess the overall definitional differences as are found in the 'fault element' for different criminal offences provided by the French Criminal Code of 1994.[14] English law's relatively broad characterisation of criminal offences also has an impact on their 'labelling': for use of the language of 'crime' or 'criminal offence' to describe parking a vehicle in a legally prohibited place, as well as murder or theft throws much more weight on the social resonance of particular offences. Of these, 'manslaughter' is a particularly striking example, for the relative seriousness with which *involuntary* manslaughter is viewed is in part a function of its application to cases of intentional killing which would count as murder in the absence of particularly excusing circumstances.[15] On the other hand, both the courts and some commentators attempt to distinguish between 'real crimes' (which require intention, such as murder, rape or theft and which tend to originate in the common law) and merely 'quasi-crime' or 'regulatory offences' without the 'disgrace of criminality' (where liability is strict or based on negligence and which are often statutory creations).[16]

(a) Offences special to the product context

There is now a great deal of quite detailed regulation concerning particular types of products (some of which reflects EC legislation) where English law supports the duties which this regulation imposes with criminal sanctions.[17] This type of control has the

---

[10] Ibid., Chap. 5.   [11] Above, p. 369.
[12] These are known as 'stipendiary magistrates' and 'magistrates' respectively.
[13] Smith and Hogan, 23 *et seq.* esp. at 25; Magistrates' Court Act 1980, ss. 17, 19, 20, Sch. 1.
[14] Art. 121-3 C. pén and cf. above, p. 387.   [15] Below, p. 411.
[16] *Sweet v Parsley* [1970] AC 132, 149–150; Smith and Hogan, 125. Cf. Blackstone's distinction between *mala per se* and *mala prohibita* in W. Blackstone, *Commentaries on the Laws of England* (Oxford, 1st. edn., 1765–1769) Book IV, *Public Wrongs*, 8.
[17] For details, see C. J. Miller, M. Mildred and C.G.J. Morse, *Product Liability and Safety Encyclopaedia* (Lexis Publishing, looseleaf) Division IV.

advantages of providing specific guidance to a manufacturer, importer or retailer so as to enable him to avoid the commission of the offence and a further advantage in leaving less room for doubt as to its having been committed so that any prosecution may be successful.[18] Since 1961 the administration has enjoyed a broad power to make regulations governing the safety of particular categories of products, a power now contained in the Consumer Protection Act 1987.[19] Under this Act, any person who supplies another with a product in breach of the regulations commits a summary offence, subject to a defence of being able to show 'due diligence'.[20] This defence, which is becoming standard in the context of product safety,[21] applies where the defendant shows that 'he took all reasonable precautions and exercised all due diligence to avoid the commission of the offence'.[22] The effect of this defence is to place a burden of proof of no negligence on the defendant of a stringent kind: he needs to show that *all* reasonable precautions and *all* due diligence have been taken.[23]

The second type of offence is based on the failure of a product to conform to a broad criterion of safety or quality. This technique was first used in relation to particular classes of products, notably food,[24] but there are now *two* broad offences in English law of supplying consumer products which fail to fulfil a requirement of reasonable safety, one under the Consumer Protection Act 1987[25] and the second under regulations of 1994 choosing to support in this way its implementation of the first EC Directive on General Product Safety,[26] though the regulations disapply the earlier provision to the extent to which it imposes general safety requirements on producers or distributors.[27] So, under the 1987 Act, it is an offence to supply consumer goods in the course of a business which fail to comply with a 'general safety requirement', which is similar but not identical to the test of 'defect' found in the Product Liability Directive;[28] and under the 1994 Regulations, it is an offence to supply 'consumer goods' which are not 'safe'.[29] The main differences between the two offences lie in the definitions of the products which they govern,[30] in the tests of safety,[31] and in those who are caught by the offences.[32] All the offences are triable summarily.[33]

Thirdly, the law governing misleading trade practices can be significant in the context of the safety of products. Since 1968, it has been an offence to apply a false

---

[18] Enforcement authorities look to a very high degree of likelihood of a conviction before bringing criminal proceedings: P. Cartwright, 'Defendants in Consumer Protection Statutes: A Search for Consistency' (1996) *MLR* 225, 227.   [19] Consumer Protection Act 1961, s. 1; 1987 Act, s. 11.

[20] 1987 Act, ss. 12(1) and (5), 39(1) and (5).

[21] 1987 Act, s. 10; Trade Descriptions Act 1968, s. 21(4)(b); Food Safety Act 1990, s. 21(1).

[22] 1987 Act, s. 39(1).

[23] Cf. the application of a similar defence under the 1987 Act, s. 12(6) in *Rotherham MBC v Raysun UK Ltd* (1989) 8 Tr L 6 and see *Tesco Supermarkets Ltd v Nattrass* [1972] AC 153.

[24] For the history see *Cranston's Consumers and the Law*, 318 *et seq.*   [25] 1987 Act, s. 10.

[26] General Product Safety Regulations 1994 SI 1994 No. 2328, r. 12 implementing Dir. 92/59/EEC of 29 Jun. 1992. At the time of writing, the UK has not implemented the General Product Safety Directive 2001/95/EC of 3 Dec. 2001.   [27] General Product Safety Regulations 1994, r. 5.

[28] 1987 Act, ss. 10(2), 46(5) and cf. below, p. 481.   [29] 1994 Regulations, r. 2 and r. 10(2).

[30] Cf. 1987 Act, s. 10(4); 1994 Regulations, r. 2.   [31] 1987 Act, ss. 10(2), 19(1),

[32] 1987 Act, s. 10(1) ('supplier' and persons preparing to supply); 1994 Regulations, 2(1) ('distributors' and 'producers'). For further discussion, see *Cranston's Consumers and the Law*, 395 *et seq.*

[33] 1987 Act, s. 12; 1994 Regulations, r. 17.

trade description on goods and to supply or offer to supply any falsely described goods.[34] These are offences of strict liability (as they require no intention to deceive), but possess a defence of 'due diligence',[35] but unlike the offences which I have so far mentioned, they are triable 'either way'.[36] However, unlike the French offences of *tromperie* and *falsification*, these offences have not played an important part in relation to product safety, in part because the 'description' of goods has not been extended to knowing silence[37] and in part because their 'primary concern ... is not with the condition or the quality of the goods themselves, but with the possibility that a buyer may be misled by a trade description which makes them look better than they really are'.[38] On occasion, though, they have been used, for example, to sanction the sale of a car for use on the road described by the trial judge as 'a potential death-trap'.[39]

(b) Offences not special to the product context

In the French context, general crimes of negligent homicide and causing personal injuries play a very important part in the prominence of claims for compensation being brought in the criminal courts by way of *action civile*.[40] Here, English law is strikingly different from the *traditional* French approach, though not quite as far from its approach after reform of the law in 2000.

(i) Murder

In the *affaire du sang contaminé*, some of the *parties civiles* argued that the administration of a product to a person knowing that it was highly likely to kill was 'poisoning' and so akin to murder, but the courts refused to find the requisite intention to kill in this situation.[41] While the matter has not been tried in the context of the supply of a lethal product, there are also similar types of difficulty in the English law approach to the *mens rea* for murder. In looking at this law, it is important to realise that, in making their formulations, English judges have very much in mind that they need to be comprehensible to laymen, as they form the basis of questions put by trial judges to juries.

A good starting point is that the requisite intention for murder is satisfied where it was the defendant's *purpose* to kill the victim or that he foresaw that death is virtually certain to follow from the act or omission in question,[42] but English law then adds (some say, unjustifiably) that a person who intends to commit 'grievous' (that is, very

---

[34] Trade Descriptions Act 1968, s. 1.   [35] Ibid., s. 24.

[36] Ibid. This is also true of the important offences governing product safety in the workplace. The Health and Safety at Work Act 1974, s. 6 (as amended) creates a general duty on manufacturers and other distributors to supply articles and substances for use at work which are safe 'so far as is reasonably practicable' and whose breach may be tried on indictment after service of 'improvement' or 'prohibition' notices (ibid., ss. 21, 22, 33(2A)). Offences against regulations under this Act are also triable either way (ibid., ss. 15(6)(a), 33(1)(c) and 33(3)). More recently, the prosecution of offences under this Act has led to trial on indictment and heavy fines in serious cases: e.g. Thames Trains was convicted of offences under this Act and fined £2 million: The Times, 6 Apr. 2004.

[37] *Cottee v Douglas Seaton (Used Cars) Ltd.* [1972] 1 WLR 1408, 1415.

[38] Ibid., 1416. Cf. above, pp. 370–1

[39] *R v Nash* (9 August, 1990) *Trading Standards Review* (1991) 24.   [40] Above, pp. 372–7.

[41] Above, pp. 395–8.   [42] Ashworth, *Principles*, 262.

serious) bodily harm and actually causes death is also guilty of murder (this being an example of 'constructive intention').[43] In *R v Maloney*[44] while Lord Bridge was careful to exclude from the *mens rea* of murder mere recklessness (where an accused foresaw to a high degree of probability that death or really serious injury would result from his act), he accepted that recklessness could provide evidence of the requisite intention from which a jury would be entitled to draw an inference of the existence of intention to kill.[45] Some writers supported this on the basis that '[b]y giving jurors this "elbow-room" in cases where death or serious harm was foreseen as certain, one naturally allows the jury to move from a fact-finding exercise to a strongly evaluative decision about whether the label of murder is appropriate for the killing'.[46] The current approach is to be found in *R v Woollin* where the proper direction to the jury was put in terms of being 'not entitled to [find] the necessary intention, unless they feel sure that death or serious bodily harm was a virtual certainty (barring unforeseen intervention) as a result of the defendant's action and that the defendant appreciated that such was the case'.[47]

How do these approaches compare to that taken in French law and how would they apply to facts such as the *affaire du sang contaminé*? First, putting aside the situation of 'constructive intention', there is a striking similarity in the approaches to the *élément moral* for murder in French law. The court found that the relevant officers of the French National Blood Transfusion Centre were aware that the continued supply of the products for which they were responsible would cause infection with HIV and that this was the causal agent of AIDS which could kill, but that their purpose in permitting the continued supply was saving money.[48] While the French discussion is complicated by the arguably distinct nature of the crime of poisoning from murder, some jurists consider that knowledge of the deadly nature of the substance administered and an intentional administration of it is sufficient,[49] which is similar to the approach in *R v Woollin* since the (known) deadliness of a substance would often make death a 'virtual certainty'.[50] The Cour de cassation, however, requires the Cour d'assises to find (in its 'sovereign assessment') an 'intention to kill', though it permits it to *infer* an intention to kill from the circumstances.[51] This approach has considerable similarity with that advocated by Lord Bridge in *Maloney*, as it leaves to the tribunal of fact the question whether an intention to kill should be inferred or (as the House of Lords in *Woollin* preferred) 'found'.

There are, moreover, echoes in English discussions of the observations made by the Cour d'appel of Paris in the *affaire du sang contaminé* which considered that it was

---

[43] Smith and Hogan, 359–60; *R. v Cunningham* [1982] AC 566; *A.–G. Ref. (No. 3 of 1994)* [1998] 1 Cr App 91, 93. This is treated in French law as the distinct crime of assault causing death: art. 222-7 C. pén.

[44] [1985] AC 905.   [45] Ibid., 925–6; *Frankland and Moore v R* [1987] AC 576 (PC).

[46] J. Horder, 'Intention in the Criminal Law—A Rejoinder' (1995) 58 *MLR* 678, 688.

[47] [1999] 1 AC 82, 96. The word in square brackets was substituted by Lord Steyn in the formula used by Lord Lane CJ in *R v Nedrick* [1986] 1 WLR 1025, 1028.   [48] Above, p. 395.

[49] Above, p. 397. English law contains a distinct offence of administering 'a noxious thing:' Offences against the Person Act 1861, s. 23. In the case of an intentional direct administration of a noxious thing there is no need for foresight of danger to life or the infliction of grievous bodily harm: *R v Cato* [1976] 1 WLR 110, although in the case of indirect injury, *advertent* recklessness is required: *R v Cunningham* [1957] 2 QB 396.   [50] Above, (this page).

[51] Paris 31 Jul. 1993, D 1994.18 note Prothais and see Crim. 18 Jun. 2003, Bull. crim. no. 127, above, pp. 372, 397–8, 400.

wrong to infer an intention to kill in a relationship such as in the case of the 'relation-ship of a manufacturer of a therapeutic product/doctor/patient' where there was no 'relationship of conflict'.[52] For example, Horder puts the case of a doctor administering to her patient a treatment which itself involves a very high risk of death, but which constitutes the only chance of cure: this would be not be murder, nor indeed would the patient's death be unlawful, for 'everything hinges on the doctor's direct intention'—to kill or to cure.[53] The (potential) value of the defendant's purposive conduct rules out criminal responsibility even in respect of an intentional action which is virtually certain to lead to death (though one may think that where death was a 'virtual certainty' a doctor would not undertake such a treatment).

How then would an English court view a case similar to the position of the officer of the National Blood Transfusion Centre in the *affaire du sang contaminé*, that is, where a defendant's direct purpose in continuing to supply a product is not to kill its recipi-ents, but to save money, but where he is aware that it is 'virtually certain' that a considerable number of its recipients will die as a result? Here, the defendant's direct purpose was not especially valuable (for example, to attempt to save life or relieve from pain[54]); in these circumstances, an English judge would have to go beyond the direc-tion as to a direct intention to kill and give a *Woollin* direction, so that the jury would be instructed that they should not convict unless they feel sure that death or serious bodily harm was a virtual certainty (barring unforeseen intervention) as a result of the defendant's action and that the defendant appreciated that such was the case. On the facts of the hypothetical case, a jury may well be entitled to convict.

Moreover, if we change the facts slightly (but significantly) it becomes apparent that there is a relationship here with manslaughter by gross negligence. Let us take a hypothetical case modelled loosely on the Ford Pinto prosecution in America.[55] A large manufacturer of motor vehicles markets a saloon car towards the lower end of the market. After some 12.5 million models of the car are put on the market, the manu-facturer realises that its fuel system design will cause an estimated 180 burn deaths, 180 serious burn injuries and 2,100 burned vehicles.[56] It further estimates that the cost to itself of these deaths and damage would be £49.5 million, whereas the cost of recall and replacement of the fuel systems would be £11 per vehicle, i.e. £137 million. The manufacturer therefore decides on a (financial) cost/benefit ratio from its point of view that it would be cheaper to allow the deaths and injuries (and pay damages) rather than to recall the product. In these circumstances, it could be argued that the manufacturer *murdered* any person who dies as a result of the fuel system of the vehicle in question, for while it was not the purpose of the manufacturer to bring about this result, it was aware that *somebody's* death would be the 'virtually certain' result of its

---

[52] Above, p. 397.   [53] *Op. cit.* n. 46, 681.

[54] On the assumption that uncontaminated blood products could have been obtained.

[55] On these proceedings see F. Cullen, W. Maakestad, and G. Cavender, 'The Ford Pinto Case and Beyond: Corporate Crime, Moral Boundaries and the Criminal Sanction' in E. Hochstedler (ed.) *Corporations as Criminals* (Sage Publications, California, 1984) 107.

[56] Cf. the memorandum of the Ford Motor Company made in respect of the Pinto fuel system design, reproduced in W. Page Keeton, D.G. Owen and J.E. Montgomery, *Products Liability and Safety, Cases and Materials* (Mineola, New York, 1980) 490.

decision not to recall the vehicles, even though this could not be said of any individual person.

However, the question can be made more difficult (and the manufacturer's position stronger) if we assume that the manufacturer's decision was not merely cost-efficient to *itself*, but also constituted 'reasonable care' under the cost/benefit analysis of the tort of negligence (which does *not* rest merely on financial utility to the defendant, but on an overall assessment of the costs (in terms of finance but also the social utility of the defendant's conduct as against the risk).[57] Where a manufacturer or supplier of a product acts reasonably in this sense, but knows that its action will be 'virtually certain' to cause someone's death (even if that person cannot be predicted or identified), is this murder?[58] The answer should perhaps be no, on the basis that if a person is judged to have acted without negligence, that is, taking all reasonable care that the law requires of a person in the circumstances, it would be wrong to say that he 'murdered' a person who died as a result. For it could be argued that the negligence formula is not merely a basis for the imposition of liability in damages: it reflects a judicial assessment of the proper decision to have been made by a person in the defendant's position and so where a defendant has acted properly, it would be pointless and unfair to punish and deter. How can a defendant's action in this situation be murder when the relevant example of the lesser offence of involuntary manslaughter requires 'gross' negligence?[59] It may instead, though, be argued that this puts too much weight on the *civil* law's understanding of negligence and not enough on the criminal law's more 'subjective' concerns.

However, if the non-negligent manufacturer in the case just outlined should not be considered to have murdered the people who are 'virtually certain' to die as a result of his design decisions, one should perhaps openly acknowledge that the reason why the fault element for murder should be restricted in the context of the manufacture and distribution of products to its primary significance of the purpose with which an action is made flows from the nature of that context. In the context of products more generally, the civil law of negligence rests on an assumption that no product can be *absolutely* safe and where a manufacturer has balanced correctly the considerations to be taken into account in deciding the appropriate level of safety, conduct which implements the resulting view should not be sanctioned *solely* on the ground that there was a high statistical likelihood of it causing death: a high probability and a likely serious harm are very important factors in deciding negligence, but have to be weighed against the cost (financial and social) of avoidance. Only where a manufacturer's conduct falls so far short of that proper balance should it be incriminated, a result which can be made in terms of 'gross negligence' under the law of manslaughter. On the other hand, the idea that the criminal law allows a manufacturer or supplier of

---

[57] Above, pp. 193–200.

[58] Cf. the facts of *Smith v Dept. of Health* [2002] EWHC 200 (QB), 67 BMLR 34, above, pp. 354–6 where the Department was held to have acted *without* negligence even though it knew that its delay in recalling the product was highly likely to cause severe illness or death.

[59] It may, though, be argued that these facts should not be murder, not because of the absence of the requisite *mens rea*, but because of the presence of some justificatory defence, such as necessity: cf. *Re A* [2000] 4 All ER 961.

a product to take *conscious* decisions which it is aware are overwhelmingly likely to lead to *some* people's deaths remains a very uncomfortable one, as it seems to put far too low a value on human life.

(ii) Manslaughter

Next to the French law of involuntary homicide, the English offence of manslaughter is a serious crime with very serious associations. For, while it can apply to cases of involuntary homicide (that is, where the defendant has no intention to kill as understood above), it also applies to many cases of voluntary homicide whose circumstances are seen as justifying a degree of diminution not merely in sentencing but in the characterisation of the offence: where there is provocation, 'diminished responsibility' or a suicide pact.[60]

Somewhat isolated examples exist in the nineteenth century law reports of the application of manslaughter to the provision of unsafe products. For example, in *R v Kempson*, in 1893 a farmer supplied the carcass of a diseased animal to market for human consumption.[61] In the circumstances, Pollock B found the farmer so grossly negligent as to be guilty of manslaughter of a person who died as a result of consuming the animal's meat.[62] However, overall manslaughter has not been a ground of conviction for the manufacture or supply of unsafe products which have caused death, for the understanding of its *mens rea* has not lent itself to application in the context of health and safety, including product safety.

After the decision of the House of Lords in *R v Adomako*,[63] there are two ways in which the requisite mental element in involuntary manslaughter may be fulfilled: by the use of 'unlawful means' and by 'gross negligence'.[64]

At the very first look, 'unlawful means' manslaughter looks rather like the French law of involuntary homicide, which sometimes allows the 'fault element' to be provided by the breach of a legal or regulatory duty, but this is a false impression. For, under this heading it is manslaughter if the defendant intended to do an act[65] which, whether he knows it or not, is unlawful and objectively dangerous in the sense of being likely to cause personal injury and direct harm is caused.[66] A clear example of this test being fulfilled is where a defendant intended to assault the victim (but not to kill), and the victim dies.[67] The courts have showed their discomfort with this form of 'constructive' *mens rea* which finds the intention for one crime in the intention for another, by defining 'unlawful' narrowly and in particular by holding that neither civil nor even *criminal* negligence is enough.[68] While some commentators have suggested that breaches of safety regulations which have caused death could be sanctioned by

---

[60] Smith and Hogan, 363 *et seq*. For the French law, see above, pp. 372–4, 387–93.

[61] (1893) 28 Law J 477. Cf. *R v Gregory* (1860) 2 F & F 153 (accident at work involving unsafe product).

[62] He was also held guilty of public nuisance, see below, pp. 414–16.   [63] [1995] 1 AC 171.

[64] Smith and Hogan, 378 *et seq*.

[65] It is less clear whether an omission of something which a defendant had to do will be enough: Smith and Hogan, 383; *R v Lowe* [1974] QB 702 and Law Commission, *Legislating the Criminal Code, Involuntary Manslaughter*, Law Com. No. 237 (1996) paras. 3.14–3.16.

[66] Smith and Hogan, 379–85.   [67] Law Com. No. 237, paras. 2.3–2.7.

[68] *Andrews v DPP* [1937] AC 576 (dangerous driving).

manslaughter under this heading,[69] the general unpopularity of 'unlawful act' manslaughter is reflected in the recommendation by the Law Commission that it should be abolished.[70]

Secondly, *Adomako* established that the *mens rea* for manslaughter may be fulfilled by showing the defendant's 'gross negligence'.[71] *Adomako* concerned an anaesthetist convicted of manslaughter in relation to his treatment of a patient during surgery, though in the Court of Appeal the case had been joined with two other medical homicide cases and one which concerned an electrician's responsibility for the death of a householder electrocuted by mis-wiring.[72] In giving judgment for the House of Lords, the Lord Chancellor, Lord Mackay held that 'ordinary principles of the law of negligence' should apply so as to ascertain whether a defendant owed the deceased a duty of care; whether there was a breach of that duty; and whether that breach caused the deceased's death.[73] However, as to the fault element in the criminal context:

[t]he essence of the matter which is supremely a jury question is whether having regard to the risk of death involved, the conduct of the defendant was so bad in all the circumstances as to amount in their judgment to a criminal act or omission.[74]

On the other hand, it is not clear quite how the gross negligence issue should be understood. The Lord Chancellor's reference to the 'ordinary principles of the law of negligence' suggests that the proper *standard of care* is objective even as regards criminal negligence, and this is confirmed by his later reference to the standard of a 'reasonably competent doctor'.[75] This has been criticised, though, on the basis that in the criminal context the standard of care ought to be more subjective, taking into account a defendant's mental and physical capabilities.[76]

However, it must be said that despite the simplification of the test of *mens rea* for manslaughter after *Adomako*, prosecutors have continued to be reluctant to charge and juries to convict in respect of deaths caused by failures in health and safety, as can be seen in a number of high-profile cases arising out of disasters.[77] Moreover, in the context of a manufacturer or supplier of a product, in order to convict a jury would have to be satisfied that a 'grossly negligent' decision was made 'to the point of criminality' in a context where the negligence itself consisted of the balancing of a complex of factors, some of which may involve scientific aspects of some uncertainty.

---

[69] N. Lacey, C. Wells and D. Meure, *Reconstructing Criminal Law* (1st. edn., 1990) 243.

[70] Law Com. No. 237, paras. 5.14–5.16.

[71] Early case law indicated that any lack of care would be enough, but the nineteenth century judges began to require 'gross negligence': *Andrews v DPP* [1937] AC 576, 581–2. Since the 1950s, special statutory offences have been available to deal with death caused by driving a motor vehicle ('motor manslaughter'): Road Traffic Act 1988, s. 1 ('causing death by dangerous driving') and s. 2 ('dangerous driving') (as substituted by Road Traffic Act 1991).

[72] *R v Prentice, R v Sullmann, R v Adomako, R v Holloway* [1994] QB 302.

[73] [1995] 1 AC 171, 187.

[74] Ibid. And see *R v Misra* [2004] EWCA Crim 2375, The Times, 13 October 2004 where it was held that the test of gross negligence manslaughter was not unacceptably uncertain for the purposes of art. 7, ECHR.   [75] Ibid. at 188.

[76] Ashworth, *Principles*, 193–6.

[77] M. Jefferson, 'Corporate Criminal Liability in the 1990s' 64 *J Crim Law* 106.

Given this, it is not surprising that there have been *no* recent prosecutions for manslaughter of manufacturers or suppliers of unsafe products which have caused death.[78]

This position contrasts strikingly with French law, both before and after the reform of the law of involuntary homicide in 1996 and 2000. Before these reforms, French courts convicted defendants for involuntary homicide on the very slightest of faults, including where they had merely broken strict safety obligations.[79] Moreover, while the reform of 1996 was intended to give exactly the 'subjective' twist to the standard of negligence in criminal cases which has been suggested for English law, in the hands of French judges this appears to make little difference.[80] At first sight the much more significant changes to the French law made in 2000 as regards injury or death caused indirectly by individuals which required *either* deliberate breach of a legal duty of safety or 'aggravated fault' look as though it is drawing closer to the English law of manslaughter by 'gross negligence':[81] they certainly have in common that the 'fault element' rests on a very serious fault assessed by bodies with considerable room for 'assessment' (the *juges du fond* and the English jury). However, here the similarities cease. For, first, while both *juges du fond* and jury have room for assessment in deciding the degree of fault serious enough to justify a conviction, they are *very* different bodies acting in *very* different institutional and procedural contexts, not least, the Tribunal correctionnel and Cour d'appel being composed of professional judges, the jury entirely lay. The different make-up of the bodies is clearly reflected in the fact that the English judges are concerned to express the law by way of formulating 'jury directions', such as the ones in *Woollin* and *Adomako*,[82] of which there is no need in the French context. Secondly, in the French context, the special faults required for involuntary homicide form an exception to a general picture where for a century the slightest fault has been enough to ground criminal responsibility (and civil liability), an exception created for a very particular purpose (the protection of public decision makers).[83] Thirdly, the relatively less serious nature of the French offence is reflected in the classification of involuntary homicide as a *délit*[84] with a maximum punishment of three years' imprisonment rising to five years maximum in its aggravated form,[85] whereas manslaughter is tried on indictment and (if the defendant does not plead guilty) by jury and bears a maximum of life imprisonment.[86] Therefore, while the formal descriptions in French or in English law of 'gross fault' sufficient to attract involuntary homicide or manslaughter may look similar, their application in the two systems is likely to be very different, though to a degree which is hard to establish given the nature of their adjudication.

---

[78] On 21 May 2003 the then Home Secretary, David Blunkett announced a new offence of 'corporate killing' with the intention to draft a bill which would rest liability on a management failure by a corporation which is one of the causes of a person's death, that failure consisting of 'conduct falling far below what can reasonably be expected of the corporation in the circumstances'. At the time of writing, this has not been brought into law. [79] Above, pp. 372–4.

[80] Above, pp. 387–8, 412.   [81] Above, pp. 388–92.

[82] Above, pp. 408, 412.   [83] Above, pp. 388–9.   [84] Above, p. 369.

[85] Art. 221-6 C. pén., above, p. 372. The aggravated form occurs where the defendant has 'manifestly deliberately' broken a particular legal duty of safety or care.

[86] Offences Against the Person Act 1861, s. 5.

Moreover, even after the legislative changes to the substantive French criminal law and to the procedural relationship between criminal responsibility and civil liability made in 2000, in many cases of involuntary homicide the French actors (*ministères publics* and judges, defendants and their insurers, and the victims themselves and their insurers) still have in mind the role of the criminal process in ensuring compensation as well as imposing penalties. And, as a result, *responsabilité civile* will remain coloured by its remaining doctrinal and procedural links with *responsabilité pénale*. By contrast, even after *Adomako*, the English definitions of the *mens rea* of manslaughter prevent the vast majority of cases of death caused by failures in health and safety from going before the criminal courts and therefore from the possibility of the courts' exercising their (strictly limited) powers to award compensation for death. This reflects English lawyers' much stronger sense of the distinctive natures of criminal responsibility and civil liability.

(iii) Negligence causing personal injuries

French law contains offences of the involuntary causing of personal injuries, graded according to the seriousness of their results, with the same *élément moral* as for involuntary homicide, without which French criminal courts could not award damages for personal injuries.[87] English and French law here are even more different than are their respective laws of homicide. For while English law possesses offences of intentional causing of personal injuries very broadly similar to the French whose seriousness depends on the degree of harm which is caused,[88] it recognises *no* crimes of negligent or even grossly negligent causing of personal injuries: the widest understanding of the fault element being what is termed *Cunningham* recklessness, that is, where the defendant was aware of an unreasonable risk.[89] This absence of any intermediate crimes of negligence causing personal injuries places the prosecution of negligence causing personal injuries into the special 'regulatory' offences of health and safety, with the possible exception of public nuisance.[90]

(iv) The crime of public nuisance

Public nuisance was the common law's answer to the control of the health and safety of the population, though it dealt and still potentially deals with a bewildering range of other situations. The enforcement of public nuisance was often by way of 'relator' action by the Attorney-General rather than by prosecution and by the end of the nineteenth century this civil mechanism had in practice supplanted the criminal route.[91] The modern definition of the crime of public nuisance is very wide: 'an act not warranted by law or an omission to discharge a legal duty, which act or omission

---

[87] Above, p. 372.

[88] So, notably, battery, assault occasioning 'actual bodily harm', 'wounding' and causing 'grievous bodily harm': Offences against the Person Act 1861, ss. 18, 20, 47.

[89] *R v Spratt* [1990] 1 WLR 1073; *R v Cunningham* [1957] 2 QB 396.

[90] This is true even of road traffic offences, where there is an offence of 'dangerous driving' which rests on the taking of a risk of personal injuries, rather than on their occurrence, above, n. 71.

[91] J.R. Spencer, 'Public Nuisance—a Critical Examination' (1989) 48 *CLJ* 55, 74. On the civil aspect of public nuisance, see above, pp. 224–5.

obstructs or causes inconvenience or damage to the public in the exercise of rights common to all [Her] Majesty's subjects'.[92] The offence is 'triable either way'[93] and punishable with an unlimited fine and a maximum of life imprisonment.[94]

Before the creation of the many special offences relating to the safety of products, public nuisance was sometimes used to prosecute those who supplied them, notably in cases relating to food. By the later nineteenth century, it was established that this offence required knowledge on the part of the supplier that the meat was diseased and an intention or belief that it would be sold for human consumption.[95] However, many other cases of the distribution of unsafe products *could* fall within the very broad definition of public nuisance and its potential for serious punishment might appear to make it appropriate where products have caused widespread or serious harm to the public.

However, there are few examples of its use for this purpose, the 'Camelford Water' case being a striking exception. There the water supply in a small town in Cornwall was contaminated when 20 tons of aluminium sulphate were accidentally emptied into a water system by a delivery driver.[96] The water was supplied at the time by a public corporation to some 20,000 people of whom some 180 people suffered ill health.[97] The corporation was prosecuted by the local authority, convicted and fined £10,000 with £25,000 costs by the Exeter Crown Court for public nuisance in respect of the supply of contaminated water,[98] rather than merely the lesser statutory offence of failing to take all reasonable care to provide a supply of wholesome water, contrary to the Water Act 1945. Clearly, in this case, the local authority which brought the prosecution considered that the case deserved the more serious label of public nuisance and trial by jury, rather than the less serious 'regulatory offence'. However, the Crown Court did not exercise its power to award compensation to those who suffered from the contamination: these claims were the subject of separate proceedings in the civil courts.[99]

However, the crime of public nuisance has been little used to sanction the supplier of unsafe products, in part because of its own uncertainties (for example, in relation to its *mens rea*),[100] its extraordinary breadth and a sense that it is redundant given modern, particular legislation.[101] So public nuisance *could* provide a general offence of 'doing anything which creates a major hazard to the physical safety or health of the public' so as to fill any accidental gaps in statutory regulation,[102] or a more serious

---

[92] Stephen's *Digest of the Criminal Law* (9th ed., 1950) 179 quoted with approval in *R v Shorrock* [1993] 3 All ER 917, 920.   [93] Magistrates' Courts Act 1980, s. 17(1), Sch. 1.

[94] Spencer, *op. cit.* n. 91, 77.

[95] *R v Jarvis, R v Crawley* (1862) 3 F & F 109. See similarly, *R v Stevenson* (1862) 3 F & F 106 (though the conviction appeared also justified on medieval statutes). In *Shillito v Thompson* [1875] 1 QBD 12 the independence of the common law offence was recognised.

[96] For the facts of the case, see the later civil proceedings which concerned the availability of exemplary damages, *AB and others v South West Water Services Ltd.* [1993] QB 507.

[97] These harms were the basis of the claims in *AB v South West Water Services Ltd.*, ibid.

[98] Exeter Crown Court, 8 January 1991, The Times 9 Jan. 1991. Cf. the much earlier case *R v Medley*, (1834) 6 C & P 292.

[99] Claims for damages for personal injuries were settled by the corporation, and in *AB and others v South West Water Services Ltd. cit.* their claim for *punitive* damages was rejected.

[100] Smith and Hogan, 775.   [101] Spencer, *op. cit.*, n. 91, 77.   [102] Ibid., at 84.

sanction of behaviour which constitute lesser statutory offences, but in general the prosecuting authorities have not seen either of these possibilities as desirable.

(c) The defendants

(i) Corporations

Since the 1840s English law has recognised that corporations as well as natural persons may be held criminally responsible,[103] but the ways in which it attributes criminal responsibility (sometimes in combination with the definitions of the crimes themselves) sometimes make its imposition problematic. English law distinguishes between the vicarious and personal criminal liability of companies and within the latter between cases where the company in law commits an offence and where offences are committed by the individuals who control the company.

First, at common law employers are vicariously criminally liable only where their employees commit the crimes of criminal libel or public nuisance, in striking contrast to their vicarious civil liability, which is imposed in respect of any tort committed in the course of employment.[104] This means, for example, that where a company employs a person who commits an act of public nuisance in the course of his employment, the company is also guilty of the crime.[105] This special treatment has been criticised as anomalous.[106]

Secondly, companies can be held to commit *in law* the conduct criminalised by a particular offence: the classic example, and one of obvious application to products, is where a company's employee *physically* sells a product to someone, but the sale is held *legally* to be his employer's. Here, if the offence in question is one of strict liability (in the sense here of lack of proof of intention or recklessness) then the company may be convicted without more.[107] However, this approach is restricted to statutory offences, is dependent on judicial construction of the statute and has been of most importance where the offence is one of strict liability, for otherwise the requisite fault element of the offence must be shown on the part of the employee/company.[108]

Thirdly, a company may be directly criminally liable in respect of offences committed by those company officers who 'represent the directing mind and will of the company and control what it does'.[109] Under this principle of identification, a company can be criminally responsible for any type of crime committed by its responsible officers. Unfortunately, it is not clear which company employees count as 'responsible officers' for this purpose, the speeches in the leading case in the House of Lords, if strictly applied, leading to different results.[110] It includes a company's managing director and

---

[103] For a general account, see Smith and Hogan, 201 *et seq.*; C. Wells, *Corporations and Criminal Responsibility* (OUP, 2nd. edn., 1998) and for its application to manslaughter: Law Com. No. 237 (1996) Part VI.   [104] Above, p. 165.

[105] *R v Great North of England Rly. Co.* (1846) 9 QB 315.

[106] Smith and Hogan, 202.   [107] *Coppen v Moore (No. 2)* [1898] 2 QB 306.

[108] Law Commission, Consultation Paper no. 135, 92.

[109] *H. L. Bolton (Engineering) Co. Ltd. v T. J. Graham & Sons Ltd.* [1957] 1 QB 159, 172, *per* Lord Denning MR; *Tesco Supermarkets Ltd. v Nattrass* [1972] AC 153, 171.

[110] *Tesco Supermarkets Ltd. v Nattrass* [1972] AC 153; Law Com. No 237, para. 6.35–6.36.

perhaps some of its other higher officers, but does not include a more junior manager who is merely in control of the way in which the company acted in a particular context or on a physical site,[111] or a mere employee or 'worker'.

This has been a very controversial route for the imposition of criminal responsibility, in particular as regards its inability to attribute criminal responsibility for manslaughter to companies in contexts of failures of health and safety.[112] This has led the Law Commission to recommend that there should be a distinct criminal offence of 'corporate killing'.[113] However, imposing corporate criminal responsibility on the basis of the *mens rea* of the 'controlling officers' also causes difficulties where an offence is one of 'strict liability' but includes a defence of due diligence, such as is found in many product safety offences.[114] For example, in *Tesco Supermarkets Ltd. v Nattrass*, a nationwide supermarket company was charged with the offence under section 11 of the Trade Descriptions Act 1968 of offering for sale at one of its stores goods at a price less than they were in fact being offered.[115] This offence did not require any dishonest intention, but it provided a defence where the 'commission of the offence was due . . . to the act or default of another person' and the defendant had taken 'all reasonable precautions and exercised all due diligence to avoid the commission of such an offence by himself or any person under his control'.[116] As the local manager of the store in question was not one of the controlling officers of the company and therefore could be 'another person' *vis-à-vis* the company, the latter could excuse itself subject to more general proof of due diligence. *Tesco* therefore encourages a large company which has set in place an appropriately 'diligent' corporate system, to devolve functions to lower managers safe in the knowledge that any failure in their implementation will not redound to the company's responsibility: indeed, some consider that 'the *Tesco* decision . . . emasculated the liability of corporations for breaches of consumer protection law'.[117]

(ii) Human defendants

While French law rejected the criminal responsibility of *personnes morales*, their *dirigeants* were left in the firing line and this remains true in those areas where the corporation remains immune, as in the case of the local authorities' powers of health and safety. This criminalisation of elected officials led to the change of the substantive definition of involuntary homicide for individual 'decision makers',[118] which has left

---

[111] *Tesco Supermarkets Ltd. v Nattrass, cit.* (the manager of a local supermarket belonging to a national company).

[112] E.g. prosecutions in respect of the sinking of the 'Herald of Free Enterprise' at Zeebrugge: *R v Coroner for East Kent, ex p Spooner* (1989) 88 Cr App Rep 10; *R v P & O European Ferries (Dover) Ltd.* (1991) 93 Cr App R 72. When this case finally went to trial, the judge directed the jury to acquit all the defendants including the company: *R v Stanley and others*, 19 October 1990 and see the Law Com. no. 135, 101. There is a considerable critical literature: see Jefferson, *op. cit.* n. 77; C.M.V. Clarkson, 'Kicking Corporate Bodies and Damning Their Souls' (1996) *MLR* 557. For the possible offence of 'corporate killing' see above, n. 78.   [113] Law Com. no. 237, Part. VIII.

[114] *Cranston's Consumers and the Law*, 329–32.   [115] [1972] AC 153.

[116] Trade Descriptions Act 1968, s. 24(1).   [117] *Cranston's Consumers and the Law*, 334.

[118] Above, pp. 387–9.

more junior employees more likely to being charged.[119] In English law, a finding of criminal responsibility on the part of a company does not preclude its officers or employees from being held liable in respect of their own criminal acts, and in regulatory offences it is often explicitly provided that a senior manager can also be liable if the company's offence was committed with his consent or as a reason of his neglect.[120] However, there has been a general tendency in health and safety contexts for any prosecutions to be brought against the company.[121]

(d) Concluding remarks

Overall, therefore, English law possesses a very considerable range of criminal offences available to sanction the supply of unsafe products, but the vast majority of those which are in practice available have four key features.

First, they are statutory offences either of strict liability or of negligence (or something in between) and therefore form part of what are often called 'regulatory offences' or 'quasi-crime'.[122] According to some observers, at the root of this distinction lies an understanding of violence as an interpersonal act of aggression committed by individuals, rather than the results of a dangerous policy, perpetrated by an institution.[123] The distinction is reinforced in English law by the arrangements for the enforcement of 'regulatory offences'.[124]

Secondly, the 'regulatory' offences are generally triable summarily, that is, by the Magistrates' Court rather than the Crown Court (the main exceptions being public nuisance and offences under the Health and Safety at Work Act[125]). This affects the extent of a court's power to order compensation.[126]

Thirdly, the ingredients of these offences (and of public nuisance) do not refer to any personal injury or death which they may cause. There is no crime of negligently causing personal injuries however serious and manslaughter requires proof of gross negligence beyond reasonable doubt. This means that there is little reason for a prosecutor to gather information or adduce evidence as to any injury which an offence may cause. As a result, the court often has only a very general understanding of the injury caused to any victims and little knowledge of its long-term prognosis, let alone its financial consequences.

Fourthly, while there is typically little difficulty in establishing the criminal responsibility of corporations in respect of regulatory offences (given that the corporation can often be held in law to have done the *actus reus*, for example, supplying an unsafe product), there is very much more difficulty in establishing their responsibility for

---

[119] Above, pp. 390–1.

[120] E.g. Consumer Protection Act 1987, s. 40(2); Food Safety Act 1990, s. 36.

[121] N. Lacey, C. Wells and O. Quick, *Reconstructing Criminal Law*: Text and Materials (LexisNexis Butterworths, 3rd. edn., 2003) 662–71; and see as to the possibilities P. Cartwright, 'Defendants in Consumer Protection Statutes: A Search for Consistency' (1996) *MLR* 225.   [122] Above, p. 405.

[123] C. Wells, 'Codification of the Criminal Law (4) Restatement or Reform' (1986) *Crim L Rev.* 314, 321.

[124] Below, p. 420.   [125] Above, pp. 415 and 407 n. 36 respectively.   [126] Below, pp. 425–6.

manslaughter even where individuals within the corporation have committed the necessary acts and possessed the necessary *mens rea*.

2. The Criminal Process and Compensation for Personal Injuries or Death

What then, is the relationship between these offences and the liability of an offender to pay compensation?

I have earlier explained that under the English law of torts as applied by the civil courts there is no necessary link between the commission of a crime and the incidence of civil liability in either direction.[127] So, the commission of an offence may or may not give rise to civil liability, this depending on whether the facts of the offence satisfy the requirements of a tort. As regards statutory offences, in the absence of express provision, the incidence of civil liability for breach of a duty (whether or not this is also sanctioned by the criminal law) often turns on the notoriously elusive criterion of implied parliamentary interpretation.[128] Even where a criminal court has convicted a person for a crime of negligence, this is no more than *evidence* (though important evidence) of negligence for the purposes of civil liability in negligence.[129]

By contrast, English criminal courts enjoy considerable powers to order compensation for the victim of a crime who has suffered personal injuries even where there would as a matter of the civil law be no liability in damages,[130] but this does not mean that the English criminal process is a significant means of victims of non-intentional criminal offences recovering compensation in any but the least serious cases. This lack of significance is explained by the location of the decision to prosecute and the marginal role of the victim, the relationship between the powers of the criminal courts to award compensation and the substantive criminal responsibilities, and most of all by judicial attitudes to the relative roles of the criminal and civil processes.

(a) The decision to prosecute and the role of the victim

In French law, the victim of a crime can trigger the commencement of criminal proceedings as well as attach himself to a prosecution brought by the public authorities, and in either event can claim *damages* for the harm which the offence has caused as a full party to the criminal proceedings.[131] None of this is true of English law.

First, as to prosecution, in English law there is a difference between constitutional tradition and modern reality, for while in theory *any* person may bring a 'private' criminal prosecution in respect of any crime,[132] in practice the decision to prosecute is

---

[127] Above, p. 202.   [128] Above, pp. 218–24.   [129] Above, pp. 202–3.

[130] Below, pp. 423–4.   [131] Above, pp. 380–3.

[132] Prosecution of Offences Act 1985, s. 6(1). For its constitutional significance see *Gouriet v Union of Post Office Workers* [1978] AC 435, 477 ('a valuable constitutional safeguard'), *per* Lord Diplock and see A. Samuels, 'Non-Crown Prosecutions: Prosecutions by Non-Police Agencies and by Private Individuals' (1986) *Crim L Rev* 33.

firmly placed in the hands of public prosecuting authorities, leaving the victim no role in the trial of offences beyond being a witness of fact. This general picture is entirely reflected in the case of offences relating to unsafe products, leaving their victims often without even the theoretical power to commence criminal proceedings and, therefore, the chance of benefiting from a compensation order.

The historical starting point was a general right in citizens to initiate criminal proceedings coupled with a responsibility in the Attorney-General to do so,[133] but in the course of the nineteenth century the police gradually came to handle the majority of prosecutions and in 1879 the office of Director of Public Prosecutions ('DPP') was created, giving statutory recognition to the importance of the public authorities in prosecution.[134] In the mid-1980s, the decision whether or not to continue criminal proceedings was removed from the police and placed in the hands of a new Crown Prosecution Service, which acts under the direction of the DPP.[135]

However, neither the police nor the Crown Prosecution Service in general see it as their role to investigate, to initiate or to continue criminal proceedings in contexts like health and safety at work or product safety,[136] though some have argued that they should particularly in relation to cases where death is caused.[137] Instead, the responsibility for enforcement of most crimes concerned with product safety is placed in the hands of regulatory authorities, notably the environmental health officers and trading standards of local authorities, who rely extensively on 'compliance strategies', in the enforcement of the law, that is, they prefer to use persuasion and negotiation and keep prosecution as a last resort for serious or recurrent offences.[138] While the prosecuting authorities take into account the harm which an offence has caused in their decision whether or not to prosecute,[139] to the extent that prosecutions are not brought by such enforcement agencies, then there can be no question of a victim of an offence being the recipient of a compensation order made by a court. Moreover, while English courts have accepted that a citizen can challenge a public prosecutorial decision *not* to prosecute an alleged offender by judicial review, they have made it very clear that they will not quash such a decision except in extreme circumstances.[140] The courts have taken a similar approach to the question whether a public prosecutor's decision to continue criminal proceedings (or to continue them on one charge rather than another) is subject to judicial review.[141]

Furthermore, the bringing of a private prosecution is not a realistic alternative for a victim of a crime arising from an unsafe product, even though the formal right to bring a private prosecution was expressly preserved when the Crown Prosecution Service was created.[142] First, many modern statutory offences are made the object of

---

[133] Sir William Holdsworth, *A History of English Law*, Vol. XV (Methuen & Co. Ltd., London, 1965) 160–1.   [134] Prosecution of Offences Act 1879, s. 2.

[135] Prosecution of Offences Act 1985 and see A. Ashworth, *The Criminal Process* (Oxford, 2nd. edn., 1998) Chap. 6.   [136] Above, pp. 405–7.

[137] E.g. D. Bergman, 'Manslaughter in the Tunnel?' (1990) NLJ 1108.

[138] P. Cartwright, *Consumer Protection and the Criminal Law* (CUP, 2001) Chap. 7.

[139] Ibid., 226.   [140] *R v Metropolitan Police Commissioner ex p Blackburn (No. 3)* [1973] 1 QB 241.

[141] *R v Chief Constable of Kent ex p L* (1991) 93 Cr App R 416; *R v IRC ex p Mead* [1993] 1 All ER 792.

[142] Prosecution of Offences Act 1985, s. 6(1). Technically, all prosecutions are 'private' except those brought by the Attorney-General, the Director of Public Prosecutions or the Crown Prosecution Service,

exclusive enforcement procedures or subjected to the requirement of obtaining the consent of either the Attorney-General or the DPP, particularly in the case of 'regulatory offences'.[143] The position regarding the prosecution of the special offences relating to unsafe products in this respect is somewhat mixed. It is clear that prosecutions for offences under the Health and Safety at Work Act[144] and the Water Act 1989[145] can be brought only by the relevant public enforcement authorities; but offences created by the Food Safety Act 1990 may (in theory) be prosecuted by persons other than the public authorities whose particular responsibility this is made.[146] In the case of the Consumer Protection Act 1987 and the General Product Safety Regulations 1994 (with certain exceptions),[147] the trading standards officers of the local authority have a duty to enforce offences against safety regulations and against the general safety requirement.[148] It is not clear whether this duty to enforce consumer protection offences excludes the right of any citizen to prosecute.[149]

Secondly, the exercise of the 'right' of private prosecution is subject to review by the public prosecution authorities. In the case of crimes triable on indictment (and therefore including manslaughter), the Attorney-General has a complete discretion[150] to enter an order of *nolle prosequi* at any time before judgment,[151] the technical effect of which is an indefinite adjournment but which in practice puts an end to the criminal proceedings.[152] This power is said to be used sparingly, where prosecution would be oppressive, for example, if the accused is seriously ill.[153] However, the DPP and the Crown Prosecution Service also have the power to take over any criminal proceedings initiated by a private individual.[154] While originally the victim of a crime could apply to the High Court if the DPP neglected to continue the proceedings,[155] this power was later abolished, partly because it left open the way for vindictive prosecutions and partly because of disuse.[156] As a result, the public prosecuting authorities have the power to take over the conduct of any criminal proceedings and

---

but the majority of these technical private prosecutions are undertaken by local authorities or other public bodies, such as the Health and Safety Executive: Home Office Evidence to the Royal Commission on Criminal Procedure, *Memorandum No. VIII, The Prosecution Process* (London, 1978) 20.

[143] Ibid., 24. The Philips Commission recommended that this practice should be reserved for situations where national interests, like security, were involved: *Royal Commission on Criminal Procedure* (chaired by Sir Cyril Philips) (the Philips Commission) Cmnd 8092 (1981), 163.

[144] Health and Safety at Work Act 1974, ss. 18 and 38.   [145] Water Industry Act 1991, s. 70(4).

[146] Food Safety Act 1990, ss. 5 and 6.

[147] R. 11(c). For example, the enforcement of cases involving food safety under the 1994 Regulations is subjected to the same enforcement as obtains under the Food Safety Act 1990: 1994 Regulations, r. 11 (c)(ii)(bb).

[148] Section 27(1) and (2). It appears that this provision was intended to be used to transfer some of these duties to the Health and Safety Executive: R. Merkin, *A Guide to the Consumer Protection Act 1987* (Financial Training, London, 1987), 76, but the Secretary of State has not exercised his powers to do so: *Consumer Safety, Report by the Secretary of State for Trade and Industry for the Period 1 April 1988–31 March 1993* (1993) 2.

[149] Cf. Merkin, *op. cit.* n. 148, 81, who asserts without argument that it is an exclusive duty to enforce.

[150] *R v Allen* (1862) 1 B & S 850, 855.

[151] J. Richardson (ed.) *Archbold: Criminal Pleading, Evidence and Practice* (2004) ('*Archbold*') para. 1–258.   [152] Samuels, *op. cit.* n. 132, 41.

[153] Ibid.   [154] Prosecution of Offences Act 1985, s. 6(2).

[155] Prosecution of Offences Act 1879, ss. 6 and 7.

[156] Prosecution of Offences Act 1908, s. 2(3) and see Home Office Evidence, *op. cit.* n. 142., 6.

then discontinue them.[157] On occasion the DPP has used the threat of his taking over a private prosecution in order to discourage its initiation, as in the case of the proceedings for manslaughter brought by the husband of one of the deceased victims of the Marchioness Riverboat disaster against the company which operated one of the two boats and against four of that company's employees.[158] Finally, the Attorney-General may apply to the High Court requesting it to forbid a person from bringing any further criminal prosecutions without its leave where that person has instituted 'vexatious prosecutions'.[159]

This picture is strikingly different from the French. For while specialist agencies exist to investigate consumer offences and appear to follow similar enforcement strategies,[160] either the direct victim or a consumers' association may trigger criminal proceedings even if the public prosecutor considers that they should not be brought: it is the *juge d'instruction* who decides whether or not proceedings should continue after investigation of the facts.[161] Moreover, there is no real equivalent in the English legal system of the possibility open to French consumers' associations of pursuing criminal prosecutions where they can show that an offence has affected the interests of consumers.[162] And the French controls on the right of victims of crime to trigger criminal proceedings do not include a power in the public prosecuting authority (the *ministère public*) to prevent their continuance.[163]

(b) Practical disincentives for private prosecution

Moreover, in English law there are two major practical disincentives on recourse to criminal proceedings by a private person, even where such a possibility is legally possible.

In French law, the victim of a crime as *partie civile* is able to take advantage of the investigative powers of the *juge d'instruction* and this constitutes a considerable advantage over the investigative process available in the civil courts.[164] By contrast, an English private prosecutor neither possesses nor can he invoke any special powers of investigation, search or seizure. Moreover, the prosecution (private or otherwise) cannot obtain an order for the disclosure of documents by a defendant relevant to the proceedings of the sort available in civil proceedings, since there is in general no obligation on the accused to disclose prior to trial more than a written statement setting out in general terms the nature of his defence and the matters on which he takes issue with the prosecution:[165] '[t]he defence have no duty to disclose information on which they

---

[157] Where no prosecution evidence has yet been heard by magistrates or where an accused has been committed for trial on indictment, the DPP may give notice to the court that he does not wish the proceedings to continue and the victim or private prosecutor (unlike the accused) has no right of appeal: Prosecution of Offences Act 1985, s. 23. The DPP may take over proceedings brought by a private person at *any* stage in the trial and offer no evidence or withdraw the prosecution, although *if* he asks the court's leave to do so, this may properly be refused: *R v Broad* (1978) 68 Cr App R 281; *R v Jenkins* (1986) 83 Cr App R 152, 154.

[158] The Times, 3 and 8 Aug. 1991. Proceedings were nevertheless brought: *R v Bow Street Metropolitan Stipendiary Magistrate, ex p South Coast Shipping Co. Ltd.* [1993] QB 645. Charges of manslaughter against the owners and managers of the Thames dredger 'Bowbelle' were later dismissed: The Times, 25 Jun. 1992.

[159] Supreme Court Act 1981, s. 42.   [160] Above, p. 381.   [161] Above, pp. 381–2.

[162] Above, p. 382.   [163] Above, pp. 382, 386–7.   [164] Above, p. 384.

[165] *Archbold*, para. 12–45 *et seq.*

do not intend to rely.'[166] A private prosecutor does not possess the considerable powers of investigation which the police or special statutory enforcement authorities possess, and does not even have the right to examine evidence taken by the relevant public authorities.[167] Finally, of course, in criminal proceedings an offence needs to be proven beyond reasonable doubt, whereas any civil claim need only be proved on the balance of probabilities.[168]

A second and very important reason for use of the criminal route to compensation by the victims of crime in France is because it is cheaper and quicker than recourse through the civil courts, the relative cheapness stemming from the fact that a significant slice of the overall cost is always borne by the State, even for cases initiated by a victim contrary to the view of the *ministère public*.[169] In England, however, cost is a major practical disincentive against private prosecution.[170] First, legal aid is not available for private prosecutions.[171] Secondly, even if a prosecution succeeds there is no *right* to the recovery of prosecution costs against the offender: the court has a discretion in the matter,[172] though a Practice Note has indicated that 'an order should be made where the court is satisfied that the offender ... has the means or ability to pay'.[173] However, the *Camelford Water case* is a striking example of the risk which a prosecutor can face. There, the local authority prosecuted and obtained a conviction for public nuisance against the supplier of contaminated water after an 18-day trial in the Crown Court.[174] However, the judge awarded the local authority only £25,000 of the £145,000 costs which it had claimed,[175] perhaps because he accepted in part the defendant's counsel's submission that his client was the object of a witch-hunt.[176]

Thirdly, where a person brings a private prosecution other than in any official capacity in respect of an indictable offence or in respect of a summary offence before the Divisional Court or the House of Lords, the court may order the payment out of central funds of such an amount which it considers reasonably sufficient to compensate him for any expenses properly incurred by him,[177] but this leaves out the prosecution of summary offences before a Magistrates' Court.[178]. Moreover, a private prosecutor, like any other party to criminal proceedings, runs the risk of being ordered to pay penal costs where another party to those proceedings incurs costs 'as a result of [his] unnecessary or improper act or omission'.[179]

(c) The restrained use of powers of the criminal courts to order compensation

Let us assume that these various hurdles to prosecution of a product offence have been overcome and its trial has come before a court. Assuming conviction, will a victim of

---

[166] M.N. Howard (gen. ed.) *Phipson on Evidence* (Sweet and Maxwell, 15th. edn., 2000) para. 9–43. For disclosure in civil proceedings, see above, p. 212–3.   [167] *R v DPP ex p Hallas* (1988) 87 Cr App Rep 340.
[168] Above, p. 208.   [169] Above, pp. 385–6.
[170] The Phillips Commission, *op. cit.* n. 143, 161.
[171] Legal Services Commission, *A Practical Guide to Criminal Defence Services* (2003) section 4.2.
[172] Prosecution of Offences Act 1985, s. 18(1).
[173] Practice Note, para. 6(4) [1991] 2 All ER 924, 928.   [174] The Times, 9 Jan. 1991.
[175] Ibid.   [176] *The Guardian*, 8 Jan. 1991, 7.   [177] Prosecution of Offences Act 1985, s. 17.
[178] This position was criticised by the Phillips Commission, *op. cit.* n. 143, 161–2.
[179] Prosecution of Offences Act 1985, s. 19(1).

such a crime be able or likely to receive compensation as a result of these proceedings? Both the Crown and Magistrates' Courts have since 1972 possessed the power to order an offender to pay to his victim compensation 'for any personal injury, loss or damage resulting from [an] offence'[180] and this power exists even in circumstances where the defendant's action would not give rise to civil liability.[181] Moreover, successive administrations have attempted to encourage the wider use of these powers,[182] developments which have 'signified a major shift in penological thinking, reflecting the growing importance attached to restitution and reparation over the more narrowly retributive aims of conventional punishment'.[183] Certainly, compensation orders have become firmly established in judicial practice as regards 'real crimes' such as violence against the person, burglary, robbery or criminal damage;[184] and are also used to compensate a consumer victim who has suffered economic loss as a result of being misled as to the *quality* of a product which he has bought.[185] There are examples of their exercise in the context of product safety, for example, in *Nestlé UK* a Magistrates' Court ordered the company to pay £120 compensation to a 20-month-old girl who had been injured by a splinter in a packet of sweets, the company also being fined £4,000.[186] However, so far these powers have been used relatively little to compensate the victims of other than such relatively minor personal injuries.[187] There are in all five reasons why this is so.

First, some victims of crimes are all but excluded from the benefit of compensation orders. While 'personal injury' has been interpreted broadly so to include fright and distress,[188] the relatives or dependents of a deceased (primary) victim of a crime are excluded from benefiting from a compensation order,[189] except in respect of funeral expenses and the payment of the fixed statutory damages recoverable for bereavement.[190] Clearly, then, in English law where a product has caused death, the deceased's dependents cannot look to the criminal process for substantial compensation.[191] Moreover, apart from this important restriction, at times the courts have taken a restrictive approach to which losses are consequential on an offence, for example rejecting a claim by the victim of an offence under the Trade Descriptions Act

---

[180] Criminal Justice Act 1972, s. 1.

[181] P.S. Atiyah, 'Compensation Orders and Civil Liability' (1979) *Crim LR* 504; *R v Chappell* (1985) 80 Cr App Rep 31.

[182] The present powers date from the Criminal Justice Act 1972, ss. 1–5, implementing recommendations made by the Advisory Council on the Penal System in its Report, *Reparation by the Offender* (1970) (the 'Widgery Report'). The powers are now contained in the Powers of the Criminal Courts (Sentencing) Act 2000 ('2000 Act') ss. 130–4 replacing the Powers of Criminal Courts Act 1973, ss. 35–8 and the Magistrates' Courts Act 1980, s. 40(1).

[183] L. Zedner, 'Victims' in M. Maguire, R. Morgan, and R. Reiner (eds.) *The Oxford Handbook of Criminology* (Oxford, 3rd. edn., 2002) 419, 440–1.

[184] Home Office, *Compensation and Support for the Victims of Crime* (2004) 12–13 and Annex B.

[185] E.g. the offence contained in the Trade Descriptions Act 1968, s. 1 on which see P.S. Atiyah, J.A. Adams and H. MacQueen, *The Sale of Goods* (Longman, 10th. edn., 2001), 294–8.

[186] 17 *Consumer Law Today* (July 1994) 3.

[187] Here, the term 'minor' is used to denote the effect of the injuries on the victim's need for medical or other care, or on the victim's ability to work.   [188] *Bond v Chief Constable of Kent* [1983] 1 WLR 40.

[189] 2000 Act, s.130 (1)(b), (9) and (10).

[190] The sum at present is £7,500: Fatal Accidents Act 1976, s. 1A(3).   [191] Cf. above, p. 410.

1968 for compensation in respect of unrecovered costs of civil proceedings against the offender which had been settled.[192]

Secondly, the victim has no *right* to compensation against the offender: a court *may* make such an order which 'shall be of such amount as the court considers appropriate, having regard to the evidence and to any representations that are made by or on behalf of the accused or the prosecutor'.[193] While it has been said that the making of an order 'is not part of the sentence of the court strictly speaking'[194] there is an 'important relationship between the sentence of the court and the desirability or otherwise of making one',[195] for a court is instructed to make a compensation order in preference to a fine where an offender's resources do not allow both.[196] Moreover, in deciding whether to make a compensation order the court should take into account much wider issues than the existence of a victim's harm and its connection to the offence, notably the moral desirability or otherwise of making him pay[197] and the offender's means.[198] In practice in many types of case it is the means of an offender which is a determining factor against an award,[199] but this is less likely to be as potent in the context of offences against product safety where the offender is a company or private business, which will often possess sufficient means to pay compensation in full. Compensation orders are backed by the same mechanism of enforcement as are fines, i.e. imprisonment on default of payment.[200] This emphasises the essentially ambiguous nature of compensation orders in English legal thinking: they clearly possess both compensatory and penal functions, with sometimes the one and sometimes the other being more prominent. It is for this reason that it is unlikely that the liability to pay a compensation order would be held capable of being insured, for it forms an aspect of a criminal court's response to an offence even where the offence was not deliberate.[201]

This ambiguous nature of the English courts' power to award compensation by criminal courts contrasts sharply with the conception of the *action civile* in French law.[202] For, although the victim's claim for compensation in a criminal court bears several special features, it remains in essence the same as an ordinary civil action (as its name bears witness). This means that the victim has a right to compensation and that there is no reason why an offender's liability to pay a victim of crime should not be covered by appropriate insurance: indeed a defendant's insurer can be represented in the criminal process so as to have a voice in its own ultimate liability.[203] Despite the double role of the *partie civile* in the French criminal process, when it comes to judgment, any award made to him is essentially no different from one made by a civil court.

A third reason for the lack of importance of compensation orders as a means of gaining compensation for personal injuries *caused by unsafe products* lies in a combination of the

---

[192] *Hammertons Cars Ltd. v Redbridge London BC* [1974] 1 WLR 484.   [193] 2000 Act, s. 130(4).

[194] *R v Brogan* [1975] 1 All ER 879, 881, *per* Scarman LJ.   [195] Ibid. at 880.

[196] 2000 Act, s. 130(12).   [197] *R v Chappell* (1985) 80 Cr App R 31, 34.

[198] 2000 Act, s. 130(11).

[199] *R v Inwood* (1975) 60 Cr App R 70 (no compensation order should be made where it is unlikely that an offender will be able to pay).

[200] Administration of Justice Act 1970, s. 41(1) Sch. 9 para.10 (as amended).

[201] Cf. the discussion in *Chitty on Contracts*, Vol. 2 para. 41–021.   [202] Above, pp. 374, 381–2.

[203] Above, p. 381.

classification of most product offences and existing jurisdictional limits on the size of awards. As I have said, while the Crown Court may make an order in *any* sum, Magistrates' Courts may only order up to £5,000.[204] Many statutory product offences, including offences against safety regulations[205] and against the general safety requirements contained in the Consumer Protection Act 1987[206] and the General Product Safety Regulations 1994[207] are triable summarily, i.e. by the Magistrates' Court alone. An upper limit of £5,000 *per* offence rules out the usefulness of compensation orders in all but cases of relatively minor injuries caused by product safety offences.

Some other statutory product offences, for example, supplying an unsafe article for use at work[208] and the crime of public nuisance are triable either way,[209] so that they *can* be tried by the Crown Court, if this appears to be more suitable to the examining Magistrates (having regard, *inter alia*, to the seriousness of the case and the punishment which they could inflict)[210] or is opted for by the accused,[211] but will otherwise most frequently be tried summarily.[212] Moreover, there is no evidence that Magistrates' Courts consider that they should use their power on convicting a person of an offence triable either way to commit that person to the Crown Court for sentence where 'the offence . . . was so serious that greater punishment should be inflicted than the court has power to impose'[213] so as to allow a greater compensation order to be imposed. In the result, where the criminal regulation of product safety is at its most developed and most stringent, as, for example, under the Consumer Protection Act, the mode of trial prevents any order for compensation exceeding £5,000!

The fourth and perhaps most important reason for the modest role of compensation orders in a field like product safety is found in the attitude of the courts themselves. For the Court of Appeal has made clear that an order should only be made in 'straightforward cases' and not upon evidence out of which arise difficult or contested questions of fact or law.[214] 'Compensation orders are not intended to be straight alternatives to civil process. In certain cases it is useful where the amounts involved are not too substantial and where the means to pay is established.'[215] Even more strikingly, Legatt LJ has observed that:

The mere fact that magistrates have power to award compensation up to a sum of £5,000 does not mean that it is always sensible for them to involve themselves in what are *essentially civil claims*.[216]

Particular difficulty arises in this respect as regards questions of causation and quantification of the victim's harm. Where offences are inchoate and do not require any resulting damage, as is the case as regards all the offences relating to product safety which we have described with the exception of manslaughter and, possibly, public

---

[204] 2000 Act, s. 131(1).   [205] 1987 Act, s. 11, 12(5).   [206] Ibid., s. 10(6).

[207] 1994 Regulations, r. 17, above, p. 406.   [208] Health and Safety at Work Act 1974, s. 6.

[209] Above, p. 415. And see the offences under the Food Safety Act 1990, ss. 7, 8, 14, 35(a).

[210] Magistrates' Courts Act 1980, s. 19 (1) and (3).   [211] Ibid., s. 20.

[212] Cf. above, p. 405.   [213] 2000 Act, s. 3(2)(a).

[214] *R v Ingram* (1975) 60 C App R 70; *R v Briscoe* (1994) 15 Cr App R (S) 699; *Holt v DPP* [1996] 2 Cr App R (S) 314, 315–16.   [215] *R v Ramsey* (1987) 9 Cr App R (S) 251, 253, *per* Stephen Brown LJ.

[216] *R v Crown Court at Liverpool ex p Cook* [1997] 1 WLR 700, 706 (emphasis added).

nuisance, there is no need for a criminal court to hear evidence as to any harm which they have caused in order to try a defendant's guilt; there is even less need to inquire into such harm if a defendant pleads guilty. But a compensation order made in the absence of evidence of any harm caused by an offender will be quashed.[217] So, while a court has a duty to give reasons why in a case where it is empowered to make a compensation order, it does not do so,[218] a lack of sufficient information about the victim's harm will pass as a justification. The Home Office has tried to address this lack of information in a number of ways, including encouraging the police and Crown Prosecutors to use a model form of record to show details of injury, loss or damage when a crime is reported to be made available to the court in deciding such an order.[219] Despite these efforts, it remains true that 'as the seriousness of the victim's injuries increases so the criminal court becomes more aware of its limitations'.[220]

The French position here could hardly be more different. There, *all* the three levels of criminal courts possess a full jurisdiction to award a sum appropriate to the compensation of a victim's harm whatever the sum might be, though in practice all but the most serious product offences which cause personal injuries or death are tried by a tribunal correctionnel.[221] In France, the criminal courts do not generally have any difficulty in deciding issues relating to compensation for personal injury, whether quantification or causation, for evidence of a victim's harm and its causal relation to the offence *must* be before the court since the various grades of involuntarily causing personal injuries require these elements to be proved before conviction, there being no such thing as a 'guilty plea' which avoids trial of the prosecution's case against a defendant.[222] And if a French court considers the evidence before it insufficient to award damages to a victim without more, it may simply defer judgment on this aspect of the case until any further *expertise* is accomplished.[223] In all, for French courts, an award of damages to a *partie civile* is part of their everyday practice, for serious cases of death or personal injuries as much as for minor ones: even while their claims are seen as 'essentially civil', this does not mean that they have to be brought before the civil courts.

The fifth reason why compensation orders have not been more used by English courts is that there is no-one represented before the court whose primary responsibility is advancing the victim's interest. It remains true that, except in the very rare cases of private prosecution, victims of crime play no active part in an English trial. This again contrasts starkly with the position of the *partie civile*, who plays a full role in the prosecution and trial of the offence, as well as being able to support his own claim for damages before the criminal court.[224]

---

[217] *R v Horsham Justices ex p Richards* [1985] 2 All ER 1114; *R v Briscoe* (1994) 15 Cr App R (S) 699.

[218] 2000 Act, s. 130(3).

[219] Home Office Circular No 20/1988, *Victims of Crime*. And see Home Office, *Compensation and Support for Victims of Crime* (2004) 13.

[220] D. Greer, *Compensation for Criminal Injuries* (Sweet and Maxwell, London, 1991) 177.

[221] Art. 2 C.P.P., above, pp. 372, 381.

[222] J.R.S. Spencer, 'French and English Criminal Procedure' in B.S.Markesinis (ed.) *The Gradual Convergence* (Oxford, 1994) 33 at 36.

[223] Art. 464 al. 4 C.P.P., and see above, p. 385 n. 199.   [224] Above, p. 381.

PART IV

THE EC PRODUCT LIABILITY AND THE CONSUMER GUARANTEES DIRECTIVES AND THEIR IMPLEMENTATION IN FRENCH AND ENGLISH LAW

16

The Creation and Maintenance of the EEC Directive on Liability for Defective Products and the Process of its Implementation in the UK and France

In this chapter, I shall look in turn at the background to the Product Liability Directive and the key decisions of the European Court of Justice in 2002 which declared that its purpose was to effect 'complete harmonisation' of the law within those matters which it governs; at the different processes of its implementation in the UK and France; and then at the review and reform of the directive at the EU level. In Chapter 17, I shall look in more detail at the provisions of the 1985 Directive, at how they were implemented in these two systems and how they are seen from the perspective of those systems.

In my present discussion, I am of course concerned with the substantive legal issues, but I am even more interested to use this Directive as a key example of the problems facing legal systems in implementing directives in an area already broadly governed by national law. While some of these problems are shared by English and French law, some are significantly different, stemming in particular from the different roles of legislation in a codified and non-codified system and from the different way in which the central distinctions between public and private law, and between civil and criminal liability are treated.

1. Creating and Maintaining the Product Liability Directive

(a) From European Convention to European Directive

As I have noted, the idea of a particular treatment for liability for products can be seen in the English context in the case law on negligence, but its distinctiveness became even more prominent in the United States, in the case law and then in section 402A of the *Second Restatement of Torts*, its core concern being with the liability of the manufacturer or supplier of a product (notably, food and manufactured goods) for personal injuries or death, whether based on negligence or defect.[1] As Advocate-General Tesauro noted in advising the European Court in *Commission v United Kingdom*, it

---

[1] American Law Institute (1977). For the English case law, see above, p. 180.

was in the United States in the 1960s that the theoretical premises of a system of producer liability uncoupled from any requirement of fault were first worked out.[2] In the course of the 1970s 'product liability' became the focus of calls for the reform of the law both in the UK and more generally in Europe. The particular spur for these calls was fundamentally social rather than economic or technically juristic, reflecting wider public concern with the plight of those suffering personal injuries as a result of products and in particular of the pharmaceutical known in the English-speaking world as Thalidomide, which was prescribed to pregnant women and which caused deformities in their offspring.[3] This public concern was clearly reflected in the report in 1978 of the Royal Commission chaired by Lord Pearson which had been asked to make recommendations for the reform of the law governing the compensation of personal injuries and death.[4] In a report which was widely viewed at the time as disappointing in its preference for the retention of civil liability as the main instrument of compensation in this area and for the piecemeal treatment of particular problems, the Royal Commission nevertheless recommended that a manufacturer's liability should be made 'strict'.[5] However, this was one of a number of the Commission's recommendations which was not given effect by Parliament, partly because possible national reform was already being overtaken by developments at a European level, partly because of the worsening economy and partly owing to the election of a Conservative government in 1979.[6]

For apart from giving prominence to the plight of victims of pharmaceutical products unable to obtain compensation because unable to prove 'fault', the tragedy of Thalidomide also emphasised the international dimension to the issues raised by product liability.[7] In the modern world of the international distribution of consumer products, a particular type of product could cause injury across a number of jurisdictions: why, it could be asked, should it make any difference *where* a victim is injured in determining the basis on which the manufacturer should be liable? More positively, if the law is to be reformed, let the reform take place at the international level.

The first result of this way of thinking was the Council of Europe Convention on Products Liability, discussed between 1972 and 1975 and agreed in 1977.[8] Its explicit concern was with the protection of consumers, by which it meant the victims of personal injuries and death,[9] by imposing liability without fault on manufacturers of defective products.[10] The Convention was prepared by a technical committee composed of government expert representatives of the Member States of the Council of

---

[2] Case C-300/95 [1997] ECR 1-2649 para. 16.   [3] Stapleton, *Product Liability*, 42–6.

[4] Royal Commission on Civil Liability and Compensation for Personal Injury (1978) Cmnd. 7054. See also English Law Commission Report No. 82, Scots Law Commission Report No. 45, *Liability for Defective Products* (1977), Cmnd. 6831.   [5] Cmnd. 7054, Chap. 22.

[6] Stapleton, *Product Liability*, 45.

[7] Explanatory Report on the European Convention on products liability in regard to personal injury and death E.T.S. No. 91 (*'Explanatory Report'*), para. 1.

[8] European Convention on products liability in regard to personal injury and death of 27 January 1977, E.T.S. No. 91 (the 'Convention'). For further comparisons between the Convention and the 1985 Directive, see Markovits, 53 *et seq.*

[9] Art. 3(1). No liability was imposed in respect of other types of harm.

[10] Art. 2(b) definition of 'producer'.

Europe and then decided upon by the Committee of Ministers of the Council of Europe as a treaty, becoming open for ratification by its Members. As a result, no Member State of the Council became bound to the Treaty merely by its conclusion: this required both ratification by the Member in question and by two other States.[11] The essentially voluntary nature of the Convention meant that those agreeing its content were not under the same pressure to make compromises between the contrasting positions on the appropriate degree of strictness of the product liability which it envisaged nor on the possibility of further defences or exclusions.[12] Moreover, there was little place for wider consultation on the content of the Convention (there were only seven meetings of the committee[13]) this being principally a 'scientific' matter for the committee of experts. While it was opened for signature in 1977, only four states have signed it.[14]

In the meanwhile, however, the EEC Commission had taken up the cause of product liability as appropriate for its own legislative programme, seeing this as a good way of showing the human side of the European Economic Community, and at the specific invitation of the Council of Ministers which had adopted a preliminary programme for a consumer protection and information policy, which asked that account should be taken of the work of the Council of Europe.[15] As a result, the EEC Commission's legislative starting point was a relatively easy one as it was able to adopt the basic approach and a good deal of the wording from an earlier draft of the European Convention.[16]

The common elements of the European Convention and the final version of the 1985 Directive are therefore very numerous. Both instruments protect all those who suffer personal injuries or death caused by a defect in a product, not distinguishing between consumers and non-consumers, those party or not party to a contract or between 'bystanders' and others.[17] Both impose liability primarily on producers of the products, which they define broadly to include manufacturers of finished or component products, importers and those who represented themselves as manufacturers;[18] but only secondarily on suppliers, the latter's liability arising if they fail to disclose the identity of the producer or their own supplier of the product.[19] Both instruments define 'products' as 'movables', whether or not incorporated into an immovable,[20] though when the Directive was first promulgated they differed as to whether or not it was necessary to include 'natural products' within the new scheme of liability.[21] Both

---

[11] Convention, art. 13.

[12] It nevertheless contained an Annex containing three possible derogations from its provisions available to signatory States: relating to the defence of contributory negligence, an overall financial limit on the liability of any individual producer and the exclusion of a *retailer's* liability in respect of primary agricultural products.   [13] *Explanatory Report,* para. 3.

[14] Austria, Belgium, France and Luxembourg.   [15] OJ No. C 92 of 25 Apr. 1975.

[16] Proposal to Council for Directive of 9 Sept. 1976, OJ No. C 241 of 14 Oct. 1976, p. 9.

[17] Convention, art. 3; 1985 Directive, arts. 1, 9(a).

[18] Convention, art. 2(a), art. 3(2); 1985 Directive, art. 3(1) and (2) (with variations).

[19] Convention, art. 3(3); 1985 Directive, art. 3(3).

[20] Convention, art. 2(a); 1985 Directive, art. 2.

[21] Convention, art. 2(a); 1985 Directive, arts. 2, 15(a). The Directive was amended in 1999, as noted below, p. 446.

instruments allow (but do not require) the inclusion of a defence of contributory negligence to be included;[22] specify that where more than one person is liable for the claimant's harm (whether or not under their special schemes of liability), they are liable in full as against the injured party;[23] provide that liability may not be excluded by contract term or notice;[24] and provide both for a three-year period within which claims must be brought starting from the time when the claimant 'became aware, or should reasonably have become aware, of the damage, the defect and the identity of the producer',[25] and for a ten-year foreclosure period from the putting into circulation of the actual product which caused the claimant's harm of all claims brought under their schemes of liability.[26] On the other hand, while the Convention was restricted to the compensation of personal injuries and death, the 1985 Directive requires the compensation of damage to 'consumer property' (as defined) with a lower threshold of 500 ECU.[27] In all, though, having overcome the differences of arrangement between the two instruments, one is first struck by how *very* similar they are.

A further and central similarity between the two instruments can be found in the basis of liability for harm caused by a defect in a product.[28] The Convention's Explanatory Report notes that there was a dispute among members of its technical committee here: while the majority agreed that 'fault' 'no longer constituted a satisfactory basis for the system of products' liability in an era of mass-production',[29] some considered that liability should be imposed in respect of 'dangerous products' (as this draws attention to the rationale of strict liability in the products' inherent risks), whereas those who preferred 'defective products' considered that this avoided 'the difficulty of deciding at the outset what products were dangerous, some products being dangerous by their very nature and others being likely to become so if defective, or if incorrectly used'.[30] After the rejection of a suggested compromise which contained *both* these concepts, liability was tied to 'defect', defined as when a product 'does not provide the safety which a person is entitled to expect having regard to all the circumstances including the presentation of the product'.[31] In coming to this position, the committee rejected the argument of one of its members that a reversed burden of proof as to fault would give an injured party enough protection, pointing out that 'the system established by the committee was not one of absolute liability but a mixed system'.[32] On the other hand, the Convention's reference to 'the safety which a person is entitled to expect' (or a person's 'legitimate expectation' as its equally authoritative French version prefers[33]) was chosen specifically instead of any reference to 'reasonableness', which, it was feared, 'could diminish the consumer's rights, since it could include considering economic factors and assessing expediency which ought not to be taken into account in determining the safety of a product'.[34]

---

[22] Convention, art. 4; 1985 Directive, art. 8(2).
[23] Convention, arts. 3(5) and 5(2); 1985 Directive, arts. 5 and 8(1).
[24] Convention, art. 8; 1985 Directive, art. 12.   [25] Convention, art. 6; 1985 Directive, art. 10.
[26] Convention, art.7; 1985 Directive, art. 11.   [27] Convention, art. 3(1); 1985 Directive, art. 9.
[28] Convention, art. 3; 1985 Directive, art. 1.   [29] *Explanatory Report*, paras. 10–11.
[30] Ibid., para. 12.   [31] Art. 2(c); *Explanatory Report*, paras. 12–15.
[32] *Explanatory Report*, para. 17.   [33] '*la sécurité à laquelle on peut légitimement s'attendre*'.
[34] *Explanatory Report*, para. 35.

The 1985 Directive followed this wording of its definition of 'defect' faithfully (or rather these wordings, the English and French versions of the Directive following their counterparts in the Convention),[35] but its drafters disagreed with the Convention's decision not to provide for any further specific explanation of 'defect'. Here, the Convention required only that regard should be had to 'all the circumstances including the presentation of the product',[36] this particular element being mentioned so as to ensure that 'defect' was not limited to 'intrinsic defects';[37] its Committee did not wish to set out any further circumstances, in particular rejecting any reference to the time at which the safety of a product must be determined (at the time of putting it into circulation rather than at the time when damage occurred) on the basis that this would implicitly admit a defence of 'development risks' which it did not wish to include.[38] This position reflects a conscious attempt on the part of the Convention's committee to avoid some aspects of the US experience of formulations of the basis of product liability, both in order to avoid the qualification of the strictness of liability which references to 'reasonable safety' or 'danger' so easily allow, and from a sense that the elaborate explanation of legal concepts is alien to the continental legislative tradition of private law.

Here, however, the Directive differed, providing that in determining the defectiveness of a product, account should be taken of all circumstances including: '(a) the presentation of the product ; (b) the use to which it could reasonably be expected that the product would be put ; [and] (c) the time when the product was put into circulation' and then adding by way of emphasis, that '[a] product shall not be considered defective for the sole reason that a better product is subsequently put into circulation'.[39] By so doing, the very open nature of 'defect' found in the Convention was given a degree of elucidation; 'reasonableness' was introduced into its application, albeit for the particular context of the expected use of the product; and most importantly the time element for assessment of the defect was explicitly set at the time of its 'putting into circulation'.

These changes represent a greater degree of compromise between those Member States who wholeheartedly supported the imposition of strict liability and those who sought something rather less strict; there was clearly a close relationship between the specification of the time at which defectiveness should be assessed and the 1985 Directive's (optional) inclusion of the controversial defence of development risks for producers.[40] Moreover, the 1985 Directive's balance of the interests of producers and persons injured by products differed in two other ways in favour of producers: by providing for defences that the defect was 'due to compliance of the product with mandatory regulations issued by the public authorities;[41] and, 'in the case of a manufacturer of a component, that the defect is attributable to the design of the product in which the component has been fitted or to the instructions given by the manufacturer of the product'.[42] These compromises reflect the different processes by which the EEC Directive and the Convention were produced, which in the case of the former was a function of the Treaty competence on which the European Commission and the Council relied as its legal basis. Moreover, this competence has also had a profound effect on the relationship of the Directive's scheme of liability and the wider laws of liability of the Member States.

---

[35] Art. 6.   [36] Art. 2(c).   [37] *Explanatory Report*, para. 36.   [38] Ibid., paras. 37–41.

[39] Art. 6.   [40] Art. 7(e).   [41] Art. 7(d).   [42] Art. 7(f).

(b) The EEC competence for the Product Liability Directive and its lasting significance

If the European Commission had little difficulty in finding draft provisions for its intended directive on product liability, it should have found rather more in identifying an appropriate competence under which to enact the requisite legislation given the absence at the time of any provision in the Treaty of Rome providing for the protection of consumers.[43] Nothing daunted, the Commission and the Council turned to article 100 of the Treaty of the time (now article 94 EC), by which directives were to be issued 'for the approximation of such legal provisions as directly affect the establishment or functioning of the Common Market'. This *vires* had two key consequences for the substantive impact of the ensuing Directive of 25 July 1985: it meant that the Directive required unanimous agreement (which in its turn led to further compromise); and it required the Directive's purposes to be skewed towards the functioning of the common market rather than the protection of consumers (which led in its turn to the European Court's decisions of 2002 holding that in the matters regulated by it, it required 'complete harmonisation' of the law).[44]

First, reliance on article 100 of the Treaty as the legal basis of the Directive meant that it required the unanimous agreement of all Member States,[45] and of course, unlike a Convention of the Council of Europe, a directive left much less room for choice in its implementation by a Member State. This requirement of unanimity was the root cause of the important substantive compromises in the Directive both in the substantive balancing between the interests of 'victims' and 'producers' and as regards the extent to which it required the harmonisation of laws in the Member States.

The extent to which the Directive itself qualified its own purported purpose in harmonisation is quite remarkable, even given its own acknowledgement that 'harmonization resulting from this cannot be total at the present stage, but opens the way towards greater harmonisation'.[46] For Member States were explicitly able to decide whether or not to include within their implementing legislation: (a) liability for 'primary agricultural products and game';[47] (b) the so-called 'development risks' defence for producers (said to be a condition of the agreement of the UK);[48] and (c) a ceiling of liability for a producer of no less than 70 million ECU for death or personal injury caused by identical items with the same defect.[49] Moreover, the Directive explicitly referred a number of questions to the laws of the Member States, including whether or to what extent the producer's liability should be reduced on the ground of the fault of the injured party;[50] the applicable rules regulating the suspension or interruption of the limitation period of three years which it required;[51] the rules governing the right of contribution or recourse of a person held liable under the Directive against

---

[43] See generally, Weatherill, *EC Consumer Law and Policy*, Chap. 1 on the evolution of the EC Treaty provisions on consumer protection.   [44] Below, pp. 440–4.

[45] Since the Single European Act of 1987, art. 100 (now art. 94) has been supplemented by art. 100A (now art. 95) which provides for qualified majority voting, on which see Weatherill, *op. cit.* n. 43, 6–9.

[46] Recital 18. Whittaker (1985) 236–37; Markovits, 98–9; Taylor, *Harmonisation communautaire*, 17–22.   [47] Arts. 2 and 15(a).

[48] Art. 7(e) and 15(b).

[49] Art. 16. Neither the UK nor France have taken advantage of this option in their implementing legislation.

[50] Art. 8(2), below, pp. 510–11.   [51] Art. 10(2).

another person also liable for the harm, whether under the Directive or not;[52] and the question whether liability should extend to the recovery of 'non-material damage'.[53] As regards other issues (such as the interpretation of the causal relationship between defect and damage,[54] the meaning of 'burden of proof',[55] and the appropriate rules regarding the assessment of damages) in principle the European Court is left with a choice as to whether to take an autonomous European interpretation or instead leave these to be decided by the laws of the Member States, or something in between.[56]

It is also in this light that the important provision in article 13 of the 1985 Directive dealing with the relationship between liability required by it and on other legal bases should be viewed. Here, the European Convention was more explicit, providing (i) that contracting States shall not adopt rules derogating from the Convention, even if more favourable to the victim;[57] but also providing that the Convention 'shall not effect [sic] any rights which a person suffering damage may have according to the ordinary rules of the law of contractual and extra-contractual liability including any rules concerning the duties of a seller who sells goods in the course of his business'[58] and permitting States to 'replace the liability of the producer, in a principal or subsidiary way, wholly or in part, in a general way, or for risks only, by the liability of a guarantee fund or other form of collective guarantee, provided that the victim shall receive protection at least equivalent to the protection he would have had under the liability scheme provided for by this Convention'.[59] So, while the Convention's scheme of liability was to remain intact, other traditional bases of liability could remain and could even be replaced by a compensation scheme resting on a basis *other than* on liability as long as it gives the consumer its minimum protection. This last caveat reflects nicely the Convention's focus on the effectiveness of an injured person's compensation rather than with a producer's liability.

Article 13 of the 1985 Directive retained only one element of these provisions, stating that:

This Directive shall not affect any rights which an injured person may have according to the rules of the law of contractual or non-contractual liability or a special liability system existing at the moment when this Directive is notified.

The second half of this provision is relatively straightforward, allowing those Member States which possessed an existing 'special liability system' to retain it, the preamble giving the example of the German law governing liability for pharmaceuticals, itself a particular response to the impact there of Thalidomide.[60] The first half of article 13 clearly *allows* a Member State to retain its existing general laws (whether of contract or non-contractual liability) even where the regime of liability required by the Directive applies, but does it *require* them to do so? The language is imperative ('[t]his Directive *shall* not affect . . .'), but this seems to fly in the face of the Directive's overriding purpose of harmonisation which would prefer the abrogation of existing bases of liability in favour of the 'harmonised' system required by the Directive. The original purpose of article 13 appears to have been to allow those Member States whose existing laws affecting liability for products were more generous to victims to maintain their existing level of

---

[52] Arts. 5 and 8(1).   [53] Art. 9 *in fine*.   [54] Art. 4.   [55] Arts. 4, 7.
[56] Below, Chap. 17, esp. pp. 492–4, 503–7.   [57] Convention, Art. 10.   [58] Ibid., art. 12.
[59] Ibid., art. 11.   [60] Recital 13.

protection, while at the same time agreeing to the introduction of a parallel system of liability at least in some respects less generous to victims.[61] As I shall explain, however, the European Court of Justice has taken a narrow interpretation of article 13 in the interests of limiting its inroad into the 'completely harmonious' nature of the regime which it declares that the Directive intended, thereby coming to a position as if the Directive had contained a provision expressly preventing any alteration of its scheme of liability even in favour of the victim as was actually provided by the Convention.[62]

This interpretation of article 13 by the European Court is directly related to the second consequence of use of article 100 EEC of the time as the 1985 Directive's legal basis, as it required it to be tied to the 'functioning of the Common Market' rather than simply the need to promote harmonisation in the interests of facilitating compensation for the victims of products or legal certainty for producers by the substantive reform of the law of product liability throughout the Member States of the European Community. So, the first recital of the preamble to the Directive asserts that the 'approximation of laws of the Member States concerning the liability of the producer for damage caused by the defectiveness of his products is necessary because the existing divergences may distort competition and affect the movement of goods within the common market'. The first and necessary justification for the enactment of the Directive was therefore economic rather than social or technically juristic; and this economic justification is fundamentally centred on the position of producers rather than claimants, as it is tied to the need to approximate the financial burden of their liability for defective products (whether borne directly or indirectly through the costs of insurance) in the interests of a 'level playing field'.

Tacked onto this economic justification asserted by the Directive's preamble, however, are arguments from the need for consumer protection, whether generally or in relation to particular provisions. So, its first recital continues that the approximation of laws is also necessary because divergences in liability 'entail a differing degree of protection of the consumer against damage caused by a defective product to his health or property'. The protection of consumers is further relied on by the preamble as the reason for requiring the imposition of what an English lawyer would see as joint and several liability on 'all producers involved in the production process', on Community importers and on all those persons 'who present themselves as producers';[63] for its definition of defectiveness in terms of 'legitimate expectation'; for its inclusion of compensation for damage to 'consumer property';[64] and for its rules preventing the exclusion of its protective effect either by exemption clause or by choice of law.[65]

On the other hand, the justification for its central decision to impose 'liability without fault' on the producer is said to be because this is 'the sole means of adequately

---

[61] Ghestin (1986), 136, referring to a Commission working document to this effect. Ghestin was a member of the scientific advisory committee advising the Council of Ministers in respect of the 1985 Directive. The Council Resolution of 19 Dec. 2002 on amendment of the liability for defective products Directive (2003/C 26/02) OJ C 26/2 4 Feb. 2003 para. 4 quotes its own joint statement of 1985 which specifically referred to the possibility for Member States of laying down rules other than those found in article 3 of the 1985 Directive for the liability of intermediaries.   [62] Below, pp. 440–4.

[63] Recital 5, 6 and 7 (on the latter see below, p. 522).

[64] On what is meant by this, see below, pp. 502–3.   [65] Recitals 12 and 13.

solving the problem, peculiar to our age of increasing technicality, of a fair apportionment of the risks inherent in modern technological production'.[66] The idea of the 'fair apportionment of risks' is also used by the preamble to justify the 'certain exonerating circumstances' (six in all) available to defendants under the Directive.[67] It appears to do little other than express in the language of fairness and risk allocation a fundamental decision of policy without any real explanation as to its more concrete reasons for coming to this view. Other aspects of the regime of liability which the Directive requires are justified merely on the basis of their 'appropriateness' or even 'reasonableness' for one reason or another or none in particular.[68] The creation of 'a uniform period of limitation for the bringing of action for compensation' (sic) is justified on the basis that it is 'in the interests both of the injured person and of the producer'.[69] Other details are imposed simply because they 'should be' the case, for example, the possibility of reliance by an injured party on claims for damages 'based on grounds of contractual liability or on grounds of non-contractual liability provisions other than that provided for in this Directive'.[70] All in all, the preamble is rich in assertion and poor in articulate justification for the positions which it reaches.

Nevertheless, we can see that in this way the European legislature pegged this directive's imposition of liability very loosely onto the economic justifications required by article 100 of the Treaty, but then used consumer protection (representing the interests of 'injured persons') and the 'fair apportionment of risks' (the interests of injured parties *balanced against* the interests of producers) as the basis for the rules which it requires. Even at the time, though, serious doubts were expressed as to the legitimacy of pegging harmonisation of producer liability to the Community's concerns with fair competition and free movement of goods, even if it is accepted that the Directive does indeed harmonise the *law* of liability within its own designated ambit.[71] For while differences in rules governing the liability of producers in respect of personal injuries and death caused by their products certainly existed, there was little evidence to suggest that these differences were reflected in differences in costs for producers of a significance to support the assertion that they 'directly affected the establishment or functioning of the internal market'.

For a number of years, it could be thought that this intellectual legerdemain had worked and that the European Commission and Council had managed to finesse the latter's competence to issue a directive so as to promote a reform of the law in the interests of EC citizens, had created a consumer dimension to EC law before its recognition in the Treaty and had achieved a new degree of juristic integration by its effect on the heartland of national private laws. However, the legal foundations of the

---

[66] Recital 2.   [67] Recital 7; art. 7.

[68] See recital 3 (the exclusion of liability for agricultural products and game, removed by amendment of the Directive by Dir. 99/34/EC of the European Parliament and of the Council of 10 May 1999 (which removes the option contained in the 1985 Directive, art. 15(1)(a)); 1985 Directive, recital 11 (the ten-year foreclosure period) and recital 17 (the optional financial ceiling).   [69] Recital 10.

[70] Recital 13.

[71] See, for example, 414 HL Deb. col. 1407 (Lord Scarman), col. 1418 (Lord Berwick); House of Lords Select Committee on the European Communities, 50th Report Session 1979–80, para. 10; Whittaker (1985) 234–5; J. Stapleton, 'Three Problems with the New Product Liability' in P. Cane and J. Stapleton (eds.), *Essays for Patrick Atiyah* (Oxford, 1991) 253, 276 *et seq.*; Stapleton, *Product Liability*, 53–60.

Directive in the need to remove distortions in competition and more generally in the needs of the internal market later exacted their revenge in the decisions of the European Court in 2002 which held that in principle its new law of product liability created not merely a minimum set of requirements for Member States, but also set a maximum beyond which they were not entitled to go.[72] As a result, the tying of competence to the economics of the internal market led to a formal (if not a substantive) limitation on the possible protections which Member States can create for consumers.

(c) The European Court's decisions of 2002: 'complete harmonisation' and its exceptions

The important question of the relationship between the 1985 Directive and existing and future national law in the area of liability for products was squarely raised before the European Court of Justice in three cases in 2002: did the Directive merely set a minimum for the liabilities of producers and others to those injured by their defective products, or did it also set a maximum, thereby creating a completely harmonised or even uniform law?[73] Two of the cases were brought by the European Commission against Member States (*Commission v France*[74] and *Commission v Greece*[75]) alleging that they had failed to implement the Directive properly on the ground that their implementing legislation went somewhat further in protecting the victims of defective products than envisaged by the Directive. The third case, *Gonzàlez Sanchez v Medicina Asturiana SA*,[76] involved a preliminary question raised by a Spanish court in litigation by a person who had contracted HIV from blood supplied by the defendant hospital. The claimant wished to rely on Spanish legislation of 1984 which could be more protective than the 1985 Directive,[77] but the defendant wished instead to rely on Spain's legislation of 1994 which implemented the Directive and precluded reliance on this earlier legislation within its scope.[78] The Spanish court asked whether article 13 of the Directive *precluded* Member States from restricting rights granted to consumers by legislation which pre-dated the enactment of the 1985 Directive.[79]

Following the advice of Advocate-General Geelhoed,[80] the European Court of Justice in its three decisions unequivocally ruled that the 1985 Directive did not merely permit the restriction of rights for consumers, but required such restriction within the domain with which it was concerned. '[T]he Directive seeks to achieve, in the matters regulated

---

[72] Below, pp. 440–4.

[73] Case C-52/00 of 25 Apr. 2002, *Commission v France* [2002] I-3827 ('Case C-52/00'); Case C-154/00 of 25 Apr. 2002, *Commission v Greece* [2002] ECR I-3879 ('Case C-154/00'); Case C-183/00 of 25 Apr. 2002, *Gonzàlez Sanchez v Medicina Asturiana SA* [2002] ECR I-3901 ('Case C-154/00' or '*Gonzàlez Sanchez*'). For earlier academic discussion of these issues see Whittaker (1985), 238; Stapleton, 'Three Problems', *op. cit.* n. 71, 278 *et seq.*; Stapleton, *Product Liability*, 60–4.   [74] Case C-52/00.

[75] Case C-154/00.   [76] Case C-183/00.

[77] Law No. 26 of 19 July 1984 for the Protection of Consumers and Users.

[78] Law No. 22 of 6 July 1994, art. 1.   [79] Case C-183/00, para. 13.

[80] Joined opinion of 18 Sept. 2001, Case C-52/00 and C-183/00 [2002] ECR I-03827.

by it, *complete harmonisation* of the laws, regulations and administrative provisions of the Member States.'[81] While the European Court dealt with particular arguments of the parties in the two cases brought by the Commission as regards those particular aspects of the implementing legislation which it criticised,[82] it set out an identical series of reasons for this general decision as to the impact of the Directive.

The Court's starting point was the first recital of the Directive, tying the Directive's purpose of approximation to the necessity to avoid the distortion of competition and the effect on the internal market which differing degrees of protection of the consumer entail, a purpose which was itself necessary to justify EC competence in enacting the Directive.[83] In this respect, the Court rejected the argument that it should take into account article 153 EC's injunction 'to ensure a high level of consumer protection' as this provision was inserted into the Treaty after the enactment of the Directive and, in any event, did not concern measures taken under the successor provisions to article 100 under which the Directive had been enacted.[84] 'Accordingly, the margin of discretion available to the Member States in order to make provision for product liability is entirely determined by the Directive itself and must be inferred from its wording, purpose and structure.'[85]

Three arguments in particular convinced the Court that this Directive should be so interpreted. First, the economic purposes of the Directive as set out in its first recital in harmonising the system of civil liability; secondly, the absence of any provision within the Directive authorising Member States to adopt or maintain more stringent provisions in the interests of consumer protection, as found, for example, in the Directive on unfair terms in consumer contracts;[86] and, thirdly, the express provision in articles 15 and 16 of the Directive allowing Member States to make 'certain derogations', which implies that they may do so 'only in regard to the matters exhaustively specified';[87] neither these derogations nor the references 'in certain cases to national law' mean that 'in regard to the matters which it regulates harmonisation is not complete'.[88]

This conclusion then coloured the view which the Court took of the significance of article 13 of the 1985 Directive.[89] The Court interpreted this article as having two distinct limbs: its second part (which refers to the Directive's not affecting 'a special liability system existing at the moment when the Directive is notified' means that the Directive does not affect the rights of injured persons under already existing laws governing liability for 'a given sector of production' as illustrated by recital 13's reference to the (German) law of liability for pharmaceuticals. However, the first part of article 13 (which refers to the Directive's not affecting 'any rights which an injured party may have according to the rules of the law of contractual or non-contractual liability') means that:

the system of rules put in place by the Directive, which in Article 4 enables the victim to seek compensation where he proves damage, the defect in the product and the causal link between

---

[81] Case C-52/00, para. 24; Case C-154/00, para. 20 (emphasis added); cf. Case C-183/00 paras. 23–32.
[82] Noted below, pp. 458–60 in relation to the French implementing legislation.   [83] Above, p. 438.
[84] I.e. arts. 94 and 95 EC.
[85] Case C-52/00 paras. 15–16; Case C-183/00 paras. 24–5; Case C-154/00 paras 11–12.
[86] Dir. 93/13/EC of 5 April 1993 art. 8.   [87] Case C-154/00 para. 16.
[88] Case C-154/00 para. 15.   [89] Quoted above, p. 437.

that defect and the damage, does not preclude the application of other systems of contractual or non-contractual liability based on other grounds, such as fault or a warranty in respect of latent defects.[90]

As regards these 'other grounds of liability', there would appear to be no limitation in terms of the timing of their enactment since article 13's phrase 'existing at the moment when this Directive is notified' does not qualify its protection of these rights.[91] In the Court's view, the Directive sets both a minimum and a maximum for the Member States in setting the liabilities which form its subject matter, but it does not prevent the application of existing or future laws affecting the rights of injured parties harmed by products on *other* legal bases. As a result, on the cases before them, the Court held both France and Greece in breach of the 1985 Directive's requirements to the extent to which their implementing measures were more protective of consumers than it allowed.

The significance of the European Court's decision in *Gonzàlez Sanchez* is more difficult to discern. The Court understood the question put to it by the Spanish court as asking whether article 13 must be interpreted as meaning that the rights conferred under legislation of a Member State on victims of damage caused by a *defective* product *may* be limited or restricted as a result of the Directive's implementation.[92] The claimant in the Spanish court had argued that Spanish implementation was not entitled to restrict her rights under previous Spanish legislation (of 1984) which, *inter alia*, imposed liability for damage caused by the correct use or consumption of goods or services, thereby imposing a liability not restricted to 'products' as such and, more importantly, where products were in fact in issue, not requiring proof of their defectiveness.[93] The European Court's reply to the Spanish court was that article 13 must be interpreted as meaning that:

the rights conferred under the legislation of a Member State on the victims of damage caused by a defective product under a general system of liability having the *same basis* as that put in place by the Directive *may* be limited or restricted as a result of the Directive's transposition into the domestic law of that State.[94]

In order for this decision to be sufficient for the Spanish court to decide its case, the European Court must be taken to have assumed that the earlier Spanish legislation *did* rest on the same basis as that put in place by the Directive, so that Spain's implementing legislation was entitled to restrict recourse by claimants to its provisions. With respect, however, the European Court did not appear to consider the question whether or not the earlier Spanish legislation did rest on the 'same ground' as the Directive for this purpose—while the relevant provision was tied to liabilities for production, it was not based on their 'defectiveness'. It could be thought that if liability for 'latent defects' in the laws of the Member States could remain unaffected by the Directive because it did not rest on the 'same ground' as the Directive and therefore fell within article 13, so could this special Spanish liability. Certainly, the European

---

[90] Case C-154/00 para. 18; Case 52/00, para. 22; Case 183/00, para. 31.
[91] Ibid. This is particularly clear in the opinion of A.-G. Geelhoed, *op. cit.* n. 80, paras. 53–54.
[92] Case C-183/00, para. 14.
[93] Law No. 26 of 19 July 1984 for the Protection of Consumers and Users, art. 28.
[94] Case C-183–00, para. 34 (emphases added).

Court's decision did not *explicitly* say that the 1985 Directive required Spain to restrict reliance on the earlier legislation as part of its proper implementation.[95]

Whatever the precise significance of the *Gonzàlez Sanchez* decision, in all three cases the European Court stated clearly that the Directive's purpose was the complete harmonisation of laws within its own ambit and terms ('in the matters regulated by it').[96] This interpretation is understandable in terms of the Court's own general approaches to legislative interpretation, for it interpreted a particular provision (article 13) of the Directive in the light of its purposes stated in its preamble which were themselves related to EC competence and wider EC principle (fair competition and free movement of goods); it looked at the preamble's gloss (notably, recital 13) to the particular provision as an aid to its interpretation; and yet it still gave a meaning to the words used by article 13. Having said this, the Court's interpretation has a number of perverse effects on the way in which its implementing legislation relates to the rest of the law of a Member State. For what it envisages is that the Directive requires that each Member State must maintain or create a special system of liability which reflects the provisions of the Directive, setting liability for producers for harm caused by defective products (as it defines all these concepts) and subject to the defences and time limits which it provides. Each Member State must possess a 'completely harmonised' set of rules for the Directive's subject matter, frozen until such time as the EC legislator itself changes the Directive's own provisions.[97] In this respect, while there has been considerable talk of reform of the Directive, very little has so far been done.[98]

However, this still leaves the question of the relationship of the Directive's implementing legislation and other laws of Member States. For example, in *Commission v France*, the Court's decision censured the expansion by the French *loi* of 1998 of liability of 'suppliers' beyond the extent required by the Directive;[99] but can the domestic law of a Member State impose liability on 'sellers' or other 'suppliers' under its law of sale or more general contract law to a more burdensome extent than the Directive requires, whether this imposition is accomplished by judicial interpretation of existing laws or by legislative change, as long as the formal implementing legislation of the Directive is left untouched? According to the Court, article 13 leaves unaffected the laws of Member States governing 'contractual and non-contractual liability' and it specifically included within these liability for latent defects (notably arising under the law of sale).[100] On the other hand, it makes little practical sense and no sense at all from the point of view of the harmonising effect of the Directive if a Member State can impose a wider liability on 'suppliers' or 'producers' simply by (a) renaming them; (b) reclassifying their liability and/or (c) making sure that the liability is imposed under some law *other than* the Directive's own implementing legislation and is expressed to rest on a legal ground distinct from the Directive's. As I shall explain, in France the question of the practical impact of the 1985 Directive as interpreted by the

---

[95] Cf. below, p. 474.   [96] Above, pp. 440–1.

[97] Cf. Stapleton, *Three Problems*, 279 who foresaw the potential problems of the 1985 Directive in this respect.   [98] Below, pp. 444–50.

[99] Art. 3(3); Case 52/00, paras. 36–40. For the *loi* of 1998, see below, pp. 458–9.

[100] This is made even more clear by the French version of the decision which refers to the '*garantie des vices cachés*'.

European Court in 2002 on existing *judicial* constructions of liability resting loosely on interpretations of the Civil Code (and therefore at first sight on 'other grounds') has become particularly prominent, being complicated by French judicial 'implementation' of the Directive in the 1990s and by French domestic understandings of the relationship between its own (national) legislation and its *jurisprudence*.[101] Moreover, if a Member State may still give effect to a more protective policy for victims of products under cover of its interpretation of domestic law, but *not* overtly in its implementing legislation of the Directive itself, this can create real problems of coherence and clarity in the fabric of the national law. As I shall explain, the problems of potential incoherence are accentuated where the implementation of other EU legislation (and notably the Consumer Guarantees Directive of 1999) may require or suggest legislative changes which impact substantively on the liability of 'producers', 'importers' and 'suppliers', though wearing their contractual denominations as various sellers in the chain of distribution.[102]

By comparison, the decisions of the European Court of Justice in 2002 on the nature of the Product Liability Directive have hardly been noticed by English commentators. Of course, at one level this can be explained by the minimalist approach to the implementation of the Directive by the United Kingdom in Part I of the Consumer Protection Act, the government of the time not wishing to impose any greater burden on business than the Directive specifically required.[103] This being the case, the minimal nature of the Directive was very much in the minds of the English draftsmen, but not the extent to which it set a maximum within its ambit. Moreover, the English law of *extra-contractual* product liability rested on (and still rests on) a general requirement of proof of negligence which looks more demanding from the point of view of a claimant than proof of the necessary elements of liability under the Consumer Protection Act 1987. And English courts have not extended the general contract law or law governing sale in any way remotely similar to that undertaken by their French counterparts, in particular as regards the extent to which liability may be relied on beyond the parties to the contract.[104]

In terms of the more general substantive sense of the European Court's decisions, it is one of the arguments of this book that the idea that the European legislature can, by requiring even a 'completely harmonised' set of rules of liability for a particular class of defendant in relation to a particular type of claim, thereby create a level playing field of costs arising from liability is fundamentally unconvincing. Even restricting one's inquiry to the impact of liability, the burden on any category of person can only be seen in the context of wider patterns of the distribution of liabilities and the pattern of their channelling within the system.[105] As long as wider patterns of liability differ as between legal systems, the creation of a formally uniform basis of liability for one category of defendant can do little in terms of their relative costs deriving from liability.

(d) Review and reform of the Product Liability Directive

The Product Liability Directive has been the subject of major official reviews at the European level on three occasions since its enactment and has been subjected to

---

[101] Below, pp. 461–5.   [102] Below, pp. 464, 507, 575–6, 662–3.   [103] Below, pp. 465–74.
[104] Above, pp. 28–9, 95–8, 158–9, 264–6.   [105] Below, Chap. 19.

considerable European Parliamentary attention (especially following the BSE crisis), but has been reformed only once and then in one fairly minor aspect.[106] The remit of the reviews has generally been to assess the practical impact of the Directive and to do so they have consulted widely and referred to liabilities of producers and suppliers in the Member States under the Directive and under domestic law, though they have not been concerned with 'liability for products' in the wider sense in which I have defined it.[107] Rather than describing the various objectives, methods and conclusions of these reports and discussions, I shall instead attempt to identify the developing themes and concerns which they display, and look at some of their key conclusions. I shall also refer to some of their views as to particular aspects of the 1985 Directive when these are themselves examined in more detail.[108]

The first report for the Commission was produced in 1995[109] partly in fulfilment of its obligation under articles 15 and 16 of the 1985 Directive to report on the application of the derogations from the Directive available to Member States.[110] Generally, the report accepted that it was rather too early to comment on the substantive impact of the Directive, in part because of the delay in its implementation in some Member States and in part because of the time lag between the enactment of legislation and the adjudication of cases; but at this stage there had been no significant increase in product

---

[106] In this discussion, the following will be referred to: C.J.S. Hodges, *Report for the Commission of the European Communities on the Application of Directive 85/374/EEC on Liability for Defective Products* (May, 1994) ('Hodges, *Report*'); EC Commission, *First Report on the Application of the Council Directive on the Approximation of Laws, Regulations and Administrative Provisions of the Member States concerning Liability for Defective Products (85/374/EEC)* Com(95)617 final (13 Dec. 1995) ('EC Commission, *First Report*'); D. Roth-Behrendt, EU Parliament, Committee on the Environment, Public Health and Consumer Protection, *Report on the Proposal for a European Parliament and Council Directive amending Council Directive 85/374/EEC* [etc.] PE 225.962fin. (28 Sep. 1998) ('Roth-Behrendt, *Report*'); *Opinion of the Economic and Social Committee on the 'Proposal for a European Parliament and Council Directive amending Council Directive 85/374/EEC* [etc.] (98/C 95/17) (30 Mar. 1998) ('*Opinion of the Economic and Social Committee*'); EU Parliamentary Decision of 23 Mar. 1999 on the common position EC No. 3/1999, OJ C 177 of 22 Jun. 1999 ('EU Parliamentary Decision 1999'); Dir. 99/34/EC of the European Parliament and of the Council of 10 May 1999 ('Amending Directive'); EC Commission, Green Paper, *Liability for Defective Products* Com(1999)396 final (28 Jul. 1999) ('EC Commission, *Green Paper*'); College of Europe, *Analysis of the Replies to the Commission Green Paper on Product Liability* (13 Sept. 2000) <http://europa.eu.int/comm/ internal_market/en/goods/prodliability.htm> ('Analysis of Replies'); D.N. MacCormick, *Report on the Commission Green Paper 'Liability for defective products'* PE 232.108 (1 Mar. 2000) ('MacCormick, *Report*'); D. Roth-Bethrendt, *Opinion for the Committee on Legal Affairs and the Internal Market* PE 232.108 ('Roth-Behrendt, *Opinion*'); European Parliament Resolution on the Commission Green Paper 'Liability for Defective Products' PE 289.426 (30 Mar. 2000) ('EU Parliament Resolution 2000'); *Report from the Commission on the Application of Directive 85/374* [etc.] Com/2000/0893 final (2001) ('EC Commission, *Second Report*'); Council Resolution of 19 Dec. 2002 on amendment of the Directive concerning liability for defective products (2003/C 26/02) OJ C 26/2 4 Feb. 2003 ('Council Resolution 2002'); Lovells, *Product Liability in the European Union: a Report for the European Commission* (Feb. 2003) (web ref. as before) ('Lovells, *Report*'); Fondazione Roselli, *Analysis of the Economic Impact of the Development Risk Clause as provided by Directive 85/374/EEC on Liability for Defective Products* April 2004 ('Roselli, *Report*').

[107] Above, pp. 5–14. Following its nature as a study into the economic effect of the development risk defence, the most recent report (the Roselli, *Report* of 2004) has looked at other mechanisms of compensation of personal injury or death (such as social security) and their potential impact on claims against producers and suppliers.   [108] Below, pp. 514, 529.

[109] EC Commission, *First Report* reflecting Hodges, *Report*.

[110] 1985 Directive, art. 16(2) and see above, p. 436.

liability claims, with the possible exception of small claims; no particular increase in insurance premiums could be attributed to the Directive and therefore no proposals for amendment should be submitted by the Commission.[111]

It was BSE ('Mad Cow Disease') which set reform of the 1985 Directive back onto the political agenda. The European Parliament had set up an ad hoc committee of inquiry into BSE in 1996 and this reported in 1997, becoming known as the Medina Report after its *rapporteur*.[112] One of its many recommendations was that the 1985 Directive should be amended so as to remove the optional derogation of Member States in relation to primary agricultural products, thereby including a person who contracted a disease from food (such as variant Creutzfeldt-Jakob disease ('vCJD') from beef) within its protective scheme.[113] At the request of the European Parliament, therefore, the Commission proposed such an amendment later the same year,[114] and on its return to the Parliament, its committees readily supported the change, in the interests of rights of citizens and the requirements of public health as well as being a 'further step towards the harmonisation of the single market and [obviating] distortions in competition between producers'.[115] However, the Committee on the Environment, Public Health and Consumer Protection wished to widen the debate considerably, and tabled a number of proposed amendments of the 1985 Directive.[116] Some of these related to aspects of the Directive which had been controversial since its inception, such as the development risks defence, the threshold of liability for compensation for property damage and the overall maximum of liability,[117] but it also introduced new elements into the debate: in its view, the experience of BSE suggested that there should be no limitation in time of liability such as the ten-year foreclosure period[118] and that Member States should be required to impose liability for 'mental damage'.[119] The committee also expressed concern as to the difficulty caused by placing the burden of proof as to defect and causation on the claimant, putting forward a 'virtually incomprehensible' form of words which would allow the inference of a causal relationship in certain circumstances.[120] Unconvinced and unwilling to allow the general compromise expressed in the Directive to be unravelled, the EU Parliament by a majority restricted itself to a decision in favour of the Commission's limited proposal for reform.[121] This was then enacted under article 95 EC, the amending Directive commencing its recitals with a reference to the 'social imperatives of product safety and compensation for damage caused by defective products which must be met within the internal market',[122] its effect on trade in agricultural products appearing much further down the list.[123]

---

[111] EC Commission, *First Report*; Hodges, *Report*, paras. 52 and 198.

[112] EU Parliament, Temporary Committee of Inquiry into BSE, *Report on alleged contraventions or maladministration in the implementation of Community law in relation to BSE, without prejudice to the jurisdiction of the Community or national courts*, M. Medina Ortega (*rapporteur*) A4-0020/97 (7 Feb. 1997).

[113] Ibid., Part AII 6(3)(b).   [114] OJ C 337 7 Nov. 1997 p. 54.

[115] *Opinion of the Economic and Social Committee*, paras. 3.2.2, 3.4; Roth-Behrendt, *Report*, para. 3 (which includes the opinions of other Parliamentary committees).

[116] Roth-Behrendt, *Report*, Legislative Proposal and Explanatory Statement.

[117] Ibid., paras. 4.2, 4.3.   [118] Ibid., para. 4.4.   [119] Ibid., para. 4.5.

[120] Ibid., para. 4.1; amendment 3. The description is that of the Committee of Legal Affairs and Citizens' Rights: Roth-Behrendt, *Report*, 26.   [121] EU Parliamentary Decision 1999.

[122] Amending Directive, recital 1.   [123] Ibid., recital 7.

However, this wider parliamentary debate was clearly influential in the Commission's decision in 1999 to issue its Green Paper on the 1985 Directive, starting a much wider consultation and review.[124] From the ensuing reports, five salient points can be seen.

First, the official view in the Green Paper and in the Commission's subsequent report was one of fundamental satisfaction with the existing terms of the 1985 Directive because these reflected a political compromise between the competing interests (or at least argumentative positions) of producers and consumers. As the Green Paper put it, the aim should be to retain the 'conciliatory approach' of the European debate (in contrast to what it saw as the position in the US)[125] and to 'maintain the balance' it proposed that the debate should be rooted in six principles: that liability should be 'objective' (i.e. without the need to prove fault); relative (i.e. the producer has certain defences, though these may be revised); limited in time; not subject to waiver by the parties; joint and several; and that the victim should prove both defect and causation.[126] All who responded to the Green Paper agreed with the need to maintain *a* balance and most agreed with these six principles.[127] In its *Second Report*, the Commission again concluded that the Directive 'functions well in practice...due to the fact that it has created a well-balanced and stable legal framework which takes into account the concerns of both the consumers and the producers'.[128] The majority of those consulted by Lovells before it reported agreed that the Directive struck an appropriate balance between the competing interests; and while consumers' representatives disagreed with this assessment, there was no consensus among them as to which aspects of the Directive should be changed.[129] Most recently, the Roselli Report has suggested that one possible way forward would be to deal with consumer concerns by creating a special compensation scheme or schemes which do not rest on the imposition of liability, leaving the balance of interests expressed in the Directive in place.[130]

Secondly, the reports reveal an increasing political and institutional dissatisfaction with reliance on 'mere positions of principle' as the basis for possible amendment of the 1985 Directive, which instead should be undertaken only after the consequences of any change can be supported by clearly established factual evidence.[131] This can be seen in particular as regards the impact of the development risks defence, which had been included by a majority of Member States, though some excluded it as regards certain types of product.[132] Here, the advocates of consumers argue that the risk of injury caused by a defect in a product should be borne by the producer, even where he could not at the time discover it, because producers profit from the marketing of the product, whereas the advocates of producers argue that the removal of the defence would tend to stifle technological innovation.[133] The evidence to the Commission

---

[124] EC Commission, *Green Paper; Analysis of Responses*; EC Commission, *Second Report*; Lovells, *Report*.
[125] EC Commission, *Green Paper*, para. 3.   [126] EC Commission, *Green Paper*, para. 3.1.
[127] *Analysis of Replies*, 11–12.   [128] EC Commission, *Second Report*, para. 2.1.1.
[129] Lovells, *Report*, 46–7.
[130] Roselli, *Report*, 5, 135 (in the context of review of the working of the development risks defence).
[131] EU Parliament Resolution 2000, paras. 2–3; EC Commission, *Second Report*, para. 4.
[132] See Lovells, *Report*, 49–50; Appendix 3, 'Article 7'.
[133] EC Commission, *Second Report*, para. 3.2.2.

indicated that the defence had been little used but it admitted that 'very little data is available'.[134] As a result of this general concern as to the basis of its decision making, two further reviews of the impact of the Directive were undertaken: a general one (the Lovells' *Report*) and a specifically economic report on the development risks defence (the Roselli *Report*). However, the Roselli *Report* itself accepted that '[i]t is very difficult to collect sound empirical evidence on the effect the [development risks defence] has on a company's innovative effect', therefore putting forward its views on the basis of theoretical prediction and survey.[135]

Thirdly, though, the institutional reports finesse the question whether the 1985 Directive has achieved its objectives. Certainly, if the Directive's purpose is interpreted as being to create a 'common basis of liability upon which all persons in the EU can claim compensation if injured by a [defective] product', then it has been successful:[136] all Member States have introduced legislation into their legal systems which create schemes of liability reflecting the Directive and, as I have described, the European Court of Justice in 2002 has protected their formal integrity forbidding 'improvement' at a national level even in the interests of consumers.[137] However, the creation of a 'common basis of liability' of this sort was not the *purpose* of the 1985 Directive, but rather the *means* by which its purposes were to be achieved, these purposes being the economic ones of avoiding distortions in competition and in the internal market owing to different costs of liability in producers and suppliers and the social one of the need for the avoidance of differing degrees of protection of consumers in Member States.[138] And it is by no means clear from the later official reports that the Directive has achieved either of these purposes. As regards the effect of the Directive itself, the responses to the *Green Paper* concluded that it does not seem to have had any impact on the level of insurance premiums,[139] the major element in the cost of liability to businesses.[140] Moreover, the report by Lovells in 2003 concluded that while there is 'some evidence' that continuing disparities in the practical functioning of the liabilities of producers and suppliers in Member States may affect the basis on which insurance cover is offered, there is no evidence that they restrict the availability of insurance in different Member States.[141] It also found that there was 'little evidence that disparities as between Member States in the practical functioning of product liability regimes create significant barriers to trade or distortions to competition in the EU'.[142] From one perspective, these conclusions as to the effect of *continuing* disparities may be said to reflect the success of the Directive, these disparities having no effect prejudicial to the internal market; but given the reality and extent of the remaining disparities which the report observes,[143] another reading would be that real differences in the law of product liability have never had a significant impact on competition or the free movement of goods.

---

[134] EC Commission, *Second Report*, para. 3.2.2.   [135] Roselli, *Report*, 3–4.
[136] Lovells, *Report*, 53.   [137] Above, pp. 440–4.   [138] Above, pp. 438–9.
[139] *Analysis of Responses*, 10.

[140] There can be other costs in terms of time spent on processing claims, loss to reputation, and putting into effect measures intended to avoid liability (e.g. the keeping of records by a mere supplier so as to pass on liability under the 1985 Directive, art. 3(3)).   [141] Lovells, *Report*, 29–30.

[142] Ibid., 28 noting that 'a few producers indicated that their businesses are affected in some ways by such disparities'.   [143] Ibid., 9 *et seq.*

Fourthly, the reports explain the various reasons for this practical disharmony in the liability of producers and suppliers, being found in the derogations allowed by the Directive itself, the different ways in which some aspects of the Directive had been implemented in the Member States,[144] and differences in the assessment of damages, and by article 13's permission to maintain existing general bases of liability for producers or suppliers.[145] All these can be accounted for within the terms of the 1985 Directive itself and its acknowledgment that its own harmonisation is not 'total' even though it is 'complete'.[146]

Of more particular interest, though, is the identification of other types of reason for the differences in the practical impact of the Directive in the Member States other than in the substantive laws of the Member States. Some are very general, such as the culture of litigation, consumer awareness and access to information in some Member States.[147] Others lie in differences in compensation of personal injuries through mechanisms other than civil liability (notably, social security payments or special compensation schemes, such as for those who suffer from AIDS as a result of receipt of contaminated blood) and the extent to which the State bears the costs of medical treatment.[148]

Finally, and most interestingly in my view, differences are said to lie in the legal procedures of Member States, including in relation to the management of multiple claims (for example, by group actions); more general access to justice;[149] and in access to technical information about particular products. Difficulties in access to information formed part of the justification for the proposal by the EU Parliament Committee for the Environment, Public Health and Consumer Protection for amendment of article 4 of the 1985 Directive's imposition of the burden of proof as to causation and defect on a claimant.[150] The Commission's *Green Paper* echoed this concern, but offered several possible solutions: the inference of a causal relationship when a claimant proves the damage or defect or of a defect when a claimant proves the existence of damage resulting from a product; setting the degree or standard of necessary proof as to damage, defect and causation at a not very high level (giving 60 per cent by way of example); imposing on producers an obligation to provide all useful documentation and information so that the victim can prove his case; and/or making the producer bear the costs of expert opinion in certain circumstances.[151] However,

---

[144] E.g. the application of the requirement that a supplier should inform a claimant of the identity of the producer within a 'reasonable time'. Whereas some Member States (e.g. the UK) had simply used these terms, others had set specific periods, varying from 1 to 3 months (Germany and Italy respectively): EC Commission, *Green Paper*, 29.   [145] Lovells, *Report*, 10 *et seq*.

[146] Cf. 1985 Directive, recital 17 and above, pp. 440–1.   [147] Lovells, *Report*, 45.

[148] EC Commission, *Green Paper*, 15–16; Roselli, *Report*, 88 *et seq*. which acknowledges the important impact of differences in social security provision or special compensation funds and their relationship with damages (including on the basis of product liability implementing the 1985 Directive) in the practical impact of the development risk defence (though this impact is of more general significance).

[149] Ibid., 31–3.

[150] Roth-Behrendt, *Report*, para. 4.1, above, p. 446. The committee took the same view on the issues' return as part of the consultation process on the EC Commission, *Green Paper*: Roth-Behrendt, *Opinion*, 2, though the Parliament's Economic and Social Committee took the opposite view: OJ C 117 of 26 Apr. 2000, para. 3.4.

[151] EC Commission, *Green Paper*, 20–2. It also noted the special problem for a claimant in some cases in determining the identity of the producer where an identical product is made by several producers, but it is

most of the responses to the *Green Paper* considered the burden of proof provided by article 4 of the Directive to be 'effective'[152] and 'delicately balanced' by the defendant's burdens of proof as to the five defences in article 7.[153]

In its *Second Report*, the Commission noted the existing mechanisms, whether of substantive law (such as inferences of causal role[154]) or of procedure in national laws which help to deal with difficulties of proof and imbalances of information, but considered that 'in general, national administrations know of no practical problems due to the rules on burden of proof'.[155] Perhaps rather more convincing is the idea that these substantive and procedural mechanisms differ very significantly from each other and reflect much wider and sometimes fundamental features of the legal system to which they belong.[156] In this respect, the Commission noted the lack of European competence under article 95 EC as regards the harmonisation of rules on group actions and that rules of civil procedure should not be created for the specific case of product liability as the problem arises in all consumer-related cases.[157]

2. The Process of Implementation of the Product Liability Directive in French Law

France was the last Member State before enlargement to introduce legislation to implement the Product Liability Directive, doing so in 1998 some 10 years later than the Directive itself required:[158] it is understandable that these provisions were thought to have suffered from 'disastrous luck'.[159] The reasons for this considerable delay are themselves revealing of the debate in *la doctrine* and at a political level and of the pervasive significance of the *affaire du sang contaminé* in French discussions of product liability and product safety. As Mme. E. Guigou, the *Garde des Sceaux* (or Minister of Justice) put it in the course of a Sénat debate in 1998:

> the drama of the contaminated blood has profoundly affected our country. There is a symbolic significance in displaying in the *loi* a principle of absolute liability, even if it has already been accepted in the *jurisprudence*.[160]

However, from the early 1990s the delay also inspired the 'judicial implementation' by the Cour de cassation of the Directive under cover of the established French technique

---

not clear which one produced the product or products in question: should the Directive impose a 'market share liability'? Ibid., 22. All responses were in the negative: *Analysis of Replies*, 14–15. Cf. below, pp. 513–14.

[152] *Analysis of Replies*, 12–13.   [153] Ibid., 13 and see Lovells, *Report*, 47.

[154] EU Commission, *Second Report*, para. 3.2.1.   [155] Ibid.

[156] See above, pp. 46–50, 205–18.   [157] EU Commission, *Second Report*, para. 3.2.10.

[158] *Loi* no. 98-389 of 19 May 1998 *relative à la responsabilité du fait des produits défectueux* ('*Loi* of 1998').

[159] R. Forni, *Rapport an nom de la commission des Lois constitutionelles* [etc.], AN No. 755 (4 Mar. 1998) ('Forni, *Rapport*), 5.

[160] Sén., Séance of 5 Feb. 1998 (available from <http://www.senat.fr/>). The president of the Sénat at the time was M. Laurent Fabius, formerly Prime Minister and himself charged with criminal offences in relation to the *affaire du sang contaminé*: above, pp. 398–400.

of *obligation de sécurité* which had long been loosely and somewhat unconvincingly pinned to the Civil Code itself.[161] At first sight, legislative implementation of the Directive might suggest that this *jurisprudence* can and ought to be abandoned, at least after a time lag to deal with cases coming before the courts on facts pre-dating the *loi* of 1998, but the decisions of the European Court of Justice in 2002, which condemned France for going too far in protecting the consumer in its legislative product liability but allowed the retention of its general laws of delict or contract, raised the question to what extent either the 1998 legislation itself or the European Court's decisions prevent French courts from relying on its earlier *jurisprudence* on product liability. These questions will remain important even after the legislative correction by the *loi* of 9 December 2004 of the *loi* of 1998 so as to accord with the European Court decision of 2002.[162] They also illustrate the very different understandings of the relationship between legislation and case law in France and in England and how these established understandings can be put to the test by the intrusion into the system of a necessary and uniform European element.

(a) How the Product Liability Directive looks to French lawyers

For French jurists the Product Liability Directive contains both familiar and unfamiliar elements. In some ways, its provisions are very familiar. In common with the Directive (and unlike English law whose law of sale does not formally rest on 'defect' and was confined strictly by privity of contract[163]), French law had long possessed in its contractual law of liability for *vice cachés* and *défaut de conformité* doctrines which tied liability to defects, whether of quality, fitness or safety and which benefited others apart from parties to the contract in question.[164] Moreover, since legislation in 1983, French law had required that 'in normal conditions of use or in other circumstances which are reasonably foreseeable by the *professionnel*, products and services must offer the safety which people are legitimately entitled to expect and must not harm human health',[165] a provision whose formulation clearly owed much to both the European Convention and an earlier draft of the Product Liability Directive, and which can be thought to have acclimatised French lawyers to a definition of defect of safety in terms of a person's legitimate expectations, even though it had no direct implications for the imposition of civil liability.[166] Moreover, for a French private lawyer of the 1980s the Product Liability Directive could not have looked at all radical. In French law, not merely was liability without fault imposed through a number of contractual techniques, but very strict liabilities were imposed on the *gardien* of things under article 1384 *aliéna* 1 of

---

[161] Below, pp. 455–7.

[162] Below, pp. 457–65. *Loi de simplification du droit* no. 2004-1343 of 9 Dec. 2004, art. 29 ('*loi* of 9 Dec. 2004). This change had been foreseen by the Sénat, *Projet de loi* No. 358 *relatif à la garantie de la conformité du bien au contrat due par le vendeur au consommateur et à la responsabilité du fait des produits deéfectueux* (Session ordinaire de 2003–2004))(16 Jun. 2004) ('*projet de loi* 2004') available at <http://www.senat.fr>. And see Case C-52/00 of 25 Apr. 2002, *Commission v France* [2002] I-3827, above, p. 440.   [163] Above, pp. 243, 264–6.

[164] Above, pp. 69–79, 95–8.

[165] *Loi* no. 83–660 of 27 Jul. 1983, now contained in Art L. 221–1 C. consom.

[166] Above, pp. 308–10.

the Civil Code, the sometimes very heated and political disputes of the early 1980s centring on whether or not the *gardien* should have a defence of *force majeure*, contributory fault in the claimant and even whether or not the claimant should prove established that the 'thing' caused his harm.[167] While French legislation in 1985 reflected something of a political and judicial interim peace in these disputes for the central context of liability for motor traffic accidents, in other contexts these disputes rumbled on, either overtly (in terms of the availability of the defences) or covertly (in their practical application).[168] In terms of its substance, therefore, at the time of the enactment of the 1985 Directive, commentators were generally cautiously welcoming, seeing it as a means of improving the position of certain victims of products and possibly helping to dispel the recurrent doctrinal debates and judicial confusion as to the lines between *vice caché* and *défaut de conformité*, but certainly not seeing it as substantively radical.[169]

On the other hand, the Product Liability Directive did and still does seem rather an alien intrusion for a French lawyer. The whole notion of the imposition of a special regime of law governing the liability of producers and, to a limited extent, suppliers of 'products' looked American in its origin (as it was) and some of the provisions of the Directive appear at least to some as drafted in a common law rather than a civilian manner, with its concepts defined rather than (following much of the Civil Code) left to juristic and judicial interpretation.[170] Moreover, the liability which it required was not merely applicable beyond the domain of contract (even as French lawyers very generously have interpreted this), but was not formally classified as either contractual or extra-contractual.[171]

(b) Abortive attempts at legislative implementation

Soon after the Directive was enacted, the *Garde des Sceaux* entrusted the task of advising on and drafting legislation for implementation to a committee chaired by the leading university jurist, M. Jacques Ghestin.[172] Given the impact of reform on *droit civil*, in principle the French Constitution required it to be effected by Parliamentary legislation (*loi*) rather than by administrative regulation (*règlement*).[173] However, the

---

[167] Above, pp. 59–61.   [168] Ibid.

[169] J. Ghestin, 'La directive communautaire et son introduction en droit français' in Ghestin, *Sécurité des consommateurs*, 111.

[170] C. Jamin, RTDCiv. 763, 764; N. Molfessis, 'Les produits en cause' in 'La responsabilité du fait des produits défectueux (loi du 19 mai 1998)' *Petites affiches, La Loi* No. 155 (28 Dec. 1998) 20 (referring to the 'Anglo-American' practice of definition in relation to 'product').

[171] C. Larroumet, 'La responsabilité du fait des produits défectueux après la loi du 19 mai 1998' D 1998.311, 312.   [172] See Ghestin (1988).

[173] The French Constitution of 1958 divides the domains of these two types of law making according to their subject matter, rather than on the basis (as in the UK) that Parliament must give authority for secondary ministerial law making: Constitution of 1958, arts. 34 and 37 and J. Bell, *French Constitutional Law* (Oxford, 1992) Chap. 3. In this respect, article 34 of the Constitution places laws which fix the 'fundamental principles of civil and commercial obligations' within the *domaine législatif*. On the other hand, art. 38 of the Constitution of 1958 empowers the government to ask Parliament to authorise it to take measures which are normally within the domain of *la loi* for a limited period. An example of this may be found in *loi* no. 2004-237 of 18 Mar. 2004 which authorised the government, *inter alia*, to take those measures necessary to implement the General Product Safety Directive of 2001, this leading to *ord.* no. 2004-670 of 9 Jul. 2004, JO Rép. fr. of 10 Jul. 2004, 12520. A further example may be found in the *ord.* of 17 Feb. 2005 which was authorised by the *loi* of 9 Dec. 2004, art. 82 and which implemented the Consumer Guarantees Directive: see below, p. 583.

bill which resulted from the Ghestin committee and which was published first in draft in 1987 never saw the light of legislative day, but became bogged down in political and juristic controversy, finally being withdrawn by the government of M. Bérégovoy at the end of 1992 after it had reached its final parliamentary stage, the report of the *Commission mixte paritaire* (joint committee of the Assemblée and the Sénat),[174] apparently on the ground of an impending general election and that the consensus reached excluded the development risks defence, a position unpopular with business and in particular with pharmaceutical manufacturers.[175] Here, I shall note the key features of this earlier legislation and account for its ultimate failure.

First, the Ghestin committee wished to use the occasion of implementing the 1985 Directive as an opportunity to undertake a wider reform of the law of liability and in particular liability arising from the law of sale. So, while the first part of the *projet de loi* provided for legislative implementation of the Directive, its following provisions provided for changes in the law governing liability of all sellers in respect of latent defects, including a presumption for a year after delivery that any defect existed at the time of sale[176] and the replacement of the *bref délai* in article 1648 of the Civil Code with a fixed prescription period of a year from the time when the buyer was aware or should have been aware of the defect.[177] Ghestin argued that this wider legislative purpose allowed French law to build on the experience of the UN Convention on Contracts for the International Sale of Goods of 1980 (the 'Vienna Convention'), to simplify the complex and at times obscure *jurisprudence* by moving towards a unique and exclusive regime of liability which could benefit both consumers and non-consumers and yet distinguish clearly between defects of conformity and of safety.[178] This much wider focus is understandable given the state of the French law of liability in sale at the time,[179] but inevitably it stirred up disputes not directly related to implementation of the 1985 Directive.

Secondly, the *projet de loi* proposed that the Directive should be implemented by adding a new title to the Civil Code, '*De la responsabilité du fait du défaut de sécurité des produits*', rather than by special legislation outside the code. The proposals would have created a second part to Title IVbis, following Titre IV *Des engagements qui se forment sans convention*, which concerns both *quasi-contrats* (articles 1371 to 1385) and *quasi-délits* (articles 1382–1386), the latter forming the legislative foundation of *la responsabilité civile*. The proposed amendments ran to 19 new additional articles, articles 1386–1 to 1396–19, reflecting the need to introduce rules reflecting the relatively detailed provisions of the Directive itself. In this respect, it is important for an English lawyer to appreciate the double significance of amendment of the Civil Code. For amendment of the Civil Code (as opposed to enactment by special *loi* outside the

---

[174] The government bill (*Projet de loi* of 1990) was introduced into the Assemblée nationale on 23 May 1990: *Projet de loi* AN no. 1395 (23 May 1990) ('*Projet de loi* 1990'). The *Commission mixte paritaire* agreed a text on 15 December 1992, but this was not submitted by the government for the approval of the two assemblies: G. Bordes, *Proposition de loi relative à la responsabilité des produits défectueux; note avant deuxième lecture*, Sén. (31 Mar. 1998) ('Bordes, note'); 1.

[175] Huet, *Principaux contrats spéciaux*, 379. [176] *Projet de loi* of 1990, art. 3.

[177] Ibid., art. 5.

[178] Ghestin (1988) and see M. Charmant, *Rapport au nom de la Commission des Lois constitutionelles, de la législation et de l'administration générale de la République* AN No. 2136 (20 Jun. 1991), 10–11.

[179] Above, pp. 69–71.

Code) has an important technical significance, the Code provides the normative framework for private law in general, and this means that any of its provisions may be used as the foundation of wider principle, going beyond their particular contents.[180] In this respect, there is a striking difference from the legislation passed in 1985 to reform, *inter alia*, liability for motor vehicle accidents. This legislation was kept outside the Civil Code, even though its provisions appeared to qualify liabilities arising from article 1384 aliéna 1 of the Code, with the result that there was for a while a dispute as to whether it had created an entirely distinct ('autonomous') basis of liability or merely amended an existing one.[181] However, there is a second and more widely symbolic or cultural significance to the amendment of the Civil Code, perhaps especially in an area so familiar, so sweepingly principled and so relatively untouched by reform as civil liability. How strange a contrast, how alien to the French legislative tradition, to have five provisions all expressed in a classically laconic style to provide all the general rules for extra-contractual liability, but 19 to provide for the particular situation of liability for defective products and expressed in a style which has a distinct flavour of the common law! At the time, the reason for the proposed partial reform of the Code was that the substantive proposals were intended to be exclusive of the general laws of delict or contract and so to govern *all* cases of liability for products suffering from defects of safety.[182] No French jurist appears to have considered the question whether implementation of the Directive by amendment of the Civil Code would be inadequate to the extent to which the former should apply to situations where French law traditionally applied administrative law (notably, as regards the liability of public hospitals).[183]

Thirdly, the exclusivity of the proposed regime of liability in respect of defects of safety in products put much more pressure on the substantive content of the legislative proposals and in two opposite directions. For it was very soon realised that existing liabilities under the law of sale imposed liability for 'development risks' on producers and business sellers to both buyers and sub-buyers and was therefore more protective than liability under the Directive if the development risk defence were retained.[184] On the other hand, it was also realised that legislation implementing the Directive would have to apply to all products as it defined them, and in particular to pharmaceutical products to which the courts had not generally extended liability *sans faute*, whether in contract or in delict.[185]

Fourthly, all this parliamentary debate as to strict liability for unsafe products was carried on at the same time as the judicial investigation and allocation of responsibility for the *affaire du sang contaminé*, the proceedings against the three ministers allegedly implicated before the Haute Cour de justice taking place in the same month in which the *projet de loi* was withdrawn.[186] While it was realised that the liabilities sought to be

---

[180] Cf. the use of particular provisions of the Civil Code to support the construction of the doctrine of *obligations d'information*, above, p. 65, or the recognition of the *exception d'inexécution*: J. Ghestin, 'L'exception d'inexécution' in Fontaine and Viney, 4.

[181] *Loi* of 5 July 1985, above, pp. 60–1. H. Groutel, 'Le fondement de la réparation instituée par la loi du 5 juillet 1985' JCP 1986. I.3244

[182] Viney and Jourdain, *Conditions*, 790.   [183] Above, pp. 144–6.   [184] Above, pp. 89–90.

[185] Above, pp. 146–7.

[186] Haute Cour de justice (*Commission d'instruction*) 5 Feb. 1993, D 1993.261 note Pradel, above, p. 398. The main proceedings in the administrative courts took place between December 1991 and the decision of the Conseil d'Etat on 9 April 1993, above, pp. 315–19. The criminal proceedings against the

imposed on the officials, politicians and the State itself rested on fault (whether criminal, civil or administrative), this made the whole topic one of the highest political sensitivity. As Larroumet later noted, this meant that the question whether France should retain the development risk defence was as much sociological as economic or legal.[187]

(c) 'Implementation' of the Product Liability Directive by the Cour de cassation

In early 1993 France was censured by the European Court for its complete failure to implement the 1985 Directive,[188] but even before this the civil courts had begun to take on the task of 'implementation' in the absence of any parliamentary text.[189] At first they did so covertly, earlier occasional judicial reliance on the 'general law' of contractual liability to avoid the *bref délai* of the *garantie légale*[190] gradually reflecting more closely the elements of the 1985 Directive's scheme. To do so, the courts took the classic (if somewhat shaky) contractual technique of *obligation de sécurité*,[191] but they gave it a twist by requiring proof of a 'defect' in the product. For example, in a decision in 1991, a couple had bought a mobile home and then a day later had been found dead in it, poisoned by carbon monoxide given out by its gas heater: according to the *expertise*, their deaths were attributable to the bad design of the heater and inadequate ventilation in the caravan.[192] Their heirs recovered damages for their deaths against the companies which had supplied them with the caravan before the *juges du fond* and the companies' argument that they should not have done so as they had claimed beyond the *bref délai* attached to the *garantie légale* was rejected by the Cour de cassation, which declared the seller could be liable 'for any failure in its *obligation de sécurité*, which consists of delivering only products exempt from any *vice* or any *défaut* of manufacture of a type to create a danger for persons or property'. While it did not say so, this definition of the seller's *obligation de sécurité* in terms of a defect of safety was clearly influenced by the 1985 Directive,[193] but while this extended *obligation de sécurité* to the contract of sale where it had not been previously established, it qualified its strictness and put it somewhere between the classic *obligation de sécurité de résultat* which requires its bearer to see that its beneficiary is safe subject only to a defence of

officers of the National Blood Transfusion Service were tried by Trib. Corr. Paris 23 Oct. 1992 and came before the Cour de cassation on 22 Jun. 1994, above, pp. 395–8.

[187] C. Larroumet, 'La responsabilité du fait des produits défectueux après la loi du 19 mai 1998' D 1998 Chron. 311 ('Larroumet, D 1998 Chron. 311'), 315 (referring to the special treatment of *corps humains* in the *loi* of 1998).

[188] Case C-293/91 *Commission v France*, of 13 Jan. 1993 [1993] ECR 1–00001.

[189] Jourdain, note, D 1995.351, 352 considered that French courts had a Community obligation to interpret its law so as to conform to EC law under the *jurisprudence* associated with Case 106/89 *Marleasing SA v La Comercial Internacional de Alimentacion SA*. [1990] ECR I-04135. This was apparently accepted by the Cour de cassation in Civ. (1) 9 Jul. 1996, Bull. civ. I no. 304 where it refused, however, to allow a defendant to take advantage of the development risk defence as this was optional on the terms of the Directive itself.

[190] Above, p. 72.   [191] Above, p. 28.

[192] Civ. (1) 11 Jun. 1991, *Soc. Zeebrugge Caravans*, Bull. civ. I no. 201, RTDCiv. 1992 114 obs. Jourdain; *Con., Conc., Cons.*, Nov. 1991, n. 11, 6 note Leveneur. See similarly Civ. (1) 20 Mar. 1989, D 1989.381 note Malaurie (exploding television); Civ. (1) 22 Jan. 1991, Bull. civ. I no. 30, RTDCiv. 1991.439 obs. Jourdain (problematic beauty cream).   [193] Jourdain, RTDCiv. 1992. 114, 115.

force majeure and an *obligation de moyens*.[194] Moreover, while use of a contractual technique had the advantage both of a degree of familiarity and ostensible legal respectability, it confined its protection to those within the domain of contract.

In 1995, the Cour de cassation went further so as to protect those not party to any contract under which the product was manufactured or supplied.[195] In this case, a child was injured when using a plastic hoop which her private school had bought. The child claimed damages against the school, the distributor from which the hoop had been bought and its manufacturer. The court below, having found 'sovereignly' that the accident was attributable to the hoop's design, held the distributor and manufacturer liable *in solidum*, though as between them, the manufacturer liable to indemnify the distributor entirely. These decisions were upheld by the Cour de cassation which declared roundly that a 'business seller is bound to deliver products exempt of any *vice* or *défaut* in manufacture of a nature to create a danger either for persons or property' and that 'he is liable for it as much to third parties as to acquirers' of products. This obligation formed the basis both of the claim by the child directly against the distributor (with whom there was no extended privity as she had not bought the hoop[196]) and the indemnity claim by the distributor against the manufacturer who was also bound 'as business seller' in the same way as the distributor.[197]

The precise legal basis of this daring extension for the benefit of third parties of liability modelled on the 1985 Directive was not clear. The Cour de cassation clearly thought that its declaration of the seller's obligation was sufficient rebuttal of the distributor's contention that the Cour d'appel had violated article 1382 of the Civil Code by holding it liable when it had committed no delictual fault; this suggests that the mere breach of this obligation constitutes delictual fault, echoing the *jurisprudence* of the 1970s.[198] However, the roots of the *obligation de sécurité* in contract still appear clearly in its tying liability to *vendeurs professionnels*.

After 1998, the Cour de cassation has appeared to prefer to base its approach squarely on the general law of contractual liability seen in article 1147 and (beyond privity of contract) on article 1384 *alinéa* 1 of the Civil Code, both provisions 'interpreted in the light of' the 1985 Directive. The effect of this has been that liability attracts the incidents of the liability under the existing and general law rather than those of the 1985 Directive, so that, notably, it applies to all those 'sellers' in the chain of distribution (whereas the Directive focuses on 'producers'), it covers all types of harm (whereas the Directive covers only personal injury, death and damage to consumer property[199]) and it attracts much longer prescription periods.[200] On the other hand, the Cour de cassation has adopted explicitly a definition of defectiveness in terms of legitimate expectation. So, for example, it has imposed liability on this basis

---

[194] Malaurie, note D 1989.381; Jourdain, obs. RTDCiv. 1991. 559, 540 and cf. above, p. 28.

[195] Civ. (1) 17 Jan. 1995, D 1995.350 note P. Jourdain.   [196] Cf. above, pp. 95–6.

[197] The Cour de cassation held that the school was bound contractually for 'the deed of the things which it makes use of in performing its contractual obligations', on which see above, p. 24.

[198] E.g. Civ (3) 5 Dec. 1972, D 1973.401 note J. Mazeaud, above, p. 51.

[199] Cf. Civ. (1) 9 Jul. 2003, Bull. civ. I no. 173 where the court refused to allow liability under art. 1147 'as interpreted in the light of the Directive' to compensate loss caused by the mere defectiveness of the product (a double-glazed window) which had caused no damage to any *other* property.

[200] Jourdain, note, D 1995.350, 353.

on the manufacturer of medicine in respect of the harm caused to a patient by the indigestible sponge in which it was wrapped,[201] and on a local blood transfusion centre in respect of blood contaminated with HIV and supplied to a patient by transfusion during treatment both to the patient herself and to members of her family for their upset caused by her infection.[202] Even after the legislative implementation of the 1985 Directive in 1998,[203] the civil courts have continued to take the same approach to deal with facts which arose before its coming into force.[204]

Apart from governing these transitional cases, it may at first be thought that legislative implementation of the Directive by the *loi* of 1998 made this *jurisprudence* redundant, interesting only to the extent to which it illustrates French judicial willingness to manipulate the concepts of private law where the French legislature has failed to act.[205] However, given its wider scope than the implementing legislation which the European Court of Justice ruled in 2002 would be lawful,[206] the status of this earlier *jurisprudence* remains significant and controversial.[207]

By way of postscript, it is interesting to note that the Conseil d'Etat has not felt the need to adapt its law governing the administrative liability of producers or suppliers so as to conform to the requirements of the Directive, a liability which is prominent as regards public liability for medical products. This can be explained in part by a general sense that the Directive belongs to *droit civil* and does not affect *droit administratif* (a sense reflected in its implementation by amendment of the *Civil* Code) and that the administrative law of liability in these circumstances was already very strict, going beyond the Directive's requirements.[208]

(d) The *loi* of 1998 and its correction by the *loi* of 9 December 2004[209]

In 1993 Mme Nicole Catala introduced a private member's bill into the Assemblée nationale aimed at implementing the 1985 Directive and taking the same text as had been approved by the *Commission mixte partaire* in 1992 with the exception of retaining the development risks defence.[210] Its progress through the French Parliament was very

---

[201] Civ. (1) 3 Mar. 1998, Bull. civ. I, no. 95, JCP 1998.II.10049 note P. Sargos and see above, Chap. 6. See also Civ. (1) 28 Apr. 1998, Bull. civ. I no. 158.

[202] Civ. (1) 28 Apr. 1998, Bull. civ. I no. 158 (expressly referring to the 1985 Directive). See similarly Civ. (1) 9 Jul. 1996, Bull. civ. I no. 304 (transfusional blood contaminated with HIV); Civ. (1) 23 Sept. 2003, Bull. civ. I, no. 188 (claim for multiple sclerosis after injection with anti-hepatitis B vaccine rejected for lack of proven defect or causation).   [203] Below, pp. 457–61.

[204] E.g. Civ. (1) 23 Sept. 2003, *cit.*

[205] Cf. the Cour de cassation's taking over the task of assessing the fairness of terms in consumer contracts while the executive failed to exercise its regulatory power to outlaw categories of term: Civ. (1) 14 May 1991, JCP 1991.11.21763 note G Paisant, D 1991.449 note Ghestin.   [206] Above, pp. 440–4.

[207] Below, pp. 461–5.   [208] Above, pp. 145–6.

[209] *Loi de simplification du droit* no. 2004–1343 of 9 Dec. 2004 ('*loi* of 9 Dec. 2004'), art. 29.

[210] *Proposition de loi* submitted by Mme Nicole Catala, No. 469 (13 Jul. 1993) ('*Proposition* Catala'). In the following, I shall refer to the following French parliamentary documents which all concern the bill on liability for defective products without giving their long titles: *Proposition de loi*, AN No. 469 ('*Proposition* No. 469'); P. Fauchon, *Rapport au nom de la commission des lois constitutionnelles* [etc.], Sén. no. 226 (21 Jan. 1998) ('Fauchon, *Rapport*'); Forni, *Rapport, op. cit.* n. 159; *Proposition de loi*, Sén. No. 360 (26 Mar. 1998); G. Bordes, *Proposition de loi relative à la responsabilité des produits défectueux; note avant deuxième lecture*, Sén. (31 Mar. 1998) ('Bordes, note').

slow at first but not quite as bumpy as had been its unsuccessful predecessor's, though there were still lively disagreements in the debates.[211] Nevertheless, the development risks defence remained a sticking point, dividing the Assemblée nationale and the Sénat.[212] As a matter of substantive arguments, those in favour of retaining the defence were concerned about its effect on French business, in terms of discouraging innovation, the consequential cost of insurance and the resulting disadvantage as compared with foreign businesses which enjoyed the benefit of the defence; those against retaining the defence pointed out that its inclusion would result in a liability *less* protective of the interests of consumers than already existed as a result of judicial interpretation of the Civil Code, and in particular that it would mean that a supplier of contaminated blood may *not* be liable to its recipient, and argued that any concerns as to the strictness of liability should be left to the courts in their assessment of the defectiveness of the product.[213] The central compromise which eventually allowed the bill to pass retained the development risks defence except where the claimant's harm is caused by 'an element of the human body or by its products',[214] but allowed a claimant to choose to claim instead under the existing law, whose *jurisprudence* did not generally recognise any defence of development risks.[215] In this way, the *loi* was seen not to reduce any existing protection while nevertheless preventing it from imposing any new liability in respect of development risks.

Even apart from this central decision, the implementation of 1998 looked distinctly unadventurous to French eyes. Soon after the bill's introduction, the proposed reforms to the law of sale had been abandoned, by this date on the basis that it would be premature given the likely enactment of a EC Directive on consumer guarantees.[216] Unsurprisingly, the *loi* included 'primary agricultural products' within its scope, because by mid-1998 the amending EC Directive requiring this had been proposed;[217] it did not include the overall financial limit on liability offered by article 10 of the Product Liability Directive as this was not within the French legal tradition (noting here a difference with Germany).[218] Otherwise, the *loi* of 1998 made four, apparently fairly minor 'improvements' on the scheme of liability set out by the Directive.

First, following the lead of the judicial implementation of the 1990s and, indeed, earlier *jurisprudence* on the contractual liability of business sellers,[219] liability was imposed on business suppliers on the same terms as on 'producers' themselves, it also being provided that this should provide the basis of a supplier's claim for contribution against 'producers', though within a prescription period of a year from the supplier's being sued.[220] This change, though, led to another. The Directive uses the notion of 'putting the product into circulation' for a number of purposes, notably the time element in article 6's definition of defect and a number of the defences in article 7,[221] but it does not define what this notion means. However, the French *loi*'s making

---

[211] See the debates in the Sénat; *Séance* of 5 Feb. 1998 and *Séance* of 21 Apr. 1998 (available from <http://www.senat.fr/>).   [212] Forni, *Rapport*, 17.

[213] Fauchon, *Rapport*, 17–20.

[214] *Loi* of 1998, art. 13, new art. 1386-12 C. civ. In the following, references will be to the new articles of the Civil Code rather than to the *loi* itself.   [215] Forni, *Rapport*, 10–11.

[216] Fauchon, *Rapport*, 21–2.   [217] Art. 1386-3 C. civ.; above, p. 446.

[218] Fauchon, *Rapport*, 23.   [219] Above, pp. 84–5.   [220] Art. 1386-8 C. civ. (as enacted).

[221] Below, pp. 481, 517–21.

suppliers liable on the same terms as 'producers' raised the possibility that every supplier could be thought to have put the product into circulation, each at different times, thereby making nonsense of the ten-year foreclosure period which commences on 'the date on which the producer put into circulation the actual product which caused the damage'.[222] To avoid this and in the interests of simplicity, the *loi* of 1998 provided that 'a product is put into circulation when a producer relinquishes it voluntarily',[223] adding that 'a product may be the subject of only one single putting into circulation'.[224] This definition for 'putting into circulation' was chosen so as to set out the intended future relationship between the new legislative product liability and liability for the 'deeds of things', 'voluntary relinquishment' serving as a touchstone of loss of *la garde*, so that before it a producer or supplier can be liable under article 1384 *alinéa* 1, after it under the new product liability.[225] While the imposition of liability on suppliers on the same terms as producers was later condemned by the European Court,[226] the related French provisions governing the 'putting into circulation' of products were neither referred to it nor discussed by it; and this is reflected by the correcting provisions of the *loi* of 9 December 2004 which places the suppliers' liability on the same restricted basis as article 3(3) of the 1985 Directive,[227] but does not touch the provision regarding 'putting into circulation'.

Secondly, in addition to excluding 'human products' from the scope of the development risks defence, the *loi* of 1998 subjected its availability and the availability of the defence that the defect resulted from conformity to mandatory rules found in article 7(d) of the Directive to a condition that, where the defect became apparent within ten years of the product's being put into circulation, the producer had taken 'measures appropriate to prevent any resulting harm'.[228] This condition provided in effect for an obligation on producers and suppliers to monitor the safety of their products after they had put them into circulation ('*une obligation de suivi des produits*') and was aimed at requiring them to provide public information about their products, their recall for repair or amendment or their withdrawal from the market, any failure to do so giving rise to civil liability.[229] This was seen as related to existing provisions which empowered relevant government ministers to order the recall of a product and was borrowed from German law to which the origin of the development risks defence was attributed and which was thought to possess such a qualification.[230] However, when this qualification on the development risks defence came before the European Court, it was held incompatible with the 'completely harmonising' nature of the Directive's scheme of liability, the court seeing the fact that the EC Directive on general product safety[231] contained a similar obligation on producers, given that it does not concern the producer's liability for products which he puts into circulation; and while

---

[222] 1985 Directive, art. 11.

[223] Art. 1386-5 C. civ. al. 1 '*lorsque le producteur s'en est dessaisi volontairement*'.

[224] Art. 1386-2 C. civ.; Forni, *Rapport*, 14; Ghestin (1998), 1203.

[225] Ghestin (1998), 1203. For *la garde* see above, pp. 52–4.   [226] Case C-52/00, paras. 36–47.

[227] *Loi* of 9 Dec. 2004, art. 29, new art. 1386-7 C. civ. which sought to achieve this result by providing that suppliers are liable on the same terms as producers 'only if the producer remains unknown'.

[228] Art. 1386-12 al. 2 C. civ. (as enacted).   [229] Fauchon, *Rapport*, No. 226, 38–40.

[230] Testu and Moitry, 12.   [231] EC 92/59/EEC of 29 Jun. 1992 on general product safety.

article 15 of the 1985 Directive allows Member States to exclude the development risks defence, it does not authorise them to cancel or amend its rules.[232]

The third improvement made by the *loi* of 1998 also reflected the Directive's earlier judicial implementation and, indeed, French general legal principle (the principle of *réparation intégrale*),[233] as it included within the scope of liability all harm to property, 'consumer' or business and without any threshold,[234] though it did exclude liability in respect of loss suffered as a result of mere defectiveness of the product itself.[235] Following in part the *jurisprudence* in sale,[236] the *loi* of 1998 further provided that as regards damage to property used by a person other than principally for his own use or consumption, any contract term excluding or limiting liability between *professionnels* should be valid.[237] Rather oddly, of these changes the EC Commission brought only the omission of the threshold for the imposition of liability to the attention of the European Court[238] and, though the Court was aware that French law had extended liability to damage to non-consumer property,[239] it was only this omission which was condemned in 2002:[240] the inclusion of liability for damage to non-consumer property was not adverted to, even though one may think it a much more significant further burden to producers than the minor sums excluded by means of the threshold. As a result, only the absence of a threshold to liability was changed by the *loi* of 9 December 2004.[241]

A fourth difference between the 1985 Directive and the new provisions of the Civil Code is that the latter specifically regulated the relationship between the new product liability and existing liabilities arising in the building context, providing that those who are liable under French law's special building law provisions[242] shall not be considered 'producers' for the purposes of the new liability.[243] In this way it was hoped to prevent the new provisions from upsetting the relatively stable law governing the liability of 'builders',[244] but some French commentators realise that it is only doubtfully compatible with the Directive itself.[245]

While I shall look at the substantive impact of the *loi* of 1998 later,[246] there are two rather more formal points. First, following the lead of the earlier bills, its implementation of the 1985 Directive took the form of the insertion of a bundle of new provisions into the Civil Code.[247] Given that the earlier reasons for this (the wider reform of the law of sale and the creation of a new unique regime of liability for unsafe products) no longer applied, this choice has been seen as debatable,[248] and it has been suggested that it would have been better to have included a statement of principle within the Code but then leave all the details to administrative regulations outside it.[249] Secondly, while

---

[232] Case C-52/00 *Commission v France*, of 25 Apr. 2002, para. 47 (text drawn from comparison of French version of judgment with confusing English version). The condition in art. 1386-12 al. 2 was removed by the *loi* of 9 Dec. 2004, art. 29.

[233] This phrase is actually used by the French version of recital 5 of the Directive, but to describe the recovery in full from any person liable *in solidum*.   [234] Art. 1386-1 C. civ. (as enacted).

[235] Art. 1386-2 C. civ. (as enacted).   [236] Above, p. 95.   [237] Art. 1386-15 al. 2. C. civ.

[238] Case C-52/00 of 25 Apr. 2002, para. 1.   [239] Ibid., para. 26.

[240] Ibid., para. 26–34.   [241] Art. 29, amending art. 1386-2 al. 2 C. civ.

[242] Above, pp. 104–7.   [243] Art. 1386-7 C.civ.   [244] Above, pp. 104–5.

[245] Huet, *Principaux contrats spéciaux*, 389 n. 1016.   [246] Below, pp. 531–8.

[247] Above, pp. 453–4.

[248] Viney and Jourdain, *Conditions*, 790; C. Jamin, RTDCiv. 1998.763, 764.

[249] Malaurie, Aynès and Stoffel-Munck, *Obligations*, 157.

some commentators are clearly relieved that the French Parliament retained the possibility of a claimant having recourse to other, established bases of liability of producers and suppliers as a matter of substance, others have decried this as 'detestable',[250] or 'deplorable' rendering the law opaque and 'showing our inability to come up with a satisfactory, and therefore unique, solution to a single problem'.[251] For some, implementation of the 1985 Directive illustrates how European harmonisation results in disharmony within internal French law.[252]

(e) The present status of earlier French *jurisprudence*

The parliamentary compromise which finally allowed the passing of the *loi* of 1998 did so on the express understanding of the existence of more protective *jurisprudence* on which a victim of a product could rely: but has this *jurisprudence*, all of which was pinned more or less to the Civil Code, survived the combined effect of the *loi* itself and the European Court's decisions of 2002? This question is crucial practically, as on this turns whether or not the new product liability has more than a limited impact;[253] it is also interesting theoretically, as it is revealing of the relationship between French legislation and *jurisprudence*.

Unfortunately, the answer remains highly controversial, though there are some areas on which most of *la doctrine* appear to agree. On one side of the argument it is said that the *loi* of 1998 itself abrogated earlier *jurisprudence*. As Larroumet put it:

> Liability for defective products was, before the new *loi*, purely a matter of *jurisprudence*. How can a judicial construction subsist once the legislator has intervened to install a new regime of liability? It is impossible, for the role of judges is to apply *la loi* and possibly to create a rule under cover of interpretation of *la loi*.[254]

For Larroumet, the position taken by the *Garde des Sceaux* by which a producer could rely on the development risks defence under the new law, but not if sued under the *droit commun*, was absurd.[255] Mazeaud also sees the force of this argument, considering that the retention of an option in a victim of a product to sue either under the new *loi* or previous *jurisprudence* 'appears difficult to reconcile with the elementary principles which govern the binding force of the new *loi* in our legal system': for if new legislation overturns existing legislation, how much more should it overturn previous *jurisprudence*?[256] However, reference to the *travaux préparatoires* of the *loi* of 1998 could be used to control

---

[250] C. Larroumet, 'Introduction' in 'La responsabilité du fait des produits défectueux (loi du 19 mai 1998)' *Petites affiches, La Loi* No. 155 (28 Dec. 1998), 3 at 7.

[251] Huet, *Principaux contrats spéciaux*, 381.   [252] Terré, Simler, Lequette, *Obligations*, 938.

[253] Viney and Jourdain, *Conditions*, 805; D. Mazeaud, 'Les victimes et les dommages réparables' in *La responsabilité du fait des produits défectueux (loi du 19 mai 1998) Petites affiches, La Loi* No. 155 (28 Dec. 1998) ('Mazeaud, *Les victimes*'), 14 at 18. S. Taylor, 'The Harmonisation of European Product Liability Rules: French and English Law' (1999) 48 *ICLQ* 419, who saw the then existing *jurisprudence* of *obligation de sécurité* and treatment of putting a defective product onto the market as delictual fault (together with the continued presence of the *garantie légale*) as marking the significant difference with English law after implementation of the Directive. The same author notes, however, in Taylor, *Harmonisation communautaire*, 41 that this case law 'ought logically to be absorbed by the new legislative scheme'.

[254] Larroumet, D 1998 Chron. 311, 316.   [255] Ibid.

[256] Mazeaud, *Les victimes*, 19 (the *jurisprudence* he has in mind is the *obligation de sécurité* of the 1990s).

the implications of this line of argument, which could be so destructive of a person's possible claims against producers and suppliers, as the abandonment of *all* the judicial constructions in favour of victims of products would fly in the face of the basis of the legislative compromise reached in the *loi* of 1998, as expressed in its retention of claimants' rights to rely on the *droit commun* either of delict or contract. And this possibility for a Member State was affirmed by the European Court in its decisions in 2002.[257]

The working out of these arguments has generally differed depending on the particular legal doctrines which the courts had earlier constructed. So, almost all French jurists agree that the *obligations de sécurité* constructed by the courts in the 1990s to implement the Directive,[258] and imposed on producers and sellers in respect of their defective products have not survived the *loi* of 1998;[259] this *jurisprudence* is in any event incompatible with the position taken by the European Court in relation to the liability of suppliers, as it imposes the same subject matter and legal basis as the 1985 Directive and yet goes beyond it.[260] On the other hand, it is agreed that a producer or supplier of a product can still be liable under the law of sale, whether under the *garantie légale* or for contractual non-conformity, a significant position given the extension of these liabilities beyond privity,[261] a position clearly acceptable to the European Court whose decisions of 2002 refer to liability for latent defects and under the general law of contract as coming within the permission granted by article 13 of the Directive.[262]

French jurists also agree that in principle the *droit commun* of delictual liability for *faute* may be imposed on either a producer or supplier (subject, it is assumed, to the operation of *non-cumul*):[263] this is specifically provided by the *loi* itself[264] and was clearly permitted by the European Court.[265] The significance of this survival is very considerable. First, it means that a person injured by a product may bring a claim as *partie civile* for damages before a criminal court, enjoying the substantive and procedural advantages which I have earlier described.[266] Secondly, ironically, it can produce the same effect as the *obligation de suivi* condemned by the European Court as an improper restriction on two of the producer's defences in article 7 of the 1985 Directive and so removed from the *loi* of 1998,[267] for a producer's failure to monitor properly the safety of his products can be liable to any person injured or whose property is damaged as a result on the basis that this constitutes *une faute délictuelle*,[268] giving rise to liability with less restrictive time limits than the new

---

[257] J. Calais-Auloy, 'Menace européenne sur la jurisprudence française concernant l'obligation de sécurité du vendeur professionnel (CJCE, 25 avril 2002)' D 2002 Chron. 2458, 2460. Above, pp. 441–2.

[258] For these doctrines, see above, pp. 455–7.

[259] Ghestin (1998), 1206; L. Leveneur, 'Le défaut' in *La responsabilité du fait des produits défectueux* (*loi du 19 mai 1998*) *Petites affiches, La Loi* No. 155 (28 Dec. 1998), 22, 33–4; Mazeaud, *Les victimes*, 19.

[260] Calais-Auloy, D 2002 Chron. 2458, 2459; Flour, Aubert and Savaux, *Fait juridique*, 304 (who are more hesitant).

[261] Mazeaud, *Les victimes*, 19; Leveneur, *Le défaut*, 34–5; Calais-Auloy, D 2002. 2458, 2460.

[262] Above, pp. 441–2.   [263] Above, p. 27.   [264] Art. 1386-18 al. 2 C. civ.

[265] Above, p. 442.

[266] F. Chabas, 'La responsabilité pour défaut de sécurité des produits, dans la loi du 19 mai 1998' GP 1998.2.1111, 1114 and see above, Chap. 14.   [267] Above, pp. 459–60; *loi* of 9 Dec. 2004, art. 29.

[268] Larroumet, D 1998 Chron. 311, 315–316 (before the ECJ's decision); Viney and Jourdain, *Conditions*, 802.

product liability.[269] Thirdly, though, the status of the *jurisprudence* of the 1970s which held that the mere putting onto the market of a defective product by a producer constituted delictual fault must be more doubtful, for while it is based on the general law,[270] it appears to fall foul of the European Court's decision just as much as the later *jurisprudence* of the 1990s on *obligation de sécurité*: both overtly impose liability on manufacturers on the ground of their putting onto the market a defective product which has caused harm. Fourthly, by contrast, it has been suggested that the courts may extend the benefit of the seller's strict contractual obligations (whether for *vice caché* or contractual non-conformity) to third parties by holding that their non-performance in itself constitutes delictual fault under articles 1382 or 1383.[271] Certainly French courts have on occasion come to this striking conclusion, thereby blurring considerably the line between contract and delict.[272] Finally, though, few jurists seem to wish to retain the liability of producers as *gardiens de la structure* under article 1384 *aliéna* 1, as the juristic splitting of *la garde* on which this would rest has been widely condemned.[273]

Perhaps most difficult is the status of the *jurisprudence* imposing on sellers and suppliers (as on a number of other *professionnels*) *obligations d'information*.[274] It may be thought to be a judicial creation governing liability of producers and suppliers in respect of defective products; this was its earliest manifestation and has remained an important context for its application, and this suggests that it should be abandoned. On the other hand, *obligations d'information* are found outside the context of unsafe defective products, find their source in the general laws of delict (pre-contractual *faute*) or contract (for non-performance of a contractual obligation), were given a legislative basis in 1992, and are linked to the general principle of good faith. All these features suggest that they may survive even as regards the liability of producers and suppliers in respect of unsafe products. If this were the case, their significance would be to allow suit beyond the restrictive periods of the *loi* of 1998, rather than to impose any stricter liability.[275]

There are, moreover, three further questions as to the relationship between the new product liability and other French bases of civil liability.

First, the European Court noted that article 13 of the Directive allowed a Member State to retain 'a special liability system existing at the moment when this Directive is notified', interpreting this to mean one governing particular categories of products and having in mind special *legislative* systems.[276] It has been argued, though, that this exception should be relied on so as to perpetuate French *jurisprudence* which applied special, more protective approaches to the victims of health products by recognising a 'true presumption of causation', even though this was done under the general law.[277] There is no reason, it is argued, why a 'special liability system' for 'health products' has to be legislative and while the relevant court decisions post-date the notification of

---

[269] Below, p. 528.   [270] Above, p. 51.   [271] Calais-Auloy, D 2002 Chron. 2458, 2460.
[272] Above, p. 29.
[273] Ghestin (1998), 1203; Calais-Auloy, D 2002 Chron. 2458, 2460 and above, p. 54.
[274] Above, pp. 65–9.   [275] L. Leveneur, 'Le défaut', in *Petites affiches*, No. 155 (28 Dec. 1988) 28, 33.
[276] Above, p. 441.
[277] N. Jonquet, A.-C. Maillois and F. Vialla, 'Les victimes de produits de santé épargnées par la CJCE: Réflexion sur la portée des arrêts du 25 avril 2002 sur la responsabilité du fait des produits de santé' D 2003 Point de vue, 1299. While the authors do not support their assertions with citation, an example may be found in Civ. (1) 9 May 2001, Bull. civ. I no. 130 (hepatitis C contracted after blood transfusion).

the Directive in 1985, the principle of the retroactive effect of *jurisprudence* means that the law actually existed prior to its formal recognition and therefore before notification.[278] In their view, acceptance of these arguments would have the advantage of allowing French law to retain and to develop a special set of liability rules for health products, without distinguishing (as does the *loi* of 1998 in relation to the development risks defence) between products derived from the human body and other health products, such as pharmaceuticals.[279] Clearly, there are a number of counter-arguments (notably, that the European Court would not consider particular judicial interpretations or applications of general rules for particular categories of products as 'a special liability system' for the purposes of article 13); and it may be thought that a French court which wished to perpetuate its strict approach to causation as regards health products could do so straightforwardly without this elaborate justification, either as a matter of liability under the *loi* of 1998 itself (which appears in principle to leave causation to the laws of Member States and the 'assessment' of their courts)[280] or under the general law which has survived it.

However, the suggestion is illustrative of the degree of dissatisfaction among French jurists with the practical and juridical effect of the product liability legislation. Again, though, the position has been further complicated by the politics of wider French legislative reform. For, as part of the package of measures introduced by *loi* in 2002 to govern medical liability, it was specifically provided that there should be a retroactive presumption of causation as to infection by hepatitis C after a patient receives contaminated blood and later contracts the disease.[281] It could be argued that this special and limited legislative reform precludes more general application of a presumption by the courts.

Secondly, French jurists accept (and the decisions of the European Court of 2002 allow) that the new legislation does not affect liability in producers or suppliers under the *garantie légale* in sale. But can this law be reformed so as to make it more protective of 'buyers' and, incidentally therefore, of the victims of products? This could be thought to provide a way around the substantive effect of the European Court's condemning of the French extensions of liability under the Directive, but the question has been overshadowed by the debate as to how French law should implement the Consumer Guarantees Directive, some fearing that legislative implementation of this second directive might weaken the palliative effect of existing contract law on the effect of the 1985 Directive.[282] As will be seen, the principal candidate for reform was the *garantie's bref délai* and provision on this was indeed tucked into the *projet de loi* of 2004,[283] despite not being required either to correct French implementation of the 1985 Directive nor to implement the 1999 Directive—and it actually found its way into law on the promulgation of the *ordonnance* of 17 February 2005.[284] Here, therefore, we can glimpse the potentially difficult relationship in French law between the two directives and their proper implementation.[285]

---

[278] N. Jonquet, A.-C. Maillois and F. Vialla, op, cit. n. 277, 1300.   [279] Ibid., 1301.
[280] Below, pp. 511–14.   [281] *Loi* no. 2002–303, art. 102, above, Chap. 6 at n. 232.
[282] Calais-Auloy, D 2002 Chron. 2458, 2460.   [283] Art. 7.
[284] Art. 3 and see below, p. 583.   [285] Below, pp. 662–3.

Thirdly, some French jurists have expressed concern about the possible wider and retrogressive effect of the *loi* of 1998 on French civil liability, both within and beyond the liabilities of producers and suppliers. In particular, some fear that the *loi*'s formal inclusion of the development risks defence may have a 'contagious effect' on liability under the *droit commun*,[286] possibly by encouraging the Cour de cassation to abandon its requirement that *force majeure* needs to be 'exterior to the thing'.[287] How can the Cour de cassation continue to refuse to allow a defence of development risks when 'a legal provision, which is actually inserted into the Civil Code, expressly states the contrary'?[288] Could a court intervene of its own initiative in the interests of *ordre public* so as to ensure that the *loi* of 1998 is applied even where a claimant relies on other laws which are to his greater advantage?[289] The decision to implement the 1985 Directive by amending the Civil Code certainly invites French courts to give it a more diffuse effect.

3. The Process of Implementation of the Product Liability Directive in English Law

The UK was one of the first Member States to implement the Product Liability Directive, doing so by the Consumer Protection Act in 1987. Apart from being much quicker, overall the process was less controversial than in France, though there were significant disagreements, notably as to the development risks defence and the position of primary agricultural products. Here, I wish to look briefly at the legal and political debate surrounding the legislation, the latter's form and relationship to English law more generally and how these compare with the *loi* of 1998. I shall then look at a particular problem raised by the 1987 Act's provisions tying consumer safety to civil liability.

(a) The legal and political debate

The idea of reforming the law of product liability so as to impose liability without fault was neither alien nor new to English lawyers in the mid-1980s, having been recommended by the Law Commissions and the Pearson Commission in 1976 and 1977 respectively.[290] At the time, product liability was seen as naturally focused on the manufacturer, whose ground of liability in respect of personal injuries and damage to property beyond privity of contract was almost exclusively in the tort of negligence.[291] This background meant that most English lawyers saw change in the law of product liability as required by the 1985 Directive as an example of law reform (changing the law to make it better or fairer) rather than merely as an instrument of EEC economic

---

[286] P. Jourdain, 'Une loi pour rien? (à propos de la loi du 19 mai 1998 relative à la responsabilité du fait des produits défectueux' Resp. civ. et assur. (1998) Chron. 4, 5.

[287] G. Viney, 'L'introduction en droit français de la directive européene du 25 juillet 1985 relative à la responsabilité du fait des produits défectueux' D 1998.Chron. 291, 298–9. There is a certain echo of this idea in Civ.(3) 28 Nov. 2002, *pourvoi* no. 00-15058, legifrance, where the court rejected the development risks defence against liability imposed on the ground of delictual fault under art. 1382 C. civ. *merely* on the ground that the *loi* of 1998 was not retroactive and did not therefore apply to the facts.   [288] Ibid.

[289] Carbonnier, *Obligations*, 479–80.   [290] Above, p. 432.   [291] Above, pp. 161–4.

policy. It is for this reason that earlier commentaries on the Directive from the point of view of English law were principally concerned with whether the change which it required was effective as a matter of law reform, assuming this to mean improving the chances of compensation of a person injured by a product as compared with the existing law.[292] This was also the focus of concern in the parliamentary debates on the Bill, centring on the development risks defence.

In the UK, the political context of implementation was a double one. While lawyers, politicians and the press had in mind the difficulties which the victims of Thalidomide encountered in their claims for compensation, this famous example of the potential liability for products did not involve any allegations against public officials or against government of the sort which made the *affaire du sang contaminé* so prominent in French political life in the mid- and later 1990s.[293] The British government in 1986 and 1987 was Conservative, the Consumer Protection Bill being introduced a few months before Margaret Thatcher was elected as Prime Minister for a third time in June 1987. The general policy of this government was expressly stated by the responsible minister, Lord Lucas, as being to implement the Directive, but not to go beyond it,[294] although in doing so the government's Bill sailed as close to the wind as it could, at times apparently trying to restrict the Directive's liability as much as could arguably be compatible with EC law.[295] This can be seen in two minor and rather obscure aspects of the implementation,[296] but is clearer in the wording of the development risks defence later brought before the European Court.[297] This suggests that the Conservative government of the day was as much concerned with the need not to impose any greater burden of liability than necessary on British industry and with a desire to keep to the limits of liability in the Directive in the interests of harmonisation of liability laws in the EEC.[298]

However, another aspect of the implementation of the Product Liability Directive in the UK reveals an apparently contrasting attitude, as it formed the first part of an Act whose second part provided important new provisions relating to the safety of products, in particular creating a general requirement of safety for all consumer products backed by criminal sanctions, and new powers in public bodies to act in the interest of product safety, whether by regulation or by intervention in the market.[299] For the government, these new provisions were justified by the need for fair competition since '[s]upplying unsafe goods is a form of unfair competition as it gives the supplier of unsafe goods an unfair advantage over a competitor who is prepared to incur the

---

[292] Whittaker (1985); J. Stapleton, 'Products Liability Reform—Real or Illusory?' (1986) 6 *OJLS* 392; C. Newdick, 'The Future of Negligence in Product Liability' (1987) 103 *LQR* 288.

[293] Above, pp. 450–1.   [294] HL Deb. Vol. 482 col. 1055.   [295] Below, p. 470.

[296] 1987 Act, s. 1(3) and 5(2).

[297] Case C-300/95 of 29 May 1997, *Commission v United Kingdom* [1997] ECR I-2649, below, pp. 495–9 (which notes that the Commission had five further points of complaint in respect of the 1987 Act which it was persuaded by the UK not to press).

[298] For possible failures to implement the Directive properly see below, p. 470 and G. Howells, 'Implications of the Implementation and Non-implementation of the EC Products Liability Directive' (1990) 41 *Northern Ireland Law Quarterly* 22.

[299] 1987 Act, Part II, on which see above, pp. 334, 406. Part III provided new provisions relating to misleading price provisions.

costs associated with ensuring that his goods are safe'.[300] These two aspects of the 1987 Act were considered complementary: Part I concerned with compensation, Part II with deterrence and punishment.[301] However, this coupling of the implementation of the 1985 Directive and reform of the law of product safety drew attention to the question of the appropriate link between the two.

Despite general parliamentary support for the Consumer Protection Bill,[302] there remained two main points of disagreement, both regarding the choices to be made by the UK under the 1985 Directive's derogations: the inclusion of primary agricultural products and the development risks defence.[303] As to the first, the government wished to exclude them from the scheme of liability on the ground that it was difficult to trace suppliers of primary goods and that they are particularly prone to hidden defects caused by environmental factors.[304] This view, reflected in the Act as enacted, has now had to be reversed as a result of amendment of the 1985 Directive in 1999.[305]

The central point of contention—and the only one to make any significant presence felt in the non-legal media—was the development risks defence. Those who opposed its inclusion considered that it would bring back negligence as the basis of liability by the back door,[306] whereas manufacturers are better able to bear this risk than are consumers: only in this way would victims of a Thalidomide-type disaster be compensated.[307] However, the government (strongly supported by the Confederation of British Industry) wished to retain the defence[308] and countered that to impose liability for development risks on producers would be a great disincentive to innovation and 'innovation benefits consumers as well as producers'.[309] It was this last argument which made Lord Denning change his mind on the issue, being impressed by the need for British companies to find new drugs without being hampered, giving the example of a new treatment for AIDS.[310]

One aspect of the parliamentary debate is particularly interesting, though, as it attempted to relate the UK's decision on the development risks defence to the burden of liability insurance. In general it was thought that the impact of the 1985 Directive would have a minimal impact on the cost of liability insurance (following the view of the Association of British Insurers) but there was more concern as to the insurability of liability for development risks[311] and the government saw the risk of producers not

---

[300] HC Deb.Vol. 115, col. 51 (27 Apr. 1987) (Mr Michael Howard MP).

[301] Dti, *Implementation of EC Directive on Product Liability, An explanatory and consultative note* (Nov. 1985) ('Dti, *Explanatory note*'), 8.

[302] HL Deb. Vol. 482 cols. 1006–07 (Bill welcomed by the opposition).

[303] The UK government decided not to exercise the option in art. 16 of the 1985 Directive to introduce an overall limit of liability on the ground that it could lead to injustice in multiple claim situations and to lengthy delays in payment of compensation awards: Dti, *Explanatory note*, 5–6.

[304] HL Deb. Vol. 483 col. 171 *et seq.*

[305] Above, p. 446 implemented in the UK by the Consumer Protection Act 1987 (Product Liability) (Modification) Order 2000, SI 2000 No. 2771 by removing s. 2(4) of the 1987 Act.

[306] HL Deb. Vol. 482 col. 1017 (Lord Abbeydale).

[307] HL Deb. Vol. 483 cols. 820–1 (Baroness Burton of Coventry).   [308] The Times, 7 Jan. 1987.

[309] The Times, 21 Nov. 1987 (reporting Mr. Michael Howard MP).

[310] HL Deb. Vol. 483 col. 826.

[311] HL Deb. Vol. 482 col. 1019 (Earl de la Warr); HL Deb. Vol. 482 col. 1049 (Lord Ezra).

being able to obtain insurance as a further reason for retaining the defence.[312] Even those who wished the defence to be excluded acknowledged that the future insurance position was uncertain and proposed by way of response that the government should be made 'insurer of last resort', for cases where the commercial market could not provide one.[313] However, the government opposed this on the ground that it constituted an 'unacceptable state intervention in the insurance market'[314] and that the defence formed part of the balance of interests between consumers and industry which had been struck in Brussels.[315] Similar reasons were adduced by the government for rejecting a later proposal that all producers should have an obligation to insure against their liability, but with a special back-up fund where this obligation was not performed similar to existing arrangements regarding road accidents.[316] In the end, the government won the day, retaining the development risks for all categories of product.

The British and French parliamentary discussions had in common, therefore, that attention was focused on the Directive's possible options (and especially on the development risks defence) rather than on the significance of the concept of 'defect', but the political and legal contexts of the French and UK implementation were radically different. In the UK in 1987, liability for unsafe products was not a highly politicised issue and the need to develop pharmaceutical products to deal with the risks of diseases such as HIV could argue for retention of the defence; in France just over a decade later, 'responsibility' for products had become very prominent in political life, ever associated with the *affaire du sang contaminé*.[317] The legal background also differed significantly: in the UK the new law looked as though it improved the position of injured parties by comparison with liability in negligence; in France, the new law risked making their position worse.[318] While in implementing the Product Liability Directive, the significance of insurance played a much larger role in the debates in the UK than in France, insurance was to become all too prominent a part of the reform of French medical liability which itself has implications for products.[319]

(b) The form of the legislation and its relationship with other English law

The UK government chose to implement the 1985 Directive by primary legislation rather than under its powers in the European Communities Act 1972, in part because it wished to introduce other provisions not required by EEC law at the same time. This meant that the implementing legislation was subjected to considerable parliamentary scrutiny and debate as well as wider public consultation.[320] In this respect, the legislation contrasts strikingly with the UK's implementation of the Consumer Guarantees Directive over a decade later which was implemented by

---

[312] The Times, 7 Jan. 1987.

[313] HL Deb. Vol. 482 cols. 821–5 (Amendment No. 54 proposed by Lord Williams of Elvel).

[314] Ibid., col. 843 (Lord Lucas).   [315] Ibid., col. 840 (Lord Lucas).

[316] Ibid., col. 872 (Amendment No. 42 proposed by Lord Airedale) opposed HL Vol. 483 col. 873 (Lord Lucas).   [317] Above, p. 450.

[318] Above, p. 458.   [319] Above, pp. 154–5.   [320] E.g. Dti, *Explanatory Note*.

secondary legislation after consultation but where there was no public debate despite the much greater range of choices for the UK which it allowed.[321]

How does implementation by statute affect the Directive's place in English law more generally? In the French system, there is an important choice in implementing a directive affecting private law between the introduction of a special *loi* and amendment of the Civil Code, a decision which can make a substantive difference to the impact of the new law.[322] Of course, the absence of a civil code precludes this dilemma for the UK legislator! Instead, the common law provides the overall framework for analysis and solution of legal problems which the Civil Code provides for France,[323] this similarity being reflected in the legitimacy as regards the common law and within the Civil Code of argument from wider legal principle and by analogy. By contrast, English statutes create exceptions or even 'isolated irruptions' in the body of this common law pattern,[324] though the truly exceptional character of a statute depends on its subject matter: some areas of English law are so widely and originally regulated that one can properly speak of their legislative codification.[325] But it remains true that civil liability, whether of contract or in tort, is dominated by the common law, statutes intervening specially to clarify, supplement or correct the general common law position. For an English common lawyer, therefore, the special nature of the liability required by the Product Liability Directive did not create any particular *formal* problem: English lawyers are used to seeing legislation parachuting into their law particular rules which are not integrated into the law more generally.

How, then, does the law created by the UK's implementation of the 1985 Directive relate it to its English surroundings? There are three questions here: first, does the style of the legislation follow the style of the Directive or a more English style? Secondly, is the new product liability entirely self-contained or are certain of its incidents regulated by existing rules, whether common law or statutory? And, thirdly, does the new product liability supplant or merely supplement existing bases of liability, whether of the common law or statutory?

First, while the Directive's style may reflect common law ways to a French lawyer,[326] they clearly did not do so to the draftsmen of the 1987 Act. In principle, a directive 'is binding, as to the result to be achieved', but leaves to the national authorities the choice of form and methods,[327] and so a directive 'does not necessarily require that its provisions be incorporated formally and verbatim in express specific legislation' as long as it is does 'guarantee the full application of the directive in a sufficiently clear and precise manner so that, where the directive is intended to create rights for individuals, the persons concerned may ascertain the full extent of their rights'.[328] In drafting the Consumer Protection Act, the government's basic purpose was 'to make

---

[321] Below, pp. 583–7.   [322] Above, pp. 453–4.   [323] Nicholas, 5–7.

[324] B. Nicholas in Harris and Tallon, Chap. 4, 'The Pre-contractual Obligation to Disclose Information, English Report' 166, 178.

[325] For example, company law in the Companies Acts or civil procedure in the Civil Procedure Rules whose Part 1.1(1) describes them as 'a new procedural code'.   [326] Above, p. 452.

[327] Art. 249 EC.

[328] Case C-71/92 of 17 Nov. 1993, *Commission v Spain*, [1993] ECR I-5923 para. 23.

clear those of [the Directive's] provisions which are unfamiliar to our law or might otherwise give rise to debate',[329] relying on its first section which required courts to construe Part I so as to ensure compliance with the Directive.[330] But the government thought that the Directive should not be attached to the Act because 'by following the provisions of this Bill . . . our national courts will arrive at a result which is the same as that to which the European Court would come in interpreting the Directive': while the reference to the Directive in section 1(1) of the Act is a reminder, the Act was intended to 'stand on its own'.[331]

So, while the French legislation generally followed the style, order and wording of the Directive very closely (at least where it did not seek substantively to improve on its provisions[332]), the 1987 Act reordered and recast the relatively simple provisions of the Directive in a style which is more prolix and less easy to read than the Directive.[333] This did not find favour with all those in Parliament. Lord Denning, for example, thought that '[t]he directive is far clearer than Part I of the Bill' adding that 'the preliminary recitals tell us exactly what the principles are at which the directive is aimed. There are none in our Bill'.[334] Moreover, others criticised the Bill's rewording of the development risks defence, which used 'wishy-washy concepts' and 'surely softens' article 7(e)'s demands in an unauthorised way.[335] Similarly, section 5(2) provides that:

a person shall not be liable for the loss of or any damage to the product itself or for the loss of or any damage to the whole or any part of any product which has been supplied with the product in question comprised in it.

While the first half of this reflects the terms of article 9(b) of the Directive, there is nothing in the Directive to justify its decidedly opaque second half, which would mean, for example, that the owner of a car damaged when its defective battery caused a crash could recover from neither the manufacturer of the car nor of the battery.[336] The government's explanation, which relied on an obscure paragraph in an earlier Commission memorandum, is not convincing.[337]

However, while the government in 1987 was able to push through its various re-workings of the Directive, its legislative strategy of domestication has not been con-spicuously successful. For in the most important decision on Part I of the 1987 Act so far, the High Court spent no time on the formulations used by the Act, but instead looked at the Directive, and at UK and continental legal commentaries.[338] This reflects an increasing tendency in the English courts as regards questions of interpretation of

---

[329] Ibid., col. 851 (Lord Lucas).   [330] 1987 Act, s. 1(1).

[331] HL Deb. col. 747 (Lord Cameron of Lochbroom, the Lord Advocate).   [332] Above, pp. 458–60.

[333] There are, e.g., *three* definitional sections, one of which constructs a definition of 'supply' which aims to fit both Parts I and II of the Act and which deals with certain aspects of the Directive's notion of 'putting a product into circulation': 1987 Act, ss. 1, 45, 46. And see, e.g., the Act's treatment of 'product', below, p. 478.

[334] HL Deb. Vol. 483 col. 746 referring to 1985 Directive, art. 4.

[335] Ibid., col. 848 (Baroness Burton of Coventry).   [336] HL Deb. Vol. 483 col. 877–8.

[337] Ibid., col. 879; EEC Commission, Explanatory Memorandum accompanying proposal of 9 Sept. 1976, Bulletin of EEC Supplement 11/76 para. 20.

[338] *A v The National Blood Authority* [2001] 3 All ER 289, below, pp. 487–92.

legislation implementing EC directives[339] and justifies the faith of the European Court in the power of the English 'legal context' to secure effectively the full application of the Directive.[340]

Secondly, and related to this, is the question of the extent to which certain of the *incidents* of the new product liability can be and should be regulated by existing rules, whether common law or statutory. Clearly, the line between interpretation of the Directive's concepts according to an autonomous European view or according to the view of the laws of the Member States depends on the terms and purposes of the Directive itself as they are interpreted by the European Court, but while some are placed explicitly within the competence of the Member States,[341] others are left unclear.[342] A national legislator, therefore, must tread carefully since any definition of the Directive's concepts or setting of the incidents of liability by national law risks trespassing onto the European competence.

The Consumer Protection Act 1987 was fairly cautious here. In some cases, it expressly linked the new liability with other special statutory provisions governing the incidents of civil liability, as in the case of claims by dependents on a person's death,[343] claims in respect of injuries to an unborn child[344] and the effect of a claimant's contributory negligence.[345] By contrast, the 1987 Act's implementation of the rules governing the time limits within which any claim must be brought took the form of elaborate new provisions inserted into the general Limitation Act 1980,[346] though the concepts which it used are governed by definitions in the 1987 Act.[347] As a result, the Limitation Act's provisions govern, for example, the suspension or renewal of limitation periods of the new product liability (but *not* its foreclosure period).[348] On the other hand, in other cases, there was thought to be no need for any overt link with existing legislation because it would simply apply to the new product liability on its own terms.[349]

The common law is also important in the regulation of the incidents of the new product liability. Sometimes, the Act brings out this relationship overtly, as in its reference to producers' and suppliers' liability under the 1987 Act being 'joint and several'.[350] Other possible connections with the common law are less obvious. The

---

[339] E.g. *Director General of Fair Trading v First National Bank* [2001] UKHL 52 esp. [8], [31]; [2002] 1 AC 481; *London Borough of Newham v Khatun* [2004] EWCA Civ. 55 [78]–[83]; [2004] 3 WLR 417 (both in the context of the 1993 Directive).

[340] Case C-300/95 of 29 May 1997 *Commission v UK* [1997] ECR I-2649, below, p. 498.

[341] E.g. the legal basis of rights of contribution or recourse (art. 5); the rules governing the suspension and interruption of its periods (art. 10(2)); and rules governing the recovery of 'non-material damage' (art. 9 *in fine*).

[342] E.g. damage resulting from death or personal injuries and damage to property (below, pp. 503–7); the causal link between 'defect' and 'damage': below, pp. 511–14.

[343] Fatal Accidents Act 1976; 1987 Act, s. 6(1) and (2).

[344] Congenital Disabilities (Civil Liability) Act 1976, s. 1; 1987 Act, s. 6(3).

[345] Law Reform (Contributory Negligence) Act 1945; 1987 Act, s. 6(4) and (5).

[346] Limitation Act 1980, ss. 11A and 14(1)A.   [347] Limitation Act 1980, s. 11A(8).

[348] E.g., the three-year limitation period of the product liability provisions is in effect suspended if the claimant is disabled at the time of the accrual of the cause of action: Limitation Act 1980, s. 28(1) and (7) and see below, pp. 528–9.

[349] E.g. Civil (Liability) Contribution Act 1987, s. 1; HL Deb. Vol. 483 cols. 783–5.

[350] 1987 Act, s. 2(5) and see below, p. 510.

1987 Act contains no provision which refers issues of causation, remoteness of damage, heads of recoverable damages or the quantification of damages to the common law,[351] but here it follows previous English statutes governing civil liability where this sort of issue is left to the common law by implication.[352] In one case, though, the extent to which the common law applies is difficult. The Directive leaves the question of recovery of 'non-material damage' to 'national provisions' and most commentators agree that this includes damages for pain and suffering, psychiatric injury or mental distress consequential on the claimant's own or another's personal injuries or (in the latter case) death.[353] The 1987 Act imposes liability for 'personal injury' and then defines this as including 'any disease and any other impairment of a person's physical *or mental* condition'.[354] Does this mean, though, that a person who suffers 'psychiatric injury' caused by a defective product can recover damages from the producer or others under the 1987 Act without reference to the sorts of restrictive criteria established at common law for the recovery of this type of harm in the tort of negligence?[355] Neither the Directive nor the 1987 Act provide a definite answer.[356]

So, while any English statute can in general be seen as an exception to the general common law position, where a statute concerns a matter which is already widely regulated by the law, it falls to be related (if not actually integrated) into the surrounding statutory and common law context. On the other hand, in reading the parliamentary debates concerning the Consumer Protection Bill and the academic discussions of the Directive, it is not suggested that the UK's implementation must in any sense be *controlled* by existing national legal principle in contrast to the French context where legislators and jurists agreed that its legal principle of full recovery for harm (the principle of *réparation intégrale*) required the imposition of liability under the *loi* of 1998 for *all* damage to property, both beyond 'consumer property' and without the threshold of liability set by article 9 of the Directive.[357] Such an argument would not have convinced in the UK context, both because statute does not need to follow any existing common law principle or statutory precedent,[358] and because of the accepted supremacy of EC law. As Lord Airedale remarked of article 9's exclusion of recovery for damage to the defective product itself: '[i]f the directive directs something which is anomalous, we have to live with it.'[359]

---

[351] Cf. HL Deb. Vol. 483 col. 876 (where this was suggested).

[352] E.g. Occupiers Liability Acts 1957 and 1984 (*Jolley v Sutton LBC* [1998] 1 Lloyd's Rep 433; [2000] 1 WLR 1082 applying the common law rules governing the quantification of damages (at trial) and remoteness of damage (HL); Animals Act 1971 (though these Acts reformed the law on common law foundations). This way of thinking could also be thought to lie behind the courts' approach to liability in the tort of breach of statutory duty, whose general incidents are fixed by the common law where not fixed by the statute in question: *Clerk and Lindsell on Torts*, para. 11–53.   [353] 1985 Directive, art. 9, below, pp. 507–8.

[354] 1987 Act, s. 45(1) 'personal injury' (emphasis added).

[355] Above, pp. 161–2.   [356] Below, pp. 507–8.

[357] Above, p. 460. When this was challenged before the European Court, the French government argued that its removal of the threshold of liability was lawful following the French principle that immunity from civil liability was contrary to *ordre public*: Case 52/00, *Commission v France*, ECR 2002 I-03827, para. 33. The Court rejected this argument.

[358] There are statutory precedents for restricting the type of harm recoverable under a statutory liability: Occupiers Liability Act 1984 (recovery by trespassers for personal injury and death but not damage to property).   [359] HL Deb. Vol. 483 col. 877.

Thirdly, how did the 1987 Act relate the new product liability to existing bases of liability? Generally, English lawyers are very tolerant of overlapping analyses of the same or similar facts, an attitude particularly prominent as regards the common law of liability. For the law of torts often provides a number of possible bases on which a person might wish to claim and in principle allows him (and *not* the court[360]) to choose on which to proceed (for example, as between public nuisance, private nuisance or the tort of negligence); and a claimant can proceed in the alternative, so as to wait and see which of the possible bases will finally be most advantageous. Similarly, a party to a contract can choose whether to claim for breach of contract or instead in tort, as long as an independent tort exists on the facts and this is not inconsistent with the contract.[361] This way of thinking can be seen as a legacy of the procedural origins of these areas of law in the forms of actions, rather than in grand, substantive legal propositions.[362]

Given this way of thinking, it did not seem odd to most English lawyers for the implementation of the 1985 Directive to add another layer to the existing law instead of creating a unique ground of liability neatly distinguished from other areas. Of course, English law distinguishes between liability in tort and in contract, but it happily includes within the latter issues of safety as well as of quality, as the statutory test of 'satisfactory quality' in the law of sale of goods explicitly recognises;[363] unlike France, there is little argument that these issues are essentially different and must be kept apart.[364] And in the law of torts, English law allows the possibility of other torts imposing liability on a manufacturer as well as the mainly relevant tort, the tort of negligence.[365] Given that article 13 of the Directive permitted Member States to retain existing liabilities, it was not even mooted that the UK's implementation should create an exclusive regime and if it had been, any argument from simplicity of regulation[366] would immediately be countered by drawing attention to the difficulty of drawing the line between the new and old liabilities and the potentially prejudicial effect such an exclusive regime would have where an injured party could otherwise sue in contract, given the latter's greater strictness.[367] So, after implementation of the Directive, a claimant can sue in negligence, for breach of contract or under the new rules provided by the 1987 Act according to the circumstances and his choice.

Again, this marks a striking contrast with France, where the implementing legislation's retention of existing bases of liability formed part of the central political compromise and became the focus of considerable subsequent dispute, both in terms of its actual effect and its desirability.[368] Overall, one gains the impression that while both English and French lawyers criticise over-complication, French lawyers value more highly

---

[360] See above, pp. 205–7.

[361] *Henderson v Merrett Syndicates Ltd.* [1995] 2 AC 145 and see *Chitty on Contracts* para. 1–116 *et seq.*

[362] See the discussion of the late eighteenth- and nineteenth-century approach to the option of claiming between contract and tort in *Chitty on Contracts* paras. 1-096–1-097, 1-105–1-108 and S. Whittaker, *The Relationship between Contract and Tort: a Comparative Study of French and English Law* (Oxford, D.phil. thesis), Chap. 8. [363] Sale of Goods Act 1979 s. 14(2), above, p. 236.

[364] Above, pp. 243–4. [365] Above, pp. 221–3, 224–5.

[366] Cf. below, p. 474 concerning the relationship between consumer safety and civil liability.

[367] Above, pp. 245–7. [368] Above, pp. 458, 460–1.

the virtues of simplicity and formal integrity in their normative regulation. Moreover, in English law there is no sense in which a new statute *implicitly* overtakes or replaces existing case law as we have seen argued in relation to the *loi* of 1998 in France:[369] English statutes do what they say they do (subject to compatibility with EU law and rights under the ECHR), but if they say nothing the implication is that the common law survives. For unlike French private law *jurisprudence*, which ultimately rests on the interpretation of legislation and in particular of the Civil Code, English common law's validity is independent of statute. Statute may be superior, but the common law came first.

(c) Consumer safety, civil liability and the European Court's decisions of 2002

Implementation of the 1985 Directive and reform of the law of consumer safety in the same Act raised squarely the question of the relationship of the regulation of safety and civil liability. Previous legislation had given the administration a power to make regulations for the safety of particular products and had provided that breach of any duty contained in these regulations would in principle give rise to civil liability.[370] On consultation before the 1987 Act, the government asked whether breach of the new general safety requirement should give rise to civil liability, given that it might be thought 'onerous and confusing and contrary to the spirit of the Directive, for producers to be subject to two concurrent provisions on strict liability . . . as well as the strict liability . . . under the law of contract'.[371] For while there is a good deal of similarity between the definition of safety for the purposes of Parts I and II of the Act, they are not the same and there are further and more significant differences in the range of products covered, the primary defendants (producers under Part I, suppliers under Part II[372]) and defences.[373] In the upshot, the government decided expressly to provide that breach of the general safety requirement should *not* give rise to civil liability, whereas breach of any obligations imposed by specific safety regulations should still do so.[374]

Uncontroversial at the time, this position may now seem open to censure given the European Court's decisions of 2002 on the completely harmonising nature of the scheme required by the Directive.[375] For the practical effect of the recognition of a power to create regulatory duties for particular products to be exercised after the Directive is to hold their *supplier* liable for failures in a product's safety in circumstances not provided by the Directive. As the European Court's decision in *Gonzàlez Sanchez* suggests, where this is the case, in principle even laws *prior* to notification of the Directive in 1985 must be corrected.[376]

However, there are two arguments which could allow the UK to retain its link between breach of safety regulations and civil liability. The first argument is that the

---

[369] Above, p. 461.
[370] Consumer Protection Act 1961, s. 3(1); Consumer Safety Act 1978, s. 6.
[371] Dti, *Consultative note*, 9–10 and see previously *The Safety of Goods* (1984) Cmnd. 9302, para. 43.
[372] 1987 Act, s. 2 and s. 10 respectively.   [373] Ibid., s. 4 and s. 39 respectively.
[374] Ibid., s. 41.   [375] Above, pp. 440–4.   [376] Case C-183/00, above, pp. 442–3.

link comes within the *second* part of article 13 of the Directive, which allows the perpetuation of existing systems of liability applicable to particular categories of products.[377] Certainly, the liabilities arising from breach of any individual regulation would concern only a particular category of product and while the regulation itself may not pre-date the Directive, the legal link between particular safety regulations and civil liability was established in English law in 1961.[378] The second argument is broader. While English law distinguishes the questions of civil liability and breach of statutory duties (whether or not they are backed with criminal sanctions),[379] some other Member States instead treat breach of any particular legislative or regulatory duty, or criminal offence as itself a civil fault of a kind capable of giving rise to liability under their general laws of delict. This position is well illustrated by French law,[380] and so a French lawyer can understandably consider that the European Court's decisions in 2002 expressly preserve the possibility for a Member State to impose liability on this ground despite the 'completely harmonious' nature of the Directive's scheme.[381] This being the case, it would be substantively pointless in terms of harmonisation for the European Court to rule that the imposition of civil liability for breach of statutory regulations governing particular products in English law fell foul of the Directive's nature simply because English law does not treat this liability as part of its 'general law', but deals with it expressly and particularly by statute. On the other hand, this practical argument may not convince the Court, whose concern in the 2002 decisions to protect the integrity of the Directive's regime appears more formal than substantive; and if it were not to, this would give a new and irrational significance to the treatment of the relationship between regulatory duties and civil liability in the laws of the Member States.

---

[377] Above, p. 441.   [378] Consumer Protection Act 1961, s. 3(1).   [379] Above, pp. 218–20.

[380] Above, p. 45.   [381] Chabas, op. cit. n. 266, 1114, above, p. 462.

17

A Closer Look at the Product Liability Directive

In this chapter I shall explore the Product Liability Directive's provisions in more detail, looking at how they have been implemented and interpreted by French and English lawyers, leaving until Chapter 18 how the liability they create affects the patterns of liability for products.[1] In the case of French law, we still have to rely on *la doctrine* given that there are only one or two decisions applying the *loi* of 1998 itself: the *jurisprudence* of the 1990s which 'implemented' the Directive can be only an approximate guide given its formal basis in other provisions of the Civil Code and its doubtful present status.[2] In the case of English law, there are a handful of decisions applying the 1987 Act, including the important decision in *A v The National Blood Authority*.[3] There are also two important decisions of the European Court itself in *Commission v United Kingdom*[4] and *Veedfald v Århus Amtskommune*.[5]

1. 'Product'

The 1985 Directive introduced into both French and English law the notion of a 'product' as a constituent element of its new special liability. The language of product itself suggests something which has been produced, that is, made by a person from one or more *other* things and this idea can be found in the preamble to the 1985 Directive, which refers to its application 'only to movables which have been industrially produced', distinguishing the position regarding 'agricultural products and game, except where they have undergone a process of an industrial nature'.[6] However, apart from its reference to 'primary agricultural products', the definition in article 2 of the Directive does not define a product in terms of its having been produced, simply stating that ' "product" means all movables . . . even though incorporated into another movable or into an immovable', adding that it 'includes electricity'. For long, the most controversial aspect of the definition was the status of 'primary agricultural goods', these being *excluded* from its definition, but capable of being included by a Member State,[7] but since the Directive's amendment in 1999 this possibility has disappeared with the

---

[1] Below, Chap. 18. [2] Above, pp. 455–7, 461–2.
[3] [2001] 3 All ER 289, below, pp. 486–92, 499–502.
[4] Case C-300/95 of 29 May 1997 [1997] ECR I-2649, below, pp. 496–9.
[5] Case C-203/99 of 10 May 2001 [2001] ECR 1-3569 ('Case C-203/99, *Veedfald*'), below, pp. 503–8.
[6] 1985 Directive, recital 3. [7] 1985 Directive, arts. 2, 15(1)(a).

result that the generality and inclusiveness of the underlying definition of product appears all the more starkly: liability is *not* tied to industrial or any other production, but instead simply to 'movable property'.[8] Unlike both the Consumer Guarantees Directive of 1999 and the General Product Safety Directive of 2001, liability under the Product Liability Directive is not even formally tied to *consumer* products.[9]

This suggests that *all movable property* attracts liability under the 1985 Directive as long as it is 'defective', so that, for example, entirely natural raw materials, such as coal, untreated spring water or untreated human blood constitute 'products' for the purposes of the Directive as much as any industrially manufactured goods.[10] It has been suggested, though, that liability for some types of products may be excluded from the Directive because they lack a 'producer' and therefore anyone liable under it, giving as examples incorporeal products and movable products incorporated into immovable property.[11]

This then raises two difficulties in relation to the Directive's definition of product: how does it relate to incorporeal property and, specifically, to electricity? and how does it relate to immovable property?

First, incorporeal property can take a number of forms, including the 'intellectual property' of copyright material or patents or computer software: is an author or publisher of a cookery book with information encouraging its readers to eat wild (poisonous) plants, or the writer of software used in the flight equipment of an aircraft liable under the Directive for the information, as itself a 'defective product'? In my view, the European Court should take different views on this sort of question according to different types of 'intellectual products', in part as a function of the borderline between liability for products and liability for services implicit within the Directive and in part on more general considerations.[12] So, for example, a distinction could be drawn between software sold ready-to-use (to which the Directive would apply) and software tailor-made by its designer for the particular purpose of its recipient.[13] By contrast, while a book with defective information affecting a person's safety could itself be considered a product so as to engender liability 'without fault' in the publisher (as the producer of the book), the information itself should not be considered a product so as to engender liability in its author as this could have damaging consequences for freedom of expression.[14] It will be seen from this example that the question of the identification of the *relevant* 'product' in a case like this is of primary importance in

---

[8] The French version of recital 3 uses the term '*biens mobiliers*'. On the Amending Directive, above, p. 446.

[9] 1999 Directive, art. 1, below, p. 589; General Product Safety Directive, art. 2(a).

[10] 1985 Directive, recital 4 refers explicitly to liability extending to suppliers of 'raw material'. Cf. C-203/99, *Veedfald*, where A.-G. Ruiz-Jarabo Colomer at para. 13 of his opinion considered that the Directive was restricted to 'movables which have been manufactured industrially' and not therefore to the case referred to the court in which a professional had prepared a product specially for a medical transplant operation. While the Court did not advert specifically to this point (which had not been referred to it) its decision held the Directive applicable to the case before it: Case C-203/99 paras. 11–18 and see below, p. 504.

[11] N. Molfessis, 'Les produits en cause' *Petites affiches, La Loi* No. 155 (28 Dec. 1998), 20 at 23–4 who gives as an example shares in a company (though it is difficult to see how their 'defects' would cause physical harm).   [12] Whittaker (1989); Stapleton, *Product Liability*, 323–36.

[13] Whittaker (1989), 135–7.

[14] Cf. ibid., 133–5. F. X. Testu and J.-H. Moitry, 'La responsabilité du fait des produits défectueux, Commentaire de la loi 98-389 du 19 mai 1998' *Dalloz Affaires* (16 Jul. 1998) *Supplément* to No. 125 ('Testu and Moitry'), 5 take a similarly nuanced view.

relation to the person who is then identified as its 'producer'. To the extent to which the Directive does apply to incorporeal movable property apart from electricity, then the 1987 Act's implementation is unhelpful and misleading, as it defines 'product' in terms of 'goods or electricity' and then defines 'goods' as *including* 'substances, growing crops and things comprised in land by virtue of being attached to it and any ship, aircraft or vehicle'.[15]

The status of electricity is particularly interesting. As a matter of legislative history, electricity appears to have been specifically included in article 2 on the ground that energy was not considered to be 'property' in some laws.[16] Opposing views can be taken as to the wider effect of this inclusion, as it can be argued either that the inclusion of electricity suggests the exclusion of other incorporeal things or that all incorporeal things are included by analogy,[17] but the European Court is likely to decide this issue as a function of the appropriateness of the application of the Directive's scheme of liability to the alleged 'product' in question in terms of its economic purposes in relation to the internal market and consumer protection.[18] If so, then, for example, gas, whether natural or industrially produced, would be included, even though its physical presence is intangible.

But *how* do electricity, gas or indeed water attract liability under the Directive? In the case of gas or water, their 'defect' may be seen easily in some physical impurity which compromises safety to the extent to which article 6 of the Directive requires.[19] But how can an electric impulse be 'defective'? Happily, the definition of defect in article 6 is functional, turning on whether the product does not provide 'the safety which a person is entitled to expect', rather than physical, requiring some material corruption.[20] From this point of view, networked electricity may be defective if, for example, its voltage or its frequency is higher or lower than the norm and causes physical harm.[21] However, would the mere interruption of an electricity supply also make it 'defective', for example, if a main generator fails to work? This may cause physical harm, for example, the loss of the content of a consumer's freezer or even personal injury (if a person relies on the public supply for kidney dialysis).[22] If one views the whole process of supply of electricity as 'the product', then an interruption in supply could render *this* product defective. Clearly, though, such an interpretation could not be restricted to cases of the accidental interruption of current, but could also apply to its deliberate interruption, for example, as a result of industrial action. This would have very considerable implications for the generators (as 'producers') and suppliers of electricity.[23]

Perhaps even more difficult is the case of 'escapes' of a product such as networked electricity or piped gas and water. In the case of a product such as a carbonated drink, bottled gas or even a pharmaceutical the 'defectiveness' of the product as put into

---

[15] 1987 Act, s. 1(2) 'product'; s. 45(1) 'goods' (emphasis added).

[16] H.C. Taschner, 'La future responsabilité du fait des produits défectueux dans la Communauté européenne' *Rev. marché commun* (1986) 257, 259.

[17] Whittaker (1989), 129; Markovits, 164; Molfessis, *op. cit.* n. 11, 22–3.

[18] Above, p. 438.   [19] For examples, see above, pp. 137–8.   [20] Below, p. 481.

[21] HL Deb. Vol. 483 cols. 868–9 (Lord Lucas).

[22] Here, there may be difficulties of contributory negligence on the part of a person who relied on a public supply for such a purpose.   [23] Cf. below, pp. 523–7 on the definition of supplier.

circulation can include attributes of its container, for example, whether the glass is strong enough, the gas-cylinder properly designed or sealed or an aspirin bottle 'child-proof'. These products are put into circulation by their producers complete with their containers and packaging which must therefore form part of the overall 'products' and can be relevant to their safety; as a result, if a bottle or gas container explodes, any physical harm caused by the product's 'escape' would clearly be recoverable under the Directive as long as the criterion of 'defectiveness' is fulfilled. It is also clear that the 'presentation of the product', which is relevant to determining its defectiveness, may include reference to wider circumstances of its marketing, such as advertising and is not restricted to looking at the physical surroundings of the product itself.[24] What, then, is the position of networked electricity, piped gas or water? Is not a consumer of these legitimately entitled to the safety of the 'overall product', which therefore should include not merely its physical characteristics but also the method of its supply? For example, if a company supplies water to a locality, and, owing to the failure of the pipes which it uses to transmit the water, it escapes and damages either his customer's or another person's property, does this make the water 'defective' and the damage recoverable? In the case of electricity, should the body who supplies it be liable where the physical apparatus by which it is supplied malfunctions and electricity short-circuits and causes a fire? Intuitively, the idea that the Directive applies to cases of this sort seems to extend its scheme of liability too far. In many legal systems these sorts of cases are treated very differently from questions of the liability of a producer for the harm caused by 'defectiveness of his product': for example, in English law, by the law of private nuisance and *Rylands v Fletcher* as well as negligence;[25] and in French law, by liability for the 'deeds of things' or for 'public works'.[26] On the other hand, cases of this type cannot be excluded from the scope of the Directive merely on the ground that they concern liability for the provision of a service, as it is clear that products supplied in the course of such a provision (for example, a medicine supplied in the course of medical treatment), are included so as to attract liability either in the producer or supplier.[27] Moreover, the 'defectiveness' of a product may involve consideration of the question whether its immediate supplier was enabled to use it carefully and appropriately (as would be the case as regards the instructions and information given to medical personnel in relation to the proper use of a medicine) and not merely of its physical characteristics (for example, the chemical composition of the medicine). Indeed, once the idea that a product's 'defect' involves some physical corruption or inadequacy is abandoned, it is more difficult to say why the surrounding circumstances of a product's supply which fail to prevent the product from harming people or property do not render it *functionally* defective; and if these are included, how can cases like escaped water or gas be excluded?

Secondly, while the Directive does not apply to immovable property as such, it expressly applies to movable property incorporated into immovable property.[28] For a French jurist, this result is achieved only by legal fiction since in general once movable property is incorporated into immovable property in an apparently permanent way, it

---

[24] Cf. below, pp. 481, 488, 490.   [25] Above, pp. 162–3.   [26] Above, pp. 52–9, 121–9.
[27] Cf. *Veedfald v Århus Amtskommune*, below, pp. 503–8.   [28] Art. 2.

loses its own identity and ceases to be movable property.[29] The Directive's rule is potentially important. Where products (such as a lift, gas pipes or roof tiles) are incorporated into a building, they can cause harm to people, the building itself, or other property, whether movable or immovable. So, for example, a person injured when a lift falls out of control, could sue the lift's manufacturer or distributor (as its supplier) under the Directive's scheme. If a gas pipe belonging to a householder breaks, causing an explosion, its manufacturer can be liable for any personal injuries or damage to 'consumer property', the latter category including immovable property as long as it is of a type ordinarily intended for private use or consumption, and was used by the injured person mainly for his own private use or consumption.[30] This means, for example, that a roof tile which breaks and allows water damage to a person's private residence could attract liability in its manufacturer.

The French and UK legislators were both clearly aware of the potentially disruptive effects of the 1985 Directive on their respective laws of construction, and this was indeed highlighted by recital 3 of the Directive itself.[31] The *loi* of 1998 tackled this problem by explicitly providing that those who are considered 'builders' under the existing legislative scheme of liability provided by article 1792 *et seq.* of the Civil Code are deemed not to be 'producers' for its purposes:[32] this can be justified on the basis that they are creating immovable property rather than a movable.[33] Here, therefore, French law has attempted to keep its legal schemes of special liability apart. However, this exclusion is problematic both to the extent to which it leaves a number of others who participate in the construction of buildings within the new product liability provisions (notably, building subcontractors who supply products to be incorporated into a building[34]) and so creates new odd differences of treatment between suppliers of building materials which do or do not count as 'builders'; and even more to the extent to which it fails properly to implement the Directive.[35] For many 'builders' will incorporate products in the course of the work which they do and where they do so, they could be 'manufacturers', 'importers' or 'suppliers' for the purposes of article 3(3) of the Directive; their work may change the nature of the product from movable to immovable property, but at the time of their *supply* it remains movable; only later is it supplied as an incorporated part of the immovable (the building).[36] In French law, the significance of this is all the greater given that the *loi* of 1998 extended the Directive's scheme of liability to *all* cases of damage to property.[37]

[29] Markovits, 169.

[30] 1985 Directive, art. 9(b). If the argument concerning the liability of the suppliers of products such as gas outlined above, p. 480, were accepted, where the gas pipe belonged to the gas supplier a person injured could sue the gas supplier in respect of the 'defective gas supply' as well as the manufacturer of the pipe in respect of the defective pipe.

[31] In France, the implications had been pointed out *very* clearly by P. Malinvaud, 'L'application de la directive communautaire sur la responsabilité du fait des produits défectueux et le droit de la construction ou le casse-tête communautaire' D 1988 Chron. 85 ('Malinvaud (1988)'); P. Malinvaud, 'La loi du 19 mai 1998 relative à la responsabilité du fait des produits défectueux et le droit de la construction' D 1999 Chron. 85 ('Malinvaud (1999)').

[32] Art. 1386-6 al. 3 C. civ. and see above, pp. 104–8 for an outline of the scheme.

[33] Malinvaud (1999), 86.   [34] Larroumet, D 1998 Chron. 311, 314 and above, pp. 106–7.

[35] This failure seems little noticed in *la doctrine*, but see Huet, *principaux contrats spéciaux*, 389, note 1016.   [36] Cf. Malinvaud (1999), 86.

[37] Above, p. 460 as to the lawfulness of this extension.

The Consumer Protection Act 1987 also attempts to reduce the impact of its scheme of liability in the building context but much more modestly than the *loi* of 1998. The Act provides that the erection of any building on land is to be treated as a supply of goods in so far as it involves the provision of any goods 'by means of their incorporation into the building':[38] so, unlike the *loi* of 1998 it sees a builder's incorporation of a product into a building as an example of its 'supply'. On the other hand, the 1987 Act also provides that there is no supply of goods comprised in land 'by the creation or disposal of an interest in the land'.[39] So, where a person sells land, he is not to be understood as supplying all the products of which it is composed so as to attract the liabilities imposed by article 3(3) of the Directive. Liability under the 1987 Act does, however, extend to damage to a building into which a product has been incorporated, even if the building is then supplied to another person: the complex exclusion of section 5(2) does not apply to products 'comprised in' buildings.[40]

2. The Standard of Liability: Defect, Fault and Development Risks

(a) Defect and fault

The concept of a defect forms the crux of the Directive's scheme of liability. So, article 4 requires the injured person to 'prove the damage, the defect and the causal relationship between defect and damage' and article 6 states that:

1. A product is defective when it does not provide the safety which a person is entitled to expect, taking all circumstances into account, including:

   (a) the presentation of the product;
   (b) the use to which it could reasonably be expected that the product would be put;
   (c) the time when the product was put into circulation.

2. A product shall not be considered defective for the sole reason that a better product is subsequently put into circulation.

The fact that the form of this provision is more reminiscent of the legislative style of common lawyers rather than of the French civil lawyer, the complex '*standard législatif*'[41] consisting of an open criterion, supported by three specified considerations (which in other language versions are to be taken into account 'notably'[42]) within an overall injunction to take 'all circumstances into account'. In looking at the French and English discussions of the definition of defect, I am struck by the extent to which they are influenced by their existing legal analyses (whether this is in terms of finding similarities or contrasts) and the striking differences in the practicalities of the processes of judicial decision making. In my view, these differences of perspective and of process will have a continuing and fundamental importance in the practical decision making of their courts and therefore of the lawyers who advise in their shadow.

---

[38] 1987 Act, s. 46(3).　　[39] Ibid., s. 46(4).　　[40] Cf. above, p. 470.
[41] Testu and Moitry, 6. Cf. above, p. 452.
[42] This is true of the French ('*notamment*') and the German versions ('*insbesondere*') of the Directive.

(i) The French approach to 'defect'

At first rather surprisingly, the notion of 'defect' has not been central to French discussions of the 1985 Directive. For most French lawyers, the language of 'defect' is all too familiar from the law of sale, where its two expressions (*vice* and *défaut de conformité*) have enjoyed a complex and controversial history which is by no means ended.[43] From this perspective, French jurists were quick to point out that the Directive's test of 'legitimate expectation' is 'objective', contrasting with contractual understandings of defect by resting on the expectations of '*le grand public*' ('people generally')[44] rather than on the consumer or injured party, and being concerned with safety, rather than with quality or fitness for purpose.[45]

But *what* standard of safety does the evaluative test of article 6 set? French lawyers generally agree that the standard is relative rather than absolute[46] and sometimes have even compared it to the standard of an 'acceptable level of safety' which governs the licensing of medicines,[47] though conceding that the Directive is more demanding.[48] The relativity of the standard can also be seen to underlie the general rejection of the suggestion that a court should 'deduce' the existence of a defect from the fact that the product has caused a claimant harm.[49] The effect of such an approach would be to draw liability under the *loi* of 1998 much closer to the traditional liability for the 'deeds of things' where the causal role of the thing attracts liability and where its defect forms the basis of establishing this causal role in some situations,[50] but the approach is generally rejected as inconsistent with article 4's requirements as to proof.[51]

The burdens of proof which the Directive requires in relation to 'defect' are not, however, completely straightforward.[52] While the basic burden of proof as to defect is on the injured party, article 7(b) provides a defence for the producer where, 'having regard to the circumstances, it is probable that the defect which caused the damage did not exist at the time when the product was put into circulation by him or that this defect came into being afterwards' and, following the position for all the defences, here the burden of proof lies on the producer.[53] So the claimant must prove the defectiveness of the product *at the time of injury* (though according to a standard appropriate to the time of putting the product into circulation[54]), but does not need to show that

---

[43] Above, pp. 69–79 and below, pp. 580–1.   [44] 1985 Directive, recital 6.

[45] Ghestin (1986) 136–7: Markovits, 183 *et seq*. L. Leveneur, 'Le défaut' in *Petites affiches*, No. 155 (28 Dec. 1998) 28, 36 Cf. 1985 Directive, recital 6.

[46] Markovits, 203, citing Taschner, *op. cit.* n. 16, 257; C. Jamin, RTDCiv. 1998.763, 765 (who criticises the test severely).

[47] Art. R. 5133 C. santé pub. implementing EC Dir. 2001/83/EC of the European Parliament and of the Council of 6 Nov. 2001 on the Community code relating to medicinal products for human use, art. 10(1)(a)(ii).

[48] Testu and Moitry, 6; Leveneur, *op. cit.* n. 45, 36 who concludes that 'it would be more in keeping with reality to call it "liability for the deeds of products not offering *sufficient* safety"' (emphasis added).

[49] This was proposed by Fauchon, *Rapport*, 34 and could be thought to be found in TGI Aix-en-Provence 2 Oct. 2001, D 2001.IR.3092 (explosion of chimney insert allowed court to find lack of safety in this product even though the cause of the accident was not established).   [50] Above, p. 57.

[51] Calais-Auloy and Steinmetz, 330; Carbonnier, *Obligations*, 483.

[52] Viney and Jourdain, *Conditions*, 770–1.

[53] 1985 Directive, art. 7: 'The producer shall not be liable *if he proves* . . .'.

[54] 1985 Directive, art. 6(1)(c).

the product was defective at the time when it was put into circulation: it is for the producer to show the contrary.

What, then, of the relationship of 'defect' to liability for '*faute*'? French lawyers accept that the 1985 Directive requires a liability that is '*sans faute*', but this means something rather different from an English lawyer's understanding of liability 'without fault' (which in this context means without negligence). As I have explained,[55] the French conception of delictual 'fault' is extremely broad and multifaceted, involving a judgment of the correctness or otherwise of the defendant's behaviour by the courts, with an objective starting point often being qualified by subjective considerations and with particular meanings in particular contexts: it has even been held that it is itself a 'fault' for a manufacturer to put an unsafely defective product onto the market.[56] The reason which most French jurists give as to why the new product liability is not technically based on *une faute* (even *une faute présumée*) is that a producer cannot escape liability by showing that the product conformed to regulatory requirements or industry standards at the time of its being put into circulation, pointing to the much more limited defence that the defect is *due* to conformity with mandatory public standards.[57] This 'reveals that the liability imposed by the law is not a liability for presumed fault, but a true liability by operation of law independent of any fault'.[58] Here, there appears to be a significant contrast with the English understanding of negligence, for a court may hold a person negligent even though their conduct followed these standards at the relevant time.[59] This suggests both that a person's behaviour can be 'negligent' even though not *fautif*,[60] as well as that it may be *fautif* and not 'negligent'.[61]

Beyond this denial of a basis of 'fault', French lawyers see the decision as to the existence of defect as '*une appréciation morale*', that is, an evaluative judgment taking into account a range of considerations, and these can include the usefulness and desirability of the product, the practical nature of any measures for the improvement of its safety and the existence of safer products.[62] This evaluation results from the requirement that the expectation must be 'legitimate', and while some French jurists see the choice of this term instead of 'reasonable' as significant (rejecting a purely 'economic' or 'contractual approach'),[63] others see no substantive difference.[64] In this respect, a product's dangerousness will not necessarily render it 'defective', as in the case of electricity or corrosive domestic products: here 'there should be no finding of defect unless the danger is shown to be higher than what would normally be expected from the type of product in question'.[65] There is, moreover, an acceptance among some French lawyers that the application of the definition of defect will involve consideration of the conduct of the producer in relation to the product, even if not of his 'fault'.[66] For a French lawyer, this does not seem so strange, given that two of the considerations which the legislation requires to be taken into account are the 'presentation of

---

[55] Above, pp. 40–6. [56] Above, p. 51. [57] 1985 Directive, art. 7(d); art. 1386-10 C. civ.
[58] Viney and Jourdain, *Conditions*, 793. Similarly, Testu and Moitry, 7, 10. [59] Above, pp. 203–4.
[60] Ibid. [61] Above, p. 160.
[62] Markovits, 201, 212; Viney and Jourdain, *Conditions*, 770.
[63] Viney and Jourdain, *Conditions*, 769 noting the *travaux préparatoires* of the European Convention, above, p. 434 . [64] Carbonnier, *Obligations*, 483.
[65] Viney and Jourdain, *Conditions*, 793. [66] Testu and Moitry, 7.

the product' (which includes its instructions, description and warnings) and its foreseeable use: both these elements evoke for them the law governing *obligations d'information*, which while occasionally demanding and certainly flexible, are typically seen as 'fault-based', founded on an *obligation de moyens*.[67] Some commentators have even argued that there is no need for the development risks defence, as the assessment of the product's defect allows the court to take into account the degree of foreseeability of the risk as part of this wider assessment:[68] the defence was not *legally* necessary, even if it is sociologically and economically explicable.[69] In all, therefore, the test of defect reflects the compromise reached in Brussels: liability is not based on 'fault', but does involve consideration by the *juges du fond* (as representative of the general public) of whether the producer should have done more.

In their discussions of defect, many jurists point out the key role of the *juges du fond*, on the clear understanding that this issue is for their 'sovereign power of assessment',[70] adding that in more complex cases, the *juges du fond* will act on the basis of an *expertise*, which is to be asked to advise on the state of technical and scientific knowledge at the time of putting the product into circulation.[71] In this respect, there is likely to be considerable continuity with the balance of roles between the *experts*, *juges du fond* and Cour de cassation already found in relation to the issues of *vice* and *défaut* in sale (both of which are for the *juges du fond*).[72] While, of course, the Cour de cassation could intervene in their assessment of 'defect' under the *loi* of 1998, for example, if a lower court 'denatured' the evidence of an *expertise* or contradicted itself, it is unlikely that it will interfere so as to control *which* circumstances are relevant, let alone in their overall balancing of considerations. As Viney and Jourdain conclude, the test of defect gives 'to the *juge* rather a large discretion' ('*une assez grande liberté*')[73] or as Jamin more critically puts it, it allows the *juges du fond* to 'do what they want according to their perception, very largely subjective, of the sociology of the time'.[74] Moreover, as Jamin also notes, the civil courts will reach their decisions on defect without possessing the means of discovering the information necessary to form a view as to whether or not the producer should have taken any further precautions, there being no equivalent to common law discovery.[75] So, while the form and focus of the test of 'defect' differs from the surrounding law, the process of its assessment remains the same: based often on a single, uncontrovertible expert opinion, very limited documentary information as to historical facts and an opaque judicial decision all but unchallengeable before the Cour de cassation.

[67] Above, p. 67.   [68] Fauchon, *Rapport*, 19–20; Carbonnier, *Obligations*, 483.

[69] Larroumet, D 1998 Chron. 311, 315 referring to the *affaire du sang contaminé* and the need not to expose French industry to greater risks than their competitors in Europe.

[70] J. Ghestin, 'La directive communautaire et son introduction en droit français' in Ghestin, *Sécurité des consommateurs*, 111, 118; Markovits, 200; Larroumet, D 1998 Chron. 311, 315.

[71] Viney and Jourdain, *Conditions*, 770; Testu and Moitry, 7.   [72] Above, pp. 78–9.

[73] Viney and Jourdain, *Conditions*, 770.

[74] C. Jamin, RTDCiv. 1998.763, 765. Similarly, Taylor (writing from the point of view of a comparison with English legal commentators' interpretation of 'defect' in terms of a cost/benefit analysis) observes that the absence of any reference to this sort of way of thinking in the Directive or the *loi* of 1998 themselves 'will permit French courts to ignore these considerations when they think that the circumstances require the victim to be compensated': *Harmonisation communautaire*, 59.   [75] Ibid. and see above, pp. 48, 78.

(ii) English approaches to defect

In contrast to France, there has been a great deal more discussion of the significance of the requirement of 'defect', both in the academic literature and, more recently, in the courts. Having set out the definition of defect provided by the Directive, many English discussions then ask whether or how the new product liability differs from liability in the tort of negligence; comparisons with a seller's liability under the Sale of Goods Act are less common as the absence of defect as the foundation of liability makes the connection less obvious than in the French context.[76]

The starting point is that, as in France, there is a general acknowledgment that the test of 'defect' does not impose an absolute standard of safety, but that it is at least *formally* different from liability in the tort of negligence. Beyond this, however, opinions differ considerably, some commentators arguing that, at least as regards the liability of manufacturers, there is little substantial difference with the tort of negligence,[77] while others argue that it does indeed impose a strict liability, it being improper for there to be any assessment of the available precautions given the forseeable risks of the type undertaken under the 'cost/benefit' analysis of the tort of negligence.[78] It is submitted that the handful of English decisions made under the Consumer Protection Act reflect this disagreement,[79] the courts being torn between the implications of the formulation of the test of 'defect' found in the Directive and its claim that it introduces 'liability without fault', which is interpreted to mean 'liability without negligence'.

For example, in *Richardson v LRC Products Ltd.*[80] the claimant sued the manufacturer of a condom used during sexual intercourse with her husband, alleging that its rupture had allowed her to become pregnant. The court considered evidence from the parties' expert witnesses as to how this rupture occurred, concentrating on invisible cracks in the fabric of the condom and on how these could have occurred either during manufacture or between use and expert assessment. In his conclusion, Kennedy J found that on balance the cracks had developed after use, but that, even if they had not, they were not the cause of the condom's fracture.[81] Moreover, while a user may expect that a condom would never fail, the learned judge held that a rupture in a condom does not itself show the existence of a 'defect' as this may occur as a result of 'inexplicable failures'; and so he found that the claimant had failed to establish a defect on the facts.[82] By contrast,

---

[76] For the English position, above, p. 243.

[77] Whittaker, (1985) 242–6; J. Stapleton, 'Products Liability Reform—Real or Illusory?' (1986) 6 *OJLS* 392; Stapleton, *Product Liability*, Chap. 10 esp. at 236, 271–2; A. Stoppa, 'The concept of defectiveness in the Consumer Protection Act 1987: a critical analysis' (1992) 12 *LS* 210 (who distinguishes the position as to manufacturing defects where liability is strict); G. Howells, *Comparative Product Liability* (Dartmouth, 1993), 36, 38; J. Stapleton, 'Products Liability in the United Kingdom: The Myths of Reform' (1999) 34 *Texas International Law Journal* 45; G. Howells, *Law of Product Liability* (Butterworths, 2000) 228 *et seq.*

[78] E.g. C. Hodges, *Product Liability: European Law and Practice* (1993) para. 3.019; E. Deards and C. Twigg-Flesner, 'The Consumer Protection Act: Proof at last that it it is protecting consumers?' (2001) 10 *Nottingham LJ* 1.

[79] *Richardson v LRC Products Ltd.* [2000] PIQR P164; *Worsely v Tambrands Ltd.* [2000] PIQR P95; *Abouzaid v Mothercare UK Ltd.* [2000] All ER (D) 2436; *Foster v Biosil* (2001) 59 BMLR 178; *A v The National Blood Authority* [2001] 3 All ER 289; *B v McDonald's Restaurants Ltd.* [2002] EWHC 490; 2002 WL 347509. *XYZ v Schering Health Care Ltd.* [2002] EWHC 1420; (2003) 70 BMLR 88 was disposed of by the court and the parties by determination of a crucial issue of fact.

[80] [2000] PIQR P164.   [81] Ibid., at P170.   [82] Ibid., at P171.

in *Abouzaid v Mothercare (UK) Ltd.*[83] the Court of Appeal held that the claimant was 'on balance' able to show a defect, but not that the defendant had been negligent. There, the claimant had as a boy aged twelve helped his mother to put his infant brother into a fleece-lined sleeping bag manufactured by the defendants and had been injured when the elastic strap slipped and its buckle hit him in the eye. The Court of Appeal upheld the decision below holding the manufacturer liable on the basis of the 1987 Act: the product was 'defective' as its design permitted the risk of injury and did not warn against it.[84] In doing so, the leading judgement of Pill LJ criticised the manufacturer's reliance on expert evidence that at the time at which the product was supplied there was no knowledge of the specific risk of an accident of the type which occurred: the nature of elastic and the vulnerability of eyes were both well known at the time and so it could not be said that the expectations of the public at large had changed between the date of the supply and of the accident.[85] But Pill LJ clearly did consider relevant to his decision as to defect the proper knowledge of the risk and the practicalities of its avoidance by the manufacturer, whether in terms of warnings or in terms of the substitution of a non-elastic material.[86] Somewhat differently, Chadwick LJ took as his starting point the question as to how the damage was caused, rather than whether or not it was foreseeable:[87] there must be no consideration of whether the cause of the damage came or ought reasonably to have come to the attention of the producer at the time of supply since the Directive's recitals made clear that it imposed 'liability without fault'.[88] He then agreed with Pill LJ's conclusion as to the existence of a defect.[89]

However, the most significant decision on the test of defect under the 1987 Act came in *A v National Blood Authority.*[90] In this case, 114 claimants sought damages in respect of their infection by the Hepatitis C virus as a result of their receipt of blood or blood products manufactured and supplied in England and Wales from 1 March 1988 (the date of the coming into force of the 1987 Act). The blood was collected from unpaid volunteers and supplied through 14 regional centres administered by a central public authority under a statutory duty, this being reorganised in 1993 into a more centralised system under the National Blood Authority (which took over liability in respect of the earlier supplies). The claims were brought exclusively on the ground of liability under the 1987 Act and two issues of law arose: whether in applying the test of 'defectiveness' under article 6 of the Directive it was proper to take into account the avoidability of a risk in relation to individual products; and whether the development risks defence of article 7(e) arose not only where the lack of knowledge of a risk prevented its discovery, but also where there was a lack of means of identifying a *known* risk in a particular example of a product.[91] If the answer to either of these questions

[83] [2000] All ER (D) 2436; C. Hodges, 'Product Liability for Old Products' (2001) NLJ 424.
[84] [2000] All ER (D) 2436 at [27].   [85] Ibid. at [24]–[25].   [86] Ibid. at [27].
[87] Ibid. at [38].   [88] Recitals 5 and 6, quoted ibid. at [44].   [89] Wright J agreed: ibid. at [53].
[90] [2001] 3 All ER 289. On which see R. Goldberg, 'Paying for Bad Blood: Strict Product Liability after the Hepatitis C Litigation' (2002) 10 *Med. L.Rev.* 165, 170 (criticising Burton J's approach as 'overly intuitive'); C. Hodges, 'Compensating Patients' (2001) 117 *LQR* 528; G. Howells and M. Mildred, 'Infected Blood: Defect and Discoverability, A First Exposition of the EC Product Liability Directive' (2001) 65 *MLR* 95; P. Giliker, 'Strict Liability for Defective Products: The Ongoing Debate' (2003) *Business L. Rev.* 87.
[91] Below, pp. 499–501.

had been in the affirmative, the factual question would have arisen as to whether the relevant blood authorities had available the means of detecting or preventing the Hepatitis C virus in particular blood products at the relevant time.

The case came before Burton J and its trial lasted three months. Although the legal questions were few, the range of sources referred to was very broad, the learned judge looking not merely at the 1985 Directive and its recitals, but also at its *travaux préparatoires*, a good deal of English and continental juristic writing, and at the English and some continental cases. Noticeably, the text of the 1987 Act did not feature at all, given its own injunction that it should be read so as to conform to the Directive and the European Court's reliance on this to correct its wording in relation to the development risks defence: 'the practical course was to go straight to the fount, the Directive itself'.[92] The factual question (which was rendered hypothetical given the judge's legal decisions) involved the investigation of the scientific literature and expert understanding of Hepatitis C, its transmission by blood and the possible means of detecting it; and to decide it the court received evidence from ten witnesses of fact and six expert witnesses and had the benefit of 16 files of documentation of the scientific literature even after a 'massive slimming-down' by the legal teams.[93] Burton J's judgment ran to just over 95,000 words, of which about two-thirds concerned the facts, for which Burton J assessed the written and oral evidence in the light of the scientific literature.[94] Viewed therefore from the point of view of the nature of the legal process, the case could not illustrate better the range of both legal and factual investigations which an English court may undertake in a suitably important case. The irony remains, however, that either the factual decision was unnecessary (given the judge's view of the law) or that the legal decisions were strictly *obiter* (given his findings of fact): the importance of the factual decision being made was in case of appeal and reversal on the law (though there was no appeal).

Perhaps surprisingly given this wealth of discussion, Burton J's conclusions on the issue of the defectiveness of the blood can be stated quite simply. It had been agreed that the standard imposed by article 6 did not rest on proof of 'fault' (as the Directive's preamble stated as much), but that it was not an absolute standard, instead requiring judicial consideration of a 'basket' of factors some of which it provided but others of which were included by the phrase 'taking all circumstances into account'.[95] The key disputed question was whether or not the avoidability of a harmful aspect of a product was a proper factor to be taken into account. In determining this question, the learned judge noted that some commentators had argued that the assessment of a product's defect would require a similar 'cost/benefit' analysis as takes place in English law in assessing negligence.[96] They had argued that the test of 'legitimate expectation' is itself circular and does not explain *how* safe the product must be, as the question of the safety which a person is *entitled* to expect is what is to be determined by the court in assessing the product's 'defectiveness'.[97] I had argued that the degree of safety which a

---

[92] [2001] 3 All ER 289 at [2] *per* Burton J., and see below, p. 498. [93] Ibid. at [97].
[94] Ibid. at [96].   [95] Ibid. at [31], [35].
[96] Whittaker (1985); Stapleton, *Product Liability*, 233–6. And see above, pp. 193–200.
[97] Whittaker (1985), 242; Stapleton, *Product Liability*, 234.

person is entitled to expect could be well caught by the language of 'reasonable safety', but Burton J rejected this on the basis that it rewrote the terms of the Directive and would defeat its purpose in imposing 'liability without fault'.[98] As a result, in his view the phrase 'taking account of all the circumstances' should be read so as to *exclude* the avoidability of the harmful aspect of the product.[99] He rejected the argument that 'the public should not "expect the unattainable"—in the sense of tests or precautions which are impossible—at least unless it is informed as to what is unattainable or impossible', as this would 'reformulate the expectation as one that the producer will not have been negligent',[100] which would render the Directive 'toothless and pointless'.[101] He supported his view by reference to the very restricted nature of the development risks defence, 'whereby a producer who has taken all possible precautions . . . remains liable unless that producer can show that the 'state of scientific and technical knowledge . . . *was not such as to enable the existence of the defect to be discovered*'.[102] Given the restricted nature of this escape from liability, a similarly restricted view of article 6 is needed to avoid this defence from being redundant.[103]

Burton J then drew two sets of distinctions between types of products in applying the test of 'legitimate expectation', though he rejected the familiar American categorisation of defects into manufacturing defects, design defects and instruction defects, on the basis that 'there is no place for them in the Directive'.[104]

First, there are products, such as knives, guns, poisons or alcohol which have 'obviously dangerous characteristics by virtue of their very nature or intended use'.[105] These products will not be held to be defective by virtue of their particular risks which are generally known to the public, as they cannot 'legitimately be expected' not to possess the characteristics in question, whether or not they are desired. Burton J was prepared to accept that drugs with advertised side-effects may fall within this category.[106]

Secondly, as regards *other* products, Burton J distinguished between 'standard' and 'non-standard products'. 'A *standard* product is one which is and performs as the producer intends. A *non-standard* product is one which is different, obviously because it is deficient or inferior in terms of safety, from the standard product'.[107] Where there is a harmful characteristic in a non-standard product, the issue of defectiveness is likely to be straightforward,[108] turning on whether its nature has been drawn to the attention of the public at large.[109] As regards standard products, any alleged defect is likely to be one of design or resulting from an allegedly flawed system and here:

the question of presentation/time/circumstances of supply/social acceptability etc. will arise . . . The sole question will be safety for the foreseeable use. If there are any comparable products on the market, then it will obviously be relevant to compare the offending product with those other products, so as to identify, compare and contrast the relevant features . . . Price is obviously a significant factor in legitimate expectation, and may well be material in the comparative process. But again . . . there is no room in the basket for: (i) what the producer could have done differently; (ii) whether the producer could or could not have done the same as the others did.[110]

[98] [2001] 3 All ER 289 at [45], [63].   [99] Ibid. at [63].   [100] Ibid. at [56].
[101] Ibid. at [69].   [102] Ibid. at [64] (original emphasis).   [103] Ibid.   [104] Ibid. at [39].
[105] Ibid. at [31].   [106] Ibid.   [107] Ibid. at [36].   [108] Ibid. at [66].
[109] Ibid. at [68].   [110] Ibid. at [71].

In coming to this view, Burton J treated as 'an anomaly' consideration of the different safety features which could have been included *now* but which could not have been included *then*, as specifically suggested by article 6(2) of the Directive, as this would 'once again go to the issue of avoidability'.[111] He also accepted that more generally it would be 'difficult' to keep out issues of 'avoidability' in assessing the defectiveness of standard products.[112]

In applying this view of the law to the facts before him, Burton J's key decision was to view the packets of blood which were infected with Hepatitis C as 'non-standard' products since they differed from the norm which was intended by their producer for use, rejecting the defendant's argument that all the blood products were equally defective (or not) because they all carried the risk of infection as 'very philosophical'.[113] He was satisfied that the problem of blood being infected by a virus (later named as Hepatitis C) was not known to the consumer at the relevant time[114] and it was not enough to have been known to medical science.[115] In the absence of such knowledge, the benefit to society or utility of the product is irrelevant to consideration of a product's defect.

This decision is certainly impressive for its sophisticated use of legal sources, for its masterly handling of the scientific complexities, and for its clear desire to make practical (European) sense of the provisions of the Directive. With respect, however, its conclusions are open to a number of criticisms.

First, the learned judge should not have relied on the recitals to the Directive which announce its purpose of imposing 'liability without fault' in order to reject recourse to any particular considerations used in determining common law negligence from use under article 6. The *text* of the Directive is careful to avoid all reference to 'fault' in relation to the basis of liability,[116] preferring to construct and define its own basis in a way which is original to the laws of all Member States. This was wise given that understandings of what 'fault' means differ significantly in the different Member States (even in the straightforward civil context[117]), as I have explained in relation to just two systems, the laws of France and England.[118] The reference in the Directive's preamble to its rejection of liability for fault as the basis for the new harmonised liability explains why this traditional and apparently shared basis for liability was rejected (as being insufficiently protective of the consumer), but it should not be used as a means of interpreting the text actually adopted since this would lead to different contrasts between the different laws of the Member States, their understandings of 'no fault' differing in mirror image to their understandings of 'fault'. Moreover, Burton J's use of an English understanding of the notion of 'fault' ('negligence') led him to reject recourse to a particular factor in the assessment of 'defect' despite article 6's explicit

---

111 Ibid. at [72].   112 Ibid. at [73].   113 Ibid. at [65].   114 Ibid. at [65].

115 Ibid. at [31].

116 Cf. art. 8(2)'s reference to the 'fault of the injured person' in providing that the liability in the producer *may* be reduced or disallowed, where the Directive appears to be content to refer both the issue of the possibility of reduction and the understanding of 'contributory fault' to the laws of the Member States: below, pp. 510–12.

117 As I have explained, 'administrative fault' may again differ: above, pp. 311–12.

118 Above, pp. 43–4, 159–60, 200–2. The ECJ has itself recognised that 'the concept of fault does not have the same content in the various legal systems' in the context of liability of Member States for infringement of EC law: Joined cases C-46/93 and C-48/93, *Brasserie du Pêcheur SA v Germany* [1996] ECR I-01029 para. 76.

injunction that *all* the circumstances should be taken into account in determining the issue of defect. And from the point of view of the jurisprudence of the European Court of 2002 (which post-dated Burton J's decision) the similarity in practice of its concept of 'defect' to English law's concept of negligence does not render the Directive pointless, as its main purpose is the construction of a harmonised scheme of liability in producers in the Member States;[119] this scheme may or may not improve the protection of consumers in any individual Member State; indeed, the European Court accepted that in some its effect might be to make it weaker.[120]

Secondly, Burton J's judgment gave insufficient consideration to the significance of two factors which are specified by article 6 to be taken into account.[121] So, the 'use to which it can reasonably be expected that the product would be put' necessarily involves a judgment as to how a producer should have designed a product so as to avoid it causing harm. In this respect, the producer must consider reasonably foreseeable *misuse* as well as use by consumers or others and balance this risk against its avoidance, notably as regards the extent to which any safety feature would compromise the product's function. Moreover, as Burton J acknowledged in treating it as 'anomalous' given his approach to avoidability, article 6 *twice* refers to the time when the product was put into circulation as relevant to the assessment of defect: first generally and then emphatically, by providing that 'a product shall not be considered defective for the sole reason that a better product is subsequently put into circulation'.[122] Burton J's view of article 6 limits these time provisions severely, leaving them concerned with the assessment of the state of consumer knowledge of a product's risks at the time of supply as distinct from later (this forming for him a key element in the judicial assessment of 'legitimate expectation').[123] But a more natural interpretation is that they make clear that a producer's conduct in relation to the risks which a product presents (including in relation to their avoidance) must be assessed as at the date of supply, rather than at the date of accident or judgment. In sum, and with respect, Burton J's interpretation distorts the significance of the words used by article 6 so as to fit a misunderstanding of the significance of the Directive's recitals.

Thirdly, and related to this is his treatment of the relevance of the 'presentation of the product'.[124] This formed the crux of Burton J's decision, as he held that the failure of the public suppliers of blood to alert the public to its risk meant that any 'non-standard' product was not socially accepted, the learned judge realising that this leads to an approach to the issue of defect akin to contract.[125] The practical impact of his decision, therefore, is to encourage the suppliers of products which contain unavoidable (even if very small) risks of harm to declare them widely. At first this may seem a necessarily good thing, increasing the level of consumer information and, therefore, choice. However, in the case of a product such as blood all examples of which contain the risk in question (from whatever producer) and which is needed by its consumers as a matter of life or death with no substitute available, it is not at all clear that informing

---

[119] European Court decisions of 2002, above, pp. 440–4.
[120] This was apparently the effect in relation to Spanish law, above, pp. 442–3.
[121] Cf. Stapleton, *Product Liability*, 244–7.   [122] Art. 6(1)(c) and (2) respectively.
[123] Above, pp. 488–9.   [124] Art. 6(1)(a).   [125] [2001] 3 All ER 289 at [66].

the public of the risk is helpful or actually enhances the consumer's choice. For even if this information were understood properly (which is unlikely), it is likely to lead to a number of people refusing to be supplied with the product, thereby creating higher risks to their health than the product itself. In this respect, a warning or instruction serves some point in terms of safety only to the extent to which it allows a person to avoid a potential danger. Burton J accepted that in relation to 'standard products' the presentation of the product could include consideration of its price, but while he restricted its relevance to the product's relative safety for foreseeable use, its most natural significance would be the extent to which a purchaser of a product had paid more for a higher degree of safety or had paid less and thereby tolerated a lesser degree of safety, even though the person injured may not be the purchaser in question. This suggests that any contractual context in which a product is manufactured or marketed remains to a degree relevant to the issue of its 'defectiveness', for its price is likely to reflect its place in the market and the product's degree of safety *may* form an aspect of this place (as in the case of more expensive motor vehicles advertised as possessing special safety features).

Fourthly, Burton J's use of a distinction between standard and non-standard products is problematic. Unless it is to be understood in terms of a broad factual cate-gorisation, of help in discussion rather than as a basis for different legal consequences, it appears unjustified given its absence from article 6 of the Directive. Moreover, the distinction is by no means uncontroversial in its application: where, as in respect of the blood, a producer knows that some examples of the product contain a harmful characteristic but he cannot detect them, is a product containing such a characteristic 'non-standard' or 'standard'? Burton J thought it 'non-standard' despite the argument of the producer that its intention as to the product (relevant to the 'standard' issue) had to be viewed overall rather than in relation to each product.[126]

Fifthly, Burton J also referred to a further possible factor in the 'basket'. The defen-dants had argued that the fact that they were required by law to produce and supply the blood products to hospitals and patients as a service to society and that they could not, unlike commercial producers, withdraw them from the market should be relevant to the assessment of 'defect'.[127] The claimants disagreed, seeing no automatic reason why this should be the case in the absence of the special defence of article 7(d), where the product's defect is due to compliance with mandatory regulation.[128] On this point, Burton J offered no conclusion, but in my view there should be no reason why the public and especially obligatory nature of a producer's supply should not affect the 'legitimate expectations' of people generally, either positively or negatively.

My final example of the application of the new product liability in England is very different both in its context and its approach. In *B v McDonald's Restaurants Ltd*[129] the claimants (of whom nearly half were children) sued the well-known fast-food restaurant for damages caused by burns from the hot drinks which they served. The court heard evidence as to the temperature of the drinks served by the defendant and of consumer preference in this respect more generally. Field J agreed with Burton J in

[126] Above, p. 489.   [127] [2001] 3 All ER 289 at [42].   [128] Ibid.
[129] [2002] EWHC 490; 2002 WL 347509.

A v The National Blood Authority, that the concept of defect did not allow consideration of the avoidability of the risk of harm (here, scalding by hot drinks),[130] but 'persons generally expect tea or coffee purchased to be consumed on the premises to be hot',[131] they realise that a spilt hot drink can cause serious scalding and therefore must take suitable care. 'They expect precautions to be taken to guard against this risk but not to the point that they are denied the basic utility of being able to buy hot drinks.'[132] So, with respect, while Field J formally rejected the avoidability of the risk in question, he then took it into account under the test of 'legitimate expectation'.

(iii) Comparative observations; the European Court's likely position

As *A v The National Blood Authority* illustrates, in English law the background of negligence which sets out a set of relevant considerations to be taken into account in determining the application of this standard of liability combines with the nature of the civil process to encourage the identification of very particular issues which are then fully argued and judicially resolved, the record of this process being exposed for further critical comment and future judicial adoption in the judgment: civil process as juristic dissection. So, while an English judge may say that the assessment of a product's defect is an issue of fact,[133] this does not prevent an English lawyer from constructing from it particular issues of law. And an English court's conclusion of an issue of law may then impact on which facts fall for investigation: so having taken the view he did as to defect, Burton J realised that this affected the role of any expert evidence which would be limited to describing 'the composition or construction of the product and its effect and consequence in use: not to consider what could or should have been done, whether in respect of its design or manufacture, to avoid the problem'.[134]

By contrast, in France judicial institutions, the nature of civil 'trials' and the style of *arrêts* and previous substantive law combine to lead to the relative submerging of particular sub-issues which may arise in relation to the decision of an issue such as 'defect' under the global evaluation of the *juges du fond*.[135] It is not, of course, that a French lawyer could not see that there is a question as to whether the avoidability of a harmful characteristic by a producer is relevant to the assessment of defect, but the civil process does not lend itself to the presentation of this question but rather to its treatment as one of fact rather than of law. It is for this reason that the concept of 'defect' has attracted relatively little attention in *la doctrine*: it is essentially a factual and judicial rather than a juristic matter.

Secondly, however, both the French and English discussions accept that dangerous products are not necessarily defective. This is a particularly striking conclusion for French lawyers, where for over a century both courts and jurists have seen the existence of a danger as a reason for the imposition of liability.[136]

Thirdly, there is a contrast between them in relation to the significance of a product's price. For a French lawyer, the test of 'defect' is objective and not 'contractual',

---

[130] [2002] EWHC 490; 2002 WL 347509 at [73].   [131] Ibid. at [80].   [132] Ibid.

[133] *Abouzaid v Mothercare UK Ltd.* [2000] All ER (D) 2436 at [40], *per* Chadwick LJ.

[134] [2001] 3 All ER 289 at [66].   [135] Above, pp. 483–4.

[136] See above, p. 53 (liability for the 'deeds of things' justified by risk even in the absence of a requirement of danger); pp. 118–21 (administrative liability for dangerous things and activities).

which suggests that its price should be irrelevant; for Burton J, price may be relevant. As I shall explain, the significance of a product's price is also controversial in relation to the Consumer Guarantee Directive's requirement of contractual conformity.[137]

How, then, would the European Court of Justice approach the issue of defect? First, it would, of course, start with the provisions of the Directive as interpreted according to its purpose in 'complete harmonisation' and in consumer protection. In considering the test of defect in the 1985 Directive, there may be a helpful analogy with its treatment of the test of 'fairness' of contract terms under article 3 of the Unfair Terms in Consumer Contracts Directive of 1993, which sets out a number of factors to be taken into account within an overall test of 'significant imbalance in the rights and obligations of the parties to the detriment of the consumer' contrary to the requirement of good faith.[138] In *Freiburger Kommunalbauten*,[139] the Court was faced with a reference by a German court under article 234 EC as to whether a clause governing interest paid on default in a consumer contract was unfair within the meaning of the 1993 Directive. Having set out the relevant provisions of the Directive and facts as found by the national court, the European Court observed that 'the question whether [a particular clause] causes a significant and unjustified imbalance for the purposes of Article 3(1) of the Directive is a matter to be decided by the national court',[140] the test in the Directive merely defining 'in a general way the factors that render unfair a contractual term that has not been individually negotiated'.[141] The Court concluded that while it 'may interpret general criteria used by the community legislature in order to define the concept of unfair terms, . . . it should not rule on the application of these general criteria to a particular term, which must be considered in the light of the particular circumstances of the case in question'[142] by the national court.[143] This decision is helpful in that it makes clear the unwillingness of the European Court in article 234 proceedings to enter issues not merely of fact but also of the application of a complex test (of 'fairness' and by analogy of 'defect') which requires the evaluation of facts in the light of a set of criteria. On the other hand, it does leave open the *possibility* that a national court could ask it to rule on whether a particular factor should or should not be used in its application of the 'general criteria' by way of the latter's interpretation.

What, therefore, would the European Court's view be if it were presented with a question by an English court as to whether the avoidability of the harm by a producer is a proper consideration in assessing 'defect'? The Court could simply dismiss this question on the basis that the issue was one for the evaluation of the national court in the light of the circumstances. But if it treated the question as one of interpretation, in my view it should not feel obliged by the references in the Directive's preamble to 'liability without fault' to constrain the range of circumstances set out in article 6 so as to exclude avoidability. As I have sought to explain, given the divergences in understanding of 'civil fault' in Member States, the rejection of particular factors which would be held relevant to 'fault' by one or other national law would pull the court in

---

[137] Above, pp. 482, 597–8.   [138] 93/13/EC.

[139] Case C-237/02 of 1 Apr. 2004 *Freiburger Kommunalbauten GmbH Baugesellschaft & Co. KG v Hofstetter* Eurtex.   [140] At para. 18.

[141] Ibid. at para. 19.   [142] Ibid. at para. 22.   [143] Ibid. at para. 25.

different ways and thereby jeopardise its primary concern with the construction of a completely harmonised scheme of liability (see above, p. 489).

On the other hand, it is likely that the Court would be concerned to ensure consistency with its own previous interpretation of the development risks defence in *Commission v United Kingdom*.[144] As will be recalled, for some French jurists the defence *is* all but redundant given the inclusive and discretionary nature of the assessment of defect.[145] By contrast, for Burton J in *A v The National Blood Authority*, the presence of what he saw as such a restricted defence argues in favour of the exclusion of the avoidability of the harmful characteristics of a product as a matter of its alleged 'defect'.[146] It is to this defence to which I must now turn.

(b) The development risks defence

(i) French perspectives

The famous development risks defence found in article 7(e) of the 1985 Directive gives to a producer a defence that 'the state of scientific and technical knowledge at the time when he put the product into circulation was not such as to enable the existence of the defect to be discovered'. I have earlier explained how this defence for long formed the sticking-point in implementing the 1985 Directive in France, how the competing arguments regarding its adoption were viewed and the double compromise (in relation to the exclusion of 'human products' from the defence and the retention of the existing law which was seen generally to impose liability for development risks) needed for the *loi* of 1998's final promulgation.[147]

More recent discussions of the defence by jurists reflect this earlier argument and then note quite briefly the impact of the European Court's decision in *Commission v United Kingdom*,[148] as regards the relativity of the 'knowledge' (which I shall discuss below), but otherwise do not cast much light on its interpretation or on its significance. Some jurists see the defence as meaning that the new product liability is very close to a presumption of fault: for 'if a producer can escape liability by proving that he was not in a position to detect the defect, his liability rests on a possible knowledge, that is, on a neglect (*une négligence*) in researching the defects affecting the product'.[149] Others consider this view 'excessive', preferring to see it as a probably very occasional limitation on the risk imposed on producers.[150] Again, the courts may take advantage of the very fluid nature of 'knowledge' and its 'accessibility' to adopt an interpretation more favourable to claimants.[151]

There are, however, two elements in the French discussions which are of particular interest. The first is the way in which they relate the defence to liability under existing law, where, apart from the special treatment given to liability of manufacturers of pharmaceuticals,[152] manufacturers' liability was seen to include liability for these development risks. This was certainly true of liability under the *garantie légale* in sale, where the nature of the *garantie* is seen to include liability for latent defects even

---

144 [2001] 3 All ER 289 at [64].   145 Above, p. 484.   146 Above, p. 488.
147 Above, p. 458.   148 Case C-300/95 [1997] ECR 1–2649.
149 Viney and Jourdain, *Conditions*, 777.   150 Flour, Aubert and Savaux, *Fait juridique*, 313.
151 Taylor, *Harmonisation communautaire*, 75.   152 Above, pp. 146–7.

though it was 'objectively impossible' for the seller to discover the nature or causes of the defect.[153] It is also true of all liabilities which arise for non-performance of an *obligation de sécurité de résultat*, where liability arises from the defendant's failure to preserve the claimant's safety and is excluded only on proof of *force majeure*. The crucial point here is that *force majeure* has been interpreted as requiring an element of 'exteriority' from the physical thing which is the subject of the obligation. In the result, it does not matter that the defendant can show that any defect in the thing was unforeseeable and could not be prevented ('absolutely impossible'), since it is not 'exterior'.[154] What this means, however, is that the development risks defence is naturally seen by French lawyers as a particular example of *force majeure*. For some, this means that the *loi* of 1998's introduction of the defence risks contaminating the defence of *force majeure* more generally;[155] but equally this association is likely to lead to the same sort of flexibility in application of the development risks defence as is found in relation to *force majeure*, which has been applied more strictly or more generously depending on its context.[156]

The second element is the relationship between the development risks defence and the nature of the French civil process. Here, Jamin has noticed the inadequacy of existing French procedures to investigate the sorts of issues which may arise under the defence:

How will the courts be able to check that the whole of world literature (for, in scientific matters, it is the world which is concerned) on this or that subject has been put before them? Will they require, moreover, that it is put to them? Will they be in a position to assess the relevance of information which has been communicated to them and will they want to? ... On all these questions, we risk having glorious arguments which are ... liable to explode our over tranquil view of the *expertise*. Perhaps it will be time to start to build a law of evidence [*la preuve*] worthy of the name, at last looking over towards American lawyers, who labour in the fields of facts and are obsessed with evidence.[157]

It is much more likely, however, that the development risks defence will not prove a spur to change in fundamental French understandings of the proper, uncontroversial and almost uncontrovertable role of the *expert*, so as to produce the sort of investigation of scientific literature and opinion of the sort which is as characteristic of the English as of the American common law where technical matters form the subject of dispute.

(ii) The European Court's decision in Commission v UK

During its parliamentary passage, the wording chosen by the UK government to implement the development risks defence was criticised as being wider than the terms of article 7(e) of the Directive,[158] giving a defence to a producer if he proves that:

the state of scientific and technical knowledge at the relevant time was not such that a producer of products of the same description as the product in question might be expected to have discovered the defect if it had existed in his products while they were under his control.[159]

---

[153] Above, pp. 89–90.   [154] Above, p. 90.   [155] Above, p. 465.

[156] See, in particular, its use in relation to traffic accidents before the *loi* of 5 Jul. 1985, above pp. 58–9. Cf. its role as an excuse for contractual non-performance owing to supervening circumstances: Nicholas, 200–05.

[157] C. Jamin, RTDCiv. 1998.763, 766–9.   [158] Above, p. 470.   [159] 1987 Act, s. 4(1)(e).

Even without this apparently greater generosity to producers provided by its reference to the state of knowledge that a producer of *products of the same description*, the defence had previously been criticised both by members of the House of Lords[160] and by academics as leading to a result not much different from that which already obtained under the tort of negligence.[161]

The European Commission brought proceedings against the UK for failure to implement the 1985 Directive as regards this defence, the Court giving judgment in 1995 in *Commission v United Kingdom*.[162] This is a significant decision: in part because of its clarification of what is meant by the 'state of scientific and technical knowledge', but even more because it illustrates the potential for confusion that may be caused in equating too readily civilian ideas of 'liability for fault' and 'objective liability' with the common law's 'liability for negligence' and 'strict liability'. This confusion then rebounded in the English context in the court's interpretation in *A v National Blood Authority* of the relationship between this defence and the Directive's conception of 'defect'.[163]

Advocate-General Tesauro's opinion set the scene, being delivered in Italian (to which reference will be made as well as to the English version for reasons which will become apparent). He emphasised that the Commission's complaint against the UK was a narrow one in that it alleged that the 1987 Act's provision was *incapable* of being interpreted by its courts in a way which conformed with the Directive: any ambiguity in the provision was therefore irrelevant to the proceedings.[164] The Commission's complaint was that the test under article 7(e) was 'objective' and makes no reference to the ability of the producer or of another producer of similar products to discover the defect, whereas the UK's implementation of the defence calls for a 'subjective assessment' in that it places emphasis on the conduct of a reasonable producer and thereby transformed the strict or no-fault liability (*la responsabilità oggettiva o senza colpa*) into one found on negligence (here, *negligenza*) of the producer.[165] However, Advocate-General Tesauro considered that this contention was unfounded, and in doing so expressed himself in the more general Italian of '*colpa*' rather than '*negligenza*', which is more linguistically similar to the English negligence. In this respect, Advocate-General Tesauro's own understanding of the differences between 'strict liability' and 'fault liability' was sophisticated. In the notes to his opinion he referred to 'strict liability' for products (using the English phrase) in the United States, the adoption of the terminology of 'unreasonably dangerous' defective products in paragraph 402A of the Restatement (Second) of Torts, and its criticism by the Californian Supreme Court as 'an element which rings of negligence';[166] but he also noted Priest's warning against 'absolute liability' for products which led in the United States to a crisis in the insurance market.[167]

---

[160] HL Deb. Vol. 414 col. 1427 (Lord Scarman).

[161] Whittaker (1985) 257–60; Stapleton, *Product Liability*, 236–42.

[162] Case C-300/95 of 29 May 1997 [1997] ECR I-2649 (which includes the opinion of A.-G. Tesauro ('Tesauro, *Opinion*')).   [163] Above, p. 488.

[164] Tesauro, *Opinion*, para. 14.   [165] Ibid. at para. 6.

[166] *Cronin v J.B.E. Olson Corp.* 8 Cal.3d 121, 501 P.2d 1153 (1972), at 1162 *per* Sullivan J (the original English, translated by Tesauro as ' "*in odore" di negligenza*': Tesauro, *Opinion*, para. 16, note 6).

[167] Tesauro, *Opinion*, para. 18, note 9 referring to G.L. Priest, 'The current insurance crisis and modern tort law' (1987) 96 *Yale Law Journal* 1521, 1589; G. Ponzanelli 'La controrivoluzione nel diritto di responsabilità da prodotti negli Stati Uniti di America' (1989) *Il Foro Italiano* IV, 119 *et seq.*

It is implicit in his opinion, that the Advocate-General considered that European lawyers had heeded and should continue to heed this warning.

In Advocate-General Tesauro's view, taking into account its development risks defence liability under the Directive is 'objective' (which he saw as the same as the common law 'strict liability'[168]) in that it sets a standard which does not depend on the ability or circumstances of the *particular* producer before a court; conversely it is 'without fault' (*senza colpa*, translated in the English version as 'without negligence') because it does not take account of these 'subjective' considerations; but it is not 'absolute'.[169] In his view, the UK's implementation of article 7(e) conforms to this way of thinking as it takes an 'objectively verifiable and assessable parameter, which is in no way influenced by consideration of the actual subjective knowledge of the producer or by his organizational and economic requirements'.[170] This view is therefore compatible with holding that the practicability and expense of measures suitable for eliminating the defect from the product and the producer's *own* knowledge are irrelevant to determining whether or not he has fulfilled the defence: the applicable standard is an 'objective' one, assessed according to the knowledge of an expert in the relevant sector.[171] For Tesauro, the defence reflects a 'fair apportionment of risk between the injured person and the producer' because it means that the latter has to bear only *quantifiable*[172] or *foreseeable* risks against which he can protect himself either by undertaking further research or by taking out liability insurance;[173] but liability remains an 'objective' one and not based on 'fault'.[174]

Secondly, Advocate-General Tesauro considered what is meant by the 'state of scientific and technical knowledge'. In his view, a producer could not simply rely on the majority of learned opinion but rather on the 'most advanced level of research'; but it would be 'unrealistic' and 'unreasonable' to include within this studies in languages and in places inaccessible to a European product manufacturer, giving as an example the Manchurian academic who published in Chinese in a local scientific journal.[175] So, 'the "state of knowledge" must be construed so as to include all data in the information circuit of the scientific community as a whole, bearing in mind, however, on the basis of a reasonableness test the actual opportunities for the information to circulate'.[176]

The European Court's judgment started by noting that recital 7 to the Directive saw the defences in article 7 as reflecting a 'fair apportionment of risk' between producers and injured persons.[177] It noted that under article 4 of the Directive, the injured party must prove the damage, the defect and the causal relationship between the two, but 'not that the producer was at fault' (*colpa* in the Italian version, *faute* in the French). The Court then agreed with its Advocate-General that the reference to 'scientific and technical knowledge' is 'not specifically directed at the practices and safety standards in use in the industrial sector in which the producer is operating, but,

---

[168] Tesauro, *Opinion*, para.16, note 6.

[169] Ibid. at paras. 18–19 (contrasting an earlier version of the 1985 Directive which provided that '[t]he producer shall be liable even if the article could not have been regarded as defective in the light of scientific and technological development at the time when he put the article into circulation' with its final version which included art. 7(e)).   [170] Ibid. at para. 26.   [171] Ibid. at para. 20.

[172] Ibid. at para. 19.   [173] Ibid. at para. 22.   [174] Ibid. at para. 27.

[175] Ibid. at paras 23–4.   [176] Ibid. at para. 24.   [177] Case C-300/95, para. 5.

unreservedly, at the state of scientific and technical knowledge, including the most advanced level of such knowledge, at the time when the product in question was put into circulation'.[178] Moreover, article 7(e) is not concerned with the 'state of knowledge of which the producer in question actually or subjectively was or could have been apprised, but the objective state of scientific and technical knowledge of which the producer is presumed to have been informed',[179] though this knowledge 'must have been accessible' at the time when the product in question was put into circulation, a point which the Court considered 'raises difficulties of interpretation'.[180] However, in applying this test to the Consumer Protection Act 1987, the Court concluded that the Commission had failed to prove its case, which 'selectively stresses particular terms used' by the provision. In its general legal context, including its provision for the correct burden of proof, the unrestricted nature of its reference to the state and degree of scientific knowledge at the material time, its lack of suggestion that the defence depends on the subjective knowledge of the producer (contrary to the Commission's allegation), and 'especially to section 1(1) of the Act' (which expressly requires a court to interpret its provisions so as to conform to the Directive as required by general EC law), the provision does not fail effectively to secure full application of the Directive.[181]

In my view, the real importance of this decision of the Court is its implicit lesson against reading into the phrase 'liability without fault' or its apparent 'equivalents' in other languages of the Member States (as in *responsabilità senza colpa* in Italian, *responsabilité sans faute* in the French) the significance of the English understanding of 'liability without negligence'. Conceptions of fault differ significantly among the laws of the Member States (and sometimes, as I have noted in relation to French law, even *within* a particular Member State[182]), not merely as between 'subjective' and 'objective' conceptions of fault but also as to what is meant by 'objective liability' *as distinct from* liability for fault, 'strict liability' as distinct from 'liability for negligence'. This being the case, a court of a Member State should not rely on its own understanding of fault in order to interpret elements of liability under the 1985 Directive *a contrario*. The European Court's decision in *Commission v UK* makes clear that liability under this Directive is 'objective' in that it rests on a standard independent of the abilities of the individual defendant and what he actually knew: but then, so, in English law, does liability in negligence.[183]

Where does the European Court's decision leave the formulation of the defence in the 1987 Act? For the Court, the standard of judging the producer's ability to detect the defect is objective in the sense that it does not depend on the resources or knowledge of the particular producer: to the extent to which the Act's reference to producers of 'products of the same description' suggests a more 'subjective' approach, then this suggestion must be resisted.[184] On the other hand, a national court will have to start

---

[178] Case C-300/95, at para. 26.   [179] Ibid. at para. 27.   [180] Ibid. at para. 29.
[181] Ibid. at paras. 33–9.   [182] Above, pp. 20–1, 42–3, 311–14 (civil and administrative faults).
[183] Above, pp. 188–9, 193–6.
[184] It is also for this reason that a non-manufacturing defendant (such as an importer or supplier) could not rely on the defence because it could not discover the defect, even though the producer could: and see Stapleton, *Product Liability*, 238.

from the particular technical context of the product in question in order to assess the *relevant* scientific and technical knowledge at 'the most advanced level' and here difficulties and uncertainties do indeed remain. For the advancement of science and technology rests on a combination of the furthering of understanding of theoretical or fundamental scientific phenomena and their radiating implications for other scientific fields and technological applications. Where the fundamental science from which a risk in the context of a particular product or category of products is later drawn is known at an earlier stage, does this mean that the 'state of scientific or technical knowledge' was present earlier or only later? Furthermore, if a risk is foreseeable but *not quantifiable*,[185] can the defence still apply? It could be argued that only a quantifiable risk (for example, knowing not merely the existence but also the prevalence of Hepatitis C in blood) provides a proper basis for insurance.

(iii) The reception of the European jurisprudence in the English courts

The proper significance of the development risks defence has come before the English courts on three occasions. In *Abouzaid*, it was noted that the defence would not be available to a producer simply on the ground that there had been no recorded history of any comparable accident at the time of supply, given that the risk in question (eye injury from a buckle attached to elastic) was known at the time.[186] Similarly dismissive was the court in *Richardson*, where it was stated that the defence would not be available to a producer in the case of a defect of a known character (there that some condoms rupture during use) merely because there is no test which is able to reveal its existence in every case.[187]

The treatment of the defence was altogether more elaborate in *A v The National Blood Authority*, which I have already discussed in relation to the notion of 'defect'.[188] The particular issue before Burton J was not whether the risk of the blood supplied being contaminated with Hepatitis C was known at the time (it was agreed that it was), but rather whether given the state of scientific and technical knowledge, the producer could have discovered the presence of this contamination in any particular batch of blood.[189] It was common ground that article 7(e) is not concerned with the conduct or knowledge of individual producers,[190] but could it protect a producer in respect of known but unavoidable risks? The claimants argued that it should not, given the Directive's purpose of consumer protection and easing the recovery of compensation; the defendants argued that it could, even if their argument as to the relevance of the avoidability of the risk of harm to the product's defectiveness was rejected, on the basis that it allowed a specific protection for producers who are non-negligent.[191] In coming to his decision, Burton J considered that the European Court in *Commission v United Kingdom*[192] intended to limit the 'escape clause' in article 7(e).[193] He also noted the Advocate-General's view that the producer must bear

---

185 Cf. above, p. 497.
186 *Abouzaid v Mothercare UK Ltd.* [2000] All ER (D) 2436 at [28]–[29] and above, p. 486.
187 *Richardson v LRC Products Ltd.* [2000] PIQR P164 at P172, above, p. 485.
188 [2001] 3 All ER 289, above, pp. 486–91.   189 Ibid. at [50].   190 Ibid. at [49].
191 Ibid. at [50]–[51].   192 Above, pp. 497–8.   193 [2001] 3 All ER 289 at [53].

foreseeable risks as he can protect himself either by stepping up experimentation and research or by taking out insurance and that the Court had referred to the producer's knowledge in relation to the risk, rather than its discoverability in a particular product.[194] For Burton J the resulting analysis was 'entirely clear':[195]

If there is a known risk, i.e., the existence of the defect is known or should have been known in the light of non-Manchurianly accessible information,[196] then the producer continues to produce and supply at his own risk. It would, in my judgment, be inconsistent with the purpose of the Directive if a producer, in the case of a known risk, continues to supply products simply because, and despite the fact that, he is unable to identify in which if any of his products that defect will occur or recur, or, more relevantly in a case such as this, where the producer is obliged to supply, continues to supply without accepting the responsibility for any injuries resulting, by insurance or otherwise.[197]

While the defence was plainly to protect producers from 'development risks' so as not to discourage innovation, in Burton J's view a risk is not a 'development risk' once it is known to the scientific community as a whole.[198]

With respect, however, the last stage of this reasoning is by no means evident: where a risk is known to the scientific community but its manifestation (the 'defect') is incapable of being detected in individual products and therefore prevented *at any cost and in any way* given the contemporary state of scientific knowledge, why should this not be thought to be a 'development risk' in that the imposition of liability would inhibit the production of innovative products? As has been said, article 7(e) refers to the discovery of the defect, not the risk.[199] Advocate-General Tesauro had suggested that the reasons why article 7(e) distinguishes between foreseeable and unforeseeable defects is that where a defect is foreseeable a producer can either take out insurance or undertake further research.[200] The first argument is not wholly convincing, as it could be said that insurance can be obtained (at least sometimes) even as regards unknown and unforseeable defects; but he rejected this as 'absolute liability'.[201] And further research may be required under a cost/benefit analysis of the sort which takes place under the tort of negligence, the cost and practicability of the research forming an element together with the foreseeable risk of a product's harm and its utility.[202] Where, however, as in *A v National Blood Transfusion Service* a producer has a legal obligation to supply a product, should liability be imposed even where the state of scientific knowledge does not permit it to prevent the harm in question? One reason why the production and supply of a particular category of product is entrusted to a public body and made a matter of obligation is that it is necessary for health, but this characteristic is not special to blood and may not have led to a public monopoly of production. Other products, most obviously medicines, should sometimes be produced and supplied despite their known risks and before the continuing research as to their

---

[194] Ibid. and see Tesauro, *Opinion*, para. 22, above, p. 497.   [195] Ibid. at [74].
[196] This phrase was used by the court to describe all data in the information circuit of the scientific community as a whole picking up A.-G. Tesauro's example: cf. above, p. 497.
[197] [2001] 3 All ER 289 at [74].   [198] Ibid. at [76].
[199] Stapleton, *Product Liability*, 237; Goldberg, *op. cit.* n. 90, 191.   [200] Ibid. at [22], above, p. 497.
[201] Ibid. at [18], above, p. 497.   [202] Whittaker (1985) 258 and see above, pp. 194–5.

avoidance is successful. Here too, further research will not avoid the risk in the products supplied in the meantime.

How then should the development risk defence be viewed and how should it be related to the Directive's general standard of liability found in its concept of defect? Burton J's view was that the development risks defence should not apply where a known risk is unavoidable except by stopping its supply and this led him to rule out the avoidability of a harmful characteristic as a factor in assessing a product's defect, unless the harmful characteristic is known to people generally and not merely to science: any other view would deny the Directive's purpose in imposing liability without fault, which he understood as liability without negligence.[203] In my view, though, the avoidability of a harmful characteristic is properly *relevant* to the assessment of a product's defect whether or not it is known to people generally, but it will not *conclude* it: this is not inconsistent with the Directive's assertion that it imposes liability without 'fault', even if it is reminiscent of the cost/benefit analysis in English negligence.[204] This leaves the defence in article 7(e) as a means by which a producer can avoid the judicial balancing of factors under article 6 by proving that at the relevant time he was unable (through the lack of the relevant scientific knowledge being available) to discover the harmful characteristic (the alleged defect) in products of the type in question, whether as regards particular examples of that type of product or more generally. Article 7(e) therefore provides a producer with a trump card, but only in limited factual circumstances which he must prove; by contrast, while the burden of proof as to 'defect' rests on the injured party, this is not purely a factual matter, but combines issues of fact with ones of an overall evaluation of those facts.[205] It may well then be easier for a producer to establish the defence provided by article 7(e) in the limited circumstances when it applies rather than successfully resist an allegation of 'defect'. But while article 7(e) relieves a producer of a particular category of 'development risk', other aspects of 'development risk' remain relevant to the overall assessment of defect.

This way of thinking is entirely consistent with the way in which a French jurist might see the relationship between 'defect' and the development risk defence. As I have explained, for some, the defence raises the same sorts of consideration (and notably the foreseeability of the risk) as are relevant to the court's assessment of the product's defect;[206] for others, the defence is reminiscent of *force majeure*.[207] In this respect, it will be recalled that French lawyers have reduced the significance of unforeseeability as an element in the definition of *force majeure*, holding it to form merely an aspect of the unavoidability of harm: so the mere fact that something is foreseeable does not prevent it constituting *force majeure* if this characteristic does not permit its avoidance.[208] Moreover, the above interpretation of article 7(e) indicates a similarity with article 7(d)'s defence that a 'defect' results from conformity with public regulatory requirements. For in practice, the latter defence allows a producer to avoid the need to argue that the public regulator's view of the matter is the right one (given a

[203] Above, pp. 487–8, 500.   [204] Above, pp. 489–90.   [205] Cf. above, pp. 483–4, 490.
[206] Above, p. 484.   [207] Above, p. 495.   [208] Above, p. 58, n. 150.

proper balance of considerations under the concept of defect) by saying that, even if there is a defect in the relevant sense, where harm is caused by following regulatory requirements no liability can ensue. For a French lawyer, this defence is seen as a particular expression of *force majeure* known as *fait du Prince*.[209]

More generally, this discussion emphasises the need for a wider appreciation of the differences in understanding in the laws of the Member States as regards such fundamental concepts as 'fault' or 'strict liability'. While the Community legislator in 1985 was careful to avoid adopting these expressions in the text of its Directive and instead adopted its own 'original' provisions (though they were directly derivative of the European Convention and, more distantly, of US law), their use in the recitals risks misunderstanding and potential distortion.

On the other hand, Jamin is right in questioning the appropriateness of the French civil process to determine the sorts of issues raised by article 7(e).[210] A common law trial such as took place in *A v The National Blood Authority* is capable of exposing for argument and evaluation the complex and sometimes controversial scientific issues of the type likely to be required by a producer's invocation of the defence in article 7(e) of the Directive, but it is difficult to see how this could effectively take place in a civil process such as the French where scientific information and advice is given to a court in a conclusive way by a single expert.

3. Claimants and Recoverable 'Damage'

The 1985 Directive did not restrict the category of person who can recover for the harm to which it applies in any way, grandly stating that 'the producer shall be liable for damage caused by a defect in his product' and referring otherwise simply to the 'the injured person'.[211] Despite its explicit concern with consumer protection, the Directive's protection is not limited to consumers, nor does it distinguish between injured persons who are or are not party to a contract. Moreover, although 'suppliers' are included within the range of those potentially liable under the Directive, there is no requirement that the person injured is the person to whom any supply took place.[212]

Instead, the Directive chose to limit recovery by designating the 'damage' for which the 'producer' is liable. Article 9 provides that:

For the purpose of Article 1, 'damage' means:

 (a) damage caused by death or by personal injuries;
 (b) damage to, or destruction of, any item of property other than the defective product itself, with a lower threshold of 500 ECU, provided that the item of property:
  (i) is of a type ordinarily intended for private use or consumption, and
  (ii) was used by the injured person mainly for his own private use or consumption.

This Article shall be without prejudice to national provisions relating to non-material damage.

---

[209] Ghestin (1998), 1209 and see below, p. 522.   [210] Above, p. 495.
[211] 1985 Directive, art. 4.   [212] Below, pp. 523–7.

I have already discussed some aspects of this provision, notably in the context of the failure of French law to implement its restrictions both as to the lower threshold of liability and as to the 'consumer' character of the property damaged,[213] and difficulties in the interpretation of the UK's implementation as regards 'non-material damage'.[214] To me, though, the first thing which is noticeable about article 9 is its use of 'damage'. In English legal usage, while 'damage' sometimes bears a more restricted meaning of physical harm, it can also be used broadly to refer to any type of harm, and this meaning of the word in the Directive is supported by the French version of article 9 using '*dommage*', an extremely broad term which includes any type of harm, physical, financial or 'moral'.[215] However, article 9 uses 'damage' in *two* senses: to refer to the harmful consequences of a physical injury ('damage *caused by* death or personal injury') and to refer to a particular type of injury ('damage *caused to*, or destruction of, any item of property') rather than to its (typically financial) consequences. This is certainly confusing and causes extra difficulty when coming to a view as to the line between the European and national competences in interpreting these concepts.

(a) The European Court's decision in *Veedfald v Århus Amtskommune*

Having said this, the decision of the European Court in *Veedfald v Århus Amtskommune*[216] gives us important general guidance as to the proper approach to article 9. In this case, the claimant had been a patient at the defendant Danish public hospital, needing a kidney transplant. His brother had donated a kidney, but after it had been treated in preparation for transplant with a liquid made by the hospital staff, it was found unsuitable for use as a result of a crystalline precipitation apparently present in the liquid used. The patient sued the hospital for damages to compensate him for the failure of the transplant operation under the Danish legislation implementing the 1985 Directive and the Danish court referred a number of questions to the European Court, including whether EC law imposes requirements as to how Member States should interpret the expressions 'damage' and 'personal injuries' in article 9 and whether damage to an organ to be transplanted into a patient constitutes 'personal injuries' to or 'damage to the property' of its intended recipient.[217]

Advocate-General Ruiz-Jarabo Colomer advised the Court that the expressions used by article 9 must be given an EC interpretation so that they are 'uniformly applied throughout the whole Community', as it defines 'in a quite detailed manner' what is meant by 'damage' for the purposes of article 1 and as the Directive's aim is harmonisation.[218] Article 9 distinguishes between two heads or categories of damage—damage caused by death or personal injuries and damage to property other than the defective product itself—and this implies that any case (apart from 'non-material damage') must come under one or other head. In the Advocate-General's view, 'damage' caused to the human organ was 'caused by personal injuries', but the question whether

---

[213] Above, p. 460.   [214] Above, p. 472.   [215] Above, p. 24.
[216] Case C-203/99 of 10 May 2001, [2001] ECR 1-3569 (which includes the opinion of A.-G. Ruiz-Jarabo Colomer ('Ruiz-Jarabo Colomer, *Opinion*')).   [217] Case C-203/99, at para. 5.
[218] Ruiz-Jarabo Colomer, *Opinion*, paras. 29–30.

this damage was caused to the organ donor or to its recipient is for the national court to decide![219] This approach would have led to many requests for interpretation by national courts and to the European Court being faced with the task of constructing a set of 'European' heads of recoverable harm resulting from death, personal injury and damage to property.

However, the European Court avoided this result by holding that these concepts are not ones on which it should take an autonomous view: neither article 1 nor article 9 of the Directive 'contains any explicit definition of the term damage', in contrast to its provisions on 'product', 'producer' and 'defect'.[220] Article 9 'indicates that "damage" must cover both damage resulting from death or from personal injuries and damage to, or destruction of, an item of property', with special conditions for the latter.[221]

Although it is left to national legislatures to determine the precise content of those two heads of damage, nevertheless, save for non-material damage whose reparation is governed solely by national law, full and proper compensation for persons injured by a defective product must be available in the case of those two heads of damage. Application of national rules may not impair the effectiveness of the Directive . . . and the national court must interpret its national law in the light of the wording and the purpose of the Directive.

A Member State cannot therefore restrict the types of material damage, resulting from death or personal injury, or from damage to or destruction of an item of property, which are to be made good.[222]

This statement of interpretative approach is of the highest significance both for the 1985 Directive itself and as a pointer towards the interpretation of other directives which use concepts which are fundamental, established in the laws of the Member States and which possess there different meanings. Rejecting its Advocate-General's view that it should take an autonomous interpretation of the concepts contained in article 9, the Court nevertheless did not simply resign them to the competence of the Member States. Instead, it referred the *interpretation* of the concepts to their laws ('for national legislatures to determine the precise content of these heads of damage'), but invoked the general principle of effectiveness to prevent a Member State from restricting the types of 'material damage' resulting from death, personal injury or damage to property: the Court has, therefore, recognised here a principle of 'full compensation',[223] but has left its working out to the Member States. As a result, there is no need for the Court to construct a European set of rules as to what 'full compensation' must mean, but beyond this, the significance of the ban on any restriction of the types of 'material damage' is less clear.

The ban could mean that it is for national law to identify the types of harm consequential, for example, on personal injury (in English law, 'loss of amenity' or 'medical expenses', 'loss of future earnings' etc.), but then for EC law to prevent *any* restriction on their recovery, even where such a restriction exists in the national law in question.

---

[219] Ruiz-Jarabo Colomer, *Opinion*, paras. 33–4.

[220] Case C-203/99, para. 25; 1985 Directive, arts. 2, 3, 6.   [221] Ibid., para. 26.

[222] Ibid., paras. 27–8 (emphasis added). Art. 9 actually provides that 'damage' *means* . . . ': see above, p. 502.

[223] The words '*un dédommagement adéquat et intégral*' are used in the French version of the Court's judgment at para. 27 appearing in English as 'full and proper compensation'.

However, this would be odd, given that in some laws the point of identifying different types of harm of this sort is in order to describe the conditions in which they are or are not available, for example, English law's denial of damages for pain and suffering while a victim of personal injuries is unconscious.[224] Clearly, the key to the European Court's likely approach is its reliance on the principle of effectiveness as the basis of its recognition of the need for 'full and proper compensation', citing its previous decision in *Hagen*,[225] where it ruled that while generally procedural rules are for national law, these rules must not be permitted by national courts to impair the effectiveness of the Brussels Convention so as to prevent a party to be joined to proceedings when the Convention allows it. Even more helpful, in my view, is the Court's jurisprudence applying the principle of effectiveness to ensure 'full compensation' for harm caused by unlawful discrimination, which suggests that a national rule which blocks compensation for a clear harm suffered by a claimant (such as a cap on liability or the denial of interest on an award[226]) is likely to be held unlawful on this ground, though it also suggests that the Court is likely to take a nuanced approach depending on the particular circumstances.[227] In the light of this, the Court is likely to hold that, while it is for national law to govern the characteristics and availability of the categories of loss resulting from personal injury, death and damage to property, it must not do so in a way which prejudices the overall effective compensation envisaged by the Directive.[228] This could be further supported from article 16 of the Directive, which provides the possibility of a financial ceiling on liability, but in restricted circumstances and to a restricted extent. In the result, a Member State which does not include recovery of a harm considered necessary for 'full and proper compensation' would have either to change its general approach (whatever its basis in public policy or public morality) *or* to take different views for compensation under the Directive and more generally.

The European Court's approach to the unusual facts presented by the Danish court also raises a number of difficult further questions. The European Court accepted that it was not its role to apply EC law to the facts of a particular case, but it clearly thought it right to advise, concluding that 'Articles 1 and 9 [of the Directive] . . . set out *exhaustively* the heads of damage that may be possible'.[229] A national court must therefore determine whether the harm in the circumstances is either (a) personal injury or death, (b) damage to property, or (c) 'non-material' damage: it cannot refuse damages on the ground that, while the other conditions of liability are fulfilled, 'the damage incurred is not such as to fall under any of the foregoing heads'.[230] But this left it for the Danish court to decide the categorisation of the harm caused by the hospital's rendering the kidney unfit to be transplanted from one of these three possibilities.

---

[224] *West v Shephard* [1964] AC 326.

[225] Case C-365/88 *Kongress Agentur Hagen GmbH v Zeehaghe BV* [1990] ECR I-1845, para. 20.

[226] Case C-271/91 *Marshall v Southampton and South West Area Health Authority II* [1993] ECR I-4367. [227] Craig and de Búrca, *EU Law*, 239–53, esp. at 47.

[228] Perhaps a clear example of inadequate compensation would be found in a rule which limited recovery under the legislation implementing the Directive in a way which is both not foreseen by it and not applicable to recovery of damages more generally in the law in question.

[229] Ibid., para. 32 (emphasis added).   [230] Ibid., para. 33.

It is understandable that the Court viewed the categories of harm in article 9 as exhaustive given the facts of the case before it and the unattractiveness of the argument put to it that the claimant could not recover because he had suffered neither personal injury nor any damage to property (the kidney not being capable of being owned).[231] However, for an English lawyer there is a very clear fourth category of 'damage' in the wide sense suggested by articles 1 and 9 which may be caused by a defective product: 'economic loss'. In this respect, the Court's decision in *Veedfald* in general allows a Member State to determine whether or not economic loss *consequential* on death, personal injury or damage to property is recoverable (this constituting a 'type of harm' *resulting from* death, personal injury or damage to property). In this respect, national laws may be very different. English law draws a series of distinctions: economic losses consequential on a claimant's *own* personal injury (or damage to his *own* property) are recoverable under the law governing the quantification of damages[232] subject to the general requirement that the damage is not too remote;[233] economic loss consequential on another person's *death* is in principle irrecoverable, but with important exceptions in the case of claims by dependants of the deceased;[234] and under the tort of negligence economic loss consequential on damage to another person's property is subjected to the restrictive approach to 'pure economic loss' generally taken by the courts.[235] By contrast, French law follows through its principle of '*réparation intégrale*';[236] the Cour de cassation has declared that the role of civil liability is to re-establish as exactly as possible the *status quo ante* destroyed by the harm and to place the action, at the expense of the person liable, in the situation where he should have found himself if the harmful act had not occurred.[237]

Where does this leave recovery under the Directive of what an English lawyer would see as 'economic loss' *not* consequential on *any* person's death, personal injury or damage to property? One important example of such a loss for an English lawyer is damage to the defective product itself and this is specifically excluded by article 9(b) of the Directive.[238] But other cases can arise where a person suffers financial loss caused by a defective product not consequential on any physical injury to persons or property: for example, a retailer may suffer loss of profits or lost business reputation caused by a producer's recall of a product which is 'defective' within the meaning of the Directive.[239] The European Court's view in *Veedfald* that the triple categorisation of 'damage' in article 9 is exhaustive suggests that this sort of case is excluded from the scope of the Directive, a result which makes sense given the Directive's clear concern with compensation for personal injuries and death and, but only to a limited extent,

---

[231] Ruiz-Jarabo Colomer, *Opinion*, para. 32.

[232] On these see *Clerk and Lindsell on Torts*, para. 29–16 *et seq.*

[233] *Spartan Steel & Alloys Ltd. v Martin & Co. (Contractors) Ltd.* [1973] QB 27 (damage to property).

[234] Fatal Accidents Act 1976, s. 1(3) of which defines 'dependent' for this purpose. The general exclusionary rule can be seen in the rejection of a business loss in *Burgess v Florence Nightingale Hospital* [1955] 1 QB 349.

[235] See esp. *Leigh & Sillivan Ltd. v Aliakmon Shipping Co. Ltd.* [1986] AC 785 and cf. above, pp. 183–5.

[236] Viney and Jourdain, *Les effets de la responsabilité*, 111 *et seq.*; Terré, Simler and Lequette, *Obligations*, 860 *et seq.*   [237] Civ. (2) 8 Apr. 1970, Bull. civ. II no. 111, RTDCiv. 1971.660 obs. Durry.

[238] *Simaan General Contracting Co. v Pilkington Glass Ltd. (No 2)* [1988] QB 758 and see above, p. 184.

[239] Cf. *Britvic Soft Drinks Ltd. v Messer UK Ltd.* [2002] 1 Lloyd's Rep. 20, above, p. 242.

damage to property. However, when this consequence of *Veedfald* is combined with the European Court's decisions of 2002 which declared the 'completely harmonising' nature of the scheme of the 1985 Directive,[240] the result is a little surprising. For the 2002 decisions made clear that a Member State is not allowed either to create or maintain liability for defective products in general (as opposed to the maintenance of an existing scheme of liability for a particular category of product) other than as provided for by the Directive. Putting this together with the exclusivity of article 9 suggests that no Member State may provide for the recovery of economic loss not consequential on physical injury or damage in its implementing legislation or otherwise in laws applicable to unsafely defective products. Such a view would, of course, mean that where a national law (such as French law) explicitly or implicitly provides that in principle *all* types of harm are recoverable (including such a pure economic loss),[241] this would be unlawful as a matter of EC law.[242]

Moreover, here we encounter a difficulty in the relationship between the 1985 Directive and *implementation* of the Consumer Guarantees Directive of 1999. For in implementing the latter, a Member State may well wish to extend its scheme of 'liability' beyond its scope, notably by including liability in damages, by benefiting all buyers (and not just consumer buyers), and/or to cover all types of property (and not just 'consumer goods') and this looks permissible given the 1999 Directive's explicit minimal character.[243] This was indeed at first planned in the case of French law,[244] and has occurred in Germany.[245] However, while the focus of the 1999 Directive is neither on the safety of goods nor on liability in damages for their defects,[246] its implementation in the laws of the Member States may well have a practical impact on liability for harm caused by unsafely defective products, in particular as regards their suppliers and even as regards 'pure economic loss'. This looks contrary to the purpose of the European Court's decisions in 2002 which interpreted the 1985 Directive as setting a maximum as well as minimum for the liability of producers and suppliers in respect of (unsafely) defective products,[247] but could be seen as permissible given the European Court's acceptance that the exception to this maximum nature of the Directive included contractual liability generally and specifically for latent defects.[248] But this would represent a compromise resting on differences of form rather than of substance, unconvincing given the economic nature of the 1985 Directive's purpose of harmonisation.

(b) 'Non-material damage'

Article 9 of the 1985 Directive expressly provides that it shall be 'without prejudice to national provisions relating to non-material damage'. This is explained in the English version of the preamble which refers to 'compensation for pain and suffering and other non-material damages' and the French version to '*la réparation du pretium*

---

[240] Above, pp. 440–1.   [241] Above, p. 460.   [242] Above, p. 441.
[243] 1999 Directive, art. 8(2), below, p. 568.   [244] Below, pp. 575–6.
[245] Zimmermann, *Liability for Non-Conformity*, 29–30.   [246] Below, pp. 565–6, 591–2.
[247] Above, p. 441.   [248] Above, p. 442.

doloris et d'autres dommages moraux[249] (which is considerably wider than the English).[250] It would appear that the reason for recovery of this category of harm being placed *entirely* within the competence of national laws was the considerable existing divergence between them. As fleshed out by the Directive's recitals, 'non-material damage' could cover quite a range of harms, including what an English lawyer would see as 'pain and suffering', and mental distress consequential on a person's own or another person's personal injury or death, but also any 'moral' or 'extra-patrimonial' harm.[251] So, in French law, *dommage moral* has even included on occasion the distress caused to its owner by the injury of a horse.[252] And in the context of the Package Travel Directive, the European Court has included within 'non-material damage' the loss of enjoyment of a holiday.[253]

This leads to the question whether the European Court should take an autonomous view of the *category* of 'non-material damage' under article 9, even though it should leave its *availability* to national law. In favour of this would be the need to distinguish it from some cases of 'harm caused by personal injury', whose recovery is not left entirely to the national law as the *Veedfald* decision makes clear.[254] Certainly, the line between 'harm caused by personal injury' falling within article 9(a) and 'non-material damage' is sometimes a difficult one. For example, English law distinguishes between psychiatric injury (formerly, nervous shock) both from personal injury (which has a physical element and which is recoverable very widely in the tort of negligence) and from grief, upset or mental distress (which are generally irrecoverable in this tort).[255] Is psychiatric injury to be considered 'personal injury' or 'non-material damage' for the purposes of article 9? For this purpose, psychiatric injury may be sub-divided. So, for example, a person may suffer psychiatric injury consequential on the death of a person killed by a defective product (for example, a person traumatised by a car accident caused by a defective brake) or consequential on the defective product itself (for example, where the recipients of human growth hormone suffered psychiatric illnesses for fear of infection by CJD).[256] The European Court could decide whether 'psychiatric injury' is or is not 'personal injury' within the meaning of the Directive without holding more generally that there is a European conception of 'non-material damage', rather in the way in which it avoided determining conceptions of the other two heads of damage in article 9(a) and 9(b); on the other hand, there is force to the argument that the question of recovery for psychiatric injury should not be left entirely to national law, but should instead by subjected to the degree of control which *Veedfald* imposed on these other categories under the principle of effectiveness.[257]

---

[249] 1985 Directive, recital 9.
[250] Cf. F. Chabas, 'La responsabilité pour défaut de sécurité des produits, dans la loi du 19 mai 1998' GP 1998.2.1111, 1114 who sees this 'inelegant expression' as referring to commercial losses.
[251] Terré, Simler, Lequette, *Obligations*, 690–2.
[252] Civ. (1) 16 Jan. 1962, D 1962.199 note Rodière, JCP 1962.II.12557 note Esmein.
[253] Case C-168/00, *Leitner v TUI Deutschland Gmbh & Co. KG*, [2003] ECR 1–2631 interpreting Dir. 90/314/ EEC on package travel, package holidays and package tours.
[254] Case C-203/99, above, p. 504.   [255] See above, pp. 161–2.
[256] The Creutzfeld-Jakob Disease Litigation, *Group B Plaintiffs v General Medical Council* [2000] BMLR 92, [2000] Lloyd's Rep. Med. 161, above, pp. 298–9.   [257] Above, p. 504.

4. 'Caused by a Defect in his Product'

While this book has not sought to address the numerous particular problems raised by the requirement of causation in existing French or English laws,[258] some consideration must nevertheless be given to how the European Court would interpret this requirement for the purposes of the 1985 Directive. Article 4 of the Directive simply states that an injured person must prove 'the causal relationship between defect and damage', and does not provide any general definition of what should be understood by a 'causal relationship', though it does provide for two situations where causation is in issue.[259]

First, article 8(1) provides that the producer's liability shall not be reduced when the damage is caused both by a defect in a product and by the act or omission of a third party. The most obvious application of this provision is where a producer is sued by the 'injured person', who has suffered damage within the meaning of the Directive. Here, the producer's liability is not to be reduced owing to the contribution of an act or omission of a third party, whether or not this would itself attract liability (on whatever legal ground), though article 8(1) further provides that where it does so the producer may exercise any right of contribution or recourse in accordance with provisions of national law.[260] This approach to contributory acts of third parties certainly accords with that existing in the English law of torts, and with the French *private* law of liability (most clearly seen where the third party act also gives rise to liability).[261] And while it contrasts with French administrative liability for *faute* (where the act of a third party (*fait d'un tiers*) can reduce a defendant's liability),[262] the Conseil d'Etat has not applied this approach to liabilities *sans faute,* which would include liability under the *loi* of 1998.[263]

However, article 8(1) *could* also be read as an injunction against the reduction of liability in the producer even when sued for contribution or a contractual indemnity by a person (co-author of the primary victim's damage) held liable other than on the basis of the Directive: its proviso that it should be 'without prejudice to the provisions of national law concerning the right of contribution or recourse' is not conclusive on this point since it refers to recourse *by* the producer *against* a third party, rather than the other way around. However, it is submitted that article 8(1) should not be interpreted in this very broad way. First, article 8(1)'s context suggests that it is concerned with the ruling out of the reduction of liability in a producer on the ground of the 'act or omission of a third party' where the producer is sued by the person claiming his liability under article 4 of the Directive, a view supported by recital 8 to the Directive which justifies the rule by reference to the need to protect consumers and by article 8(2) which by contrast *allows* the reduction of a producer's liability on the ground of the contributory fault of the injured person, a provision which could be relevant only

---

[258] For earlier discussion of particular causal issues see above, pp. 54–9 (liability for the 'deeds of things'); pp. 86–91, 247–50 (liability in the French and English laws of sale); and pp. 375–6, 388–92 (French criminal responsibility).

[259] Here, we are concerned with causation of the damage by the defect. Causation may also be seen to be relevant elsewhere, e.g., in art. 7(d) which grants a defence where the defect was due to (caused by) compliance with mandatory public regulation.   [260] 1985 Directive, art. 8(1).

[261] Above, pp. 33–4, 172–3 and below, pp. 546–7.   [262] Above, pp. 322–4.   [263] Above, p. 34.

to a claim by a primary victim. Secondly, while article 8(1)'s reference to the national law concerning rights of contribution or recourse is concerned with claims by the producer, it nevertheless suggests more generally that the Directive is not concerned to affect recourse claims, a suggestion given credence by article 5 of the Directive which provides for the 'solidary' liability of two or more persons liable for the same damage *under* the Directive 'without prejudice to the provisions of national law concerning rights of contribution or recourse'. Thirdly, the consequences of reading article 8(1) so that a producer's liability would not be reduced when himself sued for contribution or an indemnity could be distinctly perverse. Would it apply only to claims brought by way of subrogation to a primary victim's rights on the basis of the scheme of liability contained in the Directive? If so, why should the 'contributory fault' of such a defendant *not* be relevant to the liability of the producer? In conclusion, article 8(1) does not affect the rights of recourse by third parties against the producer or supplier under the Directive nor the basis of the apportionment of liability as between the two categories of co-author of the primary victim's harm, a view taken by the French[264] and apparently by the UK legislator.[265] In these circumstances, it falls to national law to govern both the legal foundation of any claim for contribution or recourse and the basis of the apportionment of liability which this may raise.

Secondly, article 8(2) states that the:

liability of the producer *may* be reduced or disallowed when, having regard to all the circumstances, the damage is caused both by a defect in the product and by the fault of the injured person or any person for whom the injured person is responsible.[266]

Here, the significance of the permissive 'may' is not completely clear. It could be thought to give to Member States an option whether or not to include a defence of 'contributory fault' in the injured person, but this may be unlikely given that where the Directive gives this sort of choice it does so by explicit possibility of derogation[267] or expressly designating that it is for the Member State.[268] Perhaps, article 8(2) should be interpreted as giving to courts a power to reduce or disallow the producer's liability in the circumstances which it sets out. In any event, the English and French legislators both included a defence of contributory fault in their implementing legislation.[269]

Article 8(2) refers to the contributory 'fault' of the injured person or of any person for whom the injured person is responsible. The terminology here follows the civilian rather than common law tradition, referring to 'fault' (as in the French *faute de la victime*) rather than the more usual English 'contributory negligence'.[270] While negligence of an injured party (a person not taking care for his own safety) can be included within

---

[264] Art. 1386-14 C. civ. provides that the producer's liability *towards the victim* is not reduced by the act of a third party which contributed to the causing of the damage.

[265] The 1987 Act provides that a producer or supplier is liable to the primary victim (who suffers the relevant type of harm) whether it was 'caused wholly or partly by a defect in a product': s. 2(1). Any claim for contribution brought by a person held liable on some legal basis apart from Part I of the Act would fall within the provisions of the Civil Liability (Contribution) Act 1978 in the absence of any provision to the contrary in the 1987 Act.   [266] Emphasis added.

[267] Art. 15.   [268] Art. 16(1) (ceiling on liability).   [269] Art. 1386-13 C. civ.; 1987 Act, s. 6(4).

[270] Above, pp. 199–200. The Law Reform (Contributory Negligence) Act 1945, s. 1 appears to use 'fault' and 'negligence' interchangeably.

what a French lawyer would see as *faute de la victime*, a French court may well take a more 'subjective' view of the matter, an English lawyer a more 'objective' view, to an extent themselves reflecting broader differences between *la faute* and negligence.[271] It is most unlikely, though, that the European Court would think it appropriate to construct an autonomous view of 'contributory fault' for the purposes of the Directive, nor to specify any of the circumstances in which such a fault should or should not be found by a court, partly because this would be to specify what article 8(2) itself leaves out and because the Court would see this sort of undertaking as trespassing too far into the assessment of the facts of the case and the application of law to them which it rightly considers to be for national courts.[272] Certainly, the defence of *faute de la victime* has been considered by French lawyers as extremely important in determining whether a liability is really *sans faute*, or something rather closer to fault, as was very visible in the context of the law governing motor vehicle accidents in the 1980s;[273] and this may explain the attempt during the passage of the *loi* of 1998 to restrict the defence of contributory fault to cases where a claimant used the product 'in abnormal conditions which the producer was not bound to have foreseen', though this restriction was not retained on the basis that it was unnecessary given the courts' ability to take into account all the circumstances in coming to their decision.[274] Certainly, where the law permits such a defence, both English and French law give the courts very considerable discretion in determining the existence of a relevant 'fault' and in its effect on liability.[275]

On the other hand, article 8(2) does specify that a court may reduce or extinguish the producer's liability on the ground of the fault of 'any person for whom the injured person is responsible'. This is an exception to the general rule provided by article 8(1), which rules out reduction of liability for an act of a 'third party' and a first question is whether 'responsible' means 'actually legally liable', 'capable of being liable', or more generally responsible.[276] For example, in English law employers are liable for the torts of their employees committed in the course of employment under the doctrine of vicarious liability, but a parent is liable only personally and not vicariously for the acts of their children.[277] And while French law recognises a general category of 'liability for the deeds of people within one's control', the actual bases of liability differ considerably within this category.[278] While an English court has allowed the contributory negligence of an employee to affect the recovery of his employer, the inclusion of this 'vicarious contributory fault' in the Directive is open to criticism.[279] With the absence of any definition of whom article 8(2) has in mind or the basis of their liability for this purpose, it is unlikely that the European Court would attempt to take an autonomous view of the issue.

As I have said, apart from these two special cases of multiple contributory causes, the 1985 Directive is silent as to what is meant by 'the causal relationship between the

---

[271] Above, pp. 42–3, 186–8.   [272] Cf. above, *Veedfald*, Case C-203/99, para. 31.

[273] Above, p. 59.   [274] AN No. 1395, 9; Fauchon, *Rapport*, Sén. No. 226, 41.

[275] Above, pp. 59, 200.

[276] Here, the change in terminology used by the English version of the Directive ('responsible' rather than 'liable') does not help as the same word ('*responsable*') is used in the French for both.

[277] Above, pp. 165–6.   [278] Above, pp. 25–6.   [279] Whittaker (1985), 252–3.

defect and the damage'. This is all too understandable given the numerous distinct questions within causation, and the very considerable differences in their treatment (at a theoretical as well as at a practical level) not merely *between* the laws of the Member States,[280] but also sometimes within them. So, for example, in French law in general criminal courts take a more generous view of the requirement of a causal connection between a defendant's (criminal) act and a claimant's damage than do the ordinary civil courts, though this has been changed by legislation in 2000 for some situations.[281] Given these differences, the European Court's decision in *Veedfald* suggests that it is likely to leave causation to be defined and interpreted by national law and to be assessed by national courts, but subject to a qualification founded on the principle of effectiveness. Here, the 'completely harmonious' character of the 1985 Directive means that 'effectiveness' would cut both ways: so, national laws must not by their interpretation of causation render ineffective either the protection of injured persons *or* the restraints on liability of producers, as these together reflect the Directive's 'fair apportionment of risk'. But, in applying this principle of effectiveness, the Court is likely to take into account the very considerable extent to which causal issues combine issues of fact and their evaluation (often at a technical level) as well as questions of law. Indeed, as I have noted, in the French law of sale, the causal relationship between the property's defect and the claimant's harm is seen in practice as one of fact for the *expert* and the *juges du fond*, although the latter must explain their decision.[282]

Here, I shall give three illustrations of how such an approach to causation under the Directive could work out in practice.

First, French courts have sometimes had recourse to the notion of a 'presumption of causation' where use of a product has been followed by an injury which suggests both its defect and its causal relevance. This became particularly visible as regards claims by those who have contracted HIV or hepatitis C after receiving blood products which were known to have been at risk of being contaminated. So, for example, where a person had established that he had developed hepatitis C after receipt of a blood transfusion and also had shown that 'he himself did not have any other means of becoming contaminated' (as regards both his lifestyle and his antecedents), the Cour de cassation held that it was for the supplier of the blood to show that the blood did not possess any defect.[283] While this sort of decision goes quite a long way in reversing the burden of proof both as to the existence of a defect and its causal relevance, it could be justified on the basis that in the circumstances the facts, *as the claimant had established them*, justified the court in drawing an inference of the existence of a defect and its causal relevance, unless the defendant showed the contrary. More difficult to justify is the legislative (and retroactive) enactment of this *jurisprudence* in 2002 for the particular case of hepatitis C, which suggests that a different legal rule as to burden of proof is to be applied, rather than merely a special approach to a category of fact.[284] This looks

---

[280] A. M. Honoré, 'Causation and Remoteness of Damage' in *Encyclopaedia of Comparative Law*, Vol. XI (ed. A. Tunc) (J.C.B. Mohr, 1981) Chap. 7; Taylor, *Harmonisation communautaire*, 83–97.

[281] Above, pp. 375–6, 388–92.   [282] Above, p. 86.

[283] Civ. (1) 9 May 2001, Bull. civ. no. 130, D 2001.2149 note P. Sargos.

[284] *Loi* no. 2002–303, art. 102 (and see above, p. 152).

directly incompatible with article 4 of the Directive and therefore contrary to the principle of effectiveness.

My second example takes as its starting point the English decision in *Fairchild*.[285] There, a person developed cancer after being exposed to carcinogenic material (asbestos dust) by two successive employers in breach of their duties in tort and, while it could be ruled out that he had developed the cancer other than by inhalation at work, owing to the limits of science he could not establish whether the condition had been caused by a single exposure or by the cumulative effect of exposure over more than one employment, or whether it was caused by the breach of duty by one employer rather than the other. Nevertheless, the House of Lords held both employers liable jointly, either on the basis that *both* employers' breaches of duty had contributed substantially to the risk of injury[286] or that, while it took liability beyond the law's normal understanding of causation,[287] any other outcome 'would be deeply offensive to instinctive notions of what justice and fairness demands'.[288] Clearly, this sort of approach could be taken by an English court in the context of product liability under the 1987 Act. Take the case, for example, of a claimant supplied with a medicine of a type manufactured by *two identified* producers in circumstances where he could prove the existence of a medical condition capable of having been caused by a characteristic of that type of product, that it had *not* been caused by some factor other than that characteristic of the product, and that he had used medicines manufactured by *both* producers, but who could not prove which of the two producers' products had caused his condition. Here, following *Fairchild*, the court could hold *both* producers liable. In these circumstances, could the producers argue that the claimant had failed to establish that either one of their respective products had caused his harm according to the normal understanding of causation in English law, and that the court had therefore upset the balance of risks put in place by the Directive? The logic of the principle of effectiveness may suggest so, but a case like *Fairchild* or my medicine example clearly involves special difficulties for normal ideas of causation, these difficulties being well-known and acknowledged in the laws of other Member States, as is the sense that they should not be allowed to bar recovery.[289]

My third illustration starts with the decision of the Dutch High Court (Hoge Raad) in 1992 which accepted a 'market share' basis for liability.[290] There, three claimants had contracted cancer after their mothers took carcinogenic medicines. The court held that they were entitled to recover jointly against all the manufacturers who had made these medicines at the time, even though the claimants could not establish whether any particular manufacturer's medicine had caused their harm, a decision incompatible with any normal understanding of causation in the sense of *conditio sine*

---

[285] *Fairchild v Glenhaven Funeral Services* [2002] UKHL 22; [2003] 1 AC 32.

[286] Ibid. at [47], *per* Lord Hoffmann. This is very much a summary of the complex judgments: see further J. Stapleton, 'Lords A'Leaping Evidentiary Gaps' (2003) 10 *Tort LR* 276.

[287] [2002] UKHL 22 at [40].   [288] Ibid. at [36], *per* Lord Nicholls.

[289] See W. Van Gerven, J. Lever, P. Larouche, *Cases, Materials and Text on National, Supranational and International Tort Law* (Hart, Oxford, 2000) 441 and 461 quoted by Lord Bingham in *Fairchild* [2002] UKHL 22 at [24]. Cf. Taylor, *Harmonisation communautaire*, 95–97.

[290] Hoge Raad 9 Oct. 1992, *B v Bayer Nederland B.V*, NJ 1994/535.

qua non:[291] for on this approach any individual manufacturer may be held liable even though it is not shown that his product contributed in any way to a claimant's harm, even to the extent of contributing to the risk of the claimants' harm (as in my second illustration based on *Fairchild*). Here, it is to be noted that the EC Commision's *Green Paper* asked whether a solution of this sort should be introduced by way of reform of the terms of the 1985 Directive,[292] but it later reported that this was not welcomed by nearly all those who responded as it would 'make persons liable although they are not involved in the damage and this deviates from a fundamental principle of liability'.[293] If this way of thinking were accepted by the European Court, it could well hold that the application by a Member State of such a 'market share liability' for the purposes of national legislation implementing the Directive compromised the effectiveness of its balance of risk between producers and consumers.

5. Defendants and Defences

The 1985 Directive's treatment of those who can be liable under its scheme ('defendants') and the defences which they may invoke is complex. There are five distinct categories of defendant discernible in article 3—manufacturers of a finished product;[294] component manufacturers; those who represent themselves as 'producers'; Community importers; and mere suppliers—and article 7 provides six express defences for them. Here, I shall look at this scheme, explaining both the range of defendants and their defences.

There are four preliminary points. First, the European Court has made clear that the defences provided by article 7 should be interpreted strictly, following its approach more generally to legislative exceptions.[295] Secondly, while article 7 refers to 'the producer', some of the defences which it creates appear to be equally relevant to defendants other than the 'producer' in the sense of the manufacturer of a finished or component product, or those who presents themselves as either; for example, article 7(a)'s defence that the producer did not put the product into circulation could apply either to an importer or a mere supplier.[296] However, this apparent difficulty can be resolved as the Directive provides that importers are 'deemed to be a producer .. and shall be responsible as a producer';[297] and 'suppliers' are to be 'treated as its producer' in certain circumstances.[298] This allows, therefore, all categories of defendant to take advantage of article 7's defences, with the exception of article 7(e) which is restricted on its terms to manufacturers of component products. Thirdly, under article 7 the burden of proof lies on the defendant to establish the exonerating circumstances which it provides, balancing in this respect the burdens of proof on the injured party

---

[291] C. von Bar, *The Common European Law of Torts* (OUP, Oxford, 2000), Vol. 2, 441–3.
[292] Com.(1999)396 final (28 Jul. 1999), 22.   [293] EC Commission, *Second Report*, para. 3.2.1.
[294] Art. 3(1)'s reference to 'finished product' is misleading as it suggests that the product has had work done to it, whereas raw materials are included. 'Final product' would be more accurate as the sense is the product as it is 'put into circulation' by the producer.   [295] Case C-203/99, *Veedfald*, para. 15.
[296] Arts. 3(2) and 3(3) respectively.   [297] Art. 3(2).   [298] Art. 3(3).

provided in article 4,[299] and seen as part of the Directive's 'fair apportionment of risk between the injured party and the producer'.[300] While there is no express provision in the Directive to this effect, it would follow from the principle of *actori incumbit probatio* (whose import is found in both the civil and the common laws)[301] that the claimant must show that the defendant against whom he claims is a 'producer' within the meaning of the Directive. Fourthly, no defendant liable under the Directive can take advantage of any contractual or non-contractual exclusion or limitation of liability.[302]

(a) Acting in the course of business, public bodies and 'putting the product into circulation'

With the exception of Community importers, the Directive does not *define* the defendants on which it imposes liability in such a way as to require that they act in the course of business, whether as producer or distributor of one sort or another,[303] differing in this respect from some more recent Directives in the area of contractual consumer protection whose ambit is restricted to cases where one of the parties acts 'for purposes relating to his trade, business or profession',[304] from the established French law applicable to *vendeurs professionnels*,[305] and from the English contractual liabilities in respect of the quality or fitness of goods.[306] Nor does the 1985 Directive specifically provide that it applies equally to public as well as private bodies.[307] Instead, article 7(c) provides that it is a defence for a producer to show that 'the product was neither manufactured by him for sale or any form of distribution for economic purpose or distributed by him in the course of his business'. This means both that the burden of proof as to the defendant's business character is shifted from the norm and that its elements will be interpreted narrowly.[308]

The proper interpretation of article 7(c) and its significance for public bodies arose in the European Court's decision in *Veedfald*, the facts of which I have already noted.[309] There, the defendant public hospital relied on article 7(c)'s defence so as to escape liability for the preparations which it produced and used in the course of providing a publicly funded service for which its patient did not pay, arguing that it was not acting for an economic purpose or in the course of a business.[310] According to

---

[299] And see above, p. 509.   [300] 1985 Directive, recital 8.

[301] In French law: art. 1315 C. civ. and Ghestin, Goubeaux and Fabre-Magnan, *Introduction* générale, 615; English law: *Constantine Line v Imperial Smelting Corpn.* [1942] AC 154, 174; M.N. Howard (gen. ed.) *Phipson on Evidence* (15th. edn., Sweet and Maxwell, 2000) para. 4–03 (C. Hollander).

[302] 1985 Directive, art. 12; art. 1386-15 al. 1 C. civ.; 1987 Act, s. 7.

[303] Art. 3(2) deems such a person to be a producer where he 'imports into the Community a product for sale, hire, leasing or any form of distribution *in the course of his business*'. Here, therefore, acting in the course of a business is made a condition of an importer's liability arising, rather than a defence under art. 7(c).

[304] E.g. Dir. 93/13/EC, art. 2(c); 1999 Directive, art. 2(c).   [305] Above, p. 85.

[306] Above, pp. 236–7.

[307] Cf. Dir. 93/13/EC art. 2(c) which refers to a 'trade, business or profession, whether publicly owned or privately owned'.   [308] Above, pp. 514–15.

[309] *Veedfald v Århus Amtskommune* Case C-203/99, [2001] ECR 1–3569, above, p. 503.

[310] Ibid., para. 20.

Advocate-General Ruiz-Jarabo Colomer, article 7(c) imposed *two* conditions—'that the product was not manufactured for economic purposes, in other words for financial gain, *and* that the product was not manufactured or distributed by the producer in the course of his business'[311]—and while the first condition had been met in the case of a fluid made to treat an organ to be transplanted, the second had not as it had been 'prepared and used by the hospital in the course of its business'.[312] The European Court agreed, holding that the fact that products are manufactured for a service for which the patient has not paid and which is financed from public funds:

cannot detract from the economic and business character of that manufacture. The activity in question is not a charitable one which could therefore be covered by the exemption from liability provided for in Article 7(c) of the Directive. Besides, the [defendant hospital] itself admitted at the hearing that, in similar circumstances, a private hospital would undoubtedly be liable for the defectiveness of the product pursuant to the provisions of the Directive.[313]

This last point was clearly addressed to the argument put to the Court that the application of the Directive's scheme of liability to public hospitals would have harmful consequences for public health care and place them at a disadvantage in relation to private health schemes.[314]

This is an important decision for the impact of the 1985 Directive on public producers and suppliers of products. For the Court did not just decide that a public body cannot rely on article 7(c) *when* it acts in the course of a business (for example, by charging for its goods or services or otherwise acting in a way that a private body would normally do), but would appear to hold also that the fact that a product is made or supplied by a public body to a person *means that* the manufacture or supply is of an economic and business character. Here, though, some care should be taken. The terminology used by some of the other language versions of article 7(c) and of the Court in its judgment suggests a rather different significance to its double condition. For example, the French version of article 7(c) allows the defence where a product is made other than for sale or any other form of distribution 'for an economic purpose of the producer' or '*dans le cadre de son activité professionnelle*'.[315] While *activité professionnelle* includes what an English lawyer would see as 'the course of his business', it also has the sense of 'professional': so, for example, the provision of medical care is a 'professional' activity as it involves a special skill, even if it is not provided in the course of a business (with a view to an economic purpose).[316] Of course, it is unlikely that the manufacture of a product by a public body is undertaken other than as a *professionnel,* since a public body is likely to have recourse to those with special skill in the provision of the products it makes and uses: but the *mere* fact that a producer is a public body or performs a public service may not be enough.

A third approach to the significance of article 7(c) for public services has been suggested by Gaumont-Prat, drawing on the jurisprudence of the European Court

---

[311] Ruiz-Jarabo Colomer, *Opinion,* para. 26 (emphasis added).   [312] Ibid.

[313] Case C-203/99, para. 21.   [314] Ibid., para. 20.

[315] Similar expressions are found in the other Romance versions of the Directive: e.g. the Italian ('*sua attività professionale*') and the Spanish ('*su actividad profesional*').   [316] Cf. above, p. 85.

under article 82 EC,[317] according to which a public hospital such as the defendant in *Veedfald* should not be able to rely on article 7(c) because it was 'engaged in an economic activity' by acting in a context which had not always been nor is necessarily carried out by a public entity.[318] However, the purposes of article 82 EC (abuse of a dominant position) are quite distant from those of the 1985 Directive, even though one of its declared purposes is the enhancement of fair competition. For the 1985 Directive's aim is the harmonisation of the laws of producer liability so as to increase the fairness of competition between those whose products are in the market: the different costs of liability cannot affect the fairness of competition if they are not capable of being passed on in terms of the cost of the products or services. The European Court in *Veedfald* was more concerned with the Directive's purpose of the protection of consumers, not wishing to deny its scheme to those who were the recipients of a free public service as opposed to a fee-paying private one. Instead, the Court interpreted the defence in article 7(c) strictly with the result that only charitable manufacturers, who can be said neither to be acting with a view to financial gain *nor* in the course of a business or profession are included. So, for example, where a charity distributes food or other products to homeless people it can invoke the defence, but it cannot do so as regards fundraising ventures such as charity shops as here the charity would be 'acting in the course of business' and possibly also with a view to financial gain.

The European Court's very extensive view in *Veedfald* of the liability of public bodies seen in relation to article 7(c) can also be seen in its interpretation of article 7(a), which provides a defence where the producer proves that he 'did not put the product into circulation'. The hospital had argued that it had not put the fluid which it had produced into circulation since it was used in the course of providing a specific medical service (the kidney transplant) within the sphere of control of the hospital;[319] against this, it was argued that the hospital had indeed put the fluid 'into circulation' because it had *used* it.[320] Interpreting article 7(a) strictly,[321] the Court held that this defence was intended primarily to cover cases in which a person other than the producer has caused the product to leave the process of manufacture and so, while it covers use of a product contrary to its producer's intention (for example, where the manufacturing process is not complete) or for private purposes, it did not apply on the facts in *Veedfald*. In this respect, the fact that the liquid had not left its producer's sphere of control was not decisive where:

the use of the product is characterised by the fact that the person for whom it is intended must bring himself within that sphere of control. Where a patient is admitted to hospital, it cannot matter whether the product used in the course of medical treatment was made in the hospital establishment or was acquired from a third party, as it might have been in this instance... Whether a product used in the provision of a service was made by a third party, by the service provider himself or by an entity linked to the service provider cannot of itself alter the fact that the product was put into circulation.[322]

---

[317] H. Gaumont-Prat, Note, JCP 2002.II.1014, p. 1637.

[318] Case C-41/90, *Höfner v Mactron GmbH*, [1991] ECR 1–1079, para. 21.

[319] Case C-203/99, para. 13.   [320] Ruiz-Jarabo Colomer, *Opinion*, para. 22.

[321] Case C-203/99, para 15.   [322] Ibid., para. 17.

In this way, the Court therefore implicitly distinguished between a case in which the product is taken from the producer's sphere of control without his consent, where article 7(a) may apply; and a case in which the product is *used* by its producer in a context where it can harm persons (or property), where article 7(a) cannot apply. So, a producer can be liable under the Directive even though neither he nor anyone else *supplied* the product to another person in the sense of transferring possession or detention of the product to that person by way of the normal mechanisms of distribution. Clearly, 'putting a product into circulation' is not the same as putting it onto the market, but includes any voluntary, non-private use of a product after its completion.

Implementation of articles 7(a) and 7(c) of the Directive in French and English law is also interesting.

The Consumer Protection Act's implementation is compatible with the interpretation given to articles 7(a) and 7(c) in *Veedfald*, though its treatment of the former is rather horribly buried in a sea of definitions and cross-references. So, section 4(1)(c) of the 1987 Act provides a defence containing both elements of article 7(c),[323] and then section 45 defines 'business' to include 'a trade or profession and the activities of a professional or trade association or of a local authority or public authority'.[324] This definition (which echoes others in modern statutes where the 'course of business' is used[325]) clearly foresaw the possible inclusion of public bodies in the production or provision of products and that the phrase 'course of business' in the 1985 Directive could also cover a professional activity. And *A v The National Blood Authority* is an example of a public body being held liable under the 1987 Act.[326]

By contrast, the 1987 Act does not use the Directive's language of 'putting into circulation', either as regards the defence in article 7(a) or more generally. Instead, a defendant can escape liability if he shows that he 'did not at any time supply the product to another'.[327] Section 46 of the Act then defines 'supply' for this and other purposes by a 500-word catalogue of situations where there is or is not a 'supply'! While this catalogue does include the provision of goods in or in connection with the performance of any statutory function[328] (which would include many public supplies), all of its examples include the transfer or provision in some way or another of the product from a defendant to another person, whether by selling, hiring, lending, furnishing or otherwise. One example of 'non-supply' is particularly striking, as section 46(9) states that 'a ship, aircraft or motor vehicle shall not be treated . . . as supplied to any person by reason only that services consisting in the carriage of goods or passengers in that ship [etc], or in its use for any other purpose . . .' So, for example, where a person builds a defective ship and then uses it to carry passengers in the course of a business, he would not be liable under the 1987 Act for any personal injury or death which the

---

[323] Unlike art. 7(c) which distinguishes between manufacturers (first limb) and manufacturers and distributors (second limb), s. 4(1)(c) of the 1987 Act distinguishes between manufacturers, 'own-branders' and EC importers on the one hand and all those who supply on the other.

[324] And Part I of the Act binds the Crown to the extent to which it can be liable under the Crown Proceedings Act 1947: 1987 Act, s. 9.

[325] E.g. Unfair Contract Terms Act 1977, s. 14(1); Sale of Goods Act 1979, s. 61(1).

[326] [2001] 3 All ER 289, above, pp. 486–9.   [327] 1987 Act, s. 46(1)(b).

[328] 1987 Act, s. 46(1)(e).

ship's defect caused. This sort of result and the Act's treatment of article 7(a) of the Directive more generally looks inconsistent with the decision in *Veedfald*, for there the hospital had *not* supplied or provided the fluid (the relevant product) to anyone in any of the many ways which section 46 indicates.[329] Indeed, it is difficult to see how the language of 'supply' used by the section 4(1)(c) can naturally be interpreted so as to conform to the European Court's understanding of article 7(a), any voluntary use of a product by its producer after its completion counting as its 'putting into circulation'. Here, therefore, an English court could have to rely heavily on its duty under section 1(1) of the Act to interpret the Act so as to conform to the Directive.[330]

However, the French implementation of the Directive here is even further away from the European Court's interpretation of article 7(a) and (c).

First, the *loi* of 1998 did not simply provide a defence for a producer of the sort found in article 7(c), but instead divided its two elements: first, by defining the category of defendants in terms of their being or acting as *professionnels*,[331] and, secondly, by creating a defence where the producer shows that the product 'was not intended for sale nor for any other form of distribution'.[332] This implementation is open to criticism both because it makes the 'business or professional' aspect of article 7(c) a matter for the claimant to prove rather than for the defendant to disprove, and because it does not specify that the 'distribution' should be 'for economic purpose' (though this could be thought to be implicit in the notion of distribution).

Secondly, and more significantly, the application of the *loi* of 1998 to the public production or supply of products is far from clear. For not merely is this not specified by the *loi*, but implementation of the Directive was effected by amendment of the *Civil Code*,[333] which more than suggests that the Directive's scheme of liability applies only where French law would hold that private law governs. While, as I have explained,[334] the line between private law and administrative law does not turn merely on the presence or absence of a public body (here, as defendant to a claim for compensation), this involvement is a very significant element. So, for example, certainly until 2002,[335] French courts allocated liabilities for the provision of public health care (including as to the products used and supplied) to the administrative courts and to administrative law, but the European Court's decision in *Veedfald* demonstrates that the Directive will sometimes govern exactly this type of case. While the Directive's final implementation by amendment of the Civil Code rather than by special *loi* took place rather by accident,[336] it seems clear from the discussion of the Directive by French jurists that its significance for public bodies and administrative law was not appreciated: the Directive's concern is with the liability of commercial undertakings and the protection of consumers, both of which are seen as *de droit privé*, an impression supported by the fact that neither of the French commentaries on *Veedfald* explain its implications for administrative law.[337] Clearly, though, this purely national understanding of the application of the Directive cannot prevail over the European Court's view as shown

---

[329] Above, p. 517.   [330] Cf. above, p. 498.

[331] Art. 1386-6 al. 1 and al. 2; art. 1386-7 al. 1 C. civ.   [332] Art. 1386-11 3° C. civ.

[333] Above, pp. 460–1.   [334] Above, p. 460.   [335] Above, pp. 142–6, 151.

[336] Above, pp. 460–1.

[337] P. Keyser, note, D 2001.3065; Gaumont-Prat, note, JCP 2002.II.10741.

in *Veedfald* that both public and private 'consumers' should be protected by the Directive's scheme of liability. As I shall explain, this scheme may be significant for public producers and suppliers of products at present governed by French *administrative* law.[338]

Thirdly, French law's implementation of article 7(a) was not straightforward. For while the *loi* of 1998 provided a defence where a producer shows that he has not put the product into circulation,[339] it adds that '[a] product is put into circulation when the producer relinquishes it voluntarily' and that 'a product may be the subject of only one single putting into circulation'.[340] The first part of this definition appears to accord very well with the European Court's understanding of article 7(a) as it sets out the very circumstance in which the Court considered that it was intended to apply, that is, where the product has been taken from the producer without his consent.[341] On the other hand, the idea of 'voluntary *relinquishment*' (*dessaisissement volontaire*) of the product (which allowed the Directive's scheme to dovetail quite nicely with existing French liability for the 'deeds of things'[342]) does not accord with the Court's view that a product can be 'put into circulation' where a producer uses it within his sphere of control: indeed, the hospital in *Veedfald* could surely not have taken advantage of the French defence on its terms.

As I have already explained, the specification in terms of timing of the French definition of 'putting into circulation' was included to avoid undue complication in the application of the foreclosure period in article 11,[343] but it causes problems in relation to the application of the *other* defences where it plays a role and to the assessment of the defect. For example, under article 7(b) it is a defence for a producer that the relevant defect did not exist at the time 'when the product was put into circulation *by him*'.[344] Where, for example, a claimant sues both a Community importer and a retailer which sells a product under its own brand (therefore representing itself as 'producer'), the importer may well wish to say that at the time he supplied it to the retailer (and so 'put it into circulation') it did not contain the defect, even if it did when the retailer 'put it into circulation', but the French definition would prevent him from doing so because only the product's *manufacturer* could rely on the defence as his would be the first (and only) 'putting into circulation' of the product—despite the fact that article 7's defences should be available to *all* those liable under the Directive.[345] It would be better to admit that each member of the chain of distribution puts the product into circulation at different times.

There is a further argument in the same direction. Under article 6(1)(c), the defect must be assessed 'at the time when the product was put into circulation'. What is the position when a manufacturer puts (first) a product into circulation which (at the time) is not 'defective', but which is imported or otherwise supplied at a time when it is 'defective' (if judged at this later time)? If an injured person claims damages from the supplier or importer under the Directive, can they escape liability by arguing that the product was not defective at the time of its *first* supply, this being when it was 'put into

---

338 Below, pp. 536–7.   339 Art. 1386-11 1° C.civ.   340 Art. 1386-5 C. civ.
341 Cf. above, pp. 517–18.   342 Above, p. 459.   343 Ibid.   344 Emphasis added.
345 Above, p. 514.

circulation'? This could be supported by article 6(2)'s emphasis that 'a product shall not be considered defective for the sole reason that a better product is subsequently put into circulation'. And this appears to have been the interpretation taken by the UK legislator, for section 3(2)(c) of the 1987 Act provides that the product's defect must be assessed taking into account 'the time when the product was supplied by its *producer* to another' 'producer' under the 1987 Act unequivocally referring to its manufacturer rather than importer, 'own-brander' or mere supplier.[346] However, this would have the odd result that all defendants except the original manufacturer could escape liability for their supply of products which are defective at the time when they supplied them, but were not when they were made. An alternative interpretation would be that the product's defect is to be assessed as at the time of its 'putting into circulation' by the defendant sued by the injured person: the reference in article 6(2) could be explained as referring to cases where a better product is put into circulation after the defendant sued has put it into circulation. This last point is, indeed, reflected in part by the 1987 Act at the point of the operation of those defences which refer to the product's 'putting into circulation,' for here the legislation does not refer to the time of supply by the producer, but rather to the 'relevant time', defined in the case of manufacturers, importers and own-branders as the time when the person who is sued supplied the product to another person.[347] Oddly, however, this is not carried through to the position of 'mere suppliers', as here the 'relevant time' is 'the time when the product was last supplied' by a manufacturer, own-brander or importer.[348]

(b) The different categories of defendant in article 3

While the manufacturer of a defective finished product was clearly seen by the Directive as the person who should primarily bear the cost of its damage, article 3 includes a number of other categories of possible defendant.

First, article 3(1) states that it is not merely the manufacturer of the finished product itself who can be liable, but also a person who 'produces' a raw material, such as wood, natural gas or the vegetable produce of market gardens, whether or not he treats these products before he puts them into circulation, in this respect following the Directive's very wide understanding of 'product' itself.[349] Manufacturers of components intended for incorporation into larger products (whether movable or immovable) are also included, though they enjoy a special defence under article 7(f) where the 'defect is attributable to the design of the product in which the component has been fitted or to the instructions given by the manufacturer of the product'.[350] This defence, therefore, allows contractual specifications stipulated by a manufacturer of a larger product (such as a motor vehicle) to the manufacturer of one of its components (such as its brakes) to form the basis of a complete defence against liability under the Directive. Both the English and French implementing legislation followed article 7(f) faithfully, if not word for word.[351]

---

[346] 1987 Act, s. 1(2) 'producer'. Taylor, *Harmonisation communautaire*, 67.

[347] 1987 Act, s. 4(1) (d) and (e), (2) achieved by reference to a special definition of the 'relevant time'.

[348] 1987 Act, s. 4(2)(b).   [349] Above, pp. 476–7.   [350] 1985 Directive, art. 7(f).

[351] Art. 1386-11 al. 2 C. civ.; 1987 Act, s. 4(1)(f).

Apart from this special defence and the 'development risks defence' which I have already discussed,[352] these manufacturers can escape liability if they prove that 'the defect is due to compliance of the product with mandatory regulations issued by the public authorities'.[353] This defence is not, of course, a defence of compliance with public standards (though such a defence has been suggested[354]): it requires that the defect itself results from the regulatory standard. But *which* 'mandatory regulations' are relevant? A manufacturer in Member State A whose product causes harm in Member State B and is sued there, could argue that this defence should protect him where the defect was caused by the 'mandatory regulations' of Member State A, even if there was no such regulation in Member State B. However, it is unlikely that such an argument would succeed, given the Court's strict approach to the interpretation of the Directive's defences, and the fact that the approach of EC law governing consumer product safety suggests that the relevant law should be the one in which a product is marketed.[355]

The 1985 Directive also assimilates to a producer a person who 'by putting his name, trade mark or other distinguishing feature on the product presents himself as producer'.[356] The example usually given in the English context is the supermarket 'own-brander' who does not manufacture the product in question, but sells it under its own brand name. This category of person is in fact not a manufacturer at all, but rather a retailer or possibly distributor, but the Directive nevertheless applies as though he were a producer. The underlying idea seems to be that a person who holds himself out as producer should bear the same risk as one, and should not be able to escape liability by identifying the real manufacturer in the way that 'suppliers' can under article 3(3).

Article 3 also imposes the Directive's scheme of liability to Community importers, as long as they import a product for 'any form of distribution in the course of business'.[357] This would apply to a person who imports a motor vehicle from outside the EU for sale in the course of business, but not to someone who does so for their *own* use, whether or not this use is in the course of business. So, a company which brings in an aircraft from outside the EU on a commercial flight or for use in the EU for commercial flights would not be liable on this ground.[358]

Two of the defences provided by article 7 may apply to such 'deemed producers', importers or suppliers somewhat differently from the way in which they would apply to a real producer. I have already noticed that article 7(b)'s defence that the defect did not exist when the producer (here, the person relying on the defence) put the product into circulation requires a different time to be used according to which of the possible defendants at the different stages of distribution attempts to use it.[359] Even more, though, the development risks defence of article 7(e) will apply differently. This defence was intended to protect the industrial or scientific innovator (that is, a manufacturer rather than a distributor of whatever type) and it is indeed difficult to see how a distributor (whether 'own-brander', importer or mere supplier) could take

---

[352] Above, pp. 494–502.   [353] Art. 7(c).   [354] Lovells, *Report*, 51.
[355] General Product Safety Directive 2001, art. 3(2).   [356] Ibid., art. 3(1).   [357] Art. 3(2).
[358] Taschner, *op. cit.* n. 16, 260.   [359] Above, pp. 520–1.

advantage of it. For the European Court has made clear that the 'state of scientific and technical knowledge' is *objective*, in the sense that it does not refer to what the particular producer (or other defendant) did know or could have known as long as the knowledge was 'accessible'.[360] In practice, a distributor is in fact much less likely to know of the risks of the products which they distribute than their real producer, as is recognised in the English law of negligence, where a distributor does not have to take the same steps as a manufacturer in order to fulfil the requirements of reasonable care.[361] By contrast, the liability of non-manufacturing defendants imposed by the Directive may well be stricter than that imposed on manufacturers, for even if the concept of 'defect' and the defence in article 7(e) apply in such a way that the manufacturer would also be liable in negligence, this would not be true of non-manufacturing defendants: EC importers, 'own-branders' and mere suppliers. Here, the product may be 'defective' and the defect discoverable (so as to rule out article 7(e)), but a *distributor* not negligent.[362]

Most difficult is the position of 'suppliers'. Article 3(3) of the Directive imposes liability 'as producer' on suppliers only if the supplier fails to inform the injured person 'within a reasonable time, of the identity of the producer, or of the person who supplied him with the product' or, where it is imported, the name of the Community importer. This provision follows the earlier European Convention which reflected a compromise between those who wished to give consumers a maximum protection by including a wide range of defendants involved in the manufacture and distribution process and those who wished to restrict liability to 'real' manufacturers.[363] The Directive itself justifies the existence of the supplier's liability simply by reference to the requirements of consumer protection,[364] but in declaring unlawful the French implementation which imposed liability on suppliers without the restrictions of article 3(3), the European Court explained that these restrictions are aimed at avoiding the multiplication of proceedings.[365] So an injured person can recover damages against a supplier of a product under the Directive only where the 'real' producer remains unidentified, either because his identity is not apparent to the injured party from the product itself or because the supplier fails to identify him within a reasonable time. As Ghestin pointed out as long ago as 1986, article 3(3) therefore intends that liability should be channelled towards the manufacturer, explaining that this was the best person to bear the risk and to insure.[366]

Who, then, are 'suppliers' and what is the basis of their liability? As to the second question, a supplier can be liable only if an injured person shows that his damage was caused by a defect in the product, since this is the basis of liability in the producer to whom he is to be assimilated. On the other hand, a supplier can escape liability merely by identifying one of the persons already mentioned within a reasonable time and this means that his liability is triggered either by a deliberate choice not to help the

---

[360] Case C-300/95, *Commission v UK*, para. 27, above p. 498.   [361] Above, p. 195.
[362] Stapleton, *Product Liability*, 242–4.
[363] European Convention, art. 3(3); *Explanatory Report*, para. 27.
[364] The *Explanatory Report*, para. 27.   [365] Case C-52/00, *Commission v France*, para. 40.
[366] Ghestin (1986), 136.

claimant (by refusing to identify his supplier when asked) or, which is much more likely, on an administrative oversight in failing to keep a record of the identity of his own supplier of the product or its manufacturer or in failing to inform the injured person within a reasonable time. From this point of view, the supplier's liability rests on a 'fault' which deprives the claimant of his proper source of recovery (the manufacturer) and the claimant's 'damage' is the financial loss which he stands to lose as a result. Certainly, in practice the most important effect of the UK's fairly faithful implementation of article 3(3)[367] has been to require those who 'supply' products whose producer is not obvious to keep careful records of their origins.

It is in the light of this purpose and the nature of the liability which article 3(3) imposes that we must interpret what is meant by 'supplier'. The Directive does not itself define this concept and so the European Court would have to choose whether to give it an autonomous interpretation or, as in the case of 'damage' under article 9, leave its interpretation to the laws of the Member States subject to an overriding control on the ground of the principle of effectiveness.[368] The French legislation does not attempt to define 'supplier', but it does refer to sellers, hirers or any other business supplier and excludes a person who merely supplies under a hire-purchase agreement.[369] Certainly, the 1987 Act includes in its defining catalogue a number of situations of 'supply' which are properly included, as in sellers, hirers, donors of prizes, and the providers of gas or water,[370] and also includes the 'effective supplier' under a hire-purchase agreement, excluding the 'ostensible supplier' (who provides the finance),[371] but its more general understanding of 'supply' for the purposes of article 3(3) appears to require the transfer of possession or, at least, detention from one person (the 'supplier') to another,[372] though the catalogue does include two cases where a person 'provides the goods', which may be rather broader.[373]

However, there are many other situations in which a person makes a product available to another person or uses a product in a context which may harm him: are these also 'supplies' so as to make him a 'supplier'? For example, does an employer 'supply' his employees with the tools or the raw materials which the latter uses in their employment or which are used to furnish their working environment? Does the owner of furnished accommodation who leases it 'supply' the products (such as the gas heater or even the glass in its doors) which he provides for his tenant? If so, is a hotel keeper in any different position? Where a train company transports passengers, does it 'supply' them with the products which are used to furnish the carriage or even with the carriage itself? Does the Directive distinguish between the case of a hospital giving medicine to one of its patients (a clear 'supply') and using a machine (such as for kidney dialysis) to treat one of its patients (which is much less clearly a 'supply')? Some of these situations

---

[367] 1987 Act, s. 3(3) which requires the injured person to request the supplier to identify one or more of the persons article 3(3) has in mind within a reasonable period 'after the damage occurs and at a time when it is not reasonably practicable for the person making the request to identify those persons'.

[368] Above, pp. 503–4.

[369] Art. 1386-7 al. 1 C. civ. After revision of this provision, these persons are simply stated to be liable under the same conditions as the producer 'only if the latter remains unknown': *loi* of 9 Dec. 2004, art. 29.

[370] 1987 Act, s. 46(1).   [371] 1987 Act, s. 46(2).

[372] 1987 Act, s. 46 and cf. above, pp. 518–19.   [373] 1987 Act, s. 46(1)(d) and (e).

can be included within the language of 'supply' without difficulty (as in the case of the employer providing products for his employees to use), but in others it seems much more difficult.[374]

Linguistically, one could distinguish first, perhaps, between a 'supplier' and a person who merely makes a product available to people for their use in the context of the provision of a service. In this respect, it is to be noticed that the General Product Safety Directive 2002 includes the situation where a product is 'made available to someone' within its controls, in *addition* to where a product is 'supplied', and this could be used to support the argument that merely making a product available for use is not a 'supply' and a person doing so therefore excluded from article 3(3) of the 1985 Directive.[375] However, in *Commission v France* the European Court rejected the argument that the 1985 Directive should be interpreted so as to allow a Member State to implement its requirements in a manner suggested by an earlier General Product Safety Directive[376] simply on the basis that it 'does not concern the producer's liability for products which he puts into circulation'.[377] Moreover, examples can be found in other EC consumer legislation where 'supplier' is used in an extremely broad sense to refer to all providers of property or services.[378]

Rather than trying to analyse the proper meaning of the word 'supplier' or of its counterparts in the other language versions of the Directive or looking for legislative analogies, the European Court is likely to look instead at the purpose for which and extent to which 'suppliers' were included within the Directive's scheme.[379] As we have seen, the reason was to help consumers either by enabling them to identify the product's real producer so as to achieve compensation from him or instead to do so from the 'supplier' himself as a back-up. The Directive's understanding is that, where a product's manufacturer cannot be known from the product itself and is not otherwise known to the injured person, the product's 'supplier' is in a much better position than the injured person to identify the manufacturer or at least to put him in touch with someone else who can do so (notably, the person who supplied him). Normally, of course, this 'supplier' will be another business at the end of the chain of contractual distribution, the retailer or (given that the Directive is not restricted to consumer products) another final seller, such as a wholesaler. Where a product causes damage and its manufacturer is not easily identifiable by the injured person, its retailer or distributor should be able to help. However, from the perspective of ability to identify the producer it could be thought that a person who *buys* a product and then uses it in the course of his business is in just as good a position to identify either the manufacturer, or at least his own supplier as is the retailer or distributor and, moreover, the final end user/purchaser may be easier for the injured party to identify than a product's retailer or distributor. This suggests that such a 'user/purchaser' should also be included as a 'supplier' for the purposes of article 3(3). So, for example, where a hotel provides a gas heater, whose defect causes the customer or another person injury, as between the

---

[374] Stapleton, *Product Liability*, 317–19.   [375] Art. 2(a) 'product' and see recitals 6 and 9.

[376] EC Dir. 92.59/EEC of 29 Jun. 1992 on general product safety.

[377] Case C-52/00, *Commission v France*, para. 47.

[378] E.g. Dir. 93/13/EC art. 2(c), on whose interpretation see *Chitty on Contracts*, para. 15–013 *et seq.*

[379] Above, pp. 523–4.

injured persons and the hotel, the latter is in a better position to identify his own supplier or the heater's manufacturer. Indeed, if the user is not to be included as a 'supplier' in this sort of case where a product is not readily identified on its face (or perhaps where it was, but has been destroyed), it is difficult to see how an injured person can otherwise jump the informational gap so as to sue the product's real manufacturer.

There is a further argument in favour of such a very wide understanding of 'supplier' for this purpose. In a 'classic' case, where a retailer sells food to a customer, who then serves it to his family, it is not merely the customer supplied with the food who can claim under the Directive: any person who suffers 'damage' caused by the food's defect can do so and can start by asking the retailer (the supplier of the food) to identify the food's 'producer'—indeed, a rule which required a 'relationship of supply' between the 'supplier' and the injured person would return liability to something very much like contract. But if this is the case, why should it matter that the 'supplier' actually 'supplied' (in the sense of provided) the product *to anybody*? For example, an employer provides one of his employees with a machine such as a lap-top computer for individual use; the machine's defect causes a fire which injures other employees: assuming that the employer 'supplied' the machine to one employee, the others would be able to claim against the employer as its 'supplier'. But should there be any distinction between this sort of case and a case where the employer uses a defective machine to heat the workplace, but does not provide it to *any* employee, and the machine causes a fire injuring employees? If, the answer to these questions is that no difference should be made, then one is led to interpret 'supplier' under article 3(3) as someone who supplies, provides *or uses* the product, subject to the defence provided by article 7(c) that this was not done in the course of business or 'for economic purposes'.[380]

Here, the European Court's decision in *Veedfald* on the notion 'putting into circulation' may be helpful.[381] There it was held that a *producer* puts a product into circulation within the meaning of article 7(a) when he uses it in a context where it may cause a person 'damage', even though it has not left his sphere of control.[382] But if as a result the product does *not* have to be the object of distribution in the marketplace for it to attract liability, should not the 'supplier's' liability be interpreted analogously, perhaps even holding that a person 'supplies' a product when he puts it into circulation within the meaning of article 7(a)? Unfortunately, the difficulty with this position is that the Directive uses different language to describe 'the supplier' and his putting the product into circulation, and their assimilation appears to make the provision of the defence in article 7(a) redundant; for if a 'supplier' has by definition put the product into circulation, why provide a defence for the situation where he has not?

Clearly, the European Court would be concerned with the practical consequences of its interpretation of 'supplier' under article 3(3). A decision holding that a supplier is any person who, being himself within the chain of distribution and therefore in a position to identify a product's manufacturer, 'uses' the product would have very significant practical consequences. For it would mean that any person unable to rely on article 7(c) could be liable under the Directive for the damage caused by the defective products which he uses *unless* he identifies his own supplier or their manufacturer

---

[380] Above, pp. 515–17.   [381] Above, pp. 517–18.   [382] Above, p. 517.

within a reasonable time of both the damage and of being asked. It could be doubted that the Directive was intended to impose liability on employers, carriers, landlords or occupiers of business premises for the harm which is caused by the defective products which they use (whether these are still movable or incorporated into an immovable) even in the restricted way which article 3(3) provides. But if the European Court adopted this wider interpretation of 'supplier' the effect would be to create something recognisably like French law's liability for the 'deeds of things', the 'supplier' substituting for the role of the *gardien*, but with the special ability to escape liability by identifying another person higher up in the product's chain of distribution.

6. Time Restrictions on Claiming

There are two important restrictions on the time within which any claim under the scheme of the Directive may be brought.[383]

First, article 10 provides for what in English law would be seen as a period of limitation of action and in French law as a period of prescription. It provides for a limitation period of three years beginning from 'the day on which the plaintiff became aware, or should reasonably have become aware, of the damage, the defect and the identity of the producer'.[384] As I have noted, article 10(2) provides that 'the laws of Member States regulating suspension or interruption of the limitation period shall not be affected by this Directive'.[385]

There are two prominent features of this provision by comparison with the general provisions of French and English law. First, the starting point from which time runs is 'subjective' in the sense that it starts when the claimant actually knew or ought to have known of all the elements which make claiming a practical possibility, rather than 'objective,' such as the time when the damage occurred or the time when any contract is breached. This is sensible as it relates a restriction on the timing of bringing proceedings to when they can reasonably be expected to be brought. In this respect, it has a good deal in common with the general French rule of prescription period for claims based on extra-contractual liability, which runs from the 'manifestation or aggravation' of the harm,[386] given that the 'manifestation of the harm' is interpreted by the courts following the traditional maxim *contra non valentem agere non currit praescriptio* and therefore so as not to start before the claimant ought to have known of the harm.[387] It is also similar to the traditional approach of French courts to the starting point for the *bref délai* of the *garantie légale* in sale, which was put at the effective

---

[383] Taylor, *Harmonisation communautaire*, 185–95.   [384] 1985 Directive, art. 10(1).

[385] For the French law, see Terré, Simler, Lequette, *Obligations*, 1369 *et seq.* There is little English law in the books on the 'interruption or suspension' of the running of periods of limitation (e.g. as to disability), but the starting point of any period will be delayed in cases of fraud, mistake or deliberate concealment by the defendant: Limitation Act 1980, s. 32. Moreover, where a defendant 'acknowledges' a debt, the limitation period starts running again (Limitation Act 1980, s. 29) and in an appropriate case he may be estopped from relying on the defence of limitation: *Wright v John Bagnall & Sons Ltd.* [1900] 2 QB 240.

[386] Art. 2270-1 C. civ.

[387] F. Chabas, *Le droit des accidents de la circulation* (Litec, Paris, 2nd. edn., 1988) 317–18.

discovery of the defect.[388] It is to be contrasted, though, with the *general* English rule for the starting point for the running of time for claims in tort which runs from the accrual of the cause of action, which is an 'objective' criterion.[389] However, this general rule does not apply to claims for personal injuries or death where the starting point is either the date of accrual of the cause of action *or* the date of knowledge of the person injured if this is later,[390] the date of knowledge for this purpose being explained as when the claimant knew various elements relating to the practicability of bringing an action and therefore including 'constructive knowledge'.[391] This was the basis of implementation of article 10 in English law.[392] Secondly, though, under the Directive the period during which a claimant must bring his action is relatively short—three years. In French law, the general rule is ten years for extra-contractual claims and for contractual claims where one of the parties is a *commerçant*,[393] though of course the *bref délai* in sale was much shorter.[394] In English law, the period for claims in tort or for breach of contract is in principle six years from the cause of action,[395] but in the case of personal injuries or death this is shortened to three years coupled with a discretion in courts to allow an action to proceed notwithstanding the expiry of the limitation period if it considers that it is just and equitable to do so, taking into account six factors.[396] This discretion has been retained as regards the limitation period for claims under Part I of the 1987 Act.[397] Although this means that a more generous period is allowed than is provided for by article 10(1) of the Directive, this discretion could be seen as a very rough English equivalent to the sorts of situation which in other laws of the Member States are dealt with by the suspension or interruption of prescription periods.[398]

Overall, therefore, the special prescription and limitation periods which the French and the UK legislator introduced in their implementing laws and which followed article 10 of the Directive have some features that are less generous than their equivalents under the general law of extra-contractual liability/torts.[399]

Secondly, however, the 1985 Directive requires the creation of a special ten-year foreclosure period. Article 11 states that its implementing legislation shall require that 'the rights conferred upon the injured person . . . shall be extinguished upon the expiry of 10 years from the date on which the producer put into circulation the actual

---

[388] Above, pp. 91–2.

[389] Limitation Act 1980, s. 2. The accrual of the cause of action varies according to the nature of the claim but in claims for torts actionable only on proof of damage, it does not begin to run until some damage actually occurs: *Clerk and Lindsell on Torts*, 33–06 *et seq.*   [390] Limitation Act 1980, s. 11(4).

[391] Ibid., s. 14; *Clerk and Lindsell on Torts*, para. 33–32 *et seq.*

[392] Limitation Act 1980, s. 11A(4).   [393] Art. 2270-1 C. civ; art. 110-4 C. com.

[394] Above, p. 92. For reform of the *bref delai*, see below, p. 583.

[395] Limitation Act 1980, ss. 2, 5. In the case of contractual claims accrual of the cause of action is generally held to be the breach of contract: *Battley v Faulkner* (1820) 3 B. & Ald. 288; *Chitty on Contracts*, para. 28–032.

[396] Limitation Act 1980, s. 33(1) and 33(3) explained in *Nash v Eli Lilly & Co.* [1993] 1 WLR 782 in the context of claims for damages in respect of the drug 'Opren'.

[397] Limitation Act 1980, s. 33(1A) (*a silentio* and not applying it to claims for damage to property).

[398] 1985 Directive, art. 10(2).

[399] In French law: art. 1386-17 C. civ. (as inserted by *loi* of 1998); in English law, Limitation Act 1987, s. 11A(4).

product which caused the damage, unless the injured person has in the meantime instituted proceedings against the producer'. This period cannot be the subject either of suspension or interruption (as can article 10's three-year prescription period) nor can it be disapplied in a court's discretion (as in the English law of limitation of actions for personal injuries or death).[400] While the period itself has been faithfully implemented in both the English and the French implementing legislation,[401] in French law its starting point has been changed by the *loi* of 1998's definition of 'putting into circulation' in terms of 'voluntary relinquishment by the producer'[402] and its provision that 'a product may be the subject of only one single putting into circulation'.[403] Taken together, the French implementation means in effect that the ten-year foreclosure period starts when the manufacturer puts the actual product which causes the harm into circulation (the first 'putting into circulation'), rather than starting from the time of its 'putting into circulation' by each distinct category of defendant ('own-brander', importer or supplier) who is in fact sued. This makes sense of the purpose of article 11, which was to create a legislative full-stop to liability in respect of any particular product after ten years, even though it requires the reference in article 11 to 'producer' to be limited to 'manufacturers' and, apparently, 'own-branders' within article 3(1) rather than the wider usage of 'producer' in other parts of the Directive to refer to any person liable under the Directive.[404] By contrast, the effect of the complicated implementation of article 11 in English law is that as regards manufacturers, 'own-branders' and EC importers, the period starts from the date of supply of the product by the defendant sued, but that as regards mere 'suppliers' it starts when the product was last supplied by a manufacturer, 'own-brander' or EC importer.[405] While the period of ten years seems quite a long time, it has been criticised as too restrictive by the European Parliament's Committee on the Environment, Public Health and Consumer Protection, particularly in the context of health risks from products such as BSE.[406]

---

[400] Above, p. 528. Hence, the Limitation Act 1980, s. 33(1A)(a). Cf. *SmithKline Beecham plc v Horne-Roberts* [2001] EWCA Civ 2006 [2002] 1 WLR 1662 where the CA held that a power in the court in the Limitation Act 1980, s. 35(3) to add a new party after the expiry of the ten-year period to proceedings commenced within that period was not incompatible with art. 11 of the 1985 Directive, relying on its recital 11's provision that it was 'without prejudice to claims pending at law'.

[401] Limitation Act 1980, s. 11A(3) as inserted by 1987 Act, s. 6(6), Sch. 1. Art. 1386-16 C. civ. does, however, oddly except the position where the producer is at fault. To the extent to which this refers to liability under the general law of arts. 1382–1383 C. civ. it is redundant.

[402] Art. 1386-5 C. civ. al. 1.   [403] Art. 1386-2 C. civ.

[404] Notably, art. 7 (defences); art. 8(2) (no reduction of liability by reason of contribution of third party to damage); art. 12 (no exclusion or limitation of liability).

[405] This is the combined effect of the Limitation Act 1980, s. 11A(3) as inserted by 1987 Act, s. 6(6), Sch. 1 and the 1987 Act, s. 4(2) defining 'relevant time'. Special provision is made for electricity where the 'relevant time' is the time 'at which it was generated, being a time before it was transmitted or distributed': 1987 Act, s. 4(2).

[406] D. Roth-Behrendt, EU Parliament, Committee on the Environment, Public Health and Consumer Protection, *Report on the proposal for a European Parliament and Council Directive amending Council Directive 85/374/EEC* [etc.] PE 225.962fin. (28 Sep. 1998) para. 4.4, above, p. 446.

18

The Patterns of Liability

In this chapter I shall attempt to explain how implementation of the Product Liability Directive has affected the patterns of liability within French and within English law. I shall do so under three main headings within each legal system.[1]

First, I shall look at the impact of the implementation of the 1985 Directive on the legal position of those whose liability for physical harm is governed by the Directive, whether death, personal injury or damage to property: manufacturers of different types, importers and 'suppliers' (the 'Directive's defendants'). Nearly 20 years after the enactment of the Product Liability Directive it remains difficult to state this with complete certainty as regards either French or English law, partly owing to unsettled issues of interpretation of the Directive itself, but partly for other reasons which differ between the two systems.

Secondly, I shall look at how these liabilities relate to the liabilities of other categories of potential defendant within the two systems, being concerned to identify whom a person who has suffered physical harm ('the primary victim' or 'primary claimant') is likely to wish to sue when harmed by a product, either as between the Directive's defendants and other categories of defendant or as well as other categories of defendant. In order to do so, I shall set out the general position or positions if they exist (whether in public or in private law) drawing on the earlier chapters of this work and then look at some important contexts in which these general frameworks are exemplified, are qualified, or where different patterns are found.

Thirdly, I am concerned to see what effect these liabilities in defendants other than those governed by the 1985 Directive have on the practical impact of liability on the Directive's defendants themselves. If someone other than a Directive defendant is held liable for the harm, where will the burden ultimately lie (putting aside for this purpose the role of liability insurers)? This requires a closer look at the rules governing 'solidarity' or joint liability in the two systems, the legal bases of claims for contribution and the apportionment of liability between 'co-authors' of the same harm. Again, I shall look at these questions in both systems, explaining any differences between the public and private laws. In this way, I hope to see (at least in part) whether or not liability is indeed channelled towards the producer of a defective product or whether instead the liabilities of other persons have a magnetic effect, both attracting liability and then at least partly retaining it.

---

[1] Cf. above, pp. 6–10.

1. French Law

(a) The impact of implementation of the 1985 Directive on producers, importers and suppliers

There are two preliminary difficulties in assessing the impact of the 1985 Directive in French law caused by the way in which it was implemented there.

First, there are a number of particular points where the *loi* of 1998 remains incompatible with the Directive's scheme of liability, quite apart from those which were censured by the European Court in 2002 and which were corrected by the *loi* of 9 December 2004,[2] notably, its inclusion of all cases of damage to property, its formal denial of any impact on 'builders' and its over-narrow definition of a product's being 'put into circulation'.[3] It is as yet not clear what will be the fate of these further incompatibilities. In principle, the European Court's decisions in 2002 mean that they are unlawful as compromising its completely harmonising scheme[4] and this could mean either that they could be brought before the European Court and censured on this ground or that a French court could interpret the *loi* in such a way as to be compatible with the Directive where this is possible. While they remain in the Civil Code, however, undenounced by *la doctrine* and uncensored by the European Court, it is more likely that they will be applied by the courts, compatible or not.

Secondly, as I have explained, implementation of the Directive by way of amendment of the Civil Code has obscured its impact on the administrative law liabilities of producers or suppliers. As I shall explain, the Directive's provisions do have implications here (the most obvious and important example being public liability for medical products), but these are closely related to other private law liabilities. Moreover, their significance would be very much more considerable if 'supplier' for the purposes of article 3(3) is to be interpreted according to the wider sense of user at the end of the chain of distribution (as I shall later explain).[5] I shall, therefore, look at these later.[6] At this stage, therefore, I shall look at the impact of the Directive on established private law liabilities of producers and suppliers, and leave until later its relationship to the administrative law affecting the production or supply of products.

Most French jurists agree that the overall substantive impact of the *loi* of 1998 on the liability of producers and suppliers depends on the uncertain fate of aspects of the previous *jurisprudence*,[7] but that a producer or supplier will remain potentially liable under the 'general law of delict' (whether for proven fault and possibly for the 'deeds of things') or under the *garantie légale* in the law of sale.[8]

Let us take the latter first. Where a person who has bought the product suffers damage, he can claim damages under the *garantie légale* against his own seller or any other seller in the change of distribution up to and including its manufacturer if the

---

[2] Above, pp. 458–60.

[3] Above, pp. 460, 480 and 520–1 (respectively). There are other points at which the *loi* can be thought incompatible: see above, p. 519 (art. 7(c)).   [4] Above, pp. 440–4.

[5] For this interpretation, see above, pp. 523–7 and below, pp. 537, 544–5.

[6] Below, pp. 536–7.   [7] Above, p. 461.   [8] Above, p. 462.

seller is *professionnel* and subject to proof of a latent defect.[9] In the vast majority of cases covered by the *loi* of 1998, an injured buyer could equally well claim under this *garantie légale*, for while 'latent defect' does not focus on a lack of safety as does 'defect' under the *loi* of 1998, it has certainly included claims of this sort.[10] There are, however, three important remaining differences between the two liabilities, quite apart from the possible difference as regards the extent of liability for property damage.[11]

First, under the *garantie légale* a 'business seller' cannot escape liability by identifying his own supplier or the product's manufacturer in the way in which the 'supplier' can under article 3(3) of the Directive (and under the *loi* of 1998 as it has been amended to conform to the European Court's decision of 2002).[12]

Secondly, while a defendant under the *garantie légale* enjoys some of the defences granted to 'producers' under the *loi* of 1998 (such as contributory fault) others are differently treated or do not exist at all. In two cases, the difference is one of burden of proof: so under the *loi* of 1998, the burden of proof rests on the defendant to show that the defect did not exist at the time of his putting the product into circulation, whereas under the *garantie légale* the buyer must show that the product was defective at the time of its delivery by the seller in question.[13] There is (or should be) a similar reversal of the burden of proof as to the issue of the 'professional' nature of the defendant's activity, which needs to be proved by the buyer under the *garantie légale*, but disproved by the producer under the Directive.[14]

More importantly, however, under the *loi* of 1998 the Directive's defendants enjoy a development risks defence for all products other than those consisting of or made from an element of the human body; this defence does not exist under the *garantie légale*, a difference whose importance was seen as crucial at the time of the *loi's* enactment.[15] To this extent, therefore, a manufacturer, importer or other member of the contractual chain bears a greater burden under the *garantie légale* than under the *loi* of 1998.

Thirdly, there are and will remain differences in time periods within which claims must be brought. As I have described, under the *loi* of 1998 a producer's liability ceases after a period of three years after the claimant becomes aware of the damage, the defect and his identity (though subject to any suspension or interruption as provided by French law generally) or after a period of ten years from the date on which the producer put the actual product which caused the claimant's damage into circulation *whichever is the shorter*.[16] At first sight, the contrast with the traditional *bref délai* which applied to claims under the *garantie légale* from 1804 to amendment by *ordonnance* in 2005 could hardly be greater, as the period within which they had to be brought was in practice being between six months and a year.[17] However, some care must be taken here, for the 'delay' only ran from the time of the *effective* discovery of the defect by a buyer (an issue within the assessment of the *juges du fond*) and this meant that the buyer could claim many years after he had purchased the product. Moreover, in implementing the Consumer Guarantees Directive, the French government also took occasion to reform

---

[9] Above, pp. 69–79, 84–5, 95–7.   [10] Above, pp. 73–4.

[11] On the terms of the *loi* of 1998 and under the *garantie légale*, liability here is the same (*réparation intégrale*) but the former is incompatible with 1985 Directive, art. 9, above, p. 460.   [12] Above, p. 459.

[13] Above, pp. 482–3 and 78 (respectively).   [14] Above, pp. 84–5 and 515, 519 respectively.

[15] Above, pp. 89, 458, 494–5.

[16] Above, pp. 527–9.   [17] Above, p. 92. *Ord.* of 17 Feb. 2005, art. 3 amending art. 1648 C. civ.

the *bref délai* in sale more generally, providing that claims must be brought within 'a period of two years from the date of the discovery of the defect'.[18] As a result, subject to practical questions of proof, a buyer injured by a product may be able to claim under the *garantie légale* after a period when the ten-year foreclosure period of the *loi* of 1998 has expired. This reform of the national law of sale may therefore have a significant impact on the relative attractiveness of claiming against a producer or supplier under the *garantie légale* rather than under the *loi* of 1998.

However, despite French law's extension of liability under the *garantie légale* by *action directe* to all buyers within the chain of distribution, its ambit does not extend to those outside the chain and so if the producer's or supplier's liability is to be sought there, it must be under the general law of delict or under the *loi* of 1998. As I have explained, it is here that the position becomes less clear.[19] The general view is that French courts should not and are not likely to impose liability on producers or suppliers under article 1384 aliéna 1 of the Civil Code, as a manufacturer can be held to be *gardien* only by invoking the much criticised distinction between the *gardien de la structure* and the *gardien du comportement*, and it is difficult to see how a supplier (such as a seller or hirer) can exercise the powers associated with *la garde* once he has parted with possession.[20]

On the other hand, a person outside the chain of supply[21] who suffers harm by an allegedly defective product and who can show *une faute délictuelle* in one of the Directive's defendants, can certainly recover damages, this claim having the advantage of a prescription period of ten years from the time of the 'manifestation or aggravation' of the claimant's harm.[22] While this prescription period compares favourably with the two time limits governing the new product liability, proof of fault in the sense of *imprudence* looks more difficult than proof of defect, particularly given the reversed burden of proof as to the existence of the defect at the relevant time under the *loi* of 1998.[23] However, the relative attractiveness of the two liabilities is actually more difficult to pin down given the diversity of conduct which has at different times been held by French courts to constitute delictual fault by French courts.[24] The breadth of this concept has certainly been used before to avoid shorter prescription periods applicable to special schemes of liability.[25]

Perhaps the interpretation of delictual fault with the most potential to subvert the restrictions on liability under the *loi* of 1998 is the idea (visible in *jurisprudence* of the 1960s and early 1970s) that it is itself *une faute* for a producer to put a defective product into circulation.[26] This interpretation has not, however, been used by French courts for a number of years and, moreover, looks inconsistent with the European Court's decision upholding the completely harmonising character of liability under the Directive.[27] Secondly, more radically and more recently, the Cour de cassation has held that a person who fails to perform a contractual obligation, including an *obligation*

---

[18] Above, p. 92 and below, p. 583.   [19] Above, pp. 462–3.

[20] Above, pp. 53–4, 463; but cf. above, pp. 523–7 on a possible wider sense of 'supplier'.

[21] A person within the chain cannot claim on these bases owing to the rule of *non-cumul*: above, pp. 96–7.

[22] Art. 2270-1 al. 1 C. civ. above, p. 34.   [23] Above, pp. 482–3.   [24] Above, pp. 42–6.

[25] E.g. Civ. 18 Dec. 1972, D 1973.272 note J. Mazeaud (architect's fault characterised as *dol* so as to apply 30 year prescription period of delict).   [26] Above, p. 51.   [27] Above, p. 463.

de résultat, thereby commits a delictual fault so as to attract liability to third parties,[28] but this rests on an idea which would, if more generally accepted, radically revise the relationship between contract and delict, denaturing contractual obligation and delictual fault and reducing the principle of the relativity of contracts to little more than a cipher.[29] Thirdly, delictual fault exists where a person commits a criminal offence, even where the criminal offence in question does not require proof of intention or even of *imprudence*, but rests on breach of a regulatory duty; and establishing criminal (and therefore delictual) fault has all the procedural and investigative advantages of the criminal process which I have outlined.[30] Of all these, therefore, it is its relationship with 'criminal fault' which is most likely to give delictual fault a continuing role in the liability of producers and suppliers to those outside the contractual chain.

However, the liability of the Directive's defendants in respect of their products may also be sought on more particular bases of liability, notably, where they are 'suppliers' in the narrow sense of a person who transfers or provides the product and in the context of buildings.

Let me start with a simple example. In established French *jurisprudence*, a person who orders dinner at a restaurant is owed an *obligation de sécurité de résultat* as to the safety of the food: if he suffers food poisoning as a result, he does not need to show any defect in the food, nor can the restaurant escape liability by showing that any defect in the food which caused his harm was unforeseeable and beyond its control.[31] However, the *jurisprudence* relating to *obligations de sécurité* is notoriously unsettled and particularised.[32] So, for example, by contrast with the restaurant, it has been held that a hairdresser owes only an *obligation de moyens* as to the products which he uses on his customers.[33] Clearly, if a supplier of a product knows the identity of his own supplier he can escape liability if sued under the *loi* of 1998 even if the product is defective, but any remaining liability to his customers under the surrounding law will depend on the court's view of the proper content of the contractual *obligation de sécurité*.

In these examples of the liability of suppliers of products, there is the additional possibility that a French court could decide that this *jurisprudence* of *obligation de sécurité* which imposes liability on the Directive's 'suppliers' beyond its terms should not survive the combination of the *loi* of 1998 and the European Court's decisions, any more than the *obligation de sécurité* which was overtly modelled on the 1985 Directive in the 1990s.[34] It is unlikely, though, given that this *jurisprudence* forms part of a much more general interpretation of the Civil Code (articles 1135 and 1147) from which French courts are likely to be loath to depart and which can be distinguished from the Directive's scheme of liability in that it does not rest on suppliers *as such* but on 'other grounds' and therefore falls within the proviso allowed by article 13 of the Directive.[35]

Another example of the way in which the liability of 'suppliers' under existing French law may relate to liability under the Directive may be found in the case of

---

[28] Civ. (1) 15 Dec. 1998, Bull. civ. I no. 368; Civ. (1) 13 Feb. 2001, Bull. civ. I no. 35, above, p. 29.
[29] Cf. Mazeaud, *Les victimes*, 16.   [30] Above, Chap. 14 esp. pp. 373–4, 384–90.
[31] Above, p. 100.   [32] Above, p. 28.   [33] Above, p. 100.   [34] Above, p. 462.
[35] Above, pp. 441–2.

those who hire out products ('owners') who are specifically included by the *loi* of 1998 as suppliers.[36] Liability under the Directive here rests on a combination of proof of a defect and a failure to identify the owner's own supplier or the producer, but this contrasts unfavourably with the range of liabilities which owners of property owe to the person who hires it, one of which is modelled on the liability of sellers under the *garantie légale*[37] and one based on an *obligation de résultat*.[38] On the one hand, following the normal logic of contractual privity, in principle only the person who hires the property can sue on this ground, unless a court finds an implicit contract for the benefit of a third party made by the owner for the third party in question.[39]

There are, however, two areas in which the liability of producers and suppliers of products is made more difficult by its interaction with other important French categories and systems of liability.

The first is found in the context of buildings. Here, the more straightforward situation is found in the manufacture or supply of products for use in construction and which are supplied or used by a person who does not count as a 'builder' for the purpose of French law's special construction liability regime,[40] for example, a manufacturer who supplies a product to a 'builder' or a building *sub*-contractor who incorporates one into the building. Apart from liability under the *loi* of 1998, this category of defendant would be liable either under the law of sale (for 'latent defect') or the general laws of either contract ('contractual non-conformity') or of delict ('fault'), the main difference in practice being the prescription periods applicable.[41] As regards these defendants, too, much of what I have said already of the relative impact of these established liabilities and the liabilities imposed by the 1985 Directive holds good.[42]

More difficult is the position of 'builders'.[43] While liability under the special construction liability regime rests on 'latent defect' as regards all categories of defendant covered, three distinct liabilities arise depending on the nature and seriousness of the defect and lasting for three different periods (ten years, two years and one year), all starting from the date of formal acceptance by the person who commissioned the building.[44] While liability under the construction regime is contractual and cannot in general be invoked by third parties to the contracts of construction, it runs with the property for the benefit of its sub-purchasers.[45] As I have earlier noted, the *loi* of 1998 formally denied the Directive's regime of liability any impact on this construction liability regime, but the legality in EC law of this denial is open to doubt.[46] In particular, while a 'builder' who incorporates a product (such as a tile or a pipe) in a building may not count as its 'producer' (in that he produces an immovable result and so not a 'product'), he may still be its 'supplier' so as to face liability on the terms provided by article 3(3) of the Directive. While *generally* a person who has suffered damage as a result of the supply of a defective building product in this way may see no advantage in claiming under the Directive's scheme of liability rather than under French law's construction liability regime, there may be particular instances where he will do so,

---

[36] Art. 1386-7 al. 1 C. civ.   [37] Above, p. 110.   [38] Above, p. 109.
[39] Above, pp. 111–12.   [40] Art. 1792-1 C. civ. *et seq.* and above, pp. 104–8.
[41] Above, pp. 106–7.   [42] Above, pp. 531–3.   [43] Above, p. 104.
[44] Above, p. 105.   [45] Above, p. 104.   [46] Above, pp. 460, 480.

notably as a function of prescription periods, either in terms of their length or when they start. As long ago as 1988 the leading construction lawyer, Malinvaud, was right to foresee the sorts of difficulties to which this type of potential overlap between the Directive's scheme of liability and the French law of construction would give rise and also right to realise that they have not gone away by the French legislator's attempt at normative tidiness.[47]

The second context is liability for medical products, an area which remains difficult to describe with any certainty owing to the complex relationship between the previous case law, the Directive of 1985, the *loi* of 1998 and French legislation of 2002 which reformed medical liability more generally and transferred part of the risk of medical liability from insurers to the State.[48] Let me attempt to assess the position according to the different potential defendants.

First, the *loi* of 1998's introduction of liability for defective products appears to have made more strict the basis of liability imposed on manufacturers of pharmaceuticals and other medicines to their consumers, as previous case law held them liable only for proven fault in the sense of lack of care. The *loi* of 1998 also made a similar change as regards the liability of dispensing pharmacists (sometimes as 'producers' though typically as 'suppliers' of pharmaceutical and other medical products) whose liability formerly rested on fault, though where they merely supply products the amendment of the *loi* so as to conform to article 3(3) of the Directive reduces its primary significance to one of record keeping.[49]

On the other hand, the position of the liability of producers of other medical products is less clear. Under the *jurisprudence* of 1995, the Cour de cassation and the Conseil d'Etat held producers of blood products (blood transfusion centres, whether public or private) liable without proof of fault or defect[50] and while (owing to the organisational changes which I have described) only the approach of the Conseil d'Etat remains relevant in this context,[51] the question arises as to the relationship between this earlier case law and liability under the 1985 Directive. The decision of the European Court in *Veedfald* makes clear that a public body who produces a product and then 'puts it into circulation' falls within the Directive's scheme of liability as its 'producer',[52] and, as a consequence, that a public body who merely supplies such a product will also do so to the limited extent which the Directive provides. But does the European Court's affirmation of the 'completely harmonising' nature of the Directive's scheme in 2002 or the enactment of the *loi* of 1998 mean that the Conseil d'Etat should abandon its former case law?[53] In interpreting article 13 of the Directive (which provides that the Directive did not affect 'any rights which an injured person may have according to the rules of the law of contractual or non-contractual liability'),

---

[47] P. Malinvaud, 'L'application de la Directive communautaire sur la responsabilité du fait des produits défectueux et le droit de la construction ou le casse-tête communautaire' D 1988 Chron. 85.

[48] Above, pp. 151–5.   [49] Above, pp. 146–8 (excluding the case law 'implementing' the 1985 Directive). On the amendment of the *loi* of 1998 see above, p. 459.

[50] CE Ass. plén. 26 May 1995, *Pavan, N'Guyen, Jouan*, Leb. 221, AJDA 1995.577–8, AJDA 1995.508 note Stahl and Chavaux, JCP 1995.II.22468 note Moreau; Civ. (1) 12 Apr. 1995, *Dupuy, Martial*, JCP 1995.II.22467 note Jourdain, above, pp. 150–1.   [51] Above, p. 151.

[52] Case C-203/99 of 10 May 2001, *Veedfald v Århus Amtskommune*, [2001] ECR 1–3569, above, pp. 515–17.   [53] Cf. the discussion above, pp. 461–5, in relation to existing private law *jurisprudence*.

the European Court distinguished between the Directive's system of liability (based on a defect in a product causally linked to damage) and contractual and non-contractual liability 'based on other grounds, such as fault or warranty in respect of latent defects'.[54] Clearly, the examples given by the Court are derived from typical (civilian) private law, but would the *jurisprudence* of the Conseil d'Etat imposing liability for risk qualify so as to fall within article 13's protection? Even if it did, would the Conseil d'Etat consider that its own *jurisprudence* had survived the legislative intervention of the French Parliament not merely in the *loi* of 1998 but also in the *loi* of May 2002 which specifically preserved liabilities in respect of medical products (having in mind the *loi* of 1998) from its general subjection of liability to fault?[55] Moreover, the contrast with the positions of the mere supplier of blood by French public or private hospitals is striking. Under the *jurisprudence* of 1995, the Cour de cassation and Conseil d'Etat imposed liability here only on the basis of proven fault, but the Directive's scheme of liability would impose liability on them for defect, subject to the possibility of the avoidance of liability by identification of their own supplier. In addition, the European Court's interpretation of article 13 of the Directive suggests that the hospitals' general liability for fault (which was confirmed by the *loi* of May 2002)[56] survives the effect of the 1985 Directive as it rests on 'another ground'.

Secondly, there remains a difficulty in fitting the scheme of liability under the 1985 Directive together with the special liability *without* fault of hospitals for nosocomial infections.[57] I have suggested that nosocomial infection is likely to include some cases involving products, but if this is the case, should the French legislation be interpreted so as to exclude these cases from the special strict liability which it imposes for the consequences of these infections? It could clearly be argued that the imposition of liability for products without proof of defect (and the other incidents of the Directive's scheme) would run counter to the completely harmonised scheme required by the Directive, but if such an interpretation were required of the French legislation as a matter of European law, it would create a difficult distinction *within* cases of nosocomial infections (those caused by and those not caused by products) which would detract from the intended strictness of liability.

Thirdly, the earlier *jurisprudence* of the Cour de cassation imposing strict liability in respect of products which hospitals or doctors use in treating their patients but which they did not supply to them in the ordinary sense did not survive the French legislation of 2002 which returned their liability to a basis on fault.[58] But if a 'supplier' of a product under article 3(3) of the Directive is interpreted to mean any person within the chain of distribution who uses a completed product as well as any person who provides it to another person, then hospitals or doctors could be affected.[59] For example, where a hospital uses an X-ray machine whose defect allegedly causes a patient harm, the latter could request the hospital to identify the hospital's own supplier or the producer of the machine within a reasonable time, in default of which it would itself be liable.[60]

However, putting aside the difficulties relating to nosocomial infections, the *general* picture as regards liability for medical products is that a claimant is likely to

---

[54] Above, pp. 441–2.   [55] Above, pp. 152–3.   [56] Above, p. 152.   [57] Above, p. 153.
[58] Above, p. 144.   [59] For this interpretation, see above, pp. 523–7.   [60] Above, p. 523.

wish to proceed against their producer or supplier under the Directive's scheme of liability, rather than against the doctor or hospital whose liability is based on fault, proven or presumed.[61]

What then is the overall verdict of French private law jurists on the impact of the *loi* of 1998 on the liability of the defendants which it includes? For some it has not done much to improve the substantive chances of recovery of the victims of defective products, though it is praised for its the abolition of the 'discrimination' between contractual and non-contractual victims.[62] For others, whether the *loi* is useful in practice will depend on the extent to which the courts continue the *jurisprudence* of the 1990s imposing an *obligation de sécurité* on producers and suppliers, but even if the *loi* takes over this task, the change would not be great.[63] Some jurists, though, are much more critical, holding the legislation to be either useless (given that it does not improve a claimant's chances of recovery)[64] or even harmful (given the risk of it contaminating the rest of the law with its 'development risks' defence).[65] From the point of view of improving consumer protection it is difficult not to agree that from the French point of view it was not worth the wait or the effort.

(b) Liability for products beyond the Directive's defendants

In the introduction to this book, I explained why I have been concerned to place the liability of producers and others liable under the 1985 Directive in the context of the liabilities of others for harm caused by products.[66] My principal concern is with the extent to which these other liabilities affect the extent to which those *potentially* liable in law under the Directive are likely to bear the burden or part of the burden of liability in fact. This is a function of two features: the first is the extent to which a claimant harmed by a possibly defective product will wish to choose to sue one or more persons other than or as well as one or more of the Directive's defendants; the second is, given this pattern of likely claims, the extent to which the Directive's defendants are likely to bear the ultimate burden of liability for the harm which their defective product has caused, a matter of the availability and effect of recourse. In this section, I shall look at the first of these questions, leaving to the following section the question of recourse.

In order to depict the patterns of claims, I shall look first at the general private law frameworks; then at particular situations which cut across the public and private law categories which I have already looked at in terms of the law *apart* from liability under the Directive to illustrate how these private frameworks relate to the wider legal contexts as well as to liability under the *loi* of 1998. Finally, I shall note the potential role of liability in the administration for any failures in the exercise of their powers of supervision of the safety of products.

---

[61] Above, pp. 151–2.   [62] Mazeaud, *Les victimes*, 19–20.

[63] Viney and Jourdain, *Conditions*, 805.

[64] C. Jamin, note, RTDCiv. 1998.763, 768 (calling the *loi 'un coup d'épée dans l'eau'*).

[65] P. Jourdain, 'Une loi pour rien? (à propos de la loi du 19 mai 1998 relative à la responsabilité du fait des produits défectueux)' (1998) *Resp. civ. et assur,* 4.   [66] Above, pp. 5–10.

(i) The general frameworks of private and administrative law

As a matter of French private law, there is broad division as to the person whom someone injured by a product (the 'claimant') may wish to sue instead of or as well as the Directive's defendants: *gardiens* within the meaning of article 1384 aliéna 1 of the Civil Code and a person with whom the claimant has a contract. Apart from this division, such a person can always claim under the *droit commun* of liability for fault under articles 1382 and 1383 where it can be established.

Liability for the 'deeds of things' under article 1384 aliéna 1 of the Civil Code has a very prominent role in French law in attracting claims for damage caused by products. As I have explained, this liability rests on a thing's *gardien*, defined as the person who possesses its 'use, direction and control' and presumed to be its owner, though this presumption may be rebutted, for example, in the case of a person who hires the thing.[67] The prominence of its role lies in the overlap between a 'thing' and a 'product,' for almost all 'products' count as 'things' for this purpose,[68] and 'things' also include immovable property and therefore 'products' incorporated into immovable property.[69] This means that a person injured by a 'product' (whether defective or not) is almost always injured by a 'thing'. Furthermore, liability under article 1384 aliéna 1 possesses a number of features which make it much more attractive to a claimant than liability under the *loi* of 1998. For in principle a person injured by a 'thing' does not have to prove either fault in its *gardien* or any defect in the thing itself,[70] which looks strikingly easier to establish than liability under the *loi* of 1998 or even liability under the *garantie légale* in sale, both of which are tied to defect. On the other hand, under the requirement that the thing must play a role in causing a claimant's harm, French courts have given expression to their overall sense of the proper attribution of responsibility,[71] and in practice distinguish between cases where the thing was in motion and impacted on the person injured, when causation is presumed; where the thing was in motion but did not impact on the person injured, when causation must be proved either by establishing a defect in the thing itself or some 'anomaly in its position or behaviour'; and where it was stationary, when the thing's 'active role' must be sought in its 'abnormality', notably by its defect or bad positioning.[72] In the complex case law to which the causal role of the thing has given rise under article 1384 aliéna 1, defectiveness can therefore become relevant, but it is neither defined nor strictly necessary given that it forms merely one possible example of the thing's 'abnormality'.[73]

A further reason why liability under article 1384 aliéna 1 is attractive from a claimant's point of view is its treatment of defences. So, while a *gardien* may escape liability by proving *force majeure*, this will not be found in any internal characteristic or defect in the thing itself, even though its presence was 'irresistible and unforeseeable'.[74] On the other hand, after a turbulent period in the mid-1980s, the law has now become settled in allowing a *gardien*'s liability to be reduced on the ground of a claimant's

---

[67] Above, p. 53. On the doctrine of 'split *garde*' and its relation to liability under the *loi* of 1998, see above, p. 54 and p. 463.

[68] The only exception to this is the possible inclusion within 'product' of incorporeal property, whereas 'things' have to be corporeal: above, pp. 52, 477–8.   [69] Above, pp. 54, 57, 479.

[70] Above, pp. 52, 57–8.   [71] Above, pp. 54–7.   [72] Above, pp. 56–7.

[73] Above, p. 57.   [74] Above, p. 58.

contributory fault,[75] as it can under the *loi* of 1998. On the other hand, a defendant to a claim under the *loi* of 1998 has the benefit of six further, special defences,[76] none of which apply to the *gardien*'s liability.

A final point of advantage of liability for the 'deeds of things' compared to liability under the *loi* of 1998 relates to their relative prescription periods, for any claim under article 1384 alinéa 1 must be brought within ten years of the damage being 'manifested or aggravated',[77] whereas any claim under the *loi* of 1998 must be brought within three years of the time when the claimant knew or ought to have known of the damage, defect and identity of the producer and within ten years of the actual product's having been put into circulation.[78]

In all, therefore, a person who has suffered physical harm caused by a product is unlikely to wish to claim under the *loi* of 1998 given the basis of liability, the narrower range of defences and the more generous prescription periods, but is likely to claim damages from its *gardien* instead. While this is little noticed in *la doctrine*,[79] in my view this is only because it is so obvious to a French lawyer as not to need stating.

But what of the position where the person who has suffered damage is himself its *gardien*? Putting aside the court's occasional recourse to the doctrine of split *garde* to enable such a person nevertheless to take advantage of article 1384 aliéna 1,[80] such a person must look to other bases of recovery. In many cases, such a person will have a contractual claim, since in many situations a person becomes its *gardien* by means of a contract, notably of sale. Where this is the case, the *gardien*/buyer can claim not merely against his own seller but against any other person in its chain of distribution,[81] though these rights rest on proof of a 'defect' or failure in information and may suffer from the two-year prescription period which replaced the *bref délai*.[82] In this situation, therefore, a claimant may have more reason to claim damages under the *loi* of 1998 rather than under the law of sale.[83] A similar position obtains where a person acquires *la garde* from its owner under a contract of hire,[84] where the bases of liability are close to those of the seller.[85]

However, contract law has a second significance for the ambit of liability for the 'deeds of things', as the rule of *non-cumul* prevents a claimant from relying on it where otherwise his contractual partner would count as its *gardien*.[86] For example, if a person is injured at a fairground when the ride which he is taking malfunctions, he cannot claim damages against the fairground operator as *gardien* of the ride but only on the contract.[87] In this way, contractual *obligations de sécurité* again become relevant to the pattern of liability, for in many types of contract where liability for the safety of the other party to the contract is set neither by its terms nor by legislation, the courts have set it by finding such an obligation.[88] Where a party to a contract suffers physical

---

[75] Above, p. 59.   [76] Above, 1985 Directive, art. 7, above, pp. 482, 492–501.

[77] Above, p. 34.   [78] Above, pp. 527–9.

[79] An exception may be found in Mazeaud, *Les victimes*, 17.   [80] Above, p. 54.

[81] Above, pp. 95–8. Clearly, such a *gardien*/ buyer will not always have such a right: he may have been given the product or have bought it from someone other than a *vendeur professionnel* and so not be able to claim damages: above, pp. 84–5.   [82] Above, pp. 65–72, and below, p. 583.

[83] The *loi* of 1998 provided a specific exception here to *non-cumul* which allows a claimant to do so: art. 1386 C. civ.   [84] See above, p. 53.

[85] Above, pp. 108–11.   [86] Above, pp. 27–8.

[87] E.g. Civ. (1) 30 Oct. 1968, JCP 1969.II.15846 note Rabbut, and see above, pp. 22, 27.

[88] Above, p. 28.

harm (whether personal injury or damage to property), is he likely to claim damages from his contractual partner under an *obligation de sécurité* rather than (or as well as) from one or more of the defendants under the *loi* of 1998? This question is difficult to answer in the abstract, as the courts have varied the content of *obligations de sécurité* from the original strict model (*obligation de résultat*) applied to contracts of carriage to one which requires proof of lack of care (*obligation de moyens*), with a number of gradations in between, such as *obligation de résultat atténuée* and the obsolescent *obligation de sécurité* modelled on the Product Liability Directive in the 1990s which required proof of a defect of safety.[89] However, it can generally be said that where an injured person enjoys the benefit of an *obligation de sécurité de résultat*, he will have little incentive to claim under the *loi* of 1998: for his injury demonstrates that the 'result' of the safety obligation is not achieved, and so liability ensues subject to the defendant establishing *force majeure* or contributory fault in the claimant.[90] And contractual claims of this sort enjoy a prescription period of ten years.[91]

In all, though, the possibility of an *obligation de sécurité* being less strict than liability for the 'deeds of things' and the relatively short time period governing liability under the *garantie légale* in sale means that an injured person may be in a *better* position if not party to a contract, either in terms of the basis of liability or the prescription period or both. In sum, where an injured person is able to claim under article 1384 alinéa 1, under the *garantie légale* in sale or under an *obligation de sécurité de résultat*, these are very likely to be more attractive bases of liability than the *loi* of 1998; but where an injured person's claim lies against a person liable only under an *obligation de moyens* or on the basis of proven delictual fault (for example, against the product's designer or repairer),[92] a claim under the *loi* of 1998 becomes more attractive.

The general patterns of French administrative law governing liability for products are more difficult to discern. While French administrative law, like its private law, distinguishes between liability for *faute* and liability *sans faute*, the treatments and distinctions underneath these headings look very different and are much more contextually sensitive.[93] Certainly, two of the key features of the private law treatment of liability for products are missing: first, there is no liability for the 'deeds of things' in French administrative law and its superficial counterpart in liability *sans faute* for dangerous things and activities on examination has only a very minor role to play in the modern law;[94] and, secondly, the distinctive law of administrative contracts has little to say about liability for products.[95] Nevertheless, two broad observations can be made at this stage.

First, the law of 'public works' can sometimes impose liability for a product. So, a person who builds and installs a product in a building which then causes damage (either to the building itself or to a person) can be liable under the law of 'public works' subject to satisfaction of the necessary public element.[96] Of much more significance, however, is that contractors working in a *travail public* often use products in their work, and when the products cause harm liability may arise in either the contractor or the public body on whose behalf the work is undertaken.[97] If there is evidence to suggest that the

[89] Above, pp. 28, 72, 100, 140, 142–3, 455–6, 462–3.   [90] Above, p. 140.
[91] Above, p. 93.   [92] Above, pp. 102–3.   [93] Above, p. 113.
[94] Above, pp. 118–21.   [95] Above, pp. 116–18.   [96] Above, pp. 122–4.
[97] Above, pp. 122–4, 129.

product was defective, is a person injured in these circumstances likely to wish to claim under the law of 'public works' or the *loi* of 1998? The answer to this depends on the particular circumstances, as these will determine both the basis of liability (fault, presumption of fault or no fault) and the range of persons who can be held liable. So, for example, if a machine which forms part of a 'public works' malfunctions and causes a fire, injuring the claimant or his property, where the claimant is a 'third party', he may well wish to claim under the law of 'public works' as he will neither have to prove fault in those responsible under this law nor any defect in the machine in question.[98] Or if a person's garden is sprayed as part of a public programme to eradicate mosquitoes with a chemical which destroys his plants, that person (again a 'third party') may prefer to sue the contractor or public body under the law of 'public works' rather than the producer of the chemical alleging that it was defective within the meaning of the *loi* of 1998.[99] But if, as sometimes, an injured person has to prove fault in a works contractor in order to recover under the law of 'public works', he may well prefer to claim instead that a product which was used in the course of the works and which caused his injuring was 'defective' under the *loi* of 1998(see above, pp. 125–6).

Secondly, claiming under the *loi* of 1998 is relatively more attractive than claiming under the general law of administrative liability which rests on proof of fault and in particular as regards cases alleging a failure in the administration properly to supervise the safety of a product manufactured or distributed by a person whose own liability is governed by private law. For while the Conseil d'Etat has provided a relatively liberal basis of liability in these circumstances—moving from *faute lourde* to (or at least towards) *faute simple*—a person injured in these circumstances is likely to wish to sue the private law person instead, both as a matter of the basis of liability and owing to other features of the two types of liability in their jurisdictional settings.[100] Liability in the administration for failure in product supervision will not, therefore, attract liability away from the Directive's defendants liability under the *loi* of 1998, except in cases where there is a problem with the ability of the Directive's defendants to pay the sums required to discharge their liability (when a public defendant's deep pockets come into their own) or where there is a symbolic or even political significance for wishing to achieve a court ruling imposing "*responsabilité*" on the administration for its actions, as in the *affaire du sang contaminé*.[101] On the other hand, in those special cases where the Conseil d'Etat imposes liability *sans faute* in respect of the use or supply of products, a person may still prefer to sue the administration rather than the Directive's defendants. However, the clearest example of this was found in the law governing the use and supply of medical products in public health care, an area of liability reworked in 2002 both for administrative and private law and generally returning liability to a basis of fault.[102]

(ii) Road accidents

My first particular example of the patterns of liability is found in the context of road accidents. If a person is injured in a road accident, does he have any reason to wish to claim that it is due to the defect of any product and so sue its producer?

---

[98] Above, p. 128.   [99] Cf. TC 4 Feb. 1974, DS 1975.214 note Despax, above, pp. 128–9.
[100] Above, pp. 312–15, 317–18, 319–25.   [101] Above, pp. 315–19.
[102] Above, pp. 145–6, 150–2, 536–7.

As I have explained, since 1957 liability for 'harm of whatever nature caused by any vehicle' was unified as between private law and administrative law and placed in the jurisdiction of the ordinary courts,[103] and since legislation in 1985 has been governed by a special regime of liability modelled closely on liability for the 'deeds of things' but distinct from it.[104] Under this regime, the victim of a 'motor vehicle accident'[105] can recover damages against its *gardien* as long as the vehicle can be shown to have been 'involved', there being no formal requirement of any causal role for the vehicle of the sort generally required under article 1384 aliéna 1, though some of the considerations taken into account by the courts as a matter of causation remain relevant to a vehicle's 'involvement'.[106] Moreover, the range of defences available to a *gardien* in this situation is very restricted: there is no defence of *force majeure*,[107] and the contributory fault of a claimant is generally relevant only if it is 'inexcusable' and the 'exclusive cause' of his injury, with the exception of drivers (whose contributory fault of any kind may reduce liability) and the young, the elderly and the significantly disabled (whose recovery will not be reduced unless they deliberately 'sought' the injury).[108] Following the general rule for delict, any claim must be brought within ten years of the 'manifestation or aggravation' of the damage.[109]

In these circumstances, it is hard to see why any person injured or whose property is damaged in a motor vehicle accident would wish to sue the producer or supplier of any vehicle involved under the *loi* of 1998: the basis of liability is much more difficult to establish (a causally relevant defect of safety as opposed to 'involvement' of a vehicle); the defences are much more numerous and contributory fault much more widely available; and the prescription period is likely to be much shorter.[110] Moreover, even if a *gardien* of a motor vehicle is himself injured in an accident, he may well be able to recover under the motor vehicle legislation as long as he can show that *another* motor vehicle is also 'involved' in the accident. In this context, therefore, in general the Directive's defendants are likely to become involved in litigation only by way of a claim for contribution or other recourse by one or more *gardiens* of the vehicles,[111] the only likely exception being where a person is prosecuted for his role in the accident and the *juge d'instruction*'s investigations lead to the inclusion in the criminal proceedings of one of the Directive's defendants for involuntary homicide or causing personal injuries.[112] Even here, however, the ultimate liability of the Directive's producers will depend on the basis of civil liability eventually imposed on them by the criminal court relative to any others also held liable.[113]

However, some road accidents can be attributed to the state of the road, its management or equipment rather than to the lack of safety of vehicles or lack of care of drivers and it is here that administrative liability could be relevant. For example, if an accident is caused by the malfunction of traffic lights at a junction, in principle a

---

[103] Above, p. 115.   [104] *Loi* of 5 July 1985 above, pp. 60–1.

[105] This means that where no motor vehicle is 'involved', liability remains under the general law of liability for the 'deeds of things', above, pp. 52–9.   [106] Above, p. 61.

[107] Above, p. 60.   [108] Ibid.   [109] Art. 2270-1 al. 1 C. civ.

[110] Under the *loi* of 1998 liability is extinguished ten years after the actual product is put into circulation, whereas the right to claim under the legislation of 1985 is prescribed ten years after the damage is 'manifested or aggravated'.   [111] Below, pp. 546–53.

[112] Above, Chap. 13.   [113] Below, pp. 546–51.

person injured could claim damages under the law of 'public works' as the traffic lights form part of an *ouvrage public*,[114] liability here resting on a presumption of fault in those responsible for the *ouvrage*.[115] If another motor vehicle is 'involved', the injured person would be better off claiming against its *gardien* under the special scheme of liability for motor vehicle accidents, but the choice between liability under the law of 'public works' and under the *loi* of 1998 looks slightly tipped in favour of the former as it rests on a presumption of fault as regards maintenance of the road overall rather than a proof of defect in a particular product. But this sort of case is likely to be distinctly marginal.

(iii) Transport accidents

The pattern of liability which I have just described for motor vehicle accidents also applies to accidents to passengers suffered during the course of motor transport (for example, by bus), but other transport accidents follow a different pattern and a key context may be found in accidents on the railways. Here, despite the existence of a strong public element in the operation of French railways, in general liability to passengers and others belongs to private law and the ordinary courts,[116] and the latter distinguish between accidents occurring during the course of the journey itself (where liability is based on a contractual *obligation de sécurité de résultat*) and accidents at the station (where liability may be imposed for the 'deed of a thing'): in either event, a person injured in this context is much more likely to prefer to claim against SNCF on one or other of these bases rather than under the *loi* of 1998 alleging that a product used by SNCF was defective. On the other hand, where exceptionally liability is imposed by the administrative courts on the basis of the law of 'public works',[117] the basis of liability depends on the status of the injured person following its standard pattern;[118] and here liability under the *loi* of 1998 may occasionally be more attractive. Both these positions would remain true even if (as I have suggested) liability could be imposed on SNCF under the *loi* of 1998 as 'supplier' of the products which it uses,[119] given that it could escape liability by identifying its own supplier or the real producer of any product used, a possibility not open to it under any of its other grounds of liability, public or private.

(iv) Accidents on premises

Unlike English law, French law does not see accidents on premises as a distinct overall category of liability, but it can still serve as a useful factual category for the purposes of depicting the patterns of liability.[120]

The French private law approach here distinguishes according to whether or not the claimant has come onto the premises under a contract. Where he has done so, the occupier (strictly, the person with whom he has made the contract) will bear an *obligation de sécurité*, sometimes *de résultat* and sometimes *de moyens*; where he has not, then liability may be imposed for the 'things' of which the occupier was *gardien*, whether these are movable products which he uses or the immovable property which he occupies.[121] With

---

[114] Above, p. 124.   [115] Above, pp. 126–7.   [116] Above, pp. 139–41.
[117] Above, p. 141.   [118] Above, pp. 124–9.   [119] Above, pp. 523–7.
[120] For English law, see above, pp. 182–3.
[121] As to liability in contract, see above, p. 111 (tenant) and Civ. (1) 19 Jul. 1983, Bull. civ. I no. 211 (hotel guest). As to liability under art. 1384 al. 1 C. civ. see above, pp. 52–9 esp. at 57.

the exception of cases where liability is held to be governed by an *obligation de sécurité de moyens*, a person injured is likely to prefer to claim under one or other of these bases of liability rather than against either the producer or 'supplier' under the *loi* of 1998, both as a matter of the basis of liability and the applicable prescription periods.

Where the premises count as an *ouvrage public* or where work done in relation to them counts as a *travail public*, liability can arise under the special administrative law of 'public works'.[122] Here, the basis of liability depends on the claimant's status for this purpose: many will be 'users' of the *ouvrage public* and so benefit from a presumption of fault in those responsible for it, but some will be 'third parties' and benefit from liability without fault.[123] This means that where an allegedly defective product forms part of an *ouvrage public* or is used by a works contractor in the course of a *travail public*, a person injured as a result may or may not prefer to claim under the law of 'public works' rather than under the *loi* of 1998. Certainly, where he benefits from the special administrative liability without fault, he is unlikely to wish to prove defect and risk the range of defences available to defendants under this *loi*; but in other cases (where liability rests on a presumption or proof of fault), liability under the *loi* of 1998 may be more attractive.

(v) Gas, electricity and water

French law is very demanding of the suppliers of networked electricity and piped gas and water.[124] As I have explained, despite the presence of a *service public* and considerable public ownership of the providers of these products (Electricité de France, Gaz de France and the more numerous providers of water), liability is generally treated as belonging to private law and the ordinary courts, with the exception of liability under the law of 'public works'. In this respect, we can discern a distinction between liability to customers and liability to non-customers.

Liability to customers is seen as contractual and belonging to private law and the ordinary courts have imposed liability based on *obligations de résultat* as to the continuity, quality and safety of the products themselves, and also the safety of the installations necessary for their supply under the general law of contractual liability.[125] So, for example, a customer who suffers injury from the content of the water supplied, or whose property is damaged when his electrical current is irregular can recover without proof of defect and within the ten-year prescription period applicable to contractual claims of this sort. This is also the case where water supplied escapes from pipes which are the responsibility of the water company, rather than of the customer.[126] Given this (and assuming that this law is unaffected by the European Court's decisions of 2002 upholding the completely harmonising nature of the Directive's scheme of liability[127]), it is unlikely that a customer injured or whose property is damaged by electricity, water or gas would wish to sue their 'producer' or 'supplier' alleging that these products were 'defective' under the *loi* of 1998.

Liability to non-customers depends on whether or not the law of 'public works' becomes involved. If it does not, liability may be imposed under article 1384 alinéa 1 on the *gardien* of gas, water or even electrical current or of any installations or apparatus

---

[122] Above, pp. 121–31. [123] Above, pp. 124–9. [124] Above, pp. 136–9.
[125] Above, pp. 137–8. [126] Above, p. 138. [127] Cf. above, p. 534.

involved in its supply. Sometimes, the *gardien* will be the public supplier of the product in question (for example, where there is a surge of power from the mains supply, the electricity itself being the 'thing') but sometimes the occupier of the premises (for example, where the malfunction or surge of power finds its origins within the sphere of the occupier's control), by way of application of the definition of *la garde* in terms of the thing's 'use, direction and control'.[128] However, where the harm is caused either by an *ouvrage public* or a *travail public*, a non-customer can claim under the law of 'public works' and will typically benefit from a liability without fault.[129] Again, the liabilities imposed on producers and suppliers of products under the *loi* of 1998 look relatively unattractive and for French law the wider interpretations of the 'defectiveness' of gas, water and electricity for the purposes of the 1985 Directive which I have discussed,[130] are likely to remain otiose.

(c) 'Solidary liability' and the potential for recourse

It can be seen, therefore, that in the French system there are a number of defendants whom a person injured or whose property has been damaged by an allegedly defective product may prefer to sue rather than, or at least as well as, the Directive's defendants. But can such a 'primary victim' of a product recover in full from such a defendant? And does the existence of these other sources of recovery of damages in respect of a product mean that liability is channelled *towards* or *away from* the producers or suppliers as defined by the 1985 Directive? The answers to these questions turn on the existence of 'solidary liability' and the availability and consequences of recourse by a defendant *other* than the producers or suppliers held liable to the product's primary victim; and, as I have already explained, here French law distinguishes between private and public law, and then again *within* public law.[131] Similarly, the question whether the policy of article 3(3) of the Directive of channelling liability towards a product's 'producer' and *away* from its mere supplier (put rather optimistically by the European Court in terms of the avoidance of the multiplication of claims[132]) is successful will also depend on the ability of such a supplier to pass on to the 'producer' its liability on some *other* legal ground.

(i) Private law

In French private law, recovery by a claimant in full against one of a number of persons civilly liable for the same harm is termed the *droit de poursuite du créancier* ('creditor's right of pursuit') and is found where the potential defendants owe *obligations solidaires* (this being termed *solidarité*) or where they owe *obligations in solidum* (sometimes termed *solidarité imparfaite*).[133] This duplication of analysis stems from the Civil Code's narrow provision for *obligations solidaires*, which exist only where they are expressly stipulated or by special legislative authority,[134] though there are some

---

[128] Above, p. 138.   [129] Ibid.   [130] Above, pp. 478–9.

[131] I have earlier argued that the 1985 Directive leaves these matters to be determined by national law, above, pp. 509–10.   [132] Above, p. 365.

[133] For useful treatments see Malaurie, Aynès and Stoffel-Munck, *Obligations*, 687 *et seq.*; Flour, Aubert and Savaux, *Fait juridique*, 162–7; P. Canin, *Les actions récursoires entre co-responsables* (Litec, Paris, 1996).

[134] Art. 1202 C. civ.

important legislative impositions of *solidarité*, for example, as regards those found jointly guilty of more serious criminal offences as to their civil liability to their victims.[135] Apart from attracting the *droit de poursuite*, *solidarité* has certain other consequences which are termed 'secondary'; for example, a claim made against any one of the persons liable interrupts the running of the prescription period for all.[136]

The law on *solidarité* has been much criticised by French writers, for its ambit is very restrictive particularly as regards extra-contractual liability and its secondary effects are considered onerous.[137] They therefore constructed the idea of *obligations in solidum*, a class of obligation which attracts the *droit de poursuite du créancier*, but applies more widely, extending to cases 'where several independent obligations arising from different sources tend to supply to the creditor the same satisfaction and therefore cannot be accumulated', and which does not formally attract the secondary effects of *solidarité*.[138] While the terminology of 'creditor' and 'satisfaction' suggests to an English lawyer a context of contractual debt, for a French lawyer this is equally appropriate to non-contractual obligations and one of its most important applications has been to civil liability, whether delictual or contractual. In the result, in private law it is established that where two or more persons are 'co-authors' of the same harm,[139] the injured party may recover in full from any one, 'without there being any room for taking into account the share in responsibility . . . as between the co-authors', this sometimes being justified on the ground that each 'co-author' has caused the injured person's entire harm,[140] but otherwise on the basis that one co-author must guarantee the other's payment.[141] The courts apply the doctrine of *obligations in solidum* where one 'co-author' is liable in delict and another liable in contract, or to two contracting parties, subject to a requirement that the defendants' actions are the cause of the claimant's same harm.[142]

Where a person has been held liable in full either under the law of *solidarité* or *obligation in solidum*, in principle he may claim contribution from any other person liable for the same harm, the amount of contribution being limited to the court's view of that person's ultimate share in the responsibility.[143] Such a claim can be made either

---

[135] Art. 375-2 & 480-1 C.P.P. See also, parental liability for harm caused by their children under art. 1384 al. 4 C. civ., above, p. 25 and liability of manufacturers of pre-fabricated parts of a building under art. 1792-4 C. civ., above, p. 104.

[136] Art. 1206 C. civ. (as very broadly interpreted). Another example is that interest accrues against all the persons liable from the time when *one* person's obligation falls due: art. 1207 C. civ.

[137] Terré, Simler and Lequette, *Obligations*, 1170; Flour and Aubert, *Rapport d'obligation*, 201–02.

[138] Malaurie, Aynès and Stoffel-Munck, *Obligations*, 699.

[139] On occasion, difficulties can arise as to whether or not the claimant has indeed suffered one, unique harm rather than several divisible ones: e.g. Paris 19 Mar. 1979, D 1979.429 note Rodière.

[140] Civ. 4 Dec. 1939, DC 1941.124 note Holleaux. See also Civ. (2) 5 Mar. 1969, Bull. civ. I no. 68; Civ. (2) 17 Mar. 1971, D 1971.494 note Chabas; Civ. (3) 5 Dec. 1984, JCP 1986.II.20543 obs. Dejean de la Bâtie.   [141] Malaurie, Aynès and Stoffel-Munck, *Obligations*, 705.

[142] Civ. (3) 5 Dec. 1972, D 1973.401 note J. Mazeaud (delict and contract); Civ. (1) 9 Oct. 1979, GP 1980.1.249 note Planqueel, *affaire Lamborghini*, D 1980.IR.222 obs. Larroumet (two contracts in chain of distribution) above, p. 97; Civ. (1) 1 Jun. 1976, JCP 1976.II.18483 (hospital and surgeon liable under different contracts with patient).

[143] Art. 1214 al.1 C. civ.; Malaurie, Aynès and Stoffel-Munck, *Obligations*, 702; Terré, Simler, Lequette, *Obligations*, 1167–9, 1173.

by bringing that other person into the original proceedings (by *appel en garantie*[144]) or by a later, separate claim (*action récursoire*). The legal basis of this claim for contribution is generally considered to be subrogation by operation of law, as this is provided for by the Civil Code as regards *solidarité*,[145] and this means that in principle a co-author as secondary claimant enjoys the rights of a primary claimant for this purpose.[146] However, the logic of subrogation is not carried through into the way in which the courts apportion liability between co-authors, for here French courts take into account both the causal role of their actions or circumstances which gives rise to liability and their relative faults. So, where both co-authors are liable on the basis of fault (including 'contractual fault'), in determining their claims for contribution the courts weigh the relative seriousness of their respective faults, making a 'moral evaluation' of their conduct and proper relative positions[147] over which the *juges du fond* possess a 'sovereign power of assessment'.[148] On the other hand, where a co-author has been held liable *without* fault (for example, as *gardien* of a thing under article 1384 aliéna 1 of the Civil Code), he can recover *in full* against any person liable on the basis of fault for the same harm to the primary claimant;[149] and conversely, a co-author held liable on the basis of fault as a matter of law cannot recover *any* contribution against a person also liable to the primary claimant without fault:[150] here judicial concern with the relative basis of liability has led to their rejection of any claim for contribution by a co-author even though the claimant has recovered in full, a position which has been seen as fair if not logical.[151] Where a co-author held liable without fault claims against another person also liable without fault, the courts share out their relative responsibility equally, this being described as following their '*parts viriles*',[152] although on occasion the Cour de cassation has required the *juges du fond* to assess the relative 'responsibility' of the co-authors of harm (each liable as *gardiens* of a thing) rather than simply dividing their liability equally.[153] Clearly, therefore, these approaches to claims for contribution between co-authors differ considerably as between liability for fault and without fault, firmly channelling liability towards a person liable for fault if one exists. For this reason, they have been criticised in the context

---

[144] Arts. 331, 334–338 N.c.pr.civ.   [145] Art. 1251 al. 3 C. civ.

[146] Art. 1251 al. 3 C. civ. One consequence of subrogation is that the claim for contribution is governed by the prescription period of the primary victim's claim: Malaurie, Aynès and Stoffel-Munck, *Obligations*, 702–03, who note that the courts have also recognised the possibility of a personal or independent right for a secondary claimant in an 'isolated decision' in 1977: Civ. (1) 7 Jun. 1977, D 1978.289 note Larroumet (the significance of this independent right was to avoid the renunciation by the primary claimant of his own action against the defendant). See further P. Jourdain, 'Droit à réparation, Lien de causalité, Pluralité des causes du dommage' in Jur.-Cl. Civ. Fasc. 162 (2002), 8.

[147] J. Boré, 'Le recours entre coobligés *in solidum*' JCP 1967.I.2126; Canin, *op. cit.* n. 133, 157 *et seq.*; Viney and Jourdain, *Conditions*, 281 *et seq.*; Taylor, *Harmonisation communautaire*, 139.

[148] Civ. (2) 14 Feb. 1979, Bull. civ. II no. 52.

[149] Civ. (3) 5 Dec. 1984, JCP 1986.II.20543 note Dejean de la Bâtie.

[150] Civ. (2) 19 Nov. 1970, JCP 1971.II.16748.

[151] Flour, Aubert and Savaux, *Fait juridique*, 167.

[152] Bénabent, *Obligations*, 466; e.g. Civ. (2) 10 May 1991, Bull. civ. II no. 134. Viney and Jourdain, *Conditions*, 283 describes this as frequently the case. Cf. Canin, *op. cit.* n. 133, 171 *et seq.* at 183 who argues that where a co-author's liability rests on *defect*, his responsibility should not be treated as the same as a person liable without fault, but who notes that this position has not generally been followed.

[153] P. Jourdain, *op. cit.* n. 146, 11–12 citing Civ. (2) 8 May 1978, JCP 1981.II.19506 note Perallat.

of liability for defective products for failing to channel liability towards the producer.[154] Finally, where one co-author is insolvent, the share of that person's liability is distributed between the others liable in accordance with the rules just set out.[155] So, for example, as between three persons liable as 'builders' or as *gardiens*, if one is insolvent, the two others are liable as between each other equally (here, half).[156]

Apart, though, from these claims for contribution which arise generally and by operation of law from the fact of payment in full of a primary claimant by a co-author, a co-author held liable in full may possess a contractual claim to recover a full or partial indemnity in respect of his liability to the primary claimant. Such a contractual claim may arise in a number of contexts, but the clearest example is the claim of a member of the contractual chain of distribution of a product, each 'buyer' having a claim against every earlier seller in respect of latent defects, all of whom are liable *in solidum*.[157] Moreover, where such a contractual claim for an indemnity exists, in principle it is exclusive of any claim in delict (following the rule of *non-cumul*), even where a co-author would wish to rely on a *subrogated* claim in delict possessed by the original claimant. For example, a manufacturer sells a television to a retailer, who then resells it to a café; the television explodes injuring the café's customers and passers-by in the street (all third parties to the contracts of sale of the television); the persons injured recover damages against the owner of the café as *gardien* of the television under article 1384 alinéa 1 of the Civil Code (without needing to prove fault or defect);[158] in these circumstances, the logic of subrogation would allow the café to sue the retailer or manufacturer of the television on the basis of any *direct delictual* liability which would have arisen in them vis-à-vis the primary victims,[159] for while a party to the contract with the retailer and possessor of an exclusively contractual *action directe* against the manufacturer,[160] the café could be said to be suing *not* as party to the contract but as subrogated to the primary victim. However, there is no example in the context of claims by buyers or sub-buyers which allows the avoidance of the contractual regime in this way, and while French courts have allowed such an argument to succeed in the context of claims by an employer against 'builders' in the law of construction,[161] their doing so has been much criticised.[162]

Out of keeping with this general picture, however, was the approach of the French legislature to recourse claims brought by 'suppliers' liable under the *loi* of 1998. Here, the legislation imposed liability on suppliers on the same terms as producers, and therefore created a special subrogated recourse for suppliers governed by 'the same rules which govern the claim of the direct victim of the defect'.[163] This suggests that a

[154] Taylor, *Harmonisation communautaire*, 142–3 (arguing that French courts should adopt a more flexible approach similar to that taken by English courts under the 1978 Act).

[155] Art. 1214 al. 2 C. civ.; P. Tourneau and L. Cadiet, *Droit de la responsabilité et des contrats* (Dalloz, 2000), 399.   [156] Civ. (1) 12 Nov. 1987, Bull. civ. I no. 290 (*a contrario*).

[157] Above, p. 96.   [158] Cf. Civ. (1) 20 Mar. 1989, Bull. civ. I no. 137.

[159] Such a claim under art. 1383 C. civ. would have the advantage of avoiding the short limitation periods governing claims by buyers: above, pp. 91–3 and below, p. 583.   [160] Above, p. 96.

[161] E.g. Civ. (1) 4 Nov. 1971, JCP 1972.II.17070 note B. Boubli; Civ. (3) 29 Jan. 1992, Bull. civ. III no. 30.

[162] Viney, *Introduction à la responsabilité*, 414–15. Civ. (2) 6 Jul. 1994, Bull. civ. II, no. 182, RTDCiv. 1995.124 no. 5 obs. Jourdain does not represent a more general acceptance of subrogation taking precedence over *non-cumul* as there was no contract between the parties to the subrogated delictual claim on the facts. See also Civ. (1) 17 Jan. 1995, D 1995.350 note Jourdain.   [163] Art. 1386-7 al. 2 C. civ.

'supplier' held liable under the *loi* of 1998 is not prevented by the rule of *non-cumul* from relying on the primary victim's rights even where his recourse claim is directed against a person within the chain of contracts distributing the product.[164] On the other hand, the *loi* of 1998 made no special provision for recourse claims against producers or suppliers liable under its provisions made by persons *other than* these two categories of defendants, and this leaves their position to be governed by French law's general approach to contribution.

How does this set of rules and practices affect claims for recourse by defendants held liable other than producers or suppliers under the meaning of the *loi* of 1998?

First, where a primary victim of a product has recovered damages in full from a person *other than* its producer or supplier within the meaning of the 1985 Directive on a legal basis of *fault* (whether delictual or contractual), then in principle any recourse by that person would obey the rules of the claim of the primary victim, following the standard analysis of recourse claims in terms of subrogation.[165] However, French courts deny *any* claim for recourse by a co-author held liable for fault against a co-author liable without fault (which would include the producer or supplier of the product liable under the *loi* of 1998) and this would mean that in these circumstances liability would remain with the first defendant. In this way, therefore, the imposition of liability for fault on other defendants has the effect of channelling liability away entirely from the producer and supplier of the product liable under the Directive. This applies to the important category of cases where a criminal court has found a defendant criminally responsible and civilly liable to the primary victim.[166]

Secondly, where, as frequently, a primary victim of a product has recovered damages in full from a person *other* than its producer or supplier within the meaning of the 1985 Directive on a legal basis *other than fault* (such as a *gardien* of the product or a person owing an *obligation de résultat* in relation to the product[167]), in principle any recourse by that person against the producer or supplier of the product will obey the rules of the claim of the primary victim, again following the standard French analysis of recourse claims in terms of subrogation.[168] In this situation, given that both the liabilities of the 'co-authors' do not rest on fault, their relative shares of liability will either be divided equally or, possibly, on the basis of the 'relative responsibilities' of the two co-authors.[169] Of course, if a *gardien* held liable could show that the damage was caused by a defect in the product for which the producer was 'responsible', he could argue that, as between the two co-authors, the producer should be liable, but, as I have said, French courts cannot be seen to have tilted the apportionment of liability towards a person liable for a defect in this way, but rather have preferred to split liability equally in the absence of fault.[170] In these circumstances, therefore, liability is again *not* likely to be ultimately borne by the Directive's defendants, but to be shared between them and any other person liable without fault to the victim of the product. In this way, therefore, the imposition of liabilities without fault on other persons has the effect of channelling liability away from the producer or supplier in part.

---

[164] Art. 1386-7 al. 2 C. civ. While the *loi* of 9 Dec. 2004, art. 29 amended the legal basis of the supplier's liability so as to conform to article 3(3) of the Directive, it left intact this special basis for recourse.
[165] Above, p. 548.   [166] Above, Chap. 14.   [167] Above, pp. 539–41.
[168] Above, p. 548.   [169] Ibid.   [170] Ibid. esp. at n. 152.

On the other hand, where a defendant who has been sued by a primary victim of a product (whether on the basis of fault or some stricter liability) is party to a contract, that defendant may possess a contractual claim for an indemnity in respect of his liability against his co-contractor. The basis of such a claim will differ according to the circumstances: sometimes it will rest on an *obligation de moyens* and here liability may be more difficult for the first defendant to establish than was his own liability for the primary victim. However, in some cases, such a contractual claim will rest on an *obligation de résultat* and so allow recovery by the first defendant without showing fault or a defect in any product implicated in the primary victim's harm. For example, where a defendant who has hired a car has been held liable as its *gardien* to a person injured in an accident in which it was involved, the hirer can recover an indemnity against the person from whom he hired it on the basis of its defect under the contract of hire. In these circumstances, any contributory fault in the hirer himself (for example, in failing to notice the car's defect, failing to maintain it or failing to take care in driving it) would reduce his recovery by way of the defence of *faute de la victime*.[171]

In a number of cases, a defendant held liable to the primary victim of the product will be able to recover under the law of sale, for (as I have explained) many *gardiens* of products (who make very attractive defendants from the point of view of a primary victim) will have bought the product from a *vendeur professionnel*.[172] For example, A buys a television set from B (a retailer); within a few months, the television explodes, injuring C. Here, C is likely to wish to sue A as *gardien* of the television, leaving it to A to claim an indemnity under his contract of sale from B; when A does so, B can oppose against his claim any contributory fault (in the maintenance or use of the television) which he can prove against A. So, even if the basis of liability of the person whom the primary victim chooses to sue does not rest on fault, any fault in that person will reduce the ultimate liability of the producer.

In the result, therefore, where the primary victim of a product chooses to sue a person (the 'first defendant') other than or as well as its producer under the *loi* of 1998, the ultimate liability of the producer is likely to be extinguished or reduced: it will be extinguished where the first defendant was held liable for fault (where French law recognises no recourse claim against a person unless the other is also liable for fault); it will be reduced where the first defendant was held liable without fault, either equally with the producer or to the extent of their respective 'responsibilities'; only where the first defendant was held liable without fault, claims a contractual indemnity and cannot himself be shown to have been at fault will liability be imposed in full on the producer. As a result, the ultimate burden of liability for defective products causing damage is a function of a combination of the existence in French law of liabilities *other than* those required by the 1985 Directive, their legal foundation and of the approach of French courts to the basis of apportionment of liability between co-authors.

(ii) Administrative law

How does this picture change when turning to persons liable in French administrative law in circumstances where the producer of a product could be liable under the *loi* of 1998?

---

[171] Above, pp. 110–11.   [172] Above, p. 540.

As has been explained, French administrative law differs significantly from the position taken by its private law, denying any general rule of 'solidary liability' in the co-authors of the same harm and granting to a public body liable to a person harmed by its *fault* the defence of *fait d'un tiers*, the effect of which is to reduce or even to exclude liability in the administration.[173] The decision as to whether to reduce liability in a public body and to what extent is based on the relative responsibilities of the public and private co-authors in the view of the *administrative* court, this possessing elements both of their comparative faults and their comparative causal roles.[174] On the other hand, where the liability of the administration is imposed without fault or under the special rules applicable to 'public works' (whether or not liability is based on fault), then the Conseil d'Etat accepts that the administration may be liable in full as against a primary victim, even if another person is also liable for the same harm as a matter of private law.[175]

How do these administrative law rules affect the patterns of liability for products and, in particular, the ultimate liability of their 'producer'?

First, I have already explained that while the Conseil d'Etat accepts that a public authority may be liable for personal injury or death caused by its failure to exercise its powers over the safety of products either on the basis of *faute simple* or *faute lourde*, there are a number of factors which combine to channel liability *away* from the public body.[176] In particular, a person injured by a product is likely to prefer to sue a person liable in private law (whether its *gardien*, its *vendeur professionnel*, or its producer) in the ordinary courts rather than sue the public authority in the administrative courts;[177] and where such a person has been held liable by the ordinary courts, the Conseil d'Etat has been very restrictive in its attitude to any claim for contribution from a public body even if the claimant can show the requisite standard of fault.[178] This means that in this sort of case any potential liability in the administration is likely to have little impact on the liability of a producer under the *loi* of 1998.

Secondly, if a person injured by a product can claim damages against the administration on the ground of a liability *without* fault, it may be thought that the primary victim of the product would prefer to sue in the administrative courts rather than in the private law courts, leaving it to the administration to recover contribution against any private person liable (such as the producer of the product). However, it is difficult to think of any practical examples of such a situation, given the marginal impact of administrative liability for dangerous things or activities and the dearth of other 'general' administrative liabilities without fault which would permit recovery in respect of harm caused by a product.[179]

Thirdly, however, the position may differ somewhat in the context of 'public works', where liability is typically imposed without proof of fault and where there are a range of defendants liable (the works contractors who undertake the work and the public bodies on whose behalf the work is done), none of whom can reduce their liability by invoking the defence of *fait d'un tiers*.[180] Where liability for 'public works' covers liability for a product, can its producer held liable in the ordinary courts claim

---

[173] Above, pp. 322–4.   [174] E.g. CE 9 Jul. 1975, *Ville de Cognac*, Leb. 413, above, p. 323.
[175] See above, pp. 34, 129.   [176] Above, pp. 321–2.   [177] Ibid.
[178] Above, pp. 326–30.   [179] Above, pp. 118–21.   [180] Above, pp. 124–9.

contribution from those liable under this special administrative law regime in the administrative courts or vice versa? Here, it would appear that in principle a public body held liable under the law of 'public works' may claim contribution against a private co-author of the primary victim's harm *in the ordinary courts* and as subrogated to the rights of the primary victim in private law.[181] Less clear, however, is the position of a person held liable as a matter of private law for damage caused by a product as regards any claim for contribution against one of the possible defendants liable under the law of public works, for example, if a person is injured when a public bridge collapses in part due to the defect of one of the materials used in its construction,[182] or a pupil is injured when his hand breaks through defective glass used in a door of his state school.[183] In principle, a private person (such as the producer of the product) may bring a recourse claim against a public body in the administrative courts by way of subrogation to the rights of primary victim,[184] but, as I have explained, such a claim risks being out of time as a result of the four-year prescription period applicable to administrative liabilities and a different view being taken by the administrative court as to the causal significance of the private person's action as compared to the public body's action.[185] Again, therefore, while the existence of administrative liabilities concurrent with liability in a producer of product could in theory reduce the impact of the producer's liability as found by an ordinary court, in fact they would not often do so.

2. English Law

I shall again look first at the impact of the 1985 Directive on the liabilities of producers, importers and suppliers before assessing more generally how these fit into the wider pattern of liabilities in English law and how these are 'shared' under the law of contribution or indemnity.

(a) The impact of implementation of the 1985 Directive on producers, importers and suppliers

In common with French law, English law also faces a degree of uncertainty as to the impact of the 1985 Directive, but this rests almost entirely on the proper interpretation to be given to 'defect' for its purposes, and, to a lesser extent, the development risks defence.[186] If the court in *A v National Blood Authority* was right to rule out from assessment of the defectiveness of a product consideration of the avoidability of a harmful aspect of a product and other factors familiar from the 'cost/benefit' analysis

---

[181] This was assumed in CE 5 Oct. 1966, *Del Carlo*, Leb. 522, above, p. 130.

[182] Cf. the facts of CE 16 Dec. 1953, *Goutines*, Leb. 552, above, pp. 126–7.

[183] Cf. the facts of CE 5 Nov. 1980, *Gentili*, RDP 1980.1108, above, p. 127.

[184] E.g. CE 22 Nov. 1985, RGTA 1986.374.

[185] As in CE Sect 16 Mar. 1962, *Cie d'assur. 'L'Urbaine et La Seine'* AJDA 1962.320. On the four year prescription period, see above, pp. 321–2. [186] Above, pp. 485–502.

of the tort of negligence, then its impact on manufacturers may be considerable.[187] If, on the other hand, the opposing view (for which I have earlier argued) is ultimately adopted, then assessment of a person's 'legitimate expectations' as to safety will lead to very similar results as assessment of a defendant's negligence as this is understood and applied by English courts.[188]

On the other hand, even if the assessment of 'defect' does allow consideration of the sorts of considerations relevant to assessment of negligence in a product's *manufacturer*, implementation of the 1985 Directive in English law has changed the basis of liability of 'Community importers' and 'own-branders' significantly. For, in assessing their negligence at common law, the courts would take into account their very limited abilities to foresee and to take action to prevent any harm caused by the products which they supply; whereas assessment of a product's 'defect' looks at the 'legitimate expectations' as to the safety of the product of people generally and (on the assumption which I have just made) their expectations would focus on the ability of a *manufacturer* to foresee and prevent harmful aspects of the product which relate to its manufacture or design.[189] Once a product is held 'defective' according to this test, under the Directive's scheme it is for the defendant (here, an importer or own-brander) to establish one of the defences allowed by article 7 in order to escape liability.

The position of 'suppliers' has also changed in English law after implementation of the 1985 Directive, but here the picture is much more complex.

First, if a person injured by a product was supplied with the product under a contract of sale or of supply (as defined by English law[190]), then he is likely to prefer to claim under the strict terms implied into these types of contract by statute: the liability is certainly as strict, there are fewer defences and, in particular, the supplier cannot escape the national contractual liability by identifying his own supplier or the producer within a reasonable time as he can escape his liability under the 1987 Act.

Secondly, if a person injured by a product was either supplied it in circumstances where English law does not recognise a contract (as in the case of statutory supplies of water or medicines and other health products under the NHS[191]) or was not himself party to the contract under which it *was* supplied in this sense, then under the general law he will have to prove the supplier's negligence in order to be able to recover.[192] Here, therefore, the special liability of 'suppliers' under the 1987 Act may be significant, for, as with importers and distributors, the supplier's liability for a 'defective' product would not need the injured party to establish the sorts of elements which would be needed for negligence *in the supplier*.[193] On the other hand, again, under the 1987 Act the supplier could escape liability by identifying his own supplier or the producer of the product.

Thirdly, exceptionally, a person injured by a product may sue its supplier on the basis of a tort which imposes liability which is stricter than negligence and where this is the case it may be more attractive than claiming against that person under the 1987 Act. This may be the case where a person supplies a product under a statutory duty whose breach is held to give rise to civil liability, for example, where a person supplies

---

[187] Above, pp. 486–9.   [188] Above, pp. 489–92.
[189] Stapleton, *Product Liability*, 242–5, above, p. 523.   [190] Above, pp. 245–6, 273.
[191] Above, pp. 278–9, 291–2.   [192] Ibid.   [193] Above, (this page).

a consumer product in breach of a statutory regulation governing its safety or where an employer breaks a regulation under the Health and Safety at Work Act.[194]

Fourthly, if the interpretation of 'supplier' as a person in the chain of distribution who uses the product is accepted,[195] the significance of the supplier's liability becomes much more significant, applying to a host of people whose liability is generally based on negligence, whether under the tort of negligence or in contract. So, for example, if an occupier of premises or a carrier of persons 'supplies' the products which he uses in his business, then he would be liable for the personal injury, death and damage to consumer property which their defects cause unless these 'suppliers' identify their own supplier or the producer of the product within a reasonable time. The practical effect of such a liability would be to impose a duty of record keeping for all those who buy or hire and then use products in the course of their business, sanctionable by liability without proof of negligence.

Fifthly, and related to this, under the Employer's Liability (Defective Equipment) Act 1969 employers are liable without proof of negligence in themselves where they provide their employees with defective 'equipment' which causes personal injury or death in the course of their employment, as long as the defect is attributable to the 'fault' of a third party (typically the manufacturer);[196] for this purpose, fault is defined as meaning 'negligence, breach of statutory duty or other act or omission which gives rise to liability in England and Wales'.[197] But can liability in a 'producer' in respect of defective equipment (the 'product') under the 1987 Act constitute 'fault' with the result that an employer is liable to any employee injured by it under the 1969 Act? This seems to follow as a matter of English statutory interpretation, but it may fall foul of the 'completely harmonised' nature of the 1985 Directive's scheme of liability as set out by the European Court in its decisions of 2002.[198] For employers often 'supply' equipment (the product) to their employees in the more narrow sense of transferring possession of it or 'providing' it (for example, an employer handing an employee a tool for use at work[199] or a car for use on the employer's business[200]) even though a contract of employment is not a contract *of* supply.[201] And if 'supplier' is interpreted to mean a person in the chain of distribution who uses the product, employers will even more frequently count as 'suppliers' within the meaning of the 1985 Directive.[202] This being so, it could be argued that as a matter of EC law the Employers' Liability (Defective Equipment) Act 1969 should be interpreted so as not to impose on 'suppliers' within the meaning of the 1985 Directive a liability more extensive than is provided for by the Directive itself. For liability under the 1969 Act imposes liability on employers ('suppliers') for defective products ('equipment') without the possibility of the employer being able to escape liability by identifying his own supplier or the producer of the product within the scheme of article 3(3).

Finally, apart from these differences based on the way in which the standard of liability of the 1987 Act in the product's 'defect' applies as compared to the standards

---

[194] Above, pp. 222, 474–5.   [195] Above, pp. 523–7.   [196] S. 1(1).

[197] Ibid., s. 1(3) and see above, p. 182.   [198] Above, pp. 440–4.

[199] As in *Davie v New Merton Board Mills Ltd.* [1959] AC 604.

[200] 'Equipment' is defined specifically to include vehicles: Employer's Liability (Defective Equipment) Act 1969, s. 1(3).   [201] Cf. above, p. 273.

[202] Above, pp. 523–7.

set by the torts of negligence and breach of statutory duty or by the law of contract, there may be particular differences generated by their different incidental effects. In English law, though, these operate very much at the margin, so, for example, any attempted exclusion of liability imposed by the 1987 Act is ineffective,[203] whereas exclusion of business liability for damage to property caused by negligence is subject to a reasonableness test.[204] Moreover, while there are minor differences between the operation of the limitation periods applicable to claims for personal injury, death and damage to property generally in English law and under the Directive's scheme (though the periods themselves and their starting points are remarkably similar[205]), the former are not subject to the foreclosure period of ten years from the time of the putting into circulation of the product which caused the harm.[206]

(b) Liability for products beyond the Directive's defendants

The wider English pattern of liabilities of which liability under the 1987 Act forms part is much simpler than the French. For in English law the general basis of liability for death, personal injuries and damage to movable property is proof of negligence (whether in tort or in contract), the principal exceptions being (a) if the claimant is party to a contract of sale or supply of goods from the defendant (where liability rests on proof of the lack of their satisfactory quality or fitness for their purpose[207]) and (b) if the claimant is able to claim in the tort of breach of statutory duty and the content of the duty is stricter than reasonable care.[208] English law does not possess anything like the French liabilities without fault for the 'deeds of things' or under contractual *obligations de sécurité de résultat*, nor under special regimes of liability such as under the law of 'public works', for motor vehicle accidents, the liability of 'builders',[209] or the liability of hospitals.[210] In English law, the differences in the context of the accident and the situation of the defendant are dealt with by variations in the standard of care,[211] and by the flexibility provided in the application of the cost/benefit analysis.[212] This even remains true of the liability of public authorities for any failure in the regulation or control of product safety: for here, if accepted at all, liability can only be based on negligence.[213]

Again, the way in which this relatively simple pattern of liabilities relates to liability under the 1987 Act depends on the interpretation to be given to 'defect'. Certainly, if 'defect' is interpreted so as to rule out consideration of some of the elements taken into account under the cost/benefit analysis in negligence,[214] then a claimant injured by an

---

[203] 1987 Act, s. 7.

[204] 1977 Act, s. 2(2). For the position regarding liability for breach of the statutory implied terms in s. 14 of the 1979 Act, see above, p. 262.

[205] In both a claimant for personal injuries and death must sue within three years of the date on which the cause of action accrued or the date of knowledge of the injured party (if later): Limitation Act 1980, s. 11 and 11A.   [206] Above, pp. 527–89.

[207] Above, pp. 235–42, 273.   [208] Above, pp. 221–3.

[209] On the marginal impact of liability without negligence under s. 1 of the Defective Premises Act 1972, see above, pp. 274–5.

[210] For the French law, see above, pp. 60–1, 104–8, 121–31, 153, 542–6.

[211] Above, pp. 188–9.   [212] Above, pp. 193–200.   [213] Above, Chap. 13.

[214] Above, pp. 486–94.

allegedly defective product is likely to wish to claim damages from its producer or supplier rather than having to prove negligence in some other person. So, for example, if a person is injured in a road or transport accident where the defect of a product can be made out (such as in one of the vehicles, the engine or signalling machinery or the software of an aeroplane's in-flight computer[215]) then he is likely to wish to claim against one of the Directive's defendants rather than allege negligence in someone else (a car driver, the train company or the airline). In sum, the general *absence* in English law of liabilities without proof of negligence to compensate death, personal injury and damage to property means that liability is *not* attracted away from the Directive's defendants in the way which it is in French law: overall, the magnetic effect is rather towards the Directive's defendants.

(c) 'Joint and several liability' and the means of recourse

This does not mean, of course, that in English law in some cases a person *other than* a 'producer' or 'supplier' may also be liable (whether in tort or in contract) to the victim of a product, though its approach is much simpler in its outline than the French, not distinguishing between the position of public authorities and other persons potentially liable.

So, in English law, when separate and independent acts or omissions which themselves satisfy the law's conditions for the imposition of liability are committed by two or more persons and cause one indivisible harm to another, the latter may recover damages in full from any one of those persons, leaving it to the latter to attempt to recover any indemnity or contribution towards the cost of this full liability.[216] Where this is the case the liabilities are usually termed 'joint and several',[217] and this applies just as much to the liabilities of a public body or a person exercising public powers as to persons more generally.[218] This rule has a very significant effect on the practical ability of a person to recover full compensation for their loss in tort,[219] but the concomitant of this protective effect is that a person liable for the claimant's harm (but whose action or omission was of relatively little significance compared to those of others) may be faced in practice with the burden of all the cost. For while (as I shall explain) the law does provide ways by which a person may recover contribution or an indemnity against others potentially also liable, those others may be not worth suing because they are insolvent and uninsured. The effect of this full liability has been criticised in some particular situations, for example, as regards the liability of auditors and in the building industry,[220] but it can also be criticised more generally

---

[215] Above, p. 477.

[216] This explanation is drawn from *Grant v Sun Shipping Co. Ltd.* [1948] AC 549, 563, *per* Lord du Parcq.

[217] The terminology, however, is complex and confusing, the common law distinguishing between 'joint', 'several' and 'joint and several' tortfeasors. For a helpful discussion see *Clerk and Lindsell on Torts*, 4–101 *et seq.*   [218] Above, pp. 172–3.

[219] Here, 'full' compensation refers to the compensation which the law considers enough to compensate the claimant's legally recoverable harms.

[220] Reform of the law so as to make accountants liable only up to their share of liability was considered and rejected by the Common Law Team of the Law Commission, *Feasibility Investigation of Joint and Several Liability* (commissioned by DTI, 1996).

on the ground that it has a distorting effect on the courts' decisions whether or not to impose liability at all as a matter of the duty of care in the tort of negligence, especially as regards public authorities.[221] However, a report considering reform of the law on joint and several liability towards a law of 'proportionate liability' saw its relationship to judicial decisions on the duty of care rather as a reason for *rejecting* reform:

[t]o remove joint and several liability would not only tend to undermine the imposition of duties of care where they have been found but might, indeed, have the effect—contrary to defendants' interests—of freeing the courts to develop the tort of negligence less conservatively.[222]

Certainly, the courts consider that the fact that a public authority is not the person 'primarily responsible' for a person's injury is a proper consideration in deciding whether to impose on it a duty of care.[223] Be that as it may, where the law *does* recognise liability, the rule remains that any person sued is liable in full towards the primary victim: all those jointly and severally liable are in a position very like each others' guarantors.

Where a person is held liable, what means of recourse does he (or his insurer) have to recoup some or all of his loss from any other person also liable? Procedurally, such a claim for recourse can be made as part of the same litigation by which the claimant sues one defendant (either where both are joined as co-defendants by a claimant[224] or by any defendant joining any other person potentially liable to the proceedings[225]) or by making a later independent claim, though the costs of the latter will be denied if bringing it subsequently is not reasonable,[226] reflecting a general policy of avoiding multiplicity of proceedings.[227] In English law, there are three possible grounds of such a claim for recourse.

First, a person held liable to the primary victim may be able claim an indemnity (which may extend to full compensation) under a contractual indemnity clause, where a particular term of a contract imposes an obligation on one of the parties to indemnify the other in respect of a defined loss, notably, by incurring liability to a third person. So, for example, in the case of a suitably drawn indemnity clause a manufacturer held liable directly to a consumer for personal injuries which his product has caused may pass on *all* the cost of this liability to the person to whom he sold the product (a wholesaler or retailer). In English law, in principle such an indemnity clause is valid,[228] though it is subject to a requirement of reasonableness as against those who 'deal as consumers'.[229]

---

[221] Cf. J. Stapleton, 'Duty of Care: Peripheral Parties and Alternative Opportunities for Deterrence' (1995) 111 *LQR* 301, 311–14.   [222] Common Law Team of the Law Commission, *op. cit.* n. 220, para. 4.20.

[223] Above, pp. 343–4.   [224] Now CPR 7.3 and see e.g. *Croston v Vaughan* [1938] 1 KB 540.

[225] CPR 20.6.

[226] Civil Liability (Contribution) Act 1978 ss. 3 and 4. See *Sweetman v Shepherd* The Times 29 Mar. 2000. On the other hand, no claim can be made against another joint and several tortfeasor after 'full and final' settlement with one: *Jameson v Central Electricity Generating Board* [1999] 2 WLR 144 (HL); *Rawlinson v North Essex HA* [2000] Lloyd's Rep Med 54 (claim against health authority barred after such a settlement with pharmaceutical manufacturer).

[227] This can now be supported by the 'overriding objective' described by the CPR 1 as 'to deal with cases justly' and including within this formula the saving of expense.

[228] *Thompson v T Lohan (Plant Hire) Ltd.* [1987] 1 WLR 649.

[229] Unfair Contract Terms Act 1977, s. 4; The Unfair Terms in Consumer Contracts Regulation 1999, r. 5 also impose a requirement of 'fairness' as regards 'consumers'. On the meaning of 'dealing as consumer' see above, p. 253. A person may recover under an indemnity clause even if the act or omission which gave rise to

Secondly, a person may be able to recover an indemnity or a partial indemnity in respect of sums paid in compensation to a primary victim as loss caused by breach of a term in a contract with another person, whether or not that person would also be liable to the primary victim directly.[230] For example, a retailer held liable to a consumer for harm caused by goods which he has sold may claim an indemnity in respect of any compensation paid to the consumer from his own seller, as long as he can establish that his own liability was caused by breach of an express term or by breach of one of the statutory implied terms as to the goods' description, quality or fitness for purpose.[231] Such a distributor may or may not also be liable directly in tort to the consumer (whether in the tort of negligence or under the Consumer Protection Act 1987), but in English law will not in principle be liable in contract for lack of privity.[232] Where a person claims to be indemnified against his own liability in this way his own negligence will *not* prevent or reduce his recovery as long as it is not so unreasonable as to break the chain of causation.[233]

Thirdly, if a person is liable together with one or more other persons in respect of the *same* damage and is held liable in full,[234] he may claim contribution under the Civil Liability (Contribution) Act 1978 from any other person also liable, to an extent which the court considers 'just and equitable having regard to the extent of that person's responsibility for the damage in question'.[235] Such a claim for contribution can be made whatever the legal basis of the liabilities of the co-authors of the primary claimant's harm: whether contractual or tortious, whether the co-authors are 'jointly liable' or otherwise,[236] and, of course, whether or not the co-author is a public body.[237] On the other hand, the condition that the liabilities must relate to the 'same damage' has been interpreted quite technically, which can be well illustrated in the product context. So, the condition is satisfied where a retailer is liable in respect of personal injuries (contractually as seller of a product to his buyer or in tort to any other person) and where the product's manufacturer is also liable to the buyer for the personal injuries

his liability constituted a criminal offence as long as it does not rest on deliberate wrong-doing: *Clerk end Lindsell on Torts*, paras. 4-128–4-29; *Spalding v Tarmac Civil Engineering Ltd.* [1967] 1 WLR 769 (HL).

[230] Such a term of indemnity has been implied: *Lister v Romford Ice and Cold Storage Co. Ltd.* [1957] AC 555 (employee's implied agreement to indemnify employer). There is also a possibility of an independent claim in the tort of negligence treating the indemnity loss as 'pure economic loss' for this purpose, see *Lambert v Lewis* [1982] AC 225, 277. There may also be a claim for a debt, i.e. a certain sum of money payable by C on the occasion of B's non-performance to A, as in the case of a contract of indemnity, such as a contract of suretyship or insurance.   [231] On these implied terms, see above, pp. 235–45.

[232] *Bostock & Co. Ltd. v Nicholson & Sons. Ltd.* [1904] 1 KB 725; *Lambert v Lewis, cit*, above, p. 264.

[233] This results from the narrow application of the defence of contributory negligence to claims for breach of contract: above, p. 248.

[234] The rule also applies where he has made a bona fide settlement or compromise of any claim: Civil Liability (Contribution) Act 1978, s. 1(4) ('1978 Act').

[235] 1978 Act, ss 1 and 2(1), repealing and extending the Law Reform (Married Women and Joint Tortfeasors) Act 1935 s 6(1)(c). At common law, there was no contribution between joint tortfeasors or several tortfeasors causing the same damage in the absence of agreement: *Merryweather v Nixon* (1799) 8 TR 186.

[236] 1978 Act, ss. 1(1), 6(1). At common law, a person is 'jointly' liable where the cause of action against each tortfeasor is the same, e.g. an employee who has committed a tort in the course of employment is jointly liable with his employer: *Clerk and Lindsell on Torts*, para. 4–108.

[237] Any claim for contribution by or against a public authority generally falls within the 1978 Act by reason of its application to 'liability': s.1(1). The 1978 Act, s. 5 specifically applies its provisions to the Crown.

caused by its negligence or under the Consumer Protection Act: here the liabilities are in respect of the same damage, the buyer's or third party's personal injuries. By contrast, where a person injured by a product recovers damages from a retailer, who then recovers a contractual indemnity (whether under an indemnity clause or by way of damages for breach of contract) from his own seller (a distributor), the distributor *cannot* claim contribution from the manufacturer or any other person liable directly to the person who suffered personal injuries: here, the liability of the manufacturer is in respect of the primary claimant's personal injuries, but the distributor's liability is in respect of an indemnity loss suffered by his own buyer under a contract: the two 'harms' are therefore not the same.[238] Clearly, the absence of a right to contribution in these circumstances throws more weight on any contractual claim for indemnity possessed by such a person (in the above example, the distributor). On the other hand, where the facts so allow, a person can choose to claim statutory contribution instead of any contractual right of indemnity which he may enjoy,[239] unless the claim for contribution is inconsistent with a valid contractual provision.[240]

What then is the legal nature of a claim to contribution under the 1978 Act? Unlike French law, English law does not overtly treat such a claim as a form of subrogation, though it follows the logic of subrogation for some purposes. First, in principle, a person may recover contribution only from a person himself liable to the primary claimant directly,[241] and cannot recover on this ground from such a person any amount greater than could have been recovered by the primary claimant directly against that co-author. So, for example, a person claiming contribution may not recover against a co-author if the latter's liability had been validly excluded or limited by contract as against the primary claimant. Similarly, where a buyer recovers damages for breach of the statutory implied term as to the quality of goods from his seller without deduction for contributory negligence,[242] any claim for contribution by that seller against the goods' manufacturer as also liable to the buyer in the tort of negligence or under the Consumer Protection Act *would* be faced with a reduction on the ground of the buyer's contributory negligence as this defence would be available to the manufacturer against the buyer.[243] On the other hand, the 1978 Act specifically provides that a person may be liable to contribution towards a person also liable for the same damage even though at the time of the claim for contribution the first liability has ceased (notably as a result of the law of limitation of actions):[244] this is incompatible with the idea that a claimant for contribution is exercising the rights of the primary claimant through a form of subrogation. Instead, in general claims for contribution

---

[238] *Clerk and Lindsell on Torts*, para. 4–127 n. 9 and cf. *Birse Construction v Haiste Ltd.* [1996] 1 WLR 675; *Royal Brompton Hospital NHS Trust v Hammond* [2002] UKHL 14; [2002] 1 WLR 1397.

[239] E.g. *Knight v Rochdale Healthcare NHS Trust* [2003] EWHC 1831 (QB) [2]; [2003] 4 All ER 416; *Bacardi-Martini Beverages Ltd. v Thomas Hardy Packaging Ltd.* [2002] EWCA Civ. 549; [2002] 2 All ER Comm. 335.

[240] This follows from the general approach to the concurrence of claims in contract and in tort, where it has been held that a claimant may choose to claim in tort even though he has a contract with the defendant as long as the tort is not inconsistent with the contract: *Henderson v Merrett Syndicates Ltd.* [1995] 2 AC 145.

[241] 1978 Act, s. 1(6).   [242] Contributory negligence does not reduce this liability: above, p. 248.

[243] *Clerk and Lindsell on Torts*, para 4–123 n. 90.

[244] 1978 Act, s. 1(3); Markesinis and Deakin's *Tort Law*, 853.

are subject to their own limitation period of two years from the date at which the claim accrues, that is, the date when the claimant is held liable or agrees to make any payment to one or more persons in compensation for the damage,[245] though this provision may have to be interpreted so as not to impose a liability to contribution on a person liable under the Consumer Protection Act 1987 beyond the foreclosure period which the 1985 Directive provides.[246]

Where a claim for contribution arises, the 1978 Act gives the court a very broad discretion as to the amount of contribution which is payable (such amount as is 'just and equitable'), specifying only that it shall have regard to 'the extent of [the co-authors] responsibility',[247] and noting that it may reduce the contribution to nothing or grant a complete indemnity.[248] For this purpose English courts take into account both the relative culpability of the tortfeasors' actions and the causal relevance of their actions or omissions. So, the fact that a person is liable strictly (and was not actually at fault) will tend to lessen his proportion of liability, and as between those 'at fault' their relative fault is relevant.[249] In this respect, relative 'fault' may refer to a range of different behaviour, from deliberate wrong-doing, through negligence to stricter liabilities, unsurprising given the range of tortious and contractual liabilities to which the statutory discretion may apply. Unlike French law, there are no rules or even settled practices according to which a person liable for negligence cannot recover against a person liable strictly or that, conversely, a person liable strictly will be able to recover in full from a person liable for negligence:[250] the relative fault or the lack of it is only one factor in the judicial assessment with which a court of appeal should not interfere unless it was clearly wrong[251] and in appropriate circumstances a deliberate wrong-doer may pay no more than a merely negligent one.[252] On the other hand, while English law does not possess a rule according to which a person liable for the same harm drops out of the calculation of proportionate responsibility if insolvent, where (as is usually the case) an insolvent person is not before the court, then his or her share is not to be taken into account.[253]

How then do these grounds of recourse (whether contractual or for contribution) affect the pattern of liabilities for products after implementation of the Product Liability Directive? As I have explained, in English law a person injured by a product whose defect is in issue may well choose to sue its producer or supplier under the 1987 Act since any other claim he may possess is very likely to require proof of negligence, with the exception of a claim under a contract of supply of the product.[254]

---

[245] Limitation Act 1980, s. 10.   [246] Above, pp. 528–9.   [247] 1978 Act, s. 2(1).
[248] Ibid., s. 2(2).
[249] *Madden v Quirk* [1989] 1 WLR 702, 709 ('blameworthiness' and 'causal potency').
[250] *Dooley v Cammell Laird & Co. Ltd.* [1951] 1 Lloyd's Rep. 271 (75/25% split). Stapleton, *Product Liability*, 300–01; Taylor, *Harmonisation communautaire*, 141. Cf. Treitel, *Law of Contract* 574 describing contribution between co-debtors where in principle a claimant may recover the amount of the debt divided by the number of the co-debtors.
[251] *Re-Source America International Ltd. v Platt Site Services Ltd.* [2004] EWCA Civ 665 [51]; (2005) WL 353356, *per* Tuckey LJ; *British Fame (Owners) v Macgregor (Owners)* [1943] AC 197; *Parkman Consulting Engineers v Cumbrian Industrials Ltd.* [2001] EWCA Civ. 1621 at [103]; 79 Con LR 112.
[252] *Downs v Chappell* [1997] 1 WLR 426, 445.   [253] *Maxfield v Llewellyn* [1961] 1 WLR 1119.
[254] Above, pp. 556–7.

Where the person actually sued by the primary victim has a contractual claim for an indemnity (whether under an indemnity clause or by way of damages for breach) then the ultimate burden of responsibility for the harm caused by the defective product is a function of this express, implied or statutory contractual allocation of risk, subject to any legislative control of an express indemnity clause.[255] For example, if a primary victim recovers damages for personal injury caused by a defective product from a retailer (whether under the law of sale of goods, negligence or as 'supplier' under the 1987 Act), then the retailer may be able to recover in full from his own supplier under his contract either under any express term or for breach of one of the statutory implied terms under the Sale of Goods Act: the statutory implied terms allow liability to be passed up the chain. Where, however, the primary victim sues someone *higher* in the chain of distribution (for example, an own-brander, importer or manufacturer of the product, again whether under the 1987 Act or the tort of negligence), the person sued can only pass on his liability *down* the chain of distribution to a person who has validly expressly agreed to indemnify him (putting aside claims for contribution under the 1978 Act). In this situation and from this perspective, then, the question whether liability remains with those liable under the 1985 Directive is a function of whether they have provided for a contractual means of their indemnity and of its validity as a matter of English law.

On the other hand, the general route to passing on the burden or some of the burden of liability is provided by the 1978 Act. Under the Act, any person liable for death, personal injury or damage to property caused by a defective product who pays the primary victim in full can claim contribution from any other person so liable, whether the liability arises in contract, in the tort of negligence or under the Consumer Protection Act. In determining the ultimate burden of liability as between those so liable an English court will take into account their relative 'fault', but also the relative causal impact of their act or omission in producing the primary victim's damage.[256] For example, where a retailer has been held liable to the primary victim under the statutory implied terms owing to a defect for which its manufacturer is also liable to the primary claimant under the 1987 Act, a court is likely to consider it 'just and equitable' that the manufacturer should bear the larger or, indeed, the whole burden of ultimate liability.[257] The court may take the same view in respect of any apportionment of liability as between an 'own-brander' and a manufacturer both liable under the 1987 Act. In both these cases, therefore, the tendency of the English approach to contribution is to channel liability for a defective product onto the manufacturer rather than leave it with a (less directly responsible) person lower down the chain of distribution. However, where a primary victim's harm is caused partly by a defect in a product and partly by the negligence of another person (whether or not that negligence forms the legal basis of that person's liability) then the presence of this negligence will tend to attract a greater proportionate share of liability. So, for example, if a retailer held strictly liable under his contract to the primary victim was also negligent, then this will tend to

---

[255] Above, p. 558. I refer in the text to the 'statutory contractual' allocation of risk, as a claim for an indemnity under contracts of sale or of transfer of goods rests on the statutory implied terms modelled on s. 14 of the 1979 Act, above, pp. 235–42, 273.   [256] Above, p. 561.

[257] It is to be recalled, though, that an *intermediate* seller cannot recover contribution under the 1978 Act for the reasons explained above, pp. 559–60.

reduce the amount which he can recover against the manufacturer. Moreover, the English approach to the allocation of the burden of liability means that a person who claims contribution against a producer or other person liable under the 1987 Act has an interest in arguing that the latter were not merely *liable* to the primary victim (so as to found the claim for contribution) but also that their *negligence* contributed to the primary victim's harm. To this extent, therefore, where another person is also liable to a primary victim, the negligence of a producer remains relevant to his ultimate share of liability even if negligence is substantively (as well as formally) irrelevant to his liability towards the primary victim.

3. The Product Liability Directive's Purposes and Harmonisation

What then do these patterns of liability have to say about the Product Liability Directive's purpose of harmonisation? It has long been acknowledged that the Directive's claim to effective harmonisation is relatively weak given its own express derogations, its retention of other grounds of liability and the likely role of national laws in the interpretation and application of key concepts which it uses.[258] As regards the retention of other bases of liability, the key difference between English and French law remains the extension of contractual liability for latent defects down the chain by *action directe*, a difference whose practical significance will be substantially affected by the replacement of its notorious *bref délai* with a fixed period of two years from the time of discovery of the defect.[259] Attention has also been drawn to the practical impact on the costs to producers of liability of different rules and practices relating to the quantification of damages for personal injuries and death and the legal effect on their calculation of social security, first party insurance or special schemes of liability.[260] However, there are two key conclusions as to its claim to harmonisation to be drawn from this discussion of the way in which the new product liability affects the wider patterns of liability in French and in English law.

First, the impact of the 1985 Directive as an instrument of harmonisation of the *protection* given to people by providing for compensation in respect of death, personal injury and damage to their consumer property caused by defective products is very weak. It is not merely that the protection given to 'consumers' in respect of these categories of harm still differs after implementation of the Directive because of other bases of claim against producers or suppliers as allowed by article 13; more importantly, a person injured by a defective product *may* have more attractive bases of claim against *other* categories of defendant on the basis of entirely distinct national laws. Here, English and French law make a striking contrast. For, in French law, such an injured person will often have a claim under article 1384 alinéa 1 against a product's *gardien* for the damage which the product has caused him or under a contractual *obligation de sécurité de résultat* without the need to prove the product's defect, without the risk of one of the Directive's six defences, with a longer prescription period, and without the

---

[258] Above, pp. 436–8, 449.   [259] Above, pp. 532–3.   [260] Above, p. 449.

ten-year foreclosure period.[261] By contrast, in modern English law, which has set its face so firmly against liabilities without proof of negligence in respect of death and personal injuries, a person injured by a product usually does not have such strict bases of liability on which to claim, with the result that proof of defect against a product's producer comes to look more attractive.[262] From the injured person's point of view, therefore, the Directive has *not* harmonised the law's protection against harm caused by defective products even if we look at just these two systems.

Secondly, conversely, the Product Liability Directive has not harmonised the burden of liability on producers and suppliers as it defines them in the interests of fair competition in the internal market. Even if implementation of the Directive had required the liability of producers and suppliers to persons harmed by a defective product to be placed on a single harmonised basis in French and English law, this would not have had the effect on the burden of liability which the Directive claimed and on which its competence rests.[263] For the ultimate burden of liability for defective products falling on producers and suppliers depends not merely on the legal basis of their liability ('fault', 'negligence', 'no fault' or 'defect') and on such factors as the quantification of damages and social security, but also on the incidence of liabilities in *other* persons: to this extent it forms the converse of the different legal grounds of recovery of damages for the victims of products. The ultimate burden of liability of producers and suppliers also depends on the availability and judicial practices of recourse by those other persons held liable for harm caused by defective products. As I have explained, the differences in French and English law here stem not so much from the legal grounds or range of recourse (which are remarkably similar, though there are some differences[264]) as in the impact of the bases of other liabilities on the assessment of the proportion of share ultimately to be borne by the producer.[265] For while both French and English courts take into account the relative faults of co-authors in sharing proportions of harm, the existence in French law of liabilities *without* fault on persons other than producers and suppliers tends to reduce the burden on producers; and where liability for fault on persons other than producers or suppliers can be established, then it extinguishes the burden on producers founded on the *loi* of 1998.[266] In English law, by contrast, while the assessment of the proportions of liability to be borne by co-authors remains more at large, the tendency of its law of contribution is to channel liability towards the manufacturer, except where another person's negligence is held as partly the cause of the primary claimant's harm.[267] Where it is, the ultimate responsibility for the harm caused by a defective product will tend to be channelled away from the manufacturer and towards the person responsible in negligence, unless the manufacturer's actions can be shown also to constitute negligence.[268] In sum, the selection by the EEC of a particular 'area' of liability for harmonisation on economic grounds (in this case 'product liability') fundamentally misunderstands the way in which the patterns of liability interrelate within legal systems and how this interrelationship affects the practical burden of liability on defendants.

---

[261] Above, pp. 539–41.   [262] Above, pp. 556–7.   [263] Above, pp. 436–40.
[264] For example, as to the time within which a claim must be brought: above, p. 560.
[265] Above, pp. 547–51 (French law); 558–61 (English law).   [266] Above, p. 550.
[267] Above, pp. 562–3.   [268] Ibid.

19

The Consumer Guarantees Directive and its Implementation in French and English Law

1. Introduction

The second European directive which impacts significantly on liability for products is the Directive on certain aspects of the sale of consumer goods and associated guarantees enacted in May 1999, which I shall refer to it as the Consumer Guarantees Directive or the 1999 Directive.[1] This directive had a long period of gestation, becoming increasingly attenuated in the process.

The idea of the harmonisation of the rules governing guarantee arrangements in sales of goods was first proposed by the Commission as part of its intended harmonisation of unfair contract terms in 1990,[2] the proposals including the imposition of a common requirement of contractual conformity of goods and requiring Member States to grant consumer buyers a number of rights against sellers, including rights of repair, replacement, rescission *and* damages.[3] However, the Council considered that this aspect of the proposed directive should be dealt with separately and invited the Commission to prepare an in-depth analysis.[4] As a result in 1996, the Commission published a Green Paper on guarantees in consumer goods and after-sales services, floating the idea that there should be a 'European Guarantee' to provide a minimum set of rights for consumer buyers.[5] While the resulting proposed directive held to the idea of a common requirement of contractual conformity,[6] and the requirement that a consumer should be given the choice of which right to exercise for non-conformity,

---

[1] Directive 1999/44/EC of the European Parliament and of the Council of 25 May 1999, OJ L171/12.

[2] Com. (90) 322 final, OJ No. C 243 of 28 September 1990, recital 3; Amended proposal for a Directive on unfair terms in consumer contracts (Com. (92) 66 of 4 Mar. 1992, OJ No. C 73, 24 Mar. 1992, art. 6) and see European Commission's Explanatory Memorandum to an earlier draft proposal for a directive on the sale of consumer goods and associated guarantees of 18 June 1996, Com. (95) 520 p. 6 ('EC Commission, *Explanatory Memorandum*'). For a highly useful discussion of the draft proposals for a directive of 1996, see House of Lords Select Committee on European Communities, *Tenth Report on Consumer Guarantees* (4 March 1997) ('HL Select Committee, *Tenth Report*').

[3] Amended proposal of 4 March 1992, art. 6.

[4] EC Commission, *Explanatory Memorandum*, § 1.

[5] Green Paper on 'Guarantees for Consumer Goods and After-Sales Service', Com. (93) 509.

[6] EC Commission, *Explanatory Memorandum*, comments on proposed art. 2.

it left out liability in damages, ostensibly on the grounds of subsidiarity.[7] And when the Directive was promulgated, its claim that it would improve consumer protection in the laws of the Member States was further weakened by its control of the buyer's choice between the rights of repair, replacement, price reduction and rescission which it provided.[8]

The other crucial and widely misunderstood aspect of the 1999 Directive related to its time elements. Here there were three questions: how long should the 'legal guarantee' last? Should there be a presumption for a set period that a subsequently discovered non-conformity in the goods existed on their delivery? And should there be a requirement that the buyer notify within a set period the seller once a lack of conformity had been discovered? In all of these questions, existing law in some of the Member States differed significantly from what was being proposed, but apart from the Directive's innovative acceptance of a presumption of anteriority of the non-conformity, its answers to these questions were fairly restrictive of the rights of consumers.[9]

Nevertheless, the 1999 Directive may still be seen as the contractual counterpart to the reforms of extra-contractual liability required by the Product Liability Directive of 1985 and it reflected a similar set of concerns for the integration of the internal market and the protection of European citizens, the first in terms of their safety, the second in terms of their financial well-being as consumers. However, there are very significant general differences between the two directives, quite apart from those which would be expected from their different remits. Moreover, the European Court's decisions of 2002 holding that the Product Liability Directive in principle requires Member States to impose both a minimum and a maximum liability on those defendants caught by its provisions,[10] means that *implementation* in a Member State of the two directives has the practical potential for conflict.[11]

In this chapter, I shall look first at very broad differences between the Product Liability and Consumer Guarantees Directives; at the debates in France and the UK concerning how the Consumer Guarantees Directive should be implemented; and finally at the substantive legal impact of this Directive on French and on English law.

2. Broad Differences between the Product Liability and Consumer Guarantees Directives

There are four broad differences between these two directives: in their overt purposes; in the parentage of their provisions; in their remedial consequence; and in the problems of integration which they cause.

---

[7] EC Commission, *Explanatory Memorandum*, comments on proposed art. 2, text at n. 47.

[8] 1999 Directive, art. 3 and see below, pp. 604–10.

[9] Below, pp. 594–5, 619–21. The 1999 Directive also allows Member States to reduce its impact on sales of second-hand goods: art. 1(3) (exclusion of second-hand goods sold at public auction); art. 7(1) § 2 (shorter periods of limitation by agreement of the parties), below, p. 589.

[10] Case C-52/00; Case C-154/00; Case C-183/00 and see above, pp. 440–4.

[11] Above, pp. 444, 464, 507, and below, pp. 662–3.

(a) The purposes of the Directives

First, while their declared purposes look similar, the Directives rest on different legal foundations and are significantly different. The Product Liability Directive was made under what was then article 100 of the EC Treaty, under which directives could be made by the Council of Ministers for the approximation of such legal provisions 'as directly affect the establishment or functioning of the Common Market'.[12] At the time, unanimity was required for such a directive and there was no distinct legal basis in the Treaties for the protection of consumers.[13] For this reason, while the preamble to the 1985 Directive did set as its purpose the protection of consumers within the EEC, its legal foundation was the distorting effect on the market of different bases of liability of those responsible for unsafe products, a legal basis which formed the main reason for the European Court's view that it required a 'complete harmonisation' within its terms.[14] By contrast, by the time of the 1999 Directive, the possible legal bases for such a directive in the Treaty had changed considerably. In particular, the protection of consumers had become recognised as an aim of European action,[15] article 153 providing that ' in order to promote the interests of consumers and to ensure a high level of consumer protection, the Community shall contribute to protecting [their] health, safety and economic interests'. One of the mechanisms to be used to do so was the adoption of measures for the approximation of laws which have as their object the establishment and functioning of the internal market under article 95 of the Treaty, which itself refers to the need as regards consumer protection measures to 'take as a base a high level of protection'[16] and provides for use of a procedure by which the Council responds to Commission proposals and the opinion of Parliament and then generally acts by qualified majority.[17] This was the legal basis on which the 1999 Directive was founded, rather than the counterpart provision of the legal basis for the 1985 Directive, article 94 EC.[18]

Nevertheless, both the main purposes set out by the 1999 Directive in its preamble are tied to the furthering of the internal market.[19] The preamble first notices the increasing importance of cross-border consumer transactions, particularly given the internet, and then claims that 'the creation of a common set of minimum rules of consumer law, valid no matter where goods are purchased within the Community, will strengthen consumer confidence and enable consumers to make the most of the internal market'.[20] In this respect, it considers that the:

main source of disputes with sellers concern the non-conformity of goods with the contract [so that it is] appropriate to approximate national legislation governing the sale of consumer goods in this respect, without however impinging on provisions and principles of national law relating to contractual and non-contractual liability.[21]

[12] Now art. 94 EC and see above, pp. 436–40.

[13] For an introduction to the evolution of consumer protection policy in the EU, see Weatherill, Chap. 1.

[14] Above, pp. 440–4.

[15] See art. 3(1)(t) EC which includes a 'contribution to the strengthening of consumer protection' as one of the Community activities.   [16] Art. 95(3) EC, art. 153(3)(a) EC.

[17] Art. 95(1), referring to art. 251 EC.

[18] 1999 Directive, recital 1. On the other hand, the 1999 Directive was not based on the independent ground of intervention for the protection of consumers provided by art. 153 (3)(b), 153(4) EC.

[19] S. Stijns and W. Van Gerven, 'Article 7 Binding Nature' in Bianca and Grundmann, *EU Sales Directive*, 235 at 238.   [20] Recital 5.

[21] Recital 6.

The preamble then summarises the main provisions of the Directive, explaining how they will ensure a 'uniform minimum set of fair rules governing the sale of consumer goods',[22] this minimal nature of the Directive being recalled explicitly towards the end of the preamble (as well as in its text).[23] Here, therefore, a minimum of consumer protection goes hand-in-hand with the opening of the internal market as it encourages consumer confidence in cross-border transactions, a theme developed in other consumer protection directives which directly concern cross-border consumer contracts.[24]

The second main purpose of the 1999 Directive, however, is even more closely tied to the internal market, as recital 3 provides that:

Whereas the laws of the Member States concerning the sale of consumer goods are somewhat disparate, with the result that national consumer goods markets differ from one another and that competition between sellers may be distorted.

And recital 4 adds, by way of aside in the course of a passage directed towards the role of consumers in cross-border transactions that 'the artificial reconstruction of frontiers and the compartmentalisation of markets should be prevented'. The problem with this second main purpose is that it has considerable potential to conflict with the minimal nature of the Directive. For, as was seen in relation to the Product Liability Directive, the converse of a higher degree of consumer protection in some national laws is a higher degree of burdens for business whose transactions are governed by those laws with a concomitant potential for the distortion of competition and the 'compartmentalisation of markets'.[25] Perhaps in this respect, the allusion in the preamble to the 1999 Directive to the possibility of 'more far-reaching harmonisation' of consumer protection at the European (and a high) level in the future (notably, as regards the imposition of liability in producers rather than merely sellers)[26] suggests that the 1999 Directive was seen as part of a process which starts by concentrating on consumer protection but also sets the foundations of further developments by which a more complete uniformity of protection is to be imposed.

(b) The parentage of the Directives' provisions

A second contrast between the 1985 and the 1999 Directives may be seen in differences in the legal parentage of their substantive contents, this being reflected in part in the style of their provisions. The 1985 Directive took as its general inspiration a sense of a common practical problem after Thalidomide and the United States law governing liability for products, as qualified and transmitted to the EEC via an earlier draft Council of Europe Convention on Products Liability.[27] Apart from this

---

[22] Recital 2.   [23] Recital 24; art. 8.
[24] See especially Dir. 97/7/EC of the European Parliament and of the Council of 20 May 1997 on the protection of consumers in respect of distance contracts; Dir. 2000/31/EC of the European Parliament and of the Council of 8 June 2000 on certain legal aspects of information society services in particular electronic contracts, in the Internal Market; Dir. 2002/65/EC of the European Parliament and of the Council of 23 September 2002 concerning the distance marketing of consumer financial services.
[25] Above, pp. 438–9, 441.   [26] Recital 23.   [27] Above, pp. 431–5.

primarily non-European influence, the remainder of the 1985 Directive's provisions have no particular intellectual flavour (except, perhaps, the flavour of compromise), though sometimes its language is distinctly unfamiliar to a common lawyer.[28]

By contrast, there are at least four distinct influences visible on the form and substance of the 1999 Directive.

First, the 1999 Directive shows the influence of the developing corpus of European legislation in the area of the protection of the economic interests of consumers. This is true of some of its definitions, for example, of 'consumer' and 'seller',[29] its means of ensuring the 'binding nature' of its provisions on parties to contracts[30] and of permitting Member States to preserve existing rights of consumers or adopting more stringent ones.[31] This reflects the Commission's growing sense that there is a need to give a greater coherence and consistency to the European legislation in the area of contract law.[32]

Secondly, a very obvious influence on the Directive's substantive provisions is that of the United Nations Convention on Contracts for the International Sale of Goods of 1980 (the 'Vienna Convention').[33] This influence, which has been well documented,[34] was particularly important in the adoption by the 1999 Directive of a unitary concept of 'contractual non-conformity' to deal with problems which in some civilian systems are dealt with either by their general law of contractual liability or special provisions governing sale (and certain other contracts) stemming ultimately from the aedilitian edicts, and which in the common law are dealt with by a combination of express and implied terms.[35] The 1999 Directive itself asserts that a seller's liability for 'contractual non-conformity' of the goods is 'the traditional solution enshrined in the legal orders of the Member States',[36] but, as I shall explain, the absorption of the traditional liability for latent defects within a new notion of contractual non-conformity became part of the argument in France as to the proper way of implementing the Directive.[37] Moreover, criticism can be aimed at use of the Vienna Convention, which was drafted as an exclusive uniform code applicable to commercial contracts in an international context and always subject to contrary intention,[38] as the basis for a directive applicable to consumer

---

[28] E.g. the reference to 'non-material damage': 1985 Directive, art. 9 *in fine*. On the other hand, the 1985 Directive's style can seem more common law in inspiration to a French lawyer, above p. 452.

[29] 1999 Directive, art. 1(2) and see below, pp. 590–1 where the qualifications are noted.

[30] 1999 Directive, art. 7 and see below, p. 623.   [31] Ibid., art. 8.

[32] Communication from the Commission to the Council and European Parliament on European Contract Law (11 July, 2001), Com. (2001) 398 final §§ 57–60.   [33] Sometimes known as 'CISG'.

[34] EC Commission, *Explanatory Memorandum*, comment on proposed art. 2; D. Staudenmayer, 'The Directive on the Sale of Goods and Associated Guarantees—A Milestone in the European Consumer and Private Law' (2000) *ERPL* 547 (particularly revealing given the author's position as competent Commission official participating in the 1999 Directive's legislative process); S.A. Kruisinga, 'What do consumer and commercial sales law have in common? A comparison of the EC Directive on consumer sales law and the UN Convention on contracts for the international sale of goods' (2001) *ERPL* 177; D. Corapi, 'La Direttiva 99/44/CE et la Convenzione di Vienna sulla vendita internazionale: verso un nuovo diritto commune della vendita?' in Università degli Studi di Padova, *L'attuazione della Direttiva 99/44/CE in Italia e in Europa* (2002), 135.   [35] Vienna Convention, art. 35(1); 1999 Directive art. 2.

[36] Recital 9.   [37] Below, pp. 580–1

[38] Vienna Convention, arts. 1, 6 (the only exception as regards contracting parties is found in art. 12): see P. Schlectriem, *Commentary on the UN Convention on the International Sale of Goods (CISG)* (OUP, 1998) 52 *et seq*.

contracts, which would *principally* apply to domestic transactions, was expressed as a supplement to existing provisions and which would be incapable of exclusion by contrary intention. So while the relationship between the 1999 Directive and the Convention may suggest that courts might refer to the case law interpreting the Convention in their decisions on the Directive, this must be done with great care for while the wording of the Directive may be traceable to the Convention, the Directive's ambit and purposes within the European legal order are fundamentally different.[39]

Thirdly, the 1999 Directive's provisions reveal quite clearly distinctive common law and civilian influences. So, even more than the Vienna Convention,[40] the 1999 Directive reveals the influence of common law ways of thinking and even more of techniques of expression. Again, the key concept of 'contractual conformity' in article 2 comes to mind, not in its terminology nor in its rather strange use of a rebuttable presumption, but in its content. For under it, contractual conformity possesses a number of elements, each one of which must be satisfied in order for the seller to escape liability.[41] Of these elements, the provision which concerns the goods' 'quality and performance' has a distinctly common law flavour, referring to the reasonable expectations of consumers and then requiring a series of considerations to be taken into account in determining whether or not these are fulfilled in the circumstances.[42] There are, moreover, three further different appeals to 'reasonableness' in the Directive's provisions.[43]

On the other hand, the influence of civilian ways of thinking is profoundly apparent in article 3 of the Directive's 'rights' of consumer buyers arising from non-conformity.[44] As I shall explain, the assumption of this complex provision is not merely that a buyer has a right to performance of the seller's obligation of contractual conformity, but that the seller has the right to perform.[45] This reflects a general principle found in both the Romanistic and the Germanic civilian families of private law that contracts are there to be performed and that this means that contractual rules should encourage performance by the parties wherever possible.[46] In the context of a seller's liability for

---

[39] C. Twigg-Flesner and R. Bradgate 'The EC Directive on certain Aspects of the sale of Consumer Goods and Associated Guarantees—All Talk and No Do?' (2000) *Web JCLI* at 4.

[40] The Vienna Convention was described by the HL Select Committee, *Tenth Report* § 83 as 'an effective marriage of the common law and the civil law.' See also Schlectriem, *op. cit.* n. 38, 5.

[41] Art. 2(2) and see below, pp. 591–604.

[42] 1999 Directive, art. 2(2)(d) and see below, pp. 509–601.

[43] See Arts. 2(3), 3(3) and 3(5). The *ord.* of 17 Feb. 2005 avoids using 'reasonableness' and replaces it with other expressions: below, pp. 595, 599, 602, 617. One should note, however, that the concept of 'disproportionality' is also used, a concept borrowed by EU law from German public law and put to much wider use. Moreover, some civil lawyers are content to see 'reasonableness' as an expression of the principle of good faith: M. Bianca, 'Article 3 Rights of the Consumer' in Bianca and Grundmann, *EU Sales Directive*, 151 at 169.

[44] F. Giardini, 'La conservazione del contratto et l'impostazione essenzialmente civilistica del legislatore comunitario nella direttiva 99/44/CE. Profili di comparazione giuridica' in Università degli Studi di Padova, *L'attuazione della Direttiva 99/44/CE in Italia e in Europa* (2002), 205; S. Whittaker 'I problemi posti dal recepimento della direttiva 1999/44/CE del 25 maggio 1999, concernente taluni aspetti della vendita di beni di consume et delle garanzie ad essi relative. Prospettive del diritto inglesi' ibid., 293 at 299; Bianca, *op. cit.* n. 43, 168; Zimmermann, *Liability for Non-Conformity*, 32–4.

[45] Below, p. 604 *et. seq.*

[46] Bianca, *op. cit.* n.43, 151 at 168 (referring to 'the principle of the conservation of the contract'). For German law, this was given effect by providing in general that an injured party must *prima facie* sue for performance rather than for a substitute for performance and in the institution of *Nachfrist*: Treitel,

defects in the property, the Directive's infusion with this idea is all the more striking given that here the Romanist tradition (as clearly seen in articles 1641 *et seq.* of the French Civil Code) treated the seller's liability for failures in function or quality differently, seeing their primary consequences as being the rescission of the contract or a reduction in the price, at the option of the buyer:[47] but these rights are placed by the Directive at the second level of remedial response.[48] For the common law, by contrast, the principle of the binding force of contracts has not been seen as a reason either for holding that specific enforcement of contractual obligations should generally be available or that the law should seek to find ways of allowing a party in default to have a second chance to perform. Quite the contrary, the primary remedy for breach of contract is said to be an award of damages and the injured party to a sufficiently major breach of contract (which is expressly defined to include the breaches of a seller's obligations concerning the quality and fitness for purpose of goods sold) has a right to terminate the contract and recover the price.[49] For the common lawyer, the buyer has the right to get out of the transaction and the right (and even the 'duty') to obtain a *substitute* performance elsewhere: there is little sense in which the seller has a right to perform.[50]

Fourthly, there is a discernible impact on the terms of the 1999 Directive of commercial practice. While the idea of a 'European Guarantee' applicable in principle to all goods purchased in the EU by consumers had earlier been abandoned,[51] one can still see its influence in the shape of the 1999 Directive's provisions on the 'legal guarantee' (which creates rights in consumers by law)[52] as opposed to its provisions on 'commercial guarantees' (provided by the seller or manufacturer and which must be 'binding').[53] While the Commission has stated that the Directive's failure to require a right in a buyer to damages reflected the requirements of subsidiarity,[54] its selection of the 'minimum rights' for consumers also reflect commercial practice, as most *manufacturers'* free guarantees are limited to the recognition of rights of replacement, return or repair of goods and do not include compensation for any loss caused by goods' failures in quality,[55] though they do not, as does the Directive, usually provide for any right of rescission at least as such.[56] The influence of commercial practice in relation to manufacturers' guarantees may also be seen in the 1999 Directive's requirement that

Remedies, 48, 51–3. For French law, this position can be seen most clearly in its treatment of *remplacement judiciaire* under art. 1144 C. civ. and *résolution judiciaire* under art. 1184 C. civ.: see S. Whittaker, 'Performance of another's obligation: French and English law contrasted' in D. Johnston and R. Zimmermann (eds.) *Unjustified Enrichment, Key Issues in Comparative Perspective* (CUP, 2002) 433. See above, p. 80.

[47] Above, p. 79. Originally, damages were available only where the seller *knew* of the defect: art. 1645 C. civ. and above, pp. 84–5.   [48] Below, p. 606.

[49] Above, pp. 250–1.

[50] This 'duty' arises under the law of mitigation of damage: see further S. Whittaker, 'Performance of another's obligation: French and English law contrasted' in D. Johnston and R. Zimmermann (eds.) *Unjustified Enrichment, Key Issues in Comparative Perspective* (CUP, 2002) 433. A qualification of uncertain ambit on this position exists in cases where a seller of goods may *re-tender* conforming goods: above, p. 251 n. 225.

[51] Above, p. 565.   [52] Arts. 2 to 5.   [53] Art. 6.   [54] Above, p. 566.

[55] This is even apparent in the definition of 'guarantee' in the 1999 Directive, art. 1(2). On manufacturers' guarantees, see above, pp. 98, 264–5 and below, pp. 624–5.

[56] Sellers' or manufacturers' guarantees do sometimes provide for the return of the price on return of the defective goods.

its 'legal guarantee' must cover any lack of conformity in new goods which becomes apparent within two years from the date of delivery.[57] This mirroring of commercial practice in its own 'uniform minimum level of consumer protection' rings true with the Directive's declared purpose of encouraging consumer confidence, the Directive requiring the laws of Member States to conform to commercial best practices.[58]

(c) The imposition of 'liability' and its remedial expression

The Product Liability Directive is concerned only with the imposition of liability in damages for harm caused by defective products (and not even harm to products caused by their own defect),[59] whereas the Consumer Guarantees Directive is concerned with the provision of remedies of repair, replacement, price reduction or rescission of the contract as a result of the defectiveness of goods but not with damages. As will be seen, though, this difference in remedies can become blurred in two ways. The first relates to the way in which the 1999 Directive may be implemented, for its full integration into either the French or the English laws of sale would have an overspill impact on liability in damages, given that this remedy is already available in both systems to sanction qualitative defects.[60] The second blurring arises from the relationship in English law between the Directive's new remedies of repair and replacement of the goods and the established use of the law of damages to form the basis for repair or replacement by the buyer at the seller's expense.[61]

There is, moreover, a further difference between the 1985 and 1999 Directives as regards the consequences of a product's defect or goods' non-conformity, for while the 1985 Directive impacts only on the legal relationship of individual parties (the producer and the person suffering harm caused by the defective product), the 1999 Directive may give rise to intervention by a public authority or a consumer association under the EC Consumer Injunctions Directive of 1998, as failures to fulfil its obligations are included as 'Community infringements' where they harm the collective interests of consumers.[62] The omission of the supply of unsafe products within the meaning of the 1985 Directive from the Consumer Injunctions Directive at first seems odd, but is explicable on the basis that the 1985 Directive is not limited to the protection of consumers and is itself buttressed by successive directives on product safety.[63]

(d) Problems of integration within national laws

At the time of its promulgation, the 1985 Directive could be seen as the first European legislation dealing with cases traditionally seen as belonging to the private laws of

---

[57] Art. 5(1), below, p. 619. In the case of second-hand goods art. 7(1) § 2 provides that Member States may allow express provision in the contract to reduce this period to one year.

[58] Art. 5(2), which permits Member States to provide that a buyer must notify the seller of any lack of conformity within two months of its detection, may also be seen to reflect commercial practice in manufacturers' guarantees. Cf. art. 39(1) of the Vienna Convention (which requires a 'reasonable time').

[59] Above, pp. 502, 506.   [60] Below, pp. 575–6, 603.   [61] Below, pp. 611–12.

[62] Dir. 98/27/EC of the European Parliament and of the Council of 19 May 1998 on injunctions for the protection of consumers' interests; 1999 Directive, art. 10.

[63] Council Dir. 92/59/EEC of 29 June 1992 on general product safety, itself repealed and replaced by Dir. 2001/95/EC of the European Parliament and of the Council of 3 December 2001 on general product safety.

Member States.[64] On the other hand, while its implementation in national laws raised questions of fit with existing general bases of liability, whether provided by civil codes or common law, generally it did not compete with existing special provisions governing the very area which it intended to harmonise.[65] As a result, it could easily be seen as creating a new special basis of liability, distinct from the ordinary and general law. This was true of French law even though the 1985 Directive was implemented into French law by amendment of the Civil Code (rather than by special *loi*) and even though many French lawyers saw its special treatment *in parallel* to existing general bases of liability as objectionable.[66] Even less was there any problem of formal fit in implementing the 1985 Directive into English law, Part I of the Consumer Protection Act 1987 merely creating a further and special layer of supposedly strict liability for an area already criss-crossed with liabilities, some contractual and some tortious, but none dedicated to liability for products.[67]

By contrast, the 1999 Directive created much more of a problem of fit for both French and English law, given that in both systems a seller's liability for qualitative defects was already the subject of considerable dedicated regulation, itself closely related to other special areas of regulation. In the French context, as we have seen, there are two main bases of liability (under the *garantie légale* and for 'contractual non-conformity' of the property)[68] and these are related, on the one hand, to the general law's treatment of contractual non-performance and, on the other, to rules governing other contracts, such as hire and construction.[69] In implementing the 1999 Directive, should the French legislature replace the traditional distinction drawn by the law of sale? If so, how should the new law relate to these other areas? Should there be a mere implementation by amendment of the *Code de la consommation* or a true integration by major amendment of the Civil Code itself? As I shall explain, problems of regulatory fit meant that implementation of the 1999 Directive was seen in some quarters as threatening the coherence of the Civil Code. Problems of the substantive fit of the 1999 Directive into English law were also significantly larger (and more present in people's minds) than they had been as regards the 1985 Directive, though not as acutely as they were in France. As I shall explain, this was due in part to the substantive similarity of the 1999 Directive's basic concept of 'non-conformity' to existing provisions in section 14 of the Sale of Goods Act 1979 but also to the apparent preparedness of the UK government (here, the effective legislator[70]) to add a further layer to what one French jurist referred to as the 'juristic "mille-feuille"'.[71] However, the result is far from satisfactory.[72]

---

[64] Whittaker (1985), 233–4.

[65] The notable exception to this is found in the case of Spanish law, the Spanish legislature having adopted particular provisions for the compensation for harm suffered as the result of goods and services: General Law No. 26 of 19 July 1984 for the Protection of Consumers and Users, arts. 25-9. Cf. Case C-183/00, above, pp. 442–3.　　　　　　　　　　　　[66] Art. 1386-1 C. civ. *et seq.*; above, pp. 460–1.

[67] Above, pp. 469–70.　　　[68] Above, pp. 69–72.　　　[69] Above, pp. 70, 105–6, 110.

[70] Above, p. 584.

[71] O. Tournafond, 'De la transposition de la directive du 25 mai 1999 à la réforme du Code civil' (2002) D Chron. 2883, at p. 2885 (so describing the French position which the author advocated).

[72] Below, pp. 611–16.

3. Implementation in French Law: Wider Reform
on a European model?

The processes by which the 1999 Directive was implemented in French and English law demonstrate a shared concern for the preservation of the integrity of the law in the face of the interpolation into existing legislative patterns of new and to an extent alien concepts and techniques, but they also illustrate differences in the constitutional routes by which implementation is to be achieved and in the nature of the arguments which are adduced in these circumstances. In the case of the 1999 Directive, there is a contrast between a lively French juristic argument and a low-key and essentially technical English debate.

The French constitutional division of law making between Parliament and the executive means that at least the principles of any changes to private law must be contained in parliamentary *loi* rather administrative *règlement*[73] and certainly all those concerned with implementation in France of the 1999 Directive apparently assumed that it would be effected by *loi*. The likely involvement of Parliament led to a much greater sensitivity in the government to political opposition, a sensitivity which in fact led to a major reversal of its initial strategy.

The government's first thoughts for implementation of the 1999 Directive attracted considerable opposition and led to an interesting juristic argument, principally between two protagonists, Mlle Geneviève Viney and M. Olivier Tournafond.[74] Their fundamental disagreement turned on whether to use implementation of the Directive as an occasion for more general reform of the law of seller's liability in the Civil Code or whether merely to enact new provisions in the *Code de la consommation* for the benefit of consumer buyers, allowing them a choice of claiming instead on the basis of the existing law of contractual non-conformity or the *garantie légale*. While the more ambitious reform looked at first more likely as it was adopted by the

---

[73] Above, p. 452.

[74] The debate may be followed in the following: M. Trochu, 'Vente et garantie des biens de consommation: directive CE No. 1999–44 du 25 mai 1999' D 2000 Chron. 119; O. Tournafond, 'Remarques critiques sur la directive européenne du 25 mai 1999 relative à certains aspects de la vente et des garanties des biens de consommation' D 2000 Chron. 159; L. Grynbaum, 'La fusion de la garantie des vices cachés et de l'obligation de délivrance opérée par la directive du 25 mai 1999' *Cont., Conc., Cons.* (May, 2000) 4; A. Ghozi, 'La conformité' in D. Fenouillet and F. Labarthe (eds.) *Faut-il recodifier le droit de la consommation?* (Paris, 2002), 103; L. Leveneur, 'Les contrats de consommation et le droit européen' *Cont., Conc., Con.* (March, 2000), 1; R. Family, 'Erreur, non-conformité, vice caché: état des questions à l'heure de la transposition de la directive 25 mai 1999' *Cont., Conc., Cons.* (Apr., 2000), 4; G. Paisant and L. Leveneur, 'Quelle transposition pour la directive du 25 mai 1999 sur les garanties dans la vente de biens de consommation?' JCP 2002.I.135; G. Viney, 'Quel domaine assigner à la loi de transposition de la directive européenne sur la vente?' JCP 2002.I.158; D. Mainguy, 'Propos dissidents sur la transposition de la directive du 25 mai 1999 sur certains aspects de la vente et des garanties des biens de consommation' JCP 2002.I.183; O. Tournafond, 'De la transposition de la directive du 25 mai 1999 à la réforme du code civil' D 2002 Chron. 2883; G. Viney, 'Retour sur la transposition de la directive du 25 mai 1999' D 2002 Chron. 3162; P. Jourdain, 'Transposition de la directive sur la vente du 25 mai 1999: Ne pas manquer une occasion de progrès' D 2003 Chron. 4; D. Mazeaud, 'La parole est à la défense' D 2003 Chron. 6; O. Tournafond, 'Transposition de la directive de 1999 sur la garantie des consommateurs, Article de foi ou réalisme législatif' D 2003 Chron. 427.

report of the ministerially appointed working group, by the middle of 2003 it had become clear that the more limited approach would be preferred, possibly coupled with a light retouching of the Civil Code's provisions governing the infamous *bref délai*,[75] and this was eventually the upshot of the discussion, the Directive being implemented in this more limited way by an *ordonnance* of 17 February 2005, that is, by government decree under a special power granted by Parliament for this purpose.[76] However, the wide-ranging arguments adduced by the opposing camps have a wider resonance for the implementation of European legislation affecting private law and are worth exploring.

(a) The Working Group's proposals

In October 2000, the French Ministry of Justice appointed a working group to advise it on implementation of the 1999 Directive chaired by Mlle Geneviève Viney of the University of Paris Panthéon-Sorbonne and consisting of other distinguished law professors, senior judges, a member of the Bar and senior officials. It reported in May 2002, together with a draft bill.[77] Its proposals were ambitious, especially given that implementation was due in the same month as the Working Group reported. The fundamental idea was to adopt the 1999 Directive's central unitary basis of 'contractual non-conformity' for the law of sale generally, applying it to all physical property (whether movable or immovable) whatever the status of the parties to the contract (whether *professionnel* or consumer) and thereby fusing the existing laws of contractual non-conformity under the 'general law of contract' and liability for latent defects under the *garantie légale*. For this purpose, the Working Group proposed that the definition of conformity (if not its exact wording) found in the 1999 Directive should be adopted,[78] as should its presumption of the existence on delivery of any failures in conformity appearing in the six months following.[79]

On the other hand, the Working Group considered that the Directive's scheme was too restrictive of the buyer's rights and proposed instead to give all buyers an option to return the property and recover the price, as long as the *défaut* is not minor; to keep the property and return part of the price; or to claim repair or replacement of the property as long as this is possible and does not constitute too great a burden on the seller.[80] In addition, it proposed that liability in damages should be imposed on

---

[75] On which, see above, pp. 91–3.

[76] *Ord.* no. 2005-136 of 17 Feb. 2005 relative à la garantie de la conformité du bien au contrat due par le vendeur au consommateur ('*Ord.* of 17 February 2005'). The powers were granted by the *loi de simplification du droit* no. 2004-1343 of 9 Dec. 2004, art. 82 made under art. 38 of the Constitution of 1958.

[77] *Rapport général du groupe de travail sur l'intégration en droit français de la directive 1999-44 du Parlement européen et du Conseil du 25 mai 1999 sur certains aspects de la vente et des garanties des biens de consommation* (in three parts) ('Working Group, *Rapport général*') published with a draft *Exposé des motifs*, an *Avant-projet de loi sur la garantie de conformité due par le vendeur* ('*Avant-projet de loi*') and a *Projet de décret modifiant la partie réglementaire du code de la consommation*, May, 2002 at <http://www.justice.gouv.fr/publicat/RappGTIDF.htm>.

[78] 1999 Directive, art. 2; *Avant projet de loi*, proposed arts. 1641, 1641-1, 1641-2 C. civ.

[79] 1999 Directive, art. 5(3); *Avant projet de loi*, proposed art. 1641-4 C. civ.

[80] *Avant-projet de loi*, proposed arts. 1644, 1644-1, 1644-2 C. civ.

the basis of the new *défaut de conformité*: on *vendeurs professionnels* whether or not they knew of the *défaut* at the time of delivery; on other sellers only if they knew of it.[81] These proposals therefore echoed the established approach of the *garantie légale* rather more than the provisions of the Directive or the existing position under the 'general law', though the Working Group was careful not to restrict the protection of consumers and so run the risk of breach of the Directive.[82] Similarly, the proposed reform denied effect to any purported exclusion of any of these rights not merely as against consumer buyers (as required by the Directive), but as against *any* buyer who was unaware of the defect on delivery and was not in the 'same speciality' of business as the seller, again following here the *jurisprudence* on the *garantie légale*.[83]

Moreover, the Working Group refused to adopt the time provisions of the Directive or of existing French analyses and instead proposed that there should be a period of five years within which a buyer of movables must 'denounce' any *défaut de conformité*, this extending to ten years for immovable property or movable property incorporated into an immovable.[84] So, the 10-year or even 30-year prescription periods of the 'general law' of contractual non-conformity and the notorious *bref délai* of the *garantie légale* would all be swept away.

Apart from other particular provisions stemming from the Directive itself which were to be implemented by changes to the *Code de la consommation*,[85] the Working Group did not propose any wider changes. So, apart from contracts for the supply of consumer goods to be manufactured or produced which the Directive includes,[86] no changes were proposed for the laws governing other contracts, even in such related areas as construction and hire. The reform was to be applied to all contracts of sale, but as little beyond sale as possible.

(b) The areas of disagreement

However, the Working Group's proposals were opposed on a number of fronts. They were criticised by some consumer groups on the basis that they would reduce the protection to consumers by forbidding their recourse to the existing 'general law' or *garantie légale*;[87] by industrialists and small businesses who feared an increase in costs; and by jurists who echoed these criticisms and added a number of specifically juristic and legal cultural grounds. Professor Tournafond soon became the most outspoken juristic critic of the proposals,[88] and agreed to a request from the Fédération des Industries Electriques, Electroniques et de Communication (FIEEC) to compose an alternative bill implementing the 1999 Directive in a restrictive way by amendment of

---

[81] *Exposé des motifs*, 3 and *Avant-projet de loi*, proposed arts. 1645, 1646 C. civ.

[82] *Exposé des motifs*, 6.   [83] *Avant-projet de loi*, proposed art. 1643 C. civ. and see above, pp. 94–5.

[84] Ibid., proposed art. 1648.

[85] These related to its provisions on exclusion by choice of law and on 'commercial guarantees': *Exposé des motifs*, 3.   [86] 1999 Directive, art. 1(4); *Avant-projet de loi*, proposed art. 1791-1 C. civ.

[87] Viney, *op. cit.* n. 74, JCP 2002.I.158, 1498. The influential Union Fédérale des Consommateurs—Que Choisir? was one opponent.

[88] O. Tournafond, *op. cit.* n. 74, D 2000 Chron. 159; D 2002 Chron. 2883; D 2003 Chron. 427.

the *Code de la consommation*,[89] the Federation and other representatives of industry feeling that 'their point of view was being neither understood nor even listened to'.[90]

In the debate which ensued, we can identify five distinct areas of disagreement: on the nature of the Directive and the proper pattern of French codification; on the French legal tradition and the Europeanisation of private law; on the value and significance of the classic conceptual distinction between 'non-conformity' and 'latent defect'; on the proper role of freedom of contract as against a social view of contract; and on the practical consequences of either method of reform. Few stones were left unturned.

(i) The nature of the 1999 Directive and the pattern of French codification

Here, there were a number of strands. A first argument used by the Working Group's opponents focused on the nature of the 1999 Directive as an instrument of consumer protection and asserted that the 'natural place' for its implementation was therefore the *Code de la consommation* rather than the Civil Code, the home of the 'general law'.[91] True, Germany had implemented the Directive by amendment of the B.G.B., but then Germany has no consumer code![92] From this starting point, the argument developed in other directions. So, distinctly unconvincingly, it was said that the amendment of the Civil Code so as to extend the Directive's protection beyond consumers would make their protection 'less special', and in some sense, therefore, 'denied'[93] and it would render the *Code de la consommation* 'an empty shell'.[94]

But the Working Group's proposals were also attacked as being too modest. The more limited (and more convincing) version of this argument noticed that its proposals were restricted (more or less) to the law of sale, whereas the distinction between contractual non-conformity and liability for defects is found elsewhere, notably in the law of hire and construction: to leave these areas unchanged would create 'incoherence' in the Civil Code or 'contamination' as the new way of thinking leaked into other areas.[95] Here, then, we see an example of the now classic dilemma for Member States faced with a directive which selects a small but central area of private law for its regulatory attentions: does one introduce a disharmonious element of regulation or permit regulatory overspill?

---

[89] O. Tournafond in cooperation with the Fédération des Industries Electriques, Electroniques et de Communication (FIEEC), 'Proposition de transposition de la directive du 25 mai 1999 sur certains aspects de la vente et des garanties des biens de consommation' published at <http://www.fieec.fr/>. This *proposition* reflected a general policy of restricting the ambit of liability whenever possible, this being reflected in the exercise of the options granted by the 1999 Directive.

[90] Tournafond, *op. cit.* n. 74, D 2002 Chron. 2883 at 2885, n. 18. The bodies included the Mouvement des Enterprises de France (MEDEF), the Chambre de Commerce et d'Industrie de Paris (CCIP) and the Confédération Générale des Petites et Moyennes Entreprises (CGPME), all of which participated in discussions on Tournafond's *proposition*.

[91] Leveneur, *op. cit.* n. 74; Paisant and Leveneur, *op. cit.* n. 74, 925; Tournafond, *op. cit.* n. 74, D 2002 Chron. 2883.

[92] Tournafond, *op. cit.* n. 74, D 2002 Chron. 2883. For the German reforms, see Zimmermann, *Liability for Non-Conformity*, 28 *et seq.*

[93] Paisant and Leveneur, *op. cit.* n. 74, 924. Cf. Mazeaud, *op. cit.* n. 74, 7 who is unconvinced by this argument.   [94] Tournafond, *op. cit.* n. 74, D 2003 Chron. 427 at 428.

[95] Tournafond, *op. cit.* n. 74, D 2002 Chron. 2883 at 2885, 2886.

A broader version of this sort of criticism was made by Tournafond, who attacked the proposals for failing properly to address the need for wider reform of the law of obligations, which he saw in terms of a 'crisis' in the law of contract and the 'torment' of the law of delict.[96] In his view, the Civil Code should be restored to the purity of its original purposes, leaving special regulation to the specialised codes, in the context, the *Code de commerce* and *Code de la consommation*. Of course, implicit in this argument was a sense that such an overhaul of the Civil Code could not be achieved within the time allotted for implementation of the 1999 Directive, which should instead be achieved by amendment of the *Code de la consommation*, and so leave sleeping 'the demons of reform of the law of sale at any price which showed themselves in 1985 on the occasion of the implementation of the product liability directive and which ended up by provoking the condemnation of France for breach of its obligations under this directive'.[97]

(ii) The French legal tradition and the Europeanisation of private law

The protagonists' attitudes to established French legal ways and the harmonisation of European private law were also very different.

The opponents of the proposed reform were accused of regarding as sacred the Code's venerable provisions governing the *garantie légale*[98] and of wishing to retain the distinction between liability for 'contractual non-conformity' and for latent defects out of sentiment.[99] While they denied these accusations,[100] the two sides do appear to have differed on whether French law, and especially the Civil Code itself, should be amended so as to reflect changing social needs or whether it should rather be preserved or perhaps even restored so as to reflect the central liberal values which it first enshrined.[101]

A similar contrast between a spirit of reform and of tradition may be seen in the extent to which French law was seen as standing to benefit from European developments, whether as represented specifically by the 1999 Directive, or at a more general level by the future results of those working towards a European Civil Code. At the specific level, the Working Group's basic assumption was that at least the fundamental and unified basis of liability adopted by the 1999 Directive provided the right model for the French law of sale more generally, even if some of its other aspects required improvement.[102] For its critics, the 1999 Directive should not be used beyond the cases where France was obliged to do so, since its unified treatment, which was itself borrowed from the Vienna Convention on *international* sales of goods, was no more appropriate as a basis for liability in sales in general than it was for consumer sales, as the rights which it provides for buyers are too restrictive.[103]

---

[96] Tournafond, *op. cit.* n. 74, D 2002 Chron. 2883, at 2889.
[97] Paisant and Leveneur, *op. cit.* n. 74, 925.   [98] Viney, *op. cit.* n. 74, JCP 2002.I.158, 1500.
[99] Jourdain, *op. cit.* n. 74, 5.   [100] Tournafond, *op. cit.* n. 74, D 2002 Chron. 2883 at 2886.
[101] Above, p. 21.   [102] See above, pp. 575–6 concerning time limits and the rights of the buyer.
[103] Mainguy, *op. cit.* n. 74, 2111–2. For Viney, the relationship with the Vienna Convention's provisions was advantageous as the Working Group's proposals would therefore allow a *rapprochement* between domestic and international sales: *op. cit.* n. 74, JCP 2002.I.158 at 1498; Tournafond, *op. cit.* n. 74, D Chron. 159, 161.

Moreover, the Directive is 'essentially impregnated with woolly concepts foreign to our legal tradition',[104] these concepts being perceptibly 'Anglo-American'.[105]

At a more general level, very different attitudes to the wider developments of European private law were revealed. Some of those opposed to the Working Group's proposed reform clearly saw it as an example of the sort of creeping Europeanisation which must be resisted so as to preserve French legal culture. So, while Mainguy accepted that the Civil Code was not untouchable, this:

does not mean that one ought to change its soul at any moment on the ground that salvation should come from a foreign rule. Let us keep ourselves from these phenomena of juristic acculturation which would wish that any grafted foreign solution should be held up as the paragon of modern legislative technique!... If... the virtues of French law should not be exaggerated, nor should those of Community law.[106]

There is more than a little suggestion here of the antipathy to European harmonisation of private law which can be seen in full flood in some French juristic reactions to Professor Von Bar's Study Group on a European Civil Code.[107] However, those who opposed the Working Group's proposals did so also on the basis that hasty changes should not be made to the Civil Code while much broader European developments were in the pipeline: the French legislator should wait and see their outcome before doing more than is required by the 1999 Directive.[108]

Here, Viney took opposite positions on both fronts. First, in her view, French lawyers should:

adopt an open attitude and display modesty. Let us not believe that we have, by a sort of right of seniority and for eternity, the best Civil Code in the world, even if this Code was, at the time of its promulgation a very fine work of which we are legitimately proud. Let us admit that at the time when it is about to attain its bicentennial, that it is no insult to the Code to examine whether it should not be reviewed with a view to taking into account the changes which have taken place in the relations between parties to contracts.[109]

Secondly, the French legislator should not hang fire waiting for further European harmonisation, but should rather join in the movement, retaining what is good but abandoning local perculiarities.[110]

This aspect of the debate about the Working Group's proposals reflects, therefore, two very different attitudes to the desirability of a wider impact of European law on French private law. Should one fight one's legal cultural corner and attempt to marginalise

---

[104] Tournafond, *op. cit.* n. 74, D 2000 Chron. 159.

[105] Grynbaum, *op. cit.* n. 74, 6 (who nevertheless supported the Working Group's proposals).

[106] *Op. cit.* n. 74, 2111. Cf. Ghozi, *op. cit.* n. 74, 105 who refers to the proposals as 'exploiting the necessity of implementation to slip in surreptiously the elements of a European Civil Code destined to replace in part the present *Code civil*'.

[107] Y. Lequette, 'Quelques remarques à propos du projet de code civil européen de M. von Bar' D 2002 Chron. 2202; Cf. P. Malinvaud, 'Réponse—hors délai—à la Commission européenne: à propos d'un code européen des contrats', D 2002 Chron. 2542.

[108] Paisant and Leveneur, *op. cit.* n. 74, 924, referring to the Communication of the Commission to the Council and European Parliament on European Contract Law, Com (11 Jul. 2001) 398 final.

[109] Viney, *op. cit.* n. 74, JCP 2002.I.158, 1501.   [110] Ibid.

the impact of any European legislation which happens to be enacted? Or rather, use the implementation of such European legislation as arises as an opportunity to keep French private law under review so that it can play a proper part in any future wider European developments? For no future European legislator will be impressed by a system of law which retains bad rules out of tradition or sentiment. Without some change, French law may lose its authority at the table of juristic Europe.

(iii) Conceptual distinctions and their technical attributes

But were the existing rules bad? Given that the Working Party had proposed 'improvements' to the 1999 Directive's approach to the relationship between buyers' rights and the period within which a claim must be brought,[111] the focus of the French debate centred firmly on the basis of liability.

For the Working Group itself, the abolition of the distinction between contractual non-conformity and latent defects was the central advantage of their proposed reforms.[112] This distinction had been the subject of sterile doctrinal controversy[113] and judicial manipulation, and had caused much wasteful litigation.[114] The creation of a unified basis of liability founded on the Directive's definition of 'non-conformity' would lead to far greater simplicity from the point of view of the users of the law themselves and this was more important than juristic dogma. 'Rather than the artificiality of a garden *à la française*, one should prefer a garden *à l'européen*, variegated and bushy, mixing up the two actions which are claimed to be essentially different'.[115]

Those opposed to the proposals responded to this in three ways. First, for them, there is a 'very real conceptual difference' between contractual non-conformity and latent defect',[116] between doing something other than what was stipulated and doing something badly, between *aliud* and *pejus*.[117] Moreover, the classic *obligation de conformité* is intimately linked to the very subject matter of the contract, its *objet*,[118] and therefore rightly forms part of the 'general law' of contractual obligation. On the other hand, liability for latent defects has always been special as it is concerned not with the difference between what a buyer orders and what is delivered, but rather with an '*anomolie*' which renders the thing sold unfit for normal use.[119] For its opponents, it was the members of the Working Group who were being dogmatic, preferring an elegant, unitary regime to a more diverse but practical one.[120] Secondly, the fact that the classic distinction has proved difficult to draw does not mean that it should be jettisoned: the law is replete with difficult but necessary distinctions.[121] Indeed,

---

[111] Above, pp. 575–6.   [112] *Rapport général, Exposé des motifs*, 2.

[113] Jourdain, *op. cit.* n. 74, 5.

[114] *Rapport général, Exposé des motifs*, 2; Viney, *op. cit.* n. 74, D 2002 Chron. 3162; Mazeaud, *op. cit.* n. 74, 7.   [115] Grynbaum, *op. cit.* n. 74, 7.

[116] Tournafond, *op. cit.* n. 74, D 2002 Chron. 2883 at 2884 ('*cette différence conceptuelle bien réelle*')

[117] Ibid. and see also Ghozi, *op. cit.* n. 74, 110–11.   [118] Ghozi, *op. cit.* n. 74, 107.

[119] Paisant and Leveneur, *op. cit.* n. 74, 924.

[120] Tournafond, *op. cit.* n. 74, D 2002 Chron. 2883, p. 2885. Tournafond later observed that 'this dogmatic way of thinking . . . reminds one of enlightened despotism and, as formerly with the Jacobins, it is dedicated to a cult of abstract reason': *op. cit.* n. 74, D 2003 Chron. 427.

[121] Paisant and Leveneur, *op. cit.* n. 74, 924.

problems with the distinction arose in practice only when courts were persuaded to attempt to assimilate the two concepts in order to avoid the *bref délai*:[122] but if the problem is the *bref délai*, *this* should be reformed, rather than tearing up the distinction.[123] Thirdly, the existing rules applicable to *obligations de conformité* and to the *garantie légale* differ for good reasons. In particular, *force majeure* applies to the former but not the latter: this difference is justified as a seller who fails to deliver or who delivers late *ought* to be excused where performance has become impossible; whereas the whole point of a *garantie* is that impossibility is no excuse.[124]

While Viney countered that such technical differences were not justified either as a matter of logic or fairness and it was therefore right for them to be swept away,[125] this last argument about the role of *force majeure* merits further attention. The 1999 Directive itself describes the seller's 'obligation of conformity' so as to include cases where different quantities or types of goods are delivered, and not merely where the stipulated goods are in the wrong condition,[126] and creates rights in consumers to demand proper performance of the seller's 'obligation of conformity', though only after the seller has had an unsuccessful first go.[127] What the opponents of the French Working Group's proposals in effect noticed was that the extension of the framework of the Directive to *all* sales would mean that these basic obligations of performance of sellers would be subject to the same strictness of regime of liability with no defence of *force majeure* as is provided for the limited 'liabilities' required by the Directive itself for consumer buyers: the extension is to all sales and would include liability in damages. But why should the seller's obligation to deliver the property as stipulated be treated differently from other contractual obligations? In this light, Tournafond's accusation that the Working Group's proposals strike at the logical underpinning of the French law of obligations looks less exaggerated.[128]

(iv) Freedom of contract or social solidarity?

A further important area of disagreement lay in the implications of the Working Group's proposed reform for freedom of contract. For its opponents, the reform's extension of the 1999 Directive's protective rules to non-consumer buyers compromised freedom of contract in an unjustified way, being based on the false assumption that all buyers are at a disadvantage and require protection,[129] whereas all French businesses want is freedom of contract![130] In Tournafond's view, '[s]ocial solidarity does not justify...the introduction into the Civil Code of *dirigiste* rules of protection',[131] especially given that French courts already have a number of techniques at their disposal for intervening in bargains.[132] It is no answer to say (as do the supporters of the Working Group's

---

[122] Ghozi, *op. cit.* n. 74, 110, who noted that since 1993 the *jurisprudence* had stabilised and see above, pp. 69–72. [123] Tournafond, *op. cit.* n. 74, D 2003 Chron. 427.

[124] Tournafond, *op. cit.* n. 74, D 2002 Chron. 2883, 2887.

[125] *Op. cit.* n. 74, D 2002 Chron. 3162 at 3163. [126] Below, p. 593. [127] Below, p. 606.

[128] *Op. cit.* n. 74, D 2003 Chron. 427, 428.

[129] Tournafond, *op. cit.* n. 74, D 2002 Chron. 2883 at 2885; D 2003 Chron. 427 at 428.

[130] Ibid., at 429. [131] Ibid.

[132] Ibid. He cites the *théorie de la cause*; good faith; contractual interpretation; defects in consent and *quasi-contrats*.

proposals[133]) that freedom of contract is preserved because the new provisions would be subject to possible contrary exclusion where the parties were in the same line of business as this just shows the need for a distinct regime for business contracts.[134]

For the Working Group's supporters, this argument from the supposed equality of business parties reflected a 'visceral attachment' to freedom of contract, whereas in reality their freedom is usually one-sided.[135] Moreover, as a matter of contractual justice, *any* buyer should have the right to receive from his seller the property in conformity with what was agreed and with what would normally be expected for property of the same type: 'is this not the essence of a contract of sale?'[136] The existing law of the time already conformed to this pattern very considerably, whether as a matter of contractual *obligations de conformité,* the *garantie légale, erreur* or *obligations d'information.*[137] In all, while appeal to freedom of contract by the Working Group's opponents had a distinctly hollow ring, it nevertheless formed an evocative rallying-cry for the opponents of change.

(v) Practical consequences of the proposed reform

Both sides appealed to the practical consequences of the reform proposed by the Working Group. For its supporters, the creation of a unique basis of liability would simplify the law for the benefit of its users, getting rid of the existing 'extraordinary complexity' and helping to reduce unnecessary litigation.[138] For its opponents, the creation of a new set of remedies for consumer buyers would not be unduly complicated: it would just give them another option.[139] Moreover, the Working Group's proposals would increase costs for businesses by introducing new rights for buyers and would have a generally unsettling effect which any major legal change possesses on transactions.[140] In particular, many buyers may prefer the replacement of goods with minor defects which would then be left on their manufacturers' hands, being difficult to sell as second-hand.[141]

(c) The outcome of the arguments and the eventual implementing legislation

While the French government's first stance had apparently been in favour of wider reform as is reflected by its creation of the Working Group, which included representatives of the Ministry of Justice, the combination of legal arguments, technical difficulty and political pressure, both from consumer groups and business, led to a much more modest approach to implementation of the 1999 Directive.

---

[133] Mazeaud, *op. cit.* n. 74, D 2003 Chron. 7 at 8. Mazeaud is a well-known exponent of the 'solidarist' vision of contract: see esp. D. Mazeaud, 'Loyauté, solidarité, fraternité: la nouvelle devise contractuelle?' in *Mélanges en hommage à François Terré: L'avenir du droit* (PUF, Dalloz & Ed. Juris-Classeur, Paris, 1999) 603.

[134] Tournafond, *op. cit.* n. 74, D 2002 Chron. 2883 at 2885.

[135] Mazeaud, *op. cit.* n. 74, D 2003 Chron. 7 at 8.

[136] Viney, *op. cit.* n. 74, JCP 2002.I.158 at 1500.   [137] Above, pp. 64–72.

[138] Viney, *op. cit.* n. 74, JCP 2002.I.158 at 1499; Jourdain, *op. cit.* n. 74, 5.

[139] Tournafond, *op. cit.* n. 74, D 2002 Chron. 2883 at 2886.

[140] Mainguy, *op. cit.* n. 74, 2111–12.   [141] Tournafond, *op. cit.* n. 74, D 2000 Chron. 159, 160.

Such a development had been half predicted by Jourdain, one of the supporters of the Working Group's proposals, who had set out an alternative 'modest' reform in addition to changing the *Code de la consommation* if the wider reforms failed for lack of political will.[142] He suggested changing the Civil Code so as to harmonise the rules on exemption clauses and on periods within which a buyer must sue, which would have the advantage of reducing the significance of the distinction between contractual non-conformity and latent defect, even though it would be maintained.[143]

However, it was a more modest approach to reform which was eventually adopted. The first clear sign of this was the publication in June 2004 by the French government of a *projet de loi* which provided for implementation of the 1999 Directive by the insertion of new provisions into the *Code de la consommation*[144] and while this *projet de loi* was not carried into law, this minimalist approach was also later taken on the Directive's final implementation by the *ordonnance* of 17 February 2005.[145] So, unlike the Working Group's proposals, the final legislation did not extend the range of contracts covered by the new provisions, did not change the hierarchy of rights available to the buyer under article 3 of the Directive, and preserved the buyer's existing rights under the Civil Code, whether under the *garantie légale* or any other contractual or extra-contractual basis.[146] On the other hand, one potentially significant reform did survive from earlier proposals, for the *ordonnance* replaced the *bref délai* of the *garantie légale* with a period of two years from the discovery of the defect.[147] While this last change is likely to be generally welcomed by French private lawyers, its amendment of an original provision of the Civil Code by *ordonnance* will certainly raise eyebrows.[148]

4. English Law: Implementation but Semi-integration

Implementation of the 1999 Directive into English law did not cause the kind of juristic or political argument which occurred in France. While the English process may, therefore, lack the rhetoric or the passion of the French, it nevertheless reveals some general points as to implementation of Directives into English private law.

---

[142] Jourdain, *op. cit.* n. 74, at 5–6.   [143] Ibid.

[144] *Projet de loi relative à la garantie de la conformité du bien au contrat due par le vendeur au consommateur et à la responsabilité du fait des produits défectueux* (16 Jun. 2004) Sén. no. 238, arts. 1–3 ('*projet de loi* of 2004'). Arts. 4–6 of the *projet de loi* proposed amendments to the Civil Code in response to the ECJ's decision in Case C-52/00, *Commission v France*, above, pp. 440–4. This was later effected by the *loi de simplification du droit* no. 2004-1343 of 9 Dec. 2004, art. 29, above, pp. 458–60.

[145] *Ord.* No. 2005-136 of 17 Feb. 2005 *relative à la garantie de la conformité du bien au contrat due par le vendeur au consommateur* ('*ordonnance* of 17 Feb. 2005').

[146] *Ord.* of 17 Feb. 2005, art. 1, creating new arts. L. 211-09–211-11, 211-13 C. consom.

[147] Ibid., art. 3, amending art. 1648 C. civ.

[148] There is, indeed, an argument for saying that the *ordonnance*'s amendment of art. 1648 C. civ. went beyond the powers entrusted to the government under the *loi de simplification du droit* n° 2004-1343 of 9 Dec. 2004, art. 82 which provides for the enactment of legislation necessary for implementation of the 1999 Directive '*ainsi que les mesures d'adaptation de la législation liées à cette transposition.*' Clearly amendment of the general time period governing liability under the *garantie légale* was not necessary for implementation of the Directive, though it could be argued that it was included within the category of 'measures

(a) The constitutional role of government in implementation of the Directive

Unlike France, legislation in the UK is either itself parliamentary or is made under powers created by Parliament.[149] As regards the introduction of EU law into the UK, section 2(2) of the European Communities Act 1972 provides that the designated minister has the power to make provision by regulation to give effect to Community obligations or rights and 'for the purpose of dealing with matters arising out of or related to any [Community] obligation or rights',[150] even if this includes the amendment of parliamentary statute. This means that in many situations it is in practice the government rather than Parliament which decides on the form and the substance of the implementation of EU directives, and work done in preparation for this is essentially undertaken within government after consultation with interested parties. For while any implementing regulations must be laid before Parliament,[151] the latter has no power of amendment and may only veto them in toto, something which is very rarely done by either House.[152] Reflecting this, the Joint Select Committee on Statutory Instruments, which scrutinises regulations made under the 1972 Act, draws the attention of the Houses to their deficiencies only on grounds which do not impinge on their merits or on the policy behind them.[153]

These features of the process of implementation of EU law were fully reflected as regards the 1999 Directive. The relevant ministry, the Department of Trade and Industry ('Dti') had made clear its general substantive policy of implementation while the Directive was still in draft, declaring that it would ensure that existing consumer protection would not be reduced,[154] a policy adopted under a Conservative government and continued under the Labour government which took office in May 1997. Throughout the subsequent consultative process this general governmental policy was an underlying given, there being no mechanism by which it could be challenged at a political level outside government.

This central policy had an important effect on the manner in which the 1999 Directive was implemented in English law, for it necessarily led to the retention of remedies available to consumer buyers under the existing law in parallel to the creation of the new rights required by the Directive itself. In particular, the two rights of termination of the contract (rejection and termination of the goods under the existing

---

to adapt legislation related to this implementation'. However, once ratified by Parliament by *loi de ratifica-tion*, an *ordonnance* acquires the status of *loi* itself and may not in general be reviewed: Chapus, *Droit administatif général*, Tome 1, 665–74 esp. at 671.

[149] There is a very small exception as regards the law-making power of chartered corporations, on which see S. Whittaker, 'Public and Private Law-making: Subordinate Legislation, Contracts and the Status of "Student Rules", (2001) 21 *OJLS* 103. For the French position, see above, pp. 307, 453.

[150] European Communities Act 1972, s. 2(2)(b).

[151] Under the European Communities Act 1972, Sch. 2 § 2 the Minister may opt whether to use the 'positive' or 'negative' procedures.

[152] A. W. Bradley and K.D. Ewing, *Constitutional and Administrative Law* (Pearson, London, 13th. edn., 2000), 657–8 (noting the exception where the parent statute otherwise provides), who observe that this is in part because members have found it impossible in recent years to obtain time to debate such a 'prayer for annulment' of statutory instruments.

[153] House of Commons Standing Orders 151(1) *in fine*.

[154] HL Select Committee, *Tenth Report*, § 66.

law and 'rescission' under the 1999 Directive) could not be amalgamated since this would have reduced a consumer buyer's protection in *some* situations under one or the other. On the other hand, the Dti wished to ensure that any changes fitted into the broader pattern of UK legislation governing contracts and so changes were made for contracts other than those governed by the Directive, presumably on the basis that these concerned 'matters arising out of or related to' the Directive's requirements.[155]

The implementing statutory instrument which resulted, the Sale and Supply of Goods to Consumers Regulations 2002, was laid before Parliament on 11 December 2002[156] and considered by the Joint Committee on Statutory Instruments in January 2003. While the Committee saw a defect in their drafting as regards the relationship of the new consumer remedies of repair and replacement,[157] the Dti disagreed and held to its own view.[158] Despite the Committee considering the Dti 'mistaken', and its drawing the 'special attention' of both Houses to the relevant provisions of regulations, the Regulations came into force unchanged at the end of March 2003.

(b) The consultative process and the technique of implementation

What has just been said should not be taken to imply a lack of consultation of interested parties before implementation of the 1999 Directive was undertaken. Even while the 1999 Directive was in draft, the House of Lords Select Committee on the European Communities investigated its implications and this work was clearly later useful to the Dti.[159] After adoption of the Directive, the Dti started a process of wide, if very rapid, consultation. So, a first consultation paper was issued in January 2001 drawing attention to the various options available under the Directive, and asking for views on these, on more technical legal matters, and information as to the estimated cost of its impact on businesses, all representations being required within three months.[160] A second round of consultation together with a draft set of regulations intended to implement the Directive took place in early 2002.[161] Following general 'Obligatory Consultation Criteria',[162] these consultation processes involved the soliciting of views from relevant interested parties (including consumers' groups, legal academics, representatives of the legal profession, and representatives of industry and retailers) and more generally via the Dti's website. The second round of consultation recorded the views which had already been expressed and made them available on request.

In looking at this process, a major contrast with its French counterpart is that there was general support for the restricted way in which the Dti proposed to implement the 1999 Directive, any disagreements tending to be based on misunderstandings of

---

[155] European Communities Act 1972, s. 2(2)(b), above, p. 584.   [156] SI 2002 No. 3045.

[157] Joint Committee on Statutory Instruments, *Ninth Report* (12 February 2003) §§ 11–15.

[158] Ibid., Appendix 4.   [159] HL Select Committee, *Tenth Report*.

[160] Dti, *EC Directive 1999/44/EC on certain aspects of the sale of consumer goods and associated guarantees, Consultation Paper* and *Regulatory Impact Assessment* (January 2001) (Dti, '*First Consultation*').

[161] Dti, Consumer Affairs Directorate, *Sale of Goods Directive*, Second Consultation (March 2002) (Dti, '*Second Consultation*') and see Dti, *Directive 1999/44/EC on certain aspects of the sale of consumer goods and associated guarantees: summary of responses to the consultation of 2002* (June, 2002).

[162] See <http://www.cabinet-office.gov.uk/servicefirst/index/consultation.htm>.

the existing position under the Sale of Goods Act 1979.[163] Instead, one can see three types of points being made.

First, there was considerable detailed, technical discussion of the way in which the provisions of the Directive compared or contrasted with existing rules of English law. So, for example, it was noticed that the definition of 'consumer' under the Directive differed slightly from that used by the Directive on unfair terms in consumer contracts of 1993, this being faithfully reflected in the UK implementing regulations:[164] was there any substantive difference and was a consistent approach preferable?[165] Similarly, while the criteria of contractual non-conformity were very similar to the formulations used by the implied terms set out in section 14 of the Sale of Goods Act 1979, there were a number of small differences: again, were these differences of substance?[166]

Secondly, views were expressed as to the way in which or the extent to which implementation of the 1999 Directive could be fitted into existing primary legislation. There had been criticism of the Dti's implementation of the Unfair Terms in Consumer Contracts Directive which was undertaken by the creation of a free-standing and additional layer of regulation,[167] distinct from both the common law and from the Unfair Contract Terms Act 1977, criticism which had been accepted to the extent that the Department commissioned research into whether and how the two legislative layers could be amalgamated to create a unified system for the control.[168] Echoing earlier comments made before the House of Lords Select Committee, there was considerable support for the substantive integration of the new rights for consumers into the structure of the Sale of Goods Act and, indeed, for ensuring that the new rights were introduced for closely related contracts, such as hire-purchase.[169] It was generally accepted that the 1999 Directive could not form the basis of a free-standing regime of protection for consumer buyers by simple 'copy-out' in a new set of regulations, as its remedial scope was limited, omitting to impose liability in damages. Nor had English law a Consumer Code into which such a new set of rules could be inserted. And given the absence of a tradition in English law for the treatment of the law of sale (as distinct from the law of sale of goods) as a unity,[170] the question whether the fundamental concepts of the Directive should be used as the basis of a wider reform of the law governing sales of immovable property or incorporeal property simply was not posed.

It is noticeable, however, that English law was able much more easily than French law to integrate the central feature of 'contractual conformity' of the 1999 Directive

---

[163] Dti, *Second Consultation*, Part 5: Summary of Responses to the First Consultation, § 4.

[164] Dir. 93/13/EC, art. 2(b); Unfair Terms in Consumer Contracts Regulations 1999, SI 1999 No. 2083, r. 3(1).   [165] Dti, *First Consultation*, Part 4, Q1.

[166] Dti, *First Consultation*, Part 4, Q4–Q6 and see below, pp. 597–8, 600.

[167] Unfair Terms in Consumer Contracts Regulations 1994, SI 1994 No. 3159; F. Reynolds (1994) 111 *LQR* 1.

[168] The initial research for the Department was undertaken by the present author in 1999. In 2001, the Parliamentary Under Secretary of State for Consumers and Corporate Affairs referred this issue and other issues relating to the reform of unfair contract terms to the Law Commissions: see the Law Commission, *Unfair Terms in Contracts*, Law Com. No. 292 (2005).

[169] HL Select Committee, *Tenth Report* § 65 referring to Professor F. Reynolds' argument against the creation of 'two, or one and a half, consumer regimes'.   [170] Above, pp. 227–8.

into its existing legislation, since article 3 was sufficiently close to the content of the implied terms in the Sale of Goods Act for the latter (as somewhat amended) to form the basis of the new consumer rights.[171] But there could be no real integration of the Directive's provisions concerning the 'rights' of consumers into the existing law of sale of goods, given their fundamentally different perspectives and contents.[172] The English legislation therefore created a distinct remedial regime for consumer buyers parallel to the existing regimes under the Sale of Goods Act *and* at common law. Overall, therefore, the Directive's requirements are only semi-integrated into the English statutory frameworks, the resulting picture being complicated and, from the point of view of a consumer, highly confusing.[173] For some, implementation of the 1999 Directive provides one more reason why English law should divide its law of sale of goods, creating distinct commercial and consumer regimes.[174]

Thirdly, the Dti was concerned to investigate the cost of increased burdens to business, both generally and as regards the possible options on implementation. In this respect, it drew on a report commissioned by the European Commission on an earlier draft of the Directive by Wilhelm Consulting, which estimated the costs of its changes for different industry sectors.[175] The Dti also received estimates from the representatives of industrial and retail enterprises, which put the cost of implementation in the region of 3–5 per cent of turnover, though small businesses thought it would be 5–10 per cent of turnover.[176] The Dti considered that these figures were too high and itself put the likely increase at an average additional recurring cost of 0.25 per cent of consumer expenditure on durable and semi-durable goods and nil for non-durables.[177] According to the Dti's estimates, the total cost of the changes would 'equate to £265 m or just over £4 per person per year in the UK'.[178] Given its view of the figures, the government held to its position that implementation of the Directive should not off-set the cost of the consumer's new rights under the Directive by reducing their existing rights.

(c) 'Scissors and paste' rather than 'copy-out'

As I have said, the combination of the decision not to reduce existing consumer protection with the need to implement the 1999 Directive rendered only partial its integration into the English statutory frameworks. It is for this reason that the resulting 2002 Regulations do not make easy reading: indeed, they make no sense at all divorced from the host statutory provisions which they amend or supplement. While I shall look later in more detail at these provisions, at this stage it is useful to set out their three-fold legislative strategy.

The first and most important amendments were made to the Sale of Goods Act 1979. Here, the Regulations amended the factors to be taken into account in determining whether goods are of 'satisfactory quality', but only where the buyer

---

[171] This difference relates to the significance of express terms, see below, pp. 592, 593.
[172] Below, pp. 611–16.   [173] Below, p. 611.
[174] M. Bridge 'What is to be done about the sale of goods?' (2003) 119 *LQR* 173.
[175] Dti, *Second Consultation 2001* Part 4, Regulatory Impact Assessment, Section 2, §§ 34 *et seq.*
[176] Ibid., § 42.   [177] Ibid., § 36   [178] Ibid., § 41.

'deals as consumer',[179] and inserted a new Part 5A to provide for the Directive's 'additional rights of buyer in consumer cases'.[180] But as Bridge has observed, 'these additional remedial provisions [are] set out in a style that jars dreadfully with those provisions of the 1979 Act dating from 1893'.[181]

Secondly, the 2002 Regulations amended a number of other statutes so as to harmonise them with the changes made to the Sale of Goods Act. So, in the case of 'contracts under which goods are transferred to consumers' (i.e. contracts for the provision of goods and services) the relevant legislation was amended so as to harmonise their implied terms, to create a presumption of non-conformity within a period of six months from delivery and to create new remedies, all of these mirroring the provisions in the 1999 Directive.[182] Furthermore, the statutes governing contracts of hire and of hire-purchase of goods, neither of which were affected by the 1999 Directive, were amended so as to harmonise their implied terms as to the quality of the goods where the buyer 'deals as consumer', though no other changes were made either as to the grounds of liability nor as to the remedies.[183]

Thirdly, in making these substantive changes the 2002 Regulations adopted the language of 'dealing as consumer' used by the Unfair Contract Terms Act 1977[184] rather than the simpler 'consumer' used by the Directive, but they amended its definition for the benefit of 'individuals' so as to conform to the Directive's own definition of 'consumer'.[185] So, for example, while section 12(1)(c) of the 1977 Act generally prevents a person buying goods from 'dealing as consumer' where the goods are not 'of a type ordinarily supplied for private use or consumption', the Regulations inserted a new section 12(1A) which provides that this subsection 'must be ignored' where the buyer is an individual.[186] Section 12 was also amended so as to exclude sales of 'second-hand goods sold by public auction at which individuals have the opportunity of attending in person', a possibility expressly allowed by the Directive.[187] The overall substantive effect of these changes is the extension of the benefit of the Directive for individual business buyers contracting outside their normal range of dealings,[188] but their formal effect is the considerable complication of the statutory definition of 'dealing as consumer'. Here too, the Directive was only half-integrated into the existing statutory framework.

[179] 2002 Regulations, r. 3, new Sale of Goods Act 1979 ('1979 Act'), ss. 14 (2D), (2E) and (2F).

[180] 2002 Regulations, r. 5, new 1979 Act, ss. 48A–48E.   [181] *Op. cit.* n. 174, 176.

[182] 2002 Regulations, rr. 7, 9 amending s. 4 and inserting ss. 11M–11S, Supply of Goods and Services Act 1982. These changes may in part have been required by art. 1(4) of the 1999 Directive, though some contracts so referred to will constitute contracts of sale in English law: S. Watterson, 'Consumer Sales Directive 1999/44/EC—The impact on English law' (2001) *ERPL* 197, 200.

[183] 2002 Regulations, r. 10 amending Supply of Goods and Services Act 1982 s. 9; 2002 Regulations, r. 13 amending Supply of Goods and Services Act 1973 s. 10.

[184] S. 12. This follows from the substantive changes to Acts which themselves provide that '[r]eferences . . . to dealing as consumer are to be construed in accordance with Part I of the Unfair Contract Terms Act 1977': e.g. 1979 Act, s. 61(5A).

[185] The definition of 'consumer' found in 2002 Regulations r. 2 refers only to the free-stranding provision in r. 15 concerning the effectiveness of consumer guarantees. All other regulations take the form of amendments of or insertions into statutes and therefore are not strictly found 'in these Regulations'.

[186] 2002 Regulations, r. 14 (2).

[187] 2002 Regulations, r. 14 (4)(b); 1999 Directive, art. 1(3) (an aspect of 'consumer goods').

[188] This substantive effect stems from the interpretation given to 'dealing as consumer', above p. 253.

5. A Closer Look at the Consumer Guarantees Directive and its Relationship to French and English Law

I wish now to look more closely at the impact of the 1999 Directive on English and on French law, both in terms of what was required and what actually occurred. Some of these issues have already been touched on, forming part of the debates as to the way in which the Directive should be implemented in either system, but others have been less prominent. I shall start with the Directive's principal provisions concerning a seller's liability for non-conformity and then look at its provisions which concern those other than the parties to a contract of sale.

(a) Initial definitions

The 1999 Directive sets the scope of its principal provisions by defining the contracts to which it applies and the status of their parties.

First, the Directive is restricted to contracts of sale of consumer goods and 'contracts for the supply of consumer goods to be manufactured' which are 'deemed' to be contracts of sale of goods for the purpose of the Directive.[189] Article 1(2)(b) defines 'consumer goods' to mean:

any tangible movable item, with the exception of:

—goods sold by way of execution or otherwise by authority of law,
—water and gas where they are not put up for sale in a limited volume or set quantity,
—electricity.

So while the Directive refers to 'consumer goods', it is not restricted to those of a type ordinarily supplied for private use or consumption.[190] As a result, the Directive applies generally to physical movable property, though not to intangible property, such as patents or shares.[191] It does, however, expressly permit Member States to exclude from their implementing laws the sale of 'second-hand goods sold at public auction where consumers have the opportunity of attending the sale in person'.[192]

On the other hand, the Directive does not define what it means by 'contract of sale' or 'selling'. Given their importance, the European Court is likely to give these notions an autonomous significance for the purposes of the 1999 Directive. In this respect, it appears to use 'contracts of sale' in a classic sense of a contract under which property (here 'consumer goods') is transferred from one party (the seller) to another (the buyer) in return for money (the price),[193] rather than the sort of loose sense in which the phrase 'sale and supply' is used in the Unfair Terms in Consumer Contracts

---

[189] Art. 1(4). Cf. above, p. 588.
[190] Cf. Unfair Contract Terms Act 1977, s. 12(1)(c); 1985 Directive, art. 9(b).
[191] Cf. above, p. 477 for the position under the 1985 Directive.   [192] Art. 1(3).
[193] Cf. L. Serrano, 'Article 1 Scope and Definitions' in Bianca and Grundmann, *European Sales Directive*, 91 at 95.   [194] Dir. 93/13/EC, art. 1.

Directive to cover all consumer contracts.[194] This narrower meaning in the 1999 Directive is clear partly from its specific inclusion of contracts for the supply of goods to be manufactured,[195] and partly from the earlier rejection of a proposed amendment by the European Parliament aimed at including other contracts for the supply of goods, including hire-purchase and barter.[196] But if 'contracts of sale' must be interpreted autonomously, then so must the underlying notion of contract itself. As I have argued elsewhere, if the European Court were to construct an autonomous conception of contract for the purposes of a particular Directive, then some legal relations not treated as contractual by the domestic law of a Member State may have to be treated as contractual in European law.[197] However, such a development would appear to be of limited impact in the context of the 1999 Directive: first, because the rejection of an amendment to include within its scope supplies of goods in the course of a 'statutory activity' suggests their exclusion;[198] and secondly, owing to the Directive's express exclusion from 'consumer goods' of gas and water (other than in limited quantities) and electricity,[199] the legal nature of whose supply varies significantly under the domestic laws of the Member States.[200] Moreover, while other situations may be envisaged in which goods are supplied by 'businesses' in the sort of public context which may render their supply non-contractual (for example, the supply of medicines by a public hospital),[201] it would be difficult to say that these supplies were *sales*, rather than forming an element in a wider supply of services, to which the 1999 Directive does not apply. On the other hand, the public nature or ownership of a seller should not be thought in itself to exclude clear contracts of sale from the ambit of the Directive, for example, the sale of lost property by a police authority.

Secondly, the 1999 Directive defines the parties to the contracts of sale which it governs. So, a 'seller' is 'any natural or legal person who, under a contract, sells consumer goods in the course of his trade, business or profession'.[202] This definition is very similar to others used by more recent consumer protection Directives, but one minor difference may be significant in relation to the question whether a person in business making a contract which does not form a regular part of his business 'acts in the course of his trade business or profession', a question on which the English and French domestic laws have differed.[203] It has been suggested that the 1999 Directive's use of the possessive ('in the course of *his* trade, business or profession') suggests

---

[195] Art. 1(4).

[196] OJ 6 April 1998, C-104/30 at 33 (amendment 13). The exclusion of contracts for the sale of goods 'sold by way of execution or otherwise by authority of law' can be explained by the presence of such a provision in art. 2(c) of the Vienna Convention and in the existing laws of some Member States, including French law: art. 1649 C. civ.

[197] S. Whittaker, 'Unfair Contract Terms, Public Services and the Construction of a European Conception of Contract' (2000) 116 *LQR* 95.

[198] OJ 6 April 1998, C-104/30 at 33 (amendment 13). Cf. Dir. 93/13/EC art. 2(c) which refers to a 'seller or supplier' 'whether publicly owned or privately owned'.

[199] 1999 Directive, art. 2(b). Cf. Vienna Convention, art. 2(f) which excludes sales of electricity.

[200] H. Hall and C. Tixador (eds.) *Rapport sur l'application de la directive 93/13 concernant les clauses abusives conclus avec les consommateurs aux prestations de service public* (1997), sections 1, 2 and 5. For French law and English law, see above, pp. 136–9, 276–9 respectively.

[201] See, e.g. above, pp. 145–6 (French law); pp. 291–2 (English law).   [202] Art. 1(2)(d).

[203] In French law, *vendeur professionnel* has been interpreted to require such a connection with the business of the seller, in English law not: above, p. 85 and pp. 236–7.

the narrower interpretation, requiring a degree of connection with the business in question.[204] The 1999 Directive does not refer to the recipient of its protections as a 'buyer', but rather as a 'consumer', defined using the familiar formulation of 'any natural person who, in contracts covered by this Directive, is acting for purposes which are not related to his trade, business or profession'.[205] On the basis of its existing case law, the European Court is likely to take a restrictive approach here, so as to exclude even non-corporate businesses acting outside their usual areas of dealing.[206]

Before the 1999 Directive, neither English or French law restricted any buyers' rights in respect of the goods' failures in quality or performance to consumers, though the latter benefited from special protections against exclusions of liability.[207] In both systems implementation of the Directive brought change here. For, as I have already explained, in English law the technique used to implement the 1999 Directive extended the new rights for buyers to non-corporate business' buyers of goods of a type which do not form a regular part of their trade.[208] While defensible as a matter of policy, this results in three categories of buyer: corporate business buyers (who cannot enjoy the Directive's new rights); non-corporate business buyers (who may enjoy these rights if acting outside their regular dealings) and non-business buyers (who may enjoy these rights). All three categories may still enjoy English law's classic remedies.[209]

In French law too, implementation of the 1999 Directive has created a second layer of buyer's rights specially for consumers in parallel to those existing under the Civil Code.[210] While French legislation has not defined 'consumer', its interpretation in the context of unfair contract terms excludes businesses acting outside their 'own speciality'.[211] In implementing the 1999 Directive, the French legislator has continued to leave 'consumer' open to judicial interpretation and it is likely that the French courts will continue to take their more restrictive approach, particularly given that this is likely to be the view of the 1999 Directive's own requirements.[212]

(b) The basis of liability: 'contractual non-conformity'

At the heart of the 1999 Directive lies its treatment of the basis of liability. Article 2(1) and 2(2) state that:

1. The seller must deliver goods to the consumer which are in conformity with the contract of sale.

---

[204] Twigg-Flesner and Bradgate, *op. cit.* n. 39, discussing 'seller'.

[205] 1999 Directive, art. 1(2)(a). Cf. 93/13/EC art. 2(b).

[206] Case 361/89 of 14 Mar. 1991 *France v Di Pinto* [1991] ECR 1–1189 § 15; Case C-269/95 of 3 Jul. 1997 *Benincasa v Dentalkit* [1997] ECR I-03767; Case C-89/91 of 19 Jan. 1993 *Shearson Lehman Hutton* [1993] ECR 1–139 §§ 20 and 22. This may be supported by the omission from the final version of the 1999 Directive of the need for a 'direct' relation between the contract and the buyer's business: see Proposal for directive on the sale of consumer goods and associated guarantees of 18 June 1996, art. 1; Trochu, *op. cit.* n. 74, 120; Serrano, *op. cit.* n. 193, 112. Cf. HL Select Committee, *Tenth Report*, §§ 119–20 where other interpretations of this earlier wording are suggested.

[207] Above, pp. 79–86, 94, 253–4, 261, 262.   [208] Above, p. 588.   [209] Below, p. 611.

[210] Above, p. 583.

[211] Grynbaum, *op. cit.* n. 74, 4. Art. L. 132-1 C. consom.; Civ. (1) 3 and 30 Jan. 1996, JCP 1996.II.22654, D 1996.228 note Paisant, above, p. 94.

[212] *Ord.* of 17 Feb. 2005, *Rapport an Président de la République* at (A), '*Le champ d'application de la nouvelle action en garantie de conformité du bien au contrat*'.

2. Consumer goods are presumed to be in conformity with the contract if they:

   (a) comply with the description given by the seller and possess the qualities of the goods which the seller has held out to the consumer as a sample or model;

   (b) are fit for any particular purpose for which the consumer requires them and which he made known to the seller at the time of conclusion of the contract and which the seller has accepted;

   (c) are fit for the purposes for which goods of the same type are normally used;

   (d) show the quality and performance which are normal in goods of the same type and which the consumer can reasonably expect, given the nature of the goods and taking into account any public statements on the specific characteristics of the goods made about them by the seller, the producer or his representative, particularly in advertising or on labelling.

The remainder of article 2 deals with the situation of the buyer's awareness of the lack of conformity, qualifications on the relevance of public statements for the purposes of article 2(d) and the significance of insufficient installation instructions.[213]

(i) The language and structure of article 2

The language and basic structure of article 2 are borrowed from the Vienna Convention, which also starts with a general declaration concerning the conformity of the goods with the contract, and then makes more detailed provision as to what this may actually mean.[214]

First, the language used is overtly and consciously contractual, rather than regulatory: the goods must conform *to the contract*, rather than apparently to a standard imposed by law. According to the preamble to the Directive this language was adopted as being common among the laws of the Member States and for its clear relationship with freedom of contract.[215] So, while the Directive does indeed require the establishment of a minimum standard for consumer goods, it does so using the classical language of contract, and thereby implicitly rejects the Romanist tradition of the aedilitian remedies or any other overtly regulatory technique.[216]

For French lawyers the Directive's unified criterion of 'contractual conformity' was a major point of disagreement, those in its favour of its wider use seeing it as attractively simple and those against both conceptually wrong-headed and substantively misguided.[217] By contrast, to an English lawyer article 2 appears to reflect the familiar distinction between express terms (article 2(1)) and implied terms (article 2(2)), this being seen in the form of the UK implementing regulations.[218] As I shall explain, however, the Directive's scheme does not exactly fit the English distinction, as it may include 'terms implied in fact' within article 2(1), whereas the established position under the Sale of Goods Act is that no terms as to the quality or fitness for any particular purpose of the goods may be implied *other than* those which it provides.[219]

---

[213] Below, pp. 601–2.   [214] Vienna Convention, art. 35.   [215] Recitals 7 and 8.

[216] S. Grundmann, 'Article 2 Conformity with the Contract' in Bianca and Grundmann, *EU Sales Directive*, 117 at 119.   [217] Above, pp. 580–1.

[218] 2002 Regulations, r. 3 (amending s. 14 Sale of Goods Act) and r. 5 (new s. 48F Sale of Goods Act).

[219] 1979 Act, s. 14(1) and see below, p. 593.

There is, furthermore, a subtle difference in the ways in which different language versions of the Directive describe a failure in goods to attain 'conformity'. Unlike the Product Liability Directive, where liability is founded on harm caused by a proven defect, the English version of the 1999 Directive does not base liability on a defect in the goods but rather on their 'lack of conformity'.[220] However, here the French version differs, for it bases liability on *'tout défaut de conformité'*, thereby adopting the existing French terminology describing a seller's failure to deliver conforming property, rather than either using some neutral expression such as *'manque de conformité'* or the highly-charged *'vice'*. The French terminology of *défaut* has associations both of defect in the English sense (which has a physical resonance even if it may apply more widely) and the much wider sense of 'default'.

Secondly, the structure of article 2(1) and 2(2) is distinctly awkward. Unlike the Vienna Convention,[221] article 2(2) does not content itself by saying when goods *will be* or *may be* held failing, but rather imposes a presumption of conformity if they satisfy the conditions set out in 2(2)(a) to 2(2)(d), a presumption which the preamble describes as rebuttable.[222] So, where a buyer establishes the factual circumstances found in any one of (a) to (d), then the presumption of conformity will be rebutted and non-conformity established: in one sense, therefore, (a) to (d) describe cumulative requirements, as recital 8 expressly states. On the other hand, recital 8 also describes these provisions as covering 'the most common situations' of contractual non-conformity, which suggests that they are merely examples (even if distinct examples) of a single concept of contractual non-conformity, rather than constituting a list of different bases of liability such as are found in the implied terms set out in sections 13, 14(2) and 14(3) of the English Sale of Goods Act. In particular, as recital 7 says, 'the goods must, above all, conform with the contractual specifications', that is, with the terms of the contract relating to them and here there is no restriction as to the nature of the terms relating to the goods. So, while terms specifically governing the quality or fitness for purpose of the goods would be included under article 2(1)'s general principle, so would terms setting out other specifications, such as their colour, age (where relevant), quantity, origin or even the time when they are to be delivered[223] (though some of these cases may also fall within article 2(2)(a)'s reference to 'the description given by the seller'). While to an English lawyer this immediately brings to mind cases of the conclusion of *express terms* of the contract of sale relating to the goods, it could also include terms implied from the circumstances where these can genuinely be said to reflect the intentions of the parties, treated in English law as 'terms implied in fact',[224] as there is no requirement in the Directive that the 'contractual specifications' be express. But the inclusion of these elements makes clear the all-encompassing nature of the concept of contractual non-conformity and that the 'examples' given in article 2(2) should not be seen as independent grounds of liability. It is for this reason that it should not be surprising that they appear to overlap.

---

[220] Art. 3(1). On neither occasion when 'defect' is used by the English version of the preamble does this refer to liability for lack of conformity: recital 21 (enforceability of express guarantees); recital 23 (producers' direct liability). For the 1985 Directive, see above, pp. 481 *et seq.*   [221] Art. 35.

[222] Recital 8.   [223] Grundmann, *op. cit.* n. 216, 122.   [224] Above, p. 157 n. 9.

Thirdly, the force of the rebuttable presumption of conformity appears to be that the burden of proof of lack of conformity rests on the buyer: for the force of a rebuttable presumption is that its subject matter is to be presumed established unless evidence shows the contrary.[225] This result would also accord both with the interpretation given to the relevant provision of the Vienna Convention and with the general maxim *actori incumbit probatio* which is common to Member States.[226] A buyer may discharge this burden by establishing that the seller has failed to perform an express or implied stipulation relating to the goods or that the case falls within one of the examples given in article 2(2).[227] This result is reflected in the English and French implementing legislation, both of which make contractual non-conformity of the goods a matter for proof by the buyer.[228]

At this stage, we need to look at article 5(3) which states that:

Unless proved otherwise, any lack of conformity which becomes apparent within six months of delivery of the goods shall be presumed to have existed at the time of delivery unless this presumption is incompatible with the nature of the goods or the nature of the lack of conformity.

This is at first confusing next to article 2(2)'s rebuttable presumption of conformity of the goods as it imposes a rebuttable presumption as to their *lack* of conformity, but the difference lies in article 5(3)'s concern not with the existence of the non-conformity, but with its timing: it is a six-month presumption of anteriority of any lack of conformity. So, while a buyer must show that the goods suffer from a lack of conformity, having done so, for a period of six months the buyer need not demonstrate that this failure existed at the time of delivery,[229] unless such a presumption is incompatible with the nature of the goods (for example, where they are perishable) or the nature of the lack of conformity (for example, where goods are second-hand).[230] While at first sight this provision is one of the most significantly consumerist of the Directive, its practical impact in the English context has been doubted given that in the circumstances to which it applies an English court would tend to draw presumptions of fact

---

[225] Cf. Grundmann, *op. cit.* n. 216, 129 who states that the burden of proof is a matter for national law.

[226] Schlectriem, *op. cit.* n. 38, 288–9 (where a buyer accepts goods without notice of a defect); Kruisinga, *op. cit.* n. 34, 186–7. For the maxim, see above, p. 515.

[227] While some of these examples involve the evaluation of the goods by reference to a complex test (notably in the case of article 2(2)(d)'s criterion of quality), it is submitted that the matter remains appropriate for the imposition of a burden of proof, rather than for a 'neutral evaluation' by the court. Cf. the Dir. 93/13/EC on unfair terms in consumer contracts where it may be argued that there is no burden of proof on either party but rather a neutral evaluation by the court as to the issue of a fairness of a contract term: *Chitty on Contracts*, paras. 15–062–15–065.

[228] In English law, this results from the inclusion of the elements of non-conformity within s. 14(2) of the 1979 Act: 2002 Regulations, r. 3. For French law, see the *ord.* of 17 Feb. 2005, art. 1, creating arts. L. 211-4, L. 211-5 C. consom.

[229] The time of 'delivery' set by art. 2(1) was chosen so as to avoid issues relating to the allocation of risk and transfer of the property in the goods, questions which are differently regulated in the Member States: see recital 14. In the case of English law, the Dti took the view that s. 20 of the 1979 Act had to be amended so as to ensure that the goods remain at the seller's risk until they are delivered: 2002 Regulations, r. 4 and see M. M. Taylor and A. Naidoo, 'The Draft Regulations to Adopt the Directive on Certain Aspects of the Sale of Consumer Goods and Associated Guarantees—Problems of the Time of Conformity for the Quality Obligation' (2002) 3 Web JCLI.   [230] Art. 5(3).

from the existence of a defect now to a defect then;[231] its impact on French practice is more difficult to judge given its treatment of the anteriority of the defect as a matter for the 'sovereign assessment' of the *juges du fond*.[232]

Fourthly, article 2(2) of the Directive structures the judicial decision as to the conformity of the goods with the contract in two ways, setting out five circumstances when goods *will* lack conformity and then for the most general standard of the goods' 'quality and performance' providing factors to be taken into account in applying the standard. To an English lawyer, this is familiar from the existing form of the Sale of Goods Act and reflects a much wider concern to structure the discretion of judges in applying broad and fundamental concepts.[233] To a French lawyer, though, these explanations of explanations can look redundant,[234] or even inflexible.[235] In this respect, while the French Working Group's draft bill simplified article 2(1) and (2) somewhat[236] and Tournafond's counterdraft all but omitted their specific elements,[237] the *ordonnance* of 17 February 2005 retains the structuring of non-conformity which the directive provides, although it re-jigs it somewhat and replaces article 2's references to 'reasonableness', perhaps owing to its 'Anglo-Saxon' connotations.[238] The retention of article 2's structure may be important, for it contrasts sharply with existing French treatments of *défaut de conformité* and *vice caché* which are left remarkably undefined by the courts, the Cour de cassation leaving their decision to the *juges du fond*, and the *juges du fond* leaving cases of any technical complexity to *experts*.[239] Whether or not the Cour de cassation chooses to make the non-application of article 2's criteria of non-conformity a basis for its own intervention in the assessment of a lower court, their inclusion within the French implementing legislation will tend to juridify their decisions on this issue. They will be a certain move away from fact towards law.

Fifthly, article 2 of the Directive makes no *general* requirement as to the seriousness of any lack of conformity for liability to arise of the sort made by French law's *garantie légale*, which applies only where the defects render the property 'unfit for the use for which it is intended, or which so diminish this use that, had he known of them, the buyer would not have acquired it, or would have acquired it only at a lesser price'.[240] Indeed, it is clear that the Directive may apply in principle to 'minor failures of conformity', because it expressly provides that they do not give rise to any right of rescission in the consumer.[241] The absence of a general criteria of seriousness follows logically from the Directive's starting point in 'contractual conformity': goods either do or do not conform to the contract's stipulations, or, in English law terms, a minor breach of contract remains a breach, even though its nature may impact on the availability of remedies. However, the explanation of the goods' 'quality and performance'

---

231 HL Select Committee, *Tenth Report*, § 37 (evidence of H. Beale and G. Howells).
232 Above, p. 76 n. 140.   233 Above, pp. 201, 235.   234 Tournafond, *op. cit.* n. 74, 161.
235 Ghozi, *op. cit.* n. 74, 118.
236 *Avant-projet de loi sur la garantie de conformité due par le vendeur*, proposed arts. 1641, 1641-1 C. civ.
237 'Proposition de transposition de la directive du 25 mai 1999 sur certains aspects de la vente et des garanties des biens de consomation' *op. cit.*, n. 89, proposed art. L. 211-3 C. consom.
238 Art. 1, new arts. L 211-5, 211-6 C. consom., below, pp. 599, 602.   239 Above, p. 78.
240 Art. 1641 C. civ. and see above, pp. 75–6.
241 1999 Directive, art. 3(6); Bianca, *op. cit.* n. 43, 164–5.

may be thought to possess its own criteria of seriousness in referring to the *normal* quality or performance given the *reasonable* expectations of consumers.[242] And the seriousness of any lack of conformity is relevant to the availability of remedies other than rescission.[243]

(ii) Compliance with description or sample

According to article 2(2)(a), the non-compliance of goods with their description or sample constitutes an example of 'contractual non-conformity'. While this provision looks very similar to the terms of section 13 of the Sale of Goods Act, the Court of Appeal has interpreted 'sales by description' within the terms of section 13 in a narrow manner, so that as regards ascertained goods it applies only to situations where the description has sufficient influence on the sale to become an essential term of the contract, the correlative of influence being reliance.[244] This view followed the approach of the general law governing the availability of termination for breach of contract, but it means that some descriptions of goods sold may count (if at all) as pre-contractual misrepresentations, rather than contractual descriptions. By contrast, there is no reason to restrict article 2(2)(a) of the 1999 Directive in such a way, so that any descriptive statement made by the *seller* to the buyer relating to the goods would found the basis of their 'non-conformity', whether or not it concerns their essential characteristics.[245] On the other hand, article 2(2)(a) may not apply to descriptions made by *manufacturers*, notably, on packaging, whereas section 13 is not so limited.[246] For while the European Court may allow any statements made *on* the goods to be found by national courts to have been implicitly adopted as part of the contract's 'specifications', it may consider that the explicit reference to labelling in article 2(2)(d) suggests their irrelevance to article 2(2)(a).[247] Given that articles 2(2)(a) to (e) are 'typical examples' of cases involving different aspects of a single concept of conformity of the goods, they should not *contrast* with each other, taking different views of the same issue, here, the relevance of labelling on the goods. Here, the French *ordonnance* of 17 February 2005 simply follows the Directive.[248]

(iii) Fitness for purpose

Article 2(2)(b) and (c) of the 1999 Directive concern the seller's liability for the fitness of the goods for their purpose, distinguishing between their normal purposes and any 'particular purpose for which the consumer requires them and which he made known to the seller at the time of conclusion of the contract and which the seller has accepted'. These two provisions are reminiscent of the implied term in section 14(3) of the Sale of Goods Act, sharing with that provision a combination of objective and subjective elements.[249] There are, however, a number of differences.

---

[242] 1999 Directive, art. 2(2)(d).
[243] Below, p. 607.   [244] Above, p. 234.   [245] Watterson, *op. cit.* n. 182, 204.
[246] Twigg-Flesner and Bradgate, *op. cit.* n. 39.
[247] The European Parliament attempted (without success) to include statements made by producers for this purpose too, but this was rejected by the Commission on the basis that it was unnecessary given art. 2(2)(d) and 2(4): OJ of 6 April 1998, C 104/30 at 34 (amendment 19).
[248] Art. 1, new arts. L 211-5 1° al. 2, 211-6 C. consom.   [249] Above, pp. 235–42.

First, neither provision in the Directive requires that the fitness for purpose be 'reasonable', a restriction which in English law forms a threshold of significance or importance of the lack of fitness and which involves the consideration of the price, the description and nature of the goods.[250] So, for example, second-hand goods are not to be expected to be as efficient as new ones in achieving their purpose.[251] Does the absence of this 'reasonableness' qualification in the Directive mean that the goods must be *absolutely fit* for their purpose?[252]

In favour of such an interpretation at a purely textual level is the contrast between the absence of 'reasonableness' here and its liberal use elsewhere in the Directive.[253] Such a strictness also fits with the remedial scheme of the Directive, which sets repair or replacement of the goods at the first level of a consumer's rights, but subjects them to a test of disproportionality and relegates reduction of price and rescission to a second level.[254] For the lack of seriousness of a lack of conformity argues against allowing replacement of the goods rather than their repair;[255] and its 'minor' character expressly excludes rescission of the contract.[256] This suggests that while *any* functional failure may constitute a 'lack of conformity', its relative insignificance *may* exclude the buyer's right of replacement and *will* exclude the right of rescission, leaving repair or reduction in the price, both of which are inherently tailored to the degree of non-conformity actually established. This connection of the definition of non-conformity and the rights provided by the Directive explains the contrast with the established position in English law under which *any* breach of the implied term in section 14(3) of the Sale of Goods Act gives rise to an unqualified right in those dealing as consumers to reject the goods and/or to recover damages,[257] so that a threshold of 'reasonableness' in the lack of fitness of goods for their purpose becomes necessary.

On the other hand, it could be argued that the 'fitness for purpose' of goods is necessarily a relative matter, in particular as a function of their place in the market. This line of argument, though, raises the question whether account can be taken of the price of the goods in assessing whether they achieved the appropriate standard of utility under the Directive. In this respect, explicit reference to the price as a factor was excluded after criticism of an earlier draft by the Economic and Social Committee[258] and by the European Parliament,[259] and this suggests that the price of the goods should be irrelevant.[260] The Committee supported its position on the basis that where 'two products are described in the same terms and the only difference is in price, consumers should not necessarily expect to have an inferior product merely because they paid less for it',[261] but this does not mean that the price should *necessarily* be irrelevant to consumer expectations of the utility of goods. Perhaps in systems like French law where the decision as to the fitness of the goods for their purpose would fall to be

---

[250] Above, pp. 240–2.   [251] Above, pp. 240–1.

[252] Twigg-Flesner and Bradgate, *op. cit.* n. 39, state that it does.   [253] Above, p. 570.

[254] 1999 Directive, art. 3 and see below, pp. 606–8.   [255] See below, p. 607.

[256] 1999 Directive, art. 3(6).

[257] As regards those not dealing as consumers, the right of rejection is qualified by reference to 'reasonableness': above, p. 253.   [258] OJ of 3 March 1997, C 66/ 05.

[259] OJ of 6 April 1998, C 104/30 at 34 (amendment 20).

[260] Grundmann, *op. cit.* n. 216, 134.   [261] OJ of 3 March 1997, C 66/ 05 § 3.8.

decided by the *juges du fond*, their 'assessment' of the fitness of the goods would take account of the price *sotto voce*.[262] On the other hand, any description of the goods may well be relevant (as in English law) to their fitness for purpose under the Directive, either to the extent to which the description defines the 'type' of the goods or the 'normality' of their use under article 2(2)(c).

Secondly, the Directive refers to the purposes for which goods of the same type are normally *used*, whereas English law requires that the goods be reasonably fit for the purpose (express or implied) for which they are *bought*.[263] Here, the wording of the Directive suggests a more objective approach than the English, allowing a court to take account of purposes to which consumers often put goods (for example, using a screwdriver to open a paint tin) but which are not the purposes for which they are supplied.[264] On the other hand, in my view no difference of substance should be seen between section 14(3)'s reference to the use for which goods are *commonly* supplied and the Directive's *normally* used, this being able to be supported from the French language version here which uses '*habituellement*', meaning usually.[265] But does normal use require the goods to be safe? In English law safety forms an important aspect of the goods' fitness for their common purpose.[266] While the 1999 Directive makes no mention of the safety of the goods, possibly considering this to be a matter for the Product Liability Directive, the examples of non-conformity given in article 2(2)(b) and (c) cannot be read in such a way as to exclude the safety of goods from their fitness for purpose.[267]

Thirdly, the Directive takes an overtly contractual approach to liability for a lack of fitness for a special purpose, requiring this to be made known by the buyer to the seller and 'accepted' by the latter: in this way, a special purpose enters the sphere of what is contractually agreed.[268] By contrast, section 14(3) of the 1979 Act does not require a seller's 'acceptance', providing instead that a buyer must make any particular purpose known expressly or impliedly.[269] While in English law a seller may escape liability 'where the circumstances show that the buyer does not rely, or that it is unreasonable for him to rely, on the skill or judgment of the seller', this is unlikely where the buyer is a consumer[270] and this could explain its absence from the Directive.[271] Nevertheless, there is a contrast between the Directive's 'contractual' approach and the English provision's focus on the seller's conclusion of the contract with knowledge of the buyer's purpose and the buyer's reliance on the seller's skill or judgment. Before implementation, the Dti noticed some of these differences between the Directive and the Sale of Goods Act, and proposed changes so as to reflect more closely the Directive's approach,[272] but fortunately the 2002 Regulations did not amend section 14(3) in this way, which would have been both fussy and needlessly complicated. To the extent,

---

[262] Cf. Twigg-Flesner and Bradgate, *op. cit.* n. 39.   [263] 1979 Act, s. 14(3)(b), above, p. 241.

[264] Twigg-Flesner and Bradgate, *op. cit.* n. 39.   [265] Cf. Ibid.   [266] 1979 Act, s. 14(2B)(d).

[267] Cf. Grundmann, *op. cit.* n. 216, 135 (safety relevant to art. 2(2)(d))   [268] Art. 2(2)(b).

[269] Sale of Goods Act, s. 14(3), above, pp. 239–40. According to Watterson, *op. cit.* n. 182, 206 there is little substantive difference between these positions if 'acceptance' by the seller may be seen 'objectively' in the seller's conduct in entering the contract knowing the buyer's special purpose.

[270] Cf. above, p. 240.   [271] Staudenmayer, *op. cit.* n. 34, 552.

[272] Dti, *Second Consultation*, Part 1, §§ 6 and 7, draft regulations, r. 3(2) and 3(5).

therefore, to which the Directive's phraseology is more restrictive than the Act's, the Act's has been allowed to prevail.

For French law, making distinct provision for a buyer's normal and special purposes within non-conformity required more change than in English law, but it may be seen to confirm the developments by which the property's unfitness for its purpose, which was originally seen as providing a threshold of seriousness of a 'latent defect', came to be seen as itself constituting a latent defect.[273] While the French Working Group's proposals would have provided that the goods must conform to 'any special use intended by the buyer which the latter has brought to the attention of the seller at the time of the making of the contract, without the seller expressing any reserve in this respect',[274] the *ordonnance* of 17 February 2005 returned to the wording of article 2(2)(b) of the Directive, linking it to the case where the goods 'show characteristics defined by the common agreement of the parties'.[275]

(iv) The 'quality and performance' of the goods

Perhaps the most interesting case of non-conformity foreseen by the Directive is found in article 2(2)(d) which requires that the goods must:

show the quality and performance which are normal in goods of the same type and which the consumer can reasonably expect, given the nature of the goods and taking into account any public statements on the specific characteristics of the goods made about them by the seller, the producer or his representative, particularly in advertising or on labelling.

To an English lawyer this provision is reminiscent of section 14(2) of the Sale of Goods Act, though before its enlargement in 1994 which added further guidance on the determination of the goods' 'satisfactory' quality. Like that provision, article 2(2)(d) appeals to an objective standard of quality,[276] both in its reference to the normality of the quality and performance and to the *reasonable* expectations of the consumer. So, unlike article 2(2)(b) and (c)'s provision governing the fitness of the goods for their purpose, article 2(2)(d) *does* qualify its requirement by reference to a test of reasonableness—here of the expectations of the consumer—and assigns to it a role similar to that of the 'satisfactory' qualification of the test of quality in the English legislation: indeed, a test based on the reasonable expectations of the buyer was mooted as a possible replacement for section 14(2)'s earlier 'merchantable quality' by the Law Commission prior to reform in 1994.[277] And after implementation, the English legislation has retained its references to 'the standard that a reasonable person would regard as satisfactory',[278] rather than adopting the language of expectation used by article 2(2)(d). Interestingly, French law has avoided the language used by the Directive here, as the *ordonnance* of 17 February 2005 preferred to express the standard to be attained as based on the buyer's *legitimate* expectation.[279] This reflects the French government's decision to avoid the language of reasonableness used by the Directive in

---

[273] Above, p. 71.   [274] *Avant-projet*, proposed art. 1641-1 al. 2.
[275] Art. 1, new art. L. 211-5 2° C. consom.   [276] Above, p. 238.
[277] Law Commission, *Sale and Supply of Goods*, Cm. 137 (1987) § 3.26.
[278] 1979 Act, s. 14(2B).   [279] Art. 1, creating new art. L. 211-5 1° al. 3 C. consom.

its implementation which I have suggested reflects a view that it is too 'Anglo-Saxon' in its connotations, but it also suggests that it considers that there is no substantive difference between a test of legitimate expectation and one of reasonable expectation.

These various formulations highlight an interesting comparison with the definition of defect under article 6 of the Product Liability Directive, which rests liability on a lack of 'the safety which a person is entitled to expect'. I have argued that there is no substantive difference between a standard of reasonable expectation and of legitimate expectation for the purposes of this directive so that the test in article 6 may require consideration of a similar set of factors as an English court would consider under negligence.[280] However, there is a significant difference in the orientation of the tests in the Consumer Guarantees Directive and the Product Liability Directive, as the test of defect in article 6 of the 1985 Directive is based on what a *person generally* is entitled to expect, whereas the test of non-conformity under article 2(2)(d) of the 1999 Directive is based on what the consumer (that is, the *buyer*) can reasonably expect. This contrast reflects the different scope of protection of the two directives, the first providing compensation in damages for personal injuries and death irrespective of contract, the second providing rights to performance and rescission based on a contract.[281]

Secondly, article 2(2)(d) of the 1999 Directive stipulates that three factors are to be taken into account in determining the normal standard of quality required. The first is not expressed as a factor at all, but is rather alluded to by its use of the phrase 'quality *and performance*'. This looks like two requirements, one as to the quality, the other as to the performance, i.e. the efficiency of the goods in doing what they are intended to do, but such an interpretation would create a second requirement of fitness for purpose in addition to the one found in article 2(2)(c),[282] but this time qualified by reference to normality and reasonableness. Instead, in my view, 'quality and performance' should be interpreted together so as to render the performance of the goods relevant with other elements to the adequacy of their quality, a position familiar to English lawyers under section 14(2) of the 1979 Act.

The second factor to be taken into account in determining the standard of quality under article 2(2)(d) is the 'nature of the goods', recital 8 giving as an example their being new or second-hand, but this leads on to the question whether the price of the goods is also relevant for this purpose. I have noted that an earlier explicit reference to price in an earlier definition of non-conformity was later dropped,[283] and this could be used as the basis for rejecting its relevance. But how can the price of goods be *always irrelevant* to their quality? Including the goods' price as relevant here would not mean that cheaper goods are not covered by the Directive or that they must not attain a certain level of quality, but merely that their price *may* be relevant to the quality which 'the consumer can reasonably expect'. This would still mean that other factors (such as advertising) may outweigh the price in the court's overall assessment of the proper level of quality.

Thirdly, the 1999 Directive introduced an element which is new to both French and English law in article 2(2)(d)'s inclusion of public statements by manufacturers as

---

[280] Above, pp. 487–8, 489–94, 501.
[281] Below, pp. 604–10 on the rights under the 1999 Directive.   [282] Above, pp. 592, 598.
[283] See the discussion, above, pp. 597–8.

relevant to the standard of quality. This was clearly a controversial part of the provision, for article 2(4) then provides that:

The seller shall not be bound by public statements, as referred to in paragraph 2(d) if he:

—shows that he was not, and could not reasonably have been, aware of the statement in question,

—shows that by the time of conclusion of the contract the statement had been corrected, or

—shows that the decision to buy the consumer goods could not have been influenced by the statement.

So while a manufacturer's statements, including advertisements and other publicity, may be relevant to what a consumer buyer may reasonably expect as to their quality and performance, this will not be the case in any of these particular circumstances. This clearly reflects a practical compromise in the legislative process leading to the Directive, but it also reflects the overall basis of liability in *contractual* non-conformity, for the circumstances in article 2(4) exclude situations where a buyer's consent to enter the contract could not or should not have been influenced by the public statements, and where any public statements were not known and could not reasonably have been known by the seller, and so form no part of his contractual consent. This reflects the idea that both the seller and the buyer have to 'accept' the basis of the goods' non-conformity.[284]

English law did not previously make manufacturer's publicity provided other than by the seller relevant to the latter's liability, and so implementation of these aspects of article 2(2)(d) was effected by the inclusion in section 14(2) of the Sale of Goods Act of a further factor stated to be of relevance where the buyer deals as consumer.[285] Indeed, it was only here that the UK legislator considered that the Directive required anything to be added to English law's existing explanation of the satisfactory quality of the goods.

What position has been taken by French lawyers to these provisions? While there is no explanation of the level of quality which is required of a seller of property in France either under the *garantie légale* or the *obligation de conformité*, one can see the courts giving effect to some of the sorts of consideration which English law expressly stipulates in section 14(2).[286] In its proposals, the French Working Group retained this open position with one exception, providing simply that the goods must 'present the qualities which a buyer can reasonably expect taking into consideration public declarations made by the seller in advertising or labelling',[287] but not retaining the complex exceptions provided by article 2(4) of the Directive which in its view 'appeared to invite business sellers to try frequently to escape their liability'; and were unnecessary given the possibility of recourse by final sellers against the person who made the public statement.[288] This extension of liability in the interests of consumer protection fitted

---

[284] Cf. above, p. 598.   [285] 2002 Regulations, r. 3, new s. 14 (2D) to (2F), 1979 Act.
[286] Above, p. 245.
[287] *Avant-projet*, proposed art. 1641-1 C. civ. According to Grynbaum, *op.cit.* n. 74, 6 the Cour de cassation was already moving in the direction of making publicity material relevant to the liability of sellers.
[288] *Rapport général*, Part II, 3.

uncomfortably with the basis of liability in the 'reasonable expectations' of the buyer which *could* not be engendered in the circumstances which article 2(4) sets out and was not retained by the *ordonnance* of 17 February 2005, which follows quite closely articles 2(2)(d) and 2(4) of the Directive. Again, though, the French legislator sought to avoid the Directive's use of 'reasonableness', replacing its reference to the statements of which the seller shows that he could not reasonably have been aware with ones of which he was not legitimately in a position to know.[289]

(v) Installation, instructions and non-conformity

While not included as an example of contractual non-conformity in article 2(2), at this stage it may be helpful to note article 2(5)'s requirement that where a product is intended to be installed by the consumer and is then installed incorrectly owing to a shortcoming in the installation instructions, then this situation will be 'deemed to be equivalent' to lack of conformity of the goods, this being coupled with a similar requirement of 'deemed lack of conformity' where the goods are installed by the seller himself. This extra provision makes sense as regards the second situation since the deeming provision extends the concept of non-conformity from the goods themselves to the provision of a service accompanying the goods,[290] but less sense as regards instructions for consumer installation or assembly, as there would be no reason why such an inadequacy in materials supplied as part of the sale and with the goods should not fall directly within one or more examples of contractual non-conformity foreseen by article 2(2). In particular, how can self-assembly goods be 'fit for their normal purpose' without instructions which permit their proper assembly? Certainly, as a matter of English law, the inadequacy of such instructions could form the basis of a claim that goods were not reasonably fit for their purpose or of satisfactory quality, without any special requirement and this is reflected in the lack of any new provision in the 2002 Regulations implementing article 2(5).[291] Apparently, the French Working Group took the same sort of view, for no special provision was included to implement article 2(5) in its proposed reform to the Civil Code, though these elements were included specifically within the *ordonnance* of 17 February 2005.[292] But there was no real need for what is sometimes known as this 'IKEA clause'.[293]

(vi) The awareness of the buyer of the lack of conformity

Article 2(3) of the 1999 Directive provides that:

There shall be deemed not to be a lack of conformity for the purposes of this Article if, at the time the contract was concluded, the consumer was aware, or could not reasonably be unaware of, the lack of conformity . . .

---

[289] *Ord.* of 17 Feb. 2005, art. 1 creating new art. L. 211-5 1° and L. 211-6 C. consom.

[290] This was implemented in the UK by 2002 Regulations, r. 9, inserting new s. 11S into the Supply of Goods and Services Act 1982.   [291] *Benjamin, Special Supplement*, § 1–193.

[292] Art. 1, creating new art. 211-4 al. 2 C. consom.

[293] This became known as the 'IKEA clause' after the well-known retailer of furniture and household accessories supplied in kit form: Staudenmayer, *op. cit.* n. 34, 553.

In the pre-existing laws of both France and England a seller is not liable to a buyer in respect of 'defects' of which the buyer was aware, though there is a difference as regards defects of which the buyer *should* have been aware, as here English law provides that a buyer cannot recover on the ground of the goods' unsatisfactory quality discoverable on examination where he examines them before the contract is made: an unreasonable failure to examine does not have this effect.[294] Here, therefore, the Directive aligns more closely with the established French position,[295] broadly providing that the seller will not be liable if the buyer either knew or ought reasonably to have known of the lack of conformity.

However, in implementing the Directive, the UK legislator retained its existing, slightly stricter approach by not introducing any new provision into the Sale of Goods Act. By contrast, having abandoned the concept of liability for *latent* defects and in the absence of any defence of *faute de la victime* as regards the liability imposed by the Directive, the French Working Group proposed an amendment to the Civil Code which would have transposed very closely the terms of article 2(3) and this approach was adopted by the *ordonnance* of 17 February 2005 in its amendment of the *Code de la consommation*.[296]

(vii) The strictness of liability under article 2

Many of the issues which I have so far discussed as regards article 2's conception of contractual non-conformity have involved consideration of its degree of strictness and whether or to what extent its requirements are qualified by concepts such as reasonableness.[297] However, there is a further sense in which liability under article 2 is 'strict', in that no fault in any sense (including negligence) in the seller need be shown by a buyer for 'liability' to be established, and that a seller cannot escape liability by showing that a 'defect of conformity' arose without fault on his part or through the fault of a third party. Moreover, given its omission of liability in damages, the question whether a seller can argue that any harm caused by the goods' lack of conformity is caused in part by other factors or by the buyer himself simply does not arise under the Directive itself.

On the other hand, the strictness of the liability arising from the Directive's definition of contractual non-conformity does indeed arise in relation to its implementation in France and in England. In England, the Directive's definition could be fitted quite easily into the statutory implied terms which now form the basis of the consumer's new rights as well as the classic rights of rejection and damages.[298] In France, by contrast, the degree of strictness of the obligation and of liability *in damages* which implementation of the Directive appeared to require formed an element in the argument as to its manner of implementation, for neither *force majeure* nor *faute de la victime* would appear relevant, even though they are under the general law.[299] This illustrates the sort of difficulty which arises in using a directive of such a partial nature as the 1999 Directive as a model for wider change, for the Directive did not envisage that its

---

[294] Above, p. 244; *Benjamin, Special Supplement*, §§ 1-073–1-074.   [295] Above, pp. 76–7.

[296] *Avant-projet*, proposed art. 1642 C. civ.; *ord.* 17 Feb. 2005, art. 1, creating new art. L. 211-8 C. consom.   [297] Above, pp. 597–600.

[298] Above, pp. 587–8.   [299] Above, pp. 580–1.

test of contractual non-conformity should give rise to liability in damages at all.[300] In this particular case, while the French Working Group's proposals would have led to 'contractual non-conformity' serving as the *exclusive* basis of liability for qualitative or performance defects even as regards claims for damages,[301] it is not entirely clear from the terms of the *ordonnance* of 17 February 2005 whether its test for contractual non-conformity may give rise to damages at all. For it declares the seller's obligation of conformity in a general way, sets out the Directive's own rights found in article 2, but then simply says that 'these provisions do not prevent ['*ne font pas obstacle*'] an award of damages',[302] without saying whether such an award would rest on the new test of contractual non-conformity (as its preamble rather suggests[303]) or only on *other* contractual or extra-contractual actions for damages which it then expressly preserves.[304]

(c) The buyer's rights

I have said that article 3 of the 1999 Directive which sets out the 'rights of the consumer' recognises not merely a creditor's right to performance but also the debtor's right to perform.[305] Moreover, at a practical level, while it does require the creation of new rights for consumers in both English and French law, it looks remarkably protective of the position of sellers, hedging the consumer's rights around with caveats and, unlike the pre-existing law in either France or England, creating an explicit 'hierarchy' of rights and sometimes even leaving a consumer with no more than a reduction in the price.[306] The reasons for these restrictions on the consumer's rights were political; in particular the hierarchy of rights resulted from concerns expressed in the European Parliament that a free right to rescission of the contracts would leave businesses with almost new goods which they would then have to repair before sale at a loss second-hand.[307] Paradoxically, however, as I shall explain, a seller may sometimes have good reasons for preferring the contract to be 'rescinded' or the price reduced rather than to have to bear the cost of repair or replacement of the goods.[308]

Before looking at this in more detail, the terminology used by the Directive is worth noting. Article 3 is entitled 'Rights of the consumer' and then states that the consumer 'shall be entitled to have the goods brought into conformity free of charge by repair or replacement'.[309] Here, then, the language used is one of rights and this is reflected in the description of the seller's position, the English version referring to the seller being 'liable', the French either 'bound' or 'responsible',[310] though in neither legal system is use of 'liability/*responsabilité*' very appropriate given the

---

[300] Above, p. 566.   [301] Above, pp. 595–6.

[302] *Ord.* of 17 Feb. 2005, art. 1, creating new art. L. 211-11 al. 2 C. consom.

[303] Ibid., *Rapport au Président de la République*, A., '*Les remèdes au défaut de la conformité*'.

[304] Ibid., art. 1 creating new art. L. 211-13 C. consom.   [305] Above, p. 570.

[306] This is true where neither replacement nor repair are available (as 'impossible' or 'disproportionate') and where a non-conformity is minor: below, p. 609.

[307] Trochu, *op. cit.* n. 74, 122, referring to European Parliament debates no. 4.515 of 9 March 1998, 12–17.

[308] Below, p. 610.   [309] Art. 3(2).

[310] 1999 Directive, art. 3(1) ('The seller shall be liable' / '*Le vendeur est tenu*'). Cf. art. 5(1) ('The seller shall be held liable under article 3'/ '*La responsabilité du vendeur prévue à l'article 3*').

absence of damages. However, later in article 3, the repair or replacement of the goods are referred to as 'remedies'[311] and the French phrase used here ('*le mode de dédommagement* or 'manner of undoing the harm') indicates that this refers to the actual making better of the effects of non-conformity, the repair, replacement, rescission of the contract or price reduction. And the rather English-sounding '*remèdes au défaut de conformité*' is used by the preamble to the French *ordonnance* of 17 February 2005 in this very sense.

Such a distinction has a familiar feel to English lawyers, who happily speak of, for example, rescission or damages as remedies and also recognise that in some situations there is a 'right to rescind' or a 'right to damages', but we should be careful not to read into the 1999 Directive's usage the very particular significance given to 'remedies' by the common law, for under the Directive there is a third stage of analysis, that is, the procedural mechanisms by which the Directive's 'remedies' are given practical effect. This third stage may be seen in recital 15 which leaves 'the detailed arrangements whereby "rescission" of the contract is effected' to national law,[312] but it also exists as regards repair or replacement of the goods, for the question arises as to *how* a recalcitrant seller should be 'forced' to repair or replace the goods. According to Staudenmayer, leaving 'the details of rescission' to Member States reflected the 'tendency of the Directive to harmonise only the really necessary rules',[313] and in giving evidence on behalf of the Commission to the House of Lords Select Committee, he observed that 'what [the Commission has] described in the Directive are the four rights of the consumer. What happens if these rights are not fulfilled or are not correctly fulfilled depends on national law'.[314] Moreover, such an allocation of responsibility reflects the general practice of European legislation of leaving matters of civil procedure and the enforcement of judgments to the laws of the Member States following the so-called 'principle of procedural autonomy'.[315] Certainly, any attempt by the Directive to construct a harmonised approach to the procedural expression of the consumer's remedies (in the Directive's sense) would have added extra complexity to an already elaborate provision and would have required the laws of some Member States to insert a mechanism both unfamiliar and jarring with its general contractual and/or procedural system. As we shall see, though, while the UK legislator felt it necessary to give effect to the consumer's new rights by creating a special statutory instance of 'specific performance', the French legislator appears content to leave the enforcement of the seller's 'remedial obligations' (if this is not too mixed an expression) to its general law of *voies d'exécution*. As I shall explain, this results in a different range of possible practical outcomes in the two legal systems. But we need to keep clear the three stages of analysis: (i) the consumer's right to (ii) a particular mode of making the non-conformity better (the 'remedy' for non-conformity) and (iii) the means by which this 'remedy' is carried into effect.

---

[311] See esp. art. 3(5).   [312] There are considerable differences here: below, p. 610 n. 329.
[313] *Op. cit.* n. 34, 555.   [314] HL Select Committee, *Tenth Report*, § 40.
[315] See notably Case 33/76 *Rewe* [1976] ECR I-1989 §§ 5 and 6, Case 45/76 *Comet BV v Produktschap voor Siergewassen* [1976] ECR I-2043, § 13, Case 78/98 *Preston v Wolverhampton Healthcare NHS Trust* [2000] ECR I-3201 § 31.

(i) The Directive's hierarchy of rights

The Directive groups the consumer's rights into two levels: the right to repair or replacement of the goods at a first level, and the right to an appropriate reduction of the price or rescission of the contract at a second. So, while article 3(2) appears to give the buyer a free choice as to which of these four rights to exercise, in fact the second level rights arise only if those at the first level fail in one of three specified ways. While this rests on the idea that the buyer should be kept wherever possible to the repair or replacement of the goods so as to protect the interest of the seller in retaining the contract and in some sense 'performing', paradoxically in some situations a seller might *prefer* the consumer to be limited to a right to rescission (involving the return of the price and the property) or price reduction.

At the first level, therefore, the Directive has in mind that the buyer asks the seller to have the goods 'brought into conformity with the contract' either by their repair or their replacement. This reflects an idea that repair and replacement are not based on new, distinct obligations but constitute a form of specific enforcement of the seller's original contractual obligation of conformity, familiar to French lawyers as *réparation en nature*.[316] However, the relationship between these two remedies in the Directive is complex, for while in principle the buyer may choose whether to require the seller to repair or to replace the goods,[317] this choice is ineffective where the remedy chosen is either 'impossible' or 'disproportionate'.

The 'impossibility' of a remedy looks the more straightforward hurdle. The Directive's preamble explains that the replacement of second-hand goods will *generally* be impossible owing to their 'specific nature'[318] and so, while it may well be impossible for a dealer to replace an antique vase, it may not be impossible for a dealer in second-hand books to replace a non-conforming copy of a book with a conforming copy from his own stock. More difficult is the question whether a seller of goods can rely on the 'impossibility' of replacement where he does not himself possess a substitute for the non-conforming goods, but where he can obtain one by purchase. In the case of new goods, it does not seem unreasonable for a retailer to be forced to purchase another item (where it is still available on the market) so as to replace non-conforming goods which he has previously supplied, but this may be less reasonable where the goods are second-hand and the market therefore less easily accessible. Perhaps, though, this sort of concern should be addressed not under the heading of impossibility but instead of 'disproportionality'.[319]

The impossibility of repair of the goods gives rise to rather different issues. A clear example of its application is where the goods are so defective that they are incapable of repair ('beyond repair'), though the line between this and the disproportionality of the cost of repair relative to the replacement of the goods may be a fine one.[320] A less clear case would be where a retailer is able to repair the goods but by doing so he would invalidate any recourse claim that he would otherwise possess against his own seller or the manufacturer: would such a consequence make it 'morally impossible' to repair

---

[316] Above, p. 81 n. 180. Cf. Stijns and Van Gerven, *op. cit.* n. 19, 248 referring to 'reparation in natura'.
[317] Recital 10.   [318] Recital 16.   [319] Below, p. 607.   [320] Ibid.

the goods? Here again, though, rather than extending the sense of 'impossibility' a better route would be to weigh this additional cost of repair to the seller against the cost of replacement as a matter of disproportionality.

This leads to the qualification that the remedy chosen by the buyer should not be disproportionate. Article 3(3) § 2 explains that:

A remedy shall be deemed to be disproportionate if it imposes costs on the seller which, in comparison with the alternative remedy, are unreasonable, taking into account:

—the value the goods would have if there were no lack of conformity;
—the significance of the lack of conformity; and
—whether the alternative remedy could be completed without significant inconvenience to the consumer.

Here, we again find in the 1999 Directive a provision which adopts an open-textured criterion and then sets out factors to be taken into account underneath. However, it does not subject the buyer's choice of remedy to a criterion of reasonableness *tout court*, but rather requires a particular cost/benefit analysis. In this respect, the significance of the 'inconvenience to the consumer' is not quite clear, for while article 3(3) § 2 includes it as a factor in the assessment, article 3(3) § 3 then requires that 'any repair or replacement *shall be completed*... without any significant inconvenience to the consumer', which suggests that where a remedy would cause such inconvenience it will not be (legally) possible. Perhaps these two provisions can be reconciled by saying that where there would be significant inconvenience to the consumer caused by the remedy which he has *not* chosen, then this factor is necessarily deemed to outweigh the costs to the seller of the chosen remedy however much they may be: but this interpretation does detract from the balancing nature of the criterion of disproportionality.

The value of the goods without the lack of conformity could work against a choice of their repair (where the costs of repair outweighs the value of goods which could be replaced more cheaply) or against a choice of replacement (where the cost of replacement of the goods is very high compared with the cost of a minor repair). The 'significance of the non-conformity' may be relevant here, for this may refer to the seriousness or otherwise of any defect,[321] but the 'significance' could also refer to the use to which the consumer intends to put the goods and whether this use is compromised by the lack of conformity in question.

A final problem arises where one of the remedies is 'impossible' (for example, repair) and the buyer chooses the other (for example, replacement). Where this is the case, how can an evaluation be made of the *relative* cost to the seller of the remedy chosen over the other remedy which *ex hypothosi* has no cost? In these circumstances one could hold there to be no disproportionality as there is no '*alternative* remedy' as envisaged by article 3(3)§ 2 with the result that the buyer's choice is effective however costly to the seller and however unreasonable given the value of the goods and the significance of the conformity—for the Directive does not allow a comparison of a first level remedy with the ones available at the second level.

---

[321] Cf. the French version here which refers to the '*l'importance du défaut de conformité*'.

All this makes clear that while the Directive talks of a choice in the buyer as between the repair or replacement of the goods, this choice is subjected to a complex evaluation of the relative interests of both parties to one or other remedy. While the preamble states that the assessment of disproportionality is 'objective',[322] its focus is on the position of the seller. In practice, the seller may either accept a consumer's choice between these two remedies or contest it on the basis of its impossibility or disproportionality, leaving it to the consumer to take the matter to court for its 'objective assessment'. So, while recital 12 says that a consumer may reject a seller's offer of any remedy, where such an offer is repair or replacement the consumer *may not* reject the offer if the other is impossible or disproportionate—or rather, if he were to reject it, he cannot proceed to the second level of remedies and would be left otherwise unaided by the Directive. Furthermore, where a seller argues that neither of the first level remedies are available and offers instead a reduction in price or rescission of the contract (either being often cheaper for a seller[323]), it may be very difficult for a consumer to reject such an offer merely on the basis that the seller's view of the impossibility and 'disproportionality' of the first stage remedies is incorrect, given that the remedies which the seller has offered are those waiting for the consumer at the second level. And in particular, a seller will typically be in a position to know the relative cost *to himself* of repair, while the buyer will not and will have difficulty in challenging the seller's figures.

A buyer's preference as between the repair and replacement of the goods will depend on a range of considerations. So, for example, where a consumer has bought a household product (such as a washing machine) which functions but not as well as described, he may wish to carry on using it and have it repaired rather than have the trouble of its removal (and un-plumbing) and of the delivery (and re-plumbing) of a replacement.[324] In other situations, a buyer may prefer to have a (brand new and 'conforming') replacement rather than repaired goods; a buyer is certainly likely to prefer replacement goods if these consist of a more recent model.[325]

The seller's preference as between repair or replacement of the goods will depend in part on the cost of the repairs (as the criterion of proportionality itself recognises), but may also depend on whether the seller has the facilities to have the goods repaired easily (with any compatible spare parts) and whether he enjoys the benefit of any arrangement either with his own distributor or with their manufacturer as regards their repair or their replacement. *Generally*, however, repair is likely to be less costly than replacement. For, while on repair the seller bears the cost of the repair itself (labour and parts) and any transport costs (depending on where the repair is effected), he does not lose the profit of *any* sale.[326] By contrast, if a seller replaces non-conforming goods, his costs will include (i) the cost of transport of the replacement to the buyer (even where in

---

[322] Recital 11.   [323] Below, p. 610.

[324] It would seem that these installation costs are not required by the Directive to be covered by the seller, as article 3(2) refers to the repair or replacement of the goods 'free of charge' *sci* by the seller, but does not require the seller to re-imburse any additional cost incurred in the process by the buyer, as would be the case typically where goods are installed under the buyer's responsibility.

[325] *Quaere* whether such a motivation should count against the buyer in any judicial discretion: cf. below, pp. 614–15.

[326] These costs may be offset by any sums recoverable from his own seller or from the manufacturer by way of recourse.

the sale itself this transport was paid for by the buyer) and of the return of the non-conforming goods to him; (ii) at least where demand exceeds supply of the goods in question, the loss of profit on one transaction;[327] set against (iii) the balance between any money obtained by way of sale of the returned (and therefore second-hand) goods.[328]

As I have said, the Directive's second level of remedies of rescission of the contract or reduction in the price are available only in three specified circumstances. Article 3(5) provides that:

The consumer may require an appropriate reduction of the price or have the contract rescinded:

—if the consumer is entitled to neither repair nor replacement, or
—if the seller has not completed the remedy within a reasonable time, or
—if the seller has not completed the remedy without significant inconvenience to the consumer.

Once any one of these conditions is satisfied, article 3(5) gives the buyer a free choice between price reduction and rescission: there is no filter similar to disproportionality as found in article 3(3), though article 3(6) excludes rescission 'if the lack of conformity is minor'.

All three general alternative conditions for these two second level remedies relate back to the 'failure' of the first level remedies of repair or replacement, either owing to their unavailability or their mishandling by the seller. The Directive clearly views rescission[329] or price reduction as more prejudicial to the seller and indeed in the case of the failure of the seller to repair or replace the goods in a reasonable time or without significant inconvenience to the consumer, as something like a sanction of bad behaviour. However, as I have suggested, the impact of these remedies may be less prejudicial to the seller, in particular as regards the contrast between replacement on the one hand and rescission or price reduction on the other.

As I have explained, replacement of the goods brings a seller double transport costs and the loss of profit on one transaction set against any sums recoverable on resale

---

[327] This is the net loss, taking into account the price paid by the seller for the replacement goods less the price which he retains under the contract. Although the seller therefore retains any profit made on the contract of sale of the non-conforming goods, he loses any profit to be made in respect of the goods with which he replaces them. It is for this reason that this loss is contingent on demand exceeding supply, for where supply exceeds demand, the availability of the extra goods (in fact used to replace the non-conforming goods) would not result in any extra profit: cf. *Charter v Sullivan* [1957] 2 QB 117 where the court denied damages representing a trader's lost profit on a sale repudiated by the buyer on the ground that he could sell all the goods of the type in question which he had available and so had suffered no loss.

[328] Again, this may be offset by any amount recoverable by way of recourse.

[329] The nature of 'rescission' which (like *résolution*, which is used by the French version of the Directive) suggests termination from the beginning, but this is not entirely clear. As has been noted, recital 15 leaves the 'details' of rescission to the national law (relating, for example, to whether or not it may be invoked where the goods cannot be returned in the same state) and both the questions of the unilateral or judicial nature of the termination and of its effect may be considered included within this allocation of responsibility. Bianca, *op. cit.* n. 43, 173 argues for the non-judicial nature of 'rescission' for the purposes of the Directive; *contra* Zimmermann, *Liability for Non-conformity*, 43; Benjamin, *Special Supplement*, § 1–142 *et seq*. The 2002 Regulations appear to interpret 'rescission' for the English context as being an act of the buyer, terminating the contract (or part of the contract), but it may be accompanied by 'such terms and conditions... as [the court] thinks just': 2002 Regulations, r. 5 new s. 48E(4)(b) 1979 Act, which refers to the buyer's having 'claimed to rescind the contract' and see also new s. 48E(6) 1979 Act.

of the (now second-hand) goods.[330] By contrast, where a contract of sale is 'rescinded', the seller's net costs consist in principle of a single cost of transport (the return of the goods), and the loss of profit on one transaction (the sale itself) set against any resale. In this light, the seller's financial position is the same for rescission as for replacement of the goods, except that the seller does not have to bear the cost of any transport of the replacement goods to the consumer. Moreover, the Directive allows Member States to provide that 'any reimbursement to the consumer may be reduced to take account of the use the consumer has had of the goods since they were delivered to him'[331] and where this is the case, a seller would be further better off than if he replaces the goods, as no similar allowance is apparently to be made to a seller in this situation.

The remedy of price reduction is more attractive in terms of cost to the seller than either the replacement of the goods or rescission, since here the seller would have to reimburse or forego 'an appropriate amount' of the price,[332] (which may sometimes be compensated by recourse against his own distributor or the manufacturer), but in principle would not lose whatever profit he made on the sale nor would he bear any transport costs.

What all this means in practice is that in general (and depending on such variables as the significance or otherwise of the cost of transport of the goods in question) from the point of view of a seller the cost of the remedies is likely to be in descending order (i) replacement of the goods; (ii) rescission of the contract; and (iii) either repair or price reduction depending on the cost of repairing the lack of conformity in question. Formally, of course, a seller is not able to choose which remedy to allow the consumer, but, as I have said, faced with a request for replacement, a seller can quite easily argue either for repair of the goods instead or that neither of the first level remedies are available and that the buyer is limited to rescission or price reduction.[333] And all that a seller need do to 'incite' a buyer to move on to the second level of remedies (rescission or price reduction) is to delay carrying out a requested repair or replacement or cause significant inconvenience to the buyer in their process, fairly safe in the knowledge that the vast majority of buyers will not choose to go to court to 'force' performance of the first level remedy. On the other hand, where a seller cannot argue that replacement of the goods is either impossible or disproportionate, then the consumer can choose replacement, which is typically the *most* costly to the seller. Finally, while the cost to the seller is made the touchstone of the availability of the first level remedies, the Directive makes no attempt to *compensate* the cost to the buyer of the lack of conformity itself, even by way of liability to reimburse 'expenses caused by the sale' of a type imposed by article 1646 of the Civil Code.[334] To this extent, the Directive's orientation is indeed towards the protection of the interests of businesses rather than of consumers.

---

[330] Above, pp. 608–9.   [331] Recital 15.

[332] The better view is that 'the appropriate amount' should relate to the relative effect of the lack of conformity on the value of the goods rather than the loss which this causes the buyer: Bradgate and Twigg-Flesner, *op. cit.* n. 39, 132 (contrasting the position here with set-off under s. 53(1)(a) of the Sale of Goods Act).   [333] Above, p. 608.

[334] Above, p. 82.

(ii) Implementation of the consumer's rights in English law

As I have explained, the UK government's decision that implementation of the Directive should not reduce the protection of consumers put a stop to any but a superficial integration of its scheme of rights for buyers with existing rights under the Sale of Goods Act.[335] Therefore, the 2002 Regulations left in place entirely the buyer's existing 'classic' remedies for breach of the implied conditions in sections 13 and 14 of the Sale of Goods Act[336] and added a second set of remedies closely, though not exactly reflecting the Directive's scheme. As a result, there is now a *three-fold* layering of remedial response to breach of the statutory implied terms: (i) the classic remedies of rejection and termination (referred to subsequently simply as 'rejection') and/or damages; (ii) repair or replacement by the seller; and (iii) 'rescission' or price reduction (terming (ii) and (iii) the 'new remedies').[337] The result takes a little explaining and could hardly be more complicated from a consumer's point of view.

First, there is a complex series of choices facing a consumer buyer as a result of implementation of the Directive, compared to the previous law's choice between rejection of the goods and/or damages. The starting point is that a consumer may choose between the classic remedies and the new remedies, as long as, of course, the respective conditions for their existence are satisfied. As a matter of their relative availability, a buyer is likely to prefer the new remedies since they benefit from the presumption of the anteriority of any defect for a period of six months[338] and are not lost by 'acceptance' of the goods.[339] On the other hand, as a matter of the substantive outcome, a buyer may well prefer to reject the goods and terminate the contract, gaining his money back in full[340] and recovering any difference in the cost of their replacement by way of damages, since this has the advantage of simplicity and relative speed. Moreover, if a buyer chooses to retain the goods or has lost the right to reject under the classic scheme, he may still have the goods repaired by a third party at the seller's expense, this being recoverable by way of damages subject to the requirement of reasonableness imposed by the law of mitigation.[341] So, even putting aside the possibility of recovery for consequential losses or damage, the classic remedies of rejection and damages allow a buyer to have the goods repaired or replaced, but by a third party in whom a buyer may have more confidence, rather than by the seller.

By contrast, if a buyer chooses to require the seller to repair or replace the goods, then the possibility of argument on the basis of the appropriateness of one or

---

[335] Above, pp. 584–5.

[336] 1979 Act, s. 11(4) (rejection of the goods and repudiation of the contract); ibid., ss. 51 and 53 (damages).

[337] It also put in place a different three-fold layer of remedial response to breach of express terms relating to the goods, that is termination for major breach of contract at common law and the further two layers of remedies contained in the Directive: 2002 Regulations r. 5 creating new s. 48F 1979 Act.

[338] 2002 Regulations, r. 5, new s. 48A(3) and (4) 1979 Act. It is to be noted that the amendments of the definition of the implied terms in s. 14 of the Sale of Goods Act apply to all remedies claimed by a individual buyer who 'deals as consumer' and not merely to the Directive's remedies.   [339] Below, p. 620.

[340] There is, though, some doubt as to whether restitution of the price is always available, above, pp. 254–5.

[341] Above, p. 256. The question would also arise as to whether a buyer who has the right to claim repair or replacement of the goods *by the seller* acts 'reasonably' by having them repaired by a third party.

other remedy immediately arises. Here, the 2002 Regulations differ from the terms of article 2 of the 1999 Directive.[342] In common with the Directive, the Regulations deny a remedy where one or both are 'impossible',[343] but their test of 'disproportionality' requires comparison of the relative cost to the seller of the remedy chosen not merely (as under the Directive) as against the other first level remedy,[344] but also as against the remedies contingently available at the second level.[345] So, for example, if a buyer chooses to require a seller to repair the goods, a court would have to assess whether its cost to the seller is unreasonable compared to the cost of replacement, the cost of 'rescission' and restitution or the cost of a reduction in the price, taking into account the same considerations as are set out in the Directive of the value of the goods if conforming, the significance of the lack of conformity and the question whether the other remedy could be effected without significant inconvenience to the buyer.[346] Moreover, this comparison of remedy must be undertaken hypothetically, since at this stage the court may be deciding a question on which the availability of one or other of these second level remedies rests. So, for example, if the buyer chooses repair in circumstances where replacement is 'impossible', the court must assess the 'disproportionality' of this choice compared with 'rescission' or price reduction, and if repair *is* held disproportionate, the buyer may not require *either* first level remedy and so the buyer reaches the second level. However, having reached the second level in this way, under the 2002 Regulations the buyer's choice is again limited. For while under the Directive at the second level the buyer's choice is free and unqualified,[347] where the buyer's first level remedy has been rejected as disproportionate, the English court is given the power by the Regulations to *substitute* what it considers to be the more appropriate remedy of each of the three other remedies available.[348] So, for example, where replacement is impossible and repair disproportionate, the court may choose to 'award rescission' or price reduction.[349] On the other hand, where a court decides the issue of 'disproportionality' or 'appropriateness', its comparison is restricted to the new consumer rights, and may *not* take into account the merits of the classic remedies of rejection and/or damages.[350]

Secondly, to a degree the Regulations lock a buyer into a particular remedial route once chosen, for they provide that if the buyer requires the seller to repair (or as the case may be, to replace) the goods, then he 'must not' claim their replacement (or if replacement were required, their repair) *nor* must he reject the goods and terminate the contract for breach of condition, until he has given the seller a reasonable time in which to perform the remedy originally required.[351] There is no equivalent provision

---

[342] Above, pp. 606–7.   [343] 2002 Regulations r. 5, new s. 48B(3)(a) 1979 Act.

[344] Ibid., new s. 48B(3)(b) 1979 Act.   [345] Ibid., new s. 48B(3)(c) 1979 Act.

[346] Ibid., new s. 48B(4) 1979 Act. For this purpose, the Regulations use the explanation of 'significant inconvenience' provided by the Directive as regards the manner in which any repair or replacement must be carried out: 2002 Regulations r. 5, new s. 48B(5) 1979 Act; 1999 Directive art. 3(3) § 3.

[347] Above, p. 609 (subject to the exclusion of rescission for minor defects).

[348] 2002 Regulations r. 5, new ss. 48C(1), 48E(3) &(4), 1979 Act and see below, p. 614.

[349] Unlike the Directive, there is no restriction of 'rescission' to 'major' non-conformity: 2002 Regulations r. 5, new s. 48C(1)(b) 1979 Act.   [350] *Benjamin, Special Supplement,* § 1–162.

[351] 2002 Regulations r. 5, new s. 48D 1979 Act.

in the Directive, but this result may be thought implicit in its setting of a reasonable time for the accomplishment of the first level remedies;[352] and as regards the classic remedy of rejection of the goods, its effect is to restrict an existing UK remedy rather than any remedy required by the Directive. On the other hand, it gives a significance and a degree of practical finality to the buyer's choice in favour of the Directive's remedies rather than rejection of the goods (it does not affect any claim for damages), for after waiting a reasonable time for repair or replacement of the goods by the seller without a satisfactory result, any attempt in the buyer to opt for rejection of the goods under the classic scheme is likely to be faced with the argument that he is deemed to have 'accepted them' by retaining 'the goods after the lapse of a reasonable time without intimating to the seller that he has rejected them'.[353] So, while waiting for repair or replacement he may not reject the goods, but in the course of waiting he may lose his right to do so! True, a court could take the seller's unreasonable delay in effecting repair or replacement into account as a matter of the general 'reasonableness' of the time taken to reject the goods by the buyer,[354] but a buyer's claim of repair or replacement by the seller nevertheless puts at risk whatever clarity might at one time have been available to the buyer under the classic right of rejection.[355]

It could be countered that this practical loss of the right of rejection of the goods does not matter given that where the seller has delayed unreasonably in putting into effect the goods' repair or replacement, the buyer may then choose either 'rescission' of the contract or a reduction in price.[356] Under the scheme of the Regulations, he may indeed do so, but 'rescission' has some features which make it sometimes less attractive to a buyer than 'rejection'. So, while 'rescission' is *not* limited to minor defects of conformity in the Regulations (unlike the Directive),[357] it allows a deduction to be made from any reimbursement to take account of the use by the buyer of the goods,[358] unlike rejection of the goods which allows recovery of the price in full;[359] and where one item of a number of goods sold under a single contract is defective, a buyer may reject the whole batch and terminate *the contract* in its entirety, whereas, following the Directive itself, 'rescission' is allowed only 'with regard to those goods', i.e. those which suffer from a lack of conformity.[360]

---

[352] Bianca, *op. cit.* n. 43, 174.   [353] 1979 Act, s. 35 and see above, pp. 252–3.

[354] Cf. *Clegg v Andersson* [2003] EWCA Civ 320 § 63 and see above, p. 253. The buyer could also point to 1979 Act, s. 35(6)(a) which provides that a 'buyer is not ... deemed to have accepted the goods merely because he asks for, or agrees to, their repair by or under an arrangement with the seller', but quite apart from the fact that this provision does not purport to help a buyer who claimed replacement of the goods rather than their repair, it may be thought inapplicable to the situation where a buyer *requires* the repair of the goods within the meaning of the Directive, rather than 'makes an arrangement'.

[355] There is a further complication in the relationship of the two termination remedies. If a buyer requires the repair or replacement of the goods and within a reasonable time the seller proceeds to perform the remedy in such a way as to cause considerable inconvenience to the buyer, the second level of remedies under the directive arise, *but not* the remedy of repudiation and termination: this appears to be frozen until after the lapse of a 'reasonable time'.   [356] 2002 Regulations r. 5, new ss. 48C(1) & 48C(2)(b) 1979 Act.

[357] Ibid., new ss. 48C(1)(b); 1999 Directive, art. 3(6).   [358] Ibid., new s. 48C(3) 1979 Act.

[359] Above, pp. 254–5.

[360] 2002 Regulations r. 5, new s. 48C(1)(b) 1979 Act; 1999 Directive, art. 3(2).

Thirdly, the 2002 Regulations retain the hierarchy of remedies of the Directive, with the twists which I have already mentioned.[361] So, a buyer reaches the second level remedies only if (i) the first level remedies are both impossible; (ii) the first level remedy chosen is disproportionate to a remedy available at the second level;[362] (iii) the seller has failed to implement a first level remedy in a reasonable time or without causing significant inconvenience to the consumer;[363] or (iv) the court considers that a second level remedy is 'appropriate' even though the claimant has chosen another remedy.[364]

When we turn to the procedural mechanisms introduced for the putting into effect of the buyer's new rights, the complexity increases. The 2002 Regulations provide that a seller of goods *must* comply with a buyer's lawful[365] requirement that he repair or replace them at his own cost within a reasonable time,[366] and that '[o]n the application of the buyer the court *may* make an order requiring specific performance' of the obligation in a seller which this creates.[367] Clearly, the Dti did not consider it sufficient for a seller's failure to comply with this obligation merely to be liable in damages to the buyer, even if this were compatible with the Directive's provisions.[368] Such a statutory example of specific performance is very unusual and even more so in that it allows judicial enforcement on pain of contempt of court of a contractual obligation which did not form one of the primary obligations of the contract contained in the agreement: the parties' may be said to have agreed to the 'conformity' of the goods (though this is debatable), but they certainly did not agree to their repair or replacement.[369] However, unless 'specific performance' were held to be entirely *sui generis* for the purposes of the Regulations (which would rather defeat the point of the use of this technical expression), it would appear to attract at least some of the general attributes of the traditional equitable remedy, notably that its availability would be discretionary and subject to equitable considerations, and this is suggested by the permissive manner in which the Regulations express the court's power.[370] The question arises, though, whether such a general equitable discretion is compatible with the express (but constrained) discretion given to the court by the Regulations to substitute another remedy *provided by the Regulations* for the remedy claimed by the seller.[371] So, the Regulations provide that where a buyer requires a seller to replace or to repair the goods, or to reduce their price by an appropriate amount, or has claimed to 'rescind' the contract, but the court decides that *another* of these four remedies is *appropriate*, the court 'may proceed ... as if the buyer had required the seller to give effect to the other remedy, or

---

[361] Above, p. 612.   [362] 2002 Regulations, r. 5 new s. 48C(2)(a) 1979 Act.

[363] Ibid., new s. 48C(2)(b) 1979 Act.   [364] Ibid., new s. 48E(3) 1979 Act.

[365] By lawful, I mean one conforming to the requirements of possibility and proportionality, see above, pp. 606–7.   [366] 2002 Regulations, r. 5 new s. 48B(2) 1979 Act.

[367] 2002 Regulations, r. 5 new s. 48E(2) 1979 Act (emphasis added).   [368] Cf. above, p. 605.

[369] This use of specific performance is likely to give rise to a degree of terminological awkwardness, in that specific performance is generally called a 'remedy', yet here is used to give effect to the 'remedies' of repair or replacement of the goods. One 'remedy' piles on top of another.

[370] '[T]he court may make an order requiring specific performance': 2002 Regulations, r. 5 new s. 48E(2) 1979 Act. For these attributes, generally see Treitel, *Law of Contracts*, 1026 *et seq*.

[371] This is linked to the Regulations' changes to the test of disproportionality: above, p. 612.

if the other remedy is rescission . . . as if the buyer had claimed to rescind the contract'.[372] Any order made by the court under these provisions may be unconditional or 'on such terms and conditions as to damages, payment of the price and otherwise as it thinks just'.[373] It has been argued, therefore, that 'specific performance' for this purpose 'operates within Pt 5A [of the 1979 Act] and that there appears to be no power to consider . . . whether an award of damages at common law (or indeed rejection at common law) would be more appropriate'.[374] This would have the result (which could be thought of as giving proper effect to the rights of repair or replacement) that the court's discretion to award specific performance for this purpose is constrained in a way which makes it differ significantly from specific performance generally, which is not normally awarded where damages would be an adequate remedy. On the other hand, it would not prevent a court's refusal of specific performance on general equitable grounds (which could come under the generally permissive nature of the power to award it), but if it did refuse, the court's choice would be restricted to the new consumer remedies (though possibly on terms). What is not clear is whether *at this stage* a consumer could opt for one or other of the classic remedies of rejection or damages despite having triggered the court's legislative discretion.[375]

In this way, the Regulations appear to have created a new form of 'specific performance', whose attributes stem partly from the common law and partly from the particular purposes for which it is used by them. As a result the Regulations appear to recognise *two* levels at which the court has a discretion to deny the replacement or repair of the goods: at the level of the existence of these rights (under the tests of impossibility and disproportionality) and at the level of procedural enforcement, the two discretions being exercisable according to distinct sets of criteria.[376]

The result is as follows. A buyer claims replacement of the goods, which the seller refuses on the ground of its disproportionality by comparison with repair. The buyer therefore goes to court asking that the court order the seller to perform its obligation to replace the goods, but the court upholds the seller's argument as to disproportionality, preferring one of the other new remedies on this ground.[377] The court then may substitute that other remedy, even if it belongs to the second level of remedies according to the Directive's scheme and even though the buyer did not ask for it! Such a substitution can be justified on the ground that to do otherwise risks a decision holding that another remedy is more appropriate and *would* have been available had it been claimed, but then denying it on the basis that it had *not* been claimed. Nor is this merely a hypothetical possibility, since in some cases rescission of the contract within

---

[372] 2002 Regulations, r. 5, new s. 48E(3) and 48(E)(4) 1979 Act. In the case of rescission, the court may reduce any reimbursement made to the buyer to take account of the use which he has had of the goods: ibid., s. 48E(5).

[373] 2002 Regulations, r. 5, new s. 48E(6) 1979 Act.

[374] *Chitty on Contracts* para. 43–124; *Benjamin, Special Supplement*, § 1–182. Cf. Treitel, *Law of Contract*, 1025 who sees damages as 'unlikely to be the most appropriate remedy for a consumer who has bought (for example) an appliance which malfunctions' and otherwise sees the Regulations' approach as 'consistent with the principles governing specific relief in English law.' [375] Cf. above, p. 612.

[376] For the criteria under 'disproportionality', see above, p. 607. For the criteria under specific performance generally, see Treitel, *loc. cit.* n. 370. [377] 2002 Regulations, r. 5, new s. 48B(3)(b) and (c).

the meaning of the Directive may be less costly for a seller than either repair or, especially, replacement of the goods.[378] So, a buyer could claim replacement, try to enforce this against an unwilling seller and then have a court in effect itself rescind the contract on such terms as it thinks fit, even if this is to the buyer's disadvantage. Again, where an English court, seized of a claim for the enforcement of a seller's obligation to repair or replace goods, holds that one of these is impossible and the other disproportionate compared to a second level remedy, the court could choose to order that second level remedy, even though the scheme of the Directive allows the buyer a free choice between them.[379] For these reasons, here the UK's implementation of the 1999 Directive appears itself to be non-conforming, for while EC law does grant Member States a general competence in the procedural putting into effect of its rights and obligations, this does not extend to the restriction of these rights themselves.

Finally, these new judicial powers of specific performance and substitution of an alternative 'appropriate' remedy apply not merely to a claim for a first level remedy based on breach of the statutory implied terms, but also to a claim for a new remedy based on breach 'in relation to the goods' of any express term.[380] The Regulations' use of specific performance for enforcement here is as alien to English law as the notion that the court should have a general power to substitute what it considers to be a more appropriate remedy for the one claimed. In sum, in relation to the buyer's rights, the Regulations introduce changes which are alien both to English law and to the 1999 Directive.

(iii) Implementation of the consumer's rights in French law

The Working Group's proposed creation of a unified basis of liability in all contracts of sale lent itself to a proposal that the remedies available should also in principle be general to all sales: no remedies were to be available only to consumer buyers.[381] It proposed, therefore, that four remedies ('*remèdes*') should be available: repair, replacement, *résolution* (which for this purpose was assumed to be by decision of the court following its general law)[382] and price reduction. While its draft legislation would have given the buyer a choice between these remedies, it proposed that the seller could refuse to reduce the price and could resist a claim for *résolution* by offering to repair or to replace the goods within a month for movable property and within three months for immovable property.[383] Otherwise, the Working Group followed the Directive, giving the buyer a choice as between repair and replacement, denying either where impossible or where it caused 'an excessive burden to the seller' and *résolution* for minor defects.[384] Moreover, it proposed that the new legislation should set out the result reached by the settled practice of the courts and declare that all *vendeurs professionnels* could also be liable in damages for loss caused by a defect of conformity, other sellers being so liable only on proof of knowledge at the time of delivery.[385]

---

[378] Above, p. 610.   [379] Above, p. 609.   [380] 2002 Regulations, r. 5, new s. 48F 1979 Act.
[381] Working Group, *Rapport général*, Part I, sections III and IV; proposed arts. 1644–1644-2 C. civ.
[382] Above, p. 82.   [383] *Avant-projet de loi*, proposed art. 1644 C. civ.
[384] Ibid., proposed art. 1644-1 C. civ.   [385] Ibid., proposed art. 1645 C. civ.

This scheme would have been not merely simpler than that found in the 2002 Regulations, but also simpler than that found in the 1999 Directive. While this may be thought surprising given the broader coverage of the proposed French legislation, it reflects the Working Group's particular concern with simplification of the law in the interests of its accessibility.[386] On the other hand, on occasion the proposed scheme risked being *less* protective for consumer buyers than the Directive required, for example, it did not adopt the Directive's test of disproportionality for first level remedies, simplifying the complex balance found in the Directive itself with a laconic reference to comparing whether either remedy imposed in relation to the other 'an excessive burden to the seller'.[387] However, given the fate of the Working Group's proposals, the question of their legality in EC law need not now be addressed.[388]

The *ordonnance* of 17 February 2005 starts by emphasising the theoretical basis of the buyer's new rights by declaring that 'the buyer has the right to demand that the property be in conformity with the contract', thereby tying the buyer's rights to the classic contractual foundation of conformity which the Directive adopts.[389] It then sets out the basic choice of the buyer in cases of non-conforming property between repair and replacement of the goods.[390] However, where the cost of the remedy chosen by the buyer is 'manifestly disproportionate' as compared to the other first level remedy or where it is impossible, the seller must instead proceed to the other first level remedy.[391] The buyer may 'return the property and recover the price or keep the property and return part of the price' only (i) where both first level remedies are impossible or (ii) where the first level remedy chosen cannot be accomplished within a period of one month from the buyer's request or cannot be accomplished without major inconvenience to the buyer.[392] No *résolution* of the contract of sale can be declared if the defect of conformity is minor.[393] As I have said, it is added somewhat ambiguously that 'these dispositions do not prevent an award of damages'.[394]

These provisions follow the scheme of the Directive very closely, differing from it principally by avoiding once again the Directive's references to 'reasonableness': first, in relation to the test of disproportionality found in article 3(3) of the Directive, the *ordonnance* preferring the more stringent test of 'manifest disproportionality'; and secondly, in relation to the period of time for the seller to give effect to a buyer's first level claim before the second level is reached by substituting a fixed period of one month. Otherwise (and unlike the 2002 Regulations), the French legislation implementing the Directive does not make any special provision in order to give procedural effect to the new remedial consequences of non-conformity of the goods, clearly relying on its general law to apply. I wish to draw attention to two consequences of this reliance.

---

[386] Above, p. 580.   [387] *Avant-projet de loi*, proposed art. 1644-1 al. 1 C. civ.

[388] Cf. Tournafond, *Proposition, Exposé des motifs*, proposed new art. L. 211-5 al. 2 C. consom. which would have allowed a *seller* to choose between repair or replacement despite this being entirely unjustified on any interpretation of the 1999 Directive.

[389] *Ord.* of 17 Feb. 2001, art. 1 creating new art. L. 211-8 C. consom. and see above, p. 592.

[390] Ibid., creating new art. L. 211-9 C. consom.

[391] Ibid., creating new art. L. 211-9 al. 2 C. consom.

[392] Ibid., creating new art. L. 211-10 al. 1 and al. 2 1° and 2° C. consom.

[393] Ibid., creating new art. L. 211-10 al. 3 C. consom.

[394] Ibid., creating new art. L. 211-11 al. 2 C. consom. above, p. 604.

First, under the general law *résolution* is in principle an act of a court by which the contract is terminated from the beginning and restitution and counter-restitution of property or money transferred under the contract is ordered at the request of a creditor of an obligation.[395] While courts are given by the Civil Code a power to refuse *résolution* so as to give a debtor more time to perform[396] and while they have taken upon themselves the power to order 'intermediate solutions',[397] they do not overtly make allowance by reduction of any reimbursement for a person's use of property to be restored after *résolution*. Here, the *ordonnance* of 17 February 2005 is somewhat unclear. At first sight it appears to create a legislative example of extra-judicial *résolution*, as it refers to the ability ('*la faculté*') to return the goods and receive back the price,[398] but then it later refers to *résolution* being 'pronounced',[399] which suggests the need for judicial intervention. Also in keeping with the general position as regards *résolution judiciaire*, there is no mention in the *ordonnance* of 17 February 2005 of any qualification of the buyer's right of reimbursement on rescission in the way which the Directive's preamble allows.[400]

Secondly, where a French civil court orders a party to perform an obligation (whether contractual or otherwise), the order may be backed by a system of monetary penalties called *astreintes*: there is no law approaching the English contempt of court.[401] Under this system, a party may apply for or a court may impose of its own initiative the payment of a money sum for every day, week or month for which a person continues in breach of a court order, the advantage being that the *astreinte* adds to a person's obligation to *do* something (notably, to repair or replace the goods) an obligation to *pay* a sum of money, which may be then enforced by way of execution against the recalcitrant person's property. French courts have a 'sovereign power of assessment' both as to the appropriateness of ordering an *astreinte* and as to its amount, it being said that this should be fixed so as to put adequate pressure on a person to obey the order.[402] What this means for the context of the provisions implementing the 1999 Directive is that while at a formal level a French court may order a seller to repair or replace non-conforming goods, the order itself will be enforceable only to the extent that a court considers it appropriate to impose an *astreinte* of sufficient size to create a real incentive for a seller to do so. So, whereas in the English context the potency of specific performance has contributed to judicial reluctance to order it,[403] in the French context, the greater liberality in granting orders of performance of obligations is accompanied by their relative weakness.

---

[395] Art. 1183 and 1184 C. civ. and see above, p. 82. The main exception is found in the practice of *clauses résolutoire expresses.*   [396] Art. 1184 al. 3 C. civ.

[397] Bell, Boyron and Whittaker, 420 *et seq.*

[398] *Ord.* of 17 Feb. 2005, art. 1 creating new art. L. 211-10 al. 1. C. consom.

[399] Ibid., creating new art. L. 211-10 al. 3 C. consom.

[400] Ibid., creating new art. L. 211-10 C. consom.; 1999 Directive, recital 15.

[401] *Loi* no. 91-650 of 9 Jul. 1991, arts. 33–7 and Bell, Boyron and Whittaker, 109 *et seq.*

[402] Terré, Simler, Lequette, *Obligations*, 1044 *et seq.*

[403] *Co-operative Insurance Society Ltd. v Argyle Stores (Holdings) Ltd.* [1998] AC 1, 12–13, *per* Lord Hoffmann.

(d) The time within which claims must be made or brought

(i) Limitation or prescription periods

Article 5(1) of the 1999 Directive states that:

The seller shall be held liable under Article 3 where the lack of conformity becomes apparent within two years as from delivery of the goods. If, under national legislation, the rights laid down in Article 3(2) are subject to a limitation period, that period shall not expire within a period of two years from the time of delivery.

The first part of this sets out the longevity of the rights required by the Directive (two years) though article 7 allows Member States to allow contracting parties to reduce this to one year in the case of second-hand goods.[404] This period starts from delivery of the goods and not the time when the consumer discovered or ought reasonably to have discovered any defect of conformity so that a consumer's rights may be lost before he knows that they exist. However, the effect of the second part of article 5(1) is that 'the total duration of [any] limitation period provided for by national law may not be shorter than two years from the time of delivery',[405] and so a Member State may provide that the two-year period starts from discovery or constructive discovery as this would extend rather than restrict the period of limitation which article 5(1) allows.[406] It needs to be emphasised that article 5 does not introduce a 'two-year' guarantee of the goods in the sense that any defect *arising* within two years after delivery will give rise to the rights set out in article 3: any non-conformity must exist on delivery, though a buyer will benefit from the presumption of its anteriority for the first six months.[407]

By comparison with previous English law, article 5 sets a period which is at once quite long and rather short. It is long compared to the rapid loss of the right to reject goods delivered in breach of the implied terms of quality and fitness for purpose as a result of the law governing 'acceptance' of the goods after a reasonable time after delivery, this being measured typically in weeks or months and not in years.[408] On the other hand, it is short compared to the standard period of the limitation of actions for breach of contract, which is set at six years from breach, this being effectively the same in this context as delivery.[409] Under the previous law, this longer period had an impact only as regards claims for damages, though these claims provided (and can continue to provide) the mechanism by which a buyer can achieve the repair or replacement of the goods.[410]

---

[404] Art. 7(1) § 2. This *may* still leave such a term challengeable under legislation implementing EC Dir. 93/13 on unfair terms in consumer contracts.

[405] 1999 Directive, recital 17. Recital 18 remarks that Member States may provide for the suspension or interruption of this period in the event of repair or replacement or negotiations with a view to amicable settlement, though this appears redundant given the minimum nature of the Directive's requirements: art. 8(2).

[406] Cf. German law's adoption of the Directive's approach here in new § 438 BGB criticised by Zimmermann, *Liability for Non-conformity*, 56–8.   [407] Above, p. 594.

[408] Above, pp. 252–3.   [409] Above, pp. 256–7.   [410] Above, pp. 255–6, 260.

Under the 2002 Regulations, the new buyers' rights for individuals who 'deal as consumers' are not lost by 'acceptance of the goods',[411] but remain valid for the full limitation period of six years from the time of their delivery.[412] Here, simplicity and the avoidance of disharmony with the limitation of actions applicable to claims for damages were preferred to the Directive's compromise expressed in the recognition of new consumer rights valid for a relatively short period.[413] In the English law context, this means that there is no advantage to a buyer in terms of timing as between the classic and the new remedies, with the exception of the difference between rejection of the goods (which remains subject to the law of 'acceptance') and 'rescission' of the contract (which remains open for six years from delivery). On the other hand, the longer a buyer enjoys goods (even if they are non-conforming) the more likely and the more substantial will be any reduction of the reimbursed price on 'rescission' for the use which has been made of them.[414]

When looking at the differences between the requirements as to the time within which claims must be brought in the previous French law and the requirements of article 5(1) of the Directive, one faces difficulties of complexity and uncertainty: complexity in that many of the grounds of avoidance of a contract on facts where 'non-conformity' could apply bear their own prescription periods or *délai* (from the 30-year prescription period of the general law to the *bref délai* of the *garantie légale*) and uncertainty given that the starting point and the duration of the *bref délai* were within the 'sovereign power of assessment' of the *juges du fond*.[415] Having said that, we can say that under the *garantie légale*, the length of time within which a claim had to be brought was normally within a few months of the effective discovery of the defect by the buyer, which might be years after the sale was concluded.[416] On the other hand, if liability can be established under the general law of contractual non-conformity, in consumer sales any claim must be brought within ten years of the time when performance was due, i.e. typically delivery of the property.[417]

The French Working Group wished to cut through most of this complexity and see created two *délais* for their proposed unitary basis of liability: five years from delivery for movables and ten years from delivery for immovables.[418] As for goods, the five-year period would have been longer than the two years required by the Directive and *usually* much longer than the *bref délai*, though the latter's starting point with the defect's discovery could occasionally make it longer. However, the *ordonnance* of 17 February 2005's much more modest approach results in two changes being made

---

[411] This follows from the insertion of the new remedies into the 1979 Act as 'additional rights' where a buyer deals as consumer and the goods do not conform to the contract of sale, the latter being then defined as being where 'there is, in relation to the goods, a breach of an express term of the contract or a term implied by section 13, 14, or 15' of the 1979 Act: 2002 Regulations, r. 5 creating new s. 48A(1) and 48F 1979 Act.

[412] This follows from the general application of the Limitation Act 1989, s. 6: Dti, *Second Consultation*, Part I, § 20.

[413] Ibid., §§ 22–3. The Law Commission has recommended a new general limitation period of 3 years from the date of reasonable discoverability which would (if adopted) also apply here: Law Commission, *Limitation of Actions*, Law Com. no. 270 (2001).

[414] 2002 Regulations, r. 5, new s. 48E(5) 1979 Act, above, p. 613.   [415] Above, pp. 91–3.

[416] Above, p. 92.   [417] Above, p. 93.   [418] *Avant-projet de loi*, proposed new art. 1648 C. civ.

to the law of *délais*. First, it follows the Directive entirely in providing that the new consumer rights must be exercised within two years of the delivery of the goods.[419] But secondly, as I have said, it also made an independent change to the national law governing the *garantie légale*, replacing the *bref délai* with a period of two years from the *discovery* of the defect.[420] This makes the *garantie légale* much more attractive in terms of timing than the new consumer rights inserted into the *Code de la consommation* and in this respect the *ordonnance* of 17 February 2005 itself allows a consumer buyer to choose freely whether to claim one of the new consumer remedies or to proceed by way of another action (whether under the *garantie légale* or any other contractual or non-contractual basis).[421] This means that a consumer buyer is likely to keep to the classic *garantie légale* except where he wishes to claim repair or replacement of the goods.

(ii) Notification by the buyer

Article 5(2) of the 1999 Directive allows Member States to require consumer buyers to inform the seller of the lack of conformity of the goods once discovered within a period of two months from the date of discovery. This provision, described as a major weakness in the Directive's protection of consumers by the responsible Commission official, was originally proposed as a counterbalance to the consumer's free choice between the remedies recognised by an earlier draft, but was nevertheless retained when the 'hierarchy of remedies' was introduced.[422] Commission opposition to this retention is reflected in its being an overt option for Member States,[423] and in a provision for the monitoring of its exercise by the Commission.[424]

Such a notification provision has formed no part of English law, although the rules on 'acceptance' have prevented a buyer from rejecting the goods after a reasonable time after their delivery.[425] On implementation of the Directive, the UK legislator decided not to include a notification requirement for the exercise of the new remedies which it created, the principal reasons being the Government's commitment to maintaining the existing classic remedies and a concern that its introduction would create a disharmony between the new remedies other than rescission and claims for damages, which were very close in practice.[426] Again, therefore, the Government's fundamental policy had a direct consequence for the UK's implementation of the Directive even as regards provisions which introduced its new and extra remedies.

French law did not either possess any such a notification requirement, though one could see the *bref délai* as having a certain similar effect. However, this similarity of effect and its restrictive nature of the notification period of two months made it unattractive both to the Working Group and the *ordonnance* of 17 February 2005, which omits it altogether.[427]

---

[419] *Ord.* of 17 Feb. 2005, art. 1 creating new art. 211-12 C. consom.

[420] Ibid., art. 3, amending art. 1648 C. civ.

[421] Ibid., art. 1, creating new art. L 211-13 C. consom.   [422] Staudenmayer, *op. cit.* n. 34, 557–8.

[423] Art. 5(2) states that 'Member States *may* provide...' This option would appear to be unnecessary given the general ability of Member States to put in place a greater consumer protection than the Directive requires under art. 8(2).   [424] Art. 5(2) §§ 2 and 3.

[425] Above, p. 252.

[426] Dti, Consumer Affaires Directorate, *Sale of Goods Directive*, Second Consultation of 2001 (June, 2001), Part I, § 25.   [427] Working Group, *Avant-projet, Exposé des motifs*, 4.

(e) Protection of the buyer's protection

In common with other directives in the area of consumer protection, the 1999 Directive makes provision so that its rules cannot be avoided by a contrary agreement in the contract.[428]

(i) *Avoidance by choice of law*

Member States are specifically required by article 7(2) to ensure that 'consumers are not deprived of the protection afforded' by the Directive as a result of a choice of the law of a non-Member State 'where the contract has a close connection with the territory of the Member States'.[429] This now standard provision[430] leaves the possibility of a seller choosing the law of a Member State other than the one with which the contract is itself most closely connected, relying principally on the Directive's own effect in ensuring a minimum standard of protection: it does not itself set a rule for the applicable law.[431] On the other hand, a consumer buyer may find himself further but differently protected from the prejudicial effect of choices of law as compared with the 'mandatory rules' of the country of his habitual place of residence by the Rome Convention[432] and possibly also by national legislation implementing the Unfair Terms in Consumer Contracts Directive 1993 where the express choice of law is not 'individually negotiated'.[433] Under English law, there is nothing in the 2002 Regulations to make particular provision for this, apparently on the assumption that the obligation to transpose article 7(2) is discharged by section 27 of the Unfair Contract Terms Act 1977.[434]

The French Working Group clearly also noticed the differences between article 7(2) of the Directive and article 5(2) of the Rome Convention and proposed a rule which borrows from both, though only for the benefit of consumers.[435] This suggestion appears to have been followed in part by the *ordonnance* of 17 February 2005, which provides that, whatever the law applicable to the contract, the buyer with habitual residence in a Member State cannot be deprived of the protection which that State gives under the Directive in circumstances very reminiscent of those found in article 5(2) of the Rome Convention.[436] It is not clear, however, that this form of implementation by explaining article 7(2)'s reference to a contract with a 'close connection with the territory of the Member States' by reference to factors in the Rome Convention is compatible with the Directive itself.[437]

---

[428] See generally, Stijns and Van Gerven, *op. cit.*, n. 19.   [429] 1999 Directive, art. 7(2).

[430] Cf. Dir. 93/13 EC on unfair terms in consumer contracts, art. 6(1); Dir. 94/47/EC ('Timeshare Directive') art. 9.   [431] Stijns and Van Gerven, *op. cit.* n. 19, 241, 258–9.

[432] Convention on the Law Applicable to Contractual Obligations of 19 June, 1980, art. 5(2); Stijns and Van Gerven, *op. cit.* n. 19, 259–60.

[433] EC Dir. 93/13 on unfair terms in consumer contracts, art. 3(1).

[434] *Benjamin, Special Supplement*, §§ 1-036–1-049 doubts whether this assumption is correct.

[435] *Avant-projet*, proposed new art. L 211-3 C. consom.

[436] *Ord.* of 17 Feb. 2005, art. 1, creating new art. L 211-18 C. consom.

[437] Cf. art. L. 135-1 C. consom. as amended in 1995 (which purported to implement Dir. 93/13/EC on unfair terms in consumer contracts art. 6(2) in France) which 'explains' that Directive's reference to 'a close connection with the laws of the Member States' in terms of the domicile of either party to the contract and whether the contract is 'proposed, concluded or performed' in one of the Member States.

(ii) Attempts to exclude or restrict the consumer's rights

Article 7(1) provides that:

Any contractual terms or agreements concluded with the seller before the lack of conformity is brought to the seller's attention which directly or indirectly waive or restrict the rights resulting from this Directive shall, as provided for by national law, not be binding on the consumer.

Again, such a provision in EC directives of consumer protection is now standard, reflecting their mandatory nature.[438] Article 7(1), however, draws a clear distinction between agreements or waivers made *before* the lack of conformity is brought to the seller's attention and afterwards. In the case of the former, the consumer's rights must be preserved and the agreement or waiver given no effect and here the Directive is drafted broadly so as to catch, for example, goods sold 'as seen' or a delivery note signed by a buyer stating that the goods were 'accepted as is'.[439] On the other hand, while the parties to a consumer contract of sale of goods may not exclude or restrict the rights which it provides for the buyer, their agreement may bear on the content of the goods' 'contractual conformity'.[440] This may happen either as a result of explicit contractual stipulations relating to the goods (whose non-fulfilment would constitute contractual non-conformity) or by a seller's descriptions, warnings or instructions which affect the goods' quality or fitness for purpose.[441] In this respect, the Directive reflects a similar tension between the substance of the contract of sale (where the Directive's preamble explicitly states that freedom of contract is preserved[442]) and particular contract terms which attempt to restrict or exclude the consequences of a seller's failure in performance (where freedom of contract is dis-applied) as is found in the Directive on unfair terms in consumer contracts, which excludes from its test of fairness terms which define the main subject matter of the contract or relate to the price/quality ratio.[443] Moreover, agreements made *after* the lack of conformity is brought by the buyer to the seller's attention would include settlements or a unilateral act of waiver of a defect by a buyer and these article 7(2) expressly leaves as effective.[444]

In its implementation of this provision in English law, the 2002 Regulations rely on their use of sections 13 to 15 of the Sale of Goods Act 1979 as the foundation of the new consumer rights, for 'as against a person dealing as consumer' a business seller cannot exclude or restrict his liability for breach of these statutory implied terms by operation of the Unfair Contract Terms Act.[445] While for this purpose, the exclusion or restriction of liability is defined by this Act very broadly,[446] this control applies only to contract terms and would not, therefore, apply to contracts of settlement nor to unilateral acts of waiver. On the other hand, exclusion of liability for breach of an *express term* relating to the goods (which is properly included by the 2002 Regulations as a possible element within 'contractual conformity')[447] is subjected by the 1977 Act

---

[438] Stijns and Van Gerven, *op. cit.* n. 19, 239.

[439] 1999 Directive, recital 22; Staudenmayer, *op. cit.* n. 34, 561.

[440] Cf. Stijns and Van Gerven, *op. cit.* n. 19, 244.   [441] Above, pp. 593, 596, 599.

[442] 1999 Directive, recital 8.   [443] Dir. 93/13/EC, art. 4(2).

[444] See also 1999 Directive, recital 12 referring to settlements. On the effect of waiver and estoppel: *Benjamin, Special Supplement*, §§ 1-165–1-173.   [445] Unfair Contract Terms Act 1977, s. 6(2).

[446] Ibid., s. 13.   [447] 2002 Regulations, r. 5, new s. 48F 1979 Act and see above, pp. 592–3.

only to a test of 'reasonableness' even where the buyer deals as consumer[448] and to this extent the UK's implementation looks inadequate to allow the Directive's protection to be as completely preserved as article 7(1) requires. For example, a consumer buyer orders a car in a particular shade of green; the seller delivers a blue car; the buyer claims its replacement under the Directive, but the seller purports to rely on a term of the contract which allows him to substitute a different coloured car if the stipulated colour is not available. Here, the buyer may need to argue that the goods were not 'conforming' by reason of the breach of an express term as to their colour, but even assuming that the 'colour variation clause' is caught by the 1977 Act,[449] it would be subject only to a test of reasonableness and not necessarily rendered ineffective.

By contrast, the French Working Group's proposals would, following its previous law, render all agreements purporting to limit the significance of the *garantie de conformité* ineffective where the seller is a *vendeur professionnel* and the buyer is not in the same 'speciality' of business as the seller, though in doing so it followed the 1999 Directive in drawing a distinction between agreements made before and after the 'denunciation' of the defect by the buyer and in specifically including 'acceptance notes'.[450] Given its restriction to consumer contracts of sale of goods, the *ordonnance* of 17 February 2005 simply followed the Directive and declares as 'not written' any agreement which 'excludes or limits, directly or indirectly' the new consumer rights which it creates.[451]

(f) Beyond the parties to the consumer contract of sale

While the main provisions of the 1999 Directive are concerned with the creation of new rights for consumers against their sellers within privity of contract, it also concerned itself with matters beyond the parties to these contracts in three ways.

The first is found in article 6, the first part of which provides that 'guarantees shall be binding on the offeror under the conditions laid down in the guarantee statement and the associated advertising'. This provision applies to any undertaking given by a seller, producer or importer of the goods 'without extra charge to reimburse the price paid or to replace, repair or handle consumer goods[452] in any way if they do not meet the specification set out in the guarantee statement or in the relevant advertising'.[453] It therefore concerns a limited range of guarantees offered by sellers or manufacturers to consumers, not applying to those which are paid for (even if they do not take the form of contracts of insurance) nor to those which go further than offering rights of refund, replacement and handling. The importance of article 6(1) is not merely to ensure that these guarantees are binding on those offering them, but that they are so on the terms which they themselves set out *and* which are set out in their relevant advertising, without the sort of qualifications on the significance of the latter found in article 2(4) for the

---

[448] Unfair Contract Terms Act 1977, s. 3.

[449] It is arguable whether or not such a clause would entitle the seller to 'render a contractual performance substantially different from that which was reasonably expected of him' within the meaning of the Unfair Contract Terms Act 1977, s. 3(2)(b)(i).   [450] *Avant-projet*, proposed new art. 1643 C. civ.

[451] *Ord.* of 17 Feb. 2005, art. 1 creating new art. L. 211-17 C. consom.

[452] As defined by art. 1(2)(b) of the 1999 Directive, see above, p. 589.

[453] 1999 Directive, art. 1(2)(d) and (e).

purposes of 'contractual conformity' between the parties.[454] Moreover, guarantees are to be 'binding' whether or not they fulfil the normal requirements for the existence of contract in the national laws of the Member States, there being a common difficulty in finding an agreement on which to found a contract where the offer of guarantee is made after the purchase of goods in the absence of any further 'acceptance' by the buyer.

The remainder of article 6 makes certain requirements concerning the content and form of any guarantees in the sense which I have just explained. So, any guarantee must contain a statement of the consumer's legal rights and express in plain and intelligible language the contents of the guarantee and the essential particulars for making claims under it, though failure in either respect must have no effect on the validity of the guarantee.[455] It is also provided that a Member State in which the consumer goods are marketed may provide that the guarantee be drafted in one or more official languages of the Community.[456] The implementation of these provisions in both English and French law have been straightforward and relatively uncontroversial.[457] In the English context, in particular, the requirement that guarantees be binding is a useful one as there had been technical doubts as to their validity as contracts.[458]

Apart from guarantees, the 1999 Directive mentions two other possible liabilities beyond the parties to the consumer contract of sale.

First, it makes provision for a review of its own application and specifies that this should include consideration of the question whether a direct liability in a producer to the consumer should be added to the existing scheme. This reflects considerable debate in the Council and European Parliament as to whether the Directive should also impose a direct liability in particular in manufacturers direct to consumers.[459] No provision was made for this in the 1999 Directive apparently on the basis that the problem to a consumer of an insolvent intermediate seller is not one particular to contracts of sale but is general to all consumer transactions.[460]

Secondly, article 4 of the 1999 Directive provides for rights of indemnity of a seller held 'liable' under its own articles 2 and 3.[461] It states:

Where the final seller is liable to the consumer because of a lack of conformity resulting from an act or omission by the producer, a previous seller in the same chain of contracts or any other intermediary, the final seller shall be entitled to pursue remedies against the person or persons liable in the contractual chain. The person or persons liable against whom the final seller may pursue remedies, together with the relevant actions and conditions of exercise, shall be determined by national law.

---

[454] Above, p. 601.

[455] Art. 6(2) and (5). It is also provided that if a consumer requests it, the guarantee should be made available in writing.   [456] Art. 6(4).

[457] 2002 Regulations, r. 5; *ord.* of 17 Feb. 2005, art. 1, creating new art. L 211-15 C. consom.

[458] Above, p. 264. The 2002 Regulations r. 15(1) declares that consumer guarantees 'take . . . effect as a contractual obligation'.

[459] See also 1999 Directive recital 23; Staudenmayer, *op. cit.* n. 34, 563; *Green Paper*, Com (93) 509 final 87 *et seq.*

[460] Staudenmayer, ibid. Another argument in favour of the direct liability was that it would allow a consumer to make a claim against a producer in his own country of residence where the direct seller was resident elsewhere, an argument described as 'hardly relevant': ibid.

[461] M. Bridge, 'Article 4 Rights of Redress' in Bianca and Grundmann, *EU Sales Directive*, 179.

While this provision does impose a requirement on Member States, its impact is distinctly diffuse. What it appears to do is to require the creation or retention for the benefit of a 'final seller' (i.e. the seller made liable under its own provisions to a 'final buyer,' i.e. a consumer) of a liability in sellers up the contractual chain of distribution, including but not limited to the producer, where the lack of conformity which formed the basis of the final seller's own liability resulted from the act or omission of *someone* in the contractual chain of distribution: it does not require the person up the chain who may be made liable to be himself so responsible. Having said that, article 4 then entrusts to national laws the rules as to whom he should be so liable, the nature of the relevant actions and the conditions of their exercise.[462]

This is really a rather strange provision. First, it is odd to find such a provision in a directive whose legal basis is partly in the protection of consumers and partly in the need for harmonisation in the internal market,[463] since it is aimed at the creation of rights for business sellers and does not require any particular rules so as to achieve even a limited harmonisation. Moreover, while it is limited to the situations where the final seller is held 'liable' only as this is understood by the 1999 Directive (i.e. to the limited range of consumer remedies), the creation of a right of indemnity creates a different type of remedy which appears to be a form of reimbursement.[464] As a matter of substance, a requirement as to a harmonised recourse action could have been one of the most important provisions of the Directive as it would have determined the channelling of liability in respect of defects of conformity in consumer goods up the chain of distribution and this could well have had a knock-on effect on other recourse claims in the Member States. But article 4 does not do this. It leaves to Member States the questions as to whether a final seller can sue only his own contractual partner (as in English law) or whether he can also sue any other seller in the chain subject only to the requirement of proof of the relevant defect when *that* seller delivered the goods (as in the French law of *action directe*).[465] Moreover, it does not even require that the legal basis of such a recourse be the same as liability under the Directive—even the definition of 'defect of conformity' may differ—and it makes no provision as to the effectiveness or otherwise of any contractual exclusions of recourse in contracts up the chain (though it had been argued that recourse should be non-excludable).[466] All article 4 requires is that a final seller must be able to claim something from someone in the chain of distribution. As Staudenmayer candidly admitted, 'the Member States have to do something, but it is left up to them, what and how they do it'.[467]

It is for these reasons not surprising that neither the UK nor the French legislator considered it necessary to make any new provision so as to implement article 4: in both English and French law a 'final seller' does have a possible right of recourse, though these are significantly different in the two.[468]

---

[462] M. Bridge, 'Article 4 Rights of Redress' in Bianca and Grundmann, *EU Sales Directive*, 179, 196.

[463] Above, pp. 567–8.   [464] Bridge, *op. cit.* n. 461, 196.   [465] Above, p. 96.

[466] Recital 9 refers to a final seller having 'renounced [the] entitlement' to pursue remedies against others in the chain of distribution. The Economic and Social Committee had proposed that it should not be excludable by contract: Trochu, *op. cit.* n. 74.   [467] Staudenmayer, *op. cit.* n. 34, 559.

[468] For English law, see Dti, *First Consultation*, 11 which asks merely whether any change should be made to the way in which the Unfair Contract Terms Act's test of reasonableness controls the validity of any

6. Concluding Remarks

The results of implementation of the Consumer Guarantees Directive in French and English law are not at all impressive. To an extent this can be attributed to failures in the respective national legislators, but in my view the problem stems from the very nature of the Directive and its relationship with national law.

Both the French and the UK national legislators were faced with implementation of a scheme of rights for contractual non-conformity of goods for the benefit of consumers which did not fit with their existing patterns of law, whether of sale in general (as in French law) or sales of goods (as in English law). In the case of French law, the real sticking point was the foundation of the buyer's rights on a unified basis of 'non-conformity' rather than distinguishing between latent defects and the established approach to non-conformity of French law; in the case of English law, it was the theoretical starting point and fundamental strategy of the rights to be provided for consumers. In both laws, however, there were a number of more minor differences between their existing schemes of liability and the one required for consumer buyers by the 1999 Directive. These differences meant that the national legislators had to choose whether or not to adopt the new way of thinking and apply it generally to their laws of sale (or at least their laws of sale of goods) without distinguishing between consumer and non-consumer buyers and thereby either preserve (in the case of English law) or establish (in the case of French law) a relatively simple framework of rights in respect of qualitative and functional defects. This was the route taken by German law,[469] but was not followed by either French law or English law.

In France, it was proposed that implementation of the 1999 Directive should furnish an opportunity for wider reform on the Directive's model, though with certain improvements (some of which had the potential to detract from the Directive's minimum character).[470] As I have explained, the plan was attacked from many sides, some more convincing than others,[471] but in the end it fell foul of a series of technical criticisms which saw it as creating an intrusive and incoherent element into the Civil Code out of keeping with French legal tradition and of political criticism from consumers (who saw it as not going far enough) and from industry (who saw it as going too far).[472] In the result, French implementation of the Directive has led to the addition of a further layer of rights for (consumer) buyers, in addition to the plethora of rights which they already enjoyed.[473] The resulting complexity is likely to be very off-putting to consumers and at the same time potentially 'contaminating' influences from abroad have been introduced, if but in the margins of French private law in the *Code de la consommation*. Ironically, however, the most important proposal for reform of French contract law made by the *ordonnance* of 17 February 2005 was not required by the Directive, for its replacement of the *bref délai* of the *garantie légale* with a fixed period of two years from the discovery of the defect[474] is likely to give a considerable

exclusion or restriction of liability in sellers up the chain of distribution. For France, see the Working Group, *Rapport Général*, Part 1, s. V.

[469] Zimmermann, *Liability for Non-Conformity*, 29 et seq. [470] Above, pp. 574–6.
[471] Above, pp. 576–82. [472] Above, pp. 582–3. [473] Above, pp. 79–86, 583.
[474] Above, p. 583.

boost to the attractiveness of this route of recovery, whether for defects of quality of the type primarily envisaged by the 1999 Directive *or* for defects of safety, even though the latter are ostensibly a matter for the Product Liability Directive of 1985.[475]

The English law legislator also faced genuine difficulties in terms of legislative strategy in implementing the 1999 Directive. As I have said, the standard of non-conformity provided by the Directive could fit quite easily with existing legislation governing contracts of sale of goods, but the scheme of rights provided for by the Directive is based on a fundamentally different view of the effects of contracts and on the most appropriate remedial strategy to balance the relative interests of contracting parties from that found in the common law. For the Directive's scheme of rights is here fundamentally civilian and rests on the primacy of performance by the debtor; whereas the fundamental view of the common law remains that the creditor should be restricted to claims for damages reflecting (where appropriate) his having obtained a substitute performance from the market. While the civilian view at first looks more protective of the rights of creditors (by giving them rights to performance), it also protects the rights of sellers to perform and (as the Directive itself provides) even grants them a second chance at performing: the policy is one of the preservation of the contract if possible. This is not the strategy of the common law, which is more concerned to satisfy the interests of the parties through financial adjustment, the injured party's claim for damages being tempered by his need to mitigate. And this common law approach is fully reflected in section 14 of the Sale of Goods Act which allows buyers to escape the contract and obtain a substitute performance elsewhere.[476]

This meant that the UK legislator had an impossible choice. It could substitute the Directive's scheme of rights for those previously provided by the law of sale of goods only in the case of consumers, but this would create disharmony with sales to other types of buyer or, if extended to all buyers, more generally in the common law and in practice lead to a diminution of protection for consumers. Or the legislator could simply add a further layer of rights for the benefit of consumers on top of those already provided by its existing scheme, but at a cost of extraordinary complexity and, at least to an extent, a mismatch in strategy between three sets of buyers' rights (at common law in respect of express terms, under the classic remedies in the Sale of Goods Act and under the new consumer rights implementing the Directive). Viewed in this light, the 2002 Regulations themselves should not bear the brunt of our criticism: rather it is the need to introduce into an area as interlinked as the buyer's remedies in sale of goods an alien system of thinking supposedly in the interests of consumers but overall of little real help to them.

[475] Above, Chap. 18.   [476] Above, pp. 251–2, 255.

PART V

GENERAL CONCLUSION

20

General Conclusion

1. The Two Directives Contrasted

I have already looked at the broad differences between the Product Liability Directive and the Consumer Guarantees Directive, in terms of their purposes and legal bases in EU law, their legal parentage, and the remedial expression of their imposition of liability.[1] There remain significant differences between the two directives: the Product Liability Directive being principally concerned with the imposition of liability in order to compensate the victim of personal injuries or death caused by an unsafe product; the Consumer Guarantees Directive being principally concerned with the provision of rights of repair or replacement of goods whose quality or fitness for purpose is inadequate.[2] This primary contrast between safety and quality could itself be seen to reflect more fundamental differences between contractual rights and extra-contractual rights (meaning by the latter, rights to damages arising from a legal basis which is independent of a contract, whether or not the right-holder happens to be a party to a contract and adopting this neutral terminology so as to avoid the language of tort or delict). Contractual rights reflect the generally positive effect which entering a contract is intended to have on the parties' legal positions and so their remedial protection can improve their position as contrasted with the *status quo ante*; extra-contractual rights reflect the negative effect of the factual circumstances from which they arise on the existing position of the right-holder and therefore are aimed at putting him back in the position he would have been in but for that negative effect.[3]

However, this series of contrasts is blurred in a number of ways as regards the two directives which form the focus of this study. First, issues of the fitness of a product for its purpose may impact on the question of its defectiveness in terms of safety under the 1985 Directive: some products (such as kitchen knives) need to be inherently dangerous in order to serve their purposes.[4] Secondly, the safety of goods is relevant to their 'fitness for purpose' within the meaning of one of the aspects of their contractual conformity under the 1999 Directive.[5] And, thirdly, while these directives themselves require the provision of different remedies (the 1985 Directive being restricted to damages, the 1999 Directive being concerned with a number of remedies *apart* from damages), the integrated implementation of the 1999 Directive in the contract laws of

---

[1] Above, pp. 566–72.   [2] Above, pp. 438, 566–68.
[3] For a development of this theme in the context of English law, see S. Whittaker, 'Privity of Contract and the Tort of Negligence: Future Directions' (1996) 16 *OJLS* 191, 207–212.   [4] Above, p. 488.
[5] Above, p. 598.

Member States may indeed have an impact on the imposition of liability in damages. This is true both of English law (which has amended—though slightly—the legal basis of liability for qualitative or functional defects, including as to damages so as to conform to the Directive) and of French law (which apparently sees the French new basis of liability for contractual non-conformity stemming from the Directive as sounding in damages).[6] Finally, the law of sale of goods (which is the concern of the 1999 Directive) forms an important basis on which a person held liable under the 1985 Directive may recover an indemnity against a person higher up the chain of distribution of the product. Again, the 1999 Directive itself does not require any particular change to the laws of the Member States in these circumstances (though it requires that there should be *some* law allowing recourse of this type), but its implementation by a Member State by way of changing the legal basis of sellers' liabilities for qualitative defects to their buyers without distinguishing between consumers and non-consumers would affect recourse claims as well as claims by the ultimate purchaser of goods.[7]

2. Fault and No Fault

French and English lawyers use the apparently very similar language of 'fault' or '*la faute*' to describe the basis on which they sometimes found liability, but the significance of this language differs significantly both within each of these systems and also between them. This has a necessary impact on the significance of the imposition of liability 'without fault', for as the significance of 'fault' changes, the absence of fault changes in its mirror image. Moreover, even where both English and French law appear to adopt the same meaning of 'fault' (notably, as regards English negligence and the French *imprudence*), a closer look at the way in which lawyers within either system use and apply these concepts reveals significant contrasts as well as a degree of commonality. These differences go beyond the formal definitions (or relative lack of definitions) of the concepts themselves and reach into the approaches and methods of the laws to the determination of the issues by courts, whether as a matter of legal or factual presumptions, judicial 'inferences' or the nature of available evidence.

In this respect, French law is particularly rich in understandings of 'fault' as the basis of liability. A good starting point is the 'general law' of liability found in articles 1382 and 1383 of the Civil Code. Here, 'fault' is used to denote the wrongfulness element of liability suitable for a very wide variety of situations, defining the scope of extra-contractual liability as well as setting the basis on which it will be imposed and thereby performing functions which in English law are fulfilled by the special rules determining the ambit of individual torts (such as the duty of care of the tort of negligence), as well as their basis of liability. Even if our discussion remains restricted to the question of the basis of liability, we find a variety of elements which can be included. So, intentional behaviour and lack of care are included, but so also is any conduct which is 'abnormal' or where one 'fails to do what one ought to do'.[8] This

---

[6] Above, pp. 587–8, 604 and see below, pp. 662–3.

[7] 1999 Directive, art. 4 and see above, pp. 625–7.   [8] Above, p. 42.

leads, in particular, to the French view that any breach of duty (professional or regulatory) in itself constitutes *une faute* so as to be capable of giving rise to liability and that any criminal fault (even if it does not itself rest on any lack of care) will constitute delictual fault.[9] It also allows it to be argued (and sometimes held) that non-performance of a contractual obligation of whatever content (whether *de moyens* or *de résultat*) in itself constitutes delictual fault so as to attract liability towards third parties.[10] However, even this does not give a proper sense of the complexity of the French treatment, which can be seen from traditional approaches to liability for products. So, apart from cases where breach of a regulatory duty, a crime or a lack of proper care count as fault,[11] French courts have also simply held (first in the 1970s and then again in the mid-1990s) that the putting onto the market by a manufacturer of a defective product *itself* constitutes a 'fault'.[12] In the last of these situations, 'fault' seems to be little more than a device to provide a foundation in the Civil Code for the imposition of liability in circumstances where a court thinks fit: so the question 'was the defendant at fault?' very easily slides into 'should the defendant be liable?' On the other hand, there is very little elucidation of what is meant by lack of care (*imprudence* or *manque de diligence*), at least to the eyes of the modern common lawyer. So, while we sometimes see references to the foreseeability of harm or dangers, there is no articulate balancing of factors of the sort which we find in the 'cost/benefit analysis' of the tort of negligence.[13] Instead, the *juges du fond* (and often in practice the *experts*) determine the issue of fault at large, 'condemning or pardoning in the name of society'.[14]

In French law, in my view, this very broad usage of the language of fault and the relatively undifferentiated understanding of *imprudence* make the drawing of the line between liability for fault and without fault very difficult except at a purely formal level. This difficulty is reflected in the way in which fault is interpreted and applied; but it is also reflected in the borderline liabilities between fault and no fault. This can be seen in a number of places in the French law (for example, in the to-ing and fro-ing of liabilities for the deeds of other people around the notion of presumptions of fault),[15] but it can be seen no more clearly than as regards liability for the 'deeds of things' under article 1384 alinéa 1. For while the formal position as to this last liability is clear (liability does not rest on proven fault, nor can a defendant escape liability by proving its absence), the courts sometimes come close to linking liability to something like a lack of proper care in their interpretation of *la garde* (including its splitting between *garde de la structure* and *garde du comportement*); in their interpretation and application of the requirement that the 'thing' must play a causal role, and in the presence or absence of the defences of *force majeure* and *faute de la victime*.[16] This impression of the relative and variable nature of the strictness of liability for the 'deeds of things' as traditionally interpreted and the rather patchy way in which it is applied is reinforced by its chaotic *jurisprudence* in the early 1980s and subsequent partial legislative reform for the context of motor accidents in 1985.[17] It is very much the lesson of the evolution of this area of the law over the last half century that the practical

---

[9] Above, pp. 45–6, 374, 393.   [10] Above, p. 29.   [11] Above, pp. 45–6.
[12] Above, p. 51.   [13] Above, pp. 189–202.   [14] Carbonnier, *Obligations*, 414, above, p. 44.
[15] Above, p. 25.   [16] Above, pp. 52–9.   [17] Above, pp. 59–61.

strictness of liability is a function of a number of elements, including the basis of liability in the traditional sense, but also of judicial attitudes to how they may be established, to causation and to defences.

The French law of contract looks at first much less complicated in this respect, reflecting its more restricted focus as compared to liability under articles 1382 *et seq*. At one level, 'contractual fault' is sometimes used to refer to any non-performance of a contractual obligation which is not excused (*'inexécution imputable'*),[18] but more prominent recently has been the division between three types of contractual obligations: *obligations de garantie*, where liability is imposed despite *force majeure* (for example, the seller's liability for latent defects[19]); *obligations de résultat*, where liability arises for failure to accomplish the obligation's subject matter, though with a defence of *force majeure* (for example, the carrier's liability to passengers[20]); and *obligations de moyens*, where liability rests on proof by the other party of a lack of care (*manque de diligence*, as in the case of many obligations to perform professional services).[21] Nevertheless, even in the contractual context the basis of liability appears more a matter of a sliding scale of strictness, with some obligations poised between *obligation de moyens* and *obligations de résultat* owing to a presumption of fault in the former[22] or the reversal of the burden of proof for the latter.[23] Moreover, as regards any particular example of liability, we find French courts nuancing the basis of liability for the circumstances. So, for example, while a seller's *obligation d'information* is classed formally as an *obligation de moyens*, in fact the courts take into account in their decisions the relative status of the parties, whether in business or consumer, and if both in business, whether of the same type.[24] And in the case of the seller's liability for defects (whether 'latent defects' under the *garantie légale*, defects of conformity under the *droit commun contractuel*, or even defects of safety under the *jurisprudence* of the 1990s[25]), the basis of liability is left to be determined according to these very open standards, assessed by the *juges du fond*, again usually on the advice of *experts*.

However, these approaches of the civil courts to the standard of liability form only part of the picture in French law.

First, French criminal courts have played a very important role in imposing liability in damages for death and personal injuries and while for this purpose the formal basis of liability remains 'civil fault' within the meaning of articles 1382 and 1383 of the Civil Code, traditionally they have taken a very strict approach to its application as regards death and personal injuries, seeing the 'speck of fault' in a defendant's action so as to impose both criminal responsibility and civil liability.[26] While French jurists consider that in doing so the criminal courts are merely applying a standard of 'ordinary fault' (*faute simple*) rather than some more demanding standard (such as those special faults required in some circumstances for criminal responsibility for death and personal injuries after the legislative reforms of 2000),[27] one is left with the impression that the greater investigative powers and, therefore, the wider range and better quality of evidence available to the criminal courts allows them more easily to find fault with a

---

[18] E.g. above, p. 28.   [19] Above, p. 89.   [20] Above, p. 140.
[21] Above, pp. 99–104, 142–3.   [22] Above, p. 67.   [23] Above, p. 101.
[24] Above, p. 67.   [25] Above, pp. 78–9, 456.   [26] Above, pp. 373–4.
[27] Above, pp. 389–93.

defendant's behaviour than their civil counterparts: as Pradel simply puts it, the chance of compensation is surer in the criminal courts than in the civil ones.[28] Of course, it is this link between civil liability and criminal responsibility which led to criticism and then reform of the basis of *criminal* responsibility in some circumstances, replacing a very open standard of negligence or breach of duty (which derived originally from the Criminal Code of 1810) with standards of deliberate breach of duties of safety or really serious fault (*une faute caractérisée*).[29]

Secondly, of course, the distinction between fault and its absence has formed the axis on which administrative liability has been constructed in French law. Here again, though, we find different treatments and understandings of 'fault' and considerable differences therefore in understandings of 'no fault'.[30] In this context, the Conseil d'Etat's declaration of independence of the basis of liability in the administration in the *arrêt Blanco* led, *inter alia*, to adoption of the Romanist distinction between *faute simple* and *faute lourde*, holding that in a number of situations liability could rest only on 'very serious fault,' though unlike the reforms of the criminal law in 2000 the Conseil d'Etat has made no attempt to describe further the characteristics which make fault more serious.[31] However, as has been seen, the significance of *faute lourde* as a means of restricting liability in the administration has dwindled very significantly over the last 20 years or so as a result of the Conseil d'Etat's greater willingness to impose liability either for *faute simple* or *sans faute*.[32] In this respect, liability in the administration for failure to intervene in the interests of the safety of products is a good example of this evolution, though it remains to be seen whether the lead given by the Conseil d'Etat in the *affaire du sang contaminé* which placed liability here on *faute simple* will be followed more generally in this sort of context.[33] Moreover, the standard of 'ordinary fault' is not a simple one at all: first, because of the assimilation of administrative illegality to fault for the purposes of liability[34] and, secondly, owing to the Conseil d'Etat's recourse to the use of rebuttable presumptions of fault.[35] While the first of these has not been important in French law in imposing liability for products, the second has sometimes been used, notably in some cases of medical liability and in the law governing liability for 'public works'.[36] This sort of blurring of the line between liability for fault and liability without fault means that French jurists remain uncertain as to the practical consequences of the legislative reform of medical liability which placed the general basis of liability, whether civil or administrative, simply on 'fault', without specifying whether this must be proved or may sometimes be presumed.[37]

In my view, when put next to French law, the English approach to 'fault' is relatively integrated, though it becomes more complex and sophisticated once one descends to the interpretation of the relatively few concepts used. First, in the context of civil liability for death and personal injuries (if not also entirely damage to property[38]), the starting point of an English lawyer is with the tort of negligence and, therefore, with

---

[28] Pradel, *Procédure pénale*, 230, above, pp. 384–5.   [29] Above, pp. 389–93.
[30] Above, pp. 19, 30–3, 310–15.   [31] Cf. above, pp. 310–11, 389.   [32] Above, pp. 31–2.
[33] Above, pp. 315–18.   [34] Above, pp. 313–14.   [35] Above, pp. 126, 145–6.
[36] Ibid.   [37] Above, p. 152.
[38] This is because damage to property may still figure in a claim for damage in private nuisance and under the rule in *Rylands v Fletcher*: above, p. 163.

the understanding of fault *as* negligence as found in that tort: other liabilities for these types of harm (whether for some variant of negligence, for other types of 'fault', or strict) are mere satellites to negligence.[39] Secondly, for this purpose 'negligence' is the subject of a complex law setting out the proper standards to be applied and then the set of proper considerations to be taken into account by a court in determining its existence.[40] In all this, 'reasonableness' appears at a number of points, but the courts have structured the discretion which this terminology allows both so as to ensure a degree of consistency in their own decision making and so as to set out the proper considerations which they consider individuals and businesses should weigh up in making their decisions on safety, considerations of the risk of injury, its likely magnitude and the financial cost of its avoidance, but also considerations of the social utility of their own activities and the rights of individuals.[41] On the other hand, this overt and structured approach to the determination of negligence leaves relatively less room for judicial reliance on presumptions: it is no accident that as negligence has become more elaborated, the maxim *res ipsa loquitur* has become less significant, the courts denying to it any substantive effect even on the burden of proof and seeing it merely as a label to describe situations where it is proper for them to infer negligence from the circumstances as established.[42]

This dominance of the tort of negligence has had an impact on other liabilities in a number of ways.

First, the understanding of negligence as a lack of reasonable care to be determined in this way led English law to reject the idea that breach of a duty of *any* content can qualify as negligence. This rejection had a particular effect on the relationship of statutory duties to civil liability, for if their breach does not in itself constitute negligence, there is no logical temptation to say that any breach of a statutory duty gives rise to liability for 'statutory' negligence.[43] This rejection therefore reinforced existing judicial approaches to the civil effect of statutory duties, according to which the question of their impact on liability was seen in terms of an interpretation of express or implied parliamentary intention, taking into account certain broad considerations but remaining essentially particular and contextual.[44]

Moreover, the understanding of negligence as a failure to take reasonable care also prevented the assimilation of breach of contractual duties to tortious negligence. For a time in the middle of the nineteenth century this sort of assimilation had looked a distinct possibility, one contractual party's 'neglect' in contractual performance being seen as negligence giving rise to an action in tort and allowing the injured party an option whether to sue in contract or in tort.[45] However, once negligence became firmly understood as a failure to take reasonable care it became seen as simply inaccurate to say that all breaches of contractual duties constitute tortious negligence: some

---

[39] Above, Chap. 9. Other types of 'fault' may be seen in relation to private nuisance, where the reasonableness of one person's interference with the use or enjoyment of another's land is determined by reference to a set of factors distinct from those employed in determining negligence. It could be thought that such an unreasonable interference is a 'fault' in a neighbour, but if so, it is a fault in a different sense from the 'fault' required of a defendant under the tort of negligence.   [40] Above, pp. 186–202.

[41] Above, pp. 193–200.   [42] Above, pp. 209–10.   [43] Above, pp. 190–1.

[44] Above, pp. 218–20.   [45] *Brown v Boorman* (1842) 3 QB 511, 526 and see above, p. 157.

would do so (where the contractual duty was itself to take reasonable care—'contractual negligence') but other, stricter duties would not.[46] This way of thinking also fits well with general attitudes to breach of contract in English law, for breach of contract has not attracted the language of fault ('contractual fault') nor does it possess the overtones of moral wrongdoing which this language would suggest. In English law, the language used to describe breach of contract usually remains quite neutral: *breach* gives rise to *liability* in damages or some other possible *remedy*. This is to be contrasted with French law, where the language is more morally loaded: *inexécution imputable* (and sometimes *la faute contractuelle*) gives rise to *responsabilité* or some other *sanction*.[47]

In English law, the strictness or otherwise of liability for breach of contract is normally a function of the content of the contract's express or implied terms, though on occasion they are supplemented by legal duties attaching to the type of contract in question.[48] Here, the liabilities imposed for breach of the statutory implied terms as to the quality and fitness for purpose in contracts of sale of goods are particularly interesting. For while they are often seen as classic examples of strict liability (and rightly so, for the buyer does not need to prove negligence, nor can the seller escape liability by showing a lack of negligence), liability is by no means absolute, for the standards which they impose in respect of the goods are relative ones: goods need only be *satisfactory* and *reasonably* fit for their purpose, as assessed according to the balancing of a set of factors. In all, therefore, decisions on a defendant's 'reasonable care' and on the 'unsatisfactory' character of goods both require judicial evaluations, but the standards which the law sets are different in focus (the defendant's behaviour, the goods themselves), as are the sets of factors to be taken into account in the evaluation.[49]

Secondly, the elucidation of negligence in terms of a balance of factors has led to the analysis of liabilities other than under the tort of negligence itself in terms of their similarity to or differences from negligence. So, in some cases the legislature has set the standard of liability as reasonable care in the circumstances, but then made particular provision requiring that this or that consideration should be taken into account in a particular way.[50] Here, the standard of liability remains 'negligence', but this is qualified or the factors relevant are nuanced.[51]

Thirdly, the courts have seen the increasing centrality of the tort of negligence in compensating death, personal injuries and damage to property as a reason for refusing to develop other bases of liability so as to impose liability for these types of harm without negligence. This can be seen particularly clearly in their restrictive attitude to the imposition of civil liability for breach of statutory duties, but also in their attitude to the interpretation of the torts of private nuisance and *Rylands v Fletcher*.[52] Moreover, where liability for harm *does* arise under *Rylands v Fletcher*, the courts have interpreted its incidents in such a way as to reduce its divergence from the negligence norm, rather

---

[46] This can be seen in the law governing the contractual provision of services, above, pp. 271–4.

[47] This analysis puts aside a further possible moral dimension to French law's response to contractual non-performance, as the Civil Code itself distinguishes between deliberate or other 'bad faith' non-performance (*l'inexécution dolosive*) and other non-performance: art. 1150–1151 C. civ. In principle, in English law, a deliberate breach of contract is treated no differently from any other: *Chitty on Contracts*, para. 1–020.

[48] Above, pp. 157–8, 270–6.   [49] Above, pp. 235–42.

[50] E.g. occupiers' liability, above, p. 182 n. 38.   [51] Cf. above, p. 197.

[52] Above, pp. 162–3, 220.

than to retain, let alone extend it.[53] From this perspective, liability under Part I of the Consumer Protection Act appears to form a very isolated island of liability without negligence.

Fourthly, English law has not generally felt any need to categorise different levels of fault in its *civil* law (though it does require gross negligence in one form of its criminal law of manslaughter[54]). In my view, this is at least in part because English courts do not approach the issue of negligence with any preconception as to the desirability or otherwise of imposing liability *so as* to provide compensation for the victim of personal injuries and death: negligence is seen as a genuine standard of liability under which the interests of claimants must be balanced against the interests of defendants and even wider public interests. So, English courts have not (at least for the most part) found 'virtual negligence' of the type which is seen as commonplace in French law where *faute simple* is seen in a 'speck of fault' so as to impose liability for personal injuries and death, whether in the criminal or the civil courts.[55] Interestingly, though, just as the Conseil d'Etat is abandoning *faute lourde* as the basis of administrative liability, English courts appear to be moving towards adopting a specially demanding approach to breach of duty before imposing civil liability on a person causing harm in the course of exercise of statutory powers.[56] This reflects a sense that if liability for negligence in these circumstances is opened up as a possibility (as a result of a degree of liberalisation in approach to the duty of care), the courts should make explicit the importance of public interest considerations in their approach to the standard of liability: the public utility of the defendant's conduct as a mere factor in the cost/benefit analysis is not enough.

Finally, parallelling their approach to denial of any necessary connection between criminal responsibility and civil liability, English courts have consistently refused to see an administrative illegality as a sufficient basis for the imposition of liability in damages (seeing the considerations which go to the *ultra vires* nature of administrative action as different from those which go to the issue of negligence) and, most recently, have attempted to divorce the two issues by rejecting administrative illegality as a necessary condition for civil liability in these circumstances.[57]

In my view, these very considerable differences in understanding of what is meant by 'fault' and, therefore, what is meant by 'no fault', even as regards just two legal systems, makes interpretation of EC legislation *by reference* to fault ill-advised. For while at a superficial level the language of fault is widely used by the laws of liability of Member States, and fault is seen to include cases where harm is caused intentionally or unintentionally through a lack of care (as we have seen in French and English law), underneath these apparent similarities differences in understanding of these concepts, in their roles and in their application abound. As I have earlier argued, the Product Liability Directive's avoidance of the language of 'fault' (negatively as well as positively) in defining its basis of liability was deliberate and sensible, reflecting a desire to steer a middle course, balancing the interests of producers and consumers and even more of setting a 'harmonised' standard of liability throughout the EC and avoiding

---

[53] Ibid. [54] Above, p. 412. [55] Above, p. 634 and cf. p. 188.
[56] Above, pp. 340, 342. [57] Above, pp. 339–40.

the traditional (and different) associations of 'fault' except to the extent that its preamble was able to say in a very general way that its provisions do not require an injured party to establish fault. It is for this reason that, with respect, the English court in *A v National Blood Transfusion Service* should not have relied on these references to fault in the preamble as a reason for denying the relevance of one or more factors for the assessment of the Directive's test of 'defect' because they are relevant to the assessment of negligence at common law.[58] Given that 'fault' and 'no fault' have many different meanings even as between the legal systems of *two* Member States, it cannot be sound reasoning to deduce from the significance given to 'fault' in one system that the Directive's standard of liability must not be the same as or similar to English negligence.

Instead, I have argued that the test of legitimate expectation of safety which article 6 of the 1985 Directive uses to define 'defect' leaves open the range of considerations which a court can properly use to determine the level of safety (and therefore the basis of liability) required in any individual situation. Certainly, a court should look at the question from the perspective of potentially injured parties (given their 'legitimate expectations'), but the particular considerations which article 6 then sets out make clear that this standard *does* take into account what may reasonably be expected of producers, whether in terms of what information they should supply with a product, how they should plan for any use to which it could reasonably be expected that the product would be put, or the timing of the assessment of defectiveness.[59] In this respect, it is to be recalled that French jurists agree that any obligation to furnish information with property (whether for the purposes of the product's safety or its utility) should be seen as an *obligation de moyens*, requiring proof of fault. They say this not so as to relieve a seller or supplier of property of liability (for their general approach is rather the contrary), but rather because they see the very nature of a decision as to what information should or should not be supplied as an issue requiring an evaluation of the seller's proper conduct, and therefore an assessment of their *faute*.[60] Now, I am not arguing from the understanding of one legal system (French law) of one of the elements of article 6 that its significance must be considered to encapsulate a test based on 'fault'. Rather, this suggests that arguments based on national law's understandings of the elements of the definition of 'defect' may insidiously argue for 'fault' as well as against it.

As I have said, article 6 sensibly avoids the language of fault or no fault and instead seeks to establish its own European definition. In doing so, it leaves a very good deal of space for the assessment of the courts of Member States, though, following what is recognisably (though not exclusively) a common law style, it seeks to cut down the judicial discretion which this creates by requiring that certain elements are to be taken into account. I have further argued that the European Court of Justice is unlikely to wish to give further elucidation to the test of 'defect' for this purpose, for example, by holding that this consideration is relevant (sometimes?) and that consideration is not relevant (again sometimes?), but instead is likely to choose to see the issue of defect as primarily one of fact and of the characterisation of fact for the decision of the courts of Member States.[61] Such an approach would certainly have echoes for lawyers from

---

[58] Above, pp. 486–8.   [59] Above, pp. 489–91.   [60] Above, p. 67.
[61] Above, pp. 493–4.

those Member States whose judicial systems have at their apex a court of 'cassation' (quashing),[62] where lawyers are familiar with the idea that certain issues of the characterisation of facts as well as of the facts themselves are for the assessment of the lower courts alone. If this way of thinking were indeed followed, it would be open to the courts of Member States to take different views as to 'the safety which a person is entitled to expect' depending on the circumstances obtaining in the Member States in question, these circumstances forming part of 'all the circumstances' which the Directive stipulates should be taken into account. In this way, the Directive as interpreted by the European Court of Justice would set a harmonised standard for the safety of products for the purposes of the imposition of liability, but the application of this standard could lead to different results in the different conditions obtaining in different Member States.

3. Judicial Institutions, Legal Procedure and Legal Substance

(a) Facts and laws

This study has argued that there is an intimate relationship between the interpretation of substantive legal rules, the legal procedure by which they are applied to facts, and the judicial institutions which decide the outcome. While the relationship or relationships between these three are neither straightforward nor uniform across different legal contexts, they can be seen very clearly in the context of liability for products.

First, there is a clear relationship between the nature of the legal rules and the judicial institutional arrangements which apply them. So, in English law, the relatively open nature of the understanding of negligence found in the nineteenth and early twentieth century flourished in a context where its decision was primarily a matter for a lay body, the jury.[63] The questions to be put to the jury needed to be relatively non-technical and simple, leaving the jury leeway to give effect to their own practical evaluation of a defendant's conduct. On the other hand, once the jury disappeared from trials for negligence (and indeed, more generally from the civil process), commentators and judges embarked on a process of elucidation of the elements to be taken into account in the assessment of negligence, reflecting the accretion of judicial examples of its application and gradually structuring the judicial discretion which it necessarily involves.[64]

By contrast, traditional French understandings of 'fault' or of 'defect' have remained remarkably broad and unstructured, the *juges du fond* having very considerable 'powers of assessment', which give room both for nuances in their interpretation and differences in their application to the facts.[65] Clearly, the division in roles between the *juges du fond* and the Cour de cassation lends itself to the retention of relatively broad and open legal concepts; but equally there is a very strong tradition within the French conception of the nature of *droit civil*, reflected to a very high degree in the

---

[62] This includes France, Belgium, Luxembourg, Italy, Greece and Spain.   [63] Above, pp. 189–90.
[64] Above, pp. 191–2.   [65] Above, pp. 40–1, 44–5, 78.

Civil Code's provisions on civil liability and to a somewhat lesser extent on contracts, which sees the role of the law to provide broad principles and rules which it is then for the judge to interpret and apply. As Portalis himself observed in his great introduction to the Civil Code of 1804:

We did not think it right to simplify the law to the point of leaving citizens without rules and without any guarantee of their most important interests. However, we managed also to avoid the dangerous ambition of wishing to regulate everything and provide for everything. Who would think that it is the very same people for whom a code is too voluminous who imperiously dare to impose on the legislator the terrible task of leaving nothing at all to the decision of judges?[66]

This passage illustrates French recognition of the tension between the quasi-constitutional need for the Civil Code (and, indeed, other legislation in the area of private law) to set out a citizen's rights and the need to keep its regulation at a certain level of generality. But it also reveals a central paradox in French thinking, which at once seeks to avoid *le gouvernement des juges* and then writes legislation in a way which leaves very considerable room for judicial discretion. In this way, the system of cassation and its concomitant acceptance of considerable 'sovereign power' in the *juges du fond* can be seen as a reflection of a particular conception of the proper limits of legal regulation.

There is in this respect, I believe, a profound difference in the way in which English lawyers see the relationship between law and fact. Their starting point in terms of normative layering and in terms of legal reasoning remains the common law, and the common law necessarily involves consideration of facts in the exploration and exposition of the law itself. So, the reason why English lawyers include cases in their exposition of the law is not merely because they like providing illustrations of the propositions which the judges expound or even that they have a taste for the practical workings out of legal concepts ('common law is pragmatic'), it is that much of the law itself can only be understood by reference to the factual context in which the legal propositions found in court judgments were set. In this way, English case law (and especially case law relating to the common law as opposed to case law relating to the interpretation of statutes) is fundamentally fact-contingent. This characteristic starts with the attributes of the doctrine of precedent itself, which holds that the binding aspect of a case (its *ratio decidendi*) is to be found in the proposition of law or propositions of law necessary for the disposal of the case on the facts, but it reaches beyond the significance of the narrow and sometimes rather formal search for *rationes decidendi*. For, in the modern law, English judges use precedents in a highly flexible manner; engaging with the substantive arguments, whether of legal principle or legal policy, but always sensitive to the normative and factual context of earlier judicial expositions of the law. It is for this reason that we find English lawyers frequently exposing the patterns of facts in which broad concepts are applied or judicial discretions exercised. It is not that these patterns necessarily create 'binding rules', to be applied when similar

---

[66] J.-E.-M. Portalis, *Discours préliminaire sur le projet de Code civil présenté le 1er pluviose an IX* [1799] repuplished in *Discours et Rapports sur le Code civil* (Centre de philosophie politique et juridique, Caen, 1989), 7.

facts present themselves: indeed, the courts may explicitly reject the rigidity of such an approach; but rather that the courts and commentators seek to explain how judicial decisions are reached, to expose and to evaluate the factors which judges do and ought to take into account. In all this, a training in the reasoning of the common law necessarily leads to an acute sensitivity to factual context.

This remains true even when an English lawyer considers the interpretation of statutes. Of course, the propositions used by statute and by statutory instrument possess an enactment force which is prior to and not contingent on factual context. On the other hand, as I have had occasion to observe earlier in this study, in general English statutes remain exceptional interventions, even if sometimes large and important ones. Moreover, they often reflect the common law and its manner of thinking in a number of ways. Statutes are enacted in the context of existing common law positions, whether this already overtly regulates the situation dealt with by the statute or silently leaves it unregulated (and therefore without a remedy). Sometimes a statute may build on existing common law starting points, whether by reforming the common law or by creating recognisably new law using or adapting the common law's concepts or approaches; sometimes a statute consciously rejects existing ways and makes a new start and creates new concepts. However, even if a statute appears to create a new *scheme* of regulation (maybe even described as a 'code'), it is not infrequent to see the common law concepts growing around the statutory scheme, pushing through its cracks or even creating cracks by the force of their own logical or substantive appeal.

Moreover, many (though by no means all) modern English statutes replicate the manner of thinking of the common law itself in the way in which they express legal propositions. Put simply, English statutes tend to descend to a considerable level of detail, seeing issues and sub-issues as distinct legal questions to be set out and answered, rather than leaving them to form part of the application of wider legal propositions; and seeing new concepts as needing to be defined and, sometimes, exemplified. So, for example, when English law created the possibility for the parties to a contract to create a right in third parties, the ensuing statute contained ten sections, totalling nearly 2,500 words:[67] the contrast with article 1121 of the Civil Code (which consists of nearly 50 words) is very striking. So too is the way in which the statutory standard of 'merchantable quality' in the Sale of Goods Act was structured and exemplified (as well as being renamed) in the latter twentieth century; here there is a striking contrast with French treatment of the notion of a latent defect which has remained almost as open and undefined in 2004 as it was two centuries previously.[68] In my view, this English tendency to see as legal questions which a French lawyer may see as ones of fact or of the application of law to fact reflects English lawyers' understanding of the common law itself, where the doctrine of precedent allows law to emerge from decisions on facts. Moreover, English courts also apply the doctrine of precedent and their more general understanding of the role of case law to their interpretation of statutes. Here, I do not so much refer to the interpretation of the words themselves (whether taking a literal, a historical or an overtly teleological approach), but rather to the growth of accretions of case law interpreting the statutory provisions,

---

[67] Contracts (Rights for Third Parties) Act 1999.   [68] Above, pp. 235–9, 245.

case law which replicates the fact-sensitivity of the courts' approach to the common law itself.

This kind of sensitivity to factual contexts in describing the law is not reflected to at all the same extent in a legal system such as the French (or at least French private law and criminal law) where the starting point of legal analysis is legislation and, moreover, legislation of the generality which we find in the Civil Code or the Criminal Code. For according to this way of thinking, the law is independent from and logically prior to facts: its validity stems from the constitutional authority of the legislator (and under the French Constitution, ultimately from the people[69]), rather than (as in the common law) from a combination of the status of its exponent (a more or less senior court), the substantive worth of its content and the latter's relationship with the factual contexts of at least *two* cases—the earlier precedent and the case before the court presently deciding. This does not mean, of course, that facts are not important in the application of French legislation nor that the context of its enactment may not be relevant to its interpretation and application.[70] But their significance is that they do (or do not) fulfil the criteria set for the application of the rule or norm which the legislation describes; this rule cannot be 'distinguished' as its validity is not factually contingent in this sense.

(b) Substantive law and legal process

There is also a relationship between the understanding and development of legal concepts and the procedural mechanisms by which their application is determined and between substantive rights and the procedural mechanisms by which they are given practical effect.

The second of these has been seen very clearly in the law governing what an English lawyer would see as remedies for breach of contract and a French lawyer the sanctions of the non-performance of contractual obligations. As the differences in terminology used by the two systems suggest, there are here a number of differences in outlook and, indeed, in substantive response to contractual non-performance, stemming partly from their different historical backgrounds and partly from the different practical strategies to which these backgrounds are related: the common law emerging from the forms of action and possessing a general commercial sense that damages are a sufficient remedy; and the modern civil law resting on a fundamental principle of *pacta sunt servanda* and giving a resulting importance to the performance of contractual obligations.[71] These differences can be seen in the fundamentally civilian approach of the Consumer Guarantees Directive and its resulting lack of fit with existing English remedial responses to breach of contract.[72] However, even where the 'same' legal response is made available to a party to a contract, the mechanisms for its putting into effect may differ. This may be seen in the case of specific enforcement of the buyer's rights to repair or replacement after implementation of this Directive, which in

---

[69] Constitution of 1958, esp. arts. 3, 24.

[70] See, e.g., the likely interpretation of the changes of the criminal law of involuntary homicide in 2000, whose main aim was the protection of elected officials, even though this was not the way in which the legislation was actually cast: above, pp. 388–91.　　　　　　　　　　　　　　　[71] Above, pp. 79–80, 250–60.

[72] Above, pp. 570–1.

English law are supported by a special form of specific performance and therefore ultimately the full rigours of contempt of court and in French law by court order itself enforceable by the relatively less stringent device of *astreintes*.[73] It may also be seen somewhat differently in the different procedural expressions and consequences of 'rescission' of the contract for non-conformity of the goods under the French and English implementations of this Directive.[74]

However, even more fundamental is the relationship between the understanding and development of legal concepts and the procedural mechanisms by which their application is determined. This relationship can be seen in a purely civil context. So, in English law, the modern elaborate definitions of negligence, 'satisfactory quality' in section 14 of the Sale of Goods Act, or 'defect' under the Consumer Protection Act are supported by the existence of procedural mechanisms for the collection of a vast range of evidence—testimonial evidence from witnesses of fact, documentary evidence and expert evidence—which allow the parties to argue and the court to assess the reality and importance of the various elements of which these definitions are constructed. In the English context, the issues to which these definitions give rise remain fundamentally controversial, a characteristic which is particularly important when they require an assessment tying scientific or technical knowledge to a legal standard. For often 'scientific fact' or perhaps more sensibly, scientific interpretations of facts may well be of decisive importance in the evaluative decisions which legal concepts of this nature require.

I have explained earlier that the French civil process has a number of attributes which distinguishes it quite sharply from its English counterpart, the most important for present purposes being the absence of a far-reaching mechanism of disclosure of documents and the essentially uncontroversial nature of expert evidence.[75] It is therefore of great interest, I believe, that some French lawyers have realised that the sorts of question which their courts will have to decide under the provisions of the Product Liability Directive (notably, as to development risks, though I would add as to defect as well) are not easily satisfied by French law's existing means of obtaining and evaluating evidence, as they assume the sorts of mechanisms for the gathering of information associated with the common law.[76] Here, then, implementation of the EC Directive introduces into the French system (if only to a very limited extent) the sort of legal issue which really requires different procedural devices.

However, in the French context, a second and more obvious context where legal substance and legal procedure have become particularly intertwined is the relationship between the criminal process, the *action civile* and the interpretation of civil fault by French courts. Here, it is widely acknowledged that French criminal courts have interpreted both criminal non-intentional fault and its requisite causal connection to a victim's harm in a very demanding way so as to maximise the chances of the victim to recover compensation in damages.[77] This effect is all the more striking in that French lawyers have rebelled against it, first, by redefining (in part and somewhat uncertainly) what can constitute *faute pénale* for this purpose,[78] but also by attempting to divorce (again in part) the historic link between *faute pénale*, *faute civile* and the imposition of

---

[73] Above, pp. 614–15, 618.   [74] Above, pp. 613, 618.   [75] Above, pp. 48–50, 211–14.
[76] Above, p. 495.   [77] Above, pp. 373–6.   [78] Above, pp. 389–93.

civil liability by either the criminal or the civil courts.[79] Nevertheless, despite this rebellion, the commission of a criminal offence still itself constitutes a 'civil fault' so as to attract liability in damages and the French criminal process remains a very important means of recovery of damages for death and personal injury, not least because the criminal courts possess investigative powers in relation to evidence without equivalent in the civil process.[80]

By contrast, in English law, the criminal courts and the criminal process have remained entirely divorced from the imposition of civil *liability*, and have been involved in the award of compensation for victims of accidental personal injuries and death only in a rather marginal way, despite the courts' possession of very considerable powers in this respect.[81] As I have explained, the reasons for this divorce lie in the substantive definitions and classifications of the crimes available for sanctioning behaviour which causes personal injury or death, in the lack of any procedural role for the victims of crime in the criminal process of a type which is played by the French *partie civile* and in the absence of a procedural mechanism by which the court can become sufficiently aware of the extent and financial consequences of the victim's harm, but most of all in a perception by English judges that a criminal court is not the proper forum for the resolution of the 'essentially civil' issues of the causal relationship between an offender's crime and the victim's harm and the latter's practical assessment. In this way, the general perception of the proper role of the criminal and civil processes is in part caused by their attributes, but in part sustains them. But it leaves the civil process as the main mechanism for the recovery of compensation by the imposition of liability in the person who caused the harm; and the courts keep very clearly distinct the questions of the incidence of crime, breach of any statutory duty and the imposition of civil liability.[82] As a result, civil liability for negligence has not been affected by (perhaps one could say, not distorted by) any direct connection with criminal responsibility or the criminal process.

(c) Law, facts and the legal characterisation of facts

Very closely related to these questions which I have been discussing are further fundamental questions as to the relationship between law and fact in the context of the process of adjudication. My starting point here is that the question whether the *characterisation* of facts (for example, a defendant's conduct as 'negligent' or a product as 'defective') is treated as a question of law, of fact or something in between (as in English law's 'secondary fact') is a function of the purpose or purposes for which the distinction between law and fact is itself drawn. In the context of the present study, I see two main legal purposes in the domestic legal systems of France and England.

First, the line between law and fact is fundamental to the allocation of the relative roles of the parties and the courts, for it is used to help in deciding which questions are subject to burdens of proof for the parties and which are for the court to determine as the public body invested with the power and duty to declare and to apply the law. In this respect, though, there has been an evolution in French thinking, moving

---

[79] Above, pp. 393–4.   [80] Above, pp. 384–5.   [81] Above, Chap. 15.
[82] Above, pp. 202–3, 219–20, 424.

somewhat away from the traditional division of function (by which it is for the parties to bring forward evidence of the facts on which they base their claims and to which the courts must then apply the law) towards a more nuanced division of function, the courts themselves seeking actively to collect evidence on which they can come to their decisions and sometimes re-classifying the basis of the parties' claims.[83] This procedural background affects significantly what it means to a French court that a party in a civil case bears the 'burden of proof' as to an issue such as the defectiveness of a product or the non-conformity of goods.

By contrast, the English understanding of the relative roles of the parties and the court to evidence, fact and law has remained relatively constant, even after the introduction of a degree of judicial interventionism in the civil process required by the Civil Procedure Rules.[84] For, it is still for the parties to put forward the claims which they wish the court to accept and to give effect, and for them to support their claims with both legal argument (which presupposes the classification of their claim in terms of a recognised legal basis), and evidence: it is not for the court to make a claimant or a defendant's case and the court does not 'share' the burden of proof on issues with the parties.[85] In this way, by contrast with the French civil process where the court is entitled to a degree of investigation of the parties' pretensions, the English civil process remains fundamentally adversarial, and the classification of a claim (in terms of one legal basis rather than another) remains a private matter for the parties.

Secondly, it will be seen from my earlier discussion that of very prominent significance for drawing the line between issues of law and issues of fact is the need to locate the judicial institution or institutions which are responsible for their authoritative and final determination. In this respect, in the French system, the *juges du fond* are empowered to decide issues of fact, of law and of the legal characterisation of facts—so much is straightforward. However, while the Cour de cassation decides issues of law, it recognises a 'sovereign power' in the *juges du fond* as to issues of fact, though it polices the way in which decisions of fact are reached. Most importantly for present purposes, the Cour de cassation allocates the final decision as to the legal characterisation of facts (whether behaviour is *fautif*, whether a product is defective) on an essentially ad hoc basis, drawing the line as a function of its own view in the context. Moreover, with a concept as broad and multi-faceted as *la faute*, some issues can be reserved by the Cour de cassation for its own final decision (for example, whether *imprudence* is sufficient to count as *une faute* in the context[86]) but leave other questions for the *juges du fond* (for example, whether the defendant's conduct amounted to *imprudence* in the circumstances). Indeed, no description of French private law is complete without an indication of how the Cour de cassation draws the line between its own competence and that of the *juges du fond*.

In the English context, the line between law and fact and the characterisation of facts used to be drawn in a similarly strict way, allocating to juries issues of fact and to judges issues of law. This left issues of the characterisation of facts (such as whether a defendant is guilty of negligence) as stretched uncomfortably between the two, the judges setting out when a person *could* be negligent and the jury deciding whether a

---

[83] Above, pp. 46–8.   [84] Above, pp. 205–10.   [85] Above, pp. 206–8.   [86] Above, p. 44.

person *was* negligent, but then at times seeking to circumscribe further the discretion of the jury by finding new issues of law or by techniques such as the withdrawal of an issue of fact from the jury on the ground of insufficient evidence.[87] While this division of function between judge and jury is all but dead in the English civil context, it is very much alive in the criminal context with the result that a description of the modern substantive criminal law where juries are involved (as in murder or manslaughter) is often put in terms of the proper questions to be put and possible explanations to be offered to a jury.[88]

However, given the demise of the jury in civil cases, judges in civil trials decide all issues—fact, law and the legal characterisation of facts. Moreover, the extent to which an English appellate court is willing to interfere with a decision of fact or of the characterisation of fact depends more on differences between the nature of decisions *at trial* and on appeal, rather than on formal distinctions between 'law', 'primary fact' and 'secondary fact'.[89] So the House of Lords seeks to impose on the Court of Appeal a degree of constraint in overturning issues such as the negligence of a defendant *not* because these are factual rather than legal but because the trial judge is seen as being likely to have been in a better position to weigh up conflicting oral evidence, assessing the likely reliability of witnesses of fact and the relative persuasiveness of experts.[90]

(d) The EU dimension to law and fact

The EU seeks to achieve its purposes of economic and social integration in a number of different ways: through the invocation of broad EC principle (for example, in its principle of non-discrimination on grounds of nationality), through taxation policy, through financial subsidies, institutional or administrative initiatives, or the recommendations and guidance of 'soft law'. However, the imposition of targeted legal requirements by the issuing of directives remains a central mechanism for the working out of its policies of integration. In this light, while the two EC directives which have been the focus of this study seek to 'harmonise' or 'approximate' the laws of the Member States, this is not their fundamental purpose; their fundamental purpose, or rather, purposes are instead to change facts, that is, to harmonise the conditions under which businesses operate and therefore compete, and to harmonise the degree of effective protection for consumers, whether as to their bodily integrity (the Product Liability Directive) or their economic interests (the Consumer Guarantees Directive).[91] In the case of these directives, these practical purposes are intended to be achieved by the 'harmonisation' of the laws of the Member States, in a way which is 'complete' within its ambit for the first, merely 'minimal' for the second.[92]

However, the EU entrusts the implementation of directives to the legislators of Member States (whether parliamentary or governmental) and the first interpretation and application of their provisions to the courts of the Member States: the role of the European Court of Justice is to ensure the proper implementation and interpretation

---

[87] Above, pp. 189–90.   [88] Above, pp. 408, 412.   [89] Above, pp. 215–16.
[90] Above, p. 216.
[91] This neat line is, of course, blurred to the extent to which the Product Liability Directive provides for recovery in respect of damage to property: above, p. 503.   [92] Above, pp. 436–44, 567–8.

of a directive. This means of course that the European Court is fundamentally concerned with issues of law and is not therefore concerned with issues of fact or the application of the law to facts (their characterisation) arising from the cases referred to it under article 234 EC: both of these are therefore left to national courts. From this point of view and for this purpose, the European Court is an appellate court exclusively on points of law. While the European Court therefore reserves to itself the right to 'interpret general criteria used by the community legislator',[93] this leaves very considerable room for disharmony of application in such important concepts as 'defect' for the purposes of the Product Liability Directive.[94] In common with the French Cour de cassation, this fairly restrained role for the 'European supreme court' is partly a function of its understanding as to what are *essentially* legal and what are factual issues, and also at least to an extent a function of practical factors such as the need to keep the number of cases coming to it manageable and a political sense that some kinds of decision are better dealt with at a national rather than at a European level.

Moreover, the European Court of Justice sometimes has a further and very different choice from those to be made by the supreme courts of Member States. For, even within the application of a European directive it sometimes has to decide the line between those issues which are to be governed by European law and by national law. In this respect, the European Court can simply decide that a particular concept should be given an 'autonomous' European interpretation (and then indicate what that interpretation should be) or that it should be left to be interpreted by the legislator or the courts of Member States according to national traditions or choices, the Court taking into account in doing so the purposes and words used by the directive. However, we have seen that the European Court sometimes chooses a half-way position, placing an issue within the competence of national legislatures or courts but then subjecting it to some degree of control by reference to the principle of effectiveness and, therefore, of its own view of the overall purposes of the EU legislation in question.[95] In this way, the line between the competence of the European Court of Justice and national legal organs is blurred, and the law itself becomes a mixture of European and national rules, the latter sometimes qualified by European principle.

4. Public Law and Private Law

This study has looked at the impact of the French and English laws of liability for products from the perspective of administrative law as well as of private law or, in the English context, of law more generally. In doing so, it is clear that in some ways the two laws remain very different, both at the levels of jurisdiction and of substantive law.

First, the jurisdictional divide between the administrative and the ordinary courts in France continues to have an important effect in the preservation of the distinctive nature of the substantive law, this being reinforced by differences in training and wider culture of the two sets of personnel which participate in the process, whether the judges who decide cases or the jurists who suggest or criticise developments. However,

---

[93] Above, p. 493. [94] Ibid. [95] Above, pp. 504–5.

the jurisdictional divide can have other effects. So, I have explained how in the case where a claimant could claim either against a private defendant in the ordinary courts or against a public defendant in the administrative courts, the jurisdictional divide together with other factors can have a practical effect on the incidence of liability, to the extent that one can legitimately speak of a practical 'irresponsibility' in the administration even where its behaviour qualifies as giving rise to liability under the rules of administrative law.[96]

Secondly, the way in which administrative law applies to a context such as liability for products is both complex and has been the subject of considerable change. True, there is a certain sense in which liability in the administration is becoming less specially administrative where the context does not involve issues which are (at least to an English lawyer) distinctively public, as in the case of liability for road accidents and for medical accidents (which were put on the same basis by legislation in 1957 and 2000 respectively) or in the case of damage done by persons who escape from control and who are likely to do harm.[97] Nevertheless, there remain considerable differences in treatment in the public and private laws: in particular, French administrative law does not possess a basis of liability without fault approaching the generality of the private law liability for the 'deeds of things', but does possess a special set of liabilities linked to 'public works'.[98]

Perhaps more interesting, though, than these differences in the substantive bases of liability in public and private law is the way in which French law (taken as a whole) uses different layers of regulation to give effect to different types of or intensities of public involvement. This can be seen very clearly in relation to its treatment of the provision of services to the public ('public services' in a very broad and non-technical sense). Here, French law distinguishes between those services which count as '*services publics*' by reference to the ultimately functional idea of the 'public interest' rather than by reference to the institutional nature of its provider: this means that the law can see the provision of services as 'public' (and therefore subject to a set of legal principles which allow the Conseil d'Etat to give effect to the concerns of the public interest) whether their provider is institutionally public or private and whatever the legal nature of the provision to their recipient.[99] However, apart from the question of the law governing institutions themselves (which follows their public or private nature), the law then distinguishes as regards the nature of the relationship between the provider of the service and its recipient betweeen services which are 'administrative' or 'industrial and commercial', this being determined by reference to a set of factors which seek to assess whether or not the provider is acting in the same sort of way and context as would a private sector supplier.[100] The decision between the two then affects the basis of liability of the provider of the service—administrative public services being governed by administrative law and 'industrial and commercial' public services being governed by private and, typically, contract law.[101] Even here, however, an exception is made for cases where liability to a non-recipient of the service (a 'third party') is involved and the harm is caused by 'public works', where liability is determined by a

---

[96] Above, pp. 319–30. [97] Above, pp. 115, 120–1, 151–2. [98] Above, pp. 118–131.
[99] Above, p. 133. [100] Above, pp. 134–5. [101] Above, p. 135.

special set of administrative law rules, the 'public' nature of the works being determined by yet another set of criteria.[102] Rather, then, than two large and separate blocks of law—public and private—French treatment of the provision of public services demonstrates its willingness to layer its regulation, applying now public, now private rules and determining 'publicness' according to different criteria for different legal purposes.

The fundamental differences with English law remain obvious. The first is the absence of a jurisdictional divide between public and private approaching that found in French law. The second, relating to differences in the two substantive laws is rather more difficult to characterise. Certainly, English law has for at least 50 years recognised a distinct 'administrative law', this centring now on the availability of judicial review of administrative action (and action which is to be assimilated to administrative action) and whose more recent history has been very closely associated with statutory powers and the doctrine of *ultra vires*. More difficult, however, is the position of areas of law where the basic framework of the law is shared with other, 'private' disputes, as in the case of liability. Here, the 'ordinary law' still applies, but it is qualified or its application affected by the public element.[103]

This sort of qualification is very well-known as regards liability in the tort of negligence for harm caused in the course of the exercise of statutory powers, where the duty of care has been used to take into account the nature of a defendant's public activities in deciding whether to allow liability for negligence and/or where decisions as to breach of duty may take into account the utility of a defendant's conduct as well as the financial cost of avoiding the harm in question as balanced against the danger.[104] Both these ways of restricting liability in the administration can be seen in English law's attitude to liability in the exercise of public powers affecting the safety of products.[105]

However, sometimes the public or, perhaps more accurately, statutory nature of a relationship can impact on liability in other, less obvious ways, as I have explained in relation to the provision of public services. English law does not possess any overarching *legal* understanding of the 'public service' or 'public services' as is found in French law, but it does take into account the public interest in the provision of particular categories of services by putting in place special institutions or rules for their supervision or regulation. Moreover, the legal relationship between the provider of a service and its recipient may either be classed as contractual, where the ordinary conditions for this concept's application apply (as in the case of the provision of gas and electricity or public transport services) or instead 'statutory', where the statutory legal framework in which the service is provided is considered inconsistent with the existence of a contract (as in the case of the provision of health care in the NHS or the provision of public water supplies).[106] One of the effects of this difference is that (apart from liability under the Consumer Protection Act) where a product is supplied in the course of provision of a contractual service, liability in its provider in respect of harm caused by the product can rest on the strict terms implied into contracts for the transfer of goods,

---

[102] Above, pp. 123–4, 136.   [103] Above, pp. 166–9, Chap. 12.
[104] Above, pp. 199, 335–44.   [105] Above, pp. 344–56.
[106] Above, Chap. 11 and see esp. pp. 276–9, 291–2.

whereas if the provision is non-contractual, liability can rest in practice only on the tort of negligence.[107]

The impact of liability under the Product Liability Directive here is particularly interesting as regards both French and English law. For the provider of a public service may be liable as 'supplier' or even as 'producer' of a product under the Product Liability Directive, whether the liability of the provider of the service would otherwise count as public or private, contractual or non-contractual as a matter of national law.[108] As the European Court stated in *Veedfald* in the context of public health care, 'the fact that products are manufactured for a specific medical service for which the patient does not pay directly but which is financed from public funds maintained out of taxpayers' contributions cannot detract from the economic and business character of that manufacturer'; as a result no defence should be accorded to a defendant on the ground that its provision of a service belonged to the public sector and did not therefore count as for 'an economic purpose or in the course of business' as 'a private hospital would undoubtedly be liable for the defectiveness of the product pursuant to the provisions of the Directive'.[109] Here, therefore, the interpretation of the 1985 Directive is true to its stated purpose of concern with the harmonisation of laws affecting the working of the internal market, rather than merely with the harmonisation of the *private* laws of Europe.[110] From this perspective, the common law's traditional lack of a formal categorisation between public and private law fits well with the EC directives' fundamental concern with the market.

5. Public Law, Criminal Law and Civil Law

French lawyers are often rather uncomfortable in placing criminal law within the framework of the dichotomy of public law and private law. At an institutional and jurisdictional level, the pull is towards private law, for it shares with *droit civil* the adjudication of the ordinary courts (the *ordre judiciaire*), at the apex of which is the Cour de cassation. On the other hand, the public interest (which is so typical a defining element within public law) is very prominent both in the substantive criminal law and even more, perhaps, in the criminal process. For while the victim of a crime (a private citizen) may be involved in the criminal process, either by instigating or by joining proceedings, the criminal proceedings themselves (the *action publique*) remain the chief concern of a public official, the *ministère public*, and the final decision whether a trial should take place and on what charges rests with a *magistrat*, the *juge d'instruction*.[111] All these features reflect the fact that a criminal case is not a matter

---

[107] Above, pp. 270–1, 291–2.

[108] Above, pp. 515–18. I have also suggested that a 'supplier' within the meaning of art. 3(3) of the 1985 Directive may extend to all those in the chain of distribution who use a product: above, pp. 523–7.) Case C-203/99 of 10 May 2001, [2001] ECR 1–3569.

[109] *Veedfald v Århus Amtskommune*, at para. 21, above, pp. 515–16.

[110] Cf. for a similar theme in relation to Dir. 93/13/EC on unfair terms in consumer contracts, see S. Whittaker, 'Unfair Contract Terms, Public Services and the Construction of a European Conception of Contract' (2000) 116 *LQR* 95. [111] Above, pp. 380–2.

merely for the parties as it is with a civil case where they dispute their own (private) interests, but is a matter for the State owing to the public interests at stake.[112] Moreover, while courts hearing criminal cases belong to the *ordre judiciaire*, criminal trials themselves differ significantly from the hearings of courts deciding civil cases, particularly in the wider recourse to oral evidence and, as regards the most serious cases, the presence of lay judges on the bench.[113] In truth, criminal law and the criminal jurisdiction fall somewhere between the public and private dichotomy or, rather better, constitute their own distinct category transcending this dichotomy altogether.

We have seen, however, a further way in which French law has found the distinction between the criminal and public domains difficult, and one where French lawyers appeared at first caught in a pincer between their own constitutional principles and the practical desires of their courts to award damages to the victims of accidents. The starting point was that French criminal courts assessed very strictly the ingredients of the offences of involuntary homicide and causing personal injuries, so as to compensate the victims of the 'crimes', present before them as *parties civiles*.[114] Their strict approach clearly spilled over into their treatment of public defendants (such as *maires*) who found themselves held guilty of involuntary homicide for minor failures in the exercise of their powers of control of health and safety, even though the criminal court (as part of the *ordre judiciaire*) was not generally entitled to impose on them or on the public bodies of which they formed part any liability in damages: the principle of the separation of powers was able to protect them from civil liability before the criminal courts (reserving this for the administrative jurisdiction and administrative law), even if not from criminal responsibility. As I have described, while 'public decision makers' (and notably *maires*) lobbied for change, most French lawyers considered that 'public decision makers' could not simply be given a special and overt legislative protection from conviction for involuntary homicide or causing personal injuries as this would breach the constitutional principle of equality before the law.[115]

In the *loi* of 2000 the French Parliament appears to have escaped the pincer of the criminal courts' desire to award compensation and constitutional principle, by changing the definition of criminal fault for the majority of cases where the actions or omissions of 'public deciders' are in issue and by partly separating the assessment of criminal and civil fault more generally.[116] Unfortunately, the legal means which the *loi* of 2000 adopted to protect human public decision makers rests on a criterion of the directness or indirectness of a defendant's action or omission in causing a victim's death or personal injuries, a criterion which is itself open to manipulation and which creates unjustifiable distinctions with the liabilities of *private* corporate defendants.[117] Moreover, the *loi* of 2000 preserved the criminal immunity of local public authorities as regards the exercise of their specially public powers,[118] as well as of the State itself.[119] In the result, while there is

---

[112] Above, p. 384.   [113] Above, pp. 369, 386.   [114] Above, pp. 372–6.
[115] Above, pp. 378, 388.   [116] Above, pp. 388–94.   [117] Above, pp. 389–93.
[118] This is defined by reference to the criterion of the legality of their delegation: above, pp. 379, 388.
[119] Above, pp. 378, 389.

no distinct substantive criminal law applicable only to public persons, the ordinary criminal law does apply specially to public decision makers and to some classes of public bodies. Nowhere can this more clearly be seen than in the provision by the Constitution of 1958 (as originally promulgated and as later amended) of a special forum for the trial of criminal offences for government ministers.[120]

By contrast, I do not think that many English lawyers would feel the need to see criminal law as part of either public law or private law, but would instead see it as distinctive from either, reflecting its fundamentally different purposes and the different nature of the judicial proceedings by which criminal offences are tried. True, criminal proceedings have in common with proceedings for judicial review (seen as typical of public law) that they oppose the administration against private bodies, but they do so in opposite directions: for proceedings for judicial review are usually brought by a citizen against the administration challenging the latter's decision making or other action; whereas criminal proceedings are brought by the administration (the Crown Prosecution Service) against citizens to establish their breaches of the criminal law. The public interest and the need to uphold citizen's rights may be central to both administrative law and criminal law, but in the same sort of very general way in which the public interest is involved in *all* law.[121]

On the other hand, we can see in English law a considerable evolution as regards the relationship between the criminal and the civil law. At a substantive level, the modern creation of numerous statutory offences (particularly in the regulatory fields of health and safety) has led to a greater divorce between crime and tort, the courts not seeing the existence of a breach of a statutory duty (whether or not backed by criminal sanctions) as necessarily a ground for the imposition of civil liability.[122] Moreover, this substantive separation is parallelled at the level of process. For historically, at a very general level common law trials of criminal and civil cases had a good deal in common, for in both proceedings were brought generally by private individuals (private prosecution being the norm before nineteenth-century reforms) and both could involve the production and examination of oral evidence, with the facts determined by verdict of a jury.[123] However, the gradual disappearance of private prosecution of offences and of trial by jury in civil cases and the increasing movement especially in civil procedure to reliance on written rather than oral evidence have served to emphasise the distinctive natures of criminal and civil trials.[124] Perhaps more important than both of these, however, is the deep sense in English lawyers that the criminal and civil laws (and so also the criminal and civil processes) exist to serve very different purposes. This, I have suggested, is the fundamental reason for the absence from the English criminal process of the victim of the crime as civil party, in contrast to the active presence of the *partie civile* in the French: English criminal courts may have the power

---

[120] Above, pp. 398–400.

[121] Cf. D. Oliver, *Common Values and the Public–Private Divide* (Butterworths, 1999) who argues not merely for the essential similarity of function of the law governing public and private powers, but that in English law these controls are based on a common set of values (though her discussion does not include the place of criminal law). [122] Above, pp. 219–20.

[123] As to these features of English civil procedure, see above, pp. 189–90, 211–12; as to private prosecution, above, pp. 419–20. [124] Above, pp. 191–2, 211–12, 420–3.

to award compensation to the victims of crimes, but they still see issues of compensation as essentially civil.[125] Overall, therefore, if the divide between English administrative and private law is relatively blurred, its divide between criminal law and other law (whether administrative or private) has become increasingly sharp.

6. European Legislation, National Laws and Implementation

Everything is connected to everything else—but as regards the modern legal systems of Europe to this trite observation must be added that while the legal institutions, legal processes, and substantive laws within Member States are connected to each other differently, they possess a common skein of legal threads tying each of them with the laws, policies and institutions of the European Union. The overall history of European Community law in general could be seen in terms of the working out of these tensions between common European norms and national legal *systems* of norms, but the tensions are particularly visible in the case of those European laws which impact on such deeply entrenched areas of national law as the law of obligations, on contracts of sale and extra-contractual liability. While EC legislation such as the Product Liability Directive or the Consumer Guarantees Directive does not simply involve the transplant of legal rules or institutions from one legal system to another (even where the legislation appears to reflect the concepts or approaches of one system or group of systems over another) since it creates a distinct and original body of law driven by the specifically European purposes for which it was enacted and principles to which it is related, nevertheless it can involve the introduction into a legal system of concepts, approaches or policies that do not fit with their indigenous surroundings. In this respect, it is noticeable that so far the EC directives which have affected the private laws of the Member States have done so in a very targeted (one could say piecemeal) fashion, creating new rights or remedies in particular circumstances, often in a way which is clearly intended to supplement other, national legal rules rather than setting out the law governing a particular situation systematically. This is conspicuously true of the Product Liability Directive, which, for all its interpretation as 'complete harmonisation' within its ambit, forms only part of the law governing manufacturers' and suppliers' liability in the laws of Member States, and even more of the Consumer Guarantees Directive which is overtly minimal in its requirements and which is more restricted both as regards the class of buyers which it protects and as regards the range of remedies which it provides than the existing laws of many if not all Member States. These directives therefore require a very considerable degree of normative integration within surrounding national laws and one of a different order given the deep roots and interconnectedness of private law within Member States.

However, perhaps paradoxically, a common law system such as English law may appear to be able to tolerate more easily the sort of norms which are parachuted in by the EC legislator, even though its historical background differs significantly from the general continental Romanist tradition. For the common law approach remains that

[125] Above, p. 426.

legislation ('statute') creates exceptional intrusions into the potentially all-embracing common law:[126] it is very much within the tradition for legislation either to supplement or to differ significantly in approach from the surrounding common law and, indeed, other statutes, since Parliament intervenes specially, for particular purposes and in particular ways. By contrast, where a legal system (such as French law) sees legislation and, in particular, codified legislation as its normative starting point, new EC-inspired laws coming into the system must either sit uncomfortably outside the existing codes (adding to substantive legal complexity and weakening the codes' claims to provide coherent and systematic schemes of regulation) or be brought within them, thereby introducing new elements which may clash with existing ways of thinking. In my view, however, this contrast between the common law and those systems whose private law is codified is not as marked as this suggests. For, even though English law may see legislation as an intervention in the common law, nevertheless modern legislators have attempted to ensure that statutes and statutory instruments connect up with the common law itself and with the surrounding pattern of other statutes: a picture of English law in terms of the common law pricked by a myriad of unrelated statutes would be a caricature.

The true extent of the sorts of difficulties faced by the English and French legislatures in implementing EC directives in areas already governed by their laws is well illustrated by the Product Liability and Consumer Guarantees Directives. The English legislator in implementing the Product Liability Directive did not face any *formal* difficulty in implementation, but was able to create easily a new basis of liability following the pattern of the Directive itself, a basis which simply sits side by side with existing (and to an extent broader) ones provided by the tort of negligence and for breach of contract: implementation of the Directive merely created a new statutory tort to add to the rather ragged bundle of other torts, some statutory and some at common law. However, at a *substantive* level, the legislation which resulted from implementation of the Product Liability Directive has appeared increasingly isolated and out of keeping with the rest of the law, whether statutory or common law. For in the second half of the twentieth century the majority of parliamentary statutes[127] and even more the courts have seen negligence as the proper basis for the imposition of liability for personal injuries and death. In the case of the courts, this vision has been reflected positively in their seeing negligent conduct causing physical harm as generally justifying the imposition of a duty of care (though particular reasons can be adduced as to why one should be denied in the circumstances) and therefore setting a minimum standard of behaviour in respect of personal safety; but it has also been reflected negatively by restricting the ambit of those established torts (of private nuisance, *Rylands v Fletcher* and breach of statutory duty) which had been used and could have been developed more widely to impose liability without negligence.[128] This second aspect should not be surprising, for if the 'negligence standard' balances the value of the defendant's activity as well as the cost of precautions against the danger which it creates, then an

---

[126] Above, pp. 223, 337, 469.

[127] E.g. Occupiers Liability Act 1957; Occupiers Liability Act 1984, above, pp. 182–3. The Employers' Liability (Defective Equipment) Act 1969 forms something of an exception, above, p. 182.

[128] Above, pp. 162–3.

absence of negligence may reflect a judicial decision that the activity in question should *not* be discouraged by the imposition of civil liability: from this perspective, the negligence standard could be seen as setting also a maximum standard of behaviour, even though one which may at times conflict with standards imposed for purposes other than of civil liability.[129] In the result, liability under Part I of the Consumer Protection Act looks very different from the generality of liabilities for personal injuries and death accepted at common law, and in a way which is (apart from its European origins) difficult to justify when put next to other situations in which the traditional arguments in favour of strict liability could equally well be canvassed.[130] In this environment, it should not be surprising that the question whether liability under Part I of the Consumer Protection Act is *substantially* different from liability in negligence remains controversial.[131]

Moreover, the English legislator faced very considerable difficulties of normative fit in implementing the Consumer Guarantees Directive, partly because the law of seller's liability in sales of goods was already the object of a developed *statutory* scheme, but even more because of the clash in remedial strategy to deal with qualitative or functional defectiveness of the goods between its existing rules, which reflected the common law stance more generally, and the scheme required by the Directive.[132] So, while the Directive's standard of 'contractual conformity' could quite easily be accommodated within section 14 of the Sale of Goods Act 1979 (with a bit of tweaking to other statutory definitions), its hierarchical system of rights clashed fundamentally with existing English law remedies for breach of the implied statutory terms of quality and fitness for purpose which give primacy to a short-lived right of rejection of the goods and a much longer-lived right to damages and do not provide any right to repair or replacement of the goods by the seller.[133] Here, the minimal nature of the 1999 Directive and UK government's declared policy of not reducing existing legal rights of consumers led to implementation of the Directive by the creation of an additional set of rights for 'consumers' (whose definition was extended) broadly in parallel to the rights already provided by the scheme of the 1979 Act and by the common law of breach of express contract terms, though at times a consumer's choice of the new scheme of rights may temporarily exclude recourse to the classic rights. The resultant layering of regulation is horribly complicated: legal implementation but only semi-integration.

If anything, however, the problems of normative fit caused by implementation of the 1985 and 1999 Directives have been more acute in French law, both at a formal and at a substantive level.

---

[129] Cf. above, pp. 202–5, 218–24. This possible conflict between the standards imposed by the law of civil liability and more generally is implicit in the English approach to the tort of breach of statutory duty. For, where a court holds that a statutory duty (typically sanctioned by the criminal law) does *not* give rise to civil liability, this has the potential to contrast with the standard set by the general law of the tort of negligence. So, a person may be liable criminally without negligence (depending on the content of the statutory offence), but liable in damages only on proof of negligence.

[130] So, for example, if it is said that liability without negligence is justified in the case of manufacturers' liability for products on the basis that they can more easily insure or otherwise spread the cost of the liability, this could equally be said of liability for motor accidents, which still rests in English law on proof of negligence. [131] Above, pp. 485–92, 499–502.

[132] Above, pp. 570–1, 587–8.   [133] Above, pp. 250–7, 604–11.

In the case of the Product Liability Directive, the first plan (the 'Ghestin *projet*') was for a rational implementation by creating an *exclusive* basis of liability for damage caused by unsafely defective products and to use implementation as an occasion for a wider reform of the law of liability for defective property by amending the law of sale on the basis of the standard of 'conformity of the property' set by the Vienna Convention.[134] Both these changes were to be effected by amendment of the Civil Code, this being acceptable because of the perceived rational relationship between the reforms and the wider Civil Code: the new product liability could be seen as a special ground of liability not altogether different from the special liabilities for animals and for the 'ruin of buildings' already provided by the code, and the amendment of the law of sale (for all buyers) would also fit there naturally.[135] From the point of view of substance, however, implementation of the Product Liability Directive itself was more problematic as a result of the generous nature of existing *jurisprudence* affecting liability for products, whether under the law of delict or contract, since this meant that a faithful and exclusive implementation appeared to reduce the protections given to French victims of products.

This substantive difficulty with the plan remained when the more ambitious reforms of the law of sale were jettisoned and did not cease to dog the process of attempted implementation in the course of the 1990s, when the *affaire du sang contaminé* made the law governing unsafe products increasingly politicised and when continued legislative inaction triggered judicial 'implementation' of the Directive under cover of interpretation of existing French concepts.[136] The resulting *loi* of 1998 reflected a rather messy compromise: in its inclusion of the development risks defence with the exception of products made from the human body, but even more in its preservation of the other grounds on which a victim of a product could claim.[137] At a formal level, the new product liability's claim to be in the Civil Code was significantly weakened, as its special and non-exclusive nature argued that it should not be seen as capable of contributing towards more general legal principle. Indeed, some authors expressed concern that it should not be allowed to contaminate the rest of the law (notably, as to *force majeure*).[138] Or, as Terré, Simler and Lequette put it, European harmonisation was achieved at the cost of internal legal disharmony.[139]

However, French law's implementation of the 1985 Directive went beyond what it required. For in an attempt to fit its implementation with general French legal principle, with its existing *jurisprudence*, and with the popular concerns of the time, the *loi* of 1998 extended liability for defective products in the Civil Code in three ways: putting the liability of suppliers on the same basis as producers (thereby fitting in with established *jurisprudence* on the liability of sellers); extending liability of all those liable for all damage to property (whatever its nature, and without any threshold of liability, both following the fundamental principle of *réparation intégrale* of the French law of liability); and by providing that two defences available to the producer under the Directive should not be available in certain circumstances in French law (this

---

[134] Above, pp. 452–5. [135] Above, pp. 453–4. [136] Above, pp. 450, 455–7.
[137] Above, pp. 457–8. [138] Above, pp. 460–1, 495, 538.
[139] Terré, Simler, Lequette, *Obligations*, 938.

reflecting a concern to impose post-marketing obligations regarding the safety of products on producers and suppliers).[140] Some (though rather oddly not all) of these extensions of liability fell foul of the European Court's decisions in 2002 which declared that the 1985 Directive required the creation of a 'completely harmonised' scheme of liability, despite its toleration in article 13 of existing liabilities based on grounds other than those set out by the Directive.[141] And after the European Court's view of the matter has been given effect by the *loi* of 9 December 2004 the legislative expression of the new product liability in France fits even less well with French legal principle and with its previous *jurisprudence*.[142]

But the problems for French law did not stop there. For the decisions of the European Court in 2002 made the question as to the status of *jurisprudence* previous to the *loi* of 1998 more acute: did this *jurisprudence* (whether intended to 'implement' the Directive or earlier developments based on traditional techniques and pinned to the Civil Code) survive the combined effect of specific French legislation in the area and the European Court's decisions?[143] Here, no clear overall answer can be given, though some particular judicial constructions look doomed (notably, the implement-ing *jurisprudence* of the 1990s) whereas others look destined for revival (notably, the *garantie légale* in sale).[144] This last point appears to have been noticed and indeed encouraged by the French government which retained a reform to the *bref délai* of the *garantié légale* in sale in its implementation of the Consumer Guarantees Directive.[145]

This brings me, then, to the implementation in France of the Consumer Guarantees Directive itself.[146] Here, we experience a certain *déja vu*, for the first *projet* (put forward by the government working group chaired by Viney), proposed using the Directive as the basis for a general reform of the law of sale recognisably similar to that proposed by Ghestin in the 1980s.[147] In the case of the 1999 Directive, the sort of extension and improvements which the *avant-projet de loi* had in mind appeared to be compatible with the Directive itself, which was overtly minimal in its requirements.[148] However, despite the fact that the subject matter of the reform did not concern the safety of products (and therefore did not impinge on the sensitivities created by the *affaire du sang contaminé*), the Viney working group's proposals attracted a very lively dispute, involving arguments as to the proper pattern of French codification (should its imple-mentation legislation amend the Civil Code or merely the *Code de la consommation*?); disputes at a conceptual level as to the nature of 'non-conformity' and 'latent defect'; tensions between those who saw the French legal tradition threatened by the creeping Europeanisation of private law; and substantive arguments between different political visions of contract law, between a 'social solidarist' vision and a more liberal vision which prioritises freedom of contract.[149] Underneath all this argumentation, there lay a genuine problem for French law: should it extend a scheme of liability conceived for sales of goods to consumers to all contracts of sale for the benefit of all categories of buyer and would it thereby create a scheme which, though 'coherent', was sometimes

---

[140] Above, pp. 458–60. The defences were those found in art. 7(d) and (e) of the 1985 Directive.
[141] Above, pp. 440–4, 460.   [142] Above, pp. 459–60.   [143] Above, pp. 461–5.
[144] Above, p. 464.   [145] Above, pp. 464, 583.   [146] Above, pp. 574–83.
[147] Above, pp. 575–6 and cf. pp. 452–5.   [148] Above, p. 568.   [149] Above, pp. 576–82.

substantively inappropriate? Or should it simply add another layer of rights limited in the way envisaged by the Directive but at a cost of complexity if not actual contradiction with existing patterns to the practical detriment of the consumers which it purported to help? In the result, the French government in the *ordonnance* of 17 February 2005 favoured the minimalist approach to implementation, the wider approach proposed by the Viney working group having become politically unpopular, being opposed both by business (on the grounds of its interference with contractual freedom) and by consumers groups (on the grounds that the new coherent scheme would sometimes be *less* protective of consumers than the existing law and *jurisprudence*).[150] Again, European harmonisation led to internal French disharmony.

7. European Harmonisation and Law Reform

Where does this leave the European harmonising effect of the two directives? At the time of the enactment of the Product Liability Directive I expressed concern that the legal harmonisation which it heralded would be more formal than substantive and that it would require a complex piece of legal rearrangement rather than genuine law reform.[151] At the time, it was clear that the Directive itself tolerated a very considerable degree of disharmony even within its own scheme. This could be seen in its explicit derogations presented for Member States, but even more in the range of important issues which are left to be determined by national law, including the causal link between the 'defect' and the 'damage' and what is properly to be treated as 'damage' for this purpose (and how its monetary equivalent is properly to be assessed), even if the national law is subjected to an overall control by the principle of effectiveness.[152] It could also be seen in the 1985 Directive's apparent tolerance of liabilities which were more generous to claimants, whether existing at the time of the Directive's promulgation or subsequent.[153]

These initial thoughts on the relative ineffectiveness of the Product Liability Directive in terms of harmonisation of laws have not been proved false by the Directive's subsequent history, even if this is restricted to the laws of just two Member States. There are three further points to be made as to the impact of this Directive on harmonisation.

First, even where legal systems share the same form of words to describe the elements of liability, their practical interpretation and application will depend on the juridical approaches followed and procedural mechanisms possessed by the courts of Member States. What I mean by 'juridical approaches' for present purposes is the extent to which lawyers within a system accept the openness of a broad concept (such as 'defect' or 'damage') or instead prefer to discover further legal issues underneath the broad concept. Here, English and French law reveal a considerable contrast. For, since the demise of the jury English lawyers have tended to seek to set out the factors which

---

[150] Above, p. 583.   [151] Whittaker (1985), 236.
[152] Above, pp. 436–7, 503–5, 508, 511–14.
[153] 1985 Directive, art. 13, above, pp. 437–8, 442–4.

a court should take into account in determining open concepts such as 'reasonable care' or 'satisfactory quality', so as to structure the judicial discretion which they entail.[154] On the other hand, French lawyers remain much more tolerant of relative uncertainty which leaves concepts like 'defect' or '*la faute*' relatively unexplained and unstructured and (at least in part) within the 'sovereign power of assessment' of the *juges du fond*.[155] In this respect, the definition of defect in the 1985 Directive (and indeed the definition of contractual conformity in the 1999 Directive) represent a compromise between the two extremes represented by English and French law in this context. However, it is likely that a French lower court will retain its existing approach to the determination of defect and so while taking the express considerations found in article 1384-4 of the Civil Code and reflecting article 6 of the Directive, will more generally continue to rely on any *expertise* and cloak its own decision beneath its 'sovereign power', whereas (as is very clearly illustrated by *A v National Blood Authority*[156]) an English court faced with all but a relatively straightforward case will seek to establish the range of relevant and, possibly, irrelevant factors to be taken into account in its decision. So, unless the European Court of Justice is given the opportunity and then chooses to take on the task of itself setting out such a 'basket of considerations', practical differences will remain underneath perfectly harmonious legal formulae.

Moreover, as my earlier reference to the role of the *expertise* in French law suggests, even where the legal questions which a court asks itself are identical, the way in which the court goes about answering them impacts significantly on the result. This study has looked at the approach of French and English courts to the determination of such issues as '*vice caché*', 'negligence' or the defectiveness of a product in terms of the relative roles of the parties and the court, the nature and range of evidential materials available and the finality of adjudication.[157] In all this, I have become increasingly convinced of the central importance of the nature of legal institutions, conceptions of the legal process and the resources of legal procedure on substantive judicial decision making.

Secondly, the Product Liability Directive's central idea that the harmonisation of the rules of liability for producers and suppliers will create or even tend to create a level playing field for producers in the internal market is fundamentally unconvincing.[158] For even if the Directive's scheme of liability were implemented in a national law in a manner which was exclusive of any other ground of liability (and, as has been said, such an exclusive approach is not required by the Directive itself), this would not mean that the practical burden of liability would fall on producers and suppliers in the same way in different national laws. For such a practical burden is a function of the patterns of liability within the national legal system, both in terms of the relative attractiveness of claims by an injured person against defendants *other* than those governed by the Directive and in terms of the availability and extent of recourse by others held liable against the Directive's defendants.[159] The Directive's claim to act as a mechanism for the channelling of liability onto producers therefore depends on the

---

[154] Above, pp. 188–200, 235–9, 245.   [155] Above, pp. 44–5, 78.
[156] [2001] 3 All ER 289, above, pp. 486–9.   [157] Above, pp. 46–50, 205–18.
[158] Above, Chap. 18.   [159] Above, pp. 538–53, 556–63.

extent to which other liabilities are imposed on other persons and then (partly or wholly) cling to them.[160] Further differences in the practical impact of liability on producers and suppliers stem from the extent to which the cost of compensation of injured parties is borne (and remains borne) by legal institutions other than individuals or businesses through the imposition of liability, notably, through social security or first party insurance, though this effect has not been the object of this present study.[161]

Thirdly, and ironically, the European Court of Justice's understandable reliance on the ostensible purpose of the Product Liability Directive in harmonising the law for economic purposes led to its decisions of 2002 which declared the Directive's 'completely harmonious' nature for the defendants which it governs on the grounds which it establishes.[162] As I have explained, the significance of these decisions has yet to be fully worked out (in particular what is meant by 'grounds other than the Directive's'),[163] but their effect can already be seen in two ways. It can be seen most vividly in the necessary pruning of the French (and Greek) implementing legislation so as to conform to the more restricted requirements of the Directive itself, with the result that the European Court's interpretation has had or will have a limiting effect on the extent of consumer protection in the two laws; the Spanish legislator had already foreseen the problem and therefore had created a hole in Spanish law's more stringent existing protection for consumers so as to conform to the Directive's scheme.[164] This, of course, reflects the necessary cost of any 'complete' harmonisation: the law is cut down as well as brought up to par. But the effect of the European Court's decisions of 2002 is worse than this, for they require the creation and the preservation of a frozen core of producer and supplier liability for defective products in the laws of the Member States, with which national law must not tamper. This means that any Member State which wishes to make any national law reform of an area of law which impacts (even to a relatively small extent) on the new product liability must still preserve this core, even if it does not fit with the rest of the reforming scheme. This has already happened in French law, where legislation in 2002 sought to place public and private medical liability on the same legal basis of 'fault', but felt it necessary specifically to retain liability in respect of defects in medical products.[165] Even more serious, though, would be the difficulty where a national parliament wished to remove a particular area from the law of liability altogether and *replace* it with a system of compensation based on social security or first party insurance: here again, the Directive's purpose in harmonising the burdens of producers throughout the EU argues for the retention of their liability, thereby risking compromising such a scheme. Indeed, it could be argued that French law's existing law governing accidents at work is partly inconsistent with the 1985 Directive, for under it employers are generally immune from liability even though they may be 'suppliers' of products which cause their employees injuries or death.[166]

The Consumer Guarantees Directive's claim to true legal harmonisation was always a more modest one, given the expressly minimal nature of its requirements.[167] Its

---

[160] Above, pp. 550–3, 561–3.   [161] Above, pp. 35–8, 173–8, 449.   [162] Above, pp. 440–4.
[163] Above, pp. 442–3.   [164] Ibid.   [165] Above, pp. 151–3.
[166] Above, pp. 61–2, 524–6.   [167] Above, p. 568.

claim was, first, that the requirement of a minimum fair basis of consumer rights in respect of the 'conformity' of goods would strengthen consumer confidence to embark on cross-border transactions and thereby promote the internal market.[168] This claim, however, is by no means borne out by the legislation produced as a result in England and France, whose complexities stemming at least in part from the Directive itself render its new rights obscure to consumers.[169] To the extent to which a non-national consumer would actually be aware of these sets of new rights, he or she is most unlikely to be encouraged to contract as a result. As I have said, the second claim of the 1999 Directive that its implementation will lead to the lessening of distortions in the market contrasts with its own explicitly minimal nature, for the construction of a minimum of 'liability' is unlikely to dissolve the existing 'compartmentalisation of markets' to which the Directive's preamble refers. With respect, both express purposes of the 1999 Directive have the empty ring of unsupported economic assertion and fine sentiment which leave an even mildly sceptical reader unconvinced and therefore easily dissatisfied when the substantive requirements of the Directive do not themselves impress either in terms of their quality or their fitness for purpose. Perhaps the EC Commission's own dissatisfaction with reliance on 'mere positions of principle' and preference for clearly established factual evidence in relation to reform of the Product Liability Directive,[170] should be more widely taken to heart.

However, in my view of most interest is the relationship between *implementation* of the Consumer Guarantees Directive and the 'completely harmonising' nature of the Product Liability Directive. As I have said, from the point of view of the European legislator, these two directives deal with different situations: the first concerns contractual liability for qualitative or stipulatory defects in consumer goods giving rise primarily to rights to their repair or replacement (but not damages); the second concerns extra-contractual liability for defects of safety in products causing personal injury, death and damage to consumer property, giving rise exclusively to liability in damages.[171] However, from the point of view of national laws, this series of contrasts is very much more blurred, it being long appreciated by national courts and commentators that the classification of liability as contract or tort may be manipulated in order to achieve particular ends; that determination of a product's fitness for its purpose or satisfactory quality may well involve consideration of its safety; and that a modern law of seller's liability should include liability in damages for consequential damage, even if its starting point is with performance of the seller's obligation. These different blurrings of the neat lines between the concerns of the 1985 and 1999 Directives can be seen in both English law and French law, but are most striking in the latter. In English law, one can see the relevance of the goods' safety to the question of breach of the statutory implied terms found in the Sale of Goods Act and to the possibility of a buyer's being able to recover damages for personal injury without proof of negligence against the seller.[172] In French law, however, the law of sale (through interpretation of the *garantie légale* and flirtation with an extensive view of 'defects of conformity') and the law of contract

---

[168] Above, pp. 567–8.   [169] Above, pp. 604–18.
[170] EC Commission, *Report from the Commission on the Application of Directive 85/374* [etc.] Com/2000/0893 final (2001), para. 4, above, p. 447.   [171] Above, p. 631.
[172] Above, pp. 239, 242, 245–6.

more generally (through use of *obligation de sécurité* and *obligations d'information*) have been used as mechanisms for the imposition of liability (typically *sans faute*) beyond privity of contract though restricted to those belonging to the chain of distribution.[173] Put simply, contract law has been a major means by which French courts have put into effect their desire to help the victims of personal injuries and death achieve compensation.

As I have said, the minimal nature of the Consumer Guarantees Directive suggests that national implementing legislation may go beyond its requirements. This has indeed been the case as regards German law,[174] and was proposed by the Viney working group in its *avant-projet de loi*, though all that remains of this more ambitious plan in the *ordonnance* of 17 February 2005 is the amendment of article 1648 of the Civil Code so as to rid the *garantie légale* of its embarrassing *bref délai*.[175] It is clear from the judgments of the European Court of Justice in 2002 that its view of the Product Liability Directive as 'completely harmonising' nevertheless permits a Member State to maintain or even to create liabilities on producers or suppliers 'on other grounds' than those required by that directive, and that these other grounds expressly included contractual liability for latent defects.[176] What this means, however, is that implementation of the 1999 Directive by way of reform of national law governing sellers' liability *in damages* necessarily has a practical impact on the effectiveness of the Product Liability Directive in harmonising the costs of liability to producers and suppliers. In this way, a lawful and sensible implementation of the 1999 Directive weakens the purpose of the creation and implementation of the 1985 Directive.

Now, of course this phenomenon could be dismissed as reflecting the weakness of the terms of both of the particular directives in question. This potential for conflict between the two would not arise if the 1999 Directive had been a maximum as well as a minimum directive and the 1985 Directive had not contained article 13 which allows (if but to an extent) the retention of some existing national liabilities, for in these circumstances the two sets of implemented liabilities would not and could not overlap. However, in my view, the phenomenon is instead symptomatic of the lack of coherence of initiatives of intervention in the market affecting contract and extra-contractual liability undertaken by the European Community,[177] a lack of coherence which the Commission has itself at least in part acknowledged.[178] However, I remain unconvinced that Commission initiatives which are aimed at creating an agreed terminology for its legislation (if this is what its proposed 'toolbox' of the 'Common Frame of Reference' amounts to[179]) will deal with the substantive problem of the

---

[173] Above, pp. 22, 27–8, 67–9, 73–4, 95–7.   [174] Zimmermann, *Liability for Non-Conformity*.
[175] Above, pp. 575–6, 583.   [176] Above, pp. 441–2.
[177] See particularly clearly W.-H. Roth, 'Transposing "Pointillist" EC Guidelines into Systematic National Codes—Problems and Consequences' (2002) 10 *ERPL* 761.
[178] This can be seen in the Communication from the Commission to the European Parliament and Council, *A More Coherent European Contract Law: An Action Plan* Com. (2003) 68 final; EC Commission, Communication from the Commission to the European Parliament and the Council: European Contract Law and the revision of the *acquis*: the way forward (2004) Com(2004) 651 final.
[179] EC Commission, Communication from the Commission to the European Parliament and the Council: European Contract Law and the revision of the *acquis*: the way forward, ibid., 3. This communication specifically denies any intention on the part of the Commission to 'propose a "European civil code" which

remarkably piecemeal and partial character of many of the directives in the area and their resulting different interaction with their surroundings once implemented in the laws of the Member States. The laws of contractual and extra-contractual liability within national legal systems *are* interrelated, and indeed form part of a complex (if not always entirely harmonious) set of norms and techniques. European legislative intervention must understand this if its unifying role is to do substantive good rather than merely create a degree of formal European legal harmony, but disharmony within national laws.

What lesson should be drawn from this rather grim conclusion? Some may say that the solution to the problems caused by piecemeal harmonisation is further and wider reform. For if the practical burden of costs is a function of the patterns of liability within a legal system and cannot be harmonised by a targeted approach dealing with particular categories of defendant in particular situations and if the 'harmonisation' of a particular legal area (whether contract or tort) can lead either to disharmony within national private laws or the risk of inappropriate regulatory spill-over, then some would argue that the law of contract or liability should be harmonised more generally. Certainly, those jurists who argue in favour of the *legislation* of a European Civil Code may take such a view,[180] though a *civil* code may still leave untouched areas of liability which in some Member States are treated as belonging to public rather than private law or are a function of the relationship between criminal responsibility and civil liability. Quite apart from any other reasons why one might wish to oppose European legislation on this scale (whether political, economic or cultural) I have very considerable doubts as to the practical effectiveness of wider legislative harmonisation of substantive law on the economic costs to market operators owing to the importance of other factors at work in the laws of the Member States. In this respect, this study has attempted to explain how judicial institutional arrangements and procedural mechanisms for the establishing of facts and their characterisation in legal terms impact on the quality of decision made and, therefore, necessarily the practical outcome of cases: as Reimann puts it 'underneath the thin veneer of harmonized blackletter rules lurks a messy reality of litigation and compensation rarely affected by it'.[181] From the practical point of view of the harmonisation of costs of liability (or conversely, of the practical effectiveness of legal remedies), there would be little point in harmonising substantive legal rules without harmonising the institutions and procedures by which these rules are given effect. This would require, however, a very much greater intervention of EC law into the very fabric of national legal systems than is at present envisaged or would, I believe, be acceptable to most lawyers, politicians or others in Member States. But without such radical change, harmonisation of substantive law risks changing national law and

---

would harmonise contract laws of Member States', but does intend to 'examine whether non-sector-specific-measures such as an optional instrument may be required to solve problems in the area of European contract law': ibid., 8. The Annex I putting forward a possible structure of the Common Frame of Reference contains headings which suggest the construction of principles or rules, rather than merely terminological definitions.

[180] E.g. Roth, *op. cit.* n. 177, (2002) 10 *ERPL* 761.

[181] M. Reimann, 'Product Liability in a Global Context: the Hollow Victory of the European Model' (2003) 11 *ERPL* 128, 151, 154.

therefore changing *some* practical outcomes without harmonising the overall effect of the application of national laws in the areas affected.

Moreover, in my view, legal change in Europe should be driven by a desire to reform the law rather than merely change it in the interests of harmonisation, but as soon as one talks of reform, it becomes obvious that substantive changes require real justifications, whether on social, economic or political grounds. The law of contracts and the law of liability (whether civil, administrative or criminal) cannot be perfected simply by the application of open-minded legal 'scientists' from a neutral standpoint (though legal scholars can do much to promote the understanding of existing laws and to expose and marshal arguments, whether technical or substantive), but must involve the weighing up of competing considerations of policy and may reflect competing tenets of principle or differing conceptions of fundamental concepts.

The highly political nature of the law of product liability has become very apparent over the two decades since the promulgation of the Product Liability Directive, even if we restrict our gaze to French law, English law and the European Communities themselves. In English law, the Conservative Government did all it could to restrict implementation of the Directive so as to minimise the cost of liability for industry in the interests of its need to innovate, but also in the interests of its continuing competitiveness *within* the EC.[182] In French law, implementation of the Product Liability Directive became embroiled in the political fall-out of the *affaire du sang contaminé*, unfairly in fact, given that the public scandal involved the supply of blood with knowledge of its high risk to life and health and that the main jurisdictional forums for the issues to which it gave rise were the criminal courts.[183] At a European level too, however, the politically controversial nature of the terms of the compromise reached in the Product Liability Directive became conspicuous: first, in the context of BSE and the Directive's optional exclusion of 'primary agricultural products' and then, much more broadly, in debates regarding the fairness of its balance between the interests of consumers and producers.[184] In this respect, the Commission's own investigations and reports into the operation of the Directive, whose soothing conclusions have been that the balance was about right, reflected more a practical sense of the difficulty in piecing together a fresh compromise rather than a general agreement on the fairness of its provisions: for while most of those consulted thought its terms fair, this did not include the consumer groups.[185]

The Consumer Guarantees Directive illustrates instead the potential for disagreements not so much as to legal policy but as to legal principle and legal strategy. For even if it is assumed that its definition of 'contractual conformity' reflects a general consensus on the appropriate standard to be imposed on sellers to their consumer customers, its provisions on the hierarchy of rights remain controversial, reflecting a civilian view of the nature of contractual obligation which can seem to a common lawyer to be less protective of the rights of a creditor (here a buyer) than the common law approach.[186] Here, then, the 1999 Directive gave priority to one conception of contract and its accompanying remedial strategy above another without any substantive justification.

---

[182] Above, pp. 466–8.   [183] Above, pp. 450, 454–5, 457–60.   [184] Above, p. 446.
[185] Above, pp. 447.   [186] Above, pp. 79–86, 258–60, 570–1, 604–10.

It remains to be seen whether the new rights which the Directive requires to be created in national laws will actually help consumers.

In my view, this experience should be drawn on in deciding how to proceed in the drawing up and enactment of European legislation within the areas of contract or extra-contractual liability, whether at a specific or at any more general level. First, the question whether a particular social or economic problem should be governed at the European rather than at a national level should be determined according to whether its nature requires a European as opposed to a national solution: arguments from a priori principle or empirical assumption should not be enough. Secondly, having decided that an issue or set of issues should be governed at the European level, there must be a genuine and more public debate as to how it should be governed, in terms of legal policy, legal principle and conceptual technique.

8. A Series of Contrasts

This book has explored a number of distinctions and contrasts within the laws of France and England and how the law stemming from two European directives has interacted with them. It has involved consideration of the relationships between contractual liability and extra-contractual liability; administrative liability and private (or at least non-administrative) liability; criminal responsibility and civil liability; and liability for fault, liability for negligence and liability without fault or negligence. It has also sought to explain certain aspects of the relationship between legal institutions, legal procedures and substantive decision making; and between law, fact and the characterisation of facts. In so doing, it has sought to go beyond the formal aspects of the harmonisation of laws which European directives require and begin to look at their substantive effect. But there are many significant aspects of the relationship between the European harmonisation of laws in areas such as contract law or civil liability and their practical application in terms of legal (and non-legal) institutions and procedures which this study has not touched on. And its focus has been restricted to just two Member States at a time when the European Union has expanded considerably and looks as though it will expand again. There is very much more work to be done.

Index